2013-2015 EDITION

IRENE C. FOUNTAS
GAY SU PINNELL

The FOUNTAS AND PINNELL

LEVELED BOOK LIST K-8+

Volume 1

Heinemann
Portsmouth, NH

Heinemann
361 Hanover Street
Portsmouth, NH 03801-3912
www.heinemann.com

Offices and agents throughout the world

Library of Congress Cataloging-in-Publication Data
Fountas, Irene C.
    The Fountas and Pinnell leveled book list K-8+ / Irene C. Fountas, Gay Su Pinnell. — 2013/2015 edition.
        volumes cm.
ISBN 978-0-325-04907-6 (v. 1) — ISBN 978-0-325-04908-3 (v. 2)
1. Reading (Elementary). 2. Reading (Middle school). 3. Book leveling. I. Pinnell, Gay Su. II. Title.
LB1573.F638 2013+
372.41—dc23   2013016740

Printed in the United States of America on acid-free paper
17 16 15   VP   3 4 5

We dedicate this extensive resource to our colleague

Carol Woodworth

with much fondness and deep appreciation.

CONTENTS

Access to the Fountas & Pinnell Leveled Books Website (LBW)

- Go to www.heinemann.com/products/LBW002119.aspx
- Click "Buy" to add the item to your shopping cart.
- Enter **FPLBW** as a coupon code
- Click "Apply Coupon" [The Heinemann website will then require that you login or create a new account first]
- Click on the blue "log in" link where you will be prompted to **Login** or **Create a New Account**
- When done, you will be brought back to your shopping cart
- Click "Checkout"
- Fill in the additional Customer Information
- Click "Continue"
- Click "Place Order"

Once completed, you will receive an email confirmation with a license key and link to the LBW. *The first time you log in,* you will need to click on the "New Subscribers" tab and enter your login info. After this initial login, you will just go to the main login window and log in.

INTRODUCTION TO THE BOOK LIST

All teachers want their students to be successful, confident readers. This process begins with sensitive and responsive reading instruction; an understanding of how books support the "learning to read" process; and access to a sufficient quantity of high-quality books at appropriate instructional levels. In our books *Guided Reading: Good First Teaching for All Children* (Heinemann 1996); *Guiding Readers and Writers: Teaching Comprehension, Genre, and Content Literacy* (Heinemann 2001); *Teaching for Comprehending and Fluency: Thinking, Talking, and Writing About Reading, K–8* (Heinemann 2006); and *Genre Study: Teaching with Fiction and Nonfiction Books* (Heinemann 2012), we describe a comprehensive language and literacy framework designed to help students develop a broad and integrated range of reading, writing, and language competencies.

Then in *Leveled Books K–8: Matching Texts to Readers for Effective Teaching* (Heinemann 2006), we focus on the texts you will need to support a rich environment for literacy teaching and learning, beginning with a description of the most effective ways to use books in the classroom. That book also describes our gradient of leveled texts and its uses. We encourage the use of leveled books for instruction in guided reading and small-group literacy intervention lessons. Our levels will help you make good choices for students at various stages of reading development. For the specific characteristics of texts at each level and the competencies students need to acquire at each level, refer to our book, *The Continuum of Literacy Learning, K–8* (Heinemann 2007).

This book—*The Fountas and Pinnell Leveled Book List, K–8*—is a reference resource of over 45,000 titles that have been through a systematic, in-depth analysis by teams of experts who are experienced in analyzing features of texts as well as in teaching guided reading. The list includes a wide variety of genres and formats, fiction and nonfiction, all leveled through this reliable process. Of course, we can't possibly level every book published. As you get to know characteristics of books at our levels, talk with colleagues about the books you have that are not yet part of this list and assign them a tentative level.

The leveling process is ongoing, including constant review and revision, as books are used by teachers in the classroom. "Leveling" is not an exact science, though it is a comprehensive analysis. A level is an approximation, not an absolute designation; not all books on a level are precisely alike. There are many variables to take into account as text difficulty is determined. A text's demands and supports cannot be reduced to a mathematical formula. The concepts of "easier" and "harder" must always be understood in relation to the complex and interrelated text factors that we describe in *Leveled Books K–8*. What's more, myriad student factors have an impact on text readability as well.

The readability of a text is influenced by the background knowledge required of the reader to understand the text, the reader's facility with word solving, the number of complex sentences embedded in the text, and so on. The specialized process of determining text difficulty is a challenge worthy of our time because the more we learn about texts, the better we understand their demands on the individual readers we teach—the first step in matching books to readers.

The most current book list can be found at *www.fountasandpinnellleveledbooks.com*. This online database version of the book list is updated constantly with hundreds of new titles as well as revisions to existing levels as they are needed. On the Leveled Books Site, you can sort by title, author, series, publisher, level, genre, short story, graphic text, and mature content with lower level text demands. Book collections continually evolve. You build your collection slowly over time as you test books with students. We hope our text gradient and this comprehensive book list will help you select texts that are "just right" for your readers.

How to Use the Book List

The list is sorted alphabetically by book title. The tabs along the page edge make it possible to quickly turn to the letter you want.

As you will see, there are six columns on each page. The contents of each column are described below.

❏ **Title:** The first column indicates the title of the book. Books are placed alphabetically by the first word of the title—unless it is *a, an,* or *the,* in which case the article follows the title. Titles beginning with a numeral are placed at the beginning of the list in order by number.

❏ **Level:** The second column indicates the level assigned to the book, from A to Z or Z+. We use the letter *A* to indicate the easiest books to read and the letter *Z* to identify the most challenging books. In addition, we have added titles recommended for high school, which are labeled Z+ and are integrated throughout the book. More detailed descriptions of the text features of each level can be found in *Leveled Books K–8.* Two other abbreviations are used in this column:

- *WB (Wordless Books):* Books without any words in them at all (books that tell a story only in pictures) are excellent for the development of oral language and so are included in our list. However, they are not "leveled" in the same sense that the other books in the list are leveled.

- *LB (Label Books):* These are books with only one word or a very short phrase on every page. As with Wordless Books, we find leveling these books inappropriate. We do not recommend label books for use in guided reading, although students may enjoy them for other purposes in the classroom.

❏ **Genre:** The third column indicates the type of book, or genre. Genre is a term that means type of

text. We have classified each book as one genre though you will find there are some books that have elements of more than one. With the wealth and variety of children's books available today, it is sometimes difficult to make a precise designation of genre for a particular text. A text may have some features of an informational text, such as describing a series of actions, but the characters in the illustrations may be animals talking or getting dressed like people. In this case, the text would be fantasy. In this list, if the material in the text or illustrations has elements of fantasy, the book is classified as fantasy. In addition, there are many "hybrid texts" that combine elements of fiction and nonfiction; for example, a group of fictional children might visit a museum and learn a great deal about fossils. The text would be realistic fiction but would provide authentic information to the reader. Where any part of the text is fiction, we have designated it as fiction. You will want to analyze texts carefully, however, to take advantage of all the text characteristics and learning opportunities.

The following codes are used to indicate genre:

- *TL—Traditional Literature*
- *RF—Realistic Fiction*
- *HF—Historical Fiction*
- *SF—Science Fiction*
- *F—Fantasy*
- *B—Biography (includes autobiography and memoir)*
- *I—Information Book*

❏ **Words:** The fourth column provides the number of words appearing in the book. Note: "250+" indicates the book contains more than 250 words.

❏ **Author/Series:** The fifth column provides the name of the author or specific reading series.

❏ **Publisher/Distributor:** The sixth column indicates the publisher's or distributor's name. A list of addresses and phone numbers for each publisher or distributor of reading series and collections can be found in Appendix A. Trade books listed with the author's name are available from a variety of distributors.

Short Story Collection

❏ You'll notice that some books are marked with an * (asterisk). The asterisk indicates that the book is a collection of short stories. Some collections contain selections in which each story is completely independent of the others. In other collections, the stories are interrelated in some way, such as short biographies or a common character or theme. These stories can often be read out of order.

Graphic Text

❏ You will also notice a category, marked with a # (pound sign). The pound sign indicates a graphic text, or a text that is written with illustrations and speech bubbles in a sequence.

Mature Content with Lower Level Text Demands:

❏ Lastly, you will also see titles marked with the ^ sign. This sign designates a text containing more sophisticated themes or mature content with lower level text demands for the reader.

The true test of any leveling system, of course, is using the texts with students over time. We have included a form following this introduction, **Evaluation Response for Text Gradient,** to gather more information about the books on our list and to provide you the opportunity to suggest new books for leveling. We want teachers in many different geographic areas to test the books and provide feedback based on their use with students in guided reading. We invite you to send feedback to us at any time. As the online database and this book are revised, we will take your comments and suggestions into consideration.

Evaluation Response for Text Gradient

Directions: Since any text gradient is always in the process of construction as it is used with varying groups of children, we expect our list to change every year. We encourage you to try the levels with your students and to provide feedback based on your own experiences. Please suggest changes to existing book levels and suggest new books for the list. Please provide the information requested below.

Name: _____ Grade Level You Teach: _____

Telephone: ( ) _____ E-mail address: _____

Address (street, city, state): _____

Book Evaluated:

Book Title: _____

Level: A B C D E F G H I J K L M N O P Q R S T U V W X Y Z Z+

Author: _____

Publisher: _____

This book is:

_____ A book listed on the gradient that I have evaluated with my class.
(Complete SECTION A and make comments in SECTION C.)

_____ A book listed on the gradient that I am recommending as a benchmark for a level.
(Complete SECTION A and make comments in SECTION C.)

_____ A new book that I suggest adding to the collection.
(Complete SECTION B and make comments in SECTION C.)

SECTION A: (for an evaluation of a book currently included in the list)

Is it appropriately placed on the level (explain)? _____
To what level should the book be moved?
A   B   C   D   E   F   G   H   I   J   K   L   M   N   O   P   Q   R   S   T   U   V   W   X   Y   Z   Z+

Are there points of difficulty that make it harder than it seems? _____

_____

Is the text supportive in ways that might not be noticeable when examining the superficial characteristics?

_____

SECTION B: (for the recommendation of a new book) Indicate recommended level: _____

How does this book support readers at this level? _____

_____

What challenges does it offer? _____

_____

SECTION C: Please place additional comments on the back or on another sheet.

Mail or fax (603–431–7840) this form to:
Leveled Book List Suggestions
c/o Heinemann
361 Hanover Street
Portsmouth, NH 03801–3912

Book List

(ORGANIZED BY TITLE)

TITLE	LEVEL	GENRE	WORD COUNT	AUTHOR / SERIES	PUBLISHER / DISTRIBUTOR
1 Is for One	E	F	82	Bookshop	Mondo Publishing
1 Potato 2 Potato	N	I	250+	Literacy 2000	Rigby
1, 2, 3 in the Box	B	RF	23	Tarlow, Ellen	Scholastic
1, 2, Kangaroo	LB	F	54	Reading Corners	Pearson Learning Group
1,000 Reasons Never to Kiss a Boy	X	RF	250+	Freeman, Martha	Holiday House
10 9 8 Polar Animals!	I	I	224	Counting Books	Capstone Press
*10 Bravest Everyday Heroes, The	T	I	250+	The 10 Books	Franklin Watts
10 Cats	LB	RF	13	Leveled Readers Language Support	Houghton Mifflin Harcourt
10 Deadliest Plants, The	T	I	250+	The 10 Books	Franklin Watts
*10 Explorers Who Changed the World	V	B	250+	Gifford, Clive	Kingfisher
10 Greatest Accidental Inventions	T	I	250+	The 10 Books	Franklin Watts
*10 Inventors Who Changed the World	V	B	250+	Gifford, Clive	Kingfisher
*10 Kings & Queens Who Changed the World	X	B	250+	Gifford, Clive	Kingfisher
*10 Leaders Who Changed the World	W	B	250+	Gifford, Clive	Kingfisher
10 Little Hot Dogs	I	F	233	Himmelman, John	Marshall Cavendish
10 Most Amazing Animal Movies, The	T	I	250+	The 10 Books	Franklin Watts
10 Most Wondrous Ancient Sites, The	V	I	250+	The 10 Books	Franklin Watts
10 p.m. Question, The	Z	RF	250+	De Goldi, Kate	Candlewick Press
10 Smartest Animals, The	T	I	250+	The 10 Books	Franklin Watts
10 Things I Can Do to Help My World	K	I	91	Walsh, Melanie	Candlewick Press
100 Days	B	RF	16	Bebop Books	Lee & Low Books Inc.
100 Days and 99 Nights	P	RF	250+	Madison, Alan	Little Brown and Company
100 Days of School	L	I	264	Harris, Trudy	Millbrook Press
100 Pets	J	RF	368	Gear Up!	Wright Group/McGraw Hill
100 Years Ago	E	I	119	Learn to Read	Creative Teaching Press
100 Years Ago	H	I	135	Twig	Wright Group/McGraw Hill
1000 Facts about Space	X	I	250+	Beasant, Pam	Scholastic
100-Pound Problem, The	L	RF	250+	Math Matters	Kane Press
100th Day of School, The	K	I	250+	Holidays and Celebrations	Picture Window Books
100th Day of School, The	H	RF	190	Medearis, Angela Shelf	Scholastic
100th Day, The	G	RF	138	Maccarone, Grace	Scholastic
100-Year-Old Secret, The	S	RF	250+	Barrett, Tracy	Henry Holt & Co.
101 Things You Wish You'd Invented ... and Some You Wish No One Had	V	I	250+	Horne, Richard & Turner, Tracey	Walker & Company
108th Sheep, The	L	F	250+	Imai, Ayano	Tiger Tales
12 Again	V	F	250+	Corbett, Sue	Penguin Group
12 Ways to Get to 11	K	I	205	Merriam, Eve	Aladdin
*13 Ghosts: Strange But True Stories	X	F	250+	Osborne, Will	Scholastic
13 Hangmen	X	F	250+	Corriveau, Art	Amulet Books
13 Monsters Who Should Be Avoided	M	F	250+	Shortsleeve, Kevin	Peachtree
13th Floor, The	P	F	250+	Storyteller-Autumn Leaves	Wright Group/McGraw Hill
13th Floor, The: A Ghost Story	U	F	250+	Fleischman, Sid	Bantam Books
14 Cows for America	S	HF	250+	Deedy, Carmen Agra	Peachtree
*145th Street	Z+	RF	250+	Myers, Walter Dean	Laurel-Leaf Books
15 Best Things About Being the New Kid, The	K	RF	585	Silly Millies	Millbrook Press
15 Facts about Atoms	S	I	654	Independent Readers Science	Houghton Mifflin Harcourt
15 Facts about Snakes	K	I	347	Rigby Focus	Rigby
15 Facts about Stars	W	I	1652	Independent Readers Science	Houghton Mifflin Harcourt
15 Facts about the Solar System	P	I	474	Independent Readers Science	Houghton Mifflin Harcourt

TITLE	LEVEL	GENRE	WORD COUNT	AUTHOR / SERIES	PUBLISHER / DISTRIBUTOR
18th Emergency, The	R	RF	250+	Byars, Betsy	Bantam Books
#1918 Flu Pandemic, The	T	I	250+	Disasters in History	Capstone Press
1963 Birmingham Church Bombing	Y	I	250+	Snapshots in History	Compass Point Books
1980s, The	R	I	1144	Leveled Readers Social Studies	Houghton Mifflin Harcourt
2 of Everything	I	RF	217	Talking Point Series	Pearson Learning Group
2 X 2 = Boo! A Set of Spooky Multiplication Stories	M	F	250+	Leedy, Loreen	Holiday House
2, 4, 6, 8 Legs	C	I	57	Literacy by Design	Rigby
2, 4, 6, 8 Legs	C	I	57	On Our Way to English	Rigby
20 Pennies	E	RF	212	Teacher's Choice Series	Pearson Learning Group
#20,000 Leagues Under the Sea	V	F	250+	Bowen, Carl (Retold)	Stone Arch Books
20,000 Leagues Under the Sea	Z+	F	250+	Verne, Jules	Scholastic
2095	P	SF	250+	Scieszka, Jon	Penguin Group
*20th Century African American Singers	U	B	2956	Reading Street	Pearson
*26 Fairmount Avenue	N	B	250+	DePaola, Tomie	G.P. Putnam's Sons Books for Young Readers
3,2,1... Lift Off!	K	RF	250+	Storyteller-Shooting Stars	Wright Group/McGraw Hill
#3.2.3 Detective Agency, The: The Disappearance of Dave Warthog	T	F	250+	Robinson, Fiona	Amulet Books
^300 Heroes: The Battle of Thermopylae	X	I	250+	Bloodiest Battles	Capstone Press
31 Ways to Change the World	P	I	250+	Taylor, Tanis	Candlewick Press
3-2-1 Blast-Off	I	RF	291	Talking Point Series	Pearson Learning Group
33 Snowfish	Z+	RF	250+	Rapp, Adam	Candlewick Press
3-D ABC: A Sculptural Alphabet	Q	I	368	Raczka, Bob	Millbrook Press
4 Kids in 5E & 1 Crazy Year	S	RF	250+	Schwartz, Virginia Frances	Holiday House
40 Nights to Knowing the Sky	Z	I	250+	Schaaf, Fred	Henry Holt & Co.
47	X	F	250+	Mosley, Walter	Little Brown and Company
5 Novels	V	F	250+	Pinkwater, Daniel	Farrar, Straus, & Giroux
50 Facts About Bison	N	I	250+	Larkin, Bruce	Wilbooks
^5010 Calling	S	SF	1496	Powell, J.	Stone Arch Books
52 Days by Camel: My Sahara Adventure	T	I	250+	Raskin, Lawrie	Annick Press
7 Facts About the Weather	I	I	231	Leveled Readers Science	Houghton Mifflin Harcourt
7 Uses for Air	B	I	46	Independent Readers Science	Houghton Mifflin Harcourt
7 Ways to Get Energy	J	I	193	Independent Readers Science	Houghton Mifflin Harcourt
89th Kitten, The	O	RF	250+	Nilsson, Eleanor	Scholastic
90 Miles to Havana	W	HF	250+	Flores-Galbis, Enrique	Roaring Brook Press
97 Ways to Train a Dragon	P	F	250+	McMullan, Kate	Scholastic

* Collection of short stories   # Graphic text
^ Mature content with lower level text demands

TITLE	LEVEL	GENRE	WORD COUNT	AUTHOR / SERIES	PUBLISHER / DISTRIBUTOR
^A Is for Arrr!	M	I	250+	Alphabet Fun	Capstone Press
A. Lincoln and Me	M	RF	250+	Borden, Louise	Scholastic
A.L.L to the Rescue	S	RF	1000	Leveled Readers/TX	Houghton Mifflin Harcourt
A-10 Thunderbolt, The	U	I	250+	Cross-Sections	Capstone Press
Aaron Rodgers	P	B	1784	Savage, Jeff/Amazing Athletes	Lerner Publishing Group
A-B-A-B-A-: A Book of Pattern Play	M	I	315	Math is CATegorical	Millbrook Press
Abandoned Lighthouse, The	J	F	250+	Lamb, Albert	Roaring Brook Press
Abarat	Z	F	250+	Barker, Clive	HarperCollins
Abby	M	RF	250+	Hanel, Wolfram	North-South Books
Abby Carnelia's One & Only Magical Power	T	F	250+	Pogue, David	Roaring Brook Press
Abby Flies	C	F	30	Brand New Readers	Candlewick Press
Abby Takes a Stand	Q	HF	250+	McKissack, Patricia	Scholastic
ABC - All About Cars	G	I	130	Factivity Series	Pearson Learning Group
ABC Bunny, The	H	F	161	Ga'g, Wanda	Scholastic
ABC I Like Me!	H	F	136	Carlson, Nancy	Puffin Books
ABC Safari	M	F	743	Lee, Karen	Sylvan Dell Publishing
ABC Who's Got Me?	E	F	40	Instant Readers	Harcourt School Publishers
Abe Lincoln	N	B	250+	Jones, Lynda/Hello Reader!	Scholastic
Abe Lincoln and the Muddy Pig	K	B	250+	Childhood of Famous Americans	Aladdin
Abe Lincoln: Log Cabin to White House	Z	B	250+	North, Sterling	Random House
Abe Lincoln's Hat	M	B	250+	Brenner, Martha	Random House
Abel's Island	T	F	250+	Steig, William	Farrar, Straus, & Giroux
Abigail Adams	S	B	250+	Amazing Americans	Wright Group/McGraw Hill
Abigail Adams	M	B	262	First Ladies	Capstone Press
Abigail Adams	S	B	3710	History Maker Bios	Lerner Publishing Group
Abigail Adams	W	B	3123	Leveled Readers	Houghton Mifflin Harcourt
Abigail Adams	W	B	3123	Leveled Readers/CA	Houghton Mifflin Harcourt
Abigail Adams	W	B	3123	Leveled Readers/TX	Houghton Mifflin Harcourt
Abigail Adams	Q	B	250+	Primary Source Readers	Teacher Created Materials
Abigail Adams, Patriot	U	B	2288	Leveled Readers Social Studies	Houghton Mifflin Harcourt
Abigail Adams: Girl of Colonial Days	R	B	250+	Wagoner, Jean Brown	Aladdin
Abigail Iris: The One and Only	P	RF	250+	Glatt, Lisa & Greenberg, Suzanne	Walker & Company
Abigail Iris: The Pet Project	P	RF	250+	Glatt, Lisa & Greenberg, Suzanne	Walker & Company
Abigail the Breeze Fairy: Rainbow Magic	L	F	250+	Meadows, Daisy	Scholastic
Abominable Snowman, The	M	F	250+	Bookweb	Rigby
Aboriginal and Inuit Worlds	T	I	3467	Take Two Books	Wright Group/McGraw Hill
About 100 Years Ago	I	I	250+	Yellow Umbrella Books	Red Brick Learning
About Amphibians: A Guide For Children	J	I	110	Sill, Cathryn	Peachtree
About Arachnids: A Guide For Children	K	I	118	Sill, Cathryn	Peachtree
About Birds: A Guide For Children	I	I	78	Sill, Cathryn	Peachtree
About Crustaceans: A Guide For Children	K	I	161	Sill, Cathryn	Peachtree
About Fish: A Guide For Children	I	I	114	Sill, Cathryn	Peachtree
About Habitats: Deserts	J	I	211	Sill, Cathryn	Peachtree
About Habitats: Grasslands	J	I	156	Sill, Cathryn	Peachtree
About Habitats: Mountains	J	I	195	About Habitats	Peachtree
About Habitats: Wetlands	J	I	205	Sill, Cathryn	Peachtree
About How Many?	M	I	250+	Early Connections	Benchmark Education
About Hummingbirds: A Guide For Children	J	I	199	Sill, Cathryn	Peachtree
About Insects: A Guide For Children	J	I	101	Sill, Cathryn	Peachtree
About Mammals: A Guide For Children	J	I	75	Sill, Cathryn	Peachtree
About Marsupials: A Guide For Children	K	I	134	Sill, Cathryn	Peachtree
About Milk	N	I	670	Springboard	Wright Group/McGraw Hill
About Mollusks: A Guide For Children	L	I	194	Sill, Cathryn	Peachtree
About Penguins: A Guide for Children	J	I	176	Sill, Cathryn	Peachtree

TITLE	LEVEL	GENRE	WORD COUNT	AUTHOR / SERIES	PUBLISHER / DISTRIBUTOR
About Pets	F	I	178	We Both Read	Treasure Bay
About Raptors: A Guide for Children	K	I	150	Sill, Cathryn	Peachtree
About Reptiles: A Guide For Children	J	I	94	Sill, Cathryn	Peachtree
About Rodents: A Guide For Children	J	I	156	Sill, Cathryn	Peachtree
About the B'nai Bagels	T	RF	250+	Konigsburg, E. L.	Dell
About the Ocean	I	I	475	We Both Read	Treasure Bay
Above and Below	C	I	41	Location	Lerner Publishing Group
Above and Below	F	I	128	Sunshine	Wright Group/McGraw Hill
Above and Below	I	I	239	Where Words	Capstone Press
Above the Rim	U	I	250+	Boldprint	Steck-Vaughn
Abracadabra	L	RF	372	Reading Unlimited	Pearson Learning Group
Abracadabra	LB	F	14	Rigby Rocket	Rigby
Abracadabra Kid, The	X	B	250+	Fleischman, Sid	Beech Tree Books
Abracadabra!	C	RF	35	InfoTrek	ETA/Cuisenaire
Abracadabra! Magic with Mouse and Mole	L	F	250+	Yee, Wong Herbert	Sandpiper Books
Abraham Lincoln	S	B	250+	Amazing Americans	Wright Group/McGraw Hill
Abraham Lincoln	P	B	250+	Early Biographies	Compass Point Books
Abraham Lincoln	M	B	235	Famous Americans	Capstone Press
Abraham Lincoln	N	B	214	First Biographies	Capstone Press
Abraham Lincoln	Q	B	250+	Gross, Ruth Belov	Scholastic
Abraham Lincoln	S	B	3783	History Maker Bios	Lerner Publishing Group
Abraham Lincoln	T	B	250+	In Their Own Words	Scholastic
Abraham Lincoln	U	B	250+	Let Freedom Ring	Red Brick Learning
Abraham Lincoln	S	B	250+	Parin d'Aulaire, Ingri & Edgar	Bantam Books
Abraham Lincoln	S	B	2747	People to Remember Series	January Books
Abraham Lincoln	Q	B	250+	Photo-Illustrated Biographies	Red Brick Learning
Abraham Lincoln	U	B	250+	Primary Source Readers	Teacher Created Materials
Abraham Lincoln	U	B	250+	Profiles of the Presidents	Compass Point Books
Abraham Lincoln: A Life of Respect	O	B	492	Pull Ahead Books	Lerner Publishing Group
Abraham Lincoln: Defender of the Union	Y	B	250+	The Civil War	Carus Publishing Company
Abraham Lincoln: Lawyer, President, Emancipator	M	B	250+	Biographies	Picture Window Books
Abraham Lincoln: President of a Divided Country	O	B	250+	Greene, Carol	Children's Press
Abraham Lincoln: Sixteenth President	R	B	250+	Getting to Know the U.S. Presidents	Children's Press
Abraham Lincoln: The Great Emancipator	R	B	250+	Stevenson, Augusta	Aladdin
Abraham's Battle: A Novel of Gettysburg	T	HF	250+	Banks, Sara Harrell	Atheneum Books
Absent Author, The	N	RF	250+	A to Z Mysteries	Random House
Absolutely Normal Chaos	V	RF	250+	Creech, Sharon	HarperTrophy
Absolutely Not!	E	F	199	Story Steps	Rigby
Absolutely True Diary of a Part-Time Indian, The	Z+	RF	250+	Alexie, Sherman	Little Brown and Company
Absolutely True Story, The: How I Visited Yellowstone Park With the Terrible Rupes	R	RF	250+	Roberts, Willo Davis	Aladdin
Abyssinian Cats	I	I	119	Cats	Capstone Press
Abyssinian Cats	Q	I	250+	Mattern, Joanne/All About Cats	Capstone Press
Acceptable Time, An	X	F	250+	L'Engle, Madeleine	Laurel-Leaf Books
Access Denied (and other eighth grade error messages)	X	RF	250+	Vega, Denise	Little Brown and Company
Accident in the Forest	M	RF	839	Springboard	Wright Group/McGraw Hill
Accident on the Bike Track	M	RF	712	Springboard	Wright Group/McGraw Hill
Accident Prone	P	RF	250+	Bookweb	Rigby
Accident, The	H	RF	313	Foundations	Wright Group/McGraw Hill
Accidental Angel (Secret Sisters)	P	RF	250+	Byrd, Sandra	WaterBrook Press

* Collection of short stories   # Graphic text
^ Mature content with lower level text demands

TITLE	LEVEL	GENRE	WORD COUNT	AUTHOR / SERIES	PUBLISHER / DISTRIBUTOR
Accidental Inventions	N	I	250+	Windows on Literacy	National Geographic
Accidental Love	W	RF	250+	Soto, Gary	Harcourt, Inc.
Accidents	D	RF	35	Visions	Wright Group/McGraw Hill
Accidents May Happen: Fifty Inventions Discovered by Mistake	T	I	250+	Jones, Charlotte Foltz	Delacorte Press
Ace Lacewing, Bug Detective	Q	F	250+	Biedrzycki, David	Charlesbridge
Ace Lacewing, Bug Detective: Bad Bugs Are My Business	Q	F	250+	Biedrzycki, David	Charlesbridge
Ace Reporter	L	RF	250+	Bookweb	Rigby
Ace: The Very Important Pig	R	F	250+	King-Smith, Dick	Alfred A. Knopf
Aches and Pains	L	F	632	Red Rocket Readers	Flying Start Books
^Achilles	W	I	250+	World Mythology	Capstone Press
Achoo! The Most Interesting Book You'll Ever Read About Germs	R	I	250+	Romanek, Trudee	Scholastic
Acid Rain	Y	I	1702	Independent Readers Science	Houghton Mifflin Harcourt
Acid Rain	U	I	250+	Our Planet In Peril	Capstone Press
Acid Rain	L	I	368	Wonder World	Wright Group/McGraw Hill
Acids and Bases	V	I	250+	Reading Expeditions	National Geographic
Acorn Is Hungry	C	F	52	Tiny Treasures	Pioneer Valley
A-Counting We Will Go	E	RF	191	Learn to Read	Creative Teaching Press
Acquaintance with Darkness, An	Y	HF	250+	Rinaldi, Ann	Harcourt
Across Five Aprils	Z	HF	250+	Hunt, Irene	Follett
Across Ice and Snow	J	I	138	Gear Up!	Wright Group/McGraw Hill
Across the Desert	G	RF	232	The Rowland Reading Program Library	Rowland Reading Foundation
Across the Lines	W	HF	250+	Reeder, Carolyn	Avon Books
Across the Oregon Trail	T	HF	250+	Storyteller-Mountain Peaks	Wright Group/McGraw Hill
Across the Seasons	C	I	75	Early Connections	Benchmark Education
Across the Stream	F	F	94	Ginsburg, Mirra	Morrow
Across the Wide and Lonesome Prairie	U	HF	250+	My America	Scholastic
Act I, Act II, Act Normal	T	RF	250+	Weston, Martha	Roaring Brook Press
Action of Subtraction, The	N	I	376	Math Is CATegorical	Millbrook Press
Action Safety	O	I	250+	Bookweb	Rigby
Action: Defense	T	I	250+	Sails	Rigby
Active Volcanoes	N	I	572	Springboard	Wright Group/McGraw Hill
Actor's Wanted	Q	RF	250+	Sails	Rigby
Ad Break	P	RF	250+	Bookweb	Rigby
Adam Canfield of the Slash	U	RF	250+	Winerip, Michael	Candlewick Press
Adam Canfield Watch Your Back!	U	RF	250+	Winerip, Michael	Candlewick Press
Adam Joshua Capers: Halloween Monster	N	RF	250+	Smith, Janice Lee	HarperTrophy
Adam Joshua Capers: Kid Next Door and Other Headaches, The	N	RF	250+	Smith, Janice Lee	HarperTrophy
Adam Joshua Capers: Monster in the Third Dresser Drawer, The	N	RF	250+	Smith, Janice Lee	HarperTrophy
Adam Joshua Capers: Nelson in Love	N	RF	250+	Smith, Janice Lee	HarperTrophy
Adam Joshua Capers: Show-and-Tell War, The	N	RF	250+	Smith, Janice Lee	HarperTrophy
Adam Joshua Capers: Superkid!	N	RF	250+	Smith, Janice Lee	HarperTrophy
Adam Joshua Capers: Turkey Trouble	N	RF	250+	Smith, Janice Lee	HarperTrophy
Adam of the Road	W	HF	250+	Gray, Elizabeth Janet	Scholastic
Adaptations	L	I	158	Windows on Literacy	National Geographic
Adaptations to Land and Water	S	I	250+	Science Support Readers	Houghton Mifflin Harcourt
Adapting to Death Valley Heat	K	I	118	Larkin, Bruce	Wilbooks
Add It Up	J	RF	311	Story Box	Wright Group/McGraw Hill
Add the Animals	D	I	74	Early Connections	Benchmark Education
Addie Meets Max	J	RF	250+	Robins, Joan	Harper & Row

TITLE	LEVEL	GENRE	WORD COUNT	AUTHOR / SERIES	PUBLISHER / DISTRIBUTOR
Addie's Bad Day	J	RF	566	Robins, Joan	HarperTrophy
Addie's Dakota Winter	T	RF	250+	Lawlor, Laurie	Pocket Books
Adding Arctic Animals	I	I	120	Yellow Umbrella Books	Red Brick Learning
Adding It Up at the Zoo	G	I	250+	Yellow Umbrella Books	Red Brick Learning
Addison Addley and the Things That Aren't There	O	RF	250+	Orca Young Readers	Orca Books
Addison Addley and the Trick of the Eye	O	RF	250+	Orca Young Readers	Orca Books
Addition	D	I	32	Early Math	Lerner Publishing Group
Addition Annie	G	RF	30	Rookie Readers	Children's Press
Addy Learns a Lesson: A School Story	Q	HF	250+	The American Girls Collection	Pleasant Company
Addy Saves the Day: A Summer Story	Q	HF	250+	The American Girls Collection	Pleasant Company
Addy's Surprise: A Christmas Story	Q	HF	250+	The American Girls Collection	Pleasant Company
Adeline's Dream	T	HF	45612	From Many Peoples	Fitzhenry & Whiteside
Adios, Anna	N	RF	250+	Giff, Patricia Reilly	Bantam Books
Adios, Coyote	K	F	250+	Rigby Literacy	Rigby
Admiral Perry	T	B	2451	Independent Readers Social Studies	Houghton Mifflin Harcourt
Adolf Hitler	Z	B	250+	A Wicked History	Scholastic
Adoration of Jenna Fox, The	Y	SF	250+	Pearson, Mary E.	Square Fish
Advances in Genetics	Y	I	250+	Navigators Science Series	Benchmark Education
#Adventues of Tom Sawyer, The	U	HF	2380	Hall, M. C. (Retold)	Stone Arch Books
Adventure at Sea	J	F	250+	Storyworlds	Heinemann
Adventure in Alaska	O	I	250+	Kramer, S. A.	Random House
Adventure in the Purple Forest	I	F	214	Spaceboy	Literacy Footprints
Adventure to the New World	T	HF	5668	Reading Street	Pearson
Adventure Travel	T	I	250+	Boldprint	Steck-Vaughn
Adventure Vacations	M	I	250+	Rigby Literacy	Rigby
Adventurers, The	O	I	250+	Scooters	ETA/Cuisenaire
Adventures in Matunaland	U	RF	8913	Reading Street	Pearson
#Adventures in Sound with Max Axiom, Super Scientist	U	I	250+	Graphic Library	Capstone Press
Adventures of a Kite	L	F	33	Jellybeans	Rigby
Adventures of a South Pole Pig	Q	F	250+	Kurtz, Chris	Houghton Mifflin Harcourt
Adventures of Ali Baba Bernstein, The	O	RF	250+	Hurwitz, Johanna	Scholastic
Adventures of Audubon, The	U	B	250+	WorldScapes	ETA/Cuisenaire
Adventures of Baby Bear, The	N	I	1173	Nature Babies	Fitzhenry & Whiteside
Adventures of Benny, The	O	F	250+	Shreve, Steve	Marshall Cavendish
Adventures of Buddy and Stuffed Buddy	F	F	152	McGougan, Kathy	Buddy Books Publishing
Adventures of Captain Underpants, The	P	F	250+	Pilkey, Dav	Scholastic
Adventures of Erik, The	O	B	956	Leveled Readers	Houghton Mifflin Harcourt
Adventures of Erik, The	O	B	956	Leveled Readers/CA	Houghton Mifflin Harcourt
Adventures of Erik, The	O	B	956	Leveled Readers/TX	Houghton Mifflin Harcourt
Adventures of George Washington, The	N	B	250+	Davidson, Margaret	Scholastic
Adventures of Granny Gatman, The	L	RF	250+	Meadows, Graham	Pearson Learning Group
Adventures of Huckleberry Finn, The	Z	HF	250+	Twain, Mark	Scholastic
Adventures of Isabel, The	L	F	271	Nash, Ogden	Sourcebooks
Adventures of Marco Polo, The	U	B	250+	Freedman, Russell	Scholastic
#Adventures of Marco Polo, The	T	B	250+	Graphic Library	Capstone Press
Adventures of Max and Ned, The	N	F	250+	Little Celebrations	Pearson Learning Group
Adventures of Ratman	M	F	250+	Weiss, Ellen; Freidman, Mel	Random House
Adventures of Sir Balin the Ill-Fated, The	R	TL	250+	Morris, Gerald	Houghton Mifflin Harcourt
Adventures of Sir Givret the Short, The	R	TL	250+	Morris, Gerald	Houghton Mifflin Harcourt
Adventures of Sir Gwain the True, The	R	TL	250+	Morris, Gerald	Houghton Mifflin Harcourt
Adventures of Sir Lancelot the Great, The	R	TL	250+	Morris, Gerald	Houghton Mifflin Harcourt

* Collection of short stories   # Graphic text
^ Mature content with lower level text demands

TITLE	LEVEL	GENRE	WORD COUNT	AUTHOR / SERIES	PUBLISHER / DISTRIBUTOR
Adventures of Snail at School	J	F	250+	Stadler, John	HarperTrophy
Adventures of Sophie Bean, The: The Red Flyer Roller Coaster	K	RF	2600	Yevchak, Kathryn	Kaeden Books
Adventures of Spider, The	R	TL	250+	Arkhurst, Joyce C.	Scholastic
Adventures of the Buried Treasure, The	L	F	250+	McArthur, Nancy	Scholastic
Adventures of the Dish and the Spoon, The	M	F	250+	Grey, Mini	Alfred A. Knopf
Adventures of the Robber Pig	K	F	250+	Storyteller-Shooting Stars	Wright Group/McGraw Hill
Adventures of the Shark Lady	Q	I	250+	McGovern, Ann	Scholastic
Adventures of Tom Sawyer, The	T	RF	5825	Oxford Bookworms Library	Oxford University Press
Adventures of Tom Sawyer, The	Z	HF	250+	Twain, Mark	Scholastic
Adventures of Tom Sawyer, The (Abridged)	S	HF	250+	Hear It Read It	Sourcebooks
Adventures on Amelia Island: A Pirate, a Princess, and Buried Treasure	R	F	250+	Wood, Jane R.	Bluefish Bay Publishing
Adventures on the High Seas	T	I	250+	Boldprint	Steck-Vaughn
Adventurous Deeds of Deadwood Jones, The	W	HF	250+	Hemphill, Helen	Front Street
Advertisements	K	I	405	Rigby Flying Colors	Rigby
Advertisements	U	I	250+	Sails	Rigby
Advice About Family: Claudia Cristina Cortez Uncomplicates Your Life	S	RF	250+	Gallagher, Diana G.	Stone Arch Books
Advice About Friends: Claudia Cristina Cortez Uncomplicates Your Life	S	RF	250+	Gallagher, Diana G.	Stone Arch Books
Advice About School: Claudia Cristina Cortez Uncomplicates Your Life	S	RF	250+	Gallagher, Diana G.	Stone Arch Books
Aeneid, The	Z+	TL	250+	Virgil	Penguin Group
*Aesop & Company: With Scenes from His Legendary Life	O	TL	250+	Bader, Barbara	Houghton Mifflin Harcourt
Aesop's Fables	K	I	209	Vocabulary Readers	Houghton Mifflin Harcourt
Aesop's Fables	K	I	209	Vocabulary Readers/CA	Houghton Mifflin Harcourt
*Afghan Dreams: Young Voices of Afghanistan	Y	I	250+	O'Brien, Tony & Sullivan, Mike	Bloomsbury Children's Books
Afghanistan	LB	I	14	Readlings	American Reading Company
Afghanistan: A Question and Answer Book	P	I	250+	Questions and Answers: Countries	Capstone Press
Afikomen Mambo	M	RF	184	Black, Rabbi Joe	Kar-Ben Publishing
Afraid	D	I	18	Feelings	Lerner Publishing Group
Africa	N	I	250+	Continents	Capstone Press
Africa	V	I	250+	Eyewitness Books	DK Publishing
Africa	N	I	442	Pull Ahead Books	Lerner Publishing Group
Africa: Geography and Environments	W	I	250+	Reading Expeditions	National Geographic
Africa: People and Places	X	I	250+	Reading Expeditions	National Geographic
African Acrostics: A Word in Edgeways	P	I	250+	Harley, Avis	Candlewick Press
*African American Athletes	T	B	2426	Reading Street	Pearson
*African Americans in History	K	I	250+	Literacy by Design	Rigby
African Animals	B	I	49	Belle River Readers	Belle River Readers, Inc.
African Art	J	I	194	Take Two Books	Wright Group/McGraw Hill
African Dance Drumbeat in Our Feet	L	RF	258	Bebop Books	Lee & Low Books Inc.
African Elephant, The	D	I	47	Bonnell, Kris/Animals in Danger	Reading Reading Books
African Elephants	O	I	1410	Early Bird Nature Books	Lerner Publishing Group
African Elephants	K	I	333	Pull Ahead Books	Lerner Publishing Group
African Giants	M	I	250+	World Quest Adventures	World Quest Learning
African Glasslands	P	I	1100	Time for Kids	Teacher Created Materials
African Hunting Dog, The	M	I	250+	Sunshine	Wright Group/McGraw Hill
African Journeys : 1850-1900	V	I	250+	Reading Expeditions	National Geographic
African Nature Reserve, An	L	I	709	Leveled Readers	Houghton Mifflin Harcourt
African Nature Reserve, An	L	I	709	Leveled Readers/CA	Houghton Mifflin Harcourt

TITLE	LEVEL	GENRE	WORD COUNT	AUTHOR / SERIES	PUBLISHER / DISTRIBUTOR
African Rhinos	K	I	425	Pull Ahead Books	Lerner Publishing Group
African Safari	V	I	250+	PM Collection	Rigby
*African-American Scientists	O	B	250+	St. John, Jetty	Red Brick Learning
African-Americans in the Colonies	U	I	250+	We The People	Compass Point Books
African-Americans in the Old West	V	I	250+	Cornerstones of Freedom	Children's Press
African-Americans in the Thirteen Colonies	V	I	250+	Cornerstones of Freedom	Children's Press
Africans in America 1619-1865	U	I	250+	Coming to America	Capstone Press
Africa's Big Three	M	I	781	Big Cat	Pacific Learning
Africa's Changing Geography	U	I	2832	Reading Street	Pearson
After All, You're Callie Boone	S	RF	250+	Mack, Winnie	Feiwel and Friends
After Dark	E	I	128	Red Rocket Readers	Flying Start Books
After Ever After	Y	RF	250+	Sonnenblick, Jordan	Scholastic
After Goldilocks	E	F	44	Instant Readers	Harcourt School Publishers
After Peaches	Q	RF	250+	Orca Young Readers	Orca Books
After School	F	I	148	Explorations	Okapi Educational Materials
After School	F	I	148	Explorations	Eleanor Curtain Publishing
After School	H	RF	199	Foundations	Wright Group/McGraw Hill
After School	D	I	107	Springboard	Wright Group/McGraw Hill
After School	D	I	58	Sunshine	Wright Group/McGraw Hill
After School Excitement	P	RF	1841	Reading Street	Pearson
After School Fun	D	RF	78	Nelson, May	Scholastic
After School Ghost Hunter	O	RF	250+	Klooz	Stone Arch Books
After the Crash	W	HF	2952	Leveled Readers	Houghton Mifflin Harcourt
After the Crash	W	HF	2952	Leveled Readers/CA	Houghton Mifflin Harcourt
After the Crash	W	HF	2952	Leveled Readers/TX	Houghton Mifflin Harcourt
After the Dancing Days	W	HF	250+	Rostkowski, Margaret I.	HarperTrophy
After the Earthquake	S	I	250+	Navigators Social Studies Series	Benchmark Education
After the Flood	G	RF	210	PM Extensions-Green	Rigby
After the Goat Man	R	RF	250+	Byars, Betsy	Puffin Books
After the High Tide	K	RF	672	PM Stars Bridge Books	Rigby
After the Rain	Z	RF	250+	Mazer, Norma Fox	Avon Books
After the Storm	G	I	130	Explorations	Okapi Educational Materials
After the Storm	G	I	130	Explorations	Eleanor Curtain Publishing
After the War	W	HF	250+	Matas, Carol	Aladdin
After Tupac & D Foster	Y	RF	250+	Woodson, Jacqueline	G.P. Putnam's Sons
Afterlife, The	Z+	F	250+	Edge	Hampton Brown
Afterlife, The	Z+	F	250+	Soto, Gary	Harcourt, Inc.
Afternoon of the Elves	S	F	250+	Lisle, Janet Taylor	Scholastic
Afternoon on the Amazon	M	F	250+	Osborne, Mary Pope	Random House
Against the Odds	P	I	250+	Layden, Joe	Scholastic
Against the Odds	Q	I	250+	Orbit Collections	Pacific Learning
Against the Odds	R	I	250+	Wildcats	Wright Group/McGraw Hill
Against the Rules	R	RF	250+	Costello, Emily	Dell
Agatha Christie, Woman of Mystery	W	B	5955	Oxford Bookworms Library	Oxford University Press
Agatha's Feather Bed: Not Just Another Wild Goose Story	O	F	250+	Deedy, Carmen Agra	Peachtree
Age of Inventions, The	U	I	250+	Reading Expeditions	National Geographic
Agency, The: A Spy in the House	Z	HF	250+	Lee, Y. S.	Candlewick Press
Agent for the Stars	W	RF	2986	Leveled Readers	Houghton Mifflin Harcourt
Agent for the Stars	W	RF	2986	Leveled Readers/CA	Houghton Mifflin Harcourt
Agent for the Stars	W	RF	2986	Leveled Readers/TX	Houghton Mifflin Harcourt
#Agent Mongoose and the Attack of the Giant Insects	U	F	250+	Twisted Journeys	Graphic Universe
#Agent Mongoose and the Beam Scheme	U	F	11377	Twisted Journeys	Graphic Universe

* Collection of short stories   # Graphic text
^ Mature content with lower level text demands

TITLE	LEVEL	GENRE	WORD COUNT	AUTHOR / SERIES	PUBLISHER / DISTRIBUTOR
*Aggie and Ben: Three Stories	J	RF	250+	Ries, Lori	Charlesbridge
Aggressive In-Line Skating	M	I	250+	To the Extreme	Capstone Press
Aggressive In-Line Skating	R	I	250+	X-Sports	Capstone Press
Agnes Macphail: Canada's Champion of the Poor	U	B	2412	Independent Readers Social Studies	Houghton Mifflin Harcourt
Agnes Parker... Girl in Progress	T	RF	250+	O'Dell, Kathleen	Puffin Books
Agnes the Sheep	R	F	250+	Taylor, William	Bantam Books
Agua, Agua, Agua	H	TL	94	Little Celebrations	Pearson Learning Group
Ah Liang's Gift	J	RF	352	Sunshine	Wright Group/McGraw Hill
Ah, Treasure	F	F	19	Voyages	SRA/McGraw Hill
AH-64 Apache Helicopter, The	U	I	250+	Cross-Sections	Capstone Press
Ah-choo!	J	RF	291	Samuels, Aurora	Sadlier-Oxford
Ahyoka and the Talking Leaves	S	HF	250+	Roop, Peter & Connie	Beech Tree Books
Aim High: Astronaut Training	S	I	1227	Reading Street	Pearson
Aimee	Z+	RF	250+	Miller, Mary Beth	Penguin Group
Air and Weather: Where'd My Hat Go?	O	I	1200	iScience	Norwood House Press
Air Disasters	W	I	7870	Disasters Up Close	Lerner Publishing Group
Air Raid - Pearl Harbor!: The Story of December 7, 1941	Z	I	250+	Taylor, Theodore	Scholastic
Air Show Jets	W	I	5063	Motor Mania	Lerner Publishing Group
Air Sports	O	I	250+	Labrecque, Ellen/Extreme Sports	Raintree
Air: A Resource Our World Depends On	V	I	250+	Managing Our Resources	Heinemann
Air: Earth Matters	L	I	250+	Bookworms	Marshall Cavendish
Air: Outside, Inside, and All Around	M	I	250+	Amazing Science	Picture Window Books
Airball: My Life in Briefs	R	RF	250+	Harkrader, L.D.	Square Fish
Airborne	X	I	250+	iOpeners	Pearson Learning Group
Aircraft Adventures	O	I	250+	Tristars	Richard C. Owen
Aircraft Carriers	T	I	250+	Land and Sea	Capstone Press
Aircraft Carriers	G	I	124	Mighty Machines	Capstone Press
Aircraft Carriers	V	I	4961	Military Hardware in Action	Lerner Publishing Group
Aircraft Carriers	N	I	414	Pull Ahead Books	Lerner Publishing Group
^Aircraft Carriers: The Nimitz Class	T	I	250+	War Machines	Capstone Press
Airedale Terriers	I	I	118	Dogs	Capstone Press
^Airmen of the U.S. Airforce	N	I	170	People of the U.S. Armed Forces	Capstone Press
#Airplane Adventure	K	RF	250+	My 1st Graphic Novel	Stone Arch Books
Airplane Adventures	S	I	250+	Dangerous Adventures	Red Brick Learning
Airplane, The	P	I	250+	Great Inventions	Red Brick Learning
Airplane, The	B	RF	21	Sunshine	Wright Group/McGraw Hill
Airplane, The	T	I	250+	Tales of Invention	Heinemann Library
Airplanes	F	I	60	Pebble Books	Capstone Press
Airplanes	M	I	250+	Transportation	Compass Point Books
Airplanes and Ships You Can Draw	R	I	1693	Ready, Set, Draw!	Millbrook Press
Airport	I	I	116	Barton, Byron	HarperCollins
Airport, The	B	I	42	Leveled Readers Language Support	Houghton Mifflin Harcourt
Ajeemah and His Son	S	HF	250+	Berry, James	HarperTrophy
Akimbo and the Baboons	P	RF	250+	McCall Smith, Alexander	Bloomsbury Children's Books
Akimbo and the Crocodile Man	P	RF	250+	McCall Smith, Alexander	Bloomsbury Children's Books
Akimbo and the Elephants	P	RF	250+	McCall Smith, Alexander	Bloomsbury Children's Books
Akimbo and the Lions	P	RF	250+	McCall Smith, Alexander	Bloomsbury Children's Books

TITLE	LEVEL	GENRE	WORD COUNT	AUTHOR / SERIES	PUBLISHER / DISTRIBUTOR
Akimbo and the Snakes	P	RF	250+	McCall Smith, Alexander	Bloomsbury Children's Books
*Akira to Zoltan: Twenty-Six Men Who Changed the World	S	B	250+	Chin-Lee, Cynthia	Charlesbridge
Aki's Special Gift	H	RF	240	Leveled Readers Language Support	Houghton Mifflin Harcourt
Aksum: Heart of Ancient Ethiopia	X	I	2568	Independent Readers Social Studies	Houghton Mifflin Harcourt
Al Capone Does My Shirts	X	HF	250+	Choldenko, Gennifer	Puffin Books
Al Capone Shines My Shoes	X	HF	250+	Choldenko, Gennifer	Penguin Group
Al Gore: Fighting For a Greener Planet	U	B	6336	Gateway Biographies	Lerner Publishing Group
Al Kalifa and the Nile	R	HF	250+	Bookweb	Rigby
Alabama	T	I	250+	Hello U.S.A.	Lerner Publishing Group
Alabama	S	I	250+	Land of Liberty	Red Brick Learning
Alabama	R	I	250+	This Land Is Your Land	Compass Point Books
Alabama Moon	W	RF	250+	Key, Watt	Square Fish
Alabama: Facts and Symbols	O	I	250+	The States and Their Symbols	Capstone Press
Aladdin & the Magic Lamp	J	TL	851	Traditional Tales	Pearson Learning Group
Aladdin and the Enchanted Lamp	T	TL	5240	Oxford Bookworms Library	Oxford University Press
Alamo Journals, The	T	HF	250+	Power Up!	Steck-Vaughn
Alamo Wars	W	RF	250+	Villareal Ray	Pinata Publishing
Alamo, The	P	I	554	Lightning Bolt Books	Lerner Publishing Group
Alamo, The	P	I	673	Pull Ahead Books	Lerner Publishing Group
Alas My Albatross Is Molting	T	I	250+	Literacy 2000	Rigby
Alaska	T	I	250+	Hello U.S.A.	Lerner Publishing Group
Alaska	S	I	250+	Land of Liberty	Red Brick Learning
Alaska	R	I	250+	This Land Is Your Land	Compass Point Books
Alaska	O	I	250+	Windows on Literacy	National Geographic
Alaska Natives	T	I	1390	Vocabulary Readers	Houghton Mifflin Harcourt
Alaska: Facts and Symbols	O	I	250+	The States and Their Symbols	Capstone Press
Alaska's Natives	T	I	1390	Vocabulary Readers/CA	Houghton Mifflin Harcourt
Alaska's Natives	T	I	1390	Vocabulary Readers/TX	Houghton Mifflin Harcourt
Alaska's Natural Resources	X	I	2811	Vocabulary Readers	Houghton Mifflin Harcourt
Alaska's Natural Resources	X	I	2811	Vocabulary Readers/CA	Houghton Mifflin Harcourt
Albatross, the Survivor	Q	I	250+	Sails	Rigby
Albert Einstein	P	B	250+	Early Biographies	Compass Point Books
Albert Einstein	N	B	189	First Biographies	Capstone Press
Albert Einstein	R	B	250+	Getting to Know the World's Greatest Inventors and Scientists	Children's Press
Albert Einstein	R	B	3418	History Maker Bios	Lerner Publishing Group
Albert Einstein and His Theory of Relativity	X	B	250+	Mission: Science	Compass Point Books
Albert Einstein: A Biography	T	B	250+	Meltzer, Milton	Holiday House
Albert Einstein: Gentle Genuis	Y	B	250+	Science Readers	Teacher Created Materials
Albert the Albatross	I	F	191	Hoff, Syd	HarperCollins
Albert the Fix-It Man	L	RF	250+	Lord, Janet	Peachtree
Albert's Raccoon	K	F	250+	I Am Reading	Kingfisher
Albie's Secret	P	F	250+	Scooters	ETA/Cuisenaire
Alcatraz	V	I	250+	Cornerstones of Freedom	Children's Press
Alchemy and Meggy Swann	X	HF	250+	Cushman, Karen	Clarion Books
Alchemyst, The: The Secrets of the Immortal Nicholas Flamel	X	F	250+	Scott, Michael	Delacorte Press
Aldo and Abby	I	RF	235	Leveled Readers	Houghton Mifflin Harcourt
Aldo and Abby	I	RF	235	Leveled Readers/CA	Houghton Mifflin Harcourt
Aldo and Abby	I	RF	235	Leveled Readers/TX	Houghton Mifflin Harcourt
Aldo Applesauce	O	RF	250+	Hurwitz, Johanna	Morrow Junior Books

* Collection of short stories   # Graphic text
^ Mature content with lower level text demands

TITLE	LEVEL	GENRE	WORD COUNT	AUTHOR / SERIES	PUBLISHER / DISTRIBUTOR
Aldo Ice Cream	O	RF	250+	Hurwitz, Johanna	Penguin Group
Aldo Peanut Butter	O	RF	250+	Hurwitz, Johanna	Penguin Group
Aleutian Islands, The	M	I	586	Gear Up!	Wright Group/McGraw Hill
Alex and the Ironic Gentleman	Y	F	250+	Kress, Adrienne	Weinstein Books
Alex Ovechkin	P	B	1924	Savage, Jeff/Amazing Athletes	Lerner Publishing Group
Alex Rodriguez	P	B	1965	Amazing Athletes	Lerner Publishing Group
Alex Rodriguez	T	B	250+	Sports Heroes	Red Brick Learning
Alex Rodriguez	U	B	250+	Sports Heroes and Legends	Lerner Publishing Group
Alex Rodriguez: Revised Edition	P	B	1898	Amazing Atheltes	Lerner Publishing Group
Alexander and the Stallion	M	HF	434	Books for Young Learners	Richard C. Owen
Alexander and the Terrible, Horrible, No Good, Very Bad Day	M	RF	250+	Viorst, Judith	Scholastic
Alexander and the Wind-Up Mouse	L	F	250+	Lionni, Leo	Scholastic
Alexander Ant Cools Off	F	F	76	Little Books	Sadlier-Oxford
Alexander Anteater's Amazing Act	K	F	724	Animal Antics A To Z	Kane Press
Alexander Graham Bell	Q	B	250+	Early Biographies	Compass Point Books
Alexander Graham Bell	N	B	250+	First Biographies	Red Brick Learning
Alexander Graham Bell	R	B	250+	Getting to Know the World's Greatest Inventors and Scientists	Children's Press
Alexander Graham Bell	R	B	3866	History Maker Bios	Lerner Publishing Group
Alexander Graham Bell	K	B	412	Leveled Readers	Houghton Mifflin Harcourt
Alexander Graham Bell	K	B	412	Leveled Readers/CA	Houghton Mifflin Harcourt
Alexander Graham Bell	K	B	412	Leveled Readers/TX	Houghton Mifflin Harcourt
Alexander Graham Bell	N	B	1890	On My Own Biography	Lerner Publishing Group
Alexander Graham Bell	P	B	250+	Photo-Illustrated Biographies	Red Brick Learning
Alexander Graham Bell	M	B	250+	Rosen Real Readers	Rosen Publishing Group
Alexander Graham Bell	X	B	250+	The Canadians	Fitzhenry & Whiteside
#Alexander Graham Bell and the Telephone	T	B	250+	Inventions and Discovery	Capstone Press
Alexander Graham Bell and the Telephone	P	B	250+	Windows on Literacy	National Geographic
Alexander Graham Bell, Teacher of the Deaf	Q	F	1930	Reading Street	Pearson
Alexander Graham Bell: A Life of Helpfulness	N	B	354	Pull Ahead Books	Lerner Publishing Group
Alexander Graham Bell: An Inventive Life	U	B	250+	MacLeod, Elizabeth	Kids Can Press
Alexander Graham Bell: Inventor of the Telephone	S	B	250+	Time For Kids Biographies	HarperCollins
^Alexander Graham Bell: The Inventor Who Changed the World	R	B	250+	Hameray Biography Series	Hameray Publishing Group
Alexander Hamilton	V	B	250+	Amazing Americans	Wright Group/McGraw Hill
Alexander the Great	W	B	250+	Demi	Marshall Cavendish
Alexander the Great	V	B	1355	Leveled Readers	Houghton Mifflin Harcourt
Alexander the Great	V	B	1355	Leveled Readers/CA	Houghton Mifflin Harcourt
Alexander the Great	V	B	1355	Leveled Readers/TX	Houghton Mifflin Harcourt
Alexander the Great	W	B	250+	Navigators Social Studies Series	Benchmark Education
Alexander, Who's Not (Do you hear me? I mean it!) Going to Move	M	RF	250+	Viorst, Judith	Scholastic
Alf	WB	RF	0	The Rowland Reading Program Library	Rowland Reading Foundation
Alfie the Apostrophe	N	F	250+	Donohue, Moira Rose	Scholastic
Alfie's Gift	L	F	250+	Literacy 2000	Rigby
Alfred	F	RF	54	Voyages	SRA/McGraw Hill
Alfred Kropp: The Seal of Solomon	Z+	F	250+	Yancey, Rick	Bloomsbury Children's Books
Alfred Kropp: The Thirteenth Skull	Z+	F	250+	Yancey, Rick	Bloomsbury Children's Books
Alfred the Curious	O	RF	250+	PM Collection	Rigby
Alfred Wegener: Uncovering Plate Tectonics	U	B	250+	Science Readers	Teacher Created Materials

A

TITLE	LEVEL	GENRE	WORD COUNT	AUTHOR / SERIES	PUBLISHER / DISTRIBUTOR
Alfred Wegner: Pioneer of Plate Tectonics	V	B	250+	Mission Science	Compass Point Books
Algonquin, The	V	I	3436	Leveled Readers Social Studies	Houghton Mifflin Harcourt
Ali Baba Bernstein, Lost and Found	O	RF	250+	Hurwitz, Johanna	Penguin Group
#Ali Baba: Fooling the Forty Thieves	U	TL	3643	Graphic Myths and Legends	Lerner Publishing Group
Ali, Hassan and the Donkey	I	TL	250+	Storyworlds	Heinemann
Alice in Rapture: Sort of	W	RF	250+	Naylor, Phyllis Reynolds	Aladdin
Alice in Wonderland	V	F	250+	Carroll, Lewis	Scholastic
Alice Ray and the Salem Witch Trials	T	HF	4471	History Speaks	Millbrook Press
Alice the Brave	Z	RF	250+	Naylor, Phyllis Reynolds	Aladdin
Alice the Tennis Fairy: Rainbow Magic	L	F	250+	Meadows, Daisy	Scholastic
Alice: Alice Alone	Z	RF	250+	Naylor, Phyllis Reynolds	Simon & Schuster
Alice's Adventures in Wonderland	S	F	6315	Oxford Bookworms Library	Oxford University Press
Alice's Diary, Living With Diabetes	S	I	250+	Gibson, Marie/Orbit Chapter Books	Pacific Learning
Alice's Funny Photo	L	RF	869	Sun Sprouts	ETA/Cuisenaire
Alicia: The Clique Summer Collection	X	RF	250+	Harrison, Lisi	Little Brown and Company
Alida's Song	Y	RF	250+	Paulsen, Gary	Random House
^Alien Abduction	R	SF	1694	Zucker, Jonny	Stone Arch Books
^Alien Abductions: The Unsolved Mystery	R	I	250+	Mysteries of Science	Capstone Press
Alien at the Zoo	E	F	85	Sunshine	Wright Group/McGraw Hill
Alien Attack - Rex Jones	P	SF	1706	Zucker, Jonny	Stone Arch Books
Alien Expedition: Alien Agent	T	SF	20052	Service, Pamela F.	Carolrhoda Books
Alien Feast	T	F	250+	Simmons, Michael	Roaring Brook Press
^Alien Implants	V	SF	250+	The Extraordinary Files	Hameray Publishing Group
Alien in the Classroom	N	F	250+	Keene, Carolyn	Pocket Books
#Alien Incident on Planet J	U	F	10827	Twisted Journeys	Graphic Universe
Alien Plant and Animal Invaders	V	I	3318	Leveled Readers Science	Houghton Mifflin Harcourt
Alien Secrets	X	F	250+	Klause, Annette Curtis	Laurel-Leaf Books
Alien Vacation	F	F	105	Instant Readers	Harcourt School Publishers
Alien Visitors and Abductions	Z	I	250+	Unsolved Mysteries	Steck-Vaughn
Alien, The	H	F	177	Windmill Books	Rigby
Alien, the Giant, and Rocketman, The	Q	RF	250+	Bookshop	Mondo Publishing
Aliens	H	RF	232	Sails	Rigby
Aliens	Z	I	3842	The Unexplained	Lerner Publishing Group
Aliens are Coming!, The	O	F	250+	McNaughton, Colin	Candlewick Press
Aliens Ate My Homework	Q	F	250+	Coville, Bruce	Pocket Books
Aliens Don't Wear Braces	M	F	250+	Dadey, Debbie; Jones, Marcia Thornton	Scholastic
Aliens for Breakfast	M	F	250+	Etra, Jonathan; Spinner, Stephanie	Random House
Aliens for Dinner	M	F	250+	Spinner, Stephanie	Random House
Aliens for Lunch	M	F	250+	Spinner, Stephanie; Etra, Jonathan	Random House
Aliens from Earth: When Animals and Plants Invade Other Ecosystems	R	I	250+	Batten, Mary	Peachtree
Aliens on the Lawn	H	F	175	Windmill Books	Rigby
Ali's Story	H	RF	236	Sunshine	Wright Group/McGraw Hill
Alison Wendlebury	J	RF	250+	Literacy 2000	Rigby
Alison's Puppy	K	RF	250+	Bauer, Marion Dane	Hyperion
Alison's Wings	K	RF	250+	Bauer, Marion Dane	Hyperion
A-List, The	Z+	RF	250+	Dean, Zoey	Little Brown and Company
All Aboard	K	RF	250+	Math Matters	Kane Press
All Aboard!	O	I	696	Red Rocket Readers	Flying Start Books
All Aboard!: Trains and Texas	S	I	250+	Literacy By Design	Rigby
All Aboard!: Trains and Texas	S	I	250+	On Our Way to English	Rigby

* Collection of short stories   # Graphic text
^ Mature content with lower level text demands

TITLE	LEVEL	GENRE	WORD COUNT	AUTHOR / SERIES	PUBLISHER / DISTRIBUTOR
All About African Elephants	K	I	326	Leveled Literacy Intervention/ Blue System	Heinemann
All About Alligators	Q	I	250+	Arnosky, Jim	Scholastic
All About Animal Babies	F	I	135	Leveled Literacy Intervention/ Green System	Heinemann
All About Ants	H	I	214	Rosen Real Readers	Rosen Publishing Group
All About Apples	E	I	35	Rosen Real Readers	Rosen Publishing Group
All About Arthropods	U	I	250+	Orbit Chapter Books	Pacific Learning
All About Astronauts	N	I	580	Leveled Literacy Intervention/ Blue System	Heinemann
All About Bats	J	I	354	Leveled Literacy Intervention/ Blue System	Heinemann
All About Bats	J	I	296	Leveled Readers	Houghton Mifflin Harcourt
All About Bats	J	I	296	Leveled Readers/CA	Houghton Mifflin Harcourt
All About Bats	J	I	296	Leveled Readers/TX	Houghton Mifflin Harcourt
All About Bats	J	I	250+	Ready Readers	Modern Curriculum
All About Bears	N	I	250+	Voyages	SRA/McGraw Hill
All About Bicycles	L	I	250+	Sunshine	Wright Group/McGraw Hill
All About Bikes	O	I	250+	iOpeners	Pearson Learning Group
All About Boats	H	I	199	Leveled Literacy Intervention/ Green System	Heinemann
All About Bugs	F	I	143	Leveled Literacy Intervention/ Blue System	Heinemann
All About Cars	M	I	250+	Trackers	Pacific Learning
All About Cats and Kittens	N	I	250+	Neye, Emily	Grosset & Dunlap
All About Chile	K	I	271	Vocabulary Readers	Houghton Mifflin Harcourt
All About Chile	K	I	271	Vocabulary Readers/CA	Houghton Mifflin Harcourt
All About Chile	K	I	271	Vocabulary Readers/TX	Houghton Mifflin Harcourt
All About Chimps	H	I	218	Leveled Literacy Intervention/ Green System	Heinemann
All About Chocolate	M	I	479	Time for Kids	Teacher Created Materials
All About Codes	Q	I	250+	Riley, Gail Blasser	Steck-Vaughn
All About Continents	N	I	575	Early Explorers	Benchmark Education
All About Danny	A	RF	33	Coulton, Mia	Maryruth Books
All About Deer	Q	I	250+	Arnosky, Jim	Scholastic
All About Dinosaurs	I	I	215	Leveled Literacy Intervention/ Blue System	Heinemann
All About Dinosaurs	C	I	34	Teacher's Choice Series	Pearson Learning Group
All About Dogs	K	I	357	Larkin, Bruce	Wilbooks
All About Dogs	L	I	551	Springboard	Wright Group/McGraw Hill
All About Dolphins	J	I	242	Leveled Literacy Intervention/ Green System	Heinemann
All About Drums	M	I	250+	Rosen Real Readers	Rosen Publishing Group
All About Eggs	P	I	250+	Sunshine	Wright Group/McGraw Hill
All About Energy	W	I	250+	Science Readers	Teacher Created Materials
All About Fireflies	L	I	319	Leveled Readers	Houghton Mifflin Harcourt
All About Fireflies	L	I	319	Leveled Readers/CA	Houghton Mifflin Harcourt
All About Fireflies	L	I	319	Leveled Readers/TX	Houghton Mifflin Harcourt
All About Frogs	Q	I	250+	Arnosky, Jim	Scholastic
All About Glass	N	I	250+	InfoTrek Plus	ETA/Cuisenaire
All About Glass	K	I	358	Red Rocket Readers	Flying Start Books
All About Grass	K	I	522	Vocabulary Readers/TX	Houghton Mifflin Harcourt
All About Hair	M	I	250+	Rigby Rocket	Rigby
All About Hair	S	I	250+	Take Two Books	Wright Group/McGraw Hill
All About Hamsters	R	I	1710	Vocabulary Readers	Houghton Mifflin Harcourt
All About Hamsters	R	I	1710	Vocabulary Readers/CA	Houghton Mifflin Harcourt

TITLE	LEVEL	GENRE	WORD COUNT	AUTHOR / SERIES	PUBLISHER / DISTRIBUTOR
All About Hand-Blown Glass	N	I	454	Time for Kids	Teacher Created Materials
All About Honeybees	I	I	194	Leveled Literacy Intervention/ Green System	Heinemann
All About Honeybees	M	I	571	Nonfiction Crimson	Pioneer Valley
All About Killer Whales	M	I	341	Larkin's Little Readers	Wilbooks
All About Light and Sound	W	I	250+	Science Readers	Teacher Created Materials
All About Manatees	Q	I	250+	Arnosky, Jim	Scholastic
All About Me	L	I	250+	iOpeners	Pearson Learning Group
All About Me	A	RF	32	Literacy by Design	Rigby
All About Me!	E	I	107	Factivity Series	Pearson Learning Group
All About Me!	J	RF	250+	Pacific Literacy	Pacific Learning
All About Meat	K	I	367	Springboard	Wright Group/McGraw Hill
All About Mechanical Engineering	Y	I	250+	Science Readers	Teacher Created Materials
All About Mice	K	I	675	Vocabulary Readers	Houghton Mifflin Harcourt
All About Mice	K	I	548	Vocabulary Readers/CA	Houghton Mifflin Harcourt
All About Mice	K	I	548	Vocabulary Readers/TX	Houghton Mifflin Harcourt
All About Miss Miller	H	RF	168	InfoTrek	ETA/Cuisenaire
All About Mitosis and Meiosis	Z	I	250+	Science Readers	Teacher Created Materials
All About Money	O	I	250+	Let's See	Compass Point Books
All About New Hampshire	O	I	234	Larkin, Bruce	Wilbooks
All About Owls	Q	I	250+	Arnosky, Jim	Scholastic
All About Panda Bears	L	I	323	Larkin's Little Readers	Wilbooks
All About Penguins	C	I	97	Leveled Literacy Intervention/ Blue System	Heinemann
All About Pine Trees	L	I	822	Leveled Readers/TX	Houghton Mifflin Harcourt
All About Pirates	L	I	250+	Trackers	Pacific Learning
All About Plants	L	I	250+	Home Connection Collection	Rigby
All About Potbellied Pigs	M	I	250+	Rigby Literacy	Rigby
All About Rattlesnakes	Q	I	250+	Aronsky, Jim	Scholastic
All About Redwood Trees	I	I	226	Leveled Literacy Intervention/ Blue System	Heinemann
All About Robots!	K	I	280	Leveled Literacy Intervention/ Blue System	Heinemann
All About Sam	Q	RF	250+	Lowry, Lois	Bantam Books
All About Schools	V	I	2084	Reading Street	Pearson
All About Seeds	Q	I	250+	Berger, Melvin	Scholastic
All About Sharks	Q	I	250+	Arnosky, Jim	Scholastic
All About Sharks	F	I	130	Leveled Literacy Intervention/ Blue System	Heinemann
All About Skyscrapers	M	I	492	Time for Kids	Teacher Created Materials
All About Sled Dogs	H	I	185	Leveled Literacy Intervention/ Blue System	Heinemann
All About Snakes	J	I	467	Gear Up!	Wright Group/McGraw Hill
All About Snakes	L	I	214	Larkin, Bruce	Wilbooks
All About Snakes	C	I	100	Leveled Literacy Intervention/ Blue System	Heinemann
All About Soccer	J	I	239	Nonfiction Set 7	Literacy Footprints
All About Spiders	H	I	146	Leveled Literacy Intervention/ Blue System	Heinemann
All About Stacy	L	RF	250+	Giff, Patricia Reilly	Bantam Books
All About Teeth	H	I	154	Healthy Teeth	Capstone Press
All About Temperature	L	I	176	Physical Science	Capstone Press
All About the Sonoran Desert	J	I	295	Leveled Literacy Intervention/ Blue System	Heinemann
All About Things People Do	K	I	250+	Rice, Melanie & Chris	Scholastic
All About Trees	H	I	177	Early Explorers	Benchmark Education

* Collection of short stories   # Graphic text
^ Mature content with lower level text demands

TITLE	LEVEL	GENRE	WORD COUNT	AUTHOR / SERIES	PUBLISHER / DISTRIBUTOR
All About Turkeys	Q	I	250+	Arnosky, Jim	Scholastic
All About Turtles	Q	I	250+	Arnosky, Jim	Scholastic
All About Volcanoes	N	I	557	Leveled Literacy Intervention/ Blue System	Heinemann
All About You	G	I	250+	Anholt, Catherine & Laurence	Scholastic
All Across America	N	I	293	Avenues	Hampton Brown
All Alone in the Universe	S	RF	250+	Perkins, Lynne Rae	Greenwillow Books
All Along the River	L	I	250+	Rookie Read About Science	Children's Press
All American Girl	Y	RF	250+	Cabot, Meg	HarperCollins
All Around Me I See	H	F	138	Steinberg, Laya	Dawn Publications
All Around Our Country	E	I	112	Hutchins, Jeannie	Scholastic
All Around Texas	O	I	177	Larkin, Bruce	Wilbooks
All Around the Cake	G	RF	159	InfoTrek	ETA/Cuisenaire
All Around the Seasons	J	I	223	Saltzberg, Barney	Candlewick Press
All Around the United States: A Travel Adventure	R	RF	250+	Pair-It Books	Steck-Vaughn
All Because of a Cup of Coffee	O	F	250+	Stilton, Geronimo	Scholastic
All But Alice	Z	RF	250+	Naylor, Phyllis Reynolds	Dell
All by Myself	H	RF	215	Cambridge Reading	Pearson Learning Group
All By Myself	E	RF	105	Foundations	Wright Group/McGraw Hill
All By Myself	E	F	157	Mayer, Mercer	Golden
All By Myself	F	F	150	Red Rocket Readers	Flying Start Books
All By Myself	E	I	60	Shutterbug Books	Steck-Vaughn
All Charged Up!	R	I	250+	On Our Way to English	Rigby
All Charged Up: A Look at Electricity	P	I	250+	Lightning Bolt Books	Lerner Publishing Group
All Clean	F	F	163	Sails	Rigby
All Creatures Great and Small	Z+	RF	250+	Herriot, James	St. Martin's Press
All Dressed Up	B	RF	38	Visions	Wright Group/McGraw Hill
All Dressed Up	H	RF	137	Voyages	SRA/McGraw Hill
All Fall Down	B	F	23	Instant Readers	Harcourt School Publishers
All Fall Down	B	F	23	Rigby Rocket	Rigby
All Fall Down	L	I	206	Spyglass Books	Compass Point Books
All Fall Down	C	F	72	Wildsmith, Brian	Oxford University Press
All for Pie, Pie for All	H	F	251	Martin, David	Candlewick Press
All for the Better: A Story of El Barrio	R	B	250+	Mohr, Nicholasa	Steck-Vaughn
All From a Bottle	N	F	250+	Phonics and Friends	Hampton Brown
*All Hallows' Eve: 13 Stories	Y	F	250+	Velde, Vivian Vande	Houghton Mifflin Harcourt
All I Did	E	RF	83	Instant Readers	Harcourt School Publishers
All I Want Is Everything: Gossip Girl	Z+	RF	250+	von Ziegesar, Cecily	Little Brown and Company
All in a Day	D	RF	78	Reading Street	Pearson
All in a Day	N	RF	194	Rylant, Cynthia	Harry N. Abrams
All in One Hour	K	TL	258	Crummel, Susan Stevens	Marshall Cavendish
All in the Family	W	I	250+	InfoQuest	Rigby
All Is Well	R	HF	250+	Litchman, Kristin Embry	Bantam Books
All Join In	D	F	38	Literacy 2000	Rigby
All Kinds of Animals	O	I	250+	It's Science	Children's Press
All Kinds of Babies	B	I	71	Literacy by Design	Rigby
All Kinds of Babies	B	I	71	On Our Way to English	Rigby
All Kinds of Books	E	I	77	Canizares, Susan; Chessen, Betsey	Scholastic
All Kinds of Clothes	I	I	395	Red Rocket Readers	Flying Start Books
All Kinds of Clothes	F	I	120	Yellow Umbrella Books	Red Brick Learning
All Kinds of Eyes	L	I	250+	Discovery World	Rigby
All Kinds of Eyes	I	I	128	Pacific Literacy	Pacific Learning

TITLE	LEVEL	GENRE	WORD COUNT	AUTHOR / SERIES	PUBLISHER / DISTRIBUTOR
All Kinds of Families	E	I	86	Reading Street	Pearson
All Kinds of Families!	L	I	250+	Hoberman, Mary Ann	Little Brown and Company
All Kinds of Family	LB	I	12	Reach	National Geographic
All Kinds of Farms	G	I	146	Yellow Umbrella Books	Red Brick Learning
All Kinds of Fish	D	F	37	Instant Readers	Harcourt School Publishers
All Kinds of Flowers	L	I	250+	Turner, Teresa	Steck-Vaughn
All Kinds of Food	D	RF	72	Carousel Readers	Pearson Learning Group
All Kinds of Food	D	I	72	Learn to Read	Creative Teaching Press
All Kinds of Homes	G	RF	116	Reading Street	Pearson
All Kinds of Jobs	WB	I	0	Reach	National Geographic
All Kinds of Kids	D	I	88	Rookie Readers	Children's Press
All Kinds of Maps	N	I	163	Windows on Literacy	National Geographic
All Kinds of Motion	K	I	193	Physical Science	Capstone Press
All Kinds of Museums	N	I	250+	Sunshine	Wright Group/McGraw Hill
All Kinds of People: What Makes Us Different	J	I	250+	Spyglass Books	Compass Point Books
All Kinds of Rocks	G	RF	136	Instant Readers	Harcourt School Publishers
All Kinds of Shoes	B	I	63	Little Readers	Houghton Mifflin Harcourt
All Kinds of Things	B	I	24	Pacific Literacy	Pacific Learning
All Kinds of Wheels	E	I	76	Pair-It Books	Steck-Vaughn
All Made Up	K	I	250+	InfoTrek Plus	ETA/Cuisenaire
All Mixed Up	G	F	105	Little Books	Sadlier-Oxford
All Night Long	E	RF	65	Visions	Wright Group/McGraw Hill
All of Me	B	RF	25	Literacy 2000	Rigby
All of the Above	U	RF	250+	Pearsall, Shelley	Scholastic
All or Nothing	L	TL	786	Rigby Flying Colors	Rigby
All Over Me!	LB	RF	24	Pair-It Books	Steck-Vaughn
All Over the World	E	RF	82	Jones, D.	Continental Press
All Pigs Are Beautiful	N	I	250+	King-Smith, Dick	Candlewick Press
All Pull Together	D	F	69	Home Connection Collection	Rigby
All Roads Lead to Rome	T	I	250+	WorldScapes	ETA/Cuisenaire
All the Colors of the World	H	I	160	Gear Up!	Wright Group/McGraw Hill
All the Lovely Bad Ones	W	F	250+	Hahn, Mary Downing	Houghton Mifflin Harcourt
All the Seasons of the Year	L	F	250+	Rose, Deborah Lee	Harry N. Abrams
All the World Loves a Puppet	P	I	250+	Lighthouse	Ginn & Co.
All the World's a Stage	O	I	250+	Literacy Tree	Rigby
All Through the Week with Cat and Dog	C	F	91	Learn to Read	Creative Teaching Press
All Through the Year	F	I	261	Visions	Wright Group/McGraw Hill
All Tied Up	S	I	250+	WorldScapes	ETA/Cuisenaire
All Together Now	J	F	250+	Jeram, Anita	Candlewick Press
All Tutus Should Be Pink	I	RF	243	Brownrigg, Sheri	Scholastic
All Wet!	B	I	28	Ready Readers	Pearson Learning Group
Allen Jay and the Underground Railroad	O	HF	250+	On My Own History	Carolrhoda Books
Allen Say, Writer and Artist	K	B	219	Leveled Readers Social Studies	Houghton Mifflin Harcourt
Alley Cat	C	RF	30	Books for Young Learners	Richard C. Owen
Alley of Shadows	T	F	250+	Brezenoff, Steve	Stone Arch Books
Allie Alligator Goes Shoe Shopping	D	F	77	Springboard	Wright Group/McGraw Hill
Allie Alligator Goes to See the King	G	F	305	Springboard	Wright Group/McGraw Hill
Allie Alligator's Adventure	I	F	435	Springboard	Wright Group/McGraw Hill
Allie Alligator's Knitting	H	F	339	Springboard	Wright Group/McGraw Hill
Allie Visits Crystal River	L	F	831	Springboard	Wright Group/McGraw Hill
Allie's Basketball Dream	K	RF	250+	Barber, Barbara E.; Ligasan, Darryl	Scholastic
Allie's Basketball Dream	K	RF	250+	Soar To Success	Houghton Mifflin Harcourt
Allies of the Night: The Saga of Darren Shan	Y	F	250+	Shan, Darren	Little Brown and Company

* Collection of short stories   # Graphic text
^ Mature content with lower level text demands

TITLE	LEVEL	GENRE	WORD COUNT	AUTHOR / SERIES	PUBLISHER / DISTRIBUTOR
Alligator Alley	M	RF	250+	Woodland Mysteries	Wright Group/McGraw Hill
Alligator Ann	B	F	15	Reading Street	Pearson
Alligator Baby	L	F	250+	Munsch, Robert	Scholastic
Alligator in the Bathtub	N	F	628	Leveled Readers	Houghton Mifflin Harcourt
Alligator Mouse and Other Disasters	K	F	250+	Voyages	SRA/McGraw Hill
Alligator Shoes	G	F	122	Dorros, Arthur	Dutton Children's Books
*Alligator Tails and Crocodile Cakes	J	F	250+	I Am Reading	Kingfisher
*Alligator Tails and Crocodile Cakes	J	F	250+	Storyteller-Shooting Stars	Wright Group/McGraw Hill
Alligator Wedding	N	F	250+	Jewell, Nancy	Henry Holt & Co.
Alligator, The	M	I	250+	Crewe, Sabrina	Steck-Vaughn
Alligators	O	I	1623	Early Bird Nature Books	Lerner Publishing Group
Alligators	J	I	140	Readlings	American Reading Company
Alligators	N	I	250+	World of Reptiles	Capstone Press
Alligators & Crocodiles	U	I	250+	The Untamed World	Steck-Vaughn
Alligators All Around	LB	F	59	Sendak, Maurice	HarperCollins
Alligators to Zebras	J	I	273	Springboard	Wright Group/McGraw Hill
All-of-a-Kind Family	Q	RF	250+	Taylor, Sydney	Bantam Books
Allosaurus	I	I	130	Dinosaur and Prehistoric Animals	Capstone Press
Allosaurus	N	I	250+	Discovering Dinosaurs	Capstone Press
All-Pro Biographies: Dan Marino	P	B	250+	Stewart, Mark	Children's Press
All-Pro Biographies: Gwen Torrence	P	B	250+	Stewart, Mark	Children's Press
All's Well That Ends Well	P	TL	250+	Storyteller-Autumn Leaves	Wright Group/McGraw Hill
All-Star Fever	M	RF	250+	Christopher, Matt	Little Brown and Company
^All-Star Pride	W	RF	250+	Orca Sports	Orca Books
Alma Flor Ada, Storyteller	F	B	75	Leveled Readers Language Support	Houghton Mifflin Harcourt
Alma Flor Ada: From a Family of Storytellers	G	B	75	Leveled Readers	Houghton Mifflin Harcourt
*Almost Astronauts: 13 Women Who Dared to Dream	Y	B	250+	Stone, Tanya Lee	Candlewick Press
Almost Home	T	RF	250+	Baskin, Nora Raleigh	Little Brown and Company
Almost Starring Skinnybones	O	RF	250+	Park, Barbara	Random House
Almost to Freedom	R	F	1782	Nelson, Vaunda Micheaux	Carolrhoda Books
*Almost Undone	T	RF	250+	Bookshop	Mondo Publishing
Alone and Together	H	RF	292	Early Connections	Benchmark Education
Alone at Recess	E	RF	136	The King School Series	Townsend Press
Alone in the Desert	T	I	250+	Drew, David	Rigby
Alone in the Storm	R	RF	250+	Leveled Readers Language Support	Houghton Mifflin Harcourt
Alone in the Wilderness!: Brennan Hawkins' Story of Survival	R	I	250+	True Tales of Survival	Capstone Press
Along Came a Spider	J	I	257	Vocabulary Readers	Houghton Mifflin Harcourt
Along Came a Spider…	J	I	257	Vocabulary Readers/CA	Houghton Mifflin Harcourt
Along Came a Spider…	J	I	257	Vocabulary Readers/TX	Houghton Mifflin Harcourt
Along Came Greedy Cat	G	F	166	Pacific Literacy	Pacific Learning
Along Comes Jake	C	RF	86	Sunshine	Wright Group/McGraw Hill
Along for the Ride	Y	RF	250+	Dessen, Sarah	Viking/Penguin
Alphabet Book	WB	I	0	Springboard	Wright Group/McGraw Hill
Alphabet Game, The	H	F	272	Story Basket	Wright Group/McGraw Hill
Alphabet Race, The	C	F	7	Visions	Wright Group/McGraw Hill
Alphabet, The	R	I	250+	Literacy 2000	Rigby
Alroy's Very Nearly Clean Bedroom	O	RF	250+	Supa Doopers	Sundance
Also Known as Harper	V	RF	250+	Leal, Ann Haywood	Henry Holt & Co.
Also Known as Rowan Pohi	Y	RF	250+	Fletcher, Ralph	Clarion Books
Alternative Energy: Beyond Fossil Fuels	W	I	250+	Green Generation	Compass Point Books

TITLE	LEVEL	GENRE	WORD COUNT	AUTHOR / SERIES	PUBLISHER / DISTRIBUTOR
Althea Gibson, Sports Hero	R	B	1395	Vocabulary Readers	Houghton Mifflin Harcourt
Althea Gibson, Sports Hero	R	B	1395	Vocabulary Readers/CA	Houghton Mifflin Harcourt
Althea Gibson: An American Hero	O	B	250+	In Step Readers	Rigby
*Altogether, One at a Time	S	RF	250+	Konigsburg, E. L.	Simon & Schuster
Alvin Ailey	P	B	250+	Pinkney, Andrea Davis	Hyperion
Alvin Ailey, an American Dancer	N	B	326	Vocabulary Readers	Houghton Mifflin Harcourt
Alvin Ailey: Master of Dance	S	B	250+	Explore More	Wright Group/McGraw Hill
Alvin Ho: Allergic to Camping, Hiking, and Other Natural Diasters	Q	RF	250+	Look, Lenore	Schwartz & Wade Books
Alvin Ho: Allergic to Girls, School and Other Scary Things	Q	RF	250+	Look, Lenore	Yearling Books
Always	H	RF	161	Stott, Ann	Candlewick Press
Always Be Safe	F	I	117	Rookie Readers	Children's Press
Always Come Home to Me	O	RF	250+	Yang, Belle	Candlewick Press
Always Elephant	M	TL	250+	Rigby Star Plus	Rigby
Always Elephant: A Traditional Tale	M	TL	250+	Rigby Literacy	Rigby
Always Learning	K	I	392	Leveled Readers	Houghton Mifflin Harcourt
Always Learning	K	I	392	Leveled Readers/CA	Houghton Mifflin Harcourt
Always Learning	K	I	392	Leveled Readers/TX	Houghton Mifflin Harcourt
Always My Dad	N	RF	250+	Wyeth, Sharon Dennis	Alfred A. Knopf
Alysha's Flat Tire	D	RF	108	Adams, Lorraine & Bruvold, Lynn	Eaglecrest Books
Am I a Snake?	C	I	51	Bonnell, Kris	Reading Reading Books
Am I Big or Small?	B	I	43	Windows on Literacy	National Geographic
Am I Ready Now?	C	RF	41	Visions	Wright Group/McGraw Hill
Am I Scary?	K	I	250+	Scooters	ETA/Cuisenaire
Amalia and the Grasshopper	K	RF	392	Tello, Jerry; Krupinski, Loretta	Scholastic
Amanda Joins the Circus	R	F	250+	Avi	Bantam Books
Amanda Miranda	Y	HF	250+	Peck, Richard	Penguin Group
*Amanda Pig and Her Big Brother Oliver	L	F	250+	Van Leeuwen, Jean	Puffin Books
Amanda Pig, Schoolgirl	K	F	250+	Van Leeuwen, Jean	Puffin Books
Amanda's Bear	G	F	154	Reading Corners	Pearson Learning Group
Amaranth Enchantment, The	X	F	250+	Berry, Julie	Bloomsbury Children's Books
#Amaterasu: Return of the Sun	V	TL	2144	Graphic Myths and Legends	Graphic Universe
Amaze Us!	S	I	250+	Wildcats	Wright Group/McGraw Hill
Amazing People	X	I	250+	Boldprint	Steck-Vaughn
Amazing ABC	LB	I	27	Kenney, Sean	Henry Holt & Co.
Amazing Adaptations	O	I	453	Independent Readers Science	Houghton Mifflin Harcourt
Amazing Adventures of Batbird, The	L	F	1252	Big Cat	Pacific Learning
Amazing Adventures of Ordinary Girl, The	P	RF	250+	Literacy by Design	Rigby
Amazing Aircraft	O	I	250+	Simon, Seymour	SeaStar Books
Amazing Amoeba, The	X	I	1290	Independent Readers Science	Houghton Mifflin Harcourt
Amazing Animal Adventures at the Poles	U	I	250+	Going Wild Series	Fitzhenry & Whiteside
Amazing Animal Adventures in Rivers	U	I	250+	Going Wild Series	Fitzhenry & Whiteside
Amazing Animal Adventures on Islands	U	I	250+	Going Wild Series	Fitzhenry & Whiteside
Amazing Animal Rescue Team, The	Q	I	250+	Blankenhorn, Rebecca	Steck-Vaughn
Amazing Animals	U	I	250+	Reading Expeditions	National Geographic
Amazing Animals	L	I	800	Reading Street	Pearson
Amazing Animals	F	I	125	Rookie Readers	Children's Press
Amazing Animals: From Performance to Preservation	T	I	250+	Explore More	Wright Group/McGraw Hill
Amazing Ant, The	M	I	250+	Story Box	Wright Group/McGraw Hill
Amazing Ants	O	I	250+	Windows on Literacy	National Geographic
Amazing Balina, The	P	TL	1000	Leveled Readers/TX	Houghton Mifflin Harcourt

* Collection of short stories   # Graphic text
^ Mature content with lower level text demands

TITLE	LEVEL	GENRE	WORD COUNT	AUTHOR / SERIES	PUBLISHER / DISTRIBUTOR
Amazing Bats	L	I	250+	Simon, Seymour	Chronicle Books
Amazing Birds of Antarctica	O	I	759	Leveled Readers	Houghton Mifflin Harcourt
Amazing Birds of Antarctica	O	I	759	Leveled Readers/CA	Houghton Mifflin Harcourt
Amazing Birds of Antarctica	O	I	759	Leveled Readers/TX	Houghton Mifflin Harcourt
Amazing Birds of the Rain Forest	M	I	250+	Pair-It Books	Steck-Vaughn
*Amazing But True Sports Stories	Q	I	250+	Hollander, Phyllis & Zander	Scholastic
Amazing DNA	Z	I	250+	Microquests	Lerner Publishing Group
Amazing Ears	I	I	145	Gear Up!	Wright Group/McGraw Hill
Amazing Earthworm, The	I	I	169	Leveled Readers Language Support	Houghton Mifflin Harcourt
Amazing Egg, The	J	I	220	Spyglass Books	Compass Point Books
Amazing Eggs	J	I	250+	Discovery World	Rigby
Amazing Fact and Puzzle Book, The	T	I	250+	Time For Kids	Time Inc.
Amazing Fish, The	G	TL	167	Pair-It Books	Steck-Vaughn
Amazing Flight of Darius Frobisher	T	F	250+	Harley, Bill	Peachtree
Amazing Geography of the West, The	Q	I	1564	Reading Street	Pearson
Amazing Grace	L	RF	250+	Hoffman, Mary	Scholastic
Amazing Grain: The Wonders of Corn	Q	I	250+	Explorer Books-Pathfinder	National Geographic
Amazing Grain: The Wonders of Corn	P	I	250+	Explorer Books-Pioneer	National Geographic
Amazing Hands	K	I	250+	Rigby Literacy	Rigby
Amazing Humpback Whales	M	I	474	Springboard	Wright Group/McGraw Hill
Amazing Impossible Erie Canal, The	S	I	250+	Harness, Cheryl	Simon & Schuster
Amazing Journeys	P	I	250+	Literacy 2000	Rigby
Amazing Journeys: Following in History's Footsteps	S	I	250+	High Five Reading	Red Brick Learning
Amazing Kangaroo, The	S	I	944	Red Rocket Readers	Flying Start Books
Amazing Lasers	M	I	250+	On Our Way to English	Rigby
Amazing Life of Benjamin Franklin, The	T	B	250+	Giblin, James Cross	Scholastic
Amazing Life of Daisy Ryan, The	Q	RF	4398	Take Two Books	Wright Group/McGraw Hill
Amazing Lifetimes	N	I	250+	Explorations	Eleanor Curtain Publishing
Amazing Lifetimes	N	I	250+	Explorations	Okapi Educational Materials
Amazing Magic Tricks: Apprentice Level	R	I	250+	Magic Tricks	Capstone Press
Amazing Magic Tricks: Beginner Level	R	I	250+	Magic Tricks	Capstone Press
Amazing Magic Tricks: Expert Level	R	I	250+	Magic Tricks	Capstone Press
Amazing Magic Tricks: Master Level	R	I	250+	Magic Tricks	Capstone Press
Amazing Magnets	C	I	53	Twig	Wright Group/McGraw Hill
Amazing Maps	Q	I	250+	Wonder World	Wright Group/McGraw Hill
Amazing Maze, The	J	RF	334	Foundations	Wright Group/McGraw Hill
Amazing Mazes	M	I	250+	Trackers	Pacific Learning
Amazing Medical Machines	W	I	250+	Connectors	Pacific Learning
Amazing Monty	M	RF	250+	Hurwitz, Johanna	Candlewick Press
Amazing Mr. Franklin, The	S	B	250+	Ashby, Ruth	Peachtree
Amazing Mr. Mulch, The	L	F	250+	Cambridge Reading	Pearson Learning Group
Amazing Mudskippers	L	I	450	Springboard	Wright Group/McGraw Hill
Amazing Nests	I	I	270	Vocabulary Readers	Houghton Mifflin Harcourt
Amazing Nests	I	I	270	Vocabulary Readers/CA	Houghton Mifflin Harcourt
Amazing Nests	I	I	270	Vocabulary Readers/TX	Houghton Mifflin Harcourt
Amazing Octopus, The	L	I	346	Leveled Readers	Houghton Mifflin Harcourt
Amazing Octopus, The	L	I	346	Leveled Readers/CA	Houghton Mifflin Harcourt
Amazing Octopus, The	L	I	346	Leveled Readers/TX	Houghton Mifflin Harcourt
Amazing Paul Bunyan, The	M	TL	250+	Windows on Literacy	National Geographic
Amazing Plants	J	I	278	Explorations	Eleanor Curtain Publishing
Amazing Plants	J	I	278	Explorations	Okapi Educational Materials
Amazing Popple Seed, The	G	F	113	Read Alongs	Rigby

A

TITLE	LEVEL	GENRE	WORD COUNT	AUTHOR / SERIES	PUBLISHER / DISTRIBUTOR
Amazing Race, The	A	RF	28	Smart Start	Rigby
Amazing Rocks	T	I	1894	Leveled Readers Science	Houghton Mifflin Harcourt
Amazing Sea Lizards	K	I	318	Explorations	Eleanor Curtain Publishing
Amazing Sea Lizards	K	I	318	Explorations	Okapi Educational Materials
Amazing Senses	P	I	250+	Scooters	ETA/Cuisenaire
Amazing Silkworm, The	M	I	250+	Windows on Literacy	National Geographic
Amazing Skyscrapers	S	I	2047	Independent Readers Social Studies	Houghton Mifflin Harcourt
Amazing Soybean, The	O	I	250+	Orbit Chapter Books	Pacific Learning
Amazing Spiders	Q	I	250+	Eyewitness Juniors	Alfred A. Knopf
Amazing Story of Adolphus Tips, The	U	HF	250+	Morpurgo, Michael	Scholastic
Amazing Tigers!	N	I	250+	Thomson, Sarah	Scholastic
Amazing Trail of Seymour Snail, The	L	F	250+	Hazen, Lynn E.	Henry Holt & Co.
Amazing Trains	L	I	482	Pair-It Books	Steck-Vaughn
Amazing Tricks	K	I	250+	Storyteller-Shooting Stars	Wright Group/McGraw Hill
Amazing Whales	K	I	250+	Rigby Rocket	Rigby
Amazing World of Caves, The	P	I	1335	Gear Up!	Wright Group/McGraw Hill
Amazing, Incredible Idea Kit, The	Q	I	1931	Reading Street	Pearson
Amazon River, The	N	I	250+	Rookie Read-About Geography	Scholastic
Amazon, The	N	I	250+	Early Connections	Benchmark Education
Amber Brown Goes Fourth	O	RF	250+	Danziger, Paula	Scholastic
Amber Brown Is Feeling Blue	O	RF	250+	Danziger, Paula	Scholastic
Amber Brown Is Green With Envy	O	RF	250+	Danziger, Paula	Scholastic
Amber Brown Is Not a Crayon	N	RF	250+	Danziger, Paula	Scholastic
Amber Brown Sees Red	O	RF	250+	Danziger, Paula	Scholastic
Amber Brown Wants Extra Credit	O	RF	250+	Danziger, Paula	Scholastic
Amber Cat, The	P	RF	250+	McKay, Hilary	Simon & Schuster
Amber Spyglass, The	Z	F	250+	Pullman, Phillip	Alfred A. Knopf
Amber the Orange Fairy: Rainbow Magic	L	F	250+	Meadows, Daisy	Scholastic
Amber Waiting	L	F	250+	Gregory, Nan	Red Deer Press
Amber's Big Dog	E	RF	208	Rigby Rocket	Rigby
Ambulance	I	I	116	Pebble Books	Capstone Press
Ambulances	G	I	119	Mighty Machines	Capstone Press
Ambulances	K	I	379	Pull Ahead Books	Lerner Publishing Group
Ambulances in Actions	M	I	250+	Transportation Zone	Capstone Press
Ambulances on the Move	J	I	288	Lightning Bolt Books	Lerner Publishing Group
Amelia Bedelia	L	F	250+	Parish, Peggy	HarperTrophy
Amelia Bedelia and the Baby	L	F	250+	Parish, Peggy	Harper & Row
Amelia Bedelia and the Surprise Shower	L	F	250+	Parish, Peggy	Harper & Row
Amelia Bedelia Goes Camping	L	F	250+	Parish, Peggy	Avon Books
Amelia Bedelia Helps Out	L	F	250+	Parish, Peggy	Avon Books
Amelia Bedelia Under Construction	L	F	250+	Parish, Herman	Scholastic
Amelia Bedelia's Family Album	L	F	250+	Parish, Peggy	Avon Books
Amelia Earhart	N	B	218	First Biographies	Capstone Press
Amelia Earhart	R	B	3465	History Maker Bios	Lerner Publishing Group
Amelia Earhart	Q	B	250+	Literacy Tree	Rigby
Amelia Earhart	P	B	250+	Parlin, John	Bantam Books
Amelia Earhart	P	B	250+	Photo-Illustrated Biographies	Red Brick Learning
Amelia Earhart: Adventure in the Sky	O	B	250+	Pennypacker, Sara	Scholastic
Amelia Earhart: Challenging the Skies	S	B	250+	Sloate, Susan	Fawcett Columbine
Amelia Earhart: Courage in the Sky	S	B	250+	Kerby, Mona	Puffin Books
^Amelia Earhart: First Lady of the Air	R	B	250+	Hameray Biography Series	Hameray Publishing Group
Amelia Earhart: Flying for Adventure	S	B	250+	Wade, Mary Dodson	Millbrook Press
#Amelia Earhart: Legendary Aviator	R	B	250+	Graphic Library	Capstone Press

* Collection of short stories   # Graphic text
^ Mature content with lower level text demands

TITLE	LEVEL	GENRE	WORD COUNT	AUTHOR / SERIES	PUBLISHER / DISTRIBUTOR
Amelia Earhart: The Legend of the Lost Aviator	T	B	250+	Tanaka, Shelley	Harry N. Abrams
Amelia Earhart: Young Aviator	R	B	250+	Gormley, Beatrice	Aladdin
Amelia Lost: The Life and Disappearance of Amelia Earhart	U	B	250+	Fleming, Candace	Schwartz & Wade Books
*Amelia to Zora: Twenty-Six Women Who Changed the World	S	B	250+	Chin-Lee, Cynthia	Charlesbridge
Amelia's Road	O	RF	250+	Soar To Success	Houghton Mifflin Harcourt
Amending the Constitution	U	I	250+	Navigators Social Studies Series	Benchmark Education
America Enters World War I	W	I	250+	Reading Expeditions	National Geographic
America Isà	M	I	250+	Borden, Louise	Margaret K. McElderry Books
*America Street: A Multicultural Anthology of Stories	R	RF	250+	Mazer, Anne	Persea Books
America Votes: How Our President Is Elected	V	I	250+	Granfield, Linda	Kids Can Press
America: A Dream	R	HF	1620	Leveled Readers	Houghton Mifflin Harcourt
American Alligator, The	R	I	250+	Wildlife of North America	Red Brick Learning
American Army of Two, An	O	HF	1665	On My Own History	Lerner Publishing Group
American Beauty	Z+	RF	250+	Dean, Zoey	Little Brown and Company
American Beavers	M	I	488	Springboard	Wright Group/McGraw Hill
American Beginnings: You're Right There!	P	HF	250+	Navigators Drama Series	Benchmark Education
American Bison	U	I	5159	Nature Watch Books	Lerner Publishing Group
American Bison, The	R	I	250+	Wildlife of North America	Red Brick Learning
American Black Bears	K	I	250+	Bears	Capstone Press
#*American Born Chinese	Z+	RF	250+	Yang, Gene Luen	Square Fish
American Cities Countdown	R	I	250+	Explore More	Wright Group/McGraw Hill
*American Dragons: Twenty-Five Asian American Voices	Z	RF	250+	Yep, Laurence	HarperTrophy
American Dream, An	Q	HF	250+	Leveled Readers Language Support	Houghton Mifflin Harcourt
American Dream: Coming to the United States, The	M	I	423	Reading Street	Pearson
*American Eyes: New Asian-American Short Stories for Young Adults	Z	RF	250+	Carlson, Lori M.	Ballantine Books
American Flag, The	S	I	250+	A True Book	Children's Press
American Flag, The	N	I	250+	American Symbols	Capstone Press
American Flag, The	Q	I	250+	Let's See	Compass Point Books
American Flag, The	P	I	700	Pull Ahead Books	Lerner Publishing Group
American Flag, The	T	I	250+	Symbols of America	Marshall Cavendish
American Fur Trade, The	V	I	2247	Leveled Readers	Houghton Mifflin Harcourt
American Fur Trade, The	V	I	2247	Leveled Readers/CA	Houghton Mifflin Harcourt
American Fur Trade, The	V	I	2200	Leveled Readers/TX	Houghton Mifflin Harcourt
American Heroes	M	I	189	Phonics Readers	Compass Point Books
American History Adds Up	T	I	250+	Navigators Math Series	Benchmark Education
American Indians in the 1800s	S	I	250+	Primary Source Readers	Teacher Created Materials
American Paint Horses	I	I	162	Horses	Capstone Press
American Patriot: Benjamin Franklin	T	B	250+	We the People	Compass Point Books
American Plague, An	Z	I	250+	Murphy, Jim	Clarion
#American Presidency, The	V	I	250+	Cartoon Nation	Capstone Press
American Quarter Horses	I	I	141	Horses	Capstone Press
American Quarter Horses Are My Favorite!	O	I	250+	My Favorite Horses	Lerner Publishing Group
American Revolution, The	T	I	250+	Bliven, Bruce, Jr.	Random House
American Revolution, The	V	I	250+	Carter, Alden R.	Franklin Watts
American Revolution, The	T	I	250+	Navigators Social Studies Series	Benchmark Education
American Revolution, The	S	I	250+	Primary Source Readers	Teacher Created Materials
American Road Trip: Famous U.S. Highways	R	I	250+	Explore More	Wright Group/McGraw Hill

TITLE	LEVEL	GENRE	WORD COUNT	AUTHOR / SERIES	PUBLISHER / DISTRIBUTOR
American Saddlebred Horses	I	I	250+	Horses	Capstone Press
American Shorthair Cats	R	I	250+	All About Cats	Capstone Press
American Shorthair Cats	I	I	124	Cats	Capstone Press
American Shorthairs Are the Best!	Q	I	1355	The Best Cats Ever	Lerner Publishing Group
*American Tall Tales	T	TL	250+	Osborne, Mary Pope	Alfred A. Knopf
American Treasures	L	I	124	Larkin, Bruce	Wilbooks
Americans of the Midwest: The Potawatomi	P	I	701	Leveled Readers Social Studies	Houghton Mifflin Harcourt
America's 13: The Original Colonies	W	I	250+	Literacy By Design	Rigby
America's Birthplace: Independence Hall	K	RF	249	Leveled Readers Social Studies	Houghton Mifflin Harcourt
America's City Parks	U	I	2811	Leveled Readers	Houghton Mifflin Harcourt
America's City Parks	U	I	2811	Leveled Readers/CA	Houghton Mifflin Harcourt
America's City Parks	U	I	2811	Leveled Readers/TX	Houghton Mifflin Harcourt
^America's Deadliest Day: The Battle of Antietam	X	I	250+	Bloodiest Battles	Capstone Press
America's First City: Caral	X	I	2654	Independent Readers Social Studies	Houghton Mifflin Harcourt
America's First Firefighters	M	I	619	Leveled Readers	Houghton Mifflin Harcourt
America's First Firefighters	M	I	619	Leveled Readers/CA	Houghton Mifflin Harcourt
America's First Firefighters	M	I	619	Leveled Readers/TX	Houghton Mifflin Harcourt
America's First Traitor: Benedict Arnold Betrays the Colonies	S	I	250+	Headlines from History	Rosen Publishing Group
America's Forests and Woodlands	V	I	250+	Bookshop	Mondo Publishing
America's Most Wanted Fifth-Graders	R	RF	250+	Lawrence, Jan; Raskin, Linda	Scholastic
America's Mountains	W	I	250+	Bookshop	Mondo Publishing
America's Mountains: Guide to Plants and Animals	V	I	250+	Wallace, Marianne D.	Fulcrum Publishing
America's Prairies and Grasslands: Guide to Plants and Animals	V	I	250+	Wallace, Marianne D.	Fulcrum Publishing
America's Seashores: Guide to Plants and Animals	V	I	250+	Wallace, Marianne D.	Fulcrum Publishing
America's Urban Parks	U	I	2657	Leveled Readers	Houghton Mifflin Harcourt
America's Urban Parks	U	I	2657	Leveled Readers/CA	Houghton Mifflin Harcourt
America's Urban Parks	U	I	2657	Leveled Readers/TX	Houghton Mifflin Harcourt
Amigo	O	F	250+	Baylor, Byrd	Aladdin
Among the Betrayed	Z	SF	250+	Haddix, Margaret Peterson	Simon & Schuster
Among the Flowers	M	I	250+	Look Once Look Again	Creative Teaching Press
Among the Hidden	Z	SF	250+	Haddix, Margaret Peterson	Aladdin
Among the Volcanoes	Y	RF	250+	Castaneda, Omar S.	Bantam Books
Amos & Boris	O	F	250+	Steig, William	Farrar, Straus, & Giroux
Amos and the Alien	R	F	250+	Paulsen, Gary	Bantam Books
Amos Binder, Secret Agent	R	F	250+	Paulsen, Gary	Bantam Books
Amos Fortune: Free Man	V	HF	250+	Yates, Elizabeth	Puffin Books
Amos Gets Famous	R	F	250+	Paulsen, Gary	Bantam Books
Amos Gets Married	R	F	250+	Paulsen, Gary	Bantam Books
Amos Goes Bananas	R	F	250+	Paulsen, Gary	Bantam Books
Amos's Killer Concert Caper	R	F	250+	Paulsen, Gary	Bantam Books
Amphibians	M	I	250+	Exploring the Animal Kingdom	Capstone Press
Amphibians	N	I	891	Rigby Flying Colors	Rigby
Amphibians: Water-to-Land Animals	N	I	250+	Amazing Science	Picture Window Books
Amphibious Ships	T	I	250+	Land and Sea	Capstone Press
#Amulet, Book One: The Stonekeeper	Q	SF	250+	Kibuishi, Kazu	Scholastic
#Amulet, Book Two: The Stonekeeper's Curse	Q	F	250+	Kibuishi, Kazu	Scholastic
Amusement Parks	V	I	250+	Boldprint	Steck-Vaughn
*Amy and Jaylen, Blue Jay in the Hay, Gail Goes Fishing	I	RF	371	Easy-for-Me Reading	Child 1st Publications
Amy Goes to School	D	RF	89	Literacy Tree	Rigby

* Collection of short stories   # Graphic text
^ Mature content with lower level text demands

TITLE	LEVEL	GENRE	WORD COUNT	AUTHOR / SERIES	PUBLISHER / DISTRIBUTOR
Amy Loves the Snow	F	RF	127	Hoban, Julia	Scholastic
Amy Loves the Sun	F	RF	122	Hoban, Julia	Scholastic
Amy Loves the Wind	F	RF	116	Hoban, Julia	Scholastic
Amy the Amethyst Fairy: Rainbow Magic	L	F	250+	Meadows, Daisy	Scholastic
Amy's Airplane	E	RF	147	Leveled Readers	Houghton Mifflin Harcourt
Amy's Airplane	E	RF	147	Leveled Readers/CA	Houghton Mifflin Harcourt
Amy's Airplane	E	RF	147	Leveled Readers/TX	Houghton Mifflin Harcourt
Amy's Light	M	RF	380	Sharing Nature with Children	Dawn Publications
Amy's True Prize	Q	HF	250+	The Little Women Journals	Avon Books
Amy's Water Wings	K	F	250+	Lighthouse	Rigby
An Upside-Down Life	I	I	199	Sails	Rigby
An Wang	J	B	193	Leveled Readers Language Support	Houghton Mifflin Harcourt
An Wang: A Mind for Computers	R	B	3495	Leveled Readers Science	Houghton Mifflin Harcourt
Ana and Adam Build a Acrostic	N	RF	1100	Poetry Builders	Norwood House Press
Anaconda	L	I	250+	A Day in the Life: Rain Forest Animals	Heinemann Library
Anacondas	M	I	250+	Snakes	Capstone Press
Anacondas	R	I	250+	Wild About Snakes	Capstone Press
Anahita's Woven Riddle	Z	HF	250+	Sayres, Meghan Nuttail	Amulet Books
Anak the Brave	L	F	250+	Sunshine	Wright Group/McGraw Hill
Ananse's Feast: An Ashanti Tale	M	TL	250+	Mollel, Tololwa M.	Clarion Books
Anansi and the Box of Stories	N	TL	1848	On My Own Folklore	Millbrook Press
Anansi Does the Impossible	O	TL	250+	Aardema, Verna	Simon & Schuster
Anansi the Spider: A Tale From the Ashanti	L	TL	250+	McDermott, Gerald	Scholastic
Anansi Weaves a Gift: An Ashanti Folktale from Ghana	K	TL	309	Gear Up!	Wright Group/McGraw Hill
Anansi's Narrow Waist	I	TL	157	Little Celebrations	Pearson Learning Group
Anastasia Again!	Q	RF	250+	Lowry, Lois	Bantam Books
Anastasia At This Address	Q	RF	250+	Lowry, Lois	Bantam Books
Anastasia At Your Service	Q	RF	250+	Lowry, Lois	Bantam Books
Anastasia Has the Answers	Q	RF	250+	Lowry, Lois	Bantam Books
Anastasia Krupnik	Q	RF	250+	Lowry, Lois	Bantam Books
Anastasia On Her Own	Q	RF	250+	Lowry, Lois	Bantam Books
Anastasia, Absolutely	Q	RF	250+	Lowry, Lois	Bantam Books
Anastasia, Ask Your Analyst	Q	RF	250+	Lowry, Lois	Bantam Books
Anastasia's Chosen Career	Q	RF	250+	Lowry, Lois	Bantam Books
Anastasia's Secret	Z+	HF	250+	Dunlap, Susanne	Bloomsbury Children's Books
Anaxander: A Man of Glory	X	TL	250+	Reading Safari	Mondo Publishing
Ancient Baghdad: City at the Crossroads of Trade	W	I	1989	Leveled Readers	Houghton Mifflin Harcourt
Ancient China	W	I	250+	Early Civilizations	Capstone Press
Ancient China	Y	I	250+	Eyewitness Books	DK Publishing
Ancient China	S	I	250+	InfoQuest	Rigby
Ancient China	Y	I	2971	Vocabulary Readers	Houghton Mifflin Harcourt
Ancient China	Y	I	2971	Vocabulary Readers/CA	Houghton Mifflin Harcourt
Ancient Civilizations	Q	I	250+	Windows on Literacy	National Geographic
Ancient Egypt	W	I	250+	Early Civilizations	Capstone Press
Ancient Egypt	Y	I	250+	Eyewitness Books	DK Publishing
^Ancient Egypt	S	I	250+	Let's See	Compass Point Books
Ancient Egypt	U	I	250+	Make It Work!	World Book
^Ancient Egypt: An Interactive History Adventure	T	HF	250+	You Choose Books	Capstone Press
Ancient Greece	W	I	250+	Early Civilizations	Capstone Press

TITLE	LEVEL	GENRE	WORD COUNT	AUTHOR / SERIES	PUBLISHER / DISTRIBUTOR
Ancient Greece	Y	I	250+	Eyewitness Books	DK Publishing
Ancient Greece	S	I	250+	Journey Into Civilization	Chelsea House
^Ancient Greece	S	I	250+	Let's See	Compass Point Books
Ancient Greece	W	I	250+	Navigators Social Studies Series	Benchmark Education
Ancient Greece and Modern Culture	X	I	2559	Reading Street	Pearson
Ancient Greeks	Q	I	250+	Worldwise	Franklin Watts
Ancient Heritage: The Arab-American Minority, An	Z	I	250+	Ashabranner, Brent	HarperCollins
Ancient Indochina	W	I	2456	Independent Readers Social Studies	Houghton Mifflin Harcourt
Ancient Inventions: Ahead of Their Time	T	I	250+	Pair-It Books	Steck-Vaughn
Ancient Life Along the Nile	W	I	3194	Reading Street	Pearson
^Ancient Mesopotamia	S	I	250+	Let's See	Compass Point Books
Ancient Mysteries	K	HF	198	Dominie Factivity Series	Pearson Learning Group
Ancient Rhymes: A Dolphin Lullaby	P	F	171	Denver, John	Dawn Publications
Ancient Romans	Q	I	250+	Worldwise	Franklin Watts
Ancient Romans, The	U	I	2005	Leveled Readers	Houghton Mifflin Harcourt
Ancient Romans, The	U	I	2005	Leveled Readers/CA	Houghton Mifflin Harcourt
Ancient Romans, The	U	I	2005	Leveled Readers/TX	Houghton Mifflin Harcourt
Ancient Rome	W	I	250+	Early Civilizations	Capstone Press
Ancient Rome	Y	I	250+	Eyewitness Books	DK Publishing
^Ancient Rome	S	I	250+	Let's See	Compass Point Books
Ancient Rome	W	I	250+	Navigators	Kingfisher
Ancient Rome	W	I	250+	Navigators Social Studies Series	Benchmark Education
Ancient Rome	Y	I	250+	Reading Expeditions	National Geographic
Ancient Times	K	HF	267	Dominie Factivity Series	Pearson Learning Group
Ancient Wonders	S	I	2308	Take Two Books	Wright Group/McGraw Hill
Ancient Worlds	T	I	250+	Boldprint	Steck-Vaughn
And Billy Went Out to Play	I	RF	227	Bookshop	Mondo Publishing
And Grandpa Sat on Friday	K	RF	250+	Voyages	SRA/McGraw Hill
And I Mean It Stanley	J	RF	184	Bonsall, Crosby	HarperCollins
And Justice for All	Y	I	250+	Power Up!	Steck-Vaughn
And Now for the Weather	T	I	250+	Bookweb	Rigby
...and Now Miguel	Z	RF	250+	Krumgold, Joseph	Scholastic
And One For All	V	RF	250+	Nelson, Theresa	Dell
And Still the Turtle Watched	Q	RF	250+	MacGill-Callahan, Sheila	Penguin Group
...And the Earth Did Not Devour Him	Z	RF	250+	Edge	Hampton Brown
And the Good Brown Earth	L	RF	250+	Henderson, Kathy	Candlewick Press
And the Teacher Got Mad	H	RF	109	City Kids	Rigby
And the Teacher Smiled	H	RF	86	City Kids	Rigby
And the Winner Is...	N	RF	250+	Storyteller Summer Skies	Wright Group/McGraw Hill
And Then Comes Halloween	M	RF	250+	Brenner, Tom	Candlewick Press
And Then It Was Sugar	N	RF	250+	Story Vines	Wright Group/McGraw Hill
And Then There Were Birds	L	TL	156	Books for Young Learners	Richard C. Owen
And Then What Happened, Paul Revere?	R	B	250+	Fritz, Jean	Bantam Books
And You Can Come Too	J	RF	224	Ohi, Ruth	Annick Press
Andi's Wool	H	I	107	Books for Young Learners	Richard C. Owen
Andrew Carnegie	R	B	250+	Amazing Americans	Wright Group/McGraw Hill
Andrew Carnegie	P	B	530	Leveled Readers Social Studies	Houghton Mifflin Harcourt
Andrew Carnegie: Builder of Libraries	P	B	250+	Community Builders	Children's Press
Andrew Carnegie: The Man Who Built Libraries	U	B	1621	Vocabulary Readers	Houghton Mifflin Harcourt
Andrew Carnegie: The Man Who Built Libraries	U	B	1621	Vocabulary Readers/CA	Houghton Mifflin Harcourt
Andrew Jackson	S	B	250+	Amazing Americans	Wright Group/McGraw Hill
Andrew Jackson	S	B	3691	History Maker Bios	Lerner Publishing Group

* Collection of short stories   # Graphic text
^ Mature content with lower level text demands

TITLE	LEVEL	GENRE	WORD COUNT	AUTHOR / SERIES	PUBLISHER / DISTRIBUTOR
Andrew Jackson	T	B	3664	Presidential Series	January Books
Andrew Jackson	U	B	250+	Profiles of the Presidents	Compass Point Books
Andrew Jackson: Seventh President	R	B	250+	Getting to Know the U.S. Presidents	Children's Press
Andrew Johnson	U	B	250+	Profiles of the Presidents	Compass Point Books
Andrew Johnson: Seventeenth President	R	B	250+	Getting to Know the U.S. Presidents	Children's Press
Andrew's Angry Words	M	F	250+	Lachner, Dorothea	North-South Books
Andriana's Birthday	N	RF	250+	InfoTrek	ETA/Cuisenaire
Androcles and the Lion	L	TL	250+	PM Tales and Plays-Silver	Rigby
Andy (That's my Name)	H	F	104	DePaola, Tomie	Aladdin
Andy and Tamika	N	RF	250+	Adler, David A.	Harcourt Trade
Andy and the Lion	M	F	250+	Daugherty, James	Puffin Books
Andy Fox at School	E	F	198	Leveled Literacy Intervention/ Blue System	Heinemann
Andy Russell, NOT Wanted by the Police	N	RF	250+	Adler, David A.	Harcourt, Inc.
Andy Shane and the Barn Sale Mystery	J	RF	250+	Jacobson, Jennifer Richard	Candlewick Press
Andy Shane and the Pumpkin Trick	K	RF	250+	Jacobson, Jennifer Richard	Candlewick Press
Andy Shane and the Queen of Egypt	K	RF	250+	Jacobson, Jennifer Richard	Candlewick Press
Andy Shane and the Very Bossy Dolores Starbuckle	K	RF	250+	Jacobson, Jennifer Richard	Candlewick Press
Andy Shane Is NOT in Love	K	RF	250+	Jacobson, Jennifer Richard	Candlewick Press
Andy Shane: Hero at Last	K	RF	250+	Jacobson, Jennifer Richard	Candlewick Press
Angel and the Soldier Boy, The	WB	F	0	Collington, Peter	Alfred A. Knopf
Angel Bites the Bullet	O	RF	250+	Delton, Judy	Houghton Mifflin Harcourt
Angel Child, Dragon Child	O	RF	250+	Surat, Michele Maria	Scholastic
Angel Factory, The	X	SF	250+	Blacker, Terence	Simon & Schuster
Angel for Solomon Singer, An	T	RF	250+	Rylant, Cynthia	Orchard Books
Angel Girl	U	HF	1391	Friedman, Laurie	Carolrhoda Books
Angel in Charge	O	RF	250+	Delton, Judy	Houghton Mifflin Harcourt
Angel Island	U	I	250+	Bookshop	Mondo Publishing
Angel Island and the Land of Promise	V	I	2595	Independent Readers Social Studies	Houghton Mifflin Harcourt
Angel Park Hoopstars: Nothing But Net	O	RF	250+	Hughes, Dean	Alfred A. Knopf
Angel Park Hoopstars: Point Guard	O	RF	250+	Hughes, Dean	Alfred A. Knopf
Angel Park Soccer Stars: Backup Goalie	O	RF	250+	Hughes, Dean	Random House
Angel Park Soccer Stars: Defense!	O	RF	250+	Hughes, Dean	Alfred A. Knopf
Angel Park Soccer Stars: Psyched!	O	RF	250+	Hughes, Dean	Random House
Angel Park Soccer Stars: Total Soccer	O	RF	250+	Hughes, Dean	Alfred A. Knopf
Angel Park Soccer Stars: Victory Goal	O	RF	250+	Hughes, Dean	Alfred A. Knopf
Angel Spreads Her Wings	O	RF	250+	Delton, Judy	Houghton Mifflin Harcourt
Angelina Trueheart and the Fox	I	RF	228	Voyages	SRA/McGraw Hill
*Angels and Other Strangers	T	RF	250+	Paterson, Katherine	HarperTrophy
Angels Don't Know Karate	M	F	250+	Dadey, Debbie; Jones, Marcia Thornton	Scholastic
Angel's Mother's Baby	O	RF	250+	Delton, Judy	Houghton Mifflin Harcourt
Angel's Mother's Boyfriend	O	RF	250+	Delton, Judy	Houghton Mifflin Harcourt
Angel's Mother's Wedding	O	RF	250+	Delton, Judy	Houghton Mifflin Harcourt
Angels on the Roof	Z	RF	250+	Moore, Martha	Bantam Books
Angry	D	I	14	Feelings	Lerner Publishing Group
Angry Bull and Other Cases, The	O	RF	250+	Simon, Seymour	Avon Books
Angry Old Woman, The	E	F	126	Adventures in Reading	Pearson Learning Group
Angus and Sadie	P	F	250+	Voigt, Cynthia	HarperCollins
Angus and the Cat	I	F	250+	Flack, Marjorie	Viking/Penguin
Angus and the Ducks	I	F	250+	Flack, Marjorie	Bantam Doubleday Dell

TITLE	LEVEL	GENRE	WORD COUNT	AUTHOR / SERIES	PUBLISHER / DISTRIBUTOR
Angus Thought He Was Big	G	F	58	Giant Step Readers	Educational Insights
Angus, Thongs and Full-Frontal Snogging: Confessions of Georgia Nicolson	Z	RF	250+	Rennison, Louise	HarperCollins
Anila's Journey	Z	HF	250+	Finn, Mary	Candlewick Press
Animal , Vegetable, or Mineral?	G	I	105	Dominie Factivity Series	Pearson Learning Group
Animal Actions	I	I	190	Home Connection Collection	Rigby
Animal Adaptations	U	I	250+	Reading Expeditions	National Geographic
Animal Adventures	N	HF	250+	Little House	HarperTrophy
Animal Adventures	M	RF	250+	Navigators Fiction Series	Benchmark Education
Animal Advertisements	N	F	250+	Sails	Rigby
Animal Ancestors	O	I	964	Big Cat	Pacific Learning
Animal Antics: The Beast Jokes Ever!	O	F	1921	Make Me Laugh!	Lerner Publishing Group
Animal Appetites	L	I	325	Gear Up!	Wright Group/McGraw Hill
Animal Armor	I	I	155	Windows on Literacy	National Geographic
Animal Art	F	F	210	Red Rocket Readers	Flying Start Books
Animal Artists	B	I	32	Little Celebrations	Pearson Learning Group
Animal Babies	R	I	250+	Kalman, Bobbie	Crabtree
Animal Babies	B	I	114	Little Red Readers	Sundance
Animal Babies	C	I	75	Rigby Rocket	Rigby
Animal Babies	E	I	114	Rookie Readers	Children's Press
Animal Babies	C	I	63	Springboard	Wright Group/McGraw Hill
Animal Babies	F	I	131	Twig	Wright Group/McGraw Hill
Animal Babies	J	I	369	Vocabulary Readers/CA	Houghton Mifflin Harcourt
Animal Band, The	K	TL	250+	PM Tales and Plays-Purple	Rigby
Animal Behaviorists	P	B	250+	Navigators Biography Series	Benchmark Education
Animal Bodies	F	I	166	PM Science Readers	Rigby
Animal Bodies	H	I	69	Windows on Literacy	National Geographic
Animal Builders	I	I	148	Little Celebrations	Pearson Learning Group
Animal Camouflage in the Desert	J	I	143	Hidden in Nature	Capstone Press
Animal Camouflage in the Forest	J	I	148	Hidden in Nature	Capstone Press
Animal Camouflage in the Ocean	J	I	135	Hidden in Nature	Capstone Press
Animal Camouflage in the Snow	J	I	134	Hidden in Nature	Capstone Press
Animal Champions	M	I	250+	Explorations	Okapi Educational Materials
Animal Champions	M	I	250+	Explorations	Eleanor Curtain Publishing
Animal Champions	O	I	250+	Jones, Teri Crawford	Pearson Learning Group
Animal Chatter	V	I	250+	High-Fliers	Pacific Learning
Animal Close-Ups	I	I	211	Explorations	Okapi Educational Materials
Animal Close-Ups	I	I	211	Explorations	Eleanor Curtain Publishing
Animal Coats	L	I	250+	Rigby Rocket	Rigby
Animal Coats	B	I	48	Sails	Rigby
Animal Communication	N	I	250+	Cambridge Reading	Pearson Learning Group
Animal Communication	S	I	250+	Pair-It Books	Steck-Vaughn
Animal Communication	L	I	569	Rigby Flying Colors	Rigby
Animal Coverings	E	I	153	Early Connections	Benchmark Education
Animal Crackers	D	F	194	Bookshop	Mondo Publishing
Animal Crackers Fly the Coop	O	F	250+	O'Malley, Kevin	Walker & Company
Animal Dazzlers: The Role of Brilliant Colors in Nature	T	I	250+	Collard, Sneed B.	Franklin Watts
Animal Defenses	M	I	423	Larkin, Bruce	Wilbooks
Animal Doctors	N	I	801	Leveled Readers	Houghton Mifflin Harcourt
Animal Doctors	N	I	801	Leveled Readers/CA	Houghton Mifflin Harcourt
Animal Doctors	N	I	801	Leveled Readers/TX	Houghton Mifflin Harcourt
Animal Ears	N	I	250+	Look Once Look Again	Creative Teaching Press
Animal Ears	I	I	250+	Yellow Umbrella Books	Red Brick Learning

* Collection of short stories   # Graphic text
^ Mature content with lower level text demands

TITLE	LEVEL	GENRE	WORD COUNT	AUTHOR / SERIES	PUBLISHER / DISTRIBUTOR
Animal Eyes	M	I	250+	Look Once Look Again	Creative Teaching Press
Animal Fair	J	F	138	Goembel, Ponder	Marshall Cavendish
Animal Families	G	I	151	Early Connections	Benchmark Education
Animal Farm	Z	F	250+	Edge	Hampton Brown
Animal Farm	Z	F	250+	inZone Books	Hampton Brown
Animal Farm	Z	F	250+	Orwell, George	Harcourt Trade
Animal Farm, An	H	I	233	Springboard	Wright Group/McGraw Hill
Animal Farmers	N	I	250+	Literacy Tree	Rigby
Animal Fathers	N	I	250+	Literacy 2000 Satellites	Rigby
Animal Feathers and Fur	M	I	250+	Look Once Look Again	Creative Teaching Press
Animal Feet	M	I	250+	Look Once Look Again	Creative Teaching Press
Animal Feet	I	I	166	Rigby Literacy	Rigby
Animal Feet	H	I	136	Rigby Star Quest	Rigby
Animal Fibers	I	I	440	Sunshine Science	Wright Group/McGraw Hill
Animal Files, The	T	I	250+	WorldScapes	ETA/Cuisenaire
Animal Friends	N	I	250+	Literacy 2000	Rigby
Animal Friends	I	I	192	Red Rocket Readers	Flying Start Books
Animal Giants	L	I	411	Yellow Umbrella Books	Red Brick Learning
Animal Graphs	F	I	139	PM Math Readers	Rigby
Animal Groups	I	I	265	Early Connections	Benchmark Education
Animal Habitats	B	I	73	Little Celebrations	Pearson Learning Group
Animal Habitats	B	I	73	Little Red Readers	Sundance
Animal Habitats	K	I	149	Windows on Literacy	National Geographic
Animal Headgear	L	I	342	Sails	Rigby
Animal Helpers	Q	I	250+	HSP/Harcourt Trophies	Harcourt, Inc.
Animal Helpers	K	I	250+	Literacy by Design	Rigby
Animal Helpers	F	I	151	PM Science Readers	Rigby
Animal Helpers	M	I	813	Reading Street	Pearson
Animal Heroes	U	I	250+	Connectors	Pacific Learning
*Animal Heroes: True Rescue Stories	T	I	8566	Markle, Sandra	Millbrook Press
Animal Hiding Places	O	I	250+	Windows on Literacy	National Geographic
Animal Homes	R	I	250+	Boldprint	Steck-Vaughn
Animal Homes	B	I	48	Early Connections	Benchmark Education
Animal Homes	L	I	250+	I Wonder Why	Kingfisher
Animal Homes	D	I	53	Instant Readers	Harcourt School Publishers
Animal Homes	E	I	170	Leveled Readers/CA	Houghton Mifflin Harcourt
Animal Homes	E	I	170	Leveled Readers/TX	Houghton Mifflin Harcourt
Animal Homes	B	I	48	Little Red Readers	Sundance
Animal Homes	A	I	35	On Our Way to English	Rigby
Animal Homes	K	I	193	Pair-It Books	Steck-Vaughn
Animal Homes	G	I	193	PM Plus Nonfiction	Rigby
Animal Homes	E	I	108	Red Rocket Readers	Flying Start Books
Animal Hospital	K	I	250+	DK Readers	DK Publishing
Animal Hospital	G	RF	193	Sunshine	Wright Group/McGraw Hill
Animal Hospital, The	B	I	24	Windows on Literacy	National Geographic
Animal House	O	F	250+	Ryan, Candance	Walker & Company
Animal Inventions	G	I	80	Sunshine	Wright Group/McGraw Hill
Animal Kingdom	W	I	250+	Mission: Science	Compass Point Books
Animal Legs	B	I	37	Discovery World	Rigby
Animal Life Cycles	Q	I	250+	Reading Expeditions	National Geographic
Animal Life Cycles	L	I	538	Science Support Readers	Houghton Mifflin Harcourt
Animal Lights	H	I	171	Sails	Rigby
Animal Look-Alikes	O	I	250+	iOpeners	Pearson Learning Group
Animal Messages	J	I	277	Red Rocket Readers	Flying Start Books

A

TITLE	LEVEL	GENRE	WORD COUNT	AUTHOR / SERIES	PUBLISHER / DISTRIBUTOR
Animal Messengers	I	I	116	Discovery Links	Newbridge
Animal Moms and Dads	E	I	121	Tarlow, Ellen	Scholastic
Animal Mothers and Babies	F	I	71	Time for Kids	Teacher Created Materials
Animal Mouths	M	I	250+	Look Once Look Again	Creative Teaching Press
Animal Mummies of Ancient Egpyt	W	I	2896	Independent Readers Social Studies	Houghton Mifflin Harcourt
Animal Mysteries	L	I	250+	Rigby Literacy	Rigby
Animal Needs:Who's New at the Zoo?	O	I	1387	iScience	Norwood House Press
Animal Neighbors	Q	I	250+	Orbit Double Takes	Pacific Learning
Animal Neighbors	I	I	250+	Vocabulary Readers	Houghton Mifflin Harcourt
Animal Noises	D	I	56	Little Red Readers	Sundance
Animal Noses	M	I	250+	Look Once Look Again	Creative Teaching Press
Animal Noses	K	I	250+	The Rowland Reading Program Libary	Rowland Reading Foundation
Animal Opposites	E	I	57	Shutterbug Books	Steck-Vaughn
Animal Pals	E	I	111	Cherrington, Janelle	Scholastic
Animal Patterns	L	I	300	Finding Patterns	Capstone Press
Animal Patterns	F	I	130	Yellow Umbrella Books	Capstone Press
Animal Pets	L	I	250+	Sunshine	Wright Group/McGraw Hill
Animal Presents	A	F	35	Rigby Star	Rigby
Animal Race	B	F	48	Little Dinosaur	Literacy Footprints
Animal Records	K	I	250+	Windows on Literacy	National Geographic
Animal Reports	L	I	277	Little Red Readers	Sundance
Animal Rescue	L	I	534	Red Rocket Readers	Flying Start Books
Animal Rights: How You Can Make a Difference	S	I	250+	Take Action	Capstone Press
Animal Scavengers	M	I	250+	Rigby Literacy	Rigby
Animal Sculpture	LB	I	24	Canizares, Susan; Chanko, Pamela	Scholastic
Animal Senses	M	I	250+	Cambridge Reading	Pearson Learning Group
Animal Senses	G	I	212	PM Science Readers	Rigby
Animal Senses	J	I	224	Spyglass Books	Compass Point Books
Animal Senses and Defenses	I	I	266	Shutterbug Books	Steck-Vaughn
Animal Senses: Sight and Hearing	T	I	250+	Sails	Rigby
Animal Senses: Smell, Taste, Touch	T	I	250+	Sails	Rigby
Animal Shapes	H	I	133	Rigby Focus	Rigby
Animal Shapes	D	I	14	Wildsmith, Brian	Oxford University Press
Animal Shelters	N	I	250+	Bookshop	Mondo Publishing
Animal Shelters	L	I	601	Reading Street	Pearson
Animal Shelters	H	I	193	Sun Sprouts	ETA/Cuisenaire
Animal Show, The	B	F	30	Sails	Rigby
Animal Sizes	G	I	163	Red Rocket Readers	Flying Start Books
Animal Skeletons	G	I	91	Alphakids	Sundance
Animal Skeletons	E	I	131	Sails	Rigby
Animal Skin and Scales	N	I	250+	Look Once Look Again	Creative Teaching Press
Animal Sounds	C	I	21	Visions	Wright Group/McGraw Hill
Animal Sports	O	I	250+	Extreme Sports	Raintree
*Animal Stories	Q	F	250+	King-Smith, Dick	Penguin Group
*Animal Stories by Young Writers	R	F	250+	Rubel, William; Mandel, Gerry	Tricycle Press
Animal Stretches	C	RF	35	Little Celebrations	Pearson Learning Group
Animal Symmetry	H	I	225	PM Math Readers	Rigby
Animal Tails	L	I	250+	Lighthouse	Rigby
Animal Tails	N	I	250+	Look Once Look Again	Creative Teaching Press
Animal Talk	A	I	45	Vocabulary Readers	Houghton Mifflin Harcourt
Animal Talk	A	I	45	Vocabulary Readers/CA	Houghton Mifflin Harcourt

* Collection of short stories   # Graphic text
^ Mature content with lower level text demands

TITLE	LEVEL	GENRE	WORD COUNT	AUTHOR / SERIES	PUBLISHER / DISTRIBUTOR
Animal Talk	A	I	45	Vocabulary Readers/TX	Houghton Mifflin Harcourt
Animal Teeth	H	I	98	Shutterbug Books	Steck-Vaughn
Animal Trackers, The	M	I	333	Independent Readers Science	Houghton Mifflin Harcourt
Animal Tracks	L	I	250+	Dorros, Arthur	Scholastic
Animal Tracks	D	I	152	Wonder World	Wright Group/McGraw Hill
Animal Treats	D	I	78	Early Connections	Benchmark Education
Animal Tricks	D	RF	115	Jasper the Cat	Pioneer Valley
Animal Tricks	H	F	102	Wildsmith, Brian	Merrimak
Animal Walk, The	B	RF	39	Rigby Literacy	Rigby
Animal Workers	M	I	759	Rigby Flying Colors	Rigby
Animal Worlds	E	I	94	Early Connections	Benchmark Education
Animal Wrestlers, The	J	TL	338	Cambridge Reading	Pearson Learning Group
Animal, the Vegetable, and John D. Jones, The	R	RF	250+	Byars, Betsy	Bantam Books
Animals	D	I	70	Foundations	Wright Group/McGraw Hill
Animals	E	I	63	Happy Baby	Priddy Books
Animals	LB	I	14	Instant Readers	Harcourt School Publishers
Animals	V	I	250+	Navigators	Kingfisher
Animals	I	I	294	Science Support Readers	Houghton Mifflin Harcourt
Animals	A	I	28	Smart Start	Rigby
Animals	I	I	149	Time for Kids	Teacher Created Materials
Animals	D	I	88	Vocabulary Readers	Houghton Mifflin Harcourt
Animals	D	I	88	Vocabulary Readers/CA	Houghton Mifflin Harcourt
Animals	D	I	88	Vocabulary Readers/TX	Houghton Mifflin Harcourt
Animals All Together	E	I	86	Windows on Literacy	National Geographic
Animals and Air	M	I	250+	Sunshine	Wright Group/McGraw Hill
Animals and Human Culture	X	I	250+	Connectors	Pacific Learning
Animals and the Environment	I	I	252	Ecology	Lerner Publishing Group
Animals and Their Adaptations	Q	I	250+	Reading Expeditions	National Geographic
Animals and Their Babies	E	I	166	Early Connections	Benchmark Education
Animals and Their Teeth	K	I	510	Sunshine	Wright Group/McGraw Hill
Animals and Their Young	N	I	484	Kratky, Lada Josefa	Hampton Brown
Animals and Us	C	RF	110	InfoTrek	ETA/Cuisenaire
Animals Are Sleeping	H	I	73	Slade, Suzanne	Sylvan Dell Publishing
Animals Armed for Survival	M	I	250+	Literacy by Design	Rigby
Animals Around the World	J	I	240	Reading Street	Pearson
Animals at Home	E	I	134	Reading Street	Pearson Learning Group
Animals at Night	I	I	215	First Start	Troll Associates
Animals at Night	L	I	520	Leveled Readers	Houghton Mifflin Harcourt
Animals at Night	D	I	161	Leveled Readers	Houghton Mifflin Harcourt
Animals at Night	D	I	161	Leveled Readers/CA	Houghton Mifflin Harcourt
Animals at Night	D	I	161	Leveled Readers/TX	Houghton Mifflin Harcourt
Animals at Night	C	I	35	Windows on Literacy	National Geographic
Animals at School	I	I	250+	Early Transitional, Set 1	Pioneer Valley
Animals at the Aquarium	H	I	257	Leveled Readers	Houghton Mifflin Harcourt
Animals at the Aquarium	H	I	257	Leveled Readers/CA	Houghton Mifflin Harcourt
Animals at the Aquarium	H	I	257	Leveled Readers/TX	Houghton Mifflin Harcourt
Animals at the Extremes	S	I	250+	Navigators Math Series	Benchmark Education
Animals at the Mall	D	F	39	Teacher's Choice Series	Pearson Learning Group
Animals at the Zoo	F	I	158	First Start	Troll Associates
Animals at Work	M	I	250+	Home Connection Collection	Rigby
Animals at Work	T	I	2814	Reading Street	Pearson
Animals Babies	J	I	369	Vocabulary Readers	Houghton Mifflin Harcourt
Animals Build	H	I	129	Discovery Links	Newbridge
Animals Building Homes	L	I	250+	Animal Behavior	Capstone Press

TITLE	LEVEL	GENRE	WORD COUNT	AUTHOR / SERIES	PUBLISHER / DISTRIBUTOR
Animals Can	A	I	27	Little Readers	Houghton Mifflin Harcourt
Animals Can Change	B	I	54	Sails	Rigby
Animals Can Help	E	I	140	Sails	Rigby
Animals Communicating	M	I	250+	Animal Behavior	Capstone Press
Animals Eat	C	I	27	We Do Too Series	Pearson Learning Group
Animals Everywhere	D	I	50	Gear Up!	Wright Group/McGraw Hill
Animals' Eyes and Ears	K	I	411	Early Connections	Benchmark Education
Animals Finding Food	L	I	250+	Animal Behavior	Capstone Press
Animals from Long Ago	G	I	141	Discovery Links	Newbridge
Animals from the Past	N	I	304	Independent Readers Science	Houghton Mifflin Harcourt
Animals Go Home	D	I	89	Literacy by Design	Rigby
Animals Go Home	D	I	89	On Our Way to English	Rigby
Animals Grow	I	I	152	Wonder World	Wright Group/McGraw Hill
Animals Grow and Change	I	I	122	Reading Street	Pearson
Animals Have Babies	C	I	42	We Do Too Series	Pearson Learning Group
Animals Have Homes	C	I	31	We Do Too Series	Pearson Learning Group
Animals Helping People	N	I	1017	Vocabulary Readers	Houghton Mifflin Harcourt
Animals Helping People	N	I	1017	Vocabulary Readers/CA	Houghton Mifflin Harcourt
Animals Helping People	N	I	1017	Vocabulary Readers/TX	Houghton Mifflin Harcourt
Animals Hide	D	I	55	Discovery Links	Newbridge
Animals Hide	B	I	64	Literacy by Design	Rigby
Animals Hide	B	I	64	On Our Way to English	Rigby
Animals Hide and Seek	C	I	56	Twig	Wright Group/McGraw Hill
Animals Hiding	B	I	61	Bookshop	Mondo Publishing
Animals' Homes	E	I	170	Leveled Readers	Houghton Mifflin Harcourt
Animals I Like to Feed	C	I	38	Little Red Readers	Sundance
Animals in a Human's World	T	I	2345	Reading Street	Pearson
Animals in Africa	B	I	47	In Step Readers	Rigby
Animals in Art	F	F	45	Pair-It Turn and Learn	Steck-Vaughn
Animals in Danger	U	I	5140	Oxford Bookworms Library	Oxford University Press
Animals in Danger	M	I	250+	Pair-It Books	Steck-Vaughn
Animals in Danger	K	I	351	Yellow Umbrella Books	Red Brick Learning
Animals in Danger!	K	I	503	Vocabulary Readers	Houghton Mifflin Harcourt
Animals in Danger!	K	I	503	Vocabulary Readers/CA	Houghton Mifflin Harcourt
Animals in Danger!	K	I	503	Vocabulary Readers/TX	Houghton Mifflin Harcourt
Animals in Fall	F	I	100	All About Fall	Capstone Press
Animals in the City	D	I	72	Sails	Rigby
Animals in the Dark	P	I	250+	Simon, Seymour	Scholastic
Animals in the Desert	D	I	31	Carousel Readers	Pearson Learning Group
Animals in the Desert	B	I	30	Sails	Rigby
Animals in the Fall	E	I	34	Preparing for Winter	Capstone Press
Animals in the Grass	E	RF	42	Reading Street	Pearson
Animals in the Grasslands	B	I	37	Sails	Rigby
Animals in the Mountains	B	I	42	Sails	Rigby
Animals in the Rain Forest	C	I	33	Vocabulary Readers	Houghton Mifflin Harcourt
Animals in the Snow	C	I	79	Sails	Rigby
Animals in the Snow	A	I	20	Vocabulary Readers	Houghton Mifflin Harcourt
Animals in the Snow	A	I	20	Vocabulary Readers/CA	Houghton Mifflin Harcourt
Animals in the Sun	C	I	44	Reading Street	Pearson
Animals in the Water	C	I	84	Sails	Rigby
Animals in the Woods	A	I	15	Leveled Readers	Houghton Mifflin Harcourt
Animals in the Woods	A	I	15	Leveled Readers/CA	Houghton Mifflin Harcourt
Animals in Winter	H	I	138	All About Winter	Capstone Press
Animals in Winter	C	I	42	Rosen Real Readers	Rosen Publishing Group

* Collection of short stories   # Graphic text
^ Mature content with lower level text demands

TITLE	LEVEL	GENRE	WORD COUNT	AUTHOR / SERIES	PUBLISHER / DISTRIBUTOR
Animals in Winter	L	I	250+	Soar To Success	Houghton Mifflin Harcourt
Animals Keep Warm	C	I	25	We Do Too Series	Pearson Learning Group
Animals Live Everywhere	H	I	250+	Phonics and Friends	Hampton Brown
Animals Love the Fair	E	F	43	Literacy 2000	Rigby
Animals Make Noises	C	I	19	We Do Too Series	Pearson Learning Group
Animals Nearby	O	I	943	Leveled Readers Science	Houghton Mifflin Harcourt
Animals of Africa	Q	I	250+	Navigators Science Series	Benchmark Education
Animals of Africa	L	I	250+	The Rowland Reading Program Library	Rowland Reading Foundation
Animals of Africa	K	I	286	Vocabulary Readers	Houghton Mifflin Harcourt
Animals of Africa	K	I	286	Vocabulary Readers/CA	Houghton Mifflin Harcourt
Animals of Alaska	J	I	147	Rosen Real Readers	Rosen Publishing Group
Animals of Alaska	S	I	517	Vocabulary Readers	Houghton Mifflin Harcourt
Animals of Asia	Q	I	250+	Navigators Science Series	Benchmark Education
Animals of Denali	Q	I	250+	Explorer Books-Pathfinder	National Geographic
Animals of Denali	P	I	250+	Explorer Books-Pioneer	National Geographic
Animals of Long Ago	N	I	250+	Ring, Susan	Scholastic
Animals of North America	Q	I	250+	Navigators Science Series	Benchmark Education
Animals of the African Grasslands	O	I	250+	Explorations	Eleanor Curtain Publishing
Animals of the African Grasslands	O	I	250+	Explorations	Okapi Educational Materials
Animals of the Amazon	R	I	683	Vocabulary Readers	Houghton Mifflin Harcourt
Animals of the Arctic and Antarctic	P	I	1242	Take Two Books	Wright Group/McGraw Hill
Animals of the Ice and Snow	O	I	250+	Literacy 2000	Rigby
Animals of the Rainforest	B	I	30	Sails	Rigby
Animals of the Redwood Forest	S	I	1484	Leveled Readers	Houghton Mifflin Harcourt
Animals of the Redwood Forest	S	I	1484	Leveled Readers/CA	Houghton Mifflin Harcourt
Animals of the Redwood Forest	S	I	1484	Leveled Readers/TX	Houghton Mifflin Harcourt
Animals of the Savanna	M	I	250+	Rosen Real Readers	Rosen Publishing Group
Animals of the Sea	S	I	250+	Navigators Math Series	Benchmark Education
Animals of the Tropical Forest	M	I	250+	Rosen Real Readers	Rosen Publishing Group
Animals of the Tropical Rain Forest	M	I	250+	Sunshine	Wright Group/McGraw Hill
Animals of the Tundra	N	I	250+	Little Celebrations	Pearson Learning Group
Animals on My Street	D	I	124	PM Science Readers	Rigby
Animals on Our Farm	F	I	162	PM Science Readers	Rigby
Animals on Show	F	I	165	PM Science Readers	Rigby
Animals on the Go	I	I	204	Green Light Readers	Harcourt
Animals on the Loose	M	F	642	Leveled Readers	Houghton Mifflin Harcourt
Animals on the Move	N	I	735	Infotrek	ETA/Cuisenaire
Animals on the Move	K	I	145	Planet Earth	Rigby
Animals on the Move	T	I	250+	PM Extensions	Rigby
Animals Play	C	I	27	We Do Too Series	Pearson Learning Group
Animals Raising Offspring	L	I	250+	Animal Behavior	Capstone Press
Animals Say	M	F	250+	Sails	Rigby
Animals Side by Side	K	I	210	Early Explorers	Benchmark Education
Animals Sleeping	L	I	250+	Animal Behavior	Capstone Press
Animals Sleeping	B	RF	61	Bookshop	Mondo Publishing
Animals Staying Safe	L	I	250+	Animal Behavior	Capstone Press
Animals Talk, Too	N	I	250+	Literacy 2000	Rigby
Animals That Build	F	I	137	Sails	Rigby
Animals That Burrow	P	I	250+	Woolley, M.; Pigdon, K.	Scholastic
Animals That Go Fast	A	I	83	Leveled Literacy Intervention/ Orange System	Heinemann
Animals That Live in the City	E	I	105	Springboard	Wright Group/McGraw Hill
Animals That Live in the Ocean	J	I	259	Springboard	Wright Group/McGraw Hill

TITLE	LEVEL	GENRE	WORD COUNT	AUTHOR / SERIES	PUBLISHER / DISTRIBUTOR
Animals That Work	A	I	14	Foundations	Wright Group/McGraw Hill
Animals Then and Now	S	I	250+	Literacy By Design	Rigby
Animals Watched, The	P	F	250+	Stewig, John Warren	Holiday House
Animals We Met	J	I	72	Larkin, Bruce	Wilbooks
Animals Went to Bed, The	B	F	32	Smart Start	Rigby
Animals With Backbones	M	I	177	Windows on Literacy	National Geographic
^Animals With No Eyes: Cave Adaptation	T	I	250+	Extreme Life	Capstone Press
Animals With Wings	L	I	363	Leveled Literacy Intervention/ Blue System	Heinemann
*Animals You Will Never Forget	R	I	250+	Pair-It Books	Steck-Vaughn
Animals, The	A	F	18	Sails	Rigby
Animated Illusions	S	I	250+	Sunshine	Wright Group/McGraw Hill
Animology: Animal Analogies	N	I	109	Berkes, Marianne	Sylvan Dell Publishing
Animorphs	U	F	250+	Applegate, K. A.	Scholastic
Ankylosaurus	N	I	250+	Discovering Dinosaurs	Capstone Press
Anna Allen Faces the White Dragon	P	I	250+	Leveled Readers Language Support	Houghton Mifflin Harcourt
Anna and the King	V	HF	250+	Landon, Margaret	HarperTrophy
Anna at Ellis Island	N	RF	250+	Windows on Literacy	National Geographic
Anna Casey's Place in the World	U	RF	250+	Fogelin, Adrian	Peachtree
Anna Is Still Here	V	HF	250+	Vos, Ida	Puffin Books
Anna, Grandpa, and the Big Storm	N	HF	250+	Stevens, Carla	Penguin Group
Annabel	H	RF	251	Story Basket	Wright Group/McGraw Hill
Annabel the Actress Starring in Gorilla My Dreams	L	RF	250+	Conford, Ellen	Simon & Schuster
Annabel-Isabel	I	RF	393	The Rowland Reading Program Library	Rowland Reading Foundation
Annabelle Swift, Kindergartner	N	RF	250+	Schwartz, Amy	Orchard Books
Anna's Art Adventure	R	F	2066	Sortland, Bjorn	Carolrhoda Books
Anna's Beetle Surprise	R	RF	1489	Leveled Readers	Houghton Mifflin Harcourt
Anna's Beetle Surprise	R	RF	1489	Leveled Readers/CA	Houghton Mifflin Harcourt
Anna's Beetle Surprise	R	RF	1489	Leveled Readers/TX	Houghton Mifflin Harcourt
Anna's Big Day	D	RF	73	Sun Sprouts	ETA/Cuisenaire
Anna's Blizzard	R	HF	250+	Hart, Alison	Peachtree
Anna's First Day	E	RF	138	Joy Starters	Pearson Learning Group
Anna's Sandwich	C	RF	33	Windmill Books	Rigby
Anna's Tree	I	RF	213	Windmill Books	Rigby
Anne Bradstreet	R	B	548	Independent Readers Science	Houghton Mifflin Harcourt
Anne Frank	V	B	250+	Epstein, Rachel	Franklin Watts
Anne Frank	V	B	3373	History Maker Bios	Lerner Publishing Group
Anne Frank Remembered: The Story of the Woman Who Helped Hide the Frank Family	Y	B	250+	Gies, Miep	Simon & Schuster
^Anne Frank: A Secret Diary	W	B	250+	Hameray Biography Series	Hameray Publishing Group
Anne Frank: Beyond the Diary	X	I	250+	Van der Rol, Ruud; Verheeven, Rian	Puffin Books
Anne Frank: Her Life in Words and Pictures	Y	B	250+	Metselaar, Menno and van der Rol, Ruund	Roaring Brook Press
Anne Frank: Life in Hiding	W	B	250+	Hurwitz, Johanna	Avon Books
Anne Frank: The Diary of a Young Girl	Y	B	250+	Frank, Anne	Bantam Books
Anne Hutchinson	V	B	250+	Amazing Ameicans	Wright Group/McGraw Hill
Anne Hutchinson	T	B	3224	History Maker Bios	Lerner Publishing Group
Anne Hutchinson: Religious Reformer	V	B	250+	Let Freedom Ring	Capstone Press
Anne of Green Gables	V	RF	250+	Montgomery, L. M.	Scholastic
Anne of Green Gables	T	RF	5860	Oxford Bookworms Library	Oxford University Press
Anne Sullivan	J	B	255	Leveled Readers	Houghton Mifflin Harcourt

TITLE	LEVEL	GENRE	WORD COUNT	AUTHOR / SERIES	PUBLISHER / DISTRIBUTOR
Anne Sullivan	J	B	255	Leveled Readers/CA	Houghton Mifflin Harcourt
Anne Sullivan	J	B	255	Leveled Readers/TX	Houghton Mifflin Harcourt
Annie and Simon	K	RF	250+	O'Neill, Catharine	Candlewick Press
Annie and Snowball and the Cozy Nest	J	RF	250+	Rylant, Cynthia	Simon & Schuster
Annie and Snowball and the Dress-Up Birthday	J	RF	250+	Rylant, Cynthia	Simon & Schuster
Annie and Snowball and the Magical House	J	RF	250+	Rylant, Cynthia	Simon & Schuster
Annie and Snowball and the Pink Surprise	J	RF	250+	Rylant, Cynthia	Simon & Schuster
Annie and Snowball and the Prettiest House	J	RF	250+	Rylant, Cynthia	Simon & Schuster
Annie and Snowball and the Shining Star	J	RF	250+	Rylant, Cynthia	Simon & Schuster
Annie and Snowball and the Teacup Club	J	RF	250+	Rylant, Cynthia	Simon & Schuster
Annie and the Old One	O	RF	250+	Miles, Miska	Little Brown and Company
Annie Bananie Moves To Barry Avenue	L	RF	250+	Komaiko, Leah	Bantam Books
Annie Glover Is Not a Tree Lover	Q	RF	250+	Beard, Darleen Bailey	Farrar, Straus, & Giroux
Annie Hoot and the Knitting Extravaganza	K	F	512	Clifton-Brown, Holly	Andersen Press USA
Annie John	Z	RF	250+	Kincaid, Jamaica	Farrar, Straus, & Giroux
Annie Oakley	R	B	2962	History Maker Bios	Lerner Publishing Group
Annie Oakley	I	B	268	My 1st Classic Story	Picture Window Books
Annie Oakley	R	B	250+	Wilson, Ellen	Aladdin
Annie Shapiro and the Clothing Workers' Strike	S	HF	4120	History Speaks	Millbrook Press
Annie's Adventures: The Sisters 8	Q	F	250+	Baratz-Logsted, Lauren	Houghton Mifflin Harcourt
Annie's Ancient Discoveries	M	RF	250+	Pair-It Turn and Learn	Steck-Vaughn
Annie's Pet	J	RF	250+	Bank Street	Bantam Books
Annie's Pictures	L	RF	460	Leveled Readers/TX	Houghton Mifflin Harcourt
Annie's Secret Diary	M	RF	250+	Little Celebrations	Pearson Learning Group
Annie's War	U	HF	250+	Sullivan, Jacqueline Levering	Eerdman's Books for Young Readers
Annika Sorenstam	P	B	1615	Amazing Athletes	Lerner Publishing Group
Annika Sorenstam	U	B	250+	Sports Heroes and Legends	Lerner Publishing Group
Anno's USA	WB	I	0	Mitsumaso, Anna	Philomel
Another Day, Another Challenge	L	RF	250+	Literacy 2000	Rigby
Another Dog	H	F	267	McAlpin, MaryAnn	Short Tales Press
Another Life	X	RF	2480	Leveled Readers	Houghton Mifflin Harcourt
Another Life	X	RF	2480	Leveled Readers/CA	Houghton Mifflin Harcourt
Another Life	X	RF	2480	Leveled Readers/TX	Houghton Mifflin Harcourt
Another Mouth to Feed	K	F	250+	Dahl, Michael	Picture Window Books
Another Point of View	P	RF	250+	Wildcats	Wright Group/McGraw Hill
Another Sneeze Louise!	E	RF	69	Potts, Cheryl A.	Kaeden Books
Another View	X	RF	3334	Leveled Readers	Houghton Mifflin Harcourt
Another View	X	RF	3334	Leveled Readers/CA	Houghton Mifflin Harcourt
Another View	X	RF	3334	Leveled Readers/TX	Houghton Mifflin Harcourt
Another Whole Nother Story	V	F	250+	Soup, Dr. Cuthbert	Bloomsbury Children's Books
Another Wonderful Day in the World of Buddy (As Told by Buddy)	E	F	165	McGougan, Kathy	Buddy Books Publishing
Ansel Adams, Photographer	R	B	1763	Leveled Readers Social Studies	Houghton Mifflin Harcourt
Anson's Way	X	HF	250+	Schmidt, Gary D.	Clarion Books
Answer the Phone, Fiona!	G	RF	119	Lighthouse	Rigby
Ant	O	I	250+	Chinery, Michael	Troll Associates
Ant and Honey Bee: A Pair of Friends at Halloween	L	F	250+	Candlewick Sparks	Candlewick Press
Ant and the Aphid, The	J	F	477	Gear Up!	Wright Group/McGraw Hill
Ant and the Chrysalis, The	K	TL	377	Springboard	Wright Group/McGraw Hill
Ant and the Dove, The	I	TL	222	Literacy by Design	Rigby
*Ant and the Dove, The	G	TL	173	New Way Blue	Steck-Vaughn

TITLE	LEVEL	GENRE	WORD COUNT	AUTHOR / SERIES	PUBLISHER / DISTRIBUTOR
Ant and the Dove, The	I	TL	250+	PM Plus Story Books	Rigby
Ant and the Dove, The	F	TL	196	Storyworlds	Heinemann
Ant and the Grasshopper, The	I	TL	231	Aesop's Fables	Pearson Learning Group
Ant and the Grasshopper, The	L	TL	250+	Little Celebrations	Pearson Learning Group
Ant and the Grasshopper, The	J	TL	250+	PM Plus Story Books	Rigby
Ant and the Grasshopper, The	L	TL	664	Reading Street	Pearson
Ant and the Grasshopper, The	J	TL	250+	Story Steps	Rigby
Ant and the Grasshopper, The: A Play	I	TL	250+	Literacy Tree	Rigby
Ant Attack!	K	RF	250+	Science Solves It!	Kane Press
Ant Can't	C	F	131	Leveled Literacy Intervention/ Green System	Heinemann
Ant Cities	O	I	250+	Dorros, Arthur	HarperCollins
Ant City	J	RF	393	PM Collection	Rigby
Ant Life Sweet	Q	F	250+	Reading Safari	Mondo Publishing
Ant, The	D	F	48	Ray's Readers	Outside the Box
Ant, The	E	F	97	Ready Readers	Pearson Learning Group
Antarctic Adventure	T	I	250+	High-Fliers	Pacific Learning
Antarctic Adventure	R	RF	250+	Reading Expeditions	National Geographic
Antarctic Adventure, An	M	I	296	Vocabulary Readers	Houghton Mifflin Harcourt
Antarctic Animals	L	I	328	Vocabulary Readers	Houghton Mifflin Harcourt
Antarctic Animals	L	I	328	Vocabulary Readers/CA	Houghton Mifflin Harcourt
Antarctic Animals	L	I	328	Vocabulary Readers/TX	Houghton Mifflin Harcourt
Antarctic Diary	M	I	250+	Voyages	SRA/McGraw Hill
Antarctic Ocean, The	N	I	250+	Oceans	Capstone Press
Antarctic Penguins	N	I	250+	PM Animal Facts: Silver	Rigby
Antarctic Seals	N	I	250+	PM Animal Facts: Silver	Rigby
Antarctica	N	I	250+	Continents	Capstone Press
Antarctica	L	I	250+	Cowcher, Helen	Square Fish
Antarctica	L	I	250+	Fowler, Allan	Scholastic
Antarctica	T	I	250+	Literacy 2000	Rigby
Antarctica	N	I	298	Pull Ahead Books	Lerner Publishing Group
Antarctica	L	I	250+	Read-About Geography	Children's Press
Antarctica	L	RF	250+	Soar To Success	Houghton Mifflin Harcourt
Antarctica	J	I	239	Sun Sprouts	ETA/Cuisenaire
Antarctica	P	I	250+	Trackers	Pacific Learning
Antarctica Adventure	S	I	250+	DK Readers	DK Publishing
Antarctica Land of Possibility	U	I	2026	Vocabulary Readers	Houghton Mifflin Harcourt
Antarctica, Land of Possibility	U	I	2026	Vocabulary Readers/CA	Houghton Mifflin Harcourt
Antarctica: Ice-Covered Continent	N	I	1016	Avenues	Hampton Brown
Antarctica: Ice-Covered Continent	N	I	250+	Phonics and Friends	Hampton Brown
Antarctica: Journey to the South Pole	X	I	250+	Myers, Walter Dean	Scholastic
Antarctica: Land of the Penguins	P	I	1315	Big Cat	Pacific Learning
Antarctica: The Frozen Continent	M	I	334	Reading Street	Pearson
Antarctica: The Last Great Wilderness	O	I	250+	Rigby Literacy	Rigby
Antartic Penguins	E	I	93	Readlings/ Marine Animals	American Reading Company
Anteaters to Zebras	LB	F	29	Fletcher, Alan	Harry N. Abrams
Anteater's Tongue, The	F	F	137	Sails	Rigby
Anthem	Z	F	250+	Edge	Hampton Brown
Anthony and the Girls	H	RF	95	Konnecke, Ole	Farrar, Straus, & Giroux
Anthony Burns: Defeat and Triumph of a Fugitive Slave	Y	B	250+	Hamilton, Virginia	Alfred A. Knopf
Anthony's New Glasses	H	RF	202	Adams, Lorraine & Bruvold, Lynn	Eaglecrest Books
Anthony's Unhappy Birthday	K	RF	560	Leveled Readers	Houghton Mifflin Harcourt
Anti-Bully Machine, The	P	F	250+	High-Fliers	Pacific Learning

* Collection of short stories   # Graphic text
^ Mature content with lower level text demands

TITLE	LEVEL	GENRE	WORD COUNT	AUTHOR / SERIES	PUBLISHER / DISTRIBUTOR
Antietam: Day of Courage and Sacrifice	Y	I	250+	The Civil War	Carus Publishing Company
Anti-Prom, The	Z+	RF	250+	McDonald, Abby	Candlewick Press
Anti-Slavery Movement, The	V	I	250+	Reading Expeditions	National Geographic
Antlers	I	I	155	Animal Spikes and Spines	Heinemann Library
Antlers	J	I	221	Windows on Literacy	National Geographic
Antoine Lavoisier: Founder of Modern Chemistry	X	B	250+	Science Readers	Teacher Created Materials
Antonia Novello: Doctor	N	B	250+	Beginning Biographies	Pearson Learning Group
Antonia Novello: Doctor for the Nation	K	B	204	Independent Readers Science	Houghton Mifflin Harcourt
Antonio's Music	J	B	250+	Emery, Joanna	Scholastic
Anton's Short Pants	D	RF	82	Bonnell, Kris	Reading Reading Books
Antonyms, Synonyms, Homonyms	Q	I	250+	Rayevsky, Kim & Robert	Holiday House
Ants	L	I	247	Ashley, Susan/Let's Read About Insects	Weekly Reader Publishing
Ants	H	I	96	Bugs, Bugs, Bugs	Red Brick Learning
Ants	B	I	16	Discovery Links	Newbridge
Ants	N	I	250+	Early Connections	Benchmark Education
Ants	E	I	50	Insects	Capstone Press
Ants	N	I	250+	Nature's Friends	Compass Point Books
Ants	E	I	127	Readlings/ Bugs	American Reading Company
Ants	A	I	98	Readlings/ Predator Bugs	American Reading Company
Ants	H	I	250+	Sunshine	Wright Group/McGraw Hill
Ants	G	I	94	Wonder World	Wright Group/McGraw Hill
Ants All Around	M	I	479	Gear Up!	Wright Group/McGraw Hill
Ants and Aphids Work Together	K	I	250+	Animals Working Together	Capstone Press
Ants and Grasshoppers, The	J	F	250+	The Wright Skills	Wright Group/McGraw Hill
Ants and the Grasshoppers, The	G	TL	144	New Way Blue	Steck-Vaughn
Ants and Their Nests	J	I	150	Animal Homes	Capstone Press
Ants Aren't Antisocial	S	I	250+	Action Packs	Rigby
Ants Everywhere	C	RF	24	Visions	Wright Group/McGraw Hill
Ants Go Home, The	B	F	60	Johns, Linda	Scholastic
Ants Go Marching, The	J	TL	250+	Traditional Songs	Picture Window Books
Ants Have a Picnic, The	I	F	181	Early Explorers	Benchmark Education
Ant's Journey, The	H	F	238	Domine Readers	Pearson Publishing Group
Ants Love Picnics, Too	B	F	27	Literacy 2000	Rigby
Ants of All Kinds	O	I	898	Vocabulary Readers	Houghton Mifflin Harcourt
Ants of All Kinds	O	I	898	Vocabulary Readers/CA	Houghton Mifflin Harcourt
Ants of All Kinds	O	I	898	Vocabulary Readers/TX	Houghton Mifflin Harcourt
Ants on a Log	E	RF	246	Leveled Literacy Intervention/ Blue System	Heinemann
Ants on a Picnic	C	F	35	Joy Readers	Pearson Learning Group
Ants, Ants, Ants	E	I	131	Sunshine	Wright Group/McGraw Hill
Ants, Aphids, and Caterpillars	S	I	1819	Vocabulary Readers	Houghton Mifflin Harcourt
Ants, Aphids, and Caterpillars	S	I	1819	Vocabulary Readers/CA	Houghton Mifflin Harcourt
Ants, The	B	RF	112	Leveled Literacy Intervention/ Blue System	Heinemann
Ants, The	B	F	30	Sails	Rigby
Anxious Hearts	Z+	RF	250+	Shaw, Tucker	Amulet Books
Any Pet Will Do	N	RF	250+	Orca Young Readers	Orca Books
Any Small Goodness: A Novel of the Barrio	X	RF	250+	Johnston, Tony	Hampton Brown
Anya's Camera	G	RF	214	PM Photo Stories	Rigby
Anybody Home?	U	I	250+	Boldprint	Steck-Vaughn
Anyone Can Eat Squid!: Simply Sarah	M	RF	250+	Naylor, Phyllis Reynolds	Marshall Cavendish
Anyone Can have a Pet	K	RF	503	PM Plus Story Books	Rigby

TITLE	LEVEL	GENRE	WORD COUNT	AUTHOR / SERIES	PUBLISHER / DISTRIBUTOR
Anything But Typical	X	RF	250+	Baskin, Nora Raleigh	Simon & Schuster
Anywhere Everywhere Bus, The	K	F	250+	Home Connection Collection	Rigby
Apache Indian Community, An	O	I	250+	Rosen Real Readers	Rosen Publishing Group
Apache Indians, The	P	I	250+	Native Peoples	Red Brick Learning
Apache, The	R	I	250+	First Reports	Compass Point Books
Apache, The: Nomadic Hunters of the Southwest	S	I	250+	American Indian Nations	Capstone Press
Apaches, The	T	I	3966	Native American Histoies	Lerner Publishing Group
Apatosaurus	O	I	250+	A True Book	Children's Press
Ape	N	RF	250+	Jenkins, Martin	Candlewick Press
Aphrodite's Blessings	Z	TL	250+	McLaren, Clemence	Atheneum Books
Apollo	K	F	208	Gregoire, Caroline	Kane/Miller Book Publishers
Apollo Moon Rocks, The	R	I	1430	Leveled Readers	Houghton Mifflin Harcourt
Apollo Moon Rocks, The	R	I	1430	Leveled Readers/CA	Houghton Mifflin Harcourt
Apollo Moon Rocks, The	R	I	1430	Leveled Readers/TX	Houghton Mifflin Harcourt
Apothecary, The	W	F	250+	Meloy, Maile	G.P. Putnam's Sons
Appalachian Trail	O	I	250+	Windows on Literacy	National Geographic
Appalachian Trail, The	H	I	205	Leveled Readers Language Support	Houghton Mifflin Harcourt
Appaloosa Horse, The	R	I	250+	Horses	Capstone Press
Appaloosa Horses	I	I	250+	Horses	Capstone Press
Appaloosas Are My Favorite!	O	I	250+	My Favorite Horses	Lerner Publishing Group
Appetite for Detention	Z+	F	250+	Tanen, Sloane	Bloomsbury Children's Books
Apple Bird, The	WB	F	0	Wildsmith, Brian	Oxford University Press
Apple Cider Making Days	L	RF	660	Purmell, Ann	Millbrook Press
Apple Farm, The	E	RF	95	Ready Readers	Pearson Learning Group
Apple Floats, An	D	I	35	Science	Outside the Box
Apple for Harriet Tubman, An	P	B	250+	Turner, Glennette Tiley	Albert Whitman & Co.
Apple Fractions	J	I	213	Rookie Read-About Math	Children's Press
Apple Harvest	F	I	93	All About Fall	Capstone Press
Apple Man, The	P	F	1094	Leveled Readers	Houghton Mifflin Harcourt
Apple Picking	B	RF	44	Bookshop	Mondo Publishing
Apple Pie	B	I	51	Leveled Literacy Intervention/ Green System	Heinemann
Apple Pie Calzones and Other Cookie Recipes	S	I	250+	Fun Food for Cool Cooks	Capstone Press
Apple Pie Family, The	E	RF	72	Pair-It Books	Steck-Vaughn
Apple Pie for Dinner, An	K	F	250+	VanHecke, Susan	Marshall Cavendish
Apple Pie Fourth of July	K	RF	250+	Wong, Janet S.	Harcourt, Inc.
Apple Pie Tree, The	K	I	250+	Zoe Hall	Scholastic
Apple Star, The	C	RF	33	First Stories	Pacific Learning
Apple Thief, The	G	F	62	Voyages	SRA/McGraw Hill
Apple Tree	I	RF	110	Book Bank	Wright Group/McGraw Hill
Apple Tree	G	RF	198	Literacy Tree	Rigby
Apple Tree Apple Tree	G	RF	340	Blocksma, Mary	Children's Press
Apple Tree Dilemma, The	R	RF	250+	Sails	Rigby
Apple Tree, An	A	I	32	Red Rocket Readers	Flying Start Books
Apple Tree, The	J	I	160	Sunshine	Wright Group/McGraw Hill
Apple Trees	D	I	62	Pebble Books	Capstone Press
Apple Trees	F	I	114	Plant Life Cycles	Lerner Publishing Group
Apple-Picking Time	J	RF	350	HSP/Harcourt Trophies	Harcourt, Inc.
Apple-Pip Princess, The	M	F	250+	Ray, Jane	Candlewick Press
Apples	LB	I	23	Berger, Samantha; Chessen, Betsey	Scholastic
Apples	A	RF	25	Leveled Readers	Houghton Mifflin Harcourt

* Collection of short stories   # Graphic text
^ Mature content with lower level text demands

TITLE	LEVEL	GENRE	WORD COUNT	AUTHOR / SERIES	PUBLISHER / DISTRIBUTOR
Apples	D	I	100	Leveled Readers	Houghton Mifflin Harcourt
Apples	D	I	100	Leveled Readers/CA	Houghton Mifflin Harcourt
Apples	A	RF	25	Leveled Readers/CA	Houghton Mifflin Harcourt
Apples	D	I	100	Leveled Readers/TX	Houghton Mifflin Harcourt
Apples	C	I	45	Williams, Deborah	Kaeden Books
Apples and How They Grow	I	I	250+	All Aboard Science Reader	Grosset & Dunlap
Apples and More Apples	E	I	97	Pair-It Books	Steck-Vaughn
Apples and Oranges: Going Bananas with Pairs	I	F	192	Pinto, Sarah	Bloomsbury Children's Books
Apples and Pumpkins	I	RF	185	Rockwell, Ann	Scholastic
Apples for America	P	B	824	Leveled Readers	Houghton Mifflin Harcourt
Apples for Sale	J	RF	354	PM Math Readers	Rigby
Apples for Santa	I	F	265	Little Elf	Literacy Footprints
Apples for the Teacher	E	RF	203	Joy Starters	Pearson Learning Group
Apples for Tiffy	F	RF	169	PM Photo Stories	Rigby
Apples Grow on a Tree	K	I	170	How Fruits and Vegetables Grow	Capstone Press
Apple's Life, An	F	I	172	Watch It Grow	Heinemann Library
Apples to Oregon	O	TL	250+	Hopkinson, Deborah & Carpenter, Nancy	Scholastic
Apples!	J	RF	503	Cambridge Reading	Pearson Learning Group
Apples, Apples, Everywhere	K	RF	906	InfoTrek	ETA/Cuisenaire
Apples, Cherries, Red Raspberries: What Is in the Fruits Group?	N	I	514	Food is CATegorical	Millbrook Press
Applesauce	D	I	45	Benchmark Rebus	Marshall Cavendish
Applesauce Season	L	RF	250+	Lipson, Eden Ross	Roaring Brook Press
Appointment with Action	P	RF	250+	Wildcats	Wright Group/McGraw Hill
Apprenticeship of Lucas Whitaker, The	U	HF	250+	DeFelice, Cynthia	Avon Books
April and Esme, Tooth Fairies	M	F	250+	Graham, Bob	Candlewick Press
April Fool's Day Mystery, The	L	RF	1182	Rigby Flying Colors	Rigby
April Fool's Day Mystery, The	M	RF	250+	Soar To Success	Houghton Mifflin Harcourt
April Morning	X	HF	250+	Fast, Howard	Bantam Books
April Showers	C	I	86	Vocabulary Readers	Houghton Mifflin Harcourt
April Showers	C	I	86	Vocabulary Readers/CA	Houghton Mifflin Harcourt
April Who? April Fools!	I	RF	197	Sunshine	Wright Group/McGraw Hill
Apron Annie in the Garden	G	RF	153	Learn to Read	Creative Teaching Press
Apron Annie's Pies	G	RF	167	Learn to Read	Creative Teaching Press
Apsaalooke (Crow) Nation, The	P	I	250+	Native Peoples	Red Brick Learning
Aquarium, The	LB	I	24	KinderReaders	Rigby
Aquarium, The	LB	I	18	Kloes, Carol	Kaeden Books
Aquarium, The	A	I	29	Leveled Readers	Houghton Mifflin Harcourt
Aquarium, The	A	I	29	Leveled Readers/CA	Houghton Mifflin Harcourt
Aquarium, The	C	RF	80	Tiny Treasures	Pioneer Valley
Arabella Miller's Tiny Caterpillar	K	RF	250+	Jarrett, Clare	Candlewick Press
Arabian Horses	I	I	141	Horses	Capstone Press
Arabian Oryx	L	I	250+	A Day in the Life: Desert Animals	Heinemann Library
Arabians Are My Favorite!	O	I	250+	My Favorite Horses	Lerner Publishing Group
Arachne	M	TL	558	Sun Sprouts	ETA/Cuisenaire
Arapaho, The: Hunters of the Great Plains	S	I	250+	American Indian Nations	Capstone Press
Arbor Day	Q	I	250+	Holiday Histories	Heinemann
Arbor Day	L	I	212	Holidays and Festivals	Heinemann Library
Arbor Day Square	N	RF	250+	Galbraith, Kathryn O.	Peachtree
Archaeological Adventures	T	I	250+	Explore More	Wright Group/McGraw Hill
Archaeologists Dig for Clues	P	I	250+	Duke, Kate	HarperCollins
Archaeology and the Ancient Past	T	I	250+	Reading Expeditions	National Geographic

* Collection of short stories # Graphic text
^ Mature content with lower level text demands

TITLE	LEVEL	GENRE	WORD COUNT	AUTHOR / SERIES	PUBLISHER / DISTRIBUTOR
Archer's Quest	Q	F	250+	Park, Linda Sue	Clarion Books
#Archie's Amazing Game	R	RF	2484	Hardcastle, Michael	Stone Arch Books
Archie's War: My Scrapbook of the First World War	X	I	250+	Williams, Maria	Candlewick Press
Archipelagoes	O	I	250+	Earthforms	Capstone Press
Architects of the Holocaust	Z	I	250+	The Holocaust	Compass Point Books
Arctic	R	I	250+	The Heinle Reading Library	Thomson Learning
Arctic and Antarctic	W	I	250+	Eyewitness Books	DK Publishing
Arctic Babies	P	I	250+	Darling, Kathy	Scholastic
Arctic Food Web, The	P	I	250+	Rigby Literacy	Rigby
Arctic Fox	L	I	250+	A Day in the Life: Polar Animals	Heinemann Library
Arctic Fox	C	I	40	Zoozoo-Animal World	Cavallo Publishing
Arctic Foxes	E	I	86	Bonnell, Kris/About	Reading Reading Books
Arctic Foxes	O	I	1412	Early Bird Nature Books	Lerner Publishing Group
Arctic Foxes	H	I	107	Polar Animals	Capstone Press
Arctic Hares	H	I	117	Polar Animals	Capstone Press
Arctic Investigations: Exploring the Frozen Ocean	T	I	250+	Young, Karen Romano	Steck-Vaughn
Arctic Journey	I	I	198	Sunshine	Wright Group/McGraw Hill
Arctic Life	M	I	250+	Robinson, F. R.	Steck-Vaughn
Arctic Ocean, The	N	I	250+	Oceans	Capstone Press
Arctic or Antarctic?	N	I	495	Red Rocket Readers	Flying Start Books
Arctic Tundra	N	I	250+	Habitats	Children's Press
Arctic Tundra and Polar Deserts	W	I	250+	Biomes Atlases	Raintree
Arctic, The	J	I	185	Early Explorers	Benchmark Education
Are All the Giants Dead?	V	F	250+	Norton, Mary	Harcourt Trade
Are Mountains Growing Taller? Questions and Answers About the Changing Earth	R	I	250+	Berger, Melvin & Gilda	Scholastic
Are Organized Sports Better for Kids Than Pickup Games? (Flipsides)	U	I	250+	Bookshop	Mondo Publishing
Are the Drums for You?	T	I	4551	Ready to Make Music	Lerner Publishing Group
Are They All the Same?	C	I	121	InfoTrek	ETA/Cuisenaire
Are They Look-Alikes?	I	I	194	Independent Readers Science	Houghton Mifflin Harcourt
Are We Hurting the Earth?	K	I	363	Early Connections	Benchmark Education
Are We There Yet?	G	RF	289	I'm Going to Read!	Sterling Publishing
Are We There Yet?	F	RF	127	Teacher's Choice Series	Pearson Learning Group
Are We There Yet?: A Journey Around Australia	N	RF	250+	Lester, Alison	Kane/Miller Book Publishers
Are We There Yet?: Using Map Scales	O	I	250+	Map Mania	Capstone Press
Are You a Ladybug?	L	I	250+	Backyard Books	Kingfisher
Are You a Ladybug?	F	I	116	Sunshine	Wright Group/McGraw Hill
Are You a Team Player?	S	I	1493	Vocabulary Readers	Houghton Mifflin Harcourt
Are You a Team Player?	S	I	1493	Vocabulary Readers/CA	Houghton Mifflin Harcourt
Are You a Team Player?	S	I	1493	Vocabulary Readers/TX	Houghton Mifflin Harcourt
Are You Afraid of . . .?	B	I	18	Little Celebrations	Pearson Learning Group
Are You Alone on Purpose?	Z	RF	250+	Werlin, Nancy	Speak
Are You Awake?	J	RF	250+	Blackall, Sophie	Henry Holt & Co.
Are You Blue Dog's Friend?	L	F	204	Rodrigue, George	Harry N. Abrams
Are You Hungry?	B	RF	49	Red Rocket Readers	Flying Start Books
Are You Living?: A Song About Living and Nonliving Things	L	I	250+	Science Songs	Picture Window Books
Are You My Mommy?	F	F	112	Dijs, Carla	Simon & Schuster
Are You My Mother?	I	F	250+	Eastman, Philip D.	Random House
Are You Ready for Bed?	K	F	250+	Johnson, Jane	Tiger Tales
Are You Ready for Fall?	J	I	389	Lightning Bolt Books	Lerner Publishing Group

* Collection of short stories   # Graphic text
^ Mature content with lower level text demands

TITLE	LEVEL	GENRE	WORD COUNT	AUTHOR / SERIES	PUBLISHER / DISTRIBUTOR
Are You Ready for Spring?	J	I	499	Lightning Bolt Books	Lerner Publishing Group
Are You Ready for Summer?	J	I	467	Lightning Bolt Books	Lerner Publishing Group
Are You Ready for Winter?	J	I	380	Lightning Bolt Books	Lerner Publishing Group
#Are You Ready To Play Outside? (Elephant & Piggie)	G	F	168	Willems, Mo	Hyperion
Are You the New Principal?	E	RF	120	Teacher's Choice Series	Pearson Learning Group
Are You There, Bear?	F	F	42	Maris, Ron	Greenwillow Books
Are You There, God? It's Me, Margaret.	T	RF	250+	Blume, Judy	Bantam Books
Are You There?	D	F	81	Sun Sprouts	ETA/Cuisenaire
Argentina	O	I	2408	A Ticket to …	Carolrhoda Books
Argentina	P	I	2461	Country Explorers	Lerner Publishing Group
Argentina: A Question and Answer Book	P	I	250+	Question and Answer Countries	Capstone Press
Arguments	K	F	398	Read Alongs	Rigby
Ariel of the Sea	U	F	250+	Calhoun, Dia	Winslow Press
Ariel Sharon	X	B	250+	A&E Biography	Lerner Publishing Group
Aristotle and Alexander	Z	I	2538	Leveled Readers	Houghton Mifflin Harcourt
Arizona	T	I	250+	Hello U.S.A.	Lerner Publishing Group
Arizona	S	I	250+	Land of Liberty	Red Brick Learning
Arizona Cardinals, The	S	I	250+	Team Spirit	Norwood House Press
Arizona Diamondbacks, The	S	I	250+	Team Spirit	Norwood House Press
Arizona Diamondbacks, The (Revised Edition)	S	I	250+	Team Spirit	Norwood House Press
Arizona: Facts and Symbols	O	I	250+	The States and Their Symbols	Capstone Press
Ark, The	O	HF	250+	Geisert, Arthur	Houghton Mifflin Harcourt
Arkadians, The	W	F	250+	Alexander, Lloyd	Puffin Books
Arkanas: Facts and Symbols	O	I	250+	The States and Their Symbols	Capstone Press
Arkansas	T	I	250+	Hello U.S.A.	Lerner Publishing Group
Arkansas	S	I	250+	Land of Liberty	Red Brick Learning
Arkansas	R	I	250+	This Land Is Your Land	Compass Point Books
Arky, the Dinosaur With Feathers	K	HF	529	PM Plus Story Books	Rigby
Arlington National Cemetery	V	I	250+	Cornerstones of Freedom	Children's Press
Armadillo	M	RF	134	Books for Young Learners	Richard C. Owen
Armadillo from Amarillo, The	N	F	800	Cherry, Lynne	Harcourt Brace
Armadillo, The	L	I	250+	Sunshine	Wright Group/McGraw Hill
Armadillo, The	R	I	250+	Wildlife of North America	Red Brick Learning
Armadillos	H	I	93	Desert Animals	Capstone Press
Armadillos	I	I	232	Sails	Rigby
Armando Asked, "Why?"	I	RF	250+	Ready Set Read	Steck-Vaughn
Armies of Ants	M	I	250+	Retan, Walter	Scholastic
Armor	M	I	641	Sun Sprouts	ETA/Cuisenaire
Armored Dinosaurs	P	I	909	Meet the Dinosaurs	Lerner Publishing Group
Army Ants	P	I	2044	Animal Scavengers	Lerner Publishing Group
Army Ants	I	I	245	Sails	Rigby
^Army Rangers, The	T	I	250+	Elite Military Forces	Capstone Press
Arnie and the Skateboard Gang	K	F	349	Carlson, Nancy	Carolrhoda Books
Arnie Goes to Camp	K	F	485	Carlson, Nancy	Carolrhoda Books
Arnold Lobel: Words and Pictures Together	L	B	375	Leveled Readers	Houghton Mifflin Harcourt
^Arnold Schwarzenegger: Athlete, Actor, Governor	R	B	250+	Hameray Biography Series	Hameray Publishing Group
Around and About	E	RF	209	Sun Sprouts	ETA/Cuisenaire
Around and Around	B	I	72	PM Plus Nonfiction	Rigby
Around and Around	J	I	424	Sails	Rigby
Around My School	E	I	60	Exploring History & Geography	Rigby
Around One Cactus: Owls, Bats, and Leaping Rats	N	I	250+	Sharing Nature with Children	Dawn Publications

TITLE	LEVEL	GENRE	WORD COUNT	AUTHOR / SERIES	PUBLISHER / DISTRIBUTOR
Around One Log	O	I	250+	Sharing Nature with Children	Dawn Publications
Around Our Way on Neighbors' Day	N	RF	250+	Brown, Tameka Fryer	Harry N. Abrams
Around the Neighborhood	E	I	74	Pair-It Books	Steck-Vaughn
Around the World	D	RF	57	Big Cat	Pacific Learning
Around the World	Q	I	1998	Take Two Books	Wright Group/McGraw Hill
Around the World in a Day	K	RF	634	InfoTrek	ETA/Cuisenaire
Around the World in a Hundred Years: From Henry the Navigator to Magellan	W	I	250+	Fritz, Jean	G.P. Putnam's Sons Books for Young Readers
#Around the World in Eighty Days	T	F	2122	Dominoes starter	Oxford University Press
Around-the-World Lunch, The	K	RF	250+	Canetti, Yanitzia	Steck-Vaughn
Art 123	O	I	195	Zuffi, Stefano	Harry N. Abrams
Art Around the World	M	I	250+	Discovery World	Rigby
Art Around the World	J	I	239	Early Connections	Benchmark Education
Art Class, The	H	RF	240	Leveled Readers	Houghton Mifflin Harcourt
Art For You	B	I	21	Shutterbug Books	Steck-Vaughn
Art Gallery	Q	I	250+	Trackers	Pacific Learning
Art in Caves	R	I	806	Leveled Readers	Houghton Mifflin Harcourt
Art in Caves	R	I	806	Leveled Readers/CA	Houghton Mifflin Harcourt
Art in Caves	R	I	806	Leveled Readers/TX	Houghton Mifflin Harcourt
Art in Sub-Saharan Africa	W	I	2877	Independent Readers Social Studies	Houghton Mifflin Harcourt
Art in the Past	Q	I	250+	Rigby Star Quest	Rigby
Art in the Renaissance	W	I	250+	Navigators Social Studies Series	Benchmark Education
Art is a...	P	I	141	Raczka, Bob	Lerner Publishing Group
Art Is All Around Us	J	I	283	Red Rocket Readers	Flying Start Books
Art Is All Around You	O	I	720	Vocabulary Readers	Houghton Mifflin Harcourt
Art Is All Around You	O	I	720	Vocabulary Readers/CA	Houghton Mifflin Harcourt
Art Lesson, The	M	B	246	DePaola, Tomie	G.P. Putnam's Sons Books for Young Readers
Art of Freedom, The: How Artists See America	P	I	69	Raczka, Bob	Millbrook Press
Art of Makeup, The: Going Behind the Mask	T	I	1752	Reading Street	Pearson
Art Riddle Contest, The	Q	RF	250+	Medearis, Angela Shelf	Steck-Vaughn
Art Scene	V	I	250+	Boldprint	Steck-Vaughn
Art Show, The	K	RF	857	Leveled Readers/TX	Houghton Mifflin Harcourt
Artemis Fowl	Y	F	250+	Colfer, Eoin	Hyperion
Artemis Fowl: The Arctic Incident	Y	F	250+	Colfer, Eoin	Hyperion
Artemis Fowl: The Graphic Novel	Y	F	250+	Colfer, Eoin & Donkin, Andrew	Hyperion
*Artful Stories	P	I	250+	Rigby Literacy	Rigby
Arthropods Everywhere!	S	I	1304	Leveled Readers	Houghton Mifflin Harcourt
Arthropods Everywhere!	S	I	1304	Leveled Readers/CA	Houghton Mifflin Harcourt
Arthropods Everywhere!	S	I	1304	Leveled Readers/TX	Houghton Mifflin Harcourt
Arthropods Rule!	S	I	1337	Leveled Readers	Houghton Mifflin Harcourt
Arthropods Rule!	S	I	1337	Leveled Readers/CA	Houghton Mifflin Harcourt
Arthropods Rule!	S	I	1337	Leveled Readers/TX	Houghton Mifflin Harcourt
#Arthur & Lancelot: The Fight for Camelot	V	TL	4365	Graphic Myths and Legends	Graphic Universe
Arthur Accused!	M	F	250+	Brown, Marc	Little Brown and Company
Arthur and the Baby	M	F	250+	Brown, Marc	Little Brown and Company
Arthur and the Big Blow-Up	M	F	250+	Brown, Marc	Little Brown and Company
Arthur and the Big Snow	J	F	250+	Brown, Marc	Little Brown and Company
Arthur and the Comet Crisis	M	F	250+	Brown, Marc	Little Brown and Company
Arthur and the Cootie-Catcher	M	F	250+	Brown, Marc	Little Brown and Company
Arthur and the Crunch Cereal Contest	M	F	250+	Brown, Marc	Little Brown and Company
Arthur and the Dog Show	J	F	250+	Brown, Marc	Little Brown and Company
Arthur and the Double Dare	M	F	250+	Brown, Marc	Little Brown and Company

* Collection of short stories   # Graphic text
^ Mature content with lower level text demands

TITLE	LEVEL	GENRE	WORD COUNT	AUTHOR / SERIES	PUBLISHER / DISTRIBUTOR
Arthur and the Forbidden City	R	F	250+	Besson, Luc	HarperTrophy
Arthur and the Lost Diary	M	F	250+	Brown, Marc	Little Brown and Company
Arthur and the No-Brainer	M	F	250+	Brown, Marc	Little Brown and Company
Arthur and the Pen-Pal Playoff	M	F	250+	Brown, Marc	Little Brown and Company
Arthur and the Poetry Contest	M	F	250+	Brown, Marc	Little Brown and Company
Arthur and the Popularity Test	M	F	250+	Brown, Marc	Little Brown and Company
Arthur and the Scare-Your-Pants-Off Club	M	F	250+	Brown, Marc	Little Brown and Company
Arthur and the TL Contest	M	F	250+	Brown, Marc	Little Brown and Company
Arthur Babysits	L	F	250+	Brown, Marc	Little Brown and Company
Arthur Goes To Camp	L	F	731	Brown, Marc	Little Brown and Company
Arthur Helps Out	J	F	250+	Brown, Marc	Little Brown and Company
Arthur Jumps into Fall	J	F	250+	Brown, Marc	Little Brown and Company
Arthur Lost and Found	L	F	250+	Brown, Marc	Little Brown and Company
Arthur Lost in the Museum	I	F	250+	Brown, Marc	Random House
Arthur Makes the Team	M	F	250+	Brown, Marc	Little Brown and Company
Arthur Meets the President	L	F	995	Brown, Marc	Little Brown and Company
Arthur Rocks with BINKY	M	F	250+	Brown, Marc	Little Brown and Company
Arthur Tells a Story	J	F	250+	Brown, Marc	Little Brown and Company
Arthur to the Rescue	J	F	250+	Brown, Marc	Little Brown and Company
Arthur Tricks the Tooth Fairy	I	F	250+	Brown, Marc	Random House
Arthur Turns Green	L	F	250+	Brown, Marc	Little Brown and Company
Arthur Writes a Story	L	F	600	Brown, Marc	Little Brown and Company
Arthur, Clean Your Room!	I	F	250+	Brown, Marc	Random House
Arthur, For the Very First Time	R	RF	250+	MacLachlan, Patricia	Bantam Books
Arthur, It's Only Rock 'n' Roll	M	F	250+	Brown, Marc	Little Brown and Company
Arthur's April Fool	K	F	250+	Brown, Marc	Little Brown and Company
Arthur's Baby	K	F	250+	Brown, Marc	Scholastic
Arthur's Back to School Day	K	F	250+	Hoban, Lillian	HarperTrophy
Arthur's Birthday	L	F	740	Brown, Marc	Little Brown and Company
Arthur's Birthday Surprise	J	F	250+	Brown, Marc	Little Brown and Company
Arthur's Camp-Out	K	F	250+	Hoban, Lillian	HarperTrophy
Arthur's Chicken Pox	L	F	801	Brown, Marc	Little Brown and Company
Arthur's Christmas	L	F	250+	Brown, Marc	Little Brown and Company
Arthur's Christmas Cookies	K	F	250+	Hoban, Lillian	HarperTrophy
Arthur's Computer Disaster	M	F	250+	Brown, Marc	Little Brown and Company
Arthur's Eyes	K	F	250+	Brown, Marc	Scholastic
Arthur's Family Vacation	L	F	785	Brown, Marc	Little Brown and Company
Arthur's Fantastic Party	I	F	254	Big Cat	Pacific Learning
Arthur's First Sleepover	L	F	878	Brown, Marc	Little Brown and Company
Arthur's Funny Money	K	F	250+	Hoban, Lillian	HarperTrophy
Arthur's Great Big Valentine	K	F	250+	Hoban, Lillian	HarperTrophy
Arthur's Halloween	L	F	250+	Brown, Marc	Little Brown and Company
Arthur's Halloween Costume	K	F	250+	Hoban, Lillian	HarperCollins
Arthur's Homework	J	F	250+	Brown, Marc	Little Brown and Company
Arthur's Honey Bear	K	F	250+	Hoban, Lillian	HarperCollins
Arthur's Jelly Beans	J	F	250+	Brown, Marc	Little Brown and Company
Arthur's Loose Tooth	K	F	250+	Hoban, Lillian	HarperCollins
Arthur's Mystery Envelope	M	F	250+	Brown, Marc	Little Brown and Company
Arthur's New Puppy	L	F	969	Brown, Marc	Little Brown and Company
Arthur's Off to School	J	F	250+	Brown, Marc	Little Brown and Company
Arthur's Pen Pal	K	F	250+	Hoban, Lillian	HarperCollins
Arthur's Pet Business	L	F	878	Brown, Marc	Little Brown and Company
Arthur's Prize Reader	K	F	250+	Hoban, Lillian	HarperTrophy
Arthur's Teacher Trouble	L	F	809	Brown, Marc	Little Brown and Company

A

TITLE	LEVEL	GENRE	WORD COUNT	AUTHOR / SERIES	PUBLISHER / DISTRIBUTOR
Arthur's Thanksgiving	L	F	250+	Brown, Marc	Little Brown and Company
Arthur's Tooth	L	F	250+	Brown, Marc	Little Brown and Company
Arthur's Tree House	J	F	250+	Brown, Marc	Little Brown and Company
Arthur's TV Trouble	L	F	250+	Brown, Marc	Little Brown and Company
Arthur's Underwear	L	F	683	Brown, Marc	Little Brown and Company
Arthur's Valentine	K	F	250+	Brown, Marc	Little Brown and Company
Artist for the Revolution, An	W	HF	3095	Leveled Readers	Houghton Mifflin Harcourt
Artist for the Revolution, An	W	HF	3095	Leveled Readers/CA	Houghton Mifflin Harcourt
Artist for the Revolution, An	W	HF	3095	Leveled Readers/TX	Houghton Mifflin Harcourt
Artist in the Woods	G	F	228	Seedlings	Continental Press
Artist, The	F	F	83	Books for Young Learners	Richard C. Owen
Artists	J	I	172	Bookworms	Marshall Cavendish
Artists All Around You	M	I	862	Leveled Readers	Houghton Mifflin Harcourt
Artists All Around You	M	I	862	Leveled Readers/CA	Houghton Mifflin Harcourt
Artists All Around You	M	I	862	Leveled Readers/TX	Houghton Mifflin Harcourt
*Artists and Their Art	Q	I	250+	Medearis, Michael	Steck-Vaughn
Artists are Everywhere	M	I	842	Leveled Readers	Houghton Mifflin Harcourt
Artists Are Everywhere	M	I	842	Leveled Readers/CA	Houghton Mifflin Harcourt
Artists Are Everywhere	M	I	842	Leveled Readers/TX	Houghton Mifflin Harcourt
Artists in Training	P	I	813	Vocabulary Readers	Houghton Mifflin Harcourt
Artists in Training	P	I	813	Vocabulary Readers/CA	Houghton Mifflin Harcourt
Artists in Training	P	I	813	Vocabulary Readers/TX	Houghton Mifflin Harcourt
Arturo's Baton	K	RF	250+	Hoff, Syd	Clarion Books
Arturo's Baton	L	RF	250+	Soar To Success	Houghton Mifflin Harcourt
As Ever, Gordy	V	HF	250+	Hahn, Mary Downing	Houghton Mifflin Harcourt
As Fast as a Fox	D	RF	69	Ready Readers	Pearson Learning Group
As Fast as You Can	B	RF	57	Red Rocket Readers	Flying Start Books
As Heavy As	F	I	170	PM Math Readers	Rigby
As Long as Grass Should Grow and Water Flow	V	I	250+	Rigby Literacy	Rigby
As Still as a Statue	K	RF	783	Sun Sprouts	ETA/Cuisenaire
As the Crow Flies: A First Book of Maps	M	I	130	Hartman, Gail	Aladdin
As Time Goes By	N	I	250+	On Our Way to English	Rigby
#As You Like It	Z	HF	250+	Manga Shakespeare	Amulet Books
Ashes for Gold	K	TL	250+	Folk Tales	Mondo Publishing
Ashes of Roses	Y	HF	250+	Auch, Mary Jane	Random House
Ashley's Elephant	J	F	250+	Zaretsky, Evan	Kaeden Books
Ashley's Great Week	F	RF	77	Larkin's Little Readers	Wilbooks
Ashley's World Record	L	F	250+	Little Celebrations	Pearson Learning Group
Ashwater Experiment, The	U	RF	250+	Koss, Amy Goldman	Scholastic
Asia	N	I	250+	Continents	Capstone Press
Asia	N	I	460	Pull Ahead Books	Lerner Publishing Group
Asian Elephants	A	I	70	Readlings/ Animals of Asia	American Reading Company
Ask Dr. K. Fisher about Creepy-Crawlies	O	I	250+	Llewellyn, Claire	Kingfisher
Ask Dr. K. Fisher about Planet Earth	O	I	250+	Llewellyn, Claire	Kingfisher
Ask Dr. K. Fisher about Reptiles	O	I	250+	Llewellyn, Claire	Kingfisher
Ask Dr. K. Fisher about Weather	O	I	250+	Llewellyn, Claire	Kingfisher
Ask Einstein!	N	RF	250+	Orbit Chapter Books	Pacific Learning
Ask Mr. Bear	J	F	613	Flack, Marjorie	Macmillan
Ask Nicely	F	F	110	Literacy 2000	Rigby
Ask the Veterinarians	O	I	250+	On Our Way to English	Rigby
Asleep	C	RF	26	Joy Readers	Pearson Learning Group
Asli's Story	S	I	250+	Jansen, Adrienne	Pacific Learning
Assassin	Y	HF	250+	Myers, Anna	Walker & Company

* Collection of short stories   # Graphic text
^ Mature content with lower level text demands

TITLE	LEVEL	GENRE	WORD COUNT	AUTHOR / SERIES	PUBLISHER / DISTRIBUTOR
Assassination at Sarajevo: The Spark That Started World War I	Y	I	250+	Snapshots in History	Compass Point Books
Assassination of Abraham Lincoln, The	V	B	250+	Cornerstones of Freedom	Children's Press
#Assassination of Abraham Lincoln, The	T	B	250+	Graphic Library	Capstone Press
Assassination of John F. Kennedy, The	V	B	250+	Cornerstones of Freedom	Children's Press
Assassination of Martin Luther King, Jr., The	V	B	250+	Cornerstones of Freedom	Children's Press
Assassin's Apprentice: Oathbreaker	Y	F	250+	Vaught, S R & Redmond, J B	Bloomsbury Children's Books
Assembly Line, The	M	I	501	Leveled Readers Social Studies	Houghton Mifflin Harcourt
Asteroid, The	M	F	752	PM Collection	Rigby
Asteroids	Q	I	250+	The Galaxy	Red Brick Learning
Asteroids, Comets, and Meteorites	M	I	250+	The Solar System	Capstone Press
Asthma	K	I	250+	Health Matters	Capstone Press
^Aston Martin	O	I	250+	Fast Cars	Capstone Press
Astro: The Steller Sea Lion	L	RF	1044	Harvey, Jeanne Walker	Sylvan Dell Publishing
Astronaut	B	I	22	Hoenecke, Karen	Kaeden Books
Astronaut Adventure	C	F	41	Phonics and Friends	Hampton Brown
Astronaut Cookbook, An	N	I	250+	First Cookbooks	Capstone Press
Astronaut, The	B	RF	30	Sunshine	Wright Group/McGraw Hill
Astronaut: Living in Space	L	I	250+	DK Readers	DK Publishing
Astronauts	M	I	250+	Community Helpers	Red Brick Learning
Astronauts	H	I	142	Exploring the Galaxy	Capstone Press
Astronauts	I	I	200	On Deck	Rigby
Astronauts	I	I	118	Phonics Readers	Compass Point Books
Astronauts	I	I	171	Wonder World	Wright Group/McGraw Hill
Astronauts and Cosmonauts	U	I	2882	Reading Street	Pearson
^Astronauts at Work	N	I	250+	Explore Space!	Red Brick Learning
Astronauts in Space	J	I	135	Windows on Literacy	National Geographic
Astronauts Take Flight	Q	I	250+	iOpeners	Pearson Learning Group
Astronauts, The	F	F	112	Foundations	Wright Group/McGraw Hill
*Astronomers	T	B	250+	Navigators Biography Series	Benchmark Education
Astronomers Through Time	S	B	250+	Science Readers	Teacher Created Materials
Astronomy: Out of This World!	W	I	250+	Green, Dan	Kingfisher
At 1600 Pennsylvania Avenue	O	I	250+	Wirth, Crystal	Scholastic
At a Fair	C	I	35	Benchmark Rebus	Marshall Cavendish
At a Fire With Firefighter Phil	C	RF	54	Run to Reading	Discovery Peak
At a Picnic	D	I	40	Benchmark Rebus	Marshall Cavendish
At Bat	D	RF	53	Reading Street	Pearson Learning Group
At Christmas	C	RF	26	Visions	Wright Group/McGraw Hill
At Grandma Ruth's House	C	F	37	Coulton, Mia	Maryruth Books
At Grandma's House	E	RF	118	Handprints D, Set 1	Educators Publishing Service
At Grandma's House	D	RF	66	Teacher's Choice Series	Pearson Learning Group
At Her Majesty's Request: An African Princess in Victorian England	X	HF	250+	Myers, Walter Dean	Scholastic
At Home and at School	B	I	32	Leveled Readers Social Studies	Houghton Mifflin Harcourt
At Home Around the World	F	I	82	Rosen Real Readers	Rosen Publishing Group
At Home by the Ocean	G	I	166	Book Worms	Marshall Cavendish
At Home in Space	V	I	2547	Leveled Readers	Houghton Mifflin Harcourt
At Home in the City	F	I	146	Book Worms	Marshall Cavendish
At Home in the Desert	G	I	182	Book Worms	Marshall Cavendish
At Home on the Farm	F	I	155	Book Worms	Marshall Cavendish
At Home on the Mountain	G	I	168	Book Worms	Marshall Cavendish
At Home on the Prairie	N	I	436	Vocabulary Readers	Houghton Mifflin Harcourt

* Collection of short stories   # Graphic text
^ Mature content with lower level text demands

TITLE	LEVEL	GENRE	WORD COUNT	AUTHOR / SERIES	PUBLISHER / DISTRIBUTOR
At Home on the Ranch	F	I	172	Book Worms	Marshall Cavendish
At Home on the Reef	M	I	526	Red Rocket Readers	Flying Start Books
At Home Sick	E	RF	121	The King School Series	Townsend Press
At Home With Marvelous Me	C	I	85	Run to Reading	Discovery Peak
At Last!	D	RF	41	Rigby Literacy	Rigby
At Last!	D	RF	65	Rigby Star	Rigby
At Lunchtime	I	I	461	Explorations	Okapi Educational Materials
At Lunchtime	I	I	461	Explorations	Eleanor Curtain Publishing
At My Grandfather's	G	RF	63	City Stories	Rigby
At My House	A	I	40	On Our Way to English	Rigby
At My School	B	I	43	Little Books for Early Readers	University of Maine
At Night	D	RF	21	Literacy Tree	Rigby
At Night	B	I	32	Sails	Rigby
At Play on the Plains and Prairie: Barn Raisings, Birthdays and Other Celebrations	P	I	250+	HSP/Harcourt Trophies	Harcourt, Inc.
At School	LB	I	12	Avenues	Hampton Brown
At School	A	I	45	Leveled Literacy Intervention/ Orange System	Heinemann
At School	A	I	28	Little Books for Early Readers	University of Maine
At School	A	I	32	Red Rocket Readers	Flying Start Books
At School	LB	I	12	Rise & Shine	Hampton Brown
At School	B	I	63	Springboard	Wright Group/McGraw Hill
At School	B	I	23	Sunshine	Wright Group/McGraw Hill
At School	B	I	29	Vocabulary Readers	Houghton Mifflin Harcourt
At School	A	I	20	Vocabulary Readers	Houghton Mifflin Harcourt
At School	A	I	20	Vocabulary Readers/CA	Houghton Mifflin Harcourt
At School	G	I	250+	Yellow Umbrella Books	Red Brick Learning
At School With Custodian Kate	C	RF	83	Run to Reading	Discovery Peak
At School With Teacher Ted	B	RF	63	Run to Reading	Discovery Peak
At the Airport	B	I	42	Leveled Readers Social Studies	Houghton Mifflin Harcourt
At the Airport	B	RF	58	Red Rocket Readers	Flying Start Books
At the Apple Farm	G	I	250+	Albanese, Rachel and Smith, Laura	Scholastic
At the Aquarium	B	I	45	Explorations	Eleanor Curtain Publishing
At the Aquarium	B	I	45	Explorations	Okapi Educational Materials
At the Aquarium	A	I	24	Leveled Readers	Houghton Mifflin Harcourt
At the Aquarium	A	I	24	Leveled Readers/CA	Houghton Mifflin Harcourt
At the Aquarium	B	RF	38	McAlpin, MaryAnn	Short Tales Press
At the Art Museum	M	I	250+	Rosen Real Readers	Rosen Publishing Group
At the Ballpark	H	RF	105	Sunshine	Wright Group/McGraw Hill
At the Barbershop	F	RF	179	Visions	Wright Group/McGraw Hill
At the Beach	D	I	39	Benchmark Rebus	Marshall Cavendish
At the Beach	B	I	30	Discovery Links	Newbridge
At the Beach	E	RF	114	InfoTrek	ETA/Cuisenaire
At the Beach	G	RF	231	Leveled Literacy Intervention/ Blue System	Heinemann
At the Beach	B	I	74	Leveled Readers Emergent	Houghton Mifflin Harcourt
At the Beach	E	RF	43	Literacy 2000	Rigby
At the Beach	A	RF	32	Literacy by Design	Rigby
At the Beach	E	RF	85	Oxford Reading Tree	Oxford University Press
At the Beach	D	I	125	PM Science Readers	Rigby
At the Beach	LB	RF	15	Rigby Literacy	Rigby
At the Beach	C	I	74	Sun Sprouts	ETA/Cuisenaire
At the Beach	A	I	78	The Places I Go	American Reading Company

* Collection of short stories   # Graphic text
^ Mature content with lower level text demands

TITLE	LEVEL	GENRE	WORD COUNT	AUTHOR / SERIES	PUBLISHER / DISTRIBUTOR
At the Beach	A	I	15	Vocabulary Readers	Houghton Mifflin Harcourt
At the Beach	A	I	15	Vocabulary Readers/CA	Houghton Mifflin Harcourt
At the Beach	D	I	43	Windows on Literacy	National Geographic
At the Car Wash	E	RF	143	Visions	Wright Group/McGraw Hill
At the Circus	K	I	300	Early Explorers	Benchmark Education
At the Circus	L	I	250+	Trackers	Pacific Learning
At the Coal Mine	L	I	317	Rigby Focus	Rigby
At the Controls: Questioning Video and Computer Games	S	I	250+	Media Literacy	Capstone Press
At the Dentist	G	I	128	Healthy Teeth	Capstone Press
At the Doctor	J	I	250+	Story Starter	Wright Group/McGraw Hill
At the Edge of the Sea	M	I	693	Sunshine	Wright Group/McGraw Hill
At the End of the Day	L	RF	250+	Pacific Literacy	Pacific Learning
At the Fair	B	I	48	Leveled Literacy Intervention/ Blue System	Heinemann
At the Fair	A	RF	20	Leveled Readers	Houghton Mifflin Harcourt
At the Fair	A	RF	20	Leveled Readers/CA	Houghton Mifflin Harcourt
At the Fair	LB	I	14	Little Books for Early Readers	University of Maine
At the Fair	D	I	116	Little Red Readers	Sundance
At the Fair	C	RF	58	Rise & Shine	Hampton Brown
At the Fair	C	F	76	Springboard	Wright Group/McGraw Hill
At the Fair	D	RF	175	Sunshine	Wright Group/McGraw Hill
At the Farm	B	I	60	Leveled Literacy Intervention/ Orange System	Heinemann
At the Farm	C	I	52	Little Red Readers	Sundance
At the Farm	M	I	250+	Look Once Look Again	Creative Teaching Press
At the Farmer's Market	H	I	137	Windows on Literacy	National Geographic
At the Firehouse with Dad	H	RF	218	Bebop Books	Lee & Low Books Inc.
At the Game	G	F	85	City Stories	Rigby
At the Garage	B	I	56	Readlings	American Reading Company
At the Horse Show	D	I	24	Books for Young Learners	Richard C. Owen
At the Ice Cream Shop	C	I	35	Vocabulary Readers	Houghton Mifflin Harcourt
At the Lake	I	RF	176	Books for Young Learners	Richard C. Owen
At the Lake	C	RF	23	KinderReaders	Rigby
At the Lake	B	I	98	Readlings	American Reading Company
At the Lake	B	I	71	The Places I Go	American Reading Company
At the Library	F	F	31	Little Celebrations	Pearson Learning Group
At the Library	C	I	69	PM Starters	Rigby
At the Market	A	I	40	Leveled Literacy Intervention/ Orange System	Heinemann
At the Movies	P	I	250+	Bookweb	Rigby
At the Museum	B	RF	28	Ready Readers	Pearson Learning Group
At the Ocean	C	RF	26	Early Emergent	Pioneer Valley
At the Ocean	A	I	29	Little Books for Early Readers	University of Maine
At the Office With Nurse Nan	B	I	63	Run to Reading	Discovery Peak
At the Park	C	I	32	Bebop Books	Lee & Low Books Inc.
At the Park	D	I	55	Benchmark Rebus	Marshall Cavendish
At the Park	F	RF	163	Early Connections	Benchmark Education
At the Park	C	RF	77	Handprints B	Educators Publishing Service
At the Park	C	I	40	Harry's Math Books	Outside the Box
At the Park	D	I	37	Hoenecke, Karen	Kaeden Books
At the Park	A	I	24	InfoTrek	ETA/Cuisenaire
At the Park	A	I	48	Leveled Literacy Intervention/ Green System	Heinemann

TITLE	LEVEL	GENRE	WORD COUNT	AUTHOR / SERIES	PUBLISHER / DISTRIBUTOR
At the Park	A	I	36	Leveled Readers	Houghton Mifflin Harcourt
At the Park	A	I	36	Leveled Readers/CA	Houghton Mifflin Harcourt
At the Park	A	I	36	Leveled Readers/TX	Houghton Mifflin Harcourt
At the Park	D	I	91	Little Red Readers	Sundance
At the Park	E	RF	29	Oxford Reading Tree	Oxford University Press
At the Park	LB	RF	14	Rigby Rocket	Rigby
At the Park	D	RF	74	Teacher's Choice Series	Pearson Learning Group
At the Park	A	I	40	The Places I Go	American Reading Company
At the Park	F	I	127	Yellow Umbrella Books	Capstone Press
At the Pet Store	I	I	177	Foundations	Wright Group/McGraw Hill
At the Plate with...Ken Griffey Jr.	T	B	250+	Christopher, Matt	Little Brown and Company
At the Playground	G	I	151	Discovery Links	Newbridge
At the Playground	B	I	54	Little Books for Early Readers	University of Maine
At the Playground	C	I	86	Little Red Readers	Sundance
At the Playground	B	I	48	Rigby Flying Colors	Rigby
At the Playground	LB	I	25	Visions	Wright Group/McGraw Hill
At the Playground	LB	I	8	Windows on Literacy	National Geographic
At the Pond	B	I	64	Early Connections	Benchmark Education
At the Pond	A	I	40	Leveled Literacy Intervention/ Orange System	Heinemann
At the Pond	A	RF	25	Leveled Readers	Houghton Mifflin Harcourt
At the Pond	B	RF	51	Leveled Readers Science	Houghton Mifflin Harcourt
At the Pond	A	RF	25	Leveled Readers/CA	Houghton Mifflin Harcourt
At the Pond	A	RF	32	Literacy by Design	Rigby
At the Pond	M	I	250+	Look Once Look Again	Creative Teaching Press
At the Pond	D	I	51	Readers for Writers	Rourke Classroom Resources
At the Pond	E	I	55	Vocabulary Readers	Houghton Mifflin Harcourt
At the Pool	C	I	64	Foundations	Wright Group/McGraw Hill
At the Pool	F	RF	87	Oxford Reading Tree	Oxford University Press
At the Pool	A	I	29	Vocabulary Readers	Houghton Mifflin Harcourt
At the Post Office	H	RF	100	City Stories	Rigby
At the Powwow	J	RF	250+	Reading Street	Pearson
At the Races	S	I	250+	NASCAR Racing	Capstone Press
At the Root of It	Q	I	250+	iOpeners	Pearson Learning Group
At the Science Center	H	I	158	Discovery Links	Newbridge
At the Seashore	N	I	250+	Look Once Look Again	Creative Teaching Press
At the Seaside	E	RF	85	Oxford Reading Tree	Oxford University Press
At the Seaside	LB	I	16	Rigby Star	Rigby
At the Store	B	I	21	Read-More Books	Pearson Learning Group
At the Store	LB	I	14	Visions	Wright Group/McGraw Hill
At the Supermarket	C	RF	60	Little Readers	Houghton Mifflin Harcourt
At the Supermarket	C	I	60	Little Red Readers	Sundance
At the Supermarket	D	I	29	Read-More Books	Pearson Learning Group
At the Supermarket	A	RF	32	Springboard	Wright Group/McGraw Hill
At the Toy Store	C	I	35	PM Plus Nonfiction	Rigby
At the Toyshop	D	RF	41	Home Connection Collection	Rigby
At the Track	E	RF	122	Ready Readers	Pearson Learning Group
At the Truckstop	LB	RF	25	Kloes, Carol	Kaeden Books
At the Vet	D	RF	83	Leveled Readers	Houghton Mifflin Harcourt
At the Vet	A	RF	30	Rigby Rocket	Rigby
At the Water Hole	K	I	236	Foundations	Wright Group/McGraw Hill
At the Water Hole	D	I	70	Little Red Readers	Sundance
At the Wildlife Park	B	I	34	Little Red Readers	Sundance

* Collection of short stories   # Graphic text
^ Mature content with lower level text demands

TITLE	LEVEL	GENRE	WORD COUNT	AUTHOR / SERIES	PUBLISHER / DISTRIBUTOR
At the Zoo	A	I	72	Animals	American Reading Company
At the Zoo	D	I	49	Benchmark Rebus	Marshall Cavendish
At the Zoo	B	I	40	Early Connections	Benchmark Education
At the Zoo	B	RF	29	Kloes, Carol	Kaeden Books
At the Zoo	A	I	40	Leveled Literacy Intervention/ Orange System	Heinemann
At the Zoo	A	RF	20	Leveled Readers	Houghton Mifflin Harcourt
At the Zoo	B	I	40	Leveled Readers Emergent	Houghton Mifflin Harcourt
At the Zoo	A	RF	20	Leveled Readers/CA	Houghton Mifflin Harcourt
At the Zoo	D	RF	37	Little Celebrations	Pearson Learning Group
At the Zoo	B	RF	54	Little Readers	Houghton Mifflin Harcourt
At the Zoo	C	I	73	Little Red Readers	Sundance
At the Zoo	M	I	250+	Look Once Look Again	Creative Teaching Press
At the Zoo	B	I	34	McAlpin, MaryAnn	Short Tales Press
At the Zoo	B	I	40	PM Starters	Rigby
At the Zoo	D	RF	116	Predictable Storybooks	SRA/McGraw Hill
At the Zoo	C	I	88	Springboard	Wright Group/McGraw Hill
At the Zoo	G	F	206	Springboard	Wright Group/McGraw Hill
At the Zoo	C	RF	64	The King School Series	Townsend Press
At the Zoo	E	I	54	Vocabulary Readers	Houghton Mifflin Harcourt
At the Zoo	B	RF	31	Windows on Literacy	National Geographic
At Work	B	I	29	Bookshop	Mondo Publishing
At Work	C	I	29	Geist, Ellen	Scholastic
At Work	B	I	54	Independent Readers Social Studies	Houghton Mifflin Harcourt
#Atalanta: The Race Against Destiny	V	TL	3435	Graphic Myths and Legends	Graphic Universe
Athena	V	I	1594	Vocabulary Readers	Houghton Mifflin Harcourt
Athena	V	I	1594	Vocabulary Readers/CA	Houghton Mifflin Harcourt
Athena	V	I	1594	Vocabulary Readers/TX	Houghton Mifflin Harcourt
^Athena	W	I	250+	World Mythology	Capstone Press
*Athletic Shorts: Six Short Stories	Y	RF	250+	Crutcher, Chris	HarperCollins
^Atlanta	U	SF	250+	The Extraordinary Files	Hameray Publishing Group
Atlanta Braves, The	S	I	4737	Team Spirit	Norwood House Press
Atlanta Braves, The (Revised Edition)	S	I	250+	Team Spirit	Norwood House Press
Atlanta Falcons, The	S	I	4650	Team Spirit	Norwood House Press
Atlanta Hawks, The	S	I	4512	Team Spirit	Norwood House Press
Atlantic	P	I	250+	Karas, G. Brian	Puffin Books
Atlantic Ocean, The	N	I	250+	Oceans	Capstone Press
^Atlantis	X	I	250+	The Unexplained	Capstone Press
Atlantis: The Lost City?	W	I	250+	DK Readers	DK Publishing
Atlas of Endangered Species	V	I	250+	Bookshop	Mondo Publishing
Atlas of Firsts: A World of Amazing Record Breakers	T	I	250+	Gifford, Clive	Kingfisher
Atoms	V	I	250+	Simply Science	Compass Point Books
Atoms and Elements	Z	I	1392	Science Support Readers	Houghton Mifflin Harcourt
Attaboy, Sam	Q	RF	250+	Lowry, Lois	Bantam Books
Attack and Defense	Q	I	250+	Explorers	Wright Group/McGraw Hill
Attack Helicopters: The AH-64 Apaches	U	I	250+	War Planes	Capstone Press
Attack of the 50-Ft. Cupid	N	SF	250+	Benton, Jim	Aladdin
Attack of the Bandit Cats	O	F	250+	Stilton, Geronimo	Scholastic
Attack of the Butt-Biting Sharks: Quentin Quirk's Magic Works	P	F	250+	Kain, Matt	Kingfisher
Attack of the Fluffy Bunnies	P	F	250+	Beaty, Andrea	Amulet Books
Attack of the Giant Squirrel!	N	F	653	Leveled Readers	Houghton Mifflin Harcourt

TITLE	LEVEL	GENRE	WORD COUNT	AUTHOR / SERIES	PUBLISHER / DISTRIBUTOR
#Attack of the Mutant Meteors	U	F	12199	Twisted Journeys	Graphic Universe
^Attack of the Paper Bats	T	F	605	Dahl, Michael	Stone Arch Books
Attack of the Runaway Robot	L	F	1253	Auto-B-Good	Rising Star Studios
Attack of the Valley Girls (Melvin Beederman, Superhero)	N	F	250+	Trine, Greg	Henry Holt & Co.
Attack on Montreal	Y	I	250+	History for Young Canadians	Fitzhenry & Whiteside
^Attack on Pearl Harbor, The: An Interactive History Adventure	V	HF	250+	You Choose Books	Capstone Press
^Attack Submarines: The Seawolf Class	T	I	250+	War Machines	Capstone Press
Attic, The	E	RF	108	The Rowland Reading Program Library	Rowland Reading Foundation
Attract and Repel: A Look at Magnets	L	I	416	Lightning Bolt Books	Lerner Publishing Group
#Attractive Story of Magnetism with Max Axiom, Super Scientist; The	V	I	250+	Graphic Library	Capstone Press
Atul's Christmas Hamster	I	I	250+	Cambridge Reading	Pearson Learning Group
Atu's Story	N	F	250+	Reading Safari	Mondo Publishing
ATV Racing	S	I	250+	Motor Sports	Red Brick Learning
Auburn Tigers, The	S	I	4500	Team Spirit College Football	Norwood House Press
Aung San Suu Kyi	V	B	1980	Leveled Readers Social Studies	Houghton Mifflin Harcourt
Aunt Clara Brown: Official Pioneer	P	B	250+	On My Own Biography	Lerner Publishing Group
Aunt Eater Loves a Mystery	J	F	250+	Cushman, Doug	HarperTrophy
Aunt Eater's Mystery Christmas	J	F	250+	Cushman, Doug	HarperTrophy
Aunt Eater's Mystery Vacation	J	F	250+	Cushman, Doug	HarperTrophy
Aunt Flossie's Hats (and Crab Cakes Later)	M	RF	250+	Howard, Elizabeth	Scholastic
Aunt Jessie	G	RF	114	Literacy 2000	Rigby
Aunt Louisa Is Coming for Lunch	G	RF	118	Windmill Books	Rigby
Aunt Maud's Mittens	H	F	200	Landman, Yael	Scholastic
Aunt Tabitha's Gift	R	RF	250+	Sails	Rigby
Aunt Victoria's Monster	R	F	250+	Storyteller-Whispering Pines	Wright Group/McGraw Hill
Aunt Wilhelmina's Will	L	RF	250+	Voyages	SRA/McGraw Hill
Auntie Maria and the Cat	F	RF	215	Sunshine	Wright Group/McGraw Hill
Aunts	F	I	42	Families	Capstone Press
Aunts	D	I	49	Pebble Books	Capstone Press
Aunts and Uncles	G	I	163	Families	Heinemann Library
Aunty Mo's Kids	I	RF	250+	Sails	Rigby
Aurelie: A Faerie Tale	U	F	250+	Tomlinson, Heather	Henry Holt & Co.
Aurora County All-Stars, The	V	RF	250+	Wiles, Deborah	Houghton Mifflin Harcourt
Austere Academy, The	V	F	250+	Snicket, Lemony	Scholastic
Austin and the Toyman	I	RF	250+	Reading Safari	Mondo Publishing
Australia	P	I	250+	A True Book	Children's Press
Australia	H	I	27	Chessen, Betsey; Chanko, Pamela	Scholastic
Australia	N	I	250+	Continents	Capstone Press
Australia	U	I	250+	Countries and Cultures	Red Brick Learning
Australia	O	I	250+	Countries of the World	Red Brick Learning
Australia	Q	I	250+	First Reports: Countries	Compass Point Books
Australia	N	I	336	Pull Ahead Books	Lerner Publishing Group
Australia ABCs: A Book About the People and Places of Australia	Q	I	250+	Country ABCs	Picture Window Books
Australia in Colors	N	I	250+	World of Colors	Capstone Press
Australian Outback Food Chain, An	U	I	7704	Follow That Food Chain	Lerner Publishing Group
Australian Shepherds	R	I	250+	All About Dogs	Capstone Press
Australia's Deserts	Q	I	250+	Theme Sets	National Geographic
Australia's First People	X	I	2579	Vocabulary Readers	Houghton Mifflin Harcourt
Australia's First People	X	I	2579	Vocabulary Readers/CA	Houghton Mifflin Harcourt
Author on My Street, The	J	RF	260	Books for Young Learners	Richard C. Owen

* Collection of short stories   # Graphic text
^ Mature content with lower level text demands

TITLE	LEVEL	GENRE	WORD COUNT	AUTHOR / SERIES	PUBLISHER / DISTRIBUTOR
Auto Mechanics	M	I	250+	Community Helpers	Red Brick Learning
Autobiography of Benjamin Franklin, The	Z+	B	250+	Franklin, Benjamin	Simon & Schuster
Autobiography of Miss Jane Pittman, The	Z+	HF	250+	Edge	Hampton Brown
Autobiography of Miss Jane Pittman, The	Z+	HF	250+	Gaines, Ernest J.	Bantam Books
Autobots Versus Decepticons	N	SF	250+	Transformers: Dark of the Moon	Little Brown and Company
Automobile, The	P	I	250+	Great Inventions	Red Brick Learning
Automobiles and How They Work	Q	I	894	Time for Kids	Teacher Created Materials
Autumn	M	I	225	Pebble Books	Red Brick Learning
Autumn Leaves	LB	I	17	Preparing for Winter	Capstone Press
Autumn Leaves	G	RF	84	Voyages	SRA/McGraw Hill
Autumn Leaves Are Falling	E	RF	125	Fleming, Maria	Scholastic
Autumn Street	V	HF	250+	Lowry, Lois	Bantam Books
AV-8B Harrier Jump Jet, The	U	I	250+	Cross-Sections	Capstone Press
Ava Tree and the Wishes Three	L	F	250+	Betancourt, Jeanne	Feiwel and Friends
Avalanche!	L	I	250+	Rosen Real Readers	Rosen Publishing Group
Avalanches	W	I	250+	Disasters Up Close	Lerner Publishing Group
Avalanches	M	I	160	Earth in Action	Capstone Press
Avalanches	M	I	668	Pull Ahead Books	Lerner Publishing Group
Avi	T	B	250+	Markham, Lois	Creative Teaching Press
Avion My Uncle Flew, The	Y	RF	250+	Fisher, Cyrus	Penguin Group
Avoiding Drugs	V	I	654	Pull Ahead Books	Lerner Publishing Group
Awake and Dreaming	S	F	250+	Person, Kit	Puffin Books
Awake in the Dark!	K	RF	875	PM Stars Bridge Books	Rigby
Award Day	G	RF	195	PM Stars	Rigby
*Awarding Greatness: Nobel, Caldecott, Pulitzer	Q	B	250+	High-Fliers	Pacific Learning
Away From Home	L	RF	250+	Literacy by Design	Rigby
Away Go the Boats	F	F	250+	Easy Stories	Norwood House Press
Away We Go!	F	I	68	Dotlich, Rebecca Kai	Hampton Brown
Away Went the Hat	I	F	260	New Way Green	Steck-Vaughn
Away West: Scraps of Time 1879	Q	HF	250+	McKissack, Patricia C.	Puffin Books
Awesome Animals	M	I	250+	Ingoglia, Gina	Golden
Awful Mess, The	H	RF	58	Rockwell, Anne	Four Winds
Awful Waffles	G	F	296	Williams, D. H.	Continental Press
Awfully Short for the Fourth Grade	Q	RF	250+	Woodruff, Elvira	Bantam Books
Awumpalema	L	TL	250+	Literacy 2000	Rigby
Awww	C	RF	35	Little Celebrations	Pearson Learning Group
Aye-Aye, The	J	I	150	Weird Animals	Capstone Press
Ayu and the Perfect Moon	K	RF	455	Avenues	Hampton Brown
A-Z Fascinating Facts About Animals	R	I	250+	Literacy 2000	Rigby
Aztec News, The	W	I	250+	The History News	Candlewick Press
Aztec People, The	L	I	236	Take Two Books	Wright Group/McGraw Hill
Aztec Warriors	S	I	250+	Fierce Fighters	Raintree
Aztec Warriors	T	I	250+	Warriors of History	Capstone Press
Aztec, Inca and Maya	Y	I	250+	Eyewitness Books	DK Publishing
Aztec, The	Q	I	250+	A True Book	Children's Press
Aztec, The	U	I	250+	Navigators Social Studies Series	Benchmark Education
Aztec, The	W	I	2193	Reading Street	Pearson
Aztecs, The	Y	I	2583	Leveled Readers	Houghton Mifflin Harcourt
Aztecs, The	Y	I	2583	Leveled Readers/CA	Houghton Mifflin Harcourt
Aztecs, The	Y	I	2583	Leveled Readers/TX	Houghton Mifflin Harcourt
Aztecs, The	Q	I	250+	Windows on Literacy	National Geographic
Aztecs, The: Life in Tenochtitlan	V	I	1654	Ancient Civilizations	Millbrook Press
Aztecs, The: Rise and Fall of a Great Empire	W	I	250+	High Five Reading	Red Brick Learning

TITLE	LEVEL	GENRE	WORD COUNT	AUTHOR / SERIES	PUBLISHER / DISTRIBUTOR
B	LB	I	14	Readlings	American Reading Company
B Is for Betsy	P	RF	250+	Haywood, Carolyn	Harcourt, Inc.
B. B. King	U	B	2632	Leveled Readers/CA	Houghton Mifflin Harcourt
B. B. King	U	B	2632	Leveled Readers/TX	Houghton Mifflin Harcourt
B.B. King	U	B	2632	Leveled Readers	Houghton Mifflin Harcourt
B-2 Spirit Stealth Bomber, The	U	I	250+	Cross-Sections	Capstone Press
Baa Baa Black Sheep	L	TL	250+	Trapani, Iza	Charlesbridge
Baba Nangko	P	F	250+	Voyages	SRA/McGraw Hill
Baba Yaga	K	TL	250+	Literacy 2000	Rigby
Baba Yaga: A Russian Folktale	N	TL	250+	Phinney, Margaret Y.	Mondo Publishing
Babar's Museum of Art	M	F	250+	De Brunhoff, Laurent	Harry N. Abrams
Babe & Me	T	F	250+	Gutman, Dan	HarperTrophy
Babe and I, The	O	HF	250+	Adler, David A.	Harcourt, Inc.
Babe Didrikson Zaharias: All-Around Athlete	N	B	1747	On My Own Biography	Lerner Publishing Group
Babe Didrikson: Athlete of the Century	R	B	250+	Knudson, R. Rozanne	Bantam Books
Babe Ruth	T	B	250+	Christopher, Matt	Little Brown and Company
Babe Ruth	Q	B	1176	Leveled Readers	Houghton Mifflin Harcourt
Babe Ruth	Q	B	1176	Leveled Readers/CA	Houghton Mifflin Harcourt
Babe Ruth	Q	B	1176	Leveled Readers/TX	Houghton Mifflin Harcourt
Babe Ruth and the Baseball Curse!	O	B	250+	Kelly, David A.	Random House
Babe Ruth: One of Baseball's Greatest	R	B	250+	Van Riper, Guernsey	Aladdin
Babe the Gallant Pig	R	F	250+	King-Smith, Dick	Random House
Babies	D	I	42	Canizares, Susan; Chanko, Pamela	Scholastic
Babies	A	I	35	On Our Way to English	Rigby
Babies in the Pouches	D	I	120	Sails	Rigby
Babies on the Bus	K	TL	336	Katz, Karen	Henry Holt & Co.
Babies on the Move	LB	I	30	Canizares, Susan; Moreton, Daniel	Scholastic
Babies!	B	I	72	Literacy by Design	Rigby
Baboon	L	I	250+	A Day in the Life: Grassland Animals	Heinemann Library
Baboon	L	I	250+	A Day in the Life: Grassland Animals	Heinemann Library
Baboon Troops	M	I	250+	Sails	Rigby
Baby	A	RF	29	Instant Readers	Harcourt School Publishers
Baby	A	I	24	Leveled Literacy Intervention/ Orange System	Heinemann
Baby	A	I	28	Little Books for Early Readers	University of Maine
Baby	T	RF	250+	MacLachlan, Patricia	Language for Learning Assoc.
Baby	A	I	24	PM Plus Starters	Rigby
Baby Animal Picture Puzzles	M	I	134	Look, Look Again	Capstone Press
Baby Animal Zoo	O	I	250+	Martin, Ann M.	Scholastic
Baby Animals	A	F	28	Avenues	Hampton Brown
Baby Animals	M	I	250+	Berger, Melvin & Gilda	Scholastic
Baby Animals	D	I	41	Discovery Links	Newbridge
Baby Animals	D	I	78	Foundations	Wright Group/McGraw Hill
Baby Animals	L	I	250+	I Wonder Why	Kingfisher
Baby Animals	B	I	44	Reading Corners	Pearson Learning Group
Baby Animals	B	I	49	Red Rocket Readers	Flying Start Books
Baby Animals	E	I	109	Rigby Focus	Rigby
Baby Animals	B	I	89	Rigby Literacy	Rigby
Baby Animals	C	I	134	Rigby Star Quest	Rigby
Baby Animals	A	I	24	Vocabulary Readers	Houghton Mifflin Harcourt

* Collection of short stories   # Graphic text
^ Mature content with lower level text demands

TITLE	LEVEL	GENRE	WORD COUNT	AUTHOR / SERIES	PUBLISHER / DISTRIBUTOR
Baby Animals at Home	C	I	64	Twig	Wright Group/McGraw Hill
Baby Animals Learn	C	I	52	Chanko, Pamela; Berger, Samantha	Scholastic
Baby Animals of the Rain Forest	J	I	294	Reading Street	Pearson
Baby Animals of the Rain Forest	B	F	55	Tiny Treasures	Pioneer Valley
Baby Animals, The	A	I	55	Leveled Literacy Intervention/ Orange System	Heinemann
Baby at Our House, The	H	RF	93	Foundations	Wright Group/McGraw Hill
Baby Bear	E	I	66	Priddy, Frank	Priddy Books
Baby Bear Climbs a Tree	F	F	147	PM Plus Story Books	Rigby
Baby Bear Goes Fishing	E	F	112	PM Story Books	Rigby
Baby Bear's Hiding Place	F	F	187	PM Plus Story Books	Rigby
Baby Bear's Present	F	F	206	PM Story Books	Rigby
Baby Bear's Ride	WB	F	0	Ready Readers	Pearson Learning Group
Baby Bear's Toys	A	F	35	Phonics and Friends	Hampton Brown
Baby Bird	G	F	251	Leveled Literacy Intervention/ Green System	Heinemann
Baby Bird	H	RF	179	The King School Series	Townsend Press
Baby Birds	D	I	51	Pebble Books	Capstone Press
Baby Birds	E	I	181	Vocabulary Readers	Houghton Mifflin Harcourt
Baby Birds	E	I	181	Vocabulary Readers/CA	Houghton Mifflin Harcourt
Baby Birds	E	I	181	Vocabulary Readers/TX	Houghton Mifflin Harcourt
Baby Birds	D	I	37	Windows on Literacy	National Geographic
Baby Brains and Robomom	M	F	250+	James, Simon	Candlewick Press
Baby Brother, The	I	RF	131	Voyages	SRA/McGraw Hill
Baby Buddy	F	RF	123	McGougan, Kathy	Buddy Books Publishing
Baby Bunny	F	I	86	Priddy, Frank	Priddy Books
Baby Bunny, The	E	RF	283	Easy Stories	Norwood House Press
Baby Can Ride	C	I	67	Leveled Readers Emergent	Houghton Mifflin Harcourt
Baby Cat	G	RF	194	Rigby Flying Colors	Rigby
Baby Chimp	A	RF	14	Twig	Wright Group/McGraw Hill
Baby Dragon	L	F	250+	Ehrlich, Amy	Candlewick Press
Baby Duck Story, A	L	I	178	Baby Animals	Capstone Press
Baby Elephant	O	I	1414	Nature Babies	Fitzhenry & Whiteside
Baby Elephant Gets Lost	D	F	90	Foundations	Wright Group/McGraw Hill
Baby Elephant Goes for a Swim	C	RF	45	Coulton, Mia	Maryruth Books
Baby Elephant Is Thirsty	H	F	188	Coulton, Mia	Maryruth Books
Baby Elephant Runs Away	D	F	58	Coulton, Mia	Maryruth Books
Baby Elephant's New Bike	G	F	187	Foundations	Wright Group/McGraw Hill
Baby Elephant's Sneeze	F	F	78	Foundations	Wright Group/McGraw Hill
Baby Elephant's Trunk	B	F	36	Coulton, Mia	Maryruth Books
Baby Elephant's Trunk	F	F	164	Red Rocket Readers	Flying Start Books
Baby Food	C	RF	21	Dunn, Tansy	Scholastic
Baby Food	L	RF	993	Rigby Gigglers	Rigby
Baby Fox	O	I	1407	Nature Babies	Fitzhenry & Whiteside
Baby Gets Dressed	LB	RF	16	Sunshine	Wright Group/McGraw Hill
Baby Grand, the Moon in July, and Me, The	P	RF	250+	Barnes, Joyce Annette	Penguin Group
Baby Grizzly	O	I	1517	Nature Babies	Fitzhenry & Whiteside
Baby Ground Squirrel	O	I	1495	Nature Babies	Fitzhenry & Whiteside
Baby Hippo	D	RF	117	PM Extensions-Yellow	Rigby
Baby in the Cart	C	RF	84	Foundations	Wright Group/McGraw Hill
Baby in the Hat, The	K	F	172	Ahlberg, Allan	Candlewick Press
Baby Is Up, The	C	RF	50	Bonnell, Kris	Reading Reading Books
Baby Island	P	RF	250+	Brink, Carol Ryrie	Simon & Schuster

* Collection of short stories   # Graphic text
^ Mature content with lower level text demands

Organized Alphabetically by Title   **51**
Storable Database at www.fountasandpinnellleveledbooks.com

TITLE	LEVEL	GENRE	WORD COUNT	AUTHOR / SERIES	PUBLISHER / DISTRIBUTOR
Baby Kangaroo	B	F	46	Sails	Rigby
Baby Kangaroo and Sneaky Snake	J	F	250+	Splash	Pacific Learning
Baby Kangaroos	L	I	256	Leveled Readers	Houghton Mifflin Harcourt
Baby Kangaroos	L	I	256	Leveled Readers/CA	Houghton Mifflin Harcourt
Baby Kangaroos	L	I	256	Leveled Readers/TX	Houghton Mifflin Harcourt
Baby Koala	O	I	1437	Nature Babies	Fitzhenry & Whiteside
Baby Lamb's First Drink	C	F	64	PM Story Books	Rigby
Baby Lion	O	I	1436	Nature Babies	Fitzhenry & Whiteside
Baby Monkey	I	F	250+	Reading Unlimited	Pearson Learning Group
Baby Owl	O	I	1463	Nature Babies	Fitzhenry & Whiteside
Baby Owl	C	F	51	Sails	Rigby
Baby Owl Goes Away	E	F	151	Sails	Rigby
Baby Owl is Scared	G	F	226	Sails	Rigby
Baby Owl's Rescue	M	RF	2175	Curtis, Jennifer Keats	Sylvan Dell Publishing
Baby Owls, The	C	RF	90	PM Extensions-Red	Rigby
Baby Panda	D	RF	97	PM Plus Story Books	Rigby
Baby Panda Is Born, A	L	I	250+	All Aboard Science Reader	Grosset & Dunlap
Baby Panda, The	D	RF	52	Reading Street	Pearson Learning Group
Baby Penguin	O	I	1118	Nature Babies	Fitzhenry & Whiteside
Baby Penguin Story, A	L	I	193	Baby Animals	Capstone Press
Baby Pictures	E	F	203	Leveled Literacy Intervention/ Green System	Heinemann
Baby Polar Bear Story, A	L	I	200	Baby Animals	Capstone Press
Baby Porcupine	O	I	1525	Nature Babies	Fitzhenry & Whiteside
Baby Rabbit Story, A	L	I	200	Baby Animals	Capstone Press
Baby Says	LB	RF	26	Steptoe, John	Morrow
Baby Sea Otter Story, A	L	I	201	Baby Animals	Capstone Press
Baby Seal	O	I	1427	Nature Babies	Fitzhenry & Whiteside
Baby Seal Story, A	L	I	220	Baby Animals	Capstone Press
Baby Shark, The	D	I	49	Windows on Literacy	National Geographic
Baby Sister for Frances, A	K	F	250+	Hoban, Lillian	Scholastic
Baby Skunk	A	RF	24	Handprints A	Educators Publishing Service
Baby Sloth	O	I	1445	Nature Babies	Fitzhenry & Whiteside
Baby Stegosaurus	J	F	717	Little Dinosaur	Literacy Footprints
Baby Talk	D	I	76	Joy Starters	Pearson Learning Group
Baby Tiger Cheats Cheetah	D	F	68	Reading Safari	Mondo Publishing
Baby Tiger's Blanket	J	F	712	Georgie Giraffe	Literacy Footprints
Baby Turtle, The	H	I	122	Big Cat	Pacific Learning
Baby Wakes Up	C	RF	50	PM Plus Story Books	Rigby
Baby Whale Rescue: The True Story of J.J.	P	I	250+	Arnold, Caroline; Hewett, Richard	Troll Associates
Baby Whales Drink Milk	M	I	250+	Soar To Success	Houghton Mifflin Harcourt
Baby Whale's Mistake	K	F	503	Red Rocket Readers	Flying Start Books
Baby Wolf	K	RF	250+	Batten, Mary/All Aboard Science Reader	Grosset & Dunlap
Baby Writer	I	RF	182	Stepping Stones	Nelson/Michaels Assoc.
Baby Zebra Helps Out	D	I	61	Bonnell, Kris	Reading Reading Books
Baby, The	E	RF	60	Burningham, John	Crowell
Baby, The	A	I	40	Leveled Literacy Intervention/ Orange System	Heinemann
Babylonians, The: Life in Ancient Babylon	V	I	1534	Ancient Civilizations	Millbrook Press
Babylonne	Z+	HF	250+	Jinks, Christine	Candlewick Press
Baby's Birthday	D	RF	53	Literacy 2000	Rigby
Baby's Dinner	E	RF	26	Literacy 2000	Rigby

* Collection of short stories   # Graphic text
^ Mature content with lower level text demands

TITLE	LEVEL	GENRE	WORD COUNT	AUTHOR / SERIES	PUBLISHER / DISTRIBUTOR
Baby-Sitter Burglaries, The	S	RF	250+	Keene, Carolyn	Pocket Books
Babysitter, The	H	RF	243	PM Extensions-Green	Rigby
Baby-Sitter, The	E	RF	69	Oxford Reading Tree	Oxford University Press
Baby-Sitters Club Mystery: Beware, Dawn!	O	RF	250+	Martin, Ann M.	Scholastic
Baby-Sitters Club Mystery: Claudia, Clue in the Photograph	O	RF	250+	Martin, Ann M.	Scholastic
Baby-Sitters Club Mystery: Claudia, Mystery at the Museum	O	RF	250+	Martin, Ann M.	Scholastic
Baby-Sitters Club Mystery: Claudia, Recipe for Danger	O	RF	250+	Martin, Ann M.	Scholastic
Baby-Sitters Club Mystery: Dawn, Disappearing Dogs	O	RF	250+	Martin, Ann M.	Scholastic
Baby-Sitters Club Mystery: Dawn, Halloween Mystery	O	RF	250+	Martin, Ann M.	Scholastic
Baby-Sitters Club Mystery: Dawn, Surfer Ghost	O	RF	250+	Martin, Ann M.	Scholastic
Baby-Sitters Club Mystery: Jessi, Jewel Thieves	O	RF	250+	Martin, Ann M.	Scholastic
Baby-Sitters Club Mystery: Kristy, Haunted Mansion	O	RF	250+	Martin, Ann M.	Scholastic
Baby-Sitters Club Mystery: Kristy, Missing Child	O	RF	250+	Martin, Ann M.	Scholastic
Baby-Sitters Club Mystery: Kristy, Missing Fortune	O	RF	250+	Martin, Ann M.	Scholastic
Baby-Sitters Club Mystery: Kristy, Vampires	O	RF	250+	Martin, Ann M.	Scholastic
Baby-Sitters Club Mystery: Mallory, Ghost Cat	O	RF	250+	Martin, Ann M.	Scholastic
Baby-Sitters Club Mystery: Mary Anne, Library Mystery	O	RF	250+	Martin, Ann M.	Scholastic
Baby-Sitters Club Mystery: Mary Anne, Secret in the Attic	O	RF	250+	Martin, Ann M.	Scholastic
Baby-Sitters Club Mystery: Mary Anne, Zoo Mystery	O	RF	250+	Martin, Ann M.	Scholastic
Baby-Sitters Club Mystery: Mystery at Claudia's House	O	RF	250+	Martin, Ann M.	Scholastic
Baby-Sitters Club Mystery: Stacey and the Mystery Money	O	RF	250+	Martin, Ann M.	Scholastic
Baby-Sitters Club Mystery: Stacey, Haunted Masquerade	O	RF	250+	Martin, Ann M.	Scholastic
Baby-Sitters Club Mystery: Stacey, Missing Ring	O	RF	250+	Martin, Ann M.	Scholastic
Baby-Sitters Club Mystery: Stacey, Mystery at the Empty House	O	RF	250+	Martin, Ann M.	Scholastic
Baby-Sitters Club Mystery: Stacey, Mystery at the Mall	O	RF	250+	Martin, Ann M.	Scholastic
Baby-Sitters Club Special Edition, The: Readers' Request	O	RF	250+	Martin, Ann M.	Scholastic
Baby-Sitters Club: Abby and the Best Kid Ever	O	RF	250+	Martin, Ann M.	Scholastic
Baby-Sitters Club: Abby, the Bad Sport	O	RF	250+	Martin, Ann M.	Scholastic
Baby-Sitters Club: Claudia and the Bad Joke	O	RF	250+	Martin, Ann M.	Scholastic
Baby-Sitters Club: Claudia and the Little Liar	O	RF	250+	Martin, Ann M.	Scholastic
Baby-Sitters Club: Claudia and the New Girl	O	RF	250+	Martin, Ann M.	Scholastic
Baby-Sitters Club: Claudia and the Phantom Phone Calls	O	RF	250+	Martin, Ann M.	Scholastic
Baby-Sitters Club: Dawn and Too Many Sitters	O	RF	250+	Martin, Ann M.	Scholastic
Baby-Sitters Club: Dawn's Big Move	O	RF	250+	Martin, Ann M.	Scholastic
Baby-Sitters Club: Dawn's Wicked Stepsister	O	RF	250+	Martin, Ann M.	Scholastic
Baby-Sitters Club: Get Well Soon, Mallory	O	RF	250+	Martin, Ann M.	Scholastic
Baby-Sitters Club: Ghost at Dawn's House, The	O	RF	250+	Martin, Ann M.	Scholastic
Baby-Sitters Club: Good-bye Stacey, Good-bye	O	RF	250+	Martin, Ann M.	Scholastic
Baby-Sitters Club: Hello, Mallory	O	RF	250+	Martin, Ann M.	Scholastic
Baby-Sitters Club: Jessi and the Bad Baby-Sitter	O	RF	250+	Martin, Ann M.	Scholastic
Baby-Sitters Club: Jessi and the Superbrat	O	RF	250+	Martin, Ann M.	Scholastic

B

* Collection of short stories   # Graphic text
^ Mature content with lower level text demands

TITLE	LEVEL	GENRE	WORD COUNT	AUTHOR / SERIES	PUBLISHER / DISTRIBUTOR
Baby-Sitters Club: Jessi Ramsey, Pet-sitter	O	RF	250+	Martin, Ann M.	Scholastic
Baby-Sitters Club: Kristy and the Snobs	O	RF	250+	Martin, Ann M.	Scholastic
Baby-Sitters Club: Kristy's Big Day	O	RF	250+	Martin, Ann M.	Scholastic
Baby-Sitters Club: Kristy's Great Idea	O	RF	250+	Martin, Ann M.	Scholastic
Baby-Sitters Club: Mary Anne and Camp BSC	O	RF	250+	Martin, Ann M.	Scholastic
Baby-Sitters Club: Mary Anne Saves the Day	O	RF	250+	Martin, Ann M.	Scholastic
Baby-Sitters Club: Welcome to the BSC, Abby	O	RF	250+	Martin, Ann M.	Scholastic
Baby-Sitter's Little Sister	O	RF	250+	Martin, Ann M.	Scholastic
Baby-Sitter's Little Sister : Karen's Accident	O	RF	250+	Martin, Ann M.	Scholastic
Baby-Sitter's Little Sister : Karen's Big Fight	O	RF	250+	Martin, Ann M.	Scholastic
Baby-Sitter's Little Sister : Karen's Big Sister	O	RF	250+	Martin, Ann M.	Scholastic
Baby-Sitter's Little Sister : Karen's Copycat	O	RF	250+	Martin, Ann M.	Scholastic
Baby-Sitter's Little Sister : Karen's Dinosaur	O	RF	250+	Martin, Ann M.	Scholastic
Baby-Sitter's Little Sister : Karen's Monsters	O	RF	250+	Martin, Ann M.	Scholastic
Baby-Sitter's Little Sister: Karen's Campout	O	RF	250+	Martin, Ann M.	Scholastic
Baby-Sitter's Little Sister: Karen's Mystery, Super Special	O	RF	250+	Martin, Ann M.	Scholastic
Baby-Sitter's Little Sister: Karen's Nanny	O	RF	250+	Martin, Ann M.	Scholastic
Baby-Sitter's Little Sister: Karen's Stepmother	O	RF	250+	Martin, Ann M.	Scholastic
Baby-Sitter's Little Sister: Karen's Two Families	O	RF	250+	Martin, Ann M.	Scholastic
Babysitting Activities: Fun with Kids of All Ages	S	I	250+	Babysitting	Capstone Press
Babysitting Basics: Caring for Kids	S	I	250+	Babysitting	Capstone Press
Babysitting Jobs: The Business of Babysitting	S	I	250+	Babysitting	Capstone Press
Babysitting Marvin's Sister	L	F	622	Pawprints Teal	Pioneer Valley
Babysitting Rules: A Guide for When You're in Charge	S	I	250+	Babysitting	Capstone Press
Babysitting Safety: Preventing Accidents and Injuries	S	I	250+	Babysitting	Capstone Press
Babysitting Skills: Traits and Training for Success	S	I	250+	Babysitting	Capstone Press
Baby-Snatcher	Z	RF	250+	Terris, Susan	Scholastic
^Back	Z	RF	250+	Orca Soundings	Orca Books
Back and Forth	E	I	54	The Way Things Move	Capstone Press
Back Home	U	RF	250+	Keller, Julia	Egmont USA
Back Home	O	RF	250+	Pinkney, Gloria Jean	Penguin Group
Back in Black	Z+	RF	250+	Dean, Zoey	Little Brown and Company
Back of Beyond: A Story about Lewis and Clark, The	S	B	8408	Creative Minds Biographies	Lerner Publishing Group
Back to Bed, Ed!	J	F	316	Braun, Sebastien	Peachtree
Back to School	L	RF	250+	Go Girl!	Feiwel and Friends
Back to School with Betsy	P	RF	250+	Haywood, Carolyn	Harcourt, Inc.
Back to School, Mallory!	O	RF	250+	Friedman, Laurie	Lerner Publishing Group
Back to the Day Lincoln Was Shot!	S	I	250+	Gormley, Beatrice	Scholastic
Back to the Dentist	M	RF	199	City Kids	Rigby
Back to the Titanic!	S	F	250+	Gormley, Beatrice	Scholastic
Back to Year Zero	V	I	250+	WorldScapes	ETA/Cuisenaire
Backhoes	F	I	118	Mighty Machines	Capstone Press
Backpack Kitty Goes to Camp	J	F	285	Masessa, Ed	Scholastic
Backstage	I	I	220	Twig	Wright Group/McGraw Hill
Backstage Pass	Q	I	250+	Bookweb	Rigby
Backup Goalie	P	RF	250+	Maddox, Jake	Stone Arch Books
Backward Bird Dog, The	R	F	250+	Wallace, Bill	Bantam Books
Backyard Angel	O	RF	250+	Delton, Judy	Houghton Mifflin Harcourt
Backyard Beasties: Jokes to Snake You Smile!	O	F	1571	Make Me Laugh!	Lerner Publishing Group
Backyard Camp-Out	L	RF	628	Leveled Readers	Houghton Mifflin Harcourt

* Collection of short stories   # Graphic text
^ Mature content with lower level text demands

TITLE	LEVEL	GENRE	WORD COUNT	AUTHOR / SERIES	PUBLISHER / DISTRIBUTOR
Backyard Hunter: The Praying Mantis	P	I	250+	Lavies, Bianca	Penguin Group
Backyard Zoo	G	I	167	Ready Readers	Pearson Learning Group
Bacon Saturday Mornings	K	RF	365	Books for Young Learners	Richard C. Owen
Bactrian Camel	L	I	250+	A Day in the Life: Desert Animals	Heinemann Library
Bad Beginning, The	V	F	250+	Snicket, Lemony	HarperTrophy
Bad Boy, Billy	G	RF	129	Cambridge Reading	Pearson Learning Group
Bad Boy: A Memoir	Y	B	250+	Myers, Walter Dean	HarperCollins
Bad Burns: True Survival Stories	Y	I	3192	Powerful Medicine	Lerner Publishing Group
Bad Chipmunk, The	I	F	197	The Rowland Reading Program Library	Rowland Reading Foundation
Bad Dad List, The	M	RF	250+	Kenna, Anna	Pacific Learning
Bad Day for Ballet	N	RF	250+	Keene, Carolyn	Pocket Books
Bad Day for Benjamin, A	L	RF	250+	Reading Unlimited	Pearson Learning Group
Bad Day for Little Dinosaur, A	E	F	153	PM Stars	Rigby
Bad Day, A	E	RF	121	Kaleidoscope Collection	Hameray Publishing Group
Bad Day, The	D	RF	93	Teacher's Choice Series	Pearson Learning Group
Bad Dream, The	E	RF	88	Teacher's Choice Series	Pearson Learning Group
Bad Girls	U	RF	250+	Voigt, Cynthia	Scholastic
Bad Girls in Love	Z+	RF	250+	Voigt, Cynthia	Simon & Schuster
Bad Hair Day	E	RF	113	Teacher's Choice Series	Pearson Learning Group
Bad Hair Days	M	I	250+	InfoTrek Plus	ETA/Cuisenaire
Bad Kitten, The	E	F	86	Bonnell, Kris	Reading Reading Books
Bad Kitty Gets a Bath	P	F	250+	Bruel, Nick	Roaring Brook Press
Bad Kitty Meets the Baby	P	F	250+	Bruel, Nick	Roaring Brook Press
Bad Luck Brad	K	RF	250+	Math Matters	Kane Press
Bad Luck of King Fred, The	O	F	250+	Literacy Tree	Rigby
Bad News for Outlaws: The Remarkable Life of Bass Reeves, Deputy U.S. Marshal	T	B	2390	Nelson, Vaunda Micheaux	Carolrhoda Books
Bad News, Good News	P	RF	250+	Storyteller-Autumn Leaves	Wright Group/McGraw Hill
Bad Spell for the Worst Witch, A	P	F	250+	Murphy, Jill	Puffin Books
Bad to the Bone: Down Girl and Sit	M	F	250+	Nolan, Lucy	Marshall Cavendish
Bad Weather, Good Weather	G	I	182	Springboard	Wright Group/McGraw Hill
Bad, Bad Day, A	E	RF	62	Hall, Kirsten	Scholastic
Bad, Badder, Baddest	U	RF	250+	Voigt, Cynthia	Scholastic
Badger in the Basement	Q	RF	250+	Daniels, Lucy	Barron's Educational
Badgers: Active at Night	M	I	250+	The Wild World of Animals	Capstone Press
Badlands	R	F	250+	Orbit Chapter Books	Pacific Learning
Bad-Luck Day	J	RF	466	Leveled Literacy Intervention/ Green System	Heinemann
Bad-Luck Penny, The	L	F	250+	O'Connor, Jane	Grosset & Dunlap
Badminton For Fun!	S	I	250+	For Fun!	Compass Point Books
Badness For Beginners: A Little Wolf and Smellybreff Adventure	L	F	664	Whybrow, Ian	Carolrhoda Books
Bad-News Report Card, The	K	RF	250+	Poydar Nancy	Holiday House
Bag of Bones, The	S	F	250+	French, Vivian	Candlewick Press
Bag of Coal, The	G	F	195	Storyworlds	Heinemann
Bagels for Kids	O	I	250+	Pacific Literacy	Pacific Learning
Bags, Cans, Pots, and Pans	C	RF	56	Ready Readers	Pearson Learning Group
*Bake a Cake and Other Stories	C	RF	94	Story Steps	Rigby
Bake Sale Battle, The	N	RF	250+	Literacy by Design	Rigby
Bake Sale Battle, The	N	RF	250+	On Our Way to English	Rigby
Bake Sale, The	K	RF	604	Leveled Readers	Houghton Mifflin Harcourt
Bake Sale, The	K	RF	604	Leveled Readers/CA	Houghton Mifflin Harcourt
Bake Sale, The	K	RF	604	Leveled Readers/TX	Houghton Mifflin Harcourt

TITLE	LEVEL	GENRE	WORD COUNT	AUTHOR / SERIES	PUBLISHER / DISTRIBUTOR
Baked Beans	K	I	221	Lighthouse	Rigby
Baked Potatoes	D	RF	73	Book Bank	Wright Group/McGraw Hill
Baker	C	I	21	Benchmark Rebus	Marshall Cavendish
Baker and the Rings, The	N	F	250+	HSP/Harcourt Trophies	Harcourt, Inc.
Baker, The	A	RF	25	Leveled Readers	Houghton Mifflin Harcourt
Baker, The	A	RF	25	Leveled Readers/CA	Houghton Mifflin Harcourt
Bakers	M	I	250+	Community Helpers	Red Brick Learning
Bakery Lady, The	M	RF	250+	Mora, Pat	Pinata Publishing
Baking	D	I	27	Harry's Math Books	Outside the Box
Baking	A	F	35	Leveled Literacy Intervention/ Orange System	Heinemann
Baking a Cake	LB	I	7	Windows on Literacy	National Geographic
Baking Bread	L	I	426	How-To Series	Benchmark Education
Baking Bread	F	I	70	Windows on Literacy	National Geographic
Baking Day	B	RF	33	Red Rocket Readers	Flying Start Books
Baking Day	C	F	35	Windmill Books	Rigby
Balance	E	I	42	Simple Tools	Lerner Publishing Group
Balance and Motion: Toying with Gravity	O	I	1200	iScience	Norwood House Press
Balancing	C	I	46	Twig	Wright Group/McGraw Hill
Balcony Garden	G	I	258	Storyteller Nonfiction	Wright Group/McGraw Hill
Bald Bandit, The	N	RF	250+	A to Z Mysteries	Random House
Bald Eagle	A	I	33	Zoozoo-Animal World	Cavallo Publishing
Bald Eagle Free Again!, The	P	I	250+	Young Readers' Series	Barron's Educational
Bald Eagle Goes Fishing, A	E	I	80	Bonnell, Kris	Reading Reading Books
Bald Eagle Is Back, The	W	I	2691	Leveled Readers	Houghton Mifflin Harcourt
Bald Eagle, The	N	I	250+	A True Book	Children's Press
Bald Eagle, The	N	I	250+	American Symbols	Capstone Press
Bald Eagle, The	P	I	556	Pull Ahead Books	Lerner Publishing Group
Bald Eagle, The	R	I	250+	Symbols of America	Marshall Cavendish
Bald Eagle, The	R	I	250+	Wildlife of North America	Red Brick Learning
Bald Eagles	Q	I	250+	Action Packs	Rigby
Bald Eagles	O	I	1941	Early Bird Nature Books	Lerner Publishing Group
Bald Eagles	L	I	420	Leveled Readers	Houghton Mifflin Harcourt
Bald Eagles	L	I	420	Leveled Readers/CA	Houghton Mifflin Harcourt
Bald Eagles	L	I	420	Leveled Readers/TX	Houghton Mifflin Harcourt
Bald Eagles	G	I	161	Readlings	American Reading Company
Baleen	O	TL	250+	Book Blazers	ETA/Cuisenaire
Balina	Q	TL	1000	Leveled Readers/TX	Houghton Mifflin Harcourt
Ball Book, The	E	I	342	Easy Stories	Norwood House Press
Ball Bounced, The	D	F	33	Tafuri, Nancy	Morrow
Ball Called Sam, A	E	RF	128	Rigby Star	Rigby
Ball Game	B	RF	16	Literacy 2000	Rigby
Ball Game, A	D	I	72	Carousel Readers	Pearson Learning Group
Ball Game, The	E	RF	45	Packard, David	Scholastic
Ball Games	B	RF	44	PM Starters	Rigby
Ball Games	B	F	77	Reading Safari	Mondo Publishing
Ball, The	C	RF	40	KinderReaders	Rigby
Ballad of Knuckles McGraw, The	Q	RF	250+	Orca Young Readers	Orca Books
Ballad of Lucky Whipple, The	V	HF	250+	Cushman, Karen	Houghton Mifflin Harcourt
Ballad of Robin Hood, The	P	TL	250+	Literacy 2000	Rigby
Ballad of the Civil War, A	T	HF	250+	Stolz, Mary	HarperTrophy
Ballerina Dreams	P	I	250+	Thompson, Lauren	Feiwel and Friends
Ballerina Girl	D	RF	77	My First Reader	Grolier
Ballet	L	I	413	Rigby Flying Colors	Rigby

* Collection of short stories   # Graphic text
^ Mature content with lower level text demands

TITLE	LEVEL	GENRE	WORD COUNT	AUTHOR / SERIES	PUBLISHER / DISTRIBUTOR
Ballet Dance	S	I	250+	Dance	Capstone Press
Ballet of the Elephants	Q	I	250+	Schubert, Leda	Roaring Brook Press
Balloon Fun	I	I	254	Springboard	Wright Group/McGraw Hill
Balloon on the Moon	L	F	250+	McCann, Dan	Walker & Company
Balloon Ride	A	F	32	Early Connections	Benchmark Education
Balloon Ride, The	F	F	245	Pearson, Mary E	Kaeden Books
Balloon Ride, The	B	RF	30	Sails	Rigby
Balloon, The	D	F	64	Carousel Readers	Pearson Learning Group
Ballooning Adventures	S	I	250+	Dangerous Adventures	Red Brick Learning
Balloons	D	RF	60	Dominie Readers	Pearson Learning Group
Balloons	B	I	55	Early Emergent	Pioneer Valley
Balloons	I	I	211	Independent Readers Science	Houghton Mifflin Harcourt
Balloons	M	I	57	iOpeners	Pearson Learning Group
Balloons	B	RF	57	PM Plus Starters	Rigby
Balloons	WB	RF	0	Rigby Literacy	Rigby
Balloons Go Pop!	C	RF	74	PM Stars	Rigby
Balloons!	D	F	56	Storyteller-First Snow	Wright Group/McGraw Hill
Balloons, The	B	RF	36	Sails	Rigby
Balloons, The	LB	RF	19	Sunshine	Wright Group/McGraw Hill
Ballots for Belva	Q	B	250+	Bardhan-Quallen, Sudipta	Harry N. Abrams
Ballroom Dancing	S	I	250+	Dance	Capstone Press
Balls	D	I	54	Rookie Readers	Children's Press
Balls	C	I	33	Windows on Literacy	National Geographic
Ballyhoo!	F	F	124	Story Basket	Wright Group/McGraw Hill
Baltimore Orioles, The	S	I	250+	Team Spirit	Norwood House Press
Baltimore Orioles, The (Revised Edition)	S	I	250+	Team Spirit	Norwood House Press
Baltimore Ravens, The	S	I	250+	Team Spirit	Norwood House Press
Balto and the Great Race	P	RF	250+	Kimmel, Elizabeth Cody	Random House
Bambi: A Life in the Woods	T	F	250+	Salten, Felix	Aladdin
#Bambino, The: The Story of Babe Ruth's Legendary 1927 Season	P	B	250+	Graphic Library	Capstone Press
Bamboo Cutter's Daughter, The	T	TL	250+	WorldScapes	ETA/Cuisenaire
Bamboo People	X	RF	250+	Perkins, Mitali	Charlesbridge
Banana Belt, The	Q	I	3033	Take Two Books	Wright Group/McGraw Hill
Banana Monster, The	D	F	54	Joy Readers	Pearson Learning Group
Banana Shake	C	RF	44	Book Bank	Wright Group/McGraw Hill
Banana Split Pizza and Other Snack Recipes	S	I	250+	Fun Food for Cool Cooks	Capstone Press
Banana-Berry Smoothies and Other Breakfast Recipes	S	I	250+	Fun Food for Cool Cooks	Capstone Press
Bananas	F	I	106	Bonnell, Kris/About	Reading Reading Books
Bananas at My Table	B	I	48	Literacy by Design	Rigby
Bananas for Breakfast	H	F	250+	Rigby Rocket	Rigby
Bananas on My Table	B	I	48	On Our Way to English	Rigby
Band	F	I	87	On Deck	Rigby
Band of Bears, A	U	I	250+	Jean-Michel Cousteau Presents	London Town Press
Band of Brave Men, A	X	I	250+	iOpeners	Pearson Learning Group
Band, The	C	I	33	Sun Sprouts	ETA/Cuisenaire
Band, The	C	RF	31	Voyages	SRA/McGraw Hill
Bandages	F	F	139	Moskowitz, Ellen	Kaeden Books
Bandit Moon	V	HF	250+	Fleischman, Sid	Dell
Bandit's Surprise	K	F	306	Rostoker-Gruber, Karen	Marshall Cavendish
Bang	F	F	55	Literacy 2000	Rigby
^Bang	Z+	RF	250+	Orca Soundings	Orca Books
Bangs and Twangs: Science Fun with Sound	T	I	250+	Science Fun with Vicki Cobb	Millbrook Press

TITLE	LEVEL	GENRE	WORD COUNT	AUTHOR / SERIES	PUBLISHER / DISTRIBUTOR
Banished, The	W	F	250+	Levin, Betty	William Morrow
Banjo Granny	L	F	250+	Busse, Sarah M. & Martin, Jacqueline B.	Houghton Mifflin Harcourt
*Bank Robbery and Jack and the Beanstalk, The	L	TL	250+	New Way Literature	Steck-Vaughn
Bank Tellers	M	I	250+	Community Workers	Compass Point Books
Bank Tellers: Then and Now	N	I	250+	Primary Source Readers	Teacher Created Materials
*Banquet for Hungry Ghosts: A Collection of Deliciously Frightening Tales	X	F	250+	Compestine, Ying Chang	Henry Holt & Co.
Bar Graphs	K	I	345	Making Graphs	Capstone Press
Barack Obama	V	B	6334	Gateway Biographies	Lerner Publishing Group
Barack Obama	T	B	3538	History Maker Bios	Lerner Publishing Group
Barack Obama	U	B	250+	Profiles of the Presidents	Compass Point Books
^Barack Obama: Making History	T	B	250+	Hameray Biography Series	Hameray Publishing Group
Barb and Dingbat's Crybaby Hotline	Z+	RF	250+	Jennings, Patrick	Holiday House
Barbara Esbensen: Words into Pictures	R	B	1043	Leveled Readers	Houghton Mifflin Harcourt
Barbara McClintock	V	B	1926	Independent Readers Science	Houghton Mifflin Harcourt
Barbecue, The	LB	RF	14	Sunshine	Wright Group/McGraw Hill
Barbers	L	I	552	Pull Ahead Books	Lerner Publishing Group
Barbie at Pet Day	H	F	206	The Joy Cowley Collection	Hameray Publishing Group
Barbie the Wild Lamb	H	F	207	The Joy Cowley Collection	Hameray Publishing Group
Barbie's Coat	G	F	223	The Joy Cowley Collection	Hameray Publishing Group
Bare Feet	B	RF	40	Visions	Wright Group/McGraw Hill
Barefoot: Escape on the Underground Railroad	S	HF	250+	Edwards, Pamela Duncan	HarperTrophy
Bargain For Frances, A	K	F	250+	Hoban, Russell	HarperTrophy
Bargains for Everyone	P	RF	1025	Leveled Readers	Houghton Mifflin Harcourt
Bark Park	K	RF	146	Ruelle, Karen Gray	Peachtree
Bark, George	H	F	229	Feiffer, Jules	Scholastic
Barker	E	RF	214	Rigby Rocket	Rigby
Barn Dance	C	F	47	Story Box	Wright Group/McGraw Hill
Barn Dance, The	B	RF	46	Leveled Readers Emergent	Houghton Mifflin Harcourt
Barn Party	K	F	250+	I Am Reading	Kingfisher
Barn Party	K	F	250+	Storyteller-Shooting Stars	Wright Group/McGraw Hill
Barn Spiders	N	I	250+	Spiders	Capstone Press
Barn, The	T	RF	250+	Avi	Avon Books
Barnaby	C	RF	100	Sails	Rigby
Barnaby Bullfrog	F	F	121	Seedlings	Continental Press
Barnaby's Birthday	J	RF	214	Voyages	SRA/McGraw Hill
Barnaby's New House, The	G	RF	135	Literacy 2000	Rigby
Barney	P	RF	250+	Literacy 2000	Rigby
Barney Bear Gets Dressed	D	F	38	Learn to Read	Creative Teaching Press
Barney Bear, World Traveler	H	F	65	Learn to Read	Creative Teaching Press
Barney Owl	E	F	154	Rigby Flying Colors	Rigby
Barney's Horse	I	HF	250+	Hoff, Syd	HarperTrophy
Barney's Lovely Lunch	K	RF	330	Windmill Books	Rigby
Barnyard Bandit, The	K	RF	371	Leveled Readers	Houghton Mifflin Harcourt
Barnyard Bandit, The	K	RF	371	Leveled Readers/CA	Houghton Mifflin Harcourt
Barnyard Bandit, The	K	RF	371	Leveled Readers/TX	Houghton Mifflin Harcourt
Barnyard Banter	K	F	137	Fleming, Denise	Henry Holt & Co.
Barnyard Baseball	C	F	19	Pair-It Books	Steck-Vaughn
Barnyard Math with Farmer Fred	G	RF	139	Learn to Read	Creative Teaching Press
Barnyard Song	F	TL	196	PM Readalongs	Rigby
Baron: Rescue Dog	I	RF	120	Books for Young Learners	Richard C. Owen
Barracudas	H	I	83	Under the Sea	Capstone Press
Barrel in the Basement, The	R	F	250+	Wallace, Barbara Brooks	Aladdin

* Collection of short stories   # Graphic text
^ Mature content with lower level text demands

TITLE	LEVEL	GENRE	WORD COUNT	AUTHOR / SERIES	PUBLISHER / DISTRIBUTOR
Barrel of Gold, A	K	F	251	Story Box	Wright Group/McGraw Hill
Barry and Bennie	H	F	251	Little Celebrations	Pearson Learning Group
Barry Bonds	P	B	1650	Amazing Athletes	Lerner Publishing Group
Barry Bonds	U	B	250+	Sports Heroes and Legends	Lerner Publishing Group
Barry Bonds: Revised Edition	P	B	250+	Amazing Athletes	Lerner Publishing Group
Barry:The Bravest Saint Bernard	M	B	250+	Step into Reading	Random House
Bartleby Speaks!	L	RF	250+	Cruise, Robin	Farrar, Straus, & Giroux
Bart's Amazing Charts	N	RF	250+	Ochiltree, Dianne	Scholastic
Baseball	P	I	250+	A True Book	Children's Press
Baseball	K	I	250+	On Deck	Rigby
Baseball	C	I	40	Readlings	American Reading Company
Baseball	G	I	98	Readlings/ Sports	American Reading Company
Baseball	LB	RF	14	Sunshine	Wright Group/McGraw Hill
#Baseball Adventure of Jackie Mitchell, Girl Pitcher vs. Babe Ruth, The	Q	HF	766	History's Kid Heroes	Lerner Publishing Group
Baseball Ballerina	J	RF	250+	Cristaldi, Kathryn	Random House
Baseball Birthday Party, The	J	RF	250+	Prager, Annabelle	Random House
Baseball Blues	S	RF	1800	Leveled Readers/TX	Houghton Mifflin Harcourt
Baseball Boys	P	RF	1146	Leveled Readers	Houghton Mifflin Harcourt
Baseball Boys	P	RF	1146	Leveled Readers/CA	Houghton Mifflin Harcourt
Baseball Boys	P	RF	1146	Leveled Readers/TX	Houghton Mifflin Harcourt
Baseball Fever	O	RF	250+	Hurwitz, Johanna	William Morrow
Baseball Firsts	P	I	1059	Vocabulary Readers	Houghton Mifflin Harcourt
Baseball Firsts	P	I	1059	Vocabulary Readers/CA	Houghton Mifflin Harcourt
Baseball Flyhawk	Q	RF	250+	Christopher, Matt	Little Brown and Company
Baseball for Fun	S	I	250+	Sports for Fun	Compass Point Books
Baseball Friends	P	RF	1214	Leveled Readers	Houghton Mifflin Harcourt
Baseball Friends	P	RF	1214	Leveled Readers/CA	Houghton Mifflin Harcourt
Baseball Friends	P	RF	1214	Leveled Readers/TX	Houghton Mifflin Harcourt
Baseball Fun	E	RF	51	Geddes, Diana	Kaeden Books
Baseball Game, The	I	F	211	Foundations	Wright Group/McGraw Hill
Baseball Game, The	L	I	358	Leveled Readers	Houghton Mifflin Harcourt
Baseball Game, The	L	I	358	Leveled Readers/CA	Houghton Mifflin Harcourt
Baseball Game, The	L	I	358	Leveled Readers/TX	Houghton Mifflin Harcourt
Baseball Heroes	U	B	250+	Good Sports	Sandpiper Books
Baseball Heroes	Q	B	1131	Reading Street	Pearson
Baseball Heroes, The	M	RF	250+	Woodland Mysteries	Wright Group/McGraw Hill
Baseball in the Barrios	P	I	250+	Horenstein, Henry	Harcourt Trade
*Baseball in April and Other Stories	U	RF	250+	Soto, Gary	Harcourt Trade
Baseball Math	N	I	250+	Early Connections	Benchmark Education
Baseball Megastars	O	I	250+	Weber, Bruce	Scholastic
Baseball Memories	S	RF	1800	Leveled Readers/TX	Houghton Mifflin Harcourt
Baseball Pals	Q	RF	250+	Christopher, Matt	Little Brown and Company
*Baseball Pitching Challenge and Other Cases, The	O	RF	250+	Simon, Seymour	Avon Books
Baseball Saved Us	O	HF	250+	Mochizuki, Ken	Scholastic
Baseball Turnaround	Q	RF	250+	Christopher, Matt	Little Brown and Company
Baseball's Best	M	F	250+	Too Cool	Pacific Learning
*Baseball's Best: Five True Stories	O	B	250+	Step into Reading	Random House
*Baseball's Greatest Pitchers	P	B	250+	Kramer, S. A.	Random House
Basement Basketball	M	RF	250+	HSP/Harcourt Trophies	Harcourt, Inc.
Basesball Fever	I	RF	453	We Both Read	Treasure Bay
Basic Heredity	Y	I	250+	Navigators Science Series	Benchmark Education
#Basics of Cell Life with Max Axiom, Super Scientist, The	W	I	250+	Graphic Library	Capstone Press

TITLE	LEVEL	GENRE	WORD COUNT	AUTHOR / SERIES	PUBLISHER / DISTRIBUTOR
Basilisk's Lair, The (Nathaniel Fludd Beastologist Book Two)	R	F	250+	LaFevers, R. L.	Houghton Mifflin Harcourt
Basil's Birds	K	F	250+	Reed, Lynn Rowe	Marshall Cavendish
Basil's Night Out	J	F	471	Gear Up!	Wright Group/McGraw Hill
Basket Ball, The	M	F	250+	Codell, Esme Raji	Harry N. Abrams
Basket Counts, The	R	RF	250+	Christopher, Matt	Little Brown and Company
Basket Full of Surprises, A	B	RF	43	Little Books	Sadlier-Oxford
Basket of Beethoven	S	RF	250+	Currie, Susan	Fitzhenry & Whiteside
^Basketball	S	I	250+	Download	Hameray Publishing Group
Basketball	M	I	250+	InfoTrek Plus	ETA/Cuisenaire
Basketball	K	I	250+	On Deck	Rigby
Basketball	C	I	47	Readlings	American Reading Company
Basketball	H	I	97	Readlings/ Sports	American Reading Company
Basketball	I	I	159	Ready Readers	Pearson Learning Group
Basketball	M	I	517	Red Rocket Readers	Flying Start Books
Basketball	C	RF	23	Visions	Wright Group/McGraw Hill
Basketball	B	I	20	Wonder World	Wright Group/McGraw Hill
Basketball Blues	L	RF	250+	Go Girl!	Feiwel and Friends
Basketball Buddies	N	RF	250+	Boyz Rule!	Mondo Publishing
Basketball for Fun	S	I	250+	Sports for Fun	Compass Point Books
Basketball Game, The	L	RF	607	Leveled Readers Science	Houghton Mifflin Harcourt
Basketball Showdown	N	RF	250+	Girlz Rock!	Mondo Publishing
Basketball War	P	SF	1946	Zucker, Jonny	Stone Arch Books
Bass Ackwards and Belly Up	Z+	RF	250+	Craft, Elizabeth & Fain, Sarah	Little Brown and Company
Basset Hounds	I	I	152	Dogs	Capstone Press
Bat	B	I	33	Zoozoo-Animal World	Cavallo Publishing
Bat 6	Z	HF	250+	Wolff, Virginia Euwer	Scholastic
Bat and Parrot	B	F	46	Sails	Rigby
Bat Bones and Spider Stew	K	RF	250+	Poploff, Michelle	Bantam Books
Bat Boy & His Violin, The	Q	RF	250+	Curtis, Gavin	Scholastic
Bat Loves the Night	M	RF	250+	Read and Wonder	Candlewick Press
Bat Scientists, The	W	I	250+	Scientists in the Field	Houghton Mifflin Harcourt
Bat, The	H	RF	256	Gear Up!	Wright Group/McGraw Hill
Bataan Death March, The	Z	I	250+	Snapshots in History	Compass Point Books
Batboy, The	U	RF	250+	Lupica, Mike	Philomel
Bat-Chen Diaries, The	X	B	13802	Shahak, Bat-Chen	Kar-Ben Publishing
Bath Day for Brutus	K	RF	347	Little Red Readers	Sundance
Bath Eyes	F	RF	154	PM Photo Stories	Rigby
Bath for a Beagle	D	RF	102	First Start	Troll Associates
Bath for Lucky, A	H	F	196	Coulton, Mia	Maryruth Books
Bath for Patches, A	E	RF	89	Carousel Readers	Pearson Learning Group
Bath Time	B	I	44	Bebop Books	Lee & Low Books Inc.
Bath Time	B	I	33	InfoTrek	ETA/Cuisenaire
Bath Time	C	I	23	Wonder World	Wright Group/McGraw Hill
Bath, The	LB	RF	14	Ready Readers	Pearson Learning Group
Bath, The	B	RF	28	Smart Start	Rigby
Bathtime for Biscuit	F	RF	148	Capucilli, Alyssa Satin	HarperCollins
Bathtub Beach	J	RF	368	Leveled Readers	Houghton Mifflin Harcourt
Bathtub Beach	J	RF	368	Leveled Readers/CA	Houghton Mifflin Harcourt
^Batista	T	B	250+	Stars of Pro Wrestling	Capstone Press
Bat-Poet, The	S	F	250+	Jarrell, Randall	HarperCollins
Bats	O	I	2473	Early Bird Nature Books	Lerner Publishing Group
Bats	O	I	250+	Gibbons, Gail	Holiday House
Bats	O	I	250+	Holmes, Kevin J.	Red Brick Learning

* Collection of short stories   # Graphic text
^ Mature content with lower level text demands

TITLE	LEVEL	GENRE	WORD COUNT	AUTHOR / SERIES	PUBLISHER / DISTRIBUTOR
Bats	P	I	250+	Literacy 2000	Rigby
Bats	O	I	250+	Nature's Friends	Compass Point Books
Bats	K	I	204	Nocturnal Animals	Capstone Press
Bats	M	I	503	Pawprints Teal	Pioneer Valley
Bats	I	I	162	Phonics Readers	Compass Point Books
Bats	M	I	250+	PM Animal Facts: Gold	Rigby
Bats	A	I	56	Readlings/ Predator Animals	American Reading Company
Bats	J	I	250+	Wood, Lily	Scholastic
Bats about Bats!	N	I	250+	Storyteller Summer Skies	Wright Group/McGraw Hill
Bats and Burglars	N	RF	250+	First Flight	Fitzhenry & Whiteside
Bats Are Thin, Bears Are Fat	I	I	103	Larkin, Bruce	Wilbooks
Bats at Bat	D	F	36	Pair-It Books	Steck-Vaughn
Bat's Big Game	K	TL	250+	MacDonald, Margaret Read	Albert Whitman & Co.
Bats in Blankets	H	I	182	Sails	Rigby
Bat's Night Out	L	RF	172	Books for Young Learners	Richard C. Owen
Bats on the Move	Q	I	865	Vocabulary Readers	Houghton Mifflin Harcourt
Bats on the Move	Q	I	865	Vocabulary Readers/CA	Houghton Mifflin Harcourt
Bats Out the Window	O	RF	250+	First Flight	Fitzhenry & Whiteside
Bats, Bats, Bats	E	I	33	Pair-It Books	Steck-Vaughn
Bats, Bats, Bats	D	I	29	Rosen Real Readers	Rosen Publishing Group
Bats, The	C	I	21	Twig	Wright Group/McGraw Hill
Bats: Creatures of the Night	L	I	250+	All Aboard Science Reader	Grosset & Dunlap
Bats: The Amazing Upside-Downers	S	I	250+	A First Book	Franklin Watts
Batter Up	G	RF	183	Adventures in Reading	Pearson Learning Group
Batter Up	C	I	8	Bebop Books	Lee & Low Books Inc.
Batter Up!	C	RF	39	Bookshop	Mondo Publishing
Batter Up!	P	RF	250+	Maddox, Jake	Stone Arch Books
Batteries	G	I	105	Early Connections	Benchmark Education
Batteries Not Required	V	I	250+	Boldprint	Steck-Vaughn
Batteries, Bulbs and Wires	R	I	250+	Young Discoverers	Kingfisher
Batting Against the Odds	Q	B	250+	WorldScapes	ETA/Cuisenaire
Battle for Iwo Jima, The	W	I	250+	Cornerstones of Freedom	Children's Press
Battle for Monmouth, The	S	I	1285	Vocabulary Readers	Houghton Mifflin Harcourt
Battle for Survival, The	P	I	250+	Sunshine	Wright Group/McGraw Hill
Battle for the Castle, The	P	F	250+	Winthrop, Elizabeth	Yearling Books
^Battle of Bull Run, The: An Interactive History Adventure	V	HF	250+	You Choose Books	Capstone Press
^Battle of Bunker Hill, The: An Interactive History Adventure	T	HF	250+	You Choose Books	Capstone Press
Battle of Chancellorsville, The	V	I	250+	Cornerstones of Freedom	Children's Press
Battle of Gettysburg, The: Turning Point of the Civil War	V	I	250+	Let Freedom Ring	Capstone Press
Battle of Lake Erie, The	Y	I	250+	History for Young Canadians	Fitzhenry & Whiteside
Battle of Leyte, The	U	I	974	Leveled Readers Social Studies	Houghton Mifflin Harcourt
Battle of Monmouth, The	S	I	1285	Vocabulary Readers/CA	Houghton Mifflin Harcourt
Battle of Monmouth, The	S	I	1285	Vocabulary Readers/TX	Houghton Mifflin Harcourt
Battle of the Alamo, The	V	I	250+	Cornerstones of Freedom	Children's Press
#Battle of the Alamo, The	T	I	250+	Graphic Library	Capstone Press
^Battle of the Alamo, The: An Interactive History Adventure	V	HF	250+	You Choose Books	Capstone Press
^Battle of the Bands	Z+	RF	250+	Orca Soundings	Orca Books
Battle of the Games	N	RF	250+	Boyz Rule!	Mondo Publishing
Battle of the Labyrinth, The	W	F	250+	Riordan, Rick	Hyperion
Battle of the Little Bighorn, The	V	I	250+	Cornerstones of Freedom	Children's Press

TITLE	LEVEL	GENRE	WORD COUNT	AUTHOR / SERIES	PUBLISHER / DISTRIBUTOR
Battle of Words, A	O	RF	250+	Literacy 2000	Rigby
Battle of Yorktown, The	V	I	250+	Let Freedom Ring	Red Brick Learning
Battle Over Rain Forest Lands, The	U	I	250+	Reading Street	Pearson
Battlefield Support	V	I	4310	Military Hardware in Action	Lerner Publishing Group
Battles at Sea	R	I	1386	Vocabulary Readers	Houghton Mifflin Harcourt
Battles at Sea	R	I	1386	Vocabulary Readers/CA	Houghton Mifflin Harcourt
Battles at Sea	R	I	1386	Vocabulary Readers/TX	Houghton Mifflin Harcourt
Battles of Lexington & Concord, The	T	I	250+	We The People	Compass Point Books
Battles of Lexington and Concord, The	V	I	250+	Let Freedom Ring	Red Brick Learning
Battles of the American Revolution: Saratoga	U	I	250+	Navigators Social Studies Series	Benchmark Education
Battles of the Civil War	U	I	250+	Primary Source Readers	Teacher Created Materials
Battles of the Civil War: Antietam	U	I	250+	Navigators Social Studies Series	Benchmark Education
Battles of the War of 1812, The	Y	I	250+	History for Young Canadians	Fitzhenry & Whiteside
Battleships	T	I	250+	Land and Sea	Capstone Press
Batty Riddles	L	F	250+	Hall, Katy & Eisenberg, Lisa	Puffin Books
Bay Run, The	C	RF	80	Foundations	Wright Group/McGraw Hill
Bay School Blogger, The	L	RF	250+	Social Studies Connects	Kane Press
B-day Box, The	Q	F	250+	Literacy by Design	Rigby
Be a Clown	C	I	29	The Candid Collection	Pearson Learning Group
Be a Good Friend!	J	I	250+	Spyglass Books	Compass Point Books
Be a Good Sport!	J	I	250+	Spyglass Books	Compass Point Books
Be a Perfect Person in Just Three Days!	N	RF	250+	Manes, Stephen	Dell
Be a Plant Scientist	L	I	250+	Take Two Books	Wright Group/McGraw Hill
Be Careful of Strangers	I	RF	362	Rigby Flying Colors	Rigby
Be Careful What You Wish For!	Q	TL	250+	Literacy by Design	Rigby
Be Careful!	I	F	236	Fried, Mary	Keep Books
Be Careful!	D	F	133	Gear Up!	Wright Group/McGraw Hill
Be Careful, Matthew!	F	RF	80	Sunshine	Wright Group/McGraw Hill
Be Careful, Ogre!	I	F	192	Sun Sprouts	ETA/Cuisenaire
Be Quiet	A	RF	25	Literacy 2000	Rigby
Be Quiet	B	RF	25	Smart Start	Rigby
Be Quiet Parrot	J	F	405	Be Nice at School	Carolrhoda Books
Be Quiet!	E	RF	95	Rigby Star	Rigby
Be Ready at Eight	K	F	250+	Parish, Peggy	Simon & Schuster
Be Safe on Your Bike	J	I	250+	Rosen Real Readers	Rosen Publishing Group
*Be the Change: People Who Have Made a Difference	T	B	250+	Power Up!	Steck-Vaughn
Be Water Wise	M	I	491	Red Rocket Readers	Flying Start Books
Bea Rocks the Flock	L	F	250+	Jamieson, Victoria	Bloomsbury Children's Books
Beach	M	I	250+	Cooper, Elisha	Orchard Books
Beach Boat, The	F	RF	168	PM Stars	Rigby
Beach Creatures	H	I	231	Pair-It Books	Steck-Vaughn
Beach Feet	D	RF	68	Books for Young Learners	Richard C. Owen
Beach House, The	F	RF	164	PM Plus Story Books	Rigby
Beach Patrol	M	F	250+	Too Cool	Pacific Learning
Beach Riddles	K	F	467	Silly Millies	Millbrook Press
Beach, The	D	RF	38	Book Bank	Wright Group/McGraw Hill
Beach, The	J	RF	292	Leveled Readers	Houghton Mifflin Harcourt
Beach, The	J	RF	292	Leveled Readers/CA	Houghton Mifflin Harcourt
Beach, The	J	RF	292	Leveled Readers/TX	Houghton Mifflin Harcourt
Beach, The	LB	I	16	Little Celebrations	Pearson Learning Group
Beach, The	B	RF	28	McAlpin, MaryAnn	Short Tales Press
Beacons of Light: Lighthouses	O	I	250+	Gibbons, Gail	Scholastic

* Collection of short stories   # Graphic text
^ Mature content with lower level text demands

TITLE	LEVEL	GENRE	WORD COUNT	AUTHOR / SERIES	PUBLISHER / DISTRIBUTOR
Beading for Fun!	S	I	250+	For Fun! Crafts	Compass Point Books
Beading: Bracelets, Barrettes, and Beyond	Q	I	250+	Crafts	Capstone Press
Beads	C	I	16	Instant Readers	Harcourt School Publishers
Beagle Brigade, The	N	I	250+	Literacy by Design	Rigby
Beagles	R	I	250+	All About Dogs	Capstone Press
Beagles	I	I	101	Dogs	Capstone Press
Beagles Are the Best!	Q	I	1286	The Best Dogs Ever	Lerner Publishing Group
Beak Book, The	D	I	48	Chanko, Pamela	Scholastic
Beaks	I	I	164	Animal Spikes and Spines	Heinemann Library
Beaks	G	I	125	Discovery Links	Newbridge
Beaks	H	I	100	Gear Up!	Wright Group/McGraw Hill
Beaks and Feet	J	I	234	Alphakids	Sundance
Beaks and Wings	L	I	250+	HSP/Harcourt Trophies	Harcourt, Inc.
Bean	N	I	250+	Life Cycles	Creative Teaching Press
Bean Bag That Mom Made, The	I	RF	270	Tadpoles	Rigby
Beanbag	K	RF	250+	Literacy 2000	Rigby
Beanpole Billy	L	F	250+	Lighthouse	Ginn & Co.
Beans	F	I	89	Life Cycles	Lerner Publishing Group
Beans	LB	I	35	Pebble Books	Capstone Press
Bean's Life, A	F	I	163	Watch It Grow	Heinemann Library
Beans on the Roof	L	RF	250+	Byars, Betsy	Bantam Books
Beany (Not Beanhead)	M	RF	250+	Wojciechowski, Susan	Candlewick Press
Beany and the Dreaded Wedding	M	RF	250+	Wojciechowski, Susan	Candlewick Press
Beany and the Magic Crystal	M	RF	250+	Wojciechowski, Susan	Candlewick Press
Beany and the Meany	M	RF	250+	Wojciechowski, Susan	Candlewick Press
Beany Goes to Camp	M	RF	250+	Wojciechowski, Susan	Candlewick Press
Bear	M	F	250+	Schoenherr, John	Scholastic
Bear and the Bees, The	J	TL	250+	PM Plus Story Books	Rigby
Bear and the Trolls, The	L	TL	250+	PM Tales and Plays-Silver	Rigby
Bear At Home	F	F	91	Blackstone, Stella	Barefoot Books
Bear at the Beach	K	F	250+	Carmichael, Clay	North-South Books
Bear Called Paddington, A	T	F	250+	Bond, Michael	Bantam Books
Bear Called Trouble, A	P	RF	250+	Bauer, Marion Dane	Clarion Books
Bear Collection, The	N	I	250+	PM Collection	Rigby
Bear Cub Grows, A	A	I	35	Early Explorers	Benchmark Education
Bear Cubs	J	I	408	Vocabulary Readers	Houghton Mifflin Harcourt
Bear Cubs	J	I	408	Vocabulary Readers/CA	Houghton Mifflin Harcourt
Bear Eats Fish, A	C	I	44	Windows on Literacy	National Geographic
Bear Escape, The	D	F	42	Pair-It Books	Steck-Vaughn
Bear Facts	E	I	41	Pair-It Books	Steck-Vaughn
Bear Flies High	M	F	250+	Rosen, Michael	Bloomsbury Children's Books
Bear for Miguel, A	K	RF	250+	Alphin, Elaine Marie	HarperTrophy
Bear Goes to Town	K	F	250+	Browne, Anthony	Doubleday Books
Bear Hug, The	J	F	250+	Bryant, Laura J.	Albert Whitman & Co.
Bear Hunt	F	RF	146	Lighthouse	Rigby
Bear in the Air	K	RF	250+	Meyers, Susan	Harry N. Abrams
Bear in the Air	I	F	367	Sun Sprouts	ETA/Cuisenaire
Bear in Trouble	I	F	439	Sails	Rigby
Bear Lived in a Cave, A	D	I	102	Little Red Readers	Sundance
Bear Man, The	J	TL	358	Reading Street	Pearson
Bear Needs a Place to Climb, A	B	I	49	Independent Readers Science	Houghton Mifflin Harcourt
Bear Needs a Place to Climb, A	B	I	49	Science Support Readers	Houghton Mifflin Harcourt
Bear Shadow	J	F	489	Asch, Frank	Simon & Schuster

TITLE	LEVEL	GENRE	WORD COUNT	AUTHOR / SERIES	PUBLISHER / DISTRIBUTOR
Bear Swims	E	F	151	Leveled Readers	Houghton Mifflin Harcourt
Bear Swims	E	F	151	Leveled Readers/CA	Houghton Mifflin Harcourt
Bear Swims	E	F	151	Leveled Readers/TX	Houghton Mifflin Harcourt
Bear That Heard Crying, The	P	HF	250+	Kinsey-Warnock, Natalie; Kinsey, Helen	Penguin Group
Bear That Wouldn't Growl, The	I	F	250+	Storyworlds	Heinemann
Bear Wakes Up	B	F	76	First Stories	Pacific Learning
Bear with Sticky Paws Goes to School, The	K	F	250+	Vulliamy, Clara	Tiger Tales
Bear with Sticky Paws Won't Go to Bed, The	K	F	250+	Vulliamy, Clara	Tiger Tales
Bear with Sticky Paws, The	K	F	250+	Vulliamy, Clara	Tiger Tales
Bear, The	LB	I	17	Carousel Earlybirds	Pearson Learning Group
Bear, The	M	I	250+	Life Cycles	Steck-Vaughn
Bear, The: An American Folk Song	K	F	250+	Bookshop	Mondo Publishing
Bear's Birthday	I	F	432	Leveled Literacy Intervention/ Green System	Heinemann
Bearded Dragons	K	I	162	Reptiles	Capstone Press
Beardream	O	F	250+	Hobbs, Will	Aladdin
Bearing Witness: Teaching About the Holocaust	Z+	I	250+	Greenbaum, Beth Aviv	Heinemann
Bears	O	I	250+	Holmes, Kevin J.	Red Brick Learning
Bears	D	F	56	Joy Readers	Pearson Learning Group
Bears	P	I	3286	Leveled Readers Science	Houghton Mifflin Harcourt
Bears	B	I	59	Storyteller Nonfiction	Wright Group/McGraw Hill
Bears and the Honey, The	D	F	86	Storyworlds	Heinemann
Bears and the Magpie, The	G	F	205	PM Plus Story Books	Rigby
Bears and Their Dens	J	I	131	Animal Homes	Capstone Press
Bears are Curious	J	I	250+	Milton, Joyce	Random House
Bear's Ball	A	F	32	Sun Sprouts	ETA/Cuisenaire
Bear's Bargain	J	F	250+	Asch, Frank	Scholastic
Bear's Bicycle, The	I	F	185	McLeod, Emilie	Little Brown and Company
Bear's Christmas	M	F	250+	Berenstain, Stan & Jan	Random House
Bear's Diet	L	RF	652	PM Collection	Rigby
Bears Have Cubs	M	I	250+	Animals and Their Young	Compass Point Books
Bears' House, The	T	RF	250+	Sachs, Marilyn	Puffin Books
Bears in the Forest	M	RF	250+	Read and Wonder	Candlewick Press
Bears in the Night	D	F	108	Berenstain, Stan & Jan	Random House
Bear's Long, Brown Tail	H	TL	332	Leveled Readers	Houghton Mifflin Harcourt
Bear's Long, Brown Tail	H	TL	332	Leveled Readers/CA	Houghton Mifflin Harcourt
Bear's Long, Brown Tail	H	TL	332	Leveled Readers/TX	Houghton Mifflin Harcourt
Bears on Hemlock Mountain, The	M	RF	250+	Dalgliesh, Alice	Aladdin
Bears on the Brain	L	RF	1119	Science Solves It!	Kane Press
Bears on Wheels	D	F	89	Berenstain, Stan & Jan	Random House
Bears' Picnic	M	F	250+	Berenstain, Stan & Jan	Random House
Bears' Picnic, The	D	F	61	Story Box	Wright Group/McGraw Hill
Bears Ride in Style, The	M	RF	735	Leveled Readers	Houghton Mifflin Harcourt
Bears Ride in Style, The	M	RF	735	Leveled Readers/CA	Houghton Mifflin Harcourt
Bears Ride in Style, The	M	RF	735	Leveled Readers/TX	Houghton Mifflin Harcourt
Bear's Tail	G	TL	292	Leveled Readers	Houghton Mifflin Harcourt
Bear's Tail	G	TL	292	Leveled Readers/CA	Houghton Mifflin Harcourt
Bear's Tail	G	TL	292	Leveled Readers/TX	Houghton Mifflin Harcourt
Bear's Tale, The	H	TL	155	Books for Young Learners	Richard C. Owen
Bears Through the Year	A	F	20	Leveled Readers	Houghton Mifflin Harcourt
Bears Through the Year	A	F	20	Leveled Readers/CA	Houghton Mifflin Harcourt
Bear's Toothache, The	J	F	216	McPhail, David	Little Brown and Company
Bear's Year, A	J	I	213	Phonics Readers	Compass Point Books

* Collection of short stories   # Graphic text
^ Mature content with lower level text demands

TITLE	LEVEL	GENRE	WORD COUNT	AUTHOR / SERIES	PUBLISHER / DISTRIBUTOR
Bears!	I	I	231	Time for Kids	HarperCollins
Bears, Bears Everywhere	D	F	52	Rookie Readers	Children's Press
Bears, Bears, Bears	I	F	250+	Little Readers	Houghton Mifflin Harcourt
Bears, Bears, Bears	D	RF	76	Step-By-Step Series	Pearson Learning Group
Bears, Bears, Bears	E	F	250+	Story Steps	Rigby
Bears, Bears, Everywhere	E	F	67	Learn to Read	Creative Teaching Press
Bears, The	A	F	30	Sails	Rigby
Bearskinner, The: A Tale of the Brothers Grimm	T	TL	250+	Schlitz, Laura Amy	Candlewick Press
Bearstone	V	RF	250+	Hobbs, Will	Hearst
Beast	X	F	250+	Napoli, Donna Jo	Atheneum Books
Beast and the Halloween Horror	M	RF	250+	Giff, Patricia Reilly	Bantam Books
^Beast Beneath the Stairs	T	F	584	Dahl, Michael	Stone Arch Books
Beast in Ms. Rooney's Room, The	M	RF	250+	Giff, Patricia Reilly	Bantam Books
Beast of Moogill, The	K	SF	596	Rigby Gigglers	Rigby
Beast, The	Z+	RF	250+	Myers, Walter Dean	Scholastic
Beast, The	M	RF	250+	PM Plus Chapter Books	Rigby
Beastly	Z	F	250+	Flinn, Alex	HarperCollins
Beat Goes On, The	Q	I	250+	Explorer Books-Pioneer	National Geographic
Beat Goes On, The	R	I	250+	Explorer Books-Pathfinder	National Geographic
Beat This	D	RF	79	Ready Readers	Pearson Learning Group
Beat, The: The Music Scene	U	I	250+	Boldprint	Steck-Vaughn
Beating Diabetes	S	I	250+	Orbit Double Takes	Pacific Learning
Beating the Cold	Q	I	250+	WorldScapes	ETA/Cuisenaire
Beating the Drought	M	RF	250+	Orbit Chapter Books	Pacific Learning
Beating the Frost	O	RF	250+	Orbit Chapter Books	Pacific Learning
Beating the Heat	Q	I	883	Leveled Readers	Houghton Mifflin Harcourt
Beating the Heat	Q	I	883	Leveled Readers/CA	Houghton Mifflin Harcourt
Beating the Heat	Q	I	883	Leveled Readers/TX	Houghton Mifflin Harcourt
Beating the Heat, Desert Style	W	I	1874	Leveled Readers	Houghton Mifflin Harcourt
Beatle Meets Destiny	Z+	RF	250+	Williams, Gabrielle	Marshall Cavendish
Beatles, The	R	B	250+	Venezia, Mike	Children's Press
Beatrice Doesn't Want To	J	F	250+	Numeroff, Laura	Candlewick Press
Beatrix Potter	J	B	135	iOpeners	Pearson Learning Group
Beatrix Potter	K	B	314	Leveled Readers	Houghton Mifflin Harcourt
Beatrix Potter	K	B	314	Leveled Readers/CA	Houghton Mifflin Harcourt
Beatrix Potter	K	B	314	Leveled Readers/TX	Houghton Mifflin Harcourt
Beatrix Potter	O	B	250+	Wallner, Alexandra	Holiday House
Beauregard the Cat	M	RF	250+	Bookshop	Mondo Publishing
Beautiful Bats	L	I	319	Glaser, Linda	Millbrook Press
Beautiful Beads	P	I	3619	Ross, Kathy	Millbrook Press
Beautiful Bugs	E	I	70	Fleming, Maria	Scholastic
Beautiful Creatures	Z	F	250+	Garcia, Kami & Stohl, Margaret	Little Brown and Company
Beautiful Darkness	Z	F	250+	Garcia, Kami & Stohl, Margaret	Little Brown and Company
Beautiful Flowers	B	I	28	Wonder World	Wright Group/McGraw Hill
Beautiful Land: A Story of the Oklahoma Land Rush	S	I	250+	Antle, Nancy	Penguin Group
Beautiful Pig	J	F	423	Read Alongs	Rigby
*Beautiful Stories of Life, The: Six Greek Myths, Retold	W	TL	250+	Rylant, Cynthia	Houghton Mifflin Harcourt
Beautiful Stranger	Z+	RF	250+	Dean, Zoey	Little Brown and Company
Beauty	V	RF	250+	Wallace, Bill	Holiday House
Beauty and the Beaks: A Turkey's Cautionary Tale	N	F	250+	Auch, Mary Jane & Herm	Holiday House
Beauty and the Beast	I	TL	258	My 1st Classic Story	Picture Window Books

B

TITLE	LEVEL	GENRE	WORD COUNT	AUTHOR / SERIES	PUBLISHER / DISTRIBUTOR
Beauty and the Beast	K	TL	250+	PM Tales and Plays-Gold	Rigby
Beauty and the Beast	K	TL	250+	Sunshine	Wright Group/McGraw Hill
Beauty and the Beast	L	TL	880	Traditional Tales	Pioneer Valley
Beauty, the Beast, and the Sisters: A Thrice-told Tale	T	TL	250+	Bookshop	Mondo Publishing
Beauty: A Retelling of the Story of Beauty and the Beast	X	F	250+	McKinley, Robin	HarperTrophy
Beaver Engineers	N	I	250+	Take Two Books	Wright Group/McGraw Hill
Beaver Tale, A	E	I	228	Twig	Wright Group/McGraw Hill
Beaver, The	M	I	250+	Crewe, Sabrina	Steck-Vaughn
Beavers	N	I	250+	Bookshop	Mondo Publishing
Beavers	I	I	218	Sails	Rigby
Beavers	H	I	119	Wetland Animals	Capstone Press
Beavers and Their Lodges	J	I	121	Animal Homes	Capstone Press
Beavers Beware!	K	I	250+	Bank Street	Bantam Books
Beaver's Legend	O	TL	974	Red Rocket Readers	Flying Start Books
Beaver's Photo	E	F	120	Springboard	Wright Group/McGraw Hill
Beaver's Tail, The	J	TL	250+	Rigby Rocket	Rigby
Bebop Under the Big Top	L	F	229	The Rowland Reading Program Libary	Rowland Reading Foundation
Bec (The Demonata Series)	Z+	F	250+	Shan, Darren	Little Brown and Company
Because a Little Bug Went Ka-Choo	I	F	250+	Stone, Rosetta	Random House
Because Daddy Did My Hair	I	RF	214	Teacher's Choice Series	Pearson Learning Group
Because I Am Your Daddy	K	RF	231	North, Sherry	Harry N. Abrams
Because I'm Little	B	RF	51	Home Connection Collection	Rigby
Because I'm Worth It: Gossip Girl	Z+	RF	250+	von Ziegesar, Cecily	Little Brown and Company
Because of Walter	N	RF	250+	Action Packs	Rigby
Because of Winn-Dixie	R	RF	250+	DiCamillo, Kate	Candlewick Press
Becky's Blue Butterfly	K	RF	664	Rigby Flying Colors	Rigby
Becky's Special Folder	I	RF	396	Rigby Flying Colors	Rigby
Becoming a Butterfly	J	I	178	Gear Up!	Wright Group/McGraw Hill
Becoming a Butterfly	H	I	83	Rosen Real Readers	Rosen Publishing Group
Becoming a Citizen	R	I	250+	A True Book	Children's Press
Becoming a Citizen	P	I	209	Vocabulary Readers	Houghton Mifflin Harcourt
Becoming a Pop Star	V	I	250+	10 Things You Need to Know About	Capstone Press
Becoming A Real Hero	T	B	1650	Leveled Readers	Houghton Mifflin Harcourt
Becoming Joe DiMaggio	T	HF	250+	Testa, Maria	Candlewick Press
Becoming Modern America	U	I	250+	Kids Discover Reading	Wright Group/McGraw Hill
Becoming Naomi Leon	V	RF	250+	Ryan, Pam Munoz	Scholastic
Bed for Paul, A	L	TL	606	Reading Street	Pearson
Bed Full of Cats, A	I	RF	250+	Green Light Readers	Harcourt
Bed Hog	F	RF	39	Noullet, Georgette	Marshall Cavendish
Bed Rest	E	I	34	Rhythm 'N' Rhyme Readers	Pearson Learning Group
Bedroom Makeover Crafts	P	I	4053	Ross, Kathy	Millbrook Press
Beds	C	I	44	Interaction	Rigby
Bedtime	C	RF	23	Books for Young Learners	Richard C. Owen
Bedtime	C	RF	83	PM Plus Story Books	Rigby
Bedtime at Aunt Carmen's	K	RF	250+	Ready Readers	Pearson Learning Group
Bedtime for Bear	C	F	12	Instant Readers	Harcourt School Publishers
Bedtime for Bear	C	F	40	Rigby Rocket	Rigby
Bedtime for Carl	A	RF	24	Bonnell, Kris	Reading Reading Books
Bedtime for Frances	K	F	250+	Hoban, Russell	Scholastic
Bedtime for Mommy	L	F	117	Rosenthal, Amy Krouse	Bloomsbury Children's Books

* Collection of short stories   # Graphic text
^ Mature content with lower level text demands

TITLE	LEVEL	GENRE	WORD COUNT	AUTHOR / SERIES	PUBLISHER / DISTRIBUTOR
Bedtime for Paulette	G	RF	212	On Our Way to English	Rigby
Bedtime Fun	B	RF	46	Bebop Books	Lee & Low Books Inc.
Bedtime Hullabaloo	N	F	250+	Conway, David	Walker & Company
Bedtime in the Jungle	H	TL	250+	Butler, John	Peachtree
Bedtime Story, A	K	RF	250+	Bookshop	Mondo Publishing
Bedtime Without Arthur	J	RF	469	Meserve, Jessica	Andersen Press USA
Bedtime!	J	I	133	Small World	Lerner Publishing Group
Bee & Bird	WB	F	0	Frazier, Craig	Roaring Brook Press
Bee in Your Ear, A	L	RF	250+	Orca Echoes	Orca Books
Bee My Valentine!	H	RF	250+	Cohen, Miriam	Bantam Books
Bee Puzzle, The	K	RF	552	Early Explorers	Benchmark Education
Bee, The	M	I	250+	Crewe, Sabrina	Steck-Vaughn
Bee, The	C	RF	26	Story Box	Wright Group/McGraw Hill
Bee-Bim Bop!	L	RF	234	Park, Linda Sue	Houghton Mifflin Harcourt
Beekeeper, The	M	I	250+	Literacy 2000	Rigby
Beekeeper's Work, A	K	I	304	Reading Street	Pearson
Beeman Interview	N	F	250+	Sails	Rigby
Beeman, The	F	F	148	Sails	Rigby
Beep, Beep	F	F	51	Start to Read	School Zone
Beep, Beep, Beep	D	F	86	Foundations	Wright Group/McGraw Hill
Beeper and Honk	C	F	33	Schaefer, Carole Lexa/Brand New Readers	Candlewick Press
Beeper and Stomp	C	F	31	Brand New Readers	Candlewick Press
Beeper and Stomp	C	F	31	Schaefer, Carole Lexa/Brand New Readers	Candlewick Press
Beeper and Winky	C	F	37	Schaefer, Carole Lexa/Brand New Readers	Candlewick Press
Beeper Bakes	C	F	34	Brand New Readers	Candlewick Press
Beeper Counts	C	F	30	Brand New Readers	Candlewick Press
Beeper Flies	C	F	31	Brand New Readers	Candlewick Press
Beeper Paints	C	F	36	Brand New Readers	Candlewick Press
Bees	O	I	250+	A True Book	Children's Press
Bees	K	I	270	Ashley, Susan/Let's Read About Insects	Weekly Reader Publishing
Bees	O	I	250+	Holmes, Kevin J.	Red Brick Learning
Bees	N	I	250+	Nature's Friends	Compass Point Books
Bees	N	I	250+	World of Insects	Capstone Press
Bees and Their Hives	J	I	112	Animal Homes	Capstone Press
Bees and Wasps	I	I	458	Sails	Rigby
Bees at Work	L	I	456	Leveled Readers	Houghton Mifflin Harcourt
Bees at Work	L	I	456	Leveled Readers/CA	Houghton Mifflin Harcourt
Bees at Work	L	I	456	Leveled Readers/TX	Houghton Mifflin Harcourt
Bee's Beautiful Garden	N	F	720	Leveled Readers	Houghton Mifflin Harcourt
Bee's Beautiful Garden	N	F	720	Leveled Readers/CA	Houghton Mifflin Harcourt
Bee's Beautiful Garden	N	F	720	Leveled Readers/TX	Houghton Mifflin Harcourt
Bees Buzzed, The	B	RF	41	Science	Outside the Box
Bee's Home, A	K	I	127	Salem, Lynn	Continental Press
Bees in My Garden	E	I	104	Flying Colors	Rigby
Bee's Life, A	H	I	100	Time for Kids	Teacher Created Materials
Bee's Life, A	F	I	158	Watch It Grow	Heinemann Library
Bees on Trees	H	F	250+	Sunshine	Wright Group/McGraw Hill
Beethoven Lives Upstairs	S	I	250+	Nichol, Barbara	Orchard Books
Beetles	H	I	115	Bugs, Bugs, Bugs!	Capstone Press
Beetles	D	I	39	Insects	Capstone Press

TITLE	LEVEL	GENRE	WORD COUNT	AUTHOR / SERIES	PUBLISHER / DISTRIBUTOR
Beetles	N	I	250+	Minibeasts	Franklin Watts
Beetles	D	I	85	Readlings/ Bugs	American Reading Company
Beetles	E	I	59	Sails	Rigby
Beetles	C	I	36	Science	Outside the Box
Beetles	Q	I	1242	Vocabulary Readers	Houghton Mifflin Harcourt
Beetles	Q	I	1242	Vocabulary Readers/CA	Houghton Mifflin Harcourt
Beetles, Lightly Toasted	Q	RF	250+	Naylor, Phyllis Reynolds	Bantam Books
Bee-Wigged	J	F	250+	Bell, Cece	Candlewick Press
Beezus & Ramona	O	RF	250+	Cleary, Beverly	Avon Books
Before I Go to School	B	I	71	Storyteller-First Snow	Wright Group/McGraw Hill
Before It Wriggles Away	O	B	250+	Meet the Author	Richard C. Owen
Before the First Flight	U	I	1718	Vocabulary Readers	Houghton Mifflin Harcourt
Before the First Flight	U	I	1718	Vocabulary Readers/CA	Houghton Mifflin Harcourt
Before the First Flight	U	I	1718	Vocabulary Readers/TX	Houghton Mifflin Harcourt
Before the Fridge	G	I	88	Seedlings	Continental Press
Before the Talkies	K	RF	402	Leveled Readers	Houghton Mifflin Harcourt
Before the Talkies	K	RF	402	Leveled Readers/CA	Houghton Mifflin Harcourt
Before the Talkies	K	RF	402	Leveled Readers/TX	Houghton Mifflin Harcourt
Before the Top Stops	C	RF	51	InfoTrek	ETA/Cuisenaire
Before They Were Famous: How Seven Artists Got Their Start	V	B	4079	Raczka, Bob	Millbrook Press
Before They Were President	M	I	583	Vocabulary Readers	Houghton Mifflin Harcourt
Before They Were President	M	I	583	Vocabulary Readers/CA	Houghton Mifflin Harcourt
Beginning Knitting: Stitches with Style	Q	I	250+	Crafts	Capstone Press
Beginning, a Middle, and an End, A: The Right Way to Write Writing	Q	F	250+	Avi	Harcourt, Inc.
Beginnings of Sports	R	I	250+	PM Nonfiction-Ruby	Rigby
Behind And In Front	C	I	48	Location	Lerner Publishing Group
Behind Castle Walls	T	I	250+	WorldScapes	ETA/Cuisenaire
Behind Every Step: Have You Got What It Takes to Be a Choreographer?	U	I	250+	On the Job	Compass Point Books
Behind Rebel Lines	T	HF	250+	Reit, Seymour	Harcourt Trade
Behind The Bedroom Wall	V	HF	250+	Williams, Laura E.	Milkweed Editions
Behind the Couch	N	F	250+	Gerstein, Mordicai	Hyperion
Behind the Rocks	E	RF	50	Wonder World	Wright Group/McGraw Hill
Behind the Scenes	R	I	250+	Literacy 2000	Rigby
Behind the Scenes	P	I	894	Vocabulary Readers	Houghton Mifflin Harcourt
Behind the Scenes	P	I	894	Vocabulary Readers/CA	Houghton Mifflin Harcourt
Behind the Scenes	P	I	894	Vocabulary Readers/TX	Houghton Mifflin Harcourt
Behind the Scenes at the Airport	R	I	250+	Explore More	Wright Group/McGraw Hill
Behind the Scenes at the Zoo	R	I	250+	Rigby Literacy	Rigby
^Behind the Scenes Fashion	T	I	250+	Download	Hameray Publishing Group
^Behind the Scenes Special Effects	T	I	250+	Download	Hameray Publishing Group
Behind the Scenes with Sammy	N	I	250+	Little Celebrations	Pearson Learning Group
Behind the Secret Window: A Memoir of a Hidden Childhood During World War II	Y	B	250+	Toll, Nelly S.	Scholastic
Behind the Wheel	S	I	250+	NASCAR Racing	Capstone Press
Being a Bug Scout	S	I	250+	Navigators How-To Series	Benchmark Education
Being a Cartoonist	O	I	250+	Trackers	Pacific Learning
Being a Good Citizen: A Book About Citizenship	J	I	250+	Way to Be!	Picture Window Books
Being a Leader	E	I	101	Citizenship	Lerner Publishing Group
Being a Spider	N	I	694	Vocabulary Readers	Houghton Mifflin Harcourt
Being a Spider	N	I	694	Vocabulary Readers/CA	Houghton Mifflin Harcourt
Being an Astronaut	I	I	133	Reading Street	Pearson

* Collection of short stories   # Graphic text
^ Mature content with lower level text demands

TITLE	LEVEL	GENRE	WORD COUNT	AUTHOR / SERIES	PUBLISHER / DISTRIBUTOR
Being Bee	T	RF	250+	Bateson, Catherine	Holiday House
Being Billy	R	RF	250+	PM Plus Chapter Books	Rigby
Being Caribou: Five Months on Foot with a Caribou Herd	U	I	250+	Heuer, Karsten	Walker & Company
Being Cooperative	K	I	250+	Way to Be!	Picture Window Books
Being Danny's Dog	U	RF	250+	Naylor, Phyllis Reynolds	Aladdin
Being Fair	F	I	102	Citizenship	Lerner Publishing Group
Being Famous	V	I	250+	10 Things You Need to Know About	Capstone Press
Being Friends	C	I	21	Rosen Real Readers	Rosen Publishing Group
Being Honest	K	I	250+	Way to Be!	Picture Window Books
Being Patriotic	J	I	224	Early Explorers	Benchmark Education
Being Responsible	F	I	77	Citizenship	Lerner Publishing Group
Being Tolerant	K	I	250+	Way to Be!	Picture Window Books
Belgian Horse, The	R	I	250+	Horses	Capstone Press
Bell of Atri	O	TL	250+	WorldScapes	ETA/Cuisenaire
Bell on the Cat, The	I	TL	235	Sun Sprouts	ETA/Cuisenaire
Bell, the Book, and the Spellbinder, The	S	F	250+	Strickland, Brad	Puffin Books
Bella & Rosie Trick or Treat	E	F	129	Bella and Rosie Series	Literacy Footprints
Bella and Rosie Play Hide and Seek	D	F	118	Bella and Rosie Series	Pioneer Valley
Bella at Midnight	V	HF	250+	Stanley, Diane	HarperTrophy
Bella Is a Bad Dog	H	F	132	Bella and Rosie Series	Pioneer Valley
Bella the Bunny Fairy: Rainbow Magic	L	F	250+	Meadows, Daisy	Scholastic
Bella: The Birthday Party	L	F	250+	Stanley, Mandy	Tiger Tales
Bella: The Fairy Ball	L	F	250+	Stanley, Mandy	Tiger Tales
Bella's Baby Bird	K	RF	514	Gear Up!	Wright Group/McGraw Hill
Bella's Birthday	D	F	59	Bella and Rosie Series	Pioneer Valley
Bella's Picnic	F	RF	273	Rigby Flying Colors	Rigby
Bella's Ride	E	RF	181	Rigby Flying Colors	Rigby
Belle of Batoche	P	HF	250+	Orca Young Readers	Orca Books
Belle Prater's Boy	V	RF	250+	White, Ruth	Bantam Books
Below the Green Pond	N	I	250+	Read All About It	Steck-Vaughn
Below Zero	O	I	250+	WorldScapes	ETA/Cuisenaire
Beltons' Imagination, The	Q	F	1505	Leveled Readers	Houghton Mifflin Harcourt
Beltons' Imagination, The	Q	F	1505	Leveled Readers/CA	Houghton Mifflin Harcourt
Beltons' Imagination, The	Q	F	1505	Leveled Readers/TX	Houghton Mifflin Harcourt
Beluga Whales Up Close	M	I	250+	First Facts-Whales and Dolphins Up Close	Capstone Press
Ben & Becky in the Haunted House	J	F	734	We Both Read	Treasure Bay
Ben and Me	S	HF	250+	Lawson, Robert	Little Brown and Company
Ben and Sooty	H	RF	152	Leveled Readers/TX	Houghton Mifflin Harcourt
Ben and the Bear	I	F	250+	Riddell, Chris	Harper & Row
Ben and the Cold	C	RF	76	Sun Sprouts	ETA/Cuisenaire
Ben and the Crab	G	RF	205	Sun Sprouts	ETA/Cuisenaire
Ben at the Theme Park	F	RF	214	Sun Sprouts	ETA/Cuisenaire
Ben Ate It	E	RF	130	Teacher's Choice Series	Pearson Learning Group
Ben Franklin Goes to Paris	R	I	1603	Vocabulary Readers	Houghton Mifflin Harcourt
Ben Franklin Goes to Paris	R	I	1603	Vocabulary Readers/CA	Houghton Mifflin Harcourt
Ben Franklin Goes to Paris	R	I	1603	Vocabulary Readers/TX	Houghton Mifflin Harcourt
Ben Franklin of Old Philadelphia	U	B	250+	Cousins, Margaret	Random House
Ben Franklin Remembers	P	B	493	Vocabulary Readers	Houghton Mifflin Harcourt
Ben Franklin, Founding Father	Q	B	1030	Vocabulary Readers	Houghton Mifflin Harcourt
Ben Franklin, Founding Father	Q	B	1030	Vocabulary Readers/CA	Houghton Mifflin Harcourt
Ben Franklin: A Man with Many Talents	O	B	250+	On Our Way to English	Rigby

B

* Collection of short stories   # Graphic text
^ Mature content with lower level text demands

TITLE	LEVEL	GENRE	WORD COUNT	AUTHOR / SERIES	PUBLISHER / DISTRIBUTOR
Ben Franklin: Scientist	J	I	266	Leveled Readers Science	Houghton Mifflin Harcourt
Ben Franklin's Big Shock	N	I	1552	On My Own History	Lerner Publishing Group
Ben Franklin's Fire Company	I	I	147	Leveled Readers Language Support	Houghton Mifflin Harcourt
Ben Lost a Tooth	E	I	31	iOpeners	Pearson Learning Group
Ben Over Night	K	RF	250+	Ellis, Sarah	Fitzhenry & Whiteside
Ben Roethlisberger	P	B	2100	Amazing Athletes	Lerner Publishing Group
Ben Runs	C	RF	66	Sun Sprouts	ETA/Cuisenaire
Ben the Bold	C	RF	71	Literacy 2000	Rigby
Ben the Cat	D	F	124	Leveled Readers	Houghton Mifflin Harcourt
Ben the Cat	D	F	124	Leveled Readers/CA	Houghton Mifflin Harcourt
Ben the Cat	D	F	124	Leveled Readers/TX	Houghton Mifflin Harcourt
Ben, the Big Brother	C	RF	48	Kaleidoscope Collection	Hameray Publishing Group
Bend and Stretch: Learning About Your Bones and Muscles	M	I	250+	Amazing Body	Picture Window Books
Bend, Stretch, and Leap	J	RF	250+	PM Plus Story Books	Rigby
Bending	C	I	32	Changing Matter	Lerner Publishing Group
Beneath Earth's Surface	O	I	250+	Rosen Real Readers	Rosen Publishing Group
Beneath Our Feet	O	I	250+	Trackers	Pacific Learning
Beneath the Mask (The Grassland Trilogy)	X	F	250+	Ward, David	Amulet Books
Beneath the Waves	Q	I	250+	InfoQuest	Rigby
Benedict Arnold	V	B	250+	Let Freedom Ring	Capstone Press
Benedict Arnold	S	B	1225	Leveled Readers	Houghton Mifflin Harcourt
Benedict Arnold	S	B	1225	Leveled Readers/CA	Houghton Mifflin Harcourt
Benedict Arnold	S	B	1225	Leveled Readers/TX	Houghton Mifflin Harcourt
Benedict Arnold at Saratoga	Y	HF	2151	Leveled Readers	Houghton Mifflin Harcourt
#Benedict Arnold: American Hero and Traitor	T	B	250+	Graphic Library	Capstone Press
Bengal Tiger, The	D	I	59	Bonnell, Kris/Animals in Danger	Reading Reading Books
Benita's Plan	M	RF	250+	On Our Way to English	Rigby
Benito's Goal	Q	RF	250+	In Step Readers	Rigby
Benjamin Banneker	T	B	250+	Amazing Americans	Wright Group/McGraw Hill
Benjamin Banneker	P	B	250+	American Lives	Heinemann
Benjamin Banneker	N	B	231	First Biographies	Capstone Press
Benjamin Banneker	S	B	3957	History Maker Bios	Lerner Publishing Group
Benjamin Banneker: An American Scientist	K	B	374	Leveled Readers Science	Houghton Mifflin Harcourt
Benjamin Banneker: Pioneering Scientist	O	B	1870	On My Own Biography	Lerner Publishing Group
Benjamin Banneker: Scientist	N	B	250+	Beginning Biographies	Pearson Learning Group
Benjamin Brown and the Great Steamboat Race	S	HF	4325	History Speaks	Millbrook Press
Benjamin Franklin	U	B	250+	Amazing Americans	Wright Group/McGraw Hill
Benjamin Franklin	N	B	250+	Biography	Benchmark Education
Benjamin Franklin	Q	B	250+	Early Biographies	Compass Point Books
Benjamin Franklin	S	B	3897	History Maker Bios	Lerner Publishing Group
Benjamin Franklin	W	B	250+	Just the Facts Biographies	Lerner Publishing Group
Benjamin Franklin	U	B	250+	Kent, Deborah	Scholastic
Benjamin Franklin	U	B	250+	Let Freedom Ring	Red Brick Learning
Benjamin Franklin	N	B	250+	Pebble Books	Capstone Press
Benjamin Franklin	Q	B	250+	Photo-Illustrated Biographies	Red Brick Learning
Benjamin Franklin	R	B	250+	Primary Source Readers	Teacher Created Materials
Benjamin Franklin: A Man with Many Jobs	O	B	250+	Greene, Carol	Children's Press
Benjamin Franklin: A Scientist by Nature	X	B	2095	Leveled Readers	Houghton Mifflin Harcourt
Benjamin Franklin: American Inventor	N	B	250+	Rosen Real Readers	Rosen Publishing Group
#Benjamin Franklin: An American Genius	T	B	250+	Graphic Library	Capstone Press
^Benjamin Franklin: From Inventor to Founder of a New Nation	T	B	250+	Hameray Biography Series	Hameray Publishing Group

* Collection of short stories   # Graphic text
^ Mature content with lower level text demands

TITLE	LEVEL	GENRE	WORD COUNT	AUTHOR / SERIES	PUBLISHER / DISTRIBUTOR
Benjamin Franklin: Writer, Inventor, Statesman	M	B	250+	Biographies	Picture Window Books
Benjamin Franklin: Young Printer	R	B	250+	Stevenson, Augusta	Aladdin
Benjamin Harrison	U	B	250+	Profiles of the Presidents	Compass Point Books
Benjamin Harrison: Twenty-third President	R	B	250+	Getting to Know the U.S. Presidents	Children's Press
Benjamin's Octopus	I	F	250+	The Rowland Reading Program Library	Rowland Reading Foundation
Benji's Pup	I	RF	439	Evangeline Nicholas Collection	Wright Group/McGraw Hill
Bennie	A	RF	29	Ray's Readers	Outside the Box
Benny	J	F	321	Posthuma, Sieb	Kane/Miller Book Publishers
#Benny and Penny and the Toy Breaker	K	F	250+	Hayes, Geoffrey	Toon Books
#Benny and Penny in Just Pretend	K	F	250+	Hayes, Geoffrey	Toon Books
#Benny and Penny in the Big No-No!	K	F	250+	Hayes, Geoffrey	Toon Books
Benny Bakes a Cake	I	RF	250+	Rice, Eve	Greenwillow Books
Benny's Baby Brother	E	RF	89	Start to Read	School Zone
Benny's School Trip	G	RF	217	Pair-It Books	Steck-Vaughn
Ben's Amazing Birthday	L	RF	250+	Cambridge Reading	Pearson Learning Group
Ben's Banana	C	F	60	Foundations	Wright Group/McGraw Hill
Ben's Bath	C	RF	56	Sun Sprouts	ETA/Cuisenaire
Ben's Bike	J	RF	414	Sails	Rigby
Ben's Boots	E	RF	101	Bonnell, Kris	Reading Reading Books
Ben's Brilliant Birthday	D	RF	63	Rigby Rocket	Rigby
Ben's Colors	C	RF	75	Sun Sprouts	ETA/Cuisenaire
Ben's Dad	E	RF	102	PM Story Books	Rigby
Ben's Dream	WB	F	0	Van Allsburg, Chris	Houghton Mifflin Harcourt
Ben's First Words	D	RF	49	Bonnell, Kris	Reading Reading Books
Ben's Fun Box	D	RF	63	New Way Red	Steck-Vaughn
Ben's Jigsaw Puzzle	D	RF	103	PM Stars	Rigby
Ben's New Trick	F	RF	219	Ready Readers	Pearson Learning Group
Ben's Pets	C	RF	30	Ready Readers	Pearson Learning Group
Ben's Red Car	B	RF	49	PM Starters	Rigby
Ben's Robot	N	F	250+	Orca Echoes	Orca Books
Ben's Story	L	RF	1060	Rigby Flying Colors	Rigby
Ben's Teddy Bear	D	RF	68	PM Story Books	Rigby
Ben's Tooth	H	RF	197	PM Story Books	Rigby
Ben's Treasure Hunt	D	RF	72	PM Story Books	Rigby
Ben's Tune	N	RF	250+	PM Collection	Rigby
*Beowulf	U	TL	250+	Literacy 2000	Rigby
Beowulf: A Tale of Blood, Heat, and Ashes	Z	TL	250+	Raven, Nicky	Candlewick Press
#Beowulf: Monster Slayer	V	TL	2727	Graphic Myths and Legends	Graphic Universe
Berenstain Bear Scouts and the Coughing Catfish	M	F	250+	Berenstain, Stan & Jan	Scholastic
Berenstain Bear Scouts, The: Ghost Versus Ghost	M	F	250+	Berenstain, Stan & Jan	Scholastic
Berenstain Bears and the Ghost of the Auto Graveyard, The	M	F	250+	Berenstain, Stan & Jan	Random House
Berenstain Bears and the Missing Honey	M	F	531	Berenstain, Stan & Jan	Random House
Berlin Wall, The	V	I	2050	Independent Readers Social Studies	Houghton Mifflin Harcourt
Berlioz The Bear	N	F	250+	Brett, Jan	Scholastic
Bermuda Triangle, The	U	I	250+	The Unexplained	Capstone Press
Bermuda Triangle, The	Z	I	250+	Unsolved Mysteries	Steck-Vaughn
^Bermuda Triangle, The: The Unsolved Mystery	R	I	250+	Mysteries of Science	Capstone Press
Bernardo de Gálvez	W	B	1818	Leveled Readers	Houghton Mifflin Harcourt
Berries for Baby Elephant	E	F	93	Coulton, Mia	Maryruth Books

TITLE	LEVEL	GENRE	WORD COUNT	AUTHOR / SERIES	PUBLISHER / DISTRIBUTOR
Berry Cake, The	G	RF	171	PM Photo Stories	Rigby
Bert and Ernie at the Pond	C	F	43	Sesame Workshop/Brand New Readers	Candlewick Press
Bert and Ernie Go Hiking	D	F	44	Sesame Workshop/Brand New Readers	Candlewick Press
Berta: A Remarkable Dog	N	RF	250+	Lottridge, Celia Barker	Groundwood Books
Bertie Beaver Goes to the City	C	F	100	Springboard	Wright Group/McGraw Hill
Bertie the Bear	I	F	250+	Allen, Pamela	Coward
Bert's Boat	E	RF	64	Rigby Star	Rigby
Beryl: A Pig's Tale	Q	F	250+	Simmons, Jane	Little Brown and Company
Bess and Bella	K	F	250+	Haas, Irene	Margaret K. McElderry Books
Bess in My Garden	E	I	104	Rigby Flying Colors	Rigby
Bessie Coleman	O	B	250+	Brager, Bruce	Scholastic
Bessie Coleman	N	B	257	First Biographies	Capstone Press
Bessie Coleman	W	B	250+	Just the Facts Biographies	Lerner Publishing Group
#Bessie Coleman: Daring Stunt Pilot	R	B	250+	Graphic Library	Capstone Press
Bessie Coleman: Daring to Fly	N	B	1706	On My Own Biography	Lerner Publishing Group
Bessie Coleman: Queen of the Sky	K	B	229	Sunshine	Wright Group/McGraw Hill
Bessie's Bed	J	F	435	Silly Millies	Millbrook Press
Bess's Log Cabin Quilt	P	HF	250+	Love, D. Anne	Bantam Books
Best Friends	WB	RF	0	Books for Young Learners	Richard C. Owen
Best Bad Thing, The	T	RF	250+	Uchida, Yoshiko	Aladdin
Best Best Friends	I	RF	250+	Chodos-Irvine, Margaret	Harcourt
Best Birthday Gift Ever, The	I	RF	249	Talking Point Series	Pearson Learning Group
Best Birthday Mole Ever Had, The	E	F	252	Ready Readers	Pearson Learning Group
Best Birthday Present, The	H	F	237	Gunderson, Kay	Keep Books
Best Birthday Present, The	K	RF	250+	Literacy 2000	Rigby
Best Blackberries, The	J	RF	410	Springboard	Wright Group/McGraw Hill
Best Boat, The	J	I	690	Leveled Readers Science	Houghton Mifflin Harcourt
Best Book for Terry Lee, The	I	RF	250+	Literacy Tree	Rigby
Best Book of the Human Body, The	Q	I	250+	Kingfisher Knowledge	Kingfisher
Best Book of Trains, The	R	I	250+	The Best Book	Kingfisher
Best Book of Weather, The	S	I	250+	The Best Book	Kingfisher
Best Bread, The	F	RF	181	Adams, Lorraine & Bruvold, Lynn	Eaglecrest Books
Best Cake, The	F	RF	162	PM Story Books	Rigby
Best Car For Us, The	I	I	161	Windows on Literacy	National Geographic
Best Children in the World, The	F	F	148	Story Box	Wright Group/McGraw Hill
Best Class Trip, The	F	RF	214	Leveled Readers	Houghton Mifflin Harcourt
Best Clown in Town, The	L	RF	250+	Bradley, Tom	Pearson Learning Group
Best Dancer, The	F	RF	166	PM Photo Stories	Rigby
Best Detective, The	N	RF	250+	Keene, Carolyn	Pocket Books
Best Diver in the World, The	M	RF	250+	Sunshine	Wright Group/McGraw Hill
Best Dog in the Whole World, The	K	RF	250+	Sunshine	Wright Group/McGraw Hill
Best Enemies	P	RF	250+	Leverich, Kathleen	Beech Tree Books
Best Enemies Again	P	RF	250+	Leverich, Kathleen	Alfred A. Knopf
Best Enemies Forever	P	RF	250+	Leverich, Kathleen	William Morrow
Best Fish Ever, The	O	RF	884	Leveled Readers	Houghton Mifflin Harcourt
Best Foot Forward	X	RF	250+	Bauer, Joan	Speak
Best Friend on Wheels	K	RF	250+	Shirley, Debra	Albert Whitman & Co.
Best Friends	F	RF	255	Adams, Lorraine & Bruvold, Lynn	Eaglecrest Books
Best Friends	B	I	28	Bebop Books	Lee & Low Books Inc.
Best Friends	E	RF	31	Fitros, Pamela	Kaeden Books

        Storable Database at www.fountasandpinnellleveledbooks.com

* Collection of short stories   # Graphic text
^ Mature content with lower level text demands

TITLE	LEVEL	GENRE	WORD COUNT	AUTHOR / SERIES	PUBLISHER / DISTRIBUTOR
Best Friends	D	RF	15	Instant Readers	Harcourt School Publishers
Best Friends	F	HF	127	Learn to Read	Creative Teaching Press
Best Friends	D	RF	68	Little Readers	Houghton Mifflin Harcourt
Best Friends	E	RF	106	Real Kids Readers	Millbrook Press
Best Friends	C	I	43	Rosen Real Readers	Rosen Publishing Group
Best Friends	C	RF	34	Windows on Literacy	National Geographic
B-E-S-T Friends	L	RF	250+	Giff, Patricia Reilly	Bantam Books
Best Friends Don't Fight	M	RF	250+	Bookshop	Mondo Publishing
Best Friends for Frances	K	F	250+	Hoban, Russell	HarperTrophy
Best Friends for Never	X	RF	250+	Harrison, Lisi	Little Brown and Company
Best Friends Forever: A World War II Scrapbook	W	HF	250+	Patt, Beverly	Marshall Cavendish
Best Friends Wear Pink Tutus	I	RF	250+	Brownrigg, Sheri	Scholastic
*Best Ghost Stories Ever, The	Z	F	250+	Krovatin, Christopher	Scholastic
Best Gift of All, The	K	F	250+	Emmett, Jonathan	Candlewick Press
Best Guess, The	I	RF	241	Foundations	Wright Group/McGraw Hill
Best Hats, The	G	RF	201	PM Plus Story Books	Rigby
Best Job for Scooter, The	J	RF	580	Leveled Readers	Houghton Mifflin Harcourt
Best Little Monkeys in the World, The	J	F	250+	Standiford, Natalie	Random House
Best Mother's Day Ever, The	M	RF	250+	Social Studies Connects	Kane Press
Best Nest	J	F	250+	Eastman, Philip D.	Random House
Best Nest, The	N	F	750	Mueller, Doris L.	Sylvan Dell Publishing
Best New Friends	G	RF	257	Leveled Literacy Intervention/ Green System	Heinemann
Best of Both Worlds	T	I	250+	WorldScapes	ETA/Cuisenaire
^Best of Pro Baseball, The	O	I	250+	Best of Pro Sports	Capstone Press
^Best of Pro Basketball, The	O	I	250+	Best of Pro Sports	Capstone Press
^Best of Pro Football, The	O	I	250+	Best of Pro Sports	Capstone Press
^Best of Pro Soccer, The	O	I	250+	Best of Pro Sports	Capstone Press
Best Older Sister, The	L	RF	250+	Choi, Sook Nyul	Bantam Books
Best Part of Me, The	P	I	250+	Ewald, Wendy	Little Brown and Company
Best Part, The	K	RF	250+	PM Story Books-Silver	Rigby
Best Pet Ever, The	K	F	250+	Roberts, Victoria	Tiger Tales
Best Pet for Al, The	G	F	203	Literacy by Design	Rigby
Best Pet Yet, The	H	RF	472	Real Kids Readers	Millbrook Press
Best Pet, The	J	RF	250+	Lighthouse	Rigby
Best Pet, The	K	I	421	Sun Sprouts	ETA/Cuisenaire
Best Place, The	C	F	77	Leveled Readers	Houghton Mifflin Harcourt
Best Place, The	C	RF	61	Literacy 2000	Rigby
Best Places, The	D	RF	68	Ready Readers	Pearson Learning Group
Best Present, The	G	RF	146	Rigby Literacy	Rigby
Best Ranger, The	K	RF	396	Leveled Readers	Houghton Mifflin Harcourt
Best School Year Ever, The	P	RF	250+	Robinson, Barbara	HarperTrophy
Best Season Ever: Katie Woo	J	RF	250+	Manushkin, Fran	Picture Window Books
Best Student, The	J	RF	390	Leveled Readers	Houghton Mifflin Harcourt
Best Student, The	J	RF	390	Leveled Readers/CA	Houghton Mifflin Harcourt
Best Student, The	J	RF	390	Leveled Readers/TX	Houghton Mifflin Harcourt
Best Tail, The	F	F	184	Red Rocket Readers	Flying Start Books
Best Teacher in Second Grade, The	J	RF	250+	Kenah, Katharine	HarperCollins
Best Teacher in the World, The	K	RF	250+	Chardiet, Bernice	Scholastic
Best Thanksgiving, The	O	HF	250+	HSP/Harcourt Trophies	Harcourt, Inc.
Best Thing About Food, The	F	I	132	Twig	Wright Group/McGraw Hill
Best Thing About Valentines, The	I	F	132	Hudson, Eleanor	Scholastic
Best Thing, The	G	I	108	Bebop Books	Lee & Low Books Inc.
Best Trade of All, The	N	RF	250+	Use Your Imagination	Steck-Vaughn

TITLE	LEVEL	GENRE	WORD COUNT	AUTHOR / SERIES	PUBLISHER / DISTRIBUTOR
Best Trick, The	G	F	275	Stone Arch Readers	Stone Arch Books
Best Way to Play, The	L	F	250+	Cosby, Bill	Scholastic
Best Web of All, The	G	F	160	Gear Up!	Wright Group/McGraw Hill
Best Wishes	O	B	250+	Meet The Author	Richard C. Owen
Best Wishes for Eddie	M	RF	250+	Nayer, Judy	Pearson Learning Group
Best Worst Day, The	L	RF	250+	Graves, Bonnie	Hyperion
Best-Loved Doll, The	L	F	250+	Caudill, Rebecca	Henry Holt & Co.
Beth's Bed	E	RF	81	Supersonics	Rigby
Beth's Snow Dancer	Q	HF	250+	The Little Women Journals	Avon Books
Betina and the Talent Show	M	RF	538	Leveled Readers/TX	Houghton Mifflin Harcourt
Betrayal of Maggie Blair, The	Z	HF	250+	Laird, Elizabeth	Houghton Mifflin Harcourt
Betrayed: (House of Night)	Z+	F	250+	Cast, P. C. & Kristin	St. Martin's Griffin
Betraying Season	Z+	F	250+	Doyle, Marissa	Henry Holt & Co.
Betsy and Billy	P	RF	250+	Haywood, Carolyn	Harcourt, Inc.
Betsy and Tacy Go Downtown	Q	HF	250+	Lovelace, Maud Hart	HarperTrophy
Betsy and Tacy Go Over the Big Hill	Q	HF	250+	Lovelace, Maud Hart	HarperTrophy
Betsy and Tacy: 60th Anniversary Edition	Q	HF	250+	Lovelace, Maud Hart	HarperTrophy
Betsy and the Boys	P	RF	250+	Haywood, Carolyn	Harcourt Trade
Betsy Ross	N	B	197	First Biographies	Capstone Press
Betsy Ross	U	B	250+	Let Freedom Ring	Red Brick Learning
Betsy Ross	L	B	250+	Pebble Books	Red Brick Learning
Betsy Ross	S	B	2058	People to Remember Series	January Books
#Betsy Ross and the American Flag	T	B	250+	Graphic Library	Capstone Press
Betsy Ross: Designer of Our Flag	R	B	250+	Weil, Ann	Aladdin
Betsy the Babysitter	F	RF	115	First Start	Troll Associates
Betta Fish	K	I	218	Colorful World of Animals	Capstone Press
Better Brown Stories, The	T	F	250+	Ahlberg, Allan	Penguin Group
Better Idea, A	J	RF	492	In Step Readers	Rigby
Better Life, A	T	RF	1066	Independent Readers Social Studies	Houghton Mifflin Harcourt
Better Look, A	H	I	106	Windows on Literacy	National Geographic
Better Off Wet: A Guide to Wetlands	O	I	250+	Windows on Literacy	National Geographic
Better Plan, A	S	RF	2617	Leveled Readers	Houghton Mifflin Harcourt
Better Plan, A	S	RF	2617	Leveled Readers/CA	Houghton Mifflin Harcourt
Better Plan, A	S	RF	2617	Leveled Readers/TX	Houghton Mifflin Harcourt
Better Than TV	J	RF	250+	Miller, Sara Swan	Bantam Books
Bettina Valentino and the Picasso Club	U	RF	250+	Daly, Niki	Farrar, Straus, & Giroux
Betty Bee Wouldn't Budge	I	F	267	Pair-It Turn and Learn	Steck-Vaughn
*Between Earth and Sky: Legends of Native American Sacred Places	Z	TL	250+	Bruchac, Joseph	Voyager Books
Between Mom and Jo	Z+	RF	250+	Peters, Julie Anne	Little Brown and Company
Between the Dragon and the Eagle	W	HF	250+	Schneider, Mical	Carolrhoda Books
*Between the Lines	U	B	250+	Rigby Literacy	Rigby
Between the Tides	E	I	52	Wonder World	Wright Group/McGraw Hill
Between the Wars	V	I	250+	Primary Source Readers	Teacher Created Materials
Between Two Worlds	T	I	250+	WorldScapes	ETA/Cuisenaire
Between Two Worlds: A Story about Pearl Buck	S	B	7415	Creative Minds Biographies	Lerner Publishing Group
Beware of the Frog	M	F	250+	Bee, William	Candlewick Press
Beware the Werepup: The Pet Sitter	O	F	250+	Sykes, Julie	Kingfisher
Beware!	N	RF	250+	Orbit Chapter Books	Pacific Learning
Beware, Princess Elizabeth	Y	HF	250+	Meyer, Carolyn	Harcourt Trade
Beyond Belief	S	I	250+	Orbit Collections	Pacific Learning
*Beyond Belief	Z	I	250+	Steiger, Brad	Scholastic

* Collection of short stories   # Graphic text
^ Mature content with lower level text demands

TITLE	LEVEL	GENRE	WORD COUNT	AUTHOR / SERIES	PUBLISHER / DISTRIBUTOR
Beyond Little Women: A Story About Louisa May Alcott	R	B	8360	Creative Minds Biographies	Carolrhoda Books
Beyond Providence	X	RF	250+	Schnur, Steven	Harcourt Brace
Beyond Reality	X	I	250+	Boldprint	Steck-Vaughn
^Beyond Repair	V	RF	250+	Peterson, Lois/Orca Currents	Orca Books
Beyond the Beyond	Q	I	250+	Wildcats	Wright Group/McGraw Hill
Beyond the Black Hole	Q	SF	250+	Bookweb	Rigby
Beyond the Burning Lands	U	F	250+	Christopher, John	Aladdin
Beyond the Grave	Z	I	7190	The Unexplained	Lerner Publishing Group
Beyond the Grave (The 39 Clues)	U	F	250+	Watson, Jude	Scholastic
Beyond the Mango Tree	V	RF	250+	Zemser, Amy Bronwen	HarperTrophy
Beyond the Myth: The Story of Joan of Arc	Z	B	250+	Brooks, Polly Schoyer	Houghton Mifflin Harcourt
Beyond the Ordinary Camera	V	I	250+	Rigby Literacy	Rigby
Beyond the Western Sea, Book II: Lord Kirkle's Money	V	HF	250+	Avi	Avon Books
Beyond: A Solar System Voyage	Z	I	250+	Benson, Michael	Harry N. Abrams
BFG, The	U	F	250+	Dahl, Roald	Penguin Group
Bibim Bap for Dinner	L	I	250+	Bebop Books	Lee & Low Books Inc.
Bicentennial Gift, The	T	RF	1906	Leveled Readers	Houghton Mifflin Harcourt
Bichons Frises	I	I	153	Dogs	Capstone Press
Bicycle Book, The	O	I	250+	PM Nonfiction-Emerald	Rigby
Bicycle for Rosaura, A	M	F	250+	Soar To Success	Houghton Mifflin Harcourt
Bicycle Man, The	P	RF	250+	Say, Allen	Houghton Mifflin Harcourt
Bicycle Patrol Officers	S	I	250+	Law Enforcement	Capstone Press
Bicycle Rider	O	B	250+	Scioscia, Mary	HarperTrophy
Bicycle, The	Q	I	250+	Great Inventions	Capstone Press
Bicycle, The	C	F	29	Story Box	Wright Group/McGraw Hill
Bicycles	N	I	250+	Windows on Literacy	National Geographic
Bicycles of the Past	M	I	250+	On Deck	Rigby
Bicycling Adventures	S	I	250+	Dangerous Adventures	Red Brick Learning
Biff's Aeroplane	E	RF	64	Oxford Reading Tree	Oxford University Press
Big Al	L	F	250+	Clements, Andrew	Scholastic
Big Al and Shrimpy	L	F	250+	Clements, Andrew	Aladdin Paperbacks
Big and Busy Body	M	I	250+	Priddy, Roger	Priddy Books
Big and Green	D	I	12	Wonder World	Wright Group/McGraw Hill
Big and Little	B	I	77	Adams, Lorraine & Bruvold, Lynn	Eaglecrest Books
Big and Little	LB	I	59	Berger, Samantha; Chanko, Pamela	Scholastic
Big and Little	B	F	40	Carousel Earlybirds	Pearson Learning Group
Big and Little	B	I	56	Early Connections	Benchmark Education
Big and Little	LB	I	21	Foundations	Wright Group/McGraw Hill
Big and Little	D	F	92	Joy Readers	Pearson Learning Group
Big and Little	LB	I	24	KinderReaders	Rigby
Big and Little	C	I	66	Little Readers	Houghton Mifflin Harcourt
Big and Little	B	I	68	PM Plus Starters	Rigby
Big and Little	B	I	38	Rigby Literacy	Rigby
Big and Little	B	I	55	Rigby Rocket	Rigby
Big and Little	B	RF	40	Storyteller	Wright Group/McGraw Hill
Big and Little	C	I	36	Sunshine	Wright Group/McGraw Hill
Big and Little	A	I	21	Time for Kids	Teacher Created Materials
Big and Little	WB	I	0	Vocabulary Readers	Houghton Mifflin Harcourt
Big and Little Dinosaurs	E	I	50	Planet Earth	Rigby
Big and Small: An Animal Opposites Book	K	I	250+	Animal Opposites	Capstone Press
Big Animals	B	F	49	Red Rocket Readers	Flying Start Books

TITLE	LEVEL	GENRE	WORD COUNT	AUTHOR / SERIES	PUBLISHER / DISTRIBUTOR
Big Animals in the Sea	A	I	24	Sails	Rigby
Big Animals, Little Animals	D	I	133	Sails	Rigby
Big Art	P	I	250+	Trackers	Pacific Learning
Big Babies	M	I	250+	Yellow Umbrella Books	Red Brick Learning
Big Baby Elephant, The	G	RF	96	Seedlings	Continental Press
Big Bad Rex	I	I	176	Erickson, Betty	Continental Press
Big Bad Wolf, The	I	RF	250+	PM Plus Story Books	Rigby
Big Bad Wolf, The	I	TL	268	Red Rocket Readers	Flying Start Books
Big Bad Wolf?	F	F	121	Rigby Rocket	Rigby
Big Balloon Festival, The	L	RF	625	PM Collection	Rigby
Big Balloon Race, The	K	RF	250+	Coerr, Eleanor	HarperTrophy
Big Barn, The	C	RF	81	Teacher's Choice Series	Pearson Learning Group
Big Barry Baker and the Bullies	J	RF	250+	Storyworlds	Heinemann
Big Barry Baker in Big Trouble	J	RF	250+	Storyworlds	Heinemann
Big Barry Baker on the Stage	J	RF	250+	Storyworlds	Heinemann
Big Barry Baker's Parcel	J	RF	250+	Storyworlds	Heinemann
Big Bear, The	B	TL	40	Avenues	Hampton Brown
Big Bear's Socks	E	F	75	Storyteller	Wright Group/McGraw Hill
Big Bed, The	I	RF	346	Pacific Literacy	Pacific Learning
Big Beet, The	L	F	250+	Ready Readers	Pearson Learning Group
Big Ben	E	RF	100	Real Kids Readers	Millbrook Press
Big Ben Helps the Town	H	F	182	Early Explorers	Benchmark Education
Big Bend Adventure	M	I	207	Windows on Literacy	National Geographic
Big Bend Treasure Hunt	S	I	250+	Literacy By Design	Rigby
Big Bend Treasure Hunt	S	I	250+	On Our Way to English	Rigby
Big Bird and Grover Move	C	F	36	Brand New Readers	Candlewick Press
Big Bird Cleans	C	F	39	Brand New Readers	Candlewick Press
Big Bird Relatives	L	I	449	Springboard	Wright Group/McGraw Hill
Big Bird Shares a Snack	C	F	45	Brand New Readers	Candlewick Press
Big Bird the Artist	C	F	34	Brand New Readers	Candlewick Press
Big Bird, The	D	RF	118	Reading Street	Pearson
Big Bird's Copycat Day	F	F	232	Lerner, Sharon	Random House
Big Black Bears	F	I	43	Rosen Real Readers	Rosen Publishing Group
Big Blue Heron	D	F	76	Kaleidoscope Collection	Hameray Publishing Group
Big Blue Sea, The	C	I	69	Scott, Janine	Scholastic
Big Blue Whale	N	RF	250+	Read and Wonder	Candlewick Press
Big Bo Peep	K	F	250+	Lighthouse	Ginn & Co.
Big Bone, The	C	F	78	Jack and Daisy	Pioneer Valley
Big Boo Bird, The	C	F	66	Joy Readers	Pearson Learning Group
Big Book of Words for Curious Kids, The	LB	I	19	Godon, Ingrid	Peachtree
Big Boots	I	RF	250+	Storyworlds	Heinemann
Big Box Fix Up, The	F	RF	198	The Rowland Reading Program Library	Rowland Reading Foundation
Big Box, The	D	F	81	Leveled Readers	Houghton Mifflin Harcourt
Big Box, The	H	RF	183	New Way Green	Steck-Vaughn
Big Box, The	E	RF	111	Real Kids Readers	Millbrook Press
Big Boy	O	TL	250+	Mollel, Tololwa M.	Houghton Mifflin Harcourt
Big Bradley	D	F	30	Ray's Readers	Outside the Box
Big Bridges	M	I	508	Vocabulary Readers	Houghton Mifflin Harcourt
Big Bridges	M	I	508	Vocabulary Readers/CA	Houghton Mifflin Harcourt
Big Bridges	M	I	508	Vocabulary Readers/TX	Houghton Mifflin Harcourt
Big Brother	C	I	49	Explorations	Okapi Educational Materials
Big Brother	C	I	49	Explorations	Eleanor Curtain Publishing
Big Brother	F	RF	191	McAlpin, MaryAnn	Short Tales Press

* Collection of short stories   # Graphic text
^ Mature content with lower level text demands

TITLE	LEVEL	GENRE	WORD COUNT	AUTHOR / SERIES	PUBLISHER / DISTRIBUTOR
^Big Brother at School	T	SF	1938	Powell, J.	Stone Arch Books
Big Brown Bear	F	F	97	Green Light Readers	Harcourt
Big Bubba Hippo	L	F	250+	Splash	Pacific Learning
Big Bug, The	E	RF	81	Reading Street	Pearson
Big Bugs	K	I	128	Big	Capstone Press
Big Bugs	M	I	250+	Simon, Seymour	Chronicle Books
Big Bulgy Fat Black Slugs	M	F	250+	Stepping Stones	Nelson/Michaels Assoc.
Big Bus, The	E	RF	54	The Rowland Reading Program Library	Rowland Reading Foundation
Big Cat Babies	I	I	282	Big Cat	Pacific Learning
Big Cat Pepper	K	RF	250+	Partridge, Elizabeth	Bloomsbury Children's Books
Big Cat Trouble	N	RF	250+	World Quest Adventures	World Quest Learning
Big Cat, Little Cat	B	I	61	Rigby Focus	Rigby
Big Cat, Little Kitty	N	F	823	Cohn, Scotti	Sylvan Dell Publishing
Big Cat, The	B	RF	25	Bonnell, Kris	Reading Reading Books
Big Cat, The	D	RF	41	Ready Readers	Pearson Learning Group
Big Catch, The	K	RF	250+	Literacy 2000	Rigby
Big Catch, The	U	RF	250+	Reading Expeditions	National Geographic
Big Catch, The	F	F	318	Stone Arch Readers	Stone Arch Books
Big Cats	S	I	250+	Boldprint	Steck-Vaughn
Big Cats	J	I	250+	Evans, Lynette	Scholastic
Big Cats	P	I	1189	Vocabulary Readers	Houghton Mifflin Harcourt
Big Cats	P	I	1189	Vocabulary Readers/CA	Houghton Mifflin Harcourt
Big Cats	P	I	1189	Vocabulary Readers/TX	Houghton Mifflin Harcourt
Big Cats Little Cats	I	I	210	Springboard	Wright Group/McGraw Hill
Big Change, A	I	RF	259	Reading Street	Pearson
Big Chase, The	A	F	14	Foundations	Wright Group/McGraw Hill
Big Chase, The	M	RF	250+	Supa Doopers	Sundance
Big Chief of the Neverwoz, The	H	F	250+	Little Celebrations	Pearson Learning Group
Big City Life	H	I	133	Shutterbug Books	Steck-Vaughn
#Big City Sights	K	RF	250+	My 1st Graphic Novel	Stone Arch Books
Big City Song	L	RF	292	Pearson, Debora	Holiday House
Big City, A	G	I	108	Larkin, Bruce	Wilbooks
Big City, The	C	RF	93	Leveled Literacy Intervention/ Blue System	Heinemann
Big Crocodile, The	G	F	61	Little Celebrations	Pearson Learning Group
Big Day, A	E	RF	120	InfoTrek	ETA/Cuisenaire
Big Dipper and You, The	Q	I	250+	Krupp, E. C.	Mulberry Books
Big Dipper, The	M	I	585	Leveled Readers Science	Houghton Mifflin Harcourt
Big Dog, Little Dog	I	F	265	Eastman, Philip D.	Random House
Big Ears	B	I	30	Sails	Rigby
Big Egg	E	F	103	Coxe, Molly	Random House
Big Elephant	A	F	26	Zoozoo-Into the Wild	Cavallo Publishing
BIG Elephants	D	I	41	Rosen Real Readers	Rosen Publishing Group
Big Enough	C	RF	49	Visions	Wright Group/McGraw Hill
Big Family, The	H	RF	250+	Sunshine	Wright Group/McGraw Hill
*Big Fat Cow That Goes Kapow, The	M	F	250+	Griffiths, Andy	Feiwel and Friends
Big Fat Manifesto	Z+	RF	250+	Vaught, Susan	Bloomsbury Children's Books
Big Fat Worm, The	G	F	250+	Van Laan, Nancy	Random House
Big Field, The	U	RF	250+	Lupica, Mike	Puffin Books
Big Fish Is Coming!, The	C	F	108	InfoTrek	ETA/Cuisenaire
Big Fish Little Fish	K	TL	250+	Folk Tales	Wright Group/McGraw Hill

B

TITLE	LEVEL	GENRE	WORD COUNT	AUTHOR / SERIES	PUBLISHER / DISTRIBUTOR
Big Fish, The	C	F	30	Brand New Readers	Candlewick Press
Big Fish, The	C	RF	82	Early Emergent	Pioneer Valley
Big Fish, The	N	RF	250+	Sunshine	Wright Group/McGraw Hill
Big Fish, The	I	RF	301	Yukish, Joe	Kaeden Books
Big Foot	X	I	4555	Monster Chronicles	Lerner Publishing Group
Big Foot	X	I	250+	The Unexplained	Capstone Press
Big Friend, Little Friend	E	RF	56	Greenfield, Eloise	Houghton Mifflin Harcourt
Big Game, The	J	F	751	Little Dinosaur	Literacy Footprints
Big Game, The	H	RF	69	Pacific Literacy	Pacific Learning
Big Giant, The	C	F	43	Sails	Rigby
Big Gold Mountain	N	RF	250+	Bookweb	Rigby
Big Green Caterpillar, The	J	RF	161	Literacy 2000	Rigby
Big Greg the Firefighter	D	RF	100	Springboard	Wright Group/McGraw Hill
Big Greg to the Rescue	K	RF	535	Springboard	Wright Group/McGraw Hill
Big Greg's Campaign	N	RF	250+	Springboard	Wright Group/McGraw Hill
Big Greg's First Ski Lesson	K	RF	696	Springboard	Wright Group/McGraw Hill
Big Gust, The	N	F	650	Leveled Readers	Houghton Mifflin Harcourt
Big Helicopter, The	E	RF	125	PM Stars	Rigby
Big Hill, The	C	F	55	PM Plus Story Books	Rigby
Big Hill, The	B	F	19	Story Box	Wright Group/McGraw Hill
Big Hippo and Little Hippo	J	F	445	Sails	Rigby
Big Hole, The	E	RF	150	Developing Books	Pioneer Valley
Big Hole, The	B	RF	39	PM Stars	Rigby
Big House, Little Mouse	B	RF	37	Handprints B	Educators Publishing Service
Big House, The	T	RF	250+	Coman, Carolyn	Puffin Books
Big Hungry Bear, The	I	F	148	Wood, Don & Audrey	Scholastic
Big Hungry Cat, The	D	RF	78	Bonnell, Kris	Reading Reading Books
Big Hunt, The	S	HF	2619	Leveled Readers	Houghton Mifflin Harcourt
Big Hunt, The	S	HF	2619	Leveled Readers/CA	Houghton Mifflin Harcourt
Big Hunt, The	S	HF	2619	Leveled Readers/TX	Houghton Mifflin Harcourt
Big Hush, The	I	RF	281	Story Box	Wright Group/McGraw Hill
Big Interview, The	R	RF	1397	Leveled Readers	Houghton Mifflin Harcourt
Big Interview, The	R	RF	1397	Leveled Readers/CA	Houghton Mifflin Harcourt
Big Interview, The	R	RF	1397	Leveled Readers/TX	Houghton Mifflin Harcourt
Big Iron Ranch	O	I	2134	In Step Readers	Rigby
Big Iron Ranch	O	I	250+	Literacy By Design	Rigby
Big Is Big (and Little, Little): A Book of Contrasts	J	I	199	Lewis, J. Patrick	Holiday House
Big Kick, The	C	RF	67	PM Story Books	Rigby
Big Kicks	K	F	250+	Kolar, Bob	Candlewick Press
Big Laugh, A	F	RF	183	Sails	Rigby
Big Laugh, The	I	F	152	Sunshine	Wright Group/McGraw Hill
Big Lie, The: A True Story	T	B	250+	Leitner, Isabella	Scholastic
Big Little Monkey	L	F	250+	Schaefer, Carole Lexa	Candlewick Press
Big Lizard, Little Lizard	C	F	97	Leveled Literacy Intervention/ Blue System	Heinemann
Big Long Animal Song	C	F	29	Little Celebrations	Pearson Learning Group
Big Machines	E	I	130	Red Rocket Readers	Flying Start Books
Big Machines	E	I	66	Rookie Readers	Children's Press
Big Mama and Grandma Ghana	J	RF	250+	Medearis, A. Shelf	Scholastic
Big Mammals	B	I	42	Little Red Readers	Sundance
Big Max	J	F	250+	Platt, Kin	HarperTrophy
Big Mess, A	J	RF	250+	On Our Way to English	Rigby

* Collection of short stories   # Graphic text
^ Mature content with lower level text demands

TITLE	LEVEL	GENRE	WORD COUNT	AUTHOR / SERIES	PUBLISHER / DISTRIBUTOR
Big Mess, The	I	F	167	Storyworlds	Heinemann
Big Mix-Up, The	G	F	70	City Stories	Rigby
Big Monster is Running Away	C	F	41	Rigby Rocket	Rigby
Big Mouse, Little Mouse	I	F	370	Sails	Rigby
Big Mouth & Ugly Girl	Z+	RF	250+	Oates, Joyce Carol	HarperCollins
Big Mouths	B	I	37	Sails	Rigby
Big Move, A	E	RF	65	Reading Street	Pearson
Big Nap, The: A Chet Gecko Mystery	Q	F	250+	Hale, Bruce	Harcourt, Inc.
Big Ned and the Eggs	L	TL	690	Sun Sprouts	ETA/Cuisenaire
Big Noodle, The	D	F	110	Joy Starters	Pearson Learning Group
Big Nothing, The	Y	RF	250+	Fogelin, Adrian	Peachtree
Big or Little?	B	I	35	Bebop Books	Lee & Low Books Inc.
Big or Little?	D	I	64	Dominie Factivity Series	Pearson Learning Group
Big or Little?	I	RF	250+	Stinson, Kathy	Pearson Learning Group
Big or Small?	B	I	30	Yellow Umbrella Books	Red Brick Learning
Big Orange Splot, The	L	F	250+	Pinkwater, Daniel Manus	Scholastic
Big Pancake, The	I	TL	312	Storyworlds	Heinemann
Big Party, The	L	F	692	Early Explorers	Benchmark Education
Big Picture, The	R	I	250+	Bennett, Mary	Pacific Learning
Big Pig and Little Pig	D	F	83	Green Light Readers	Harcourt
Big Pig, Little Pig	E	F	54	Little Celebrations	Pearson Learning Group
Big Predators	J	I	125	Big	Capstone Press
Big Prize, The	K	F	401	Adventures in Reading	Pearson Learning Group
Big Race, The	L	RF	250+	Home Connection Collection	Rigby
Big Race, The	N	F	250+	Pye, Trevor	Pacific Learning
Big Race, The	H	RF	250+	Start to Read	School Zone
Big Rain Coming	L	RF	141	Germein, Katrina	Clarion Books
Big Red and the Car Wash	G	F	250+	Sails	Rigby
Big Red Apple, The	H	F	250+	Momentum Literacy Program	Troll Associates
Big Red Comes to Stay	F	RF	298	Sails	Rigby
Big Red Fire Engine	G	F	158	First Start	Troll Associates
Big Red Tomatoes	I	I	168	Windows on Literacy	National Geographic
Big Rex and Friends	F	I	95	Priddy, Frank	Priddy Books
Big Rig Bugs	L	F	72	Cyrus, Kurt	Walker & Company
Big Rigs	L	I	113	On Deck	Rigby
Big Rigs	L	I	488	Pull Ahead Books	Lerner Publishing Group
Big Rigs	M	I	250+	Transportation	Compass Point Books
Big Rigs on the Move	K	I	372	Lightning Bolt Books	Lerner Publishing Group
Big Rocks, Little Rocks	E	I	180	Early Connections	Benchmark Education
Big Rocks, Small Rocks	C	I	49	Dominie Factivity Series	Pearson Learning Group
Big Roller Coasters	K	I	142	Big	Capstone Press
Big Roundup, The	G	I	121	Wonder World	Wright Group/McGraw Hill
Big Sale, The	H	RF	486	Real Kids Readers	Millbrook Press
Big Sea Animals	B	I	79	PM Plus Starters	Rigby
Big Seed, The	E	RF	83	New Way	Steck-Vaughn
Big Shapes and Little Shapes	C	I	99	PM Math Readers	Rigby
Big Shrink, The	L	F	250+	Cambridge Reading	Pearson Learning Group
Big Sister	C	RF	44	Visions	Wright Group/McGraw Hill
Big Sky Country	T	RF	250+	Reading Expeditions	National Geographic
Big Small	B	I	70	Bookworms	Marshall Cavendish
Big Smelly Bear	J	F	250+	Teckentrup, Britta	Scholastic
Big Snapper, The	O	RF	250+	Orca Young Readers	Orca Books
Big Sneeze, The	K	F	131	Brown, Ruth	Lothrop
Big Sneeze, The	D	F	112	Foundations	Wright Group/McGraw Hill

TITLE	LEVEL	GENRE	WORD COUNT	AUTHOR / SERIES	PUBLISHER / DISTRIBUTOR
Big Snow	M	F	250+	Hader, Berta & Elmer	Scholastic
Big Snow, The	E	RF	150	Developing Books	Pioneer Valley
Big Snow, The	J	I	150	Early Connections	Benchmark Education
Big Snowball Fight	C	RF	15	Bebop Books	Lee & Low Books Inc.
Big Snowball, The	G	F	250+	Storyworlds	Heinemann
Big Spider	I	TL	250+	Rigby Star	Rigby
Big Spider, A	H	I	271	Sails	Rigby
Big Splash, The	B	F	33	Big Cat	Pacific Learning
Big Splash, The	W	RF	250+	Ferraiolo, Jack D.	Amulet Books
Big Storm, The	Q	I	250+	Hiscock, Bruce	Aladdin
Big Storm, The	F	F	123	Leveled Literacy Intervention/ Green System	Heinemann
Big Surprise, The	H	RF	123	Pacific Literacy	Pacific Learning
Big Surprise, The	B	F	29	Storyworlds	Heinemann
Big Tease, The	I	RF	250+	Story Box	Wright Group/McGraw Hill
Big Teeth, No Teeth	D	I	153	Sails	Rigby
Big Tennis Match, A	I	I	122	Vocabulary Readers	Houghton Mifflin Harcourt
Big Things	A	I	33	PM Starters	Rigby
Big Things	C	I	81	Sails	Rigby
Big Things	D	I	88	Springboard	Wright Group/McGraw Hill
Big Toe Robbery, The	N	F	250+	PM Collection	Rigby
Big Toe, The	E	F	123	Story Box	Wright Group/McGraw Hill
Big Tracks, Little Tracks	L	I	250+	Let's-Read-and-Find-Out Science	HarperTrophy
*Big Tree Gang, The	M	F	250+	Orca Echoes	Orca Books
Big Trucks	J	I	148	Big	Capstone Press
Big Tug	D	F	80	Leveled Readers	Houghton Mifflin Harcourt
Big Tunnels	K	I	331	Red Rocket Readers	Flying Start Books
Big Wave, The	Q	RF	250+	Buck, Pearl S.	Scholastic
Big Wheel, The	M	HF	250+	Windows on Literacy	National Geographic
Big Yellow Castle, The	E	RF	135	PM Plus Story Books	Rigby
Big Yellow Sunflower	I	I	93	Fold Out and Find Out	Candlewick Press
Big, Bad Cook, The	J	TL	250+	Literacy Tree	Rigby
Big, Big Box, A	B	RF	35	Ready Readers	Pearson Learning Group
Big, Big Trucks	H	I	162	Start to Read	School Zone
Big, Big Wall, The	E	F	92	Green Light Readers	Harcourt
Big, Bigger, Biggest	C	RF	32	Rigby Star Quest	Rigby
Big, Bigger, Biggest	LB	I	58	Shutterbug Books	Steck-Vaughn
Big, Bigger, Biggest	C	I	31	Windows on Literacy	National Geographic
Big, Bigger, Biggest!	N	I	182	Coffelt, Nancy	Henry Holt & Co.
Big, Brown Box, The	E	RF	93	Voyages	SRA/McGraw Hill
Big, Brown Pot, The	J	F	250+	Mahy, Margaret	Scholastic
Big, Fat, Wide Mouth	G	F	183	Story Box	Wright Group/McGraw Hill
Big, Hit, The	D	RF	120	PM Plus Story Books	Rigby
Big, Small, or Just Right?	C	F	40	Leveled Readers Language Support	Houghton Mifflin Harcourt
Bigfoot Backpacking Bonanza	Q	F	250+	Wiley & Grampa's Creature Features	Little Brown and Company
Bigfoot Doesn't Square Dance	M	F	250+	Dadey, Debbie; Jones, Marcia Thornton	Scholastic
^Bigfoot: The Unsolved Mystery	R	I	250+	Mysteries of Science	Capstone Press
Bigger and Bigger	C	I	49	Twig	Wright Group/McGraw Hill
Bigger Burger, A	I	RF	253	Story Box	Wright Group/McGraw Hill
Bigger or Smaller?	F	I	112	Sunshine	Wright Group/McGraw Hill
Bigger Than? Smaller Than?	D	I	123	Early Connections	Benchmark Education

* Collection of short stories   # Graphic text
^ Mature content with lower level text demands

TITLE	LEVEL	GENRE	WORD COUNT	AUTHOR / SERIES	PUBLISHER / DISTRIBUTOR
Biggest Bear in the Woods, The	K	F	250+	Little Celebrations	Pearson Learning Group
Biggest Cake in the World, The	F	F	120	Pacific Literacy	Pacific Learning
Biggest Fish, The	I	RF	254	PM Story Books-Orange	Rigby
Biggest Klutz in Fifth Grade, The	V	RF	250+	Wallace, Bill	Simon & Schuster
Biggest Land Animal, The	J	I	376	Sails	Rigby
Biggest Pool of All, The	K	RF	250+	Sunshine	Wright Group/McGraw Hill
Biggest Pumpkin Ever, The	L	F	250+	Kroll, Steven	Scholastic
Biggest Sandwich Ever, The	E	F	87	Pair-It Books	Steck-Vaughn
Bigggest, Smallest, Fastest, Slowest	I	I	248	Literacy by Design	Rigby
Big-Hearted Monkey and the Crocodile, The	K	TL	250+	World Quest Adventures	World Quest Learning
Big-Hearted Monkey and the Lion, The	K	TL	250+	World Quest Adventures	World Quest Learning
Bighorn Sheep	C	I	107	Vocabulary Readers	Houghton Mifflin Harcourt
Bighorn Sheep	C	I	107	Vocabulary Readers/CA	Houghton Mifflin Harcourt
Bighorn Sheep, The	R	I	250+	Wildlife of North America	Red Brick Learning
Bigmama's	L	RF	250+	Crews, Donald	Greenwillow Books
Bike Daredevils	N	RF	250+	Boyz Rule!	Mondo Publishing
Bike For Alex, A	I	RF	250+	PM Plus Story Books	Rigby
Bike for Brad, A	K	RF	510	PM Story Books	Rigby
Bike for Russ, A	C	RF	37	Handprints B	Educators Publishing Service
Bike Lesson	I	F	250+	Berenstain, Stan & Jan	Random House
Bike Parade, The	LB	RF	16	Literacy 2000	Rigby
Bike Race, The	B	RF	48	Sails	Rigby
Bike Ride, The	D	RF	100	Emergent	Pioneer Valley
Bike Ride, The	D	RF	72	Leveled Readers Language Support	Houghton Mifflin Harcourt
Bike Ride, The	E	RF	118	Springboard	Wright Group/McGraw Hill
Bike That Spike Likes, The	E	RF	91	Ready Readers	Pearson Learning Group
Bike Trail, The	J	RF	250+	Windows on Literacy	National Geographic
Bike Trip, The	D	RF	60	Leveled Readers	Houghton Mifflin Harcourt
Bike, The	A	RF	16	Kaleidoscope Collection	Hameray Publishing Group
Bike, The	LB	I	14	Twig	Wright Group/McGraw Hill
Biker City	T	F	4274	Masters, Anthony	Stone Arch Books
Bikes	F	I	133	Discovery Links	Newbridge
Bikes	G	RF	156	Foundations	Wright Group/McGraw Hill
Bikes	D	I	45	Gear Up!	Wright Group/McGraw Hill
Bikes	B	I	78	Readlings	American Reading Company
Bikes	D	I	62	Sails	Rigby
Bikes at Work	D	I	123	Sails	Rigby
Biking Safely	K	RF	250+	On Our Way to English	Rigby
Bill	I	RF	166	Sunshine	Wright Group/McGraw Hill
Bill and Pete Go Down the Nile	P	F	250+	dePaola, Tomie	Scholastic
Bill and Ted at the Store	D	F	50	Joy Readers	Pearson Learning Group
Bill Clinton	T	B	3837	History Maker Bios	Lerner Publishing Group
Bill Clinton: Forty-second President	R	B	250+	Getting to Know the U.S. Presidents	Children's Press
Bill Clinton: Forty-Second President of the U.S.	O	B	250+	Greene, Carol	Children's Press
Bill Cosby's Little Bill: The Best Way to Play	L	F	250+	Cosby, Bill	Scholastic
Bill Gates	V	B	250+	A&E Biography	Lerner Publishing Group
Bill Gates	U	B	250+	Amazing Americans	Wright Group/McGraw Hill
Bill Gates	X	B	250+	Just the Facts Biographies	Lerner Publishing Group
^Bill Gates: Building and Giving Back	S	B	250+	Hameray Biography Series	Hameray Publishing Group
Bill Gates: Helping People Use Computers	P	B	250+	Community Builders	Children's Press

B

TITLE	LEVEL	GENRE	WORD COUNT	AUTHOR / SERIES	PUBLISHER / DISTRIBUTOR
Bill of Rights in Translation, The: What It Really Means	V	I	250+	Kids' Translations	Capstone Press
Bill of Rights, The	S	I	250+	A True Book	Children's Press
Bill of Rights, The	V	I	250+	Cornerstones of Freedom	Children's Press
Bill of Rights, The	O	I	364	Independent Readers Social Studies	Houghton Mifflin Harcourt
Bill of Rights, The	W	I	250+	Reading Expeditions	National Geographic
Bill Pickett, Rodeo King	V	B	3134	Leveled Readers	Houghton Mifflin Harcourt
Billie the Hippo	N	I	250+	Pacific Literacy	Pacific Learning
Billie's Book	F	I	110	Sunshine	Wright Group/McGraw Hill
Billions of Bugs	N	I	250+	On Our Way to English	Rigby
Bill's Baby	E	RF	41	Tadpoles	Rigby
Bill's First Day	D	RF	110	Early Explorers	Benchmark Education
Bill's Trip	E	RF	77	Dominie Phonics Reader	Pearson Learning Group
Billy and the Basketball	E	RF	106	Award Reading	School Specialty Publishing
Billy at School	F	RF	163	PM Plus Story Books	Rigby
Billy Can Count	D	RF	122	PM Plus Story Books	Rigby
Billy Goats Gruff	F	TL	381	Hunia, Fran	Ladybird Books
Billy Goats Gruff and the Troll, The	G	TL	279	Traditional Tales	Pioneer Valley
Billy Goats Gruff, The	I	TL	300	Sun Sprouts	ETA/Cuisenaire
Billy Hooten: Owl Boy	Q	F	250+	Sniegoski, Thomas E.	Yearling Books
Billy Is Hiding	D	RF	97	PM Plus Story Books	Rigby
Billy Magee's New Car	J	RF	391	Foundations	Wright Group/McGraw Hill
Billy Ray Pyle's Style	J	RF	191	Dominie Readers	Pearson Learning Group
Billy the Ghost and Me	L	F	250+	Greer, Gery; Ruddick, Bob	HarperTrophy
Billy, the Number Champ	J	RF	377	PM Math Readers	Rigby
Billy, the Pet Bird	H	RF	371	Leveled Readers/TX	Houghton Mifflin Harcourt
Billy's Pen	D	RF	166	Leveled Literacy Intervention/ Blue System	Heinemann
Billy's Biscuits	I	RF	222	Dominie Readers	Pearson Learning Group
Billy's Box	G	F	207	Cambridge Reading	Pearson Learning Group
Billy's Sticker Book	I	RF	372	PM Math Readers	Rigby
Billy's Truck Diary	N	I	250+	Sunshine	Wright Group/McGraw Hill
Bingo	D	TL	179	PM Readalongs	Rigby
B-I-N-G-O	C	RF	41	Tiger Cub	Peguis
Bingo and the Bone	C	F	41	Storyworlds	Heinemann
Bingo and the Ducks	E	RF	121	PM Stars	Rigby
Bingo Goes to School	F	RF	171	PM Plus Story Books	Rigby
Bingo Wants to Play	C	F	45	Storyworlds	Heinemann
Bingo's Birthday	E	RF	116	PM Plus Story Books	Rigby
Bingo's Ice-Cream Cone	D	RF	88	PM Plus Story Books	Rigby
*Bink & Gollie	M	RF	250+	DiCamillo, Kate & McGhee, Alison	Candlewick Press
*Bink & Gollie: Two For One	M	RF	250+	DiCamillo, Kate & McGhee, Alison	Candlewick Press
Binky Rules	M	F	250+	Brown, Marc	Little Brown and Company
Binxie Gets Lost	L	F	819	Leveled Readers	Houghton Mifflin Harcourt
Binxie Gets Lost	L	F	819	Leveled Readers/CA	Houghton Mifflin Harcourt
Binxie Gets Lost	L	F	819	Leveled Readers/TX	Houghton Mifflin Harcourt
Biodiversity Hotspots	Y	I	250+	Independent Readers Science	Houghton Mifflin Harcourt
Biography of Benjamin Banneker, A	O	B	733	Gear Up!	Wright Group/McGraw Hill
Biography of Faith Ringgold, A	J	B	132	Vocabulary Readers	Houghton Mifflin Harcourt
Biology: Life as We Know It	Z	I	250+	Green, Dan	Kingfisher
Biomes	V	I	1420	Independent Readers Science	Houghton Mifflin Harcourt
Bionic Hand, The	U	I	4306	A Great Idea	Norwood House Press

* Collection of short stories   # Graphic text
^ Mature content with lower level text demands

TITLE	LEVEL	GENRE	WORD COUNT	AUTHOR / SERIES	PUBLISHER / DISTRIBUTOR
Bionics	Y	I	250+	Cool Science	Lerner Publishing Group
Biosphere, The	U	I	1845	Science Support Readers	Houghton Mifflin Harcourt
Bippity Bop Barbershop	M	RF	250+	Tarpley, Natasha Anastasia	Little Brown and Company
Birchbark House, The	T	HF	250+	Erdrich, Louise	Hyperion
Bird	V	I	250+	Eyewitness Books	DK Publishing
Bird and a Bug, A	F	RF	47	Windows on Literacy	National Geographic
Bird and the Worm, The	D	F	73	Tiny Treasures	Pioneer Valley
Bird Barn, The	I	I	241	Foundations	Wright Group/McGraw Hill
Bird Beaks	H	I	90	Windows on Literacy	National Geographic
Bird Beaks	I	I	180	Wonder World	Wright Group/McGraw Hill
Bird Behavior: Living Together	M	I	631	Sunshine	Wright Group/McGraw Hill
Bird Can Fly, A	G	I	209	Florian, Douglas	Hampton Brown
Bird Chain, The	M	F	250+	Voyages	SRA/McGraw Hill
Bird Eggs	F	I	50	Pebble Books	Capstone Press
Bird Fact File	M	I	792	Rigby Flying Colors	Rigby
Bird Families	F	I	60	Pebble Books	Capstone Press
Bird Feeder, The	D	I	55	Coulton, Mia	Kaeden Books
Bird Feeder, The	C	I	31	Storyteller-First Snow	Wright Group/McGraw Hill
Bird Feeder, The	C	RF	40	Sun Sprouts	ETA/Cuisenaire
Bird Feeders, The	H	RF	311	Leveled Literacy Intervention/ Blue System	Heinemann
Bird Flies By, A	E	I	87	Windows on Literacy	National Geographic
Bird for You, A: Caring for Your Bird	M	I	250+	Pet Care	Picture Window Books
Bird Has Feathers, A	C	I	27	Science	Outside the Box
Bird Hotel	I	F	358	Sails	Rigby
Bird in a Box	V	HF	250+	Pinkney, Andrea Davis	Little Brown and Company
Bird in the Basket, The	M	TL	250+	Beveridge, Barbara	Pacific Learning
Bird Is a Bird, A	D	F	116	Sails	Rigby
Bird Lady, The	J	I	250+	Story Steps	Rigby
Bird Life	B	I	37	Red Rocket Readers	Flying Start Books
Bird Nests	C	I	48	Little Celebrations	Pearson Learning Group
Bird Nests	F	I	78	Pebble Books	Capstone Press
Bird on the Bus, A	E	RF	115	Leveled Readers	Houghton Mifflin Harcourt
Bird Race	I	TL	195	Leveled Readers	Houghton Mifflin Harcourt
Bird Rescue, The	L	F	757	Arctic Adventures	Pioneer Valley
Bird Song	I	F	99	Storyteller-Night Crickets	Wright Group/McGraw Hill
Bird Table, The	H	RF	166	Book Bank	Wright Group/McGraw Hill
Bird Talk: Kok, Kok	B	F	42	Little Celebrations	Pearson Learning Group
Bird That Could Think, The	I	F	250+	PM Plus Story Books	Rigby
Bird Watchers	L	I	250+	Storyteller-Lightning Bolts	Wright Group/McGraw Hill
Bird Watching	J	RF	475	PM Plus Story Books	Rigby
Bird, The	K	RF	852	Rigby Flying Colors	Rigby
Bird, The	A	F	30	Sails	Rigby
Birdie for Now	O	RF	250+	Orca Young Readers	Orca Books
Birds	D	I	39	All About Pets	Red Brick Learning
Birds	F	I	54	Birds Series	Pearson Learning Group
Birds	M	I	68	Exploring the Animal Kingdom	Capstone Press
Birds	A	I	32	Leveled Literacy Intervention/ Orange System	Heinemann
Birds	F	I	50	Literacy 2000	Rigby
Birds	N	I	250+	Nature's Friends	Compass Point Books
Birds	B	I	18	Rigby Focus	Rigby
Birds	LB	I	12	Vocabulary Readers	Houghton Mifflin Harcourt
Birds	F	I	68	Windows on Literacy	National Geographic

* Collection of short stories   # Graphic text
^ Mature content with lower level text demands

TITLE	LEVEL	GENRE	WORD COUNT	AUTHOR / SERIES	PUBLISHER / DISTRIBUTOR
Birds and How They Grow	N	I	250+	National Geographic Society	National Geographic
Birds and Their Nests	J	I	175	Animal Homes	Capstone Press
Birds at My Barn, The	L	RF	230	Books for Young Learners	Richard C. Owen
Birds At My Feeder	R	I	250+	Kalman, Bobbie	Crabtree
Bird's Bad Day	C	F	36	Instant Readers	Harcourt School Publishers
Birds' Feet	C	I	86	Sails	Rigby
Birds in the Bushes: A Story About Margaret Morse Nice	R	B	8996	Creative Minds Biographies	Carolrhoda Books
Birds in Winter	D	I	34	Gear Up!	Wright Group/McGraw Hill
Birds Need Trees	D	I	63	Teacher's Choice Series	Pearson Learning Group
Birds' Nests	J	I	111	Wonder World	Wright Group/McGraw Hill
Birds of a Feather	N	RF	250+	Literacy 2000	Rigby
Birds of Flight	T	I	2158	Reading Street	Pearson
Birds of Prey	S	I	250+	Peterson Field Guides	Houghton Mifflin Harcourt
Birds of Prey	M	I	250+	Storyteller-Lightning Bolts	Wright Group/McGraw Hill
Birds of Prey	O	I	250+	Woolley, M.; Pigdon, K.	Mondo Publishing
Birds of Prey in North America	U	I	2249	Vocabulary Readers	Houghton Mifflin Harcourt
Birds of Prey in North America	U	I	2249	Vocabulary Readers/CA	Houghton Mifflin Harcourt
Birds of Prey: A Look at Daytime Raptors	U	I	250+	Collard III, Sneed B.	Franklin Watts
Birds of the City	M	I	840	Sunshine	Wright Group/McGraw Hill
Birds on Stage	H	F	153	Romay, Saturnino	Scholastic
Birds That Can't Fly!	M	I	651	Reading Street	Pearson
Birds That Hunt	N	I	276	Larkin, Bruce	Wilbooks
Birds Under the Water	D	I	116	Sails	Rigby
Birds, Bees, and Sailing Ships	I	F	243	Sunshine	Wright Group/McGraw Hill
Birds: Winged and Feathered Animals	M	I	250+	Amazing Science	Picture Window Books
Bird's-Eye View	J	RF	393	PM Collection	Rigby
Bird's-Eye View, A	K	I	250+	People, Spaces & Places	Rand McNally
Bird's-Eye View, A	H	I	402	Sails	Rigby
Bird-Watcher	O	I	250+	Wonder World	Wright Group/McGraw Hill
Bird-Watching	S	I	250+	iOpeners	Pearson Learning Group
Birdwing	V	F	250+	Martin, Rafe	Scholastic
Birdwoman Interview	M	RF	250+	Sails	Rigby
Birman Cats	R	I	250+	All About Cats	Capstone Press
Birman Cats	I	I	102	Cats	Capstone Press
Birmingham 1963: How a Photograph Rallied Civil Rights Support	Y	I	250+	Captured History	Compass Point Books
Birth of a Killer (The Saga of Larten Crepsley)	X	F	250+	Shan, Darren	Little Brown and Company
Birth of a Warrior	Y	HF	250+	Ford, Michael	Walker & Company
Birth of an Island, The	K	I	231	Avenues	Hampton Brown
Birth of Earth	U	I	250+	News Extra	Richard C. Owen
Birthday	N	RF	250+	Steptoe, John	Henry Holt & Co.
Birthday Ball, The	U	F	250+	Lowry, Lois	Houghton Mifflin Harcourt
Birthday Balloons	F	RF	182	PM Extensions-Blue	Rigby
Birthday Balloons	D	F	104	Rigby Literacy	Rigby
Birthday Bear	D	F	91	Sun Sprouts	ETA/Cuisenaire
Birthday Bike for Brimhall, A	K	RF	250+	Delton, Judy	Bantam Books
Birthday Bird, The	F	RF	82	Books for Young Learners	Richard C. Owen
Birthday Book	H	RF	93	Story Box	Wright Group/McGraw Hill
Birthday Buddy, The	M	RF	250+	Windows on Literacy	National Geographic
Birthday Bug, The	B	RF	53	Story Steps	Rigby
Birthday Cake	D	RF	27	Literacy 2000	Rigby
Birthday Cake for Ben, A	C	RF	59	PM Extensions-Red	Rigby
Birthday Cake, The	G	RF	107	Rigby Focus	Rigby

* Collection of short stories   # Graphic text
^ Mature content with lower level text demands

TITLE	LEVEL	GENRE	WORD COUNT	AUTHOR / SERIES	PUBLISHER / DISTRIBUTOR
Birthday Cake, The	H	F	201	Story Box	Wright Group/McGraw Hill
Birthday Cake, The	LB	F	22	Sunshine	Wright Group/McGraw Hill
Birthday Candles	C	RF	52	Carousel Readers	Pearson Learning Group
Birthday Candles	F	RF	145	InfoTrek	ETA/Cuisenaire
Birthday Car, The	E	RF	176	Fairy Tales and Folklore	Norwood House Press
Birthday Celebrations	E	I	111	Early Connections	Benchmark Education
Birthday Celebrations	D	I	80	Factivity Series	Pearson Learning Group
Birthday Cookies	I	RF	250+	HSP/Harcourt Trophies	Harcourt, Inc.
Birthday Dig, The	R	F	1216	Leveled Readers	Houghton Mifflin Harcourt
Birthday Disaster	Q	RF	250+	Literacy 2000	Rigby
Birthday Dog	I	RF	250+	Sunshine	Wright Group/McGraw Hill
Birthday Flood, The	P	RF	250+	Storyteller	Wright Group/McGraw Hill
Birthday Flowers, The	D	RF	71	Early Explorers	Benchmark Education
Birthday for Frances, A	K	F	250+	Hoban, Russell	Scholastic
Birthday Girl, The	M	RF	250+	Orca Echoes	Orca Books
Birthday in the Woods, A	F	F	199	Salem, Lynn; Stewart, Josie	Continental Press
Birthday Invitation, The	L	RF	1075	Rigby Flying Colors	Rigby
Birthday Kitten, The	E	RF	149	PM Photo Stories	Rigby
Birthday Party for Cornelius, A	N	RF	250+	Leveled Readers Language Support	Houghton Mifflin Harcourt
Birthday Party, A	C	RF	47	Early Emergent	Pioneer Valley
Birthday Party, A	F	RF	109	Sunshine	Wright Group/McGraw Hill
Birthday Party, The	O	F	797	Leveled Readers	Houghton Mifflin Harcourt
Birthday Party, The	LB	I	16	Rise & Shine	Hampton Brown
Birthday Party, The	LB	RF	15	Sunshine	Wright Group/McGraw Hill
Birthday Party, The	D	RF	95	The King School Series	Townsend Press
Birthday Pinata, The	H	RF	128	Handprints D	Educators Publishing Service
Birthday Present for Mom, A	F	I	98	In Step Readers	Rigby
Birthday Present for Mom, A	J	RF	529	Rigby Flying Colors	Rigby
Birthday Present for Spaceboy, A	E	F	130	Spaceboy	Literacy Footprints
Birthday Present, The	E	F	86	Leveled Readers Language Support	Houghton Mifflin Harcourt
Birthday Presents	F	RF	162	PM Plus Story Books	Rigby
Birthday Room, The	V	RF	250+	Henkes, Kevin	William Morrow
Birthday Song, The	D	F	183	Leveled Literacy Intervention/ Blue System	Heinemann
Birthday Surprise	H	RF	265	Leveled Readers	Houghton Mifflin Harcourt
Birthday Surprise, A	H	RF	157	Developing Books, Set 2	Pioneer Valley
Birthday Surprise, The	H	RF	237	On Our Way to English	Rigby
Birthday Surprise, The	D	RF	101	Red Rocket Readers	Flying Start Books
*Birthday Surprises: Ten Great Stories to Unwrap	R	RF	250+	Hurwitz, Johanna	William Morrow
Birthday Tree, The	P	F	250+	Fleischman, Paul	Candlewick Press
Birthday Wishes	L	RF	250+	Voyages	SRA/McGraw Hill
Birthday, A	C	F	39	New Way	Steck-Vaughn
Birthday, The	C	RF	30	Harry's Math Books	Outside the Box
Birthday, The	A	I	23	Little Books for Early Readers	University of Maine
Birthday, The	B	RF	36	Sails	Rigby
Birthdays	C	RF	59	Foundations	Wright Group/McGraw Hill
Birthdays	K	I	250+	Holidays and Celebrations	Picture Window Books
Birthdays	K	I	59	Purkis, Sallie	Nelson/Michaels Assoc.
Birthdays	I	I	147	Sunshine	Wright Group/McGraw Hill
Birthdays Around the World	M	I	250+	Early Connections	Benchmark Education
Birthdays Around the World	J	I	375	Leveled Readers	Houghton Mifflin Harcourt

TITLE	LEVEL	GENRE	WORD COUNT	AUTHOR / SERIES	PUBLISHER / DISTRIBUTOR
Birthdays Around the World	J	I	375	Leveled Readers/CA	Houghton Mifflin Harcourt
Birthdays Around the World	J	I	375	Leveled Readers/TX	Houghton Mifflin Harcourt
Birthdays Around the World	N	I	795	Reading Street	Pearson
Birthdays Around the World	J	I	178	Vocabulary Readers	Houghton Mifflin Harcourt
Birthdays Around the World	J	I	178	Vocabulary Readers/CA	Houghton Mifflin Harcourt
Birthdays in Many Cultures	I	I	108	Life Around the World	Capstone Press
Birthmarked	Z	SF	250+	O'Brien, Caragh M.	Roaring Brook Press
Birthstones	O	I	250+	Windows on Literacy	National Geographic
Bisa's First Gallop	J	RF	439	Springboard	Wright Group/McGraw Hill
Biscuit	F	RF	132	Capucilli, Alyssa Satin	HarperTrophy
Biscuit and the Little Pup	F	F	152	Capucilli, Alyssa Satin	HarperTrophy
Biscuit Finds a Friend	F	RF	114	Capucilli, Alyssa Satin	HarperTrophy
Biscuit Visits the Big City	F	RF	150	Capucilli, Alyssa Satin	Scholastic
Bison Are Back!, The	P	RF	743	Leveled Readers	Houghton Mifflin Harcourt
Bite of the Gold Bug, The: A Story of the Alaskan Gold Rush	S	I	250+	DeClements, Barthe	Penguin Group
Bitter End	Z+	RF	250+	Brown, Jennifer	Little Brown and Company
Bitty Fish	J	F	277	Let's Read Together	Kane Press
Bizarre, Creepy Hoaxes	T	I	250+	Horrible Things	Capstone Press
Black	B	I	26	Colors	Lerner Publishing Group
Black and White	B	I	23	Reading Safari	Mondo Publishing
Black and White	D	I	77	Storyteller Nonfiction	Wright Group/McGraw Hill
Black and White	C	I	32	Voyages	SRA/McGraw Hill
Black and White Airmen: Their True History	Y	B	250+	Fleischman, John	Houghton Mifflin Harcourt
Black Beans and Lamb, Poached Eggs and Ham: What Is in the Meat and Beans Group?	N	I	344	Food is CATegorical	Millbrook Press
Black Bear Cub	L	F	250+	Lind, Alan	Scholastic
Black Bear Rescue	Q	RF	250+	Reading Expeditions	National Geographic
Black Bears	E	I	50	Pebble Books	Capstone Press
Black Bears	Q	I	1272	Vocabulary Readers	Houghton Mifflin Harcourt
Black Bears	Q	I	1272	Vocabulary Readers/CA	Houghton Mifflin Harcourt
Black Bears	Q	I	1272	Vocabulary Readers/TX	Houghton Mifflin Harcourt
#Black Beauty	T	F	2520	Owens, L.L. (Retold)	Stone Arch Books
Black Beauty and the Thunderstorm	J	F	250+	Hill, Susan (Retold)	Square Fish
Black Beauty Stolen!	K	F	250+	Hill, Susan (Retold)	Macmillan
Black Beauty: The Autobiography of a Horse (Abridged)	S	F	14600	Hear It Read It	Sourcebooks
Black Beauty: The Greatest Horse Story Ever Told	S	F	250+	DK Readers	DK Publishing
Black Book of Secrets, The	X	RF	250+	Higgins, F. E.	Feiwel and Friends
Black Boy	Z	RF	250+	Wright, Richard	HarperPerennial
Black Cat and Poodle Dog	J	F	334	Sails	Rigby
Black Cat Goes Away	J	F	403	Sails	Rigby
Black Cat Stays Out	I	F	302	Sails	Rigby
Black Circle, The (The 39 Clues)	U	F	250+	Carman, Patrick	Scholastic
Black Diamond: Story of the Negro Baseball Leagues	W	I	250+	McKissack, Patricia & Fred	Scholastic
*Black Eagles: African Americans in Aviation	X	B	250+	Haskins, Jim	Scholastic
Black Elk: A Man with a Vision	N	B	250+	Rookie Biographies	Children's Press
Black Elk's Vision: A Lakota Story	U	B	250+	Nelson, S. D.	Harry N. Abrams
Black Everywhere	J	I	282	Lightning Bolt Books	Lerner Publishing Group
Black Gold	R	RF	250+	Henry, Marguerite	Aladdin
Black Gold	S	I	250+	Orbit Chapter books	Pacific Learning
Black Heart: Vampirates	Z+	F	250+	Somper, Justin	Little Brown and Company
Black Hearts in Battersea	V	HF	250+	Aiken, Joan	Houghton Mifflin Harcourt

* Collection of short stories   # Graphic text
^ Mature content with lower level text demands

TITLE	LEVEL	GENRE	WORD COUNT	AUTHOR / SERIES	PUBLISHER / DISTRIBUTOR
*Black Heroes of the American Revolution	X	B	250+	Davis, Burke	Harcourt Trade
Black Holes	Q	I	250+	A True Book	Children's Press
Black Jack: The Ballard of Jack Johnson	Q	B	250+	Smith, Charles R. Jr	Roaring Brook Press
Black Kitten, The	E	RF	115	Handprints C, Set 2	Educators Publishing Service
Black Mambas	M	I	250+	Snakes	Capstone Press
Black Pearl, The	X	RF	250+	O'Dell, Scott	Bantam Books
*Black Pioneers of Science and Invention	Y	B	250+	Haber, Louis	Harcourt Trade
Black Ships Before Troy: The Story of the Iliad	Y	TL	250+	Sutcliff, Rosemary	Laurel-Leaf Books
Black Snowman, The	P	F	250+	Mendez, Phil	Scholastic
Black Stallion, The	T	RF	250+	Farley, Walter	Language for Learning Assoc.
Black Star, Bright Dawn	V	RF	250+	O'Dell, Scott	Ballantine Books
Black Storm Comin'	W	HF	250+	Wilson, Diane Lee	Aladdin
Black Swan's Breakfast	G	RF	147	Book Bank	Wright Group/McGraw Hill
Black Tooth the Pirate	G	RF	198	Take Two Books	Wright Group/McGraw Hill
Black Velvet Mystery, The	N	RF	250+	Keene, Carolyn	Pocket Books
Black Water: Pendragon	X	F	250+	MacHale, D.J.	Aladdin
Black Widow Spiders	N	I	250+	Spiders	Capstone Press
Black: Seeing Black All Around Us	L	I	250+	Colors	Capstone Press
Black-and-White Ruffed Lemurs	H	I	94	Seedlings	Continental Press
Blackbeard: Pirate for Hire	O	F	250+	McElligott, Matthew	Walker & Company
Blackbeard's Last Stand	T	HF	250+	High-Fliers	Pacific Learning
Blackbeard's Sword: The Pirate King of the Carolinas	T	HF	2565	O'Donnell, Liam	Stone Arch Books
Blackberries	D	F	107	PM Story Books	Rigby
Blackberries in the Dark	N	RF	250+	Jukes, Mavis	Alfred A. Knopf
Blackberry Banquet	K	F	189	Pierce, Terry	Sylvan Dell Publishing
Blackberry Stew	M	RF	1459	Monk, Isabell	Carolrhoda Books
Blackbird Diary	N	I	996	Rigby Flying Colors	Rigby
Blackbirds	L	I	250+	Sunshine	Wright Group/McGraw Hill
Blackbird's Nest	G	RF	71	Pacific Literacy	Pacific Learning
Blackboard Bear	J	F	117	Alexander, Martha	Penguin Group
Blackbriar	X	F	250+	Sleator, William	Marshall Cavendish
Black-Eyed Susan	Q	HF	250+	Armstrong, Jennifer	Alfred A. Knopf
Blackfeet, The	R	I	250+	First Reports	Compass Point Books
Blackfeet, The: People of the Dark Moccasins	S	I	250+	American Indian Nations	Capstone Press
Blackout!	P	RF	250+	Bookweb	Rigby
Blackwater Swamp	T	RF	250+	Wallace, Bill	Language for Learning Assoc.
Blair's Deer	K	RF	250+	Phonics and Friends	Hampton Brown
Blanche Bruce of Mississippi	K	B	413	Leveled Readers Social Studies	Houghton Mifflin Harcourt
Blank Sheet of Paper, The	J	RF	379	Springboard	Wright Group/McGraw Hill
Blanket, The	E	RF	65	Burningham, John	Crowell
Blast Off Kid, The	K	RF	250+	Math Matters	Kane Press
Blast Off with Ellen Ochoa!	M	B	250+	Greetings	Rigby
Blast Off!	H	F	155	Dominie Math Series	Pearson Publishing Group
Blast Off!	N	I	250+	Home Connection Collection	Rigby
Blast Off!	F	I	95	Ready Readers	Pearson Learning Group
Blast to the Past	N	SF	250+	Orbit Chapter Books	Pacific Learning
Blat, the Alley Cat	H	F	300	Sails	Rigby
^Blazer Drive	U	RF	250+	Orca Sports	Orca Books
Blazing a Cattle Trail	T	I	2747	Leveled Readers	Houghton Mifflin Harcourt
Blazing a Cattle Trail	T	I	2747	Leveled Readers/CA	Houghton Mifflin Harcourt

TITLE	LEVEL	GENRE	WORD COUNT	AUTHOR / SERIES	PUBLISHER / DISTRIBUTOR
Blazing a Cattle Trail	T	I	2747	Leveled Readers/TX	Houghton Mifflin Harcourt
Bless Me, Ultima	Z	RF	250+	Anaya, Rudolfo	Warner Books
Bless This Mouse	Q	F	250+	Lowry, Lois	Houghton Mifflin Harcourt
Blessing's Dead	X	HF	250+	Edwardson, Debby Dahl	Farrar, Straus, & Giroux
Blimps	O	I	250+	A True Book	Children's Press
Blind Boone: Piano Prodigy	V	B	250+	Trailblazer Biographies	Carolrhoda Books
Blind Man's Buff	H	RF	331	Red Rocket Readers	Flying Start Books
Blind Men and the Elephant, The	K	TL	250+	Backstein, Karen	Scholastic
Blind Outlaw, The	P	RF	250+	Rounds, Glen	Scholastic
Bliss	Z+	RF	250+	Myracle, Lauren	Amulet Books
Blister	S	RF	250+	Shreve, Susan	Scholastic
Blizzard	S	HF	250+	Duey, Kathleen	Simon & Schuster
Blizzard of the Blue Moon	N	RF	250+	Osborne, Mary Pope	Scholastic
Blizzards	G	I	84	Bonnell, Kris/About	Reading Reading Books
Blizzards	W	I	7777	Disasters Up Close	Lerner Publishing Group
Blizzards	S	I	250+	Natural Disasters	Capstone Press
Blizzards	M	I	666	Pull Ahead Books	Lerner Publishing Group
Blizzards	N	I	250+	Weather Update	Capstone Press
Blizzards!	M	HF	250+	Hopping, Lorraine Jean	Scholastic
Block Party, The	H	I	127	Learn to Read	Creative Teaching Press
Blockhead: The Life of Fibonacci	S	B	250+	D'Agnese, Joseph	Henry Holt & Co.
Blocks	C	RF	60	Early Emergent	Pioneer Valley
Blonde Ambition	Z+	RF	250+	Dean, Zoey	Little Brown and Company
Blood	U	I	250+	Discovery Links	Newbridge
Blood	T	I	250+	Theme Sets	National Geographic
Blood	J	I	241	Twig	Wright Group/McGraw Hill
Blood and Guts: The Basics of Mixed Martial Arts	T	I	250+	The World of Mixed Martial Arts	Capstone Press
Blood Bank	P	I	250+	Sun Sprouts	ETA/Cuisenaire
Blood Beast (The Demonata Series)	Z+	F	250+	Shan, Darren	Little Brown and Company
Blood Captain: Vampirates	Z+	F	250+	Somper, Justin	Little Brown and Company
Blood Is Thicker	Y	RF	250+	Langan, Paul & Blackwell, D.M.	Townsend Press
Blood on the River: James Town 1607	W	HF	250+	Carbone, Elisa	Scholastic
Bloodhounds	R	I	250+	All About Dogs	Capstone Press
Bloodhounds	I	I	147	Dogs	Capstone Press
Bloodsuckers: Bats, Bugs and Other Bloodthirsty Creatures	W	I	250+	High Five Reading	Red Brick Learning
Blood-Sucking, Man-Eating Monsters	T	I	250+	Horrible Things	Capstone Press
Bloody Book of Blood, The	S	I	250+	The Amazingly Gross Human Body	Capstone Press
Bloom!: A Little Book About Finding Love	K	F	236	Van Lieshout, Maria	Feiwel and Friends
Bloomability	V	RF	250+	Creech, Sharon	HarperCollins
Blossom	J	F	225	Voyages	SRA/McGraw Hill
Blossom Promise, A	R	RF	250+	Byars, Betsy	Bantam Books
Blossoms and the Green Phantom, The	R	RF	250+	Byars, Betsy	Dell
Blossom's Babies	I	F	250+	Book Bus	Creative Edge
Blossoms Meet the Vulture Lady, The	R	RF	250+	Byars, Betsy	Bantam Books
Blow Out: Verbs in Action	K	I	250+	Bookworms	Marshall Cavendish
*Blow, Wind, Blow! And Other Stories	D	RF	114	Story Steps	Rigby
Blowing in the Wind	T	I	250+	Literacy 2000	Rigby
Blowing in the Wind	E	I	45	Shutterbug Books	Steck-Vaughn
Blown Away	U	RF	250+	Reading Expeditions	National Geographic
Blown Away: Forces of Nature	S	I	250+	Kids Discover Reading	Wright Group/McGraw Hill
Blubber	T	RF	250+	Blume, Judy	Bantam Books

* Collection of short stories   # Graphic text
^ Mature content with lower level text demands

TITLE	LEVEL	GENRE	WORD COUNT	AUTHOR / SERIES	PUBLISHER / DISTRIBUTOR
Blue	C	F	51	Bonnell, Kris	Reading Reading Books
Blue	B	I	63	Bookworms	Marshall Cavendish
Blue	B	I	26	Colors	Lerner Publishing Group
Blue All Around	A	I	66	Color My World	American Reading Company
Blue Birthday, A	J	RF	250+	Literacy by Design	Rigby
Blue Bug and the Bullies	D	F	18	Poulet, Virginia	Children's Press
Blue Bug Goes to School	D	F	57	Poulet, Virginia	Children's Press
Blue Bug Goes to the Library	F	F	59	Poulet, Virginia	Children's Press
Blue Bug's Book of Colors	E	F	49	Poulet, Virginia	Children's Press
Blue Bug's Vegetable Garden	D	F	27	Poulet, Virginia	Children's Press
Blue Day	C	RF	35	Literacy 2000	Rigby
Blue Door, The	X	HF	250+	Rinaldi, Ann	Scholastic
Blue Everywhere	J	I	292	Lightning Bolt Books	Lerner Publishing Group
Blue Flame: Book One of the Perfect Fire Trilogy	Y	HF	250+	Grant, K.M.	Walker & Company
Blue Ghost, The	M	F	250+	Bauer, Marion Dane	Random House
Blue Goo	I	F	65	Rigby Star	Rigby
Blue Gorph, The	P	F	250+	Scooters	ETA/Cuisenaire
Blue Heron	W	RF	250+	Avi	Avon Books
Blue Highway	Z+	RF	250+	Tullson, Diane	Fitzhenry & Whiteside
Blue Hill Meadows, The	M	RF	250+	Rylant, Cynthia	Harcourt Trade
Blue House Dog, The	S	RF	250+	Blumenthal, Deborah	Peachtree
Blue Ice	U	RF	250+	Salata, Estelle	Fitzhenry & Whiteside
Blue Jay, The	H	RF	173	Little Readers	Houghton Mifflin Harcourt
Blue Jay's Home	L	F	250+	Pair-It Turn and Learn	Steck-Vaughn
Blue Kangaroo, The	H	F	361	Leveled Readers	Houghton Mifflin Harcourt
Blue Layer, The	N	I	250+	Voyages	SRA/McGraw Hill
Blue Lollipops	G	RF	250+	Stepping Stones	Nelson/Michaels Assoc.
Blue Mittens, The	I	RF	250+	Mann, Rachel	Scholastic
^Blue Moon	T	RF	250+	Orca Soundings	Orca Books
Blue Moon Effect, The	Q	F	250+	Extreme Monsters	Penny Candy Press
Blue Moon: The Immortals	Z+	F	250+	Noel, Alyson	St. Martin's Griffin
Blue Morpho Butterflies	M	I	668	Springboard	Wright Group/McGraw Hill
Blue or Gray?	W	I	250+	Reading Expeditions	National Geographic
Blue Ribbon Blues	M	RF	250+	Spinelli, Jerry	Random House
Blue Stone, The: A Journey Through Life	R	F	250+	Liao, Jimmy	Little Brown and Company
Blue Sue	G	F	121	Ready Readers	Pearson Learning Group
Blue Sword, The	Y	F	250+	McKinley, Robin	Puffin Books
Blue Whales	U	I	250+	The Untamed World	Steck-Vaughn
Blue Whales Up Close	M	I	250+	First Facts-Whales and Dolphins Up Close	Capstone Press
Blue Willow	V	RF	250+	Gates, Doris	Puffin Books
Blue: Seeing Blue All Around Us	L	I	250+	Colors	Capstone Press
Blueberries for Sal	M	RF	250+	McCloskey, Robert	Scholastic
Blueberries from Maine	A	RF	28	Little Books for Early Readers	University of Maine
Blueberries Grow on a Bush	K	I	166	How Fruits and Vegetables Grow	Capstone Press
Blueberry Muffins	D	RF	191	Story Box	Wright Group/McGraw Hill
Blueberry Queen	M	RF	250+	Kylie Jean	Picture Window Books
Bluebird Out My Window	L	RF	633	Leveled Readers Science	Houghton Mifflin Harcourt
Blue-Eyed Daisy, A	W	RF	250+	Rylant, Cynthia	Simon & Schuster
Bluefish	W	RF	250+	Schmatz, Pat	Candlewick Press
Blue-Green Housefly, The	H	F	124	Domine Readers	Pearson Publishing Group
Blue-green Mystery, The	P	RF	1563	Gear Up!	Wright Group/McGraw Hill
Blues Go Birding Across America, The	N	F	3700	Sharing Nature with Children	Dawn Publications

* Collection of short stories   # Graphic text
^ Mature content with lower level text demands

TITLE	LEVEL	GENRE	WORD COUNT	AUTHOR / SERIES	PUBLISHER / DISTRIBUTOR
Blues Go Birding at Wild America's Shores, The	N	F	250+	Sharing Nature with Children	Dawn Publications
Blues Go Extreme Birding, The	N	F	250+	Sharing Nature with Children	Dawn Publications
Bluish	S	RF	250+	Hamilton, Virginia	Scholastic
BMX Bikes	Q	I	250+	Wild Rides!	Capstone Press
^BMX & Mountain Biking	S	I	250+	Download	Hameray Publishing Group
BMX Billy	G	RF	93	Literacy 2000	Rigby
BMX Bully	P	RF	4609	Maddox, Jake	Stone Arch Books
BMX Champ	M	F	250+	Too Cool	Pacific Learning
BMX Freestyle	M	I	250+	Horsepower	Capstone Press
BMX Racing	M	I	250+	To the Extreme	Capstone Press
BMX Racing	S	I	250+	X-Sports	Capstone Press
BMX Winner, The	F	RF	219	Handprints D, Set 2	Educators Publishing Service
Bo and Peter	C	RF	44	Franco, Betsy	Scholastic
Bo Meets Grandma	I	RF	401	McAlpin, MaryAnn	Short Tales Press
Bo Peep's Sheep	C	TL	39	Pair-It Books	Steck-Vaughn
Boa Constrictors	J	I	250+	Rain Forest Animals	Red Brick Learning
Boa Constrictors	M	I	250+	Snakes	Capstone Press
Board Rebel	P	RF	250+	Maddox, Jake	Stone Arch Books
Board Sports	O	I	250+	Extreme Sports	Raintree
Boards and More	I	RF	250+	Phonics Readers Plus	Steck-Vaughn
Boat	W	I	250+	Eyewitness Books	DK Publishing
Boat Race, The	J	F	366	Leveled Readers	Houghton Mifflin Harcourt
Boat Race, the	J	F	366	Leveled Readers/CA	Houghton Mifflin Harcourt
Boat Race, The	J	F	366	Leveled Readers/TX	Houghton Mifflin Harcourt
Boat Ride with Lillian Two Blossom	N	F	250+	Polacco, Patricia	Philomel
Boat Ride, The	C	F	38	PM Stars	Rigby
Boat Rides	C	I	100	Vocabulary Readers	Houghton Mifflin Harcourt
Boat Rides	C	I	100	Vocabulary Readers/CA	Houghton Mifflin Harcourt
Boat Trip, The	D	F	70	Carousel Earlybirds	Pearson Learning Group
Boat, The	LB	RF	14	Pacific Literacy	Pacific Learning
Boat, The	A	F	30	Sails	Rigby
Boat, The	A	RF	28	Sunshine	Wright Group/McGraw Hill
Boats	C	I	100	Pebble Books	Capstone Press
Boats	E	I	275	Rigby Flying Colors	Rigby
Boats	M	I	250+	Robbins, Ken	Scholastic
Boats	G	I	84	Rockwell, Anne	Penguin Group
Boats	G	I	260	Sails	Rigby
Boats	M	I	250+	Transportation	Compass Point Books
Boats	D	I	57	Twig	Wright Group/McGraw Hill
Boats Afloat	M	I	752	Sunshine	Wright Group/McGraw Hill
Boats of the Past	M	I	250+	On Deck	Rigby
Boats on the River, The	M	F	250+	Flack, Marjorie	Troll Associates
Boats, Boats, Boats	D	I	44	My First Reader	Grolier
Boats, Boats, Boats	L	I	250+	Yellow Umbrella Books	Red Brick Learning
Bob	J	F	488	Pearson, Tracy Campbell	Farrar, Straus, & Giroux
Bob and Billy	I	F	434	Sails	Rigby
Bobbie and the Baby	C	RF	62	Literacy by Design	Rigby
Bobbie and the Baby	C	RF	62	Rigby Literacy	Rigby
Bobbie and the Kite	WB	RF	0	Rigby Literacy	Rigby
Bobbie and the Monster	B	RF	24	Rigby Literacy	Rigby
Bobbie and the Parade	C	RF	49	Rigby Literacy	Rigby
Bobbie and the Play	F	RF	164	Literacy By Design	Rigby
Bobbie and the Play	F	RF	164	Rigby Literacy	Rigby

* Collection of short stories   # Graphic text
^ Mature content with lower level text demands

TITLE	LEVEL	GENRE	WORD COUNT	AUTHOR / SERIES	PUBLISHER / DISTRIBUTOR
Bobbie Goes on Vacation	F	RF	240	Rigby Literacy	Rigby
Bobbie's Airplane	E	RF	64	Oxford Reading Tree	Oxford University Press
Bobbie's New Coat	F	RF	189	Literacy By Design	Rigby
Bobbie's New Coat	F	RF	189	Rigby Literacy	Rigby
Bobby Baboon's Banana Be-Bop	J	F	505	Animal Antics A To Z	Kane Press
Bobby's New Apartment	M	RF	1350	Reading Street	Pearson
Bobby's Zoo	E	RF	54	Rookie Readers	Children's Press
Bobcat Tells a Tale	J	F	250+	Leveled Readers/TX	Houghton Mifflin Harcourt
Bobcats	O	I	1392	Early Bird Nature Books	Lerner Publishing Group
Bobo and the New Neighbor	I	F	250+	Page, Gail	Bloomsbury Children's Books
Bobo's Magic Wishes	L	F	250+	Little Readers	Houghton Mifflin Harcourt
Bob's Springtime Birthday	J	F	277	Dominie Readers	Pearson Learning Group
Body Art: A Quiz	T	I	250+	Trackers	Pacific Learning
Body Battles	P	I	250+	Gelman, Rita G.	Scholastic
Body Beasts	R	I	250+	Explorer Books-Pathfinder	National Geographic
Body Beasts	P	I	250+	Explorer Books-Pioneer	National Geographic
Body Check	R	RF	250+	Christopher, Matt	Little Brown and Company
Body Dictionary, A	S	I	250+	High-Fliers	Pacific Learning
Body Numbers	K	I	250+	Discovery World	Rigby
Body Parts Work Together	I	I	119	Instant Readers	Harcourt School Publishers
Body Systems	T	I	250+	The News	Richard C. Owen
Body Systems: Skeletal and Muscular	S	I	250+	Navigators Science Series	Benchmark Education
Body Systems: The Respiratory and Circulatory Systems	S	I	250+	Navigators Science Series	Benchmark Education
Body Tour, The	P	I	250+	InfoTrek Plus	ETA/Cuisenaire
Body Works	O	I	527	Avenues	Hampton Brown
#Boffin Boy and the Invaders From Space	Q	SF	250+	Orme, David	Ransom Publishing
#Boffin Boy and the Lost City	Q	SF	250+	Orme, David	Ransom Publishing
#Boffin Boy and the Red Wolf	Q	SF	250+	Orme, David	Ransom Publishing
#Boffin Boy and the Time Warriors	Q	SF	250+	Orme, David	Ransom Publishing
#Boffin Boy and the Wizard of Edo	Q	SF	250+	Orme, David	Ransom Publishing
Bog Child	Z+	HF	250+	Dowd, Siobhan	David Fickling Books
Bogeymen Don't Play Football	M	F	250+	Dadey, Debbie; Jones, Marcia Thornton	Scholastic
Boggart and the Monster, The	U	F	250+	Cooper, Susan	Aladdin
Boggart, The	U	F	250+	Cooper, Susan	Simon & Schuster
Boggywooga	I	F	274	Sunshine	Wright Group/McGraw Hill
Bogle's Card	H	F	244	Sunshine	Wright Group/McGraw Hill
Bogle's Feet	I	F	280	Sunshine	Wright Group/McGraw Hill
Bokuden and the Bully	N	TL	1483	On My Own Folklore	Millbrook Press
Bolivia	Q	I	250+	First Reports: Countries	Compass Point Books
Bomb Detection Squads	S	I	250+	Law Enforcement	Capstone Press
Bomb, The	Z	HF	250+	Taylor, Theodore	Avon Books
Bombed House, The	T	HF	250+	Zucker, Jonny	Stone Arch Books
Bombers	J	I	105	Mighty Machines	Capstone Press
Bombers	V	I	4552	Military Hardware in Action	Lerner Publishing Group
Bommyknocker Tree, The	R	RF	250+	PM Extensions	Rigby
Bonanza Girl	T	HF	250+	Beatty, Patricia	Scholastic
Bon-Bon the Downtown Cow	K	F	838	Appleton-Smith, Laura	Flyleaf Publishing
Bone Dance	X	RF	250+	Brooks, Martha	Random House
Bone Detectives	W	I	1818	Reading Street	Pearson
Bone Dog	L	F	250+	Rohmann, Eric	Roaring Brook Press
Bone for Buddy, A	H	RF	327	Red Rocket Readers	Flying Start Books

TITLE	LEVEL	GENRE	WORD COUNT	AUTHOR / SERIES	PUBLISHER / DISTRIBUTOR
Bone Magician, The	X	F	250+	Higgins, F. E.	Feiwel and Friends
Bone Museum, The	M	RF	250+	Sunshine	Wright Group/McGraw Hill
Bone Tree, The	N	F	250+	Voyages	SRA/McGraw Hill
#Bone: Crown Of Horns	W	F	250+	Smith, Jeff	Scholastic
#Bone: Eyes of the Storm	W	F	250+	Smith, Jeff	Scholastic
#Bone: Ghost Circles	W	F	250+	Smith, Jeff	Scholastic
#Bone: Old Man's Cave	W	F	250+	Smith, Jeff	Scholastic
#Bone: Out From Boneville	W	F	250+	Smith, Jeff	Scholastic
#Bone: Rock Jaw, Master of the Eastern Border	W	F	250+	Smith, Jeff	Scholastic
#Bone: The Dragonslayer	W	F	250+	Smith, Jeff	Scholastic
#Bone: The Great Cow Race	W	F	250+	Smith, Jeff	Scholastic
#Bone: Treasure Hunters	W	F	250+	Smith, Jeff	Scholastic
Bones	J	I	182	Rigby Focus	Rigby
Bones	C	I	56	Rigby Literacy	Rigby
Bones	L	I	545	Sun Sprouts	ETA/Cuisenaire
Bones	T	I	250+	The News	Richard C. Owen
Bones	T	I	250+	Theme Sets	National Geographic
Bones and Muscles	X	I	250+	Reading Expeditions	National Geographic
Bones and the Clown Mix-Up Mystery	J	RF	250+	Alder, David A.	Puffin Books
Bones and the Dinosaur Mystery	J	RF	250+	Adler, David A.	Puffin Books
Bones for Lunch	K	F	221	Sunshine	Wright Group/McGraw Hill
Bones!	O	F	250+	High-Fliers	Pacific Learning
Bones, Bones, Dinosaur Bones	H	I	126	Barton, Byron	Thomas Y. Crowell
Bongos, Maracas, and Xylophones	I	I	210	Vocabulary Readers	Houghton Mifflin Harcourt
Bongos, Maracas, and Xylophones	I	I	210	Vocabulary Readers/CA	Houghton Mifflin Harcourt
Bongos, Maracas, and Xylophones	I	I	210	Vocabulary Readers/TX	Houghton Mifflin Harcourt
Bonnie on the Beach	H	RF	198	Little Readers	Houghton Mifflin Harcourt
Bony Back: The Adventure of Stegosaurus	N	I	250+	Dinosaur World	Picture Window Books
Bony-Legs	K	TL	250+	Cole, Joanna	Scholastic
Boo!	B	RF	41	Handprints B	Educators Publishing Service
Boo!: A Ghost Story That Could Be True	J	F	315	Johnston, Tony	Scholastic
Boo, Katie Woo	J	RF	250+	Manushkin, Fran	Picture Window Books
Boodil My Dog	Q	RF	250+	Lindenbaum, Pija	Henry Holt & Co.
Booford Summer, The	R	RF	250+	Smith, Susan Mathias	Clarion Books
Boogie-Woogie Man, The	D	F	101	Story Box	Wright Group/McGraw Hill
Boogly, The	E	F	61	Literacy 2000	Rigby
Boo-Hoo	E	F	149	Story Box	Wright Group/McGraw Hill
Boo-Hoo Moo	N	F	250+	Palatini, Margie	HarperCollins
Book	X	I	250+	Eyewitness Books	DK Publishing
Book About Planets and Stars, A	R	I	250+	Reigot, Betty Polisar	Scholastic
Book About Your Skeleton, A	M	I	250+	Gross, Ruth Belov	Scholastic
Book Club, The	H	RF	247	Leveled Readers Language Support	Houghton Mifflin Harcourt
Book Making and Paper Making: Be Your Own Publisher	Q	I	250+	Crafts	Capstone Press
Book of a Thousand Days	W	TL	250+	Hale, Shannon	Bloomsbury Children's Books
*Book of Black Heroes from A to Z	P	B	250+	Hudson, Wade; Wesley, Valerie Wilson	Scholastic
Book of Boats, A	H	I	106	Gear Up!	Wright Group/McGraw Hill
Book of Dreams, The	Y	F	250+	Melling, O.R.	Amulet Books
Book of Hours, A	O	I	250+	Cambridge Reading	Pearson Learning Group
Book of Letters, A	L	RF	250+	Wilson-Max, Ken	Scholastic
Book of Monsters, The	P	I	250+	Sunshine	Wright Group/McGraw Hill

Organized Alphabetically by Title
Storable Database at www.fountasandpinnellleveledbooks.com

* Collection of short stories   # Graphic text
^ Mature content with lower level text demands

TITLE	LEVEL	GENRE	WORD COUNT	AUTHOR / SERIES	PUBLISHER / DISTRIBUTOR
*Book of Monsters: Tales to Give You the Creeps	T	F	250+	Coville, Bruce	Scholastic
Book of Shadow Boxes, The: A Story of the ABC's	L	F	250+	Seeley, Laura L.	Peachtree
*Book of Spine Tinglers: Tales To Make You Shiver	T	F	250+	Coville, Bruce	Scholastic
Book of Story Beginnings, The	W	F	250+	Kladstrup, Kristin	Candlewick Press
Book of Three, The	U	F	250+	Alexander, Lloyd	Bantam Books
Book of Tormod, The: A Templar's Appentice	W	F	250+	Black, Kat	Scholastic
Book Steps	T	I	250+	Bookweb	Rigby
^Book that Dripped Blood, The	T	F	835	Dahl, Michael	Stone Arch Books
Book Thief, The	Z+	HF	250+	Zusack, Markus	Alfred A. Knopf
Book Week	E	RF	71	Oxford Reading Tree	Oxford University Press
#Booker T Washington: Great American Educator	T	B	250+	Graphic Library	Capstone Press
Booker T. Washington	N	B	250+	First Biographies	Steck-Vaughn
Booker T. Washington	N	B	1634	On My Own Biography	Lerner Publishing Group
Booker T. Washington	P	B	250+	Photo-Illustrated Biographies	Red Brick Learning
Booker T. Washington: Educator and Leader	P	B	250+	Great African Americans	Capstone Press
Books	C	RF	21	Beginning Literacy	Scholastic
Books	D	RF	145	Leveled Literacy Intervention/ Green System	Heinemann
Books	B	I	21	Smart Start	Rigby
Books	B	RF	29	Sunshine	Wright Group/McGraw Hill
Books for Oliver	P	RF	250+	Bookshop	Mondo Publishing
Bookstore Cat	I	RF	207	Little Readers	Houghton Mifflin Harcourt
Bookstore Cat	I	F	217	Step into Reading	Random House
Bookworm Who Hatched, A	O	B	250+	Meet The Author	Richard C. Owen
Boom and Bust	Q	I	250+	Orbit Chapter Books	Pacific Learning
Boom Boom Bay!	D	RF	130	Avenues	Hampton Brown
Boom Boom Bay!	D	RF	130	Phonics and Friends	Hampton Brown
Boom!	N	I	250+	Gutner, Howard	Scholastic
Boomtowns of the West	S	I	250+	Kalman, Bobbie	Crabtree
Boonsville Bombers, The	N	RF	250+	Herzig, Alison	Puffin Books
Booooo!	E	RF	90	Rigby Star	Rigby
Boo's Surprise	K	F	250+	Byars, Betsy	Henry Holt & Co.
Boot Balancers Wanted	O	F	250+	Sails	Rigby
Boot Camp	S	RF	250+	Orca Young Readers	Orca Books
Bootlace Soup	J	TL	250+	Voyages	SRA/McGraw Hill
Boots	C	RF	57	Schreiber, Anne; Doughty, Arbo	Scholastic
Boots and Shoes	D	I	68	Cooper, Anne	Kaeden Books
Boots and Shoes	B	I	74	Leveled Literacy Intervention/ Green System	Heinemann
Boots for the King	D	F	93	Sun Sprouts	ETA/Cuisenaire
Boots for Toots	C	F	41	Pacific Literacy	Pacific Learning
Bootscooting	B	I	38	First Stories	Pacific Learning
Bootsie Barker Ballerina	K	HF	250+	Bottner, Barbara	HarperTrophy
Boring Day, The	D	RF	81	Emergent Books	Pioneer Valley
Boring Old Bed	J	F	250+	Lighthouse	Rigby
Boring Old Bed	I	RF	211	Sunshine	Wright Group/McGraw Hill
Boris and the Snoozebox	M	F	250+	Hodgkinson, Leigh	Tiger Tales
Boris and the Wrong Shadow	M	F	250+	Hodgkinson, Leigh	Tiger Tales
Boris Bad Enough	G	F	167	Kraus, Robert	Simon & Schuster
Born Blue	Z+	RF	250+	Nolan, Han	Harcourt
Born to be a Butterfly	H	I	250+	DK Readers	DK Publishing

TITLE	LEVEL	GENRE	WORD COUNT	AUTHOR / SERIES	PUBLISHER / DISTRIBUTOR
Born to Be Giants: How Baby Dinosaurs Grew to Rule the World	R	I	250+	Judge, Lita	Roaring Brook Press
Born To Trot	R	RF	250+	Henry, Marguerite	Aladdin
Born Too Short	Z+	RF	250+	Elish, Dan	Simon & Schuster
Born with a Bang: The Universe Tells Our Cosmic Story	W	I	2903	Sharing Nature with Children	Dawn Publications
Borning Room, The	Y	HF	250+	Fleischman, Paul	HarperCollins
Borreguita and the Coyote	O	TL	250+	Aardema, Verna	Scholastic
Borrowers Afield, The	S	F	250+	Norton, Mary	Harcourt, Inc.
Borrowers Afloat, The	S	F	250+	Norton, Mary	Sandpiper Books
Borrowers Aloft, The	S	F	250+	Norton, Mary	Harcourt, Inc.
Borrowers Avenged, The	S	F	250+	Norton, Mary	Houghton Mifflin Harcourt
Borrowers, The	S	F	250+	Norton, Mary	Harcourt Trade
Bo's Bows	F	F	245	Phonics Readers	Scholastic
Boss	C	F	48	Foundations	Wright Group/McGraw Hill
Boss For A Day	I	RF	250+	DePaola, Tomie	Grosset & Dunlap
Boss of the World: Katie Woo	J	RF	250+	Manushkin, Fran	Picture Window Books
Boss, The	H	RF	281	Leveled Literacy Intervention/ Blue System	Heinemann
Boss, The	E	RF	76	The Rowland Reading Program Library	Rowland Reading Foundation
Bossy and Wag	D	F	63	Sun Sprouts	ETA/Cuisenaire
Bossy Bear	J	TL	669	Red Rocket Readers	Flying Start Books
Bossy Bettina	F	RF	97	Literacy 2000	Rigby
Bossy Pig, The	G	F	240	Leveled Literacy Intervention/ Green System	Heinemann
Boston Celtics, The	S	I	4620	Team Spirit	Norwood House Press
Boston Coffee Party, The	L	HF	250+	Rappaport, Doreen	HarperCollins
Boston Jane: An Adventure	W	HF	250+	Holm, Jennifer L.	Yearling Books
#Boston Massacre, The	T	I	250+	Graphic Library	Capstone Press
Boston Massacre, The	V	I	250+	Let Freedom Ring	Red Brick Learning
^Boston Massacre, The: An Interactive History Adventure	T	HF	250+	You Choose Books	Capstone Press
Boston Massacre, The: Five Colonists Killed by British Soldiers	S	I	250+	Headlines from History	Rosen Publishing Group
Boston Red Sox, The	S	I	250+	Team Spirit	Norwood House Press
Boston Red Sox, The (Revised Edition)	S	I	250+	Team Spirit	Norwood House Press
Boston Tea Party, The	V	I	250+	Cornerstones of Freedom	Children's Press
#Boston Tea Party, The	T	I	250+	Graphic Library	Capstone Press
Boston Tea Party, The	V	I	250+	Let Freedom Ring	Red Brick Learning
Boston Tea Party, The	T	I	250+	We The People	Compass Point Books
Boston Tea Party, The: Angry Colonists Dump British Tea	S	I	250+	Headlines from History	Rosen Publishing Group
Boston Tea Party: Rebellion in the Colonies	T	I	250+	Adventures in Colonial America	Troll Associates
Boston Terriers Are the Best!	Q	I	1482	The Best Dogs Ever	Lerner Publishing Group
Botanist Danny	E	F	59	Coulton, Mia	Maryruth Books
Both Sides of the Story	L	RF	701	Gear Up!	Wright Group/McGraw Hill
Bot's Bits	G	F	99	Supersonics	Rigby
Botticelli	R	B	250+	Venezia, Mike	Children's Press
Bottle Garden, A	E	I	52	Wonder World	Wright Group/McGraw Hill
Bottle Mystery, The	M	I	250+	Sun Sprouts	ETA/Cuisenaire
Bottlenose Dolphins	O	I	961	Leveled Readers	Houghton Mifflin Harcourt
Bottlenose Dolphins	O	I	961	Leveled Readers/CA	Houghton Mifflin Harcourt
Bottlenose Dolphins	O	I	961	Leveled Readers/TX	Houghton Mifflin Harcourt
Bottlenose Dolphins Up Close	M	I	250+	First Facts-Whales and Dolphins Up Close	Capstone Press

* Collection of short stories   # Graphic text
^ Mature content with lower level text demands

TITLE	LEVEL	GENRE	WORD COUNT	AUTHOR / SERIES	PUBLISHER / DISTRIBUTOR
Bottles, Boxes, and Bins	C	I	36	Twig	Wright Group/McGraw Hill
Bouncer Bear	P	RF	890	Red Rocket Readers	Flying Start Books
Bouncer Comes to Stay	I	RF	250+	Storyworlds	Heinemann
Bouncy Balls	I	RF	389	InfoTrek	ETA/Cuisenaire
Bouncy Mouse	J	F	250+	Let's Read Together	Kane Press
Bound for Oregon	S	HF	250+	Van Leeuwen, Jean	Puffin Books
Bound for Rock Bottom	W	F	2705	Leveled Readers	Houghton Mifflin Harcourt
Bound for Rock Bottom	W	F	2705	Leveled Readers/CA	Houghton Mifflin Harcourt
Bound for Rock Bottom	W	F	2705	Leveled Readers/TX	Houghton Mifflin Harcourt
*Bound for the North Star: True Stories of Fugitive Slaves	Z	B	250+	Fradin, Dennis Brindell	Houghton Mifflin Harcourt
Bound to Be Bad: Ivy & Bean	M	RF	250+	Barrows, Annie	Chronicle Books
Boundaries Washed Away	O	RF	250+	On Our Way to English	Rigby
Boundary Busters	V	I	250+	Boldprint	Steck-Vaughn
Boundless Grace	M	RF	250+	Hoffman, Mary	Scholastic
Bouquet, The	A	RF	38	Carousel Earlybirds	Pearson Learning Group
Bow Down, Shadrach	R	RF	250+	Cowley, Joy	Wright Group/McGraw Hill
Bowhunting	S	I	250+	The Great Outdoors	Capstone Press
Bowled Over!	N	RF	250+	PM Plus Chapter Books	Rigby
Bowling at Home	F	RF	151	PM Stars	Rigby
Bowling Buddies	N	RF	250+	Girlz Rock!	Mondo Publishing
Bowman's Store: A Journey to Myself	Z	B	250+	Bruchac, Joseph	Lee & Low Books Inc.
Box Can Be Many Things, A	E	RF	51	Rookie Readers	Children's Press
Box House, The	G	RF	194	Sails	Rigby
Box of Butterflies, A	K	RF	250+	Leveled Readers Language Support	Houghton Mifflin Harcourt
Box, A	D	I	118	Leveled Literacy Intervention/ Green System	Heinemann
Box, The	A	RF	31	First Stories	Pacific Learning
Box, The	C	RF	30	Leveled Readers Language Support	Houghton Mifflin Harcourt
Boxcar Children Return, The	O	RF	250+	Warner, Gertrude Chandler	Albert Whitman & Co.
Boxcar Children Special: The Mystery at Snowflake Inn	O	RF	250+	Warner, Gertrude Chandler	Albert Whitman & Co.
Boxcar Children Special: The Mystery at the Ballpark	O	RF	250+	Warner, Gertrude Chandler	Albert Whitman & Co.
Boxcar Children Special: The Mystery at the Fair	O	RF	250+	Warner, Gertrude Chandler	Albert Whitman & Co.
Boxcar Children Special: The Pilgrim Village Mystery	O	RF	250+	Warner, Gertrude Chandler	Albert Whitman & Co.
Boxcar Children: Amusement Park Mystery, The	O	RF	250+	Warner, Gertrude Chandler	Albert Whitman & Co.
Boxcar Children: Animal Shelter Mystery, The	O	RF	250+	Warner, Gertrude Chandler	Albert Whitman & Co.
Boxcar Children: Basketball Mystery, The	O	RF	250+	Warner, Gertrude Chandler	Albert Whitman & Co.
Boxcar Children: Benny Uncovers a Mystery	O	RF	250+	Warner, Gertrude Chandler	Albert Whitman & Co.
Boxcar Children: Bicycle Mystery	O	RF	250+	Warner, Gertrude Chandler	Albert Whitman & Co.
Boxcar Children: Black Pearl Mystery, The	O	RF	250+	Warner, Gertrude Chandler	Albert Whitman & Co.
Boxcar Children: Blue Bay Mystery	O	RF	250+	Warner, Gertrude Chandler	Albert Whitman & Co.
Boxcar Children: Boxcar Children, The	O	RF	250+	Warner, Gertrude Chandler	Albert Whitman & Co.
Boxcar Children: Bus Station Mystery	O	RF	250+	Warner, Gertrude Chandler	Albert Whitman & Co.
Boxcar Children: Caboose Mystery	O	RF	250+	Warner, Gertrude Chandler	Albert Whitman & Co.
Boxcar Children: Camp-Out Mystery, The	O	RF	250+	Warner, Gertrude Chandler	Albert Whitman & Co.
Boxcar Children: Canoe Trip Mystery, The	O	RF	250+	Warner, Gertrude Chandler	Albert Whitman & Co.
Boxcar Children: Castle Mystery, The	O	RF	250+	Warner, Gertrude Chandler	Albert Whitman & Co.
Boxcar Children: Cereal Box Mystery, The	O	RF	250+	Warner, Gertrude Chandler	Albert Whitman & Co.
Boxcar Children: Chocolate Sundae Mystery, The	O	RF	250+	Warner, Gertrude Chandler	Albert Whitman & Co.

TITLE	LEVEL	GENRE	WORD COUNT	AUTHOR / SERIES	PUBLISHER / DISTRIBUTOR
Boxcar Children: Deserted Library Mystery, The	O	RF	250+	Warner, Gertrude Chandler	Albert Whitman & Co.
Boxcar Children: Dinosaur Mystery, The	O	RF	250+	Warner, Gertrude Chandler	Albert Whitman & Co.
Boxcar Children: Disappearing Friend Mystery, The	O	RF	250+	Warner, Gertrude Chandler	Albert Whitman & Co.
Boxcar Children: Firehouse Mystery, The	O	RF	250+	Warner, Gertrude Chandler	Albert Whitman & Co.
Boxcar Children: Ghost Ship Mystery, The	O	RF	250+	Warner, Gertrude Chandler	Albert Whitman & Co.
Boxcar Children: Growling Bear Mystery, The	O	RF	250+	Warner, Gertrude Chandler	Albert Whitman & Co.
Boxcar Children: Haunted Cabin Mystery, The	O	RF	250+	Warner, Gertrude Chandler	Albert Whitman & Co.
Boxcar Children: Lighthouse Mystery, The	O	RF	250+	Warner, Gertrude Chandler	Albert Whitman & Co.
Boxcar Children: Mike's Mystery	O	RF	250+	Warner, Gertrude Chandler	Albert Whitman & Co.
Boxcar Children: Mountain Top Mystery	O	RF	250+	Warner, Gertrude Chandler	Albert Whitman & Co.
Boxcar Children: Mystery at Snowflake Inn, The	O	RF	250+	Warner, Gertrude Chandler	Albert Whitman & Co.
Boxcar Children: Mystery at the Alamo, The	O	RF	250+	Warner, Gertrude Chandler	Albert Whitman & Co.
Boxcar Children: Mystery at the Ballpark, The	O	RF	250+	Warner, Gertrude Chandler	Albert Whitman & Co.
Boxcar Children: Mystery at the Dog Show, The	O	RF	250+	Warner, Gertrude Chandler	Albert Whitman & Co.
Boxcar Children: Mystery at the Fair	O	RF	250+	Warner, Gertrude Chandler	Albert Whitman & Co.
Boxcar Children: Mystery Behind the Wall	O	RF	250+	Warner, Gertrude Chandler	Albert Whitman & Co.
Boxcar Children: Mystery Bookstore, The	O	RF	250+	Warner, Gertrude Chandler	Albert Whitman & Co.
Boxcar Children: Mystery Cruise, The	O	RF	250+	Warner, Gertrude Chandler	Albert Whitman & Co.
Boxcar Children: Mystery Girl, The	O	RF	250+	Warner, Gertrude Chandler	Albert Whitman & Co.
Boxcar Children: Mystery Horse, The	O	RF	250+	Warner, Gertrude Chandler	Albert Whitman & Co.
Boxcar Children: Mystery in San Francisco, The	O	RF	250+	Warner, Gertrude Chandler	Albert Whitman & Co.
Boxcar Children: Mystery in the Cave, The	O	RF	250+	Warner, Gertrude Chandler	Albert Whitman & Co.
Boxcar Children: Mystery in the Old Attic, The	O	RF	250+	Warner, Gertrude Chandler	Albert Whitman & Co.
Boxcar Children: Mystery in the Sand	O	RF	250+	Warner, Gertrude Chandler	Albert Whitman & Co.
Boxcar Children: Mystery in Washington, DC, The	O	RF	250+	Warner, Gertrude Chandler	Albert Whitman & Co.
Boxcar Children: Mystery of the Hidden Beach	O	RF	250+	Warner, Gertrude Chandler	Albert Whitman & Co.
Boxcar Children: Mystery of the Lost Mine, The	O	RF	250+	Warner, Gertrude Chandler	Albert Whitman & Co.
Boxcar Children: Mystery of the Lost Village, The	O	RF	250+	Warner, Gertrude Chandler	Albert Whitman & Co.
Boxcar Children: Mystery of the Missing Cat, The	O	RF	250+	Warner, Gertrude Chandler	Albert Whitman & Co.
Boxcar Children: Mystery of the Mixed-Up Zoo, The	O	RF	250+	Warner, Gertrude Chandler	Albert Whitman & Co.
Boxcar Children: Mystery of the Stolen Boxcar, The	O	RF	250+	Warner, Gertrude Chandler	Albert Whitman & Co.
Boxcar Children: Mystery of the Stolen Music, The	O	RF	250+	Warner, Gertrude Chandler	Albert Whitman & Co.
Boxcar Children: Mystery on Stage, The	O	RF	250+	Warner, Gertrude Chandler	Albert Whitman & Co.
Boxcar Children: Mystery on the Train, The	O	RF	250+	Warner, Gertrude Chandler	Albert Whitman & Co.
Boxcar Children: Mystery Ranch	O	RF	250+	Warner, Gertrude Chandler	Albert Whitman & Co.
Boxcar Children: Outer Space Mystery, The	O	RF	250+	Warner, Gertrude Chandler	Albert Whitman & Co.
Boxcar Children: Pizza Mystery, The	O	RF	250+	Warner, Gertrude Chandler	Albert Whitman & Co.
Boxcar Children: Schoolhouse Mystery	O	RF	250+	Warner, Gertrude Chandler	Albert Whitman & Co.
Boxcar Children: Snowbound Mystery	O	RF	250+	Warner, Gertrude Chandler	Albert Whitman & Co.
Boxcar Children: Soccer Mystery, The	O	RF	250+	Warner, Gertrude Chandler	Albert Whitman & Co.
Boxcar Children: Surprise Island	O	RF	250+	Warner, Gertrude Chandler	Albert Whitman & Co.
Boxcar Children: The Box that Watch Found	O	RF	250+	Warner, Gertrude Chandler	Albert Whitman & Co.
Boxcar Children: The Creature in Ogopogo Lake	O	RF	250+	Warner, Gertrude Chandler	Albert Whitman & Co.
Boxcar Children: The Ghost in the First Row	O	RF	250+	Warner, Gertrude Chandler	Albert Whitman & Co.
Boxcar Children: The Giant Yo-Yo Mystery	O	RF	250+	Warner, Gertrude Chandler	Albert Whitman & Co.
Boxcar Children: The Rock 'n' Roll Mystery	O	RF	250+	Warner, Gertrude Chandler	Albert Whitman & Co.
Boxcar Children: The Seattle Puzzle	O	RF	250+	Warner, Gertrude Chandler	Albert Whitman & Co.

* Collection of short stories   # Graphic text
^ Mature content with lower level text demands

TITLE	LEVEL	GENRE	WORD COUNT	AUTHOR / SERIES	PUBLISHER / DISTRIBUTOR
Boxcar Children: The Secret of the Mask	O	RF	250+	Warner, Gertrude Chandler	Albert Whitman & Co.
Boxcar Children: The Vanishing Passenger	O	RF	250+	Warner, Gertrude Chandler	Albert Whitman & Co.
Boxcar Children: Woodshed Mystery, The	O	RF	250+	Warner, Gertrude Chandler	Albert Whitman & Co.
Boxcar Children: Yellow House Mystery, The	O	RF	250+	Warner, Gertrude Chandler	Albert Whitman & Co.
Boxers	R	I	250+	All About Dogs	Capstone Press
Boxers	I	I	109	Dogs	Capstone Press
Boxers Are the Best!	Q	I	1732	The Best Dogs Ever	Lerner Publishing Group
Boxes	A	RF	38	Davidson, Avelyn	Scholastic
Boxes	E	F	103	Foundations	Wright Group/McGraw Hill
Boxes	H	F	153	Literacy 2000	Rigby
Boxes for Katje	S	HF	250+	Fleming, Candace	Farrar, Straus, & Giroux
Boxes of Fun	D	RF	95	Story Steps	Rigby
Boxes, Boxes, Boxes	E	RF	63	Stewart, Josie; Salem, Lynn	Continental Press
Boxes, Cans, and Balls	E	I	171	PM Math Readers	Rigby
Boy	T	B	250+	Dahl, Roald	Puffin Books
Boy and His Donkey, A	K	F	250+	Literacy 2000	Rigby
Boy and the Elk Dogs, The	T	TL	1688	Leveled Readers	Houghton Mifflin Harcourt
Boy and the Goats, The	F	TL	346	Fairy Tales and Folklore	Norwood House Press
Boy and the Lion, The	H	TL	166	Aesop	Wright Group/McGraw Hill
Boy and the Wolf, The	I	TL	200	Book Bank	Wright Group/McGraw Hill
Boy at the Park, The	J	RF	578	PM Stars Bridge Books	Rigby
Boy Called Slow, A	S	B	250+	Bruchac, Joseph	G.P. Putnam's Sons Books for Young Readers
Boy in Motion: Rick Hansen's Story	N	B	250+	Manson, Ainslie	Greystone Books
Boy in the Burning House, The	X	RF	250+	Wynne-Jones, Tim	Macmillan
Boy in the Doghouse, A	N	RF	250+	Duffey, Betsy	Simon & Schuster
Boy Named Beckoning: The True Story of Dr. Carlos Montezuma, Native American Hero, A	S	B	3611	Capaldi, Gina	Carolrhoda Books
Boy Named Boomer, A	K	B	250+	Esiason, Boomer	Scholastic
Boy of a Thousand Faces, The	R	RF	250+	Selznick, Brian	HarperCollins
Boy of the Three-Year Nap, The	N	TL	250+	Soar To Success	Houghton Mifflin Harcourt
Boy Who Ate Dog Biscuits, The	N	RF	250+	Sachs, Betsy	Random House
Boy Who Climbed into the Moon, The	P	F	250+	Almond, David	Candlewick Press
Boy Who Cried Bigfoot, The	N	F	250+	The Zack Files	Grosset & Dunlap
Boy Who Cried Wolf, The	I	TL	460	Aesop	Wright Group/McGraw Hill
Boy Who Cried Wolf, The	J	TL	460	Aesop's Fables	Pearson Learning Group
Boy Who Cried Wolf, The	K	TL	250+	Hennessy, B. G.	Simon & Schuster
Boy Who Cried Wolf, The	L	TL	250+	Literacy Tree	Rigby
Boy Who Cried Wolf, The	J	TL	140	Littledale, Freya	Scholastic
Boy Who Cried Wolf, The	K	TL	250+	PM Tales and Plays-Purple	Rigby
Boy Who Cried Wolf, The	L	TL	970	Reading Street	Pearson
Boy Who Cried Wolf, The	D	TL	97	Storyworlds	Heinemann
Boy Who Cried Wolf, The	H	TL	324	Sunshine	Wright Group/McGraw Hill
Boy Who Dared, The	Y	HF	250+	Bartoletti, Susan Campbell	Scholastic
Boy Who Lost His Face, The	R	RF	250+	Sachar, Louis	Alfred A. Knopf
Boy Who Owned the School, The	U	RF	250+	Paulsen, Gary	Bantam Books
Boy Who Reversed Himself, The	Y	SF	250+	Sleator, William	Puffin Books
Boy Who Saved Baseball, The	U	RF	250+	Ritter, John H.	Penguin Group
Boy Who Saved Cleveland, The	Q	HF	250+	Giblin, James Cross	Henry Holt & Co.
Boy Who Spoke Dog, The	S	F	250+	Morgan, Clay	Puffin Books
Boy Who Stretched to the Sky, The	M	F	463	Book Bank	Wright Group/McGraw Hill
Boy Who Thought He Was a Teddy Bear, The	L	F	250+	Willis, Jeanne	Peachtree
Boy Who Tried to Hide, The	I	TL	219	Storyteller-Night Crickets	Wright Group/McGraw Hill
Boy Who Turned Into a T.V. Set, The	L	F	250+	Manes, Stephen	Avon Books

TITLE	LEVEL	GENRE	WORD COUNT	AUTHOR / SERIES	PUBLISHER / DISTRIBUTOR
Boy Who Was Raised by Librarians, The	O	RF	250+	Morris, Carla	Peachtree
Boy Who Went to the North Wind, The	L	TL	250+	Literacy 2000	Rigby
Boy Who Would Not Say His Name, The	J	RF	250+	Vreeken, Elizabeth	Pearson Publishing Group
Boy, a Dog, and a Frog, A	WB	F	0	Mayer, Mercer	Dial/Penguin
Boy2Girl	Y	RF	250+	Blacker, Terence	Square Fish
Boyfriend Rules of Good Behavior, The	Y	RF	250+	Bateson, Catherine	Holiday House
Boys Against Girls	S	RF	250+	Naylor, Phyllis Reynolds	Bantam Books
*Boys and Girls	D	RF	62	Williams, Deborah	Kaeden Books
Boys are Dogs	R	RF	250+	Margolis, Leslie	Bloomsbury Children's Books
Boys Don't Dance!	M	RF	250+	PM Plus Chapter Books	Rigby
Boys R Us: The Clique	X	RF	250+	Harrison, Lisi	Little Brown and Company
Boys Start the War and the Girls Get Even, The	S	RF	250+	Naylor, Phyllis Reynolds	Bantam Books
*Boys Who Rocked the World: From King Tut to Tiger Woods	U	B	250+	Carlsmith, L.; Mann, B.; McCann, M. R.; & Strelow, E.	Beyond Words
Boys Will Be	X	I	250+	Brooks, Bruce	Hyperion
Boy's Will, A	T	HF	250+	Haugaard, Erik Christian	Houghton Mifflin Harcourt
Bozo	H	RF	94	Wonder World	Wright Group/McGraw Hill
Bozo the Clone	N	SF	250+	The Zack Files	Grosset & Dunlap
Bracelet, The	R	HF	250+	Uchida, Yoshiko	Philomel
Brachiosaurus	N	I	250+	Discovering Dinosaurs	Capstone Press
Brachiosaurus in the River	L	F	200	Wesley & The Dinosaurs	Wright Group/McGraw Hill
Brad and Butter Play Ball!	N	RF	250+	Hughes, Dean	William Morrow
Brad and His Brilliant Ideas	K	RF	826	Rigby Flying Colors	Rigby
Brad's Birthday Cake	H	RF	200	PM Stars	Rigby
Brady	V	HF	250+	Fritz, Jean	Puffin Books
Brahman and the Ungrateful Tiger, The	Q	TL	250+	PM Plus Chapter Books	Rigby
Braiding Hair: Beyond the Basics	Q	I	250+	Crafts	Capstone Press
Braids	D	RF	24	Visions	Wright Group/McGraw Hill
Braids for Naya	G	RF	89	City Stories	Rigby
Brain	V	I	250+	You And Your Body	Troll Associates
Brain Block	M	F	250+	Rigby Gigglers	Rigby
Brain Drain	Q	I	250+	WorldScapes	ETA/Cuisenaire
Brain Finds a Leg, The	V	RF	250+	Chatterton, Martin	Peachtree
Brain Matter	T	I	250+	Sails	Rigby
Brain, The	Q	I	668	Time for Kids	Teacher Created Materials
Brain-in-a-Box	M	F	250+	Matthews, Steve	Sundance
*Brainstorm!: The Stories of Twenty American Kid Inventors	V	B	250+	Tucker, Tom	Farrar, Straus, & Giroux
Brainwaves	W	I	250+	Boldprint	Steck-Vaughn
Brainy Brain	N	I	250+	InfoTrek Plus	ETA/Cuisenaire
Brand New Butterfly, A	L	I	186	Literacy 2000	Rigby
Brand New Ideas	T	I	250+	The News	Richard C. Owen
Brand-New Day with Mouse and Mole, A	L	F	250+	Yee, Wong Herbert	Sandpiper Books
Brand-New School, Brave New Ruby	N	RF	250+	Barnes, Derrick	Scholastic
Brandon's New School	F	RF	163	Developing Books, Set 3	Pioneer Valley
Brasilia	P	I	250+	Leveled Readers	Houghton Mifflin Harcourt
Brat Princess	T	F	250+	Hopkins, Cathy	Kingfisher
Bratfest at Tiffany's: The Clique	X	RF	250+	Harrison, Lisi	Little Brown and Company
Brave As	P	RF	250+	Orbit Chapter Books	Pacific Learning
Brave Baby, The	I	TL	321	Big Cat	Pacific Learning
Brave Ben	K	RF	162	Literacy 2000	Rigby
Brave Bessie: Queen of the Skies	S	HF	1889	Reading Street	Pearson

* Collection of short stories   # Graphic text
^ Mature content with lower level text demands

TITLE	LEVEL	GENRE	WORD COUNT	AUTHOR / SERIES	PUBLISHER / DISTRIBUTOR
Brave Charlotte and the Wolves	L	F	250+	Stohner, Anu	Bloomsbury Children's Books
Brave Dave and the Dragons	C	F	46	Reed, Janet	Scholastic
#Brave Escape of Ellen and William Craft, The	S	B	250+	Graphic Library	Capstone Press
Brave Father Mouse	E	RF	92	PM Story Books	Rigby
Brave Fire Truck	E	F	89	Stone Arch Readers	Stone Arch Books
Brave Grace	D	RF	127	Red Rocket Readers	Flying Start Books
*Brave Hope, Chip's Tricks	K	F	305	Easy-for-Me Reading	Child 1st Publications
Brave Irene	S	F	250+	Steig, William	Farrar, Straus, & Giroux
Brave Little Monster	M	F	250+	Baker, Ken	Scholastic
Brave Little Mouse	I	F	249	Story Steps	Rigby
Brave Little Snail	D	RF	110	Rigby Flying Colors	Rigby
Brave Little Tailor, The	J	TL	250+	PM Tales and Plays Turquoise	Rigby
Brave Little Tailor, The: A German Folktale	O	TL	660	Leveled Readers	Houghton Mifflin Harcourt
Brave Maddie Egg	M	RF	250+	Standiford, Natalie	Random House
Brave Past, A	V	I	1931	Leveled Readers	Houghton Mifflin Harcourt
Brave Pilot, A	U	B	660	Vocabulary Readers	Houghton Mifflin Harcourt
Brave Settlers in a Strange Land	Q	I	1013	Reading Street	Pearson
Brave Taco	E	F	129	Leveled Literacy Intervention/ Green System	Heinemann
Brave Thing to Do, A	K	RF	623	Gear Up!	Wright Group/McGraw Hill
Brave Triceratops	G	F	178	PM Story Books	Rigby
Bravest Dog Ever, The: The True Story of Balto	L	B	250+	Standiford, Natalie	Random House
Bravo Amelia Bedelia!	L	F	250+	Parish, Herman	Avon Books
Bravo Zulu, Samantha	U	RF	250+	Duble, Kathleen Benner	Peachtree
Brazil	P	I	250+	A True Book	Children's Press
Brazil	O	I	250+	Countries of the World	Red Brick Learning
Brazil	Q	I	250+	First Reports: Countries	Compass Point Books
Brazil in Colors	N	I	250+	World of Colors	Capstone Press
Brazil: A Question and Answer Book	P	I	250+	Questions and Answers: Countries	Capstone Press
Bread	D	I	43	Benchmark Rebus	Marshall Cavendish
Bread	D	RF	69	Sunshine	Wright Group/McGraw Hill
Bread and Butter	K	I	351	Red Rocket Readers	Flying Start Books
Bread and Cheese	J	RF	457	InfoTrek	ETA/Cuisenaire
Bread and Jam for Frances	K	F	250+	Hoban, Russell	Scholastic
Bread and Roses, Too	W	HF	250+	Paterson, Katherine	Houghton Mifflin Harcourt
Bread and Roses: How an Orphan Girl Helped American Women Win the Vote	R	HF	250+	Navigators Fiction Series	Benchmark Education
Bread for Life	O	I	250+	Orbit Chapter Books	Pacific Learning
Bread for the Ducks	D	RF	109	PM Plus Story Books	Rigby
Bread Is for Eating	M	RF	250+	Gershator, David & Phillis	Henry Holt & Co.
Bread Song	Q	RF	250+	Bookshop	Mondo Publishing
Bread, Bread, Bread	F	I	95	Morris, Ann	Scholastic
Breadwinner, The	Z	RF	250+	Ellis, Deborah	Groundwood Books
Break with Charity, A: A Story About the Salem Witch Trials	X	HF	250+	Rinaldi, Ann	Harcourt Trade
Breakdancing	S	I	250+	Dance	Capstone Press
Breakfast	C	RF	35	Foundations	Wright Group/McGraw Hill
Breakfast	C	I	37	Little Books for Early Readers	University of Maine
Breakfast	D	RF	23	Voyages	SRA/McGraw Hill
Breakfast Around the World	S	I	1894	Leveled Readers Social Studies	Houghton Mifflin Harcourt
Breakfast Around the World	N	I	846	Time for Kids	Teacher Created Materials
Breakfast Around the World	J	I	101	Twig	Wright Group/McGraw Hill
Breakfast at the Farm	B	RF	56	Bookshop	Mondo Publishing

TITLE	LEVEL	GENRE	WORD COUNT	AUTHOR / SERIES	PUBLISHER / DISTRIBUTOR
Breakfast at the Zoo	F	F	157	Red Rocket Readers	Flying Start Books
*Breakfast Bird and Other Animal Stories	M	F	250+	Bookshop	Mondo Publishing
Breakfast for Bears	I	F	477	Leveled Readers	Houghton Mifflin Harcourt
Breakfast for Pickles	C	RF	62	Pickles the Dog Series	Pioneer Valley
Breakfast for Us	C	I	35	Bonnell, Kris	Reading Reading Books
Breakfast in Bed	G	F	36	Tadpoles	Rigby
Breakfast in Bed	C	RF	10	Voyages	SRA/McGraw Hill
Breakfast in the Bathtub	D	RF	94	InfoTrek	ETA/Cuisenaire
Breakfast in the Rainforest: A Visit with Mountain Gorillas	U	I	250+	Sobol, Richard	Candlewick Press
Breakfast on the Farm	D	I	73	Storyteller Nonfiction	Wright Group/McGraw Hill
Breakfast Time	G	F	250+	Bookshop	Mondo Publishing
Breakfast Time	R	I	1714	Leveled Readers Language Support	Houghton Mifflin Harcourt
Breakfast with John	C	RF	29	Books for Young Learners	Richard C. Owen
Breaking News	U	I	250+	News Extra	Richard C. Owen
Breaking Stuff	L	I	250+	The Rowland Reading Program Library	Rowland Reading Foundation
Breaking Through	W	B	250+	Edge	Hampton Brown
Breaking Through	Z	B	250+	Jimenez, Francisco	Houghton Mifflin Harcourt
*Breaking Up Is Hard to Do	Z+	RF	250+	Burnham, Niki & Clark, Terri, Hopkins, Ellen Sandoval, Lynda	Graphia
Breakthrough!	U	I	250+	Boldprint	Steck-Vaughn
Breath of Air, A	T	I	1356	Leveled Readers Science	Houghton Mifflin Harcourt
Breath of Fresh Air, A	P	RF	961	Leveled Readers	Houghton Mifflin Harcourt
Breath of the Dragon	P	RF	250+	Giles, Gail	Bantam Books
Breathe In, Breathe Out: Learning About Your Lungs	M	I	250+	Amazing Body	Picture Window Books
Breathing	L	I	106	Bookshop	Mondo Publishing
Breathing Under Water	C	I	39	Sunshine	Wright Group/McGraw Hill
Breathing Underwater	Z+	RF	250+	Flinn, Alex	HarperCollins
Breathing Underwater: Adventures in Chemistry	Y	RF	1752	Leveled Readers Science	Houghton Mifflin Harcourt
Breathless	Z+	RF	250+	Warman, Jessica	Walker & Company
Bremen Town Band	J	TL	250+	Reading Safari	Mondo Publishing
Bremen Town Musicians	K	TL	567	Sun Sprouts	ETA/Cuisenaire
Bremen-Town Musicians, The	K	TL	741	Gross, Ruth Belov	Scholastic
Brendan the Navigator: A History Mystery about the Discovery of America	R	HF	250+	Fritz, Jean	Penguin Group
Brenda's Birthday	A	RF	18	Story Box	Wright Group/McGraw Hill
Brenda's Private Swing	K	RF	250+	Chardiet, Bernice; Maccarone, Grace	Scholastic
Brer Rabbit at the Well	I	TL	268	Leveled Readers	Houghton Mifflin Harcourt
Brer Rabbit at the Well	I	TL	268	Leveled Readers/CA	Houghton Mifflin Harcourt
Brer Rabbit at the Well	I	TL	268	Leveled Readers/TX	Houghton Mifflin Harcourt
Brett Favre	P	B	2369	Amazing Athletes	Lerner Publishing Group
Brett Favre	T	B	250+	Sports Heroes	Red Brick Learning
Brett Got Wet	C	RF	50	Gear Up!	Wright Group/McGraw Hill
Brewster Rooster	J	F	250+	Underwood, Barbara J.	Kaeden Books
Brian Fixit	H	RF	317	Springboard	Wright Group/McGraw Hill
Brian Urlacher	P	B	2247	Amazing Athletes	Lerner Publishing Group
Brian's Brilliant Career	P	RF	250+	Literacy 2000	Rigby
Brian's Song	Z	B	250+	Blinn, William	Bantam Books
Brian's Winter	R	RF	250+	Paulsen, Gary	Bantam Books
Bricks, Wood, and Stones	D	I	54	Windows on Literacy	National Geographic
Bridesmaids Club	T	RF	250+	Hopkins, Cathy	Kingfisher

* Collection of short stories   # Graphic text
^ Mature content with lower level text demands

TITLE	LEVEL	GENRE	WORD COUNT	AUTHOR / SERIES	PUBLISHER / DISTRIBUTOR
Bridge Building: Bridge Designs and How They Work	V	I	250+	High Five Reading	Red Brick Learning
Bridge Is Too Small, The	H	RF	250+	Reading Safari	Mondo Publishing
Bridge of Grass, A	N	RF	715	Gear Up!	Wright Group/McGraw Hill
Bridge to Terabithia	T	RF	250+	Paterson, Katherine	HarperTrophy
Bridge, The	M	I	250+	Cambridge Reading	Pearson Learning Group
Bridge, The	J	F	250+	Reading Safari	Mondo Publishing
Bridge, The	B	F	32	Story Box	Wright Group/McGraw Hill
Bridges	D	I	49	Canizares, Susan; Moreton, Daniel	Scholastic
Bridges	M	I	250+	Explorations	Okapi Educational Materials
Bridges	M	I	250+	Explorations	Eleanor Curtain Publishing
Bridges	Q	I	730	Gear Up!	Wright Group/McGraw Hill
Bridges	R	I	250+	InfoTrek	ETA/Cuisenaire
Bridges	E	I	137	Sails	Rigby
Bridges	D	RF	62	Seedlings	Continental Press
Bridges	N	I	250+	Wildcats	Wright Group/McGraw Hill
Bridges - Across the Gap	R	I	250+	Wonder World	Wright Group/McGraw Hill
Bridging Beyond	X	F	250+	Duble, Kathleen Benner	Penguin Group
Bridging the Gap	Q	I	250+	Orbit Chapter Books	Pacific Learning
Bridle the Wind	Y	RF	250+	Aiken, Joan	Harcourt
Bright Eyes, Brown Skin	I	I	54	Hudson, Cheryl Willis & Ford, Bernette G.	Just Us Books
Bright Idea, A	X	I	250+	iOpeners	Pearson Learning Group
Bright Ideas	Q	I	250+	Explorers	Wright Group/McGraw Hill
Bright Ideas About Light	R	I	250+	In Step Readers	Rigby
Bright Lights and Shadowy Shapes	L	I	250+	Spyglass Books	Compass Point Books
Bright Paddles	P	HF	250+	Downi, Mary Alice	Fitzhenry & Whiteside
Bright Path: Young Jim Thorpe	N	B	250+	Brown, Don	Square Fish
Bright Shadow	T	F	250+	Avi	Aladdin
Brighty of the Grand Canyon	R	RF	250+	Henry, Marguerite	Aladdin
Brigid Beware	L	RF	250+	Leverich, Kathleen	Random House
Brigid Bewitched	L	RF	250+	Leverich, Kathleen	Random House
Brigid the Bad	L	RF	250+	Leverich, Kathleen	Random House
Brilliant Bees	L	I	1475	Glaser, Linda	Millbrook Press
Brilliant Blunders	T	I	250+	Connectors	Pacific Learning
Brilliant Bugologist, The	N	RF	250+	Orbit Chapter Books	Pacific Learning
Brilliant Fall of Gianna Z., The	T	RF	250+	Messner, Kate	Walker & Company
Brilliant Mind, A	W	B	250+	WorldScapes	ETA/Cuisenaire
Bring Me Your Horses	J	I	250+	Phonics and Friends	Hampton Brown
Bringing the Rain to Kapiti Plain	J	TL	739	Aardema, Verna	Scholastic
Bringing the Sea Back Home	L	F	250+	Literacy 2000	Rigby
Bringing Up Baby Chimp	N	I	495	Independent Readers Science	Houghton Mifflin Harcourt
Brinker's Isle	T	RF	2475	Leveled Readers	Houghton Mifflin Harcourt
Bristol Motor Speedway	S	I	250+	NASCAR Racing	Capstone Press
Brith The Terrible	M	F	250+	Literacy 2000	Rigby
British Redcoats	T	I	250+	Warriors of History	Capstone Press
Brittany the Basketball Fairy: Rainbow Magic	L	F	250+	Meadows, Daisy	Scholastic
Broad Stripes and Bright Stars	R	I	250+	Explorer Books-Pathfinder	National Geographic
Broad Stripes and Bright Stars	P	I	250+	Explorer Books-Pioneer	National Geographic
Broccoli Tapes, The	S	RF	250+	Slepian, Jan	Scholastic
Broken Blade, The	T	HF	250+	Durbin, William	Yearling Books

TITLE	LEVEL	GENRE	WORD COUNT	AUTHOR / SERIES	PUBLISHER / DISTRIBUTOR
Broken Bones	K	I	250+	Health Matters	Capstone Press
Broken Bones	J	I	250+	Sunshine	Wright Group/McGraw Hill
Broken Bridge, The	Z	RF	250+	Pullman, Philip	Alfred A. Knopf
Broken Clock, The	E	RF	174	Leveled Literacy Intervention/ Blue System	Heinemann
Broken Flower Pot, The	G	RF	203	PM Plus Story Books	Rigby
Broken Plate, The	I	RF	198	Foundations	Wright Group/McGraw Hill
Broken Window	G	RF	136	New Way Blue	Steck-Vaughn
*Broken Window and Other Cases, The	O	RF	250+	Simon, Seymour	Avon Books
Bronco Charlie and the Pony Express	U	B	1824	Leveled Readers	Houghton Mifflin Harcourt
Bronco Charlie and the Pony Express	M	HF	1867	On My Own History	Lerner Publishing Group
Brontë Story, The	W	B	19600	Oxford Bookworms Library	Oxford University Press
Brontorina	L	F	250+	Howe, James	Candlewick Press
Bronto's New House	H	F	342	Springboard	Wright Group/McGraw Hill
Brontosaurus, Beaver	I	F	130	Springboard	Wright Group/McGraw Hill
Bronx Masquerade	Z+	RF	250+	Edge	Hampton Brown
Bronx Masquerade	Z+	RF	250+	Grimes, Nikki	Dial/Penguin
Bronze Bow, The	U	HF	250+	Speare, Elizabeth George	Houghton Mifflin Harcourt
Brooke and Her Crayons	H	RF	283	Leveled Readers	Houghton Mifflin Harcourt
Brookfield Days	N	HF	250+	Little House	HarperTrophy
Brooklyn Bridge	U	HF	250+	Hesse, Karen	Feiwel and Friends
Brooklyn Bridge, The	Q	I	1294	Vocabulary Readers	Houghton Mifflin Harcourt
Brooklyn Bridge, The	Q	I	1294	Vocabulary Readers/CA	Houghton Mifflin Harcourt
Brooklyn Bridge: Eighth Wonder of the World, The	Z	I	3473	Leveled Readers	Houghton Mifflin Harcourt
Brooklyn Dodgers, The	J	I	323	Vocabulary Readers	Houghton Mifflin Harcourt
Brooklyn Dodgers, The	J	I	323	Vocabulary Readers/CA	Houghton Mifflin Harcourt
Brooklyn Dodgers, The	J	I	323	Vocabulary Readers/TX	Houghton Mifflin Harcourt
Brooms Are for Flying!	H	F	55	Rex, Michael	Square Fish
Brother Love	E	RF	116	Rigby Rocket	Rigby
Brother To Shadows	Z	SF	250+	Norton, Andre	Avon Books
Brother Who Gave Rice, The	L	TL	250+	Yang, Dori Jones	Hampton Brown
Brotherhood of the Traveling Underpants, The (Melvin Beederman, Superhero)	N	F	250+	Trine, Greg	Henry Holt & Co.
Brothers	F	I	63	Families	Capstone Press
Brothers	B	I	36	Pebble Books	Capstone Press
Brothers	E	I	65	Talk About Books	Pearson Learning Group
Brothers and Sisters	G	I	145	Families	Heinemann Library
Brothers are Forever	L	RF	536	Leveled Readers	Houghton Mifflin Harcourt
Brothers Grimm, The	X	B	2435	Leveled Readers	Houghton Mifflin Harcourt
Brothers Grimm, The	X	B	2435	Leveled Readers/CA	Houghton Mifflin Harcourt
Brothers Grimm, The	X	B	2435	Leveled Readers/TX	Houghton Mifflin Harcourt
Brothers in Arms	Z	RF	250+	Langan, Paul & Alirez, Ben	Townsend Press
Brown	B	I	26	Colors	Lerner Publishing Group
Brown Bear	C	I	40	Zoozoo-Animal World	Cavallo Publishing
Brown Bear Figures it Out!	K	F	250+	Phonics and Friends	Hampton Brown
Brown Bear Gets in Shape	K	F	250+	I Am Reading	Kingfisher
Brown Bear, Brown Bear	C	F	185	Martin, Bill	Henry Holt & Co.
Brown Bears	O	I	1363	Early Bird Nature Books	Lerner Publishing Group
Brown Bears	E	I	45	Pebble Books	Capstone Press
Brown Bears	K	I	250+	PM Animal Facts: Turquoise	Rigby
Brown Bears	G	I	159	Readlings	American Reading Company
Brown Bears	A	I	70	Readlings/ Predator Animals	American Reading Company
Brown Cow Frowned, The	F	F	102	Seedlings	Continental Press

* Collection of short stories   # Graphic text
^ Mature content with lower level text demands

TITLE	LEVEL	GENRE	WORD COUNT	AUTHOR / SERIES	PUBLISHER / DISTRIBUTOR
Brown Everywhere	K	I	283	Lightning Bolt Books	Lerner Publishing Group
Brown Mouse Gets Some Corn	F	F	158	PM Plus Story Books	Rigby
Brown Mouse Plays a Trick	F	F	155	PM Plus Story Books	Rigby
Brown Sunshine of Sawdust Valley	O	RF	250+	Henry, Marguerite	Aladdin
Brown: Seeing Brown All Around Us	L	I	250+	Colors	Capstone Press
Brownie	C	RF	38	Seedlings	Continental Press
Brownie and Spottie	I	F	250+	Reading Safari	Mondo Publishing
Brownie Math	I	I	206	Rosen Real Readers	Rosen Publishing Group
Brr!	A	RF	29	Bonnell, Kris	Reading Reading Books
Bruce Larkin Goes to Alaska	N	I	977	Larkin, Bruce	Wilbooks
Bruce Larkin's Brain Busters: Volume 10	O	I	250+	Larkin, Bruce	Wilbooks
Bruce Larkin's Brain Busters: Volume 3	O	I	250+	Larkin, Bruce	Wilbooks
Bruce Larkin's Favorite Jokes: Volume 6	O	I	250+	Larkin, Bruce	Wilbooks
Bruce Larkin's Favorite Jokes: Volume 9	O	I	250+	Larkin, Bruce	Wilbooks
Bruce, Phil, and Adonna Head for the Mountains	N	I	889	Larkin, Bruce	Wilbooks
Bruises	Z	RF	250+	De Vries, Anke	Bantam Books
*Bruno for Real	M	RF	250+	Orca Echoes	Orca Books
Bruno's Birthday	E	RF	32	Literacy 2000	Rigby
Brushes	E	I	109	Rigby Literacy	Rigby
Brushing Teeth	G	I	147	Healthy Teeth	Capstone Press
Brushing Well	D	I	42	Dental Health	Capstone Press
Brutus Learns to Fetch	F	RF	155	Little Red Readers	Sundance
Bryce Canyon National Park	O	I	250+	A True Book	Children's Press
Bubble Booth, The	I	RF	152	InfoTrek	ETA/Cuisenaire
Bubble Gum	B	RF	21	Carousel Readers	Pearson Learning Group
Bubble Gum	H	RF	66	City Kids	Rigby
Bubble Gum	E	RF	81	Kaleidoscope Collection	Hameray Publishing Group
Bubble Gum Can Be Trouble	E	RF	147	Visions	Wright Group/McGraw Hill
Bubble Gum Contest, The	J	F	737	Spaceboy	Literacy Footprints
Bubble Trouble	K	RF	1317	Science Solves It!	Kane Press
Bubbles	M	I	250+	Cambridge Reading	Pearson Learning Group
Bubbles	C	I	34	Discovery Links	Newbridge
Bubbles	B	I	48	Leveled Literacy Intervention/ Green System	Heinemann
Bubbles	I	RF	236	Leveled Readers Science	Houghton Mifflin Harcourt
Bubbles	C	RF	33	Literacy 2000	Rigby
Bubbles	C	RF	31	Sunshine	Wright Group/McGraw Hill
Bubbles Everywhere	C	I	41	Twig	Wright Group/McGraw Hill
Bubbles Float, Bubbles Pop!	M	I	250+	Science Starts	Capstone Press
Bubbles in the Sky	C	RF	57	PM Stars	Rigby
Bubbles on the Bus	I	RF	250+	The Story Basket	Wright Group/McGraw Hill
Bubbling Crocodile	K	F	250+	Pacific Literacy	Pacific Learning
Buck Fever	Y	RF	250+	Willis, Cynthia Chapman	Feiwel and Friends
Buck Leonard, Baseball Hero	Q	B	250+	Leveled Readers Language Support	Houghton Mifflin Harcourt
Buck Leonard, Baseball's Greatest Gentleman	R	B	1419	Leveled Readers	Houghton Mifflin Harcourt
Buck Stops Here, The	T	I	250+	Provensen, Alice	Harcourt Brace
Buckle My Shoe	C	RF	31	Sunshine	Wright Group/McGraw Hill
Buck's Way	L	F	359	Reading Street	Pearson
Bud in the Mud	E	RF	111	Reading Street	Pearson Learning Group
Bud on the Beach	E	RF	61	Rigby Star	Rigby
Bud the Mud Bug	D	F	72	Reading Street	Pearson
Bud the Pup	E	RF	95	Reading Street	Pearson Learning Group

TITLE	LEVEL	GENRE	WORD COUNT	AUTHOR / SERIES	PUBLISHER / DISTRIBUTOR
Bud, Not Buddy	U	RF	250+	Curtis, Christopher Paul	Random House
Buddha Boy	X	RF	250+	Koja, Kathe	Puffin Books
Buddha's Diamonds, The	T	RF	250+	Marsden, Carolyn & Niem, Thay Phap	Candlewick Press
Buddhism	Y	I	250+	World Religions	Compass Point Books
Buddies	F	F	177	Instant Readers	Harcourt School Publishers
Buddy	Q	RF	1522	Leveled Readers	Houghton Mifflin Harcourt
Buddy and Bailey	E	F	95	McGougan, Kathy	Buddy Books Publishing
Buddy and the Walking School Bus	H	F	210	McGougan, Kathy	Buddy Books Publishing
Buddy at School	H	RF	195	McGougan, Kathy	Buddy Books Publishing
Buddy at the Beach	D	F	86	McGougan, Kathy	Buddy Books Publishing
Buddy Biscuit, Buddy Biscuit, What Did You Do?	E	RF	99	McGougan, Kathy	Buddy Books Publishing
Buddy Boy and His Skateboard	E	RF	148	Kaleidoscope Collection	Hameray Publishing Group
Buddy Gets Dirty	C	RF	50	McGougan, Kathy	Buddy Books Publishing
Buddy Goes on a Walk	D	RF	74	McGougan, Kathy	Buddy Books Publishing
Buddy Goes Trick-or-Treating	E	F	129	McGougan, Kathy	Buddy Books Publishing
Buddy Has a Playdate!	H	F	207	McGougan, Kathy	Buddy Books Publishing
Buddy Likes to Ride	E	F	140	Red Rocket Readers	Flying Start Books
Buddy Likes toà	B	F	32	McGougan, Kathy	Buddy Books Publishing
Buddy Meets Another Buddy	H	F	152	McGougan, Kathy	Buddy Books Publishing
Buddy on the Farm	I	F	172	McGougan, Kathy	Buddy Books Publishing
Buddy Plays Ball	D	F	76	McGougan, Kathy	Buddy Books Publishing
Buddy Rides	D	RF	94	McGougan, Kathy	Buddy Books Publishing
Buddy the TV Star	H	F	164	McGougan, Kathy	Buddy Books Publishing
Buddy Visits a Shelter	I	F	196	McGougan, Kathy	Buddy Books Publishing
Buddy Works	D	F	66	McGougan, Kathy	Buddy Books Publishing
Buddy: The Puppy Place	N	RF	250+	Miles, Ellen	Scholastic
Buddy: The First Seeing Eye Dog	M	I	250+	Moore, Eva	Scholastic
Buddy's Bath	E	RF	131	Literacy by Design	Rigby
Buddy's Birthday	I	F	181	McGougan, Kathy	Buddy Books Publishing
Buddy's Boo-Boo	E	F	153	McGougan, Kathy	Buddy Books Publishing
Buddy's Christmas	G	F	122	McGougan, Kathy	Buddy Books Publishing
Buddy's Friend	K	RF	585	Red Rocket Readers	Flying Start Books
Buddy's Friends	F	F	91	McGougan, Kathy	Buddy Books Publishing
Buddy's Mountain Vacation	K	F	1030	McGougan, Kathy	Buddy Books Publishing
Buddy's Rules	E	F	98	McGougan, Kathy	Buddy Books Publishing
Buddy's Summer Diary	F	F	248	McGougan, Kathy	Buddy Books Publishing
Buddy's Toys	C	I	33	McGougan, Kathy	Buddy Books Publishing
Budgeting	T	I	250+	How Economics Works	Lerner Publishing Group
Budgie & Boo	K	F	250+	McPhail, David	Harry N. Abrams
Budgie's Dream	J	F	250+	Story Starter	Wright Group/McGraw Hill
Buds and Blossoms: A Book About Flowers	M	I	250+	Growing Things	Picture Window Books
Buffalo Before Breakfast	M	F	250+	Osborne, Mary Pope	Random House
Buffalo Bill and the Pony Express	K	B	250+	Coerr, Eleanor	HarperTrophy
Buffalo Bill's Wild West Show	V	B	1750	Leveled Readers	Houghton Mifflin Harcourt
Buffalo Bills, The	S	I	250+	Team Spirit	Norwood House Press
Buffalo Gal	U	RF	250+	Wallace, Bill	Simon & Schuster
Buffalo Hunt	W	I	250+	Freedman, Russell	Holiday House
Buffalo Hunt	S	HF	2489	Leveled Readers	Houghton Mifflin Harcourt
Buffalo Hunt	S	HF	2489	Leveled Readers/CA	Houghton Mifflin Harcourt
Buffalo Hunt	S	HF	2489	Leveled Readers/TX	Houghton Mifflin Harcourt
Buffalo Soldiers and the Western Frontier	R	I	250+	On Deck	Rigby
#Buffalo Soldiers of the American West, The	T	I	250+	Graphic Library	Capstone Press

* Collection of short stories   # Graphic text
^ Mature content with lower level text demands

TITLE	LEVEL	GENRE	WORD COUNT	AUTHOR / SERIES	PUBLISHER / DISTRIBUTOR
Buffalo Woman	N	TL	250+	Goble, Paul	Aladdin
Buffalo, The	M	I	250+	Crewe, Sabrina	Steck-Vaughn
Buffalo's Homework	N	F	250+	Springboard	Wright Group/McGraw Hill
Buffy	B	F	28	Literacy 2000	Rigby
Buffy's Tricks	G	RF	97	Literacy 2000	Rigby
Bug Bus, The	K	F	250+	Sunshine	Wright Group/McGraw Hill
Bug Business	T	I	250+	Power Up!	Steck-Vaughn
Bug Club, The	G	F	118	Get Readyà Get SetàRead!	Barron's Educational
Bug Eyes	C	I	60	Bonnell, Kris	Reading Reading Books
Bug in the Jug Wants a Hug, The	J	F	159	Sounds Like Reading	Lerner Publishing Group
Bug Off!	L	F	250+	Dussling, Jennifer	Grosset & Dunlap
Bug on the Beam	N	RF	250+	Literacy by Design	Rigby
Bug Parts	A	RF	17	Leveled Readers	Houghton Mifflin Harcourt
Bug Parts	A	RF	17	Leveled Readers/CA	Houghton Mifflin Harcourt
Bug Party	F	I	131	Twig	Wright Group/McGraw Hill
Bug Safari	N	RF	250+	Barner, Bob	Holiday House
Bug School, The	C	F	66	Reading Safari	Mondo Publishing
Bug Watching	B	I	25	Twig	Wright Group/McGraw Hill
Bug, a Bear, and a Boy Go for a Ride, A	E	F	82	McPhail, David	Scholastic
Bug, a Bear, and a Boy, A	F	F	250+	McPhail, David	Scholastic
Bugged!	K	RF	1732	Science Solves It!	Kane Press
Buggy Riddles	I	F	221	Little Books	Sadlier-Oxford
Bug-head and Me	M	RF	250+	Literacy By Design	Rigby
Bug-head and Me	M	RF	250+	Rigby Literacy	Rigby
Bugliest Bug, The	N	F	250+	Shields, Carol Diggory	Candlewick Press
Bugs	P	I	250+	Animals Are Amazing	Carus Publishing Company
Bugs	A	I	32	Handprints A	Educators Publishing Service
Bugs	O	I	250+	Parker, Nancy Winslow; Wright, Joan Richards	Mulberry Books
Bugs and Beetles	D	I	173	Reading Safari	Mondo Publishing
Bugs and More Bugs	A	I	36	Animals	American Reading Company
Bugs and Other Insects	O	I	250+	Kalman, Bobbie	Crabtree
*Bugs And Other Stories	F	RF	250+	Story Steps	Rigby
Bugs Are Insects	M	I	250+	Rockwell, Anne	HarperCollins
Bugs Beware!	T	I	250+	Literacy by Design	Rigby
Bugs Beware!	T	I	250+	On Our Way to English	Rigby
Bugs for Breakfast	F	F	158	PM Plus Story Books	Rigby
Bugs for Dinner	A	I	35	Leveled Readers	Houghton Mifflin Harcourt
Bugs for Dinner	A	I	35	Leveled Readers/CA	Houghton Mifflin Harcourt
Bugs for Lunch	J	RF	193	Facklam, Margery	Charlesbridge
Bugs in My Backyard	D	I	55	Bonnell, Kris	Reading Reading Books
Bugs in My Hair?	L	RF	250+	Stier, Catherine	Albert Whitman & Co.
Bugs in the Garden	B	RF	59	Literacy by Design	Rigby
Bugs on the Menu	M	I	250+	Sails	Rigby
Bugs!	R	I	250+	Boldprint	Steck-Vaughn
Bugs!	O	F	250+	Greenberg, David T.	Little Brown and Company
Bugs!	L	I	250+	Phonics and Friends	Hampton Brown
Bugs!	C	F	32	Rookie Readers	Children's Press
Bugs!	A	I	20	Vocabulary Readers	Houghton Mifflin Harcourt
Bugs!	A	I	20	Vocabulary Readers/CA	Houghton Mifflin Harcourt
Bugs! Bugs! Bugs!	M	I	250+	DK Readers	DK Publishing
BugZ	S	F	250+	Power Up!	Steck-Vaughn
Build It Strong!	M	I	250+	First Science	Children's Press

TITLE	LEVEL	GENRE	WORD COUNT	AUTHOR / SERIES	PUBLISHER / DISTRIBUTOR
Build Your Own Weather Station	I	I	250+	Leveled Readers Science	Houghton Mifflin Harcourt
Build Your Own Web Site	X	I	250+	iOpeners	Pearson Learning Group
Build, Build, Build	M	I	470	Sunshine	Wright Group/McGraw Hill
Builders	J	I	158	Bookworms	Marshall Cavendish
Builder's Day, A	J	I	417	Springboard	Wright Group/McGraw Hill
Building	V	I	250+	Eyewitness Books	DK Publishing
Building a Bridge	K	I	158	Construction Zone	Capstone Press
Building a Case	N	I	379	Vocabulary Readers	Houghton Mifflin Harcourt
Building a Castle	L	I	250+	Early Connections	Benchmark Education
Building a Doghouse	M	I	250+	On Our Way to English	Rigby
Building a Dream	V	HF	250+	Reading Expeditions	National Geographic
Building a Dream: Mary Bethune's School	R	B	250+	Kelso, Richard	Steck-Vaughn
Building a House	H	I	83	Avenues	Hampton Brown
Building a House	H	I	83	Barton, Byron	Morrow
Building a House	J	I	119	Construction Zone	Capstone Press
Building a House	G	I	197	PM Plus Nonfiction	Rigby
Building a Nest	N	I	512	Springboard	Wright Group/McGraw Hill
Building a Road	I	I	106	Construction Zone	Capstone Press
Building a Skyscraper	J	I	110	Construction Zone	Capstone Press
Building a Tree House	N	I	250+	Infotrek Plus	ETA/Cuisenaire
Building an Ice Hotel	U	I	250+	iOpeners	Pearson Learning Group
Building Beavers	K	I	407	Pull Ahead Books	Lerner Publishing Group
Building Big Bridges	O	I	466	Red Rocket Readers	Flying Start Books
Building Blocks	T	I	250+	WorldScapes	ETA/Cuisenaire
Building Bridges	V	I	250+	iOpeners	Pearson Learning Group
Building Bridges	S	I	250+	Navigators Science Series	Benchmark Education
Building High	O	I	1510	Big Cat	Pacific Learning
Building Homes, Building Hope	O	I	250+	Sunshine	Wright Group/McGraw Hill
Building Lady Liberty	K	I	450	Leveled Readers Social Studies	Houghton Mifflin Harcourt
#Building of the Transcontinental Railroad	T	I	250+	Graphic Library	Capstone Press
Building on Nature: The Life of Antoni Gaudi	N	B	250+	Rodriguez, Rachel	Henry Holt & Co.
Building Quiz	Q	I	250+	Trackers	Pacific Learning
Building Roads	F	I	151	Red Rocket Readers	Flying Start Books
Building Shapes	G	I	30	Canizares, Susan; Berger, Samantha	Scholastic
Building Strong Bridges	M	I	250+	Twig	Wright Group/McGraw Hill
Building the Capital City	V	I	250+	Cornerstones of Freedom	Children's Press
#Building the Great Wall of China: An Isabel Soto History Adventure	S	F	250+	Graphic Expeditions	Capstone Press
Building the Hoover Dam	W	I	1878	Leveled Readers Science	Houghton Mifflin Harcourt
Building the Railroad	K	I	250+	Twig	Wright Group/McGraw Hill
Building the Three Gorges Dam	W	I	250+	Science Missions	Raintree
Building the Transcontinental Railroad	U	I	250+	Reading Expeditions	National Geographic
Building Things	F	I	24	Sunshine	Wright Group/McGraw Hill
Building Tiny Transistors	V	I	250+	Reading Expeditions	National Geographic
Building with Blocks	LB	RF	20	Sunshine	Wright Group/McGraw Hill
Buildings	C	I	61	Chessen, Betsey; Chanko, Pamela	Scholastic
Buildings	Q	I	250+	InfoTrek	ETA/Cuisenaire
Buildings	F	I	85	Leveled Readers Science	Houghton Mifflin Harcourt
Buildings	G	I	327	Sails	Rigby
Buildings and Structures	Y	I	250+	From Fail to Win! Learning from Bad Ideas	Raintree
Buildings of Distinction: Exploring State Capitols	R	I	250+	Explore More	Wright Group/McGraw Hill

* Collection of short stories   # Graphic text
^ Mature content with lower level text demands

TITLE	LEVEL	GENRE	WORD COUNT	AUTHOR / SERIES	PUBLISHER / DISTRIBUTOR
Buildings on My Street	F	RF	109	Foundations	Wright Group/McGraw Hill
Buildings That Go Up, Up, Up	I	I	133	Shutterbug Books	Steck-Vaughn
Built Below Sea Level: New Orleans	T	I	250+	Shockwave	Children's Press
Built for Speed Aircraft	T	I	250+	Graham, Ian	Steck-Vaughn
Built Like That	S	I	250+	PM Plus Nonfiction	Rigby
Built to Last	U	I	250+	InfoQuest	Rigby
Built to Last: Famous Structures of the World	U	I	250+	Explore More	Wright Group/McGraw Hill
Bull and the Firetruck, The	I	F	250+	Johnston, Tony	Scholastic
Bull Harris and the Purple Ooze	M	F	250+	Supa Doopers	Sundance
Bull in a China Shop, A	K	F	250+	Literacy 2000	Rigby
^Bull Rider	T	RF	250+	Orca Soundings	Orca Books
Bull Riding	N	RF	250+	Boyz Rule!	Mondo Publishing
Bull Run	Y	HF	250+	Fleischman, Paul	HarperCollins
^Bull Shark	N	I	250+	Shark Zone	Capstone Press
Bull Shark	J	I	129	Sharks	Capstone Press
Bulldog George	K	RF	250+	Voyages	SRA/McGraw Hill
Bulldogs	R	I	250+	All About Dogs	Capstone Press
Bulldogs	I	I	133	Dogs	Capstone Press
Bulldogs Are the Best!	Q	I	1564	The Best Dogs Ever	Lerner Publishing Group
Bulldozer, The	D	I	48	Sunshine	Wright Group/McGraw Hill
Bulldozers	F	I	94	Mighty Machines	Capstone Press
Bullies	V	I	250+	10 Things You Need to Know About	Capstone Press
^Bull's Eye	Z+	RF	250+	Orca Soundings	Orca Books
Bull's-eye!	F	RF	87	Oxford Reading Tree	Oxford University Press
Bully Bear	F	F	139	Rigby Literacy	Rigby
Bully Bear	F	F	144	Rigby Star	Rigby
Bully Book, The: How to Deal with the Mean Crowd	S	I	250+	Power Up!	Steck-Vaughn
Bully Cat	I	F	324	Sails	Rigby
Bully Cat and Fat Cat	J	F	400	Sails	Rigby
Bully Cat and the Birds	G	F	158	Sails	Rigby
Bully Cat's Mistake	F	F	190	Sails	Rigby
Bully Dinosaur	E	F	118	Little Dinosaur	Literacy Footprints
Bully for You, Teddy Roosevelt!	X	B	250+	Fritz, Jean	Penguin Group
Bully of Barkham Street	R	RF	250+	Stolz, Mary	HarperTrophy
Bully, The	Y	RF	250+	Langan, Paul	Townsend Press
Bully, The	L	RF	250+	PM Story Books	Rigby
Bumble Bear	F	F	89	Start to Read	School Zone
Bumble Bee	D	I	53	Pacific Literacy	Pacific Learning
Bumble Bee, The	E	RF	55	Szymanek, Susie	Kaeden Books
Bumble Bees	I	I	123	Bugs, Bugs, Bugs	Capstone Press
Bumble Bees	E	I	56	Insects	Capstone Press
Bumblebee Queen, The	M	I	250+	Sayre, April Pulley	Charlesbridge
Bumblebees	P	I	1958	Early Bird Nature Books	Lerner Publishing Group
Bumblebee's Best Friend	M	SF	250+	Transformers: Dark of the Moon	Little Brown and Company
Bump	F	I	217	Sun Sprouts	ETA/Cuisenaire
Bump!	C	F	12	KinderReaders	Rigby
Bump! Thump! Splat!	D	RF	40	Brand New Readers	Candlewick Press
Bump, Bump, Bump	D	RF	51	Cat on the Mat	Oxford University Press
Bumper Cars, The	C	RF	94	PM Extensions-Red	Rigby
Bumper Cars, The	B	RF	36	Sails	Rigby
Bumpity, Bumpity, Bump	F	RF	62	Parker, Carol	Continental Press
Bumps in the Night	L	F	250+	Allard, Harry	Bantam Books

TITLE	LEVEL	GENRE	WORD COUNT	AUTHOR / SERIES	PUBLISHER / DISTRIBUTOR
Bumpy Snowman, The	H	RF	334	Leveled Readers	Houghton Mifflin Harcourt
Bumpy Snowman, The	H	RF	334	Leveled Readers/CA	Houghton Mifflin Harcourt
Bumpy Snowman, The	H	RF	334	Leveled Readers/TX	Houghton Mifflin Harcourt
Bumpy the Frog	K	F	250+	Beers, Steven	Kaeden Books
Bun, The	I	TL	421	Storyteller-Moon Rising	Wright Group/McGraw Hill
Bundle Up!	LB	I	21	Reach	National Geographic
Bundle Up!	B	RF	35	Science	Outside the Box
Bungee Hero	S	RF	4080	Bertagna, J.	Stone Arch Books
Bungy 70528	O	RF	250+	Belcher, Angie	Pacific Learning
Bunker 10	X	SF	250+	Henderson, J. A.	Harcourt, Inc.
Bunker's Cove	S	HF	1125	Leveled Readers	Houghton Mifflin Harcourt
Bunnicula	Q	F	250+	Howe, James	Avon Books
Bunnicula Strikes Again!	Q	F	250+	Howe, James	Simon & Schuster
Bunnies in the Bathroom	Q	RF	250+	Baglio, Ben M.	Scholastic
Bunny and the Monster	F	F	161	Leveled Literacy Intervention/ Green System	Heinemann
Bunny Hop, The	I	F	250+	Slater, Teddy	Scholastic
Bunny Magic	I	RF	176	Books for Young Learners	Richard C. Owen
Bunny Opposites	LB	F	14	Pair-It Books	Steck-Vaughn
Bunny Runs Away	K	F	250+	Chardiet, Bernice; Maccarone, Grace	Scholastic
Bunny to Love, A	I	RF	444	Adams, Lorraine & Bruvold, Lynn	Eaglecrest Books
Bunny, Bunny	D	F	40	My First Reader	Grolier
Bunny's Recess	A	I	35	Little Books for Early Readers	University of Maine
Bunrakkit	K	F	250+	Sunshine	Wright Group/McGraw Hill
Burger Time	L	I	250+	Voyages	SRA/McGraw Hill
Burglar Next Door, The	I	RF	599	Rigby Flying Colors	Rigby
^Burglar Who Bit the Big Apple, The	Q	RF	250+	Brezenoff, Steve/Field Trip Mysteries	Stone Arch Books
Burglars' Ball, The	N	F	250+	Wonder World	Wright Group/McGraw Hill
Buried Eye, The	M	F	250+	Woodland Mysteries	Wright Group/McGraw Hill
Buried in Ice: The Mystery of a Lost Arctic Expedition	U	I	250+	Beattie, Owen & Geiger, John	Scholastic
Buried in the Backyard	M	RF	930	Science Solves It!	Kane Press
Buried Onions	Z+	F	250+	Soto, Gary	Harcourt, Inc.
Buried Treasure	O	I	250+	Rigby Focus	Rigby
Buried Treasure	N	RF	1480	Take Two Books	Wright Group/McGraw Hill
Buried Treasures: Uncovering Secrets of the Past	Z	I	250+	Compoint, Stephane	Harry N. Abrams
Burly Reid	S	RF	250+	Sails	Rigby
Burn	Z+	RF	250+	Phillips, Suzanne	Little Brown and Company
Burning Questions of Bingo Brown, The	U	RF	250+	Byars, Betsy	Puffin Books
^Burning Secrets	S	F	250+	Brezenoff, Steve	Stone Arch Books
Burning Up: Losing Our Ozone Layer	R	I	250+	On Deck	Rigby
Burning, The: Guardians of Ga'Hoole	V	F	250+	Lasky, Kathryn	Scholastic
Burps, Boogers, and Bad Breath	K	I	246	Spyglass Books	Compass Point Books
Burro's Tortillas	O	TL	816	Fields, Terri	Sylvan Dell Publishing
Burrows	E	I	51	Storyteller-Setting Sun	Wright Group/McGraw Hill
Burrows, Tunnels, and Chambers	N	I	250+	Sails	Rigby
Bus Driver	C	I	26	Work People Do	Lerner Publishing Group
Bus Driver's Birthday, The	G	RF	234	Springboard	Wright Group/McGraw Hill
#Bus Ride Bully	K	RF	250+	My 1st Graphic Novel	Stone Arch Books
Bus Ride, The	C	RF	52	Gear Up!	Wright Group/McGraw Hill
Bus Ride, The	C	F	164	Little Celebrations	Pearson Learning Group
Bus Ride, The	C	F	175	Reading Unlimited	Pearson Learning Group

* Collection of short stories   # Graphic text
^ Mature content with lower level text demands

TITLE	LEVEL	GENRE	WORD COUNT	AUTHOR / SERIES	PUBLISHER / DISTRIBUTOR
Bus Ride, The	F	RF	99	Storyteller-Setting Sun	Wright Group/McGraw Hill
Bus Stop, The	G	RF	110	Hellen, Nancy	Orchard Books
Bus, The	C	I	46	Twig	Wright Group/McGraw Hill
Buses	K	I	403	Pull Ahead Books	Lerner Publishing Group
Bush Bunyip, The	J	F	250+	Bookshop	Mondo Publishing
Bush Tucker	M	I	250+	Sunshine	Wright Group/McGraw Hill
Bushfire in the Koala Reserve	K	RF	250+	PM Plus Story Books	Rigby
Bushwhacker: A Civil War Adventure, The	V	HF	250+	Garrity, Jennifer Johnson	Peachtree
Business Basics	U	I	250+	In Step Readers	Rigby
Business Sense	W	I	3237	Vocabulary Readers	Houghton Mifflin Harcourt
Business Sense	W	I	3237	Vocabulary Readers/CA	Houghton Mifflin Harcourt
Business Sense	W	I	3237	Vocabulary Readers/TX	Houghton Mifflin Harcourt
Business Without Borders: Globalization	Y	I	250+	The Global Marketplace	Heinemann Library
Buster	M	F	250+	Bookshop	Mondo Publishing
Buster	C	I	36	Twig	Wright Group/McGraw Hill
*Buster and Phoebe: The Great Bone Game	K	F	250+	Bechtold, Lisze	Houghton Mifflin Harcourt
Buster and the Dance Contest	J	F	586	Brown, Marc	Little Brown and Company
Buster and the Giant Pumpkin	J	F	498	Brown, Marc	Little Brown and Company
Buster and the Great Swamp	J	F	615	Brown, Marc	Little Brown and Company
Buster Baxter, Cat Saver	M	F	250+	Brown, Marc	Little Brown and Company
Buster Catches a Wave	J	F	417	Brown, Marc	Little Brown and Company
Buster Changes His Luck	J	F	250+	Brown, Marc	Little Brown and Company
Buster Climbs the Walls	K	F	1093	Brown, Marc	Little Brown and Company
Buster Hits the Trail	K	F	250+	Brown, Marc	Little Brown and Company
Buster Hunts for Dinosaurs	J	F	506	Brown, Marc	Little Brown and Company
Buster Makes the Grade	M	F	250+	Brown, Marc	Little Brown and Company
Buster McCluster	E	F	71	Wonder World	Wright Group/McGraw Hill
Buster McCluster has Chicken Pox	E	RF	77	Wonder World	Wright Group/McGraw Hill
Buster on the Farm	J	F	589	Brown, Marc	Little Brown and Company
Buster on the Town	J	F	250+	Brown, Marc	Little Brown and Company
Buster Plays Along	K	F	250+	Brown, Marc	Little Brown and Company
Buster the Balloon	E	F	70	Mathtales	Mimosa
*Buster: The Very Shy Dog	K	F	250+	Bechtold, Lisze	Houghton Mifflin Harcourt
Buster's Dino Dilemma	M	F	250+	Brown, Marc	Little Brown and Company
Buster's New Friend	M	F	250+	Brown, Marc	Little Brown and Company
Buster's Sugartime	J	F	642	Brown, Marc	Little Brown and Company
Busy Animals at Night	D	I	183	Leveled Readers	Houghton Mifflin Harcourt
Busy Animals at Night	D	I	183	Leveled Readers/CA	Houghton Mifflin Harcourt
Busy Animals at Night	D	I	183	Leveled Readers/TX	Houghton Mifflin Harcourt
Busy Ants	L	I	392	Pull Ahead Books	Lerner Publishing Group
Busy Ants and the Lazy Ants, The	J	F	375	InfoTrek	ETA/Cuisenaire
Busy Baby	J	RF	250+	Sunshine	Wright Group/McGraw Hill
Busy Beaver, A	I	I	323	Leveled Readers	Houghton Mifflin Harcourt
Busy Beaver, A	I	I	323	Leveled Readers/CA	Houghton Mifflin Harcourt
Busy Beaver, A	I	I	323	Leveled Readers/TX	Houghton Mifflin Harcourt
Busy Beavers	K	RF	80	Dabcovich, Lydia	Scholastic
Busy Beavers	I	I	123	Reading Street	Pearson
Busy Beavers, The	I	RF	362	PM Story Books-Orange	Rigby
Busy Bees	K	F	1137	InfoTrek	ETA/Cuisenaire
Busy Bees	M	I	514	Leveled Readers	Houghton Mifflin Harcourt
Busy Bees	L	I	417	Leveled Readers	Houghton Mifflin Harcourt
Busy Bees	L	I	417	Leveled Readers/CA	Houghton Mifflin Harcourt
Busy Bees	L	I	417	Leveled Readers/TX	Houghton Mifflin Harcourt
Busy Bees	K	I	177	Rosen Real Readers	Rosen Publishing Group

TITLE	LEVEL	GENRE	WORD COUNT	AUTHOR / SERIES	PUBLISHER / DISTRIBUTOR
Busy Bees	LB	RF	12	Voyages	SRA/McGraw Hill
Busy Bird	LB	F	14	Pacific Literacy	Pacific Learning
Busy Body Book, The	O	I	250+	Rockwell, Lizzy	Scholastic
Busy Buzzers: Bees in Your Backyard	M	I	250+	Backyard Bugs	Picture Window Books
Busy Dad	A	RF	24	Mom and Dad Series	Pioneer Valley
Busy Fingers	H	RF	87	Bowie, C.W.	Charlesbridge
Busy Guy, A	K	RF	72	Rookie Readers	Children's Press
Busy Mosquito, The	C	F	112	Foundations	Wright Group/McGraw Hill
Busy People	C	RF	40	Little Celebrations	Pearson Learning Group
Busy Street	E	RF	67	Tadpoles	Rigby
Busy Toes	LB	RF	69	Bowie, C.W.	Charlesbridge
Busy Tree, The	K	I	234	Ward, Jennifer	Marshall Cavendish
Busy Week, A	D	RF	49	Pair-It Books	Steck-Vaughn
Busy, Lively, Sleepy, and Quiet Pond, The	J	I	416	Reading Street	Pearson
*Busybody Nora	N	RF	250+	Hurwitz, Johanna	Penguin Group
But Excuse Me That Is My Book	M	RF	250+	Child, Lauren	Dial/Penguin
But Granny Did!	D	RF	58	Voyages	SRA/McGraw Hill
But I Knew Better	H	RF	242	Home Connection Collection	Rigby
But I Want It!	J	RF	250+	On Our Way to English	Rigby
But I'll Be Back Again	V	B	250+	Rylant, Cynthia	Beech Tree Books
Butch, the Outdoor Cat	E	RF	65	Carousel Readers	Pearson Learning Group
Butler Gets a Break, The	T	F	250+	Venuti, Kristin Clark	Egmont USA
Butter Man, The	O	RF	250+	Alalou, Elizabeth & Ali	Charlesbridge
Buttercup Moon	F	RF	61	Book Bank	Wright Group/McGraw Hill
Butterflies	K	I	208	Ashley, Susan/Let's Read About Insects	Weekly Reader Publishing
Butterflies	I	I	94	Bugs, Bugs, Bugs	Capstone Press
Butterflies	O	I	250+	Holmes, Kevin J.	Red Brick Learning
Butterflies	E	I	47	Insects	Capstone Press
Butterflies	C	I	16	Instant Readers	Harcourt School Publishers
Butterflies	F	I	101	Life Cycles	Lerner Publishing Group
Butterflies	O	I	250+	Nature's Friends	Compass Point Books
Butterflies	I	I	250+	Neye, Emily	Grosset & Dunlap
Butterflies	K	I	213	Nonfiction Set 7	Literacy Footprints
Butterflies	L	I	416	Reading Street	Pearson
Butterflies	E	I	79	Sails	Rigby
Butterflies	F	I	168	Vocabulary Readers	Houghton Mifflin Harcourt
Butterflies	F	I	168	Vocabulary Readers/CA	Houghton Mifflin Harcourt
Butterflies	F	I	168	Vocabulary Readers/TX	Houghton Mifflin Harcourt
Butterflies	N	I	250+	World of Insects	Capstone Press
Butterflies & Caterpillars	N	I	250+	Berger, Melvin & Gilda	Scholastic
Butterflies and Moths	L	I	250+	Early Connections	Benchmark Education
Butterflies and Moths	N	I	250+	Kalman, Bobbie	Crabtree
Butterflies and Moths	O	I	250+	Leveled Reader Library	Macmillan/McGraw Hill
Butterflies in My Garden	G	RF	177	Bookshop	Mondo Publishing
Butterflies of the Sea	L	I	250+	Marine Life for Young Readers	Pearson Learning Group
Butterflies!	O	I	725	Leveled Readers	Houghton Mifflin Harcourt
Butterfly	Z+	RF	250+	Hartnett, Sonya	Candlewick Press
Butterfly	G	I	84	Joy Starters	Pearson Learning Group
Butterfly	B	I	39	Zoozoo-Animal World	Cavallo Publishing
Butterfly and Me, The	F	RF	41	Reading Links	Steck-Vaughn
Butterfly and Moth	W	I	250+	Eyewitness Books	DK Publishing
Butterfly Colors	F	I	52	Pebble Books	Capstone Press
Butterfly Day	K	RF	250+	Pacific Literacy	Pacific Learning

* Collection of short stories   # Graphic text
^ Mature content with lower level text demands

TITLE	LEVEL	GENRE	WORD COUNT	AUTHOR / SERIES	PUBLISHER / DISTRIBUTOR
Butterfly Eggs	F	I	57	Pebble Books	Capstone Press
Butterfly Farm Burglar, The	M	RF	250+	Woodland Mysteries	Wright Group/McGraw Hill
Butterfly Grows, A	J	I	172	Green Light Readers	Sandpiper Books
Butterfly House, The	D	RF	113	Rigby Flying Colors	Rigby
Butterfly in the Garden, The	B	RF	41	Windows on Literacy	National Geographic
Butterfly in the Sky, The	E	I	92	Benchmark Rebus	Marshall Cavendish
Butterfly Net, The	I	I	141	Storyteller	Wright Group/McGraw Hill
Butterfly Notes	M	RF	250+	PM Plus Chapter Books	Rigby
Butterfly Pyramid, The	N	TL	250+	Story Vines	Wright Group/McGraw Hill
Butterfly Quilt, The	J	RF	313	Reading Street	Pearson
Butterfly Report, The	D	I	86	Rigby Flying Colors	Rigby
Butterfly Robber, The	I	F	293	Sails	Rigby
Butterfly Survival	K	I	329	Vocabulary Readers	Houghton Mifflin Harcourt
Butterfly Survival	K	I	329	Vocabulary Readers/CA	Houghton Mifflin Harcourt
Butterfly Tree	O	RF	1042	Markle, Sandra	Peachtree
Butterfly, The	M	I	250+	Crewe, Sabrina	Steck-Vaughn
Butterfly, The	C	I	21	Science	Outside the Box
Butterfly's Life, A	K	I	250+	Burke, Melissa Blackwell	Steck-Vaughn
Butterfly's Life, A	K	I	346	Red Rocket Readers	Flying Start Books
Butterfly's Life, A	H	I	99	Time for Kids	Teacher Created Materials
Butterfly's Life, A	F	I	177	Watch It Grow	Heinemann Library
Button Soup	K	RF	250+	Bank Street	Bantam Books
Buttons	C	RF	81	First Stories	Pacific Learning
Buttons Buttons	LB	I	26	Learn to Read	Creative Teaching Press
Buttons for General Washington	M	HF	250+	On My Own History	Carolrhoda Books
Buying and Building Airplanes	O	I	608	Gear Up!	Wright Group/McGraw Hill
Buzby	J	F	250+	Hoban, Julia	HarperTrophy
Buzz	I	RF	228	Wong, Janet S.	Harcourt
Buzz and Bingo in the Fairy Tale Forest	N	F	774	Big Cat	Pacific Learning
Buzz and Bingo in the Starry Sky	N	SF	1271	Big Cat	Pacific Learning
Buzz Beaker and the Outer Space Trip	J	F	449	Stone Arch Readers	Stone Arch Books
Buzz Beaker and the Speed Secret	J	F	459	Stone Arch Readers	Stone Arch Books
Buzz Beaker and the Super Fast Car	J	F	427	Stone Arch Readers	Stone Arch Books
Buzz Bradley & the Invisible Fort	P	RF	250+	Howe, Jeff	Llumina Press
Buzz Is Part of a Bee, A	E	RF	162	Rookie Readers	Children's Press
Buzz Said the Bee	G	F	62	Lewison, Wendy	Scholastic
Buzz!: A Book About Insects	M	I	250+	Berger, Melvin & Gilda	Scholastic
Buzz, Bee, Buzz!	D	I	33	Bookworms	Marshall Cavendish
Buzz, Buzz, Buzz	H	F	162	Barton, Byron	Macmillan
Buzzing Bee	LB	F	28	Rigby Star	Rigby
Buzzing Bees	LB	RF	69	Mathtales	Mimosa
Buzzing Bumblebees	K	I	440	Pull Ahead Books	Lerner Publishing Group
Buzzing Flies	C	RF	45	Sunshine	Wright Group/McGraw Hill
Buzzing Rattlesnakes	K	I	323	Pull Ahead Books	Lerner Publishing Group
Buzzy Fly	C	F	72	Gear Up!	Wright Group/McGraw Hill
Buzzzzzz Said the Bee	G	F	147	Lewison, Cheyette	Scholastic
By E-mail with Love	Q	RF	250+	Leveled Readers	Houghton Mifflin Harcourt
By Lakes and Rivers	N	I	250+	Animal Trackers	Crabtree
By Land, Sea and Air	N	I	250+	Explorations	Okapi Educational Materials
By Land, Sea and Air	N	I	250+	Explorations	Eleanor Curtain Publishing
By Myself or with My Friends	E	RF	200	Learn to Read	Creative Teaching Press
By Sea to America	S	HF	250+	Literacy By Design	Rigby
By the Great Horn Spoon!	V	HF	250+	Fleischman, Sid	Little Brown and Company
By the Light of the Halloween Moon	L	F	250+	Stutson, Caroline	Marshall Cavendish

TITLE	LEVEL	GENRE	WORD COUNT	AUTHOR / SERIES	PUBLISHER / DISTRIBUTOR
By the Sea	B	I	65	Leveled Readers	Houghton Mifflin Harcourt
By the Sea	B	I	65	Leveled Readers/CA	Houghton Mifflin Harcourt
By the Sea	I	I	251	PM Science Readers	Rigby
By the Seashore	N	I	250+	Animal Trackers	Crabtree
By the Shores of Silver Lake	Q	HF	250+	Wilder, Laura Ingalls	HarperTrophy
By the Stream	E	RF	73	Oxford Reading Tree	Oxford University Press
By the Tree	D	RF	75	Ready Readers	Pearson Learning Group
Bye, Bye, Bali Kai	U	RF	250+	Luger, Harriett	Harcourt Brace
Bye-Bye, Baby!	K	RF	250+	Morris, Richard	Walker & Company
Bye-Bye, Big Bad Bullybug!	J	F	115	Emberley, Ed	Little Brown and Company
Bystander	U	RF	250+	Preller, James	Feiwel and Friends

B

* Collection of short stories   # Graphic text
^ Mature content with lower level text demands

TITLE	LEVEL	GENRE	WORD COUNT	AUTHOR / SERIES	PUBLISHER / DISTRIBUTOR
C	LB	I	14	Readlings	American Reading Company
C and P Pies, The	I	RF	257	Take Two Books	Wright Group/McGraw Hill
C. W. Post: A Pioneer in His Time	X	B	2121	Leveled Readers	Houghton Mifflin Harcourt
C.A.L.I.F.O.R.N.I.A	P	I	859	Springboard	Wright Group/McGraw Hill
Cabbage Caterpillar	I	F	221	Sunshine	Wright Group/McGraw Hill
Cabbage Princess, The	K	TL	250+	Literacy 2000	Rigby
Cabin Faced West, The	R	HF	250+	Fritz, Jean	Bantam Books
Cabin in the Hills, The	J	RF	349	PM Collection	Rigby
Cabinet of Wonders, The	X	F	250+	Rutkoski, Marie	Farrar, Straus, & Giroux
Cabot: John Cabot and the Journey to North America	U	B	250+	Exploring the World	Compass Point Books
Cacti	J	I	305	Rigby Flying Colors	Rigby
Cactus Town	C	RF	43	Sunshine	Wright Group/McGraw Hill
Cactuses	K	I	237	Windows on Literacy	National Geographic
Caddie Woodlawn	R	HF	250+	Brink, Carol Ryrie	Bantam Books
Cafeteria Contest, The	O	RF	1286	Leveled Readers	Houghton Mifflin Harcourt
Cafeteria Contest, The	O	RF	1286	Leveled Readers/CA	Houghton Mifflin Harcourt
Cafeteria Contest, The	O	RF	1286	Leveled Readers/TX	Houghton Mifflin Harcourt
Cage, The	Z	B	250+	Sender, Ruth Minsky	Simon & Schuster
Cages	W	RF	250+	Kehret, Peg	Puffin Books
Cairo by Camel	U	I	250+	WorldScapes	ETA/Cuisenaire
Cajun Country	S	I	2013	Leveled Readers Social Studies	Houghton Mifflin Harcourt
Cake	D	I	38	Benchmark Rebus	Marshall Cavendish
Cake for Mom, A	D	RF	63	Home Connection Collection	Rigby
Cake for Our Sister, A	F	RF	114	Larkin's Little Readers	Wilbooks
Cake Girl	J	F	332	Lucas, David	Farrar, Straus, & Giroux
Cake That Mack Ate, The	H	TL	189	Robart, Rose; Kovalski, Maryann	Little Brown and Company
Cake Walk	M	RF	250+	Books for Young Learners	Richard C. Owen
Cake, The	E	RF	121	Early Connections	Benchmark Education
Cake, The	M	RF	250+	Read Alongs	Rigby
Cake, The	E	RF	250+	Story Steps	Rigby
Cake, The	C	I	40	Sun Sprouts	ETA/Cuisenaire
Cakes and Miracles: A Purim Tale	N	RF	250+	Goldin, Barbara Diamond	Marshall Cavendish
Cal Ripken Jr.	U	B	250+	Sports Heroes and Legends	Lerner Publishing Group
#Calamity Jack	U	F	250+	Hale, Shannon & Dean	Bloomsbury Children's Books
Calamity Jane	N	B	2003	On My Own Folklore	Lerner Publishing Group
Calamity Kate	Q	RF	250+	Deary, Terry	HarperTrophy
Calcium	Q	I	250+	A True Book	Children's Press
Calder Game, The	U	RF	250+	Balliett, Blue	Scholastic
Caleb's Choice	S	HF	250+	Wisler, Clifton G.	Penguin Group
Calendar	K	RF	55	Livingston, Myra Cohn	Holiday House
Calendar, The	K	I	263	Red Rocket Readers	Flying Start Books
Calendar, The	N	I	180	Take Two Books	Wright Group/McGraw Hill
Calendar's Trick, The	E	F	88	Reading Safari	Mondo Publishing
Calick's Three Friends	G	F	142	McAlpin, MaryAnn	Short Tales Press
Calico Bush	W	HF	250+	Field, Rachel	Simon & Schuster
Calico Captive	S	HF	250+	Speare, Elizabeth George	Yearling Books
Calico Cat at School	G	F	86	Charles, Donald	Children's Press
Calico Cat at the Zoo	F	F	88	Charles, Donald	Children's Press
Calico Cat Meets Bookworm	G	F	90	Charles, Donald	Children's Press
Calico Cat's Rainbow	E	F	78	Charles, Donald	Children's Press
Calico the Cat	F	F	82	Charles, Donald	Children's Press
California	T	I	250+	Hello U.S.A.	Lerner Publishing Group

C

TITLE	LEVEL	GENRE	WORD COUNT	AUTHOR / SERIES	PUBLISHER / DISTRIBUTOR
California	S	I	250+	Land of Liberty	Red Brick Learning
California	Q	I	250+	One Nation	Capstone Press
California	T	I	250+	Sea To Shining Sea	Children's Press
California	T	I	250+	Theme Sets	National Geographic
California	R	I	250+	This Land Is Your Land	Compass Point Books
California Blue	Y	RF	250+	Klass, David	Scholastic
California Dreaming	Z+	RF	250+	Dean, Zoey	Little Brown and Company
California Gold Rush, The	V	I	250+	Cornerstones of Freedom	Children's Press
California Gold Rush, The	V	I	250+	Let Freedom Ring	Red Brick Learning
California Gold Rush, The	T	I	250+	McNeer, May	Random House
California Gold Rush, The	U	I	250+	Pair-It Books	Steck-Vaughn
California Gold Rush, The	T	I	250+	We The People	Compass Point Books
California Gold Rush, The: A Letter Home	P	HF	392	Reading Street	Pearson
^California Gold Rush, The: An Interactive History Adventure	T	HF	250+	You Choose Books	Capstone Press
California Missions Projects and Layouts	X	I	21000	Exploring California Missions	Lerner Publishing Group
California or Bust!	N	HF	250+	Stamper, Judith	Scholastic
California: Facts and Symbols	O	I	250+	The States and Their Symbols	Capstone Press
Call 911	C	I	22	Twig	Wright Group/McGraw Hill
Call 911!	L	F	670	Harrison, Pat	Blueberry Hill Books
Call It Courage	X	RF	250+	Sperry, Armstrong	Aladdin
Call Me Fizz	S	RF	250+	Scooters	ETA/Cuisenaire
Call Me Francis Tucket	V	HF	250+	Paulsen, Gary	Yearling Books
Call Me Hope	W	RF	250+	Olson Gretchen	Little Brown and Company
Call Me Ruth	R	RF	250+	Sachs, Marilyn	Beech Tree Books
Call Mr. Vasquez, He'll Fix It!	K	I	250+	Our Neighborhood	Children's Press
Call of the Selkie	Q	RF	250+	Action Packs	Rigby
Call of the Wild	Y	F	250+	London, Jack	Signet Classics
Call of the Wild, The	U	F	10965	Oxford Bookworms Library	Oxford University Press
Call Waiting	Y	RF	250+	Stine, R. L.	Scholastic
Called To a Cause	R	B	250+	Power Up!	Steck-Vaughn
Called To a Cause	R	B	250+	Power Up!	Steck-Vaughn
Callie Cat, Ice Skater	K	F	250+	Spinelli, Eileen	Albert Whitman & Co.
Callie's Rules	S	RF	250+	Zucker, Naomi	Egmont USA
Callie's Scrapbook	K	RF	687	InfoTrek	ETA/Cuisenaire
Calvin Coconut Touble Magnet	O	RF	250+	Salisbury, Graham	Yearling Books
Calvin Cooidge: Thirtieth President	R	B	250+	Getting to Know the U.S. Presidents	Children's Press
Calvin Coolidge	U	B	250+	Profiles of the Presidents	Compass Point Books
Cam in the Cave	J	RF	461	Sails	Rigby
Cam Jansen and the Chocolate Fudge Mystery	L	RF	250+	Adler, David A.	Puffin Books
Cam Jansen and the Ghostly Mystery	L	RF	250+	Adler, David A.	Puffin Books
Cam Jansen and the Mystery at the Haunted House	L	RF	250+	Adler, David A.	Puffin Books
Cam Jansen and the Mystery at the Monkey House	L	RF	250+	Adler, David A.	Puffin Books
Cam Jansen and the Mystery of Flight 54	L	RF	250+	Adler, David A.	Puffin Books
Cam Jansen and the Mystery of the Babe Ruth Baseball	L	RF	250+	Adler, David A.	Puffin Books
Cam Jansen and the Mystery of the Carnival Prize	L	RF	250+	Adler, David A.	Puffin Books
Cam Jansen and the Mystery of the Circus Clown	L	RF	250+	Adler, David A.	Puffin Books
Cam Jansen and the Mystery of the Dinosaur Bones	L	RF	250+	Adler, David A.	Puffin Books

* Collection of short stories   # Graphic text
^ Mature content with lower level text demands

TITLE	LEVEL	GENRE	WORD COUNT	AUTHOR / SERIES	PUBLISHER / DISTRIBUTOR
Cam Jansen and the Mystery of the Gold Coins	L	RF	250+	Adler, David A.	Puffin Books
Cam Jansen and the Mystery of the Monkey House	L	RF	250+	Adler, David A.	Puffin Books
Cam Jansen and the Mystery of the Monster Movie	L	RF	250+	Adler, David A.	Puffin Books
Cam Jansen and the Mystery of the Stolen Corn Popper	L	RF	250+	Adler, David A.	Puffin Books
Cam Jansen and the Mystery of the Stolen Diamonds	L	RF	250+	Adler, David A.	Puffin Books
Cam Jansen and the Mystery of the Television Dog	L	RF	250+	Adler, David A.	Puffin Books
Cam Jansen and the Mystery of the U.F.O.	L	RF	250+	Adler, David A.	Puffin Books
Cam Jansen and the Scary Snake Mystery	L	RF	250+	Adler, David A.	Puffin Books
Cam Jansen and the Secret Service Mystery	L	RF	250+	Adler, David A.	Scholastic
Cam Jansen and the Triceratops Pops Mystery	L	RF	250+	Adler, David A.	Puffin Books
Cam the Camel	K	F	334	Leveled Readers	Houghton Mifflin Harcourt
Cam the Camel	K	F	334	Leveled Readers/CA	Houghton Mifflin Harcourt
Cam the Camel	K	F	334	Leveled Readers/TX	Houghton Mifflin Harcourt
Cam the Cow	B	F	32	Reading Street	Pearson
Cambodian New Year	M	I	395	Nonfiction Set 9	Literacy Footprints
Camel Ben	F	RF	32	Books for Young Learners	Richard C. Owen
Camel Called Bump-Along, A	K	F	373	Evangeline Nicholas Collection	Wright Group/McGraw Hill
Camel Fair	Q	I	1394	Big Cat	Pacific Learning
Camels	H	I	108	Desert Animals	Capstone Press
Camels	H	I	123	Sails	Rigby
Camels and Their Cousins	L	I	250+	Storyteller Chapter Books	Wright Group/McGraw Hill
Camel's Hump	I	TL	274	Leveled Readers	Houghton Mifflin Harcourt
Camel's Hump	I	TL	274	Leveled Readers/CA	Houghton Mifflin Harcourt
Camel's Hump	I	TL	274	Leveled Readers/TX	Houghton Mifflin Harcourt
Camels of Asia	A	I	36	Readlings/ Animals of Asia	American Reading Company
Camels: Ships of the Desert	T	I	667	Vocabulary Readers	Houghton Mifflin Harcourt
Camera, The	Q	I	250+	Great Inventions	Capstone Press
Camera, The	T	I	250+	Tales of Invention	Heinemann Library
Cameras on the Battlefield: Photos of War	W	I	250+	High Five Reading	Red Brick Learning
Camilla	Y	RF	250+	L'Engle, Madeleine	Farrar, Straus, & Giroux
Camille's Team	K	F	250+	I See I Learn	Charlesbridge
Camouflage	M	I	250+	Cambridge Reading	Pearson Learning Group
Camouflage	B	I	56	Nonfiction Set 2	Literacy Footprints
Camouflage	K	I	202	Rigby Focus	Rigby
Camouflage	H	I	154	Sunshine	Wright Group/McGraw Hill
Camp Alien: Alien Agent	T	F	20053	Service, Pamela F.	Carolrhoda Books
Camp Big Paw	J	RF	250+	Cushman, Doug	HarperTrophy
Camp Can't: The Complicated Life of Claudia Cristina Cortez	S	RF	250+	Gallagher, Diana G.	Stone Arch Books
Camp K-9	K	F	250+	Rodman, Mary Ann	Peachtree
Camp Knock Knock	K	RF	250+	Duffey, Betsy	Bantam Books
Camp Knock Knock Mystery, The	K	RF	250+	Duffey, Betsy	Bantam Books
Camp Sink or Swim	M	RF	250+	Davis, Gibbs	Random House
^Camp Wild	T	RF	250+	Orca Currents	Orca Books
C-A-M-P! Camp!	K	I	595	Vocabulary Readers	Houghton Mifflin Harcourt
C-A-M-P! Camp!	K	I	595	Vocabulary Readers/CA	Houghton Mifflin Harcourt
Campfire Mallory	O	RF	17381	Friedman, Laurie	Carolrhoda Books
Camping	C	F	29	Brand New Readers	Candlewick Press
Camping	C	RF	49	Foundations	Wright Group/McGraw Hill
Camping	D	RF	64	Hooker, Karen	Kaeden Books

TITLE	LEVEL	GENRE	WORD COUNT	AUTHOR / SERIES	PUBLISHER / DISTRIBUTOR
Camping	F	RF	71	Leveled Readers	Houghton Mifflin Harcourt
Camping	B	RF	19	Literacy 2000	Rigby
Camping	I	I	200	Rigby Star Quest	Rigby
Camping	E	RF	76	Storyteller	Wright Group/McGraw Hill
Camping	E	RF	264	Sunshine	Wright Group/McGraw Hill
Camping	S	I	250+	The Great Outdoors	Capstone Press
Camping at School	L	RF	522	Gear Up!	Wright Group/McGraw Hill
Camping Chaos	N	RF	250+	Girlz Rock!	Mondo Publishing
Camping In	K	RF	589	Springboard	Wright Group/McGraw Hill
Camping in the Woods	Q	I	250+	Sails	Rigby
Camping in the Yard	G	RF	171	Joy Starters	Pearson Learning Group
Camping Is Fun!	F	RF	112	Reading Street	Pearson Learning Group
Camping Is Fun!	D	RF	86	Windows on Literacy	National Geographic
Camping Out	J	F	250+	Coulton, Mia	Maryruth Books
Camping Out	H	RF	218	Sun Sprouts	ETA/Cuisenaire
Camping Out	E	RF	141	Visions	Wright Group/McGraw Hill
Camping Out	C	I	59	Vocabulary Readers	Houghton Mifflin Harcourt
Camping Out	C	I	59	Vocabulary Readers/CA	Houghton Mifflin Harcourt
Camping Outside	F	RF	95	Book Bank	Wright Group/McGraw Hill
Camping Trip, The	L	F	740	Arctic Adventures	Pioneer Valley
Camping Trip, The	E	RF	71	Leveled Readers Language Support	Houghton Mifflin Harcourt
Camping Under the Stars	A	I	21	Vocabulary Readers	Houghton Mifflin Harcourt
Camping Under the Stars	A	I	21	Vocabulary Readers/CA	Houghton Mifflin Harcourt
Camping with Claudine	K	RF	250+	Literacy 2000	Rigby
Camping with Dad	J	RF	316	Sails	Rigby
Camping with Grandma	M	RF	250+	Reading Safari	Mondo Publishing
Camping with Our Dad	L	RF	250+	Sunshine	Wright Group/McGraw Hill
Campout, The	H	RF	298	Rigby Flying Colors	Rigby
Can a Cow Hop?	D	I	40	Ready Readers	Pearson Learning Group
Can a Fox Wear Polka-Dotted Socks?	D	F	51	Dominie Readers	Pearson Learning Group
Can a Hippo Hop?	E	I	140	Tidd, Louise Vitellaro	Kaeden Books
Can an Old Dog Learn New Tricks?: And Other Questions about Animals	U	I	4427	Is That a Fact?	Lerner Publishing Group
Can Do, Jenny Archer	M	RF	250+	Conford, Ellen	Random House
Can Dogs Talk?	B	F	19	Bonnell, Kris	Reading Reading Books
Can Hank Sing?	F	F	83	Reading Street	Pearson
Can I Bring My Pterodactyl to School, Ms. Johnson?	M	F	250+	Grambling, Lois G.	Charlesbridge
Can I Have a Dinosaur?	L	RF	250+	Literacy 2000	Rigby
Can I Have a Lick?	C	RF	69	Carousel Readers	Pearson Learning Group
Can I Have a Pet?	A	RF	36	Bebop Books	Lee & Low Books Inc.
Can I Help?	F	F	250+	Janovitz, Marilyn	North-South Books
Can I Play Outside?	H	RF	121	Literacy 2000	Rigby
Can I Play?	C	F	30	The Book Project	Sundance
Can It Rain Cats and Dogs?	R	I	250+	Berger, Melvin & Gilda	Scholastic
Can Lightening Strike the Same Place Twice?: And Other Questions about Earth, Weather, and the Environment	U	I	4325	Is That a Fact?	Lerner Publishing Group
Can Rats Swim from Sewers into Toilets?: And Other Questions about Your Home	U	I	4858	Is That a Fact?	Lerner Publishing Group
Can Turtle Fly?	K	TL	250+	Bruchac, Joseph	Hampton Brown
Can We Be Friends?	C	I	71	Bonnell, Kris	Reading Reading Books
Can We Do It?	E	RF	79	Reading Street	Pearson
Can We Go?	C	RF	25	Cherrington, Janelle	Scholastic

* Collection of short stories   # Graphic text
^ Mature content with lower level text demands

TITLE	LEVEL	GENRE	WORD COUNT	AUTHOR / SERIES	PUBLISHER / DISTRIBUTOR
Can We Have a Pet?	E	RF	139	Early Explorers	Benchmark Education
Can We Play?	C	F	95	McGougan, Kathy	Buddy Books Publishing
Can We Save the Tiger?	S	I	250+	Jenkins, Martin	Candlewick Press
Can You Believe?: Hurricanes	Q	I	250+	Markle, Sandra	Scholastic
Can You Cuddle Like a Koala?	J	F	141	Butler, John	Peachtree
Can You Do This?	B	F	20	The Book Project	Sundance
Can You Eat a Fraction?	M	I	250+	Yellow Umbrella Books	Capstone Press
Can You Find a Pattern?	B	I	41	Gear Up!	Wright Group/McGraw Hill
Can You Find It?	B	I	34	Ready Readers	Pearson Learning Group
Can You Find It? America	K	I	250+	Falken, Linda	Harry N. Abrams
Can You Find the Pattern?	D	I	113	Visions	Wright Group/McGraw Hill
Can You Fly High, Wright Brothers?	O	B	250+	Berger, Melvin & Gilda	Scholastic
Can You Fly?	C	I	51	Foundations	Wright Group/McGraw Hill
Can You Growl Like a Bear?	K	I	277	Butler, John	Peachtree
Can You Guess?	G	I	185	InfoTrek	ETA/Cuisenaire
Can You Guess?	K	I	196	Yellow Umbrella Books	Capstone Press
Can You Hear A Rainbow? The Story of a Deaf Boy Named Chris	N	RF	250+	Heelan, Jamee Riggio	Peachtree
Can You Hear it?	Q	I	250+	Lach, William	Harry N. Abrams
Can You Imagine?	O	B	250+	Meet The Author	Richard C. Owen
Can You Read a Map?	C	F	38	Learn to Read	Creative Teaching Press
Can You See An Insect?	J	I	171	Windows on Literacy	National Geographic
Can You See Me?	C	I	48	Foundations	Wright Group/McGraw Hill
Can You See Me?	B	I	72	Rigby Flying Colors	Rigby
Can You See the Eggs?	C	I	87	PM Starters	Rigby
Can You See the Wagon?	A	I	40	On Our Way to English	Rigby
Can You See?	B	F	30	Sails	Rigby
Can You Spot It?	E	RF	79	Reading Street	Pearson
Can You Tell a Bee from a Wasp?	L	I	679	Lightning Bolt Books	Lerner Publishing Group
Can You Tell a Butterfly from a Moth?	L	I	574	Lightning Bolt Books	Lerner Publishing Group
Can You Tell a Cheetah from a Leopard?	L	I	651	Lightning Bolt Books	Lerner Publishing Group
Can You Tell a Coyote from a Wolf?	L	I	659	Lightning Bolt Books	Lerner Publishing Group
Can You Tell a Cricket from a Grasshopper?	L	I	555	Lightning Bolt Books	Lerner Publishing Group
Can You Tell a Dolphin from a Porpoise?	L	I	575	Lightning Bolt Books	Lerner Publishing Group
Can You Tell a Frog from a Toad?	M	I	622	Lightning Bolt Books	Lerner Publishing Group
Can You Tell a Gecko from a Salamander?	L	I	629	Lightning Bolt Books	Lerner Publishing Group
Can You Tell a Horse from a Pony?	M	I	651	Lightning Bolt Books	Lerner Publishing Group
Can You Tell a Seal from a Sea Lion?	L	I	659	Lightning Bolt Books	Lerner Publishing Group
Can You Tell an Alligator from a Crocodile?	L	I	593	Lightning Bolt Books	Lerner Publishing Group
Can You Tell an Ostrich from an Emu?	M	I	617	Lightning Bolt Books	Lerner Publishing Group
Can You Top That?	H	RF	250+	Bebop Books	Lee & Low Books Inc.
Canada	H	I	68	Canizares, Susan; Berger, Samantha	Scholastic
Canada	O	I	250+	Countries of the World	Red Brick Learning
Canada	Q	I	250+	First Reports: Countries	Compass Point Books
Canada	L	I	331	Time for Kids	Teacher Created Materials
Canada ABCs: A Book About the People and Places of Canada	Q	I	250+	Country ABCs	Picture Window Books
Canada Celebrates Multiculturalism	T	I	250+	Kalman, Bobbie	Crabtree
Canada Geese Quilt, The	P	RF	250+	Kinsey-Warnock, Natalie	Bantam Books
Canada Under Siege	Y	I	250+	History for Young Canadians	Fitzhenry & Whiteside
Canada: A Question and Answer Book	P	I	250+	Questions and Answers: Countries	Capstone Press
Canada: The Culture	T	I	250+	Kalman, Bobbie	Crabtree

* Collection of short stories   # Graphic text
^ Mature content with lower level text demands

TITLE	LEVEL	GENRE	WORD COUNT	AUTHOR / SERIES	PUBLISHER / DISTRIBUTOR
Canada: The Land	T	I	250+	Kalman, Bobbie	Crabtree
Canada: The People	T	I	250+	Kalman, Bobbie	Crabtree
Canada's Birds	N	I	250+	Hughes Susan	Scholastic
Canada's Wetland Animals	M	I	250+	Donaldson, Chelsea	Scholastic
*Canadian Disasters	W	I	250+	Schmidt, Rene	Scholastic
*Canadian Greats	R	B	250+	Trottier, Maxine	Scholastic
Canal Boat Cat	J	F	250+	Storyworlds	Heinemann
Canals	J	I	257	Sails	Rigby
Canary Caper, The	N	RF	250+	A to Z Mysteries	Random House
Candle Making: Work with Wicks and Wax	Q	I	250+	Crafts	Capstone Press
Candlelight	G	RF	231	PM Story Books	Rigby
Candlelight Service	O	RF	250+	Literacy 2000	Rigby
Candles to Lasers	S	I	1164	Take Two Books	Wright Group/McGraw Hill
Candy Corn Contest, The	L	RF	250+	Giff, Patricia Reilly	Bantam Books
Candy Creations from the "Candy Queen"	N	I	250+	Bookshop	Mondo Publishing
Candy Store, The	I	RF	230	InfoTrek	ETA/Cuisenaire
Candy, the Old Car	H	F	234	PM Plus Story Books	Rigby
Candyfloss	U	RF	250+	Wilson, Jacqueline	Roaring Brook Press
Candymakers, The	U	RF	250+	Mass, Wendy	Little Brown and Company
Cannonball Chris	L	RF	250+	Marzollo, Jean	Random House
Canoe Diary	O	I	250+	Orbit Chapter Books	Pacific Learning
Canoeing	S	I	250+	The Great Outdoors	Red Brick Learning
Can't You Make Them Behave, King George?	R	I	250+	Fritz, Jean	G.P. Putnam's Sons Books for Young Readers
Can't You See We're Reading?	D	RF	71	Stepping Stones	Nelson/Michaels Assoc.
Can't You Sleep, Little Bear?	L	F	250+	Waddell, Martin	Candlewick Press
Canterville Ghost, The	U	F	6100	Oxford Bookworms Library	Oxford University Press
Canyon Hunters	P	I	250+	Landform Adventurers	Raintree
Canyon Is Deep, The	G	I	40	Windows on Literacy	National Geographic
Canyons	V	F	250+	Paulsen, Gary	Laurel-Leaf Books
Cape for Daisy, A	H	F	235	Jack and Daisy	Pioneer Valley
Cape of Rushes, The	M	TL	250+	Cambridge Reading	Pearson Learning Group
Caper of the Crown Jewels, The	P	SF	250+	Secret Agent Jack Stalwart	Weinstein Books
Capitol Building, The	N	I	511	Lightning Bolt Books	Lerner Publishing Group
Capitol, The	V	I	250+	Cornerstones of Freedom	Children's Press
Capitol, The	S	I	250+	Symbols of America	Marshall Cavendish
Capoeira: Game! Dance! Martial Art!	T	I	250+	Ancona, George	Lee & Low Books Inc.
Caps for Sale	K	F	675	Slobodkina, Esphyr	Harper & Row
Caps, Hats, Socks, and Mittens: A Book About the Four Seasons	I	I	250+	Borden, Louise	Scholastic
Capsize!	P	RF	250+	Bookweb	Rigby
Captain America to the Rescue!	K	F	250+	Marvel Super Hero Squad	Little Brown and Company
Captain Bluefin's Underwater Ride	J	I	250+	Phonics Readers Plus	Steck-Vaughn
Captain B's Boat	G	F	158	Sunshine	Wright Group/McGraw Hill
Captain Bumble	K	F	510	Story Box	Wright Group/McGraw Hill
Captain Cat	H	F	250+	Hoff, Syd	HarperTrophy
Captain Ebenezer	E	F	190	Joy Starters	Pearson Learning Group
Captain Felonius	L	F	250+	Literacy 2000	Rigby
Captain Foot and the Treasure	I	F	282	InfoTrek	ETA/Cuisenaire
Captain Gallant	M	SF	763	Springboard	Wright Group/McGraw Hill
Captain Grey	U	HF	250+	Avi	HarperTrophy
^Captain Jake	M	F	250+	Orca Echoes	Orca Books
Captain Kind: Kindness	K	F	1218	Salerno, Tony Character Classics	Character Building Company

* Collection of short stories   # Graphic text
^ Mature content with lower level text demands

TITLE	LEVEL	GENRE	WORD COUNT	AUTHOR / SERIES	PUBLISHER / DISTRIBUTOR
Captain Orinocos Onion	K	RF	250+	Voyages	SRA/McGraw Hill
Captain Pepper's Pets	L	F	250+	I Am Reading	Kingfisher
Captain Small Pig	K	F	250+	Waddell, Martin	Peachtree
Captains Courageous	Z+	HF	250+	Kipling, Rudyard	Bantam Books
Captivate	Z+	F	250+	Jones, Carrie	Bloomsbury Children's Books
Captive or Free: Zoos in Debate	W	I	2516	Reading Street	Pearson
Capture of Detroit, The	Y	I	250+	History for Young Canadians	Fitzhenry & Whiteside
Capture, The: Guardians of Ga'Hoole	V	F	250+	Lasky, Kathryn	Scholastic
#Captured by Pirates	U	F	12000	Twisted Journeys	Graphic Universe
Captured Off Guard: The Attack on Pearl Harbor	T	HF	250+	Lemke, Donald	Stone Arch Books
Capybara	L	I	250+	A Day in the Life: Rain Forest Animals	Heinemann Library
Car	W	I	250+	Eyewitness Books	DK Publishing
Car Accident, The	F	RF	161	Foundations	Wright Group/McGraw Hill
Car Followed Us, A	D	RF	54	Books for Young Learners	Richard C. Owen
Car Ride, The	A	RF	41	Little Red Readers	Sundance
Car Trip, A	C	RF	64	PM Stars	Rigby
Car Trouble	L	RF	724	PM Collection	Rigby
Car Wash Kid	D	RF	55	Rookie Readers	Children's Press
Car Wash, The	G	RF	214	Handprints D	Educators Publishing Service
Car Wash, The	K	RF	544	Red Rocket Readers	Flying Start Books
Car Wash, The	G	I	98	Windows on Literacy	National Geographic
Car, The	T	I	250+	Tales of Invention	Heinemann Library
Caracas, Venezuela: Communities Around the World	S	I	250+	Reading Expeditions	National Geographic
Cara's Letters	R	RF	250+	PM Chapter Books	Rigby
Caravan Boy	X	HF	3258	Leveled Readers	Houghton Mifflin Harcourt
Card, The	Y	HF	11100	Oxford Bookworms Library	Oxford University Press
Cardboard Box, A	K	TL	250+	Ready to Read	Pacific Learning
Cardturner, The	X	RF	250+	Sachar, Louis	Delacorte Press
Careers	G	I	121	Benger, Wendy	Kaeden Books
Careers-Day Surprise	Q	RF	2177	Take Two Books	Wright Group/McGraw Hill
Careful Counting	E	F	162	Red Rocket Readers	Flying Start Books
Careful Crocodile, The	I	HF	271	PM Story Books-Orange	Rigby
Careful Mouse, A	E	RF	73	Larkin's Little Readers	Wilbooks
Cargo Cat	G	F	222	Sails	Rigby
Caribbean Cats	M	RF	250+	Books for Young Learners	Richard C. Owen
Caribbean, The	M	I	349	Time for Kids	Teacher Created Materials
Caribou	H	I	120	Polar Animals	Capstone Press
Caribou (Reindeer)	N	I	250+	PM Animal Facts: Silver	Rigby
Caribou Journey, A	Q	I	250+	Miller, Debbie S.	Little Brown and Company
Caring	L	I	250+	Character Education	Red Brick Learning
Caring	C	I	47	Interaction	Rigby
Caring	K	I	250+	Way to Be!	Picture Window Books
Caring for Earth	P	I	250+	PM Extensions	Rigby
Caring for Earth	H	I	80	Windows on Literacy	National Geographic
Caring for Eggs and Babies	E	I	113	Sails	Rigby
Caring for Our Lizard	G	I	133	Learn to Read	Creative Teaching Press
Caring for Our Pets	C	I	74	Early Connections	Benchmark Education
Caring for Our World	N	I	250+	Rigby Star Quest	Rigby
Caring for Outdoor Places	M	I	1001	Rigby Flying Colors	Rigby
Caring for Wild Animals	P	I	250+	Trackers	Pacific Learning

TITLE	LEVEL	GENRE	WORD COUNT	AUTHOR / SERIES	PUBLISHER / DISTRIBUTOR
Caring for Your Bird	K	I	250+	Positively Pets	Capstone Press
Caring for Your Cat	K	I	250+	Positively Pets	Capstone Press
Caring for Your Dog	I	I	250+	All About Dogs	Literacy Footprints
Caring for Your Dog	K	I	250+	Positively Pets	Capstone Press
Caring for Your Ferret	K	I	250+	Positively Pets	Capstone Press
Caring for Your Fish	K	I	250+	Positively Pets	Capstone Press
Caring for Your Gerbil	K	I	250+	Positively Pets	Capstone Press
Caring for Your Guinea Pig	K	I	250+	Positively Pets	Capstone Press
Caring for Your Hamster	K	I	250+	Positively Pets	Capstone Press
Caring for Your Hermit Crab	K	I	250+	Positively Pets	Capstone Press
Caring for Your Horse	K	I	250+	Positively Pets	Capstone Press
Caring for Your Pet Bird	O	I	1360	Reading Street	Pearson
Caring For Your Pets: A Book About Veterinarians	I	I	175	Community Workers	Picture Window Books
Caring for Your Rabbit	K	I	250+	Positively Pets	Capstone Press
Caring for Your Snake	K	I	250+	Positively Pets	Capstone Press
Carl and the Baby Duck	G	F	159	Day, Alexandra	Square Fish
Carl and the Kitten	G	F	136	Day, Alexandra	Macmillan
Carl and the Puppies	H	F	151	Day, Alexandra	Square Fish
Carl and the Sick Puppiy	G	F	154	Day, Alexandra	Square Fish
Carl Goes Shopping	WB	F	0	Day, Alexandra	Green Tiger Press
Carl Goes to Daycare	WB	F	0	Day, Alexandra	Green Tiger Press
Carl the Complainer	M	RF	250+	Social Studies Connects	Kane Press
Carla Crow's Pie	I	F	288	Springboard	Wright Group/McGraw Hill
Carla Gets a Pet	I	RF	250+	Ready Readers	Pearson Learning Group
Carla's Big Splash	A	RF	19	Beckley, Kimberly	Kaeden Books
Carla's Bookcase	F	RF	198	On Our Way to English	Rigby
Carla's Breakfast	G	RF	225	Harper, Leslie	Kaeden Books
Carla's Corner	J	RF	646	Leveled Readers	Houghton Mifflin Harcourt
Carla's New Glasses	I	RF	207	Coulton, Mia	Kaeden Books
Carla's Ribbons	G	RF	212	Harper, Leslie	Kaeden Books
Carla's Talent Show	J	RF	388	Beckley, Kimberly	Kaeden Books
Carla's Wheels	I	RF	200	Story Box	Wright Group/McGraw Hill
Carlita Ropes the Twister	L	F	363	Pair-It Books	Steck-Vaughn
Carlo and the Really Nice Librarian	I	F	250+	Spanyol, Jessica	Candlewick Press
Carlo Watches the Boys	M	RF	1002	Leveled Readers	Houghton Mifflin Harcourt
Carlo Watches the Boys	M	RF	1002	Leveled Readers/CA	Houghton Mifflin Harcourt
Carlo Watches the Boys	M	RF	1002	Leveled Readers/TX	Houghton Mifflin Harcourt
Carlos and his Friends	M	RF	250+	Sunflower	Intercultural Center for Research in Education
Carlos and Juan Visit Yellowstone	D	RF	70	Larkin's Little Readers	Wilbooks
Carlos Goes Camping	D	RF	99	In Step Readers	Rigby
Carlos Goes Camping	D	RF	99	Literacy by Design	Rigby
Carlos Picks a Pet	I	RF	427	Reading Street	Pearson
Carlos's Big Yawn	G	RF	228	Springboard	Wright Group/McGraw Hill
Carlota's Cooking Class	L	RF	250+	On Our Way to English	Rigby
Carl's Afternoon in the Park	WB	F	0	Day, Alexandra	Green Tiger Press
Carl's Birthday	WB	F	0	Day, Alexandra	Green Tiger Press
Carl's High Jump	K	RF	250+	PM Plus Story Books	Rigby
Carly Patterson	P	B	1934	Amazing Athletes	Lerner Publishing Group
Carlyles, The	Z+	RF	250+	von Ziegesar, Cecily	Little Brown and Company
Carmelita's Cabbage	H	F	240	Springboard	Wright Group/McGraw Hill
Carmen's Colors	LB	RF	14	Bebop Books	Lee & Low Books Inc.
Carmen's Star Party	J	RF	250+	Phonics and Friends	Hampton Brown

* Collection of short stories   # Graphic text
^ Mature content with lower level text demands

TITLE	LEVEL	GENRE	WORD COUNT	AUTHOR / SERIES	PUBLISHER / DISTRIBUTOR
Carnival	P	I	250+	Holidays and Festivals	Compass Point Books
Carnival Horse, The	K	RF	499	PM Plus Story Books	Rigby
Carnival King	T	HF	250+	High-Fliers	Pacific Learning
Carnival Time!	S	I	250+	WorldScapes	ETA/Cuisenaire
Carnival, The	F	RF	82	Oxford Reading Tree	Oxford University Press
Carnivals Around the World	I	I	116	Lighthouse	Rigby
Carnivorous Carnival, The	V	F	250+	Snicket, Lemony	Scholastic
Carnivorous Plants: Plants That Eat Insects	O	I	250+	Literacy by Design	Rigby
Carole: The Inside Story	R	RF	250+	Bryant, Bonnie	Skylark
Carolina Crow Girl	T	F	250+	Hobbs, Valerie	Puffin Books
Carolina Panthers, The	S	I	250+	Team Spirit	Norwood House Press
Carolina's Story: Sea Turtles Get Sick Too!	M	I	514	Rathmell, Donna	Sylvan Dell Publishing
Caroline's Treats	R	RF	1184	Leveled Readers	Houghton Mifflin Harcourt
Caroline's Treats	R	RF	1184	Leveled Readers/CA	Houghton Mifflin Harcourt
Caroline's Treats	R	RF	1184	Leveled Readers/TX	Houghton Mifflin Harcourt
Carpe Diem	Z+	RF	250+	Cornwell, Autumn	Square Fish
Carpenter	D	I	20	Work People Do	Lerner Publishing Group
Carpenters	M	I	250+	Community Helpers	Red Brick Learning
Carpenters	L	I	250+	Community Workers	Compass Point Books
Carpenters	M	I	477	Pull Ahead Books	Lerner Publishing Group
Carpenter's Tools, A	D	I	63	Nonfiction Set 3	Literacy Footprints
Carrie Measures Up	K	RF	927	Math Matters	Kane Press
Carrier-Based Jet Fighters: The F-14 Tomcats	V	I	250+	War Planes	Capstone Press
Carrot Seed, The	G	F	101	Krauss, Ruth	Harper & Row
Carrot Soup	H	TL	142	Literacy Tree	Rigby
Carrot, The	C	F	48	Leveled Readers Language Support	Houghton Mifflin Harcourt
Carrots	B	I	51	Pebble Books	Capstone Press
Carrots Don't Talk!	J	F	250+	Ready Readers	Pearson Learning Group
Carrots Grow Underground	K	I	152	How Fruits and Vegetables Grow	Capstone Press
Carrots, Peas, and Beans	F	RF	142	Sunshine	Wright Group/McGraw Hill
Carry it All!	C	I	51	Little Celebrations	Pearson Learning Group
Carry Me	WB	I	0	Big Cat	Pacific Learning
Carry Me	D	F	94	Red Rocket Readers	Flying Start Books
Carry Me!: Animal Babies on the Move	I	I	81	Stockdale, Susan	Peachtree
Carry on, Mr. Bowditch	Y	B	250+	Latham, Jean Lee	Houghton Mifflin Harcourt
Carry On: Verbs in Action	K	I	250+	Bookworms	Marshall Cavendish
Carrying	J	I	126	Small World	Lerner Publishing Group
Carrying Babies	D	I	98	Sails	Rigby
Carrying the Load	T	I	250+	Connectors	Pacific Learning
Carry-Out Food	D	RF	56	Tadpoles	Rigby
Cars	LB	I	24	Big Cat	Pacific Learning
Cars	Q	I	250+	Early Connections	Benchmark Education
Cars	B	I	30	Little Readers	Houghton Mifflin Harcourt
Cars	C	I	30	Little Readers	Houghton Mifflin Harcourt
Cars	F	I	72	Rockwell, Anne	Dutton Children's Books
Cars	LB	I	18	Transportation	Capstone Press
Cars of the Past	M	I	182	On Deck	Rigby
Cars!	F	I	56	Independent Readers Social Studies	Houghton Mifflin Harcourt
Cars, Trucks, and Motorcycles You Can Draw	R	I	1695	Ready, Set, Draw!	Millbrook Press
Cars: Rushing! Honking! Zooming!	L	F	217	Hubbel, Patricia	Marshall Cavendish
Cartier: Jacques Cartier in Search of the Northwest Passage	U	B	250+	Exploring the World	Compass Point Books

TITLE	LEVEL	GENRE	WORD COUNT	AUTHOR / SERIES	PUBLISHER / DISTRIBUTOR
Cartoonist, The	S	RF	250+	Byars, Betsy	Puffin Books
Carved in Stone: Borglum and Mount Rushmore	W	I	2997	Leveled Readers	Houghton Mifflin Harcourt
Cascarones Are for Fun	M	I	534	Reading Street	Pearson
Case for Jenny Archer, A	M	RF	250+	Conford, Ellen	Random House
Case of Capital Intrigue, The	S	RF	250+	Keene, Carolyn	Pocket Books
Case of Hermie the Missing Hamster, The	M	RF	250+	A Jigsaw Jones Mystery	Scholastic
Case of Jake's Escape, The	I	RF	962	Appleton-Smith, Laura	Flyleaf Publishing
Case of the Amazing Zelda, The: The Milo and Jazz Mysteries	L	RF	250+	Montgomery, Lewis B.	Kane Press
Case of the Captured Queen	S	RF	250+	Keene, Carolyn	Pocket Books
Case of the Carnival Cash, The	R	RF	250+	Power Up!	Steck-Vaughn
Case of the Cat's Meow, The	K	RF	250+	Bonsall, Crosby	HarperTrophy
Case of the Christmas Snowman, The	M	RF	250+	A Jigsaw Jones Mystery	Scholastic
Case of the Class Clown, The	M	RF	250+	A Jigsaw Jones Mystery	Scholastic
Case of the Clothing Culprit, The	R	F	2228	Leveled Readers	Houghton Mifflin Harcourt
Case of the Clothing Culprit, The	R	F	2228	Leveled Readers/CA	Houghton Mifflin Harcourt
Case of the Cool-Itch Kid, The	L	RF	250+	Giff, Patricia Reilly	Bantam Books
Case of the Dangerous Solution, The	S	RF	250+	Keene, Carolyn	Pocket Books
Case of the Detective in Disguise, The	M	RF	250+	A Jigsaw Jones Mystery	Scholastic
Case of the Diamond Dog Collar, The	S	RF	1385	Leveled Readers	Houghton Mifflin Harcourt
Case of the Diamond Dog Collar, The	S	RF	1385	Leveled Readers/CA	Houghton Mifflin Harcourt
Case of the Dirty Bird, The	O	RF	250+	Paulsen, Gary	Bantam Books
Case of the Disappearing Bones	N	RF	250+	Supa Doopers	Sundance
Case of the Disappearing Daughter, The	N	RF	3338	Damian Drooth Supersleuth	Stone Arch Books
Case of the Double Cross, The	K	RF	250+	Bonsall, Crosby	HarperTrophy
Case of the Dumb Bells, The	K	RF	250+	Bonsall, Crosby	HarperTrophy
Case of the Elevator Duck, The	M	RF	250+	Berends, Polly Berrien	Random House
Case of the Floating Crime, The	S	RF	250+	Keene, Carolyn	Pocket Books
Case of the Food Fight, The	M	RF	250+	A Jigsaw Jones Mystery	Scholastic
Case of the Furry Thing, The	G	RF	267	Ready Readers	Pearson Learning Group
Case of the Ghostwriter, The	M	RF	250+	A Jigsaw Jones Mystery	Scholastic
Case of the Groaning Ghost, The	M	RF	250+	A Jigsaw Jones Mystery	Scholastic
Case of the Haunted, Haunted House, The: The Milo and Jazz Mysteries	L	RF	250+	Montgomery, Lewis B.	Kane Press
Case of the Hungry Stranger, The	K	RF	1358	Bonsall, Crosby	HarperTrophy
Case of the Invisible Cat, The	Q	RF	250+	Parker, A. E.	Scholastic
Case of the July 4th Jinx, The: The Milo & Jazz Mysteries	L	RF	250+	Montgomery, Lewis B.	Kane Press
Case of the Left-Handed Lady, The: An Enola Holmes Mystery	U	HF	250+	Springer, Nancy	Puffin Books
Case of the Lion Dance	U	RF	250+	Yep, Laurence	HarperTrophy
Case of the Measled Cowboy, The	Q	F	250+	Erickson, John R.	Puffin Books
Case of the Midnight Rustler, The	Q	F	250+	Erickson, John R.	Puffin Books
Case of the Missing Cat, The	Q	F	250+	Erickson, John R.	Puffin Books
Case of the Missing Cookie, The	M	RF	873	Leveled Readers	Houghton Mifflin Harcourt
Case of the Missing Cookie, The	M	RF	873	Leveled Readers/CA	Houghton Mifflin Harcourt
Case of the Missing Cutthroats, The	S	RF	250+	George, Jean Craighead	HarperTrophy
Case of the Missing Dog Collar, The	S	F	1385	Leveled Readers	Houghton Mifflin Harcourt
Case of the Missing Fish, The	I	RF	119	Reading Street	Pearson
Case of the Missing Grass, The	O	F	1041	Leveled Readers	Houghton Mifflin Harcourt
Case of the Missing Grass, The	O	F	1041	Leveled Readers/CA	Houghton Mifflin Harcourt
Case of the Missing Grass, The	R	I	1310	Leveled Readers/TX	Houghton Mifflin Harcourt

* Collection of short stories   # Graphic text
^ Mature content with lower level text demands

TITLE	LEVEL	GENRE	WORD COUNT	AUTHOR / SERIES	PUBLISHER / DISTRIBUTOR
Case of the Missing Homework, The	H	RF	181	Literacy by Design	Rigby
Case of the Missing Iguana, The	P	RF	2374	Reading Street	Pearson
Case of the Missing Key, The	P	F	1198	Leveled Readers	Houghton Mifflin Harcourt
Case of the Missing Moose, The: The Milo & Jazz Mysteries	L	RF	250+	Montgomery, Lewis B.	Kane Press
Case of the Missing Snacks, The	J	RF	454	Sunshine	Wright Group/McGraw Hill
Case of the Mistaken Identity, The (The Brixton Brothers)	Q	RF	250+	Barnett, Mac	Simon & Schuster
Case of the Nervous Newsboy, The	N	RF	250+	Hildick, E. W.	Sundance
Case of the Poisoned Pig, The: The Milo and Jazz Mysteries	L	RF	250+	Montgomery, Lewis B.	Kane Press
Case of the Pop Star's Wedding, The	N	RF	250+	Damian Drooth Supersleuth	Stone Arch Books
Case of the Purloined Professor, The	S	F	250+	Cox, Judy	Marshall Cavendish
Case of the Purple Pool, The: The Milo & Jazz Mysteries	L	RF	6552	Montgomery, Lewis B.	Kane Press
Case of the Sabotaged School Play, The	R	RF	250+	Singer, Marilyn	Bantam Books
Case of the Scaredy Cats, The	K	RF	250+	Bonsall, Crosby	HarperTrophy
Case of the Secret Valentine, The	M	RF	250+	A Jigsaw Jones Mystery	Scholastic
Case of the Smelly Water	R	RF	250+	Reading Expeditions	National Geographic
Case of the Smiling Shark, The	N	RF	250+	High-Fliers	Pacific Learning
Case of the Snowboarding Superstar, The	M	RF	250+	A Jigsaw Jones Mystery	Scholastic
Case of the Spooky Sleepover, The	M	RF	250+	A Jigsaw Jones Mystery	Scholastic
Case of the Stinky Science Project, The	M	RF	250+	A Jigsaw Jones Mystery	Scholastic
Case of the Stinky Socks, The: The Milo and Jazz Mysteries	L	RF	250+	Montgomery, Lewis B.	Kane Press
Case of the Stolen Baseball Cards, The	M	RF	250+	A Jigsaw Jones Mystery	Scholastic
Case of the Talking Trousers, The	O	F	250+	High-Fliers	Pacific Learning
Case of the Twin Teddy Bears, The	S	RF	250+	Keene, Carolyn	Pocket Books
Case of the Two Masked Robbers, The	K	F	250+	Hoban, Lillian	HarperTrophy
Case of Vampire Vivian, The	L	RF	1406	Science Solves It!	Kane Press
Case That Time Forgot, The	S	RF	250+	Barrett, Tracy,	Henry Holt & Co.
Casey and the Nest	J	F	966	Georgie Giraffe	Literacy Footprints
Casey Jones	N	B	1875	On My Own Folklore	Lerner Publishing Group
Casey Little Yo-Yo Queen	O	RF	250+	Orca Young Readers	Orca Books
Casey's Art Project	J	RF	417	Springboard	Wright Group/McGraw Hill
Casey's Case	Q	RF	250+	Literacy 2000	Rigby
Casey's Code	Q	RF	250+	Riley, Gail Blasser	Steck-Vaughn
Casey's Lamb	D	I	75	Literacy by Design	Rigby
Casey's Lamb	D	I	75	On Our Way to English	Rigby
Cashiers	E	I	30	Work People Do	Lerner Publishing Group
Cass	WB	RF	0	The Rowland Reading Program Library	Rowland Reading Foundation
Cass Becomes a Star	L	B	250+	Literacy 2000	Rigby
Cass Is Ill	C	RF	27	The Rowland Reading Program Library	Rowland Reading Foundation
Cassandra's Sister	Y	HF	250+	Bennett, Veronica	Candlewick Press
Cassidy's Magic	S	F	250+	Literacy 2000	Rigby
Cassie Binegar	T	RF	250+	MacLachlan, Patricia	HarperTrophy
Cassie's Castle	L	RF	250+	Rigby Literacy	Rigby
Cassie's Word Quilt	I	RF	109	Ringgold, Faith	Alfred A. Knopf
Cast Your Vote	Q	RF	250+	Orbit Chapter Books	Pacific Learning
Casting Nets	I	I	107	Reading Street	Pearson
Castle	L	I	135	Bookworms	Marshall Cavendish
Castle	E	I	37	Exploring History & Geography	Rigby
Castle	X	I	250+	Eyewitness Books	DK Publishing

TITLE	LEVEL	GENRE	WORD COUNT	AUTHOR / SERIES	PUBLISHER / DISTRIBUTOR
Castle	X	I	250+	Macaulay, David	Scholastic
Castle Corona, The	U	F	250+	Creech, Sharon	HarperCollins
Castle in the Attic, The	R	F	250+	Winthrop, Elizabeth	Bantam Books
Castle of Llyr, The	W	F	250+	Alexander, Lloyd	Dell
Castle Under Attack	K	F	250+	DK Readers	DK Publishing
Castle, The	H	RF	286	Storyworlds	Heinemann
Castles	M	I	231	Big Cat	Pacific Learning
Castles	F	I	89	Nonfiction Set 4	Literacy Footprints
Castles	Q	I	250+	Tristars	Richard C. Owen
Castles	M	I	250+	Usborne Beginners	Usborne Publishing Ltd.
*Castles in the Air	O	TL	250+	Literacy by Design	Rigby
Castles: Towers, Dungeons, Moats, and More	U	I	250+	High Five Reading	Red Brick Learning
Cat	V	I	250+	Eyewitness Books	DK Publishing
Cat Among the Pigeons	X	HF	250+	Golding, Julia	Roaring Brook Press
Cat and Dog	WB	F	0	Big Cat	Pacific Learning
Cat and Dog	C	F	71	Learn to Read	Creative Teaching Press
Cat and Dog	B	RF	41	Leveled Readers	Houghton Mifflin Harcourt
Cat and Dog	C	F	31	Sails	Rigby
Cat and Dog at School	F	F	101	Learn to Read	Creative Teaching Press
Cat and Dog Go into Space, A	C	F	27	Bonnell, Kris	Reading Reading Books
Cat and Dog Go Shopping	G	F	127	Learn to Read	Creative Teaching Press
Cat and Dog Go To Town	C	F	32	Reading Street	Pearson
Cat and Dog Have Lunch, A	B	F	78	Bonnell, Kris	Reading Reading Books
Cat and Dog Make the Best, Biggest, Most Wonderful Cheese Sandwich	G	F	250+	Learn to Read	Creative Teaching Press
Cat and Dog Play Hide and Seek	B	F	27	Big Cat	Pacific Learning
Cat and Dog Talk	H	I	399	Sails	Rigby
Cat and Dog: The Super Snack	F	F	161	Learn to Read	Creative Teaching Press
Cat and Mouse	C	F	31	Brand New Readers	Candlewick Press
Cat and Mouse	B	F	75	PM Starters	Rigby
Cat and Mouse in a Haunted House	O	F	250+	Stilton, Geronimo	Scholastic
Cat and Rat	M	TL	250+	Young, Ed	Henry Holt & Co.
Cat and Rat Fall Out	J	TL	250+	Lighthouse	Rigby
Cat and the King, The	D	F	30	Literacy 2000	Rigby
Cat and the Mice, The	I	F	526	Book Bank	Wright Group/McGraw Hill
Cat at School?, A	D	RF	58	Independent Readers Social Studies	Houghton Mifflin Harcourt
Cat Ate My Gymsuit, The	U	RF	250+	Danziger, Paula	G.P. Putnam's Sons Books for Young Readers
Cat Bath	C	RF	41	Brand New Readers	Candlewick Press
Cat Burglar of Pethaven Drive, The	N	F	250+	Literacy 2000	Rigby
Cat Burglar, The	M	RF	250+	Krailing, Tessa	Barron's Educational
Cat Called Tim, A	L	RF	250+	New Way Literature	Steck-Vaughn
Cat Called, The	B	F	18	Ray's Readers	Outside the Box
Cat Came Back, The	I	TL	250+	Little Celebrations	Pearson Learning Group
Cat Came Back, The	B	TL	22	Ready Readers	Pearson Learning Group
Cat Chat	F	F	85	Ready Readers	Pearson Learning Group
Cat Concert	J	F	250+	Literacy 2000	Rigby
Cat Crazy	O	RF	250+	Baglio, Ben M.	Scholastic
Cat Culture	P	I	250+	Storyteller - Whispering Pines	Wright Group/McGraw Hill
*Cat Diaries	N	F	250+	Byars, Betsy, Duffey, Betsy & Myers, Laurie	Henry Holt & Co.
Cat for Keeps, A	L	RF	250+	Cambridge Reading	Pearson Learning Group
Cat for You, A: Caring for Your Cat	M	I	250+	Pet Care	Picture Window Books

* Collection of short stories   # Graphic text
^ Mature content with lower level text demands

TITLE	LEVEL	GENRE	WORD COUNT	AUTHOR / SERIES	PUBLISHER / DISTRIBUTOR
Cat Games	E	F	229	Ziefert, Harriet	Puffin Books
Cat Goes Fiddle-i-fee	F	TL	333	Galdone, Paul	Houghton Mifflin Harcourt
Cat in the Bag	E	RF	85	Rookie Reader	Children's Press
Cat in the Hat	J	F	250+	Seuss, Dr.	Random House
Cat in the Tree, A	F	F	79	Oxford Reading Tree	Oxford University Press
Cat Named Ben, A	D	F	131	Leveled Readers	Houghton Mifflin Harcourt
Cat Named Ben, A	D	F	131	Leveled Readers/CA	Houghton Mifflin Harcourt
Cat Named Ben, A	D	F	131	Leveled Readers/TX	Houghton Mifflin Harcourt
Cat on the Chimney, The: Solving Problems with Technology	S	I	250+	Drew, David	Rigby
Cat on the Mat	B	F	37	Wildsmith, Brian	Oxford University Press
*Cat on the Mat Is Flat, The	I	F	250+	Griffiths, Andy	Square Fish
Cat on the Move	A	F	30	Phonics and Friends	Hampton Brown
Cat on the Roof	H	RF	250+	Story Box	Wright Group/McGraw Hill
Cat O'Nine Tails	Y	HF	250+	Golding, Julia	Roaring Brook Press
Cat Out of the Bag	O	F	250+	High-Fliers	Pacific Learning
Cat Party	B	F	37	Sails	Rigby
Cat Prints	C	RF	25	Pair-It Books	Steck-Vaughn
Cat Running	U	RF	250+	Snyder, Zilpha Keatley	Bantam Books
Cat Show, The	C	F	43	Sails	Rigby
Cat Snacks	D	F	36	Potato Chip Books	American Reading Company
Cat Tails	D	I	40	Books for Young Learners	Richard C. Owen
Cat Talk	N	I	250+	Orbit Chapter Books	Pacific Learning
Cat That Broke the Rules, The	G	F	192	Ready Readers	Pearson Learning Group
Cat That Sat, The	D	RF	66	Start to Read	School Zone
Cat Traps	D	F	93	Coxe, Molly	Random House
Cat Tricks	E	RF	41	Potato Chip Books	American Reading Company
Cat Walk	R	F	250+	Stolz, Mary	Bantam Books
Cat Wants to Play, The	C	F	31	Coulton, Mia	Maryruth Books
Cat Whispers	H	RF	250+	Rigby Literacy	Rigby
Cat Who Couldn't Meow, The	J	RF	575	Rappaport, Doreen	January Books
Cat Who Loved Red, The	D	F	63	Salem, Lynn; Stewart, Josie	Continental Press
Cat Who Went To Heaven, The	S	F	250+	Coatsworth, Elizabeth	Aladdin
Cat Who Wore a Pot on Her Head, The	N	F	250+	Slepian, Jan; Seidler, Ann	Scholastic
Cat with No Tail, The	I	TL	137	Books for Young Learners	Richard C. Owen
Cat with the Yellow Star: Coming of Age in Terezin, The	Z	B	250+	Rubin, Susan Goldman	Holiday House
Cat!	S	I	250+	Kroll, Virginia L.	Dawn Publications
Cat, The	A	I	40	InfoTrek	ETA/Cuisenaire
Cat, The	A	I	28	Leveled Readers Science	Houghton Mifflin Harcourt
Cat, The	A	I	42	Little Books for Early Readers	University of Maine
Cat, The	E	RF	46	Potato Chip Books	American Reading Company
Cat, The	C	RF	23	Smart Start	Rigby
Catalyst	Z	RF	250+	Anderson, Laurie Halse	Penguin Group
Catastrophe!	Z	I	250+	Boldprint	Steck-Vaughn
Catastrophic Storms	T	I	250+	Navigators Science Series	Benchmark Education
Catch It!	E	F	73	Pair-It Turn and Learn	Steck-Vaughn
Catch It!	A	RF	25	Rigby Star	Rigby
Catch It, Marvin	E	RF	61	Windmill Books	Rigby
Catch Me If You Can	L	RF	250+	Go Girl!	Feiwel and Friends
Catch Me If You Can!	F	F	180	Green Light Readers	Harcourt
Catch Me If You Can!: The Roadrunner	M	I	250+	Sunshine	Wright Group/McGraw Hill
Catch Me, Cat	C	F	131	Sails	Rigby
Catch That Ball!	F	RF	114	Reading Street	Pearson

TITLE	LEVEL	GENRE	WORD COUNT	AUTHOR / SERIES	PUBLISHER / DISTRIBUTOR
Catch That Bus!	F	RF	119	Reading Street	Pearson
Catch That Cat!	LB	RF	16	Rookie Readers	Children's Press
Catch That Frog	E	F	131	Reading Unlimited	Pearson Learning Group
Catch That Goat!	I	F	293	Alakija, Polly	Barefoot Books
Catch That Pass!	Q	RF	250+	Christopher, Matt	Little Brown and Company
Catch the Cookie	J	F	250+	Little Celebrations	Pearson Learning Group
Catcher With a Glass Arm	P	RF	250+	Christopher, Matt	Little Brown and Company
Catcher's Mask, The	M	RF	250+	Christopher, Matt	Little Brown and Company
Catching	B	I	35	Teacher's Choice Series	Pearson Learning Group
Catching Sunlight: A Book About Leaves	M	I	250+	Growing Things	Picture Window Books
Catching Air!	S	RF	250+	PM Chapter Books	Rigby
Catching Cam's Balloon	L	RF	250+	Scooters	ETA/Cuisenaire
Catching Fire	Z	F	250+	Collins, Suzanne	Scholastic
Catching Some Respect	T	RF	3009	Leveled Readers	Houghton Mifflin Harcourt
Catching Spring	O	RF	250+	Orca Young Readers	Orca Books
*Catching the Sun	M	TL	250+	Take Two Books	Wright Group/McGraw Hill
Catching the Velociraptor: Dinosaur Cove	N	F	250+	Stone, Rex	Scholastic
Catching the Wind	N	I	250+	iOpeners	Pearson Learning Group
Catching Waves	R	RF	250+	Christopher, Matt	Little Brown and Company
Caterpillar Can't Wait!	I	F	241	Early Explorers	Benchmark Education
Caterpillars	M	I	114	Bookshop	Mondo Publishing
Caterpillars	P	I	250+	Mini Pets	Steck-Vaughn
Caterpillars	N	I	250+	Minibeasts	Franklin Watts
Caterpillars	F	I	54	Pebble Books	Capstone Press
Caterpillar's Adventure	F	F	69	Story Box	Wright Group/McGraw Hill
Catherine the Counter	E	RF	86	Sunshine	Wright Group/McGraw Hill
Catherine, Called Birdy	X	HF	250+	Cushman, Karen	Clarion
Catnapper, The	J	F	398	Leveled Readers	Houghton Mifflin Harcourt
Catnapper, The	J	F	398	Leveled Readers/CA	Houghton Mifflin Harcourt
Catnapper, The	N	I	323	Leveled Readers/TX	Houghton Mifflin Harcourt
Cats	D	I	43	All About Pets	Red Brick Learning
Cats	A	I	21	Big Cat	Pacific Learning
Cats	O	I	1981	Early Bird Nature Books	Lerner Publishing Group
Cats	K	I	338	Nonfiction Set 9	Literacy Footprints
Cats	J	I	250+	PM Animal Facts: Orange	Rigby
Cats	LB	I	14	Readlings	American Reading Company
Cats	A	I	24	Vocabulary Readers	Houghton Mifflin Harcourt
Cats	C	I	45	Williams, Deborah	Kaeden Books
Cats	I	I	137	Wonder World	Wright Group/McGraw Hill
Cats and Dogs	N	I	250+	Quick Draw	Kingfisher
Cats and Kids	F	I	136	Silly Millies	Millbrook Press
Cats and Kittens	F	I	44	Reading Unlimited	Pearson Learning Group
Cats and Mice	H	F	51	Gelman, Rita	Scholastic
*Cats and Other Stories	J	F	250+	Story Steps	Rigby
Cats' Burglar, The	K	F	250+	Parish, Peggy	Hearst
Cat's Day, A	B	I	23	Twig	Wright Group/McGraw Hill
Cat's Diary	M	F	250+	Sails	Rigby
Cat's Dream, A	A	F	20	Handprints A	Educators Publishing Service
Cats Everywhere	F	RF	51	Books for Young Learners	Richard C. Owen
Cat's Eye Corner	T	F	250+	Griggs, Terry	Raincoast Books
Cats Have Kittens	M	I	250+	Animals and Their Young	Compass Point Books
Cats in Krasinski Square, The	V	HF	250+	Hesse, Karen	Scholastic
Cat's Meow, The	O	F	250+	Soto, Gary	Scholastic

* Collection of short stories   # Graphic text
^ Mature content with lower level text demands

TITLE	LEVEL	GENRE	WORD COUNT	AUTHOR / SERIES	PUBLISHER / DISTRIBUTOR
Cats of Roxville Station, The	S	F	250+	George, Jean Craighead	Dutton Children's Books
Cats of the Clan: Warriors	U	F	250+	Hunter, Erin	HarperCollins
Cats of the Night	K	RF	379	Book Bank	Wright Group/McGraw Hill
Cats on the Farm	H	I	71	Pebble Books	Red Brick Learning
Cat's Party	F	F	39	Sunshine	Wright Group/McGraw Hill
Cat's Surprise Party	I	F	376	Leveled Readers	Houghton Mifflin Harcourt
Cat's Trip	G	F	158	Ready Readers	Pearson Learning Group
Cat's Whiskers, A	I	I	250+	Windows on Literacy	National Geographic
Cats You Can Draw	R	I	1568	Ready, Set, Draw!	Millbrook Press
Cats!	D	RF	50	Rookie Readers	Children's Press
Cats, Cats, Cats	Q	I	250+	Literacy 2000	Rigby
Cats, Cats, Cats	B	I	14	Pair-It Books	Steck-Vaughn
Cats, Cats, Cats	G	RF	217	Story Basket	Wright Group/McGraw Hill
Catten, The	K	F	769	Jellybeans	Rigby
Cattle	L	I	250+	PM Animal Facts: Purple	Rigby
Cattle Drive!	V	I	2940	Vocabulary Readers	Houghton Mifflin Harcourt
Cattle Drive!	V	I	2940	Vocabulary Readers/CA	Houghton Mifflin Harcourt
Cattle Drive!	V	I	2940	Vocabulary Readers/TX	Houghton Mifflin Harcourt
Catwings	N	F	250+	Le Guin, Ursula K.	Scholastic
Catwings Return	N	F	250+	Le Guin, Ursula K.	Scholastic
Caty the Caterpillar	H	RF	175	Leveled Readers	Houghton Mifflin Harcourt
Caty the Caterpillar	H	RF	175	Leveled Readers/CA	Houghton Mifflin Harcourt
Caty the Caterpillar	H	RF	175	Leveled Readers/TX	Houghton Mifflin Harcourt
Caught by the Sea	N	RF	250+	Keating, Rosemary	Pacific Learning
Caught in a Flash	P	I	250+	Orbit Chapter Books	Pacific Learning
Caught in the Storm	H	RF	250+	Home Connection Collection	Rigby
Caught Out	S	I	250+	WorldScapes	ETA/Cuisenaire
Causes of the Revolution	S	I	250+	Primary Source Readers	Teacher Created Materials
Cave Bear	N	I	250+	Extinct Monsters	Capstone Press
Cave Crawlers	O	I	250+	Landform Adventurers	Raintree
Cave Creatures	Q	I	872	Independent Readers Science	Houghton Mifflin Harcourt
Cave Dwellers	O	I	2005	Take Two Books	Wright Group/McGraw Hill
Cave Explorers, The	N	RF	250+	Windows on Literacy	National Geographic
Cave In	S	HF	250+	Duey, Kathleen; Bale, Karen A.	Simon & Schuster
^Cave of the Bookworms, The	T	F	250+	Dahl, Michael	Stone Arch Books
^Cave That Shouldn't Collapse, The	Q	RF	250+	Brezenoff, Steve/Field Trip Mysteries	Stone Arch Books
Cave, The	C	RF	67	Book Bank	Wright Group/McGraw Hill
Cave, The	T	F	250+	Book Blazers	ETA/Cuisenaire
Caves	M	I	250+	Discovery World	Rigby
Caves	R	I	250+	Early Bird Earth Science	Lerner Publishing Group
Caves	N	I	250+	Earthforms	Capstone Press
Caves	K	I	360	Red Rocket Readers	Flying Start Books
Caves	D	I	80	Sails	Rigby
Caves	G	I	79	Seedlings	Continental Press
Caves	I	I	155	Storyteller	Wright Group/McGraw Hill
Caves	P	I	1719	Take Two Books	Wright Group/McGraw Hill
Caves	G	I	210	The Rowland Reading Program Library	Rowland Reading Foundation
Caves	R	I	250+	The Wonders of Our World	Crabtree
Caves	O	I	250+	Windows on Literacy	National Geographic
Caves	R	I	250+	Wood, Jenny	Scholastic
Caves and Caverns	O	I	250+	Gibbons, Gail	Harcourt Trade
Caves: Wonders of Nature	L	I	250+	Bookworms	Marshall Cavendish

C

TITLE	LEVEL	GENRE	WORD COUNT	AUTHOR / SERIES	PUBLISHER / DISTRIBUTOR
Caving Adventures	S	I	250+	Dangerous Adventures	Red Brick Learning
Cay, The	V	HF	250+	Taylor, Theodore	Avon Books
CD and the Giant Cat	V	SF	250+	Action Packs	Rigby
Cecil the Caterpillar	E	F	130	Lighthouse	Rigby
Cecil the Caterpillar	E	F	130	Lighthouse	Ginn & Co.
Ceiling of Stars, A	U	RF	250+	Creel, Ann Howard	Pleasant Company
Celebrate Art	M	I	228	Twig	Wright Group/McGraw Hill
Celebrate the 50 States!	N	I	250+	Leedy, Loreen	Holiday House
Celebrating	J	I	125	Small World	Lerner Publishing Group
Celebrating Chanukah: Eight Nights	J	I	188	Learn to Read	Creative Teaching Press
Celebrating Chinese New Year: Nick's New Year	J	I	142	Learn to Read	Creative Teaching Press
Celebrating Christmas: Christmas Decorations	J	I	165	Learn to Read	Creative Teaching Press
Celebrating Cinco de Mayo: Fiesta Time!	J	I	41	Learn to Read	Creative Teaching Press
Celebrating Easter: The Easter Egg Hunt	J	I	166	Learn to Read	Creative Teaching Press
Celebrating Father's Day: Father's Day is for Special People	F	RF	115	Learn to Read	Creative Teaching Press
Celebrating Martin Luther King, Jr. Day: Dreaming of Change	J	I	152	Learn to Read	Creative Teaching Press
Celebrating Mother's Day: Mom's Memory Box	E	F	100	Learn to Read	Creative Teaching Press
Celebrating Patriotic Holidays: Honoring America	H	I	175	Learn to Read	Creative Teaching Press
Celebrating President's Day	H	I	181	Learn to Read	Creative Teaching Press
Celebrating Thanksgiving: Giving Thanks	F	I	145	Learn to Read	Creative Teaching Press
Celebrating the New Year	K	I	234	Take Two Books	Wright Group/McGraw Hill
Celebrating Valentine's Day: My Special Valentines	F	RF	137	Learn to Read	Creative Teaching Press
Celebrations	G	I	37	Berger, Samantha; Moreton, Daniel	Scholastic
Celebrations	G	I	107	Storyteller-Moon Rising	Wright Group/McGraw Hill
Celebrations	L	I	199	Yellow Umbrella Books	Capstone Press
Celebrations Around the World	J	I	205	Early Connections	Benchmark Education
Celebrations!	L	I	250+	Trackers	Pacific Learning
Celebrities That Care	S	I	250+	High-Fliers	Pacific Learning
Celebrity	X	I	250+	Boldprint	Steck-Vaughn
Celery Stalks at Midnight, The	R	F	250+	Howe, James	Atheneum Books
Celeste's Harlem Renaissance	X	HF	250+	Tate, Eleanora	Little Brown and Company
Celestial Globe, The	X	F	250+	Rutkoski, Marie	Farrar, Straus, & Giroux
Celia	K	RF	182	Leveled Readers	Houghton Mifflin Harcourt
Celia and Ali	I	RF	137	Leveled Readers Language Support	Houghton Mifflin Harcourt
Celia Cruz: The Queen of Salsa Music	P	B	250+	In Step Readers	Rigby
Celia's Gift	M	RF	231	On Our Way To English	Rigby
Cell Scientists: Discovering How Cells Work	Y	B	250+	Science Readers	Teacher Created Materials
Cells	R	I	1649	Leveled Readers Science	Houghton Mifflin Harcourt
Cells	Y	I	1831	Science Support Readers	Houghton Mifflin Harcourt
Cells	J	I	96	Wonder World	Wright Group/McGraw Hill
Cement Tent	G	F	358	First Start	Troll Associates
Center Court Sting	R	RF	250+	Christopher, Matt	Little Brown and Company
Center Field	Z+	RF	250+	Lipsyte, Robert	HarperCollins
*Centerburg Tales: More Adventures of Homer Price	Q	RF	250+	McCloskey, Robert	Puffin Books
Centerfield Ballhawk	M	RF	250+	Christopher, Matt	Little Brown and Company
Centipede's New Shoes	D	F	78	Reading Safari	Mondo Publishing
Central Coast Missions in California	X	I	5221	Exploring California Missions	Lerner Publishing Group

TITLE	LEVEL	GENRE	WORD COUNT	AUTHOR / SERIES	PUBLISHER / DISTRIBUTOR
^Central Intelligence Agency, The: Stopping Terrorists	S	I	250+	Line of Duty	Capstone Press
Centuries of Horsepower: Horses at Work	T	I	250+	Explore More	Wright Group/McGraw Hill
Cephalopods	N	I	250+	Pacific Literacy	Pacific Learning
Cervantes, A Life of Adventure	W	B	2165	Vocabulary Readers	Houghton Mifflin Harcourt
Cervantes, A Life of Adventure	W	B	2165	Vocabulary Readers/CA	Houghton Mifflin Harcourt
Cervantes, A Life of Adventure	W	B	2165	Vocabulary Readers/TX	Houghton Mifflin Harcourt
Cesar Chavez	V	B	250+	Amazing Ameicans	Wright Group/McGraw Hill
Cesar Chavez	N	B	262	Biography	Benchmark Education
Cesar Chavez	Q	B	250+	Early Biographies	Compass Point Books
Cesar Chavez	M	B	262	Famous Americans	Capstone Press
Cesar Chavez	M	B	295	Independent Readers Social Studies	Houghton Mifflin Harcourt
Cesar Chavez	W	B	250+	Just the Facts Biographies	Lerner Publishing Group
Cesar Chavez	Y	B	2023	Leveled Readers	Houghton Mifflin Harcourt
Cesar Chavez	O	B	1890	On My Own Biography	Lerner Publishing Group
Cesar Chavez	P	B	262	Photo-Illustrated Biographies	Red Brick Learning
Cesar Chavez	Y	B	250+	Rodriguez, Consuelo	Chelsea House
Cesar Chavez	M	B	250+	Rookie Biographies	Children's Press
#Cesar Chavez : Fighting for Farmworkers	T	B	250+	Edge	Hampton Brown
^Cesar Chavez: Fighter for Workers' Rights	T	B	250+	Hameray Biography Series	Hameray Publishing Group
Cesar Chavez: Fighter in the Field	T	B	250+	High Five Reading	Red Brick Learning
#Cesar Chavez: Fighting for Farmworkers	T	B	250+	Graphic Library	Capstone Press
Cesar Chavez: Labor Leader	N	B	250+	Beginning Biographies	Pearson Learning Group
Cesar Chavez: The Farm Workers' Friend	N	B	250+	Literacy by Design	Rigby
Cesar Chavez: The Farm Workers' Friend	N	B	250+	On Our Way to English	Rigby
Cezar's Pollution Solution	P	RF	1270	Leveled Readers	Houghton Mifflin Harcourt
Cezar's Pollution Solution	P	RF	1270	Leveled Readers/CA	Houghton Mifflin Harcourt
Cezar's Pollution Solution	P	RF	1270	Leveled Readers/TX	Houghton Mifflin Harcourt
Chad and the Big Egg	F	F	204	Leveled Readers	Houghton Mifflin Harcourt
Chain of Giving, The	K	TL	250+	Rigby Rocket	Rigby
Chains	Z	HF	250+	Anderson, Laurie Halse	Scholastic
Chair For My Mother, A	M	RF	250+	Williams, Vera B.	Scholastic
Chairs, Chairs, Chairs!	E	I	70	Rookie Readers	Children's Press
Chalk	WB	F	0	Thomson, Bill	Marshall Cavendish
Chalk Talk	C	I	69	Storyteller-First Snow	Wright Group/McGraw Hill
Chalkbox Kid, The	N	RF	250+	Bulla, Clyde Robert	Random House
Challenge at Second Base	Q	RF	250+	Christopher, Matt	Little Brown and Company
Challenge of Change, The	U	I	250+	WorldScapes	ETA/Cuisenaire
Challenger Disaster, The	U	I	250+	Cornerstones of Freedom	Children's Press
Challenger, The: The Explosion on Liftoff	R	I	250+	Disaster!	Capstone Press
Challenges of Storm Chasing, The	S	I	1877	Reading Street	Pearson
Chameleon	Z+	RF	250+	Smith, Charles R. Jr.	Candlewick Press
Chameleon Wore Chartreuse, The: A Chet Gecko Mystery	Q	F	250+	Hale, Bruce	Harcourt, Inc.
Chameleon, Chameleon	J	RF	136	Cowley, Joy	Scholastic
Chameleons	D	RF	73	Reading Street	Pearson
Chameleons	K	I	167	Reptiles	Capstone Press
Chameleons	I	I	289	Sails	Rigby
Chameleons	L	I	201	Twig	Wright Group/McGraw Hill
Chameleons Are Cool	M	I	250+	Read and Wonder	Candlewick Press
Chameleon's Colors	L	F	250+	Tashiro, Chisato	Scholastic
Chameleons of the Rain Forest	N	I	250+	Pacific Literacy	Pacific Learning
Chameleons' Rainbow	M	F	250+	Use Your Imagination	Steck-Vaughn

C

TITLE	LEVEL	GENRE	WORD COUNT	AUTHOR / SERIES	PUBLISHER / DISTRIBUTOR
Champ	Q	RF	250+	Jones, Marcia	Scholastic
Champ	M	HF	1015	Leveled Readers	Houghton Mifflin Harcourt
Champ	M	HF	1015	Leveled Readers/CA	Houghton Mifflin Harcourt
Champ	M	HF	1015	Leveled Readers/TX	Houghton Mifflin Harcourt
Champ	I	RF	274	Story Box	Wright Group/McGraw Hill
Champ of Hoover Dam	M	HF	869	Leveled Readers	Houghton Mifflin Harcourt
Champ of Hoover Dam	M	HF	869	Leveled Readers/CA	Houghton Mifflin Harcourt
Champ of Hoover Dam	M	HF	869	Leveled Readers/TX	Houghton Mifflin Harcourt
Champion Billy Mills	P	B	725	Leveled Readers	Houghton Mifflin Harcourt
Champion Crackups: More Than 140 Sensational Sports Jokes	P	F	250+	Sidesplitters	Kingfisher
Champion of Change, A	S	B	1341	Leveled Readers	Houghton Mifflin Harcourt
Champion of Change, A	S	B	1341	Leveled Readers/CA	Houghton Mifflin Harcourt
Champion of Change, A	S	B	1341	Leveled Readers/TX	Houghton Mifflin Harcourt
Champion of Children, The: The Story of Janusz Korczak	S	B	250+	Bogacki, Tomek	Farrar, Straus, & Giroux
Champions	C	I	13	Twig	Wright Group/McGraw Hill
Champions of the Wilderness	V	B	250+	Earth Heroes	Dawn Publications
Champions on Ice	S	I	1880	Leveled Readers	Houghton Mifflin Harcourt
Champions on Ice	S	I	1880	Leveled Readers/CA	Houghton Mifflin Harcourt
Champions on Ice	S	I	1880	Leveled Readers/TX	Houghton Mifflin Harcourt
Champ's Story: Dogs Get Cancer Too!	P	RF	250+	North, Sherry	Sylvan Dell Publishing
Chan Li's Pot of Gold	T	HF	2705	Leveled Readers	Houghton Mifflin Harcourt
Chan Li's Pot of Gold	T	HF	2705	Leveled Readers/CA	Houghton Mifflin Harcourt
Chan Li's Pot of Gold	T	HF	2705	Leveled Readers/TX	Houghton Mifflin Harcourt
Chance to Dance, The	Q	B	250+	WorldScapes	ETA/Cuisenaire
Chancey of the Maury River	S	F	250+	Amateau, Gigi	Candlewick Press
Chancy and the Grand Rascal	R	F	250+	Fleischman, Sid	Beech Tree Books
Change for Zoe, A	K	RF	250+	Home Connection Collection	Rigby
Change in Plans, A	L	F	250+	On Our Way to English	Rigby
Change in the Community	P	I	250+	PM Extensions	Rigby
Change the Locks	S	RF	250+	French, Simon	Scholastic
Changes	WB	I	0	Book Bank	Wright Group/McGraw Hill
Changes All Around Us	M	I	250+	Windows on Literacy	National Geographic
Changes Around Us	J	I	176	Instant Readers	Harcourt School Publishers
Changes for Addy	Q	HF	250+	The American Girls Collection	Pleasant Company
Changes for Addy: A Winter Story	Q	HF	250+	The American Girls Collection	Pleasant Company
Changes for Felicity: A Winter Story	Q	HF	250+	The American Girls Collection	Pleasant Company
Changes for Josefina: A Winter Story	Q	HF	250+	The American Girls Collection	Pleasant Company
Changes for Kirsten: A Winter Story	Q	HF	250+	The American Girls Collection	Pleasant Company
Changes for Molly: A Winter Story	Q	HF	250+	The American Girls Collection	Pleasant Company
Changes for Samantha: A Winter Story	Q	HF	250+	The American Girls Collection	Pleasant Company
Changes in Materials	J	I	441	Science Support Readers	Houghton Mifflin Harcourt
Changes in Seasons	I	I	250+	Phonics Readers Plus	Steck-Vaughn
Changes, Changes	WB	I	0	Hutchins, Pat	Aladdin
Change-Up: Mystery at the World Series	V	RF	250+	Feinstein, John	Yearling Books
Chang-Ho Visits America	J	RF	596	InfoTrek	ETA/Cuisenaire
Changing and Growing	H	I	315	Sails	Rigby
Changing Caterpillar, The	G	I	56	Books for Young Learners	Richard C. Owen
Changing Chameleon, The	H	RF	147	Domine Readers	Pearson Publishing Group
Changing Colors	B	I	16	Pair-It Books	Steck-Vaughn
Changing Colors	M	I	247	Vocabulary Readers	Houghton Mifflin Harcourt
Changing Cultures	P	I	250+	PM Extensions	Rigby
Changing Earth	T	I	250+	The News	Richard C. Owen

* Collection of short stories   # Graphic text
^ Mature content with lower level text demands

TITLE	LEVEL	GENRE	WORD COUNT	AUTHOR / SERIES	PUBLISHER / DISTRIBUTOR
Changing Earth, The	Q	I	250+	Exploring the Earth	Capstone Press
Changing Earth, The	P	I	250+	iOpeners	Pearson Learning Group
Changing Earth, The	N	I	201	Windows on Literacy	National Geographic
Changing Land, The	I	I	64	Pacific Literacy	Pacific Learning
#Changing Places	T	RF	2220	Dominoes starter	Oxford University Press
Changing Schools	F	RF	53	City Stories	Rigby
Changing Seasons	S	I	1936	Leveled Readers Science	Houghton Mifflin Harcourt
Changing Seasons	I	I	106	Shutterbug Books	Steck-Vaughn
Changing Shape	I	I	143	Rigby Literacy	Rigby
Changing Shape	J	I	200	Rigby Star Quest	Rigby
Changing Shores	O	I	250+	iOpeners	Pearson Learning Group
Changing the Past	Y	SF	3387	Leveled Readers	Houghton Mifflin Harcourt
Changing the Past	Y	SF	3387	Leveled Readers/CA	Houghton Mifflin Harcourt
Changing the Past	Y	SF	3387	Leveled Readers/TX	Houghton Mifflin Harcourt
Changing the Rules	S	RF	1908	Leveled Readers	Houghton Mifflin Harcourt
Changing Times	Q	RF	250+	Treasured Horses Collection	Scholastic
Changing to Survive: Bird Adaptations	S	I	2536	Reading Street	Pearson
Changing Weather	G	I	145	Early Connections	Benchmark Education
*Changing Woman and Her Sisters: Stories of Goddesses from Around the World	V	TL	250+	Tchana, Katrin Hyman	Holiday House
Chang's Paper Pony	L	RF	250+	Coerr, Eleanor	HarperTrophy
Chano	H	RF	124	Literacy 2000	Rigby
Chaos in the Kitchen	K	F	250+	Home Connection Collection	Rigby
Characteristics of Matter	U	I	2036	Science Support Readers	Houghton Mifflin Harcourt
Charge of the Triceratops: Dinosaur Cove	N	F	250+	Stone, Rex	Scholastic
Charged Up: The Story of Electricity	Q	I	250+	Science Works	Picture Window Books
Chariot Race, The	Q	HF	1676	Take Two Books	Wright Group/McGraw Hill
Charlemagne	X	B	2629	Leveled Readers Language Support	Houghton Mifflin Harcourt
Charlemagne and the Holy Roman Empire	Y	B	3083	Leveled Readers Social Studies	Houghton Mifflin Harcourt
Charles	C	RF	48	Learn to Read	Creative Teaching Press
Charles Darwin	W	HF	250+	Gibbons, Alan	Kingfisher
Charles Darwin and the Beagle Adventure	Z	B	250+	Wood, A.J. & Twist, Clinton	Candlewick Press
Charles Darwin and the Mystery of Mysteries	Z	B	250+	Eldredge, Niles, & Pearson, Susan	Roaring Brook Press
#Charles Darwin and the Theory of Evolution	V	B	250+	Inventions and Discovery	Capstone Press
Charles Dickens and the Street Children of London	Z	B	250+	Warren, Andrea	Houghton Mifflin Harcourt
Charles Drew: Doctor	N	B	250+	Beginning Biographies	Pearson Learning Group
Charles Lindbergh	P	B	250+	Early Biographies	Compass Point Books
Charles Lindbergh	P	B	250+	Photo-Illustrated Biographies	Red Brick Learning
Charles M. Schulz	L	B	186	First Biographies	Red Brick Learning
Charley Skedaddle	U	HF	250+	Beatty, Patricia	Troll Associates
Charlie	L	F	250+	Literacy 2000	Rigby
Charlie and the Chocolate Factory	R	F	250+	Dahl, Roald	Bantam Books
Charlie and the Great Glass Elevator	R	F	250+	Dahl, Roald	Bantam Books
Charlie Best	J	F	250+	Voyages	SRA/McGraw Hill
Charlie Bone and the Beast	U	F	250+	Nimmo, Jenny	Orchard Books
Charlie Bone and the Blue Boa	U	F	250+	Nimmo, Jenny	Orchard Books
Charlie Bone and the Castle of Mirrors	U	F	250+	Nimmo, Jenny	Orchard Books
Charlie Bone and the Hidden King	U	F	250+	Nimmo, Jenny	Orchard Books
Charlie Bone and the Invisible Boy	U	F	250+	Nimmo, Jenny	Orchard Books
Charlie Bone and the Shadow	U	F	250+	Nimmo, Jenny	Orchard Books
Charlie Bone and the Shadow of Badlock	U	F	250+	Nimmo, Jenny	Orchard Books

C

* Collection of short stories   # Graphic text
^ Mature content with lower level text demands

TITLE	LEVEL	GENRE	WORD COUNT	AUTHOR / SERIES	PUBLISHER / DISTRIBUTOR
Charlie Bone and the Time Twister	U	F	250+	Nimmo, Jenny	Orchard Books
Charlie Bone and the Wilderness Wolf	U	F	250+	Nimmo, Jenny	Orchard Books
Charlie Cook's Favorite Book	L	F	250+	Donaldson, Julia	Dial/Penguin
Charlie Is a Chicken	P	RF	250+	Smith, Jane Denitz	HarperTrophy
Charlie Malarkey and the Singing Moose	R	F	250+	Kennedy, William & Brendan	Puffin Books
Charlie Needs a Cloak	I	HF	187	DePaola, Tomie	Prentice-Hall
Charlie Small 1: Gorilla City	R	F	250+	Small, Charlie	David Fickling Books
Charlie Small 2: Perfumed Pirates of Perfidy	R	F	250+	Small, Charlie	David Fickling Books
Charlie Small 3: The Puppet Master	R	F	250+	Small, Charlie	David Fickling Books
Charlie Small 4: The Daredevil Desperados of Destiny	R	F	250+	Small, Charlie	David Fickling Books
Charlie Strong and His Favourite Song	G	RF	120	Breakthrough	Longman/Bow
Charlie Takes a Shot	W	RF	2507	Leveled Readers	Houghton Mifflin Harcourt
Charlie the Bridesmaid	K	RF	250+	Rigby Literacy	Rigby
Charlie the Bridesmaid	K	RF	250+	Rigby Star	Rigby
Charlie, the Pancake Pirate	M	F	250+	Wonder World	Wright Group/McGraw Hill
Charlie's Bad Hair Day	E	F	120	Harrison, Pat	Blueberry Hill Books
Charlie's Black Hen	E	RF	89	Seedlings	Continental Press
Charlie's Boat	E	RF	109	Red Rocket Readers	Flying Start Books
Charlie's Great Race	K	RF	867	PM Plus Story Books	Rigby
Charlie's P.E. Gear	E	RF	102	Lighthouse	Rigby
Charlie's PE Kit	E	RF	114	Lighthouse	Ginn & Co.
Charlie's Story	W	RF	250+	Friel, Maeve	Peachtree
Charlie's Visit	I	RF	315	Red Rocket Readers	Flying Start Books
Charlotte Bobcats, The	S	I	250+	Team Spirit	Norwood House Press
Charlotte the Sunflower Fairy: Rainbow Magic	L	F	250+	Meadows, Daisy	Scholastic
Charlotte's Web	R	F	250+	White, E. B.	HarperTrophy
Charlotte's Web Page	P	RF	250+	Action Packs	Rigby
^Charmed	Z+	RF	250+	Orca Soundings	Orca Books
Charters of Freedom	Y	I	2738	Independent Readers Social Studies	Houghton Mifflin Harcourt
Charters of Freedom, The	T	I	250+	Literacy by Design	Rigby
Charting Your Course	T	I	250+	iOpeners	Pearson Learning Group
Charts and Graphs	F	I	123	Shutterbug Books	Steck-Vaughn
Chase, The	D	I	52	Bonnell, Kris	Reading Reading Books
Chase, The	C	RF	36	Brand New Readers	Candlewick Press
Chase, The	F	F	85	Oxford Reading Tree	Oxford University Press
Chasing Boys	Y	RF	250+	Tayleur, Karen	Walker & Company
Chasing Degas	N	HF	250+	Montanari, Eva	Harry N. Abrams
Chasing Lincoln's Killer	Z	HF	250+	Swanson, James	Scholastic
Chasing Normal	U	RF	250+	Papademetriou, Lisa	Hyperion
Chasing Orion	X	HF	250+	Lasky, Kathryn	Candlewick Press
Chasing Redbird	V	RF	250+	Creech, Sharon	HarperCollins
Chasing Storms	R	I	1373	Leveled Readers	Houghton Mifflin Harcourt
Chasing Storms	R	I	1373	Leveled Readers/CA	Houghton Mifflin Harcourt
Chasing the Shadow	O	F	250+	The Adventures of Sam X	Stone Arch Books
Chasing the Train	P	HF	768	Leveled Readers	Houghton Mifflin Harcourt
Chasing Tornadoes	P	I	250+	Gold, Becky	Pearson Learning Group
Chasing Tornadoes!	P	I	250+	Rigby Literacy	Rigby
Chasing Vermeer	T	RF	250+	Balliett, Blue	Scholastic
^Chat Room	W	RF	250+	Orca Currents	Orca Books
Chato and the Party Animals	Q	F	250+	Soto, Gary	Puffin Books
Chattering Chipmunks	K	I	341	Pull Ahead Books	Lerner Publishing Group
Cheap Jeep	J	RF	324	Dominie Readers	Pearson Learning Group

* Collection of short stories   # Graphic text
^ Mature content with lower level text demands

TITLE	LEVEL	GENRE	WORD COUNT	AUTHOR / SERIES	PUBLISHER / DISTRIBUTOR
Cheaper, Faster, Better	W	I	3253	Reading Street	Pearson
Cheat, The	W	RF	250+	Koss, Amy Goldman	Speak
Check it Out!	B	I	24	Little Celebrations	Pearson Learning Group
Check It Out!	M	RF	250+	Social Studies Connects	Kane/Miller Book Publishers
Check it Out!: Reading, Finding, Helping	I	RF	194	Hubbell, Patricia	Marshall Cavendish
Check Out the Library	N	I	839	Vocabulary Readers	Houghton Mifflin Harcourt
Check Out the Library	N	I	839	Vocabulary Readers/CA	Houghton Mifflin Harcourt
Check Out the Library	N	I	839	Vocabulary Readers/TX	Houghton Mifflin Harcourt
Checkout!	P	I	250+	Bookweb	Rigby
Checks and Balances: A Look at the Powers of Government	S	I	1522	Searchlight Books	Lerner Publishing Group
Cheer All-Stars: Best of the Best	T	I	250+	Cheerleading	Capstone Press
Cheer Basics: Rules to Cheer By	S	I	250+	Cheerleading	Capstone Press
Cheer Challenge	P	RF	250+	Maddox, Jake	Stone Arch Books
Cheer Competitions:Impressing the Judges	T	I	250+	Cheerleading	Capstone Press
Cheer Essentials: Uniforms and Equipment	S	I	250+	Cheerleading	Capstone Press
Cheer Gear	M	I	157	Cheerleading	Capstone Press
Cheer Professionals: Cheer as a Career	T	I	250+	Cheerleading	Capstone Press
Cheer Skills	M	I	198	Cheerleading	Capstone Press
Cheer Skills: Beginning Tumbling and Stunting	S	I	250+	Cheerleading	Capstone Press
Cheer Spirit: Revving Up the Crowd	S	I	250+	Cheerleading	Capstone Press
Cheer Squad: Building Spirit and Getting Along	S	I	250+	Cheerleading	Capstone Press
Cheer Tryouts: Making the Cut	S	I	250+	Cheerleading	Capstone Press
Cheerful King, The	K	F	351	Little Books	Sadlier-Oxford
Cheerleaders in Action	M	I	186	Cheerleading	Capstone Press
Cheerleaders, The	D	F	36	Reading Safari	Mondo Publishing
Cheerleading	F	I	56	On Deck	Rigby
Cheerleading for Fun!	S	I	250+	Activities for Fun	Compass Point Books
Cheers and Chants	M	I	130	Cheerleading	Capstone Press
Cheers for the Cheetahs	N	RF	889	Reading Street	Pearson
Cheers, Chants, and Signs: Getting the Crowd Going	T	I	250+	Cheerleading	Capstone Press
Cheese, Please?	C	RF	62	Story Steps	Rigby
Cheesecake Cupcakes and Other Cake Recipes	S	I	250+	Fun Food for Cool Cooks	Capstone Press
Cheese-Colored Camper, A	O	F	250+	Stilton, Geronimo	Scholastic
Cheetah Conservation	R	I	250+	Storyteller-Whispering Pines	Wright Group/McGraw Hill
Cheetah Cubs	L	I	250+	All Aboard Science Reader	Grosset & Dunlap
Cheetahs	I	I	139	African Animals	Capstone Press
Cheetahs	O	I	2085	Early Bird Nature Books	Lerner Publishing Group
Cheetahs	U	I	5682	Nature Watch	Lerner Publishing Group
Cheetahs	G	RF	140	Seedlings	Continental Press
Chefs	J	I	170	Bookworms	Marshall Cavendish
Chefs	L	I	250+	Community Workers	Compass Point Books
Chefs	J	I	239	On Deck	Rigby
Chemical Changes	X	I	250+	Reading Expeditions	National Geographic
Chemical Changes	V	I	983	Science Support Readers	Houghton Mifflin Harcourt
Chemical Compounds	Y	I	1404	Science Support Readers	Houghton Mifflin Harcourt
Chemical Secret	X	RF	10150	Oxford Bookworms Library	Oxford University Press
Chemistry in Medicine	W	I	250+	Navigators Science Series	Benchmark Education
Chemistry in the Kitchen	W	I	250+	Navigators Science Series	Benchmark Education
Chen's Christmas Tree	E	RF	166	Developing Books	Pioneer Valley
Cherokee Indians, The	P	I	250+	Native Peoples	Red Brick Learning
Cherokee Little People, The	I	TL	250+	Rigby Star	Rigby

TITLE	LEVEL	GENRE	WORD COUNT	AUTHOR / SERIES	PUBLISHER / DISTRIBUTOR
Cherokee Little People, The: A Native American Tale	I	TL	250+	Rigby Literacy	Rigby
Cherokee, The	R	I	250+	First Reports	Compass Point Books
Cherokee, The: Native Basket Weavers	R	I	250+	America's First Peoples	Capstone Press
Cherokees, The	T	I	4165	Native American Histoies	Lerner Publishing Group
Cherries and Cherry Pits	M	RF	250+	Williams, Vera B.	Houghton Mifflin Harcourt
Cherries, The	H	F	286	Leveled Literacy Intervention/ Green System	Heinemann
Cherry Blossom Cat	J	F	250+	Storyworlds	Heinemann
Cherry Blossom Festival, The	S	I	250+	WorldScapes	ETA/Cuisenaire
Cherry Blossoms Everywhere	M	I	370	Independent Readers Social Studies	Houghton Mifflin Harcourt
Cherry Tree, The	R	F	1684	Leveled Readers	Houghton Mifflin Harcourt
Cherry Tree, The	R	F	1684	Leveled Readers/CA	Houghton Mifflin Harcourt
Cherry Tree, The	R	F	1684	Leveled Readers/TX	Houghton Mifflin Harcourt
Chesapeake Bay	R	I	1192	Leveled Readers Social Studies	Houghton Mifflin Harcourt
Chesapeake Bay Wetlands	P	I	1082	Time for Kids	Teacher Created Materials
Cheshire Cheese Cat, The: A Dickens of a Tale	W	F	250+	Deedy, Carmen Agra & Wright, Randall	Peachtree
Chess Rumble	V	RF	250+	Neri, G.	Lee & Low Books Inc.
Chester	I	RF	397	Red Rocket Readers	Flying Start Books
Chester A. Arthur	U	B	250+	Profiles of the Presidents	Compass Point Books
Chester A. Arthur: Twenty-first President	R	B	250+	Getting to Know the U.S. Presidents	Children's Press
Chester Cricket's New Home	S	F	250+	Selden, George	Bantam Books
Chester Cricket's Pigeon Ride	S	F	250+	Selden, George	Bantam Books
Chester Greenwood's Big Idea	N	I	642	Leveled Literacy Intervention/ Blue System	Heinemann
Chester the Wizard	M	F	250+	Reading Unlimited	Pearson Learning Group
Chester The Worldly Pig	M	F	250+	Peet, Bill	Houghton Mifflin Harcourt
Chester's Good Idea	M	B	250+	Leveled Readers Language Support	Houghton Mifflin Harcourt
Chester's Way	M	F	250+	Henkes, Kevin	Scholastic
Chestnut	O	HF	250+	McGeorge, Constance W.	Peachtree
Chevrolet Corvette	O	I	250+	Fast Cars	Capstone Press
Chew, Chew, Chew	C	RF	24	Literacy 2000	Rigby
Cheyenne, The	P	I	250+	A New True Book	Children's Press
Cheyenne, The	R	I	250+	First Reports	Compass Point Books
Cheyenne, The: People of the Central Plains	S	I	250+	Theme Sets	National Geographic
Chicago American Giants, The	S	I	1058	Reading Street	Pearson
Chicago Bears, The	S	I	250+	Team Spirit	Norwood House Press
Chicago Blackhawks, The	S	I	4930	Team Spirit	Norwood House Press
Chicago Bulls, The	S	I	250+	Team Spirit	Norwood House Press
Chicago Cubs, The	S	I	5128	Team Spirit	Norwood House Press
Chicago Cubs, The (Revised Edition)	S	I	250+	Team Spirit	Norwood House Press
Chicago Defender and the Great Migration, The	Y	I	2694	Reading Street	Pearson
Chicago Fire, The	P	I	250+	Gutner, Howard	Scholastic
Chicago White Sox, The	S	I	4630	Team Spirit	Norwood House Press
Chicago White Sox, The (Revised Edition)	S	I	250+	Team Spirit	Norwood House Press
Chicago Winds	K	I	173	Evangeline Nicholas Collection	Wright Group/McGraw Hill
Chick and the Duckling, The	D	F	112	Ginsburg, Mirra	Macmillan
Chick Catches Dinner	J	F	451	Sun Sprouts	ETA/Cuisenaire
Chick Challenge	O	RF	250+	Baglio, Ben M.	Scholastic
Chick That Wouldn't Hatch, The	F	F	173	Green Light Readers	Harcourt
Chicken	M	I	250+	Life Cycles	Creative Teaching Press

* Collection of short stories   # Graphic text
^ Mature content with lower level text demands

TITLE	LEVEL	GENRE	WORD COUNT	AUTHOR / SERIES	PUBLISHER / DISTRIBUTOR
Chicken	B	I	29	Zoozoo-Animal World	Cavallo Publishing
Chicken and Egg Chores	C	RF	27	Little Books for Early Readers	University of Maine
Chicken and the Egg, The	E	I	68	Sun Sprouts	ETA/Cuisenaire
Chicken Boy	W	RF	250+	Dowell, Frances O'Roark	Aladdin Paperbacks
Chicken Butt!	K	F	144	Perl, Erica S.	Harry N. Abrams
Chicken Feed	E	RF	67	Joy Readers	Pearson Learning Group
Chicken Foot Farm	X	RF	250+	Estevis, Anne	Pinata Publishing
Chicken for Dinner	C	RF	27	Story Box	Wright Group/McGraw Hill
Chicken in the Middle of the Road	J	RF	250+	Bookshop	Mondo Publishing
Chicken Licken	I	TL	698	Big Cat	Pacific Learning
Chicken Licken	H	TL	171	Rigby Star	Rigby
Chicken Licken	I	TL	346	Sunshine	Wright Group/McGraw Hill
Chicken Licken	H	TL	233	Supersonics	Rigby
Chicken Little	K	TL	250+	Emberley, Rebecca & Ed	Roaring Brook Press
Chicken Little	E	TL	256	Leveled Literacy Intervention/ Blue System	Heinemann
Chicken Little	I	TL	258	My 1st Classic Story	Picture Window Books
Chicken Little	I	TL	250+	PM Traditional Tales-Orange	Rigby
Chicken Little	E	TL	107	Sunshine	Wright Group/McGraw Hill
Chicken Little	L	TL	587	Traditional Tales & More	Rigby
Chicken Pox	K	I	250+	Health Matters	Capstone Press
Chicken Pox	H	RF	220	Little Readers	Houghton Mifflin Harcourt
Chicken School	E	F	82	Joy Starters	Pearson Learning Group
Chicken Soup	B	I	38	Fitros, Pamela	Kaeden Books
Chicken Soup	K	F	250+	Van Leeuwen, Jean	Harry N. Abrams
Chicken Soup with Rice	M	F	310	Sendak, Maurice	HarperCollins
Chicken Sunday	N	RF	250+	Polacco, Patricia	Scholastic
Chicken Surprise	I	RF	347	PM Stars Bridge Books	Rigby
Chickens	D	I	23	Books for Young Learners	Richard C. Owen
Chickens	G	I	105	Bookshop	Mondo Publishing
Chickens	F	I	99	Farm Animals	Lerner Publishing Group
Chickens	B	I	24	Pebble Books	Capstone Press
Chickens	L	I	250+	PM Animal Facts: Purple	Rigby
Chickens and Chicks	B	I	31	Animal Families	Lerner Publishing Group
Chickens and the Fox, The	D	F	50	Coulton, Mia	Maryruth Books
Chickens Are Here!, The	D	I	50	Vocabulary Readers	Houghton Mifflin Harcourt
Chickens Aren't the Only Ones	L	I	250+	Heller, Ruth	Scholastic
Chickens Have Chicks	M	I	250+	Animals and Their Young	Compass Point Books
Chicken's Life, A	F	I	135	Watch It Grow	Heinemann Library
Chickens on the Farm	G	I	59	Pebble Books	Capstone Press
Chickens on the Farm	F	I	68	Vocabulary Readers	Houghton Mifflin Harcourt
Chickens on the Move	K	RF	250+	Math Matters	Kane Press
Chickens On Vacation	G	F	169	Seedlings	Continental Press
Chicken's Ride	G	RF	199	Adams, Lorraine	Eaglecrest Books
Chickens to the Rescue	I	F	159	Himmelman, John	Henry Holt & Co.
Chickerella	N	TL	250+	Auch, Mary Jane and Herm	Holiday House
Chick-in-a-Box	K	RF	250+	Voyages	SRA/McGraw Hill
Chick's Adventure	I	F	363	Sun Sprouts	ETA/Cuisenaire
Chicks are Hatching, The	D	F	81	Gilbert the Pig	Pioneer Valley
Chicks Don't Say Quack	D	F	86	Sun Sprouts	ETA/Cuisenaire
Chicks Versus Bunnies (Hop)	M	F	250+	Paul, Cinco & Daurio, Ken	Little Brown and Company
Chick's Walk	A	F	14	Story Box	Wright Group/McGraw Hill
Chico	D	RF	86	Literacy by Design	Rigby
Chico	D	RF	86	On Our Way to English	Rigby

TITLE	LEVEL	GENRE	WORD COUNT	AUTHOR / SERIES	PUBLISHER / DISTRIBUTOR
Chief Great Raven	N	TL	250+	Orbit Double Takes	Pacific Learning
Chief Joseph	S	B	3585	History Maker Bios	Lerner Publishing Group
Chief Joseph	Y	B	2199	Leveled Readers	Houghton Mifflin Harcourt
Chief Joseph of the Nez Percé	P	B	250+	Photo-Illustrated Biographies	Red Brick Learning
Chief Justice John Marshall	U	B	250+	Bookshop	Mondo Publishing
Chief Rhino to the Rescue	K	F	250+	Lloyd, Sam	Henry Holt & Co.
Chief Seattle	T	B	250+	Amazing Americans	Wright Group/McGraw Hill
^Chief Sitting Bull: Brave Freedom Fighter	S	B	250+	Hameray Biography Series	Hameray Publishing Group
Chief Washakie	U	B	2073	Leveled Readers	Houghton Mifflin Harcourt
Chief Washakie	U	B	2073	Leveled Readers/CA	Houghton Mifflin Harcourt
Chief Washakie	U	B	2073	Leveled Readers/TX	Houghton Mifflin Harcourt
Chihuahua Chase, The	Q	RF	250+	Cannon, A.E.	Farrar, Straus, & Giroux
Chihuahuas	R	I	250+	All About Dogs	Capstone Press
Chihuahuas	I	I	158	Dogs	Capstone Press
Chihuahuas Are the Best!	Q	I	1378	The Best Dogs Ever	Lerner Publishing Group
Child Called "It", A	Z+	B	250+	Pelzer, Dave	Health Communications
Child in Prison Camp, A	X	HF	250+	Takashima, Shizuye	Tundra Books
Child of the Owl	W	RF	250+	Yep, Laurence	HarperTrophy
Child of the Wolves	U	RF	250+	Hall, Elizabeth	Bantam Books
Childhood in Pre-War Japan	V	I	1832	Reading Street	Pearson
Children	C	I	45	Pebble Books	Capstone Press
Children	F	I	67	People	Capstone Press
Children Around the World	M	I	250+	People, Spaces & Places	Rand McNally
Children Around the World	P	I	250+	Rigby Focus	Rigby
Children as Young Scientists	K	I	393	Early Connections	Benchmark Education
Children at Play	F	I	101	Little Red Readers	Sundance
Children of Ancient Greece	P	I	250+	Rosen Real Readers	Rosen Publishing Group
*Children of Christmas: Stories for the Season	R	RF	250+	Rylant, Cynthia	Orchard Books
Children of Clay: A Family of Pueblo Potters	S	I	250+	Swentzell, Rina	Lerner Publishing Group
Children of Green Knowe, The	T	F	250+	Boston, L. M.	Harcourt Trade
Children of Sierra Leone, The	J	I	142	Books For Young Learners	Richard C. Owen
Children of the Dust Bowl	Y	I	250+	Stanley, Jerry	Crown Publishers
*Children of the Earth and Sky	P	I	250+	Krensky, Stephen	Scholastic
Children of the Fire	P	HF	250+	Robinet, Harriette	Aladdin
Children of the Great Depression	X	I	250+	Freedman, Russell	Sandpiper Books
Children of the Holocaust	Z	I	250+	The Holocaust	Compass Point Books
Children of the Longhouse	S	HF	250+	Bruchac, Joseph	Penguin Group
Children of the New Forest, The	T	HF	6605	Oxford Bookworms Library	Oxford University Press
Children of the River	X	RF	250+	Crew, Linda	Bantam Books
Children of the Sierra Madre, The	U	I	250+	Staub, Frank	Carolrhoda Books
Children of the Wild West	X	I	250+	Freedman, Russell	Clarion
Children's Clothing of the 1800's	S	I	250+	Historic Communities	Crabtree
Children's Farm, The	I	I	390	Explorations	Okapi Educational Materials
Children's Farm, The	I	I	390	Explorations	Eleanor Curtain Publishing
Children's Forest, The	Q	I	250+	Explorer Books-Pathfinder	National Geographic
Children's Forest, The	P	I	250+	Explorer Books-Pioneer	National Geographic
Child's Day, A	T	I	250+	Historic Communities	Crabtree
Child's Day, A	C	RF	34	Sunshine	Wright Group/McGraw Hill
Child's Life in Korea, A	M	I	638	Reading Street	Pearson
Child's Portrait of Shakespeare, A	Q	B	250+	Burdett, Lois	Firefly Books
Childtimes: A Three-Generation Memoir	X	B	250+	Greenfield, Eloise; Little, Lessie Jones	HarperTrophy
Chile	P	I	1769	Country Explorers	Lerner Publishing Group
Chile	Q	I	250+	First Reports: Countries	Compass Point Books

* Collection of short stories   # Graphic text
^ Mature content with lower level text demands

TITLE	LEVEL	GENRE	WORD COUNT	AUTHOR / SERIES	PUBLISHER / DISTRIBUTOR
Chile Peppers	E	I	115	On Our Way to English	Rigby
Chili for Lindy	J	RF	250+	Leveled Readers Language Support	Houghton Mifflin Harcourt
Chili Pepper Pinata, The	H	RF	257	Story Box	Wright Group/McGraw Hill
*Ch'i-lin Purse, The: A Collection of Ancient Chinese Stories	T	TL	250+	Edge	Hampton Brown
^Chill	U	RF	250+	Orca Soundings	Orca Books
Chill Wind	Z	RF	250+	McDonald, Janet	Farrar, Straus, & Giroux
Chimp Communities	U	I	1618	Leveled Readers Science	Houghton Mifflin Harcourt
Chimp Math: Learning About Time From a Baby Chimpanzee	Q	I	250+	Nagda, Ann Whitehead & Bickel, Cindy	Henry Holt & Co.
Chimpanzees	O	I	2307	Early Bird Nature Books	Lerner Publishing Group
Chimpanzees	S	I	1605	Leveled Readers Science	Houghton Mifflin Harcourt
Chimpanzees	H	I	86	Rain Forest Animals	Capstone Press
Chimpanzees	I	I	200	Sails	Rigby
Chimpanzees	M	I	250+	The Wild World of Animals	Capstone Press
Chimpanzees of Happytown, The	M	F	250+	Andreae, Giles	Scholastic
Chimps Don't Wear Glasses	J	F	183	Numeroff, Laura	Scholastic
China	O	I	2373	A Ticket to ...	Carolrhoda Books
China	P	I	250+	A True Book	Children's Press
China	O	I	250+	Countries of the World	Red Brick Learning
China	Q	I	250+	First Reports: Countries	Compass Point Books
China	P	I	250+	Many Cultures, One World	Capstone Press
China	W	I	250+	Primary Source Readers	Teacher Created Materials
China	LB	I	14	Readlings	American Reading Company
China	W	I	250+	Theme Sets	National Geographic
China ABCs: A Book About the People and Places of China	Q	I	250+	Country ABCs	Picture Window Books
China in Colors	N	I	250+	World of Colors	Capstone Press
China Teacup, The	M	F	250+	Voyages	SRA/McGraw Hill
China, America, and Me	T	I	2309	Reading Street	Pearson
China: A Question and Answer Book	P	I	250+	Questions and Answers: Countries	Capstone Press
China: Civilizations Past to Present	S	I	250+	Reading Expeditions	National Geographic
China: Everyday Kids Now and Then	S	HF	250+	Reading Expeditions	National Geographic
China: Now and Then	T	I	1387	Reading Street	Pearson
China: The Culture	T	I	250+	Kalman, Bobbie	Crabtree
China: The Land	T	I	250+	Kalman, Bobbie	Crabtree
China: The People	T	I	250+	Kalman, Bobbie	Crabtree
Chinampa, The	K	RF	405	Take Two Books	Wright Group/McGraw Hill
China's Amazing Buildings	T	I	498	Vocabulary Readers	Houghton Mifflin Harcourt
China's Bravest Girl: The Legend of Hua Mu Lan	O	TL	250+	Chin, Charlie	Children's Press
China's Gifts to the World	Q	I	1352	Reading Street	Pearson
China's Huang River	S	I	2036	Independent Readers Social Studies	Houghton Mifflin Harcourt
Chinchillas	S	I	250+	Keeping Unusual Pets	Heinemann Library
Chinese Americans: An Imigration History	W	I	2660	Reading Street	Pearson
Chinese Civilization	Y	I	250+	Reading Expeditions	National Geographic
Chinese Foods and Recipes	P	I	250+	Rosen Real Readers	Rosen Publishing Group
Chinese Immigrants 1850-1900	U	I	250+	Coming to America	Capstone Press
^Chinese Immigrants in America: An Interactive History Adventure	V	HF	250+	You Choose Books	Capstone Press
Chinese Immigration	V	I	250+	Theme Sets	National Geographic
Chinese Kites	LB	I	15	Twig	Wright Group/McGraw Hill

TITLE	LEVEL	GENRE	WORD COUNT	AUTHOR / SERIES	PUBLISHER / DISTRIBUTOR
Chinese New Year	K	I	264	Avenues	Hampton Brown
Chinese New Year	J	I	176	Holidays and Celebrations	Capstone Press
Chinese New Year	O	I	250+	Holidays and Festivals	Compass Point Books
Chinese New Year	J	I	130	Holidays and Festivals	Heinemann Library
Chinese New Year	N	I	1679	On My Own Holidays	Lerner Publishing Group
Chinese New Year	D	I	33	Pacific Literacy	Pacific Learning
Chinese New Year	N	I	812	Springboard	Wright Group/McGraw Hill
Chinese New Year	F	I	79	Vocabulary Readers	Houghton Mifflin Harcourt
Chinese New Year, The	J	TL	250+	Troughton, Joanna	Pearson Learning Group
Chinese, The: Life in China's Golden Age	V	I	2381	Ancient Civilizations	Millbrook Press
Chin's Lunch	G	RF	188	On Our Way to English	Rigby
Chipmunk at Hollow Tree Lane	K	F	250+	Sherrow, Victoria	Scholastic
Chipmunks Do What Chipmunks Do	I	F	138	Leveled Readers/TX	Houghton Mifflin Harcourt
Chipmunk's New Home	I	F	300	Leveled Readers	Houghton Mifflin Harcourt
Chipmunk's New Home	I	F	300	Leveled Readers/CA	Houghton Mifflin Harcourt
Chipmunk's New Home	I	F	300	Leveled Readers/TX	Houghton Mifflin Harcourt
Chip's Dad	K	RF	250+	Rigby Literacy	Rigby
Chisholm Trail, The	V	I	250+	Cornerstones of Freedom	Children's Press
Chloe Doe	Z+	RF	250+	Phillips, Suzanne	Little Brown and Company
Chloe the Chameleon	F	F	250+	Warren, Celia	Scholastic
Chloe the Topaz Fairy: Rainbow Magic	L	F	250+	Meadows, Daisy	Scholastic
Chocolate	O	I	250+	Tristars	Richard C. Owen
Chocolate	N	I	250+	What's For Lunch?	Children's Press
Chocolate	L	I	191	Windows on Literacy	National Geographic
Chocolate by Hershey: A Story about Milton S. Hershey	R	B	250+	Burford, Betty	Carolrhoda Books
Chocolate Cake, The	J	RF	250+	PM Plus Story Books	Rigby
Chocolate Cake, The	B	RF	23	Story Box	Wright Group/McGraw Hill
Chocolate Chill-Out Cake and Other Yummy Desserts	R	I	250+	Kids Dish	Picture Window Books
Chocolate Chip Cookies	LB	I	12	Preiss, Leah Palmer	Henry Holt & Co.
Chocolate Chip Cookies	B	I	32	Ready Readers	Pearson Learning Group
Chocolate Factory, The	G	I	153	Red Rocket Readers	Flying Start Books
Chocolate Fever	O	F	250+	Smith, Robert	Bantam Books
Chocolate Flier, The	R	I	250+	Action Packs	Rigby
Chocolate Maker's Secrets, The	N	I	250+	Sun Sprouts	ETA/Cuisenaire
Chocolate Touch, The	N	F	250+	Catling, Patrick Skene	Bantam Books
Chocolate Trail, The	N	I	250+	Rigby Focus	Rigby
Chocolate Tree, The	N	TL	2178	On My Own Folklore	Millbrook Press
Chocolate!	P	I	250+	Action Packs	Rigby
Chocolate, Chocolate, Chocolate	E	RF	106	Visions	Wright Group/McGraw Hill
Chocolate...Yum!	M	I	579	Springboard	Wright Group/McGraw Hill
Chocolate-Chip Muffins	J	RF	204	Sunshine	Wright Group/McGraw Hill
Chocolate-Covered Contest, The	S	RF	250+	Keene, Carolyn	Pocket Books
Choctaws, The	T	I	3586	Native American Histoies	Lerner Publishing Group
Choice for Sarah, A	K	RF	250+	PM Plus Story Books	Rigby
Chomp	L	I	250+	Berger, Melvin	Scholastic
Chomp	W	RF	250+	Hiaasen, Carl	Alfred A. Knopf
Choo Choo Clickety-Clack!	K	I	286	Mayo, Margaret	Carolrhoda Books
Chook, Chook	E	RF	42	Sunshine	Wright Group/McGraw Hill
Choose Me!	H	F	204	Reading Corners	Pearson Learning Group
Choosing a Kitten	I	RF	394	Adams, Lorraine	Eaglecrest Books
Choosing a Pet	A	I	31	Leveled Readers	Houghton Mifflin Harcourt
Choosing a Pet	A	I	31	Leveled Readers/CA	Houghton Mifflin Harcourt

* Collection of short stories   # Graphic text
^ Mature content with lower level text demands

TITLE	LEVEL	GENRE	WORD COUNT	AUTHOR / SERIES	PUBLISHER / DISTRIBUTOR
Choosing a Puppy	E	RF	158	PM Extensions-Yellow	Rigby
Choosing a Trip	L	I	672	Sun Sprouts	ETA/Cuisenaire
Choosing Eyeglasses with Mrs. Koutris	J	I	299	Our Neighborhood	Children's Press
Choosing Up Sides	V	RF	250+	Ritter, John H.	Puffin Books
Chop and Pop	F	I	99	Reading Safari	Mondo Publishing
Chop, Simmer, Season	LB	I	21	Brandenburg, Alexa	Harcourt Brace
Choppers	M	I	250+	Horsepower	Capstone Press
Choppers	W	I	5275	Motor Mania	Lerner Publishing Group
Chopsticks	H	RF	222	On Our Way to English	Rigby
Chores	D	RF	50	Windows on Literacy	National Geographic
Chorus	F	I	77	On Deck	Rigby
Chorus of Frogs, A	U	I	250+	Wild Life Series	London Town Press
Chosen One, The	Z	RF	250+	Williams, Carol Lynch	Macmillan
Chosen: (House of Night)	Z	F	250+	Cast, P. C. & Kristin	St. Martin's Griffin
Chow Chows	Q	I	250+	All About Dogs	Capstone Press
^Chris Jericho	T	B	250+	Stars of Pro Wrestling	Capstone Press
Chris Paul	P	B	2241	Amazing Athletes	Lerner Publishing Group
^Christa McAuliffe	N	B	250+	Explore Space!	Capstone Press
Christa McAuliffe: Teacher in Space	W	B	250+	Naden, Corinne J.; Blue, Rose	Millbrook Press
Christian the Lion	M	I	250+	Bourke, Anthony & Rendall, John	Henry Holt & Co.
Christianity	Y	I	250+	World Religions	Compass Point Books
Christina's Ghost	R	F	250+	Wright, Betty Ren	Bantam Books
Christmas	H	I	129	All About Winter	Capstone Press
Christmas	Q	I	250+	Celebrate!	Capstone Press
Christmas	F	I	106	Fiesta Holiday Series	Pearson Learning Group
Christmas	J	I	133	Holidays and Celebrations	Capstone Press
Christmas	M	I	250+	Holidays and Celebrations	Picture Window Books
Christmas	O	I	250+	Holidays and Festivals	Compass Point Books
Christmas	K	I	122	Holidays and Festivals	Heinemann Library
Christmas	P	I	250+	Let's See	Compass Point Books
Christmas	LB	I	16	Smart Start	Rigby
Christmas Around the World	N	I	1699	On My Own Holidays	Lerner Publishing Group
Christmas at Wapos Bay	T	RF	250+	From Many Peoples	Fitzhenry & Whiteside
Christmas Carol, A	U	F	250+	Dickens, Charles	Scholastic
Christmas Carol, A	U	F	10385	Oxford Bookworms Library	Oxford University Press
Christmas Catastrophe	O	F	250+	Stilton, Geronimo	Scholastic
Christmas Eve Blizzard	M	RF	784	Vlahakis, Andrea	Sylvan Dell Publishing
Christmas Fun: A Spot-It Challenge	J	I	250+	Spot It	Capstone Press
Christmas in Many Cultures	I	I	125	Life Around the World	Capstone Press
Christmas in Prague	W	RF	4720	Oxford Bookworms Library	Oxford University Press
Christmas in the Big Woods	J	HF	250+	Wilder, Laura Ingalls	HarperCollins
Christmas in the Trenches	T	HF	250+	McCutcheon, John	Peachtree
Christmas Santa Almost Missed, The	G	F	158	First Start	Troll Associates
Christmas Shopping	E	RF	48	Literacy 2000	Rigby
Christmas Spurs, The	R	RF	250+	Wallace, Bill	Bantam Books
Christmas Surprise	G	RF	145	First Start	Troll Associates
Christmas Tale, A	O	F	250+	Stilton, Geronimo	Scholastic
Christmas Toy Factory, The	O	F	250+	Stilton, Geronimo	Scholastic
Christmas Tree Farm	N	RF	250+	Purmell, Ann	Holiday House
Christmas Tree, The	F	RF	163	PM Story Books	Rigby
Christmas: Season of Peace and Joy	M	I	250+	Holidays and Culture	Capstone Press
Christmas: Why We Celebrate It the Way We Do	P	I	250+	Hintz, Martin & Kate	Red Brick Learning
Christopher Columbus	M	B	250+	First Biographies	Red Brick Learning
Christopher Columbus	S	B	3543	History Maker Bios	Lerner Publishing Group

C

* Collection of short stories   # Graphic text
^ Mature content with lower level text demands

TITLE	LEVEL	GENRE	WORD COUNT	AUTHOR / SERIES	PUBLISHER / DISTRIBUTOR
Christopher Columbus	T	B	250+	In Their Own Words	Scholastic
Christopher Columbus	S	B	250+	Primary Source Readers	Teacher Created Materials
Christopher Columbus	M	B	250+	Step into Reading	Random House
Christopher Columbus: A Great Explorer	O	B	250+	Greene, Carol	Children's Press
#Christopher Columbus: Famous Explorer	R	B	250+	Graphic Library	Capstone Press
Christopher Reeve: A Life Worth Living	Q	B	1518	Gear Up!	Wright Group/McGraw Hill
Christopher Reeve: Still a Hero	R	B	250+	Leveled Readers Language Support	Houghton Mifflin Harcourt
Christophe's Story	Q	RF	250+	Cornwell, Nicki	Frances Lincoln
Christy's First Dive	J	RF	250+	Leveled Readers Language Support	Houghton Mifflin Harcourt
Chronicles of Harris Burdick, The	V	F	250+	Van Allsburg, Chris	Houghton Mifflin Harcourt
Chrysanthemum	M	F	250+	Henkes, Kevin	Scholastic
Chu Ju's House	W	RF	250+	Whelan, Gloria	Scholastic
Chug the Tractor	F	F	203	PM Story Books	Rigby
Chug, Chug, Chug!	F	RF	137	Reading Street	Pearson
Chumash, The	T	I	4147	Native American Histoies	Lerner Publishing Group
Chunk of Cheese, A	F	F	215	Leveled Readers	Houghton Mifflin Harcourt
Chunk of Cheese, A	F	F	215	Leveled Readers/CA	Houghton Mifflin Harcourt
Chunk of Cheese, A	F	F	215	Leveled Readers/TX	Houghton Mifflin Harcourt
Church	LB	I	17	Visions	Wright Group/McGraw Hill
Cicadas	J	I	87	Pebble Books	Red Brick Learning
Cincinnati Bengals, The	S	I	250+	Team Spirit	Norwood House Press
Cincinnati Reds, The	S	I	250+	Team Spirit	Norwood House Press
Cincinnati Reds, The (Revised Edition)	S	I	250+	Team Spirit	Norwood House Press
Cinco de Mayo	E	I	120	Fiesta Holiday Series	Pearson Learning Group
Cinco de Mayo	Q	I	250+	Holiday Histories	Heinemann
Cinco de Mayo	J	I	144	Holidays and Celebrations	Capstone Press
Cinco de Mayo	O	I	250+	Holidays and Festivals	Compass Point Books
Cinco de Mayo	M	I	229	Holidays and Festivals	Heinemann Library
Cinco de Mayo	N	I	1731	On My Own Holidays	Lerner Publishing Group
Cinderella	L	TL	250+	Eilenberg, Max	Candlewick Press
Cinderella	J	TL	250+	Jumbled Tumbled Tales & Rhymes	Rigby
Cinderella	K	TL	250+	Once Upon a Time	Wright Group/McGraw Hill
Cinderella	K	TL	250+	PM Tales and Plays-Gold	Rigby
Cinderella	L	TL	849	Traditional Tales	Pioneer Valley
Cinderella	I	TL	580	Traditional Tales	Pearson Learning Group
Cinderella at the Ball	F	TL	269	Fairy Tales and Folklore	Norwood House Press
Cinderella Dressed in Yellow	E	F	81	Learn to Read	Creative Teaching Press
Cinderella Society, The	Z	RF	250+	Cassidy, Kay	Egmont USA
*Cinderfella's Big Night and Other Fractured Fairy Tales	P	TL	250+	Action Packs	Rigby
Cindy and the Football Boots	M	RF	250+	Lighthouse	Ginn & Co.
Cinnabar and the Island of Shadows: The Fairy Chronicles	Q	F	11700	Sweet, J.H.	Sourcebooks
Circle	B	I	32	Shapes	Lerner Publishing Group
Circle of Gold	R	RF	250+	Boyd, Candy Dawson	Bantam Books
Circle of Quiet, A	Z	B	250+	L'Engle, Madeleine	HarperCollins
Circle of Time, A	Y	RF	250+	Montes, Marisa	Harcourt Trade
Circle Story, A	L	RF	250+	HSP/Harcourt Trophies	Harcourt, Inc.
Circle Unbroken	S	RF	250+	Raven, Margot Thesis	Square Fish
Circle Unbroken, A	V	HF	250+	Leveled Readers Language Support	Houghton Mifflin Harcourt
Circles	D	I	27	Bookworms	Marshall Cavendish

* Collection of short stories   # Graphic text
^ Mature content with lower level text demands

TITLE	LEVEL	GENRE	WORD COUNT	AUTHOR / SERIES	PUBLISHER / DISTRIBUTOR
Circles	C	I	56	Dominie Readers	Pearson Learning Group
Circles Around Town	J	I	253	Shapes Around Town	Capstone Press
Circles Everywhere	A	I	40	On Our Way to English	Rigby
Circles: Seeing Circles All Around Us	L	I	198	Shapes	Capstone Press
*Circuit, The	Z	B	250+	Francisco, Jimenez	Houghton Mifflin Harcourt
Circular Movement	E	I	43	The Way Things Move	Capstone Press
Circulatory System, The	S	I	250+	A True Book	Children's Press
Circulatory System, The	P	I	2175	Early Bird Body Systems	Lerner Publishing Group
Circulatory System, The	M	I	171	Human Body Systems	Red Brick Learning
Circus	B	I	20	Twig	Wright Group/McGraw Hill
Circus Book, The	I	I	250+	Reading Unlimited	Pearson Learning Group
Circus Clown, The	A	RF	31	Literacy 2000	Rigby
Circus Detective, The	R	RF	250+	Book Blazers	ETA/Cuisenaire
Circus Fish	F	F	80	Coulton, Mia	Maryruth Books
Circus Fun	E	RF	280	Easy Stories	Norwood House Press
Circus Fun	G	RF	219	Momentum Literacy Program	Troll Associates
Circus Mystery, The	M	RF	250+	Woodland Mysteries	Wright Group/McGraw Hill
Circus Ship, The	M	F	250+	Dusen, Chris Van	Candlewick Press
Circus Train, The	A	F	48	Little Red Readers	Sundance
Circus Tricks	H	I	236	Scooters	ETA/Cuisenaire
Circus, The	WB	I	0	Carle, Eric	HarperCollins
Circus, The	LB	I	31	Literacy 2000	Rigby
Circus, The	D	RF	42	Wonder World	Wright Group/McGraw Hill
Cirque Du Freak: The Saga of Darren Shan	X	F	250+	Shan, Darren	Little Brown and Company
Cities Around the World	M	I	250+	Pair-It Books	Steck-Vaughn
Cities Below the Sea	O	I	250+	WorldScapes	ETA/Cuisenaire
Cities of Splendor: The Facts and the Fables	R	TL	250+	Landscapes of Legend	Children's Press
Cities Then, Cities Now	M	I	406	Leveled Readers Social Studies	Houghton Mifflin Harcourt
Cities: The Building of America	Q	I	250+	Thompson, Gare	Children's Press
Cities: Then and Now	O	I	250+	People, Spaces & Places	Rand McNally
Citizen's Movements	U	I	2079	Reading Street	Pearson
Citizens of the World	T	I	2642	Independent Readers Social Studies	Houghton Mifflin Harcourt
*Citizens Who Made a Difference	P	B	250+	Navigators Social Studies Series	Benchmark Education
#Citizenship	V	I	250+	Cartoon Nation	Capstone Press
Citizenship	L	I	250+	Everyday Character Education	Capstone Press
Citizenship	J	I	103	Government	Lerner Publishing Group
City and Country	G	I	268	Vocabulary Readers	Houghton Mifflin Harcourt
City and Country	G	I	268	Vocabulary Readers/CA	Houghton Mifflin Harcourt
City and the Country, The	B	I	48	Leveled Readers Emergent	Houghton Mifflin Harcourt
City Animals	G	RF	102	Higgins, Malcom	Houghton Mifflin Harcourt
City Boy	X	RF	250+	Michael, Jan	Clarion Books
City Buildings	G	I	133	Discovery Links	Newbridge
City Buried in Time, A	U	I	1429	Vocabulary Readers	Houghton Mifflin Harcourt
City Buried in Time, A	U	I	1429	Vocabulary Readers/CA	Houghton Mifflin Harcourt
City Buried in Time, A	U	I	1429	Vocabulary Readers/TX	Houghton Mifflin Harcourt
City Bus, The	B	RF	21	Visions	Wright Group/McGraw Hill
City by the Lake	N	I	250+	Early Connections	Benchmark Education
City Cat	J	F	250+	Storyworlds	Heinemann
City Cat and the Country Cat, The	E	F	152	Ready Readers	Pearson Learning Group
City Divided, A	X	I	250+	Power Up!	Steck-Vaughn
City Dog, Country Dog	O	F	250+	Crummel, Susan & Donohue, Dorothy	Marshall Cavendish
City Dog, Country Dog	H	RF	203	Literacy by Design	Rigby

TITLE	LEVEL	GENRE	WORD COUNT	AUTHOR / SERIES	PUBLISHER / DISTRIBUTOR
City Friends, Country Friends	L	RF	908	Reading Street	Pearson
City Fun	F	RF	250+	Let's Play	Norwood House Press
City Garden, A	G	RF	77	City Stories	Rigby
City Garden, A	C	I	111	Leveled Readers	Houghton Mifflin Harcourt
City Garden, A	C	I	111	Leveled Readers/CA	Houghton Mifflin Harcourt
City Green	L	RF	250+	DiSalvo-Ryan, DyAnne	Scholastic
City in the Cliffs	Q	HF	1454	Leveled Readers	Houghton Mifflin Harcourt
City in the Cliffs	Q	HF	1454	Leveled Readers/CA	Houghton Mifflin Harcourt
City in the Cliffs	Q	HF	1454	Leveled Readers/TX	Houghton Mifflin Harcourt
City in the Clouds: The Secrets of Droon	O	F	250+	Abbott, Tony	Scholastic
City Life	C	I	32	Rosen Real Readers	Rosen Publishing Group
City Life and Country Life	E	F	66	Moriarty, Julie	Scholastic
City Life: Then and Now	T	I	2253	Reading Street	Pearson
City Lights	N	RF	250+	Orbit Double Takes	Pacific Learning
City Lights	LB	RF	16	Visions	Wright Group/McGraw Hill
City Mouse and Country Mouse	D	TL	87	Learn to Read	Creative Teaching Press
City Mouse and Country Mouse	I	TL	168	Reading Street	Pearson
City Mouse and the Country Mouse, The	K	TL	636	Leveled Literacy Intervention/ Blue System	Heinemann
City Mouse-Country Mouse	J	TL	198	Wallner, John	Scholastic
City Noises	D	RF	37	Instant Readers	Harcourt School Publishers
City of Ember, The	W	F	250+	DuPrau, Jeanne	Random House
City of Gold & Lead, The	V	F	250+	Christopher, John	Aladdin
City of Ruins	X	SF	250+	Williams, Mark London	Candlewick Press
City of the Beasts	Z	F	250+	Allende, Isabel	HarperTrophy
City of the Inca	S	B	250+	WorldScapes	ETA/Cuisenaire
City on a Lake, The	R	I	642	Vocabulary Readers	Houghton Mifflin Harcourt
City or Country	H	I	88	Pair-It Turn and Learn	Steck-Vaughn
City Park	N	I	250+	Habitats	Children's Press
City Park, A	I	RF	59	Leveled Readers	Houghton Mifflin Harcourt
City Parks	L	I	650	Vocabulary Readers/TX	Houghton Mifflin Harcourt
City Patterns	J	I	270	Finding Patterns	Capstone Press
City Places, Country Places	K	RF	633	InfoTrek	ETA/Cuisenaire
City Scenes	E	RF	24	Pacific Literacy	Pacific Learning
City Senses	C	I	85	Twig	Wright Group/McGraw Hill
City Shapes	G	I	176	Yellow Umbrella Books	Red Brick Learning
City Sights	G	I	250+	Phonics and Friends	Hampton Brown
City Sounds	G	RF	142	Marzollo, Jean	Scholastic
City Storm	E	I	180	Twig	Wright Group/McGraw Hill
City Tales	L	RF	250+	Smith, Geof	Scholastic
City Through the Ages	U	I	250+	Steele, Philip	Troll Associates
City Transportation	L	I	459	Rigby Flying Colors	Rigby
City, The	C	I	98	Vocabulary Readers	Houghton Mifflin Harcourt
City, The	C	I	98	Vocabulary Readers/CA	Houghton Mifflin Harcourt
Civil Rights Marches	V	I	250+	Cornerstones of Freedom	Children's Press
Civil Rights Movement	U	I	250+	Primary Source Readers	Teacher Created Materials
Civil Rights Movement in America, The	V	I	250+	Cornerstones of Freedom	Children's Press
Civil Rights Movement, The	V	I	250+	Reading Expeditions	National Geographic
Civil Rights Movement, The	V	I	1916	Reading Street	Pearson
^Civil Rights Movement, The: An Interactive History Adventure	V	HF	250+	You Choose Books	Capstone Press
Civil War is Coming	T	I	250+	Primary Source Readers	Teacher Created Materials
Civil War Leaders	T	B	250+	Primary Source Readers	Teacher Created Materials
Civil War on Sunday	M	F	250+	Osborne, Mary Pope	Random House

* Collection of short stories   # Graphic text
^ Mature content with lower level text demands

TITLE	LEVEL	GENRE	WORD COUNT	AUTHOR / SERIES	PUBLISHER / DISTRIBUTOR
^Civil War Spies	U	I	250+	Spies	Capstone Press
Civil War Spy: Elizabeth Van Lew	T	B	250+	We the People	Compass Point Books
Civil War, The	V	I	250+	America Goes to War	Red Brick Learning
Civil War, The	T	I	250+	Reading Expeditions	National Geographic
^Civil War, The: An Interactive History Adventure	V	HF	250+	You Choose Books	Capstone Press
Civilizations - Yesterday, Today	W	I	250+	Connectors	Pacific Learning
Claiming Georgia Tate	Z+	HF	250+	Amateau, Gigi	Candlewick Press
Clap for the Show	I	RF	250+	Phonics and Friends	Hampton Brown
Clap Your Hands!	B	I	22	Pair-It Books	Steck-Vaughn
Clara and the Bookwagon	K	RF	250+	Levinson, Nancy Smiler	HarperTrophy
Clara and the Bossy	K	F	684	Ohi, Ruth	Annick Press
Clara Barton	N	B	203	First Biographies	Capstone Press
Clara Barton	S	B	3920	History Maker Bios	Lerner Publishing Group
Clara Barton	M	B	320	Independent Readers Social Studies	Houghton Mifflin Harcourt
Clara Barton	S	B	2411	People to Remember Series	January Books
Clara Barton	P	B	250+	Photo-Illustrated Biographies	Red Brick Learning
#Clara Barton: Angel of the Battlefield	S	B	250+	Graphic Library	Capstone Press
Clara Barton: Angel of the Battlefield	M	B	250+	Rosen Real Readers	Rosen Publishing Group
Clara Barton: Founder of the American Red Cross	R	B	250+	Stevenson, Augusta	Aladdin
Clara Morgan and the Oregon Trail Journey	S	HF	4109	History Speaks	Millbrook Press
Clarence Cochran, A Human Boy	R	F	250+	Loizeaux, William	Macmillan
Clarence the Crocodile	L	F	250+	New Way Literature	Steck-Vaughn
Clarice Bean Spells Trouble	R	RF	250+	Child, Lauren	Scholastic
Clarice Bean, Don't Look Now	Q	RF	250+	Child, Lauren	Candlewick Press
Class Calender	H	I	81	Windows on Literacy	National Geographic
Class Clown	O	RF	250+	Hurwitz, Johanna	Scholastic
Class Photograph, The	J	RF	462	PM Math Readers	Rigby
Class Picture Day	I	RF	204	Buckless, Andrea	Scholastic
Class Play with Ms. Vanilla, A	I	RF	234	Ehrlich, Fred	Puffin Books
Class Play, The	J	RF	250+	Little Readers	Houghton Mifflin Harcourt
Class President	O	RF	250+	Hurwitz, Johanna	Scholastic
Class Rules	G	RF	143	Windows on Literacy	National Geographic
Class Store, The	F	I	164	Early Connections	Benchmark Education
Class Teddy Bear	F	RF	106	Windows on Literacy	National Geographic
Class Three at Sea	N	F	430	Jarman, Julia	Carolrhoda Books
Class Trip from the Black Lagoon, The	N	F	250+	Black Lagoon Adventures	Scholastic
Class Trip to the Cave of Doom	P	F	250+	McMullan, Kate	Grosset & Dunlap
Class Trip, The	G	RF	115	Maccarone, Grace	Scholastic
Class, The	F	RF	93	Reading Street	Pearson
Classification Clues	V	I	250+	Reading Expeditions	National Geographic
Classifying Living Things	Q	I	250+	Reading Expeditions	National Geographic
Classroom Animals	I	I	328	Explorations	Okapi Educational Materials
Classroom Animals	I	I	328	Explorations	Eleanor Curtain Publishing
Classroom Caterpillars, The	H	RF	216	PM Plus Story Books	Rigby
Classroom Fun	LB	I	17	Reach	National Geographic
Classroom Pets	K	I	250+	Literacy by Design	Rigby
Classroom Rules	F	I	190	On Our Way to English	Rigby
Classroom Zone, The	O	F	250+	The Funny Zone	Norwood House Press
Clatter Bash! A Day of the Dead Celebration	LB	F	60	Keep, Richard	Peachtree
Claude Monet: Sunshine and Waterlilies	S	B	250+	Kelley, True	Grosset & Dunlap
Claudette Colvin: Twice Toward Justice	Z	B	250+	Hoose, Phillip	Farrar, Straus, & Giroux

TITLE	LEVEL	GENRE	WORD COUNT	AUTHOR / SERIES	PUBLISHER / DISTRIBUTOR
Claudine's Concert	L	RF	250+	Literacy 2000	Rigby
Claws	I	I	160	Animal Spikes and Spines	Heinemann Library
Claws	I	I	228	Sails	Rigby
Clay	M	I	250+	Materials	Capstone Press
Clay Art	F	I	62	Chanko, Pamela; Chessen, Betsey	Scholastic
Clay Creatures	I	I	213	Literacy by Design	Rigby
Clay Creatures	I	I	213	Rigby Literacy	Rigby
Clay Dog, The	L	HF	250+	Lighthouse	Rigby
Clay Marble, The	V	RF	250+	Ho, Minfong	Farrar, Straus, & Giroux
Clay Things, Play Things	J	I	250+	Phonics Readers	Scholastic
Clay Today!	C	RF	37	Learn to Read	Creative Teaching Press
Clean Air	P	I	250+	Independent Readers Social Studies	Houghton Mifflin Harcourt
Clean Air	V	I	250+	Sally Ride Science	Roaring Brook Press
Clean and Clear	P	I	806	Independent Readers Social Studies	Houghton Mifflin Harcourt
Clean and Healthy	I	I	199	Rosen Real Readers	Rosen Publishing Group
Clean Beaches	I	I	155	Early Connections	Benchmark Education
Clean Energy	V	I	250+	Sally Ride Science	Roaring Brook Press
Clean House for Mole and Mouse, A	H	F	201	Ziefert, Harriet	Scholastic
Clean Machine, The	L	RF	250+	Home Connection Collection	Rigby
Clean My Teeth!	C	F	51	Sails	Rigby
Clean Out the Fridge, Fred	I	F	250+	Popcorn	Sundance
Clean Up Time	B	RF	57	Red Rocket Readers	Flying Start Books
Clean Up Your Room	B	RF	35	Visions	Wright Group/McGraw Hill
Clean Water	V	I	250+	Sally Ride Science	Roaring Brook Press
Clean Your Room, Nick!	D	RF	107	Kaleidoscope Collection	Hameray Publishing Group
Clean Your Room, Tanya!	L	RF	250+	Scooters	ETA/Cuisenaire
Cleaning Day	C	RF	26	Bebop Books	Lee & Low Books Inc.
Cleaning My Room	I	I	189	Early Connections	Benchmark Education
Cleaning Teeth	D	I	37	Wonder World	Wright Group/McGraw Hill
Cleaning Up	A	I	26	Early Connections	Benchmark Education
Cleaning Up the Park	H	I	153	Home Connection Collection	Rigby
Clean-Sweep Campers	M	RF	250+	Math Matters	Kane Press
Clean-Up Day	H	RF	179	Instant Readers	Harcourt School Publishers
Clean-Up Day	K	RF	720	PM Stars-Bridge Books	Rigby
Clean-Up Day	D	RF	72	Rigby Rocket	Rigby
Clean-Up Team, The	G	RF	159	InfoTrek	ETA/Cuisenaire
Clean-Up Time	F	RF	226	Handprints D, Set 1	Educators Publishing Service
Cleared for Takeoff: Have You Got What It Takes to Be an Airline Pilot?	T	I	250+	On the Job	Compass Point Books
Clearing the Dust	V	HF	2327	Leveled Readers	Houghton Mifflin Harcourt
Clementine	O	RF	250+	Pennypacker, Sara	Hyperion
Clementine	L	TL	101	Traditional Songs	Picture Window Books
Clementine's Letter	O	RF	250+	Pennypacker, Sara	Hyperion
^Cleopatra	T	B	250+	Ancient Egypt	Capstone Press
Cleopatra	X	B	250+	Green, Robert	Franklin Watts
Cleopatra	W	B	2055	Independent Readers Social Studies	Houghton Mifflin Harcourt
Cleopatra	T	B	250+	Stanley, Diane; Vennema, Peter	Mulberry Books
Cleopatra and the King's Enemies	N	B	250+	Young Princesses Around the World	Aladdin
Cleopatra: Egypt's Last and Greatest Queen	Y	B	250+	Sterling Biographies	Sterling Publishing
Cleveland Browns, The	S	I	250+	Team Spirit	Norwood House Press

* Collection of short stories   # Graphic text
^ Mature content with lower level text demands

TITLE	LEVEL	GENRE	WORD COUNT	AUTHOR / SERIES	PUBLISHER / DISTRIBUTOR
Cleveland Cavaliers, The	S	I	4452	Team Spirit	Norwood House Press
Cleveland Indians, The	S	I	250+	Team Spirit	Norwood House Press
Cleveland Indians, The (Revised Edition)	S	I	250+	Team Spirit	Norwood House Press
Clever Ali	S	TL	250+	Farmer, Nancy	Orchard Books
Clever and Quirky Creatures	S	I	250+	Story Surfers	ETA/Cuisenaire
Clever Animals	J	I	332	Vocabulary Readers/TX	Houghton Mifflin Harcourt
Clever Beatrice	M	TL	250+	Willey, Margaret	Atheneum Books
Clever Bird	K	F	250+	Little Celebrations	Pearson Learning Group
Clever Brown Mouse	G	F	199	PM Plus Story Books	Rigby
Clever Calculations	X	I	250+	WorldScapes	ETA/Cuisenaire
Clever Camouflage	J	I	335	Red Rocket Readers	Flying Start Books
Clever Chick	G	F	250+	Rigby Star	Rigby
Clever Coyote and Other Wild Dogs	L	I	250+	Storyteller Chapter Books	Wright Group/McGraw Hill
Clever Crustaceans	S	I	250+	Underwater Encounters	Hameray Publishing Group
Clever Fox	D	RF	114	PM Plus Story Books	Rigby
Clever Hamburger	K	F	560	Jellybeans	Rigby
Clever Happy Monkey	C	F	28	Joy Readers	Pearson Learning Group
Clever Jackals, The	H	TL	231	PM Stars	Rigby
Clever Joe	B	RF	53	Storyworlds	Heinemann
Clever Little Bird	D	F	73	Storyteller-Setting Sun	Wright Group/McGraw Hill
Clever Lollipop	P	F	250+	King-Smith, Dick	Candlewick Press
Clever Mr. Brown	K	F	397	Story Box	Wright Group/McGraw Hill
Clever Penguins, The	G	I	174	PM Story Books	Rigby
Clever Raccoons	K	I	388	Pull Ahead Books	Lerner Publishing Group
Clever Tortoise, The	H	TL	202	Cambridge Reading	Pearson Learning Group
Clever Trevor	K	RF	1117	Science Solves It!	Kane Press
Clever Trick, A	K	TL	674	Springboard	Wright Group/McGraw Hill
Clever, Crow, The	H	TL	223	PM Plus Story Books	Rigby
Click	E	RF	41	Books for Young Learners	Richard C. Owen
Click!	G	RF	250+	Foundations	Wright Group/McGraw Hill
Click, Clack, Moo Cows That Type	M	F	250+	Cronin, Doreen	Scholastic
Click: A Story about George Eastman	R	B	5614	Creative Minds Biographies	Carolrhoda Books
Cliff Can't Come	F	RF	276	Leveled Readers	Houghton Mifflin Harcourt
Cliff Climbers	P	I	250+	Landform Adventurers	Raintree
Clifford Can	E	F	55	Blevins, Wiley	Scholastic
Clifford, the Big Red Dog	J	F	241	Bridwell, Norman	Scholastic
Clifford, the Firehouse Dog	J	F	250+	Bridwell, Norman	Scholastic
Clifford, the Small Red Puppy	J	F	499	Bridwell, Norman	Scholastic
Clifford's First Halloween	J	F	250+	Bridwell, Norman	Scholastic
Clifford's Good Deeds	J	F	250+	Bridwell, Norman	Scholastic
Clifford's Puppy Days	J	F	308	Bridwell, Norman	Scholastic
Climate	P	I	250+	Reading Expeditions	National Geographic
Climate Change in the Past	Y	I	2922	Leveled Readers	Houghton Mifflin Harcourt
Climate Change in the Past	Y	I	2922	Leveled Readers/CA	Houghton Mifflin Harcourt
Climate Change in the Past	Y	I	2922	Leveled Readers/TX	Houghton Mifflin Harcourt
Climate Fever: Stopping Global Warming	T	I	250+	Green Generation	Compass Point Books
Climbers	F	I	128	Sails	Rigby
Climbing	G	I	84	Benchmark Rebus	Marshall Cavendish
Climbing	C	F	34	Literacy 2000	Rigby
Climbing	B	I	48	PM Starters	Rigby
Climbing Everest	W	I	250+	iOpeners	Pearson Learning Group
Climbing Mount Everest	R	I	250+	Windows On Literacy	National Geographic
Climbing the Continents: Everest, McKinley, Kilimanjaro	W	I	3847	Leveled Readers Social Studies	Houghton Mifflin Harcourt

TITLE	LEVEL	GENRE	WORD COUNT	AUTHOR / SERIES	PUBLISHER / DISTRIBUTOR
Climbing the Stairs	Y	HF	250+	Venkatraman, Padma	Speak
Climbing to Success	S	I	250+	Explorer Books-Pathfinder	National Geographic
Climbing to Success	P	I	250+	Explorer Books-Pioneer	National Geographic
Climbing Tree Frogs	L	I	386	Pull Ahead Books	Lerner Publishing Group
Clinging Sea Horses	L	I	356	Pull Ahead Books	Lerner Publishing Group
Clinic	D	I	32	Community Buildings	Lerner Publishing Group
Clique, The	X	RF	250+	Harrison, Lisi	Little Brown and Company
Cliques	V	I	250+	10 Things You Need to Know About	Capstone Press
Cloak of the Wind	P	HF	250+	Voyages in Time	Wright Group/McGraw Hill
*Cloaked in Red	W	TL	250+	Velde, Vivian Vande	Marshall Cavendish
Clock Struck One, The: A Time-Telling Tale	K	F	285	Harris, Trudy	Millbrook Press
Clock That Couldn't Tell Time, The	H	F	310	Carousel Readers	Pearson Learning Group
Clock Watch	B	I	76	Early Connections	Benchmark Education
Clocks and Calendars	H	I	165	Measuring Time	Heinemann Library
Clocks and More Clocks	J	RF	374	Hutchins, Pat	Scholastic
Clockwork	Z	F	250+	Pullman, Philip	Scholastic
Cloning Pets	Z	I	250+	Science Missions	Raintree
Close Call, A	M	RF	250+	Kenna, Anna	Pacific Learning
Close to Famous	T	RF	250+	Bauer, Joan	Viking/Penguin
Close to Home: A Story of the Polio Epidemic	R	I	250+	Weaver, Lydia	Bantam Books
Close Up on Careers	T	I	250+	InfoQuest	Rigby
Close Your Eyes	E	RF	131	Foundations	Wright Group/McGraw Hill
Closer and Closer	LB	I	13	Twig	Wright Group/McGraw Hill
Closet in the Hall, The	D	F	84	Wonder World	Wright Group/McGraw Hill
Closet Under the Stairs, The	I	RF	214	Story Box	Wright Group/McGraw Hill
Clot & Scab: Gross Stuff About Our Scrapes, Bumps, and Bruises	U	I	4522	Gross Body Science	Millbrook Press
Cloth	G	I	90	Materials	Lerner Publishing Group
Clothes	B	I	51	Early Explorers	Benchmark Education
Clothes	C	I	25	Interaction	Rigby
Clothes	F	I	103	Talk About Books	Pearson Learning Group
Clothes	D	RF	63	Voyages	SRA/McGraw Hill
Clothes	C	I	18	We Are Alike and Different	Lerner Publishing Group
Clothes	L	I	386	Wonder World	Wright Group/McGraw Hill
Clothes & Crafts in Ancient Egypt	T	I	250+	Balkwill, Richard	Dillon Press
Clothes & Crafts in Ancient Greece	T	I	250+	Steele, Philip	Dillon Press
Clothes & Crafts in Aztec Times	T	I	250+	Dawson, Imogen	Dillon Press
Clothes & Crafts in Roman Times	T	I	250+	Steele, Philip	Dillon Press
Clothes & Crafts in the Middle Ages	T	I	250+	Dawson, Imogen	Dillon Press
Clothes & Crafts in Victorian Times	T	I	250+	Steele, Philip	Dillon Press
Clothes Around the World	J	I	214	Vocabulary Readers	Houghton Mifflin Harcourt
Clothes in Many Cultures	I	I	79	Life Around the World	Capstone Press
Clothes Long Ago	K	I	264	Early Explorers	Benchmark Education
Clothes That Help	I	I	252	Sails	Rigby
Clothes Then and Now	L	I	353	Early Explorers	Benchmark Education
Clothes: From Fur to Fair Trade	U	I	250+	Timeline History	Heinemann Library
Clothing	C	I	23	Basic Human Needs	Lerner Publishing Group
Cloud Book, The	N	I	250+	DePaola, Tomie	Scholastic
Cloud Catcher	P	F	250+	Action Packs	Rigby
Cloud Forest	P	I	1313	Big Cat	Pacific Learning
Cloud Forest Food Chain, A: A Who-Eats-What Adventure in Africa	U	I	7729	Follow That Food Chain	Lerner Publishing Group
Cloud Tea Monkeys	Q	TL	250+	Peet, Mal & Graham, Elspeth	Candlewick Press

* Collection of short stories   # Graphic text
^ Mature content with lower level text demands

TITLE	LEVEL	GENRE	WORD COUNT	AUTHOR / SERIES	PUBLISHER / DISTRIBUTOR
Clouds	A	RF	47	Bookshop	Mondo Publishing
Clouds	D	RF	40	Costain, Meredith	Scholastic
Clouds	J	I	246	Early Connections	Benchmark Education
Clouds	L	I	345	Gear Up!	Wright Group/McGraw Hill
Clouds	C	I	67	Handprints C, Set 1	Educators Publishing Service
Clouds	J	I	204	Independent Readers Science	Houghton Mifflin Harcourt
Clouds	L	I	40	iOpeners	Pearson Learning Group
Clouds	C	RF	92	Leveled Literacy Intervention/ Green System	Heinemann
Clouds	N	I	250+	Literacy 2000	Rigby
Clouds	C	RF	44	Science	Outside the Box
Clouds	H	I	108	Sunshine	Wright Group/McGraw Hill
Clouds	H	I	132	Twig	Wright Group/McGraw Hill
Clouds	B	RF	42	Voyages	SRA/McGraw Hill
Clouds	I	I	249	Weather	Capstone Press
Clouds of Terror	L	HF	250+	Soar To Success	Houghton Mifflin Harcourt
Clouds of Terror	L	HF	250+	Welsh, Catherine A.	Carolrhoda Books
Clouds Tell the Weather	E	F	89	Bonnell, Kris	Reading Reading Books
Clouds, Rain, and Fog	K	I	488	Sunshine	Wright Group/McGraw Hill
Cloudy	B	I	27	Weather	Lerner Publishing Group
Cloudy Day Sunny Day	E	RF	108	Green Light Readers	Harcourt
Cloudy Day, A	E	I	90	Weather	Lerner Publishing Group
Cloudy With a Chance of Meatballs	M	F	250+	Barrett, Judi	Atheneum Books
Clover Twig and the Magical Cottage	S	F	250+	Umansky, Kaye	Roaring Brook Press
Clown	WB	I	0	Blake, Quentin	Henry Holt & Co.
Clown	C	RF	146	Sails	Rigby
Clown and Elephant	C	F	38	Story Box	Wright Group/McGraw Hill
Clown Around	F	F	67	Early Readers	Compass Point Books
Clown Face	LB	RF	14	Twig	Wright Group/McGraw Hill
Clown Fish	J	I	123	Under the Sea	Capstone Press
Clown Fish and Sea Anemones Work Together	K	I	250+	Animals Working Together	Capstone Press
Clown in the Gown Drives the Car with the Star, The	J	F	177	Sounds Like Reading	Lerner Publishing Group
Clown in the Well, The	D	F	140	Story Box	Wright Group/McGraw Hill
Clown Is Sick	I	F	350	Sails	Rigby
Clown Paints His House	E	RF	143	Sails	Rigby
Clown, The	LB	I	31	First Stories	Pacific Learning
Clown, The	LB	I	13	Smart Start	Rigby
Clown, The	LB	I	29	Urmston, Kathleen; Evans, Karen	Kaeden Books
Clownfish Goes for a Swim	D	I	68	Bonnell, Kris	Reading Reading Books
Clowning Around	L	I	250+	Rigby Literacy	Rigby
Clowns	K	I	289	Rigby Flying Colors	Rigby
Clown's Clothes	B	RF	54	Sails	Rigby
Clown's Party	C	RF	115	Sails	Rigby
Clowns with Frowns Parade, The	I	F	291	Springboard	Wright Group/McGraw Hill
Clubhouse, The	K	RF	659	PM Collection	Rigby
Cluck!	H	I	151	The Rowland Reading Program Library	Rowland Reading Foundation
Cluck! Quack! Moo!	F	RF	209	Sun Sprouts	ETA/Cuisenaire
Clucky	I	F	250+	PM Plus Story Books	Rigby
Clue at the Bottom of the Lake, The	Q	RF	250+	Gregory, Kristiana	Scholastic
Clue at the Zoo, The	L	RF	250+	Giff, Patricia Reilly	Bantam Books
Clue Club, The	M	RF	660	Leveled Readers	Houghton Mifflin Harcourt

C

TITLE	LEVEL	GENRE	WORD COUNT	AUTHOR / SERIES	PUBLISHER / DISTRIBUTOR
Clue in the Castle, The	M	RF	250+	Woodland Mysteries	Wright Group/McGraw Hill
Clue in the Glue, The	N	RF	250+	Keene, Carolyn	Pocket Books
Clue of the Gold Doubloons, The	S	RF	250+	Keene, Carolyn	Pocket Books
Clue of the Linoleum Lederhosen, The	U	F	250+	Anderson, M. T.	Harcourt
Clue, Jr.: The Case of the Chocolate Fingerprints	O	RF	250+	Hinter, Parker C.	Scholastic
#Clues in the Attic	K	RF	250+	My 1st Graphic Novel	Stone Arch Books
Clues in the Car Wash	O	RF	250+	Klooz	Stone Arch Books
Clues in the Woods	N	RF	250+	Parish, Peggy	Yearling Books
Clues to Crime	T	I	250+	The News	Richard C. Owen
Clumsy Clinton	M	RF	894	Springboard	Wright Group/McGraw Hill
Clyde Klutter's Room	I	F	146	Sunshine	Wright Group/McGraw Hill
Clyde the Otter	J	F	250+	Reading Safari	Mondo Publishing
Clyde Tombaugh and the Search for Planet X	N	B	250+	Wetterer, Margaret K.	Carolrhoda Books
Coach Amos	R	RF	250+	Paulsen, Gary	Bantam Books
Coach Hyatt Is a Riot!	O	RF	250+	Gutman, Dan	HarperTrophy
Coach Kaputo	R	RF	1476	Leveled Readers	Houghton Mifflin Harcourt
Coach Kaputo	R	RF	1476	Leveled Readers/CA	Houghton Mifflin Harcourt
Coaches	L	I	547	Pull Ahead Books	Lerner Publishing Group
Coal Miner's Son, A	U	RF	2652	Leveled Readers Science	Houghton Mifflin Harcourt
Coast to Coast	N	I	250+	People, Spaces & Places	Rand McNally
Coasts	J	I	273	Landforms	Lerner Publishing Group
Coasts: The Land Around Us	S	I	250+	Reading Expeditions	National Geographic
Coastwatcher, The	U	HF	250+	Weston, Elise	Peachtree
Coat Full of Bubbles, A	G	RF	72	Books for Young Learners	Richard C. Owen
Coats	A	I	32	Ray's Readers	Outside the Box
Cobber Dog and Old Mary	K	F	509	Springboard	Wright Group/McGraw Hill
Cobra Cat	J	F	250+	Storyworlds	Heinemann
^Cobra Strike	U	RF	250+	Orca Sports	Orca Books
Cobras	A	I	70	Readlings/ Predator Animals	American Reading Company
Cobras	M	I	250+	Snakes	Capstone Press
^Cobras on the Hunt	N	I	250+	Killer Animals	Capstone Press
Cobsdown Cat Case, The	L	RF	250+	Rigby Rocket	Rigby
Cobwebs, Elephants, and Stars	M	F	779	Sunshine	Wright Group/McGraw Hill
Cocci, Spirilla, & Other Bacteria	Y	I	250+	Kingdom Classification	Compass Point Books
Cock-A-Doodle-Do	F	RF	160	Brandenberg, Franz	Greenwillow Books
Cocker Spaniels	I	I	146	Dogs	Capstone Press
Cocker Spaniels Are the Best!	Q	I	1336	The Best Dogs Ever	Lerner Publishing Group
Cockroach Cooties	O	RF	250+	Yep, Laurence	Hyperion
Cockroaches	P	I	2529	Early Bird Nature Books	Lerner Publishing Group
Cockroaches	I	I	60	Pebble Books	Red Brick Learning
Cockroaches	I	I	283	Sails	Rigby
Cockroaches	N	I	250+	World of Insects	Capstone Press
Coconut Lunches	J	RF	564	Sunshine	Wright Group/McGraw Hill
Coconut Seed or Fruit?	N	I	250+	iOpeners	Pearson Learning Group
Cocoons and Cases	C	I	59	Rigby Literacy	Rigby
Coco's Bell	H	RF	224	PM Plus Story Books	Rigby
Code Breakers	Q	RF	1520	Powell, J.	Stone Arch Books
Code in the Tree, The	F	RF	191	Leveled Readers	Houghton Mifflin Harcourt
Code in the Tree, The	F	RF	191	Leveled Readers/CA	Houghton Mifflin Harcourt
Code Talker	Y	HF	250+	Edge	Hampton Brown
Code Talkers, The	W	I	2207	Reading Street	Pearson
Code that No One Broke, The	L	I	90	Independent Readers Social Studies	Houghton Mifflin Harcourt

Organized Alphabetically by Title
Storable Database at www.fountasandpinnellleveledbooks.com

* Collection of short stories   # Graphic text
^ Mature content with lower level text demands

TITLE	LEVEL	GENRE	WORD COUNT	AUTHOR / SERIES	PUBLISHER / DISTRIBUTOR
Code, The	U	I	250+	Edge	Hampton Brown
Code, The: The 5 Secrets of Teen Success	U	I	250+	Asgedom, Mawi	Hampton Brown
Codes and Signals	N	I	250+	Cambridge Reading	Pearson Learning Group
Cody Meets Theo	J	RF	456	PM Stars Bridge Books	Rigby
Cody's Snake Tale	M	RF	250+	Windows on Literacy	National Geographic
Coffin Quilt, The: The Feud between the Hatfields and the McCoys	Y	HF	250+	Rinaldi, Ann	Harcourt, Inc.
Cogs in the Wheel	V	I	250+	InfoQuest	Rigby
Coin Magic	L	I	250+	How-To Series	Benchmark Education
Coins	A	I	32	On Our Way to English	Rigby
Cold and Hot	B	RF	24	Bebop Books	Lee & Low Books Inc.
Cold As Ice	T	RF	250+	Keene, Carolyn	Pocket Books
Cold Case: Dinosaurs	U	I	2718	Reading Street	Pearson
Cold Day, A	E	I	71	Pebble Books	Capstone Press
Cold Day, Hot Chocolate	E	RF	110	On Our Way to English	Rigby
Cold Day, The	F	RF	80	Oxford Reading Tree	Oxford University Press
Cold Hands, Warm Heart	Z	RF	250+	Wolfson, Jill	Henry Holt & Co.
Cold Little Duck, Duck, Duck	K	F	204	Peters, Lisa Westberg	Greenwillow Books
Cold Place, A	B	I	43	Sails	Rigby
Cold Places	M	I	388	Sails	Rigby
Cold Shoulder Road	V	RF	250+	Aiken, Joan	Bantam Books
Cold War Leaders	U	B	250+	Primary Source Readers	Teacher Created Materials
^Cold War Spies	X	I	250+	Spies	Capstone Press
Cold War, The	W	I	250+	Primary Source Readers	Teacher Created Materials
Cold, The	D	RF	96	Leveled Literacy Intervention/ Blue System	Heinemann
Coldest Place on Earth, The	T	I	5500	Oxford Bookworms Library	Oxford University Press
Coldest Places, The	H	I	224	PM Science Readers	Rigby
Colds	K	I	250+	Health Matters	Capstone Press
Cole, the Midwest Giant	M	F	977	Springboard	Wright Group/McGraw Hill
Colibri	W	RF	250+	Cameron, Ann	Farrar, Straus, & Giroux
Colin Powell	X	B	250+	A&E Biography	Lerner Publishing Group
Colin Powell	S	B	4022	History Maker Bios	Lerner Publishing Group
Colin Powell	K	B	250+	Welcome Books	Children's Press
Colin Powell, American Leader	H	B	77	Leveled Readers Social Studies	Houghton Mifflin Harcourt
Colin Powell: It Can Be Done!	U	B	250+	High Five Reading	Red Brick Learning
Colin Powell: Straight to the Top	S	B	250+	Blue, Rose; Naden, Corinne J.	Millbrook Press
Collages	M	I	250+	Start with Art	Heinemann Library
Collapse! The Science of Structural Engineering Failures	X	I	250+	Headline Science	Compass Point Books
Collecting Badges	J	I	250+	Stepping Stones	Nelson/Michaels Assoc.
Collecting Cones	I	I	127	Wonder World	Wright Group/McGraw Hill
Collecting Dreams	O	RF	2391	Reading Street	Pearson
Collecting Leaves	K	I	250+	Stepping Stones	Nelson/Michaels Assoc.
Collecting Shapes	J	I	250+	Stepping Stones	Nelson/Michaels Assoc.
Collecting Things Is Fun!	G	RF	134	Learn to Read	Creative Teaching Press
Collection for Kate, A	K	RF	250+	Math Matters	Kane Press
Collections	E	RF	54	Ballinger, Margaret; Gosset, Rachel	Scholastic
Collections	J	RF	250+	Voyages	SRA/McGraw Hill
Collies	I	I	120	Dogs	Capstone Press
Colombia	P	I	1845	Country Explorers	Lerner Publishing Group
Colonial Adventure, The	N	HF	1007	Reading Street	Pearson

TITLE	LEVEL	GENRE	WORD COUNT	AUTHOR / SERIES	PUBLISHER / DISTRIBUTOR
Colonial Crafts	T	I	250+	Historic Communities	Crabtree
Colonial Families	K	I	250+	Rosen Real Readers	Rosen Publishing Group
Colonial Life	S	I	250+	A True Book	Children's Press
Colonial Life	S	I	250+	Historic Communities	Crabtree
Colonial Life	W	I	250+	Reading Expeditions	National Geographic
Colonial New England	O	I	457	Reading Street	Pearson
Colonial Teachers	L	I	250+	Rosen Real Readers	Rosen Publishing Group
Colonial Times	T	I	250+	Navigators Social Studies Series	Benchmark Education
Colonial Times 1600-1700	T	I	250+	Masoff, Joy	Scholastic
Colonial Times from A to Z	T	I	250+	Kalman, Bobbie	Crabtree
Colonial Town, A: Williamsburg	T	I	250+	Historic Communities	Crabtree
Colonialism and Native Peoples	W	I	2595	Reading Street	Pearson
Colony of Massachusetts, The	T	I	250+	The Library of the Thirteen Colonies and The Lost Colony	Rosen Publishing Group
Colony of New York, The	T	I	250+	The Library of the Thirteen Colonies and The Lost Colony	Rosen Publishing Group
Colony of Pennsylvania, The	T	I	250+	The Library of the Thirteen Colonies and The Lost Colony	Rosen Publishing Group
Colony of Virginia, The	T	I	250+	The Library of the Thirteen Colonies and The Lost Colony	Rosen Publishing Group
Color	M	I	250+	Early Connections	Benchmark Education
Color	P	I	250+	Our Physical World	Capstone Press
Color and Size	G	I	27	Windows on Literacy	National Geographic
Color Around Us	V	I	250+	PM Plus	Rigby
Color Camouflage	J	I	201	Spot-It	Capstone Press
Color It My Way	G	RF	123	Story Steps	Rigby
Color Me Dark	V	HF	250+	Dear America	Scholastic
Color Me Even, Color Me Odd	K	RF	250+	Read-it! Readers	Picture Window Books
Color My World	K	I	250+	InfoTrek Plus	ETA/Cuisenaire
Color of His Own, A	I	F	239	Lionni, Leo	Scholastic
Color of Life, The	Q	B	250+	WorldScapes	ETA/Cuisenaire
Color of Light, The	M	I	558	Leveled Readers Science	Houghton Mifflin Harcourt
Color Wizard, The	J	F	250+	Bank Street	Bantam Books
Colorado	T	I	250+	Hello U.S.A.	Lerner Publishing Group
Colorado	S	I	250+	Land of Liberty	Red Brick Learning
Colorado	T	I	250+	Sea To Shining Sea	Children's Press
Colorado	R	I	250+	This Land Is Your Land	Compass Point Books
Colorado Is the Centennial State	O	I	218	Larkin, Bruce	Wilbooks
Colorado River, The	T	I	250+	Waterways of the World	Franklin Watts
Colorado Rockies, The	S	I	250+	Team Spirit	Norwood House Press
Colorado Rockies, The (Revised Edition)	S	I	250+	Team Spirit	Norwood House Press
Colorado: Facts and Symbols	O	I	250+	The States and Their Symbols	Capstone Press
Colorful Animals	D	I	142	Sails	Rigby
Colorful Animals	M	I	250+	Sunshine	Wright Group/McGraw Hill
Colorful Coral Reefs	I	I	195	Early Explorers	Benchmark Education
Colorful Facts	N	I	561	Leveled Readers Science	Houghton Mifflin Harcourt
Colorful Ghost, The	E	F	135	TOTTS	Tott Publications
Colorful Peacocks	L	I	333	Pull Ahead Books	Lerner Publishing Group
Colors	A	I	20	Belle River Readers	Belle River Readers, Inc.
Colors	G	RF	118	Big Cat	Pacific Learning
Colors	F	I	198	Foundations	Wright Group/McGraw Hill
Colors	LB	I	51	Happy Baby	Priddy Books
Colors	B	I	40	InfoTrek	ETA/Cuisenaire
Colors	LB	I	9	Leveled Readers Language Support	Houghton Mifflin Harcourt

* Collection of short stories   # Graphic text
^ Mature content with lower level text demands

TITLE	LEVEL	GENRE	WORD COUNT	AUTHOR / SERIES	PUBLISHER / DISTRIBUTOR
Colors	A	I	9	Little Red Readers	Sundance
Colors	B	RF	11	McAlpin, MaryAnn	Short Tales Press
Colors	B	I	38	Science	Outside the Box
Colors	LB	I	29	Shutterbug Books	Steck-Vaughn
Colors	A	I	16	Time for Kids	Teacher Created Materials
Colors	LB	I	6	Vocabulary Readers	Houghton Mifflin Harcourt
Colors ABC Numbers	LB	I	258	Bright Baby	Priddy Books
Colors Around Me	LB	I	7	Reading Street	Pearson
Colors at the Zoo	B	I	59	Little Books	Sadlier-Oxford
Colors in the City	LB	I	61	Urmston, Kathleen; Evans, Karen	Kaeden Books
Colors of Australia	P	I	250+	Colors of the World	Carolrhoda Books
Colors of Fall	K	I	250+	Colors All Around	Capstone Press
Colors of Fall, The	A	I	26	Gear Up!	Wright Group/McGraw Hill
Colors of Germany	P	I	250+	Colors of the World	Carolrhoda Books
Colors of Ghana	P	I	250+	Colors of the World	Carolrhoda Books
Colors of Horses	E	I	49	Brand, Mona	Kaeden Books
Colors of India	P	I	250+	Colors of the World	Carolrhoda Books
Colors of Insects	L	I	250+	Colors All Around	Capstone Press
Colors of Kenya	P	I	250+	Colors of the World	Carolrhoda Books
Colors of Leaves, The	I	F	561	Leveled Readers/TX	Houghton Mifflin Harcourt
Colors of Mexico	P	I	250+	Colors of the World	Carolrhoda Books
Colors of My Day, The	F	I	147	Learn to Read	Creative Teaching Press
Colors of Sports	K	I	250+	Colors All Around	Capstone Press
Colors of the Ocean	L	I	250+	Colors All Around	Capstone Press
Colors of Weather	K	I	250+	Colors All Around	Capstone Press
Colossal Fossil Freakout, The (Splurch Academy)	Q	F	250+	Berry, Julie & Gardner, Sally	Grosset & Dunlap
Colours	LB	I	8	Pienkowski, Jan	Penguin Group
Columbia	U	I	250+	Countries and Cultures	Red Brick Learning
Columbian Exchange, The	Z	I	2956	Leveled Readers	Houghton Mifflin Harcourt
Columbian Exchange, The	Z	I	2956	Leveled Readers/CA	Houghton Mifflin Harcourt
Columbian Exchange, The	Z	I	2956	Leveled Readers/TX	Houghton Mifflin Harcourt
Columbus and the Americas	S	I	250+	Reading Expeditions	National Geographic
Columbus Day	I	I	122	American Holidays	Lerner Publishing Group
Columbus Day	Q	I	250+	Holiday Histories	Heinemann
Columbus Day	N	I	2221	On My Own Holidays	Lerner Publishing Group
Comanche Indians, The	P	I	250+	Native Peoples	Red Brick Learning
Comanche Warriors	T	I	250+	Warriors of History	Capstone Press
Combat Rescue Helicopters: The MH-53 Pave Lows	V	I	250+	War Planes	Capstone Press
Combining Shapes	C	I	29	Early Math	Lerner Publishing Group
Come	A	F	20	Sails	Rigby
Come and Have Fun	I	F	250+	Hurd, Edith Thacher	HarperCollins
Come and Have Fun	A	F	49	KinderReaders	Rigby
Come and Play	B	F	104	Bookshop	Mondo Publishing
Come and Play	B	F	34	Interaction	Rigby
Come and Play	C	RF	62	McAlpin, MaryAnn	Short Tales Press
Come and Play	B	RF	84	Rigby Flying Colors	Rigby
Come and Play	D	F	104	Story Steps	Rigby
Come and Play, Cats!	C	RF	45	Early Emergent	Pioneer Valley
Come and Play, Sarah!	D	RF	49	Sunshine	Wright Group/McGraw Hill
Come and See!	G	RF	134	Foundations	Wright Group/McGraw Hill
Come Back, Amelia Bedelia	L	F	250+	Parish, Peggy	Harper & Row
Come Back, Pip!	J	RF	355	PM Plus Story Books	Rigby

TITLE	LEVEL	GENRE	WORD COUNT	AUTHOR / SERIES	PUBLISHER / DISTRIBUTOR
Come Closer	L	I	250+	Trackers	Pacific Learning
Come for a Swim!	D	F	107	Leveled Readers	Houghton Mifflin Harcourt
Come for a Swim!	D	F	107	Leveled Readers/CA	Houghton Mifflin Harcourt
Come for a Swim!	F	RF	129	Sunshine	Wright Group/McGraw Hill
Come Here Spinner!	K	F	250+	Foundations	Wright Group/McGraw Hill
Come Here, Big Cat	D	RF	94	Bonnell, Kris	Reading Reading Books
Come Here, Puppy	B	F	56	Bella and Rosie Series	Literacy Footprints
Come Here, Puppy!	C	RF	39	Handprints B	Educators Publishing Service
Come Here, Tiger!	D	RF	62	Green Light Readers	Harcourt
Come in the Grass	A	F	24	Sails	Rigby
Come In!	B	F	20	The Book Project	Sundance
Come Meet Some Seals	I	I	118	Little Books	Sadlier-Oxford
Come Morning	V	HF	250+	Guccione, Leslie Davis	Lerner Publishing Group
Come On Down	K	I	250+	World Quest Adventures	World Quest Learning
Come On Up	A	F	16	KinderReaders	Rigby
Come On!	B	RF	22	Sunshine	Wright Group/McGraw Hill
Come On, Mom	D	RF	56	New Way	Steck-Vaughn
Come On, Tim	G	RF	198	PM Story Books	Rigby
Come Out and Play Little Mouse	H	F	198	Kraus, Robert	Morrow
Come Play With Me	D	RF	69	Leveled Readers	Houghton Mifflin Harcourt
Come Play With Me	C	F	36	Little Readers	Houghton Mifflin Harcourt
Come Sing, Jimmy Jo	V	RF	250+	Paterson, Katherine	Penguin Group
Come to Mexico	M	I	250+	Yellow Umbrella Books	Red Brick Learning
Come to My House	C	F	56	Joy Readers	Pearson Learning Group
Come to My House!	F	RF	131	Sunshine	Wright Group/McGraw Hill
Come to My Party	D	RF	84	Windows on Literacy	National Geographic
Come to Nicodemus	S	HF	1859	Leveled Readers	Houghton Mifflin Harcourt
Come to Nicodemus	S	HF	1859	Leveled Readers/CA	Houghton Mifflin Harcourt
Come to Nicodemus	S	HF	1859	Leveled Readers/TX	Houghton Mifflin Harcourt
Come to School, Dear Dragon	E	F	301	Dear Dragon	Norwood House Press
Come to the Library	B	I	46	Red Rocket Readers	Flying Start Books
Come with Me	E	RF	60	Potato Chip Books	American Reading Company
Come with Me	C	RF	25	Story Box	Wright Group/McGraw Hill
Come! Sit! Speak!	H	RF	57	Rookie Readers	Children's Press
Comeback Challenge, The	Q	RF	250+	Christopher, Matt	Little Brown and Company
Comeback Dog, The	O	RF	250+	Thomas, Jane Resh	Bantam Books
Comeback of the Home Run Kid	P	RF	250+	Christopher, Matt	Little Brown and Company
Comet Dust	U	I	2489	Leveled Readers	Houghton Mifflin Harcourt
Comet Dust	U	I	1671	Leveled Readers/CA	Houghton Mifflin Harcourt
Comet Dust	U	I	1671	Leveled Readers/TX	Houghton Mifflin Harcourt
Comet in Moominland	S	F	250+	Jansson, Tove	Farrar, Straus, & Giroux
Comets	U	I	250+	A First Book	Franklin Watts
Comets	S	I	250+	Sails	Rigby
Comets	Q	I	250+	The Galaxy	Red Brick Learning
Comets	P	I	250+	Trail Blazers	Ransom Publishing
Comets and Meteor Showers	Q	I	250+	A True Book	Children's Press
Comets, Asteroids, and Meteoroids	S	I	250+	Our Solar System	Compass Point Books
Comfort	Z+	RF	250+	Dean, Carolee	Houghton Mifflin Harcourt
Comic Books: From Superheroes to Manga	R	I	250+	High Five Reading	Red Brick Learning
Comic-Book Facts	T	I	250+	Power Up!	Steck-Vaughn
Coming Distractions: Questioning Movies	S	I	250+	Media Literacy	Capstone Press
Coming Home	U	HF	1920	Leveled Readers	Houghton Mifflin Harcourt
Coming of Hoole, The: Guardians of Ga'Hoole	V	F	250+	Lasky, Kathryn	Scholastic

* Collection of short stories   # Graphic text
^ Mature content with lower level text demands

TITLE	LEVEL	GENRE	WORD COUNT	AUTHOR / SERIES	PUBLISHER / DISTRIBUTOR
Coming to America	L	I	185	Vocabulary Readers	Houghton Mifflin Harcourt
Coming to Ellis Island	N	I	172	In Step Readers	Rigby
Commander Toad and the Big Black Hole	K	F	250+	Yolen, Jane	G.P. Putnam's Sons Books for Young Readers
Commander Toad and the Dis-Asteroid	K	F	250+	Yolen, Jane	G.P. Putnam's Sons Books for Young Readers
Commander Toad and the Intergalactic Spy	K	F	250+	Yolen, Jane	G.P. Putnam's Sons Books for Young Readers
Commander Toad and the Planet of the Grapes	K	F	250+	Yolen, Jane	G.P. Putnam's Sons Books for Young Readers
Commander Toad and the Space Pirates	K	F	250+	Yolen, Jane	G.P. Putnam's Sons Books for Young Readers
Commander Toad And The Voyage Home	K	F	250+	Yolen, Jane	G.P. Putnam's Sons Books for Young Readers
Commander Toad in Space	K	F	250+	Yolen, Jane	Scholastic
Communication	J	I	231	Early Explorers	Benchmark Education
Communication	N	I	250+	Literacy 2000	Rigby
Communication	K	I	462	Red Rocket Readers	Flying Start Books
Communication Connection	S	I	250+	Kids Discover Reading	Wright Group/McGraw Hill
Communication in the U.S.A., Then & Now	P	I	739	Time for Kids	Teacher Created Materials
Communication Then and Now	I	I	99	Early Explorers	Benchmark Education
Communication Then and Now	P	I	250+	Lighthouse	Ginn & Co.
Communication Then and Now	I	I	123	Then and Now	Lerner Publishing Group
Communities	D	I	42	Pebble Books	Capstone Press
Communities	F	I	89	People	Capstone Press
Communities	I	I	63	Windows on Literacy	National Geographic
Communities	E	I	59	Wonder World	Wright Group/McGraw Hill
Communities	I	I	42	Yellow Umbrella Books	Red Brick Learning
Communities Across America Today	R	I	250+	Reading Expeditions	National Geographic
Communities Everywhere	P	I	250+	PM Extensions	Rigby
Communities Helping Communities	P	I	250+	Navigators Social Studies Series	Benchmark Education
Communities Need Each Other	M	I	287	Larkin, Bruce	Wilbooks
Communities Then and Now	M	I	620	Early Explorers	Benchmark Education
Community Cares, A	J	RF	591	InfoTrek	ETA/Cuisenaire
Community Garden, The	J	RF	419	Leveled Readers	Houghton Mifflin Harcourt
Community Garden, The	J	RF	419	Leveled Readers/CA	Houghton Mifflin Harcourt
Community Garden, The	J	RF	419	Leveled Readers/TX	Houghton Mifflin Harcourt
Community Has Homes, A	G	I	126	Early Explorers	Benchmark Education
Community Helpers	J	I	301	Reading Street	Pearson
Community Jobs	I	I	207	Early Connections	Benchmark Education
Community Leaders: Then and Now	N	I	250+	Primary Source Readers	Teacher Created Materials
Community of Washington, D.C., The	O	I	250+	Navigators Social Studies Series	Benchmark Education
Community Places	B	I	37	Reach	National Geographic
Community Service	F	I	80	On Deck	Rigby
Community Teamwork	O	I	1100	Vocabulary Readers/TX	Houghton Mifflin Harcourt
Community, A	K	I	238	Larkin, Bruce	Wilbooks
Commuter	M	I	343	Independent Readers Social Studies	Houghton Mifflin Harcourt
Comparing Data	M	I	169	Windows on Literacy	National Geographic
Comparing in Nature	I	I	156	Early Explorers	Benchmark Education
Comparing Sizes and Weights	H	I	52	Windows on Literacy	National Geographic
Comparing Two Cities	H	I	113	Early Explorers	Benchmark Education
Compass	D	I	31	Simple Tools	Lerner Publishing Group
Composting	N	I	755	Vocabulary Readers	Houghton Mifflin Harcourt
Composting	N	I	755	Vocabulary Readers/CA	Houghton Mifflin Harcourt

C

* Collection of short stories   # Graphic text
^ Mature content with lower level text demands

Organized Alphabetically by Title   **153**
Storable Database at www.fountasandpinnellleveledbooks.com

TITLE	LEVEL	GENRE	WORD COUNT	AUTHOR / SERIES	PUBLISHER / DISTRIBUTOR
Composting - Worms Tell All	P	I	250+	InfoTrek	ETA/Cuisenaire
Compound, The	Y	SF	250+	Bodeen, S. A.	Square Fish
Computer Buttons	I	F	250+	Sunshine	Wright Group/McGraw Hill
Computer Error	L	F	250+	Rigby Literacy	Rigby
^Computer Evidence	Q	I	250+	Forensic Crime Solvers	Capstone Press
Computer Game, The	D	RF	75	Literacy by Design	Rigby
Computer Game, The	E	RF	75	Rigby Literacy	Rigby
Computer Game, The	E	RF	85	Rigby Star	Rigby
Computer Keys	E	F	85	Reading Safari	Mondo Publishing
Computer Nut, The	R	SF	250+	Byars, Betsy	Bantam Books
Computer Pals	J	RF	365	InfoTrek	ETA/Cuisenaire
Computer Pigs	M	TL	250+	Reading Safari	Mondo Publishing
Computer Projects	P	I	250+	Infotrek Plus	ETA/Cuisenaire
Computer Virus	M	RF	250+	Rigby Gigglers	Rigby
Computer Zone, The	O	F	1674	The Funny Zone	Norwood House Press
Computer, The	P	I	250+	Great Inventions	Red Brick Learning
Computer, The	T	I	250+	Tales of Invention	Heinemann Library
Computer, The: Passport to the Digital Age	R	I	250+	On Deck	Rigby
Computers and Movies	S	I	1271	Vocabulary Readers	Houghton Mifflin Harcourt
Computers and Movies	S	I	1271	Vocabulary Readers/CA	Houghton Mifflin Harcourt
Computers and Movies	S	I	1271	Vocabulary Readers/TX	Houghton Mifflin Harcourt
Computers Are for Everyone	K	I	464	Sunshine	Wright Group/McGraw Hill
Computers Can Help	G	I	86	Shutterbug Books	Steck-Vaughn
Comsats and Phone Calls	P	I	487	Springboard	Wright Group/McGraw Hill
Comstock Lode, The	U	I	2086	Leveled Readers Social Studies	Houghton Mifflin Harcourt
Conceived in Liberty: The Gettysburg Address	X	I	2069	Leveled Readers	Houghton Mifflin Harcourt
Concert Night	K	RF	250+	Literacy 2000	Rigby
Concert, The	B	I	49	Rigby Flying Colors	Rigby
Concord	R	I	250+	HSP/Harcourt Trophies	Harcourt, Inc.
Concrete	H	I	123	Books for Young Learners	Richard C. Owen
Concrete Jungle	L	RF	250+	Pacific Literacy	Pacific Learning
Concrete Mixers	G	I	110	Mighty Machines	Capstone Press
Concrete Mixers	K	I	110	Pebble Books	Capstone Press
Concrete Mixers	L	I	510	Pull Ahead Books	Lerner Publishing Group
Condoleezza Rice: Strength of Conviction	T	B	250+	Explore More	Wright Group/McGraw Hill
Condor Rescue	Q	RF	250+	Reading Expeditions	National Geographic
Cone	C	I	33	Solid Shapes	Lerner Publishing Group
Cones	K	I	226	3-D Shapes	Capstone Press
Cones All Around	E	I	85	Early Explorers	Benchmark Education
Confederate Commander: General Robert E. Lee	T	B	250+	We the People	Compass Point Books
Confederate General: Stonewall Jackson	T	B	250+	We the People	Compass Point Books
Confederate Girl, A	U	I	250+	Diaries and Memoirs	Capstone Press
Confetti Girl	V	RF	250+	Lopez, Diana	Little Brown and Company
Confucius	X	B	250+	Primary Source Readers	Teacher Created Materials
Confucius, Teacher for a Troubled Time	X	I	2349	Leveled Readers	Houghton Mifflin Harcourt
Confucius, Teacher for a Troubled Time	X	I	2349	Leveled Readers/CA	Houghton Mifflin Harcourt
Confucius, Teacher for a Troubled Time	X	I	2349	Leveled Readers/TX	Houghton Mifflin Harcourt
Confucius: The Golden Rule	Y	HF	250+	Russell Freedman	Scholastic
Congratulations, Miss Malarkey!	L	RF	250+	Finchler, Judy & O'Malley, Kevin	Walker & Company
Congress	S	I	250+	A True Book	Children's Press
Congress and Parliament	W	I	1803	Leveled Readers Social Studies	Houghton Mifflin Harcourt
Congress of the United States, The	W	I	250+	American Civics	Red Brick Learning
Congress, The: A Look at the Legislative Branch	S	I	1754	Searchlight Books	Lerner Publishing Group

* Collection of short stories   # Graphic text
^ Mature content with lower level text demands

TITLE	LEVEL	GENRE	WORD COUNT	AUTHOR / SERIES	PUBLISHER / DISTRIBUTOR
Connecticut	T	I	250+	Hello U.S.A.	Lerner Publishing Group
Connecticut	S	I	250+	Land of Liberty	Red Brick Learning
Connecticut	T	I	250+	Sea To Shining Sea	Children's Press
Connecticut	R	I	250+	This Land Is Your Land	Compass Point Books
Connecticut Colony, The	R	I	250+	The American Colonies	Capstone Press
Connecticut: Facts and Symbols	O	I	250+	The States and Their Symbols	Capstone Press
Connecting to the Internet	O	I	250+	Rigby Literacy	Rigby
Connie's Dance	M	RF	361	Windmill Books	Rigby
Connor and Clara Build a Concrete Poem	N	RF	1100	Poetry Builders	Norwood House Press
^Conquering England: The Battle of Hastings	X	I	250+	Bloodiest Battles	Capstone Press
Conquering Mount Everest	S	I	250+	Navigators Social Studies Series	Benchmark Education
Conrad Saves Pinger Park	L	RF	489	Winans, Carvin	Marimba Books
Consideration	L	I	250+	Character Education	Red Brick Learning
Consideration	K	I	250+	Everyday Character Education	Capstone Press
Constance and the Great Escape	L	F	250+	Le Gall, Pierre	Sterling Publishing
Constance and Tiny	L	F	250+	Le Gall, Pierre	Sterling Publishing
Constantinople in the Center of the World	Z	I	2840	Independent Readers Social Studies	Houghton Mifflin Harcourt
Constellations	Q	I	250+	A True Book	Children's Press
Constellations	Q	I	250+	The Galaxy	Capstone Press
Constitution and the Bill of Rights, The	T	I	250+	Primary Source Readers	Teacher Created Materials
Constitution Day	J	I	115	American Holidays	Lerner Publishing Group
Constitution, The	S	I	250+	A True Book	Children's Press
Constitution, The	V	I	250+	Cornerstones of Freedom	Children's Press
Constitution, The	W	I	250+	Reading Expeditions	National Geographic
Constitutional Convention, The	T	I	1267	Leveled Readers Social Studies	Houghton Mifflin Harcourt
Construction Alphabet Book, The	M	I	250+	Pallotta, Jerry	Charlesbridge
Construction Crews	J	I	115	Construction Zone	Capstone Press
Construction Tools	I	I	113	Construction Zone	Capstone Press
Construction Workers	M	I	250+	Community Helpers	Red Brick Learning
Contact	T	F	250+	Reading Safari	Mondo Publishing
Contemporary Age, The	R	I	250+	Journey Through History	Barron's Educational
Contender, The	Z+	RF	250+	Lipsyte, Robert	HarperTrophy
Contest Between the Sun and the Wind, The: An Aesop's Fable	M	TL	250+	Forest, Heather	August House Publishers
Contest, The	K	RF	250+	PM Plus Story Books	Rigby
Continents, The	M	I	250+	Spyglass Books	Compass Point Books
Controlling Traffic	V	I	250+	PM Collection	Rigby
Conversation Club, The	L	F	250+	Stanley, Diane	Aladdin
Coo Coo Caroo	G	F	57	Books for Young Learners	Richard C. Owen
Coober Pedy, Australia: Communities Around the World	S	I	250+	Reading Expeditions	National Geographic
Cook	D	I	20	Work People Do	Lerner Publishing Group
Cook: Captain James Cook Charts the Pacific Ocean	U	B	250+	Exploring the World	Compass Point Books
Cookcamp, The	V	RF	250+	Paulsen, Gary	Bantam Books
Cookie	X	RF	250+	Wilson, Jacqueline	Roaring Brook Press
Cookie and Elmo Eat Their Colors	C	F	37	Brand New Readers	Candlewick Press
Cookie Count!	M	I	250+	Early Connections	Benchmark Education
Cookie House, The	F	TL	310	Fairy Tales and Folklore	Norwood House Press
Cookie Jar, The	G	RF	106	Sunshine	Wright Group/McGraw Hill
Cookie Monster and the Parade	D	F	29	Brand New Readers	Candlewick Press
Cookie Monster Cleans Up	C	F	35	Brand New Readers	Candlewick Press
Cookie Monster's Bed	C	F	48	Brand New Readers	Candlewick Press

C

TITLE	LEVEL	GENRE	WORD COUNT	AUTHOR / SERIES	PUBLISHER / DISTRIBUTOR
Cookie Problem, The	E	RF	103	The King School Series	Townsend Press
Cookies	D	I	43	Benchmark Rebus	Marshall Cavendish
Cookies	D	RF	18	Little Celebrations	Pearson Learning Group
Cookies	LB	I	15	Twig	Wright Group/McGraw Hill
Cookies for a Royal Snack	G	F	136	Dominie Math Stories	Pearson Learning Group
Cookies for Danny	D	F	58	Coulton, Mia	Maryruth Books
Cookies for Santa	H	F	217	Little Elf	Literacy Footprints
Cookies to Share	E	RF	45	Pair-It Books	Steck-Vaughn
Cookie's Week	F	RF	84	Ward, Cindy	G.P. Putnam's Sons Books for Young Readers
Cooking	B	RF	30	Sails	Rigby
Cooking at School	G	RF	68	City Kids	Rigby
Cooking Catastrophe	N	RF	250+	Girlz Rock!	Mondo Publishing
Cooking Contest, The	K	RF	904	Early Connections	Benchmark Education
Cooking Dinner	G	I	86	Windows on Literacy	National Geographic
*Cooking Pot	L	TL	250+	Story Box	Wright Group/McGraw Hill
Cooking Pot, The	I	TL	250+	Storyworlds	Heinemann
Cooking Pot, The	F	F	132	Sunshine	Wright Group/McGraw Hill
Cooking Spaghetti	I	RF	150	City Kids	Rigby
Cooking Thanksgiving Dinner	E	RF	126	Early Emergent	Pioneer Valley
Cook-Out, The	E	RF	78	Oxford Reading Tree	Oxford University Press
Cook's Catastrophe!, The	M	F	250+	Tristars	Richard C. Owen
Cool	K	RF	137	Books for Young Learners	Richard C. Owen
^Cool BMX Racing Facts	N	I	203	Cool Sports Facts	Capstone Press
Cool Boy Stuff You Can Draw	R	I	1695	Ready, Set, Draw!	Millbrook Press
^Cool Brands	T	I	250+	Download	Hameray Publishing Group
Cool Cars and Trucks	J	I	264	Kenney, Sean	Henry Holt & Co.
Cool Cat	WB	F	0	Hogrogian, Nonny	Roaring Brook Press
Cool Cat, A	O	RF	250+	Leveled Readers	Houghton Mifflin Harcourt
Cool Clive	M	RF	250+	High-Fliers	Pacific Learning
Cool Clive and the Bubble Trouble	M	RF	250+	High-Fliers	Pacific Learning
Cool Clive and the Little Pest	M	RF	250+	High-Fliers	Pacific Learning
Cool Crabs	H	I	258	Sails	Rigby
Cool Crazy Crickets to the Rescue, The	L	RF	250+	Elliott, David	Candlewick Press
Cool Customs	K	I	250+	Spyglass Books	Compass Point Books
Cool Dog, School Dog	K	F	177	Bowers, Tim	Marshall Cavendish
Cool Drink of Water, A	H	I	96	Kerley, Barbara	National Geographic
Cool Girl Stuff You Can Draw	R	I	1665	Ready, Set, Draw!	Millbrook Press
Cool in the Summer	E	I	63	Windows on Literacy	National Geographic
Cool Off	C	RF	37	Bookshop	Mondo Publishing
^Cool Pro Wrestling Facts	N	I	179	Cool Sports Facts	Capstone Press
Cool School	O	F	250+	Sails	Rigby
Cool School, A	G	RF	138	City Stories	Rigby
^Cool Skateboarding Facts	N	I	179	Cool Sports Facts	Capstone Press
^Cool Stock Car Racing Facts	N	I	202	Cool Sports Facts	Capstone Press
Cool Stuff 2.0 and How It Works	Z	I	250+	Woodford, Chris & Woodcock, Jon	DK Publishing
Cool Tools	I	I	238	Sails	Rigby
Cool Tools	B	I	42	Shutterbug Books	Steck-Vaughn
Cool Tools	K	I	250+	Spyglass Books	Compass Point Books
Cool Treasure, The	N	RF	250+	Orbit Chapter Books	Pacific Learning
Cool Zone with the Pain & the Great One	M	RF	250+	Blume, Judy	Delacorte Press
Coolest Rock, The	L	I	945	Avenues	Hampton Brown
Coolest Rock, The	L	I	250+	Chanek, Sherilin	Hampton Brown

* Collection of short stories   # Graphic text
^ Mature content with lower level text demands

TITLE	LEVEL	GENRE	WORD COUNT	AUTHOR / SERIES	PUBLISHER / DISTRIBUTOR
Cooling	C	I	26	Changing Matter	Lerner Publishing Group
Cooling Off	D	RF	104	Reading Corners	Pearson Learning Group
Cooped Up	K	RF	250+	Pacific Literacy	Pacific Learning
Cooperation	L	I	250+	Everyday Character Education	Capstone Press
Copán: City of the Maya	Z	I	3688	Leveled Readers	Houghton Mifflin Harcourt
Copper Lady, The	M	HF	250+	On My Own History	Carolrhoda Books
Copperheads	M	I	250+	Snakes	Capstone Press
Copy Crocs, The	L	F	250+	Bedford, David	Peachtree
Copycat	C	F	54	Story Box	Wright Group/McGraw Hill
Cora at Camp	M	RF	250+	Leveled Readers Language Support	Houghton Mifflin Harcourt
Cora at Camp Blue Waters	N	RF	772	Leveled Readers	Houghton Mifflin Harcourt
Coral	L	I	250+	Marine Life For Young Readers	Pearson Learning Group
Coral in Crisis	S	I	1272	Leveled Readers	Houghton Mifflin Harcourt
Coral in Crisis	S	I	1272	Leveled Readers/CA	Houghton Mifflin Harcourt
Coral Reef	N	I	250+	Habitats	Children's Press
Coral Reef Diary	K	I	595	Explorations	Eleanor Curtain Publishing
Coral Reef Diary	K	I	595	Explorations	Okapi Educational Materials
Coral Reef Food Chain, A: A Who-Eats-What Adventure in the Caribbean Sea	U	I	7440	Follow That Food Chain	Lerner Publishing Group
Coral Reef Hunters	N	I	250+	Soar To Success	Houghton Mifflin Harcourt
Coral Reef, A	I	I	153	Rigby Focus	Rigby
Coral Reef, The	L	I	250+	Books for Young Learners	Richard C. Owen
Coral Reef, The	H	I	186	Discovery Links	Newbridge
Coral Reef: Inside Australia's Great Barrier Reef	P	I	250+	Cambridge Reading	Pearson Learning Group
Coral Reefs	Q	I	250+	Explorer Books-Pathfinder	National Geographic
Coral Reefs	P	I	250+	Explorer Books-Pioneer	National Geographic
Coral Reefs	Q	I	250+	First Reports	Compass Point Books
Coral Reefs	P	I	250+	Gibbons, Gail	Holiday House
Coral Reefs	H	I	206	Leveled Readers	Houghton Mifflin Harcourt
Coral Reefs	H	I	206	Leveled Readers/CA	Houghton Mifflin Harcourt
Coral Reefs	H	I	206	Leveled Readers/TX	Houghton Mifflin Harcourt
Coral Reefs	I	I	266	Vocabulary Readers	Houghton Mifflin Harcourt
Coral Reefs	I	I	266	Vocabulary Readers/CA	Houghton Mifflin Harcourt
Coral Reefs	I	I	266	Vocabulary Readers/TX	Houghton Mifflin Harcourt
Coral Reefs: Colorful Underwater Habitats	N	I	250+	Amazing Science	Picture Window Books
Coral Reefs: Wonders of Nature	L	I	250+	Bookworms	Marshall Cavendish
Coraline	W	F	250+	Gaiman, Neil	HarperCollins
Corals	G	I	51	Ocean Life	Capstone Press
Corals	K	I	133	Under the Sea	Capstone Press
Corduroy	K	F	250+	Freeman, Don	Scholastic
Coretta Scott King	R	B	3995	History Maker Bios	Lerner Publishing Group
Coretta Scott King: Civil Rights Activist	P	B	250+	On Deck	Rigby
Corey's Christmas Wish	M	RF	250+	Pony Tails	Skylark
Cork	K	RF	473	Gear Up!	Wright Group/McGraw Hill
Cork & Fuzz: Finders Keepers	J	F	250+	Chaconas, Dori	Puffin Books
Cork & Fuzz: Short and Tall	J	F	250+	Chaconas, Dori	Puffin Books
Cork & Fuzz: The Collectors	J	F	250+	Chaconas, Dori	Puffin Books
Corkscrew, The	Q	RF	250+	WorldScapes	ETA/Cuisenaire
Corky Cub's Crazy Caps	K	F	638	Animal Antics A To Z	Kane Press
Cormorant, The	P	RF	250+	Tristars	Richard C. Owen
Corn	E	I	90	Bonnell, Kris/About	Reading Reading Books
Corn	L	I	612	Rigby Flying Colors	Rigby
Corn	K	I	221	Windows on Literacy	National Geographic

C

TITLE	LEVEL	GENRE	WORD COUNT	AUTHOR / SERIES	PUBLISHER / DISTRIBUTOR
Corn	L	I	401	Yellow Umbrella Books	Red Brick Learning
Corn Bread for Everyone!	J	RF	250+	On Our Way to English	Rigby
Corn for Sale	F	I	128	Literacy by Design	Rigby
Corn Husk Doll, The	K	RF	250+	Schiller, Melissa	Scholastic
Corn Is Maize: The Gift of the Indians	O	I	250+	Aliki	Steck-Vaughn
Corn Snakes	M	I	250+	Snakes	Capstone Press
Corn That Kay Grew, The	D	RF	80	Windows on Literacy	National Geographic
Corn: An American Indian Gift	M	I	690	Pair-It Books	Steck-Vaughn
Corn: from Table to Table	H	I	171	Discovery Links	Newbridge
Cornelius Vanderbilt and the Railroad Industry	R	B	250+	On Deck	Rigby
Corner of the Universe, A	Y	RF	250+	Martin, Ann M.	Scholastic
Cornfield Volcano, The	N	HF	250+	Windows on Literacy	National Geographic
Coronado and the Cities of Gold	Y	B	2051	Leveled Readers	Houghton Mifflin Harcourt
Coronado: Francisco Vasquez de Coronado Explores the Southwest	U	B	250+	Exploring the World	Compass Point Books
Coronado's Golden Quest	R	B	250+	Weisberg, Barbara	Steck-Vaughn
Corps of Discovery, The	S	I	1000	Leveled Readers/TX	Houghton Mifflin Harcourt
Corps of Discovery, The	Q	I	250+	Literacy by Design	Rigby
Corps of the Bare-Boned Plane, The	X	RF	250+	Horvath, Polly	Farrar, Straus, & Giroux
Corrie's Important Decision	V	I	250+	Leveled Readers Language Support	Houghton Mifflin Harcourt
Corrie's Secret	W	I	1726	Leveled Readers	Houghton Mifflin Harcourt
Corvettes	T	I	250+	High Performance	Red Brick Learning
Cosmic Clock, The	Y	I	250+	High-Fliers	Pacific Learning
Cosmic Joker, The	Z	I	250+	Unsolved Mysteries	Steck-Vaughn
Cost of Dinner, The	N	I	332	Early Explorers	Benchmark Education
Costa Rica	O	I	2503	A Ticket to ...	Carolrhoda Books
Costa Rica	P	I	2216	Country Explorers	Lerner Publishing Group
Costa Rica: A Question and Answer Book	P	I	250+	Question and Answer Countries	Capstone Press
Costume	W	I	250+	Eyewitness Books	DK Publishing
Costume Box, The	B	F	55	Leveled Readers	Houghton Mifflin Harcourt
Costume Box, The	B	F	55	Leveled Readers/CA	Houghton Mifflin Harcourt
Costume Parade, The	E	RF	57	Learn to Read	Creative Teaching Press
Costume Party	C	RF	64	Early Connections	Benchmark Education
Costume Party	A	RF	32	Joy Readers	Pearson Learning Group
Costume Party, The	J	RF	145	City Kids	Rigby
Costume Party, The	A	RF	35	Handprints A	Educators Publishing Service
Costume Party, The	M	F	577	Leveled Literacy Intervention/ Blue System	Heinemann
Costume Party, The	B	RF	15	Sunshine	Wright Group/McGraw Hill
Costume, The	A	RF	20	Leveled Readers	Houghton Mifflin Harcourt
Costume, The	A	RF	20	Leveled Readers/CA	Houghton Mifflin Harcourt
Costumes	C	RF	23	Oxford Reading Tree	Oxford University Press
Costumes	C	I	36	Pebble Books	Capstone Press
Costumes on Show	K	I	378	Rigby Flying Colors	Rigby
Cottle Street	N	RF	250+	Action Packs	Rigby
Cotton Comes From Plants	K	I	161	Windows on Literacy	National Geographic
Cotton Gin, The	R	I	250+	Theme Sets	National Geographic
Cotton Plant to Cotton Shirt	L	I	250+	Early Connections	Benchmark Education
Cottontail Rabbits	K	I	371	Pull Ahead Books	Lerner Publishing Group
Couch was a Castle, The	H	F	138	Ohi, Ruth	Annick Press
Cougars	O	I	1475	Early Bird Nature Books	Lerner Publishing Group
Cougars	R	I	250+	Predators in the Wild	Capstone Press

* Collection of short stories   # Graphic text
^ Mature content with lower level text demands

TITLE	LEVEL	GENRE	WORD COUNT	AUTHOR / SERIES	PUBLISHER / DISTRIBUTOR
Cougars	G	I	132	Readlings	American Reading Company
Could It Be?	J	RF	250+	Bank Street	Bantam Books
Could We Live on the Moon?	O	I	250+	iOpeners	Pearson Learning Group
Council of Evil: Villain.net	W	F	250+	Briggs, Andy	Walker & Company
Count and See	WB	I	0	Hoban, Tana	Macmillan
Count Down to Fall	M	I	809	Hawk, Frank	Sylvan Dell Publishing
Count Karlstein	Y	F	250+	Pullman, Philip	Alfred A. Knopf
Count of Monte Cristo, The	Z+	HF	10960	Dominoes three	Oxford University Press
Count On Me!	Q	I	250+	Orbit Collections	Pacific Learning
Count on Pablo	K	RF	250+	Math Matters	Kane Press
Count on Your Body	K	I	250+	Rigby Literacy	Rigby
Count on Your Body	K	I	250+	Rigby Star Quest	Rigby
Count the Animals	LB	I	10	Windows on Literacy	National Geographic
Count the Kittens	B	I	38	Tiny Treasures	Pioneer Valley
Count to a Million	V	I	250+	Pallotta, Jerry	Scholastic
Count with Me	A	I	49	Little Books	Sadlier-Oxford
Count Your Chickens	G	I	123	Yellow Umbrella Books	Red Brick Learning
Count Your Money with the Polk Street School	M	RF	250+	Giff, Patricia Reilly	Bantam Books
Count Your Way Through Afghanistan	P	I	619	Count Your Way Books	Carolrhoda Books
Count Your Way Through Africa	P	I	1257	Count Your Way Books	Carolrhoda Books
Count Your Way Through Brazil	Q	I	1095	Count Your Way Books	Carolrhoda Books
Count Your Way Through China	P	I	967	Count Your Way Books	Carolrhoda Books
Count Your Way Through Egypt	P	I	828	Count Your Way Books	Carolrhoda Books
Count Your Way Through France	P	I	990	Count Your Way Books	Carolrhoda Books
Count Your Way Through Greece	P	I	1060	Count Your Way Books	Carolrhoda Books
Count Your Way Through India	P	I	1026	Count Your Way Books	Carolrhoda Books
Count Your Way Through Iran	P	I	700	Count Your Way Books	Carolrhoda Books
Count Your Way Through Ireland	P	I	1288	Count Your Way Books	Carolrhoda Books
Count Your Way Through Israel	Q	I	1086	Count Your Way Books	Carolrhoda Books
Count Your Way Through Italy	P	I	891	Count Your Way Books	Carolrhoda Books
Count Your Way Through Japan	P	I	749	Count Your Way Books	Carolrhoda Books
Count Your Way Through Kenya	P	I	544	Count Your Way Books	Carolrhoda Books
Count Your Way Through Korea	P	I	991	Count Your Way Books	Carolrhoda Books
Count Your Way Through Mexico	P	I	1097	Count Your Way Books	Carolrhoda Books
Count Your Way Through Russia	P	I	507	Count Your Way Books	Carolrhoda Books
Count Your Way Through South Africa	P	I	700	Count Your Way Books	Carolrhoda Books
Count Your Way Through the Arab World	P	I	936	Count Your Way Books	Carolrhoda Books
Count Your Way Through Zimbabwe	P	I	618	Count Your Way Books	Carolrhoda Books
Count!	H	RF	70	Fleming, Denise	Scholastic
Countdown	G	F	70	Literacy Tree	Rigby
Countdown	X	HF	250+	Wiles, Deborah	Scholastic
Countdown to a Space Shuttle Launch	W	I	250+	Literacy By Design	Rigby
Countdown to the Year 1000	P	F	250+	McMullan, Kate	Scholastic
Countdown: a play	J	F	250+	Story Box	Wright Group/McGraw Hill
Counterfeit Tackle, The	P	RF	250+	Christopher, Matt	Little Brown and Company
Countess Below the Stairs, A	Z+	HF	250+	Ibbotson, Eva	Speak
Countess Veronica	Q	RF	250+	Robinson, Nancy K.	Scholastic
Counting	C	I	33	Early Math	Lerner Publishing Group
Counting	G	I	66	Windows on Literacy	National Geographic
Counting Around Town	D	RF	84	Early Connections	Benchmark Education
Counting Colors	K	I	234	Priddy, Roger	Priddy Books
Counting Down	C	RF	93	PM Math Readers	Rigby
Counting in the City	D	I	90	Math Around Us	Heinemann Library
Counting Insects	K	I	230	Early Connections	Benchmark Education

TITLE	LEVEL	GENRE	WORD COUNT	AUTHOR / SERIES	PUBLISHER / DISTRIBUTOR
Counting Many Ways	J	I	250+	Yellow Umbrella Books	Capstone Press
Counting Money	G	I	122	Early Connections	Benchmark Education
Counting Money	E	I	107	Money	Lerner Publishing Group
Counting My Collections	F	I	126	Early Connections	Benchmark Education
Counting on a Win	K	RF	250+	Read-it! Readers	Picture Window Books
Counting One to Five	B	I	64	Early Connections	Benchmark Education
Counting Pencils	A	I	32	Early Explorers	Benchmark Education
Counting Pets by Twos	I	I	234	Counting Books	Capstone Press
Counting Seeds	C	I	63	Early Connections	Benchmark Education
Counting Stars	F	I	144	Early Connections	Benchmark Education
Counting to 100	J	I	247	Gear Up!	Wright Group/McGraw Hill
Counting with Apollo	K	F	285	Gregoire, Caroline	Kane/Miller Book Publishers
Countries of the World	Q	I	250+	High-Fliers	Pacific Learning
Country Artist: A Story About Beatrix Potter, The	R	B	6783	Creative Minds Biographies	Carolrhoda Books
Country Fair	J	HF	250+	Wilder, Laura Ingalls	HarperCollins
Country Family	G	RF	262	Instant Readers	Harcourt School Publishers
Country Mouse and a Town Mouse, A	G	TL	196	Traditional Tales	Pioneer Valley
Country Mouse and the Town Mouse, The	F	TL	200	Reed, Janet	Scholastic
Country Vet	N	I	250+	Infotrek Plus	ETA/Cuisenaire
Courage	K	I	250+	Everyday Character Education	Capstone Press
Courage of Helen Keller, The	N	B	250+	Rosen Real Readers	Rosen Publishing Group
Courage of Sarah Noble, The	O	HF	250+	Dalgliesh, Alice	Aladdin
Courage to Fly	O	RF	1170	Harrison, Troon	Red Deer Press
Courage to Ride: Ridgeview Riding Club	P	RF	250+	Kelly, Bernadette,	Stone Arch Books
Courtney's Twos	C	RF	30	Harry's Math Books	Outside the Box
Cousin Kira	J	RF	250+	Sunshine	Wright Group/McGraw Hill
Cousins	F	I	56	Families	Capstone Press
Cousins	G	I	152	Families	Heinemann Library
Cousins	T	RF	250+	Hamilton, Virginia	Language for Learning Assoc.
Cousins	D	I	41	Pebble Books	Capstone Press
Cousins in the Castle	U	F	250+	Wallace, Barbara Brooks	Aladdin
Cover Story: Have You Got What It Takes to Be a Magazine Editor?	T	I	250+	On the Job	Compass Point Books
Covers	E	RF	30	Little Celebrations	Pearson Learning Group
Cow	O	I	250+	Older, Jules	Charlesbridge
Cow	B	I	40	Zoozoo-Animal World	Cavallo Publishing
*Cow in the Garden and Other Stories, The	H	F	158	New Way Literature	Steck-Vaughn
Cow Jumped Over the Moon, The	C	F	33	Rigby Rocket	Rigby
*Cow of No Color, The: Riddle Stories and Justice Tales From Around the World	U	TL	250+	Jaffe, Nina; Zeitlin, Steve	Henry Holt & Co.
Cow That Got Her Wish, The	I	F	250+	Easy Stories	Norwood House Press
Cow That Got Her Wish, The	I	F	250+	Hillert, Margaret	Pearson Publishing Group
Cow Up a Tree	H	F	215	Read Alongs	Rigby
Cow Who Clucked, The	J	F	250+	Fleming, Denise	Henry Holt & Co.
Cowboy	X	I	250+	Eyewitness Books	DK Publishing
Cowboy Days	N	HF	926	Reading Street	Pearson
Cowboy Jake	I	RF	174	Sunshine	Wright Group/McGraw Hill
Cowboy Slim	O	RF	250+	Danneberg, Julie	Charlesbridge
Cowboy Trade, The	S	I	250+	Rounds, Glen	Holiday House
Cowboy, The	C	RF	35	Step-By-Step Series	Pearson Learning Group
Cowboys	T	I	250+	Sandler, Martin W.	HarperTrophy
Cowboys and Cattle Drives	W	I	250+	Reading Expeditions	National Geographic

* Collection of short stories   # Graphic text
^ Mature content with lower level text demands

TITLE	LEVEL	GENRE	WORD COUNT	AUTHOR / SERIES	PUBLISHER / DISTRIBUTOR
Cowboys of the Wild West	X	I	250+	Freedman, Russell	Clarion
Cowboys on a Ranch	H	I	210	On Our Way to English	Rigby
Cowgirl Aunt of Harriet Bean, The	O	RF	250+	Smith, Alexander McCall	Bloomsbury Children's Books
Cowgirl Kate and Cocoa	J	F	250+	Silverman, Erica	Harcourt
Cowgirl Kate and Cocoa: Partners	J	F	250+	Silverman, Erica	Harcourt
Cowgirl Kate and Cocoa: Rain or Shine	K	F	250+	Silverman, Erica	Harcourt
Cowgirl Kate and Cocoa: Spring Babies	K	F	250+	Silverman, Erica	Sandpiper Books
Cowhands and Cattle Trails	S	I	250+	Navigators Social Studies Series	Benchmark Education
Cowpokes and Desperadoes	O	RF	250+	Paulsen, Gary	Bantam Books
Cows	G	I	97	Farm Animals	Lerner Publishing Group
Cows and Calves	B	I	33	Animal Families	Lerner Publishing Group
Cows Are in the Corn, The	F	RF	131	Young, James	Scholastic
Cows Have Calves	M	I	250+	Animals and Their Young	Compass Point Books
Cows in the Garden	G	F	163	PM Story Books	Rigby
Cow's Lunch	L	RF	363	Leveled Readers	Houghton Mifflin Harcourt
Cow's Lunch	L	RF	363	Leveled Readers/CA	Houghton Mifflin Harcourt
Cow's Lunch	L	RF	363	Leveled Readers/TX	Houghton Mifflin Harcourt
Cows on the Farm	G	I	56	Pebble Books	Capstone Press
*Cow-Tail Switch and Other West African Stories, The	U	TL	250+	Courlander, Harold & Herzog, George	Square Fish
Coyote	L	I	250+	A Day in the Life: Grassland Animals	Heinemann Library
Coyote	L	I	250+	A Day in the Life: Grassland Animals	Heinemann Library
Coyote and the Rabbit	M	TL	1018	Leveled Readers/TX	Houghton Mifflin Harcourt
Coyote and the Rabbit, The	H	TL	243	Leveled Literacy Intervention/ Blue System	Heinemann
Coyote Girl	M	TL	250+	Cambridge Reading	Pearson Learning Group
*Coyote in Trouble	L	TL	250+	Beveridge, Barbara	Pacific Learning
*Coyote Not-So-Clever	N	TL	250+	Beveridge, Barbara	Pacific Learning
Coyote Plants a Peach Tree	I	TL	233	Books for Young Learners	Richard C. Owen
*Coyote, Fox, and Wolf Tales	K	TL	250+	Storyteller-Lightning Bolts	Wright Group/McGraw Hill
Coyote, The	R	I	250+	Wildlife of North America	Red Brick Learning
Coyote: A Trickster Tale From The American Southwest	M	TL	400	McDermott, Gerald	Voyager Books
Coyotes	L	I	250+	Story Box	Wright Group/McGraw Hill
Crab at the Bottom of the Sea, The	H	TL	141	Literacy 2000	Rigby
Crab Hunt, The	G	RF	179	PM Photo Stories	Rigby
Crab Moon	N	RF	250+	Horowitz, Ruth	Candlewick Press
Crab, The	E	RF	71	Phonetic Connections	Benchmark Education
Crabbing Time	I	RF	75	Books for Young Learners	Richard C. Owen
Crabby Cat and the Doctor	F	F	130	Joy Starters	Pearson Learning Group
Crabby Cat at School	E	F	142	Joy Starters	Pearson Learning Group
Crabby Cat's Exercise	D	F	65	Joy Starters	Pearson Learning Group
Crabby Cat's Party	D	F	99	Joy Starters	Pearson Learning Group
Crabby Cat's Phone Call	F	F	139	Joy Starters	Pearson Learning Group
Crabby Cat's Shopping	C	F	39	Joy Starters	Pearson Learning Group
Crabby Cat's Test	F	F	97	Joy Starters	Pearson Learning Group
Crabby Cat's Vacation	F	F	132	Joy Starters	Pearson Learning Group
Crabby Cat's Watch	G	F	167	Joy Starters	Pearson Learning Group
Crabs	E	I	46	Ocean Life	Capstone Press
Crabs	L	I	501	Sunshine	Wright Group/McGraw Hill
Crabs	H	I	111	Under the Sea	Capstone Press

TITLE	LEVEL	GENRE	WORD COUNT	AUTHOR / SERIES	PUBLISHER / DISTRIBUTOR
Crabs	M	I	272	Wonder World	Wright Group/McGraw Hill
Crabs for Dinner	H	RF	231	Adams, Lorraine & Bruvold, Lynn	Eaglecrest Books
Crabs on a Rock	D	RF	77	Sun Sprouts	ETA/Cuisenaire
Crabs, Shrimp & Lobsters	L	I	322	Marine Life For Young Readers	Pearson Learning Group
^Cracked	T	RF	250+	Orca Currents	Orca Books
Cracked Up to Be	Z+	RF	250+	Summers, Courtney	St. Martin's Griffin
Cracker Jack, The	D	F	25	Sunshine	Wright Group/McGraw Hill
Cracker Jackson	T	RF	250+	Byars, Betsy	Puffin Books
CrackerJack Halfback	Q	RF	250+	Christopher, Matt	Little Brown and Company
Cracking the Code	V	I	250+	High-Fliers	Pacific Learning
Cracking the Code	Z	I	3314	Leveled Readers Science	Houghton Mifflin Harcourt
Cracking the Code	V	I	250+	WorldScapes	ETA/Cuisenaire
Cracking the German Code	W	I	2141	Reading Street	Pearson
Cracking the Wall: The Struggles of the Little Rock Nine	R	I	1403	On My Own History	Lerner Publishing Group
Craft Makers	A	I	24	Early Connections	Benchmark Education
Craft Stick Project, The	L	RF	250+	On Our Way to English	Rigby
Crafts	G	I	50	Chessen, Betsey; Chanko, Pamela	Scholastic
Crafts and Games Around the World	U	I	250+	iOpeners	Pearson Learning Group
Crafts for Kids Who Are Learning About Dinosaurs	P	I	3383	Ross, Kathy	Millbrook Press
Crafts for Kids Who Are Learning About Insects	P	I	3725	Ross, Kathy	Millbrook Press
Crafty Jackal	L	TL	250+	Folk Tales	Wright Group/McGraw Hill
Cranberries: Fruit of the Bogs	T	I	250+	Burns, Diane L.	Carolrhoda Books
Crane Wife, The	M	TL	620	Pair-It Books	Steck-Vaughn
Cranes	I	I	228	Leveled Literacy Intervention/ Blue System	Heinemann
Cranes	G	I	105	Mighty Machines	Capstone Press
Cranes	K	I	105	Pebble Books	Capstone Press
Cranes	L	I	454	Pull Ahead Books	Lerner Publishing Group
Cranes	N	I	250+	Take Two Books	Wright Group/McGraw Hill
Cranky Old Magician, The	J	F	522	Rigby Gigglers	Rigby
Crash	A	RF	29	First Stories	Pacific Learning
Crash	V	RF	250+	Spinelli, Jerry	Alfred A. Knopf
Crash Cars	D	RF	48	Kaleidoscope Collection	Hameray Publishing Group
#Crash Course in Forces and Motion with Max Axiom, Super Scientist; A	V	I	250+	Graphic Library	Capstone Press
Crawfish Hunt	N	RF	250+	Boyz Rule!	Mondo Publishing
Crawl, Caterpillar, Crawl!	C	RF	24	Pair-It Books	Steck-Vaughn
Crawl, Ladybug, Crawl!	D	I	32	Bookworms	Marshall Cavendish
Crayfish	O	I	2507	Early Bird Nature Books	Lerner Publishing Group
Crayfish Thief, The	O	RF	1875	Take Two Books	Wright Group/McGraw Hill
Crayola Counting Book, The	G	I	102	Learn to Read	Creative Teaching Press
Crazy	Z	RF	250+	Nolan, Han	Houghton Mifflin Harcourt
Crazy Cats	A	I	42	Little Books for Early Readers	University of Maine
Crazy Chewing Gum	K	RF	250+	Rigby Gigglers	Rigby
Crazy Critter's Cooking Convention, The	K	F	232	Springboard	Wright Group/McGraw Hill
Crazy Fish	T	RF	250+	Mazer, Norma Fox	Avon Books
Crazy Hair Day	L	F	250+	Saltzberg, Barney	Candlewick Press
Crazy Horse	S	I	515	Vocabulary Readers	Houghton Mifflin Harcourt
Crazy Horse: The Horses of Half Moon Ranch	S	RF	20000	Oldfield, Jenny	Sourcebooks
Crazy Lady!	U	RF	250+	Conly, Jane Leslie	HarperCollins
*Crazy Loco	Y	RF	250+	Edge	Hampton Brown
Crazy Miss Maisey's Alphabet Pets	K	F	250+	Storyteller-Lightning Bolts	Wright Group/McGraw Hill

* Collection of short stories   # Graphic text
^ Mature content with lower level text demands

TITLE	LEVEL	GENRE	WORD COUNT	AUTHOR / SERIES	PUBLISHER / DISTRIBUTOR
Crazy Quilt, The	G	F	148	Little Celebrations	Pearson Learning Group
Crazy Quilt, The	G	RF	148	Little Readers	Houghton Mifflin Harcourt
Crazy Wheels	I	I	215	Sails	Rigby
Creaky Old House	O	RF	250+	Ashman, Linda	Sterling Publishing
Creamed Tuna Fish & Peas on Toast	K	RF	250+	Stead, Philip Christian	Roaring Brook Press
#Creation of the U.S. Constitution, The	T	I	250+	Graphic Library	Capstone Press
Creative Impulse	R	I	250+	Orbit Collections	Pacific Learning
Creative Kitchen Crafts	P	I	4790	Ross, Kathy	Millbrook Press
Creativity	P	RF	250+	Steptoe, John	Clarion Books
Creature Chase - Rex Jones	P	F	1576	Zucker, Jonny	Stone Arch Books
Creature Features	E	RF	172	Windows on Literacy	National Geographic
Creature Features: Exploring Animal Characteristics	W	I	250+	Literacy By Design	Rigby
Creature from Beneath the Ice and Other Cases, The	O	RF	250+	Simon, Seymour	Avon Books
Creature of Cassidy's Creek, The	N	RF	250+	PM Collection	Rigby
Creatures of the Dark	N	I	250+	Literacy 2000	Rigby
Creatures of the Deep	T	I	250+	Boldprint	Steck-Vaughn
Creatures of the Deep	O	I	842	Vocabulary Readers	Houghton Mifflin Harcourt
Creatures of the Deep	O	I	842	Vocabulary Readers/CA	Houghton Mifflin Harcourt
Creatures of the Extreme	T	I	250+	Connectors	Pacific Learning
Creatures of the Night	M	I	250+	Murdock & Ray	Mondo Publishing
Creatures of the Night	M	I	250+	Rigby Focus	Rigby
Creatures of the Reef	S	I	250+	Belcher, Angie	Pacific Learning
Creek, The	T	I	4374	Native American Histoies	Lerner Publishing Group
Creek, The: Farmers of the Southeast	S	I	250+	American Indian Nations	Capstone Press
Creep Show	L	F	250+	Dussling, Jennifer	Grosset & Dunlap
Creepiest Animals, The	K	I	250+	EXtreme Animals	Capstone Press
Creepiest, Crawliest Places	M	I	651	Leveled Readers	Houghton Mifflin Harcourt
Creepiest, Crawliest Places	M	I	651	Leveled Readers/CA	Houghton Mifflin Harcourt
^Creeping Bookends, The	T	F	250+	Dahl, Michael	Stone Arch Books
Creeping Tide, The	M	RF	250+	Science Solves It!	Kane Press
Creepy Castle	G	F	208	Storyworlds	Heinemann
Creepy Caterpillar	E	F	118	Little Readers	Houghton Mifflin Harcourt
Creepy Crawlies	B	RF	38	Carousel Earlybirds	Pearson Learning Group
Creepy Crawlies	P	I	250+	Literacy 2000	Rigby
Creepy Crawlies	L	I	250+	Trackers	Pacific Learning
Creepy Crawlies	F	I	35	Voyages	SRA/McGraw Hill
Creepy- Crawlies	L	I	250+	I Wonder Why	Kingfisher
Creepy Creatures	Q	I	250+	Explorers	Wright Group/McGraw Hill
Creepy Creatures (Goosebumps)	U	F	250+	Stine, R. L.	Scholastic
Creepy Customers	L	F	250+	I Am Reading	Kingfisher
Creepy Monsters, Sleepy Monsters: A Lullaby	K	F	72	Yolen, Jane	Candlewick Press
Creepy Sea Creatures	S	I	250+	Underwater Encounters	Hameray Publishing Group
Cricket Bat Mystery, The	I	RF	250+	Storyworlds	Heinemann
*Cricket Boy and Other Stories, The	L	TL	250+	New Way Literature	Steck-Vaughn
Cricket in Times Square, The	S	F	250+	Selden, George	Bantam Books
Cricket Song, A	F	RF	54	Appleton-Smith, Laura	Flyleaf Publishing
Cricket the Dog	I	I	250+	All About Dogs	Literacy Footprints
Crickets	H	I	89	Bugs, Bugs, Bugs!	Red Brick Learning
Crickets	D	I	48	Insects	Capstone Press
Crickets on the Go	D	F	56	Little Celebrations	Pearson Learning Group

TITLE	LEVEL	GENRE	WORD COUNT	AUTHOR / SERIES	PUBLISHER / DISTRIBUTOR
Crime At the Chat Café	S	RF	250+	Keene, Carolyn	Pocket Books
Crime Busters	W	I	250+	Boldprint	Steck-Vaughn
Crime for Christmas, A	S	RF	250+	Keene, Carolyn	Pocket Books
Crime in the Queen's Court	S	RF	250+	Keene, Carolyn	Pocket Books
Crime Scene Clues	X	I	250+	Independent Readers Science	Houghton Mifflin Harcourt
^Crime Scene Investigators: Uncovering the Truth	S	I	250+	Line of Duty	Capstone Press
Crime Solvers	W	I	250+	Orbit Chapter Books	Pacific Learning
*Crinkum Crankum	M	F	250+	Pacific Literacy	Pacific Learning
Crisis	Z+	I	250+	Boldprint	Steck-Vaughn
Crispin: At the Edge of the World	W	HF	250+	Avi	Hyperion
Crispin: The Cross of Lead	W	HF	250+	Avi	Hyperion
Crispus Attucks: Black Leader of Colonial Patriots	R	B	250+	Millender, Dharathula H.	Aladdin
Criss Cross	W	RF	250+	Perkins, Lynne Rae	Greenwillow Books
Critics in Hollywood	V	I	1799	Leveled Readers	Houghton Mifflin Harcourt
Critics in Hollywood	V	I	1799	Leveled Readers/CA	Houghton Mifflin Harcourt
Critics in Hollywood	V	I	1799	Leveled Readers/TX	Houghton Mifflin Harcourt
Critter Race	G	F	118	Reese, Bob	Children's Press
Critter Sitter	M	F	250+	Richards, Chuck	Walker & Company
Crittercam	N	I	250+	Windows on Literacy	National Geographic
Crocheting for Fun!	S	I	250+	For Fun! Crafts	Compass Point Books
Crocodaddy	L	F	250+	Norman, Kim	Sterling Publishing
Crocodile	C	I	42	Zoozoo-Animal World	Cavallo Publishing
Crocodile and a Whale, A	E	RF	127	PM Plus Story Books	Rigby
Crocodile in the Garden, A	L	F	250+	Ready to Read	Pacific Learning
Crocodile in the Library, A	L	F	250+	Pacific Literacy	Pacific Learning
Crocodile Lake	K	F	322	Pacific Literacy	Pacific Learning
Crocodile Rescue	Q	RF	250+	Reading Expeditions	National Geographic
Crocodile Tears: Alex Rider	X	RF	250+	Horowitz, Anthony	Penguin Group
Crocodile Vs. Wildebeest	L	I	250+	Predator Vs. Prey	Raintree
Crocodiles	P	I	2023	Animal Predators	Lerner Publishing Group
Crocodiles	L	I	250+	Sunshine	Wright Group/McGraw Hill
Crocodiles	N	I	250+	World of Reptiles	Capstone Press
Crocodiles are Dangerous	J	I	217	Breakthrough	Longman Group UK
Crocodile's Bag	K	F	250+	Storyteller- Shooting Stars	Wright Group/McGraw Hill
Crocodile's Christmas Jandals, The	L	F	250+	Pacific Literacy	Pacific Learning
^Crocodiles on the Hunt	N	I	250+	Killer Animals	Capstone Press
Crocodile's Smile	E	F	86	Seedlings	Continental Press
Crocodilians	O	I	250+	Literacy 2000	Rigby
Crocodilians	U	I	250+	Short, Joan; Bird, Bettina	Mondo Publishing
Crocodilians: Reminders of the Age of Dinosaurs	S	I	250+	A First Book	Franklin Watts
Crocs!	O	F	250+	Greenberg, David T.	Little Brown and Company
Crooked Kind of Perfect	U	RF	250+	Urban, Linda	Houghton Mifflin Harcourt
Crops	P	I	250+	Avenues	Hampton Brown
Crosby Crocodile's Disguise	K	F	250+	LIteracy 2000	Rigby
Cross My Heart and Hope to Spy	W	RF	250+	Carter, Ally	Hyperion
^Crossbow	T	RF	250+	Orca Currents	Orca Books
Cross-Country Cousins	O	RF	919	Leveled Readers	Houghton Mifflin Harcourt
Cross-Country Cousins	O	RF	919	Leveled Readers/CA	Houghton Mifflin Harcourt
Cross-Country Cousins	O	RF	919	Leveled Readers/TX	Houghton Mifflin Harcourt
Cross-Country Race	C	RF	33	Windmill Books	Rigby
Cross-Country Race, The	H	RF	246	PM Story Books	Rigby

* Collection of short stories   # Graphic text
^ Mature content with lower level text demands

TITLE	LEVEL	GENRE	WORD COUNT	AUTHOR / SERIES	PUBLISHER / DISTRIBUTOR
Crossing Bok Chitto	T	TL	250+	Tingle, Tim	Cinco Puntos Press
Crossing Borders: Stories of Immigrants	T	I	250+	iOpeners	Pearson Learning Group
Crossing Jordan	X	RF	250+	Fogelin, Adrian	Peachtree
Crossing Safety	F	I	46	Safety	Lerner Publishing Group
Crossing Stones	Y	HF	250+	Frost, Helen	Farrar, Straus, & Giroux
Crossing the Atlantic: One Family's Story	N	I	250+	iOpeners	Pearson Learning Group
Crossing the Creek	C	F	35	Learn to Read	Creative Teaching Press
Crossing the Ocean	K	I	374	Vocabulary Readers	Houghton Mifflin Harcourt
Crossing the Ocean	K	I	374	Vocabulary Readers/CA	Houghton Mifflin Harcourt
Crossing the Street	G	RF	142	City Stories	Rigby
Crow and the Pitcher, The	I	TL	265	Aesop's Fables	Pearson Learning Group
Crow Said No	K	F	250+	Haight, Angela B.	Kaeden Books
Crow, The	Y	F	250+	Croggon, Alison	Candlewick Press
*Crowded Dock and Other Cases, The	O	RF	250+	Simon, Seymour	Avon Books
Crowfoot	X	B	250+	The Canadians	Fitzhenry & Whiteside
Crow-Girl, The	S	RF	250+	Bredsdorff, Bodil	Farrar, Straus, & Giroux
Crows of Pearlblossom, The	M	F	250+	Huxley, Aldous	Harry N. Abrams
Cruise Control	T	RF	250+	Reading Safari	Mondo Publishing
Cruisers	T	I	250+	Land and Sea	Capstone Press
Cruising the Caribbean	U	I	250+	WorldScapes	ETA/Cuisenaire
Crunch	U	RF	250+	Connor, Leslie	HarperCollins
Crunch and Munch	K	I	535	Big Cat	Pacific Learning
Crunching Numbers	U	I	250+	Reading Expeditions	National Geographic
Crunchy Munchy	G	F	189	Bookshop	Mondo Publishing
^Crush	Z+	RF	250+	Orca Soundings	Orca Books
Crust & Spray: Gross Stuff in Your Eyes, Ears, Nose, and Throat	U	I	3972	Gross Body Science	Millbrook Press
Cry of the Crow, The	S	RF	250+	George, Jean Craighead	HarperTrophy
*Crying Rocks and Other Cases, The	O	RF	250+	Simon, Seymour	Avon Books
Cryobiology	Y	I	6679	Cool Science	Lerner Publishing Group
Crypted Hunters	Y	SF	250+	Smith, Roland	Hyperion
Crystal Cave, The	Z+	TL	250+	Stewart, Mary	HarperCollins
Crystal Doors Book I: Island Realm	W	F	250+	Moesta, Rebecca & Anderson, Kevin J.	Little Brown and Company
Crystal Doors Book II: Ocean Realm	W	F	250+	Moesta, Rebecca & Anderson, Kevin J.	Little Brown and Company
Crystal Doors Book III: Sky Realm	W	F	250+	Moesta, Rebecca & Anderson, Kevin J.	Little Brown and Company
Crystal the Snow Fairy: Rainbow Magic	L	F	250+	Meadows, Daisy	Scholastic
Crystal Unicorn, The	N	RF	250+	PM Collection	Rigby
Crystals	S	I	250+	Let's Rock	Heinemann Library
Crystals	L	I	661	Sun Sprouts	ETA/Cuisenaire
Cuauhtemoc	R	B	1543	Leveled Readers Language Support	Houghton Mifflin Harcourt
Cuauhtemoc, the Last Aztec Ruler	S	B	1598	Leveled Readers Social Studies	Houghton Mifflin Harcourt
Cub in the Cupboard	Q	RF	250+	Baglio, Ben M.	Scholastic
Cub Saves the Day	H	RF	156	Leveled Readers	Houghton Mifflin Harcourt
Cub Saves the Day	H	RF	156	Leveled Readers/CA	Houghton Mifflin Harcourt
Cub Saves the Day	H	RF	156	Leveled Readers/TX	Houghton Mifflin Harcourt
Cuba	O	I	250+	Countries of the World	Red Brick Learning
Cuba	P	I	1515	Country Explorers	Lerner Publishing Group
Cuba	Q	I	250+	First Reports: Countries	Compass Point Books
Cuba 15	W	RF	250+	Osa, Nancy	Delacorte Press
Cuban Americans	U	I	1590	Reading Street	Pearson
Cubby's Gum	J	F	250+	Ready Readers	Pearson Learning Group

TITLE	LEVEL	GENRE	WORD COUNT	AUTHOR / SERIES	PUBLISHER / DISTRIBUTOR
Cube	C	I	32	Solid Shapes	Lerner Publishing Group
Cubes	K	I	252	3-D Shapes	Capstone Press
Cuckoo Bird, The	I	I	236	Sails	Rigby
Cuckoo Child, The	Q	F	250+	King-Smith, Dick	Hyperion
Cuckoo Feathers: Simply Sarah	M	RF	250+	Naylor, Phyllis Reynolds	Marshall Cavendish
Cuckoo's Sacrifice, The: A Tale From the Yucatán	T	TL	1900	Leveled Readers	Houghton Mifflin Harcourt
Culpepper's Canyon	O	RF	250+	Paulsen, Gary	Bantam Books
Cultural Clothes	P	I	1543	Take Two Books	Wright Group/McGraw Hill
Cultural Games	L	I	373	Take Two Books	Wright Group/McGraw Hill
Cultural Instruments	Q	I	1414	Take Two Books	Wright Group/McGraw Hill
Culture Clash	Q	I	250+	Explorer Books-Pioneer	National Geographic
Culture Clash	R	I	250+	Explorer Books-Pathfinder	National Geographic
Cumberland Gap, The	S	I	1262	Leveled Readers Social Studies	Houghton Mifflin Harcourt
Cunning Creatures	K	I	250+	Home Connection Collection	Rigby
Cupboard Full of Summer, A	J	RF	234	Pacific Literacy	Pacific Learning
Cupcake Queen, The	V	RF	250+	Hepler, Heather	Speak
Cupcake Thief, The	M	RF	250+	Social Studies Connects	Kane Press
Cupcake, The	F	RF	151	The King School Series	Townsend Press
Cupcakes	E	F	68	Leveled Readers	Houghton Mifflin Harcourt
Cupcakes	J	RF	665	Rigby Flying Colors	Rigby
Cupids Don't Flip Hamburgers	M	F	250+	Dadey, Debbie; Jones, Marcia Thornton	Scholastic
Cupid's Valentine	J	F	608	Dolgin, Phyllis	January Books
Curious About Animals That Dig	D	I	82	Vocabulary Readers	Houghton Mifflin Harcourt
Curious About Animals that Dig	D	I	82	Vocabulary Readers/CA	Houghton Mifflin Harcourt
Curious About Playing Ball	A	I	25	Vocabulary Readers	Houghton Mifflin Harcourt
Curious About Playing Ball	A	I	25	Vocabulary Readers/CA	Houghton Mifflin Harcourt
Curious About School	B	I	65	Vocabulary Readers	Houghton Mifflin Harcourt
Curious About School	B	I	65	Vocabulary Readers/CA	Houghton Mifflin Harcourt
Curious About School	B	I	65	Vocabulary Readers/TX	Houghton Mifflin Harcourt
Curious About School Helpers	G	I	203	Vocabulary Readers	Houghton Mifflin Harcourt
Curious About School Helpers	G	I	203	Vocabulary Readers/CA	Houghton Mifflin Harcourt
Curious About the Animal Park	A	I	20	Vocabulary Readers	Houghton Mifflin Harcourt
Curious About the Animal Park	A	I	20	Vocabulary Readers/CA	Houghton Mifflin Harcourt
Curious About What Kids Can Do	D	I	124	Vocabulary Readers	Houghton Mifflin Harcourt
Curious About What Kids Can Do	D	I	124	Vocabulary Readers/CA	Houghton Mifflin Harcourt
Curious Cases	S	I	250+	Orbit Collections	Pacific Learning
Curious Cat	E	F	95	Little Celebrations	Pearson Learning Group
Curious Charlotte	L	RF	250+	Windows on Literacy	National Geographic
Curious Garden, The	M	RF	250+	Brown, Peter	Little Brown and Company
Curious George and the Animals	A	F	29	Leveled Readers	Houghton Mifflin Harcourt
Curious George and the Animals	A	F	29	Leveled Readers/CA	Houghton Mifflin Harcourt
Curious George and the Hungry Animals	A	F	23	Leveled Readers	Houghton Mifflin Harcourt
Curious George and the Hungry Animals	A	F	23	Leveled Readers/CA	Houghton Mifflin Harcourt
Curious George and the Newspapers	F	F	137	Leveled Readers	Houghton Mifflin Harcourt
Curious George and the Newspapers	F	F	137	Leveled Readers/CA	Houghton Mifflin Harcourt
Curious George at the Library	I	F	281	Leveled Readers	Houghton Mifflin Harcourt
Curious George at the Library	I	F	281	Leveled Readers/CA	Houghton Mifflin Harcourt
Curious George at the Library	I	F	281	Leveled Readers/TX	Houghton Mifflin Harcourt
Curious George Finds Out About School	C	F	51	Leveled Readers	Houghton Mifflin Harcourt
Curious George Finds Out About School	C	F	51	Leveled Readers/CA	Houghton Mifflin Harcourt
Curious George Finds Out About School	C	F	51	Leveled Readers/TX	Houghton Mifflin Harcourt
Curious George Gets a Medal	L	F	250+	Rey, H. A.	Scholastic

C

* Collection of short stories   # Graphic text
^ Mature content with lower level text demands

TITLE	LEVEL	GENRE	WORD COUNT	AUTHOR / SERIES	PUBLISHER / DISTRIBUTOR
Curious George Goes for a Ride	B	F	35	Leveled Readers	Houghton Mifflin Harcourt
Curious George Goes for a Ride	B	F	35	Leveled Readers/CA	Houghton Mifflin Harcourt
Curious George Goes to the Zoo	J	F	250+	Platt, Cynthia	Houghton Mifflin Harcourt
Curious George in the Big City	J	F	250+	Rey, Margret & H.A.	Scholastic
Curious George Likes to Ride	B	F	44	Leveled Readers	Houghton Mifflin Harcourt
Curious George Likes to Ride	B	F	44	Leveled Readers/CA	Houghton Mifflin Harcourt
Curious George Rides a Bike	K	F	250+	Rey, Margret	Scholastic
Curious George Visits Animal Friends	A	F	26	Leveled Readers	Houghton Mifflin Harcourt
Curious George Visits Animal Friends	A	F	26	Leveled Readers/CA	Houghton Mifflin Harcourt
Curious George Visits School	C	F	88	Leveled Readers	Houghton Mifflin Harcourt
Curious George Visits School	C	F	88	Leveled Readers/CA	Houghton Mifflin Harcourt
Curious George Visits School	C	F	88	Leveled Readers/TX	Houghton Mifflin Harcourt
Curious George Visits the Woods	E	F	91	Leveled Readers	Houghton Mifflin Harcourt
Curious George Visits the Woods	E	F	91	Leveled Readers/CA	Houghton Mifflin Harcourt
Curious George's Day at School	C	F	87	Leveled Readers	Houghton Mifflin Harcourt
Curious George's Day at School	C	F	87	Leveled Readers/CA	Houghton Mifflin Harcourt
Curious George's Day at School	C	F	87	Leveled Readers/TX	Houghton Mifflin Harcourt
Curious Kat	P	RF	250+	Leveled Readers	Houghton Mifflin Harcourt
Curious Kids Go on Vacation	LB	I	19	Godon, Ingrid	Peachtree
Curious Kids Go to Preschool	LB	I	22	Godon, Ingrid	Peachtree
Curly and His Friends	LB	F	15	Rigby Literacy	Rigby
Curly and the Big Berry	D	F	94	Rigby Rocket	Rigby
Curly and the Cherries	WB	F	0	Rigby Literacy	Rigby
Curly and the Honey	F	F	113	Rigby Star	Rigby
Curly and the Log	C	F	38	Rigby Rocket	Rigby
Curly Finds a Home	B	F	30	Rigby Literacy	Rigby
Curly Is Hungry	B	F	41	Rigby Literacy	Rigby
Curly Is Hungry	B	F	41	Rigby Star	Rigby
Curly to the Rescue	E	F	107	Rigby Literacy	Rigby
Curly to the Rescue	E	F	127	Rigby Star	Rigby
Curlylocks and the Three Bears: A Play	F	TL	194	Rigby Literacy	Rigby
Current in Your Home, The	T	I	554	Leveled Readers Science	Houghton Mifflin Harcourt
Curse Dark as Gold, A	Y	F	250+	Bunce, Elizabeth C.	Scholastic
Curse of Being Pharaoh, The	P	RF	250+	Orbit Chapter Books	Pacific Learning
#Curse of King Tut's Tomb, The	U	I	250+	Graphic Library	Capstone Press
*Curse of The Ancient Mask and Other Case Files, The: Saxby Smart, Private Detective	S	RF	250+	Cheshire, Simon	Roaring Brook Press
Curse of the Bizarro Beetle (Splurch Academy)	Q	F	250+	Berry, Julie & Gardner, Sally	Grosset & Dunlap
Curse of the Bologna Sandwich, The (Melvin Beederman, Superhero)	N	F	250+	Trine, Greg	Henry Holt & Co.
*Curse of the Campfire Weenies and Other Warped and Creepy Tales, The	T	F	250+	Lubar, David	Tom Doherty
Curse of the Cheese Pyramid, The	O	F	250+	Stilton, Geronimo	Scholastic
Curse of the Cobweb Queen, The	L	F	250+	Hayes, Geoffrey	Random House
Curse of the Kitty Litter	Q	F	250+	Wiley & Grampa's Creature Features	Little Brown and Company
Curse of the Mummy, The	T	HF	8726	Dominoes one	Oxford University Press
Curse of the Squirrel, The	N	F	250+	Yep, Laurence	Random House
Curse of the Wendigo, The:	T	F	250+	Welvaert, Scott R.	Stone Arch Books
^Curtains! A High School Musical Mystery	S	RF	250+	Dahl, Michael	Stone Arch Books
Cuss	U	HF	250+	Franklin, Kristine	Candlewick Press
Custard	E	RF	82	Wonder World	Wright Group/McGraw Hill
Custard's Cat Flap	F	F	198	Sails	Rigby
Custodian	D	I	24	Work People Do	Lerner Publishing Group

C

TITLE	LEVEL	GENRE	WORD COUNT	AUTHOR / SERIES	PUBLISHER / DISTRIBUTOR
Custodian Kate Fixing Things at School	A	I	40	Run to Reading	Discovery Peak
Custodians	M	I	250+	Community Helpers	Red Brick Learning
Custodians	K	I	304	Pull Ahead Books	Lerner Publishing Group
Custom Cars	W	I	6333	Motor Mania	Lerner Publishing Group
Custom Cars: The Ins and Outs of Tuners, Hot Rods, and Other Muscle Cars	T	I	250+	Velocity-RPM	Capstone Press
Customs Service	S	I	250+	Law Enforcement	Capstone Press
Cut	Z+	RF	250+	McCormick, Patricia	Scholastic
*Cut From the Same Cloth: American Women of Myth, Legend, and Tall Tale	T	TL	250+	San Souci, Robert D.	Puffin Books
Cuts, Scrapes, Scabs, and Scars	S	I	250+	My Health	Franklin Watts
Cut-Throat Pirates - Rex Jones	P	F	1837	Zucker, Jonny	Stone Arch Books
Cutting	C	I	26	Changing Matter	Lerner Publishing Group
Cutting and Sticking	K	RF	250+	Cambridge Reading	Pearson Learning Group
Cutting Machines	G	I	132	Sunshine	Wright Group/McGraw Hill
Cutting Our Food	B	I	40	Early Connections	Benchmark Education
Cuttlebone	L	I	429	Sun Sprouts	ETA/Cuisenaire
Cyberpals: According to Kaley	S	RF	11817	Regan, Dian Curtis	Darby Creek Publishing
Cyberspace	S	SF	250+	Wildcats	Wright Group/McGraw Hill
Cybil War, The	S	RF	250+	Byars, Betsy	Scholastic
Cycle of Nature, A - Migrating Journeys	U	I	250+	Connectors	Pacific Learning
Cycle of Your Life, The	T	I	203	Health and Your Body	Capstone Press
Cycler	Z+	F	250+	McLaughlin, Lauren	Random House
Cycles and Patterns in Space	P	I	2000	Science Support Readers	Houghton Mifflin Harcourt
Cyclops Doesn't Roller-Skate	M	F	250+	Dadey, Debbie; Jones, Marcia Thornton	Scholastic
Cylinder	E	I	31	Solid Shapes	Lerner Publishing Group
Cylinders	K	I	237	3-D Shapes	Capstone Press
Cynthia Rylant, Author	J	B	137	Vocabulary Readers	Houghton Mifflin Harcourt
Cyril the Dragon	M	F	250+	Sun Sprouts	ETA/Cuisenaire
Cyrus the Unsinkable Sea Serpent	M	F	250+	Peet, Bill	Houghton Mifflin Harcourt

* Collection of short stories   # Graphic text
^ Mature content with lower level text demands

TITLE	LEVEL	GENRE	WORD COUNT	AUTHOR / SERIES	PUBLISHER / DISTRIBUTOR
D	LB	I	14	Readlings	American Reading Company
D.W. All Wet	J	F	217	Brown, Marc	Little Brown and Company
D.W. Flips!	J	F	245	Brown, Marc	Little Brown and Company
D.W. Rides Again!	K	F	250+	Brown, Marc	Little Brown and Company
D.W. Says Please and Thank You	K	F	250+	Brown, Marc	Little Brown and Company
D.W. the Big Boss	J	F	250+	Brown, Marc	Little Brown and Company
D.W. the Picky Eater	L	F	250+	Brown, Marc	Little Brown and Company
D.W. Thinks Big	K	F	250+	Brown, Marc	Little Brown and Company
D.W., Go to Your Room!	J	F	250+	Brown, Marc	Little Brown and Company
D.W.'s Guide to Perfect Manners	K	F	250+	Brown, Marc	Little Brown and Company
D.W.'s Guide to Preschool	J	F	250+	Brown, Marc	Little Brown and Company
D.W.'s Library Card	K	F	250+	Brown, Marc	Little Brown and Company
Da Gama: Vasco da Gama Sails Around the Cape of Good Hope	U	B	250+	Exploring the World	Compass Point Books
Da Vinci	R	B	250+	Venezia, Mike	Children's Press
Da Wild, Da Crazy, Da Vinci	P	F	250+	Scieszka, Jon	Penguin Group
Dabble Duck	K	RF	250+	Ellis, Anne Leo	HarperTrophy
Dabbling in Dough	K	I	250+	Book Bank	Wright Group/McGraw Hill
Dachshunds	I	I	136	Dogs	Capstone Press
Dachshunds Are the Best!	Q	I	1458	The Best Dogs Ever	Lerner Publishing Group
Dad	B	I	37	InfoTrek	ETA/Cuisenaire
Dad	A	RF	24	Leveled Literacy Intervention/ Orange System	Heinemann
Dad	B	RF	21	Little Readers	Houghton Mifflin Harcourt
Dad	A	I	24	PM Starters	Rigby
Dad and Beth Clean Up	E	RF	113	Book Bus	Creative Edge
Dad and Fif Fan	D	RF	31	Reading Street	Pearson
Dad and I	C	RF	59	Avenues	Hampton Brown
Dad and I	A	RF	40	On Our Way to English	Rigby
Dad and I	C	RF	59	Rise & Shine	Hampton Brown
Dad and Pop	H	RF	150	Bennett, Kelly	Candlewick Press
Dad and the Bike Race	J	RF	416	Sails	Rigby
Dad and the Cake	I	F	308	Sails	Rigby
Dad and the Go-Cart	H	RF	317	Sails	Rigby
Dad and the Grizzly Bear	I	RF	274	Sails	Rigby
Dad and the Mosquito	I	RF	246	Sunshine	Wright Group/McGraw Hill
Dad and the Skateboard	F	RF	202	Sails	Rigby
Dad and Wag	D	RF	52	Phonics and Friends	Hampton Brown
Dad at the Beach	I	F	318	Sails	Rigby
Dad at the Fair	I	RF	345	Sails	Rigby
Dad at the Park	C	RF	117	Sails	Rigby
Dad Cooks Breakfast	H	RF	195	Windmill Books	Rigby
Dad Didn't Mind at All	F	RF	134	Literacy 2000	Rigby
Dad Goes Fishing	J	F	453	Sails	Rigby
Dad Goes to School	A	RF	43	Mom and Dad Series	Pioneer Valley
Dad Still Smiles	L	RF	212	Books for Young Learners	Richard C. Owen
Dad, Jackie, and Me	Q	HF	250+	Uhlberg, Myron	Peachtree
Daddy Book, The	H	I	171	Parr, Todd	Little Brown and Company
Daddy Is a Cozy Hug	N	RF	278	Greene, Rhonda Gowler	Walker & Company
Daddy Long-Leg Spiders	N	I	250+	Spiders	Capstone Press
Daddy Longlegs Blues, The	P	F	250+	Ornstein, Mike	Sterling Publishing
Daddy Saved the Day	M	RF	250+	Greetings	Rigby
Daddy Works Out	D	RF	39	Visions	Wright Group/McGraw Hill
Dad's Bathtime	E	RF	114	Literacy Tree	Rigby

TITLE	LEVEL	GENRE	WORD COUNT	AUTHOR / SERIES	PUBLISHER / DISTRIBUTOR
Dad's Bike	E	RF	52	Literacy 2000	Rigby
Dad's Dinner	E	RF	159	Sails	Rigby
Dad's Favorite Tie	A	RF	35	Bonnell, Kris	Reading Reading Books
Dad's Flowers	C	RF	36	Windows on Literacy	National Geographic
Dad's Garden	Q	RF	1000	Leveled Readers/TX	Houghton Mifflin Harcourt
Dad's Garden	D	RF	25	Literacy 2000	Rigby
Dad's Hamburger	D	RF	51	Bonnell, Kris	Reading Reading Books
Dad's Headache	F	RF	86	Sunshine	Wright Group/McGraw Hill
Dad's New Path	F	RF	218	Foundations	Wright Group/McGraw Hill
Dad's Pasta	L	RF	250+	Sails	Rigby
Dad's Phone	F	RF	142	Springboard	Wright Group/McGraw Hill
Dad's Pizza	D	RF	77	Windows on Literacy	National Geographic
Dad's Promise	L	RF	250+	Cambridge Reading	Pearson Learning Group
Dad's Ship	C	RF	42	PM Stars	Rigby
Dad's Shirt	F	RF	38	Joy Readers	Pearson Learning Group
Dad's Surprise	J	RF	202	Foundations	Wright Group/McGraw Hill
Dad's Turkey Sandwich	A	RF	26	Mom and Dad Series	Pioneer Valley
Daemon Hall	X	F	250+	Nance, Andrew	Henry Holt & Co.
Daffodil Spring	M	I	456	Leveled Readers/TX	Houghton Mifflin Harcourt
Daffodils for You	D	RF	90	Adams, Lorraine & Bruvold, Lynn	Eaglecrest Books
Daily Life Around the World	P	I	250+	Navigators Social Studies Series	Benchmark Education
Daily Life in a Plains Indian Village: 1868	U	I	250+	Terry, Michael Bad Hand	Clarion
Daily Life in the Pilgrim Colony 1636	U	I	250+	Erickson, Paul	Clarion Books
Daily Life of the Cherokee, The	N	I	647	Vocabulary Readers	Houghton Mifflin Harcourt
Daily Life of the Cherokee, The	N	I	647	Vocabulary Readers/CA	Houghton Mifflin Harcourt
Daily Life of the Cherokee, The	N	I	647	Vocabulary Readers/TX	Houghton Mifflin Harcourt
Daily Meow, The	M	F	250+	Sails	Rigby
Dairy	F	I	93	Food Groups	Lerner Publishing Group
Dairy Group, The	H	I	97	The Food Guide Pyramid	Capstone Press
Daisy	J	RF	250+	Stepping Stones	Nelson/Michaels Assoc.
Daisy Dawson and the Big Freeze	N	F	250+	Voake, Steve	Candlewick Press
Daisy Dawson and the Secret Pond	N	F	250+	Voake, Steve	Candlewick Press
Daisy Dawson at the Beach	N	F	250+	Voake, Steve	Candlewick Press
Daisy Dawson Is on Her Way!	N	F	250+	Voake, Steve	Candlewick Press
Daisy Dawson on the Farm	N	F	250+	Voake, Steve	Candlewick Press
Daisy Divine, Dancing Dog	M	F	763	Leveled Readers	Houghton Mifflin Harcourt
Daisy Takes a Swim	I	RF	307	Red Rocket Readers	Flying Start Books
Daisy to the Rescue	K	F	375	Jack and Daisy	Pioneer Valley
Daisy's Airplane Trip	J	F	362	Jack and Daisy	Pioneer Valley
Daisy's Bell	G	F	211	Jack and Daisy	Pioneer Valley
Daisy's Party Dresses	A	F	29	Tiny Treasures	Pioneer Valley
Daisy's Tiny Things	B	I	47	Tiny Treasures	Pioneer Valley
Dalai Lama: A Life of Compassion, The	P	B	609	Pull Ahead Books	Lerner Publishing Group
Dale Earnhardt	Q	B	250+	NASCAR Racing	Capstone Press
Dale Earnhardt Jr.	P	B	1843	Amazing Athletes	Lerner Publishing Group
Dale Earnhardt Jr.	T	B	250+	Christopher, Matt	Little Brown and Company
Dale Earnhardt Jr.	U	B	250+	Sports Heroes and Legends	Lerner Publishing Group
Dallas Cowboys, The	S	I	4427	Team Spirit	Norwood House Press
Dallas Mavericks, The	S	I	250+	Team Spirit	Norwood House Press
Dallas Shapes Up	T	RF	250+	On Our Way to English	Rigby
Dalmatians	I	I	132	Dogs	Capstone Press
Dalmatians	I	RF	70	Salem, Lynn	Continental Press
Dalmations	F	I	70	Seedlings	Continental Press
Damage	Z+	RF	250+	Jenkins, A.M.	HarperCollins

* Collection of short stories   # Graphic text
^ Mature content with lower level text demands

TITLE	LEVEL	GENRE	WORD COUNT	AUTHOR / SERIES	PUBLISHER / DISTRIBUTOR
Dame Shirley and the Gold Rush	R	B	250+	Rawls, Jim	Steck-Vaughn
Dan and Dan	E	RF	96	Real Kids Readers	Millbrook Press
Dan and His Brothers	C	RF	105	Leveled Readers	Houghton Mifflin Harcourt
Dan and His Brothers	C	RF	105	Leveled Readers/CA	Houghton Mifflin Harcourt
Dan and the Parrot	H	F	230	The Joy Cowley Collection	Hameray Publishing Group
Dan Did It!	C	RF	28	Reading Street	Pearson
Dan Gets Dressed	B	RF	42	Story Box	Wright Group/McGraw Hill
Dan Goes Home	E	F	153	Story Basket	Wright Group/McGraw Hill
Dan the Dunce	J	TL	539	Tales from Hans Andersen	Wright Group/McGraw Hill
Dan the Flying Man	C	F	60	Story Box	Wright Group/McGraw Hill
Dance	W	I	250+	Eyewitness Books	DK Publishing
Dance Around the World	O	I	211	Gear Up!	Wright Group/McGraw Hill
Dance at Grandpa's	J	HF	250+	Wilder, Laura Ingalls	HarperCollins
Dance Day	M	RF	1392	Gear Up!	Wright Group/McGraw Hill
Dance Fever	P	I	250+	Trackers	Pacific Learning
Dance for Fun!	S	I	250+	Activities for Fun	Compass Point Books
Dance Hall of the Dead	Z	RF	250+	Edge	Hampton Brown
Dance My Dance	L	TL	250+	Foundations	Wright Group/McGraw Hill
Dance of the Swan: A Story about Anna Pavlova	S	B	8434	Creative Minds Biographies	Lerner Publishing Group
Dance Team	S	I	250+	Dance	Capstone Press
Dance to the Beat	D	I	83	Big Cat	Pacific Learning
Dance Trap: The Complicated Life of Claudia Cristina Cortez	S	RF	250+	Gallagher, Diana G.	Stone Arch Books
Dance With Me	I	F	89	Smith, Charles R. Jr.	Candlewick Press
Dance Wth Rosie	N	RF	250+	Giff, Patricia Reilly	Penguin Group
Dance, Dance, Dance!	G	I	124	Red Rocket Readers	Flying Start Books
Dance, The	C	F	35	Learn to Read	Creative Teaching Press
Dances We Do, The	G	I	131	Twig	Wright Group/McGraw Hill
Dancin' Down	I	RF	193	Evangeline Nicholas Collection	Wright Group/McGraw Hill
Dancing	D	I	27	Canizares, Susan; Chessen, Betsey	Scholastic
Dancing	E	I	42	Instant Readers	Harcourt School Publishers
Dancing	C	RF	38	Visions	Wright Group/McGraw Hill
Dancing Around the World	T	I	250+	iOpeners	Pearson Learning Group
Dancing Around the World	I	I	210	Leveled Readers	Houghton Mifflin Harcourt
Dancing Around the World	I	I	210	Leveled Readers/CA	Houghton Mifflin Harcourt
Dancing Carl	U	RF	250+	Paulsen, Gary	Aladdin
Dancing Dinosaurs	E	F	45	Little Celebrations	Pearson Learning Group
Dancing Dragon, The	I	F	236	Bookshop	Mondo Publishing
Dancing Fly, The	F	F	108	Sunshine	Wright Group/McGraw Hill
Dancing Gingerbread	H	RF	236	PM Photo Stories	Rigby
Dancing in Soot	L	RF	250+	Cambridge Reading	Pearson Learning Group
Dancing in the Cadillac Light	T	HF	250+	Holt, Kimberly Willis	G.P. Putnam's Sons
Dancing Naked	Z+	RF	250+	Hrdlitschka, Shelley	Orca Books
Dancing on the Edge	Z	RF	250+	Nolan, Han	Harcourt School Publishers
Dancing Queen	L	RF	250+	Go Girl!	Feiwel and Friends
Dancing Queen	T	F	250+	Hopkins, Cathy	Kingfisher
Dancing Shoes	B	F	23	Literacy 2000	Rigby
Dancing to Freedom: The True Story of Mao's Last Dancer	S	B	250+	Cunxin, Li	Walker & Company
Dancing to the Beat	P	I	250+	PM Plus Nonfiction	Rigby
Dancing to the River	J	TL	250+	Cambridge Reading	Pearson Learning Group
Dancing with Jacques	P	HF	250+	Voyages in Time	Wright Group/McGraw Hill
Dancing with Katya	P	HF	250+	Chaconas, Dori	Peachtree

TITLE	LEVEL	GENRE	WORD COUNT	AUTHOR / SERIES	PUBLISHER / DISTRIBUTOR
Dancing with Manatees	N	I	250+	McNulty, Faith	Scholastic
Dancing with the Indians	M	HF	250+	Medearis, Angela	Scholastic
Dandelion	M	F	250+	Freeman, Don	Puffin Books
*Dandelion and Other Stories	H	F	250+	Story Steps	Rigby
Dandelion Danny	D	F	76	Coulton, Mia	Maryruth Books
Dandelion Seed, The	M	F	252	Sharing Nature with Children	Dawn Publications
Dandelion Year	H	I	136	Little Celebrations	Pearson Learning Group
Dandelion, The	E	RF	99	Sunshine	Wright Group/McGraw Hill
Dandelions	F	I	90	Bonnell, Kris/About	Reading Reading Books
Dandelions	Q	I	1672	Early Bird Nature Books	Lerner Publishing Group
Dandelions	F	I	101	Plant Life Cycles	Lerner Publishing Group
Dandelions: Stars in the Grass	K	I	216	Posada, Mia	Carolrhoda Books
Danger	C	RF	66	Story Box	Wright Group/McGraw Hill
Danger At Sand Cave	N	HF	1505	On My Own History	Lerner Publishing Group
Danger at the Breaker	N	HF	1871	On My Own History	Lerner Publishing Group
Danger At Work	W	I	250+	Boldprint	Steck-Vaughn
Danger Box, The	U	RF	250+	Balliett, Blue	Scholastic
Danger Guys	N	RF	250+	Abbott, Tony	HarperTrophy
Danger Guys Blast Off	N	RF	250+	Abbott, Tony	HarperTrophy
Danger Guys on Ice	N	RF	250+	Abbott, Tony	HarperTrophy
Danger in Quicksand Swamp	W	RF	250+	Wallace, Bill	Simon & Schuster
^Danger in the Dark	W	F	250+	Dark Man	Ransom Publishing
Danger in the Dark: A Houdini & Nate Mystery	R	HF	250+	Lalicky, Tom	Farrar, Straus, & Giroux
Danger in the Parking Lot	J	RF	250+	PM Plus Story Books	Rigby
Danger on Ice	S	I	250+	Power Up!	Steck-Vaughn
Danger on Midnight River	O	RF	250+	Paulsen, Gary	Bantam Books
Danger on Panther Peak	R	RF	250+	Wallace, Bill	Pocket Books
Danger on Parade	T	RF	250+	Keene, Carolyn	Pocket Books
Danger! Children at Work	V	I	1784	Reading Street	Pearson
Danger, Landslides!	Q	I	250+	Leveled Readers Language Support	Houghton Mifflin Harcourt
Danger: Dynamite!	Q	HF	250+	Capeci, Anne	Peachtree
Danger: The World Is Getting Hot!	V	I	1483	Reading Street	Pearson
Dangerous Animals	R	I	250+	Explorers	Wright Group/McGraw Hill
*Dangerous Comet and Other Cases, The	O	RF	250+	Simon, Seymour	Avon Books
Dangerous Days of Daniel X, The	Y	F	250+	Patterson, James & Michael Ledwidge	Little Brown and Company
Dangerous Droughts	L	I	250+	Rosen Real Readers	Rosen Publishing Group
Dangerous Dues	Z+	I	250+	What's the Issue?	Compass Point Books
Dangerous Jobs	L	I	373	Sails	Rigby
Dangerous Mission of Emily Geiger, The	T	I	1273	Leveled Readers	Houghton Mifflin Harcourt
Dangerous Neighbors	W	HF	250+	Kephart, Beth	Egmont USA
Dangerous Path, A: Warriors, Book 5	U	F	250+	Hunter, Erin	HarperCollins
Dangerous Plants	F	I	115	Explorations	Okapi Educational Materials
Dangerous Plants	F	I	115	Explorations	Eleanor Curtain Publishing
Dangerous Professions of the Past	O	I	250+	Rigby Focus	Rigby
Dangerous Skies	Z	RF	250+	Staples, Suzanne Fisher	Macmillan
Dangerous Trip, A	S	HF	1359	Leveled Readers	Houghton Mifflin Harcourt
Dangerous Trip, A	S	HF	1359	Leveled Readers/CA	Houghton Mifflin Harcourt
Dangerous Trip, A	S	HF	1359	Leveled Readers/TX	Houghton Mifflin Harcourt
Dangerous Waters	Q	I	250+	Leveled Readers	Houghton Mifflin Harcourt
Dangerous Waves	P	I	915	Vocabulary Readers	Houghton Mifflin Harcourt
Dangerous Waves	P	I	915	Vocabulary Readers/CA	Houghton Mifflin Harcourt
Dangerous Waves	P	I	915	Vocabulary Readers/TX	Houghton Mifflin Harcourt

* Collection of short stories   # Graphic text
^ Mature content with lower level text demands

TITLE	LEVEL	GENRE	WORD COUNT	AUTHOR / SERIES	PUBLISHER / DISTRIBUTOR
Dangerous Wishes	U	F	250+	Sleator, William	Penguin Group
Danica Patrick	P	B	2160	Amazing Athletes	Lerner Publishing Group
Daniel	F	RF	161	Literacy 2000	Rigby
Daniel and His Walking Stick	L	RF	250+	McCormick, Wendy	Peachtree
Daniel and the Great Bearded One	W	F	250+	Bookshop	Mondo Publishing
Daniel Boone	R	B	3586	History Maker Bios	Lerner Publishing Group
Daniel Boone	N	B	1889	On My Own Biography	Lerner Publishing Group
Daniel Boone	T	B	3234	People to Remember Series	January Books
Daniel Boone: Frontier Scout	V	B	250+	Let Freedom Ring	Capstone Press
Daniel Boone: Man of the Forests	O	B	250+	Greene, Carol	Children's Press
Daniel Boone's Great Escape	T	B	250+	Spradlin, Michael P.	Walker & Company
Daniel Inouye: Hero from Hawaii	W	B	3114	Leveled Readers	Houghton Mifflin Harcourt
Daniel Inouye: Senator from Hawaii	P	B	799	Leveled Readers Social Studies	Houghton Mifflin Harcourt
#Daniel X: Alien Hunter	W	F	250+	Patterson, James & Gout, Leopoldo	Little Brown and Company
Danielle the Daisy Fairy: Rainbow Magic	L	F	250+	Meadows, Daisy	Scholastic
Daniel's Basketball Team	E	RF	80	Carousel Readers	Pearson Learning Group
Daniel's Dog	K	RF	250+	Bogart, Jo Allen	Scholastic
Daniel's Duck	K	HF	250+	Bulla, Clyde Robert	HarperTrophy
Daniel's Pet	F	RF	76	Green Light Readers	Harcourt
Daniel's Story	Z	HF	250+	Matas, Carol	Scholastic
Danny and Abby Are Friends	E	RF	109	Coulton, Mia	Maryruth Books
Danny and Abby Play Hospital	E	F	60	Coulton, Mia	Maryruth Books
Danny and Abby Play Tag	E	F	74	Coulton, Mia	Maryruth Books
Danny and Bee's Book of Opposites	D	F	41	Coulton, Mia	Maryruth Books
Danny and Bee's Safety Rules	F	RF	106	Coulton, Mia	Maryruth Books
Danny and Dad Go Shopping	C	I	69	Coulton, Mia	Maryruth Books
Danny and Dad Read	D	F	61	Coulton, Mia	Maryruth Books
Danny and the Bully	H	F	344	Coulton, Mia	Maryruth Books
Danny and the Corn Maze	D	F	47	Coulton, Mia	Maryruth Books
Danny and the Dinosaur	J	F	250+	Hoff, Syd	Scholastic
Danny and the Dinosaur Go to Camp	H	F	250+	Hoff, Syd	HarperTrophy
Danny and the Four Seasons	C	RF	55	Coulton, Mia	Maryruth Books
Danny and the Little Worm	F	F	174	Coulton, Mia	Maryruth Books
Danny and the Monarch Butterfly	I	I	282	Coulton, Mia	Maryruth Books
Danny at the Car Wash	E	RF	124	Coulton, Mia	Maryruth Books
Danny Can Sort	C	I	42	Coulton, Mia	Maryruth Books
Danny Dragon Goes to the City	D	F	64	Reading Safari	Mondo Publishing
Danny Drives Too Fast	E	RF	160	Reading Safari	Mondo Publishing
Danny Gets Fit	E	RF	177	Coulton, Mia	Maryruth Books
Danny Goes For a Walk	C	F	50	Coulton, Mia	Maryruth Books
Danny Likes Red	B	RF	28	Coulton, Mia	Maryruth Books
Danny Likes to Help	D	F	60	Coulton, Mia	Maryruth Books
Danny Looks for Abby	E	RF	120	Coulton, Mia	Maryruth Books
Danny Makes a Mask	C	F	67	Coulton, Mia	Maryruth Books
Danny Paints a Picture	F	F	117	Coulton, Mia	Maryruth Books
Danny the Dinosaur	B	F	31	Coulton, Mia	Maryruth Books
Danny, Bee and the Skunk	E	F	71	Coulton, Mia	Maryruth Books
Danny, Champion of the World	T	RF	250+	Dahl, Roald	Language for Learning Assoc.
Danny's Bee (the beginning)	LB	RF	5	Coulton, Mia	Maryruth Books
Danny's Big Adventure	J	F	250+	Coulton, Mia	Maryruth Books
Danny's Big Jump	L	RF	250+	Take Two Books	Wright Group/McGraw Hill
Danny's Birthday Wishes	D	F	46	Coulton, Mia	Maryruth Books

D

TITLE	LEVEL	GENRE	WORD COUNT	AUTHOR / SERIES	PUBLISHER / DISTRIBUTOR
Danny's Castle	D	F	61	Coulton, Mia	Maryruth Books
Danny's Desert Rats	X	RF	250+	Naylor, Phyllis Reynolds	Aladdin
Danny's Dinner	G	F	142	Coulton, Mia	Maryruth Books
Danny's Dollars	D	RF	88	Reading Corners	Pearson Learning Group
Danny's Drawing Book	K	F	250+	Heap, Sue	Candlewick Press
Danny's Drums	F	F	109	Pair-It Turn and Learn	Steck-Vaughn
Danny's Favorite Shapes	F	F	95	Coulton, Mia	Maryruth Books
Danny's Five Little Pumpkins	C	F	51	Coulton, Mia	Maryruth Books
Danny's Five Senses	D	RF	52	Coulton, Mia	Maryruth Books
Danny's Game of Sink or Float	D	F	92	Coulton, Mia	Maryruth Books
Danny's Garden	E	F	84	Coulton, Mia	Maryruth Books
Danny's Groundhog Day	F	RF	126	Coulton, Mia	Maryruth Books
Danny's Hair Is Everywhere	D	RF	38	Coulton, Mia	Maryruth Books
Danny's New Toy	E	RF	70	Coulton, Mia	Maryruth Books
Danny's Party	B	RF	21	Coulton, Mia	Maryruth Books
Danny's Rocket	G	F	131	Coulton, Mia	Maryruth Books
Danny's Special Tree	M	F	400	Coulton, Mia	Maryruth Books
Danny's Timeline	D	F	73	Coulton, Mia	Maryruth Books
Danny's Window	C	RF	62	Coulton, Mia	Maryruth Books
Dan's Box	G	F	105	Cambridge Reading	Pearson Learning Group
Dan's Lost Hat	G	F	208	The Joy Cowley Collection	Hameray Publishing Group
Dan's Old Van	H	F	145	Supersonics	Rigby
Darby	T	HF	250+	Fuqua, Jonathon Scott	Candlewick Press
Darcy and Gran Don't Like Babies	K	RF	250+	Cutler, Jane	Scholastic
Darcy Devlin and the Mystery Boy	Q	RF	250+	PM Plus Chapter Books	Rigby
Darcy Goes for a Ride	L	I	250+	InfoTrek Plus	ETA/Cuisenaire
*Dare to Be Scared: Thirteen Stories to Chill and Thrill	V	F	250+	San Souci, Robert D.	Cricket Books
^Daredevil Club	T	RF	250+	Orca Currents	Orca Books
Daredevil on Ice	M	F	250+	Too Cool	Pacific Learning
Daredevils	Q	HF	250+	Capeci, Anne	Peachtree
Daring Cell Defenders	Z	I	250+	Microquests	Lerner Publishing Group
Daring Escape of Ellen Craft, The	P	B	1893	On My Own History	Lerner Publishing Group
Daring Rescue of Marlon the Swimming Pig, The	P	F	250+	Saunders, S.	Random House
Daring Riders of the Pony Express, The	U	I	1853	Vocabulary Readers	Houghton Mifflin Harcourt
Daring Riders of the Pony Express, The	U	I	1853	Vocabulary Readers/CA	Houghton Mifflin Harcourt
Dark and Full of Secrets	N	RF	250+	Carrick, Carol	Houghton Mifflin Harcourt
Dark and Stormy Night, A	G	F	160	Little Red Readers	Sundance
Dark Canoe, The	X	RF	29300	O'Dell, Scott	Sourcebooks
^Dark Dreams of Hell, The	W	F	250+	Dark Man	Ransom Publishing
^Dark Fire of Doom, The	W	F	250+	Dark Man	Ransom Publishing
^Dark Fire of Doom, The	W	F	250+	Dark Man	Stone Arch Books
Dark Frigate, The	W	HF	250+	Hawes, Charles Boardman	Little Brown and Company
^Dark Glass, The	W	F	250+	Dark Man	Ransom Publishing
Dark Is Rising, The	X	F	250+	Cooper, Susan	Macmillan
Dark Life	W	SF	250+	Falls, Kat	Scholastic
^Dark Never Hides, The	W	F	250+	Dark Man	Ransom Publishing
^Dark Never Hides, The	W	F	250+	Dark Man	Stone Arch Books
Dark Night, Sleepy Night	F	I	123	Ziefert, Harriet	Puffin Books
Dark Planet, The	U	F	250+	Carman, Patrick	Little Brown and Company
Dark River: Warriors, Power of Three	U	F	250+	Hunter, Erin	HarperCollins
^Dark Side of Magic, The	W	F	250+	Dark Man	Ransom Publishing
Dark Side of the Creek, The	M	RF	250+	Sunshine	Wright Group/McGraw Hill

* Collection of short stories   # Graphic text
^ Mature content with lower level text demands

TITLE	LEVEL	GENRE	WORD COUNT	AUTHOR / SERIES	PUBLISHER / DISTRIBUTOR
Dark Stairs	V	RF	250+	Byars, Betsy	Puffin Books
Dark Water Rising	W	HF	250+	Hale, Marian	Henry Holt & Co.
^Dark Waters of Time, The	W	F	250+	Dark Man	Ransom Publishing
Dark, Dark Tale, A	F	F	115	Brown, Ruth	Penguin Group
Darkest Hour, The: Warriors, Book 6	U	F	250+	Hunter, Erin	HarperCollins
Darkling Curse, The: Something Wickedly Weird	R	F	250+	Mould, Chris	Roaring Brook Press
Darkness Before Dawn	Z+	RF	250+	Draper, Sharon M.	Simon & Schuster
Darkness into Light	S	I	1482	Reading Street	Pearson
Darkness Under the Water, The	Z	HF	250+	Kanell, Beth	Candlewick Press
Dark's Tale	S	F	250+	Grabien, Deborah	Egmont USA
*Dark-Thirty: Southern Tales of the Supernatural	R	F	250+	McKissack, Patricia C.	Alfred A. Knopf
Darkwood	U	F	250+	Breen, M. E.	Bloomsbury Children's Books
Darlene and the Art Show	N	RF	963	Leveled Readers/TX	Houghton Mifflin Harcourt
Darren Dwayne DeBakery and His Amazing Inventions	R	F	250+	Pair-It Books	Steck-Vaughn
Darryl the Doorman	F	RF	85	City Stories	Rigby
^Darwin Expedition, The	Z+	RF	250+	Orca Soundings	Orca Books
Dash of Science, A	W	I	250+	Literacy By Design	Rigby
Dash, the Young Meerkat	K	RF	250+	PM Plus Story Books	Rigby
Dashing Through the Snow: The Story of the Jr. Iditarod	U	I	250+	Bookshop	Mondo Publishing
Daughter of the Mountains	V	HF	250+	Rankin, Louise	Penguin Group
Daughter of the Sun	H	RF	210	Storyteller-Night Crickets	Wright Group/McGraw Hill
Daughter of Venice	X	HF	250+	Napoli, Donna Jo	Random House
Daughter of Winter	X	HF	250+	Collins, Pat Lowery	Candlewick Press
Daughters of Liberty	S	B	1620	Independent Readers Social Studies	Houghton Mifflin Harcourt
Daughters, The	Z	RF	250+	Philbin, Joanna	Little Brown and Company
David Beckham	P	B	250+	Amazing Athletes	Lerner Publishing Group
David Beckham	O	B	928	Leveled Readers	Houghton Mifflin Harcourt
David Beckham	O	B	928	Leveled Readers/CA	Houghton Mifflin Harcourt
David Beckham	O	B	928	Leveled Readers/TX	Houghton Mifflin Harcourt
David Beckham	U	B	250+	Sports Heroes and Legends	Lerner Publishing Group
David Beckham Soccer Superstar	O	B	953	Leveled Readers/CA	Houghton Mifflin Harcourt
David Beckham Soccer Superstar	O	B	953	Leveled Readers/TX	Houghton Mifflin Harcourt
David Beckham, Soccer Superstar	O	B	953	Leveled Readers	Houghton Mifflin Harcourt
David Inside Out	Z+	RF	250+	Bantle, Lee	Henry Holt & Co.
David McCord: Poet	Q	B	407	Vocabulary Readers	Houghton Mifflin Harcourt
David Mortimore Baxter: Chicken!	P	RF	250+	Tayleur, Karen	Stone Arch Books
David Mortimore Baxter: Excuses!	P	RF	8776	Tayleur, Karen	Stone Arch Books
David Mortimore Baxter: Haunted!	P	RF	250+	Tayleur, Karen	Stone Arch Books
David Mortimore Baxter: Liar!	P	RF	9827	Tayleur, Karen	Stone Arch Books
David Mortimore Baxter: Manners!	P	RF	10673	Tayleur, Karen	Stone Arch Books
David Mortimore Baxter: Promises!	P	RF	10748	Tayleur, Karen	Stone Arch Books
David Mortimore Baxter: Secrets!	P	RF	10548	Tayleur, Karen	Stone Arch Books
David Mortimore Baxter: Spies!	P	RF	250+	Tayleur, Karen	Stone Arch Books
David Mortimore Baxter: The Truth!	P	RF	10667	Tayleur, Karen	Stone Arch Books
David Mortimore Baxter: Wild!	P	RF	250+	Tayleur, Karen	Stone Arch Books
David Ortiz	P	B	2023	Amazing Athletes	Lerner Publishing Group
David Ortiz: Revised Edition	P	B	2265	Amazing Athletes	Lerner Publishing Group
David Wiggles	F	RF	54	City Stories	Rigby
David's Cold	E	I	151	Little Celebrations	Pearson Learning Group
David's Drawings	I	RF	250+	Falwell, Cathryn	Lee & Low Books Inc.

D

* Collection of short stories   # Graphic text
^ Mature content with lower level text demands

TITLE	LEVEL	GENRE	WORD COUNT	AUTHOR / SERIES	PUBLISHER / DISTRIBUTOR
Davin	R	F	250+	Gordon, Dan; Gordon, Zaki	Bantam Books
DaVinci's Designs	V	B	1669	Reading Street	Pearson
Davis Buys a Dog	K	RF	299	Reading Street	Pearson
Davy Crockett	R	B	3885	History Maker Bios	Lerner Publishing Group
Davy Crockett	T	B	250+	In Their Own Words	Scholastic
Davy Crockett	S	B	2184	People to Remember Series	January Books
Davy Crockett	P	B	250+	Photo-Illustrated Biographies	Red Brick Learning
Davy Crockett and the Wild Cat	H	F	148	Instant Readers	Harcourt School Publishers
^Davy Crockett: A True American Hero	S	B	250+	Hameray Biography Series	Hameray Publishing Group
Davy Crockett: Frontier Hero	V	B	2127	Leveled Readers	Houghton Mifflin Harcourt
Davy Crockett: His Life and Legend	S	B	250+	Power Up!	Steck-Vaughn
Dawn of Fear	X	HF	250+	Cooper, Susan	Simon & Schuster
^Dawn of the Zombies	W	F	250+	The Extraordinary Files	Hameray Publishing Group
Dawn; Warriors, The New Prophecy	U	F	250+	Hunter, Erin	HarperCollins
Day and Night	H	I	128	Discovering Nature's Cycles	Lerner Publishing Group
Day and Night	G	I	115	Discovery Links	Newbridge
Day and Night	I	I	228	Gear Up!	Wright Group/McGraw Hill
Day and Night	M	TL	250+	Orbit Chapter Books	Pacific Learning
Day and Night	J	I	188	Patterns in Nature	Capstone Press
Day and Night	D	I	102	Rigby Rocket	Rigby
Day and Night	T	I	250+	The News	Richard C. Owen
Day and Night	D	I	102	Twig	Wright Group/McGraw Hill
Day at a Time, A	LB	I	27	Shutterbug Books	Steck-Vaughn
Day at a Zoo, A	M	I	250+	Time Goes By	Millbrook Press
Day at an Airport, A	M	I	250+	Time Goes By	Millbrook Press
Day at an Indian Market, A	L	I	250+	The Big Picture	Capstone Press
Day at Rainbow Lake, A	I	I	250+	Phonics Readers Plus	Steck-Vaughn
Day at School, A	A	F	15	Leveled Readers	Houghton Mifflin Harcourt
Day at School, A	A	I	21	Leveled Readers Emergent	Houghton Mifflin Harcourt
Day at School, A	A	F	15	Leveled Readers/CA	Houghton Mifflin Harcourt
Day at School, A	C	RF	38	Sunshine	Wright Group/McGraw Hill
Day at the Beach, A	E	RF	207	Rigby Flying Colors	Rigby
Day at the Fair, A	B	RF	42	Bebop Books	Lee & Low Books Inc.
Day at the Fair, A	N	I	250+	Books for Young Learners	Richard C. Owen
Day at the Market, A	J	I	250+	Explorations	Eleanor Curtain Publishing
Day at the Market, A	J	I	250+	Explorations	Okapi Educational Materials
Day at the Park, A	C	RF	105	Leveled Literacy Intervention/ Green System	Heinemann
Day at the Pond, A	I	I	193	InfoTrek	ETA/Cuisenaire
Day at the Races, A	H	RF	85	Bauer, Roger	Kaeden Books
Day at the Races, A	M	RF	250+	Michaels, Eric	Pearson Learning Group
Day at the Trout Farm, A	L	I	653	Rigby Flying Colors	Rigby
Day Buzzy Stopped Being Busy, The	G	F	147	First Start	Troll Associates
Day Camp	B	I	48	Early Connections	Benchmark Education
Day Dirk Yeller Came to Town, The	N	F	250+	Casanova, Mary	Farrar, Straus, & Giroux
Day for J. J. and Me, A	M	RF	371	Evangeline Nicholas Collection	Wright Group/McGraw Hill
Day for Night	Q	I	947	Reading Street	Pearson
Day I Chose My Family, The	I	F	292	Springboard	Wright Group/McGraw Hill
Day I Had to Play with My Sister, The	G	RF	139	Bonsall, Crosby	HarperCollins
Day I Lost My Bus Pass, The	J	RF	131	City Kids	Rigby
Day I Tore My Shorts, The	I	RF	209	City Kids	Rigby
Day in a City, A	M	I	250+	Time Goes By	Millbrook Press
Day in Africa, A	A	I	24	Bonnell, Kris	Reading Reading Books

* Collection of short stories   # Graphic text
^ Mature content with lower level text demands

TITLE	LEVEL	GENRE	WORD COUNT	AUTHOR / SERIES	PUBLISHER / DISTRIBUTOR
Day in Japan, A	G	I	54	Moreton, Daniel; Berger, Samantha	Scholastic
Day in San Juan, A	M	I	621	Vocabulary Readers/CA	Houghton Mifflin Harcourt
Day in Space, A	L	SF	250+	Lord, Suzanne; Epstein, Jolie	Scholastic
Day in the Life of a Ballet Dancer, A	O	I	824	Time for Kids	Teacher Created Materials
Day in the Life of a Colonial Cabinetmaker, A	S	I	250+	The Library of Living and Working in Colonial Times	Rosen Publishing Group
Day in the Life of a Colonial Dressmaker, A	S	I	250+	The Library of Living and Working in Colonial Times	Rosen Publishing Group
Day in the Life of a Colonial Glassblower, A	S	I	250+	The Library of Living and Working in Colonial Times	Rosen Publishing Group
Day in the Life of a Colonial Sea Captain, A	S	I	250+	The Library of Living and Working in Colonial Times	Rosen Publishing Group
Day in the Life of a Colonial Soldier, A	S	I	250+	The Library of Living and Working in Colonial Times	Rosen Publishing Group
Day in the Life of a Colonial Surveyor, A	S	I	250+	The Library of Living and Working in Colonial Times	Rosen Publishing Group
Day in the Life of a Computer, A	K	I	250+	On Our Way to English	Rigby
Day in the Life of a Cowhand, A	N	I	803	Time for Kids	Teacher Created Materials
Day in the Life of a Firefighter, A	N	I	818	Time for Kids	Teacher Created Materials
Day in the Life of a Garbage Collector, A	K	I	250+	Community Helpers at Work	Capstone Press
Day in the Life of a Librarian, A	L	I	250+	Community Helpers at Work	Capstone Press
Day in the Life of a Vet, A	M	I	1215	Reading Street	Pearson
Day in the Life of a Zoo Keeper, A	L	I	250+	Community Helpers at Work	Capstone Press
Day in the Life of Peter and Eve, A	V	HF	1974	Reading Street	Pearson
Day in the Life of the Great Plains, A	Q	I	1287	Leveled Readers Social Studies	Houghton Mifflin Harcourt
Day in the Salt Marsh, A	M	I	538	Kurtz, Kevin	Sylvan Dell Publishing
Day in Town, A	K	RF	206	Story Box	Wright Group/McGraw Hill
Day It Rained Forever, The: A Story of the Johnstown Flood	S	I	250+	Gross, Virginia T.	Penguin Group
Day Jimmy's Boa Ate the Wash, The	K	F	250+	Noble, Trinka H.	Scholastic
Day Leo Said I Hate You!, The	M	RF	250+	Harris, Robie H.	Little Brown and Company
Day Martin Luther King, Jr., Died, The	M	RF	250+	Story Vines	Wright Group/McGraw Hill
Day Martin Luther King, Jr., Was Shot, The	Y	B	250+	Haskins, Jim	Scholastic
Day Miss Francie Got Skunked, The	N	RF	250+	DeFord, Diane	Pearson Learning Group
Day No Pigs Would Die, A	Z	HF	250+	Peck, Robert Newton	Random House
Day of Ahmed's Secret, A	M	RF	250+	Heide, Florence Perry; Gilliland, Judith Heide	Scholastic
^Day of Judgement	Y	SF	250+	The Extraordinary Files	Hameray Publishing Group
Day of Pleasure, A: Stories of a Boy Growing Up in Warsaw	W	B	250+	Singer, Isaac Bashevis	Farrar, Straus, & Giroux
Day of the Black Blizzard, The	M	HF	1422	On My Own History	Millbrook Press
Day of the Blizzard	Q	I	250+	Moskin, Marietta	Scholastic
Day of the Dead	N	I	1630	On My Own Holidays	Lerner Publishing Group
Day of the Dead, The	I	RF	250+	Greetings	Rigby
Day of the Dragon King	M	F	250+	Osborne, Mary Pope	Random House
Day of the Iguana	R	RF	250+	Winkler, Henry and Oliver, Lin	Grosset & Dunlap
Day of the Pelican, The	X	HF	250+	Paterson, Katherine	Clarion Books
Day of the Rain, The	L	F	250+	Cowley, Joy	Pearson Learning Group
Day of the Snow, The	L	F	250+	Cowley, Joy	Pearson Learning Group
Day of the Storm	M	F	250+	Sun Sprouts	ETA/Cuisenaire
Day of the Tornadoes	P	I	552	Vocabulary Readers	Houghton Mifflin Harcourt
Day of the Wind, The	L	F	250+	Cowley, Joy	Pearson Learning Group
Day on the Mountain, A	P	I	560	Kurtz, Kevin	Sylvan Dell Publishing
Day Shopping, A	E	RF	157	Foundations	Wright Group/McGraw Hill
Day the Earth Shook, The	T	I	1889	Leveled Readers Science	Houghton Mifflin Harcourt

TITLE	LEVEL	GENRE	WORD COUNT	AUTHOR / SERIES	PUBLISHER / DISTRIBUTOR
Day the Fifth Grade Disappeared, The	Q	F	250+	Fields, Terri	Scholastic
Day the Gorilla Came to School, The	I	RF	293	Sunshine	Wright Group/McGraw Hill
Day the Sky Fell Down, The	H	F	226	Lighthouse	Rigby
Day the Sky Turned Green, The	M	F	250+	Reeves, Barbara	Pearson Learning Group
Day the Women Got the Vote, The: A Photo History of the Women's Rights Movement	Y	B	250+	Sullivan, George	Scholastic
Day to Remember, A	J	RF	280	Take Two Books	Wright Group/McGraw Hill
Day With a Mail Carrier, A	J	I	187	Welcome Books	Children's Press
Day With a Mechanic, A	J	I	147	Welcome Books	Children's Press
Day with Air Traffic Controllers, A	J	I	145	Welcome Books	Children's Press
Day with Aunt Eva, A	K	RF	509	Pair-It Turn and Learn	Steck-Vaughn
Day with Belugas, A	Q	I	250+	WorldScapes	ETA/Cuisenaire
Day with Dad, A	L	RF	250+	Holmberg, Bo R.	Candlewick Press
Day with Emily Emeryboard	K	F	250+	Foundations	Wright Group/McGraw Hill
Day with Firefighters, A	H	I	171	Welcome Books	Children's Press
Day with My Dad, A	C	RF	88	Fiesta Series	Pearson Learning Group
Day With My Family, A	J	RF	250+	Parker, David	Scholastic
Day With Nurse Nan, A	E	RF	100	Run to Reading	Discovery Peak
Day with Paramedics, A	F	I	147	Kottke, Jan	Scholastic
Day with the Dogs, A	M	RF	1037	Reading Street	Pearson
Day with the Mayor, A	N	RF	704	Leveled Readers Social Studies	Houghton Mifflin Harcourt
Day with Wilbur Robinson, A	N	RF	250+	Joyce, William	HarperTrophy
Day with Your Dog, A	C	I	32	Rosen Real Readers	Rosen Publishing Group
Day, A	F	I	109	Calendars	Lerner Publishing Group
Day, A	H	I	134	The Calendar	Capstone Press
Day, Gogo Went to Vote, The	P	RF	250+	Sisulu, Elinor Batezat	Little Brown and Company
Day, Night	B	RF	42	Reading Safari	Mondo Publishing
Day, The	LB	F	12	Sails	Rigby
Days at the Beach	E	I	85	Sun Sprouts	ETA/Cuisenaire
Days of Adventure	E	F	47	Bookshop	Mondo Publishing
Days of Courage: The Little Rock Story	R	I	250+	Kelso, Richard	Steck-Vaughn
Days of Decision: An Oral History of Conscientious Objectors in the Military During the Vietnam War	Z+	B	250+	Gioglio, Gerald R.	The Broken Rifle Press
Days of the Knights: A Tale of Castles and Battles	V	HF	250+	DK Readers	DK Publishing
Days of the Week	G	I	168	Measuring Time	Heinemann Library
Days of the Week	E	I	166	PM Math Readers	Rigby
Days of the Week, The	A	RF	54	InfoTrek	ETA/Cuisenaire
Days to Remember	R	I	250+	iOpeners	Pearson Learning Group
*Days With Frog and Toad	K	F	250+	Lobel, Arnold	HarperTrophy
Dayton and the Happy Tree	M	RF	1237	Sunshine	Wright Group/McGraw Hill
Dazzle of Hummingbirds, A	U	I	250+	Wild Life Series	London Town Press
Dazzle's First Day: Butterfly Meadow	M	F	250+	Moss, Olivia	Scholastic
Dazzle's New Friend: Butterfly Meadow	M	F	250+	Moss, Olivia	Scholastic
Dazzling Book Report, The (Fancy Nancy)	J	RF	250+	O'Connor, Jane	HarperCollins
Dazzling Designs	R	I	250+	WorldScapes	ETA/Cuisenaire
Dazzling Dragonflies: A Life Cycle Story	M	I	355	Glaser, Linda	Millbrook Press
DC Super Heroes: The Ultimate Pop-Up Book	X	F	250+	Reinhart, Matthew	Little Brown and Company
^D-Day: The Battle of Normandy	X	I	250+	Bloodiest Battles	Capstone Press
De Soto: Hernando de Soto Explores the Southeast	U	B	250+	Exploring the World	Compass Point Books
Dead & the Gone, The	Z+	F	250+	Pfeffer, Susan Beth	Harcourt
^Dead Cool	Q	F	4627	Clover, Peter	Stone Arch Books

Organized Alphabetically by Title
Storable Database at www.fountasandpinnellleveledbooks.com

* Collection of short stories   # Graphic text
^ Mature content with lower level text demands

TITLE	LEVEL	GENRE	WORD COUNT	AUTHOR / SERIES	PUBLISHER / DISTRIBUTOR
Dead Drop, The: Gilda Joyce	W	F	250+	Allison, Jennifer	Puffin Books
Dead End in Norvelt	Y	HF	250+	Gantos, Jack	Farrar, Straus, & Giroux
Dead Girls Don't Write Letters	W	RF	250+	Giles, Gail	Millbrook Press
Dead Letter	S	RF	250+	Byars, Betsy	Puffin Books
Dead Man's Island	Y	RF	5215	Oxford Bookworms Library	Oxford University Press
^Dead Man's Map	S	RF	250+	Peschke, M.	Stone Arch Books
^Dead Wings	T	F	250+	Dragonblood	Stone Arch Books
Deadbolts and Dinkles	N	RF	250+	Tapp, Kathy Kennedy	Mondo Publishing
^Dead-End Job	Z+	RF	250+	Orca Soundings	Orca Books
Deadliest Dinosaurs, The	P	I	1106	Meet the Dinosaurs	Lerner Publishing Group
^Deadly Doll, The	R	F	250+	Burke, J.	Stone Arch Books
Deadly Dungeon, The	N	RF	250+	A to Z Mysteries	Random House
Deadly Perils and How to Avoid Them	V	I	250+	Turner, Tracy	Walker & Company
Deadly Sea Creatures	N	I	1308	Take Two Books	Wright Group/McGraw Hill
Deadwood, South Dakota: A Frontier Community	P	I	250+	Navigators Social Studies Series	Benchmark Education
Dealing with Dragons	U	F	250+	Wrede, Patricia	Harcourt
Dear America: Letters From Vietnam	Z+	I	250+	Edelman, Bernard	Pocket Books
Dear Benjamin Banneker	U	B	250+	Pinkney, Andrea Davis	Voyager Books
Dear Butterflies . . .	L	RF	414	Leveled Readers	Houghton Mifflin Harcourt
Dear Calvin	O	RF	250+	PM Plus Chapter Books	Rigby
Dear Cousin	W	HF	3804	Leveled Readers	Houghton Mifflin Harcourt
Dear Cousin	W	HF	3804	Leveled Readers/CA	Houghton Mifflin Harcourt
Dear Cousin	W	HF	3804	Leveled Readers/TX	Houghton Mifflin Harcourt
Dear Deer: A Book of Homophones	N	F	243	Barretta, Gene	Henry Holt & Co.
Dear Diary	M	RF	712	Leveled Readers/TX	Houghton Mifflin Harcourt
Dear Diary	N	RF	250+	Literacy 2000 Satellites	Rigby
Dear Dr. Bell... Your Friend, Helen Keller	W	B	250+	St. George, Judith	Scholastic
Dear Dragon Goes Camping	E	F	273	Dear Dragon	Norwood House Press
Dear Dragon Goes to the Bank	F	F	285	Hillert, Margaret/Dear Dragon	Norwood House Press
Dear Dragon Goes to the Carnival	E	F	273	Dear Dragon	Norwood House Press
Dear Dragon Goes to the Firehouse	E	F	174	Dear Dragon	Norwood House Press
Dear Dragon Goes to the Library	E	F	250+	Dear Dragon	Norwood House Press
Dear Dragon Goes to the Market	E	F	211	Dear Dragon	Norwood House Press
Dear Dragon Goes to the Zoo	E	F	205	Dear Dragon	Norwood House Press
Dear Dragon Helps Out	F	F	144	Hillert, Margaret/Dear Dragon	Norwood House Press
Dear Dragon's A is for Apple	E	F	250+	Dear Dragon	Norwood House Press
Dear Dragon's Colors 1, 2, 3	E	F	248	Dear Dragon	Norwood House Press
Dear Dragon's Day with Father	F	F	250+	Dear Dragon	Norwood House Press
Dear Fish	M	F	250+	Gall, Chris	Little Brown and Company
Dear Future	Q	RF	250+	Literacy 2000	Rigby
Dear Grandma	M	I	264	Storyteller Nonfiction	Wright Group/McGraw Hill
Dear Juno	M	RF	250+	Park, Soyung	Scholastic
Dear Levi: Letters from the Overland Trail	T	HF	250+	Woodruff, Elvira	Alfred A. Knopf
Dear Mabel!	H	RF	138	Little Celebrations	Pearson Learning Group
Dear Mr. Blueberry	L	F	250+	James, Simon	Aladdin Paperbacks
Dear Mr. Henshaw	Q	RF	250+	Cleary, Beverly	HarperCollins
Dear Mrs. Parks: A Dialogue with Today's Youth	V	I	250+	Parks, Rosa	Lee & Low Books Inc.
Dear Papa	S	HF	250+	Ylvisaker, Anne	Candlewick Press
Dear Pop	N	RF	250+	Wonder World	Wright Group/McGraw Hill
Dear Prime Minister	O	I	250+	Roberts, Chris	Fitzhenry & Whiteside
Dear Primo: A Letter to My Cousin	M	RF	250+	Tonatiuh, Duncan	Harry N. Abrams
Dear Sam, Dear Ben	Q	RF	250+	Book Blazers	ETA/Cuisenaire
Dear Santa	B	F	50	Literacy 2000	Rigby

D

TITLE	LEVEL	GENRE	WORD COUNT	AUTHOR / SERIES	PUBLISHER / DISTRIBUTOR
Dear Tom	H	RF	153	Wonder World	Wright Group/McGraw Hill
Dear Tooth Fairy	K	F	250+	Ruelle, Karen Gray	Holiday House
Dear Zoo	F	F	115	Campbell, Rod	Macmillan
Dearly, Nearly, Insincerely: What is an Adverb?	O	I	362	Words Are CATegorical	Millbrook Press
Death Be Not Proud	Z+	B	250+	Gunther, John	HarperCollins
Death by Eggplant	T	RF	250+	O'Keefe, Susan Heyboer	Roaring Brook Press
Death in the Freezer	Z+	RF	6180	Oxford Bookworms Library	Oxford University Press
Death Mountain	U	RF	250+	Shahan, Sherry	Peachtree
Death of Issac Brock, The	Y	I	250+	History for Young Canadians	Fitzhenry & Whiteside
Death of Karen Silkwood, The	X	I	5585	Oxford Bookworms Library	Oxford University Press
Death of Tecumseh, The	Y	I	250+	History for Young Canadians	Fitzhenry & Whiteside
Death Valley	S	HF	250+	Duey, Kathleen; Bale, Karen A.	Simon & Schuster
Death Valley	Q	I	1571	Vocabulary Readers	Houghton Mifflin Harcourt
Death Valley	Q	I	1571	Vocabulary Readers/CA	Houghton Mifflin Harcourt
Death Valley Desert	P	I	1097	Time for Kids	Teacher Created Materials
^Death Wind	Z+	RF	250+	Orca Soundings	Orca Books
Death's Door	V	RF	250+	Byars, Betsy	Puffin Books
Death's Shadow (The Demonata Series)	Z+	F	250+	Shan, Darren	Little Brown and Company
Deathwatch	Z+	RF	250+	White, Robb	Bantam Books
Deborah Sampson, Soldier of the American Revolution	P	B	250+	Leveled Readers Language Support	Houghton Mifflin Harcourt
Deborah Sampson: Soldier of the Revolution	S	B	1207	Leveled Readers	Houghton Mifflin Harcourt
Debra's Dog	H	F	157	Tadpoles	Rigby
*Deb's Secret Wish and Other Stories	H	F	250+	New Way Literature	Steck-Vaughn
December Secrets	L	RF	250+	Giff, Patricia Reilly	Bantam Books
Deception: Haunting Emma	Z+	F	250+	Nichols, Lee	Bloomsbury Children's Books
Decision at Fort Laramie	W	HF	3450	Leveled Readers/CA	Houghton Mifflin Harcourt
Decision at Fort Laramie	W	HF	3450	Leveled Readers/TX	Houghton Mifflin Harcourt
Decisions at Fort Laramie	W	HF	3450	Leveled Readers	Houghton Mifflin Harcourt
^Deck of Monsters, A	S	F	250+	Zucker, Jonny	Stone Arch Books
Declaration of Independence and Benjamin Franklin of Pennsylvania, The	R	B	250+	Framers of the Declaration of Independence	Rosen Publishing Group
Declaration of Independence and John Adams of Massachusetts, The	R	B	250+	Framers of the Declaration of Independence	Rosen Publishing Group
Declaration of Independence and Richard Henry Lee of Virginia, The	R	B	250+	Framers of the Declaration of Independence	Rosen Publishing Group
Declaration of Independence and Robert Livingston of New York, The	R	B	250+	Framers of the Declaration of Independence	Rosen Publishing Group
Declaration of Independence and Roger Sherman of Connecticut, The	R	B	250+	Framers of the Declaration of Independence	Rosen Publishing Group
Declaration of Independence and Thomas Jefferson of Virginia, The	R	B	250+	Framers of the Declaration of Independence	Rosen Publishing Group
Declaration of Independence in Translation, The: What It Really Means	V	I	250+	Kids' Translations	Capstone Press
Declaration of Independence, The	S	I	250+	A True Book	Children's Press
Declaration of Independence, The	Q	I	250+	American Symbols	Picture Window Books
Declaration of Independence, The	V	I	250+	Cornerstones of Freedom	Children's Press
Declaration of Independence, The	V	I	250+	Let Freedom Ring	Red Brick Learning
Declaration of Independence, The	Q	RF	250+	Mazer, Anne	Scholastic
Declaration of Independence, The	T	I	250+	Primary Source Readers	Teacher Created Materials
Declaration of Independence, The	W	I	250+	Reading Expeditions	National Geographic
Declaration of Independence, The	T	I	250+	Symbols of America	Marshall Cavendish
Declaration of Independence, The	T	I	250+	We The People	Compass Point Books
Declaration, The	Z+	SF	250+	Malley, Gemma	Bloomsbury Children's Books

* Collection of short stories   # Graphic text
^ Mature content with lower level text demands

TITLE	LEVEL	GENRE	WORD COUNT	AUTHOR / SERIES	PUBLISHER / DISTRIBUTOR
Declaring Independence	T	I	250+	Reading Expeditions	National Geographic
Decoding Data	T	I	250+	Reading Expeditions	National Geographic
Dede and the Dinosaur	K	F	232	Cumpiano, Ina	Hampton Brown
DeDe Takes Charge!	O	RF	250+	Hurwitz, Johanna	Morrow
Dee and Me	G	RF	189	Ready Readers	Pearson Learning Group
Deena's Lucky Penny	K	RF	250+	Math Matters	Kane Press
Deep and Dark and Dangerous	U	F	250+	Hahn, Mary Downing	Houghton Mifflin Harcourt
Deep Blue Lake, A	V	I	2270	Leveled Readers	Houghton Mifflin Harcourt
Deep Blue Sea, The	G	I	195	Wood, Audrey	Scholastic
Deep Diving Adventures	S	I	250+	Dangerous Adventures	Red Brick Learning
Deep Down Popular	T	RF	250+	Stone, Phoebe	Scholastic
Deep Freeze	Q	I	250+	Explorer Books-Pathfinder	National Geographic
Deep Freeze	P	I	250+	Explorer Books-Pioneer	National Geographic
Deep in the Desert	O	I	1476	Donald, Rhonda Lucas	Sylvan Dell Publishing
Deep in the Forest	WB	TL	0	Turkle, Brinton	Dutton Children's Books
Deep in the Heart of High School	Z	RF	250+	Goldbach, Veronica	Farrar, Straus, & Giroux
Deep in the Jungle	S	I	250+	WorldScapes	ETA/Cuisenaire
Deep in the Woods	E	RF	164	Carousel Readers	Pearson Learning Group
Deep Ocean, The	T	I	250+	Connectors	Pacific Learning
Deep Sea, The	G	I	152	Ready Readers	Pearson Learning Group
Deep Space Hijack: Superman	P	F	250+	DC Superheroes	Stone Arch Books
Deep Trouble	Z	RF	5197	Dominoes one	Oxford University Press
Deep Waters: Zac Power	O	F	250+	Larry, H. I.	Feiwel and Friends
Deer	F	I	98	Animal Life Cycles	Lerner Publishing Group
Deer	H	I	80	Woodland Animals	Capstone Press
Deer	C	I	34	Zoozoo-Animal World	Cavallo Publishing
Deer and the Crocodile, The	G	F	178	Literacy 2000	Rigby
Deer Family, The	K	I	412	Vocabulary Readers	Houghton Mifflin Harcourt
Deer Family, The	K	I	412	Vocabulary Readers/CA	Houghton Mifflin Harcourt
Deer Have Fawns	M	I	250+	Animals and Their Young	Compass Point Books
Deer Hunting	S	I	250+	The Great Outdoors	Capstone Press
Deer in the Wood, The	J	HF	250+	Wilder, Laura Ingalls	HarperCollins
Deer Report, The	J	RF	765	The Fawn	Pioneer Valley
Defenders, The	T	B	250+	McGovern, Ann	Language for Learning Assoc.
Defending Irene	U	RF	250+	Nitz, Kristen Wolden	Peachtree
Defense of Thaddeus A. Ledbetter, The	W	RF	250+	Gosselink, John	Amulet Books
Defiance	T	RF	250+	Hobbs, Valerie	Square Fish
Define Normal	Y	RF	250+	Peters, Julie Anne	Little Brown and Company
Defining the Laws of Motion	W	I	250+	Reading Expeditions	National Geographic
Definitely Cool	X	RF	250+	Wilkinson, Brenda	Scholastic
Definitely Different	I	RF	102	Voyages	SRA/McGraw Hill
Definitely, Positively, Absolutely NO!	D	F	147	Story Basket	Wright Group/McGraw Hill
Deforestation and Desertification	U	I	250+	Navigators Science Series	Benchmark Education
Delaware	T	I	250+	Hello U.S.A.	Lerner Publishing Group
Delaware	S	I	250+	Land of Liberty	Red Brick Learning
Delaware	T	I	250+	Sea to Shining Sea	Children's Press
Delaware	R	I	250+	This Land Is Your Land	Compass Point Books
Delaware Colony, The	R	I	250+	The American Colonies	Capstone Press
Delaware People, The	P	I	250+	Native Peoples	Red Brick Learning
Delaware, The	T	I	4094	Native American Histoies	Lerner Publishing Group
Delaware: Facts and Symbols	O	I	250+	The States and Their Symbols	Capstone Press
Delicious Hullabaloo	P	F	250+	Mora, Pat	Pinata Publishing
Delivering Justice	U	B	250+	Haskins, Jim	Candlewick Press

D

TITLE	LEVEL	GENRE	WORD COUNT	AUTHOR / SERIES	PUBLISHER / DISTRIBUTOR
Delivering Your Mail: A Book About Mail Carriers	H	I	120	Community Workers	Picture Window Books
^Delta Force, The	T	I	250+	Elite Military Forces	Capstone Press
^Deltas	N	I	190	Natural Wonders	Capstone Press
Dem Bones	O	I	250+	Barner, Bob	Chronicle Books
Demanding Justice: A Story About Mary Ann Shadd Cary	R	B	8711	Creative Minds Biographies	Carolrhoda Books
#Demeter & Persephone: Spring Held Hostage	V	TL	5053	Graphic Myths and Legends	Graphic Universe
Demeter and Persephone	T	TL	250+	Bookshop	Mondo Publishing
#Democracy	V	I	250+	Cartoon Nation	Capstone Press
Demolition	J	I	118	Construction Zone	Capstone Press
Demolition	V	I	250+	iOpeners	Pearson Learning Group
Demolition Derby Cars	Q	I	250+	Wild Rides!	Capstone Press
Demon Apocalypse (The Demonata Series)	Z+	F	250+	Shan, Darren	Little Brown and Company
Demon Thief (The Demonata Series)	Z+	F	250+	Shan, Darren	Little Brown and Company
Demons of the Ocean: Vampirates	Z+	F	250+	Somper, Justin	Little Brown and Company
Den of Thieves	X	HF	250+	Golding, Julia	Roaring Brook Press
Den, The	B	RF	34	Rigby Star	Rigby
Denali National Park	K	I	390	Springboard	Wright Group/McGraw Hill
Denali National Park and Preserve	O	I	250+	A True Book	Children's Press
Dennis Tito: First Space Tourist	Q	I	250+	Rosen Real Readers	Rosen Publishing Group
Denny Davidson, Detective	M	F	250+	Tristars	Richard C. Owen
Dentist, The	G	I	201	PM Nonfiction-Blue	Rigby
Dentist, The	D	RF	77	Rigby Star	Rigby
Dentists	M	I	250+	Community Helpers	Red Brick Learning
Dentists	M	I	565	Pull Ahead Books	Lerner Publishing Group
Dentist's Dream, A	O	RF	250+	Tristars	Richard C. Owen
Denver Broncos, The	S	I	250+	Team Spirit	Norwood House Press
Denver Nuggets, The	S	I	4342	Team Spirit	Norwood House Press
Deputy Dan and the Bank Robbers	L	RF	250+	Rosenbloom, Joseph	Random House
Deputy Dan Gets His Man	L	RF	250+	Rosenbloom, Joseph	Random House
Derek Jeter	P	B	1955	Amazing Athletes	Lerner Publishing Group
Derek Jeter	R	B	250+	Sports Heroes	Red Brick Learning
Derek Jeter (Revised Edition)	P	B	1690	Amazing Athletes	Lerner Publishing Group
Desert	V	I	250+	Eyewitness Books	DK Publishing
Desert	F	I	96	Habitats	Lerner Publishing Group
Desert	H	I	133	Reading Street	Pearson
Desert Animals	D	I	50	Benchmark Rebus	Marshall Cavendish
Desert Animals	J	I	195	Rosen Real Readers	Rosen Publishing Group
Desert Animals	I	I	134	Spyglass Books	Compass Point Books
Desert Animals	P	I	250+	Theme Sets	National Geographic
Desert Animals	E	I	186	Vocabulary Readers	Houghton Mifflin Harcourt
Desert Animals	E	I	186	Vocabulary Readers/CA	Houghton Mifflin Harcourt
Desert Animals	E	I	186	Vocabulary Readers/TX	Houghton Mifflin Harcourt
Desert Birds	N	I	250+	A New True Book	Children's Press
Desert Climate	R	I	250+	Theme Sets	National Geographic
Desert Clowns	J	I	283	On Our Way to English	Rigby
Desert Dance	G	RF	184	Little Celebrations	Pearson Learning Group
Desert Day	C	I	23	Twig	Wright Group/McGraw Hill
Desert Food Chain, A	U	I	6718	Follow That Food Chain	Lerner Publishing Group
Desert Food Chains	T	I	250+	Protecting Food Chains	Heinemann Library
Desert Food Webs	Q	I	2376	Early Bird Food Webs	Lerner Publishing Group
Desert Friends	E	I	48	Ray's Readers	Outside the Box
Desert Giant: The World of the Saguaro Cactus	R	I	250+	Bash, Barbara	Scholastic

* Collection of short stories   # Graphic text
^ Mature content with lower level text demands

TITLE	LEVEL	GENRE	WORD COUNT	AUTHOR / SERIES	PUBLISHER / DISTRIBUTOR
Desert Iguanas	K	I	381	Pull Ahead Books	Lerner Publishing Group
Desert Is My Mother, The	L	F	126	Mora, Pat	Pinata Publishing
Desert Journal	T	I	250+	PM Plus Nonfiction	Rigby
Desert Life	K	I	129	Independent Readers Science	Houghton Mifflin Harcourt
Desert Life	J	I	230	Literacy by Design	Rigby
Desert Life	N	I	250+	Mann, Rachel	Scholastic
Desert Machine, The	K	I	202	Sunshine	Wright Group/McGraw Hill
^Desert Pirates, The	P	F	250+	Masters, Anthony	Stone Arch Books
Desert Plants	N	I	250+	Life in the World's Biomes	Capstone Press
Desert Rain	K	I	214	Windows on Literacy	National Geographic
Desert Rose and Her Highfalutin Hog	L	F	250+	Jackson, Alison	Walker & Company
Desert Run, The	P	I	250+	Orbit Chapter Books	Pacific Learning
Desert Treasure	M	RF	250+	Pair-It Books	Steck-Vaughn
Desert, The	C	I	34	Carousel Readers	Pearson Learning Group
Desert, The	A	I	32	Literacy by Design	Rigby
Desert, The	A	I	32	On Our Way to English	Rigby
Desert: Inside Australia's Simpson Desert	P	I	250+	Cambridge Reading	Pearson Learning Group
Deserts	O	I	250+	A True Book	Children's Press
Deserts	K	I	212	Early Connections	Benchmark Education
Deserts	Q	I	250+	Ecosystems	Red Brick Learning
Deserts	I	I	154	Explorations	Eleanor Curtain Publishing
Deserts	I	I	154	Explorations	Okapi Educational Materials
Deserts	Q	I	250+	First Reports	Compass Point Books
Deserts	O	I	250+	Gibbons, Gail	Holiday House
Deserts	N	I	250+	Habitats of the World	Pearson Learning Group
Deserts	M	I	250+	PM Plus Nonfiction	Rigby
Deserts	R	I	250+	The Wonders of Our World	Crabtree
Deserts	S	I	250+	Theme Sets	National Geographic
Deserts and Semideserts	W	I	250+	Biomes Atlases	Raintree
Deserts Are Not Deserted	R	I	250+	WorldScapes	ETA/Cuisenaire
Deserts of the World	Q	I	1288	Leveled Readers Science	Houghton Mifflin Harcourt
Deserts: The Land Around Us	S	I	250+	Reading Expeditions	National Geographic
Deserts: Wonders of Nature	L	I	250+	Bookworms	Marshall Cavendish
Design All Around Us	Q	I	250+	PM Plus Nonfiction	Rigby
Designated Ugly Fat Friend, The	Z+	RF	250+	Keplinger, Kody	Little Brown and Company
Designed for Living	P	I	250+	InfoQuest	Rigby
Designs	E	I	15	Little Celebrations	Pearson Learning Group
Desk for Doc, A	H	RF	172	The Rowland Reading Program Library	Rowland Reading Foundation
Desmond D. Duck: Respect	K	F	1395	Salerno, Tony Character Classics	Character Building Company
Desperate Journey	V	HF	250+	Murphy, Jim	Scholastic
Desperate Road to Freedom, A	U	HF	250+	Dear Canada	Scholastic
Dessert First	O	RF	250+	Durand, Hallie	Atheneum Books
Destination America: How Immigration Shaped Our Nation	T	I	250+	Explore More	Wright Group/McGraw Hill
Destination Disaster	P	RF	250+	Action Packs	Rigby
Destination Freedom	S	I	250+	McGovern, Kate	Harcourt School Publishers
Destination Hawaii	T	I	250+	WorldScapes	ETA/Cuisenaire
Destination Planet Blobb	N	F	250+	Sails	Rigby
Destination: Mars	Y	I	2966	Reading Street	Pearson
^Destiny in the Dark	W	F	250+	Dark Man	Ransom Publishing
^Destiny in the Dark	W	F	250+	Dark Man	Stone Arch Books
Destroyers	T	I	250+	Land and Sea	Capstone Press

D

* Collection of short stories   # Graphic text
^ Mature content with lower level text demands

Organized Alphabetically by Title   **183**
Storable Database at www.fountasandpinnellleveledbooks.com

TITLE	LEVEL	GENRE	WORD COUNT	AUTHOR / SERIES	PUBLISHER / DISTRIBUTOR
Destroyers	J	I	84	Mighty Machines	Capstone Press
^Destroyers: The Arleigh Burke Class	T	I	250+	War Machines	Capstone Press
Detective Business, The	J	F	590	Georgie Giraffe	Literacy Footprints
*Detective Dinosaur	J	F	250+	Skofield, James	HarperTrophy
Detective Dog	H	F	198	The Story Basket	Wright Group/McGraw Hill
Detective Dog and the Search for Cat	E	F	142	Learn to Read	Creative Teaching Press
#Detective Files	U	RF	250+	Bowkett, Steve	Stone Arch Books
#Detective Frankenstein	U	F	250+	Twisted Journeys	Graphic Universe
Detective LaRue: Letters from the Investigation	N	F	250+	Teague, Mark	Scholastic
Detective Max	LB	RF	32	Pair-It Books	Steck-Vaughn
*Detective Stories	Z	RF	250+	Pullman, Philip	Kingfisher
Detective Work	O	I	250+	Trackers	Pacific Learning
Detective's Duel	O	RF	250+	Klooz	Stone Arch Books
Detectives of the Past	T	I	250+	WorldScapes	ETA/Cuisenaire
Detective's Tools, A	O	I	797	Vocabulary Readers	Houghton Mifflin Harcourt
Detective's Tools, The	O	I	797	Vocabulary Readers/CA	Houghton Mifflin Harcourt
Detector Dog	O	I	250+	Bookweb	Rigby
*Determined to Be First	S	B	250+	Rigby Literacy	Rigby
^Determining the Cause of Death	T	I	250+	Crime Solvers	Capstone Press
Detour for Emmy	Z+	RF	250+	Reynolds, Marilynn	Morning Glory Press
Detriot Tigers, The (Revised Edition)	S	I	250+	Team Spirit	Norwood House Press
Detroit Lions, The	S	I	4479	Team Spirit	Norwood House Press
Detroit Pistons, The	S	I	4656	Team Spirit	Norwood House Press
Detroit Tigers, The	S	I	250+	Team Spirit	Norwood House Press
Developing Flu Vaccines	Z	I	250+	Science Missions	Raintree
Devil's Arithmetic, The	Y	F	250+	Yolen, Jane	Puffin Books
Devil's Bridge	R	RF	250+	DeFelice, Cynthia	Avon Books
Devil's Highway, The	T	HF	250+	Applegate, Stan	Peachtree
Devouring, The	Z	F	250+	Holt, Simon	Little Brown and Company
Dewberry and the Lost Chest of Paragon: The Fairy Chronicles	Q	F	13300	Sweet, J.H.	Sourcebooks
Dewey the Library Cat: A True Story	R	B	250+	Myron, Vicki with Witter, Bret	Little Brown and Company
DeWitt and Lila Wallace: Charity for All	P	B	250+	Community Builders	Children's Press
Dex Is a Hero	S	SF	1492	Leveled Readers	Houghton Mifflin Harcourt
Dex Is a Hero	S	SF	1492	Leveled Readers/CA	Houghton Mifflin Harcourt
Dex Is a Hero	S	SF	1492	Leveled Readers/TX	Houghton Mifflin Harcourt
Dexter Bexley and the Big Blue Beastie	M	F	250+	Stewart, Joel	Holiday House
Diabetes	S	I	250+	My Health	Scholastic
Dial L for Loser: The Clique	X	RF	250+	Harrison, Lisi	Little Brown and Company
Dial M for Mongoose: A Chet Gecko Mystery	R	F	250+	Hale, Bruce	Sandpiper Books
Diamond Champs, The	P	RF	250+	Christopher, Matt	Little Brown and Company
Diamond Hunter	T	SF	250+	Sails	Rigby
Diamond of Doom, The	M	RF	250+	Woodland Mysteries	Wright Group/McGraw Hill
Diamond of Drury Lane, The	X	HF	250+	Golding, Julia	Square Fish
Diamond Takers: The Lady Violet Mysteries	W	HF	250+	Wallace, Karen	Simon & Schuster
Diamonds	T	I	250+	Navigators Science Series	Benchmark Education
Dian and the Gorillas	W	B	10000	Dominoes three	Oxford University Press
Dian Fossey and the Mountain Gorillas	N	B	1723	On My Own Biography	Lerner Publishing Group
^Diana	W	I	250+	World Mythology	Capstone Press
Diana Made Dinner	E	RF	81	Carousel Readers	Pearson Learning Group
Diana Princess of Wales	T	B	250+	Queens and Princesses	Capstone Press
Diary Disaster	N	RF	250+	Girlz Rock!	Mondo Publishing
Diary of a Chav	Z+	RF	250+	Dent, Grace	Little Brown and Company
Diary of a Dog	J	F	495	Sun Sprouts	ETA/Cuisenaire

* Collection of short stories   # Graphic text
^ Mature content with lower level text demands

TITLE	LEVEL	GENRE	WORD COUNT	AUTHOR / SERIES	PUBLISHER / DISTRIBUTOR
Diary of a Fairy Godmother	T	F	250+	Codell, Esme Raji	Hyperion
Diary of a Honeybee	L	I	250+	Literacy 2000	Rigby
Diary of a Hurricane	S	RF	3402	Leveled Readers Science	Houghton Mifflin Harcourt
Diary of a Pioneer Boy	Q	HF	250+	Massie, Elizabeth	Steck-Vaughn
Diary of a Sunflower	L	I	250+	Story Steps	Rigby
Diary of a Wimpy Kid	T	RF	250+	Kinney, Jeff	Amulet Books
Diary of a Wimpy Kid Do-It-Yourself Book	T	RF	250+	Kinney, Jeff	Amulet Books
Diary of a Wimpy Kid: Dog Days	T	RF	250+	Kinney, Jeff	Amulet Books
Diary of a Wimpy Kid: Rodrick Rules	T	RF	250+	Kinney, Jeff	Amulet Books
Diary of a Wimpy Kid: The Last Straw	T	RF	250+	Kinney, Jeff	Amulet Books
Diary of Anne Frank, The	Y	B	250+	Frank, Anne	Pocket Books
Dia's Story Cloth: The Hmong People's Journey of Freedom	R	I	250+	Cha, Dia	Lee & Low Books Inc.
Dicey's Song	X	RF	250+	Voigt, Cynthia	Ballantine Books
Dick Whittington	L	TL	250+	PM Tales and Plays-Silver	Rigby
Dickens: His Work and His World	V	B	250+	Rosen, Michael	Candlewick Press
Dictionary About Maps, A	N	I	394	In Step Readers	Rigby
Dictionary of Animals	K	I	270	Literacy by Design	Rigby
Dictionary of Dogs	N	I	250+	InfoTrek Plus	ETA/Cuisenaire
Dictionary of Snake Facts, A	J	I	250+	Literacy by Design	Rigby
Dictionary of Space, A	H	I	181	On Our Way to English	Rigby
Did a Dinosaur Drink This Water?	P	I	250+	Wells, Robert E.	Albert Whitman & Co.
Did Castles Have Bathrooms?: And Other Questions about the Middle Ages	U	I	5288	Is That a Fact?	Lerner Publishing Group
Did Dinosaurs Eat People?: And Other Questions Kids Have About Dinosaurs	O	I	250+	Kids' Questions	Picture Window Books
Did Greek Soldiers Really Hide Inside the Trojan Horse?: And Other Questions about the Ancient World	U	I	5309	Is That a Fact?	Lerner Publishing Group
Did I Scare You?	H	RF	238	Sun Sprouts	ETA/Cuisenaire
Did President Grant Really Get a Ticket for Speeding in a Horse- Drawn Carriage?: And Other Questions about U.S. Presidents	U	I	4884	Is That a Fact?	Lerner Publishing Group
Did You Carry The Flag Today, Charley?	N	RF	250+	Caudill, Rebecca	Bantam Books
Did You Hear About Jake?	I	RF	383	Real Kids Readers	Millbrook Press
Did You Hear Wind Sing Your Name?	N	TL	182	Bookshop	Mondo Publishing
Did You Hear?	M	RF	250+	On Our Way to English	Rigby
Did You Invent the Phone Alone, Alexander Graham Bell?	P	B	250+	Berger, Melvin & Gilda	Scholastic
Did You Know?	G	I	22	Learn to Read	Creative Teaching Press
Did You Know?	L	I	250+	Sunshine	Wright Group/McGraw Hill
Did You Know?: Fun Facts About Firefighters	G	I	115	Run to Reading	Discovery Peak
Did you say, "Fire"?	G	F	158	Pacific Literacy	Pacific Learning
Did You See Chip?	I	RF	250+	Yee, Wong Herbert	Scholastic
Diddle Diddle Dumpling	E	F	54	Seedlings	Continental Press
Diego Rivera	O	B	250+	First Biographies	Steck-Vaughn
Diego Rivera	R	B	250+	Venezia, Mike	Children's Press
Diego Rivera: An Artist's Life	L	B	250+	Pair-It Books	Steck-Vaughn
Diego's Moving Day	F	RF	192	On Our Way to English	Rigby
Different Beat, A	U	RF	250+	Boyd, Candy Dawson	Penguin Group
Different Communities	K	I	275	Larkin, Bruce	Wilbooks
Different Dogs	C	I	38	Windows on Literacy	National Geographic
Different Dragons	P	RF	250+	Little, Jean	Penguin Group
Different Drawing, A	M	RF	705	Reading Street	Pearson
Different Faces from Different Places	I	I	148	Twig	Wright Group/McGraw Hill

TITLE	LEVEL	GENRE	WORD COUNT	AUTHOR / SERIES	PUBLISHER / DISTRIBUTOR
Different Fish	E	I	40	Reading Street	Pearson
Different Foods, Different Cultures	O	I	250+	InfoTrek	ETA/Cuisenaire
Different Game, A	Q	RF	250+	Orca Young Readers	Orca Books
Different Homes Around the World	K	I	200	Rigby Literacy	Rigby
Different Kinds of Homes	C	I	44	Windows on Literacy	National Geographic
Different Places, Different Faces	Q	I	250+	InfoQuest	Rigby
Different Seasons	B	I	37	Leveled Readers Science	Houghton Mifflin Harcourt
Different Tune, A	G	F	86	Start to Read	School Zone
Difficult Day, The	J	RF	304	Read Alongs	Rigby
Difficult Origami	R	I	250+	Origami	Capstone Press
Dig	C	F	20	KinderReaders	Rigby
Dig Dig Digging	J	I	250+	Mayo, Margaret	Scholastic
Dig In	I	I	96	iOpeners	Pearson Learning Group
Dig In: Verbs in Action	K	I	250+	Bookworms	Marshall Cavendish
Dig, Dig	A	RF	12	Cat on the Mat	Oxford University Press
Digby	I	RF	250+	Little Readers	Houghton Mifflin Harcourt
*Digby and Kate	K	F	250+	Baker, Barbara	Puffin Books
Digestive System, The	S	I	250+	A True Book	Children's Press
Digestive System, The	P	I	1957	Early Bird Body Systems	Lerner Publishing Group
Digestive System, The	L	I	173	Human Body Systems	Red Brick Learning
Digestive System, The	S	I	250+	Time for Kids	Teacher Created Materials
Digestive Tale, A	P	I	250+	Infotrek Plus	ETA/Cuisenaire
Digger Pig and the Turnip	G	TL	195	Green Light Readers	Harcourt
Digging Armadillos	K	I	366	Pull Ahead Books	Lerner Publishing Group
Digging Deep	T	I	250+	WorldScapes	ETA/Cuisenaire
Digging Dinosaurs	P	I	250+	Nayer, Judy	Pearson Learning Group
Digging for Dinner	H	F	181	Fried, Mary	Keep Books
Digging for Dinosaurs	P	I	250+	Lighthouse	Ginn & Co.
Digging into the Ice Age	S	RF	250+	Reading Expeditions	National Geographic
Digging into the Past	T	I	250+	Kids Discover Reading	Wright Group/McGraw Hill
Digging to China	H	F	108	Books for Young Learners	Richard C. Owen
Digging Tunnels	J	I	143	Construction Zone	Capstone Press
Digging Up Dinosaurs!	O	I	848	Vocabulary Readers	Houghton Mifflin Harcourt
Digging Up Dinosaurs!	O	I	848	Vocabulary Readers/CA	Houghton Mifflin Harcourt
Digging Up Secrets	Q	RF	250+	Reading Expeditions	National Geographic
Digging Up Tyrannosaurus Rex	P	I	250+	Horner, John; Lessem, Don	Crown Publishers
Digital Revolutionaries: The Men and Women Who Brought Computing to Life	Y	I	250+	Lohr, Steve	Roaring Brook Press
Dillon Dillon	S	RF	250+	Banks, Kate	Farrar, Straus, & Giroux
Dilly Dog's Dizzy Dancing	K	F	567	Animal Antics A To Z	Kane Press
Dilly Duck and Dally Duck	D	F	139	PM Plus Story Books	Rigby
Dimples Delight	M	RF	250+	Orca Echoes	Orca Books
Dine, The	T	I	1900	Reading Street	Pearson
Dingoes at Dinnertime	M	F	250+	Osborne, Mary Pope	Random House
Dinner	E	F	191	Joy Starters	Pearson Learning Group
Dinner	A	F	21	KinderReaders	Rigby
Dinner	E	RF	154	Rigby Flying Colors	Rigby
Dinner	B	F	30	Sails	Rigby
Dinner at Aunt Connie's House	Q	F	250+	Ringgold, Faith	Scholastic
Dinner by Five	F	RF	215	Ready Readers	Pearson Learning Group
Dinner for Maisy	H	RF	239	Leveled Literacy Intervention/ Green System	Heinemann
Dinner for Two Hundred	S	RF	2471	Leveled Readers	Houghton Mifflin Harcourt
Dinner for Two Hundred	S	RF	2471	Leveled Readers/CA	Houghton Mifflin Harcourt

* Collection of short stories   # Graphic text
^ Mature content with lower level text demands

TITLE	LEVEL	GENRE	WORD COUNT	AUTHOR / SERIES	PUBLISHER / DISTRIBUTOR
Dinner for Two Hundred	S	RF	2471	Leveled Readers/TX	Houghton Mifflin Harcourt
Dinner Time	I	F	500	Gilbert the Pig	Pioneer Valley
Dinner Time	A	I	28	On Our Way to English	Rigby
Dinner Time	J	F	132	Pienkowski, Jan	Candlewick Press
Dinner Time	C	RF	37	Storyworlds	Heinemann
Dinner!	LB	RF	19	Sunshine	Wright Group/McGraw Hill
Dino at the Park	E	RF	131	PM Photo Stories	Rigby
Dino Baseball	K	F	554	Wheeler, Lisa,	Carolrhoda Books
Dino Info	N	I	776	Springboard	Wright Group/McGraw Hill
Dino World	I	I	203	Sun Sprouts	ETA/Cuisenaire
Dino-Dinners	P	I	250+	Manning, Mick and Granstrom, Brita	Holiday House
Dinosaur	M	I	250+	Cambridge Reading	Pearson Learning Group
Dinosaur	W	I	250+	Eyewitness Books	DK Publishing
Dinosaur	B	I	17	Science	Outside the Box
Dinosaur	U	I	250+	Stansbie, Stephanie	Little Brown and Company
Dinosaur Alphabet Book, The	O	I	250+	Pallotta, Jerry	Charlesbridge
Dinosaur Babies	L	I	250+	Penner, Lucille Recht	Random House
Dinosaur Bones Don't Rot	I	I	147	Reading Street	Pearson
Dinosaur Breakout	T	F	250+	Silverthorne, Judith	Fitzhenry & Whiteside
Dinosaur Canyon	N	F	250+	In Step Readers	Rigby
Dinosaur Chase, The	I	HF	240	PM Story Books-Orange	Rigby
Dinosaur Club, The	I	RF	373	Red Rocket Readers	Flying Start Books
Dinosaur Connection, The	O	I	250+	Literacy Tree	Rigby
Dinosaur Dan	G	F	197	Springboard	Wright Group/McGraw Hill
Dinosaur Dance, The	B	F	52	Little Books	Sadlier-Oxford
Dinosaur Days	L	I	250+	Milton, Joyce	Random House
Dinosaur Days	K	RF	250+	Ready Readers	Pearson Learning Group
Dinosaur Days	B	I	71	Red Rocket Readers	Flying Start Books
Dinosaur Detective	O	I	250+	Wildcats	Wright Group/McGraw Hill
Dinosaur Detectives	K	F	250+	Pacific Literacy	Pacific Learning
Dinosaur Detectives	L	I	328	Reading Street	Pearson
Dinosaur Detectives	O	I	250+	Windows on Literacy	National Geographic
Dinosaur Dig	L	RF	250+	Windows on Literacy	National Geographic
Dinosaur Dinners	K	I	250+	DK Readers	DK Publishing
Dinosaur Discoveries	P	I	250+	Gibbons, Gail	Holiday House
Dinosaur Discoveries	S	I	250+	WorldScapes	ETA/Cuisenaire
Dinosaur Discovery	I	I	250+	Story Steps	Rigby
Dinosaur Extremes	L	I	156	Windows on Literacy	National Geographic
Dinosaur Fan, The	F	F	125	Windmill Books	Rigby
Dinosaur Fossils	I	I	370	Vocabulary Readers	Houghton Mifflin Harcourt
Dinosaur Fossils	I	I	370	Vocabulary Readers/CA	Houghton Mifflin Harcourt
Dinosaur Fossils	I	I	370	Vocabulary Readers/TX	Houghton Mifflin Harcourt
Dinosaur Fun Facts	E	I	84	Pair-It Books	Steck-Vaughn
Dinosaur Girl	N	RF	250+	Literacy Tree	Rigby
Dinosaur Herds	H	I	101	Reading Street	Pearson
Dinosaur Hideout	T	RF	250+	Silverthorne, Judith	Fitzhenry & Whiteside
Dinosaur Hunt (Max Spaniel)	I	F	164	Catrow, David	Orchard Books
Dinosaur Hunt, The	G	RF	155	Rigby Literacy	Rigby
Dinosaur Hunt, The	G	F	131	Windmill Books	Rigby
Dinosaur Hunters	O	I	250+	McMullan, Kate	Random House
Dinosaur Hunters	I	RF	252	Red Rocket Readers	Flying Start Books
Dinosaur Hunting	N	I	579	Leveled Readers Science	Houghton Mifflin Harcourt
Dinosaur in Trouble	G	F	121	First Start	Troll Associates

D

* Collection of short stories   # Graphic text
^ Mature content with lower level text demands

TITLE	LEVEL	GENRE	WORD COUNT	AUTHOR / SERIES	PUBLISHER / DISTRIBUTOR
Dinosaur Morning	J	I	225	The Story Basket	Wright Group/McGraw Hill
Dinosaur Mountain	S	I	250+	Ray, Deborah Kogan	Farrar, Straus, & Giroux
Dinosaur Named Sue, A	P	I	250+	Robinson, Fay	Scholastic
Dinosaur Nests	J	I	349	Sails	Rigby
Dinosaur Olympics	N	I	250+	Scooters	ETA/Cuisenaire
Dinosaur on the Motorway	K	F	231	Wesley & the Dinosaurs	Wright Group/McGraw Hill
Dinosaur Party	B	F	27	Smart Start	Rigby
Dinosaur Reports	L	I	324	Little Red Readers	Sundance
Dinosaur Reports	K	F	577	Red Rocket Readers	Flying Start Books
Dinosaur Roar!	LB	F	59	Strickland, Paul & Henrietta	Scholastic
Dinosaur Rock	A	F	28	Big Cat	Pacific Learning
Dinosaur Show and Tell	G	RF	212	Pair-It Books	Steck-Vaughn
Dinosaur Snack, A	D	F	74	Little Dinosaur	Literacy Footprints
Dinosaur Stakeout	T	F	250+	Silverthorne, Judith	Fitzhenry & Whiteside
Dinosaur Time	K	I	250+	Parish, Peggy	HarperTrophy
Dinosaur Times	D	RF	43	Sunshine	Wright Group/McGraw Hill
Dinosaur Who Lived in My Backyard, The	I	F	250+	Hennessy, Brendan G.	Scholastic
Dinosaur Zoo, The	J	F	250+	Literacy Tree	Rigby
Dinosaur!	O	I	250+	Trail Blazers	Ransom Publishing
Dinosaur, The	F	F	131	Joy Readers	Pearson Learning Group
Dinosaur, The	A	F	14	Sunshine	Wright Group/McGraw Hill
Dinosaurs	S	I	250+	Boldprint	Steck-Vaughn
Dinosaurs	K	I	193	Bookshop	Mondo Publishing
Dinosaurs	M	I	250+	Gibbons, Gail	Holiday House
Dinosaurs	L	I	250+	I Wonder Why	Kingfisher
Dinosaurs	E	I	37	Instant Readers	Harcourt School Publishers
Dinosaurs	F	I	115	Maccarone, Grace	Scholastic
Dinosaurs	R	RF	250+	PM Plus Chapter Books	Rigby
Dinosaurs	C	I	100	Sails	Rigby
Dinosaurs	H	I	117	Sunshine	Wright Group/McGraw Hill
Dinosaurs	M	I	250+	Trackers	Pacific Learning
Dinosaurs & Other Reptiles	I	I	123	Planet Earth	Rigby
Dinosaurs Alive and Well!: A Guide to Good Health	O	I	250+	Brown, Laurie Krasny & Marc	Little Brown and Company
Dinosaurs and Other Prehistoric Creatures You Can Draw	R	I	1840	Ready, Set, Draw!	Millbrook Press
Dinosaurs Before Dark	M	F	250+	Osborne, Mary Pope	Random House
Dinosaur's Cold, The	J	F	244	Literacy 2000	Rigby
Dinosaurs Dance	E	F	17	Rookie Readers	Children's Press
Dinosaurs Dancing	F	F	115	Learn to Read	Creative Teaching Press
Dinosaur's Day	L	I	250+	DK Readers	DK Publishing
Dinosaurs Divorce: A Guide for Changing Families	N	I	250+	Brown, Laurie Krasny & Marc	Little Brown and Company
Dinosaurs Galore	D	F	34	Eaton, Audrey; Kennedy, Jane	Continental Press
Dinosaurs Go Green!: A Guide to Protecting Our Planet	O	I	250+	Brown, Laura Krasny & Marc	Little Brown and Company
Dinosaurs in Your Backyard	T	I	250+	Brewster, Hugh	Harry N. Abrams
Dinosaurs of Waterhouse Hawkins, The	S	I	250+	Kerley, Barbara	Scholastic
Dinosaurs on the Beach	O	RF	250+	Orca Young Readers	Orca Books
Dinosaurs on the Motorway	K	F	250+	Wesley & the Dinosaurs	Wright Group/McGraw Hill
Dinosaurs, Dinosaurs	G	I	96	Barton, Byron	HarperCollins
Dinosaurs: Giant Jigsaws	S	I	250+	Sails	Rigby
Dinotrux	M	F	250+	Gall, Chris	Little Brown and Company
Diogenes	N	F	250+	Usher, M.D.	Farrar, Straus, & Giroux

* Collection of short stories   # Graphic text
^ Mature content with lower level text demands

TITLE	LEVEL	GENRE	WORD COUNT	AUTHOR / SERIES	PUBLISHER / DISTRIBUTOR
Diplodocus in the Garden, A	K	F	210	Wesley & the Dinosaurs	Wright Group/McGraw Hill
Diplodocus	N	I	250+	Discovering Dinosaurs	Red Brick Learning
Dipper and the Old Wreck	F	F	207	Storyworlds	Heinemann
Dipper Gets Stuck	F	F	200	Storyworlds	Heinemann
Dipper in Danger	F	F	192	Storyworlds	Heinemann
Dipper to the Rescue	F	F	216	Storyworlds	Heinemann
Dippy Dinner Drippers, The	H	F	181	Sunshine	Wright Group/McGraw Hill
Dirk Nowitzki	P	B	2337	Amazing Athletes	Lerner Publishing Group
Dirk Nowitzki: Revised Edition	P	B	1758	Amazing Athletes	Lerner Publishing Group
Dirt Bike Racer	S	RF	250+	Christopher, Matt	Little Brown and Company
Dirt Bike Runaway	S	RF	250+	Christopher, Matt	Little Brown and Company
Dirt Bikes	M	I	250+	Horsepower	Capstone Press
Dirt Bikes	Q	I	250+	Wild Rides!	Capstone Press
Dirt: The Scoop on Soil	M	I	250+	Amazing Science	Picture Window Books
Dirty and Wet Dogs	J	F	590	Bella and Rosie Series	Literacy Footprints
Dirty Animals	E	F	168	Red Rocket Readers	Flying Start Books
Dirty Beasts	O	F	250+	Dahl, Roald	Penguin Group
Dirty Clean	B	I	71	Bookworms	Marshall Cavendish
Dirty Dog	A	RF	19	Rigby Rocket	Rigby
Dirty Gertie	K	RF	250+	Read-it! Readers	Picture Window Books
Dirty Hippo	B	F	46	Zoozoo-Into the Wild	Cavallo Publishing
Dirty Larry	D	RF	53	Rookie Readers	Children's Press
Dirty Little Secrets	Z+	RF	250+	Omololu, C. J.	Walker & Company
Dirty Mike	C	RF	54	InfoTrek	ETA/Cuisenaire
Dirty Socks Don't Win Games	R	RF	250+	Marney, Dean	Scholastic
Disability Rights Movement, The	W	I	250+	Cornerstones of Freedom	Children's Press
Disappearing Acts	S	RF	250+	Byars, Betsy	Puffin Books
Disappearing Bike Shop, The	Q	SF	250+	Woodruff, Elvira	Bantam Books
*Disappearing Cookies and Other Cases, The	O	RF	250+	Simon, Seymour	Avon Books
Disappearing Dinosaurs	M	I	473	Red Rocket Readers	Flying Start Books
*Disappearing Ice Cream and Other Cases, The	O	RF	250+	Simon, Seymour	Avon Books
*Disappearing Snowball and Other Cases, The	O	RF	250+	Simon, Seymour	Avon Books
Disaster Around the Indian Ocean	P	I	990	Springboard	Wright Group/McGraw Hill
Disaster in the Mountains!: Colby Coombs' Story of Survival	S	I	250+	True Tales of Survival	Capstone Press
Disaster of the Hindenburg, The: The Last Flight of the Greatest Airship Ever Built	Z	I	250+	Tanaka, Shelley	Scholastic
Disaster Plan	T	I	250+	Bookweb	Rigby
Disaster, The	R	RF	1309	Leveled Readers	Houghton Mifflin Harcourt
Disasters at Sea	W	I	8571	Disasters Up Close	Lerner Publishing Group
Disasters: Natural and Man-Made Catastrophes Through the Centuries	W	I	250+	Guiberson, Brenda Z.	Henry Holt & Co.
Discount Diva	T	F	250+	Hopkins, Cathy	Kingfisher
Discover Dinosaurs	J	I	198	Red Rocket Readers	Flying Start Books
Discover the Rain Forest	L	I	348	Yellow Umbrella Books	Red Brick Learning
Discovering Dinosaurs	K	I	211	Spyglass Books	Compass Point Books
Discovering Dinosaurs	M	F	335	Little Books	Sadlier-Oxford
Discovering Emily	O	HF	250+	Orca Young Readers	Orca Books
Discovering India	O	I	250+	Trackers	Pacific Learning
Discovering Jupiter: The Amazing Collision in Space	T	I	250+	Berger, Melvin	Scholastic
Discovering Nature's Laws: A Story About Isaac Newton	T	B	8285	Creative Minds Biographies	Carolrhoda Books
Discovering Radioactivity	V	I	250+	Reading Expeditions	National Geographic
Discovering the Past	S	I	250+	Literacy 2000	Rigby

D

TITLE	LEVEL	GENRE	WORD COUNT	AUTHOR / SERIES	PUBLISHER / DISTRIBUTOR
Discovering the Titanic	O	I	250+	Trumbore, Cindy	Pearson Learning Group
Discovering with Harry Hoggart	P	I	250+	Sails	Rigby
Discovery in Egypt	S	RF	250+	Literacy By Design	Rigby
Discovery of the Americas, The	S	I	250+	Maestro, Betsy & Giulio	William Morrow
Discovery: Past, Present, Future	T	I	250+	Kids Discover Reading	Wright Group/McGraw Hill
Discus Dynamo	M	F	250+	Too Cool	Pacific Learning
Disease and the Body	S	I	250+	Reading Expeditions	National Geographic
Disease Detectives	U	I	250+	Connectors	Pacific Learning
Disease Detectives	O	I	250+	Infotrek Plus	ETA/Cuisenaire
Disease Detectives on the Case	V	I	250+	Explore More	Wright Group/McGraw Hill
Dishy-Washy	E	F	92	Story Basket	Wright Group/McGraw Hill
Dissolving	C	I	31	Changing Matter	Lerner Publishing Group
*Distant Stars and Other Cases, The	O	RF	250+	Simon, Seymour	Avon Books
Ditching School	J	RF	128	City Kids	Rigby
Dive In!	F	RF	133	Ready Readers	Pearson Learning Group
Dive to the Deep Ocean: Voyages of Exploration and Discovery	W	I	250+	Kovacs, Deborah	Steck-Vaughn
Dive!: My Adventures in the Deep Frontier	V	B	250+	Earle, Sylvia A.	Scholastic
Dive, The	K	RF	488	Leveled Readers	Houghton Mifflin Harcourt
Diver, The	B	RF	30	Sunshine	Wright Group/McGraw Hill
Divers' Dream	P	I	250+	Pacific Literacy	Pacific Learning
Divers of the Deep Sea	S	I	250+	Windows on Literacy	National Geographic
Divers, The	C	I	25	Wonder World	Wright Group/McGraw Hill
Divided Loyalties	T	HF	250+	Reading Expeditions	National Geographic
Dividing the Strawberries	E	I	93	In Step Readers	Rigby
Diving	G	RF	164	Story Box	Wright Group/McGraw Hill
Diving at the Pool	M	RF	519	PM Plus Story Books	Rigby
Diving Beetles: Underwater Insect Predators	T	I	2695	Insect World	Lerner Publishing Group
Diving Deep	I	I	120	Gear Up!	Wright Group/McGraw Hill
Diving for Treasure	M	I	284	Books for Young Learners	Richard C. Owen
Diwali	K	I	150	Holidays and Festivals	Heinemann Library
Diwali: Hindu Fesival of Lights	M	I	250+	Holidays and Culture	Capstone Press
Dixie in Danger: The Pet Sitter	O	F	250+	Sykes, Julie	Kingfisher
Dizzy	S	B	250+	Winter, Jonah	Arthur A. Levine Books
Dizzy Izzy (Jon Scieszka's Trucktown)	H	F	95	Scieszka, Jon	Aladdin
Dizzy Lizzy	E	RF	37	Literacy 2000	Rigby
Django: World's Greatest Jazz Guitarist	S	B	250+	Christensen, Bonnie	Roaring Brook Press
Do Animals Have a Sixth Sense?	M	I	377	Reading Street	Pearson
Do Animals Have Feelings Too?	S	I	250+	Sharing Nature with Children	Dawn Publications
Do Animals Live in Plants?	F	I	56	Instant Readers	Harcourt School Publishers
Do Animals Migrate?	M	I	250+	I Like Reading About Animals!	Enslow Publishers, Inc.
Do Animals Think?	N	I	250+	Trackers	Pacific Learning
Do Bears Buzz?: A Book About Animal Sounds	M	I	250+	Animals All Around	Picture Window Books
Do Bed Bugs Bite?	N	I	250+	Why In the World?	Capstone Press
Do Bees Make Butter?: A Book About Things Animals Make	M	I	250+	Animals All Around	Picture Window Books
Do Cows Eat Cake?: A Book About What Animals Eat	M	I	250+	Animals All Around	Picture Window Books
Do Dogs Make Dessert?: A Book About How Animals Help Humans	M	I	250+	Animals All Around	Picture Window Books
Do Ducks Live in the Desert?: A Book About Where Animals Live	M	I	250+	Animals All Around	Picture Window Books
Do Elephants Talk?	Q	I	250+	Explorer Books-Pathfinder	National Geographic
Do Elephants Talk?	P	I	250+	Explorer Books-Pioneer	National Geographic

TITLE	LEVEL	GENRE	WORD COUNT	AUTHOR / SERIES	PUBLISHER / DISTRIBUTOR
Do Frogs Have Fur?: A Book About Animal Coats and Coverings	M	I	250+	Animals All Around	Picture Window Books
Do Goldfish Gallop?: A Book About Animal Movement	M	I	250+	Animals All Around	Picture Window Books
Do I Have To?	Q	I	250+	Kids Talk	Picture Window Books
Do I Need It? Or Do I Want It?: Making Budget Choices	L	I	503	Lightning Bolt Books	Lerner Publishing Group
Do Ladybugs Go to School?	E	F	75	Visions	Wright Group/McGraw Hill
Do Not Open This Book!	F	F	134	Story Basket	Wright Group/McGraw Hill
Do Not Quit, Quinn!	E	RF	91	Reading Street	Pearson Learning Group
Do Not Spill!	C	RF	79	Reading Street	Pearson
Do Not Touch	B	I	51	Reading Safari	Mondo Publishing
Do Parrots Have Pillows?: A Book About Where Animals Sleep	M	I	250+	Animals All Around	Picture Window Books
Do Penguins Have Puppies?: A Book About Animal Babies	M	I	250+	Animals All Around	Picture Window Books
Do People Really Have Tiny Insects Living in Their Eyelashes?: And Other Questions about the Microscopic World	U	I	5244	Is That a Fact?	Lerner Publishing Group
Do Pigs Sit in Trees?	J	F	250+	Zelasney, Jean	Pearson Learning Group
Do Plants Grow Under Water?	J	I	271	Early Explorers	Benchmark Education
Do Salamanders Spit?: A Book About How Animals Protect Themselves	M	I	250+	Animals All Around	Picture Window Books
Do Something for Your Family	I	I	183	Do Something About It!	ABDO Publishing Company
Do Squirrels Swarm?: A Book About Animal Groups	M	I	250+	Animals All Around	Picture Window Books
Do Stars Have Points?	R	I	250+	Berger, Melvin & Gilda	Scholastic
Do That, Do This!	H	RF	151	Supersonics	Rigby
Do the Funky Pickle	U	RF	250+	Spinelli, Jerry	Scholastic
Do Tornadoes Really Twist?	S	I	250+	Berger, Melvin	Scholastic
Do Unto Others: A Book About Manners	M	F	250+	Keller, Laurie	Square Fish
Do We Have Enough?	A	RF	42	InfoTrek	ETA/Cuisenaire
Do We Need It? Do We Want It?	G	I	111	Early Connections	Benchmark Education
Do Whales Have Wings?: A Book About Animal Bodies	M	I	250+	Animals All Around	Picture Window Books
Do You Know about Amphibians?	L	I	338	Lightning Bolt Books	Lerner Publishing Group
Do You Know about Birds?	K	I	370	Lightning Bolt Books	Lerner Publishing Group
Do You Know about Fish?	L	I	422	Lightning Bolt Books	Lerner Publishing Group
Do You Know about Insects?	L	I	370	Lightning Bolt Books	Lerner Publishing Group
Do You Know about Mammals?	L	I	461	Lightning Bolt Books	Lerner Publishing Group
Do You Know about Reptiles?	L	I	416	Lightning Bolt Books	Lerner Publishing Group
Do You Know Me?	Q	RF	250+	Farmer, Nancy	Penguin Group
Do You Know the Monkey Man?	Y	RF	250+	Butler, Dori Hillestad	Peachtree
Do You Know Where Your Water Has Been?: The Disgusting Story Behind What You're Drinking	S	I	250+	Sanitation Investigation	Capstone Press
Do You Know Why?	C	I	56	Little Celebrations	Pearson Learning Group
Do You Like Cats?	K	I	250+	Bank Street	Bantam Books
Do You Like Grapes?	B	RF	31	Science	Outside the Box
Do You Like My Pet?	A	F	35	Phonics and Friends	Hampton Brown
Do You Read Me?	W	I	250+	24/7 Science Behind the Scenes	Scholastic
Do You Remember When?	D	RF	198	Visions	Wright Group/McGraw Hill
Do You See Mouse?	G	F	201	Crume, Marion	Ginn & Co.
Do You Share?	F	I	132	Are You a Good Friend?	Weekly Reader Publishing
Do You Take Turns?	G	I	141	Are You a Good Friend?	Weekly Reader Publishing
Do You Want to Be My Friend?	A	F	8	Carle, Eric	Penguin Group

D

TITLE	LEVEL	GENRE	WORD COUNT	AUTHOR / SERIES	PUBLISHER / DISTRIBUTOR
Doaks of Montana, The	T	HF	2426	Reading Street	Pearson
Doc	WB	RF	0	The Rowland Reading Program Library	Rowland Reading Foundation
Doc's Costume Contest	G	RF	193	The Rowland Reading Program Library	Rowland Reading Foundation
Doc's Tree House	F	RF	96	The Rowland Reading Program Library	Rowland Reading Foundation
Doctor	C	I	24	Work People Do	Lerner Publishing Group
Doctor Boondoggle	D	F	51	Story Box	Wright Group/McGraw Hill
Doctor DeSoto	N	F	250+	Steig, William	Scholastic
Doctor Foster	D	F	68	Seedlings	Continental Press
Doctor Has the Flu, The	H	RF	106	Ready Readers	Pearson Learning Group
Doctor Witch's Animal Hospital	L	F	250+	I Am Reading	Kingfisher
Doctor, The	G	I	179	PM Nonfiction-Blue	Rigby
Doctors	J	I	169	Bookworms	Marshall Cavendish
Doctors	M	I	250+	Community Helpers	Red Brick Learning
Doctors	L	I	250+	Community Workers	Compass Point Books
Doctors	L	I	463	Pull Ahead Books	Lerner Publishing Group
Doctor's Busy Day, A	L	I	250+	Rosen Real Readers	Rosen Publishing Group
Doctor's Office, The	K	I	272	Pebble Books	Capstone Press
Doctors: Then and Now	P	I	250+	Primary Source Readers	Teacher Created Materials
Documents of Freedom: A Look at the Declaration of Independence, the Bill of Rights, and the U.S. Constitution	S	I	1508	Searchlight Books	Lerner Publishing Group
^Dodge Viper	O	I	250+	Fast Cars	Capstone Press
Dodger for President	S	F	250+	Sonnenblick, Jordan	Feiwel and Friends
Dodsworth in London	M	F	250+	Egan, Tim	Sandpiper Books
Dodsworth in New York	L	F	250+	Egan, Tim	Houghton Mifflin Harcourt
Dodsworth in Paris	M	F	250+	Egan, Tim	Houghton Mifflin Harcourt
Dodsworth in Rome	M	F	250+	Egan, Tim	Houghton Mifflin Harcourt
Does a Babysitter Know What to Do?	F	RF	177	Reading Street	Pearson
Does a Kangaroo Have a Mother Too?	F	I	214	Carle, Eric	Scholastic
Does a Penguin Have Fur?	D	RF	74	Rigby Literacy	Rigby
Does a Sea Cow Say Moo?	M	F	250+	Harshman, Terry Webb	Bloomsbury Children's Books
Does a Ten-Gallon Hat Really Hold Ten Gallons?: And Other Questions about Fashion	U	I	4711	Is That a Fact?	Lerner Publishing Group
Does an Apple a Day Keep the Doctor Away?: And Other Questions About Your Health and Body	U	I	4635	Is That a Fact?	Lerner Publishing Group
Does it Really Take Seven Years to Digest Swallowed Gum?: And Other Questions You've Always Wanted to Ask	U	I	4261	Is That a Fact?	Lerner Publishing Group
Does Third Grade Last Forever?	O	RF	250+	Schanback, Mindy	Troll Associates
Dog	V	I	250+	Eyewitness Books	DK Publishing
Dog	B	RF	37	Pacific Literacy	Pacific Learning
Dog and Bear: Three To Get Ready	K	F	250+	Seeger, Laura Vaccaro	Roaring Brook Press
Dog and Cat	F	RF	62	My First Reader	Grolier
Dog and the Bone, The	E	TL	67	Leveled Readers	Houghton Mifflin Harcourt
Dog Biscuit	M	RF	250+	Cooper, Helen	Farrar, Straus, & Giroux
Dog Blue	J	RF	250+	Dunbar, Polly	Candlewick Press
Dog Called Bear, A	K	RF	438	PM Story Books	Rigby
Dog Called Kitty, A	R	RF	250+	Wallace, Bill	Pocket Books
Dog Called Mischief, A	D	RF	42	Cat on the Mat	Oxford University Press
Dog Control	T	RF	2354	Leveled Readers	Houghton Mifflin Harcourt
Dog Control	T	RF	2354	Leveled Readers/CA	Houghton Mifflin Harcourt

* Collection of short stories   # Graphic text
^ Mature content with lower level text demands

TITLE	LEVEL	GENRE	WORD COUNT	AUTHOR / SERIES	PUBLISHER / DISTRIBUTOR
Dog Control	T	RF	2354	Leveled Readers/TX	Houghton Mifflin Harcourt
Dog Day!, A	LB	RF	21	Smart Start	Rigby
Dog Days	N	RF	250+	Orca Young Readers	Orca Books
Dog Family, The	J	I	250+	Story Steps	Rigby
Dog Food	C	F	57	Bonnell, Kris	Reading Reading Books
Dog for a Day, A	M	RF	250+	High-Fliers	Pacific Learning
Dog for Each Day, A	G	RF	107	Rookie Readers	Children's Press
Dog for Life, A	T	F	250+	Matthews, L.S.	Yearling Books
Dog for Mrs. Muddle Mud-Puddle, A	H	F	194	Story Box	Wright Group/McGraw Hill
Dog for You, A: Caring for Your Dog	M	I	250+	Pet Care	Picture Window Books
Dog from Outer Space, The	I	SF	250+	Lighthouse	Rigby
Dog Gone	T	RF	250+	Willis, Cynthia Chapman	Square Fish
Dog Helpers	M	I	495	Vocabulary Readers	Houghton Mifflin Harcourt
Dog Helpers	M	I	495	Vocabulary Readers/CA	Houghton Mifflin Harcourt
Dog Helpers	J	I	495	Vocabulary Readers/TX	Houghton Mifflin Harcourt
Dog I Share, The	N	RF	250+	Orbit Chapter Books	Pacific Learning
Dog in the Freezer, The	W	F	250+	Mazer, Harry	Simon & Schuster
Dog Named Honey, A	F	I	46	iOpeners	Pearson Learning Group
Dog on Barkham Street, A	R	RF	250+	Stolz, Mary	HarperTrophy
Dog on the Loose	N	RF	250+	Girlz Rock!	Mondo Publishing
Dog on Vacation	B	F	69	First Stories	Pacific Learning
Dog Safety Rules	C	RF	91	InfoTrek	ETA/Cuisenaire
Dog School	E	RF	133	Explorations	Eleanor Curtain Publishing
Dog School	E	I	133	Explorations	Okapi Educational Materials
Dog School	I	RF	224	Story Steps	Rigby
Dog School	LB	RF	11	TOTTS	Tott Publications
Dog Sense	W	RF	250+	Collard, Sneed B.	Peachtree
Dog Show, The	K	RF	250+	Cambridge Reading	Pearson Learning Group
Dog Show, The	F	I	131	Foundations	Wright Group/McGraw Hill
Dog Show, The	B	RF	35	Rigby Star	Rigby
Dog Sled Ride, The	I	RF	374	Adams, Lorraine & Bruvold, Lynn	Eaglecrest Books
Dog Tales	R	I	250+	Boldprint	Steck-Vaughn
Dog Talk	J	I	324	Leveled Readers	Houghton Mifflin Harcourt
Dog Talk	J	I	324	Leveled Readers/CA	Houghton Mifflin Harcourt
Dog Talk	J	I	324	Leveled Readers/TX	Houghton Mifflin Harcourt
Dog that Pitched a No-Hitter, The	L	F	250+	Christopher, Matt	Little Brown and Company
Dog that Stole Football Plays, The	L	F	250+	Christopher, Matt	Little Brown and Company
Dog that Stole Home, The	L	F	250+	Christopher, Matt	Little Brown and Company
Dog to Walk, A	F	RF	178	Developing Set 4	Pioneer Valley
Dog Walk	K	F	250+	Bourne, Miriam Anne	Pearson Learning Group
^Dog Walker	W	RF	250+	Orca Currents	Orca Books
Dog Walker, Inc.	P	RF	1640	Leveled Readers	Houghton Mifflin Harcourt
Dog Walker, Inc.	P	RF	1640	Leveled Readers/CA	Houghton Mifflin Harcourt
Dog Walker, Inc.	P	RF	1640	Leveled Readers/TX	Houghton Mifflin Harcourt
Dog Walker, The	D	RF	100	Reed, Janet	Scholastic
Dog Went for a Walk	D	RF	51	Voyages	SRA/McGraw Hill
Dog Whisperer: The Rescue	T	RF	250+	Edwards, Nicholas	Square Fish
Dog Who Came to Dinner, The	J	RF	250+	Taylor, Sydney	Pearson Publishing Group
Dog Who Sang at the Opera, The	N	F	250+	West, Jim & Izen, Marshall	Harry N. Abrams
Dog Who Thought He Was Santa, The	R	F	250+	Wallace, Bill	Holiday House
Dog Who Wanted to Be a Tiger!, The	M	F	250+	Little Celebrations	Pearson Learning Group
Dog Years	R	RF	250+	Warner, Sally	Alfred A. Knopf
Dog, The	G	RF	56	Burningham, John	Crowell
Dogerella	I	TL	250+	Boelts, Maribeth	Random House

D

TITLE	LEVEL	GENRE	WORD COUNT	AUTHOR / SERIES	PUBLISHER / DISTRIBUTOR
Dog-Gone Hollywood	L	F	250+	Sharmat, Marjorie Weinman	Random House
Doggy Dare	O	RF	250+	Baglio, Ben M.	Scholastic
Doghouse Discounts	Q	RF	250+	In Step Readers	Rigby
Dogs	D	I	44	All About Pets	Red Brick Learning
Dogs	F	I	116	Foundations	Wright Group/McGraw Hill
Dogs	I	I	116	Hutchins, Pat	Wright Group/McGraw Hill
Dogs	B	I	79	Leveled Readers	Houghton Mifflin Harcourt
Dogs	B	I	79	Leveled Readers/CA	Houghton Mifflin Harcourt
Dogs	B	I	79	Leveled Readers/TX	Houghton Mifflin Harcourt
Dogs	B	RF	27	Levin, Amy	Scholastic
Dogs	J	I	250+	PM Animal Facts: Orange	Rigby
Dogs	LB	I	14	Readlings	American Reading Company
Dogs and Puppies	B	I	35	Animal Families	Lerner Publishing Group
Dogs and Puppies	G	I	210	Dominie Factivity Series	Pearson Learning Group
Dogs Are My Favorite Things	J	RF	246	Bookshop	Mondo Publishing
Dogs at School	F	F	94	Books for Young Learners	Richard C. Owen
Dogs at Work	Q	I	250+	Explorer Books-Pathfinder	National Geographic
Dogs at Work	P	I	250+	Explorer Books-Pioneer	National Geographic
Dogs at Work	J	I	250+	Little Readers	Houghton Mifflin Harcourt
Dogs at Work	I	I	153	Reading Street	Pearson
Dogs at Work	K	I	469	Red Rocket Readers	Flying Start Books
Dogs at Work	N	I	250+	Windows on Literacy	National Geographic
Dog's Best Friend, A	M	RF	647	Pair-It Books	Steck-Vaughn
Dog's Diary	M	F	250+	Sails	Rigby
Dogs Dogs Dogs	R	I	250+	Literacy 2000	Rigby
Dogs Don't Tell Jokes	O	RF	250+	Sachar, Louis	Alfred A. Knopf
Dogs Don't Wear Sneakers	H	F	172	Numeroff, Laura	Aladdin
Dog's Guide to Humans, The	M	F	250+	Bookweb	Rigby
Dogs Have Paws	J	RF	250+	Ross, Jan	Pearson Publishing Group
Dogs Have Puppies	M	I	250+	Animals and Their Young	Compass Point Books
Dogs Learn Every Day	C	I	38	Vocabulary Readers	Houghton Mifflin Harcourt
Dog's Life, A	F	I	109	Watch It Grow	Heinemann Library
Dog's Life, A	WB	I	0	Windows on Literacy	National Geographic
Dog's Life, A: The Autobiography of a Stray	S	F	250+	Martin, Ann M.	Scholastic
Dogs Love to Play Ball	I	F	159	Books for Young Learners	Richard C. Owen
Dogs on the Bed	M	F	250+	Bluemle, Elizabeth	Candlewick Press
Dogs on the Farm	I	I	85	Pebble Books	Red Brick Learning
Dog's Party	I	F	628	Leveled Readers	Houghton Mifflin Harcourt
Dogs That Help People	N	I	824	Leveled Readers	Houghton Mifflin Harcourt
Dogs That Help People	N	I	824	Leveled Readers/CA	Houghton Mifflin Harcourt
Dogs That Help People	N	I	824	Leveled Readers/TX	Houghton Mifflin Harcourt
Dogs to the Rescue	R	I	1154	Leveled Readers	Houghton Mifflin Harcourt
Dogs to the Rescue	R	I	1154	Leveled Readers/CA	Houghton Mifflin Harcourt
Dogs to the Rescue	R	I	1154	Leveled Readers/TX	Houghton Mifflin Harcourt
Dogs to the Rescue	H	I	105	Reading Street	Pearson
Dogs You Can Draw	R	I	1729	Ready, Set, Draw!	Millbrook Press
Dogs, Dogs, Dogs	H	I	183	Appleton-Smith, Laura	Flyleaf Publishing
Dogs: From Tip to Tail	J	I	202	The Rowland Reading Program Libary	Rowland Reading Foundation
Dogsong	V	RF	250+	Paulsen, Gary	Simon & Schuster
Dogstar	J	F	250+	Literacy 2000	Rigby
Dogtag Summer	Y	HF	250+	Partridge, Elizabeth	Bloomsbury Children's Books
#Dogtown Diner	D	F	80	Dogtown Comics	American Reading Company

* Collection of short stories   # Graphic text
^ Mature content with lower level text demands

TITLE	LEVEL	GENRE	WORD COUNT	AUTHOR / SERIES	PUBLISHER / DISTRIBUTOR
#Dogtown's Got Talent	D	F	87	Dogtown Comics	American Reading Company
Dogwood Tree, The	J	I	363	Vocabulary Readers	Houghton Mifflin Harcourt
Dogwood Tree, The	J	I	363	Vocabulary Readers/CA	Houghton Mifflin Harcourt
Doing Jobs Together	F	RF	194	Early Connections	Benchmark Education
Doing My Job	H	I	188	Early Connections	Benchmark Education
Doing the Dishes	L	RF	136	City Kids	Rigby
Doll Hospital, The	C	RF	57	The Rowland Reading Program Library	Rowland Reading Foundation
Doll in the Garden, The: A Ghost Story	T	F	250+	Hahn, Mary Downing	Clarion Books
Doll People, The	S	F	250+	Martin, Ann M. & Godwin, Laura	Hyperion Paperbacks for Children
Dollar Bill in Translation, The: What It Really Means	V	I	250+	Kids' Translations	Capstone Press
Dollar Bill's Journey, A	M	I	250+	Follow-It!	Picture Window Books
Dollar, The	I	RF	169	Books for Young Learners	Richard C. Owen
Dollars and Cents	K	I	226	Early Explorers	Benchmark Education
Dolley Madison	N	B	197	First Biographies	Capstone Press
Dolley Madison	S	B	3435	History Maker Bios	Lerner Publishing Group
Dolley Madison Saves George Washington	Q	B	250+	Brown, Don	Houghton Mifflin Harcourt
#Dolley Madison Saves History	T	B	250+	Graphic Library	Capstone Press
Dolley Madison, First Lady	L	B	330	Leveled Readers Social Studies	Houghton Mifflin Harcourt
Dolley Madison: First Lady	U	B	250+	Let Freedom Ring	Capstone Press
Dollhouse Murders, The	S	F	250+	Wright, Betty Ren	Scholastic
Doll's House, The	R	RF	250+	Godden, Rumer	Penguin Group
Dolly Madison, First Lady	J	B	250+	Leveled Readers Social Studies	Houghton Mifflin Harcourt
Dolly's Car	H	RF	192	Handprints C, Set 2	Educators Publishing Service
Dolores Huerta, Civil Rights Leader	U	B	1655	Leveled Readers Social Studies	Houghton Mifflin Harcourt
Dolphin	L	I	250+	A Day in the Life: Sea Animals	Heinemann Library
Dolphin	L	I	250+	Morris, Robert A.	HarperTrophy
Dolphin Adventure	P	RF	250+	Grover, Wayne	Beech Tree Books
Dolphin Caller, The	R	RF	250+	PM Chapter Books	Rigby
Dolphin Dreaming	M	RF	250+	PM Extensions	Rigby
Dolphin on the Wall, The	K	RF	250+	PM Story Books-Silver	Rigby
Dolphin Rescue	Q	RF	250+	Reading Expeditions	National Geographic
Dolphin Song	T	F	250+	St. John, Lauren	Puffin Books
Dolphin Treasure	P	RF	250+	Grover, Wayne	Beech Tree Books
Dolphin Vs. Fish	L	I	250+	Predator Vs. Prey	Raintree
Dolphin, The	P	I	250+	Animal Close-Ups	Charlesbridge
Dolphins	K	I	111	Bookshop	Mondo Publishing
Dolphins	O	I	1474	Early Bird Nature Books	Lerner Publishing Group
Dolphins	O	I	250+	Holmes, Kevin J.	Red Brick Learning
Dolphins	N	I	250+	Kalman, Bobbie	Crabtree
Dolphins	I	I	44	Pebble Books	Red Brick Learning
Dolphins	T	I	250+	PM Plus Nonfiction	Rigby
Dolphins	Q	I	1073	Reading Street	Pearson
Dolphins	F	I	136	Readlings/Marine Animals	American Reading Company
Dolphins	Q	I	250+	Storyteller-Raging Rivers	Wright Group/McGraw Hill
Dolphins	U	I	250+	The Heinle Reading Library	Thomson Learning
Dolphins	I	I	91	Under the Sea	Capstone Press
Dolphins	J	I	111	Wonder World	Wright Group/McGraw Hill
Dolphins	N	I	250+	World of Mammals	Capstone Press
Dolphins at Daybreak	M	F	250+	Osborne, Mary Pope	Random House

D

TITLE	LEVEL	GENRE	WORD COUNT	AUTHOR / SERIES	PUBLISHER / DISTRIBUTOR
Dolphin's First Day: The Story of a Bottlenose Dolphin	N	I	250+	Zoehfeld, Kathleen Weidnetz	Scholastic
Dolphins!	L	I	250+	Bokoske, Sharon	Random House
Dolphins, The	L	RF	721	PM Collection	Rigby
Dome, The	T	SF	250+	Power Up!	Steck-Vaughn
Domes of Mars, The	U	SF	6559	Reading Street	Pearson
Dominic	R	F	250+	Steig, William	Farrar, Straus, & Giroux
Dominican Republic, The: A Question and Answer Book	P	I	250+	Questions & Answers: Countries	Capstone Press
Dominic's Collections	L	RF	894	Rigby Gigglers	Rigby
Dominoes	P	I	250+	Games Around the World	Compass Point Books
Dom's Dragon	E	RF	176	Take Two Books	Wright Group/McGraw Hill
Dom's Handplant	L	RF	250+	Literacy 2000	Rigby
Don't Go In The Cellar	O	F	250+	Strong, Jeremy	Stone Arch Books
Don't Shoot! Chase R's Top Ten Reasons NOT to Move to the Country	V	RF	250+	Rosen, Michael J.	Candlewick Press
Dona Felisa Rincon de Gautier: Mayor of San Juan	N	B	250+	Beginning Biographies	Pearson Learning Group
Donald Quixote	Q	RF	1300	Leveled Readers	Houghton Mifflin Harcourt
Donald Quixote	Q	RF	1300	Leveled Readers/CA	Houghton Mifflin Harcourt
Donald Quixote	Q	RF	1300	Leveled Readers/TX	Houghton Mifflin Harcourt
Donald's Garden	K	RF	250+	Reading Unlimited	Pearson Learning Group
Donavan's Word Jar	N	RF	250+	DeGross, Monalisa	HarperCollins
Donkey	M	RF	250+	Literacy 2000	Rigby
Donkey in the Lion's Skin, The	G	TL	56	Aesop	Wright Group/McGraw Hill
Donkey in the Lion's Skin, The	G	TL	213	PM Plus Story Books	Rigby
Donkey of Gallipoli, The	T	HF	250+	Greenwood, Mark	Candlewick Press
Donkey Rescue	M	RF	250+	Krailing, Tessa	Barron's Educational
Donkey Rides	I	RF	375	Red Rocket Readers	Flying Start Books
Donkey Work	H	I	129	Wonder World	Wright Group/McGraw Hill
Donkeys	M	I	250+	Voyages	SRA/McGraw Hill
Donkey's Tale, The	J	TL	250+	Bank Street	Bantam Books
Donna O'Neeshuck Was Chased by Some Cows	L	RF	250+	Grossman, Bill	HarperTrophy
Donner Party, The	T	I	250+	Werther, Scott P.	Scholastic
Don't Be Late	D	F	111	Gibson, Akimi	Scholastic
Don't Be Late!	L	RF	250+	Cambridge Reading	Pearson Learning Group
Don't Be My Valentine: A Classroom Mystery	J	RF	250+	Lexau, Joan M.	HarperTrophy
Don't Be Silly	E	F	76	Teacher's Choice Series	Pearson Learning Group
Don't Bug Me!	T	RF	2224	Leveled Readers	Houghton Mifflin Harcourt
Don't Call Me Beanhead!	M	RF	250+	Wojciechowski, Susan	Candlewick Press
Don't Cut Down This Tree	G	F	129	Voyages	SRA/McGraw Hill
Don't Eat the Stick	I	F	250+	Sunshine	Wright Group/McGraw Hill
Don't Eat Too Much Turkey	J	TL	250+	Cohen, Miriam	Bantam Books
Don't Forget	E	RF	80	Literacy Tree	Rigby
Don't Forget Fun	L	RF	250+	Little Celebrations	Pearson Learning Group
Don't Forget the Bacon	M	RF	174	Hutchins, Pat	Puffin Books
Don't Get Lost	E	RF	105	Emergent Set 4	Pioneer Valley
Don't Go Out	F	F	179	Take Two Books	Wright Group/McGraw Hill
Don't Interrupt!	I	RF	225	Windmill Books	Rigby
Don't Kid Yourself: Relatively Great (Family) Jokes!	O	F	2212	Make Me Laugh!	Lerner Publishing Group
*Don't Kiss the Frog!: Princess Stories with Attitude	R	F	250+	Waters, Fiona	Kingfisher
Don't Leave Anything Behind!	C	RF	26	Literacy 2000	Rigby
Don't Let Go!	E	RF	114	The King School Series	Townsend Press

* Collection of short stories   # Graphic text
^ Mature content with lower level text demands

TITLE	LEVEL	GENRE	WORD COUNT	AUTHOR / SERIES	PUBLISHER / DISTRIBUTOR
Don't Let Ted Have Bubble Gum!	I	RF	250+	Phonics Readers Plus	Steck-Vaughn
Don't Let the Cat Out!	F	RF	109	Independent Readers Social Studies	Houghton Mifflin Harcourt
Don't Let the Pigeon Stay Up Late!	K	F	193	Willems, Mo	Scholastic
Don't Lick the Dog: Making Friends with Dogs	K	RF	254	Wahman, Wendy	Henry Holt & Co.
Don't Look Behind You	Z	RF	250+	Duncan, Lois	Little Brown and Company
Don't Look Down!	H	I	120	Storyteller	Wright Group/McGraw Hill
Don't Look Now	K	F	36	Briant, Ed	Roaring Brook Press
Don't Make a Vompa Mad!	M	SF	250+	Scooters	ETA/Cuisenaire
Don't Panic!	E	RF	122	Book Bank	Wright Group/McGraw Hill
Don't Panic!	T	F	250+	Power Up!	Steck-Vaughn
Don't Quit, Frits!	F	RF	172	The Rowland Reading Program Library	Rowland Reading Foundation
Don't Scare the Fish	J	RF	498	Red Rocket Readers	Flying Start Books
Don't Sit on My Lunch!	L	RF	250+	Klein, Abby	Scholastic
Don't Smile	F	RF	125	Red Rocket Readers	Flying Start Books
Don't Splash Me!	A	RF	24	Windmill Books	Wright Group/McGraw Hill
*Don't Split the Pole: Tales of Down-Home Folk Wisdom	S	RF	250+	Tate, Eleanora E.	Bantam Books
Don't Stomp on That Bug	J	I	250+	Literacy by Design	Rigby
Don't Stomp on That Bug	J	I	250+	Rigby Literacy	Rigby
Don't Talk to Me About the War	U	HF	250+	Adler, David A.	Puffin Books
Don't Talk to Strangers	E	I	157	Rosen Real Readers	Rosen Publishing Group
Don't Tell!	G	RF	82	Little Books	Sadlier-Oxford
Don't Throw It Away	J	I	330	Springboard	Wright Group/McGraw Hill
Don't Throw It Away!	I	RF	235	InfoTrek	ETA/Cuisenaire
Don't Throw It Away!	F	I	90	Wonder World	Wright Group/McGraw Hill
Don't Throw Your Spinach	I	RF	155	Story Box	Wright Group/McGraw Hill
Don't Touch	I	RF	250+	Kline, Suzy	Penguin Group
Don't Touch	I	I	177	Sails	Rigby
Don't Touch It, Lily	K	F	250+	Popcorn	Sundance
Don't Try This at Home	S	I	250+	Story Surfers	ETA/Cuisenaire
Don't Wake the Baby	B	RF	18	Literacy 2000	Rigby
Don't Wake the Baby!	E	RF	127	All Aboard Reading	Grosset & Dunlap
Don't Worry	J	RF	339	Literacy 2000	Rigby
Don't You Forget About Me	Z+	RF	250+	von Ziegesar, Cecily	Little Brown and Company
Don't You Laugh at Me!	E	F	167	Sunshine	Wright Group/McGraw Hill
Dooby Dooby Moo	M	F	250+	Cronin, Doreen & Lewin, Betsy	Atheneum Books
Doodler, The	T	RF	2012	Leveled Readers	Houghton Mifflin Harcourt
Doohickey and the Robot	O	F	250+	High-Fliers	Pacific Learning
Doomed Queen Anne	Z	HF	250+	Meyer, Carolyn	Harcourt Trade
Doomed to Dance: Ivy & Bean	M	RF	250+	Barrows, Annie	Chronicle Books
Doomed to Disappear? Endangered Species	T	I	250+	Navigators Science Series	Benchmark Education
^Doomsday Virus, The	T	SF	250+	Barlow, Steve	Stone Arch Books
Door in the Wall, The	U	HF	250+	De Angeli, Marguerite	Bantam Books
Door to Time, The	R	F	250+	Moore, Ulysses	Scholastic
Doorbell Rang, The	J	RF	283	Hutchins, Pat	Greenwillow Books
Doors	D	I	83	Sails	Rigby
^Doorway to Darkness	S	SF	250+	Banks, John	Stone Arch Books
Dora's Decision	M	RF	250+	On Our Way To English	Rigby
Dora's Soapbox Car	J	RF	250+	On Our Way to English	Rigby
Dora's Time to Shine	O	RF	250+	Literacy by Design	Rigby
Dora's Time to Shine	O	RF	250+	On Our Way to English	Rigby
Doris Free	U	HF	250+	Bookshop	Mondo Publishing

D

TITLE	LEVEL	GENRE	WORD COUNT	AUTHOR / SERIES	PUBLISHER / DISTRIBUTOR
Dormia	Y	F	250+	Halpern, Jake & Kujawinski, Peter	Sandpiper Books
Dorothea Dix: Social Reformer	U	B	250+	Let Freedom Ring	Capstone Press
Dorothea Lange	T	B	250+	Amazing Americans	Wright Group/McGraw Hill
Dorothea Lange: Faces of the Great Depression	Q	B	250+	On Our Way to English	Rigby
Dory Story	M	F	588	Pallotta, Jerry	Charlesbridge
Do's and Don'ts	G	RF	127	Parr, Todd	Little Brown and Company
Dot	F	RF	122	The Rowland Reading Program Library	Rowland Reading Foundation
Dot in Larryland: The Big Little Book of an Odd-Sized Friendship	O	F	250+	Marx, Patricia	Bloomsbury Children's Books
Dot, The	L	RF	250+	Reynolds, Peter H.	Candlewick Press
Dots, Dots, Dots	B	RF	25	Reading Street	Pearson
Dotty	N	F	250+	Perl, Erica S.	Harry N. Abrams
Dotty's Dots	I	RF	296	Reading Street	Pearson
Double Act	L	RF	1038	Rigby Flying Colors	Rigby
Double Danger	S	F	250+	Hager, Mandy	Pacific Learning
Double Dutch	E	RF	191	Visions	Wright Group/McGraw Hill
Double Eagle	X	RF	250+	Collard III, Sneed B.	Peachtree
Double It Daily	L	RF	639	Dominie Math Stories	Pearson Learning Group
Double Life of Pocahontas, The	U	B	250+	Fritz, Jean	Language for Learning Assoc.
Double Play	V	RF	3662	Leveled Readers	Houghton Mifflin Harcourt
Double Play	V	RF	3662	Leveled Readers/CA	Houghton Mifflin Harcourt
Double Play	U	RF	4526	Reading Street	Pearson
Double Play at Short	Q	RF	250+	Christopher, Matt	Little Brown and Company
Double Spell	S	F	250+	Lunn, Janet	Tundra Books
Double Switch	M	RF	250+	Orbit Chapter Books	Pacific Learning
Double the Animals	M	I	250+	Yellow Umbrella Books	Red Brick Learning
Double Trouble	T	RF	250+	Hopkins, Cathy	Kingfisher
Double Trouble	Q	RF	250+	Leveled Readers Language Support	Houghton Mifflin Harcourt
Double Trouble	M	TL	250+	Literacy 2000	Rigby
Double Trouble	L	RF	890	Reading Street	Pearson
Double Trouble	L	RF	250+	Sunshine	Wright Group/McGraw Hill
Double Trouble in Walla Walla	O	F	960	Clements, Andrew	Carolrhoda Books
Double Trouble Squared	U	F	250+	Lasky, Kathryn	Harcourt, Inc.
Double Troubles	N	RF	250+	Hicks, Betty	Roaring Brook Press
*Double-Dare to Be Scared: Another Thirteen Chilling Tales	V	F	250+	San Souci, Robert D.	Scholastic
Doug Flutie	U	B	250+	Sports Heroes and Legends	Lerner Publishing Group
Dough Boy	Z+	RF	250+	Marino, Peter	Holiday House
Doughnut Danger	K	F	250+	I Am Reading	Kingfisher
Douglas Fir	N	I	250+	Habitats	Children's Press
Douglas Florian	K	B	250+	Leveled Readers Language Support	Houghton Mifflin Harcourt
Douglas Florian, Poet and Artist	M	B	484	Leveled Readers	Houghton Mifflin Harcourt
Douglas MacArthur	T	B	3624	History Maker Bios	Lerner Publishing Group
Dove Dream	Z+	RF	250+	Rumbaut, Hendle	Houghton Mifflin Harcourt
Dove Isabeau	T	F	250+	Yolen, Jane	Harcourt Brace
Dovey Coe	U	RF	250+	Dowell, Frances O'Roark	Aladdin Paperbacks
Do-Whacky-Do	H	F	249	Read Alongs	Rigby
^Down	Z+	RF	250+	Orca Soundings	Orca Books
Down a Dark Hall	W	F	250+	Duncan, Lois	Little Brown and Company
Down and Out Down Under	O	F	250+	Stilton, Geronimo	Scholastic

* Collection of short stories   # Graphic text
^ Mature content with lower level text demands

TITLE	LEVEL	GENRE	WORD COUNT	AUTHOR / SERIES	PUBLISHER / DISTRIBUTOR
Down at the Billabong	F	RF	93	Voyages	SRA/McGraw Hill
Down at the River	E	RF	51	Pacific Literacy	Pacific Learning
Down by the Bay	E	RF	121	Little Celebrations	Pearson Learning Group
Down by the Pond	F	I	131	Leveled Literacy Intervention/ Blue System	Heinemann
Down by the Pond	B	F	72	On Our Way to English	Rigby
Down by the Pond	I	I	118	Story Box	Wright Group/McGraw Hill
Down by the Sea	G	RF	173	PM Plus Story Books	Rigby
Down by the Stream	E	I	97	Independent Readers Science	Houghton Mifflin Harcourt
Down by the Swamp	F	RF	50	Little Celebrations	Pearson Learning Group
*Down Garrapata Road	Z	RF	250+	Edge	Hampton Brown
Down in the Sea	C	I	87	Bonnell, Kris	Reading Reading Books
Down in the Woods	I	F	155	Storyteller-Moon Rising	Wright Group/McGraw Hill
Down on the Farm	B	RF	59	Green Light Readers	Harcourt
Down on the Farm	E	F	244	Learn to Read	Creative Teaching Press
Down on the Ice	P	I	250+	Alchin, Rupert	Pacific Learning
Down Sand Mountain	X	HF	250+	Watkins, Steve	Candlewick Press
Down the Back of the Chair	O	F	250+	Mahy, Margaret	Clarion
Down the Chimney with Googol and Googolplex	L	SF	250+	Orca Echoes	Orca Books
Down the Columbia	R	HF	1516	Leveled Readers	Houghton Mifflin Harcourt
Down the Columbia	R	HF	1516	Leveled Readers/CA	Houghton Mifflin Harcourt
Down the Columbia	R	HF	1516	Leveled Readers/TX	Houghton Mifflin Harcourt
Down the Hill	C	RF	32	KinderReaders	Rigby
Down the Hill	C	RF	94	New Way Red	Steck-Vaughn
Down the Laser Beam	P	SF	1752	Take Two Books	Wright Group/McGraw Hill
Down the Nile	Q	I	250+	Windows on Literacy	National Geographic
Down the Path	B	F	43	Leveled Literacy Intervention/ Blue System	Heinemann
Down the Rabbit Hole	W	RF	250+	Abrahams, Peter	HarperTrophy
Down the River	C	RF	85	Leveled Literacy Intervention/ Blue System	Heinemann
Down the Side of the Sofa	B	RF	66	Lighthouse	Ginn & Co.
Down the Street	E	RF	66	Little Celebrations	Pearson Learning Group
Down the Well	E	F	200	Sun Sprouts	ETA/Cuisenaire
Down to a Science	S	I	250+	Boldprint	Steck-Vaughn
Down to a Sunless Sea: The Strange World of Hydrothermal Vents	W	I	250+	Madin, Kate	Steck-Vaughn
Down to Town	A	F	26	Sunshine	Wright Group/McGraw Hill
Down Under Vacation	P	I	250+	Trackers	Pacific Learning
Downhill BMX	M	I	250+	To the Extreme	Capstone Press
Downhill Fun: A Counting Book About Winter	J	I	123	Know Your Numbers	Picture Window Books
Downhill Race, The	D	F	45	Bonnell, Kris	Reading Reading Books
Downhill Skiing For Fun!	S	I	250+	For Fun!	Compass Point Books
Downtown Lost & Found	E	F	55	New Reader Series	Bungalo Books
Dowser's Son, The	W	F	250+	Holt, Kimberly Willis	Henry Holt & Co.
Dozen Dizzy Dogs, A	G	F	157	Bank Street	Bantam Books
Dozen Dogs, A	F	F	228	Ziefert, Harriet	Random House
Dozen Eggs, A	LB	RF	14	Harry's Math Books	Outside the Box
Dr. Ben Carson: From Setbacks to Success	T	B	250+	Explore More	Wright Group/McGraw Hill
Dr. Brad Has Gone Mad!	O	RF	250+	Gutman, Dan	HarperTrophy
Dr. Carbles Is Losing His Marbles!	O	RF	250+	Gutman, Dan	HarperTrophy
Dr. Charles Drew and the Blood Banks	S	B	1515	Independent Readers Science	Houghton Mifflin Harcourt
Dr. Faucet and the Case of the Missing Drops	L	F	650	Gear Up!	Wright Group/McGraw Hill
Dr. Green	G	RF	141	Little Readers	Houghton Mifflin Harcourt

D

TITLE	LEVEL	GENRE	WORD COUNT	AUTHOR / SERIES	PUBLISHER / DISTRIBUTOR
Dr. Jekyll and Mr. Hyde	W	F	250+	Edge	Hampton Brown
#Dr. Jekyll and Mr. Hyde (Adapted)	Z	F	250+	Klimowski, Andrzej & Schejbal, Danusia	Sterling Publishing
Dr. Jekyll, Orthodontist	N	RF	250+	The Zack Files	Grosset & Dunlap
Dr. Jenner and the Speckled Monster	Y	I	250+	Edge	Hampton Brown
Dr. MacTavish's Creature	N	RF	250+	PM Collection	Rigby
Dr. Martin Luther King Jr.'s I Have a Dream Speech in Translation: What it Really Means	V	I	250+	Kids' Translations	Capstone Press
Dr. Quinn, Medicine Woman	T	B	250+	McKenna, Colleen O'Shaughnessy	Language for Learning Assoc.
Dr. Seuss	L	B	184	First Biographies	Red Brick Learning
Dr. Seuss	R	B	3272	History Maker Bios	Lerner Publishing Group
Dr. Seuss and His Stories	N	B	250+	Sunshine	Wright Group/McGraw Hill
Dr. Sharma Is a Veterinarian	F	I	98	InfoTrek	ETA/Cuisenaire
Dr. Tran to the Rescue	H	I	173	Dominie Factivity Series	Pearson Publishing Group
#Dracula	W	F	250+	Burgan, Michael (Retold)	Stone Arch Books
Dracula	W	F	250+	Edge	Hampton Brown
Dracula	W	F	7875	Oxford Bookworms Library	Oxford University Press
Dracula	Y	TL	250+	Raven, Nicky	Candlewick Press
Dracula	Z+	F	250+	Stoker, Bram	Bantam Books
Dracula Doesn't Drink Lemonade	M	F	250+	Dadey, Debbie; Jones, Marcia Thornton	Scholastic
Dracula vs. Grampa at the Monster Truck Spectacular	Q	F	250+	Wiley & Grampa's Creature Features	Little Brown and Company
Drag Racers	W	I	6405	Motor Mania	Lerner Publishing Group
Dragon	I	F	161	Pacific Literacy	Pacific Learning
Dragon Bones	O	F	250+	Hindman, Paul	Random House
Dragon Breath	L	F	250+	O'Connor, Jane	Grosset & Dunlap
Dragon Cauldron	W	F	250+	Yep, Laurence	HarperCollins
^Dragon Cowboy	T	F	250+	Dragonblood	Stone Arch Books
Dragon Emperor, The	N	TL	1727	On My Own Folklore	Millbrook Press
Dragon Family, The	J	F	250+	Scooters	ETA/Cuisenaire
Dragon Feet	K	F	153	Books For Young Learners	Richard C. Owen
Dragon Fire	P	F	250+	Cowley, Joy	Pacific Learning
Dragon Flight	U	F	250+	George, Jessica Day	Bloomsbury Children's Books
Dragon for Sale	Q	F	250+	MacDonald, Marianne	Troll Associates
Dragon Gets By	I	F	250+	Pilkey, Dav	Orchard Books
*Dragon Hunt, The	F	F	53	New Way Red	Steck-Vaughn
Dragon in the Family, A	Q	F	250+	Koller, Jackie French	Pocket Books
Dragon in the Ghetto Caper, The	T	RF	250+	Konigsburg, E. L.	Aladdin
Dragon Inside, The	S	RF	250+	Power Up!	Steck-Vaughn
*Dragon King's Palace, The	T	TL	250+	Literacy 2000	Rigby
Dragon Kiss	U	F	250+	Baker, E.D.	Bloomsbury Children's Books
Dragon Legends	S	TL	250+	Dragons	Capstone Press
Dragon Life	S	I	250+	Dragons	Capstone Press
Dragon New Year, The: A Chinese Legend	R	TL	250+	Bouchard, David	Peachtree
Dragon of Doom, The	P	F	250+	Coville, Bruce	Aladdin Paperbacks
Dragon of Krakow, The: A Polish Folktale	L	TL	366	Leveled Readers	Houghton Mifflin Harcourt
Dragon of Lonely Island, The	R	F	250+	Rupp, Rebecca	Scholastic
Dragon of the Lost Sea	W	F	250+	Yep, Laurence	HarperCollins
Dragon of Trelian, The	X	F	250+	Knudsen, Michelle	Candlewick Press
Dragon Parade: A Chinese New Year Story	O	I	250+	Chin, Steven A.	Steck-Vaughn

* Collection of short stories   # Graphic text
^ Mature content with lower level text demands

TITLE	LEVEL	GENRE	WORD COUNT	AUTHOR / SERIES	PUBLISHER / DISTRIBUTOR
Dragon Prince, The: A Chinese Beauty and the Beast Tale	P	TL	250+	Yep, Laurence	HarperCollins
Dragon Princess, The	U	F	250+	Baker, E. D.	Bloomsbury Children's Books
Dragon Quest	Q	F	250+	Koller, Jackie French	Pocket Books
Dragon Rider	V	F	250+	Funke, Cornelia	Scholastic
Dragon Slayer	P	F	250+	Cowley, Joy	Pacific Learning
Dragon Slippers	U	F	250+	George, Jessica Day	Bloomsbury Children's Books
Dragon Spear	U	F	250+	George, Jessica Day	Bloomsbury Children's Books
Dragon Steel	W	F	250+	Yep, Laurence	HarperCollins
Dragon Trouble	Q	F	250+	Koller, Jackie French	Pocket Books
Dragon Trouble	N	F	250+	Supa Doopers	Sundance
Dragon War	W	F	250+	Yep, Laurence	HarperCollins
Dragon Who Came to Dinner, The	K	F	250+	The Wright Skills	Wright Group/McGraw Hill
Dragon Who Had the Measles,The	J	F	250+	Literacy 2000	Rigby
Dragon with a Cold	J	F	250+	Sunshine	Wright Group/McGraw Hill
Dragon!	E	F	68	Wonder World	Wright Group/McGraw Hill
Dragon, The	D	F	29	Math Stories	Pearson Learning Group
Dragon, The	I	F	250+	Story Box	Wright Group/McGraw Hill
Dragon, The	C	F	130	Sunshine	Wright Group/McGraw Hill
Dragon's Lullaby, A	M	F	670	Leveled Literacy Intervention/ Blue System	Heinemann
Dragonatomy	S	I	250+	Dragons	Capstone Press
Dragonflies	F	I	110	Animal Life Cycles	Lerner Publishing Group
Dragonflies	F	I	104	Bonnell, Kris/About	Reading Reading Books
Dragonflies	G	I	53	Books for Young Learners	Richard C. Owen
Dragonflies	H	I	133	Bugs, Bugs, Bugs!	Capstone Press
Dragonflies	E	I	39	Insects	Capstone Press
Dragonflies	I	I	218	Sails	Rigby
Dragonflies	N	I	250+	World of Insects	Capstone Press
Dragonflies Are Super Bugs	G	I	101	Seedlings	Continental Press
Dragonfly	Y	F	250+	Golding, Julia	Marshall Cavendish
Dragonfly and the Web of Dreams: The Fairy Chronicles	Q	F	13600	Sweet, J.H.	Sourcebooks
*Dragonfly Dreams and Other Stories	I	F	250+	Story Steps	Rigby
Dragonfly Pool, The	W	HF	250+	Ibbotson, Eva	Puffin Books
Dragonfly's Tale	N	TL	250+	Rodanas, Kristina	Clarion
Dragonling, The	Q	F	250+	Koller, Jackie French	Pocket Books
Dragons	X	I	5067	Monster Chronicles	Lerner Publishing Group
Dragons	Q	I	250+	Mythical Creatures	Raintree
Dragons and Kings	Q	F	250+	Koller, Jackie French	Pocket Books
Dragon's Birthday, The	K	F	250+	Literacy 2000	Rigby
Dragon's Blood	X	F	250+	Yolen, Jane	Harcourt Trade
Dragon's Coming After You, The	H	F	156	Voyages	SRA/McGraw Hill
Dragons Don't Cook Pizza	M	F	250+	Dadey, Debbie; Jones, Marcia Thornton	Scholastic
Dragons Don't Read Books	M	RF	250+	Bookshop	Mondo Publishing
Dragon's Dream	C	F	34	Learn to Read	Creative Teaching Press
Dragon's Eye: Dragonology Chronicles Volume One	W	F	250+	Steer, Dugald A.	Candlewick Press
Dragon's Fat Cat	I	F	250+	Pilkey, Dav	Orchard Books
Dragons Galore	N	F	250+	Wildcats	Wright Group/McGraw Hill
Dragon's Gate	W	HF	250+	Yep, Laurence	HarperCollins

TITLE	LEVEL	GENRE	WORD COUNT	AUTHOR / SERIES	PUBLISHER / DISTRIBUTOR
Dragon's Halloween	I	F	250+	Pilkey, Dav	Orchard Books
Dragon's Heart	X	F	250+	Yolen, Jane	Houghton Mifflin Harcourt
Dragon's Lunch	F	F	85	Ready Readers	Pearson Learning Group
Dragon's Merry Christmas	I	F	250+	Pilkey, Dav	Orchard Books
Dragon's Milk: The Dragon Chronicles	V	F	250+	Fletcher, Susan	Aladdin
Dragons of Blueland, The	L	F	250+	Gannett, Ruth	Random House
Dragons of Darkness	X	F	250+	Michaelis, Antonia	Amulet Books
Dragons of Krad	Q	F	250+	Koller, Jackie French	Pocket Books
Dragon's Scales, The	J	F	250+	Albee, Sarah	Random House
Dragon's Tail, A: Jane and the Dragon	O	F	250+	Baynton, Martin	Candlewick Press
Dragon's View, A	S	F	2317	Leveled Readers	Houghton Mifflin Harcourt
Dragon's View, A	S	F	2317	Leveled Readers/CA	Houghton Mifflin Harcourt
Dragon's View, A	S	F	2317	Leveled Readers/TX	Houghton Mifflin Harcourt
Dragonsong	V	F	250+	McCaffrey, Anne	Bantam Books
Dragonwings	W	HF	250+	Yep, Lawrence	HarperTrophy
Dragsters	M	I	250+	Horsepower	Capstone Press
Dragsters	L	I	113	On Deck	Rigby
^Dragsters	N	I	184	Rev It Up!	Capstone Press
Dragsters	T	I	250+	The World's Fastest	Red Brick Learning
Dragsters	Q	I	250+	Wild Rides!	Red Brick Learning
Drama Club	F	I	60	On Deck	Rigby
Drama Queen	M	RF	250+	Kylie Jean	Picture Window Books
Drat That Cat!	I	F	250+	Cambridge Reading	Pearson Learning Group
Draw Me a Story	P	B	250+	Winter, Max	Scholastic
Draw Your Own Cartoons	N	I	250+	Infotrek Plus	ETA/Cuisenaire
Drawbridge	E	I	29	Books for Young Learners	Richard C. Owen
Drawing	A	RF	40	Leveled Literacy Intervention/ Orange System	Heinemann
Drawing	B	I	48	Leveled Readers	Houghton Mifflin Harcourt
Drawing	B	I	48	Leveled Readers/CA	Houghton Mifflin Harcourt
Drawing	B	I	48	Leveled Readers/TX	Houghton Mifflin Harcourt
Drawing	M	I	250+	Start with Art	Heinemann Library
Drawing Lessons from a Bear	K	F	250+	McPhail, David	Little Brown and Company
Drawing, Sketching, and Cartooning: Techniques for Drawing People, Places, Pets, and Cartoon Characters	S	I	250+	Bookshop	Mondo Publishing
Dread Mountain	T	F	250+	Rodda, Emily	Scholastic
Dreadful Acts	U	F	250+	Ardagh, Philip	Scholastic
Dreadful Dinosaurs	N	F	250+	Springboard	Wright Group/McGraw Hill
Dreadful Future of Blossom Culp, The	U	SF	250+	Peck, Richard	Bantam Books
Dreadful Revenge of Ernest Gallen, The	U	F	250+	Collier, James Lincoln	Bloomsbury Children's Books
Dream Around the World	G	F	138	Instant Readers	Harcourt School Publishers
Dream Boat	M	RF	250+	Action Packs	Rigby
Dream Catcher	M	RF	159	Books for Young Learners	Richard C. Owen
Dream Catcher, The	H	RF	230	Adams, Lorraine & Bruvold, Lynn	Eaglecrest Books
Dream Catchers	M	RF	176	Storyteller-Night Crickets	Wright Group/McGraw Hill
Dream Come True, A	O	B	250+	Meet The Author	Richard C. Owen
Dream Comes True, A	N	B	250+	On Our Way to English	Rigby
Dream Eater, The	N	F	250+	Garrison, Christian	Aladdin
Dream Factory	Z+	RF	250+	Barkley, Brad & Helper, Heather	Speak
Dream Horse	C	F	47	Pair-It Books	Steck-Vaughn
Dream in the Wishing Well	H	F	250+	Van Allen, Roach	SRA/McGraw Hill
Dream of Flight, The	O	I	250+	Rigby Focus	Rigby

Organized Alphabetically by Title
Storable Database at www.fountasandpinnellleveledbooks.com

* Collection of short stories   # Graphic text
^ Mature content with lower level text demands

TITLE	LEVEL	GENRE	WORD COUNT	AUTHOR / SERIES	PUBLISHER / DISTRIBUTOR
Dream Stealer, The	N	F	250+	Fleischman, Sid	HarperCollins
Dream Team, The	I	RF	250+	Lighthouse	Rigby
Dream Weaver	W	HF	3045	Leveled Readers	Houghton Mifflin Harcourt
Dream, The	F	RF	54	Oxford Reading Tree	Oxford University Press
Dreamacres	L	I	758	InfoTrek	ETA/Cuisenaire
Dreamer Behind the Dome, The: Judge Roy Hofheinz	O	I	250+	On Our Way to English	Rigby
Dreamer, The	V	RF	250+	Ryan, Pam Munoz & Sis, Peter	Scholastic
*Dreamers and Doers	S	B	250+	On Our Way to English	Rigby
Dreamhunter	Z	F	250+	Knox, Elizabeth	Square Fish
Dreaming	B	RF	23	Smart Start	Rigby
Dreaming in Black and White	Z	HF	250+	Jung, Reinhardt	Penguin Group
Dreaming Place, The	S	RF	250+	PM Plus Chapter Books	Rigby
Dreamquest: Tales of Slumberia	X	F	250+	Hartinger, Brent	Tom Doherty
Dreams	E	RF	93	Book Bank	Wright Group/McGraw Hill
Dreams	F	RF	41	Dominie Readers	Pearson Learning Group
Dreams	T	HF	250+	Reading Safari	Mondo Publishing
Dreams	G	RF	98	Sunshine	Wright Group/McGraw Hill
Dreams of Flying	O	I	250+	Rigby Literacy	Rigby
Dred Scott and the Supreme Court	S	I	250+	Navigators Social Studies Series	Benchmark Education
Dred Scott Decision, The	X	I	250+	Cornerstones of Freedom	Children's Press
Dred Scott v. Sandford	Y	I	250+	Snapshots in History	Compass Point Books
Dress Up	D	RF	80	Carousel Readers	Pearson Learning Group
Dress Up	B	RF	49	Leveled Readers	Houghton Mifflin Harcourt
Dress Up	B	RF	49	Leveled Readers/CA	Houghton Mifflin Harcourt
Dress Up	B	RF	49	Leveled Readers/TX	Houghton Mifflin Harcourt
Dressed for School Success	P	I	731	Reading Street	Pearson
Dressed Up Dogs	A	F	25	Bonnell, Kris	Reading Reading Books
Dressed-Up Sammy	E	F	91	Urmston, Kathleen; Evans, Karen	Kaeden Books
Dressing Up	G	RF	104	Breakthrough	Longman
Dressing Up	B	I	50	InfoTrek	ETA/Cuisenaire
Dressing Up	A	RF	12	Jellybeans	Rigby
Dressing Up	B	RF	66	Leveled Readers	Houghton Mifflin Harcourt
Dressing Up	B	RF	66	Leveled Readers/CA	Houghton Mifflin Harcourt
Dressing Up	C	RF	31	Literacy 2000	Rigby
Dressing Up	A	F	32	PM Starters	Rigby
Dressing Up	B	RF	25	Smart Start	Rigby
Dressing Up	I	RF	222	Stepping Stones	Nelson/Michaels Assoc.
Dressing Up	LB	RF	12	Sunshine	Wright Group/McGraw Hill
Dressing-Up Box, The	C	RF	61	Book Bank	Wright Group/McGraw Hill
Dress-Up	E	RF	104	Real Kids Readers	Millbrook Press
Dress-Up Corner, The	H	RF	68	City Kids	Rigby
Dress-Up Day	A	RF	32	Red Rocket Readers	Flying Start Books
Drew and the Homeboy Question	U	RF	250+	Armstrong, Robb	HarperTrophy
Dribble, Dribble, Shoot	F	RF	198	Handprints D, Set 2	Educators Publishing Service
Drier Than a Bone	S	RF	250+	Reading Safari	Mondo Publishing
Drift Cars	M	I	250+	Horsepower	Capstone Press
Drift House: The First Voyage	U	F	250+	Peck, Dale	Bloomsbury Children's Books
Drinking Gourd, The	M	HF	250+	Monjo, F. N.	HarperTrophy
Drinking Water	H	I	79	The Food Guide Pyramid	Capstone Press
Drip Drip Drip	C	F	33	Brand New Readers	Candlewick Press

D

TITLE	LEVEL	GENRE	WORD COUNT	AUTHOR / SERIES	PUBLISHER / DISTRIBUTOR
Drip! Drop!	G	RF	251	The Rowland Reading Program Library	Rowland Reading Foundation
Drip! Drop!: How Water Gets to Your Tap	O	I	250+	Seuling, Barbara	Holiday House
Drip, The	D	RF	103	Leveled Literacy Intervention/ Blue System	Heinemann
Driscoll and the Singing Fish	Q	F	1005	Leveled Readers	Houghton Mifflin Harcourt
Drita My Homegirl	T	RF	250+	Lombard, Jenny	Scholastic
Drive in the Country, A	L	RF	250+	Rosen, Michael J.	Candlewick Press
Drive Toward the Future	U	I	250+	In Step Readers	Rigby
Drive Toward the Future	U	I	250+	Literacy by Design	Rigby
Drive-By	W	RF	250+	Ewing, Lynne	HarperCollins
Driving	F	I	45	Benchmark Rebus	Marshall Cavendish
Driving Mom Crazy	H	RF	131	City Stories	Rigby
Driving on Mars	T	I	936	Leveled Readers	Houghton Mifflin Harcourt
Driving Tin Lizzie	K	HF	250+	Windows on Literacy	National Geographic
Drooling and Dangerous: The Riot Brothers Return!	O	RF	250+	Amato, Mary	Holiday House
Drop Around the World, A	P	I	1248	McKinney, Barbara Shaw	Dawn Publications
Drop by Drop	R	I	250+	Explorer Books-Pathfinder	National Geographic
Drop by Drop	Q	I	250+	Explorer Books-Pioneer	National Geographic
Drop in the Ocean, A: The Story of Water	Q	I	250+	Science Works	Picture Window Books
Drop of Water, A	S	I	250+	Wick, Walter	Scholastic
Drought and Wildfire	V	I	3297	Vocabulary Readers	Houghton Mifflin Harcourt
Drought and Wildfire	V	I	3297	Vocabulary Readers/CA	Houghton Mifflin Harcourt
Drought and Wildfire	V	I	3297	Vocabulary Readers/TX	Houghton Mifflin Harcourt
Drought Marker, The	M	F	250+	Literacy 2000	Rigby
Droughts	W	I	250+	Disasters Up Close	Lerner Publishing Group
Droughts	Q	I	250+	Natural Disasters	Red Brick Learning
Droughts	S	I	250+	Theme Sets	National Geographic
Droughts	O	I	250+	Weather Update	Capstone Press
Drowned Maiden's Hair, A	W	HF	250+	Schlitz, Laura A.	Candlewick Press
Drowning in a Bottle: Teens and Alcohol Abuse	Z	I	250+	What's the Issue?	Compass Point Books
Drum Beats On, The	O	I	250+	Cherrington, Janelle	Scholastic
Drum Dancers: An Inuit Story	Q	RF	873	Leveled Readers	Houghton Mifflin Harcourt
Drum, The	D	TL	117	Instant Readers	Harcourt School Publishers
Drummer Boy, The	S	I	1164	Leveled Readers	Houghton Mifflin Harcourt
Drummer Boy, The	Q	B	250+	WorldScapes	ETA/Cuisenaire
Drummer Hoff	J	TL	173	Emberly, Barbara	Prentice-Hall
Drummers, The	H	RF	80	Gould, Carol	Kaeden Books
Drums	K	I	280	InfoTrek Plus	ETA/Cuisenaire
Drums Around the World	G	I	192	Dominie Factivity Series	Pearson Learning Group
Drums: The Beat Goes on	L	I	250+	HSP/Harcourt Trophies	Harcourt, Inc.
Druscilla's Halloween	M	F	844	Walker, Sally M.	Carolrhoda Books
Dry and Snug and Warm	G	RF	64	Book Bank	Wright Group/McGraw Hill
Drylongso	V	RF	250+	Hamilton, Virginia	Harcourt Trade
Duck	K	F	250+	Cecil, Randy	Candlewick Press
*Duck & Company	K	F	250+	Caple, Kathy	Holiday House
Duck and Goose and the Perfect Puddle	F	F	73	Seedlings	Continental Press
Duck and Goose Give a Party	E	F	110	Seedlings	Continental Press
Duck and Goose Have a Picnic	G	F	125	Seedlings	Continental Press
Duck and Goose in the Rain	E	F	88	Seedlings	Continental Press
Duck and Goose Play with Frog	F	F	98	Seedlings	Continental Press
Duck and Hen	H	F	193	Sunshine	Wright Group/McGraw Hill
Duck and Pig	C	F	101	Sails	Rigby

* Collection of short stories   # Graphic text
^ Mature content with lower level text demands

TITLE	LEVEL	GENRE	WORD COUNT	AUTHOR / SERIES	PUBLISHER / DISTRIBUTOR
Duck and Rooster	C	F	81	Sails	Rigby
Duck and Rooster Go Out	F	F	193	Sails	Rigby
Duck and Rooster Go to School	H	F	365	Sails	Rigby
Duck and Rooster in Trouble	G	F	192	Sails	Rigby
Duck Feet	L	RF	751	Rigby Flying Colors	Rigby
Duck Goes to the Farm	J	F	373	Leveled Readers	Houghton Mifflin Harcourt
Duck Hunting	S	I	250+	The Great Outdoors	Capstone Press
Duck in the Gun, The	M	F	250+	Literacy 2000	Rigby
Duck in the Truck	J	F	250+	Alborough, Jez	Kane/Miller Book Publishers
Duck Magic	N	I	250+	Literacy 2000 Satellites	Rigby
Duck Pond, The	G	RF	276	Leveled Readers	Houghton Mifflin Harcourt
Duck Tents	K	F	301	Berry, Lynne	Henry Holt & Co.
Duck with the Broken Wing, The	F	RF	189	PM Extensions-Blue	Rigby
Duck, Duck, Goose!	E	F	92	My First Reader	Grolier
Duck-Billed Dinosaurs	P	I	1159	Meet the Dinosaurs	Lerner Publishing Group
Duckling Diary	O	RF	250+	Baglio, Ben M.	Scholastic
Ducklings Grow Up	E	I	77	Early Explorers	Benchmark Education
Ducks	F	I	98	Life Cycles	Lerner Publishing Group
Ducks	D	F	94	Story Box	Wright Group/McGraw Hill
Ducks	D	I	54	Vocabulary Readers	Houghton Mifflin Harcourt
Ducks	D	I	54	Vocabulary Readers/CA	Houghton Mifflin Harcourt
Ducks	D	I	54	Vocabulary Readers/TX	Houghton Mifflin Harcourt
Ducks Crossing	M	RF	250+	Orbit Chapter Books	Pacific Learning
Ducks Have Ducklings	M	I	250+	Animals and Their Young	Compass Point Books
Ducks in a Row	I	F	250+	Houran, Lori Haskins	HarperCollins
Ducks in Muck	B	F	48	Step into Reading	Random House
Ducks on the Farm	I	I	91	Pebble Books	Red Brick Learning
Ducks on the Run	I	RF	250+	PM Plus Story Books	Rigby
Ducks, The	H	RF	326	Rigby Flying Colors	Rigby
Duel! Burr and Hamilton's Deadly War of Words	S	B	250+	Fradin, Dennis Brindell	Walker & Company
Dugout Rivals	Q	RF	250+	Bowen, Fred	Peachtree
Duke and Duchess	I	RF	250+	Reading Safari	Mondo Publishing
Duke Ellington	T	B	250+	Amazing Americans	Wright Group/McGraw Hill
Duke Ellington	Q	B	250+	Pinkey, Andrea Davis	Scholastic
Duke Ellington	R	B	250+	Venezia, Mike	Children's Press
Duke Ellington: A Life in Music	Q	B	905	Leveled Readers	Houghton Mifflin Harcourt
Duke Ellington: Man of Music	P	B	250+	Leveled Readers Language Support	Houghton Mifflin Harcourt
Duke Kahanamoku	U	B	250+	Amazing Americans	Wright Group/McGraw Hill
Duke the Mule	H	F	59	Easy Phonics Readers	Teacher Created Materials
Duma and the Lion	I	F	250+	Storyworlds	Heinemann
Dumb Bunnies, The	J	F	250+	Pilkey, Dav	Scholastic
Dump Trucks	F	I	119	Mighty Machines	Capstone Press
Dump Trucks	L	I	356	Pull Ahead Books	Lerner Publishing Group
Dump Trucks on the Move	K	I	369	Lightning Bolt Books	Lerner Publishing Group
Dumpling Soup	M	RF	250+	Rattigan, Jama Kim	Little Brown and Company
Dumpsideary Jelly	H	RF	250+	Momentum Literacy Program	Troll Associates
Dunc and Amos and the Red Tattoos	R	RF	250+	Paulsen, Gary	Bantam Books
Dunc and Amos Go to the Dogs	R	RF	250+	Paulsen, Gary	Bantam Books
Dunc and Amos Hit the Big Top	R	RF	250+	Paulsen, Gary	Bantam Books
Dunc and Amos Meet the Slasher	R	RF	250+	Paulsen, Gary	Bantam Books
Dunc and the Flaming Ghost	R	F	250+	Paulsen, Gary	Bantam Books
Dunc and the Greased Sticks of Doom	R	RF	250+	Paulsen, Gary	Bantam Books
Dunc and the Haunted Castle	R	RF	250+	Paulsen, Gary	Bantam Books

D

TITLE	LEVEL	GENRE	WORD COUNT	AUTHOR / SERIES	PUBLISHER / DISTRIBUTOR
Dunc and the Scam Artists	R	RF	250+	Paulsen, Gary	Bantam Books
Dunc Breaks the Record	R	RF	250+	Paulsen, Gary	Bantam Books
Dunc Gets Tweaked	R	RF	250+	Paulsen, Gary	Bantam Books
Duncan the Dancing Duck	J	F	250+	Hoff, Syd	Clarion Books
Dunces Anonymous	R	RF	250+	Jaimet, Kate	Orca Books
Dunc's Doll	R	RF	250+	Paulsen, Gary	Bantam Books
Dunc's Dump	R	RF	250+	Paulsen, Gary	Bantam Books
Dunc's Halloween	R	RF	250+	Paulsen, Gary	Bantam Books
Dunc's Undercover Christmas	R	RF	250+	Paulsen, Gary	Bantam Books
Dunderheads Behind Bars, The	O	F	250+	Fleischman, Paul	Candlewick Press
Dune Buggies	M	I	250+	Horsepower	Capstone Press
Dunk	Y	RF	250+	Lubar, David	Graphia
Dunkin' Dazza's Daring Dribble	O	RF	250+	Supa Doopers	Sundance
Dunkin' Dazza's Soaring Slammer	O	RF	250+	Supa Doopers	Sundance
Durban, South Africa: Communities Around the World	S	I	250+	Reading Expeditions	National Geographic
Durinda's Danger: The Sisters 8	Q	F	250+	Baratz-Logsted, Lauren	Houghton Mifflin Harcourt
During the Day	A	I	32	Springboard	Wright Group/McGraw Hill
DuSable - Chicago's First Citizen	T	B	1522	Leveled Readers Social Studies	Houghton Mifflin Harcourt
Dust Bowl Days	W	I	250+	Reading Expeditions	National Geographic
Dust Bowl Lands	O	I	1206	Leveled Readers Language Support	Houghton Mifflin Harcourt
Dust Bowl Survivors	W	I	250+	Literacy by Design	Rigby
Dust Bowl Through the Lens, The: How Photography Revealed and Helped to Remedy a National Disaster	X	I	250+	Sandler, Martin W.	Walker & Company
Dust Bowl, The	P	I	1204	Leveled Readers Social Studies	Houghton Mifflin Harcourt
^Dust Bowl, The: An Interactive History Adventure	T	HF	250+	You Choose Books	Capstone Press
Dust from Comets	U	I	1735	Leveled Readers	Houghton Mifflin Harcourt
Dust from Comets	U	I	1735	Leveled Readers/CA	Houghton Mifflin Harcourt
Dust from Comets	U	I	1735	Leveled Readers/TX	Houghton Mifflin Harcourt
Dust from Old Bones	X	HF	250+	Forrester, Sandra	William Morrow
Dusted and Busted!	W	I	250+	24/7 Science Behind the Scenes	Scholastic
Dustland	V	F	250+	Hamilton, Virginia	Scholastic
Dusty's Big Day	H	RF	290	Handprints D	Educators Publishing Service
Dutch Colonies in the Americas	S	I	250+	On Deck	Rigby
Dwight D. Eisenhower	S	B	250+	Amazing Americans	Wright Group/McGraw Hill
Dwight D. Eisenhower	S	B	3605	History Maker Bios	Lerner Publishing Group
Dwight D. Eisenhower	U	B	250+	Profiles of the Presidents	Compass Point Books
Dwight D. Eisenhower: Thirty-fourth President	R	B	250+	Getting to Know the U.S. Presidents	Children's Press
Dwight Howard	P	B	2186	Amazing Athletes	Lerner Publishing Group
Dwyane Wade	Q	B	2059	Amazing Athletes	Lerner Publishing Group
Dying to Cross: The Worst Immigrant Tragedy in American History	Z+	I	250+	Edge	Hampton Brown
Dying to Meet You: 43 Old Cemetery Road: Book One	U	F	250+	Klise, Kate	Harcourt
Dylan: The Clique Summer Collection	X	RF	250+	Harrison, Lisi	Little Brown and Company
Dynamic Dance	S	I	250+	InfoQuest	Rigby
Dynamic Duos	P	F	250+	Moore, David	Scholastic

* Collection of short stories   # Graphic text
^ Mature content with lower level text demands

TITLE	LEVEL	GENRE	WORD COUNT	AUTHOR / SERIES	PUBLISHER / DISTRIBUTOR
*E is for Elisa	N	RF	250+	Hurwitz, Johanna	Puffin Books
E-(t)mail	R	F	250+	Bookshop	Mondo Publishing
EA-6B Prowler, The	U	I	250+	Cross-Sections	Capstone Press
Each Little Bird That Sings	U	RF	250+	Wiles, Deborah	Harcourt, Inc.
Each Peach, Pear, Plum	G	TL	115	Ahlberg, Allan & Janet	Penguin Group
Eagle and the Moon Gold, The	K	TL	250+	Avenues	Hampton Brown
Eagle Blue: A Team, a Tribe, and a High School Basketball Season in Arctic Alaska	Z	I	250+	D'Orso, Michael	Bloomsbury Children's Books
Eagle Feather	M	RF	250+	Bulla, Clyde Robert	Puffin Books
Eagle Feathers	N	TL	250+	Story Vines	Wright Group/McGraw Hill
Eagle Flies High, An	G	I	142	Ready Readers	Pearson Learning Group
Eagle Has Landed, The	O	I	250+	Merchant, Peter	Scholastic
Eagle in the Sky	L	RF	250+	Little Celebrations	Pearson Learning Group
Eagle of the Ninth	Z	HF	250+	Sutcliff, Rosemary	Farrar, Straus, & Giroux
Eagle Song	S	RF	250+	Bruchac, Joseph	Puffin Books
Eagle Watchers	N	RF	765	Leveled Readers	Houghton Mifflin Harcourt
Eagle, The	D	RF	72	Adams, Lorraine & Bruvold, Lynn	Eaglecrest Books
Eagles	S	I	2123	Animal Predators	Lerner Publishing Group
Eagles	L	I	425	Time for Kids	Teacher Created Materials
Eagles and Birds of Prey	V	I	250+	Eyewitness Books	DK Publishing
*Eagle's Reflection and Other Northwest Coast Stories	P	TL	250+	Challenger, James Robert	Heritage House
Eagles, Hawks, and Falcons	O	I	992	Take Two Books	Wright Group/McGraw Hill
Eagles: Birds of Prey	M	I	250+	The Wild World of Animals	Red Brick Learning
Ear Book	E	I	119	Perkins, Al	Random House
Ear Infections	K	I	250+	Health Matters	Capstone Press
Ear, the Eye, and the Arm, The	Y	SF	250+	Farmer, Nancy	Puffin Books
Earl and Eggster Float Away	M	F	918	Leveled Readers	Houghton Mifflin Harcourt
Earl and Eggster Float Away	M	F	918	Leveled Readers/CA	Houghton Mifflin Harcourt
Earl and Eggster Float Away	M	F	918	Leveled Readers/TX	Houghton Mifflin Harcourt
Earl and His Egg	L	F	1014	Leveled Readers	Houghton Mifflin Harcourt
Earl and His Egg	L	F	1014	Leveled Readers/CA	Houghton Mifflin Harcourt
Earl and His Egg	L	F	1014	Leveled Readers/TX	Houghton Mifflin Harcourt
Earl the Squirrel	K	F	250+	Freeman, Don	Scholastic
Earliest American, The	S	I	250+	Kids Discover Reading	Wright Group/McGraw Hill
Early American Indian Tribes	T	I	250+	Primary Source Readers	Teacher Created Materials
Early American Industrial Revolution, 1793-1850, The	V	I	250+	Let Freedom Ring	Capstone Press
Early Bird's Alarm Clock, The	J	F	250+	Pair-It Books	Steck-Vaughn
Early Congresses	T	I	250+	Primary Source Readers	Teacher Created Materials
Early Humans	Y	I	250+	Reading Expeditions	National Geographic
Early in the Morning	D	RF	55	Rise & Shine	Hampton Brown
Early in the Morning	C	RF	56	Windows on Literacy	National Geographic
Early Inventions	M	I	250+	Rigby Focus	Rigby
Early Winter, An	T	RF	250+	Bauer, Marion Dane	Houghton Mifflin Harcourt
Earning Money	T	I	250+	How Economics Works	Lerner Publishing Group
Earning Money	L	I	250+	Learning About Money	Capstone Press
Earning Money	O	I	250+	Let's See	Compass Point Books
Earning Money	E	I	104	Money	Lerner Publishing Group
Earning Money My Own Way	L	RF	625	Reading Street	Pearson
Ear-Rings from Frankfurt	T	RF	6422	Oxford Bookworms Library	Oxford University Press
Ears	B	I	21	Animal Traits	Lerner Publishing Group
Ears	E	I	74	Rigby Literacy	Rigby
Ears	C	I	37	Rise & Shine	Hampton Brown

TITLE	LEVEL	GENRE	WORD COUNT	AUTHOR / SERIES	PUBLISHER / DISTRIBUTOR
Ears	I	I	166	Sails	Rigby
Earth	Q	I	250+	A True Book	Children's Press
Earth	Q	I	1908	Early Bird Astronomy	Lerner Publishing Group
Earth	J	I	148	Exploring the Galaxy	Capstone Press
Earth	T	I	250+	Mission: Science	Compass Point Books
Earth	S	I	250+	Our Solar System	Compass Point Books
Earth	N	I	842	Our Universe	Lerner Publishing Group
Earth	H	I	122	Space	Lerner Publishing Group
Earth	Q	I	250+	The Galaxy	Capstone Press
Earth	M	I	250+	The Solar System	Capstone Press
Earth and I, The	J	RF	84	Asch, Frank	Harcourt
Earth and Moon	G	I	250+	Sunshine	Wright Group/McGraw Hill
Earth at Risk	V	I	250+	Sunshine	Wright Group/McGraw Hill
Earth Book, The	I	I	250+	Parr, Todd	Little Brown and Company
Earth Cycles	M	I	499	Cycles	Millbrook Press
Earth Day	F	I	111	American Holidays	Lerner Publishing Group
Earth Day	M	I	250+	Holiday Histories	Heinemann
Earth Day	J	I	153	Holidays and Festivals	Heinemann Library
Earth Day	N	I	1559	On My Own Holidays	Lerner Publishing Group
Earth Day	P	I	250+	Windows on Literacy	National Geographic
^Earth Evidence	W	I	250+	Forensic Crime Solvers	Capstone Press
*Earth Heroes: Champions of the Ocean	W	B	32785	Hodgkins, Fran	Dawn Publications
Earth in Space	N	I	250+	Reading Expeditions	National Geographic
Earth in Space, The	T	I	250+	Straightforward Science	Franklin Watts
Earth Is Mostly Ocean, The	M	I	250+	Rookie Read About Science	Children's Press
Earth Materials: The Mystery Rocks	R	I	1808	iScience	Norwood House Press
Earth Movement	R	I	1473	Reading Street	Pearson
Earth Movers	A	I	60	Readlings	American Reading Company
Earth on Turtle's Back, The	L	TL	508	Early Connections	Benchmark Education
Earth Rocks!	N	I	402	Pair-It Turn and Learn	Steck-Vaughn
*Earth Scientists: From Mercator to Evans	U	B	250+	Mission Science	Compass Point Books
Earth to Matthew	U	RF	250+	Danziger, Paula	PaperStar
Earth, Sun, Moon	S	I	250+	Reading Expeditions	National Geographic
Earth, The	B	I	35	On Our Way to English	Rigby
Earth, The	H	I	112	Windows on Literacy	National Geographic
Earth: Fast Changes	R	I	250+	Navigators Science Series	Benchmark Education
Earth: Measuring Its Changes	R	I	250+	Navigators Science Series	Benchmark Education
Earth: Slow Changes	R	I	250+	Navigators Science Series	Benchmark Education
Earth: The Inside Story	V	I	2030	Reading Street	Pearson
Earth: The Water Planet	T	I	250+	Navigators Science Series	Benchmark Education
Earthborn	Z	F	250+	Card, Orson Scott	Tor
Earthfall	Z	F	250+	Card, Orson Scott	Tor
Earth-Friendly Crafts: Clever Ways to Reuse Everyday Items	P	I	2850	Ross, Kathy	Millbrook Press
Earth-Friendly Design	X	I	10486	Saving Our Living Earth	Lerner Publishing Group
Earth-Friendly Energy	Y	I	10298	Saving Our Living Earth	Lerner Publishing Group
Earth-Friendly Waste Management	Y	I	10669	Saving Our Living Earth	Lerner Publishing Group
Earthlings in Space	U	SF	250+	Sunshine	Wright Group/McGraw Hill
Earthmovers	G	I	121	Mighty Machines	Capstone Press
Earthmovers	K	I	377	Pull Ahead Books	Lerner Publishing Group
Earthmovers on the Move	K	I	377	Lightning Bolt Books	Lerner Publishing Group
Earthquake	S	HF	250+	Duey, Kathleen; Bale, Karen A.	Simon & Schuster
Earthquake	M	RF	415	Jellybeans	Rigby
Earthquake	O	HF	250+	Lee, Milly	Farrar, Straus, & Giroux

* Collection of short stories   # Graphic text
^ Mature content with lower level text demands

TITLE	LEVEL	GENRE	WORD COUNT	AUTHOR / SERIES	PUBLISHER / DISTRIBUTOR
Earthquake	E	RF	40	Wonder World	Wright Group/McGraw Hill
Earthquake Alaska	U	HF	2192	Leveled Readers	Houghton Mifflin Harcourt
Earthquake in the Third Grade	N	RF	250+	Myers, Laurie	Clarion
Earthquake Scientists	T	I	1579	Vocabulary Readers	Houghton Mifflin Harcourt
Earthquake Scientists	T	I	1579	Vocabulary Readers/CA	Houghton Mifflin Harcourt
Earthquake Terror	X	RF	250+	Kehret, Peg	Puffin Books
Earthquake!	N	RF	250+	Bookweb	Rigby
Earthquake!	S	HF	2376	Leveled Readers	Houghton Mifflin Harcourt
Earthquake!	S	I	2075	Leveled Readers Science	Houghton Mifflin Harcourt
Earthquake!	V	I	250+	WorldScapes	ETA/Cuisenaire
Earthquake!: A Story of Old San Francisco	S	I	250+	Kudlinski, Kathleen V.	Penguin Group
Earthquake!: San Francisco, 1906	R	I	250+	Wilson, Kate	Steck-Vaughn
Earthquake!: The Disaster that Rocked San Francisco	R	HF	1753	Reading Street	Pearson
Earthquakes	Q	I	250+	A True Book	Children's Press
Earthquakes	O	I	250+	Branley, Franklyn M.	HarperCollins
Earthquakes	W	I	250+	Disasters Up Close	Lerner Publishing Group
Earthquakes	R	I	250+	Early Bird Earth Science	Lerner Publishing Group
Earthquakes	M	I	154	Earth in Action	Capstone Press
Earthquakes	T	I	250+	Earth Science	Franklin Watts
Earthquakes	R	I	250+	Explorers	Wright Group/McGraw Hill
Earthquakes	P	I	250+	InfoTrek Plus	ETA/Cuisenaire
Earthquakes	S	I	250+	Natural Disasters	Capstone Press
Earthquakes	M	I	763	Pull Ahead Books	Lerner Publishing Group
Earthquakes	S	I	250+	Simon, Seymour	Mulberry Books
Earthquakes	R	I	250+	The Wonders of Our World	Crabtree
Earthquakes	L	I	390	Time for Kids	Teacher Created Materials
Earthquakes and Tsunamis	O	I	250+	PM Plus Story Books	Rigby
Earthquakes and Volcanoes	Q	I	250+	Theme Sets	National Geographic
Earthquakes That Shook America	U	I	250+	Explore More	Wright Group/McGraw Hill
Earth's Changing Land	Q	I	250+	Reading Expeditions	National Geographic
Earth's Crust	R	I	1863	Early Bird Earth Systems	Lerner Publishing Group
Earth's Land and Water	J	I	234	Yellow Umbrella Books	Capstone Press
Earth's Place in Space	V	I	2535	Reading Street	Pearson
Earth's Riches	M	I	386	Gear Up!	Wright Group/McGraw Hill
Earth's Riches	P	I	250+	WorldScapes	ETA/Cuisenaire
Earth's Seasons & Cycles	S	I	250+	Time for Kids	Teacher Created Materials
Earth's Structure	T	I	2279	Science Support Readers	Houghton Mifflin Harcourt
Earth's Water Cycle	H	I	111	Discovering Nature's Cycles	Lerner Publishing Group
Earth's Water Cycle	M	I	757	Early Explorers	Benchmark Education
#Earth-Shaking Facts About Earthquakes with Max Axiom, Super Scientist; The	U	I	250+	Graphic Library	Capstone Press
Earthworm, The	H	I	157	Wonder World	Wright Group/McGraw Hill
Earthworms	O	I	250+	Holmes, Kevin J.	Red Brick Learning
Earthworms	J	I	185	Leveled Readers	Houghton Mifflin Harcourt
Earthworms	K	I	212	Rigby Focus	Rigby
Earthworms	I	I	156	Take Two Books	Wright Group/McGraw Hill
Earthworm's Life, An	K	I	250+	Himmelman, John	Scholastic
Earthworm's Life, An	K	I	250+	Nature Upclose	Children's Press
East Asia: Geography and Environments	W	I	250+	Reading Expeditions	National Geographic
East Asia: People and Places	X	I	250+	Reading Expeditions	National Geographic
East Meets West: Japan and America	M	I	396	Reading Street	Pearson
East of the Sun & West of the Moon	P	TL	250+	Mayer, Mercer	Aladdin
East of the Sun and West of the Moon	R	TL	250+	Hague, Kathleen & Michael	Harcourt Trade

TITLE	LEVEL	GENRE	WORD COUNT	AUTHOR / SERIES	PUBLISHER / DISTRIBUTOR
Easter	E	I	112	Fiesta Holiday Series	Pearson Learning Group
Easter	M	I	250+	Holidays and Celebrations	Picture Window Books
Easter	J	I	127	Holidays and Celebrations	Capstone Press
Easter	K	I	145	Holidays and Festivals	Heinemann Library
Easter Around the World	N	I	1494	On My Own Holidays	Lerner Publishing Group
Easter Bunny That Ate My Sister, The	Q	F	250+	Marney, Dean	Scholastic
Easter Bunny's Lost Egg	G	F	174	First Start	Troll Associates
Easter Island Odyssey	T	RF	250+	Reading Safari	Mondo Publishing
Easter Island: Giant Stone Statues Tell of a Rich and Tragic Past	W	I	250+	Arnold, Caroline	Houghton Mifflin Harcourt
Easy Cheese	J	I	271	Red Rocket Readers	Flying Start Books
Easy Origami	R	I	250+	Origami	Capstone Press
Eat and Run!	L	I	289	Vocabulary Readers	Houghton Mifflin Harcourt
Eat Fresh Food: Awesome Recipes for Teen Chefs	U	I	250+	Gold, Rozanne	Bloomsbury Children's Books
Eat It, Print It	B	I	70	Rigby Literacy	Rigby
Eat Right!: How You Can Make Good Food Choices	U	I	6703	Health Zone	Lerner Publishing Group
Eat Right, Feel Good	K	I	250+	Rosen Real Readers	Rosen Publishing Group
Eat to Win	T	I	250+	The News	Richard C. Owen
Eat Up!	G	RF	95	Sunshine	Wright Group/McGraw Hill
Eat Up, Chick!	I	F	274	Sun Sprouts	ETA/Cuisenaire
Eat Up, Gemma	I	RF	463	Hayes, Sarah	Sundance
Eat Your Broccoli	D	RF	72	Books for Young Learners	Richard C. Owen
Eat Your Peas, Louise	E	RF	83	Rookie Readers	Children's Press
Eat Your Peas, Please!	G	F	84	Pair-It Turn and Learn	Steck-Vaughn
Eat Your Vegetables	J	I	157	iOpeners	Pearson Learning Group
Eat Your Vegetables! Drink Your Milk!	P	I	250+	My Health	Franklin Watts
Eat Your Veggies	K	RF	704	Springboard	Wright Group/McGraw Hill
Eat!	M	RF	250+	Kroll, Steven	Hyperion
Eating	A	RF	29	Foundations	Wright Group/McGraw Hill
Eating	J	I	123	Small World	Lerner Publishing Group
Eating Apples	LB	I	17	Apples	Capstone Press
Eating Breakfast	B	I	18	Rosen Real Readers	Rosen Publishing Group
Eating Fish	B	I	37	Sails	Rigby
Eating Food	I	I	392	Sails	Rigby
Eating Green	C	F	88	Bonnell, Kris	Reading Reading Books
Eating Healthy Meals	P	I	1219	Vocabulary Readers	Houghton Mifflin Harcourt
Eating Healthy Meals	P	I	1219	Vocabulary Readers/CA	Houghton Mifflin Harcourt
Eating Lunch at School	I	RF	170	City Kids	Rigby
Eating Mud	D	I	35	Bonnell, Kris	Reading Reading Books
Eating Out	C	RF	31	Sunshine	Wright Group/McGraw Hill
Eating Right	H	I	151	The Food Guide Pyramid	Capstone Press
Eating Right	I	I	250+	Time for Kids	Teacher Created Materials
Eating Well	M	I	457	Pull Ahead Books	Lerner Publishing Group
Eating Well	H	I	214	Yellow Umbrella Books	Red Brick Learning
Eats	R	I	250+	Boldprint	Steck-Vaughn
Ebenezer and the Sneeze	D	RF	77	Story Box	Wright Group/McGraw Hill
Echohawk	X	HF	250+	Durrant, Lynda	Bantam Books
Echolocation: Animals Making Sound Waves	U	I	2125	Reading Street	Pearson
Eclipse	Z+	F	250+	Meyer, Stephanie	Little Brown and Company
Eclipses: Nature's Blackouts	T	I	250+	Aronson, Billy	Franklin Watts
Ecological Disasters	W	I	250+	Navigators Science Series	Benchmark Education
*Ecologists: From Woodward to Miranda	W	B	250+	Mission: Science	Compass Point Books

* Collection of short stories   # Graphic text
^ Mature content with lower level text demands

TITLE	LEVEL	GENRE	WORD COUNT	AUTHOR / SERIES	PUBLISHER / DISTRIBUTOR
Ecology: Earth's Balancing Act	T	I	250+	Kids Discover Reading	Wright Group/McGraw Hill
#Economix: How Our Economy Works (and Doesn't Work) in Words and Pictures	Z+	I	250+	Goodwin, Michael	Abrams Comicarts
Ecosystems	U	I	250+	Mission: Science	Compass Point Books
Ecosystems	T	I	250+	Pair-It Books	Steck-Vaughn
Ecosystems	U	I	250+	Reading Expeditions	National Geographic
Ecosystems of the Rain Forests	T	I	1790	Reading Street	Pearson
Ecosystems: Changing and Conserving	R	I	250+	ConceptLinks	Millmark Education
Ecosystems: Energy Flow and Use	R	I	250+	ConceptLinks	Millmark Education
Ecosystems: Food Chains and Food Webs	R	I	250+	ConceptLinks	Millmark Education
Ecosystems: Populations and Communities	R	I	250+	ConceptLinks	Millmark Education
Ed and Me	L	RF	250+	McPhail, David	Harcourt Brace
Ed Makes Shapes	F	RF	133	Early Connections	Benchmark Education
Eddie and Little Sam	C	F	39	Brand New Readers	Candlewick Press
Eddie and the Fire Engine	P	RF	250+	Haywood, Carolyn	Beech Tree Books
Eddie and the Jets	U	RF	26549	Attanas, John	Darby Creek Publishing
Eddie Digs a Hole	B	F	28	Brand New Readers	Candlewick Press
Eddie Elephant's Exciting Egg-Sitting	J	F	512	Animal Antics A To Z	Kane Press
Eddie in a Jam	C	F	31	Brand New Readers	Candlewick Press
Eddy's Hair	G	RF	322	Sails	Rigby
Edgar Allan Poe	X	B	250+	Just the Facts Biographies	Lerner Publishing Group
Edgar Badger's Balloon Day	K	F	864	Kulling, Monica	Mondo Publishing
Edgar Badger's Butterfly Day	K	F	250+	Kulling, Monica	Mondo Publishing
Edgar Badger's Fishing Day	K	F	250+	Kulling, Monica	Mondo Publishing
Edgar Badger's Fix-it Day	K	F	250+	Kulling, Monica	Mondo Publishing
Edge	T	B	250+	Stars of Pro Wrestling	Capstone Press
Edge of the Clearing, The	K	RF	760	Gear Up!	Wright Group/McGraw Hill
Edge of the Sword, The	Y	HF	250+	Tingle, Rebecca	Scholastic
Edible Pyramid, The: Good Eating Every Day	L	I	244	Leedy, Loreen	Holiday House
Edison's Gold	T	RF	250+	Watson, Geoff	Egmont USA
Edmond Went Splash	B	F	69	First Stories	Pacific Learning
^Edmund Hillary: Explorer on Top of the World	R	B	250+	Hameray Biography Series	Hameray Publishing Group
Edna Bakes Cookies	D	F	37	Brand New Readers	Candlewick Press
Edna Dances	C	F	25	Brand New Readers	Candlewick Press
Edna's Flowers	D	F	41	Brand New Readers	Candlewick Press
Edna's New Coat	D	F	39	Brand New Readers	Candlewick Press
Educating Arthur	J	F	250+	Soar To Success	Houghton Mifflin Harcourt
Edward and the Pirates	M	F	250+	McPhail, David	Little Brown and Company
Edward's Eyes	S	RF	250+	MacLachlan, Patricia	Aladdin
Edward's Night Light	M	RF	622	Reading Corners	Pearson Learning Group
Edwin and Emily	K	RF	250+	Williams, Suzanne	Hyperion
Edwina Victorious	O	RF	250+	Bonners, Susan	Farrar, Straus, & Giroux
Eeek! Look at This!	C	I	66	Rigby Star Quest	Rigby
Eek!	D	F	103	Lester the Lion Series	Pioneer Valley
Eek! Look at This!	C	I	66	Rigby Literacy	Rigby
Eels	I	I	200	Sails	Rigby
Eels	H	I	113	Under the Sea	Capstone Press
Eency Weency Spider	I	F	250+	Bank Street	Bantam Books
Eenie, Meanie, Murphy, NO!	S	RF	250+	McKenna, Colleen O'Shaughnessy	Scholastic
Eensy-Weensy Spider, The	K	TL	250+	Hoberman, Mary Ann	Little Brown and Company
Eeny, Meeny, Miney Mole	M	F	250+	Yolen, Jane	Harcourt Brace

E

TITLE	LEVEL	GENRE	WORD COUNT	AUTHOR / SERIES	PUBLISHER / DISTRIBUTOR
Effect of Gamma Rays on Man-in-the-Moon Marigolds, The	Z+	RF	250+	Zindel, Paul	Bantam Books
Effie	K	F	250+	Allison, Beverly	Scholastic
Egg	K	F	250+	Logan, Dick	Cypress
Egg Incubators	T	I	250+	Sails	Rigby
Egg Is Quiet, An	N	I	250+	Aston, Dianna	Scholastic
Egg Saga, The	N	RF	250+	Sails	Rigby
Egg To Chick	J	I	250+	Selsam, Millicent E.	HarperTrophy
Egg Watching	Q	RF	2840	Reading Street	Pearson
Egg, The	C	F	48	Joy Readers	Pearson Learning Group
Eggs	L	I	250+	HSP/Harcourt Trophies	Harcourt, Inc.
Eggs	F	F	81	Joy Starters	Pearson Learning Group
Eggs	C	I	87	Leveled Literacy Intervention/ Green System	Heinemann
Eggs	L	I	250+	Rigby Literacy	Rigby
Eggs	B	I	56	Sails	Rigby
Eggs	U	RF	250+	Spinelli, Jerry	Little Brown and Company
Eggs	C	I	30	Windows on Literacy	National Geographic
Eggs and Baby Birds	M	I	539	Sunshine	Wright Group/McGraw Hill
Eggs and Dandelions	F	F	182	PM Stars	Rigby
Eggs for Breakfast	D	I	126	PM Nonfiction-Red	Rigby
Eggs from the Chicken to You!	L	I	565	Rigby Flying Colors	Rigby
Eggs in the Hay	D	RF	69	Windows on Literacy	National Geographic
Eggs in the Sun	J	RF	384	Sails	Rigby
Eggs!	B	RF	28	Ready Readers	Pearson Learning Group
Eggs, Eggs, Eggs	H	I	248	Sails	Rigby
Eggs, Eggs, Eggs	J	I	188	Wonder World	Wright Group/McGraw Hill
Eggs, Larvae, and Flies	K	I	450	Sunshine	Wright Group/McGraw Hill
#Eggs, Legs, Wings: A Butterfly Life Cycle	M	I	250+	First Graphics	Capstone Press
Eggshell Garden, The	LB	RF	14	Sunshine	Wright Group/McGraw Hill
Egypt	P	I	2018	Country Explorers	Lerner Publishing Group
Egypt	Q	I	250+	First Reports: Countries	Compass Point Books
Egypt	W	I	250+	Primary Source Readers	Teacher Created Materials
Egypt (Ancient Civilizations)	W	I	250+	Theme Sets	National Geographic
Egypt (Cultures and Celebrations)	R	I	250+	Theme Sets	National Geographic
Egypt ABCs: A Book About the People and Places of Egypt	Q	I	250+	Country ABCs	Picture Window Books
Egypt Game, The	X	RF	250+	Snyder, Zilpha Keatley	Bantam Books
Egypt in Colors	N	I	250+	World of Colors	Capstone Press
Egypt in the Past and Present	S	I	250+	Reading Expeditions	National Geographic
Egypt, Nubia, and Kush	W	I	250+	Navigators Social Studies Series	Benchmark Education
Egypt: A Question and Answer Book	P	I	250+	Questions and Answers: Countries	Capstone Press
Egypt: Civilizations Past to Present	S	I	250+	Reading Expeditions	National Geographic
Egypt: Everyday Kids Now and Then	S	HF	250+	Reading Expeditions	National Geographic
Egypt: The Culture	U	I	250+	Kalman, Bobbie	Crabtree
Egypt: The Land	U	I	250+	Kalman, Bobbie	Crabtree
Egypt: The People	U	I	250+	Kalman, Bobbie	Crabtree
Egyptian Gods and Goddesses	N	I	250+	All Aboard Reading	Grosset & Dunlap
Egyptian Maus Are the Best!	Q	I	1327	The Best Cats Ever	Lerner Publishing Group
Egyptian News, The	W	I	250+	The History News	Candlewick Press
Egyptian Town	U	I	250+	Steedman, Scott	Franklin Watts
Egyptians, The: Life in Ancient Egypt	V	I	2010	Ancient Civilizations	Millbrook Press
Egypt's Greatest Treasure	Q	HF	250+	Lighthouse	Ginn & Co.

* Collection of short stories   # Graphic text
^ Mature content with lower level text demands

TITLE	LEVEL	GENRE	WORD COUNT	AUTHOR / SERIES	PUBLISHER / DISTRIBUTOR
Eidi	S	RF	250+	Bredsdorff, Bodil	Farrar, Straus, & Giroux
Eiffel Tower, The	M	I	191	Windows on Literacy	National Geographic
Eight Friends in All	D	RF	64	Ready Readers	Pearson Learning Group
Eight Little Legs	H	RF	137	Gravelle, Karen	Kaeden Books
*Eight Tales of Terror	Z+	F	250+	Poe, Edgar Allan	Scholastic
Eight Wild Nights: A Family Hanukkah Tale	N	RF	509	Cleary, Brian P	Kar-Ben Publishing
Eileen Collins: First Woman in Space	V	B	2488	Leveled Readers	Houghton Mifflin Harcourt
Einstein, Father of Physics	Z	B	250+	Independent Readers Science	Houghton Mifflin Harcourt
Einstein: Champion of the World	N	RF	250+	Trussell-Cullen, Alan	Pacific Learning
EJ and the Bully	L	F	1338	Auto-B-Good	Rising Star Studios
El Barrio	O	RF	373	Chocolate, Debbi	Henry Holt & Co.
*EL Bronx Remembered	Z	RF	250+	Mohr, Nicholas	HarperTrophy
El Camino Real	S	RF	2361	Leveled Readers	Houghton Mifflin Harcourt
El Camino Real	S	RF	2361	Leveled Readers/CA	Houghton Mifflin Harcourt
El Camino Real	S	RF	2361	Leveled Readers/TX	Houghton Mifflin Harcourt
El Chino	P	B	250+	Say, Allen	Houghton Mifflin Harcourt
El Greco	R	B	250+	Venezia, Mike	Children's Press
El Nino	I	RF	250+	Reading Safari	Mondo Publishing
El Sid and the Flea	V	RF	2632	Leveled Readers	Houghton Mifflin Harcourt
Elaine	J	I	250+	Stepping Stones	Nelson/Michaels Assoc.
Elaine and the Flying Frog	M	RF	250+	Chang, Heidi	Scholastic
Elbert's Bad Word	M	RF	250+	Wood, Audrey	Harcourt Trade
Eleanor	S	B	250+	Cooney, Barbara	Puffin Books
Eleanor Everywhere: The Life of Eleanor Roosevelt	O	B	250+	Step into Reading	Random House
Eleanor Roosevelt	U	B	250+	Blevins, Wiley	Scholastic
Eleanor Roosevelt	P	B	250+	Early Biographies	Compass Point Books
Eleanor Roosevelt	M	B	229	First Ladies	Capstone Press
Eleanor Roosevelt	S	B	3773	History Maker Bios	Lerner Publishing Group
Eleanor Roosevelt	N	B	250+	Pebble Books	Capstone Press
Eleanor Roosevelt	P	B	250+	Photo-Illustrated Biographies	Red Brick Learning
Eleanor Roosevelt	R	B	250+	Primary Source Readers	Teacher Created Materials
Eleanor Roosevelt: A Life of Discovery	W	B	250+	Freedman, Russell	Clarion
Eleanor Roosevelt: A Lifetime of Giving	Q	B	250+	Literacy by Design	Rigby
^Eleanor Roosevelt: A Modern First Lady	T	B	250+	Hameray Biography Series	Hameray Publishing Group
Eleanor Roosevelt: Fighter for Social Justice	O	B	250+	Childhood of Famous Americans	Aladdin
Eleanor Roosevelt: First Lady of the World	R	B	250+	Faber, Doris	Penguin Group
#Eleanor Roosevelt: First Lady of the World	T	B	250+	Graphic Library	Capstone Press
Eleanor Roosevelt: More Than a First Lady	P	B	250+	On Deck	Rigby
Eleanor's Story: An American Girl in Hitler's Germany	Y	B	250+	Garner, Eleanor Ramrath	Peachtree
Election Connection	T	I	250+	Ring, Susan	Chronicle Books
Election Day	Q	I	250+	Holiday Histories	Heinemann
Election Day	M	I	255	Holidays and Festivals	Heinemann Library
Election Day	H	RF	250+	McNamara, Margaret	Aladdin
Elections in the United States	W	I	250+	American Civics	Red Brick Learning
Electric Eels	O	I	2314	Early Bird Nature Books	Lerner Publishing Group
Electric Mischief	W	I	250+	Bartholomew, Alan	Kids Can Press
*Electric Spark and Other Cases, The	O	RF	250+	Simon, Seymour	Avon Books
Electricity	Q	I	2246	Early Bird Energy	Lerner Publishing Group
^Electricity	P	I	250+	Our Physical World	Capstone Press
Electricity	S	I	250+	Reading Expeditions	National Geographic
Electricity	Y	I	250+	Reading Street	Pearson
Electricity	R	I	1437	Science Support Readers	Houghton Mifflin Harcourt

E

TITLE	LEVEL	GENRE	WORD COUNT	AUTHOR / SERIES	PUBLISHER / DISTRIBUTOR
Electricity	O	I	250+	Sunshine	Wright Group/McGraw Hill
Electricity Adds Up	W	I	250+	Navigators Math Series	Benchmark Education
Electricity at Home	U	I	250+	Theme Sets	National Geographic
Electricity at Play	U	I	250+	Theme Sets	National Geographic
Electricity at School	U	I	250+	Theme Sets	National Geographic
Electricity at Work	U	I	250+	Theme Sets	National Geographic
Electricity Makes Things Work	N	I	250+	PM Plus Nonfiction	Rigby
Electricity Mystery, The	W	I	250+	Literacy By Design	Rigby
Electricity: Bulbs, Batteries, and Sparks	N	I	250+	Amazing Science	Picture Window Books
*Electrifying Cows and Other Cases, The	O	RF	250+	Simon, Seymour	Avon Books
Electrifying Personalities	S	B	250+	Navigators Biography Series	Benchmark Education
Electromagnetism	X	I	250+	Mission Science	Compass Point Books
Elements in Nature	V	I	1001	Leveled Readers Science	Houghton Mifflin Harcourt
Elements in Our Universe	Z	I	2755	Reading Street	Pearson
Elements, The	V	I	841	Leveled Readers Science	Houghton Mifflin Harcourt
Elena in America	O	HF	575	Leveled Readers	Houghton Mifflin Harcourt
Elena Makes Tortillas	A	I	18	Pacific Literacy	Pacific Learning
Elena's Two Homes	M	HF	250+	Leveled Readers Language Support	Houghton Mifflin Harcourt
Elena's Wish	J	RF	708	Leveled Readers	Houghton Mifflin Harcourt
Elena's Wish	J	RF	708	Leveled Readers/CA	Houghton Mifflin Harcourt
Elena's Wish	J	RF	708	Leveled Readers/TX	Houghton Mifflin Harcourt
Elephant	V	I	250+	Eyewitness Books	DK Publishing
Elephant	C	I	41	Zoozoo-Into the Wild	Cavallo Publishing
Elephant and Envelope	G	F	158	Start to Read	School Zone
Elephant and Mouse	B	F	50	Sails	Rigby
Elephant and the Bad Baby, The	J	F	250+	Hayes, Sarah	Sundance
Elephant and the Six Wise Men, The	L	TL	692	Rigby Flying Colors	Rigby
Elephant and Tiger	J	F	486	Leveled Literacy Intervention/ Blue System	Heinemann
Elephant Costume, The	A	RF	29	Leveled Readers	Houghton Mifflin Harcourt
Elephant Costume, The	A	RF	29	Leveled Readers/CA	Houghton Mifflin Harcourt
Elephant Dancer, The: A Story of Ancient India	O	HF	250+	Historical Tales	Picture Window Books
Elephant for the Holidays, An	I	F	118	Sunshine	Wright Group/McGraw Hill
Elephant in the Garden, An	Y	HF	250+	Morpurgo, Michael	Feiwel and Friends
Elephant in the House, An	J	F	546	Read Alongs	Rigby
Elephant in Trouble	H	F	98	First Start	Troll Associates
Elephant Man, The	V	HF	5400	Oxford Bookworms Library	Oxford University Press
Elephant on My Roof	L	F	250+	Harris, Erin	Red Cygnet Press
Elephant Orphanage, The	M	I	308	Pawprints Teal	Pioneer Valley
Elephant Play	E	F	35	Sun Sprouts	ETA/Cuisenaire
Elephant Rescue	J	RF	250+	Leveled Readers Language Support	Houghton Mifflin Harcourt
Elephant Run	Y	HF	250+	Smith, Roland	Hyperion
Elephant That Forgot, The	I	F	250+	Storyworlds	Heinemann
Elephant Trick	B	F	30	Sails	Rigby
Elephant Tricks	F	F	147	Sun Sprouts	ETA/Cuisenaire
Elephant Walk	C	RF	50	Rigby Literacy	Rigby
Elephant Walk	C	RF	51	Rigby Star	Rigby
Elephant Walk	L	I	250+	Storyteller Chapter Books	Wright Group/McGraw Hill
Elephant Walk	C	F	44	Sunshine	Wright Group/McGraw Hill
Elephants	I	I	125	African Animals	Capstone Press
Elephants	I	I	224	Foundations	Wright Group/McGraw Hill
Elephants	N	I	250+	Meadows, Graham; Vial, Claire	Pearson Learning Group

* Collection of short stories   # Graphic text
^ Mature content with lower level text demands

TITLE	LEVEL	GENRE	WORD COUNT	AUTHOR / SERIES	PUBLISHER / DISTRIBUTOR
Elephants	C	F	224	Phonics and Friends	Hampton Brown
Elephants	K	I	250+	PM Animal Facts: Turquoise	Rigby
Elephants	U	I	250+	The Untamed World	Steck-Vaughn
Elephants Are Coming, The	E	F	138	Little Readers	Houghton Mifflin Harcourt
Elephants Can't Hop	C	F	75	Sails	Rigby
Elephants Swim	L	I	108	Riley, Linda Capus	Houghton Mifflin Harcourt
Elephant's Trunk, An	C	F	31	Little Celebrations	Pearson Learning Group
Elephant's Trunk, An	D	I	49	Windows on Literacy	National Geographic
Elephant's Trunk, The	E	I	60	Seedlings	Continental Press
Elevator	D	F	90	Story Box	Wright Group/McGraw Hill
Eleven	U	RF	250+	Giff, Patricia Reilly	Yearling Books
Eleven	T	RF	250+	Myracle, Lauren	Puffin Books
Eleven Kids, One Summer	O	RF	250+	Martin, Ann M.	Scholastic
Eleven on a Team	H	RF	326	PM Math Readers	Rigby
Elf Realm: The Low Road	Y	F	250+	Kirk, Daniel	Amulet Books
Eli Explores God's World	I	RF	81	Eli's Books	Child 1st Publications
Eli Goes Fishing	I	RF	86	Eli's Books	Child 1st Publications
Eli Hears Music	I	RF	107	Eli's Books	Child 1st Publications
Eli Makes Cookies	I	RF	74	Eli's Books	Child 1st Publications
Eli Manning	P	B	1909	Amazing Athletes	Lerner Publishing Group
Eli Manning	U	B	250+	Sports Heroes and Legends	Lerner Publishing Group
Eli Meets His Shadow	G	RF	61	Eli's Books	Child 1st Publications
Eli Picks Berries	J	RF	183	Eli's Books	Child 1st Publications
Eli the Good	Z	HF	250+	House, Silas	Candlewick Press
Eli Whitney	R	B	250+	Amazing Americans	Wright Group/McGraw Hill
Eli Whitney	R	B	3896	History Maker Bios	Lerner Publishing Group
#Eli Whitney and the Cotton Gin	S	B	250+	Graphic Library	Capstone Press
Eli Whitney: American Inventor	U	B	250+	Let Freedom Ring	Capstone Press
Elie Wiesel: A Holocaust Survivor Cries Out for Peace	X	B	250+	High Five Reading	Red Brick Learning
Elijah McCoy	U	B	250+	Independent Readers Science	Houghton Mifflin Harcourt
Elijah McCoy: Inventor	N	B	250+	Beginning Biographies	Pearson Learning Group
Elijah of Buxton	W	HF	250+	Curtis, Christopher Paul	Scholastic
Eli's Cross Day	I	RF	94	Eli's Books	Child 1st Publications
Eli's Fall Day	I	RF	117	Eli's Books	Child 1st Publications
Eli's Spring Day	I	RF	84	Eli's Books	Child 1st Publications
Eli's Summer Day	J	RF	107	Eli's Books	Child 1st Publications
Eli's Winter Day	H	RF	102	Eli's Books	Child 1st Publications
*Elisa in the Middle	N	RF	250+	Hurwitz, Johanna	Penguin Group
Elisha Otis's Ups and Downs	U	I	1759	Leveled Readers	Houghton Mifflin Harcourt
Elissa and the Stone	R	RF	250+	PM Plus Chapter Books	Rigby
Eliza and the Dragonfly	M	RF	250+	Sharing Nature with Children	Dawn Publications
Eliza Pinckney	M	B	325	Independent Readers Social Studies	Houghton Mifflin Harcourt
Eliza the Hypnotizer	M	RF	250+	Granger, Michele	Scholastic
Elizabeth Blackwell	N	B	200	First Biographies	Capstone Press
Elizabeth Blackwell: A Life of Diligence	O	B	464	Pull Ahead Books	Lerner Publishing Group
#Elizabeth Blackwell: America's First Woman Doctor	R	B	250+	Graphic Library	Capstone Press
Elizabeth Blackwell: First Woman Doctor	O	B	250+	Greene, Carol	Children's Press
Elizabeth Blackwell: First Woman Doctor	Q	B	250+	High-Fliers	Pacific Learning
Elizabeth Blackwell: Girl Doctor	O	B	250+	Henry, Joanne Landers	Simon & Schuster
Elizabeth Cady Stanton	P	B	250+	Photo-Illustrated Biographies	Red Brick Learning

E

* Collection of short stories   # Graphic text
^ Mature content with lower level text demands

TITLE	LEVEL	GENRE	WORD COUNT	AUTHOR / SERIES	PUBLISHER / DISTRIBUTOR
Elizabeth Cady Stanton and Susan B. Anthony: Fighting Together for Women's Rights	P	B	250+	On Deck	Rigby
#Elizabeth Cady Stanton: Women's Rights Pioneer	T	B	250+	Graphic Library	Capstone Press
Elizabeth Leads the Way: Elizabeth Cady Stanton and the Right to Vote	O	B	250+	Stone, Tanya Lee	Henry Holt & Co.
Elizabeth the First: Queen of England	O	B	250+	Greene, Carol	Children's Press
Elizabeth's Stormy Ride	N	HF	815	Leveled Readers	Houghton Mifflin Harcourt
Elizabeth's Stormy Ride	N	HF	815	Leveled Readers/CA	Houghton Mifflin Harcourt
Elizabeth's Stormy Ride	N	HF	815	Leveled Readers/TX	Houghton Mifflin Harcourt
Elizabeti's Doll	M	RF	250+	Bebop Books	Lee & Low Books Inc.
Elizabite: Adventures of a Carnivorous Plant	K	F	250+	Rey, H. A.	Houghton Mifflin Harcourt
Eliza's Freedom Road	S	HF	250+	Nolen, Jerdine	Simon & Schuster
Eliza's Kindergarten Pet	L	RF	250+	McGinty, Alice B.	Marshall Cavendish
Elk Hunters, The	N	TL	434	Reading Street	Pearson
Ella and the Toy Rabbit	D	RF	108	PM Stars	Rigby
Ella Enchanted	U	F	250+	Levine, Gail Carson	HarperTrophy
Ella Kazoo Will NOT Brush Her Hair!	L	F	250+	Fox, Lee	Walker & Company
Ella Minnow Pea	Z	F	250+	Dunn, Mark	MacAdam/Cage Publishing
Ella the Rose Fairy: Rainbow Magic	L	F	250+	Meadows, Daisy	Scholastic
Ella the Superstar	I	F	239	Big Cat	Pacific Learning
Ella's Time Line	H	RF	101	Windows on Literacy	National Geographic
Ella's Trip to Israel	L	RF	453	Newman, Vivian	Kar-Ben Publishing
Ellen Craft's Escape from Slavery	S	HF	3752	History Seaks	Millbrook Press
Ellen Ochoa	L	B	250+	Biography	Benchmark Education
Ellen Ochoa	N	B	703	Leveled Readers Science	Houghton Mifflin Harcourt
Ellen Ochoa	G	B	250+	Welcome Books	Children's Press
Ellen Ochoa, Astronaut	M	B	726	Leveled Readers Science	Houghton Mifflin Harcourt
Ellen Ochoa: Reaching for the Stars	T	B	250+	Explore More	Wright Group/McGraw Hill
Ellen Tebbits	P	RF	250+	Cleary, Beverly	Dell
Ellie	Z	RF	250+	Borntrager, Mary Christner	Herald Press
Ellie and the Steel Drum	S	B	1344	Leveled Readers	Houghton Mifflin Harcourt
Ellie and the Steel Drum	S	B	1344	Leveled Readers/CA	Houghton Mifflin Harcourt
Ellie and the Steel Drum	S	B	1344	Leveled Readers/TX	Houghton Mifflin Harcourt
Ellie Brader Hates Mr. G.	R	RF	250+	Johnston, Janet	Pocket Books
Ellie McDoodle: Best Friends Fur-Ever	Q	RF	250+	Barshaw, Ruth McNally	Bloomsbury Children's Books
Ellie McDoodle: Have Pen, Will Travel	P	RF	250+	Barshaw, Ruth McNally	Bloomsbury Children's Books
Ellie McDoodle: New Kid in School	P	RF	250+	Barshaw, Ruth McNally	Bloomsbury Children's Books
Ellie's New Home	O	RF	250+	Orca Young Readers	Orca Books
Ellis Island	S	I	250+	A True Book	Children's Press
Ellis Island	V	I	250+	Cornerstones of Freedom	Children's Press
Ellis Island	N	I	250+	Early Connections	Benchmark Education
Ellis Island	N	I	263	Independent Readers Social Studies	Houghton Mifflin Harcourt
Ellis Island	V	I	250+	Jango-Cohen, Judith	Scholastic
Ellis Island	S	I	250+	Symbols of America	Marshall Cavendish
Ellis Island	U	I	250+	We The People	Compass Point Books
Ellis Island: Welcome to America	P	I	250+	Rosen Real Readers	Rosen Publishing Group
Elm River Airport	K	RF	603	Gear Up!	Wright Group/McGraw Hill
Elm Tree, The	K	RF	483	Gear Up!	Wright Group/McGraw Hill
Elmer	K	F	250+	McKee, David	Lothrop, Lee & Shepard
Elmer and Rose	L	F	514	McKee, David	Andersen Press USA

* Collection of short stories   # Graphic text
^ Mature content with lower level text demands

TITLE	LEVEL	GENRE	WORD COUNT	AUTHOR / SERIES	PUBLISHER / DISTRIBUTOR
Elmer and the Dragon	M	F	250+	Gannett, Ruth	Random House
Elmer and the Hippos	K	F	508	McKee, David	Andersen Press USA
Elmer's Special Day	K	F	452	McKee, David	Andersen Press USA
Elmo and the Cookies	C	F	35	Brand New Readers	Candlewick Press
Elmo Gets Dressed	C	F	40	Brand New Readers	Candlewick Press
Elmo's Elephant	L	RF	250+	Book Blazers	ETA/Cuisenaire
Elmo's Shoes	C	F	53	Brand New Readers	Candlewick Press
Eloise Greenfield: Poetry to Grow On	P	B	886	Leveled Readers	Houghton Mifflin Harcourt
Eloise Greenfield: The Music of Poetry	O	B	250+	Leveled Readers Language Support	Houghton Mifflin Harcourt
Elsewhere	Y	F	250+	Zevin, Gabrielle	Farrar, Straus, & Giroux
Elsie Piddock Skips in Her Sleep	T	F	250+	Farjeon, Eleanor	Candlewick Press
Elves and the Shoemaker, The	F	TL	214	Folk Tales	Pioneer Valley
#Elves and the Shoemaker, The	N	TL	250+	Graphic Spin	Stone Arch Books
Elves and the Shoemaker, The	J	TL	300	PM Tales and Plays-Turquoise	Rigby
Elves and the Shoemaker, The	I	TL	250+	Storyworlds	Heinemann
Elves and the Shoemaker, The: A Tale by the Brothers Grimm	K	TL	250+	Rigby Literacy	Rigby
*Elves and the Shoemaker, The	K	TL	622	New Way Orange	Steck-Vaughn
Elves and the Shoemakers, The	J	TL	250+	Rigby Star	Rigby
Elves Don't Wear Hard Hats	M	F	250+	Dadey, Debbie; Jones, Marcia Thornton	Scholastic
#Elvis	U	B	250+	Graphic Library	Capstone Press
Elvis and the Camping Trip	E	F	60	Rigby Star	Rigby
Elvis and the Scooter	C	F	83	Rigby Rocket	Rigby
Elvis and the Space Junk	I	F	250+	Rigby Star	Rigby
Elvis the Turnip and Me	N	F	250+	The Zack Files	Gosset & Dunlap
E-Mail Muddles the Mystery	N	RF	250+	Reading Safari	Mondo Publishing
E-Mail Pals	M	RF	250+	InfoTrek	ETA/Cuisenaire
E-Mails from the Teacher	N	RF	915	Leveled Readers	Houghton Mifflin Harcourt
E-Mails from the Teacher	N	RF	915	Leveled Readers/CA	Houghton Mifflin Harcourt
E-Mails from the Teacher	N	RF	915	Leveled Readers/TX	Houghton Mifflin Harcourt
Emako Blue	Z	RF	250+	Edge	Hampton Brown
Emancipation Proclamation, The	V	I	250+	Cornerstones of Freedom	Children's Press
Emancipation Proclamation, The	W	I	250+	Reading Expeditions	National Geographic
Emancipation Proclamation, The: Hope of Freedom for the Slaves	V	I	250+	Let Freedom Ring	Capstone Press
Emerald Cathedral, The	V	I	1983	Leveled Readers	Houghton Mifflin Harcourt
Emerald Throne, The	T	F	250+	Baldry, Cherith	Mondo Publishing
Emergencies	E	I	31	Safety	Lerner Publishing Group
Emergency	I	I	377	Red Rocket Readers	Flying Start Books
Emergency Medical Technicians	J	I	223	On Deck	Rigby
Emergency Vehicles	K	I	250+	PM Plus	Rigby
Emergency Workers	L	I	250+	Rigby Focus	Rigby
Emergency!	K	F	250+	Mayo, Margaret	Carolrhoda Books
EMI and the Rhino Scientist	W	I	250+	Scientists in the Field	Houghton Mifflin Harcourt
Emil	J	RF	250+	Stepping Stones	Nelson/Michaels Assoc.
Emil and Karl	Y	HF	250+	Glatshteyn, Yankev	Square Fish
Emilio and the River	J	RF	403	Sunshine	Wright Group/McGraw Hill
Emily and Alice	L	RF	250+	Champion, Joyce	Harcourt Trade
Emily Arrow Promises to Do Better This Year	M	RF	250+	Giff, Patricia Reilly	Bantam Books
Emily at School	L	RF	250+	Williams, Suzanne	Hyperion
Emily Can't Sleep	F	RF	124	Early Emergent, Set 2	Pioneer Valley
Emily Carr	X	B	250+	The Canadians	Fitzhenry & Whiteside
Emily Dickinson: American Poet	O	B	250+	Greene, Carol	Children's Press

TITLE	LEVEL	GENRE	WORD COUNT	AUTHOR / SERIES	PUBLISHER / DISTRIBUTOR
Emily Eyefinger	M	F	250+	Ball, Duncan	Aladdin
Emily Geiger's Dangerous Mission	T	I	1273	Leveled Readers/CA	Houghton Mifflin Harcourt
Emily Geiger's Dangerous Mission	T	I	1273	Leveled Readers/TX	Houghton Mifflin Harcourt
Emily Loved Yellow	I	RF	99	Sunshine	Wright Group/McGraw Hill
Emily Murphy	X	B	250+	The Canadians	Fitzhenry & Whiteside
Emily Rodda's Raven Hill Mysteries: Dirty Tricks	T	RF	250+	Rodda, Emily & Rowe, Kate	Scholastic
Emily the Emerald Fairy: Rainbow Magic	L	F	250+	Meadows, Daisy	Scholastic
Emily Windsnap and the Castle in the Mist	S	F	250+	Kessler, Liz	Candlewick Press
Emily Windsnap and the Monster from the Deep	S	F	250+	Kessler, Liz	Candlewick Press
Emily Windsnap and the Siren's Secret	S	F	250+	Kessler, Liz	Candlewick Press
Emily's Babysitter	C	RF	67	Emergent	Pioneer Valley
Emily's Balloon	I	RF	180	Sakai, Komako	Chronicle Books
Emily's Dream	P	HF	250+	Orca Young Readers	Orca Books
Emily's Runaway Imagination	P	F	250+	Cleary, Beverly	Avon Books
Emma	W	RF	10770	Dominoes two	Oxford University Press
Emma	L	RF	250+	Kesselman, Wendy	HarperTrophy
Emma Dilemma and the Camping Nanny	Q	RF	250+	Hermes, Patricia	Marshall Cavendish
Emma Dilemma and the New Nanny	Q	RF	250+	Hermes, Patricia	Marshall Cavendish
Emma Dilemma and the Soccer Nanny	Q	RF	250+	Hermes, Patricia	Marshall Cavendish
Emma Dilemma and the Two Nannies	Q	RF	250+	Hermes, Patricia	Marshall Cavendish
Emma Dilemma, the Nanny and the Secret Ferret	Q	RF	250+	Hermes, Patricia	Marshall Cavendish
Emma Dilemma, the Nanny, and the Best Horse Ever	Q	RF	250+	Hermes, Patricia	Marshall Cavendish
Emma Rides on the Erie Canal	T	HF	1904	Leveled Readers	Houghton Mifflin Harcourt
Emma the Easter Fairy: Rainbow Magic	L	F	250+	Meadows, Daisy	Scholastic
Emma, the Birthday Clown	M	RF	1887	Sunshine	Wright Group/McGraw Hill
Emma-Jean Lazarus Fell in Love	R	RF	250+	Tarshis, Lauren	Puffin Books
Emma-Jean Lazarus Fell Out of a Tree	R	RF	250+	Tarshis, Lauren	Dial/Penguin
Emmaline and the Bunny	M	F	250+	Hannigan, Katherine	Greenwillow Books
Emma's Emu	N	F	250+	First Flight	Fitzhenry & Whiteside
Emma's Friendwich	K	F	250+	I See I Learn	Charlesbridge
Emma's Problem	H	RF	190	Literacy 2000	Rigby
Emma's River	R	HF	250+	Hart, Alison	Peachtree
Emma's Strange Pet	J	RF	250+	Little, Jean	HarperTrophy
Emmy and the Home for Troubled Girls	T	F	250+	Jonell, Lynne	Henry Holt & Co.
Emmy and the Incredible Shrinking Rat	T	F	250+	Jonell, Lynne	Henry Holt & Co.
Emperor and the Nightingale, The	L	TL	250+	Literacy 2000	Rigby
Emperor Penguin	L	I	250+	A Day in the Life: Polar Animals	Heinemann Library
Emperor Penguins	K	I	250+	All Aboard Science Reader	Grosset & Dunlap
Emperor Penguins	L	I	420	Pull Ahead Books	Lerner Publishing Group
Emperor Penguins	S	I	912	Red Rocket Readers	Flying Start Books
Emperor Penguins	J	I	597	Vocabulary Readers	Houghton Mifflin Harcourt
Emperor Penguins	J	I	597	Vocabulary Readers/CA	Houghton Mifflin Harcourt
Emperor Penguins	J	I	597	Vocabulary Readers/TX	Houghton Mifflin Harcourt
Emperor's Birthday Suit, The	K	TL	250+	Wheeler, Cindy	Random House
Emperor's Code, The (The 39 Clues)	U	F	250+	Korman, Gordon	Scholastic
Emperor's Egg, The	O	I	250+	Read and Wonder	Candlewick Press
Emperor's New Clothes, The	K	TL	250+	Gross, Ruth Belov (Retold)	Scholastic
Emperor's New Clothes, The	K	TL	250+	Literacy by Design	Rigby
Emperor's New Clothes, The	J	TL	250+	Rigby Literacy	Rigby
Emperor's New Clothes, The	J	TL	571	Tales from Hans Andersen	Wright Group/McGraw Hill

* Collection of short stories   # Graphic text
^ Mature content with lower level text demands

TITLE	LEVEL	GENRE	WORD COUNT	AUTHOR / SERIES	PUBLISHER / DISTRIBUTOR
Emperor's New Clothes, The	M	TL	788	Traditional Tales	Pioneer Valley
Emperor's Painting, The: A Story of Ancient China	O	HF	250+	Historical Tales	Picture Window Books
Empire Builders	T	I	250+	Rigby Focus	Rigby
Empire State Building, The	N	I	495	Lightning Bolt Books	Lerner Publishing Group
Empty City, The: Survivors	U	F	250+	Hunter, Erin	HarperCollins
Empty Envelope, The	N	RF	250+	A to Z Mysteries	Random House
Empty Lot, The	M	RF	606	Leveled Readers	Houghton Mifflin Harcourt
Empty Lunch Box, The	C	RF	73	Storyworlds	Heinemann
Empty Pot, The	M	TL	250+	Demi	Henry Holt & Co.
EMTs	K	I	170	Bookworms	Marshall Cavendish
EMTs	M	I	401	Pull Ahead Books	Lerner Publishing Group
Emu Who Wanted to Be a Horse, The	J	F	250+	Voyages	SRA/McGraw Hill
Enchanted Horse, The	R	F	250+	Nabb, Magdalen	Hyperion
Encyclofact, The	I	I	124	Reading Safari	Mondo Publishing
*Encyclopedia Brown Boy Detective	P	RF	250+	Sobol, Donald J.	Bantam Books
*Encyclopedia Brown Carries On	P	RF	250+	Sobol, Donald J.	Bantam Books
*Encyclopedia Brown Finds the Clues	P	RF	250+	Sobol, Donald J.	Bantam Books
*Encyclopedia Brown Gets His Man	P	RF	250+	Sobol, Donald J.	Bantam Books
*Encyclopedia Brown Keeps the Peace	P	RF	250+	Sobol, Donald J.	Bantam Books
*Encyclopedia Brown Lends a Hand	P	RF	250+	Sobol, Donald J.	Bantam Books
*Encyclopedia Brown Saves the Day	P	RF	250+	Sobol, Donald J.	Bantam Books
*Encyclopedia Brown Sets the Pace	P	RF	250+	Sobol, Donald J.	Bantam Books
*Encyclopedia Brown Shows the Way	P	RF	250+	Sobol, Donald J.	Bantam Books
*Encyclopedia Brown Solves Them All	P	RF	250+	Sobol, Donald J.	Bantam Books
*Encyclopedia Brown Takes the Cake	P	RF	250+	Sobol, Donald J.	Bantam Books
*Encyclopedia Brown Takes the Case	P	RF	250+	Sobol, Donald J.	Bantam Books
*Encyclopedia Brown Tracks Them Down	P	RF	250+	Sobol, Donald J.	Bantam Books
*Encyclopedia Brown: Case of Pablo's Nose	P	RF	250+	Sobol, Donald J.	Scholastic
*Encyclopedia Brown: Case of the Dead Eagles	P	RF	250+	Sobol, Donald J.	Bantam Books
*Encyclopedia Brown: Case of the Disgusting Sneakers	P	RF	250+	Sobol, Donald J.	Bantam Books
*Encyclopedia Brown: Case of the Midnight Visitor	P	RF	250+	Sobol, Donald J.	Bantam Books
*Encyclopedia Brown: Case of the Mysterious Handprints	P	RF	250+	Sobol, Donald J.	Bantam Books
*Encyclopedia Brown: Case of the Secret Pitch	P	RF	250+	Sobol, Donald J.	Bantam Books
*Encyclopedia Brown: Case of the Sleeping Dog	P	RF	250+	Sobol, Donald J.	Scholastic
*Encyclopedia Brown: Case of the Slippery Salamander	P	RF	250+	Sobol, Donald J.	Scholastic
*Encyclopedia Brown: Case of the Treasure Hunt	P	RF	250+	Sobol, Donald J.	Bantam Books
*Encyclopedia Brown: Case of the Two Spies	P	RF	250+	Sobol, Donald J.	Bantam Books
*Encyclopedia Brown's Book of Strange But True Crimes	P	RF	250+	Sobol, Donald J.; Sobol, Rose	Scholastic
Encyclopedia Mythologica: Gods & Heroes	Y	I	250+	Reinhart, Matthew & Sabuda, Robert	Candlewick Press
Encyclopedia of a Rain Forest	N	I	250+	Rigby Literacy	Rigby
Encyclopedia of Animals, An	M	I	250+	Literacy by Design	Rigby
Encyclopedia of Animals, An	M	I	250+	On Our Way to English	Rigby
Encyclopedia of Birds, An	N	I	1021	In Step Readers	Rigby
Encyclopedia of Fantastic Fish	L	I	250+	Rigby Literacy	Rigby
Encyclopedia of Fantastic Fish	L	I	250+	Rigby Star Quest	Rigby
Encyclopedia of Fossils, An	O	I	250+	Literacy by Design	Rigby
Encyclopedia of Fossils, An	O	I	250+	On Our Way to English	Rigby
Encyclopedia of Life in the Smokies, An	P	I	250+	In Step Readers	Rigby

E

TITLE	LEVEL	GENRE	WORD COUNT	AUTHOR / SERIES	PUBLISHER / DISTRIBUTOR
Encyclopedia of New Year's Celebrations Around the World	T	I	250+	Literacy by Design	Rigby
Encyclopedia of Rocks, An	P	I	250+	Literacy by Design	Rigby
Encyclopedia of Tiny Creatures	J	I	250+	Discovery World	Rigby
End of the American Revolution	O	I	556	Leveled Readers Language Support	Houghton Mifflin Harcourt
End of the Beginning, The: Being the Adventures of a Small Snail (and an Even Smaller Ant)	Q	F	250+	Avi	Harcourt, Inc.
End of the Ice Age, The	U	I	2221	Independent Readers Science	Houghton Mifflin Harcourt
^End of the Line, The	T	F	250+	Crew, Gary	Stone Arch Books
End, The	C	RF	106	Tiger Cub	Peguis
Endangered Animals	N	I	250+	A New True Book	Children's Press
Endangered Animals	K	I	148	Early Connections	Benchmark Education
Endangered Animals	K	I	280	McNulty, Faith	Scholastic
Endangered Animals	T	I	1448	Reading Street	Pearson
Endangered Birds	O	I	250+	Wonder World	Wright Group/McGraw Hill
Endangered Desert Animals	R	I	250+	Taylor, Dave	Crabtree
Endangered Forest Animals	R	I	250+	Taylor, Dave	Crabtree
Endangered Grassland Animals	R	I	250+	Taylor, Dave	Crabtree
Endangered Island Animals	R	I	250+	Taylor, Dave	Crabtree
Endangered Mammals	P	I	250+	Rigby Focus	Rigby
Endangered Mountain Animals	R	I	250+	Taylor, Dave	Crabtree
Endangered Ocean Animals	R	I	250+	Taylor, Dave	Crabtree
Endangered or Extinct!	U	I	250+	The News	Richard C. Owen
Endangered Savannah Animals	R	I	250+	Taylor, Dave	Crabtree
Endangered Species	T	I	250+	Reading Expeditions	National Geographic
Endangered Wetland Animals	R	I	250+	Taylor, Dave	Crabtree
Endless Puzzle, The	J	RF	416	Leveled Readers	Houghton Mifflin Harcourt
Endless Steppe, The	Y	B	250+	Hautzig, Esther	HarperTrophy
Ends of the Earth	S	I	250+	The News	Richard C. Owen
Endurance: Shackleton's Antarctic Expedition	S	I	250+	Orbit Chapter Books	Pacific Learning
Endurance: Shipwreck and Survival on a Sea of Ice	T	I	250+	High Five Reading	Red Brick Learning
Enduro Racing	Q	I	250+	Dirt Bikes	Capstone Press
Energized!	S	I	250+	Reading Expeditions	National Geographic
Energy	X	I	250+	Mission: Science	Compass Point Books
^Energy	P	I	250+	Our Physical World	Capstone Press
Energy	P	I	250+	Sails	Rigby
Energy	Y	I	250+	The Heinle Reading Library	Thomson Learning
Energy and Me	U	I	250+	The News	Richard C. Owen
Energy and Weather	T	I	1828	Science Support Readers	Houghton Mifflin Harcourt
Energy at the Airport	W	I	250+	Theme Sets	National Geographic
Energy at the Sports Arena	W	I	250+	Theme Sets	National Geographic
Energy Chain	S	I	250+	Bookweb	Rigby
Energy Contest, The	K	RF	564	In Step Readers	Rigby
Energy for the Future	O	I	250+	Rigby Focus	Rigby
Energy in Ecosystems	Q	I	1106	Science Support Readers	Houghton Mifflin Harcourt
Energy in the Factory	W	I	250+	Theme Sets	National Geographic
Energy in the Home	W	I	250+	Theme Sets	National Geographic
Energy Resources	V	I	1964	Science Support Readers	Houghton Mifflin Harcourt
Energy Stars, The	U	RF	250+	Reading Expeditions	National Geographic
Energy That Warms Us, The: A Look at Heat	M	I	250+	Lightning Bolt Books	Lerner Publishing Group
Energy We See, The: A Look at Light	N	I	250+	Lightning Bolt Books	Lerner Publishing Group
Energy: Heat, Light, and Fuel	M	I	250+	Amazing Science	Picture Window Books

E

* Collection of short stories   # Graphic text
^ Mature content with lower level text demands

TITLE	LEVEL	GENRE	WORD COUNT	AUTHOR / SERIES	PUBLISHER / DISTRIBUTOR
Enforcing Rules	M	I	549	Early Explorers	Benchmark Education
Engelbert the Hero	H	F	113	Little Celebrations	Pearson Learning Group
Engelbert's Exercises	E	F	23	Little Celebrations	Pearson Learning Group
Engines	E	I	81	Sunshine	Wright Group/McGraw Hill
England	Q	I	250+	First Reports: Countries	Compass Point Books
England	P	I	250+	Many Cultures, One World	Capstone Press
England: A Question and Answer Book	P	I	250+	Questions and Answers: Countries	Capstone Press
English Channel, The	M	I	433	Reading Street	Pearson
English Colonies in the Armericas	S	I	250+	On Deck	Rigby
English Springer Spaniels	I	I	139	Dogs	Capstone Press
Enigma: A Magical Mystery	S	F	250+	Base, Graeme	Harry N. Abrams
Enormous Crocodile, The	N	F	250+	Dahl, Roald	Penguin Group
Enormous Egg, The	R	F	250+	Butterworth, Oliver	Little Brown and Company
Enormous Egg, The	C	F	52	Learn to Read	Creative Teaching Press
Enormous Turnip, The	H	TL	250+	Green Light Readers	Harcourt
Enormous Turnip, The	H	TL	431	Hunia, Fran	Ladybird Books
Enormous Turnip, The	H	TL	250+	Storyworlds	Heinemann
Enormous Turnip, The	H	TL	250+	Tolstoy, Alexei	Collins Publishing Group
Enormous Watermelon, The	H	TL	304	Traditional Tales & More	Rigby
Enrique Esparza and the Battle of the Alamo	S	HF	3957	History Speaks	Millbrook Press
Entertainment Then and Now	U	I	1627	Vocabulary Readers	Houghton Mifflin Harcourt
Entertainment Then and Now	U	I	1627	Vocabulary Readers/CA	Houghton Mifflin Harcourt
Entomologist Danny	F	F	77	Coulton, Mia	Maryruth Books
Environment, The	Y	I	250+	From Fail to Win! Learning from Bad Ideas	Raintree
Environmental Disasters	W	I	8442	Disasters Up Close	Lerner Publishing Group
Environmentalism: How You Can Make a Difference	S	I	250+	Take Action	Capstone Press
Environmentally Friendly World	L	F	929	Early Connections	Benchmark Education
E-Pals	L	RF	347	Reading Street	Pearson
E-Pals Across the World	P	I	250+	Literacy by Design	Rigby
Epic	X	SF	250+	Kostick, Conor	Penguin Group
Equal Parts	I	I	233	Shutterbug Books	Steck-Vaughn
Equal Shmequal	L	F	250+	Kroll, Virginia	Charlesbridge
Equality in American Schools	X	I	1597	Reading Street	Pearson
Eragon	Y	F	250+	Paolini, Christopher	Alfred A. Knopf
Erana's Land: A Story from New Zealand	S	RF	250+	Reading Expeditions	National Geographic
Ereth's Birthday	S	F	250+	Avi	HarperTrophy
Eric's Birthday	H	RF	77	City Stories	Rigby
Eric's Greek Travel Diary	T	RF	250+	PM Extensions	Rigby
Eric's Thai Travel Diary	T	RF	250+	PM Extensions	Rigby
Erie Canal, The	N	I	550	Lightning Bolt Books	Lerner Publishing Group
Erik and the Three Goats	H	F	257	Ready Readers	Pearson Learning Group
Erik's Story: From Sweden to Minnesota	T	HF	250+	Reading Expeditions	National Geographic
Erin Meets Tiffy	D	RF	104	PM Photo Stories	Rigby
Erin Rides Tiffy	F	RF	154	PM Photo Stories	Rigby
Er-Lang and the Suns: A Tale from China	M	TL	250+	Folk Tales	Mondo Publishing
Ernesto the Engine	C	F	50	Reading Safari	Mondo Publishing
Ernie and the Nighttime Noises	B	F	28	Brand New Readers	Candlewick Press
Ernie and the Tracks	C	F	31	Brand New Readers	Candlewick Press
Erosion	R	I	1896	Early Bird Earth Systems	Lerner Publishing Group
Erosion	M	I	250+	Early Connections	Benchmark Education
Erosion	Q	I	250+	Exploring the Earth	Capstone Press

TITLE	LEVEL	GENRE	WORD COUNT	AUTHOR / SERIES	PUBLISHER / DISTRIBUTOR
Erosion	L	I	300	Independent Readers Social Studies	Houghton Mifflin Harcourt
Erosion Shapes the Earth	N	I	882	Pair-It Turn and Learn	Steck-Vaughn
Erosion: The Changing Shape of the Land	M	I	250+	Explorations	Okapi Educational Materials
Erosion: The Changing Shape of the Land	M	I	250+	Explorations	Eleanor Curtain Publishing
Errol the Peril	Q	F	250+	Literacy 2000	Rigby
Ersatz Elevator, The	V	F	250+	Snicket, Lemony	Scholastic
Eruption	R	I	250+	Wildcats	Wright Group/McGraw Hill
Eruption of Mount St. Helens, The	V	HF	250+	Reading Expeditions	National Geographic
Eruption: Storm Runners	U	RF	250+	Smith, Roland	Scholastic
Eruptions!	P	I	729	Red Rocket Readers	Flying Start Books
Escalator Escapade	N	RF	250+	Girlz Rock!	Mondo Publishing
Escalator, The	A	RF	23	Story Box	Wright Group/McGraw Hill
Escape	T	I	250+	Trackers	Pacific Learning
Escape by Night: A Civil War Adventure	T	HF	250+	Myers, Laurie	Henry Holt & Co.
Escape from Castle Cant	S	F	250+	Bath, K.P.	Little Brown and Company
Escape from Death Valley	M	I	419	Books for Young Learners	Richard C. Owen
#Escape From Pyramid X	U	F	11500	Twisted Journeys	Graphic Universe
Escape From Slavery: Five Journeys to Freedom	Q	B	250+	Rappaport, Doreen	HarperTrophy
Escape from the Comics	Q	RF	250+	Bookweb	Rigby
^Escape from the Dark	W	F	250+	Dark Man	Stone Arch Books
^Escape from the Dark	W	F	250+	Dark Man	Ransom Publishing
Escape from the Deep	O	SF	1715	Take Two Books	Wright Group/McGraw Hill
Escape from the Nazis	Y	I	1620	Vocabulary Readers	Houghton Mifflin Harcourt
Escape from the Nazis	Y	I	1620	Vocabulary Readers/CA	Houghton Mifflin Harcourt
Escape from the Nazis	Y	I	1620	Vocabulary Readers/TX	Houghton Mifflin Harcourt
^Escape from the Pop-Up Prison	T	F	250+	Dahl, Michael	Stone Arch Books
Escape from the Tower	W	HF	250+	WorldScapes	ETA/Cuisenaire
Escape From the Zoo	E	F	108	Springboard	Wright Group/McGraw Hill
Escape from Vesuvius	U	HF	250+	PM Plus	Rigby
Escape of the Deadly Dinosaur, The	P	SF	250+	Secret Agent Jack Stalwart	Weinstein Books
Escape the Mask (The Grassland Trilogy)	X	F	250+	Ward, David	Amulet Books
Escape to Canada	P	I	513	Vocabulary Readers	Houghton Mifflin Harcourt
Escape to Freedom	V	HF	250+	Davis, Ossie	Puffin Books
Escape to Freedom: The Underground Railroad	S	I	250+	Navigators Social Studies Series	Benchmark Education
Escape!	V	I	250+	InfoQuest	Rigby
Escape!	N	SF	250+	Orbit Chapter Books	Pacific Learning
e-search	S	F	250+	Storyteller-Autumn Leaves	Wright Group/McGraw Hill
ESP	Z	I	8314	The Unexplained	Lerner Publishing Group
ESP TV	R	SF	250+	Rodgers, Mary	HarperTrophy
Esperanza Rising	V	HF	250+	Ryan, Pam Munoz	Scholastic
Estuary Food Chain, An: A Who-Eats-What Adventure in North America	U	I	6445	Follow That Food Chain	Lerner Publishing Group
Ethan Frome	Z	RF	10700	Oxford Bookworms Library	Oxford University Press
Ethan's Bike	C	RF	43	Brand New Readers	Candlewick Press
Ethan's Birds	C	RF	38	Brand New Readers	Candlewick Press
Ethan's Cat	C	RF	41	Brand New Readers	Candlewick Press
Ethan's Lunch	C	RF	30	Brand New Readers	Candlewick Press
Ethel the Emu	K	RF	1700	Wiley, Pamela	Kaeden Books
Ethiopia: A Question and Answer Book	P	I	250+	Questions & Answers: Countries	Capstone Press
Ettabetta's Pen Pal	F	RF	184	The Rowland Reading Program Library	Rowland Reading Foundation

* Collection of short stories   # Graphic text
^ Mature content with lower level text demands

Eugenie Clark Shark Lady	N	I	566	Leveled Literacy Intervention/ Blue System	Heinemann
Eureka!	Q	I	250+	Orbit Collections	Pacific Learning
Eureka! It's an Airplane	T	I	250+	Bendick, Jeanne	Scholastic
Eureka! It's Television!	T	I	250+	Bendick, Jeanne & Robert	Scholastic
Eureka! Stories of Everyday Inventions	P	I	250+	Literacy 2000	Rigby
Europe	N	I	250+	Continents	Capstone Press
Europe	N	I	330	Pull Ahead Books	Lerner Publishing Group
Europe and Russia: Geography and Environments	W	I	250+	Reading Expeditions	National Geographic
Europe and Russia: People and Places	X	I	250+	Reading Expeditions	National Geographic
Europe: Geography of Conquest	X	I	1830	Leveled Readers Social Studies	Houghton Mifflin Harcourt
Eva	Z	F	250+	Dickenson, Eva	Laurel-Leaf Books
Eva and Max	C	RF	27	Appleton-Smith, Laura	Flyleaf Publishing
Eva Perón: First Lady of the People	P	B	250+	Great Hispanics	Capstone Press
Eva the Beekeeper	J	I	250+	iOpeners	Pearson Learning Group
Evangeline Mudd's Great Mink Rescue	U	F	250+	Elliott, David	Candlewick Press
Eva's Lost and Found Report	K	F	250+	On Our Way to English	Rigby
Eve Shops	F	RF	146	Ready Readers	Pearson Learning Group
Evelyn Cisneros: Prima Ballerina	P	B	250+	Great Hispanics	Capstone Press
Even Bread Has a Home	M	F	1888	Take Two Books	Wright Group/McGraw Hill
Even Steven and Odd Todd	K	F	250+	Cristaldi, Kathryn	Scholastic
Evening Meals Around the World	M	I	250+	Meals Around the World	Picture Window Books
Evening Song	L	RF	115	Books for Young Learners	Richard C. Owen
Ever-After Bird, The	Y	HF	250+	Rinaldi, Ann	Houghton Mifflin Harcourt
Everafter War, The: The Sisters Grimm	U	F	250+	Buckley, Michael	Amulet Books
Everest	V	I	250+	PM Collection	Rigby
Everest Adventures	T	I	250+	WorldScapes	ETA/Cuisenaire
Everest Challenge	Q	I	489	Vocabulary Readers	Houghton Mifflin Harcourt
Everglades	T	I	250+	George, Jean Craighead	HarperTrophy
Everglades, The	M	I	250+	Early Connections	Benchmark Education
Everglades, The	M	I	427	Lightning Bolt Books	Lerner Publishing Group
Evergreens	E	I	81	Bonnell, Kris/About	Reading Reading Books
Everlasting Now, The	U	HF	250+	Harrell Banks, Sara	Peachtree
Evermore: The Immortals	Z+	F	250+	Noel, Alyson	St. Martin's Griffin
Every Bird Has a Beak	E	I	49	Birds Series	Pearson Learning Group
Every Bird Has Feathers	E	I	50	Birds Series	Pearson Learning Group
Every Bird Has Two Feet	E	I	46	Birds Series	Pearson Learning Group
Every Body Tells a Story	R	I	250+	Explorers	Wright Group/McGraw Hill
Every Cat	F	RF	91	Instant Readers	Harcourt School Publishers
Every Cloud Has a Silver Lining	Q	RF	250+	Mazer, Anne	Scholastic
Every Day But Sunday	E	RF	83	Home Connection Collection	Rigby
Every Flower is Beautiful	K	TL	250+	Turner, Teresa	Steck-Vaughn
Every Girl Tells a Story: A Celebration of Girls Speaking Their Minds	W	I	250+	Jones, Carolyn	Simon & Schuster
Every Kind of Wish	K	RF	664	Leveled Readers	Houghton Mifflin Harcourt
Every Kind of Wish	K	RF	664	Leveled Readers/CA	Houghton Mifflin Harcourt
Every Kind of Wish	K	RF	664	Leveled Readers/TX	Houghton Mifflin Harcourt
*Every Living Thing	R	RF	250+	Rylant, Cynthia	Aladdin
Every Monday	C	F	52	Pair-It Books	Steck-Vaughn
Every Morning	A	I	30	Twig	Wright Group/McGraw Hill
Every Mother Bird Builds a Nest	E	I	62	Birds Series	Pearson Learning Group
Every Shape and Size	G	I	97	Wonder World	Wright Group/McGraw Hill
Every Soul a Star	U	RF	250+	Mass, Wendy	Little Brown and Company

E

TITLE	LEVEL	GENRE	WORD COUNT	AUTHOR / SERIES	PUBLISHER / DISTRIBUTOR
Every Tree Has a Life Cycle	E	I	92	Early Explorers	Benchmark Education
Everybody Bakes Bread	M	RF	1828	Dooley, Norah	Carolrhoda Books
Everybody Brings Noodles	M	RF	1887	Dooley, Norah	Carolrhoda Books
Everybody Cooks Rice	M	RF	1041	Dooley, Norah	Scholastic
Everybody Dances	T	I	250+	Literacy 2000	Rigby
Everybody Eats Bread	J	I	241	Literacy 2000	Rigby
Everybody Makes Soup	M	RF	2416	Dooley, Norah	Carolrhoda Books
Everybody Says	G	RF	70	Rookie Readers	Children's Press
Everybody Wears Braids	B	RF	30	Bebop Books	Lee & Low Books Inc.
Everybody Wins!	M	RF	250+	Math Matters	Kane Press
Everybody Wins! The Story of Special Olympics	S	I	1734	Reading Street	Pearson
Everybody Works	I	I	82	Shelley Rotner's Early Childhood Library	Millbrook Press
Everyday	D	I	45	Bonnell, Kris	Reading Reading Books
Everyday Forces	M	I	250+	Discovery World	Rigby
Everyday Hero	I	I	249	Vocabulary Readers	Houghton Mifflin Harcourt
Everyday Hero	I	I	249	Vocabulary Readers/CA	Houghton Mifflin Harcourt
Everyday Hero	I	I	249	Vocabulary Readers/TX	Houghton Mifflin Harcourt
Everyday Inventions	N	I	641	Vocabulary Readers	Houghton Mifflin Harcourt
Everyday Inventions	N	I	641	Vocabulary Readers/CA	Houghton Mifflin Harcourt
Everyday Inventions	N	I	641	Vocabulary Readers/TX	Houghton Mifflin Harcourt
Everyday Machines	J	I	188	Rigby Focus	Rigby
Everyday Math	D	I	102	Early Connections	Benchmark Education
Everyday Patterns	F	I	110	Early Connections	Benchmark Education
Everyone	J	F	553	Sun Sprouts	ETA/Cuisenaire
Everyone Can Help	K	I	250+	HSP/Harcourt Trophies	Harcourt, Inc.
Everyone Eats	C	I	44	Discovery Links	Newbridge
Everyone Eats Bread	G	I	139	Yellow Umbrella Books	Red Brick Learning
Everyone Else's Parents Said Yes	U	RF	250+	Danziger, Paula	PaperStar
Everyone Is a Scientist	I	I	197	Yellow Umbrella Books	Red Brick Learning
Everyone Is Coming	B	I	21	On Our Way to English	Rigby
Everyone Is Reading	H	RF	225	Cambridge Reading	Pearson Learning Group
Everyone Is Special	K	RF	155	Dominie Readers	Pearson Learning Group
Everyone Knows About Cars	L	I	176	Bookshop	Mondo Publishing
Everyone Says Sh-h-h!	E	RF	93	Rigby Literacy	Rigby
Everyone Says Sh-h-h-h!	E	RF	93	Literacy By Design	Rigby
Everyone Uses Math	G	I	211	Yellow Umbrella Books	Red Brick Learning
Everyone Uses Services	L	I	252	Larkin, Bruce	Wilbooks
Everyone Wears Wool	A	I	21	Pair-It Books	Steck-Vaughn
Everything Beautiful	Z+	RF	250+	Howell, Simone	Bloomsbury Children's Books
Everything Cat: What Kids Really Want to Know About Cats	R	I	250+	Crisp, Marty	NorthWord Press
Everything Changes	L	I	250+	Discovery World	Rigby
Everything Dog: What Kids Really Want to Know About Dogs	R	I	250+	Crisp, Marty	NorthWord Press
Everything for a Dog	T	F	250+	Martin, Ann M.	Feiwel and Friends
Everything Is Fine	Z+	RF	250+	Ellis, Ann Dee	Little Brown and Company
Everything Is Made of Matter	M	I	250+	Windows on Literacy	National Geographic
Everything Is Matter!	L	I	226	Yellow Umbrella Books	Capstone Press
Everything Machine, The	L	F	250+	Novak, Matt	Roaring Brook Press
Everything New Under the Sun	Q	RF	250+	Mazer, Anne	Scholastic
Everything on a Waffle	V	RF	250+	Horvath, Polly	Farrar, Straus, & Giroux

* Collection of short stories   # Graphic text
^ Mature content with lower level text demands

TITLE	LEVEL	GENRE	WORD COUNT	AUTHOR / SERIES	PUBLISHER / DISTRIBUTOR
Everything You Need to Know About Science	S	I	250+	Goldsmith, Mike	Kingfisher
Everywhere	R	RF	250+	Brooks, Bruce	Scholastic
Everywhere You Look	H	I	191	Sunshine	Wright Group/McGraw Hill
Evidence of Plate Tectonics	W	I	2446	Science Support Readers	Houghton Mifflin Harcourt
Evie the Mist Fairy: Rainbow Magic	L	F	250+	Meadows, Daisy	Scholastic
Evil Genius	Z	SF	250+	Jinks, Catherine	Houghton Mifflin Harcourt
Evil Queen Tut and the Great Ant Pyramids	N	F	250+	The Zack Files	Grosset & Dunlap
Evolution of Calpurnia Tate, The	Y	HF	250+	Kelly, Jaqueline	Henry Holt & Co.
Evolution, Me & Other Freaks of Nature	Y	RF	250+	Brande, Robin	Alfred A. Knopf
Evvy's Civil War	X	HF	250+	Brenaman, Miriam	G.P. Putnam's Sons Books for Young Readers
Exactly Right	I	RF	250+	Reading Safari	Mondo Publishing
Excavating a Castle	T	RF	250+	Reading Expeditions	National Geographic
Excuses, Excuses	E	RF	104	Tadpoles	Rigby
Exercise Time	O	F	250+	Sails	Rigby
Exercising	L	I	390	Pull Ahead Books	Lerner Publishing Group
Exile: Guardians of Ga'Hoole	V	F	250+	Lasky, Kathryn	Scholastic
^Exit Point	Z+	RF	250+	Orca Soundings	Orca Books
Exodus	Y	SF	250+	Bertagna, Julie	Walker & Company
Exotic Cats	R	I	250+	All About Cats	Capstone Press
Exotic Cats	I	I	104	Cats	Capstone Press
Exotic Tropical Fish	L	I	250+	Marine Life for Young Readers	Pearson Learning Group
Expanding the Nation	U	I	250+	Primary Source Readers	Teacher Created Materials
Expect the Unexpected	Q	I	250+	Orbit Double Takes	Pacific Learning
Expeditions in the Americas : 1492-1700	V	I	250+	Reading Expeditions	National Geographic
Experiment with Movement	Q	I	250+	Murphy, Bryan	Scholastic
Experiment with Water	Q	I	250+	Murphy, Bryan	Scholastic
Experiments on Myself	R	I	250+	High-Fliers	Pacific Learning
Experiments with Electricity	S	I	250+	A True Book	Children's Press
Experiments with Liquids	P	I	250+	Taylor-Butler, Christine/My Science Investigations	Heinemann Library
Experiments with Magnets and Metal	P	I	250+	Taylor-Butler, Christine/My Science Investigations	Heinemann Library
Experiments with Plants	P	I	250+	Taylor-Butler, Christine/My Science Investigations	Heinemann Library
Experiments with Rocks	P	I	250+	Taylor-Butler, Christine/My Science Investigations	Heinemann Library
Experiments with Soil	P	I	250+	Taylor-Butler, Christine/My Science Investigations	Heinemann Library
Experiments with Sound	S	I	3457	Take Two Books	Wright Group/McGraw Hill
Exploration	V	I	250+	High-Fliers	Pacific Learning
Exploration	M	I	160	Windows on Literacy	National Geographic
Exploration and Conquest: The Americas After Columbus, 1500-1620	T	I	250+	Maestro, Betsy & Giulio	William Morrow
Exploration: Questing for Knowledge	R	I	250+	Explore More	Wright Group/McGraw Hill
Explore	Z	I	250+	Caller, Sean, Gifford, Clive & Goldsmith, Dr. Mike	Kingfisher
Explore the Deciduous Forest	Q	I	250+	Explore the Biomes	Capstone Press
Explore the Desert	Q	I	250+	Explore the Biomes	Capstone Press
Explore the Galaxy	N	I	580	Reading Street	Pearson
Explore the Grasslands	Q	I	250+	Explore the Biomes	Capstone Press
Explore the Midwest	Q	I	250+	Reading Expeditions	National Geographic
Explore the Northeast	Q	I	250+	Reading Expeditions	National Geographic
Explore the Ocean	Q	I	250+	Explore the Biomes	Capstone Press
Explore the Southeast	Q	I	250+	Reading Expeditions	National Geographic

E

TITLE	LEVEL	GENRE	WORD COUNT	AUTHOR / SERIES	PUBLISHER / DISTRIBUTOR
Explore the Southwest	Q	I	250+	Reading Expeditions	National Geographic
Explore the Tropical Rain Forest	Q	I	250+	Explore the Biomes	Capstone Press
Explore the Tundra	Q	I	250+	Explore the Biomes	Capstone Press
Explore the West	Q	I	250+	Reading Expeditions	National Geographic
Explore the Wild West	S	I	250+	Explorer Books-Pathfinder	National Geographic
Explore the Wild West	R	I	250+	Explorer Books-Pioneer	National Geographic
Explore Your World	V	I	250+	iOpeners	Pearson Learning Group
Explore!	I	I	150	Avenues	Hampton Brown
Explorer	X	I	250+	Eyewitness Books	DK Publishing
Explorer of Glaciers	U	B	2110	Leveled Readers	Houghton Mifflin Harcourt
Explorer of Glaciers	U	B	2110	Leveled Readers/CA	Houghton Mifflin Harcourt
Explorer of Glaciers	U	B	2110	Leveled Readers/TX	Houghton Mifflin Harcourt
Explorer of the Gobi	X	B	3142	Leveled Readers	Houghton Mifflin Harcourt
Explorer of the Gobi	X	B	3142	Leveled Readers/CA	Houghton Mifflin Harcourt
Explorer of the Gobi	X	B	3142	Leveled Readers/TX	Houghton Mifflin Harcourt
Explorer, The	F	RF	73	City Stories	Rigby
Explorers News	W	I	250+	The History News	Candlewick Press
Explorers of the Americas	T	B	250+	Navigators Social Studies Series	Benchmark Education
Explorers, The (Dinotopia)	T	F	250+	Ciencin, Scott	Random House
Explorers: Searching for Adventure	M	I	250+	Pair-It Books	Steck-Vaughn
*Explorers: Women in Profile	T	B	250+	Hacker, Carlotta	Crabtree
Exploring a Park	H	I	65	Vocabulary Readers	Houghton Mifflin Harcourt
Exploring an Ocean Tide Pool	W	I	250+	Bendick, Jeanne	Henry Holt & Co.
Exploring Antarctica	P	I	745	Leveled Readers	Houghton Mifflin Harcourt
Exploring Antarctica	P	I	745	Leveled Readers/CA	Houghton Mifflin Harcourt
Exploring Antarctica	P	I	745	Leveled Readers/TX	Houghton Mifflin Harcourt
Exploring Black Holes	R	I	1262	Searchlight Books	Lerner Publishing Group
Exploring Brazil	X	I	2434	Reading Street	Pearson
Exploring Caves	Q	I	250+	Explorer Books-Pathfinder	National Geographic
Exploring Caves	P	I	250+	Explorer Books-Pioneer	National Geographic
Exploring Dangers in Space: Asteroids, Space Junk, and More	Q	I	1311	Searchlight Books	Lerner Publishing Group
Exploring Earth's Oceans	Z	I	2880	Vocabulary Readers	Houghton Mifflin Harcourt
Exploring Earth's Oceans	Z	I	2880	Vocabulary Readers/CA	Houghton Mifflin Harcourt
Exploring Ecosystems	Q	I	250+	Reading Expeditions	National Geographic
#Exploring Ecosystems with Max Axiom, Super Scientist	U	I	250+	Graphic Library	Capstone Press
Exploring Exoplanets	R	I	1198	Searchlight Books	Lerner Publishing Group
Exploring Flowers	E	I	119	Let's Look at Plants	Lerner Publishing Group
Exploring Fossils	K	I	242	Windows on Literacy	National Geographic
Exploring Freshwater Habitats	P	I	250+	Snowball, Diane	Mondo Publishing
Exploring Land Habitats	P	I	250+	Phinney, Margaret Yatsevitch	Mondo Publishing
Exploring Leaves	E	I	94	Let's Look at Plants	Lerner Publishing Group
Exploring Mars	X	I	7261	Cool Science	Lerner Publishing Group
Exploring Mars	W	I	2853	Reading Street	Pearson
Exploring Mars: The Red Planet	O	I	250+	In Step Readers	Rigby
Exploring Mars: The Red Planet	O	I	250+	Literacy by Design	Rigby
Exploring Medicine	V	I	250+	Kids Discover Reading	Wright Group/McGraw Hill
Exploring National Parks	L	I	250+	Rigby Literacy	Rigby
Exploring New Worlds	T	I	250+	News Extra	Richard C. Owen
Exploring Roots	E	I	100	Let's Look at Plants	Lerner Publishing Group
Exploring Saltwater Habitats	P	I	250+	Smith, Sue	Mondo Publishing
Exploring Saturn	L	I	250+	Rosen Real Readers	Rosen Publishing Group
Exploring Seeds	E	I	123	Let's Look at Plants	Lerner Publishing Group

* Collection of short stories   # Graphic text
^ Mature content with lower level text demands

TITLE	LEVEL	GENRE	WORD COUNT	AUTHOR / SERIES	PUBLISHER / DISTRIBUTOR
Exploring Space	R	I	250+	Explorers	Wright Group/McGraw Hill
Exploring Space	Y	I	250+	High-Fliers	Pacific Learning
Exploring Space	T	I	250+	Reading Expeditions	National Geographic
Exploring Space	I	I	250+	Sunshine	Wright Group/McGraw Hill
Exploring Space Robots	Q	I	1193	Searchlight Books	Lerner Publishing Group
Exploring Space Travel	Q	I	1430	Searchlight Books	Lerner Publishing Group
Exploring Stems	E	I	103	Let's Look at Plants	Lerner Publishing Group
Exploring the Everglades	O	I	250+	Windows on Literacy	National Geographic
Exploring the Frozen North	X	I	250+	Berton, Pierre	Fitzhenry & Whiteside
Exploring the Grand Canyon	Q	I	250+	Rosen Real Readers	Rosen Publishing Group
Exploring the International Space Station	Q	I	1310	Searchlight Books	Lerner Publishing Group
Exploring the Internet	N	I	520	Red Rocket Readers	Flying Start Books
Exploring the Mysteries of Space	U	I	2893	Reading Street	Pearson
Exploring the New World	S	I	250+	Primary Source Readers	Teacher Created Materials
^Exploring the New World: An Interactive History Adventure	U	HF	250+	You Choose Books	Capstone Press
Exploring the Titanic	Q	I	250+	Ballard, Robert D.	Scholastic
Exploring the World	O	I	250+	Literacy by Design	Rigby
Exploring the World	O	I	250+	On Our Way to English	Rigby
Exploring Tide Pools	O	I	250+	Windows on Literacy	National Geographic
#Exploring Titanic: An Isabel Soto History Adventure	R	F	250+	Graphic Expeditions	Capstone Press
Exploring Tree Habitats	P	I	250+	Seifert, Patti	Mondo Publishing
Exploring with Lewis and Clark	O	I	250+	People, Spaces & Places	Rand McNally
Exploring with Science	T	I	1675	Reading Street	Pearson
#Explosive World of Volcanoes with Max Axiom, Super Scientist; The	T	I	250+	Graphic Library	Capstone Press
Exposed	Z+	RF	250+	Vaught, Susan	Bloomsbury Children's Books
^Exposure	Z+	RF	250+	Orca Soundings	Orca Books
Expressway Jewels	M	RF	368	Evangeline Nicholas Collection	Wright Group/McGraw Hill
Extinct	S	I	2101	Leveled Readers Science	Houghton Mifflin Harcourt
Extinct and Endangered	T	I	250+	Boldprint	Steck-Vaughn
Extinct and Endangered Animals	Q	I	2014	Take Two Books	Wright Group/McGraw Hill
Extinct and Endangered Animals You Can Draw	R	I	1579	Ready, Set, Draw!	Millbrook Press
Extra Credit	U	RF	250+	Clements, Andrew	Simon & Schuster
Extraordinary Adventures of Ordinary Basil, The	R	F	250+	Miller, Wiley	Blue Sky Press
*Extraordinary American Indians	W	B	250+	Avery, Susan; Skinner, Linda	Children's Press
Extraordinary Animals!	Q	I	250+	Tristars	Richard C. Owen
*Extraordinary Black Americans: From Colonial to Contemporary Times	W	B	250+	Altman, Susan	Children's Press
Extraordinary Endangered Animals	V	I	250+	Silhol, Sandrine & GuTrive, Gadlle	Harry N. Abrams
Extraordinary House, The	L	F	762	Springboard	Wright Group/McGraw Hill
*Extraordinary Jewish Americans	W	B	250+	Brooks, Philip	Children's Press
Extraordinary Life of Thomas Peters	U	B	2250	Leveled Readers	Houghton Mifflin Harcourt
Extraordinary Life of Thomas Peters, The	U	B	2250	Leveled Readers/CA	Houghton Mifflin Harcourt
Extraordinary Life of Thomas Peters, The	U	B	2250	Leveled Readers/TX	Houghton Mifflin Harcourt
Extraordinary Life, An: The Story of a Monarch Butterfly	V	I	250+	Pringle, Laurence	Orchard Books
*Extraordinary People with Disabilities	W	B	250+	Kent, Deborah; Quinlan, Kathryn A.	Children's Press
Extra-Ordinary Princess, The	W	F	250+	Ebbitt, Carolyn Q.	Bloomsbury Children's Books
Extraordinary Volcanoes	Q	I	250+	Gaff, Jackie & Polt, Gabrielle	Scholastic
*Extraordinary Women in Politics	W	B	250+	Gulatta, Charles	Children's Press

E

TITLE	LEVEL	GENRE	WORD COUNT	AUTHOR / SERIES	PUBLISHER / DISTRIBUTOR
*Extraordinary Women Journalists	W	B	250+	Price-Groff, Claire	Children's Press
*Extraordinary Women of Medicine	W	B	250+	Stille, Darlene R.	Children's Press
*Extraordinary Women of the American West	W	B	250+	Alter, Judy	Children's Press
*Extraordinary Women Scientists	W	B	250+	Stille, Darlene R.	Children's Press
*Extraordinary Young People	W	B	250+	Brill, Marlene Targ	Children's Press
Extreme Animals: The Toughest Creatures on Earth	S	I	250+	Davies, Nicola	Candlewick Press
Extreme Challenge!	Q	I	250+	Explorer Books-Pathfinder	National Geographic
Extreme Challenge!	P	I	250+	Explorer Books-Pioneer	National Geographic
Extreme Destinations	Y	I	250+	Boldprint	Steck-Vaughn
Extreme Earth	L	I	250+	Trackers	Pacific Learning
Extreme Environments	V	I	250+	Literacy By Design	Rigby
Extreme Environments - Challenges to Survival	U	I	250+	Connectors	Pacific Learning
Extreme Freestyle Motocross Moves	S	I	250+	Behind the Moves	Capstone Press
Extreme Lives	N	I	250+	Wildcats	Wright Group/McGraw Hill
Extreme Machines	U	I	250+	DK Readers	DK Publishing
Extreme Mountain Biking Moves	S	I	250+	Behind the Moves	Capstone Press
Extreme Racer	M	RF	696	Springboard	Wright Group/McGraw Hill
Extreme Rock Climbing Moves	S	I	250+	Behind the Moves	Capstone Press
Extreme Scientists	T	I	250+	Connectors	Pacific Learning
Extreme Solutions	Q	I	1478	Leveled Readers	Houghton Mifflin Harcourt
Extreme Solutions	Q	I	1478	Leveled Readers/CA	Houghton Mifflin Harcourt
Extreme Sports	R	I	250+	Bookweb	Rigby
Extreme Sports	T	I	250+	High-Fliers	Pacific Learning
Extreme Sports	Q	I	250+	In Step Readers	Rigby
Extreme Sports	O	I	978	Leveled Readers	Houghton Mifflin Harcourt
Extreme Sports	O	I	978	Leveled Readers/CA	Houghton Mifflin Harcourt
Extreme Sports	R	I	250+	PM Nonfiction-Ruby	Rigby
Extreme Sports	L	I	250+	The Rowland Reading Program Library	Rowland Reading Foundation
Extreme Sports	P	I	250+	Wildcats	Wright Group/McGraw Hill
Extreme Surfing	M	I	250+	To the Extreme	Capstone Press
Extreme U.S.A.	R	I	250+	Literacy by Design	Rigby
Extreme Wakeboarding Moves	S	I	250+	Behind the Moves	Capstone Press
Extreme Weather	R	I	250+	Explore More	Wright Group/McGraw Hill
Extreme Weather	S	I	250+	Reading Expeditions	National Geographic
Extreme!	O	I	250+	Scooters	ETA/Cuisenaire
Exxon Valdez, The:The Oil Spill off the Alaskan Coast	R	I	250+	Disaster!	Capstone Press
Eye and Ear Pollution	V	I	250+	Connectors	Pacific Learning
Eye Doctor, The	D	I	50	Little Celebrations	Pearson Learning Group
Eye for an Eye, An	T	HF	250+	Roop, Peter & Connie	Jamestown Publishers
Eye for Color, An: The Story of Josef Albers	M	B	250+	Wing, Natasha	Henry Holt & Co.
^Eye in the Graveyard, The	T	F	250+	Dahl, Michael	Stone Arch Books
Eye in the Sky	P	F	250+	Orbit Chapter Books	Pacific Learning
Eye of the Law, The	T	I	250+	Connectors	Pacific Learning
^Eye of the Monster	T	F	250+	Dragonblood	Stone Arch Books
Eye on Invention	S	I	250+	WorldScapes	ETA/Cuisenaire
Eye on the Ball	S	I	250+	InfoQuest	Rigby
Eye on the Wild: A Story about Ansel Adams	R	B	8848	Creative Minds Biographies	Carolrhoda Books
Eye Spy	P	I	250+	Wildcats	Wright Group/McGraw Hill
Eye Tricks	N	I	250+	Trackers	Pacific Learning
Eye Wonder	W	I	250+	Rigby Literacy	Rigby
Eyeball Collector, The	Y	F	250+	Higgins, F. E.	Feiwel and Friends

* Collection of short stories   # Graphic text
^ Mature content with lower level text demands

TITLE	LEVEL	GENRE	WORD COUNT	AUTHOR / SERIES	PUBLISHER / DISTRIBUTOR
Eyedropper	C	I	23	Simple Tools	Lerner Publishing Group
Eyes	B	I	21	Animal Traits	Lerner Publishing Group
Eyes	I	I	211	Explorations	Eleanor Curtain Publishing
Eyes	I	I	211	Explorations	Okapi Educational Materials
Eyes	B	I	48	Sails	Rigby
Eyes	C	I	64	Wonder World	Wright Group/McGraw Hill
Eyes are Everywhere	E	I	131	Ready Readers	Pearson Learning Group
Eyes for Evidence: Have You Got What It Takes to Be a Forensic Scientist?	U	I	250+	On the Job	Compass Point Books
Eyes in the Sky	R	I	250+	Literacy 2000	Rigby
Eyes Like Stars	Z	F	250+	Mantchev, Lisa	Feiwel and Friends
Eyes of the Amaryllis, The	V	RF	250+	Babbitt, Natalie	Farrar, Straus, & Giroux
Eyes of the Jungle	S	RF	4816	Take Two Books	Wright Group/McGraw Hill
Eyes of Wisdom: The Buffalo Woman Trilogy Book One	Z	HF	250+	Merrifield, Heyoka	Atria Books
Eyes on the Sky	T	I	250+	Kids Discover Reading	Wright Group/McGraw Hill
Eyewitness!	Q	RF	250+	Tristars	Richard C. Owen

E

TITLE	LEVEL	GENRE	WORD COUNT	AUTHOR / SERIES	PUBLISHER / DISTRIBUTOR
F	LB	I	14	Readlings	American Reading Company
F is for Fabuloso	W	RF	250+	Lee, Marie G.	Avon Books
F/A-22 Raptor, The	U	I	250+	Cross-Sections	Capstone Press
Fab Four from Liverpool, The	U	B	1862	Leveled Readers	Houghton Mifflin Harcourt
Fabled Fourth Graders of Aesop Elementary School, The	Q	RF	250+	Fleming, Candace	Yearling Books
*Fables	N	TL	250+	Lobel, Arnold	HarperCollins
Fables	D	I	40	Vocabulary Readers	Houghton Mifflin Harcourt
*Fables by Aesop	K	TL	250+	Reading Unlimited	Pearson Learning Group
Fabric Painting for Fun!	S	I	250+	For Fun! Crafts	Compass Point Books
Fabric: It's Got You Covered	O	I	1226	iScience	Norwood House Press
Fabulous and Monstrous Beasts	W	I	250+	Weber, Belinda	Kingfisher
Fabulous Animal Families	K	I	250+	Home Connection Collection	Rigby
Fabulous Creatures - Are They Real?	Q	I	1708	Big Cat	Pacific Learning
Fabulous Female Athletes	Q	B	1653	Reading Street	Pearson
Fabulous Fish	K	I	178	Rigby Focus	Rigby
Fabulous Fishes	J	I	71	Stockdale, Susan	Peachtree
Fabulous Freckles	K	RF	250+	Literacy 2000	Rigby
Fabulous Frogs	L	I	271	Glaser, Linda	Millbrook Press
Fabulous Fruits	D	I	121	Fiesta Series	Pearson Learning Group
Fabulous Principal Pie, The	G	F	250+	Start to Read	School Zone
*Fabulous Spotted Egg, The	T	TL	250+	Literacy 2000	Rigby
Fabumouse School Adventure, A	O	F	250+	Stilton, Geronimo	Scholastic
Fabumouse Vacation for Geronimo, A	O	F	250+	Stilton, Geronimo	Scholastic
^Face in the Dark Mirror, The	W	F	250+	Dark Man	Stone Arch Books
^Face in the Dark Mirror, The	W	F	250+	Dark Man	Ransom Publishing
Face in the Dark, The	D	RF	64	Storyteller-Setting Sun	Wright Group/McGraw Hill
Face on the Milk Carton, The	Y	RF	250+	Cooney, Caroline B.	Bantam Books
Face Painting	B	RF	24	Rigby Rocket	Rigby
Face Painting	G	RF	90	Wonder World	Wright Group/McGraw Hill
Face Sandwich, The	LB	RF	16	Sunshine	Wright Group/McGraw Hill
Face to Face	W	RF	250+	Bauer, Marion Dane	Bantam Books
Face to Face	P	RF	250+	Bookweb	Rigby
Face to the Sky	P	RF	250+	Greetings	Rigby
Face-Off	Q	RF	250+	Christopher, Matt	Little Brown and Company
Face-Off	P	RF	4301	Maddox, Jake	Stone Arch Books
Faceoff!	T	I	250+	Boldprint	Steck-Vaughn
Faces	D	I	250+	Little Celebrations	Pearson Learning Group
Faces	B	RF	27	Sunshine	Wright Group/McGraw Hill
Faces on Mount Rushmore	D	I	36	Leveled Readers Social Studies	Houghton Mifflin Harcourt
Facing My Music	Q	RF	250+	Pair-It Books	Steck-Vaughn
Facing the Flood	Q	RF	250+	Kleinhenz, Sydnie Meltzer	Steck-Vaughn
Facing the Lion	X	B	250+	Edge	Hampton Brown
Facing West: A Story of the Oregon Trail	S	I	250+	Kudlinski, Kathleen V.	Penguin Group
Fact Finding	X	I	250+	Connectors	Pacific Learning
Fact or Fiction?	S	I	250+	Connectors	Pacific Learning
Factory Through the Ages	U	I	250+	Steele, Philip	Troll Associates
Facts About 50 States	Q	I	250+	Rigby Literacy	Rigby
Facts About Cerebral Palsy, The	P	I	250+	Literacy by Design	Rigby
Facts About Earthquakes	O	I	250+	Rosen Real Readers	Rosen Publishing Group
Facts About Forest Fires	J	I	250+	Rosen Real Readers	Rosen Publishing Group
Facts About Honeybees	K	I	575	Rigby Flying Colors	Rigby
Facts About Magnets	L	I	237	Leveled Readers Science	Houghton Mifflin Harcourt
Facts About Tornadoes	L	I	250+	Rosen Real Readers	Rosen Publishing Group

* Collection of short stories   # Graphic text
^ Mature content with lower level text demands

TITLE	LEVEL	GENRE	WORD COUNT	AUTHOR / SERIES	PUBLISHER / DISTRIBUTOR
Facts and Fictions of Minna Pratt, The	U	RF	250+	MacLachlan, Patricia	HarperTrophy
Facts and Fun About the Presidents	S	I	250+	Sullivan, George	Scholastic
*Facts of Life: Stories	W	RF	250+	Soto, Gary	Houghton Mifflin Harcourt
Facts on Film: How to Make a Documentary	U	I	250+	Bookshop	Mondo Publishing
Fade to Blue	Z+	F	250+	Beaudoin, Sean	Little Brown and Company
Fading Forests: The Destruction of Our Rainforests	O	I	250+	On Deck	Rigby
Fahrenheit 451	Z+	SF	250+	Bradbury, Ray	Ballantine Books
Fair Cow	M	F	250+	Helakoski, Leslie	Marshall Cavendish
Fair Day	J	RF	184	City Kids	Rigby
Fair Day U.S.A.	N	I	250+	Discovery Links	Newbridge
Fair Is Fair!	L	RF	250+	Math Matters	Kane Press
Fair Share	K	I	332	Yellow Umbrella Books	Red Brick Learning
Fair Swap, A	K	TL	250+	PM Story Books-Silver	Rigby
Fair Weather	T	HF	250+	Peck, Richard	Scholastic
Fair, Brown and Trembling	S	TL	250+	WorldScapes	ETA/Cuisenaire
Fair, The	A	RF	40	First Stories	Pacific Learning
Fairest	V	F	250+	Levine, Gail Carson	HarperTrophy
Fairies	Q	I	250+	Mythical Creatures	Raintree
Fairies and Elves	U	I	250+	Fantasy Chronicles	Lerner Publishing Group
Fairies and Magical Creatures	V	I	250+	Reinhart, Matthew and Sabuda, Robert	Candlewick Press
Fairies and Princesses	N	I	250+	Quick Draw	Kingfisher
Fairies!: A True Story	M	I	250+	Step Into Reading	Random House
Fairy World Crafts	P	I	3881	Ross, Kathy	Millbrook Press
Fairy's Guide to Understanding Humans, A	S	F	250+	Meacham, Margaret	Holiday House
Fairy-Tale Detectives, The: The Sisters Grimm	U	F	250+	Buckley, Michael	Scholastic
Faith's Journey	S	HF	1263	Leveled Readers	Houghton Mifflin Harcourt
Fake Cape Caper, The (Melvin Beederman, Superhero)	N	F	250+	Trine, Greg	Henry Holt & Co.
Fake Mustache	S	F	250+	Angleberger, Tom	Amulet Books
Falcon, The	N	RF	250+	PM Collection	Rigby
Falcon's Feathers, The	N	RF	250+	A to Z Mysteries	Random House
Falcons Nest on Skyscrapers	P	I	250+	Soar To Success	Houghton Mifflin Harcourt
Fall	B	I	12	Discovery Links	Newbridge
Fall	A	I	22	Little Books for Early Readers	University of Maine
Fall	E	I	54	Seasons	Lerner Publishing Group
Fall	E	I	73	Sunshine	Wright Group/McGraw Hill
Fall Changes	L	I	320	Leveled Readers	Houghton Mifflin Harcourt
Fall Changes	L	I	320	Leveled Readers/CA	Houghton Mifflin Harcourt
Fall Changes	L	I	320	Leveled Readers/TX	Houghton Mifflin Harcourt
Fall Colors	C	I	53	Bonnell, Kris	Reading Reading Books
Fall Colors	D	I	23	Windows on Literacy	National Geographic
Fall Down: Verbs in Action	K	I	250+	Bookworms	Marshall Cavendish
Fall Fair Contest	J	RF	511	InfoTrek	ETA/Cuisenaire
Fall Harvest	LB	I	16	Little Books for Early Readers	University of Maine
Fall Harvest	E	I	39	Preparing for Winter	Capstone Press
Fall Harvest	I	I	179	Vocabulary Readers/TX	Houghton Mifflin Harcourt
Fall Leaves	J	I	222	Leveled Readers	Houghton Mifflin Harcourt
Fall of Tenochtitlan	X	I	3489	Leveled Readers Social Studies	Houghton Mifflin Harcourt
Fallen Angels	Z+	HF	250+	Myers, Walter Dean	Scholastic
Falling From Grace	Z	RF	250+	Godwin, Jane	Holiday House
Falling Off a Log	Q	RF	1290	Leveled Readers	Houghton Mifflin Harcourt
Fallout	Z+	HF	250+	Krisher, Trudy	Holiday House

F

TITLE	LEVEL	GENRE	WORD COUNT	AUTHOR / SERIES	PUBLISHER / DISTRIBUTOR
Fallout: Nuclear Disasters in Our World	R	I	250+	On Deck	Rigby
Fame, Glory, and Other Things on My To Do List	W	RF	250+	Rallison, Janette	Walker & Company
Families	J	I	128	Avenues	Hampton Brown
Families	H	I	160	Early Connections	Benchmark Education
Families	B	I	49	Interaction	Rigby
Families	D	I	60	Pebble Books	Capstone Press
Families	F	I	75	People	Capstone Press
Families	C	I	32	Rosen Real Readers	Rosen Publishing Group
Families	J	F	184	Storyteller-Night Crickets	Wright Group/McGraw Hill
Families	F	I	132	Twig	Wright Group/McGraw Hill
Families	C	I	94	Vocabulary Readers	Houghton Mifflin Harcourt
Families	C	I	94	Vocabulary Readers/CA	Houghton Mifflin Harcourt
Families	LB	I	8	Windows on Literacy	National Geographic
Families	G	I	46	Windows on Literacy	National Geographic
Families	F	I	159	Yellow Umbrella Books	Capstone Press
Families and Feasts	I	I	196	PM Plus Nonfiction	Rigby
Families Are Different	K	RF	250+	Pellegrini, Nina	Scholastic
Families Have Rules	D	I	71	Early Explorers	Benchmark Education
Families in Many Cultures	I	I	114	Life Around the World	Capstone Press
Families in the City	D	I	134	Vocabulary Readers	Houghton Mifflin Harcourt
Families in the City	D	I	134	Vocabulary Readers/CA	Houghton Mifflin Harcourt
Families of 1608 Ash Street, The	L	RF	571	Leveled Readers	Houghton Mifflin Harcourt
Families of the Deep Blue Sea	P	I	250+	Mallory, Kenneth	Charlesbridge
Families Share	E	RF	72	Learn to Read	Creative Teaching Press
Families Work and Play Together	F	I	130	Early Connections	Benchmark Education
Family	N	RF	250+	Monk, Isabell	Carolrhoda Books
Family Affairs: Secrets of My Hollywood Life	Y	RF	250+	Calonita, Jen	Little Brown and Company
Family Bike Ride	C	RF	55	Handprints C, Set 1	Educators Publishing Service
Family Birthday, A	C	RF	55	Gear Up!	Wright Group/McGraw Hill
Family Book, The	H	I	177	Parr, Todd	Little Brown and Company
Family Counts	B	RF	19	Avenues	Hampton Brown
Family Counts	B	RF	19	Rise & Shine	Hampton Brown
Family Dinner	Q	RF	250+	Cutler, Jane	Farrar, Straus, & Giroux
Family Feelings	C	I	14	Reach	National Geographic
Family Fun	A	RF	24	Handprints A	Educators Publishing Service
Family Fun	E	I	40	Shutterbug Books	Steck-Vaughn
Family Fun	B	I	69	Social Studies	Newmark Learning
Family Fun	A	I	20	Vocabulary Readers	Houghton Mifflin Harcourt
Family Fun	A	I	20	Vocabulary Readers/CA	Houghton Mifflin Harcourt
Family Greene, The	Y	HF	250+	Rinaldi, Ann	Harcourt, Inc.
Family Life in the U.S.A., Then & Now	P	I	744	Time for Kids	Teacher Created Materials
Family Names	D	RF	36	Visions	Wright Group/McGraw Hill
Family Night	K	RF	561	InfoTrek	ETA/Cuisenaire
Family of Beavers, A	J	RF	141	Books for Young Learners	Richard C. Owen
Family of Five, A	C	F	26	Pair-It Books	Steck-Vaughn
Family on Lake Street, The	F	RF	159	Teacher's Choice Series	Pearson Learning Group
Family Pets	F	I	61	Families	Capstone Press
Family Pets	C	I	37	Pebble Books	Capstone Press
Family Photo	L	RF	909	InfoTrek	ETA/Cuisenaire
Family Photos	F	RF	106	Literacy 2000	Rigby
Family Picnic	B	RF	18	Bebop Books	Lee & Low Books Inc.

Organized Alphabetically by Title
Storable Database at www.fountasandpinnellleveledbooks.com

* Collection of short stories   # Graphic text
^ Mature content with lower level text demands

TITLE	LEVEL	GENRE	WORD COUNT	AUTHOR / SERIES	PUBLISHER / DISTRIBUTOR
Family Picture, A	R	RF	1570	Leveled Readers	Houghton Mifflin Harcourt
Family Pictures	A	RF	32	Leveled Literacy Intervention/ Green System	Heinemann
Family Quilt, The	J	RF	250+	Windows on Literacy	National Geographic
Family Reunion	G	RF	243	Visions	Wright Group/McGraw Hill
#Family Secret, A	Y	HF	250+	Heuvel, Eric	Farrar, Straus, & Giroux
Family Soccer	D	RF	55	Geddes, Diana	Kaeden Books
Family Table, The	J	RF	274	Leveled Readers Language Support	Houghton Mifflin Harcourt
Family Ties	Z	I	250+	Boldprint	Steck-Vaughn
Family Time	B	I	16	Pair-It Books	Steck-Vaughn
Family Traditions and Celebrations	N	I	1431	Reading Street	Pearson
Family Tree	S	RF	250+	Ayres, Katherine	Bantam Books
Family Tree, The	K	RF	250+	PM Plus Story Books	Rigby
Family Tree, The	G	F	213	Ready Readers	Pearson Learning Group
Family Under the Bridge, The	R	RF	250+	Savage Carlson, Natalie	Scholastic
Family Work and Fun	B	I	38	Little Red Readers	Sundance
Family, The	A	F	24	Sails	Rigby
Family, The	E	RF	55	Sunshine	Wright Group/McGraw Hill
*Famous Animals	Q	I	250+	Literacy Tree	Rigby
*Famous Children	O	I	250+	Literacy 2000	Rigby
Famous Faces	X	I	250+	InfoQuest	Rigby
Famous Feet	E	F	34	Instant Readers	Harcourt School Publishers
Famous Friendships	Z	I	2538	Independent Readers Social Studies	Houghton Mifflin Harcourt
Famous Immigrants	T	B	250+	Primary Source Readers	Teacher Created Materials
Famous Landmarks	I	I	163	Early Explorers	Benchmark Education
Famous Places	N	I	250+	Windows on Literacy	National Geographic
Famous Places Around the World	N	I	200	Larkin, Bruce	Wilbooks
Famous Rocks	Q	I	578	Independent Readers Science	Houghton Mifflin Harcourt
Famous Trials	Z	I	250+	Boldprint	Steck-Vaughn
Famous Trios in World Literature	Z	I	3306	Vocabulary Readers	Houghton Mifflin Harcourt
Famous Trios in World Literature	Z	I	3306	Vocabulary Readers/CA	Houghton Mifflin Harcourt
*Famous Women Athletes	S	B	2630	Reading Street	Pearson
Fancy Dance	H	RF	155	Bebop Books	Lee & Low Books Inc.
Fancy Dress	B	RF	28	Rigby Star	Rigby
Fancy Dress Parade, The	H	RF	171	Stepping Stones	Nelson/Michaels Assoc.
Fancy Feet	L	RF	250+	Giff, Patricia Reilly	Bantam Books
Fancy Feet	M	I	250+	Yellow Umbrella Books	Red Brick Learning
Fancy Nancy and the Boy from Paris	J	RF	250+	O'Connor, Jane	HarperCollins
Fancy Nancy and the Mean Girl	J	RF	250+	O'Connor, Jane	HarperCollins
Fancy Nancy: The 100th Day of School	J	RF	250+	O'Connor, Jane	HarperCollins
Fanfare for Food	O	I	497	Vocabulary Readers	Houghton Mifflin Harcourt
Fangs	F	I	100	Sails	Rigby
Fangs and Me	N	RF	250+	Gilmore, Rachna	Fitzhenry & Whiteside
Fangs and Teeth	M	I	250+	Sails	Rigby
Fanny	M	F	250+	Hobbie, Holly	Little Brown and Company
Fans and Umbrellas	E	TL	107	Joy Readers	Pearson Learning Group
Fantail, Fantail	D	F	67	Pacific Literacy	Pacific Learning
Fantastic Animal Features	Q	I	250+	Parker, Heather	Steck-Vaughn
Fantastic Cake, The	E	RF	169	Story Box	Wright Group/McGraw Hill
Fantastic Field Trip, A	O	SF	1854	Reading Street	Pearson
Fantastic Fish	B	I	37	Gear Up!	Wright Group/McGraw Hill
Fantastic Flying Squirrel, The	G	I	127	Big Cat	Pacific Learning

F

TITLE	LEVEL	GENRE	WORD COUNT	AUTHOR / SERIES	PUBLISHER / DISTRIBUTOR
Fantastic Forest, The	R	I	250+	Explorer Books-Pathfinder	National Geographic
Fantastic Forest, The	P	I	250+	Explorer Books-Pioneer	National Geographic
Fantastic Frogs	I	I	156	Sails	Rigby
Fantastic Frogs!	J	I	204	Robinson, Fay	Scholastic
Fantastic Fungi	K	I	234	Rigby Focus	Rigby
Fantastic Mr. Fox	P	F	250+	Dahl, Roald	Penguin Group
Fantastic Pumpkin, The	H	F	216	Rigby Literacy	Rigby
Fantastic Rocks	H	I	128	Shutterbug Books	Steck-Vaughn
Fantastic Secret of Owen Jester, The	R	RF	250+	O'Connor, Barbara	Farrar, Straus, & Giroux
Fantastic Washing Machine	J	F	250+	Sunshine	Wright Group/McGraw Hill
*Fantastic Water Pot and Other Cases, The	O	RF	250+	Simon, Seymour	Avon Books
Fantastical Creatures and Magical Beasts	U	I	250+	Fantasy Chronicles	Lerner Publishing Group
Fantasy	V	I	250+	Boldprint	Steck-Vaughn
Fantasy	X	F	250+	Boos, Ben	Candlewick Press
Far Away	C	I	32	Avenues	Hampton Brown
Far Away at Home	T	RF	5638	Reading Street	Pearson
Far Away Moon	G	I	80	Pacific Literacy	Pacific Learning
Far from Home	W	RF	2000	Leveled Readers/TX	Houghton Mifflin Harcourt
Far North	V	RF	250+	Hobbs, Will	Avon Books
Far Out!	Q	I	250+	Orbit Collections	Pacific Learning
Faraway Farm	H	RF	171	Whybrow, Ian	Carolrhoda Books
Farewell to Boyhood	O	I	250+	WorldScapes	ETA/Cuisenaire
Farewell to Manzanar	Z	B	250+	Edge	Hampton Brown
Farewell to Manzanar	Z	B	250+	Houston, Jeanne; Houston, James D.	Houghton Mifflin Harcourt
Farewell, My Lunchbag: A Chet Gecko Mystery	Q	F	250+	Hale, Bruce	Harcourt, Inc.
Far-Flung Places	T	I	250+	Connectors	Pacific Learning
Farley Frog	B	F	33	Pair-It Books	Steck-Vaughn
Farm	W	I	250+	Eyewitness Books	DK Publishing
Farm Alarm	E	F	103	Early Connections	Benchmark Education
Farm Animals	LB	I	9	Beginning Words Books	American Reading Company
Farm Animals	A	I	28	Belle River Readers	Belle River Readers, Inc.
Farm Animals	L	I	250+	I Wonder Why	Kingfisher
Farm Animals	A	I	28	Nonfiction Set 1	Literacy Footprints
Farm Animals	A	I	24	Vocabulary Readers	Houghton Mifflin Harcourt
Farm Animals	E	I	100	World of Farming	Heinemann Library
Farm Chores	D	RF	35	Early Emergent, Set 4	Pioneer Valley
Farm Concert, The	C	F	74	Story Box	Wright Group/McGraw Hill
Farm Day	D	F	36	Little Celebrations	Pearson Learning Group
Farm Feet	B	I	40	Bonnell, Kris	Reading Reading Books
Farm for Wild Animals, A	K	I	161	Vocabulary Readers	Houghton Mifflin Harcourt
Farm Friends	B	I	72	Red Rocket Readers	Flying Start Books
Farm Friends	K	I	197	Spyglass Books	Compass Point Books
Farm in Spring, The	C	I	69	PM Starters	Rigby
Farm Life Long Ago	L	I	436	Pair-It Books	Steck-Vaughn
Farm Machines	F	I	109	World of Farming	Heinemann Library
Farm Patterns	J	I	308	Finding Patterns	Capstone Press
Farm Picture Pops	M	I	250+	Priddy, Roger	Priddy Books
Farm Products	I	I	156	Larkin, Bruce	Wilbooks
Farm Stand Mystery, The	J	RF	310	Early Explorers	Benchmark Education
Farm Through the Ages	U	I	250+	Steele, Philip	Troll Associates
Farm Tractors	H	I	79	Mighty Machines	Capstone Press
Farm Tractors	L	I	416	Pull Ahead Books	Lerner Publishing Group
Farm Tractors on the Move	K	I	416	Lightning Bolt Books	Lerner Publishing Group

* Collection of short stories   # Graphic text
^ Mature content with lower level text demands

TITLE	LEVEL	GENRE	WORD COUNT	AUTHOR / SERIES	PUBLISHER / DISTRIBUTOR
Farm Work	D	F	80	Early Connections	Benchmark Education
Farm, The	A	F	46	InfoTrek	ETA/Cuisenaire
Farm, The	B	I	79	Leveled Readers Emergent	Houghton Mifflin Harcourt
Farm, The	LB	I	14	Literacy 2000	Rigby
Farm, The	A	I	28	Little Books for Early Readers	University of Maine
Farm, The	A	I	42	Little Readers	Houghton Mifflin Harcourt
Farm, The	I	I	228	Pebble Books	Capstone Press
Farm, The	LB	I	14	Ready Readers	Pearson Learning Group
Farm, The	LB	F	12	Sails	Rigby
Farm, The	LB	I	14	Smart Start	Rigby
Farm, The	LB	I	21	Sunshine	Wright Group/McGraw Hill
Farmer and His Two Lazy Sons, The	I	TL	250+	Aesop's Fables	Pearson Learning Group
Farmer and the Skunk	E	F	139	Tiger Cub	Peguis
Farmer Boy	Q	HF	250+	Wilder, Laura Ingalls	HarperTrophy
Farmer Boy Birthday, A	J	HF	250+	Wilder, Laura Ingalls	HarperCollins
Farmer Boy Days	M	HF	250+	Wilder, Laura Ingalls	HarperTrophy
Farmer Brown and Dapple Gray	J	RF	166	Books for Young Learners	Richard C. Owen
Farmer Brown's Garden	C	F	48	Windmill Books	Rigby
Farmer Dan's Ducks	D	F	126	Leveled Literacy Intervention/ Green System	Heinemann
Farmer Didn't Wake Up, The	F	F	185	Learn to Read	Creative Teaching Press
Farmer Duck	K	F	250+	Waddell, Martin	Candlewick Press
Farmer Had a Pig, A	G	TL	149	Tiger Cub	Peguis
Farmer in the Dell	E	F	114	Parkinson, Kathy	Whitman
Farmer in the Dell, The	F	TL	159	PM Readalongs	Rigby
Farmer in the Dell, The	K	TL	250+	Traditional Songs	Picture Window Books
Farmer in the Soup, The	K	TL	250+	Littledale, Freya	Scholastic
Farmer Joe's Hot Day	J	F	406	Richards, Nancy W.	Scholastic
Farmer McFuddy's Garden	K	F	609	Mills, Tania	Kaeden Books
Farmer Mike	E	RF	52	Leveled Readers	Houghton Mifflin Harcourt
Farmer Upsy-Daisy	E	F	129	Start to Read	School Zone
Farmers	M	I	250+	Community Helpers	Red Brick Learning
Farmers	M	I	250+	Community Workers	Compass Point Books
Farmer's Journey, The	M	RF	250+	Little Celebrations	Pearson Learning Group
Farmer's Market	C	I	38	Avenues	Hampton Brown
Farmers, The	A	RF	28	Leveled Literacy Intervention/ Green System	Heinemann
Farmers: Then and Now	P	I	250+	Primary Source Readers	Teacher Created Materials
Farming	N	I	582	Avenues	Hampton Brown
Farming in the 1800s	U	I	2188	Reading Street	Pearson
Farms	F	I	153	Foundations	Wright Group/McGraw Hill
Farms	F	RF	102	Sunshine	Wright Group/McGraw Hill
Farms	N	I	606	Wonders	Hampton Brown
Farmyard Fiasco, A	H	F	186	Book Bank	Wright Group/McGraw Hill
*Far-Out Frisbee and Other Cases, The	O	RF	250+	Simon, Seymour	Avon Books
Farther and Faster	I	I	204	Early Explorers	Benchmark Education
Farthest Shore, The	Z	F	250+	Le Guin, Ursula	Bantam Books
Farwalker's Quest, The	Y	F	250+	Sensel, Joni	Bloomsbury Children's Books
Fascinating Faces	J	I	99	Literacy Tree	Rigby
Fascinating Families	O	I	717	Leveled Readers	Houghton Mifflin Harcourt
Fashion	V	I	250+	10 Things You Need to Know About	Capstone Press
Fashion Careers: Finding the Right Fit	V	I	250+	The World of Fashion	Capstone Press

F

TITLE	LEVEL	GENRE	WORD COUNT	AUTHOR / SERIES	PUBLISHER / DISTRIBUTOR
Fashion Crafts: Create Your Own Style	Q	I	250+	Crafts	Capstone Press
Fashion Design School: Learning the Skills to Succeed	V	I	250+	The World of Fashion	Capstone Press
Fashion Design: The Art of Style	V	I	250+	The World of Fashion	Capstone Press
Fashion History: Looking Great Through the Ages	V	I	250+	The World of Fashion	Capstone Press
Fashion Modeling: Being Beautiful, Selling Clothes	V	I	250+	The World of Fashion	Capstone Press
Fashion Trends: How Popular Style Is Shaped	V	I	250+	The World of Fashion	Capstone Press
Fasi Sings and Fasi's Fish	I	RF	204	Pacific Literacy	Pacific Learning
Fast and Faster	B	I	24	Windows on Literacy	National Geographic
Fast and Faster!	D	I	77	Yellow Umbrella Books	Red Brick Learning
*Fast and Funny	J	RF	1499	Story Box	Wright Group/McGraw Hill
Fast and Furious	Q	I	250+	InfoQuest	Rigby
Fast and Noisy	E	RF	152	Red Rocket Readers	Flying Start Books
Fast and Slow	F	I	55	Pair-It Turn and Learn	Steck-Vaughn
Fast and Slow	B	F	48	Springboard	Wright Group/McGraw Hill
Fast and Slow: An Animal Opposites Book	K	I	250+	Animal Opposites	Capstone Press
Fast Athletes	C	I	104	Careers Series	Benchmark Education
Fast Food	E	RF	112	Foundations	Wright Group/McGraw Hill
Fast Food	M	I	250+	InfoTrek Plus	ETA/Cuisenaire
Fast Food Felicity	L	F	250+	Bookweb	Rigby
Fast Food for Butterflies	I	I	170	Storyteller-Moon Rising	Wright Group/McGraw Hill
Fast Forward: Cities of the Future	U	I	250+	Explore More	Wright Group/McGraw Hill
Fast Fox, A	F	F	247	Leveled Literacy Intervention/ Blue System	Heinemann
Fast Machines	D	RF	146	Foundations	Wright Group/McGraw Hill
Fast 'n' Snappy	M	F	1751	Schnetzler, Pattie	Carolrhoda Books
Fast Sam	D	F	46	The Rowland Reading Program Library	Rowland Reading Foundation
Fast Sam, Cool Clyde, and Stuff	Y	RF	250+	Myers, Walter Dean	Puffin Books
Fast Slow	B	I	70	Bookworms	Marshall Cavendish
Fast Track	W	RF	250+	Redline Racing Series	Fitzhenry & Whiteside
Fast Track to Success	T	I	250+	WorldScapes	ETA/Cuisenaire
Fast, Faster, Fastest	C	I	66	Twig	Wright Group/McGraw Hill
Fast, Not Last	H	F	233	Sunshine	Wright Group/McGraw Hill
^Fastback Beach	W	RF	250+	Orca Soundings	Orca Books
Fast-Draw Freddie	D	F	50	Rookie Readers	Children's Press
Fasten It	G	I	91	Factivity Series	Pearson Learning Group
Faster! Faster!	H	F	285	Leveled Readers	Houghton Mifflin Harcourt
Fastest Animals, The	L	I	250+	EXtreme Animals	Capstone Press
Fastest Dinosaurs, The	P	I	1070	Meet the Dinosaurs	Lerner Publishing Group
Fastest Gazelle, The	E	RF	146	Literacy 2000	Rigby
*Fastest Ketchup in the Cafeteria and Other Cases, The	O	RF	250+	Simon, Seymour	Avon Books
Fastest, Longest, Biggest, Lightest	O	I	1769	Reading Street	Pearson
Fat Cat	I	TL	250+	Kent, Jack	Scholastic
Fat Cat Sat on the Mat, The	G	F	250+	Karlin, Nurit	HarperTrophy
Fat Cat Tompkin	I	F	196	Voyages	SRA/McGraw Hill
Fat Cat's Chair	F	F	140	PM Stars	Rigby
Fat Ducks	G	F	253	Sails	Rigby
*Fat Man in a Fur Coat and Other Bear Stories	T	RF	250+	Schwartz, Alvin	Farrar, Straus, & Giroux
Fat Pig, The	I	TL	250+	Tiger Cub	Peguis
Fate of Achilles, The	W	TL	1891	Leveled Readers	Houghton Mifflin Harcourt
Fate of Achilles, The	W	TL	1891	Leveled Readers/CA	Houghton Mifflin Harcourt

* Collection of short stories   # Graphic text
^ Mature content with lower level text demands

TITLE	LEVEL	GENRE	WORD COUNT	AUTHOR / SERIES	PUBLISHER / DISTRIBUTOR
Fate of Achilles, The	W	TL	1891	Leveled Readers/TX	Houghton Mifflin Harcourt
Father Animals	D	I	79	Bonnell, Kris/About	Reading Reading Books
Father Bear Comes Home	I	F	331	Minarik, Else H.	HarperCollins
Father Bear Goes Fishing	D	F	98	PM Story Books	Rigby
Father Bear's Surprise	H	RF	224	PM Extensions-Green	Rigby
Father Eusebio Francisco Kino: Changing the Colonial Southwest	W	I	2436	Independent Readers Science	Houghton Mifflin Harcourt
Father Fights Back: Franklin Delano Roosevelt and Polio	M	B	250+	Twig	Wright Group/McGraw Hill
Father Fox's Christmas Rhymes	M	F	250+	Watson, Clyde	Square Fish
Father of the Constitution: A Story about James Madison	S	B	8998	Creative Minds Biographies	Lerner Publishing Group
Father Turk	X	B	250+	WorldScapes	ETA/Cuisenaire
*Father Water, Mother Woods	V	RF	250+	Paulsen, Gary	Bantam Books
Father Who Walked on Hands, The	K	RF	344	Literacy 2000	Rigby
Father Who Walked on His Hands, The	H	RF	250+	Mahy, Margaret	Scholastic
Fathers	F	I	46	Families	Capstone Press
Fathers	B	I	26	Pebble Books	Capstone Press
Father's Arcane Daughter	V	RF	250+	Konigsburg, E. L.	Aladdin
Father's Garden, A	P	RF	1000	Leveled Readers/TX	Houghton Mifflin Harcourt
Fatima	Q	RF	250+	Bookshop	Mondo Publishing
Fats, Oils, and Sweets	F	I	107	Food Groups	Lerner Publishing Group
Fats, Oils, and Sweets	I	I	190	The Food Guide Pyramid	Capstone Press
Faulty Hearts: True Survival Stories	Z	I	4494	Powerful Medicine	Lerner Publishing Group
Favorite Books	H	RF	251	PM Math Readers	Rigby
Favorite Fables	J	TL	667	Leveled Readers/TX	Houghton Mifflin Harcourt
Favorite Games Around the World	Q	I	250+	Sunshine	Wright Group/McGraw Hill
*Favorite Greek Myths	Y	TL	250+	Osborne, Mary Pope	Scholastic
*Favorite Medieval Tales	S	TL	250+	Osborne, Mary Pope	Scholastic
Favorite Places	C	I	75	Explorations	Eleanor Curtain Publishing
Favorite Places	C	I	75	Explorations	Okapi Educational Materials
Favorite Things	A	I	28	Vocabulary Readers	Houghton Mifflin Harcourt
Favorite Things	A	I	28	Vocabulary Readers/CA	Houghton Mifflin Harcourt
Favorite Things	A	I	28	Vocabulary Readers/TX	Houghton Mifflin Harcourt
Fawn in the Forest, The	H	RF	227	PM Plus Story Books	Rigby
Fawn, The	E	F	69	Reading Street	Pearson
Fawn, The	J	RF	701	The Fawn	Pioneer Valley
Fayim's Incredible Journey	T	RF	250+	High-Fliers	Pacific Learning
#FBI, The	T	I	250+	Cartoon Nation	Capstone Press
^Fear in the Dark	W	F	250+	Dark Man	Ransom Publishing
^Fear in the Dark	W	F	250+	Dark Man	Stone Arch Books
Fear Itself (Benjamin Pratt and the Keepers of the School)	S	RF	250+	Clements, Andrew	Simon & Schuster
Fear of White Water	S	RF	250+	Leveled Readers Language Support	Houghton Mifflin Harcourt
*Fearless Explorer and Other Cases, The	O	RF	250+	Simon, Seymour	Avon Books
Fearless Feats	U	I	250+	Connectors	Pacific Learning
Fearsome Four, The	M	RF	250+	Bookweb	Rigby
Feast For 10	E	RF	97	Falwell, Cathryn	Scholastic
Feast or Famine?	V	I	250+	WorldScapes	ETA/Cuisenaire
Feast, The	E	F	58	Leveled Readers	Houghton Mifflin Harcourt
Feather Brain	O	F	250+	Orca Young Readers	Orca Books
Featherbys	S	RF	250+	Steele, Mary	Peachtree
Feathered Dinosaurs	P	I	1180	Meet the Dinosaurs	Lerner Publishing Group
Feathered Friends	F	RF	147	Sails	Rigby

F

TITLE	LEVEL	GENRE	WORD COUNT	AUTHOR / SERIES	PUBLISHER / DISTRIBUTOR
Feathered Hunters of the Night	Q	I	959	Vocabulary Readers	Houghton Mifflin Harcourt
Feathered Hunters of the Night	Q	I	959	Vocabulary Readers/CA	Houghton Mifflin Harcourt
Feathered Hunters of the Night	Q	I	959	Vocabulary Readers/TX	Houghton Mifflin Harcourt
Feathers	E	I	101	Body Coverings	Lerner Publishing Group
Feathers	C	I	39	Bonnell, Kris	Reading Reading Books
Feathers	C	I	104	Sails	Rigby
Feathers	K	RF	250+	Storyteller-Lightning Bolts	Wright Group/McGraw Hill
Feathers	X	RF	250+	Woodson, Jaqueline	Puffin Books
Feathers and Flight	Q	I	250+	Explorers	Wright Group/McGraw Hill
Feathers and Flight	I	I	790	Sunshine	Wright Group/McGraw Hill
*Feathery Fables	P	TL	250+	Action Packs	Rigby
^Federal Bureau of Investigation, The: Hunting Criminals	S	I	250+	Line of Duty	Capstone Press
Feed Me! An Aesop Fable	I	TL	250+	Bank Street	Bantam Books
Feed the Ducks	F	RF	172	Red Rocket Readers	Flying Start Books
Feeding	A	I	40	Sun Sprouts	ETA/Cuisenaire
Feeding Our Pets	A	I	25	Leveled Readers	Houghton Mifflin Harcourt
Feeding Our Pets	A	I	25	Leveled Readers/CA	Houghton Mifflin Harcourt
Feeding the Baby	C	I	51	Home Connection Collection	Rigby
Feeding the Lambs	H	RF	61	PM Plus Nonfiction	Rigby
Feeding the Otters	K	I	250+	On Our Way to English	Rigby
Feeding the World	T	I	250+	Reading Expeditions	National Geographic
Feeding Time	C	RF	55	Carousel Readers	Pearson Learning Group
Feeding Time	K	I	250+	DK Readers	DK Publishing
Feeding Time	A	RF	35	Rigby Rocket	Rigby
Feeding Time	B	I	54	Windows on Literacy	National Geographic
Feeding Time at the Zoo	L	I	250+	Scooters	ETA/Cuisenaire
Feeding Time at the Zoo	D	RF	73	Windmill Books	Rigby
Feel Good Book, The	H	I	242	Parr, Todd	Little Brown and Company
Feel The G's: The Science of Gravity and G-Forces	X	I	250+	Headline Science	Compass Point Books
Feel the Power: Energy All Around	K	I	250+	Spyglass Books	Compass Point Books
Feel, Think, Move	U	I	2136	Reading Street	Pearson
Feeling	G	I	205	PM Science Readers	Rigby
Feeling Angry	F	I	70	Emotions	Red Brick Learning
Feeling Funny	J	F	250+	Sunshine	Wright Group/McGraw Hill
Feeling Great!	S	I	250+	Orbit Collections	Pacific Learning
Feeling Happy	F	I	57	Emotions	Red Brick Learning
Feeling Lucky	L	RF	916	Dominie Math Stories	Pearson Learning Group
Feeling Sad	F	I	62	Emotions	Red Brick Learning
Feeling Scared	F	I	62	Emotions	Red Brick Learning
Feeling Shy	G	RF	154	The King School Series	Townsend Press
Feelings	LB	I	12	Canizares, Susan	Scholastic
Feelings	G	F	43	Dominie Readers	Pearson Learning Group
Feelings	E	I	133	Rigby Rocket	Rigby
Feelings	D	RF	39	Rise & Shine	Hampton Brown
Feelings	P	I	250+	Sunshine	Wright Group/McGraw Hill
Feelings	A	I	24	Windows on Literacy	National Geographic
Feelings Book, The	I	I	179	Parr, Todd	Little Brown and Company
Feet	B	I	21	Animal Traits	Lerner Publishing Group
Feet	H	F	76	Book Bank	Wright Group/McGraw Hill
Feet	A	I	14	Foundations	Wright Group/McGraw Hill
Feet	D	RF	18	Story Box	Wright Group/McGraw Hill

* Collection of short stories   # Graphic text
^ Mature content with lower level text demands

TITLE	LEVEL	GENRE	WORD COUNT	AUTHOR / SERIES	PUBLISHER / DISTRIBUTOR
Feet First: The Story of Shoes	S	I	250+	Discovery Links	Newbridge
Feet!	LB	I	28	Ray's Readers	Outside the Box
Feisty Old Woman Who Lived in the Cozy Cave	J	F	301	Foundations	Wright Group/McGraw Hill
Felicia the Critic	P	RF	250+	Conford, Ellen	Little Brown and Company
Felicity Learns a Lesson	Q	HF	250+	The American Girls Collection	Pleasant Company
Felicity Saves the Day	Q	HF	250+	The American Girls Collection	Pleasant Company
Felicity's Surprise	Q	HF	250+	The American Girls Collection	Pleasant Company
Felina's New Home	M	F	1098	Wlodarski, Loran	Sylvan Dell Publishing
Felipe the Flamingo	M	F	4340	Conway, Jill Ker	Fulcrum Publishing
Felita	P	RF	250+	Mohr, Nicholas	Dell
Felix, the Very Hungry Fish	C	F	32	Little Books	Sadlier-Oxford
Fell	Z	F	250+	Clement-Davies, David	Amulet Books
Fence, The	B	F	44	Bookshop	Mondo Publishing
Fence, The	A	RF	24	Handprints A	Educators Publishing Service
Fennec Fox	L	I	250+	A Day in the Life: Desert Animals	Heinemann Library
Ferdinand Magellan	S	B	3385	History Maker Bios	Lerner Publishing Group
Ferdinand Saves the Day	N	RF	888	Leveled Readers	Houghton Mifflin Harcourt
Ferdinand Saves the Day	N	RF	888	Leveled Readers/CA	Houghton Mifflin Harcourt
Ferdinand Saves the Day	N	RF	888	Leveled Readers/TX	Houghton Mifflin Harcourt
Fergus and Bridey	K	F	250+	Little Celebrations	Pearson Learning Group
Fergus and the Princess	M	F	250+	Rigby Literacy	Rigby
Fern and Burt	H	F	250+	Ready Readers	Pearson Learning Group
Fern Goes Away	F	F	208	Sails	Rigby
Fern the Green Fairy: Rainbow Magic	L	F	250+	Meadows, Daisy	Scholastic
Fernitickles	R	HF	250+	Literacy 2000	Rigby
Fern's Purple Birthday	I	F	250+	Phonics Readers Plus	Steck-Vaughn
Ferns, Mosses & Other Spore-Producing Plants	Y	I	250+	Kingdom Classification	Compass Point Books
^Ferrari	O	I	250+	Fast Cars	Capstone Press
Ferret Fun	O	RF	250+	Baglio, Ben M.	Scholastic
Ferret in the Bedroom, Lizards in the Fridge	T	RF	250+	Wallace, Bill	Language for Learning Assoc.
Ferret Rescue	Q	RF	250+	Reading Expeditions	National Geographic
Ferrets	S	I	250+	Keeping Unusual Pets	Heinemann Library
Ferry, The	C	RF	27	Sunshine	Wright Group/McGraw Hill
Festival Foods Around the World	M	I	250+	Stull, Becky	Steck-Vaughn
Festival Fun	N	I	250+	Wildcats	Wright Group/McGraw Hill
Festival in Valencia	L	RF	301	Leveled Readers	Houghton Mifflin Harcourt
Festival, The	D	I	146	Fiesta Series	Pearson Learning Group
Festival, the	B	I	37	Windows on Literacy	National Geographic
Festivals	F	I	40	Berger, Samantha; Chanko, Pamela	Scholastic
Festivals and Feasts	O	I	250+	InfoQuest	Rigby
Festus the Clownfish Finds a Home	Q	F	250+	Pair-It Books	Steck-Vaughn
Fever 1793	Z	HF	250+	Anderson, Laurie Halse	Simon & Schuster
Fibers from Plants	I	I	392	Sunshine	Wright Group/McGraw Hill
Fibers in Fashion	U	I	250+	PM Plus	Rigby
Fibers Made by People	M	I	442	Sunshine	Wright Group/McGraw Hill
Fibonacci's Cows	U	I	250+	Storyteller-Mountain Peaks	Wright Group/McGraw Hill
*Fiddle and the Gun, The	M	F	250+	Literacy 2000	Rigby
Fiddle Maker, The	P	RF	4745	Take Two Books	Wright Group/McGraw Hill
Fidel Castro	X	B	250+	A&E Biography	Lerner Publishing Group
Field Day with Alex, A	D	F	96	Javernick, Ellen	Kaeden Books
Field Full of Horses, A	M	I	250+	Read and Wonder	Candlewick Press

F

TITLE	LEVEL	GENRE	WORD COUNT	AUTHOR / SERIES	PUBLISHER / DISTRIBUTOR
Field Guide to Aliens, A: Intergalatic Worrywarts, Bubblonauts, Silver-Slurpers, and Other Extraterrestrials	V	SF	250+	Olander, Johan	Marshall Cavendish
Field Guide to Dangerous Animals	N	I	250+	Infotrek Plus	ETA/Cuisenaire
Field Mouse and the Dinosaur Named Sue, The	L	F	250+	Wahl, Jan	Scholastic
Field of Gold	H	TL	172	Rigby Star	Rigby
Field Trip to Niagara Falls	O	F	250+	Stilton, Geronimo	Scholastic
Field Trip, The	L	RF	853	Springboard	Wright Group/McGraw Hill
Fields of Home	T	HF	250+	Conlon-McKenna, Marita	The O'Brien Press
Fields of Hope	V	I	250+	WorldScapes	ETA/Cuisenaire
Fiesta	LB	I	43	Guy, Ginger Foglesong	Greenwillow Books
Fiesta	D	RF	50	Javernick, Ellen	Kaeden Books
Fiesta Fiasco	M	F	250+	Paul, Ann Whitford	Holiday House
Fiesta Time	C	I	28	Little Celebrations	Pearson Learning Group
Fiesta!	M	I	250+	Festivals and Holidays	Children's Press
Fife and Drum Boys	S	HF	1584	Leveled Readers	Houghton Mifflin Harcourt
Fife and Drum Boys	S	HF	1584	Leveled Readers/CA	Houghton Mifflin Harcourt
Fife and Drum Boys	S	HF	1584	Leveled Readers/TX	Houghton Mifflin Harcourt
FiFi's Bath	K	RF	436	Leveled Readers	Houghton Mifflin Harcourt
FiFi's Bath	K	RF	436	Leveled Readers/CA	Houghton Mifflin Harcourt
FiFi's Bath	K	RF	436	Leveled Readers/TX	Houghton Mifflin Harcourt
Fifth Grade: Here Comes Trouble	S	RF	250+	McKenna, Colleen O'Shaughnessy	Scholastic
Fifth of March, The	Y	HF	250+	Rinaldi, Ann	Harcourt, Inc.
Fig Pudding	R	RF	250+	Fletcher, Ralph	Clarion
Figaro	K	F	250+	Voyages	SRA/McGraw Hill
Fight for Freedom	V	I	250+	Reading Expeditions	National Geographic
Fight For Freedom: The American Revolutionary War	X	I	250+	Bobrick, Benson	Scholastic
Fight for Right, The	V	I	250+	Power Up!	Steck-Vaughn
Fight in the Schoolyard, The	K	RF	129	City Kids	Rigby
Fight on the Hill, The	I	F	336	Read Alongs	Rigby
Fighter Planes	G	I	115	Mighty Machines	Capstone Press
Fighter Planes	V	I	4968	Military Hardware in Action	Lerner Publishing Group
Fighter Planes	N	I	470	Pull Ahead Books	Lerner Publishing Group
Fighting Disease	X	I	250+	Reading Expeditions	National Geographic
Fighting Fire with Fire	W	I	2951	Leveled Readers	Houghton Mifflin Harcourt
Fighting Fire with Fire	W	I	2951	Leveled Readers/CA	Houghton Mifflin Harcourt
Fighting Fire With Fire	M	I	250+	Rigby Literacy	Rigby
Fighting Fires	G	I	198	Leveled Literacy Intervention/ Blue System	Heinemann
Fighting Fires Then and Now	L	I	381	Leveled Readers	Houghton Mifflin Harcourt
Fighting Fish	O	I	250+	Life Cycles	Creative Teaching Press
Fighting for Equal Rights: A Story About Susan B. Anthony	R	B	8730	Creative Minds Biographies	Carolrhoda Books
Fighting for Freedom	Q	B	250+	WorldScapes	ETA/Cuisenaire
Fighting for History	R	I	250+	Explorer Books-Pathfinder	National Geographic
Fighting for History	Q	I	250+	Explorer Books-Pioneer	National Geographic
Fighting Ground, The	V	HF	250+	Avi	HarperTrophy
Fighting Tackle	R	RF	250+	Christopher, Matt	Little Brown and Company
Figure in the Shadows, The	S	F	250+	Bellairs, John	Penguin Group
Fiji Facts and Figures	O	I	250+	WorldScapes	ETA/Cuisenaire
Fiji Flood, The	M	F	250+	Woodland Mysteries	Wright Group/McGraw Hill
Filbert the Fly	C	F	28	Literacy 2000	Rigby
Film	Z	I	250+	Eyewitness Books	DK Publishing
Final Cut, The	Q	RF	250+	Bowen, Fred	Peachtree

Organized Alphabetically by Title
Storable Database at www.fountasandpinnellleveledbooks.com

* Collection of short stories   # Graphic text
^ Mature content with lower level text demands

TITLE	LEVEL	GENRE	WORD COUNT	AUTHOR / SERIES	PUBLISHER / DISTRIBUTOR
Final Freedom, The	V	RF	250+	Wallace, Bill	Pocket Books
Finally	U	RF	250+	Mass Wendy	Scholastic
Fina's Story: From Mexico to Texas	U	HF	250+	Reading Expeditions	National Geographic
*Finch Family Summer	M	F	250+	Sunshine	Wright Group/McGraw Hill
Finches' Fabulous Furnace, The	O	F	250+	Drury, Roger	Scholastic
Find a Caterpillar	E	I	102	Book Bank	Wright Group/McGraw Hill
Find a Stranger, Say Goodbye	X	RF	250+	Lowry, Lois	Dell
Find It	C	RF	63	Carousel Earlybirds	Pearson Learning Group
Find It on the Map	G	I	61	Shutterbug Books	Steck-Vaughn
Find Out About It!	T	I	250+	iOpeners	Pearson Learning Group
Find the Bug	A	RF	29	Leveled Readers	Houghton Mifflin Harcourt
Find the Bug	A	RF	29	Leveled Readers/CA	Houghton Mifflin Harcourt
Find the Cat!	I	F	256	Stone Arch Readers	Stone Arch Books
FInd the Prize	E	RF	39	Independent Readers Social Studies	Houghton Mifflin Harcourt
Find the Shapes	B	I	36	InfoTrek	ETA/Cuisenaire
Find the Wild Animal	F	I	108	Foley, Cate	Scholastic
Find Yourself a Friend	F	RF	261	Visions	Wright Group/McGraw Hill
Finders Keepers	H	RF	191	The King School Series	Townsend Press
Finders Keepers?	T	I	250+	WorldScapes	ETA/Cuisenaire
Finding a Dinosaur Named Sue	N	I	615	Reading Street	Pearson
Finding a Way: Six Historic U.S. Routes	W	I	250+	iOpeners	Pearson Learning Group
Finding a Wooly Mammoth	F	I	120	Independent Readers Science	Houghton Mifflin Harcourt
Finding Africa	K	I	277	Early Explorers	Benchmark Education
Finding Aunt Maria	N	RF	250+	Windows on Literacy	National Geographic
Finding Buck McHenry	S	RF	250+	Slote, Alfred	Scholastic
Finding Chance	S	RF	250+	Bookshop	Mondo Publishing
^Finding Elmo	S	RF	250+	Orca Currents	Orca Books
Finding Family	T	HF	250+	Bolden, Tonya	Bloomsbury Children's Books
Finding Gold	N	I	848	Leveled Readers Science	Houghton Mifflin Harcourt
Finding Home Again	U	RF	250+	Reading Expeditions	National Geographic
Finding Miracles	Y	RF	250+	Edge	Hampton Brown
Finding My Hat	Z	RF	250+	Son, John	Scholastic
Finding My Place	Z	HF	250+	Jones, Tracie L.	Farrar, Straus, & Giroux
Finding Out About the Past	H	I	155	Windows on Literacy	National Geographic
Finding Providence: The Story of Roger Williams	P	B	250+	Avi	HarperTrophy
Finding Shapes and Solids	M	I	437	Early Explorers	Benchmark Education
Finding Talent	L	RF	250+	Literacy by Design	Rigby
Finding Talent	L	RF	250+	On Our Way to English	Rigby
Finding the First Vaccines	V	I	250+	Reading Expeditions	National Geographic
^Finding the Murder Weapon	T	I	250+	Crime Solvers	Capstone Press
Finding the Party	J	RF	613	Leveled Readers	Houghton Mifflin Harcourt
Finding the Party	J	RF	613	Leveled Readers/CA	Houghton Mifflin Harcourt
Finding the Party	J	RF	613	Leveled Readers/TX	Houghton Mifflin Harcourt
Finding the Pharaohs	V	I	250+	WorldScapes	ETA/Cuisenaire
Finding the Titanic	Q	I	250+	Ballard, Robert D.	Scholastic
Finding Your Way	R	I	250+	Orbit Chapter Books	Pacific Learning
Fine Lines	O	B	250+	Meet The Author	Richard C. Owen
Fine Print: A Story about Johann Gutenberg	S	B	7897	Creative Minds Biographies	Lerner Publishing Group
Finger Puppet, The	B	RF	18	Sunshine	Wright Group/McGraw Hill
Finger Puppets, Finger Plays	I	I	268	Storyteller-Night Crickets	Wright Group/McGraw Hill

F

TITLE	LEVEL	GENRE	WORD COUNT	AUTHOR / SERIES	PUBLISHER / DISTRIBUTOR
Fingernail Art: Dazzling Fingers and Terrific Toes	Q	I	250+	Crafts	Capstone Press
Fingerprint Family	C	I	24	Rigby Literacy	Rigby
Fingers and Thumbs	E	I	108	Sails	Rigby
Fingertips of Duncan Dorfman, The	W	RF	250+	Wolitzer, Meg	Dutton Children's Books
Finicky Fish	L	RF	250+	Rigby Gigglers	Rigby
Finland: A Question and Answer Book	P	I	250+	Questions & Answers: Countries	Capstone Press
Finn Family Moomintroll	S	F	250+	Jansson, Tove	Farrar, Straus, & Giroux
Finn MacCool and Big Head MacTavish	J	TL	250+	Lighthouse	Ginn & Co.
^Finn Reeder, Flu Fighter: How I Survived a Worldwide Pandemic, the School Bully, and the Craziest Game of Dodge Ball Ever	S	RF	250+	Stevens, Eric	Stone Arch Books
Fins, Wings, and Legs	J	I	250+	iOpeners	Pearson Learning Group
Fire	S	HF	250+	Duey, Kathleen; Bale, Karen A.	Simon & Schuster
Fire	S	HF	250+	Duey, Kathleen; Bale, Karen A.	Aladdin
Fire and Ash	P	I	250+	WorldScapes	ETA/Cuisenaire
Fire and Ice: Warriors, Book 2	U	F	250+	Hunter, Erin	Avon Books
^Fire and Snow: A Tale of the Alaskan Gold Rush	Q	HF	250+	Gunderson, J	Stone Arch Books
Fire and Water	E	TL	127	Story Box	Wright Group/McGraw Hill
Fire and Wind	L	TL	250+	PM Story Books-Silver	Rigby
Fire at the Triangle Factory	P	HF	250+	On My Own History	Carolrhoda Books
Fire at the Zoo, A	I	F	229	Sunshine	Wright Group/McGraw Hill
Fire Boats	I	I	188	Community Vehicles	Capstone Press
Fire Bug Connection, The	S	RF	250+	George, Jean Craighead	HarperTrophy
Fire Cat, The	J	F	250+	Averill, Esther	HarperTrophy
Fire Drill	E	RF	136	Jacobs, Paul DuBois & Swender, Jennifer	Henry Holt & Co.
Fire Engines	I	I	184	Community Vehicles	Capstone Press
Fire Escape	L	I	250+	InfoTrek Plus	ETA/Cuisenaire
Fire Fighter!	L	I	250+	DK Readers	DK Publishing
Fire Fighter, The	A	I	25	Leveled Readers	Houghton Mifflin Harcourt
Fire Fighter, The	A	I	25	Leveled Readers/CA	Houghton Mifflin Harcourt
Fire Fighters	M	I	250+	Community Helpers	Red Brick Learning
Fire Fighters	L	I	250+	Community Workers	Compass Point Books
Fire in the Hills	Y	HF	250+	Myers, Anna	Puffin Books
Fire in the Jungle	J	F	458	Red Rocket Readers	Flying Start Books
Fire in the Sky	R	I	1215	Leveled Readers	Houghton Mifflin Harcourt
Fire in the Sky	R	I	1215	Leveled Readers/CA	Houghton Mifflin Harcourt
Fire in the Sky	R	HF	250+	Ransom, Candice F.	Carolrhoda Books
Fire in the Wind	U	RF	250+	Levin, Betty	Beech Tree Books
Fire in Wild Wood	G	F	214	Storyworlds	Heinemann
Fire of Ares, The	Y	HF	250+	Ford, Michael	Walker & Company
Fire on the Farm	M	RF	250+	PM Plus Chapter Books	Rigby
Fire on Toytown Hill, The	F	F	166	PM Plus Story Books	Rigby
Fire Safety	F	I	40	Safety	Lerner Publishing Group
Fire Safety Day	M	RF	749	Leveled Readers	Houghton Mifflin Harcourt
Fire Safety in Action	I	I	164	Fighting Fire	Capstone Press
Fire Station	D	I	33	Community Buildings	Lerner Publishing Group
Fire Station, The	J	I	237	Pebble Books	Capstone Press
Fire Stations in Action	I	I	149	Fighting Fire	Capstone Press
Fire Thief Fights Back, The	V	F	250+	Deary, Terry	Kingfisher
Fire Trucks	G	I	127	Mighty Machines	Capstone Press
Fire Trucks	K	I	327	Pull Ahead Books	Lerner Publishing Group
Fire Trucks	M	I	250+	Transportation	Compass Point Books

* Collection of short stories   # Graphic text
^ Mature content with lower level text demands

TITLE	LEVEL	GENRE	WORD COUNT	AUTHOR / SERIES	PUBLISHER / DISTRIBUTOR
Fire Trucks in Action	I	I	131	Fighting Fire	Capstone Press
Fire Trucks in Action	L	I	250+	Transportation Zone	Capstone Press
Fire Trucks on the Move	K	I	351	Lightning Bolt Books	Lerner Publishing Group
Fire Zenith, The	R	F	250+	Sails	Rigby
Fire!	Q	I	250+	Bookweb	Rigby
Fire!	I	RF	224	Breakthrough	Longman
Fire!	M	RF	250+	Rigby Flying Colors	Rigby
Fire!	K	F	250+	Rigby Literacy	Rigby
Fire! Fire!	I	I	384	Big Cat	Pacific Learning
Fire! Fire!	P	I	250+	Orbit Chapter Books	Pacific Learning
Fire! Fire!	E	RF	164	PM Story Books	Rigby
Fire! Fire!	L	I	250+	Storyteller Chapter Books	Wright Group/McGraw Hill
Fire! Fire!	O	I	250+	Wildcats	Wright Group/McGraw Hill
Fire! in Yellowstone: A True Adventure	O	I	250+	Soar To Success	Houghton Mifflin Harcourt
Fire! The Beginnings of the Labor Movement	R	HF	250+	Goldin, Barbara Diamond	Puffin Books
Fire, Bed & Bone	X	HF	250+	Branford, Henrietta	Candlewick Press
Fire, The	D	RF	120	Sails	Rigby
*Fire-Bird, The	U	TL	250+	Literacy 2000	Rigby
Fireboats in Action	I	I	156	Fighting Fire	Capstone Press
Firedog!	G	RF	217	Leveled Readers	Houghton Mifflin Harcourt
Firedog!	G	RF	217	Leveled Readers/CA	Houghton Mifflin Harcourt
Firedog!	G	RF	217	Leveled Readers/TX	Houghton Mifflin Harcourt
Firefighter	D	I	31	Benchmark Rebus	Marshall Cavendish
Firefighter	C	I	23	Work People Do	Lerner Publishing Group
Firefighter Phil and His Equipment	LB	I	24	Run to Reading	Discovery Peak
Firefighter Wears a Helmet, A	F	I	79	Windows on Literacy	National Geographic
Firefighters	E	RF	250+	Bookshop	Mondo Publishing
Firefighters	L	I	250+	Mitten, Christopher	Scholastic
Firefighters	J	I	167	Nonfiction Set 7	Literacy Footprints
Firefighters	K	I	470	Pull Ahead Books	Lerner Publishing Group
Firefighters	L	I	623	Sun Sprouts	ETA/Cuisenaire
Firefighters	T	I	250+	The News	Richard C. Owen
Firefighters in America	M	I	619	Leveled Readers	Houghton Mifflin Harcourt
Firefighters in America	M	I	619	Leveled Readers/CA	Houghton Mifflin Harcourt
Firefighters in America	M	I	619	Leveled Readers/TX	Houghton Mifflin Harcourt
Firefighters, The	K	RF	250+	Whiting, Sue	Candlewick Press
Firefighters: Then and Now	M	I	250+	Primary Source Readers	Teacher Created Materials
Firefighting Then and Now	T	I	2226	Leveled Readers	Houghton Mifflin Harcourt
Firefighting Then and Now	T	I	2226	Leveled Readers/CA	Houghton Mifflin Harcourt
Fireflies	L	I	232	Ashley, Susan/Let's Read About Insects	Weekly Reader Publishing
Fireflies	H	I	135	Bugs, Bugs, Bugs!	Capstone Press
Fireflies	Q	I	2704	Early Bird Nature Books	Lerner Publishing Group
Fireflies	L	I	289	Leveled Readers	Houghton Mifflin Harcourt
Fireflies	L	I	289	Leveled Readers/CA	Houghton Mifflin Harcourt
Fireflies	L	I	289	Leveled Readers/TX	Houghton Mifflin Harcourt
Fireflies	F	I	85	Little Celebrations	Pearson Learning Group
Fireflies	O	I	250+	Nature's Friends	Compass Point Books
Fireflies	E	I	49	Pebble Books	Capstone Press
Fireflies	E	I	57	Vocabulary Readers	Houghton Mifflin Harcourt
Fireflies in the Night	M	I	250+	Hawes, Judy	HarperTrophy
Fireflies!	L	I	250+	Twig	Wright Group/McGraw Hill
Firefly and the Quest of the Black Squirrel: The Fairy Chronicles	Q	F	12800	Sweet, J.H.	Sourcebooks

TITLE	LEVEL	GENRE	WORD COUNT	AUTHOR / SERIES	PUBLISHER / DISTRIBUTOR
Firefly at Stonybrook Farm	N	I	250+	Pfeffer, Wendy	Smithsonian
Firefly Friend	D	RF	116	Rookie Readers	Children's Press
Firefly Letters, The	Z	HF	250+	Engle, Margarita	Henry Holt & Co.
Firefly Moutain	P	RF	250+	Thomas, Patricia	Peachtree
Firefly Named Torchy, A	L	F	250+	Waber, Bernard	Houghton Mifflin Harcourt
Firegirl	V	RF	250+	Abbott, Tony	Little Brown and Company
Firehouse	A	I	36	Vocabulary Readers	Houghton Mifflin Harcourt
Firehouse	A	I	36	Vocabulary Readers/CA	Houghton Mifflin Harcourt
Firehouse	A	I	36	Vocabulary Readers/TX	Houghton Mifflin Harcourt
Firehouse Sal	F	RF	52	Rookie Readers	Children's Press
Firelight Secrets	O	RF	250+	PM Collection	Rigby
Fires	W	I	250+	Disasters Up Close	Lerner Publishing Group
Fires in the Wild	U	I	250+	Sails	Rigby
Firestar's Quest: Warriors Manga	U	F	250+	Hunter, Erin	HarperCollins
Firestorm	Z+	F	250+	Klass, David	Square Fish
Firetalking	O	B	250+	Meet The Author	Richard C. Owen
Firewing	Y	F	250+	Oppel, Kenneth	Aladdin
Firework-Maker's Daughter, The	V	F	250+	Pullman, Philip	Scholastic
Fireworks	C	RF	29	Joy Readers	Pearson Learning Group
Fireworks	U	I	250+	Where's the Science Here?	Lerner Publishing Group
Fireworks at the FBI	N	RF	250+	Roy, Ron	Random House
Fireworks for All	K	F	250+	Martha Speaks	Houghton Mifflin Harcourt
Fireworks!	P	I	889	Leveled Readers Science	Houghton Mifflin Harcourt
First 100 Animals	LB	I	137	Bright Baby	Priddy Books
First Aid	F	I	44	Canizares, Susan; Chanko, Pamela	Scholastic
First American Colonies	R	I	250+	World Discovery History Readers	Scholastic
First American Flag, The	N	I	250+	Our American Story	Picture Window Books
First Americans, The	O	I	250+	People, Spaces & Places	Rand McNally
^First and Final Voyage, The: The Sinking of the Titanic	Q	HF	250+	Peters, Stephanie	Stone Arch Books
First and Last	C	I	44	Teacher's Choice Series	Pearson Learning Group
First and Ten	V	RF	250+	South Side Sports	Orca Books
First Apple	N	RF	250+	Russell, Ching Yueng	Penguin Group
First Art Class, The	G	RF	250+	Leveled Readers Language Support	Houghton Mifflin Harcourt
First Big Game, The	N	HF	821	Reading Street	Pearson
First Book About Africa: An Introduction for Young Readers	Q	I	250+	Ellis, Veronica Freeman	Just Us Books
First Boy	U	RF	250+	Schmidt, Gary	Square Fish
First Builders, The	O	I	250+	Orbit Chapter Books	Pacific Learning
First Cars	L	I	371	Red Rocket Readers	Flying Start Books
First Civilizations, The	Y	I	250+	Reading Expeditions	National Geographic
First Collier, The: Guardians of Ga'Hoole	V	F	250+	Lasky, Kathryn	Scholastic
First Cowboys, The	Q	I	1180	Vocabulary Readers	Houghton Mifflin Harcourt
First Cowboys, The	Q	I	1180	Vocabulary Readers/CA	Houghton Mifflin Harcourt
First Day	C	RF	64	InfoTrek	ETA/Cuisenaire
First Day Back at School	H	RF	132	City Kids	Rigby
First Day For Carlos	P	RF	764	Leveled Readers	Houghton Mifflin Harcourt
First Day Jitters	L	RF	250+	Danneberg, Julie	Charlesbridge
First Day of School	D	RF	60	Carousel Readers	Pearson Learning Group
First Day of School	LB	RF	16	Visions	Wright Group/McGraw Hill
First Day of School, The	A	RF	28	Bookshop	Mondo Publishing

* Collection of short stories   # Graphic text
^ Mature content with lower level text demands

TITLE	LEVEL	GENRE	WORD COUNT	AUTHOR / SERIES	PUBLISHER / DISTRIBUTOR
First Day of School, The	G	RF	262	Handprints D	Educators Publishing Service
First Day of Second Grade	H	RF	263	Leveled Readers	Houghton Mifflin Harcourt
First Day of Second Grade	H	RF	263	Leveled Readers/CA	Houghton Mifflin Harcourt
First Day of Second Grade	H	RF	263	Leveled Readers/TX	Houghton Mifflin Harcourt
First Day of Winter, The	I	RF	250+	Fleming, Denise	Scholastic
First Dinosaur Picture Atlas	R	I	250+	Burnie, David	Kingfisher
First Dog Fala	R	B	250+	Montgomery, Michael G.	Peachtree
First Emperor, The	W	I	1617	Vocabulary Readers	Houghton Mifflin Harcourt
First Emperor, The	W	I	1617	Vocabulary Readers/CA	Houghton Mifflin Harcourt
First Emperor, The	W	I	1617	Vocabulary Readers/TX	Houghton Mifflin Harcourt
First Family on Mars, The	P	SF	250+	Orbit Double Takes	Pacific Learning
First Family: The Roosevelts	U	B	2374	Independent Readers Social Studies	Houghton Mifflin Harcourt
First Fire Company, The	J	I	182	Leveled Readers	Houghton Mifflin Harcourt
First Fire, The	K	F	250+	Little Celebrations	Pearson Learning Group
First Fire: A Traditional Native American Tale	K	TL	250+	Rigby Literacy	Rigby
First Flight	Q	I	250+	Explorer Books-Pathfinder	National Geographic
First Flight	P	I	250+	Explorer Books-Pioneer	National Geographic
First Flight	J	RF	250+	PM Plus Story Books	Rigby
First Flight	L	I	356	Red Rocket Readers	Flying Start Books
First Flight	K	B	250+	Shea, George	HarperTrophy
First Flight: The Story of the Wright Brothers	R	B	250+	DK Readers	DK Publishing
First Four Years, The	R	HF	250+	Wilder, Laura Ingalls	HarperTrophy
*First French Kiss and Other Traumas	Z+	RF	250+	Bagdasarian, Adam	Farrar, Straus, & Giroux
First Geologists, The	U	B	250+	Science Readers	Teacher Created Materials
First Grade Stinks!	K	RF	250+	Rodman, Mary Ann	Peachtree
First Grade Takes a Test	J	RF	250+	Cohen, Miriam	Bantam Books
First Hot-Air Balloons, The	M	I	250+	Take Two Books	Wright Group/McGraw Hill
First Humans, The	U	I	1814	Leveled Readers Social Studies	Houghton Mifflin Harcourt
First in Line	D	RF	77	Teacher's Choice Series	Pearson Learning Group
First in Space	R	I	250+	WorldScapes	ETA/Cuisenaire
First Journeys	X	I	250+	iOpeners	Pearson Learning Group
First Ladies	U	B	250+	Cornerstones of Freedom	Children's Press
*First Ladies of the White House	U	B	250+	Skarmeas, Nancy	Ideals Publications Inc.
*First Ladies: Women Who Called the White House Home	U	B	250+	Gormley, Beatrice	Scholastic
First Lady of Track, The	O	I	885	Vocabulary Readers	Houghton Mifflin Harcourt
First Lady of Track, The	O	I	885	Vocabulary Readers/CA	Houghton Mifflin Harcourt
First Lady of Track, The	O	I	885	Vocabulary Readers/TX	Houghton Mifflin Harcourt
First Marathon, The	Q	B	250+	Reynolds, Susan	Albert Whitman & Co.
First Men on the Moon, The	R	B	3856	History Maker Bios	Lerner Publishing Group
#First Moon Landing, The	S	I	250+	Graphic Library	Capstone Press
First Moon Landing, The	M	I	250+	The Solar System	Capstone Press
First Morning, The	N	TL	250+	Literacy 2000	Rigby
First of First Ladies: Martha Washington	T	B	250+	We the People	Compass Point Books
First Olympians, The	Y	I	2437	Vocabulary Readers	Houghton Mifflin Harcourt
First Olympians, The	Y	I	2437	Vocabulary Readers/CA	Houghton Mifflin Harcourt
First On The Moon	Y	I	250+	Hehner, Barbara	Hyperion
First Part Last, The	Z+	RF	250+	Johnson, Angela	Simon & Schuster
First People, The	T	I	1962	Leveled Readers Language Support	Houghton Mifflin Harcourt
First Pooch: The Obamas Pick a Pet	N	RF	250+	Weatherford, Carole Boston	Marshall Cavendish
First Rainbow, The: A Zapotec Myth, The	O	TL	250+	On Our Way to English	Rigby

F

TITLE	LEVEL	GENRE	WORD COUNT	AUTHOR / SERIES	PUBLISHER / DISTRIBUTOR
First Sleepover	F	RF	154	The King School Series	Townsend Press
First Snow	WB	RF	0	McCully, Emily Arnold	Harper & Row
First Son and President: A Story about John Quincy Adams	S	B	8707	Creative Minds Biographies	Lerner Publishing Group
First Thanksgiving, The	M	I	250+	Rogers, Lou	Pearson Learning Group
First Thanksgiving, The	M	I	250+	Step into Reading	Random House
First Thanksgiving, The	R	I	250+	The Library of the Pilgrims	Rosen Publishing Group
First Things	LB	RF	18	Home Connection Collection	Rigby
First Things	N	RF	250+	Stepping Stones	Nelson/Michaels Assoc.
First to the Top	L	I	304	Red Rocket Readers	Flying Start Books
First Woman Doctor, The	P	B	880	Leveled Readers	Houghton Mifflin Harcourt
First Woman Doctor, The	P	B	880	Leveled Readers/CA	Houghton Mifflin Harcourt
First Woman Doctor, The	P	B	880	Leveled Readers/TX	Houghton Mifflin Harcourt
First Woman Doctor, The	T	B	250+	Rachel Baker	Scholastic
First Year Letters	M	RF	250+	Danneberg, Julie	Charlesbridge
First Year, The	N	HF	922	Reading Street	Pearson
First, Second, Third	D	I	28	Shutterbug Books	Steck-Vaughn
First, Second, Third	C	I	24	Windows on Literacy	National Geographic
First, Take the Flour	L	I	186	Rigby Literacy	Rigby
First-Aid Handbook	S	I	250+	iOpeners	Pearson Learning Group
Firsts in Forecasting	T	I	1439	Vocabulary Readers	Houghton Mifflin Harcourt
Firsts in Forecasting	T	I	1439	Vocabulary Readers/CA	Houghton Mifflin Harcourt
Fish	D	I	34	All About Pets	Red Brick Learning
Fish	M	I	250+	Exploring the Animal Kingdom	Capstone Press
Fish	W	I	250+	Eyewitness Books	DK Publishing
Fish	L	I	298	Marine Life For Young Readers	Pearson Learning Group
Fish	O	I	250+	Nature's Friends	Compass Point Books
Fish	D	I	58	Sun Sprouts	ETA/Cuisenaire
Fish	D	I	58	Wonder World	Wright Group/McGraw Hill
Fish and the Cat, The	C	F	91	Sun Sprouts	ETA/Cuisenaire
Fish Bowl, The	C	I	48	Sun Sprouts	ETA/Cuisenaire
Fish Can Swim	E	I	102	Reading Street	Pearson
Fish Colors	LB	I	6	Vocabulary Readers	Houghton Mifflin Harcourt
Fish Colours	C	I	37	Rigby Rocket	Rigby
Fish Face	M	RF	250+	Giff, Patricia Reilly	Bantam Books
Fish Facts	D	I	55	Rigby Rocket	Rigby
Fish Facts	C	I	27	Shutterbug Books	Steck-Vaughn
Fish for Dinner	M	RF	250+	PM Extensions	Rigby
Fish for Dinner	C	RF	93	Sails	Rigby
Fish for Lunch, A	D	F	62	Rigby Star	Rigby
Fish for Sale	K	RF	250+	Supa Doopers	Sundance
Fish For the Grand Lady	Q	RF	250+	Bootman, Colin	Holiday House
Fish for You, A: Caring for Your Fish	M	I	250+	Pet Care	Picture Window Books
Fish from the Rainbow	I	F	239	Sunshine	Wright Group/McGraw Hill
^Fish Gut Experiment, The	T	F	250+	Starke, R.	Stone Arch Books
Fish Guts	J	RF	439	Rigby Gigglers	Rigby
Fish is Fish	L	F	250+	Lionni, Leo	Scholastic
Fish Makes Faces	C	F	35	Brand New Readers	Candlewick Press
Fish Named Goggles, A	H	RF	218	PM Photo Stories	Rigby
Fish on the Move	P	I	1061	Leveled Readers	Houghton Mifflin Harcourt
Fish on the Move	P	I	1061	Leveled Readers/CA	Houghton Mifflin Harcourt
Fish on the Move	P	I	1061	Leveled Readers/TX	Houghton Mifflin Harcourt
Fish Picture, A	B	RF	58	First Stories	Pacific Learning
Fish Print	B	I	25	Bebop Books	Lee & Low Books Inc.

F

* Collection of short stories   # Graphic text
^ Mature content with lower level text demands

TITLE	LEVEL	GENRE	WORD COUNT	AUTHOR / SERIES	PUBLISHER / DISTRIBUTOR
Fish Stew for Supper	C	I	56	First Stories	Pacific Learning
Fish Story, A	C	I	51	Coulton, Mia	Maryruth Books
Fish Swims	C	F	32	Brand New Readers	Candlewick Press
Fish Tank, The	C	I	91	Leveled Literacy Intervention/ Blue System	Heinemann
Fish That Hide	L	I	250+	Marine Life For Young Readers	Pearson Learning Group
Fish That Migrate	P	I	1039	Leveled Readers	Houghton Mifflin Harcourt
Fish That Migrate	P	I	1039	Leveled Readers/CA	Houghton Mifflin Harcourt
Fish That Migrate	P	I	1039	Leveled Readers/TX	Houghton Mifflin Harcourt
Fish Tricks	S	I	250+	Underwater Encounters	Hameray Publishing Group
Fish, Not Fish	S	I	250+	Underwater Encounters	Hameray Publishing Group
Fish: Finned and Gilled Animals	N	I	250+	Amazing Science	Picture Window Books
Fisherman and the Golden Fish, The	J	TL	553	Pawprints Teal	Pioneer Valley
Fishers: Then and Now	N	I	250+	Primary Source Readers	Teacher Created Materials
Fishing	G	RF	180	Foundations	Wright Group/McGraw Hill
Fishing	C	RF	15	Instant Readers	Harcourt School Publishers
Fishing	C	I	35	KinderReaders	Rigby
Fishing	C	I	100	Leveled Literacy Intervention/ Blue System	Heinemann
Fishing	B	I	41	Little Books for Early Readers	University of Maine
Fishing	C	RF	63	PM Starters	Rigby
Fishing	B	F	40	Reed, Janet	Scholastic
Fishing	C	RF	35	Story Box	Wright Group/McGraw Hill
Fishing	E	RF	47	Wonder World	Wright Group/McGraw Hill
Fishing	D	RF	48	Yukish, Joe	Kaeden Books
Fishing Adventure, The	H	F	232	Arctic Stories	Pioneer Valley
Fishing Bears	K	I	321	Pull Ahead Books	Lerner Publishing Group
Fishing Contest, The	E	RF	84	Literacy Tree	Rigby
Fishing Contest, The	H	RF	250+	Yukish, Joe	Kaeden Books
Fishing Family	L	I	281	Independent Readers Science	Houghton Mifflin Harcourt
Fishing Fanatic	M	F	250+	Too Cool	Pacific Learning
Fishing Fun	I	RF	250+	Bebop Books	Lee & Low Books Inc.
Fishing Game, The	D	RF	69	Windows on Literacy	National Geographic
Fishing in the City	K	F	625	Pawprints Teal	Pioneer Valley
Fishing Is Fun	G	I	207	Rigby Flying Colors	Rigby
Fishing Off the Wharf	M	RF	274	Pacific Literacy	Pacific Learning
Fishing Trip, The	E	RF	121	Adams, Lorraine & Bruvold, Lynn	Eaglecrest Books
Fishing Trip, The	B	RF	74	Literacy by Design	Rigby
Fishing Trip, The	K	RF	250+	PM Plus Story Books	Rigby
Fishing Trip, The	D	RF	89	Springboard	Wright Group/McGraw Hill
Fishing with Sam	U	RF	2764	Leveled Readers	Houghton Mifflin Harcourt
Fishing with Sam	U	RF	2764	Leveled Readers/CA	Houghton Mifflin Harcourt
Fishing with Sam	U	RF	2764	Leveled Readers/TX	Houghton Mifflin Harcourt
Fishing with the Birds	N	I	250+	WorldScapes	ETA/Cuisenaire
Fishing!	C	RF	40	Sails	Rigby
Fishy Alphabet Story	F	F	126	Wylie, Joanne & David	Children's Press
Fishy Color Story	D	F	142	Wylie, Joanne & David	Children's Press
Fishy Colors	B	I	64	Color My World	American Reading Company
Fishy Mystery, The	N	RF	250+	Orbit Chapter Books	Pacific Learning
Fishy Names	B	I	41	Bonnell, Kris	Reading Reading Books
Fishy Scales	I	F	107	Mathtales	Mimosa
Fishy Story, A	L	F	174	Books for Young Learners	Richard C. Owen
Fishy Story, A	C	F	102	Pair-It Books	Steck-Vaughn

F

TITLE	LEVEL	GENRE	WORD COUNT	AUTHOR / SERIES	PUBLISHER / DISTRIBUTOR
Fishy, Flashy Fourth, The	M	RF	250+	Woodland Mysteries	Wright Group/McGraw Hill
Fitness	C	F	60	Foundations	Wright Group/McGraw Hill
Fitness and Training	N	I	667	Vocabulary Readers	Houghton Mifflin Harcourt
Fitness and Training	N	I	667	Vocabulary Readers/CA	Houghton Mifflin Harcourt
Fitness For Fun!	S	I	250+	For Fun!	Compass Point Books
Fitness Is Fun	I	I	193	Red Rocket Readers	Flying Start Books
Fitness Test, The	H	RF	343	The Rowland Reading Program Library	Rowland Reading Foundation
Fitting In	T	I	250+	WorldScapes	ETA/Cuisenaire
Five	LB	I	17	Count on It!	Marshall Cavendish
Five and Five Are Ten	F	I	128	PM Math Readers	Rigby
Five Beans	H	I	197	Sun Sprouts	ETA/Cuisenaire
Five Bears All in a Den	E	F	88	Reading Street	Pearson
Five Birds and Five Mice	D	RF	108	PM Math Readers	Rigby
Five Boxes	F	RF	203	In Step Readers	Rigby
*Five Brave Explorers	Q	B	250+	Hudson, Wade	Scholastic
*Five Brilliant Scientists	Q	B	250+	Jones, Lynda	Scholastic
Five Children and It	R	F	5945	Oxford Bookworms Library	Oxford University Press
Five Danny Dogs	F	F	122	Coulton, Mia	Maryruth Books
Five Days to Go!	K	RF	250+	Rigby Literacy	Rigby
Five Ducks	D	RF	89	Joy Readers	Pearson Learning Group
*Five Funny Frights	K	RF	250+	Bauer, Judith	Scholastic
Five Funny Uncles	I	RF	269	Story Box	Wright Group/McGraw Hill
Five Little Dinosaurs	E	F	113	Ready Readers	Pearson Learning Group
Five Little Dogs	D	F	123	Bella and Rosie Series	Literacy Footprints
Five Little Foxes and the Snow	I	F	250+	Johnston, Tony	G.P. Putnam's Sons
Five Little Monkeys	F	TL	81	Bookshelf	Scholastic
Five Little Monkeys	F	F	81	Bookshop	Mondo Publishing
Five Little Monkeys	G	F	160	Cambridge Reading	Pearson Learning Group
Five Little Monkeys Going to the Zoo	E	F	201	Valerie Cutteridge's First Grade	Continental Press
Five Little Monkeys Jumping on the Bed	E	TL	200	Christelow, Eileen	Houghton Mifflin Harcourt
Five Little Monsters	D	F	146	Learn to Read	Creative Teaching Press
Five Little Monsters Went to School	E	F	65	Learn to Read	Creative Teaching Press
Five Little Speckled Frogs	G	RF	180	Tiger Cub	Peguis
Five Lives of Our Cat Zook, The	S	RF	250+	Rocklin, Joanne	Amulet Books
Five Lost Aunts of Harriet Bean, The	O	RF	250+	Smith, Alexander McCall	Bloomsbury Children's Books
*Five Notable Inventors	Q	B	250+	Hudson, Wade	Scholastic
Five Senses	G	I	122	Dominie Factivity Series	Pearson Learning Group
Five Senses	D	RF	101	Sun Sprouts	ETA/Cuisenaire
Five Senses, The	C	I	53	Rigby Focus	Rigby
Five Senses, The	K	I	280	Story Box	Wright Group/McGraw Hill
Five Senses, The	S	I	250+	Time for Kids	Teacher Created Materials
Five Silly Fishermen	G	TL	250+	Edwards, Roberta	Random House
Five Stars for Emily	O	RF	250+	Orca Young Readers	Orca Books
Five Stops	E	RF	104	Reading Street	Pearson Learning Group
*Five True Dog Stories	M	I	250+	Davidson, Margaret	Scholastic
*Five True Horse Stories	M	I	250+	Davidson, Margaret	Scholastic
Five-Dog Night, The	P	RF	250+	Christelow, Eileen	Clarion
Fix It	C	I	35	InfoTrek	ETA/Cuisenaire
Fix It	I	F	171	McPhail, David	Penguin Group
Fix It, Fox	E	F	62	Ready Readers	Pearson Learning Group
Fixing Things	L	I	250+	Explorations	Okapi Educational Materials
Fixing Things	L	I	250+	Explorations	Eleanor Curtain Publishing

* Collection of short stories   # Graphic text
^ Mature content with lower level text demands

TITLE	LEVEL	GENRE	WORD COUNT	AUTHOR / SERIES	PUBLISHER / DISTRIBUTOR
Fix-It Bear	G	F	287	The Joy Cowley Collection	Hameray Publishing Group
Fix-Its, The	N	RF	250+	Windows on Literacy	National Geographic
Fizz and Splutter	E	F	92	Story Box	Wright Group/McGraw Hill
Fizzkid the Inventor	J	F	250+	Rigby Literacy	Rigby
Fizzywhiz Kid, The	T	RF	250+	Williams, Maiya	Amulet Books
Flabby Cat and Slobby Dog	L	F	620	Willis, Jeanne & Ross, Tony	Andersen Press USA
Flag	W	I	250+	Eyewitness Books	DK Publishing
Flag Book, The	N	I	792	InfoTrek	ETA/Cuisenaire
Flag Day	J	I	113	American Holidays	Lerner Publishing Group
Flag Day	Q	I	250+	Holiday Histories	Heinemann
Flag Day	L	I	116	National Holidays	Red Brick Learning
Flag For All, A	I	RF	250+	Rookie Choices	Children's Press
Flag For Our Country, A	N	I	250+	Spencer, Eve	Steck-Vaughn
Flag Throwers, The	R	I	250+	WorldScapes	ETA/Cuisenaire
Flag We Love, The	Q	I	250+	Ryan, Pam Munoz	Charlesbridge
Flag With Fifty-Six Stars: A Gift from the Survivors of Mauthausen, The	Y	I	250+	Rubin, Susan Goldman	Holiday House
Flag, The	B	I	56	Early Explorers	Benchmark Education
Flag, The	C	I	31	Leveled Readers Language Support	Houghton Mifflin Harcourt
Flags	R	I	250+	Action Packs	Rigby
Flags	U	I	250+	iOpeners	Pearson Learning Group
Flags	D	RF	41	Windows on Literacy	National Geographic
Flags Around the World	J	I	193	Early Explorers	Benchmark Education
Flags Everywhere!	B	I	25	Independent Readers Social Studies	Houghton Mifflin Harcourt
Flags of the World	U	I	250+	Bednar, Sylvie	Harry N. Abrams
Flakes and Flurries: A Book About Snow	M	I	250+	Amazing Science	Picture Window Books
Flamenco, Ole!	U	I	1729	Vocabulary Readers	Houghton Mifflin Harcourt
Flamenco, Olé!	U	I	1729	Vocabulary Readers/CA	Houghton Mifflin Harcourt
Flaming Arrows	T	HF	250+	Steele, William O.	Harcourt Trade
Flamingo Chick Grows Up, A	K	I	447	Baby Animals	Lerner Publishing Group
Flamingoes	N	I	250+	All Aboard Science Reader	Grosset & Dunlap
Flamingos	K	I	198	Colorful World of Animals	Capstone Press
Flamingos	N	I	250+	Take Two Books	Wright Group/McGraw Hill
Flap and Sing: Birds	E	I	100	Douglas, Ian	Scholastic
Flap, Flap, Fly	C	F	93	Leveled Literacy Intervention/ Orange System	Heinemann
Flash	Z+	RF	250+	Cadnum, Michael	Farrar, Straus, & Giroux
Flash Flood	N	RF	853	Reading Street	Pearson
Flash Flood!	O	I	1784	Independent Readers Science	Houghton Mifflin Harcourt
Flash Point	Y	RF	250+	Collard, Sneed B.	Peachtree
Flash, Firefly, Flash!	D	I	35	Bookworms	Marshall Cavendish
Flash: The Puppy Place	N	RF	250+	Miles, Ellen	Scholastic
Flashcards of My Life	R	RF	250+	Harper, Charise Mericle	Little Brown and Company
Flashlights	J	I	250+	Sunshine	Wright Group/McGraw Hill
Flat Broke	V	RF	250+	Paulsen, Gary	Wendy Lamb Books
Flat Hat, The	C	I	24	KinderReaders	Rigby
Flat Stanley	M	F	250+	Brown, Jeff	HarperTrophy
Flatboat Mondays	U	I	2452	Independent Readers Social Studies	Houghton Mifflin Harcourt
Flavors and Fragrances	T	I	1987	Leveled Readers Science	Houghton Mifflin Harcourt
Flawless	Y	RF	250+	Chapman, Lara	Bloomsbury Children's Books
Flawless (Pretty Little Liars)	Z+	RF	250+	Shepard, Sara	HarperCollins

F

TITLE	LEVEL	GENRE	WORD COUNT	AUTHOR / SERIES	PUBLISHER / DISTRIBUTOR
Flea and Big Bill	E	F	126	Sails	Rigby
Flea and Robber Cat	G	F	185	Sails	Rigby
Flea at the Football Game	I	F	248	Sails	Rigby
Flea Gets Wet	C	F	106	Sails	Rigby
Flea Goes Out!	E	F	151	Sails	Rigby
Flea Story, A	L	F	250+	Lionni, Leo	Scholastic
Flea Treat	L	F	250+	Rigby Rocket	Rigby
Fledgling, The	U	F	250+	Langton, Jane	Scholastic
^Flesh-Eating Machines: Maggots in the Food Chain	T	I	250+	Extreme Life	Capstone Press
Flicking the Switch	O	I	250+	Pacific Literacy	Pacific Learning
Flies	O	I	250+	A True Book	Children's Press
Flies	F	I	56	Pebble Books	Capstone Press
Flies for Dinner	C	I	37	Gear Up!	Wright Group/McGraw Hill
Flies for Lunch	D	F	35	Brand New Readers	Candlewick Press
Flight #116 Is Down!	Z	RF	250+	Cooney, Caroline B.	Scholastic
Flight Deck	C	I	30	Wonder World	Wright Group/McGraw Hill
Flight from Bear Canyon	P	RF	250+	Orca Young Readers	Orca Books
Flight from Big Tangle	P	RF	250+	Orca Young Readers	Orca Books
Flight of the Dragons, The	S	F	250+	French, Vivian	Candlewick Press
Flight of the Phoenix (Nathaniel Fludd Beastologist Book One)	R	F	250+	LaFevers, R. L.	Houghton Mifflin Harcourt
Flight of the Quetzalcoatlus: Dinosaur Cove	N	F	250+	Stone, Rex	Scholastic
Flight of the Swallows	N	I	606	Vocabulary Readers	Houghton Mifflin Harcourt
Flight of the Swallows	N	I	606	Vocabulary Readers/CA	Houghton Mifflin Harcourt
Flight of the Swallows	N	I	606	Vocabulary Readers/TX	Houghton Mifflin Harcourt
Flight of the Union, The	L	B	250+	On My Own History	Carolrhoda Books
Flight Path	P	I	250+	InfoQuest	Rigby
Flight: The Journey of Charles Lindbergh	R	I	250+	Burleigh, Robert	G.P. Putnam's Sons Books for Young Readers
Flip Flop	G	RF	70	Books for Young Learners	Richard C. Owen
Flip, Flap, Flop	I	F	252	Sunshine	Wright Group/McGraw Hill
Flipped	U	RF	250+	Van Draanen, Wendelin	Random House
Flip's Trick	H	RF	134	Ready Readers	Pearson Learning Group
Flips, Twists, and Somersaults	T	RF	250+	Reading Safari	Mondo Publishing
Float and Sink	E	I	44	Forces and Motion	Lerner Publishing Group
Floating	E	I	69	Benchmark Rebus	Marshall Cavendish
Floating	C	I	29	Little Blue Readers	Sundance
Floating	K	RF	250+	Sunshine	Wright Group/McGraw Hill
Floating and Paddling	N	I	250+	Take Two Books	Wright Group/McGraw Hill
Floating and Sinking	J	I	221	Alphakids	Sundance
Floating and Sinking	J	I	168	Bookshop	Mondo Publishing
^Floating and Sinking	P	I	250+	Our Physical World	Capstone Press
Floating and Sinking	H	I	168	Sunshine	Wright Group/McGraw Hill
Floating Circus, The	W	HF	250+	Zimmer, Tracie Vaughn	Bloomsbury Children's Books
Floating Island, The	X	F	250+	Haydon, Elizabeth	Tom Doherty
Floating Jellyfish	L	I	390	Pull Ahead Books	Lerner Publishing Group
Floating Markets of Bangkok, The	L	I	250+	Sunshine	Wright Group/McGraw Hill
Floating on Air	Q	F	1332	Leveled Readers	Houghton Mifflin Harcourt
Floating on Airships	V	I	2715	Vocabulary Readers	Houghton Mifflin Harcourt
Floating on Airships	V	I	2715	Vocabulary Readers/CA	Houghton Mifflin Harcourt
Flood	S	HF	250+	Duey, Kathleen; Bale, Karen A.	Simon & Schuster
Flood	H	RF	170	Story Box	Wright Group/McGraw Hill

* Collection of short stories   # Graphic text
^ Mature content with lower level text demands

TITLE	LEVEL	GENRE	WORD COUNT	AUTHOR / SERIES	PUBLISHER / DISTRIBUTOR
Flood!	K	RF	250+	Rigby Literacy	Rigby
Flood, The	H	RF	237	PM Story Books	Rigby
Flood, The	I	I	138	Wonder World	Wright Group/McGraw Hill
Floods	O	I	250+	A True Book	Children's Press
Floods	W	I	250+	Disasters Up Close	Lerner Publishing Group
Floods	M	I	171	Earth in Action	Capstone Press
Floods	R	I	1142	Leveled Readers	Houghton Mifflin Harcourt
Floods	M	I	708	Pull Ahead Books	Lerner Publishing Group
Floods	S	I	250+	Theme Sets	National Geographic
Floppy the Hero	F	F	74	Oxford Reading Tree	Oxford University Press
Floppy's Bath	E	F	55	Oxford Reading Tree	Oxford University Press
Flora the Dress-Up Fairy: Rainbow Magic	L	F	250+	Meadows, Daisy	Scholastic
Flora the Fly Saves the Spiders	J	F	353	Leveled Readers	Houghton Mifflin Harcourt
Flora the Fly Saves the Spiders	J	F	353	Leveled Readers/CA	Houghton Mifflin Harcourt
Flora the Fly Saves the Spiders	J	F	353	Leveled Readers/TX	Houghton Mifflin Harcourt
Flora the Frog	K	RF	250+	Isherwood, Shirley	Peachtree
Flora to the Rescue	H	F	250+	Storyworlds	Heinemann
Flora, a Friend for the Animals	J	RF	337	Sunshine	Wright Group/McGraw Hill
Florence Griffith-Joyner: Olympic Champion	K	B	184	Leveled Readers	Houghton Mifflin Harcourt
Florence Griffith-Joyner: Olympic Runner	J	B	184	Leveled Readers Language Support	Houghton Mifflin Harcourt
Florence Kelley	P	B	250+	Saller, Carol	Carolrhoda Books
Florence Nightingale	S	B	3969	History Maker Bios	Lerner Publishing Group
Florence Nightingale	P	B	1996	On My Own Biography	Lerner Publishing Group
Florence Nightingale	N	B	228	Pebble Books	Capstone Press
Florence Nightingale	T	B	3005	People to Remember Series	January Books
Florence Nightingale	P	B	250+	Photo-Illustrated Biographies	Red Brick Learning
#Florence Nightingale: Lady with the Lamp	R	B	250+	Graphic Library	Capstone Press
Florida	T	I	250+	Hello U.S.A.	Lerner Publishing Group
Florida	S	I	250+	Land of Liberty	Red Brick Learning
Florida	Q	I	250+	One Nation	Capstone Press
Florida	R	I	250+	This Land Is Your Land	Compass Point Books
Florida Everglades, The	P	I	712	Gear Up	Wright Group/McGraw Hill
Florida Everglades: Its Plants & Animals	O	I	670	Reading Street	Pearson
Florida Is the Sunshine State	O	I	231	Larkin, Bruce	Wilbooks
Florida Marlins, The	S	I	250+	Team Spirit	Norwood House Press
Florida Marlins, The	S	I	250+	Team Spirit	Norwood House Press
Florida: Facts and Symbols	O	I	250+	The States and Their Symbols	Capstone Press
Flossie and the Fox	O	F	250+	McKissack, Patricia	Scholastic
Flossing Teeth	G	I	142	Healthy Teeth	Capstone Press
Flour	K	I	174	Wonder World	Wright Group/McGraw Hill
Flower Box, The	LB	I	14	Twig	Wright Group/McGraw Hill
Flower Colors	A	I	24	Color My World	American Reading Company
Flower Farms	L	I	445	Rigby Flying Colors	Rigby
Flower for a Bee, A	D	F	71	Bonnell, Kris	Reading Reading Books
Flower Garden	J	RF	146	Bunting, Eve	Scholastic
Flower Girl, The	C	RF	90	PM Extensions-Red	Rigby
Flower Girls # 1: Violet	L	RF	250+	Leverich, Kathleen	HarperTrophy
Flower Girls # 2: Daisy	L	RF	250+	Leverich, Kathleen	HarperTrophy
Flower Girls # 3: Heather	L	RF	250+	Leverich, Kathleen	HarperTrophy
Flower Girls # 4: Rose	L	RF	250+	Leverich, Kathleen	HarperTrophy
Flower Necklace, The	N	RF	250+	PM Extensions	Rigby
Flower of Sheba, The	L	TL	250+	Orgel, Doris; Schecter, Ellen	Bantam Books
^Flower Power	S	RF	250+	Orca Currents	Orca Books

TITLE	LEVEL	GENRE	WORD COUNT	AUTHOR / SERIES	PUBLISHER / DISTRIBUTOR
Flower Robber, The	G	RF	173	Sails	Rigby
Flower, The	A	I	32	Leveled Literacy Intervention/ Orange System	Heinemann
Flower, The	A	I	20	Vocabulary Readers	Houghton Mifflin Harcourt
Flower, The	A	I	20	Vocabulary Readers/CA	Houghton Mifflin Harcourt
Flowers	A	I	27	Bookshop	Mondo Publishing
Flowers	B	I	31	Explorations	Eleanor Curtain Publishing
Flowers	B	I	31	Explorations	Okapi Educational Materials
Flowers	A	I	27	Hoenecke, Karen	Kaeden Books
Flowers	E	I	29	Parts of Plants	Lerner Publishing Group
Flowers	L	I	270	Pebble Books	Capstone Press
Flowers	I	I	118	Plant Parts	Capstone Press
Flowers and Plants	N	I	250+	Quick Draw	Kingfisher
Flowers For Algernon	Z	RF	250+	Keyes, Daniel	Harcourt Trade
Flowers for Grandma	E	RF	131	PM Stars	Rigby
Flowers for Grandma	LB	RF	8	Windows on Literacy	National Geographic
Flowers for Mom	E	RF	88	Carousel Readers	Pearson Learning Group
Flowers for Mrs. Falepau	M	RF	857	Book Bank	Wright Group/McGraw Hill
Flowers Have Colors	B	I	29	Cherrington, Janelle	Scholastic
Flowers Like Worms	C	F	45	Bonnell, Kris	Reading Reading Books
Flows & Quakes and Spinning Winds	K	I	250+	Home Connection Collection	Rigby
Flu	K	I	250+	Health Matters	Capstone Press
Fluffy Chicks	E	RF	50	Book Bank	Wright Group/McGraw Hill
Fluffy Rodriguez	H	RF	189	Seedlings	Continental Press
Fluffy: Scourge of the Sea	Q	F	250+	Bateman, Teresa	Charlesbridge
Fluffy's Accident	F	RF	136	Adams, Lorraine & Bruvold, Lynn	Eaglecrest Books
Fluffy's Trip	K	F	250+	Sunshine	Wright Group/McGraw Hill
Flunking of Joshua T. Bates, The	Q	RF	250+	Shreve, Susan	Alfred A. Knopf
Flush	W	RF	250+	Hiaasen, Carl	Yearling Books
Flutey Family Fruitcake, The	K	F	250+	Storyteller-Lightning Bolts	Wright Group/McGraw Hill
Flutter: The Story of Four Sisters and One Incredible Journey	T	RF	250+	Moulton, Erin E.	Philomel
Fly Away	H	RF	195	Reading Street	Pearson
Fly Away Home	A	F	28	Big Cat	Pacific Learning
Fly Away Home	P	RF	250+	Bunting, Eve	Clarion Books
Fly Away Home	I	I	250+	Wonder World	Wright Group/McGraw Hill
Fly Away, Children	S	I	548	Vocabulary Readers	Houghton Mifflin Harcourt
Fly Facts	M	I	423	Big Cat	Pacific Learning
Fly Fishing	S	I	250+	The Great Outdoors	Capstone Press
Fly Guy Meets Fly Girl	I	F	230	Arnold, Tedd	Scholastic
Fly High	B	RF	24	Visions	Wright Group/McGraw Hill
Fly Homer Fly	N	F	250+	Peet, Bill	Houghton Mifflin Harcourt
Fly Like a Bird	R	I	1212	Reading Street	Pearson
Fly Like the Eagle	K	RF	603	Rigby Flying Colors	Rigby
Fly Spy	I	RF	350	InfoTrek	ETA/Cuisenaire
Fly to the Rescue!	J	F	384	Leveled Readers	Houghton Mifflin Harcourt
Fly to the Rescue!	J	F	384	Leveled Readers/CA	Houghton Mifflin Harcourt
Fly to the Rescue!	J	F	384	Leveled Readers/TX	Houghton Mifflin Harcourt
Fly Trap	L	F	250+	Anastasio, Dina	Grosset & Dunlap
Fly, Butterfly	F	I	49	Discovery Links	Newbridge
Fly, Butterfly, Fly!	D	I	34	Bookworms	Marshall Cavendish
Fly, The	D	F	78	Story Steps	Rigby
Fly-Away Umbrella, The	M	F	250+	Voyages	SRA/McGraw Hill
Flyer Flew, The: The Invention of the Airplane	O	I	1815	On My Own Science	Lerner Publishing Group

* Collection of short stories   # Graphic text
^ Mature content with lower level text demands

TITLE	LEVEL	GENRE	WORD COUNT	AUTHOR / SERIES	PUBLISHER / DISTRIBUTOR
Flyers	I	RF	250+	Rigby Literacy	Rigby
Flyers	I	RF	250+	Rigby Star	Rigby
Flyers and Swimmers	B	I	39	Sails	Rigby
Fly-Fishing with Grandpa	O	RF	1029	Leveled Readers	Houghton Mifflin Harcourt
Flying	D	I	76	Benchmark Rebus	Marshall Cavendish
Flying	C	I	49	Crews, Donald	Mulberry Books
Flying	A	F	40	Leveled Literacy Intervention/ Green System	Heinemann
Flying	H	F	226	Leveled Readers	Houghton Mifflin Harcourt
Flying	H	F	226	Leveled Readers/CA	Houghton Mifflin Harcourt
Flying	H	F	226	Leveled Readers/TX	Houghton Mifflin Harcourt
Flying	H	F	75	Luthardt, Kevin	Peachtree
Flying	C	F	26	Story Box	Wright Group/McGraw Hill
Flying Ace: The Story of Amelia Earhart	Q	B	250+	Eyewitness Readers	DK Publishing
Flying Across the Ocean: Yesterday and Today	T	I	1752	Reading Street	Pearson
Flying Against the Wind: A Story about Beryl Markham	R	B	8214	Creative Minds Biographies	Carolrhoda Books
Flying and Floating	B	I	64	Little Red Readers	Sundance
Flying Balloons	B	I	69	Literacy by Design	Rigby
Flying Brown Pelicans	K	I	421	Pull Ahead Books	Lerner Publishing Group
Flying Car, The	J	RF	519	Pair-It Turn and Learn	Steck-Vaughn
Flying Doctor, The	H	F	246	Springboard	Wright Group/McGraw Hill
Flying Doctor, The	M	RF	250+	Windows on Literacy	National Geographic
Flying Fingers	K	RF	250+	Literacy 2000	Rigby
Flying Fish, The	H	RF	215	PM Extensions-Green	Rigby
Flying Flea, Callie, and Me, The	S	F	250+	Wallace, Carol & Bill	Pocket Books
Flying Football, The	I	RF	250+	Cambridge Reading	Pearson Learning Group
*Flying Free: America's First Black Aviators	T	B	250+	Hart, Philip S.	Lerner Publishing Group
Flying Free: Corey's Underground Railroad Diary	Q	HF	250+	Wyeth, Sharon Dennis	Scholastic
Flying Giants of Dinosaur Time	P	I	1090	Meet the Dinosaurs	Lerner Publishing Group
Flying High	R	RF	250+	Orbit Double Takes	Pacific Learning
Flying High	F	RF	250+	Predictable Storybooks	SRA/McGraw Hill
Flying in an Airplane	H	F	272	Leveled Readers	Houghton Mifflin Harcourt
Flying in an Airplane	H	F	272	Leveled Readers/CA	Houghton Mifflin Harcourt
Flying in an Airplane	H	F	272	Leveled Readers/TX	Houghton Mifflin Harcourt
Flying into History	P	I	846	Leveled Readers/CA	Houghton Mifflin Harcourt
Flying into History	P	I	846	Leveled Readers/TX	Houghton Mifflin Harcourt
Flying into Histroy	P	I	846	Leveled Readers	Houghton Mifflin Harcourt
Flying into the 21st Century	T	I	2565	Reading Street	Pearson
Flying Jewels	I	I	178	On Our Way to English	Rigby
Flying Lessons	W	HF	250+	Matthews, Kezi	Cricket Books
Flying Machines	J	I	270	Sails	Rigby
Flying Monkey, The	B	F	55	Red Rocket Readers	Flying Start Books
Flying Mosquitoes	L	I	383	Pull Ahead Books	Lerner Publishing Group
Flying Over Brooklyn	O	F	250+	Uhlberg, Myron	Peachtree
Flying Saucer	I	RF	250+	Phonics Readers Plus	Steck-Vaughn
Flying Solo	S	RF	250+	Fletcher, Ralph	Bantam Books
Flying Spider	C	F	112	Sails	Rigby
Flying Squirrels	K	I	413	Pull Ahead Books	Lerner Publishing Group
Flying Tree, The	I	RF	323	PM Stars Bridge Books	Rigby
Flying Trunk,The	M	TL	644	Tales from Hans Andersen	Wright Group/McGraw Hill
*Flying With the Eagle, Racing the Great Bear: Stories from Native North America	U	TL	250+	Bruchac, Joseph	Troll Associates

TITLE	LEVEL	GENRE	WORD COUNT	AUTHOR / SERIES	PUBLISHER / DISTRIBUTOR
*Flying-Saucer People and Other Cases, The	O	RF	250+	Simon, Seymour	Avon Books
Fly-Right Kite, The	J	RF	250+	Windows on Literacy	National Geographic
Focus: Different Ways of Seeing	T	I	250+	Power Up!	Steck-Vaughn
#Foiled	Y	F	250+	Yolen, Jane	Roaring Brook Press
Folk Dancer	C	I	36	The Candid Collection	Pearson Learning Group
Folk Tales, Fables and Fairy Tales	L	I	204	Take Two Books	Wright Group/McGraw Hill
Folktales Around the World	N	I	757	Vocabulary Readers	Houghton Mifflin Harcourt
Folktales Around the World	N	I	757	Vocabulary Readers/CA	Houghton Mifflin Harcourt
*Folktales from Asia	O	TL	250+	Bookshop	Mondo Publishing
*Folktales from China	N	TL	250+	Lawson, Barbara	Scholastic
*Folktales from Ecosystems Around the World	Q	TL	250+	Pair-It Books	Steck-Vaughn
*Folktales of the Midwest	R	TL	250+	Reading Expeditions	National Geographic
*Folktales of the Northeast	R	TL	250+	Reading Expeditions	National Geographic
*Folktales of the Southeast	R	TL	250+	Reading Expeditions	National Geographic
*Folktales of the Southwest	R	TL	250+	Reading Expeditions	National Geographic
*Folktales of the West	R	TL	250+	Reading Expeditions	National Geographic
Follow a River	L	I	198	iOpeners	Pearson Learning Group
Follow Me!	I	F	250+	Ziefert, Harriet	Puffin Books
Follow Me!: How People Track Animals	P	I	1722	Reading Street	Pearson
Follow Me, Be a Bee	N	I	250+	Emerson, Dhanna	Houghton Mifflin Harcourt
Follow Me, Be a Bee	K	I	428	Independent Readers Science	Houghton Mifflin Harcourt
Follow Me, Mittens	G	RF	170	Schaefer, Lola M.	HarperTrophy
Follow My Leader	H	RF	96	Cambridge Reading	Pearson Learning Group
Follow That Car!	R	I	250+	Power Up!	Steck-Vaughn
Follow That Clue!	L	RF	250+	Social Studies Connects	Kane Press
Follow That Fin!: Studying Dolphin Behavior	T	I	250+	Samuels, Amy	Steck-Vaughn
Follow That Fish	K	F	250+	Bank Street	Bantam Books
Follow That Spy!	P	RF	250+	Action Packs	Rigby
Follow the Appalachian Trail	I	I	129	Leveled Readers Social Studies	Houghton Mifflin Harcourt
Follow the Leader	C	RF	62	First Stories	Pacific Learning
Follow the Leader	B	RF	32	Independent Readers Social Studies	Houghton Mifflin Harcourt
Follow the Leader	X	RF	2911	Leveled Readers	Houghton Mifflin Harcourt
Follow the Leader	X	RF	2911	Leveled Readers/CA	Houghton Mifflin Harcourt
Follow the Leader	X	RF	2911	Leveled Readers/TX	Houghton Mifflin Harcourt
Follow the Leader	D	RF	75	Teacher's Choice Series	Pearson Learning Group
Follow the Leader	B	RF	15	Windmill Books	Wright Group/McGraw Hill
Follow the Line	I	I	67	Ljungkvist, Laura	Viking/Penguin
Follow the Money!	N	I	250+	Leedy, Loreen	Holiday House
Follow the Sun	D	RF	60	Leveled Readers Science	Houghton Mifflin Harcourt
Follower, The	P	F	494	Thompson, Richard	Fitzhenry & Whiteside
Following Rules	E	I	73	Citizenship	Lerner Publishing Group
Food	C	I	24	Basic Human Needs	Lerner Publishing Group
Food	G	I	33	Windows on Literacy	National Geographic
Food & Feasts Between the Two World Wars	T	I	250+	Steele, Philip	Dillon Press
Food & Feasts in Ancient Egypt	T	I	250+	Balkwill, Richard	Dillon Press
Food & Feasts in Ancient Greece	T	I	250+	Steele, Philip	Dillon Press
Food & Feasts in Ancient Rome	T	I	250+	Steele, Philip	Dillon Press
Food & Feasts in the Middle Ages	T	I	250+	Dawson, Imogen	Dillon Press
Food & Feasts in Tudor Times	T	I	250+	Balkwill, Richard	Dillon Press
Food & Feasts With the Aztecs	T	I	250+	Dawson, Imogen	Dillon Press
Food & Feasts With the Vikings	T	I	250+	Martell, Hazel	Dillon Press
Food Allergies	K	I	250+	Health Matters	Capstone Press
Food and Festivals: Israel	O	I	250+	Randall, Ronne	Steck-Vaughn

TITLE	LEVEL	GENRE	WORD COUNT	AUTHOR / SERIES	PUBLISHER / DISTRIBUTOR
Food and Festivals: Italy	O	I	250+	Pirotta, Saviour	Steck-Vaughn
Food and Recipes of the Pilgrims	R	I	250+	Cooking Throughout American History	Rosen Publishing Group
Food and Recipes of the Thirteen Colonies	R	I	250+	Cooking Throughout American History	Rosen Publishing Group
Food and Recipes of the Westward Expansion	R	I	250+	Cooking Throughout American History	Rosen Publishing Group
Food Around the World	I	I	298	Early Connections	Benchmark Education
Food Around the World	G	I	95	Factivity Series	Pearson Learning Group
Food Around the World	K	I	341	Red Rocket Readers	Flying Start Books
Food Around the World	L	I	250+	The Big Picture	Capstone Press
Food Around the World	L	I	250+	Trackers	Pacific Learning
Food Chain	K	I	160	Pair-It Turn and Learn	Steck-Vaughn
Food Chains	O	I	677	Leveled Readers Science	Houghton Mifflin Harcourt
Food Chains	O	I	250+	Rigby Focus	Rigby
Food Chains and Webs	P	I	974	Springboard	Wright Group/McGraw Hill
Food Comes From Farms	F	I	75	Windows on Literacy	National Geographic
Food Comes from the Sun	I	I	104	Larkin, Bruce	Wilbooks
Food for a Mouse	C	I	94	Sails	Rigby
Food for Animals	H	I	223	Explorations	Eleanor Curtain Publishing
Food for Animals	H	I	223	Explorations	Okapi Educational Materials
Food for Healthy Teeth	E	I	40	Dental Health	Capstone Press
Food for the World	W	I	250+	Rigby Literacy	Rigby
Food for Thought	U	I	250+	WorldScapes	ETA/Cuisenaire
Food for Thought	I	I	250+	Yellow Umbrella Books	Red Brick Learning
Food for You	H	I	232	Leveled Readers	Houghton Mifflin Harcourt
Food for You	F	I	85	Leveled Readers Science	Houghton Mifflin Harcourt
Food for You	H	I	232	Leveled Readers/CA	Houghton Mifflin Harcourt
Food for You	H	I	232	Leveled Readers/TX	Houghton Mifflin Harcourt
Food Found All Around	L	I	220	Spyglass Books	Compass Point Books
Food from Another Country	H	I	91	Windows on Literacy	National Geographic
Food from Farms	E	I	121	World of Farming	Heinemann Library
Food from Farms, Ranches, and Orchards	L	I	397	Larkin, Bruce	Wilbooks
Food from Plants	D	RF	66	Rigby Literacy	Rigby
Food from Plants	H	I	37	Windows on Literacy	National Geographic
Food from the Farm	D	RF	78	Home Connection Collection	Rigby
Food from the Sea	K	I	256	Larkin, Bruce	Wilbooks
Food from the Water	I	I	416	Sails	Rigby
Food from the World	J	I	251	Rigby Focus Forward	Rigby
Food in Colonial America	K	I	140	Welcome Books	Children's Press
Food in the Forest	G	I	120	Book Worms	Marshall Cavendish
Food in the Ocean	J	I	267	Early Explorers	Benchmark Education
Food Is Fun	H	RF	250+	PM Plus Poetry	Rigby
Food Is Matter	K	I	199	Early Explorers	Benchmark Education
Food Journey, The	K	I	116	Home Connection Collection	Rigby
Food Patterns	J	I	263	Finding Patterns	Capstone Press
Food Pyramid, The	L	I	155	Spyglass Books	Compass Point Books
Food Science	Y	I	7194	Cool Science	Lerner Publishing Group
Food Service Workers	M	I	250+	Community Helpers	Red Brick Learning
Food to Eat	B	I	29	Little Readers	Houghton Mifflin Harcourt
Food Trappers	I	I	165	Wonder World	Wright Group/McGraw Hill
Foods	C	I	18	We Are Alike and Different	Lerner Publishing Group
Foods of Mexico	S	I	1398	Vocabulary Readers	Houghton Mifflin Harcourt
Foods of Mexico	S	I	1398	Vocabulary Readers/CA	Houghton Mifflin Harcourt

F

TITLE	LEVEL	GENRE	WORD COUNT	AUTHOR / SERIES	PUBLISHER / DISTRIBUTOR
Foods of Mexico	S	I	1398	Vocabulary Readers/TX	Houghton Mifflin Harcourt
Foolish Goose	F	F	141	Start To Read	School Zone
Foolish Gretel	O	HF	250+	Armstrong, Jennifer	Random House
Fool's Girl, The	Z	HF	250+	Rees, Celia	Bloomsbury Children's Books
Fool's Gold	T	RF	250+	Reading Safari	Mondo Publishing
Foot Book	E	F	108	Seuss, Dr.	Random House
Football	C	I	44	Readlings	American Reading Company
Football	J	I	122	Readlings	American Reading Company
Football	O	I	250+	Trail Blazers	Ransom Publishing
Football	B	I	28	Visions	Wright Group/McGraw Hill
Football Book, The	I	RF	242	Breakthrough	Longman
Football Double Threat	Q	RF	250+	Christopher, Matt	Little Brown and Company
Football Fever	H	RF	51	Pacific Literacy	Pacific Learning
Football for Fun	S	I	250+	Sports for Fun	Compass Point Books
Football Friends	L	RF	250+	Marzollo, Jean, Dan & Dave	Scholastic
Football Fugitive	Q	RF	250+	Christopher, Matt	Little Brown and Company
Football Genius	V	F	250+	Green, Tim	HarperCollins
Football Legend	M	F	250+	Too Cool	Pacific Learning
Football Nightmare	Q	RF	250+	Christopher, Matt	Little Brown and Company
Football, Game, The	B	RF	36	Award Reading	School Specialty Publishing
Footfree and Fancyloose	Z	RF	250+	Craft, Elizabeth and Fain, Sarah	Little Brown and Company
Footprints	H	RF	96	Book Bus	Creative Edge
Footprints	H	F	241	Leveled Literacy Intervention/ Blue System	Heinemann
Footprints	G	RF	96	Literacy Tree	Rigby
Footprints	C	I	69	Rigby Focus	Rigby
Footprints in the Garden	J	RF	250+	Literacy by Design	Rigby
Footprints in the Park	M	RF	748	Springboard	Wright Group/McGraw Hill
Footprints in the Sand	D	RF	42	Benjamin, Cynthia	Scholastic
Footprints in the Snow	D	RF	39	Benjamin, Cynthia	Scholastic
Footprints on the Moon	M	RF	250+	Haddon, Mark	Candlewick Press
Footwork: The Story of Fred and Adele Astaire	P	B	250+	Orgill, Roxane	Candlewick Press
For a Better Life	T	B	250+	Power Up!	Steck-Vaughn
For a Good Cause	Q	I	250+	Discovery Links	Newbridge
For Baby (For Bobbie)	O	RF	185	Denver, John	Dawn Publications
For Boys Only: The Biggest, Baddest Book Ever	V	I	250+	Aronson, Marc & Newquist, HP	Feiwel and Friends
For Breakfast	LB	I	22	Visions	Wright Group/McGraw Hill
For Girls Only: Every Thing Great About Being a Girl	W	I	250+	Dower, Laura	Feiwel and Friends
For Good Measure: The Ways We Say How Much, How Far, How Heavy, How Big, How Old	T	I	250+	Robbins, Ken	Roaring Brook Press
For My Birthday	B	RF	48	Lighthouse	Rigby
For the Birds!	R	I	250+	Boldprint	Steck-Vaughn
For the Feet	E	I	146	Sails	Rigby
For The Life of Laetitia	Y	RF	250+	Hodge, Merle	Farrar, Straus, & Giroux
For the Love of Pooch	N	RF	250+	Literacy 2000	Rigby
For the Love of Turtles	M	RF	250+	Greetings	Rigby
For You Are a Kenyan Child	N	RF	250+	Cunnane, Kelly	Atheneum Books
Forbidden Schoolhouse, The	X	I	250+	Edge	Hampton Brown
Force and Motion	I	I	55	Windows on Literacy	National Geographic
Forced Out	O	I	889	Independent Readers Science	Houghton Mifflin Harcourt
Forces and Motion	W	I	250+	Mission Science	Compass Point Books

* Collection of short stories   # Graphic text
^ Mature content with lower level text demands

TITLE	LEVEL	GENRE	WORD COUNT	AUTHOR / SERIES	PUBLISHER / DISTRIBUTOR
Forces and Motion in Sports	V	I	250+	Navigators Science Series	Benchmark Education
Forces and Motion on Earth	V	I	250+	Navigators Science Series	Benchmark Education
Forces and Movement	S	I	250+	Straightforward Science	Franklin Watts
Forces of Nature	M	I	517	Red Rocket Readers	Flying Start Books
Forces That Move	Q	I	250+	Reading Expeditions	National Geographic
^Ford Mustang	O	I	250+	Fast Cars	Capstone Press
Forecasting the Weather	K	I	235	Gear Up!	Wright Group/McGraw Hill
Forecasting the Weather	T	I	2435	Reading Street	Pearson
Forensic Science	X	I	7703	Cool Science	Lerner Publishing Group
Forensic Science: Putting the Pieces Together	X	I	250+	Explore More	Wright Group/McGraw Hill
Forensics: Chemistry and Crime	T	I	250+	Navigators Science Series	Benchmark Education
Forest	F	I	101	Habitats	Lerner Publishing Group
Forest Animals	P	I	250+	Theme Sets	National Geographic
Forest Born	X	F	250+	Hale, Shannon	Bloomsbury Children's Books
Forest Bright, Forest Night	L	I	470	Ward, Jennifer	Dawn Publications
Forest Community, A	Q	I	250+	Massie, Elizabeth	Steck-Vaughn
Forest Fire	I	I	347	Rigby Flying Colors	Rigby
Forest Fire!	O	I	769	Leveled Readers Science	Houghton Mifflin Harcourt
Forest Fire!	J	I	250+	On Our Way to English	Rigby
Forest Fire, A	D	RF	103	Red Rocket Readers	Flying Start Books
Forest Fires	S	I	250+	Natural Disasters	Capstone Press
Forest Fires	M	I	648	Pull Ahead Books	Lerner Publishing Group
Forest Fires	O	I	250+	Windows on Literacy	National Geographic
Forest Fires: Run for Your Life!	T	I	250+	Bookshop	Mondo Publishing
Forest Food Webs	Q	I	1850	Early Bird Food Webs	Lerner Publishing Group
Forest Giants	N	I	250+	InfoQuest	Rigby
Forest Mammals	R	I	250+	Kalman, Bobbie	Crabtree
Forest of Secrets: Warriors, Book 3	U	F	250+	Hunter, Erin	Avon Books
Forest Stew	H	F	239	Leveled Readers	Houghton Mifflin Harcourt
Forest Stew	H	F	239	Leveled Readers/CA	Houghton Mifflin Harcourt
Forest Stew	H	F	239	Leveled Readers/TX	Houghton Mifflin Harcourt
#Forest Surprise, The	K	RF	250+	My 1st Graphic Novel	Stone Arch Books
Forest, The	L	I	250+	Cambridge Reading	Pearson Learning Group
Forest, The	A	I	32	Literacy by Design	Rigby
Forest, The	A	I	34	On Our Way to English	Rigby
Forest, The	E	I	74	Reading Street	Pearson
Forests	N	I	250+	Habitats of the World	Pearson Learning Group
Forests	M	I	250+	PM Plus Nonfiction	Rigby
Forests	R	I	250+	The Wonders of Our World	Crabtree
Forest's Life, A: From Meadow to Mature Woodland	T	I	250+	A First Book	Franklin Watts
Forests, Grasslands, Deserts	M	I	250+	People, Spaces & Places	Rand McNally
Forever Amber Brown	O	RF	250+	Danziger, Paula	Scholastic
Forever Changes	Z+	RF	250+	Halpin, Brendan	Farrar, Straus, & Giroux
Forever Friends	X	RF	250+	Boyd, Candy Dawson	Puffin Books
Forever Green	P	I	846	Vocabulary Readers	Houghton Mifflin Harcourt
Forever Green	P	I	846	Vocabulary Readers/CA	Houghton Mifflin Harcourt
Forever Green	P	I	846	Vocabulary Readers/TX	Houghton Mifflin Harcourt
Forged By Fire	Z	RF	250+	Draper, Sharon M.	Aladdin
Forgery and Frauds	W	I	250+	Mauro, Paul	Scholastic
Forget It!	L	RF	250+	Rigby Literacy	Rigby
Forgetful Bee, The	E	F	80	Reading Safari	Mondo Publishing
Forgetful Fran	J	RF	250+	Sunshine	Wright Group/McGraw Hill

TITLE	LEVEL	GENRE	WORD COUNT	AUTHOR / SERIES	PUBLISHER / DISTRIBUTOR
Forgetful Fred	E	RF	78	Tadpoles	Rigby
Forgetful Frits	G	RF	252	The Rowland Reading Program Library	Rowland Reading Foundation
Forgiveness	M	I	250+	Character Education	Red Brick Learning
Forgotten Door, The	T	SF	250+	Key, Alexander	Language for Learning Assoc.
Forgotten Heroes, The: The Story of the Buffalo Soldiers	X	I	250+	Cox, Clinton	Scholastic
Forgotten Hiding Place, The	M	RF	250+	Woodland Mysteries	Wright Group/McGraw Hill
Forgotten Princess, The	L	TL	250+	Literacy 2000	Rigby
Forgotten Voyager: The Story of Amerigo Vespucci	V	B	250+	Trailblazer Biographies	Carolrhoda Books
Forklifts	L	I	371	Pull Ahead Books	Lerner Publishing Group
Formation of the Continents	X	I	2046	Reading Street	Pearson
Forms of Energy	R	I	1168	Science Support Readers	Houghton Mifflin Harcourt
Forms of Transportation	M	I	478	Larkin, Bruce	Wilbooks
Formula One	P	I	250+	Trail Blazers	Ransom Publishing
Formula One Cars	M	I	250+	Horsepower	Capstone Press
Formula One Cars	Q	I	250+	Wild Rides!	Capstone Press
Formula One Race Cars	K	I	431	Lightning Bolt Books	Lerner Publishing Group
Formula One Race Cars	W	I	6230	Motor Mania	Lerner Publishing Group
Formula One Race Cars	N	I	498	Pull Ahead Books	Lerner Publishing Group
Fort Life	T	I	250+	Historic Communities	Crabtree
Fort Sumter	V	I	250+	Cornerstones of Freedom	Children's Press
Fort Sumter: Where the Civil War Began	Q	I	250+	Rosen Real Readers	Rosen Publishing Group
Fort, The	I	F	250+	Coulton, Mia	Maryruth Books
Fortune Branches Out, A	R	RF	250+	Mahy, Margaret	Bantam Books
*Fortune's Friend: Tales of Rivalry and Riches	Q	TL	250+	Literacy 2000	Rigby
Fortune's Magic Farm	S	F	250+	Selfors, Suzanne	Little Brown and Company
Fortune-Tellers, The	O	TL	250+	Alexander, Lloyd	Puffin Books
Forty Acres and Maybe a Mule	V	HF	250+	Robinet, Harriette Gillem	Scholastic
Forty-Three Cats	K	RF	232	Sunshine	Wright Group/McGraw Hill
Forward, Shakespeare!	N	RF	250+	Orca Young Readers	Orca Books
Fossil Fuel Power	V	I	250+	Energy at Work	Capstone Press
Fossil Fuels	R	I	250+	Early Bird Earth Science	Lerner Publishing Group
Fossil Fuels	M	I	250+	Rigby Focus	Rigby
Fossil Fuels: A Resource Our World Depends On	V	I	250+	Managing Our Resources	Heinemann
Fossil Hunters	Q	I	1048	Vocabulary Readers	Houghton Mifflin Harcourt
Fossil Hunters	Q	I	1048	Vocabulary Readers/CA	Houghton Mifflin Harcourt
Fossil Hunters, The	J	I	207	Instant Readers	Harcourt School Publishers
Fossil Hunters, The	M	RF	250+	Orca Echoes	Orca Books
Fossil Hunting	L	I	170	Rigby Focus	Rigby
Fossil Seekers	U	I	250+	iOpeners	Pearson Learning Group
Fossilized	T	I	3782	Take Two Books	Wright Group/McGraw Hill
Fossils	R	I	1526	Early Bird Earth Systems	Lerner Publishing Group
Fossils	L	I	250+	Early Connections	Benchmark Education
Fossils	Q	I	250+	Exploring the Earth	Capstone Press
Fossils	S	I	250+	Let's Rock	Heinemann Library
Fossils	R	I	1272	Leveled Readers Science	Houghton Mifflin Harcourt
Fossils	Q	I	250+	On Deck	Rigby
Fossils	M	I	497	Red Rocket Readers	Flying Start Books
Fossils	P	I	250+	Simply Science	Compass Point Books
Fossils	K	I	238	Windows on Literacy	National Geographic
Fossils Alive!	Q	I	250+	Pair-It Books	Steck-Vaughn

* Collection of short stories   # Graphic text
^ Mature content with lower level text demands

TITLE	LEVEL	GENRE	WORD COUNT	AUTHOR / SERIES	PUBLISHER / DISTRIBUTOR
Fossils Tell of Long Ago	O	I	250+	Soar To Success	Houghton Mifflin Harcourt
Fossils: Pictures from the Past	Q	I	250+	Pair-It Books	Steck-Vaughn
Foster Parents	H	I	170	Families	Heinemann Library
Foster's Famous Farm	J	RF	353	Leveled Readers	Houghton Mifflin Harcourt
Foster's Famous Farm	J	RF	353	Leveled Readers/CA	Houghton Mifflin Harcourt
Foster's Famous Farm	J	RF	353	Leveled Readers/TX	Houghton Mifflin Harcourt
Foster's Farm	J	RF	323	Leveled Readers	Houghton Mifflin Harcourt
Foster's Farm	J	RF	323	Leveled Readers/CA	Houghton Mifflin Harcourt
Foster's Farm	J	RF	323	Leveled Readers/TX	Houghton Mifflin Harcourt
Foster's War	V	HF	250+	Reeder, Carolyn	Scholastic
Foul Play on the Sidelines	R	RF	250+	Costello, Emily	Dell
Foul Play: Jokes That Won't Strike Out	O	F	1775	Make Me Laugh!	Lerner Publishing Group
*Foundling and Other Tales of Prydain, The	T	F	250+	Alexander, Lloyd	Puffin Books
Fountains of Life: The Story of Deep-Sea Vents	S	I	250+	A First Book	Franklin Watts
Four	LB	I	17	Count on It!	Marshall Cavendish
Four A's, The	Q	RF	250+	Wildcats	Wright Group/McGraw Hill
Four Cars	C	I	96	PM Math Readers	Rigby
Four Cheerful Chipmunks	H	F	250+	Phonics and Friends	Hampton Brown
Four Days in the Life of Zoe Coznaut	L	SF	250+	Foundations	Wright Group/McGraw Hill
Four Faces in Rock	M	I	300	Early Connections	Benchmark Education
*Four Friends and Other Stories, The	L	TL	250+	New Way Literature	Steck-Vaughn
Four Frogs	A	RF	25	Leveled Readers	Houghton Mifflin Harcourt
Four Frogs	A	RF	25	Leveled Readers/CA	Houghton Mifflin Harcourt
Four Getters and Arf, The	G	F	123	Little Celebrations	Pearson Learning Group
Four Good Friends	F	TL	274	Fairy Tales and Folklore	Norwood House Press
Four Great Cities	W	I	250+	iOpeners	Pearson Learning Group
Four Great Inventions of Ancient China	W	I	2534	Independent Readers Social Studies	Houghton Mifflin Harcourt
Four Ice Creams	C	RF	61	PM Starters	Rigby
Four Mice Deep in the Jungle	O	F	250+	Stilton, Geronimo	Scholastic
*Four on the Shore	J	F	250+	Marshall, Edward	Puffin Books
Four Pictures By Emily Carr	X	B	250+	Debon, Nicolas	Groundwood Books
Four Seasons, The	E	I	154	Early Connections	Benchmark Education
Four Seasons, The	C	RF	20	Learn to Read	Creative Teaching Press
Four Seasons, The	S	I	1820	Leveled Readers Science	Houghton Mifflin Harcourt
Four Seasons, The	C	I	57	Windows on Literacy	National Geographic
Four Stops on the Sante Fe Trail	S	I	1224	Vocabulary Readers	Houghton Mifflin Harcourt
Four Stops on the Sante Fe Trail	S	I	1224	Vocabulary Readers/CA	Houghton Mifflin Harcourt
Four Stops on the Sante Fe Trail	S	I	1224	Vocabulary Readers/TX	Houghton Mifflin Harcourt
Four Very Big Beans	E	RF	79	Instant Readers	Harcourt School Publishers
*Four-Legged Friends	N	TL	250+	Literacy 2000	Rigby
Fourteen Marbles	J	RF	181	PM Math Readers	Rigby
Fourth Grade Celebrity	Q	RF	250+	Giff, Patricia Reilly	Bantam Books
Fourth Grade Is a Jinx	P	RF	250+	McKenna, Colleen	Scholastic
Fourth Grade Wizards, The	Q	RF	250+	DeClements, Barthe	Penguin Group
Fourth Little Pig, The	K	TL	250+	Ready Set Read	Steck-Vaughn
Fourth of July, The	G	I	120	Fiesta Holiday Series	Pearson Learning Group
Fourth of July, The	F	I	153	Ready Readers	Pearson Learning Group
Fourth of July, The	I	I	206	Rosen Real Readers	Rosen Publishing Group
Fourth of July, The	H	I	142	Shutterbug Books	Steck-Vaughn
Fourth of July, The	T	I	250+	Symbols of America	Marshall Cavendish
Fourth of July, The	B	I	17	Windows on Literacy	National Geographic
Fourth-Graders Don't Believe in Witches	P	F	250+	Fields, Terri	Scholastic
Fowler's Family Tree	J	F	418	Storyteller	Wright Group/McGraw Hill

F

TITLE	LEVEL	GENRE	WORD COUNT	AUTHOR / SERIES	PUBLISHER / DISTRIBUTOR
Fox	J	I	250+	See How They Grow	DK Publishing
*Fox All Week	J	F	250+	Marshall, Edward	Puffin Books
Fox and Crow	I	TL	333	Leveled Readers	Houghton Mifflin Harcourt
Fox and Crow	I	TL	333	Leveled Readers/CA	Houghton Mifflin Harcourt
Fox and Crow	I	TL	333	Leveled Readers/TX	Houghton Mifflin Harcourt
Fox and Crow, The	H	TL	201	Alphakids	Sundance
*Fox and His Friends	J	F	250+	Marshall, Edward	Puffin Books
Fox and the Crow, The	I	TL	250+	Aesop's Fables	Pearson Learning Group
Fox and the Crow, The	J	F	240	Instant Readers	Harcourt School Publishers
Fox and the Crow, The	M	TL	614	Leveled Readers	Houghton Mifflin Harcourt
Fox and the Crow, The	J	TL	250+	PM Plus Story Books	Rigby
Fox and The Crow, The	K	TL	250+	Ready Readers	Pearson Learning Group
Fox and the Crow, The	H	TL	148	Sun Sprouts	ETA/Cuisenaire
Fox and the Goat, The	J	TL	365	Aesop's Fables	Pearson Learning Group
Fox and the Grapes, The	G	TL	60	Jumbled Tumbled Tales & Rhymes	Rigby
Fox and the Gulls, The	M	TL	499	Leveled Literacy Intervention/ Blue System	Heinemann
Fox and the Little Red Hen, The	L	TL	250+	Traditional Tales & More	Rigby
Fox and the Rabbit, The	C	TL	48	Storyworlds	Heinemann
Fox and the Stork	H	F	149	New Way Blue	Steck-Vaughn
Fox and the Stork, The	H	TL	250+	Green Light Readers	Harcourt
Fox and the Stork, The	K	TL	399	Rigby Flying Colors	Rigby
Fox and the Stork, The	C	TL	51	Storyworlds	Heinemann
*Fox at School	J	F	250+	Marshall, Edward	Puffin Books
*Fox Be Nimble	J	F	250+	Marshall, James	Puffin Books
Fox Fables	J	F	250+	Sunshine	Wright Group/McGraw Hill
Fox Gets a Note	G	F	152	Gear Up!	Wright Group/McGraw Hill
*Fox in Love	J	F	250+	Marshall, Edward	Puffin Books
Fox in the Forest	E	F	105	Early Explorers	Benchmark Education
Fox in the Frost	Q	RF	250+	Baglio, Ben M.	Scholastic
Fox in the Moon, The	M	TL	250+	Quintana, Juan & Ryall, Michael	Hampton Brown
Fox Lives Here, A	I	I	160	Ready Readers	Pearson Learning Group
*Fox on Stage	J	F	250+	Marshall, James	Puffin Books
Fox on the Box, The	C	RF	36	Little Readers	Houghton Mifflin Harcourt
Fox on the Box, The	C	RF	36	Start to Read	School Zone
Fox on the Job	J	F	250+	Marshall, James	Puffin Books
*Fox on Wheels	J	F	250+	Marshall, Edward	Puffin Books
*Fox Outfoxed	J	F	250+	Marshall, James	Puffin Books
Fox Steals Home, The	Q	RF	250+	Christopher, Matt	Little Brown and Company
Fox Who Foxed, The	H	F	212	PM Story Books	Rigby
Fox, The	C	RF	24	Books for Young Learners	Richard C. Owen
Foxes	R	I	1967	Animal Predators	Lerner Publishing Group
Foxes	M	I	250+	PM Animal Facts: Gold	Rigby
Foxes	H	I	164	Sails	Rigby
Foxes and Their Dens	J	I	146	Animal Homes	Capstone Press
Foxes: Clever Hunters	M	I	250+	The Wild World of Animals	Red Brick Learning
Fox's Box	D	I	72	Dominie Phonics Reader	Pearson Learning Group
Fox's Cave	I	TL	323	Red Rocket Readers	Flying Start Books
Fox's Hungry Day	H	RF	227	On Our Way to English	Rigby
Foxy Fox	J	F	278	Let's Read Together	Kane Press
Fraction Action	N	F	250+	Leedy, Loreen	Holiday House
Fraction Fun	Q	I	250+	Adler, David A.	Holiday House
Fractions	D	I	42	Early Math	Lerner Publishing Group

Organized Alphabetically by Title
Storable Database at www.fountasandpinnellleveledbooks.com

* Collection of short stories   # Graphic text
^ Mature content with lower level text demands

TITLE	LEVEL	GENRE	WORD COUNT	AUTHOR / SERIES	PUBLISHER / DISTRIBUTOR
Fractions = Trouble!	M	RF	250+	Mills, Claudia	Farrar, Straus, & Giroux
Fractions Everywhere!	J	I	178	Windows on Literacy	National Geographic
Fractions: Making Fair Shares	M	I	250+	Exploring Math	Capstone Press
Fraidy Cats	J	F	250+	Krensky, Stephen	Scholastic
Frail Snail on the Trail, The	J	F	167	Sounds Like Reading	Lerner Publishing Group
Frame by Frame	T	I	250+	Boldprint	Steck-Vaughn
Framed	V	RF	250+	Boyce, Frank Cottrell	HarperCollins
Frame-Up on the Bowery: A Houdini and Nate Mystery	T	HF	250+	Lalicki, Tom	Farrar, Straus, & Giroux
Fran That Time Forgot, The	N	SF	250+	Benton, Jim	Aladdin
France	U	I	250+	Countries and Cultures	Red Brick Learning
France	O	I	250+	Countries of the World	Red Brick Learning
France	P	I	2269	Country Explorers	Lerner Publishing Group
France: A Question and Answer Book	P	I	250+	Questions and Answers: Countries	Capstone Press
Frances Frog's Forever Friend	J	F	566	Animal Antics A To Z	Kane Press
Frances Hodgson Burnett: Beyond the Secret Garden	U	B	250+	Carpenter, Angelica Shirley; Shirley, Jean	Lerner Publishing Group
Frances the Fairy Dressmaker	L	F	736	Early Connections	Benchmark Education
Francie	W	RF	250+	English, Karen	Farrar, Straus, & Giroux
Francine, Believe It or Not	M	F	250+	Brown, Marc	Little Brown and Company
Francis Frog Meets a Space Snake	H	F	250+	Reading Safari	Mondo Publishing
Francis Marion	S	B	2216	People to Remember Series	January Books
Francis Scott Key and "The Star-Spangled Banner"	M	I	250+	Bookshop	Mondo Publishing
Francis Scott Key: Patriotic Poet	U	B	250+	Let Freedom Ring	Capstone Press
Francisco Goya	R	B	250+	Venezia, Mike	Children's Press
Francisco's Collection	H	RF	250+	Pacific Literacy	Pacific Learning
Frank and Sam's Summer at Aramoana	M	RF	250+	Voyages	SRA/McGraw Hill
Frank Ghery	W	B	250+	A&E Biography	Lerner Publishing Group
Frank Lloyd Wright	O	B	346	Independent Readers Social Studies	Houghton Mifflin Harcourt
Frank the Fish Gets His Wish	I	F	250+	Appleton-Smith, Laura	Flyleaf Publishing
#Frank Zamboni and the Ice-Resurfacing Machine	T	B	250+	Inventions and Discovery	Capstone Press
#Frankenstein	X	SF	250+	Burgan, Michael (Retold)	Stone Arch Books
Frankenstein	W	SF	250+	High-Fliers	Pacific Learning
Frankenstein	X	I	5158	Monster Chronicles	Lerner Publishing Group
Frankenstein	U	SF	9685	Oxford Bookworms Library	Oxford University Press
Frankenstein	Z+	SF	250+	Shelley, Mary	Penguin Group
Frankenstein Doesn't Plant Petunias	M	F	250+	Dadey, Debbie; Jones, Marcia Thornton	Scholastic
Frankenstein Doesn't Slam Hockey Pucks	M	F	250+	Dadey, Debbie; Jones, Marcia Thornton	Scholastic
Frankenstein Moved on to the 4th Floor	M	RF	250+	Levy, Elizabeth	Harper & Row
Frankie Stein	L	F	250+	Schaefer, Lola M.	Marshall Cavendish
Frankie Stein Starts School	M	F	250+	Schaefer, Lola M.	Marshall Cavendish
Frankie's Facts	K	RF	443	Leveled Readers	Houghton Mifflin Harcourt
Frankie's Facts	K	RF	443	Leveled Readers/CA	Houghton Mifflin Harcourt
Frankie's Facts	K	RF	443	Leveled Readers/TX	Houghton Mifflin Harcourt
Franklin Chang-Diaz in Space	M	B	250+	Vocabulary Readers	Houghton Mifflin Harcourt
Franklin D. Roosevelt	S	B	3374	History Maker Bios	Lerner Publishing Group
Franklin D. Roosevelt	N	B	223	Pebble Books	Capstone Press
Franklin D. Roosevelt	Q	B	250+	Photo-Illustrated Biographies	Red Brick Learning
Franklin D. Roosevelt	U	B	250+	Profiles of the Presidents	Compass Point Books

TITLE	LEVEL	GENRE	WORD COUNT	AUTHOR / SERIES	PUBLISHER / DISTRIBUTOR
Franklin D. Roosevelt: Thirty-second President	R	B	250+	Getting to Know the U.S. Presidents	Children's Press
Franklin Delano Roosevelt	R	B	250+	Amazing Americans	Wright Group/McGraw Hill
Franklin Delano Roosevelt	W	B	250+	Freedman, Russell	Clarion
Franklin Goes To School	K	F	250+	Bourgeois, Paulette; Clark, Brenda	Scholastic
Franklin Pierce	U	B	250+	Profiles of the Presidents	Compass Point Books
Franklin Pierce: Fourteenth President	R	B	250+	Getting to Know the U.S. Presidents	Children's Press
Franklin Plays the Game	K	F	250+	Bourgeois, Paulette; Clark, Brenda	Scholastic
Franklin's Valentines	K	F	250+	Bourgeois, Paulette & Jennings, Sharon	Scholastic
Franny Parker	U	RF	250+	McKinnon, Hannah Roberts	Macmillan
Frantastic Voyage	N	SF	250+	Benton, Jim	Aladdin
Freak Out!: Animals Beyond Your Wildest Imagination	N	I	250+	All Aboard Science Reader	Grosset & Dunlap
Freak the Mighty	W	RF	250+	Philbrick, Rodman	Scholastic
Freaky Flowers	S	I	250+	Plants and Fungi	Franklin Watts
Freaky Friday	R	F	250+	Rodgers, Mary	HarperTrophy
Freaky Frogs	P	I	250+	Explorer Books-Pioneer	National Geographic
Freaky Frogs	R	I	250+	Explorer Books-Pathfinder	National Geographic
Freckle Juice	M	RF	250+	Blume, Judy	Bantam Books
Freckleface Strawberry	K	RF	250+	Moore, Julianne	Bloomsbury Children's Books
Freckleface Strawberry and the Dodgeball Bully	K	RF	250+	Moore, Julianne	Bloomsbury Children's Books
Fred and the Ball	G	RF	171	Rigby Flying Colors	Rigby
Fred and Zack in the Sandbox	F	RF	61	Appleton-Smith, Laura	Flyleaf Publishing
Fred Fixes a Faucet	I	F	250+	Popcorn	Sundance
Fred Goes Shopping	I	F	250+	Popcorn	Sundance
Fred Helps, Too	F	RF	218	Rigby Flying Colors	Rigby
Fred Joins the Band	I	F	250+	Popcorn	Sundance
Fred Plays a Trick	H	RF	237	Rigby Flying Colors	Rigby
Fred Said	D	RF	35	Sunshine	Wright Group/McGraw Hill
Fred Stays with Me!	I	RF	352	Coffelt, Nancy	Little Brown and Company
Freda Plans a Picnic	K	F	250+	I See I Learn	Charlesbridge
Freda's Signs	K	F	528	Reading Street	Pearson
Freddie the Frog	D	F	132	First Start	Troll Associates
Freddie the Frog	G	F	250+	Supersonics	Rigby
Freddie's Spaghetti	F	RF	250+	Doyle, Charlotte	Random House
Freddy Adu	P	B	1742	Amazing Athletes	Lerner Publishing Group
Freddy Frog's Note	H	F	253	Ready Readers	Pearson Learning Group
Freddy the Frog	F	F	94	Dominie Readers	Pearson Learning Group
Freddy's Train Ride	K	RF	573	Pair-It Books	Steck-Vaughn
Frederick Douglass	T	B	250+	Amazing Americans	Wright Group/McGraw Hill
Frederick Douglass	P	B	250+	Early Biographies	Compass Point Books
Frederick Douglass	N	B	257	First Biographies	Red Brick Learning
Frederick Douglass	S	B	3743	History Maker Bios	Lerner Publishing Group
Frederick Douglass	P	B	250+	Photo-Illustrated Biographies	Red Brick Learning
Frederick Douglass: Fights For Freedom	M	B	250+	Davidson, Margaret	Language for Learning Assoc.
Frederick Douglass: Freedom Fighter	N	B	250+	Beginning Biographies	Pearson Learning Group
Frederick Douglass: His Story Made History	U	B	2008	Leveled Readers	Houghton Mifflin Harcourt
Frederick Douglass: The Last Days of Slavery	R	B	250+	Miller, William	Lee & Low Books Inc.
Fred's Big Lunch	I	F	250+	Popcorn	Sundance

* Collection of short stories   # Graphic text
^ Mature content with lower level text demands

TITLE	LEVEL	GENRE	WORD COUNT	AUTHOR / SERIES	PUBLISHER / DISTRIBUTOR
Fred's Cold	I	F	250+	Popcorn	Sundance
Fred's Doghouse	H	RF	288	Rigby Flying Colors	Rigby
Fred's Little Snack	I	F	250+	Popcorn	Sundance
Fred's Polka-Dot Sock	I	F	250+	Popcorn	Sundance
Fred's Weekend	I	F	250+	Popcorn	Sundance
Fred's Wish for Fish	E	RF	128	Landman, Yael	Scholastic
Free at Last	S	B	250+	DK Readers	DK Publishing
Free Baseball	T	HF	250+	Corbett, Sue	Puffin Books
Free Black Communities in the Time of Slavery	W	I	3120	Leveled Readers Social Studies	Houghton Mifflin Harcourt
Free Black Girl Before the Civil War, A	U	I	250+	Diaries and Memoirs	Capstone Press
Free Climb	Q	RF	250+	Maddox, Jake	Stone Arch Books
Free Fall	Q	I	250+	Basalaj, Kathy	Pacific Learning
Free Fall	WB	F	0	Wiesner, David	Lothrop, Lee & Shepard
Free Throw	P	RF	4509	Maddox, Jake	Stone Arch Books
Free to Fly	E	RF	96	Gibson, Kathleen	Continental Press
*Free?: Stories about Human Rights	Y	RF	250+	Amnesty International	Candlewick Press
Freedom	M	RF	250+	Rigby Literacy	Rigby
Freedom Crossing	R	HF	250+	Clark, Margaret Goff	Scholastic
Freedom Debate	W	I	250+	WorldScapes	ETA/Cuisenaire
Freedom Fighters: The Massachusetts 54th Regiment	V	I	2052	Leveled Readers Social Studies	Houghton Mifflin Harcourt
Freedom of Speech and Assembly in the United States	X	I	2852	Reading Street	Pearson
Freedom Quilt	M	HF	300	Books for Young Learners	Richard C. Owen
Freedom Readers	R	I	250+	Explorer Books-Pathfinder	National Geographic
Freedom Readers	Q	I	250+	Explorer Books-Pioneer	National Geographic
Freedom Seeker: A Story about William Penn	S	B	9841	Creative Minds Biographies	Lerner Publishing Group
Freedom Sings: A Tale of the Underground Railroad	R	HF	250+	Robbins, Trina	Stone Arch Books
Freedom Songs: A Tale of the Underground Railroad	T	HF	250+	Moore, Yvette	Language for Learning Assoc.
Freedom Trail, The	P	I	859	Leveled Readers Language Support	Houghton Mifflin Harcourt
Freedom Train	T	B	250+	Sterling, Dorothy	Scholastic
Freedom Walkers: The Story of the Montgomery Bus Boycott	X	I	250+	Freedman, Russell	Holiday House
Freedom's Fire	U	HF	250+	Bookshop	Mondo Publishing
Freedom's Wings: Corey's Underground Railroad Diary	Q	HF	250+	Wyeth, Sharon Dennis	Scholastic
Freeman's Fax Machine, The	J	F	250+	Reading Safari	Mondo Publishing
Freewill	Z+	RF	250+	Lynch, Chris	Harper Tempest
Freeze Tag	G	RF	112	City Stories	Rigby
Freeze, Goldilocks!	M	F	250+	Pacific Literacy	Pacific Learning
Freezing and Melting	H	I	101	Water	Lerner Publishing Group
Freight Trains	M	I	250+	Transportation	Compass Point Books
Freight Trains in Action	M	I	250+	Transportation Zone	Capstone Press
French Colonies in the Americas	S	I	250+	On Deck	Rigby
French Roots in North America	S	I	1612	Reading Street	Pearson
Frenzy of Sharks, A	U	I	250+	Jean-Michel Cousteau Presents	London Town Press
Fresh Air	O	RF	250+	Leveled Readers Language Support	Houghton Mifflin Harcourt
Fresh Fall Leaves	E	RF	50	Franco, Betsy	Scholastic
Fresh from the Farm!	M	I	727	Rigby Flying Colors	Rigby
Freshwater Fishing	S	I	250+	The Great Outdoors	Capstone Press
Freshwater Giants: Hippopotamus, River Dolphins, and Manatees	S	I	250+	Perry, Phyllis J.	Franklin Watts

F

TITLE	LEVEL	GENRE	WORD COUNT	AUTHOR / SERIES	PUBLISHER / DISTRIBUTOR
Freshwater Habitats	N	I	250+	Habitats of the World	Pearson Learning Group
Freshwater Pond, A	T	I	250+	Small Worlds	Crabtree
Freshwater Seas: The Great Lakes	S	I	1905	Independent Readers Social Studies	Houghton Mifflin Harcourt
Friction	Z+	RF	250+	Frank, E.R.	Simon & Schuster
^Friction	P	I	250+	Our Physical World	Capstone Press
Frida Kahlo	R	B	250+	Venezia, Mike	Children's Press
Frida Kahlo: Mexican Painter	R	B	250+	The Heinle Reading Library	Thomson Learning
Frida Kahlo: Painter of Strength	P	B	250+	Great Hispanics	Capstone Press
Frida María: A Story of the Old Southwest	M	RF	250+	Lattimore, Deborah Nourse	Harcourt Trade
Friday Afternoon Fun	J	RF	393	PM Stars Bridge Books	Rigby
Friday Pizza	I	RF	334	Pair-It Turn and Learn	Steck-Vaughn
Friedrich	Z	HF	250+	Richter, Hans Peter	Puffin Books
Friend for Baby Kangaroo, A	L	F	250+	Splash	Pacific Learning
Friend for Ben, A	K	RF	250+	Literacy by Design	Rigby
Friend for Dear Dragon, A	E	F	279	Dear Dragon	Norwood House Press
Friend for Dragon, A	I	F	250+	Pilkey, Dav	Orchard Books
Friend for Glory, A	J	F	212	McAlpin, MaryAnn	Short Tales Press
Friend for Jasper, A	J	F	584	Jasper the Cat	Pioneer Valley
Friend for Jellyfish, A	E	F	121	Bonnell, Kris	Reading Reading Books
Friend for Kate, A	I	RF	250+	Cambridge Reading	Pearson Learning Group
Friend for Little White Rabbit, A	E	F	113	PM Story Books	Rigby
Friend for Max, A	G	RF	228	PM Plus Story Books	Rigby
Friend for Me, A	A	I	48	First Stories	Pacific Learning
Friend for Peanut, A	E	RF	88	Emergent Set 4	Pioneer Valley
Friend in the Wild, A	T	RF	250+	Storyteller-Whispering Pines	Wright Group/McGraw Hill
Friend, A	G	RF	57	Literacy 2000	Rigby
Friendliness	L	I	250+	Character Education	Red Brick Learning
Friendliness	K	I	250+	Everyday Character Education	Capstone Press
Friendly Crocodile, The	I	F	218	Hiris, Monica	Kaeden Books
Friendly Field Trip, A	P	RF	1000	Leveled Readers/TX	Houghton Mifflin Harcourt
Friendly Snowman	F	F	134	First Start	Troll Associates
Friendly Snowman	F	F	144	Joyce, William	Scholastic
Friends	U	I	250+	Boldprint	Steck-Vaughn
Friends	F	RF	57	Bookshop	Mondo Publishing
Friends	I	I	313	Early Connections	Benchmark Education
Friends	D	I	134	Fiesta Series	Pearson Learning Group
Friends	D	F	98	Joy Starters	Pearson Learning Group
Friends	A	F	80	Leveled Literacy Intervention/ Green System	Heinemann
Friends	I	I	302	Leveled Readers	Houghton Mifflin Harcourt
Friends	A	I	21	Leveled Readers Emergent	Houghton Mifflin Harcourt
Friends	I	I	302	Leveled Readers/CA	Houghton Mifflin Harcourt
Friends	I	I	302	Leveled Readers/TX	Houghton Mifflin Harcourt
Friends	B	RF	36	Little Readers	Houghton Mifflin Harcourt
Friends	G	RF	195	Reading Unlimited	Pearson Learning Group
Friends	B	I	21	Rigby Literacy	Rigby
Friends	B	I	30	Rigby Star Quest	Rigby
Friends	D	I	60	Sun Sprouts	ETA/Cuisenaire
Friends	A	I	20	Vocabulary Readers	Houghton Mifflin Harcourt
Friends	A	I	20	Vocabulary Readers/CA	Houghton Mifflin Harcourt
Friends	G	RF	250+	Well-Being Series	Pearson Learning Group
Friends Along the Way	W	I	1500	Leveled Readers/TX	Houghton Mifflin Harcourt
Friends and Competitors	X	B	2333	Leveled Readers	Houghton Mifflin Harcourt

* Collection of short stories   \# Graphic text
^ Mature content with lower level text demands

TITLE	LEVEL	GENRE	WORD COUNT	AUTHOR / SERIES	PUBLISHER / DISTRIBUTOR
Friends and Family	Q	I	250+	Orbit Collections	Pacific Learning
Friends Are Forever	K	F	585	Literacy 2000	Rigby
Friends Are Fun	C	I	34	Red Rocket Readers	Flying Start Books
Friends Forever	L	RF	250+	HSP/Harcourt Trophies	Harcourt, Inc.
Friends Forever	K	F	250+	I Am Reading	Kingfisher
Friends Forever	K	RF	559	Leveled Readers	Houghton Mifflin Harcourt
Friends Forever	I	TL	250+	Ready Readers	Pearson Learning Group
Friends Go Together	D	RF	36	Pair-It Books	Steck-Vaughn
Friends of the Earth	J	RF	264	InfoTrek	ETA/Cuisenaire
Friends on a Field Trip	O	RF	1000	Leveled Readers/TX	Houghton Mifflin Harcourt
Friends on Earth	E	F	186	Bonnell, Kris	Reading Reading Books
Friends Online	I	RF	318	Leveled Readers	Houghton Mifflin Harcourt
Friends or Enemies?	R	I	250+	Leveled Readers Language Support	Houghton Mifflin Harcourt
Friends or Foes?	N	TL	250+	WorldScapes	ETA/Cuisenaire
Friends Share	C	I	34	Vocabulary Readers	Houghton Mifflin Harcourt
Friends Who Share	C	I	118	Leveled Readers	Houghton Mifflin Harcourt
Friends Who Share	C	I	118	Leveled Readers/CA	Houghton Mifflin Harcourt
Friends Who Share	C	I	118	Leveled Readers/TX	Houghton Mifflin Harcourt
Friends with Wings	R	RF	1249	Leveled Readers	Houghton Mifflin Harcourt
Friends with Wings	R	RF	1249	Leveled Readers/CA	Houghton Mifflin Harcourt
Friends with Wings	R	RF	1249	Leveled Readers/TX	Houghton Mifflin Harcourt
Friends, The	Z	RF	250+	Edge	Hampton Brown
Friends, The	Z	RF	250+	Guy, Rosa	Bantam Books
Friends, The	T	RF	250+	Yumoto, Kazumi	Yearling Books
Friendship According to Humphrey	Q	F	250+	Birney, Betty G.	Puffin Books
Friendship and the Gold Cadillac, The	S	HF	250+	Taylor, Mildred	Bantam Books
Friendship Garden, The	S	RF	2232	Leveled Readers	Houghton Mifflin Harcourt
Friendship Garden, The	S	RF	2232	Leveled Readers/CA	Houghton Mifflin Harcourt
Friendship Garden, The	S	RF	2232	Leveled Readers/TX	Houghton Mifflin Harcourt
Friendship Garden, The	K	RF	250+	Little Celebrations	Pearson Learning Group
Friendship in Action	O	I	250+	Literacy Tree	Rigby
Friendship Pact, The	Q	RF	250+	Pfeffer, Susan Beth	Scholastic
Friendship Rules!	I	I	256	Vocabulary Readers	Houghton Mifflin Harcourt
Friendship Rules!	I	I	256	Vocabulary Readers/CA	Houghton Mifflin Harcourt
Friendship Rules!	I	I	256	Vocabulary Readers/TX	Houghton Mifflin Harcourt
Friendship Salad	D	RF	42	Instant Readers	Harcourt School Publishers
Friendship, The	S	HF	250+	Taylor, Mildred	Puffin Books
Fright Zone, The	O	F	1685	The Funny Zone	Norwood House Press
Frightened	B	F	42	Story Box	Wright Group/McGraw Hill
Frightened Scarecrow, The	L	F	896	Springboard	Wright Group/McGraw Hill
Frightful's Mountain	U	RF	250+	George, Jean Craighead	Puffin Books
Frindle	R	RF	250+	Clements, Andrew	Aladdin
Frisky and the Cat	D	F	117	Storyworlds	Heinemann
Frisky and the Ducks	D	F	90	Storyworlds	Heinemann
Frisky Plays a Trick	D	F	102	Storyworlds	Heinemann
Frisky Wants to Sleep	C	F	66	Storyworlds	Heinemann
Frito Jumps In	D	RF	34	Step-By-Step Series	Pearson Learning Group
Frits Had a Frog	F	RF	177	The Rowland Reading Program Library	Rowland Reading Foundation
Frits Visits Grandpop	D	RF	94	The Rowland Reading Program Library	Rowland Reading Foundation
Frog	B	RF	50	Sails	Rigby
Frog	C	I	39	Zoozoo-Into the Wild	Cavallo Publishing

TITLE	LEVEL	GENRE	WORD COUNT	AUTHOR / SERIES	PUBLISHER / DISTRIBUTOR
Frog Alert	K	I	452	Explorations	Eleanor Curtain Publishing
Frog Alert	K	I	452	Explorations	Okapi Educational Materials
Frog and the Fly, The	D	F	33	Cat on the Mat	Oxford University Press
*Frog and Toad All Year	K	F	250+	Little Readers	Houghton Mifflin Harcourt
*Frog and Toad Are Friends	K	F	250+	Lobel, Arnold	Harper & Row
*Frog and Toad Together	K	F	250+	Little Readers	Houghton Mifflin Harcourt
*Frog and Toad Together	K	F	1927	Lobel, Arnold	HarperCollins
Frog Bog	M	I	250+	Explorations	Eleanor Curtain Publishing
Frog Bog	M	I	250+	Explorations	Okapi Educational Materials
Frog Catchers of Fairfax, The	L	F	856	InfoTrek	ETA/Cuisenaire
Frog Day	J	RF	442	Storyteller	Wright Group/McGraw Hill
Frog Food	A	F	38	Leveled Literacy Intervention/ Green System	Heinemann
Frog Friends	K	F	415	Reading Street	Pearson
Frog Fun	C	I	45	Bonnell, Kris	Reading Reading Books
Frog Goes to Dinner	WB	F	0	Mayer, Mercer	Dial/Penguin
Frog Has a Sticky Tongue, A	H	I	176	Windows on Literacy	National Geographic
Frog Hollow	K	RF	797	PM Stars Bridge Books	Rigby
Frog in a Bog	M	RF	250+	Himmelman, John	Charlesbridge
Frog in the Pond, The	G	I	75	Benchmark Rebus	Marshall Cavendish
Frog in the Pond, The	H	RF	175	Rookie Readers	Children's Press
Frog in the Throat, A	J	F	250+	Waddell, Martin	Sundance
Frog on His Own	WB	F	0	Mayer, Mercer	Dial/Penguin
Frog or Toad?	I	I	241	Ready Readers	Pearson Learning Group
Frog Prince, The	I	TL	250+	Jumbled Tumbled Tales & Rhymes	Rigby
Frog Prince, The	K	TL	250+	Literacy by Design	Rigby
Frog Prince, The	H	TL	250+	My 1st Classic Story	Picture Window Books
Frog Prince, The	J	TL	542	Pawprints Teal	Pioneer Valley
Frog Prince, The	I	TL	250+	Storyworlds	Heinemann
Frog Prince, The	K	TL	250+	Tarcov, Edith H.	Scholastic
Frog Prince, The	I	TL	572	Traditional Tales	Pearson Learning Group
Frog Princess, The	K	TL	206	Literacy 2000	Rigby
Frog Princess, The	N	TL	250+	WorldScapes	ETA/Cuisenaire
Frog Princess, The: A Tlingit Legend from Alaska	O	TL	250+	Kimmel, Eric A.	Holiday House
Frog Report	O	I	250+	Windows on Literacy	National Geographic
Frog Report, The	K	I	184	Rigby Focus	Rigby
Frog Scientist, The	W	I	250+	Scientists in the Field	Houghton Mifflin Harcourt
Frog Someday, A	H	F	192	Early Explorers	Benchmark Education
Frog Songs	J	F	377	Leveled Literacy Intervention/ Blue System	Heinemann
Frog Under the Tree, The	G	RF	194	PM Photo Stories	Rigby
Frog Who Thought He Was a Horse, The	L	F	250+	Literacy 2000	Rigby
Frog Who Would Be King, The	N	TL	250+	Walker, Kate	Mondo Publishing
Frog, The	D	RF	69	Adams, Lorraine & Bruvold, Lynn	Eaglecrest Books
Frog, The	M	I	250+	Crewe, Sabrina	Steck-Vaughn
Frogfish, The	J	I	130	Weird Animals	Capstone Press
Froggy Learns to Swim	J	F	250+	London, Jonathan	Scholastic
Froggy Tale, A	I	F	250+	Literacy 2000	Rigby
Frogs	N	I	250+	Bookshop	Mondo Publishing
Frogs	N	I	250+	Gibbons, Gail	Holiday House
Frogs	O	I	250+	Holmes, Kevin J.	Red Brick Learning
Frogs	C	F	36	Joy Readers	Pearson Learning Group

F

* Collection of short stories   # Graphic text
^ Mature content with lower level text demands

TITLE	LEVEL	GENRE	WORD COUNT	AUTHOR / SERIES	PUBLISHER / DISTRIBUTOR
Frogs	F	I	94	Life Cycles	Lerner Publishing Group
Frogs	N	I	250+	Nature's Friends	Compass Point Books
Frogs	C	I	34	Pair-It Books	Steck-Vaughn
Frogs	D	I	28	Pebble Books	Capstone Press
Frogs	G	I	192	Rigby Flying Colors	Rigby
Frogs	G	I	100	Storyteller-First Snow	Wright Group/McGraw Hill
Frogs	A	I	13	Twig	Wright Group/McGraw Hill
Frogs	K	I	170	Windows on Literacy	National Geographic
Frogs	K	I	311	Wonder World	Wright Group/McGraw Hill
Frogs and Tadpoles	L	I	913	Sun Sprouts	ETA/Cuisenaire
Frogs and Toads	P	I	250+	Crabapples	Crabtree
Frogs and Toads	G	I	323	Sails	Rigby
Frogs and Toads	J	I	187	Shutterbug Books	Steck-Vaughn
Frogs and Turtles	A	I	58	InfoTrek	ETA/Cuisenaire
Frogs Can Jump	C	I	41	Book Bank	Wright Group/McGraw Hill
Frog's Day	E	F	101	Instant Readers	Harcourt School Publishers
Frogs in the House	J	F	355	Sails	Rigby
Frogs in the Pond	D	I	122	PM Science Readers	Rigby
Frog's Life, A	L	I	246	Reading Street	Pearson
Frog's Life, A	K	I	409	Red Rocket Readers	Flying Start Books
Frog's Life, A	G	I	100	Time for Kids	Teacher Created Materials
Frog's Life, A	F	I	151	Watch It Grow	Heinemann Library
Frog's Lunch	E	F	89	Lillegard, Dee	Scholastic
Frogs of Betts, The	N	RF	250+	Supa Doopers	Sundance
Frogs on a Log	D	F	113	Bonnell, Kris	Reading Reading Books
Frogs on a Log	D	F	75	Teacher's Choice Series	Pearson Learning Group
Frogs Play	B	F	28	Zoozoo-Into the Wild	Cavallo Publishing
Frogs: Fascinating... and Fragile	T	I	250+	PM Plus Nonfiction	Rigby
From a Tree	K	I	351	Rigby Focus	Rigby
From Acorn to Oak Tree	I	I	199	Welcome Books	Children's Press
From Apples to Applesauce	M	I	250+	From Farm to Table	Capstone Press
From Assembly Lines to Home Offices: How Work Has Changed	K	I	283	Lightning Bolt Books	Lerner Publishing Group
From Axes to Zippers: Simple Machines	Q	I	250+	Navigators Social Studies Series	Benchmark Education
From Barbadoes to Brooklyn: The Story of Shirley Chisholm	S	B	2374	Leveled Readers Social Studies	Houghton Mifflin Harcourt
From Bee to Honey	J	I	102	Take Two Books	Wright Group/McGraw Hill
From Beginning to End: A Song About Life Cycles	M	I	250+	Science Songs	Picture Window Books
From Big Bands to Rap	S	I	3915	Take Two Books	Wright Group/McGraw Hill
From Blossom to Fruit	E	I	44	Pebble Books	Capstone Press
From Bud to Blossom	D	I	40	Pebble Books	Capstone Press
From Camel Cart to Canoe	L	I	250+	Sunshine	Wright Group/McGraw Hill
From Cane to Crystals	R	I	250+	Orbit Chapter Books	Pacific Learning
From Cane to Sugar	L	I	250+	From Farm to Table	Capstone Press
From Cane to Sugar	M	I	350	Start to Finish	Lerner Publishing Group
From Caves to Canvas	V	I	250+	Navigators Social Studies Series	Benchmark Education
From Cells to Systems	S	I	250+	Reading Expeditions	National Geographic
From Cement to Bridge	L	I	400	Start to Finish	Lerner Publishing Group
From Chalkboards to Computers: How Schools Have Changed	K	I	374	Lightning Bolt Books	Lerner Publishing Group
From Chili to Chocolate	S	I	250+	WorldScapes	ETA/Cuisenaire
From Clay to Bricks	L	I	289	Start to Finish	Lerner Publishing Group
From Cloth to American Flag	L	I	320	Start to Finish	Lerner Publishing Group

F

TITLE	LEVEL	GENRE	WORD COUNT	AUTHOR / SERIES	PUBLISHER / DISTRIBUTOR
From Cocoa Bean to Chocolate	L	I	301	Start to Finish	Lerner Publishing Group
From Corn to Cereal	L	I	250+	From Farm to Table	Capstone Press
From Cotton Plant to Cotton Shirt	L	I	250+	Early Connections	Benchmark Education
From Cotton to Blue Jeans	Q	I	250+	Theme Sets	National Geographic
From Cotton to T-Shirt	K	I	311	Start to Finish	Lerner Publishing Group
From Cow to Milk Carton	M	I	250+	Take Two Books	Wright Group/McGraw Hill
From Cows to Ice Cream	Q	I	250+	Theme Sets	National Geographic
From Cub to King	J	I	316	Leveled Readers	Houghton Mifflin Harcourt
From Cub to King	J	I	316	Leveled Readers/CA	Houghton Mifflin Harcourt
From Cuneiform to Computers	V	I	250+	High-Fliers	Pacific Learning
From Day to Night	B	I	23	On Our Way to English	Rigby
From Drummers to Satellites	R	I	250+	Take Two Books	Wright Group/McGraw Hill
From Earth to Art	U	I	250+	Rigby Literacy	Rigby
From Egg to Butterfly	J	I	262	Start to Finish	Lerner Publishing Group
From Egg to Butterfly	L	I	261	Windows on Literacy	National Geographic
From Egg to Butterfly (Revised Edition)	J	I	265	Start to Finish	Lerner Publishing Group
From Egg to Chicken	K	I	268	Start to Finish	Lerner Publishing Group
From Egg to Robin	D	I	31	Canizares, Susan; Chessen, Betsey	Scholastic
From Egg to Snake: Following the Life Cycle	M	I	250+	Amazing Science	Picture Window Books
From Eggs	A	I	32	Red Rocket Readers	Flying Start Books
From Farm to Store	J	I	181	Phonics Readers	Compass Point Books
From Farm to Table	K	I	252	Early Explorers	Benchmark Education
From Field to Florist	I	I	142	Windows on Literacy	National Geographic
From Flower to Honey	J	I	274	Start to Finish	Lerner Publishing Group
From Flower to Honey (Revised Edition)	J	I	275	Start to Finish	Lerner Publishing Group
From Foal to Horse	M	I	337	Start to Finish	Lerner Publishing Group
From Foal to Horse (Revised Edition)	M	I	338	Start to Finish	Lerner Publishing Group
From Fruit to Jelly	L	I	302	Start to Finish	Lerner Publishing Group
From Geek to Goddess	T	F	250+	Hopkins, Cathy	Kingfisher
From Grain to Pita	M	I	1331	Take Two Books	Wright Group/McGraw Hill
From Grass to Milk	M	I	300	Start to Finish	Lerner Publishing Group
From Here to There	M	I	250+	Sails	Rigby
From Here to There	G	I	179	Yellow Umbrella Books	Red Brick Learning
From Here to There: Transportation Timelines	P	I	250+	Discovery World	Rigby
From Hive to Home	J	I	200	Windows on Literacy	National Geographic
From Hubble to Hubble Astronomers and Outer Space	S	B	250+	Science Readers	Teacher Created Materials
From Idea to Book	K	I	407	Start to Finish	Lerner Publishing Group
From Idea to Law: The Legislative Process	S	I	1625	Leveled Readers Social Studies	Houghton Mifflin Harcourt
From Iron to Car	L	I	339	Start to Finish	Lerner Publishing Group
From Kernel to Corn	L	I	364	Start to Finish	Lerner Publishing Group
From Kernel to Corn (Revised Edition)	L	I	355	Start to Finish	Lerner Publishing Group
From Lava to Life: The Universe Tells Our Earth Story	W	I	3586	Sharing Nature with Children	Dawn Publications
From Maple Tree to Syrup	L	I	274	Start to Finish	Lerner Publishing Group
From Maple Trees to Maple Syrup	M	I	250+	From Farm to Table	Capstone Press
From Marbles to Video Games: How Toys Have Changed	J	I	366	Lightning Bolt Books	Lerner Publishing Group
From Metal to Airplane	K	I	278	Start to Finish	Lerner Publishing Group
From Milk to Cheese	M	I	332	From Farm to Table	Capstone Press
From Milk to Cheese	M	I	318	Start to Finish	Lerner Publishing Group
From Milk to Ice Cream	M	I	250+	From Farm to Table	Capstone Press
From Milk to Ice Cream	L	I	365	Leveled Literacy Intervention/ Blue System	Heinemann

* Collection of short stories   # Graphic text
^ Mature content with lower level text demands

TITLE	LEVEL	GENRE	WORD COUNT	AUTHOR / SERIES	PUBLISHER / DISTRIBUTOR
From Milk to Ice Cream	K	I	347	Start to Finish	Lerner Publishing Group
From Oil to Gas	K	I	314	Start to Finish	Lerner Publishing Group
From One to Eight	F	I	171	PM Math Readers	Rigby
From Oranges to Orange Juice	M	I	250+	From Farm to Table	Capstone Press
From Oscar Micheaux to the Oscars	X	I	2858	Reading Street	Pearson
From Paper Airplanes to Outer Space	O	B	250+	Meet The Author	Richard C. Owen
From Parking Lot to Garden	R	I	1236	Vocabulary Readers	Houghton Mifflin Harcourt
From Parking Lot to Garden	R	I	1236	Vocabulary Readers/CA	Houghton Mifflin Harcourt
From Parking Lot to Garden	R	I	1236	Vocabulary Readers/TX	Houghton Mifflin Harcourt
From Peanut to Peanut Butter	L	I	357	Start to Finish	Lerner Publishing Group
From Peanuts to Peanut Butter	M	I	250+	From Farm to Table	Capstone Press
From Plan to House	K	I	252	Take Two Books	Wright Group/McGraw Hill
From Pup to Rat: Following the Life Cycle	M	I	250+	Amazing Science	Picture Window Books
From Pyramids to Skyscrapers: Building in the Americas	R	I	250+	Navigators Social Studies Series	Benchmark Education
From Raider to Peacemaker	U	I	1307	Leveled Readers	Houghton Mifflin Harcourt
From Raider to Peacemaker	U	I	1307	Leveled Readers/CA	Houghton Mifflin Harcourt
From Raider to Peacemaker	U	I	1307	Leveled Readers/TX	Houghton Mifflin Harcourt
From Rock to Rap	P	I	121	Trackers	Pacific Learning
From Rock to Road	J	I	241	Start to Finish	Lerner Publishing Group
From Rocks to Sand: The Story of a Beach	J	I	224	Wonder World	Wright Group/McGraw Hill
From Russia with Lunch: A Chet Gecko Mystery	R	F	250+	Hale, Bruce	Sandpiper Books
From Salt to Silk: Precious Goods	U	I	2867	Reading Street	Pearson
From Sand to Glass	K	I	352	Start to Finish	Lerner Publishing Group
From Sea to Salt	M	I	322	Start to Finish	Lerner Publishing Group
From Seed to Apple Tree: Following the Life Cycle	M	I	250+	Amazing Science	Picture Window Books
From Seed to Pine Tree: Following the Life Cycle	N	I	250+	Amazing Science	Picture Window Books
From Seed to Plant	M	I	250+	Gibbons, Gail	Holiday House
From Seed to Pumpkin	F	I	148	Kottke, Jan	Scholastic
From Seedling to Tree	E	I	78	Rigby Star Quest	Rigby
From Seeds to Plants	E	RF	80	Reading Street	Pearson
From Sheep to Sweater	J	I	266	Leveled Readers	Houghton Mifflin Harcourt
From Sheep to Sweater	J	I	266	Leveled Readers/CA	Houghton Mifflin Harcourt
From Sheep to Sweater	J	I	266	Leveled Readers/TX	Houghton Mifflin Harcourt
From Sheep to Sweater	L	I	308	Start to Finish	Lerner Publishing Group
From Sheep to Sweater	B	I	28	Tarlow, Ellen	Scholastic
From Shoot to Apple	J	I	271	Start to Finish	Lerner Publishing Group
From Shoot to Apple (Revised Edition)	J	I	274	Start to Finish	Lerner Publishing Group
From Sky to Sea	H	I	40	Pacific Literacy	Pacific Learning
From Spain to America	T	I	1096	Reading Street	Pearson
From Tadpole to Frog	L	I	327	Start to Finish	Lerner Publishing Group
From Tadpole to Frog (Revised Edition)	L	I	327	Start to Finish	Lerner Publishing Group
From Tadpole to Frog: Following the Life Cycle	N	I	250+	Amazing Science	Picture Window Books
From Texas to California	L	RF	250+	On Our Way to English	Rigby
From the Air	E	I	107	Wonder World	Wright Group/McGraw Hill
From the Earth	J	I	186	Discovery Links	Newbridge
From the Farm to the Table	D	I	26	Rosen Real Readers	Rosen Publishing Group
From the Garden: A Counting Book About Growing Food	J	I	118	Know Your Numbers	Picture Window Books
From the Lake to Your Faucet	M	I	250+	On Our Way to English	Rigby
From the Mixed-up Files of Mrs. Basil E. Frankweiler	S	RF	250+	Konigsburg, E. L.	Bantam Books

F

TITLE	LEVEL	GENRE	WORD COUNT	AUTHOR / SERIES	PUBLISHER / DISTRIBUTOR
From the Model T to Hybrid Cars: How Transportation Has Changed	K	I	345	Lightning Bolt Books	Lerner Publishing Group
From the Mountain to the Ocean	K	I	99	Independent Readers Social Studies	Houghton Mifflin Harcourt
From the Notebooks of Melanin Sun	Z	RF	250+	Woodson, Jacqueline	Scholastic
From the Sea	O	I	250+	Rigby Focus	Rigby
From the Skyscraper	E	I	82	Windows on Literacy	National Geographic
From Tomato to Ketchup	L	I	250+	From Farm to Table	Capstone Press
From Trails to Highways	Q	I	919	Leveled Readers	Houghton Mifflin Harcourt
From Trails to Highways	Q	I	919	Leveled Readers/CA	Houghton Mifflin Harcourt
From Trails to Highways	Q	I	919	Leveled Readers/TX	Houghton Mifflin Harcourt
From Tree to House	J	I	319	Start to Finish	Lerner Publishing Group
From Tree to Me	N	I	250+	Windows on Literacy	National Geographic
From Tree to Paper	K	I	278	Start to Finish	Lerner Publishing Group
From Tree to Table	K	I	338	Start to Finish	Lerner Publishing Group
From Tree to Table	E	I	89	Yellow Umbrella Books	Red Brick Learning
From Trees to Paper	Q	I	250+	Theme Sets	National Geographic
From Typewriters to Computers	K	I	312	Vocabulary Readers	Houghton Mifflin Harcourt
From Typewriters to Computers	K	I	312	Vocabulary Readers/CA	Houghton Mifflin Harcourt
From Typewriters to Computers	K	I	312	Vocabulary Readers/TX	Houghton Mifflin Harcourt
From Typewriters to Text Messages: How Communication Has Changed	K	I	320	Lightning Bolt Books	Lerner Publishing Group
From Washboards to Washing Machines: How Homes Have Changed	J	I	350	Lightning Bolt Books	Lerner Publishing Group
From Wax to Crayon	L	I	303	Start to Finish	Lerner Publishing Group
From Wheat to Bread	M	I	250+	From Farm to Table	Capstone Press
From Wheat to Bread	K	I	305	Start to Finish	Lerner Publishing Group
From Wheat to Bread	Q	I	250+	Theme Sets	National Geographic
From Wheels to Wings	J	I	149	Shutterbug Books	Steck-Vaughn
From Zeus to Aliens	V	I	250+	Power Up!	Steck-Vaughn
Frost in the Night, A: A Girlhood on the Eve of the Third Reich	X	B	250+	Baer, Edith	Sunburst
Frosty: The Adventures of a Morgan Horse	S	RF	250+	Feld, Ellen F.	Willow Bend Publishing
Frown, The	K	RF	228	Read Alongs	Rigby
Frozen Fear: Zac Power	O	F	250+	Larry, H. I.	Feiwel and Friends
Frozen in Time	Q	I	250+	Book Blazers	ETA/Cuisenaire
Frozen Man	T	I	250+	Getz, David	Henry Holt & Co.
Frozen Music	L	TL	432	Books for Young Learners	Richard C. Owen
Frozen Secrets: Antarctica Revealed	Y	I	26036	Walker, Sally M.	Carolrhoda Books
Frozen Wasteland, The	S	RF	250+	Reading Safari	Mondo Publishing
Fruit	A	I	28	Leveled Readers Emergent	Houghton Mifflin Harcourt
Fruit	K	I	551	Rigby Flying Colors	Rigby
Fruit	B	I	20	Rise & Shine	Hampton Brown
Fruit Facts	E	I	198	Rosen Real Readers	Rosen Publishing Group
Fruit for Fly	E	F	103	Bonnell, Kris	Reading Reading Books
Fruit for You	A	RF	32	Red Rocket Readers	Flying Start Books
Fruit Group, The	H	I	96	The Food Guide Pyramid	Capstone Press
Fruit Pops	H	I	89	Windows on Literacy	National Geographic
Fruit Salad	A	I	25	Early Connections	Benchmark Education
Fruit Salad	B	I	24	Early Emergent	Pioneer Valley
Fruit Salad	D	I	18	Hoenecke, Karen	Kaeden Books
Fruit Salad	LB	I	15	Literacy 2000	Rigby
Fruit Salad	B	I	27	Rigby Rocket	Rigby
Fruit Salad	A	I	37	Sun Sprouts	ETA/Cuisenaire
Fruit Salad	LB	I	7	Windows on Literacy	National Geographic

* Collection of short stories   # Graphic text
^ Mature content with lower level text demands

F

TITLE	LEVEL	GENRE	WORD COUNT	AUTHOR / SERIES	PUBLISHER / DISTRIBUTOR
Fruit Salad	D	I	37	Wonder World	Wright Group/McGraw Hill
Fruit Trees	C	I	67	Bonnell, Kris/About	Reading Reading Books
Fruit Trees	LB	I	24	Visions	Wright Group/McGraw Hill
Fruits	F	I	87	Food Groups	Lerner Publishing Group
Fruits	I	I	149	Healthy Eating	Heinemann Library
Fruits	H	I	114	Plant Parts	Capstone Press
Fudge	O	RF	250+	Graeber, Charlotte Towner	Simon & Schuster
Fudge-a-Mania	Q	RF	250+	Blume, Judy	Bantam Books
Full Court Dreams	P	RF	250+	Maddox, Jake	Stone Arch Books
Full Court Fever	Q	RF	250+	Bowen, Fred	Peachtree
Full Court Press	S	RF	250+	Orca Young Readers	Orca Books
Full House: An Invitation to Fractions	J	F	250+	Dodds, Dayle Ann	Candlewick Press
Full House: Club Stephanie	Q	RF	250+	Herman, Gail	Pocket Books
Full House; Stephanie	Q	RF	250+	Herman, Gail	Pocket Books
Full of Air	E	I	97	Gear Up!	Wright Group/McGraw Hill
Full Throttle	W	RF	250+	Redline Racing Series	Fitzhenry & Whiteside
Full, Full, Full of Love	K	RF	250+	Cooke, Trish	Candlewick Press
Fun	D	RF	45	Yannone, Deborah	Kaeden Books
Fun All Year	A	I	25	Leveled Readers	Houghton Mifflin Harcourt
Fun All Year	A	I	25	Leveled Readers/CA	Houghton Mifflin Harcourt
Fun and Food to Eat	D	F	68	Leveled Readers Language Support	Houghton Mifflin Harcourt
Fun and Games	O	I	250+	Orbit Chapter Books	Pacific Learning
Fun and Games	O	I	250+	Rigby Focus	Rigby
Fun and Games, Then and Now	C	I	42	Independent Readers Social Studies	Houghton Mifflin Harcourt
Fun and Games: A Spot-It Challenge	J	I	250+	Spot It	Capstone Press
Fun at Camp	H	RF	178	First Start	Troll Associates
Fun at Camp	A	F	35	Leveled Readers	Houghton Mifflin Harcourt
Fun at Camp	A	F	35	Leveled Readers/CA	Houghton Mifflin Harcourt
Fun at School	C	RF	50	Foundations	Wright Group/McGraw Hill
Fun at School	B	I	40	Leveled Literacy Intervention/ Orange System	Heinemann
Fun at the Amusement Park	G	RF	176	Frankford, Marilyn	Kaeden Books
Fun at the Beach	A	I	28	Early Explorers	Benchmark Education
Fun at the Beach	E	RF	88	Rigby Focus	Rigby
Fun at the Park	A	I	32	Red Rocket Readers	Flying Start Books
Fun Baseball Game, A	H	I	376	Leveled Readers	Houghton Mifflin Harcourt
Fun Baseball Game, A	H	I	376	Leveled Readers/CA	Houghton Mifflin Harcourt
Fun Baseball Game, A	H	I	376	Leveled Readers/TX	Houghton Mifflin Harcourt
Fun Club Goes to a Dairy Farm, The	H	I	233	Leveled Literacy Intervention/ Blue System	Heinemann
Fun Club Goes to the Aquarium, The	K	I	635	Leveled Literacy Intervention/ Blue System	Heinemann
Fun Club Goes to the Post Office, The	I	I	230	Leveled Literacy Intervention/ Blue System	Heinemann
Fun Club Goes to the Vet Clinic, The	I	I	258	Leveled Literacy Intervention/ Blue System	Heinemann
Fun Days	F	RF	250+	Let's Play	Norwood House Press
Fun Days!	D	RF	79	Literacy by Design	Rigby
Fun Days!	D	RF	79	On Our Way to English	Rigby
Fun Facts About Fossils	S	I	1129	Leveled Readers Science	Houghton Mifflin Harcourt
Fun Food	C	I	29	Home Connection Collection	Rigby
Fun for All Seasons	A	RF	24	Literacy by Design	Rigby
Fun for Everyone	K	RF	250+	On Our Way to English	Rigby

F

TITLE	LEVEL	GENRE	WORD COUNT	AUTHOR / SERIES	PUBLISHER / DISTRIBUTOR
Fun For Families	D	I	28	Reading Street	Pearson
Fun for Hugs	I	RF	307	Leveled Literacy Intervention/ Green System	Heinemann
Fun for Pickles	J	F	608	Pickles the Dog Series	Pioneer Valley
Fun in Colonial Times	R	I	1431	Vocabulary Readers	Houghton Mifflin Harcourt
Fun in Colonial Times	R	I	1431	Vocabulary Readers/CA	Houghton Mifflin Harcourt
Fun in Colonial Times	R	I	1431	Vocabulary Readers/TX	Houghton Mifflin Harcourt
Fun in July	A	I	20	Vocabulary Readers	Houghton Mifflin Harcourt
Fun in July	A	I	20	Vocabulary Readers/CA	Houghton Mifflin Harcourt
Fun in the Mud	G	RF	182	Foundations	Wright Group/McGraw Hill
Fun in the Snow	C	F	56	Bella and Rosie Series	Pioneer Valley
Fun in the Snow	D	I	76	Leveled Readers	Houghton Mifflin Harcourt
Fun on the Sled	G	RF	269	Adams, Lorraine & Bruvold, Lynn	Eaglecrest Books
Fun on the Slide	C	RF	37	Early Emergent	Pioneer Valley
Fun Pets	H	I	190	Vocabulary Readers	Houghton Mifflin Harcourt
Fun Pets	H	I	190	Vocabulary Readers/CA	Houghton Mifflin Harcourt
Fun Pets	H	I	190	Vocabulary Readers/TX	Houghton Mifflin Harcourt
Fun Place to Eat, A	E	RF	90	Ready Readers	Pearson Learning Group
Fun Run, The	C	RF	27	Rigby Star	Rigby
Fun Things to Make and Do	I	I	250+	Discovery World	Rigby
Fun with Balls!	B	I	44	Bonnell, Kris	Reading Reading Books
Fun with Fingerprints	K	I	250+	How-To Series	Benchmark Education
Fun with Fingerprints	M	I	250+	Sunshine	Wright Group/McGraw Hill
Fun with Fives	J	I	200	Early Explorers	Benchmark Education
Fun with Fizz and Frost	P	I	250+	Storyteller-Raging Rivers	Wright Group/McGraw Hill
Fun with Fractions	P	I	250+	Rosen Real Readers	Rosen Publishing Group
Fun With Friends	A	RF	21	Bookshop	Mondo Publishing
Fun With Friends	A	I	28	Gear Up!	Wright Group/McGraw Hill
Fun with Friends	LB	RF	18	Rise & Shine	Hampton Brown
Fun with Fruit	B	I	37	Storyteller	Wright Group/McGraw Hill
Fun with Hats	B	F	38	Bookshop	Mondo Publishing
Fun With Magnets	M	I	250+	Early Connections	Benchmark Education
Fun with Magnets	L	I	394	Rigby Focus	Rigby
Fun with Magnets	D	I	38	Rosen Real Readers	Rosen Publishing Group
Fun with Mo and Toots	C	F	41	Pacific Literacy	Pacific Learning
Fun with My Family	B	RF	56	Windows on Literacy	National Geographic
Fun with Paper	A	I	29	Gear Up!	Wright Group/McGraw Hill
Fun With Plaster	H	I	150	Rigby Focus	Rigby
Fun with Science	O	I	801	Reading Street	Pearson
Fun with Science	L	I	433	Vocabulary Readers/TX	Houghton Mifflin Harcourt
Fun With Shadows	M	I	250+	iOpeners	Pearson Learning Group
Fun with Simple Machines	C	RF	28	Tarlow, Ellen	Scholastic
Fun Zone	N	F	250+	Sails	Rigby
Fun, Fun, Fun	D	I	71	Leveled Readers	Houghton Mifflin Harcourt
Fungi	M	I	326	Take Two Books	Wright Group/McGraw Hill
Funky Chicken Enchiladas and Other Mexican Dishes	R	I	250+	Kids Dish	Picture Window Books
Funky Flamingos	I	I	202	Sails	Rigby
Funny Baby Monkey, The	E	RF	87	Seedlings	Continental Press
Funny Baby, The	F	TL	217	Fairy Tales and Folklore	Norwood House Press
Funny Bananas: The Mystery in the Museum	N	RF	250+	McHargue, Georgess	Dell
Funny Bones	J	F	250+	Ahlberg, Allan & Janet	Viking/Penguin
Funny Cars	M	I	250+	Horsepower	Capstone Press
Funny Dog Facts	L	I	250+	Scooters	ETA/Cuisenaire

F

TITLE	LEVEL	GENRE	WORD COUNT	AUTHOR / SERIES	PUBLISHER / DISTRIBUTOR
Funny Ears	E	I	77	Rigby Star Quest	Rigby
Funny Face	A	RF	11	InfoTrek	ETA/Cuisenaire
Funny Face	M	RF	250+	Rigby Gigglers	Rigby
Funny Faces	Q	I	250+	Rigby Literacy	Rigby
Funny Faces and Funny Places	D	I	45	Ready Readers	Pearson Learning Group
Funny Faces, Wacky Wings, and Other Silly Big Bird Things	J	I	387	Silly Millies	Millbrook Press
Funny Fish	E	F	130	Big Cat	Pacific Learning
Funny Fish	I	I	211	Sails	Rigby
Funny Fish	C	I	86	Springboard	Wright Group/McGraw Hill
Funny Fish Story	E	F	152	Rookie Readers	Children's Press
Funny Garden, A	I	RF	234	Reading Street	Pearson
Funny Insects	D	I	117	Sails	Rigby
Funny Lunch (Max Spaniel)	I	F	213	Catrow, David	Orchard Books
Funny Man, A	E	F	244	Jensen, Patricia	Scholastic
Funny Old Man and the Funny Old Woman, The	M	F	250+	Bookshop	Mondo Publishing
Funny Ride, The	F	RF	250+	Let's Play	Norwood House Press
Funny Talk and More	I	F	250+	Bookshop	Mondo Publishing
Funny Things	A	I	40	Leveled Literacy Intervention/ Orange System	Heinemann
Funny Ways to Sleep	E	I	70	Bonnell, Kris	Reading Reading Books
Funny, Funny Clown Face, The	M	F	250+	Sunshine	Wright Group/McGraw Hill
Fur	E	I	104	Body Coverings	Lerner Publishing Group
Fur	D	RF	32	Mark, Jan	Harper & Row
Fur	J	I	287	Springboard	Wright Group/McGraw Hill
Fur	U	I	250+	Theme Sets	National Geographic
Fur and Feathers	M	F	764	Halfmann, Janet	Sylvan Dell Publishing
Fur Traders of New France	X	I	2576	Independent Readers Social Studies	Houghton Mifflin Harcourt
Fur, Feathers, and Flippers: How Animals Live Where They Do	T	I	250+	Lauber, Patricia	Scholastic
Fur, Feathers, or Skin	I	I	354	Sails	Rigby
Fur, Feathers, Scales, Skin	H	I	173	Discovery Links	Newbridge
Furball to the Rescue	E	F	133	Rigby Rocket	Rigby
Furry	B	I	19	Little Celebrations	Pearson Learning Group
Furry Baby Bear, The	E	RF	91	Seedlings	Continental Press
Fussy Heron	F	TL	177	PM Stars	Rigby
Fussy Wolf	D	F	60	Sun Sprouts	ETA/Cuisenaire
Future of NASA, The	U	I	1498	Leveled Readers	Houghton Mifflin Harcourt
Future of NASA, The	U	I	1498	Leveled Readers/CA	Houghton Mifflin Harcourt
Future of NASA, The	U	I	1498	Leveled Readers/TX	Houghton Mifflin Harcourt
Future Space Explorers: The Ultimate Camp Adventure	L	I	250+	On Our Way to English	Rigby
*Future-Telling Lady and Other Stories, The	S	RF	250+	Berry, James	HarperTrophy
Fuzz and the Glass Eye	M	RF	250+	Literacy Tree	Rigby
Fuzz, Feathers, Fur	E	I	131	Twig	Wright Group/McGraw Hill
Fuzzy on Parade	I	RF	402	PM Stars Bridge Books	Rigby

F

TITLE	LEVEL	GENRE	WORD COUNT	AUTHOR / SERIES	PUBLISHER / DISTRIBUTOR
G	LB	I	14	Readlings	American Reading Company
G is for Googol	U	I	250+	Schwartz, David M.	Scholastic
Gabby and the Christmas Tree	G	F	113	Developing Books, Set 2	Pioneer Valley
Gabby Is Hungry	C	RF	78	Emergent	Pioneer Valley
Gabby Runs Away	G	RF	223	Developing Books, Set 1	Pioneer Valley
Gabby Visits Buster	C	RF	39	Early Emergent	Pioneer Valley
Gabriella the Snow Kingdom Fairy: Rainbow Magic	L	F	250+	Meadows, Daisy	Scholastic
Gabrielle Lyon and the Fossil Hunt	P	I	250+	On Our Way to English	Rigby
Gabrielle's Team	G	RF	250+	Reading Safari	Mondo Publishing
Gabriel's Horses	V	HF	250+	Hart, Alison	Peachtree
Gabriel's Journey	V	HF	250+	Hart, Alison	Peachtree
Gabriel's Triumph	V	HF	250+	Hart, Alison	Peachtree
Gadget War, The	N	RF	250+	Duffey, Betsy	Penguin Group
Gadgets and Inventions	Y	I	250+	From Fail to Win! Learning from Bad Ideas	Raintree
Gai See: What You Can See in Chinatown	O	RF	250+	Thong, Roseanne	Harry N. Abrams
Gaia Warriors	W	I	250+	Davies, Nicola	Candlewick Press
Gail & Me	L	RF	250+	Literacy 2000	Rigby
Gail Devers: A Runner's Dream	M	B	250+	Pair-It Books	Steck-Vaughn
Galapagos Giants	P	I	250+	Orbit Double Takes	Pacific Learning
Galapagos Islands, The	R	I	250+	Rosen Real Readers	Rosen Publishing Group
Galapagos Tortoises	O	I	1561	Early Bird Nature Books	Lerner Publishing Group
Galapßgos Island Food Chain, A: A Who-Eats-What Adventure	U	I	7767	Follow That Food Chain	Lerner Publishing Group
Galaxies	Q	I	250+	A True Book	Children's Press
Galaxies	S	I	250+	Simon, Seymour	Mulberry Books
Galaxies Await	T	I	250+	Boldprint	Steck-Vaughn
Galaxies, Galaxies!	S	I	250+	Gibbons, Gail	Holiday House
Gale and Brian, Friends Forever	S	I	1984	Vocabulary Readers	Houghton Mifflin Harcourt
Gale and Brian, Friends Forever	S	I	1984	Vocabulary Readers/CA	Houghton Mifflin Harcourt
Galileo	W	I	2592	Leveled Readers	Houghton Mifflin Harcourt
Galileo	W	I	2592	Leveled Readers/CA	Houghton Mifflin Harcourt
Galileo	W	I	2592	Leveled Readers/TX	Houghton Mifflin Harcourt
Galileo Galilee, Astronomer	Q	B	455	Independent Readers Science	Houghton Mifflin Harcourt
Galileo Galilei: A Life of Curiosity	P	B	456	Pull Ahead Books	Lerner Publishing Group
Galileo, Messenger of Modern Science	Z	B	3428	Leveled Readers	Houghton Mifflin Harcourt
Galileo: Man of Science	R	B	250+	Rosen Real Readers	Rosen Publishing Group
Galileo's Journal 1609-1610	S	HF	250+	Pettenati, Jeanne K.	Charlesbridge
Galileo's Telescope	X	I	2796	Leveled Readers	Houghton Mifflin Harcourt
Galileo's Telescope	X	I	2796	Leveled Readers/CA	Houghton Mifflin Harcourt
Galileo's Telescope	X	I	2796	Leveled Readers/TX	Houghton Mifflin Harcourt
Gallo and Zorro	J	TL	369	Literacy 2000	Rigby
Galway, Ireland: Communities Around the World	S	I	250+	Reading Expeditions	National Geographic
Game Chaos	L	RF	250+	Go Girl!	Feiwel and Friends
Game for Jamie, A	M	RF	572	Sunshine	Wright Group/McGraw Hill
Game for Scruffy, A	D	RF	109	PM Photo Stories	Rigby
Game of Bowling, A	G	RF	295	PM Math Stories	Rigby
Game On: Have You Got What It Takes to Be a Video Game Developer?	U	I	250+	On the Job	Compass Point Books
Game Show, The	K	RF	610	InfoTrek	ETA/Cuisenaire
Game with Shapes, A	D	I	74	PM Math Readers	Rigby
Game-Day Gigglers: Winning Jokes to Score Some Laughs	O	F	2287	Make Me Laugh!	Lerner Publishing Group

* Collection of short stories   # Graphic text
^ Mature content with lower level text demands

TITLE	LEVEL	GENRE	WORD COUNT	AUTHOR / SERIES	PUBLISHER / DISTRIBUTOR
^Gamer	O	F	250+	Durant, Alan	Stone Arch Books
^Gamer: Next Level	O	F	250+	Durant, Alan	Stone Arch Books
Games	B	I	28	Berger, Samantha; Moreton, Daniel	Scholastic
Games	C	RF	69	Berger, Samantha; Moreton, Daniel	Scholastic
Games	W	I	250+	Boldprint	Steck-Vaughn
Games	A	F	28	KinderReaders	Rigby
Games Around the World	D	I	110	Dominie Factivity Series	Pearson Learning Group
Games Around the World	N	I	873	Time for Kids	Teacher Created Materials
Games at School	D	I	121	Vocabulary Readers	Houghton Mifflin Harcourt
Games at School	D	I	121	Vocabulary Readers/CA	Houghton Mifflin Harcourt
Games from Long Ago	T	I	250+	Historic Communities	Crabtree
Games Kids Play	N	I	250+	Windows on Literacy	National Geographic
Games We Play	Q	I	1368	Leveled Readers	Houghton Mifflin Harcourt
Games We Play	Q	I	1368	Leveled Readers/CA	Houghton Mifflin Harcourt
Games We Play	Q	I	1368	Leveled Readers/TX	Houghton Mifflin Harcourt
Games We Play	J	I	250+	PM Plus Nonfiction	Rigby
Games We Play	A	I	32	Red Rocket Readers	Flying Start Books
Games: From Dice to Gaming	U	I	250+	Timeline History	Heinemann Library
Gampy's Lamps	P	RF	1296	Leveled Readers	Houghton Mifflin Harcourt
Gannets	L	I	250+	Sunshine	Wright Group/McGraw Hill
Garage Sale, The	D	RF	44	Harry's Math Books	Outside the Box
Garbage	C	I	51	Wonder World	Wright Group/McGraw Hill
Garbage Can Concert, The	L	F	604	Pawprints Teal	Pioneer Valley
Garbage Collectors	M	I	250+	Community Helpers	Red Brick Learning
Garbage Helps Our Garden Grow: A Compost Story	K	I	431	Glaser, Linda	Millbrook Press
Garbage King, The	Y	RF	250+	Laird, Elizabeth	Barron's Educational
Garbage Trucks	I	I	131	Mighty Machines	Capstone Press
Garbage Trucks	K	I	444	Pull Ahead Books	Lerner Publishing Group
Garbage, Waste, Dumps, and You; The Disgusting Story Behind What We leave Behind	S	I	250+	Sanitation Investigation	Capstone Press
Garden Birthday	LB	F	15	Instant Readers	Harcourt School Publishers
Garden Colors	LB	F	15	Pair-It Books	Steck-Vaughn
Garden in a Bottle, A	K	I	370	Springboard	Wright Group/McGraw Hill
Garden in Your Bedroom, A	O	I	250+	Sunshine	Wright Group/McGraw Hill
Garden Is Fun, A	B	RF	36	Bonnell, Kris	Reading Reading Books
Garden Lunch	F	F	151	Early Explorers	Benchmark Education
Garden of Abdul Gasazi, The	P	F	250+	Van Allsburg, Chris	Houghton Mifflin Harcourt
Garden of Eden Motel, The	W	RF	250+	Hamilton, Morse	William Morrow
Garden of Happiness, The	O	RF	1100	Tamar, Erika	Harcourt, Brace, and Company
Garden on Green Street, The	L	RF	250+	Meish Goldish	Scholastic
Garden Tools	J	I	165	Spyglass Books	Compass Point Books
Garden Wall, The	M	RF	250+	Tildes, Phyllis Limbacher	Imagination Stage
Garden Zoo	E	RF	102	Joy Starters	Pearson Learning Group
Garden, A	A	I	40	Foundations	Wright Group/McGraw Hill
Garden, A	LB	F	12	Sails	Rigby
Garden, The	G	RF	21	Hoenecke, Karen	Kaeden Books
Garden, The	LB	I	14	Instant Readers	Harcourt School Publishers
Garden, The	A	I	27	Leveled Readers	Houghton Mifflin Harcourt
Garden, The	B	RF	63	Leveled Readers Emergent	Houghton Mifflin Harcourt
Garden, The	A	I	27	Leveled Readers/CA	Houghton Mifflin Harcourt
Garden, The	G	RF	107	Reading Street	Pearson

G

* Collection of short stories   # Graphic text
^ Mature content with lower level text demands

Organized Alphabetically by Title   **275**
Storable Database at www.fountasandpinnellleveledbooks.com

TITLE	LEVEL	GENRE	WORD COUNT	AUTHOR / SERIES	PUBLISHER / DISTRIBUTOR
Gardener, The	Z	SF	250+	Bodeen, S. A.	Feiwel and Friends
Gardener, The	M	RF	250+	Stewart, Sarah	Farrar, Straus, & Giroux
Gardening	D	RF	77	Foundations	Wright Group/McGraw Hill
Gardening with Grandpa	K	RF	310	Reading Street	Pearson
Gardens of the Sea	I	I	195	Sails	Rigby
Gardens on Green Street, The	I	RF	174	TOTTS	Tott Publications
Garfield and the Beast in the Basement	Q	F	250+	Davis, Jim	Troll Associates
Garfield and the Mysterious Mummy	Q	F	250+	Davis, Jim	Troll Associates
Gargoyles Don't Drive School Buses	M	F	250+	Dadey, Debbie; Jones, Marcia Thornton	Scholastic
Gargoyles On Guard	K	I	269	Books for Young Learners	Richard C. Owen
Garrett Morgan: Inventor	N	B	250+	Beginning Biographies	Pearson Learning Group
Garter Snakes	M	I	250+	Snakes	Capstone Press
Gary Soto	Y	B	2464	Leveled Readers	Houghton Mifflin Harcourt
Gases	J	I	93	What Earth Is Made Of	Lerner Publishing Group
Gasp!	L	F	250+	Bookshop	Mondo Publishing
*Gaston the Giant	K	F	331	New Way Orange	Steck-Vaughn
Gateway Arch, The	N	I	492	Lightning Bolt Books	Lerner Publishing Group
^Gathering Blood Evidence	T	I	250+	Crime Solvers	Capstone Press
Gathering Blue	X	F	250+	Lowry, Lois	Houghton Mifflin Harcourt
Gathering of Days, A: A New England Girl's Journal, 1830-32	U	HF	250+	Blos, Joan	Aladdin
*Gathering of Flowers, A	Z	RF	250+	Thomas, Joyce Carol	HarperTrophy
Gathering of Gargoyles, A	Y	F	250+	Pierce, Meredith Ann	Little Brown and Company
Gathering, The	V	F	250+	Hamilton, Virginia	Harcourt Brace
Gathering: A Northwoods Counting Book	Q	I	250+	Bowen, Betsy	Houghton Mifflin Harcourt
Gator Girls, The	L	F	250+	Calmenson, Stephanie & Cole	Beech Tree Books
Gator or Croc?	K	I	250+	Rookie Read About Science	Children's Press
Gator's Out, Said the Trout	E	F	71	Dominie Readers	Pearson Learning Group
^Gears Go, Wheels Roll	N	I	250+	Science Starts	Capstone Press
Gecko That Came to School, The	H	RF	302	Leveled Literacy Intervention/ Green System	Heinemann
Geckos	S	I	250+	Keeping Unusual Pets	Heinemann Library
Geckos	K	I	183	Reptiles	Capstone Press
Geckos	N	I	250+	World of Reptiles	Capstone Press
Gecko's Story	F	F	61	Books for Young Learners	Richard C. Owen
*Geektastic: Stories from the Nerd Herd	Z+	RF	250+	Black, Holly & Castelluccci, Cecil	Little Brown and Company
Geena's Project	H	I	212	Springboard	Wright Group/McGraw Hill
Gee's Bend Quilts, The	X	I	2901	Leveled Readers	Houghton Mifflin Harcourt
Gee's Bend Quilts, The	X	I	2901	Leveled Readers/CA	Houghton Mifflin Harcourt
Gee's Bend Quilts, The	X	I	2901	Leveled Readers/TX	Houghton Mifflin Harcourt
Geese on the Farm	I	I	69	On the Farm	Red Brick Learning
Geezer in the Freezer, The	M	F	250+	Wright, Randall	Bloomsbury Children's Books
Gem of a Tale, A	P	I	1500	Reading Street	Pearson
Gemini Summer	V	RF	250+	Lawrence, Iain	Yearling Books
Gemma the Gymnastics Fairy: Rainbow Magic	L	F	250+	Meadows, Daisy	Scholastic
Gems	Q	I	250+	On Deck	Rigby
^Gene Machine	X	SF	250+	The Extraordinary Files	Hameray Publishing Group
General Butterfingers	O	RF	250+	Gardiner, John Reynolds	Puffin Books
General Robert E. Lee	S	B	1921	Leveled Readers Language Support	Houghton Mifflin Harcourt
Genetic Disorders	Z	I	250+	Navigators Science Series	Benchmark Education
Genetic Engineering	Z	I	250+	Cool Science	Lerner Publishing Group
Genghis Khan: A Dog Star is Born	L	RF	250+	Sharmat, Marjorie Weinman	Random House

* Collection of short stories   # Graphic text
^ Mature content with lower level text demands

TITLE	LEVEL	GENRE	WORD COUNT	AUTHOR / SERIES	PUBLISHER / DISTRIBUTOR
Genie of the Bike Lamp	P	F	250+	Storyteller-Mountain Peaks	Wright Group/McGraw Hill
^Genie, The	O	F	250+	Hooper, M.	Stone Arch Books
Genies Don't Ride Bicycles	M	F	250+	Dadey, Debbie; Jones, Marcia Thornton	Scholastic
*Genies, Meanies, and Magic Rings	U	TL	250+	Mitchell, Stephen	Walker & Company
Genius Squad	Z	SF	250+	Jinks, Catherine	Houghton Mifflin Harcourt
Gentle and Friendly Sea Lions	S	I	1000	Leveled Readers/TX	Houghton Mifflin Harcourt
Gentle Annie: The True Story of a Civil War Nurse	R	I	250+	Shura, Mary Frances	Scholastic
Gentle Giant Octopus	M	I	250+	Read and Wonder	Candlewick Press
Gentle Giant, The	K	F	565	Red Rocket Readers	Flying Start Books
Gentle Lions of the Sea	T	I	1000	Leveled Readers/TX	Houghton Mifflin Harcourt
Gentle Manatees	K	I	381	Pull Ahead Books	Lerner Publishing Group
Gentle Redwood Giants	S	I	1776	Leveled Readers	Houghton Mifflin Harcourt
Gentle Redwood Giants	S	I	1776	Leveled Readers/CA	Houghton Mifflin Harcourt
Gentle Redwood Giants	S	I	1776	Leveled Readers/TX	Houghton Mifflin Harcourt
Gentlehands	Z	RF	250+	Kerr, M. E.	HarperTrophy
Gentleman Outlaw and Me - Eli, The: A Story of the Old West	T	HF	250+	Hahn, Mary Downing	Avon Books
Geoffrey the Dinosaur	D	F	36	Sunshine	Wright Group/McGraw Hill
Geographic Information Systems: Locating Ourselves	T	I	1493	Leveled Readers Social Studies	Houghton Mifflin Harcourt
Geography Affects Communities	M	I	295	Larkin, Bruce	Wilbooks
Geography Bee, The	V	RF	3165	Leveled Readers	Houghton Mifflin Harcourt
Geography Bee, The	V	RF	3165	Leveled Readers/CA	Houghton Mifflin Harcourt
Geography Bee, The	V	RF	3165	Leveled Readers/TX	Houghton Mifflin Harcourt
Geography of an Empire: Ancient Rome	X	I	2392	Independent Readers Social Studies	Houghton Mifflin Harcourt
Geography of Canada	T	I	250+	Navigators Social Studies Series	Benchmark Education
Geography of Girlhood, The	Z+	RF	250+	Smith, Kirsten	Little Brown and Company
Geography of Mexico	T	I	250+	Navigators Social Studies Series	Benchmark Education
Geography of South America	T	I	250+	Navigators Social Studies Series	Benchmark Education
Geography of War, The: The Battle of Salamis	Y	I	2877	Independent Readers Social Studies	Houghton Mifflin Harcourt
Geography Shapes Our World	T	I	1701	Reading Street	Pearson
Geologist Danny	E	F	75	Coulton, Mia	Maryruth Books
George and Martha	L	F	250+	Marshall, James	Houghton Mifflin Harcourt
George and Martha Back in Town	L	F	250+	Marshall, James	Houghton Mifflin Harcourt
George and Martha Encore	L	F	250+	Marshall, James	Houghton Mifflin Harcourt
George and Martha Full of Surprises	L	F	250+	Marshall, James	Houghton Mifflin Harcourt
George and Martha One Fine Day	L	F	250+	Marshall, James	Houghton Mifflin Harcourt
George and Martha One More Time	L	F	250+	Marshall, James	Sandpiper Books
George and Martha Rise and Shine	L	F	250+	Marshall, James	Houghton Mifflin Harcourt
George and Martha Round and Round	L	F	250+	Marshall, James	Houghton Mifflin Harcourt
George and Martha The Best of Friends	L	F	250+	Marshall, James	Sandpiper Books
George and Martha Two Great Friends	L	F	250+	Marshall, James	Sandpiper Books
George and the Whopper	L	F	250+	Rigby Literacy	Rigby
George Armstrong Custer	P	B	250+	Early Biographies	Compass Point Books
George at the Zoo	H	F	250+	Voyages	SRA/McGraw Hill
George Bush: Forty-first President	R	B	250+	Getting to Know the U.S. Presidents	Children's Press
George C. Marshall	T	B	4008	History Maker Bios	Lerner Publishing Group
George Catlin, Frontier Painter	Y	B	3371	Leveled Readers	Houghton Mifflin Harcourt
George Eastman	S	B	3213	History Maker Bios	Lerner Publishing Group
#George Eastman and the Kodak Camera	R	B	250+	Graphic Library	Capstone Press

G

TITLE	LEVEL	GENRE	WORD COUNT	AUTHOR / SERIES	PUBLISHER / DISTRIBUTOR
George Goes to Town	M	F	250+	Literacy by Design	Rigby
George H. W. Bush	U	B	250+	Profiles of the Presidents	Compass Point Books
George H.W. Bush	T	B	3602	History Maker Bios	Lerner Publishing Group
George Handel	R	B	250+	Venezia, Mike	Children's Press
George Most Wanted	M	F	250+	Orca Echoes	Orca Books
George Rogers Clark and the American Revolution in the Midwest	V	B	2534	Leveled Readers Social Studies	Houghton Mifflin Harcourt
George S. Patton Jr.	T	B	3807	History Maker Bios	Lerner Publishing Group
George Shrinks	H	F	114	Joyce, William	Scholastic
George the Drummer Boy	K	HF	250+	Benchley, Nathaniel	HarperTrophy
George the Joker	K	RF	640	Red Rocket Readers	Flying Start Books
George W. Bush	W	B	250+	A&E Biography	Lerner Publishing Group
George W. Bush	X	B	250+	Just the Facts Biographies	Lerner Publishing Group
George W. Bush	U	B	250+	Profiles of the Presidents	Compass Point Books
George W. Bush: Forty-third President	R	B	250+	Getting to Know the U.S. Presidents	Children's Press
George Washington	U	B	250+	Amazing Americans	Wright Group/McGraw Hill
George Washington	P	B	250+	Early Biographies	Compass Point Books
George Washington	M	B	270	Famous Americans	Capstone Press
George Washington	N	B	196	First Biographies	Capstone Press
George Washington	S	B	250+	History Maker Bios	Lerner Publishing Group
George Washington	E	B	69	Independent Readers Social Studies	Houghton Mifflin Harcourt
George Washington	O	B	250+	Judson, Clara Ingram	Pearson Learning Group
George Washington	U	B	250+	Let Freedom Ring	Red Brick Learning
George Washington	S	B	2444	People to Remember Series	January Books
George Washington	Q	I	250+	Photo-Illustrated Biographies	Red Brick Learning
George Washington	Q	B	250+	Primary Source Readers	Teacher Created Materials
George Washington	U	B	250+	Profiles of the Presidents	Compass Point Books
George Washington	P	B	799	Time for Kids	Teacher Created Materials
George Washington Carver	T	B	250+	Amazing Americans	Wright Group/McGraw Hill
George Washington Carver	M	B	250+	Biography	Benchmark Education
George Washington Carver	Q	B	250+	Early Biographies	Compass Point Books
George Washington Carver	T	B	3716	History Maker Bios	Lerner Publishing Group
George Washington Carver	O	B	967	Leveled Readers	Houghton Mifflin Harcourt
George Washington Carver	M	B	521	Leveled Readers	Houghton Mifflin Harcourt
George Washington Carver	O	B	967	Leveled Readers/CA	Houghton Mifflin Harcourt
George Washington Carver	O	B	967	Leveled Readers/TX	Houghton Mifflin Harcourt
George Washington Carver	N	B	1406	On My Own Biography	Lerner Publishing Group
George Washington Carver	N	B	224	Pebble Books	Capstone Press
George Washington Carver	S	B	2851	People to Remember Series	January Books
George Washington Carver	P	B	250+	Photo-Illustrated Biographies	Red Brick Learning
George Washington Carver: A Life of Devotion	N	B	391	Pull Ahead Books	Lerner Publishing Group
George Washington Carver: Agriculture Pioneer	R	B	250+	Science Readers	Teacher Created Materials
George Washington Carver: Scientist and Inventor	P	B	250+	Great African Americans	Capstone Press
George Washington Carver: Scientist and Teacher	O	B	250+	Greene, Carol	Children's Press
George Washington Carver: The Peanut Wizard	Q	B	250+	Driscoll, Laura	Grosset & Dunlap
George Washington Elected: How America's First President Was Chosen	S	I	250+	Headlines from History	Rosen Publishing Group
George Washington: A Life of Leadership	O	B	530	Pull Ahead Books	Lerner Publishing Group
George Washington: A Picture Book Biography	R	B	250+	Giblin, James Cross	Scholastic

* Collection of short stories   # Graphic text
^ Mature content with lower level text demands

TITLE	LEVEL	GENRE	WORD COUNT	AUTHOR / SERIES	PUBLISHER / DISTRIBUTOR
George Washington: Farmer, Soldier, President	M	B	250+	Biographies	Picture Window Books
George Washington: First President	R	B	250+	Getting to Know the U.S. Presidents	Children's Press
George Washington: First President of the U.S.	N	B	250+	Rookie Biographies	Children's Press
^George Washington: First President of the United States	T	B	250+	Hameray Biography Series	Hameray Publishing Group
#George Washington: Leading a Nation	T	B	250+	Graphic Library	Capstone Press
George Washington: Our First President	M	B	250+	Jackson, Garnet	Scholastic
George Washington: Our First President	M	B	200	Rosen Real Readers	Rosen Publishing Group
George Washington: The Man Who Would Not Be King	U	B	250+	Krensky, Stephen	Scholastic
George Washington: Young Leader	O	B	250+	Childhood of Famous Americans	Aladdin
George Washington: Young Leader	R	B	250+	Santrey, Laurence	Troll Associates
George Washington's Breakfast	P	B	250+	Fritz, Jean	G.P. Putnam's Sons Books for Young Readers
George Washington's First Victory	K	B	250+	Childhood of Famous Americans	Aladdin
George Washington's Invisible Enemy	W	I	2874	Leveled Readers	Houghton Mifflin Harcourt
George Washington's Invisible Enemy	W	I	2874	Leveled Readers/CA	Houghton Mifflin Harcourt
George Washington's Invisible Enemy	W	I	2874	Leveled Readers/TX	Houghton Mifflin Harcourt
George Washington's Mother	M	B	250+	Fritz, Jean	Scholastic
George Washington's Socks	T	F	250+	Woodruff, Elvira	Scholastic
George Washington's Teeth	N	HF	250+	Chandra, Deborah & Comora, Madeleine	Square Fish
George's Cosmic Treasure Hunt	U	F	250+	Hawking, Lucy & Stephen	Simon & Schuster
George's Marvelous Medicine	P	F	250+	Dahl, Roald	Penguin Group
George's Secret Key to the Universe	U	F	250+	Hawking, Lucy & Stephen	Simon & Schuster
George's Show and Tell	E	RF	133	Early Emergent	Pioneer Valley
George's Story	G	RF	133	Developing Books	Pioneer Valley
Georgia	T	I	250+	Hello U.S.A.	Lerner Publishing Group
Georgia	S	I	250+	Land of Liberty	Red Brick Learning
Georgia	Q	I	250+	One Nation	Capstone Press
Georgia	T	I	250+	Sea to Shining Sea	Children's Press
Georgia	R	I	250+	This Land Is Your Land	Compass Point Books
Georgia Colony, The	R	I	250+	The American Colonies	Capstone Press
Georgia Is the Peach State	O	I	221	Larkin, Bruce	Wilbooks
Georgia O'Keeffe	M	B	250+	On My Own Biography	Carolrhoda Books
Georgia O'Keeffe	R	B	250+	Venezia, Mike	Children's Press
Georgia Rises: A Day in the Life of Georgia O'Keefe	S	HF	250+	Lasky, Katherine	Farrar, Straus, & Giroux
Georgia the Guinea Pig Fairy: Rainbow Magic	L	F	250+	Meadows, Daisy	Scholastic
Georgia: Facts and Symbols	O	I	250+	The States and Their Symbols	Capstone Press
Georgia's Greatness: The Sisters 8	Q	F	250+	Baratz-Logsted, Lauren	Houghton Mifflin Harcourt
Georgie Giraffe, the Detective	E	F	96	Georgie Giraffe	Literacy Footprints
Georgina and the Dragon	K	F	250+	Rigby Rocket	Rigby
Geothermal Power	X	I	250+	Energy at Work	Capstone Press
Gerald R. Ford	T	B	3660	History Maker Bios	Lerner Publishing Group
Gerald R. Ford	U	B	250+	Profiles of the Presidents	Compass Point Books
Gerald R. Ford: Thirty-eighth President	R	B	250+	Getting to Know the U.S. Presidents	Children's Press
Geraldine's Big Snow	I	F	250+	Keller, Holly	Scholastic
Gerard Giraffe: Private Investigator	M	F	250+	Foundations	Wright Group/McGraw Hill
Gerbil Genius	O	RF	250+	Baglio, Ben M.	Scholastic
Gerbilitis	P	RF	250+	Soar To Success	Houghton Mifflin Harcourt

G

TITLE	LEVEL	GENRE	WORD COUNT	AUTHOR / SERIES	PUBLISHER / DISTRIBUTOR
Gerbilitis	P	RF	250+	Spinner, Stephanie; Weiss, Ellen	HarperTrophy
Germ Warfare	T	I	250+	Bookweb	Rigby
^German Immigrants in America: An Interactive History Adventure	V	HF	250+	You Choose Books	Capstone Press
German Shepards	I	I	149	Dogs	Capstone Press
German Sheperds	R	I	250+	All About Dogs	Capstone Press
German Shepherds Are the Best!	Q	I	1774	The Best Dogs Ever	Lerner Publishing Group
German-Jewish Immigration	V	I	250+	Theme Sets	National Geographic
Germany	O	I	250+	Countries of the World	Red Brick Learning
Germany	Q	I	1638	Country Explorers	Lerner Publishing Group
Germany	Q	I	250+	First Reports: Countries	Compass Point Books
Germany ABCs: A Book About the People and Places of Germany	Q	I	250+	Country ABCs	Picture Window Books
Germany: A Question and Answer Book	P	I	250+	Questions and Answers: Countries	Capstone Press
Germs	L	I	250+	Twig	Wright Group/McGraw Hill
Germ's Journey, A	M	I	250+	Follow-It!	Picture Window Books
Germs Make Me Sick!	O	I	250+	Berger, Melvin	Scholastic
Germs!	W	I	250+	WorldScapes	ETA/Cuisenaire
Germs! Germs! Germs!	L	F	250+	Katz, Bobbi	Scholastic
Geronimo	R	B	3449	History Maker Bios	Lerner Publishing Group
Geronimo	U	B	1903	Leveled Readers Social Studies	Houghton Mifflin Harcourt
Geronimo and the Gold Medal Mystery	O	F	250+	Stilton, Geronimo	Scholastic
Geronimo Stilton, Secret Agent	O	F	250+	Stilton, Geronimo	Scholastic
Geronimo: A Novel	Y	HF	250+	Bruchac, Joseph	Scholastic
Geronimo's Valentine	O	F	250+	Stilton, Geronimo	Scholastic
Gershwin's Rhapsoday in Blue	S	B	250+	Celenza, A. H.	Charlesbridge
Gertie Gorilla's Glorious Gift	K	F	520	Animal Antics A To Z	Kane Press
Gertie's Green Thumb	O	F	250+	Dexter, Catherine	Dell
Gertrude McClatter Finds Some Friends	J	F	250+	Reading Safari	Mondo Publishing
Get A Grip, Pip!	P	RF	250+	Literacy 2000	Rigby
Get Down Danny	C	RF	32	Coulton, Mia	Maryruth Books
Get Dressed!	E	I	52	Chwast, Seymour	Harry N. Abrams
Get Dressed!	J	I	129	Small World	Lerner Publishing Group
Get It!	C	RF	50	The Rowland Reading Program Library	Rowland Reading Foundation
Get Lost Becka!	E	RF	102	Start to Read	School Zone
Get Lost!	F	RF	219	Foundations	Wright Group/McGraw Hill
Get Me Out of Here!	M	F	250+	Rigby Rocket	Rigby
Get Moving!	A	I	32	Red Rocket Readers	Flying Start Books
Get on Board: The Story of the Underground Railroad	V	I	250+	Haskins, Jim	Scholastic
Get On Out of Here, Philip Hall	Y	RF	250+	Greene, Bette	Puffin Books
Get on the Train	C	F	42	Gear Up!	Wright Group/McGraw Hill
Get Ready for Second Grade, Amber Brown	K	RF	250+	Danziger, Paula	Puffin Books
Get Ready to Race	H	F	98	Instant Readers	Harcourt School Publishers
Get Ready!	B	I	22	On Our Way to English	Rigby
Get Set and Go	J	F	250+	Real Reading	Steck-Vaughn
Get Set for a Pet Hen	D	RF	31	Reading Street	Pearson
Get Set, Go!	E	RF	97	Reading Street	Pearson
Get Stronger	D	I	66	Little Celebrations	Pearson Learning Group
^Get That Ghost to Go!	O	F	5931	MacPhail, C.	Stone Arch Books
Get That Pest!	F	F	179	Green Light Readers	Harcourt
Get the Ball, Slim	E	RF	94	Real Kids Readers	Millbrook Press
Get the Fruit!	WB	F	0	Big Cat	Pacific Learning

* Collection of short stories   # Graphic text
^ Mature content with lower level text demands

TITLE	LEVEL	GENRE	WORD COUNT	AUTHOR / SERIES	PUBLISHER / DISTRIBUTOR
Get the Message	S	I	250+	Discovery Links	Newbridge
Get the Message	J	I	110	iOpeners	Pearson Learning Group
Get the Picture?	Q	I	250+	PM Plus Nonfiction	Rigby
Get Up	D	F	28	Potato Chip Books	American Reading Company
Get Up and Go: Being Active	K	I	204	How to Be Healthy!	Capstone Press
Get Up!	D	RF	70	Reading Street	Pearson
Get Well Soon	Z+	RF	250+	Halpern, Julie	Square Fish
Getting a Game	J	RF	250+	Reading Safari	Mondo Publishing
Getting Along	K	I	250+	InfoTrek	ETA/Cuisenaire
Getting Along - Contests, Conflicts, and Combats	V	I	250+	Connectors	Pacific Learning
Getting Around	LB	I	12	Beginning Word Books	American Reading Company
Getting Around	F	I	182	Chessen, Betsey; Moreton, Daniel	Scholastic
Getting Around	H	I	211	Momentum Literacy Program	Troll Associates
Getting Around	Q	I	250+	Orbit Collections	Pacific Learning
Getting Away With Murder: The True Story of the Emmett Till Case	Z+	I	250+	Crowe, Chris	Ideals Children's Books
Getting Cold! Getting Hot!	K	RF	753	Sunshine	Wright Group/McGraw Hill
Getting Dressed	B	RF	40	Carousel Earlybirds	Pearson Learning Group
Getting Dressed	A	I	31	Leveled Literacy Intervention/ Green System	Heinemann
Getting Dressed	LB	RF	16	Sunshine	Wright Group/McGraw Hill
Getting Elected: A Look at Running for Office	R	I	1490	Searchlight Books	Lerner Publishing Group
Getting Energy from Food	K	I	283	Vocabulary Readers	Houghton Mifflin Harcourt
Getting Energy from Food	K	I	283	Vocabulary Readers/CA	Houghton Mifflin Harcourt
Getting Fit	C	I	15	Wonder World	Wright Group/McGraw Hill
Getting Glasses	G	I	82	Wonder World	Wright Group/McGraw Hill
Getting Home	A	I	24	Windows on Literacy	National Geographic
Getting in the Game	Z	RF	250+	Fitzgerald, Dawn	Square Fish
Getting Lincoln's Goat	V	RF	250+	Goldman, E. M.	Bantam Books
Getting Near to Baby	V	RF	250+	Couloumbis, Audrey	Penguin Group
Getting Ready	A	I	42	Leveled Literacy Intervention/ Orange System	Heinemann
Getting Ready	B	I	29	Little Books for Early Readers	University of Maine
Getting Ready	A	I	32	Red Rocket Readers	Flying Start Books
Getting Ready	WB	I	0	Windows on Literacy	National Geographic
Getting Ready for School	I	I	270	Early Explorers	Benchmark Education
Getting Ready for School	E	RF	109	Foundations	Wright Group/McGraw Hill
Getting Ready for School	C	I	109	Little Red Readers	Sundance
Getting Ready for School	B	I	72	Vocabulary Readers	Houghton Mifflin Harcourt
Getting Ready for School	B	I	72	Vocabulary Readers/CA	Houghton Mifflin Harcourt
Getting Ready for the Ball	C	F	27	Literacy 2000	Rigby
Getting Ready for Winter	C	F	43	Gear Up!	Wright Group/McGraw Hill
Getting Rest	L	I	350	Pull Ahead Books	Lerner Publishing Group
Getting Rid of Katherine	Q	RF	250+	Wright, Betty Ren	Troll Associates
Getting Samantha to Smile	I	RF	287	The Rowland Reading Program Library	Rowland Reading Foundation
Getting the Lay of the Land	P	I	997	Reading Street	Pearson
Getting the Mail	G	RF	213	Voyages	SRA/McGraw Hill
Getting the Message	Q	I	250+	Orbit Collections	Pacific Learning
Getting the Message Across	U	I	250+	Connectors	Pacific Learning
Getting There	LB	I	10	Beginning Word Books	American Reading Company
Getting There	B	I	71	Johns, Edwin	Scholastic
Getting There	P	I	250+	Literacy by Design	Rigby
Getting There	B	I	36	Wonder World	Wright Group/McGraw Hill

G

TITLE	LEVEL	GENRE	WORD COUNT	AUTHOR / SERIES	PUBLISHER / DISTRIBUTOR
Getting to Grandpa's	K	RF	441	HSP/Harcourt Trophies	Harcourt, Inc.
Getting to Know Sharks	K	I	379	Little Books	Sadlier-Oxford
Getting to Know Your Neighbors	M	RF	250+	On Our Way To English	Rigby
Getting to Know Your Toilet: The Disgusting Story Behind Your Home's Strangest Feature	S	I	250+	Sanitation Investigation	Capstone Press
Getting to the Message	Q	I	250+	PM Plus Nonfiction	Rigby
Getting Together	R	I	250+	InfoQuest	Rigby
Getting Water	H	I	409	Sails	Rigby
Gettysburg Address in Translation, The: What It Really Means	V	I	250+	Kids' Translations	Capstone Press
Gettysburg Address, The	V	I	250+	Cornerstones of Freedom	Children's Press
Gettysburg Address, The	T	I	250+	Lincoln, Abraham	Houghton Mifflin Harcourt
Gettysburg: Bold Battle in the North	Y	I	250+	The Civil War	Carus Publishing Company
Get-Up Machine, The	I	F	115	Sunshine	Wright Group/McGraw Hill
Geysers	P	I	250+	A True Book	Children's Press
Geysers: When Earth Roars	U	I	250+	A First Book	Franklin Watts
Ghana	O	I	250+	Countries of the World	Red Brick Learning
Ghana	P	I	2470	Country Explorers	Lerner Publishing Group
Ghana: Ancient Empire	Y	I	2070	Leveled Readers Social Studies	Houghton Mifflin Harcourt
Ghost and Mrs. Hobbs, The	T	F	250+	DeFelice, Cynthia	Farrar, Straus, & Giroux
Ghost and the Sausage, The	I	F	250+	Story Box	Wright Group/McGraw Hill
Ghost Belonged to Me, The	V	F	250+	Peck, Richard	Penguin Group
Ghost Cadet	T	SF	250+	Alphin, Elaine Marie	Language for Learning Assoc.
Ghost Canoe	X	HF	250+	Hobbs, Will	Avon Books
Ghost Children, The	T	RF	250+	Bunting, Eve	Clarion Books
Ghost Comes Calling, The	Q	F	250+	Wright, Betty	Scholastic
Ghost Dog	M	F	250+	Allen, Eleanor	Scholastic
^Ghost Dog, The	S	F	250+	Warren, C	Stone Arch Books
Ghost Fox, The	P	F	250+	Yep, Laurence	Scholastic
Ghost Horse	M	F	250+	Stanley, George Edward	Random House
*Ghost Hunt: Chilling Tales of the Unknown	U	I	250+	Hawes, Jason & Wilson, Grant	Little Brown and Company
Ghost in Tent 19, The	M	F	250+	O'Connor, Jim	Random House
^Ghost in the Screen	W	F	250+	The Extraordinary Files	Hameray Publishing Group
Ghost in the Tokaido Inn, The	U	F	250+	Hoobler, Dorothy & Thomas	Penguin Group
Ghost Letters	W	F	250+	Alter, Stephen	Bloomsbury Children's Books
Ghost Medicine	Z	RF	250+	Smith, Andrew	Feiwel and Friends
Ghost Named Wanda, A	N	F	250+	The Zack Files	Grosset & Dunlap
Ghost of Crutchfield Hall, The	U	F	250+	Hahn, Mary Downing	Sandpiper Books
Ghost of Fossil Glen, The	U	F	250+	DeFelice, Cynthia	Farrar, Straus, & Giroux
Ghost of Popcorn Hill, The	N	F	250+	Wright, Betty Ren	Scholastic
Ghost on Saturday Night, The	Q	HF	250+	Fleischman, Sid	Beech Tree Books
Ghost School	M	F	250+	Clifford, Eth	Scholastic
Ghost School	Q	F	10091	Purkiss, S.	Stone Arch Books
Ghost Sonata, The: Gilda Joyce	W	F	250+	Allison, Jennifer	Puffin Books
Ghost Town at Sundown	M	F	250+	Osborne, Mary Pope	Random House
Ghost Town Mystery, The	M	RF	250+	Social Studies Connects	Kane Press
Ghost Town Treasure	M	RF	250+	Bulla, Clyde Robert	Penguin Group
Ghost Train	Q	HF	250+	Capeci, Anne	Peachtree
Ghost Tree, The	K	RF	250+	Voyages	SRA/McGraw Hill
Ghost Wolf	N	RF	250+	Orca Echoes	Orca Books
Ghost Zone, The	O	F	1227	The Funny Zone	Norwood House Press

* Collection of short stories   # Graphic text
^ Mature content with lower level text demands

TITLE	LEVEL	GENRE	WORD COUNT	AUTHOR / SERIES	PUBLISHER / DISTRIBUTOR
Ghost, The	A	RF	26	Story Box	Wright Group/McGraw Hill
Ghost, the White House, and Me, The	R	RF	250+	St. George, Judith	Holiday House
Ghostgirl	Z	F	250+	Hurley, Tonya	Little Brown and Company
Ghostgirl: Homecoming	Z	F	250+	Hurley, Tonya	Little Brown and Company
Ghosthunters and the Gruesome Invincible Lightning Ghost!	Q	F	250+	Funke, Cornelia	Scholastic
Ghosthunters and the Incredibly Revolting Ghost!	Q	F	250+	Funke, Cornelia	Scholastic
Ghosthunters and the Muddy Monster of Doom!	Q	F	250+	Funke, Cornelia	Scholastic
Ghosthunters and the Totally Moldy Baroness!	Q	F	250+	Funke, Cornelia	Scholastic
Ghostmobile, The	S	F	250+	Tapp, Kathy Kennedy	Scholastic
^Ghosts	X	I	250+	The Unexplained	Capstone Press
Ghosts Away	R	F	10285	Purkiss, S.	Stone Arch Books
Ghosts Beneath Our Feet	Q	F	250+	Wright, Betty Ren	Scholastic
Ghosts Don't Eat Potato Chips	M	F	250+	Dadey, Debbie; Jones, Marcia Thornton	Scholastic
Ghosts of Cougar Island, The	N	RF	250+	Parish, Peggy	Yearling Books
Ghosts of Flight 401	Z	I	250+	Unsolved Mysteries	Steck-Vaughn
^Ghost's Revenge, The	T	F	9889	Peschke, M.	Stone Arch Books
Ghosts' Secret, The	D	F	79	TOTTS	Tott Publications
*Ghosts!: Ghostly Tales from Folklore	J	TL	250+	Schwartz, Alvin	HarperTrophy
^Ghosts: The Unsolved Mystery	R	I	250+	Mysteries of Science	Capstone Press
Ghouls Don't Scoop Ice Cream	M	F	250+	Dadey, Debbie; Jones, Marcia Thornton	Scholastic
GIA and the One Hundred Dollars Worth of Bubblegum	J	F	169	Asch, Frank	Scholastic
Giant and the Boy, The	C	F	44	Sunshine	Wright Group/McGraw Hill
Giant and the Frippit, The	H	F	250+	Rigby Literacy	Rigby
Giant Anteaters	O	I	2097	Early Bird Nature Books	Lerner Publishing Group
Giant Balloons	J	I	185	Rigby Focus	Rigby
Giant Bugs Were Real!	I	I	54	Seedlings	Continental Press
Giant Forest, The	H	F	269	Leveled Readers	Houghton Mifflin Harcourt
Giant Forest, The	H	F	269	Leveled Readers/CA	Houghton Mifflin Harcourt
Giant Forest, The	H	F	269	Leveled Readers/TX	Houghton Mifflin Harcourt
Giant Games	K	F	767	Avenues	Hampton Brown
Giant Games	K	F	250+	Phonics and Friends	Hampton Brown
Giant Gingerbread Man, The	G	TL	248	Alphakids	Sundance
Giant Grass	J	I	250+	Story Steps	Rigby
Giant Ground Sloth	J	I	132	Dinosaurs and Prehistoric Animals	Capstone Press
Giant Humanlike Beasts	Z	I	250+	Unsolved Mysteries	Steck-Vaughn
Giant in the Bed, The	H	F	253	New Way Green	Steck-Vaughn
Giant in the Forest, A	J	F	250+	Reading Unlimited	Pearson Learning Group
Giant Jack's Boots	M	F	420	Book Bank	Wright Group/McGraw Hill
Giant Jam Sandwich, The	K	F	250+	Vernon Lord, John	Houghton Mifflin Harcourt
Giant Jumperee	J	F	250+	Literacy by Design	Rigby
Giant Jumperee, The: A Play	J	F	250+	Rigby Literacy	Rigby
Giant Jumperee, The: A Play	J	F	250+	Rigby Star	Rigby
^Giant Kangaroo	N	I	250+	Extinct Monsters	Capstone Press
Giant Meat-Eating Dinosaurs	P	I	940	Meet the Dinosaurs	Lerner Publishing Group
Giant Octopuses	L	I	399	Pull Ahead Books	Lerner Publishing Group
Giant Panda, The	D	I	78	Bonnell, Kris/Animals in Danger	Reading Reading Books
Giant Pandas	K	I	250+	Bears	Capstone Press
Giant Pandas	O	I	1904	Early Bird Nature Books	Lerner Publishing Group
Giant Pandas	G	I	72	Pebble Books	Capstone Press

* Collection of short stories   # Graphic text
^ Mature content with lower level text demands

G

TITLE	LEVEL	GENRE	WORD COUNT	AUTHOR / SERIES	PUBLISHER / DISTRIBUTOR
Giant Pandas	K	I	345	Pull Ahead Books	Lerner Publishing Group
Giant Pandas	U	I	250+	The Untamed World	Steck-Vaughn
Giant Pandas	R	I	250+	Theme Sets	National Geographic
Giant Pandas: Gifts from China	I	I	250+	Rookie Read-About Science	Children's Press
Giant Plant-Eating Dinosaurs	P	I	1035	Meet the Dinosaurs	Lerner Publishing Group
Giant Rhinoceros	J	I	137	Dinosaurs and Prehistoric Animals	Capstone Press
^Giant Ripper Lizard	N	I	250+	Extinct Monsters	Capstone Press
Giant Rock of Yosemite, The: A Sierra Miwok Tale	Q	F	1028	Leveled Readers	Houghton Mifflin Harcourt
Giant Seeds, The	K	RF	507	PM Plus Story Books	Rigby
Giant-Sized Day, A	I	F	245	Ready Readers	Pearson Learning Group
Giant Snakes	O	I	1347	Take Two Books	Wright Group/McGraw Hill
*Giant Soup	J	F	419	Pacific Literacy	Pacific Learning
Giant, The	LB	F	20	Joy Readers	Pearson Learning Group
Giant, The	M	F	250+	Voyages	SRA/McGraw Hill
Giants	F	F	52	Blaxland, Wendy	Scholastic
Giant's Boy, The	H	F	89	Sunshine	Wright Group/McGraw Hill
Giant's Breakfast, The	B	F	42	Literacy 2000	Rigby
Giant's Cake	M	F	250+	Learning Media	Pacific Learning
Giant's Cake, The	H	F	162	Literacy 2000	Rigby
Giant's Cake, The	I	F	280	Sun Sprouts	ETA/Cuisenaire
Giant's Day Out, The	B	F	26	Smart Start	Rigby
Giants Don't Go Snowboarding	M	F	250+	Dadey, Debbie; Jones, Marcia Thornton	Scholastic
Giant's Fire, The	J	F	351	Springboard	Wright Group/McGraw Hill
Giant's Job, The	H	F	180	Stewart, Josie; Salem, Lynn	Continental Press
Giant's Pizza, The	C	RF	28	Joy Readers	Pearson Learning Group
Giant's Rice, The	C	F	28	Joy Readers	Pearson Learning Group
Giant's Stew, The	I	F	259	Sunshine	Wright Group/McGraw Hill
Giants, Monsters & Mythical Beasts	O	I	250+	Literacy 2000	Rigby
Giants, Trolls and Ogres	U	I	5494	Fantasy Chronicles	Lerner Publishing Group
Giant-Size Hamburger, A	C	F	38	Wonder World	Wright Group/McGraw Hill
Gib Got It	B	F	28	Reading Street	Pearson
Gib Rides Home	V	RF	250+	Snyder, Zilpha Keatley	Bantam Books
Gibbon Island	K	RF	444	PM Plus Story Books	Rigby
Gibbons, the Singing Apes	J	I	250+	Literacy by Design	Rigby
Giddy Up	C	RF	49	Cat on the Mat	Oxford University Press
Giddyoocha!	I	F	297	Story Box	Wright Group/McGraw Hill
Giddyup Lucky	F	RF	128	Coulton, Mia	Maryruth Books
Gift for Abuela, A	K	RF	670	Gear Up!	Wright Group/McGraw Hill
Gift for Grandpa, A	S	RF	1440	Leveled Readers	Houghton Mifflin Harcourt
Gift for Grandpa, A	S	RF	1440	Leveled Readers/CA	Houghton Mifflin Harcourt
Gift for Grandpa, A	S	RF	1440	Leveled Readers/TX	Houghton Mifflin Harcourt
Gift for Mama, A	N	RF	250+	Hautzig, Esther	Penguin Group
Gift for Yoshi, A	J	RF	282	Leveled Readers	Houghton Mifflin Harcourt
*Gift From Zeus, A: Sixteen Favorite Myths	X	TL	250+	Steig, Jeanne	HarperCollins
Gift of Crayons, A	G	RF	226	Leveled Readers Language Support	Houghton Mifflin Harcourt
Gift of Light, The: A Japanese Myth	Y	TL	2018	Leveled Readers	Houghton Mifflin Harcourt
Gift of Magic, A	W	F	250+	Duncan, Lois	Laurel-Leaf Books
Gift of the Girl Who Couldn't Hear, The	U	RF	250+	Shreve, Susan	Beech Tree Books
Gift of the Magi	X	HF	250+	Henry, O.	Candlewick Press
Gift of the Pirate Queen, The	S	RF	250+	Giff, Patricia Reilly	Yearling Books

* Collection of short stories   # Graphic text
^ Mature content with lower level text demands

G

TITLE	LEVEL	GENRE	WORD COUNT	AUTHOR / SERIES	PUBLISHER / DISTRIBUTOR
Gift That Wasn't Perfect, The	K	RF	892	Denholtz, Roni S.	January Books
Gift to Share, A	K	RF	544	Pair-It Books	Steck-Vaughn
Gift, The	WB	RF	0	Prater, J.	Wright Group/McGraw Hill
Gift, The	Q	RF	2340	Reading Street	Pearson
Gift, The	N	TL	250+	Story Vines	Wright Group/McGraw Hill
Gifted: Better Late Than Never	Y	F	250+	Kaye, Marilyn	Kingfisher
Gifted: Here Today, Gone Tomorrow	X	F	250+	Kaye, Marilyn	Kingfisher
Gifted: Out of Sight, Out of Mind	Y	F	250+	Kaye, Marilyn	Kingfisher
Gift-Giver, The	S	RF	250+	Hansen, Joyce	Houghton Mifflin Harcourt
Gifts	C	RF	91	The Rowland Reading Program Library	Rowland Reading Foundation
Gifts for Dad	H	RF	178	Urmston, Kathleen; Evans, Karen	Kaeden Books
Gifts for Everyone	B	F	35	Rigby Literacy	Rigby
Gifts from Greece	Q	I	250+	InfoQuest	Rigby
Gifts from the Gods: Ancient Words & Wisdom from Greek & Roman Gods	W	TL	250+	Lunge-Larsen, Lise	Houghton Mifflin Harcourt
Gifts of the Dineh	Q	RF	1301	Leveled Readers	Houghton Mifflin Harcourt
Gifts to Make	K	I	509	Pair-It Books	Steck-Vaughn
Gifts, The	B	RF	34	Story Box	Wright Group/McGraw Hill
Gifts, The	I	RF	250+	The Rowland Reading Program Library	Rowland Reading Foundation
Giganotosaurus	J	I	130	Dinosaurs and Prehistoric Animals	Capstone Press
*Gigantic Ants and Other Cases, The	O	RF	250+	Simon, Seymour	Avon Books
Gigantic Bell, The	K	TL	250+	PM Plus Story Books	Rigby
Gigantic George	H	F	224	Little Celebrations	Pearson Learning Group
Giggle Belly	G	RF	108	Rookie Readers	Children's Press
Giggle Box, The	E	F	176	Story Box	Wright Group/McGraw Hill
Gila Monster	L	I	250+	A Day in the Life: Desert Animals	Heinemann Library
Gila Monsters	O	I	2003	Early Bird Nature Books	Lerner Publishing Group
Gila Monsters	K	I	180	Reptiles	Capstone Press
Gilbert de la frogponde: A Swamp Story	M	F	250+	Rae, Jennifer	Peachtree
Gilbert Galaxy, Space Hero	L	SF	250+	Rigby Gigglers	Rigby
Gilbert Goes on a Picnic	F	F	152	Gilbert the Pig	Pioneer Valley
Gilbert in the Snow	I	F	706	Gilbert the Pig	Pioneer Valley
Gilbert the Pig Goes on a Diet	E	F	118	Gilbert the Pig	Pioneer Valley
Gilbert the Pig Has an Adventure	H	F	262	Gilbert the Pig	Pioneer Valley
Gilbert the Pig Wears a Dress	E	F	124	Gilbert the Pig	Pioneer Valley
Gilbert the Prize Winning Pig	B	RF	20	Gilbert the Pig	Pioneer Valley
Gilbert the Special Pig	H	F	238	Gilbert the Pig	Pioneer Valley
Gilda Joyce, Psychic Investigator	W	F	250+	Allison, Jennifer	Puffin Books
Gillian's Nines	C	RF	29	Harry's Math Books	Outside the Box
Gimme Cracked Corn & I Will Share	O	F	250+	O'Malley, Kevin	Walker & Company
Gina's Puppy	L	RF	250+	Windows on Literacy	National Geographic
Ginger	I	RF	232	Little Readers	Houghton Mifflin Harcourt
Ginger	D	RF	43	Parker, Ant	Mondo Publishing
Ginger Brown: The Nobody Boy	L	RF	250+	Wyeth, Sharon Dennis	Random House
Ginger Brown: Too Many Houses	L	RF	250+	Wyeth, Sharon Dennis	Random House
Ginger Pye	U	RF	250+	Estes, Eleanor	Scholastic
Gingerbread	Z+	RF	250+	Cohn, Rachel	Simon & Schuster
Gingerbread	I	I	134	Windows on Literacy	National Geographic
Gingerbread Boy	F	TL	137	New Way Red	Steck-Vaughn
Gingerbread Boy, The	C	TL	107	Folk Tales	Pioneer Valley
Gingerbread Boy, The	L	TL	1097	Galdone, Paul	Clarion

G

TITLE	LEVEL	GENRE	WORD COUNT	AUTHOR / SERIES	PUBLISHER / DISTRIBUTOR
Gingerbread Boy, The	C	TL	107	Traditional Tales	Pioneer Valley
Gingerbread Boy, The	G	TL	250+	Ziefert, Harriet	Puffin Books
Gingerbread Man	I	TL	250+	Hunia, Fran	Ladybird Books
Gingerbread Man, The	J	TL	250+	Aylesworth, Jim	Scholastic
Gingerbread Man, The	G	TL	139	Cambridge Reading	Pearson Learning Group
Gingerbread Man, The	G	TL	250+	Cherrington, Janelle	Scholastic
Gingerbread Man, The	E	F	79	Instant Readers	Harcourt School Publishers
Gingerbread Man, The	H	TL	447	Leveled Literacy Intervention/ Green System	Heinemann
Gingerbread Man, The	H	TL	250+	Literacy 2000	Rigby
Gingerbread Man, The	F	TL	180	Little Readers	Houghton Mifflin Harcourt
Gingerbread Man, The	K	TL	250+	McCafferty, Catherine	School Specialty Publishing
Gingerbread Man, The	I	TL	180	Rose, Rita	Scholastic
Gingerbread Man, The	I	TL	250+	Storyworlds	Heinemann
Gingerbread Man, The	H	TL	197	Sunshine	Wright Group/McGraw Hill
Gingerbread Man, The	I	TL	250+	Tiger Cub	Peguis
Gingerbread Man, The	I	TL	544	Traditional Tales	Pearson Learning Group
Gingerbread Man, The	J	TL	535	Traditional Tales & More	Rigby
Gingerbread Men, The	D	I	37	Sunshine	Wright Group/McGraw Hill
Ginger's War	S	HF	250+	Sunshine	Wright Group/McGraw Hill
Giraffe	C	I	41	Zoozoo-Into the Wild	Cavallo Publishing
Giraffe and the Pelly and Me, The	P	F	250+	Dahl, Roald	Penguin Group
Giraffe Calf Grows Up, A	K	I	429	Baby Animals	Lerner Publishing Group
Giraffe Goes Skating	E	F	101	Springboard	Wright Group/McGraw Hill
Giraffe Goes to Paris, A	P	HF	250+	Holmes, Mary Tavener & Harris, John	Marshall Cavendish
Giraffe Grows Up	D	I	72	Little Celebrations	Pearson Learning Group
Giraffe Made Her Laugh, The	E	F	70	Learn to Read	Creative Teaching Press
Giraffe Who Was Afraid of Heights, The	L	F	676	Ufer, David A.	Sylvan Dell Publishing
Giraffe, The	P	I	250+	Animal Close-Ups	Charlesbridge
Giraffes	I	I	137	African Animals	Capstone Press
Giraffes	P	I	250+	Crabapples	Crabtree
Giraffes	O	I	2038	Early Bird Nature Books	Lerner Publishing Group
Giraffes	N	I	250+	Meadows, Graham; Vial, Claire	Pearson Learning Group
Giraffes	D	I	63	Nonfiction Set 3	Literacy Footprints
Giraffes	O	I	250+	Take Two Books	Wright Group/McGraw Hill
Giraffes	L	I	318	Windows on Literacy	National Geographic
Giraffes Can't Dance	M	F	250+	Andreae, Giles	Scholastic
Giraffe's Neck	E	TL	109	Leveled Readers	Houghton Mifflin Harcourt
Giraffe's Neck	E	TL	109	Leveled Readers/CA	Houghton Mifflin Harcourt
Giraffe's Neck	E	TL	109	Leveled Readers/TX	Houghton Mifflin Harcourt
Giraffe's Sad Tale (With a Happy Ending)	H	F	250+	Ada, Alma Flor	Hampton Brown
Girl and the Wolf, The	N	RF	1038	Leveled Readers	Houghton Mifflin Harcourt
Girl and the Wolf, The	N	RF	1038	Leveled Readers/CA	Houghton Mifflin Harcourt
Girl and the Wolf, The	N	RF	1038	Leveled Readers/TX	Houghton Mifflin Harcourt
Girl Called Al, A	P	RF	250+	Greene, Constance C.	Puffin Books
Girl Called Boy, A	U	F	250+	Hurmence, Belinda	Clarion
Girl From Yamhill, A	W	B	250+	Cleary, Beverly	Bantam Books
Girl in a Cage	X	HF	250+	Yolen, Jane; Harris, Robert J.	Scholastic
Girl in the Golden Bower, The	Q	TL	250+	Yolen, Jane	Little Brown and Company
Girl in the Window, The	U	RF	250+	Yeo, Wilma	Scholastic
Girl Named Amira, A	X	RF	2450	Leveled Readers	Houghton Mifflin Harcourt
Girl Named Amira, A	X	RF	2450	Leveled Readers/CA	Houghton Mifflin Harcourt
Girl Named Amira, A	X	RF	2450	Leveled Readers/TX	Houghton Mifflin Harcourt

G

* Collection of short stories   # Graphic text
^ Mature content with lower level text demands

TITLE	LEVEL	GENRE	WORD COUNT	AUTHOR / SERIES	PUBLISHER / DISTRIBUTOR
Girl Named Disaster, A	X	RF	250+	Farmer, Nancy	Penguin Group
Girl Named Helen Keller, A	K	B	250+	Lundell, Margo	Scholastic
Girl Overboard	Y	RF	250+	Headley, Justina Chen	Little Brown and Company
Girl Pirates	N	RF	250+	Girlz Rock!	Mondo Publishing
Girl Saves Giant	M	RF	250+	Wonder World	Wright Group/McGraw Hill
^Girl Who Breathed Fire, The	T	F	250+	Dragonblood	Stone Arch Books
Girl Who Chased Away Sorrow, The: The Diary of Sarah Nita, a Navajo Girl	U	HF	250+	Dear America	Scholastic
Girl Who Climbed to the Moon, The	L	TL	604	Sunshine	Wright Group/McGraw Hill
Girl Who Could Fly, The	V	F	250+	Forester, Victoria	Feiwel and Friends
Girl Who Helped the Wolf, The	N	RF	999	Leveled Readers	Houghton Mifflin Harcourt
Girl Who Helped the Wolf, The	N	RF	999	Leveled Readers/CA	Houghton Mifflin Harcourt
Girl Who Helped the Wolf, The	N	RF	999	Leveled Readers/TX	Houghton Mifflin Harcourt
Girl Who Knew It All, The	Q	RF	250+	Giff, Patricia Reilly	Bantam Books
Girl Who Loved Meerkats, The	M	F	250+	World Quest Adventures	World Quest Learning
Girl Who Loved the Wind, The	Q	TL	250+	Yolen, Jane	HarperTrophy
Girl Who Loved Wild Horses, The	N	TL	250+	Goble, Paul	Scholastic
*Girl Who Married the Moon, The: Tales from Native North America	U	TL	250+	Bruchac, Joseph; Ross, Gayle	Troll Associates
Girl Who Owned a City, The	X	F	250+	Nelson, O. T.	Laurel-Leaf Books
Girl Who Struck Out Babe Ruth, The	N	B	1715	On My Own History	Lerner Publishing Group
Girl With the Silver Eyes, The	U	F	250+	Roberts, Willo Davis	Scholastic
Girl Wonder: A Baseball Story in Nine Innings	P	HF	250+	Hopkinson, Deborah	Aladdin Paperbacks
GirlForce: A Girl's Guide to the Body and Soul	Z+	I	250+	Goldstein, Nikki	Bloomsbury Children's Books
Girls Acting Catty	S	RF	250+	Margolis, Leslie	Bloomsbury Children's Books
Girls' Basketball: Making Your Mark on the Court	R	I	250+	Girls Got Game	Capstone Press
Girls' Figure Skating: Ruling the Rink	R	I	250+	Girls Got Game	Capstone Press
Girl's Golf: Teeing Up	R	I	250+	Girls Got Game	Capstone Press
Girl's Ice Hockey:Dominating the Rink	R	I	250+	Girls Got Game	Capstone Press
Girls of Many Lands	W	HF	250+	Croutier, Alev Lytle	Pleasant Company
Girls on Film	Z+	RF	250+	Dean, Zoey	Little Brown and Company
Girl's Skateboarding: Skating to Be the Best	R	I	250+	Girls Got Game	Capstone Press
Girl's Snowboarding:Showing Off Your Style	R	I	250+	Girls Got Game	Capstone Press
Girls' Soccer: Going for the Goal	R	I	250+	Girls Got Game	Capstone Press
Girls' Softball: Winning on the Diamond	R	I	250+	Girls Got Game	Capstone Press
Girls' Tennis: Conquering the Court	R	I	250+	Girls Got Game	Capstone Press
*Girls Think of Everything: Stories of Ingenious Inventions by Women	S	I	250+	Thimmesh, Catherine	Houghton Mifflin Harcourt
*Girls to the Rescue, Book 1	Q	RF	250+	Lansky, Bruce	Meadowbrook Press
*Girls to the Rescue, Book 2	Q	RF	250+	Lansky, Bruce	Meadowbrook Press
*Girls to the Rescue, Book 3	Q	RF	250+	Lansky, Bruce	Meadowbrook Press
*Girls to the Rescue, Book 4	Q	RF	250+	Lansky, Bruce	Meadowbrook Press
*Girls to the Rescue, Book 5	Q	RF	250+	Lansky, Bruce	Meadowbrook Press
*Girls to the Rescue, Book 6	Q	RF	250+	Lansky, Bruce	Meadowbrook Press
*Girls to the Rescue, Book 7	Q	RF	250+	Lansky, Bruce	Meadowbrook Press
Girls' Volleyball: Setting Up Success	R	I	250+	Girls Got Game	Capstone Press
Girls, The	Y	RF	250+	Koss, Amy Goldman	Scholastic
Girls, The	Z+	RF	250+	Shaw, Tucker	Amulet Books
Girl-Son, The	R	HF	250+	Neuberger, Anne E.	Carolrhoda Books
Give and Take	D	RF	122	Literacy by Design	Rigby
Give It a Push! Give It a Pull!: A Look at Forces	L	I	431	Lightning Bolt Books	Lerner Publishing Group
Give Me a Hug	B	RF	28	Sunshine	Wright Group/McGraw Hill

G

TITLE	LEVEL	GENRE	WORD COUNT	AUTHOR / SERIES	PUBLISHER / DISTRIBUTOR
Give Me Liberty: The Story of the Declaration of Independence	V	I	250+	Freedman, Russell	Holiday House
Give My Regrets to Broadway: A Chet Gecko Mystery	R	F	250+	Hale, Bruce	Harcourt, Inc.
Giver, The	Y	F	250+	Lowry, Lois	Bantam Books
Giving Thanks A Native American Good Morning Message	M	RF	305	Swamp, Chief Jake	Scholastic
Giving Thanks Around the World	K	I	350	Reading Street	Pearson
Giving Tree, The	N	F	250+	Silverstein, Shel	HarperCollins
Giving Up the Ghost	V	F	250+	Sinykin, Sheri	Peachtree
Gizmos' Party, The	J	F	250+	Rigby Literacy	Rigby
Gizmos' Party, The	J	F	250+	Rigby Star	Rigby
Gizmos' Trip, The	J	F	250+	Rigby Literacy	Rigby
Gizmos' Trip, The	J	F	250+	Rigby Star	Rigby
Glaciers	R	I	250+	Early Bird Earth Science	Lerner Publishing Group
Glaciers	T	I	250+	Gallant, Roy A.	Franklin Watts
Glaciers	V	I	2117	Leveled Readers Social Studies	Houghton Mifflin Harcourt
Glaciers Are Melting, The	N	F	793	Love, Donna	Sylvan Dell Publishing
Glad Golly	LB	RF	20	The Rowland Reading Program Library	Rowland Reading Foundation
Glad Monster, Sad Monster: A Book About Feelings	I	F	171	Miranda, Anne	Little Brown and Company
Gladiators	W	HF	250+	Forward, Toby	Candlewick Press
Gladiators	T	I	250+	Warriors of History	Capstone Press
Gladiators and Roman Soldiers	S	I	250+	Fierce Fighters	Raintree
Gladly, Here I Come	R	RF	250+	Cowley, Joy	Wright Group/McGraw Hill
Gladys and Max Love Bob	M	RF	459	Book Bank	Wright Group/McGraw Hill
Glass	M	I	250+	Materials	Capstone Press
Glass	G	I	112	Rigby Focus	Rigby
Glass	P	I	250+	Windows on Literacy	National Geographic
Glass Blowing	M	I	663	Reading Street	Pearson
Glass Café, The	Z	RF	250+	Paulsen, Gary	Random House
Glass Slipper for Rosie, A	N	RF	250+	Giff, Patricia Reilly	Penguin Group
Glass-Bottomed Boat, The	L	RF	854	Springboard	Wright Group/McGraw Hill
Glasses	D	RF	19	Visions	Wright Group/McGraw Hill
Glasses for D.W.	I	F	250+	Brown, Marc	Random House
Gleam and Glow	P	HF	250+	Bunting, Eve	Harcourt, Inc.
Glenda	P	F	250+	Udry, Janice May	HarperTrophy
Glenda Glinka: Witch-At-Large	P	F	250+	Udry, Janice May	HarperTrophy
Glenda the Lion	E	F	88	Ready Readers	Pearson Learning Group
Glessner House: An American Home and Family	T	I	250+	Rigby Literacy	Rigby
Glide, Wriggle, Zoom	M	I	250+	Pacific Literacy	Pacific Learning
Gliders and Sliders	H	I	198	Sails	Rigby
Gliding Garter Snakes	K	I	400	Pull Ahead Books	Lerner Publishing Group
Glitter Trouble	C	RF	32	Learn to Read	Creative Teaching Press
Glitz Girls, The	R	RF	250+	Literacy by Design	Rigby
Global Alert	Q	I	250+	Navigators Social Studies Series	Benchmark Education
Global Energy	Y	I	2359	Independent Readers Science	Houghton Mifflin Harcourt
Global Warming	U	I	250+	Our Planet in Peril	Capstone Press
Global Warming	V	I	250+	Reading Expeditions	National Geographic
Globes	C	I	11	Geography	Lerner Publishing Group
Gloria Rising	N	RF	250+	Cameron, Ann	Random House
Glorious Days, Dreadful Days: The Battle of Bunker Hill	R	I	250+	Kirby, Philippa	Steck-Vaughn

Organized Alphabetically by Title
Storable Database at www.fountasandpinnellleveledbooks.com

* Collection of short stories   # Graphic text
^ Mature content with lower level text demands

TITLE	LEVEL	GENRE	WORD COUNT	AUTHOR / SERIES	PUBLISHER / DISTRIBUTOR
Glorious Flight, The: Across the Channel with Louis Blériot	O	B	250+	Provensen, Alice & Martin	Puffin Books
Glory Be	S	HF	250+	Scattergood, Augusta	Scholastic
Glory Field, The	X	HF	250+	Myers, Walter Dean	Scholastic
Glory Gate	U	SF	250+	Storyteller-Mountain Peaks	Wright Group/McGraw Hill
Glory Girl, The	S	RF	250+	Byars, Betsy	Penguin Group
Gloves	E	RF	103	Story Box	Wright Group/McGraw Hill
Glow from Lighthouse Cove, The	S	RF	2501	Leveled Readers	Houghton Mifflin Harcourt
Glow Stone, The	Z	RF	250+	Dreyer, Ellen	Peachtree
Gluepots	K	RF	205	Book Bank	Wright Group/McGraw Hill
Glum Princess, The	H	RF	250+	The Rowland Reading Program Library	Rowland Reading Foundation
Glumly	Q	F	250+	Literacy 2000	Rigby
Gnu Named Blue, A	K	F	250+	Phonics and Friends	Hampton Brown
Go and Get It!	C	RF	68	Rigby Rocket	Rigby
Go and Hush the Baby	K	RF	250+	Byars, Betsy	Viking/Penguin
Go Annie, Go!	K	RF	250+	Pacific Literacy	Pacific Learning
Go Away Dog	I	RF	250+	Nodset, Joan	HarperCollins
Go Away!	B	I	36	Sails	Rigby
Go Away!	H	RF	216	The King School Series	Townsend Press
Go Away, Tooth Decay	T	I	250+	Leveled Readers Language Support	Houghton Mifflin Harcourt
Go Back to Bed!	L	RF	627	Guy, Ginger Foglesong	Carolrhoda Books
Go Back to Sleep	E	RF	74	Literacy 2000	Rigby
Go Dog Go	E	F	250+	Eastman, Philip D.	Random House
Go Fish	O	RF	250+	Stolz, Mary	Scholastic
Go Fly a Kite!	T	I	250+	WorldScapes	ETA/Cuisenaire
Go for the Gold	S	I	250+	Explorer Books-Pathfinder	National Geographic
Go for the Gold	R	I	250+	Explorer Books-Pioneer	National Geographic
Go Free or Die: A Story About Harriet Tubman	R	B	250+	Ferris, Jeri	Carolrhoda Books
Go Green	R	RF	1542	Leveled Readers	Houghton Mifflin Harcourt
Go Green	R	RF	1542	Leveled Readers/CA	Houghton Mifflin Harcourt
Go Green	R	RF	1542	Leveled Readers/TX	Houghton Mifflin Harcourt
Go Home, Chick!	B	F	77	Literacy by Design	Rigby
Go Home, Daisy	F	RF	100	Hill, Barbara	Scholastic
Go Left or Right	E	RF	142	Red Rocket Readers	Flying Start Books
Go Sea It!	A	I	16	Little Celebrations	Pearson Learning Group
Go Teddy!	B	I	27	Windows on Literacy	National Geographic
Go to Bed!	D	RF	45	Joy Readers	Pearson Learning Group
Go to Bed, Oscar!	F	RF	214	The Joy Cowley Collection	Hameray Publishing Group
Go To School	A	F	21	Reading Street	Pearson
Go to Sleep, Dear Dragon	E	F	313	Dear Dragon	Norwood House Press
Go Turtle! Go Hare!	D	TL	100	Leveled Readers	Houghton Mifflin Harcourt
Go Turtle! Go Hare!	D	TL	100	Leveled Readers/CA	Houghton Mifflin Harcourt
Go Turtle! Go Hare!	D	TL	100	Leveled Readers/TX	Houghton Mifflin Harcourt
Go West!	S	I	250+	Reading Expeditions	National Geographic
Go!	D	RF	44	Little Readers	Houghton Mifflin Harcourt
Go! Go! Go!	C	I	20	Munro, Roxie	Sterling Publishing
Go, Gina!	I	RF	519	Rigby Flying Colors	Rigby
Go, Go, Go	LB	RF	12	Handprints A	Educators Publishing Service
Go, Go, Go	A	I	23	Little Books for Early Readers	University of Maine
Go, Go, Go	A	RF	17	Story Box	Wright Group/McGraw Hill
Go, Go, Go!	A	I	24	On Our Way to English	Rigby

TITLE	LEVEL	GENRE	WORD COUNT	AUTHOR / SERIES	PUBLISHER / DISTRIBUTOR
Go, Meg, Go!	D	RF	70	Pair-It Turn and Learn	Steck-Vaughn
Goal!	H	RF	232	Lighthouse	Rigby
Goalie from Nowhere, The	O	F	250+	High-Fliers	Pacific Learning
Goalkeeper in Charge	Q	RF	250+	Christopher, Matt	Little Brown and Company
Goat and the Rock, The: A Tale from Tibet	N	TL	250+	On Our Way to English	Rigby
Goat Goes to Town, The	H	RF	131	Bebop Books	Lee & Low Books Inc.
Goat in the Chile Patch, The	H	TL	250+	Kratky, Lada Josefa	Hampton Brown
Goat in the Garden	Q	RF	250+	Baglio, Ben M.	Scholastic
Goat in the Garden, The	G	TL	227	Leveled Literacy Intervention/ Green System	Heinemann
*Goat Monster and Other Stories, The	L	F	250+	New Way Literature	Steck-Vaughn
*Goat on Soap, Joe Glow, Colt and Mole	K	F	451	Easy-for-Me Reading	Child 1st Publications
Goat Who Wouldn't Come Home, The	G	F	184	Seedlings	Continental Press
Goat, The	C	RF	17	KinderReaders	Rigby
Goat, The	B	F	40	Sails	Rigby
Goats	F	I	93	Farm Animals	Lerner Publishing Group
Goats	L	I	250+	PM Animal Facts: Purple	Rigby
Goat's Beard, The	H	F	325	Sails	Rigby
Goats in the Turnip Field, The	I	TL	250+	PM Plus Story Books	Rigby
Goats on the Farm	I	I	67	Pebble Books	Red Brick Learning
Goats, The	Y	RF	250+	Cole, Brock	Farrar, Straus, & Giroux
Goats, The	A	F	24	Sails	Rigby
Gobble Gobble	M	RF	169	Sharing Nature with Children	Dawn Publications
Gobble Up the Moon	J	F	289	Gear Up!	Wright Group/McGraw Hill
Gobble! Gobble! Munch!	F	F	64	Rhythm 'N' Rhyme Readers	Pearson Learning Group
Gobble, Gobble, Gone	D	F	58	Little Celebrations	Pearson Learning Group
#Goblin King, The	U	F	11290	Twisted Journeys	Graphic Universe
Goblin Shark	J	I	122	Sharks	Capstone Press
Goblins Don't Play Video Games	M	RF	250+	Dadey, Debbie; Jones, Marcia Thornton	Scholastic
Go-cart Day	K	RF	165	City Kids	Rigby
Gocart Genius	M	F	250+	Too Cool	Pacific Learning
Go-Cart Team, The	O	I	250+	PM Nonfiction-Emerald	Rigby
Go-Cart, The	E	RF	47	Oxford Reading Tree	Oxford University Press
Go-Carts, The	B	RF	46	PM Starters	Rigby
God of Mischief, The	U	F	250+	Bajoria, Paul	Little Brown and Company
^Gods and Goddesses of Ancient Egypt	S	I	250+	Ancient Egypt	Capstone Press
Godzilla Ate My Homework	O	F	250+	Jones, Marcia	Scholastic
Goggly Gookers	H	F	100	Story Basket	Wright Group/McGraw Hill
Goha and His Donkey	I	F	114	Books for Young Learners	Richard C. Owen
Going Along With Lewis and Clark	T	I	250+	Fifer, Barbara	Montana Magazine
Going Back to Harlem	P	I	522	Vocabulary Readers	Houghton Mifflin Harcourt
Going Bowling	J	I	338	Springboard	Wright Group/McGraw Hill
Going Camping	F	RF	238	Leveled Literacy Intervention/ Blue System	Heinemann
Going Fast	N	I	449	Big Cat	Pacific Learning
Going Fast	D	I	116	Leveled Readers	Houghton Mifflin Harcourt
Going Fast	D	I	116	Leveled Readers/CA	Houghton Mifflin Harcourt
Going Fast	H	I	197	Sails	Rigby
Going Faster	D	I	78	Early Explorers	Benchmark Education
Going Fishing	E	F	99	Arctic Stories	Pioneer Valley
Going Fishing	G	RF	117	Cambridge Reading	Pearson Learning Group
Going Fishing	F	F	240	Leveled Readers	Houghton Mifflin Harcourt
Going Fishing	E	RF	26	Literacy 2000	Rigby

G

TITLE	LEVEL	GENRE	WORD COUNT	AUTHOR / SERIES	PUBLISHER / DISTRIBUTOR
Going Fishing	I	RF	250+	Momentum Literacy Program	Troll Associates
Going Fishing	B	F	22	Ready Readers	Pearson Learning Group
Going Fishing	C	RF	30	Visions	Wright Group/McGraw Hill
Going Fishing	F	RF	26	Voyages	SRA/McGraw Hill
Going Fishing	I	I	161	Windows on Literacy	National Geographic
Going for a Hay Ride	A	I	26	Leveled Readers	Houghton Mifflin Harcourt
Going for a Hay Ride	A	I	26	Leveled Readers/CA	Houghton Mifflin Harcourt
Going for a Hike	A	I	20	Vocabulary Readers	Houghton Mifflin Harcourt
Going for a Hike	A	I	20	Vocabulary Readers/CA	Houghton Mifflin Harcourt
Going for a Ride	C	RF	52	Early Emergent	Pioneer Valley
Going for a Ride	B	I	67	Leveled Readers Emergent	Houghton Mifflin Harcourt
Going for a Ride	B	RF	40	Little Books for Early Readers	University of Maine
Going for a Walk	F	RF	82	DeRegniers, Beatrice Schenk	Harper & Row
Going for Gold	O	B	250+	WorldScapes	ETA/Cuisenaire
Going for Gold!	P	B	250+	Eyewitness Readers	DK Publishing
Going Green	R	I	250+	High-Fliers	Pacific Learning
Going Here and There	D	RF	124	Early Connections	Benchmark Education
Going Home	T	RF	250+	Mohr, Nicholas	Penguin Group
Going Home	O	I	930	Sharing Nature with Children	Dawn Publications
Going in the Car	B	RF	24	Sunshine	Wright Group/McGraw Hill
Going Live in 3, 2, 1: Have You Got What It Takes to Be a TV Producer?	T	I	250+	On the Job	Compass Point Books
Going Lobstering	O	I	250+	Pallotta, Jerry; Bolster, Rob	Charlesbridge
Going Nowhere Faster	Z	RF	250+	Beaudoin, Sean	Little Brown and Company
Going on a Airplane	C	I	83	Vocabulary Readers/CA	Houghton Mifflin Harcourt
Going on a Dinosaur Dig	K	I	342	Reading Street	Pearson
Going on a Field Trip	I	RF	288	Visions	Wright Group/McGraw Hill
Going on a Train Ride	C	RF	76	Leveled Literacy Intervention/ Orange System	Heinemann
Going on an Airplane	C	I	83	Vocabulary Readers	Houghton Mifflin Harcourt
Going on Safari	M	I	250+	Pacific Literacy	Pacific Learning
Going on Vacation	B	RF	51	Leveled Literacy Intervention/ Orange System	Heinemann
Going on Vacation	A	I	40	PM Plus Starters	Rigby
Going Out	D	RF	94	Foundations	Wright Group/McGraw Hill
Going Out	A	F	42	KinderReaders	Rigby
Going Out	B	RF	48	PM Plus Starters	Rigby
Going Outside	A	RF	35	Adams, Lorraine & Bruvold, Lynn	Eaglecrest Books
Going Outside	M	F	118	Voyages	SRA/McGraw Hill
Going Places	K	I	410	Early Connections	Benchmark Education
Going Places	B	F	49	First Stories	Pacific Learning
Going Places	R	I	250+	Orbit Collections	Pacific Learning
Going Places	P	RF	250+	Orca Young Readers	Orca Books
Going Places	C	I	32	Rosen Real Readers	Rosen Publishing Group
Going Places	E	I	101	Sails	Rigby
Going Places	L	I	250+	The Rowland Reading Program Library	Rowland Reading Foundation
Going Shopping	F	I	112	Bookshop	Mondo Publishing
Going Shopping	D	RF	92	Carousel Readers	Pearson Learning Group
Going Shopping	F	RF	99	Leveled Readers Social Studies	Houghton Mifflin Harcourt
Going Shopping	B	RF	31	Rigby Literacy	Rigby
Going Shopping	B	F	24	Sails	Rigby
Going Sledding	A	I	31	Leveled Literacy Intervention/ Orange System	Heinemann
Going Solo	T	B	250+	Dahl, Roald	Puffin Books

G

TITLE	LEVEL	GENRE	WORD COUNT	AUTHOR / SERIES	PUBLISHER / DISTRIBUTOR
Going Solo	T	I	250+	iOpeners	Pearson Learning Group
Going Swimming	J	RF	210	City Kids	Rigby
Going Swimming	J	I	250+	Explorations	Eleanor Curtain Publishing
Going Swimming	J	I	250+	Explorations	Okapi Educational Materials
Going the Distance	T	RF	1626	Leveled Readers	Houghton Mifflin Harcourt
Going to a Football Game	I	RF	131	City Kids	Rigby
Going to America	K	HF	250+	Leveled Readers Language Support	Houghton Mifflin Harcourt
Going to America	N	RF	250+	Orbit Chapter Books	Pacific Learning
Going to Be a Butterfly	L	I	250+	Sunshine	Wright Group/McGraw Hill
Going to Bed	B	F	36	Sails	Rigby
Going to Grandma's	I	RF	136	Tarlton, John	Scholastic
Going to Grandma's Farm	C	RF	56	Rookie Readers	Children's Press
Going to Grandma's House	D	RF	122	Joy Starters	Pearson Learning Group
Going to Grandpa's House	C	RF	37	Frankford, Marilyn	Kaeden Books
Going to Kindergarten	G	I	106	Factivity Series	Pearson Learning Group
Going to Lucy's House	E	RF	151	Sunshine	Wright Group/McGraw Hill
Going to School	I	F	476	Bella and Rosie Series	Literacy Footprints
Going to School	H	RF	250+	Cambridge Reading	Pearson Learning Group
Going to School	F	I	171	Foundations	Wright Group/McGraw Hill
Going to School	C	I	45	Gear Up!	Wright Group/McGraw Hill
Going to School	O	I	21	iOpeners	Pearson Learning Group
Going to School	B	I	77	Leveled Literacy Intervention/ Blue System	Heinemann
Going to School	B	I	40	Leveled Readers	Houghton Mifflin Harcourt
Going to School	A	RF	28	Leveled Readers Emergent	Houghton Mifflin Harcourt
Going to School	B	I	40	Leveled Readers/CA	Houghton Mifflin Harcourt
Going to School	LB	RF	21	Smart Start	Rigby
Going to School	C	I	43	Story Box	Wright Group/McGraw Hill
Going to School	C	I	50	Sunshine	Wright Group/McGraw Hill
Going to School	D	I	104	Vocabulary Readers	Houghton Mifflin Harcourt
Going to School	D	I	104	Vocabulary Readers/CA	Houghton Mifflin Harcourt
Going to School	D	I	104	Vocabulary Readers/TX	Houghton Mifflin Harcourt
Going to School	C	I	30	Windows on Literacy	National Geographic
Going to the Bank	J	I	317	Foundations	Wright Group/McGraw Hill
Going to the Beach	C	RF	75	Carousel Readers	Pearson Learning Group
Going to the Beach	E	I	30	Little Red Readers	Sundance
Going to the Beach	LB	RF	30	Pacific Literacy	Pacific Learning
Going to the Beach	C	I	60	Rigby Flying Colors	Rigby
Going to the Beach	E	RF	49	Rookie Readers	Children's Press
Going to the City	J	I	250+	People, Spaces & Places	Rand McNally
Going to the Dentist	F	I	122	Dental Health	Capstone Press
Going to the Doctor	F	RF	101	City Stories	Rigby
Going to the Hairdresser	J	I	227	Foundations	Wright Group/McGraw Hill
Going to the Hospital	H	RF	335	Foundations	Wright Group/McGraw Hill
Going to the Hospital	J	I	250+	Growing Up	Heinemann Library
Going to the Moon	C	F	75	Springboard	Wright Group/McGraw Hill
Going to the Movies	L	I	432	Rigby Flying Colors	Rigby
Going to the Park	C	RF	41	Home Connection Collection	Rigby
Going to the Park with Grandaddy	C	RF	30	Visions	Wright Group/McGraw Hill
Going to the Pool	D	RF	55	Pair-It Books	Steck-Vaughn
Going to the South Pole	O	I	843	Leveled Readers	Houghton Mifflin Harcourt
Going to the South Pole	O	I	843	Leveled Readers/CA	Houghton Mifflin Harcourt
Going to the South Pole	O	I	843	Leveled Readers/TX	Houghton Mifflin Harcourt

* Collection of short stories   # Graphic text
^ Mature content with lower level text demands

TITLE	LEVEL	GENRE	WORD COUNT	AUTHOR / SERIES	PUBLISHER / DISTRIBUTOR
Going to the Symphony	G	I	132	Twig	Wright Group/McGraw Hill
Going to the Vet	D	I	46	Sunshine	Wright Group/McGraw Hill
Going to Town	B	RF	63	Springboard	Wright Group/McGraw Hill
Going to Town	J	HF	250+	Wilder, Laura Ingalls	HarperCollins
Going to Town With Mom and Dad	D	RF	85	Early Connections	Benchmark Education
Going to Visit Grandfather	J	RF	289	McAlpin, MaryAnn	Short Tales Press
Going Up	B	RF	41	Red Rocket Readers	Flying Start Books
Going Up	P	I	250+	Scooters	ETA/Cuisenaire
Going Up and Down	B	RF	51	Early Emergent	Pioneer Valley
Going Up the Mountain	K	I	251	Windows on Literacy	National Geographic
Going up the Wall	N	I	250+	Pacific Literacy	Pacific Learning
Going Up?	B	F	26	Little Celebrations	Pearson Learning Group
Going West	N	I	250+	Discovery Links	Newbridge
Going West	O	HF	250+	Van Leeuwen, Jean	Penguin Group
Going West	N	I	428	Vocabulary Readers	Houghton Mifflin Harcourt
Going West	J	HF	250+	Wilder, Laura Ingalls	HarperCollins
Going West: Trials and Tradeoffs	S	I	2572	Independent Readers Social Studies	Houghton Mifflin Harcourt
Going Wild at the Zoo	R	I	1320	Leveled Readers	Houghton Mifflin Harcourt
Going Wild at the Zoo	R	I	1320	Leveled Readers/CA	Houghton Mifflin Harcourt
Going Wild at the Zoo	R	I	1320	Leveled Readers/TX	Houghton Mifflin Harcourt
Going, Going, Gone! with the Pain & the Great One	M	RF	250+	Blume, Judy	Delacorte Press
Go-Kart Rush	Q	RF	4681	Maddox, Jake	Stone Arch Books
Go-Karts	Q	I	250+	Wild Rides!	Capstone Press
Gold	T	I	250+	Navigators Science Series	Benchmark Education
Gold	Q	I	250+	Trackers	Pacific Learning
Gold	Q	I	250+	Windows on Literacy	National Geographic
Gold and Earth's Treasures	U	I	250+	The News	Richard C. Owen
Gold Cadillac, The	S	HF	250+	Taylor, Mildred D.	Puffin Books
Gold Dust Kids, The	R	HF	250+	Sunshine	Wright Group/McGraw Hill
Gold Dust Letters, The	S	RF	250+	Lisle, Janet Taylor	Avon Books
Gold Fever!	N	HF	250+	Step into Reading	Random House
Gold for Chan Li	T	HF	2647	Leveled Readers	Houghton Mifflin Harcourt
Gold for Chan Li	T	HF	2647	Leveled Readers/CA	Houghton Mifflin Harcourt
Gold for Chan Li	T	HF	2647	Leveled Readers/TX	Houghton Mifflin Harcourt
Gold Miner's Daughter, The: A Melodramatic Fairy Tale	N	TL	250+	Hopkins, Jackie Mims	Peachtree
Gold Mountain	R	HF	250+	Pair-It Books	Steck-Vaughn
Gold Rush of 1849, The	S	I	1192	Reading Street	Pearson
Gold Rush!	T	I	250+	Navigators Social Studies Series	Benchmark Education
Gold Rush, The: California or Bust!	Q	I	250+	On Deck	Rigby
Gold! Gold! Gold!	C	F	37	Dominie Math Stories	Pearson Learning Group
Golden Age of Baghdad, The	W	I	2406	Reading Street	Pearson
^Golden Age of Pirates, The: An Interactive History Adventure	T	HF	250+	You Choose Books	Capstone Press
Golden Age of Sail, The	P	I	1200	Vocabulary Readers/TX	Houghton Mifflin Harcourt
^Golden Book of Death, The	T	F	250+	Dahl, Michael	Stone Arch Books
Golden Compass, The	Z	F	250+	Pullman, Philip	Ballantine Books
Golden Dragon	J	F	250+	Supersonics	Rigby
Golden Fish, The	N	TL	250+	WorldScapes	ETA/Cuisenaire
Golden Fleece and the Heroes Who Lived Before Achilles, The	X	TL	250+	Colum, Padraic	Scholastic
Golden Fleece, The	Y	TL	250+	Colum, Padraic	Aladdin Paperbacks

G

TITLE	LEVEL	GENRE	WORD COUNT	AUTHOR / SERIES	PUBLISHER / DISTRIBUTOR
Golden Flower: A Taino Myth From Puerto Rico, The	M	TL	250+	Jaffe, Nina	Pinata Publishing
Golden Games	Q	I	250+	Zemanski, Stella	Scholastic
Golden Gate Bridge, The	N	I	579	Lightning Bolt Books	Lerner Publishing Group
Golden Gate Bridge, The	Q	I	250+	Windows on Literacy	National Geographic
Golden Glove, The	O	RF	250+	Bowen, Fred	Peachtree
Golden Goblet, The	V	RF	250+	McGraw, Eloise Jarvis	Scholastic
Golden Goose, The	M	TL	250+	Literacy 2000	Rigby
Golden Goose, The	L	TL	731	Sunshine	Wright Group/McGraw Hill
Golden Land, The	L	HF	505	Leveled Readers	Houghton Mifflin Harcourt
Golden Lasso, The	H	F	250+	Home Connection Collection	Rigby
Golden Locket, The	M	F	250+	Greene, Carol	Harcourt Brace
Golden Retrievers	R	I	250+	All About Dogs	Capstone Press
Golden Retrievers	I	I	104	Dogs	Capstone Press
Golden Retrievers Are the Best!	Q	I	1481	The Best Dogs Ever	Lerner Publishing Group
Golden Rule, The	O	RF	250+	Cooper, Ilene	Harry N. Abrams
Golden Rule, The	K	I	360	Vocabulary Readers	Houghton Mifflin Harcourt
Golden Rule, The	K	I	360	Vocabulary Readers/CA	Houghton Mifflin Harcourt
Golden State Warriors, The	S	I	4595	Team Spirit	Norwood House Press
Golden Sword of Dragonwalk	Q	F	250+	Stine, R. L.	Scholastic
Golden Touch, The	K	TL	783	Gear Up!	Wright Group/McGraw Hill
Golden Tree, The: Guardians of Ga'Hoole	V	F	250+	Lasky, Kathryn	Scholastic
Golden Year, The	T	HF	3713	Reading Street	Pearson
Goldfish	J	I	250+	PM Animal Facts: Orange	Rigby
Goldfish	K	I	159	Watch It Grow	Capstone Press
Goldfish Charlie and the Case of the Missing Planet	R	SF	250+	Mazer, Anne	Troll Associates
Goldie and the Fawn	J	RF	632	The Fawn	Pioneer Valley
Goldie and the Three Bears	G	TL	365	Leveled Literacy Intervention/ Green System	Heinemann
Goldie the Sunshine Fairy: Rainbow Magic	L	F	250+	Meadows, Daisy	Scholastic
Goldie: The Puppy Place	N	RF	250+	Miles, Ellen	Scholastic
Goldilocks	I	TL	250+	Jumbled Tumbled Tales & Rhymes	Rigby
Goldilocks	G	TL	244	Sunshine	Wright Group/McGraw Hill
Goldilocks	C	TL	19	Tarlow, Ellen	Scholastic
Goldilocks and the Three Bears	WB	TL	0	Big Cat	Pacific Learning
Goldilocks and the Three Bears	N	TL	250+	Guarnaccia, Steven	Harry N. Abrams
Goldilocks and the Three Bears	E	TL	184	Hunia, Fran	Ladybird Books
Goldilocks and the Three Bears	G	TL	250+	Literacy Tree	Rigby
Goldilocks and the Three Bears	C	TL	54	Little Books	Sadlier-Oxford
Goldilocks and The Three Bears	M	TL	250+	Marshall, James	Scholastic
Goldilocks and the Three Bears	K	TL	250+	New Way Literature	Steck-Vaughn
Goldilocks and the Three Bears	K	TL	250+	Once Upon a Time	Wright Group/McGraw Hill
Goldilocks and The Three Bears	H	TL	250+	PM Tales and Plays-Turquoise	Rigby
Goldilocks and the Three Bears	M	TL	1102	Reading Street	Pearson
Goldilocks and the Three Bears	F	TL	200	Shapiro, Sara	Scholastic
Goldilocks and the Three Bears	G	TL	265	Storyteller Nonfiction	Wright Group/McGraw Hill
Goldilocks and the Three Bears	H	TL	250+	Traditional Tales & More	Rigby
Goldilocks Comes Back	F	TL	134	Pair-It Books	Steck-Vaughn
Goldsmith's Daughter, The	Y	HF	250+	Landman, Tanya	Candlewick Press
Goldsworthy and Mort Blast Off	L	F	250+	Little Celebrations	Pearson Learning Group
Golf for Fun!	S	I	250+	Sports for Fun	Compass Point Books
Golf Legends	N	RF	250+	Boyz Rule!	Mondo Publishing

* Collection of short stories   # Graphic text
^ Mature content with lower level text demands

TITLE	LEVEL	GENRE	WORD COUNT	AUTHOR / SERIES	PUBLISHER / DISTRIBUTOR
Golfing Giant	M	F	250+	Too Cool	Pacific Learning
Goliath and the Burglar	L	RF	250+	Dicks, Terrance	Barron's Educational
Goliath and the Buried Treasure	L	RF	250+	Dicks, Terrance	Barron's Educational
Goliath and the Cub Scouts	L	RF	250+	Dicks, Terrance	Barron's Educational
Goliath at the Dog Show	L	RF	250+	Dicks, Terrance	Barron's Educational
Goliath at the Seaside	L	RF	250+	Dicks, Terrance	Barron's Educational
^Goliath Bird-Eating Spiders and Other Extreme Bugs	T	I	250+	Extreme Life	Capstone Press
Goliath Goes to Summer School	L	RF	250+	Dicks, Terrance	Barron's Educational
Goliath on Vacation	L	RF	250+	Dicks, Terrance	Barron's Educational
Goliath's Birthday	L	RF	250+	Dicks, Terrance	Barron's Educational
Goliath's Christmas	L	RF	250+	Dicks, Terrance	Barron's Educational
Goliath's Easter Parade	L	RF	250+	Dicks, Terrance	Barron's Educational
Golly	WB	RF	0	The Rowland Reading Program Library	Rowland Reading Foundation
Golly and the Flip-Flop Flap	G	F	177	The Rowland Reading Program Library	Rowland Reading Foundation
Golly Sisters Go West, The	K	RF	250+	Byars, Betsy	HarperTrophy
Golly Sisters Ride Again, The	K	RF	250+	Byars, Betsy	HarperTrophy
Golly's Trick	F	F	190	The Rowland Reading Program Library	Rowland Reading Foundation
Gollywhopper Eggs, The: A Play	K	F	250+	Windows on Literacy	National Geographic
Gone Fishing	N	RF	250+	Boyz Rule!	Mondo Publishing
Gone Fishing	G	RF	180	Long, Erlene	Houghton Mifflin Harcourt
Gone Fishing: Ocean Life by the Numbers	T	I	250+	McLimans, David	Walker & Company
*Gone from Home	W	RF	250+	Johnson, Angela	Alfred A. Knopf
Gone Wild: An Endangered Animal Alphabet	S	I	250+	McLimans, David	Walker & Company
Gone-Away Lake	V	RF	250+	Enright, Elizabeth	Harcourt Trade
Gonna Bird, The	H	F	209	Storyteller-Night Crickets	Wright Group/McGraw Hill
Good As New	L	RF	250+	Douglass, Barbara	Scholastic
Good Bad Cat, The	D	RF	65	Little Readers	Houghton Mifflin Harcourt
Good Bad Cat, The	D	RF	65	Start to Read	School Zone
Good Bad Day, The	I	RF	451	Real Kids Readers	Millbrook Press
Good Big Brother, A	F	RF	216	Reading Street	Pearson
Good Boy, Andrew!	E	RF	85	Literacy 2000	Rigby
*Good Catch!, A	E	RF	191	New Way Red	Steck-Vaughn
Good Choices for Cat and Dog	E	F	97	Learn to Read	Creative Teaching Press
Good Citizen	J	RF	372	Leveled Readers	Houghton Mifflin Harcourt
Good Citizen	J	RF	372	Leveled Readers/CA	Houghton Mifflin Harcourt
Good Citizen	J	RF	372	Leveled Readers/TX	Houghton Mifflin Harcourt
Good Citizen Sarah	K	RF	250+	The Way I Act	Albert Whitman & Co.
Good Citizens	K	I	463	Early Explorers	Benchmark Education
Good Citizens	K	I	292	Larkin's Little Readers	Wilbooks
Good Citizens Can Help	A	I	21	Early Explorers	Benchmark Education
Good Dessert, A	J	F	250+	Leveled Readers Language Support	Houghton Mifflin Harcourt
Good Dog	C	RF	43	Sun Sprouts	ETA/Cuisenaire
Good Dog!	N	I	250+	Harcourt Trophies	Harcourt, Inc.
Good Dog!	P	I	1932	Vocabulary Readers	Houghton Mifflin Harcourt
Good Dog!	P	I	1932	Vocabulary Readers/CA	Houghton Mifflin Harcourt
Good Dog!	J	I	251	Yellow Umbrella Books	Red Brick Learning
Good Dog, Aggie	J	RF	250+	Ries, Lori	Charlesbridge
Good Dog, Bonita	N	RF	250+	Giff, Patricia Reilly	Bantam Books
Good Dog, Carl	WB	F	0	Day, Alexandra	Green Tiger Press
Good Dog, The	S	F	250+	Avi	Simon & Schuster

G

TITLE	LEVEL	GENRE	WORD COUNT	AUTHOR / SERIES	PUBLISHER / DISTRIBUTOR
Good Dog, The	D	F	125	Leveled Literacy Intervention/ Green System	Heinemann
Good Dogs, Guide Dogs	N	I	911	Leveled Readers	Houghton Mifflin Harcourt
Good Dogs, Guide Dogs	N	I	911	Leveled Readers/CA	Houghton Mifflin Harcourt
Good Dogs, Guide Dogs	O	I	911	Leveled Readers/TX	Houghton Mifflin Harcourt
Good Driving, Amelia Bedelia	L	F	250+	Parish, Peggy	Harper & Row
Good Earth, The	Z+	HF	250+	Buck, Pearl S.	Simon & Schuster
Good Fires, Bad Fires	L	I	885	Sun Sprouts	ETA/Cuisenaire
Good Food	C	I	57	Kaleidoscope Collection	Hameray Publishing Group
Good Food	F	I	78	Leveled Readers Science	Houghton Mifflin Harcourt
Good for You	D	F	44	Sunshine	Wright Group/McGraw Hill
Good Fortune	U	B	250+	Wong, Li Keng	Peachtree
Good Friends	L	F	482	Leveled Literacy Intervention/ Blue System	Heinemann
Good Friends	A	I	21	Shutterbug Books	Steck-Vaughn
Good Friends	H	I	169	Vocabulary Readers	Houghton Mifflin Harcourt
Good Friends	H	I	169	Vocabulary Readers/CA	Houghton Mifflin Harcourt
Good Fun Farm	J	F	532	Big Cat	Pacific Learning
Good Gauley!	O	I	250+	Literacy by Design	Rigby
Good Girl	B	F	18	Ready Readers	Pearson Learning Group
Good Grief . . . Third Grade	O	RF	250+	McKenna, Colleen	Scholastic
Good Hat for a Cat, A	E	F	104	Bonnell, Kris	Reading Reading Books
Good Home, A	C	F	77	Leveled Readers Language Support	Houghton Mifflin Harcourt
Good Idea, A	H	RF	250+	Leveled Readers Language Support	Houghton Mifflin Harcourt
Good Ideas for People	G	I	125	Sails	Rigby
Good Job, Ajay!	L	F	250+	I See I Learn	Charlesbridge
Good Job, Little Bear	K	F	250+	Waddell, Martin	Candlewick Press
Good Job, Sam!	D	F	108	Leveled Readers	Houghton Mifflin Harcourt
Good Job, Sam!	D	F	108	Leveled Readers/CA	Houghton Mifflin Harcourt
Good Knee for a Cat, A	I	RF	205	Pacific Literacy	Pacific Learning
Good Knight	J	RF	264	Rymill, Linda R.	Scholastic
Good Luck Elephant	I	F	171	Sunshine	Wright Group/McGraw Hill
Good Luck, Martha	K	F	250+	Martha Speaks	Houghton Mifflin Harcourt
Good Manners	H	RF	222	Well-Being Series	Pearson Learning Group
Good Master, The	S	RF	250+	Seredy, Kate	Scholastic
Good Masters! Sweet Ladies!: Voices From a Medieval Village	Z	I	250+	Schlitz, Laura Amy	Candlewick Press
Good Morning Duck and Goose	F	F	123	Seedlings	Continental Press
Good Morning Isabel	G	RF	143	Literacy 2000	Rigby
Good Morning Mrs. Martin	K	F	156	Book Bank	Wright Group/McGraw Hill
Good Morning!	C	F	51	Science	Outside the Box
Good Morning, Monday	H	RF	77	Keenan, Sheila	Scholastic
Good Morning, Who's Snoring?	E	F	127	Story Steps	Rigby
Good Neighbor Nicholas	M	RF	250+	The Way I Act Books	Albert Whitman & Co.
Good Neighbors	E	RF	104	InfoTrek	ETA/Cuisenaire
Good News	F	RF	61	Avenues	Hampton Brown
Good News	I	TL	250+	Brenner, Barbara	Bantam Books
Good Night	M	RF	753	Leveled Readers	Houghton Mifflin Harcourt
Good Night	E	RF	114	Start to Read	School Zone
Good Night Sky	D	RF	32	Seedlings	Continental Press
Good Night!	D	F	73	Leveled Readers Language Support	Houghton Mifflin Harcourt
Good Night, Baby Ruby	I	RF	121	Henry, Rohan	Harry N. Abrams

* Collection of short stories   # Graphic text
^ Mature content with lower level text demands

TITLE	LEVEL	GENRE	WORD COUNT	AUTHOR / SERIES	PUBLISHER / DISTRIBUTOR
Good Night, City Lights	F	RF	74	City Stories	Rigby
Good Night, Good Knight	I	F	250+	Thomas, Shelley Moore	Puffin Books
Good Night, Little Brother	F	RF	69	Literacy 2000	Rigby
Good Night, Little Bug	D	F	54	Ready Readers	Pearson Learning Group
Good Night, Little Kitten	D	F	78	My First Reader	Grolier
Good Night, Maman	W	HF	250+	Mazer, Norma Fox	Houghton Mifflin Harcourt
Good Night, Mr. Tom	Z	HF	250+	Magorian, Michelle	HarperTrophy
Good Night's Sleep, A	P	RF	1091	Leveled Readers	Houghton Mifflin Harcourt
Good Old Mom	C	RF	34	Oxford Reading Tree	Oxford University Press
Good Old Wood	L	I	293	Gear Up!	Wright Group/McGraw Hill
Good Pick, A	I	RF	258	Early Explorers	Benchmark Education
Good Place for a City, A	N	I	194	Windows on Literacy	National Geographic
Good Place to Live, A	G	I	97	Windows on Literacy	National Geographic
Good Shopper, A	M	I	311	Larkin, Bruce	Wilbooks
Good Soil	G	I	259	Dominie Factivity Series	Pearson Publishing Group
Good Sport: Games, Sports, and Festivals	S	I	250+	Kids Discover Reading	Wright Group/McGraw Hill
Good Sports	H	I	206	Foundations	Wright Group/McGraw Hill
Good Sports	R	B	250+	InfoQuest	Rigby
Good Times Book, The	K	RF	851	Rigby Flying Colors	Rigby
Good to Eat	H	I	152	Rigby Focus	Rigby
Good to Eat	B	I	31	Twig	Wright Group/McGraw Hill
Good Vibrations: Experimenting with Sound	K	I	250+	Rigby Literacy	Rigby
Good Work, Amelia Bedelia	L	F	250+	Parish, Peggy	Avon Books
Good, the Bad, and Everything Else, The	R	RF	250+	Action Packs	Rigby
Good, the Bad, and the Goofy, The	P	SF	250+	Scieszka, Jon	Penguin Group
Goodbye Gabby	I	RF	400	Early Transitional, Set 1	Pioneer Valley
Goodbye Goose	L	F	264	Books for Young Learners	Richard C. Owen
Good-Bye Marianne	T	B	250+	Watts, Irene N.	Tundra Books
Good-Bye My Wishing Star	S	RF	250+	Grove, Vicki	Scholastic
Good-bye Perky	E	RF	54	Twig	Wright Group/McGraw Hill
Goodbye Season, The	X	HF	250+	Hale, Marian	Henry Holt & Co.
Good-bye Summer, Hello Fall	H	I	169	Ready Readers	Pearson Learning Group
Goodbye to Angel Island	R	HF	1055	Leveled Readers	Houghton Mifflin Harcourt
Goodbye to Goldie: Katie Woo	J	RF	250+	Manushkin, Fran	Picture Window Books
Good-bye to the Fast Cat	K	RF	250+	The Rowland Reading Program Libary	Rowland Reading Foundation
Good-Bye, Billy Radish	V	HF	250+	Skurzynski, Gloria	Aladdin
Good-Bye, Chicken Little	Q	RF	250+	Byars, Betsy	HarperTrophy
Good-Bye, Fox	D	F	27	Instant Readers	Harcourt School Publishers
Good-Bye, Lucy	D	RF	60	Sunshine	Wright Group/McGraw Hill
Good-bye, Sheepie	M	RF	250+	Burleigh, Robert	Marshall Cavendish
Good-Bye, Vietnam	V	RF	250+	Whelan, Gloria	Alfred A. Knopf
Good-bye, Zoo	C	RF	48	Ready Readers	Pearson Learning Group
Good-Byes	J	I	184	Shelley Rotner's Early Childhood Library	Millbrook Press
Good-for-Nothing Dog, The	M	RF	250+	Woodland Mysteries	Wright Group/McGraw Hill
Goodness Gracious	I	I	190	Literacy 2000	Rigby
Goodness Me, Mr. Magee!	F	F	251	Sails	Rigby
Goodnight	F	F	131	Rigby Rocket	Rigby
Goodnight	D	RF	83	Voyages	SRA/McGraw Hill
Goodnight Bobbie	LB	RF	15	Rigby Literacy	Rigby
Goodnight Goodnight	H	F	185	Literacy Tree	Rigby
Goodnight Josie	LB	RF	15	Rigby Star	Rigby
Goodnight Moon	H	F	130	Brown, Margaret Wise	HarperCollins

G

TITLE	LEVEL	GENRE	WORD COUNT	AUTHOR / SERIES	PUBLISHER / DISTRIBUTOR
Goodnight Peter	G	RF	107	Windmill Books	Wright Group/McGraw Hill
Goodnight!	D	RF	61	Joy Readers	Pearson Learning Group
Goodnight, Gorilla	LB	F	25	Rothmann, Peggy	G.P. Putnam's Sons Books for Young Readers
Goodnight, Little Monster	L	F	246	Ketteman, Helen	Marshall Cavendish
Goodnight, Owl	I	F	181	Hutchins, Pat	Aladdin
Goodnight, Owl!	I	F	196	Hutchins, Pat	Macmillan
Goodnight-Loving Trail, The	U	I	2736	Leveled Readers	Houghton Mifflin Harcourt
Goodnight-Loving Trail, The	U	I	2736	Leveled Readers/CA	Houghton Mifflin Harcourt
Goodnight-Loving Trail, The	U	I	2736	Leveled Readers/TX	Houghton Mifflin Harcourt
Goods and Services	N	I	909	Reading Street	Pearson
Goody Hall	V	RF	250+	Babbitt, Natalie	Farrar, Straus, & Giroux
Gooey Chewy Contest, The	L	F	1512	Bookshop	Mondo Publishing
Gooney Bird and the Room Mother	N	RF	250+	Lowry, Lois	Houghton Mifflin Harcourt
Gooney Bird Greene	N	RF	250+	Lowry, Lois	Dell
Gooney Bird Is So Absurd	N	RF	250+	Lowry, Lois	Houghton Mifflin Harcourt
Gooney Bird on the Map	N	RF	250+	Lowry, Lois	Houghton Mifflin Harcourt
Gooney the Fabulous	N	RF	250+	Lowry, Lois	Houghton Mifflin Harcourt
Goooaaalll!	P	RF	250+	Sails	Rigby
Goose Chase	D	F	43	Ready Readers	Pearson Learning Group
Goose Girl, The	X	F	250+	Hale, Shannon	Bloomsbury Children's Books
Goose on the Loose	Q	RF	250+	Baglio, Ben M.	Scholastic
Goose That Laid the Golden Egg, The	G	TL	73	Aesop	Wright Group/McGraw Hill
Goose Who Acted Like a Cow, The	J	F	250+	Phonics and Friends	Hampton Brown
Gooseberry Park	P	F	250+	Rylant, Cynthia	Scholastic
Goosebumps: It Came From Beneath the Sink	T	F	250+	Stine, R. L.	Language for Learning Assoc.
Goose's Gold, The	N	RF	250+	A to Z Mysteries	Random House
Gopher to the Rescue: A Volcano Recovery Story	M	F	701	Jennings, Terry Catasus	Sylvan Dell Publishing
Gordon Gets Even	M	RF	250+	Lighthouse	Ginn & Co.
Gordon Grizwald's Grumpy Goose	L	F	250+	Read it! Readers	Picture Window Books
Gorganzola Zombies in the Park	O	F	250+	Levy, Elizabeth	HarperTrophy
Gorgo Meets Her Match	K	HF	453	PM Story Books	Rigby
Gorilla	B	I	33	Zoozoo-Animal World	Cavallo Publishing
Gorilla Doctors: Saving Endangered Great Apes	W	I	250+	Scientists in the Field	Houghton Mifflin Harcourt
Gorilla Families	L	I	250+	Rosen Real Readers	Rosen Publishing Group
Gorilla Games	B	F	27	Phonics and Friends	Hampton Brown
Gorilla Guardian	L	RF	250+	World Quest Adventures	World Quest Learning
Gorilla, Monkey, and Ape	V	I	250+	Eyewitness Books	DK Publishing
Gorillas	T	I	250+	Burgel, Paul H.; Hartwig, M.	Carolrhoda Books
Gorillas	M	I	541	Nonfiction Indigo	Pioneer Valley
Gorillas	J	I	250+	Pebble Books	Red Brick Learning
Gorillas	I	I	173	Sails	Rigby
Gorillas	H	I	185	Seedlings	Continental Press
Gorillas	U	I	250+	The Untamed World	Steck-Vaughn
Gorillas and Chimpanzees	S	I	4454	Take Two Books	Wright Group/McGraw Hill
Gorilla's Story	K	RF	250+	Blackford, Harriet	Sterling Publishing
Gorillas: Gentle Giants of the Forest	L	I	250+	Milton, Joyce	Random House
Gossamer	V	F	250+	Lowry, Lois	Yearling Books
Gossip Girl	Z+	RF	250+	von Ziegesar, Cecily	Little Brown and Company
Gotcha Box, The	A	RF	30	Story Box	Wright Group/McGraw Hill
Gotcha!	L	RF	250+	Science Solves It!	Kane Press

* Collection of short stories   # Graphic text
^ Mature content with lower level text demands

TITLE	LEVEL	GENRE	WORD COUNT	AUTHOR / SERIES	PUBLISHER / DISTRIBUTOR
Government in Action	T	I	250+	Reading Expeditions	National Geographic
Government Leaders: Then and Now	Q	I	250+	Primary Source Readers	Teacher Created Materials
Government Rules	U	I	250+	News Extra	Richard C. Owen
Government Services	K	I	100	Government	Lerner Publishing Group
Go-With Words	F	I	133	Rookie Readers	Children's Press
Gowler's Horn	Z	RF	250+	Misfits Inc.	Peachtree
GPS Mystery, The	R	RF	250+	Take Two Books	Wright Group/McGraw Hill
Grab Bag, The	C	RF	85	PM Plus Story Books	Rigby
Grab Hands and Run	V	RF	250+	Temple, Frances	HarperTrophy
Grab It!	C	RF	45	Leveled Readers Language Support	Houghton Mifflin Harcourt
Grabbing Bird, The	L	F	250+	Cambridge Reading	Pearson Learning Group
Grace	U	HF	250+	Walsh, Jill Paton	Farrar, Straus, & Giroux
Grace Darling	T	HF	6685	Oxford Bookworms Library	Oxford University Press
Grace Hopper: Computer Pioneer	P	B	250+	On Deck	Rigby
Grace the Pirate	O	F	250+	High-Fliers	Pacific Learning
Grace the Pirate	O	F	250+	Lasky, Kathryn	Hyperion
Grace's Letter to Lincoln	P	HF	250+	Roop, Peter & Connie	Hyperion
Gracie the Lighthouse Cat	K	HF	563	Brown, Ruth	Andersen Press USA
Graciela Finds the Fair	Q	RF	250+	On Our Way to English	Rigby
Gracie's Cat	I	RF	250+	Cambridge Reading	Pearson Learning Group
Graduation of Jake Moon, The	U	RF	250+	Park, Barbara	Scholastic
Graffiti	L	RF	688	Rigby Flying Colors	Rigby
Graffiti	I	RF	168	Sunshine	Wright Group/McGraw Hill
Graham Hawkes: Underwater Pilot	U	B	1492	Leveled Readers	Houghton Mifflin Harcourt
Grain Group, The	H	I	108	The Food Guide Pyramid	Capstone Press
Grain of Rice, A	P	TL	250+	Pittman, Helena Clare	Bantam Books
Grains	F	I	88	Food Groups	Lerner Publishing Group
Grains	I	I	157	Healthy Eating	Heinemann Library
Grampa's Zombie BBQ	Q	F	250+	Wiley & Grampa's Creature Features	Little Brown and Company
Gramp's Favorite Gift	S	RF	1481	Leveled Readers	Houghton Mifflin Harcourt
Gramp's Favorite Gift	S	RF	1481	Leveled Readers/CA	Houghton Mifflin Harcourt
Gramp's Favorite Gift	S	RF	1481	Leveled Readers/TX	Houghton Mifflin Harcourt
Gram's Hat	D	RF	76	Leveled Readers	Houghton Mifflin Harcourt
Grams, Her Boyfriend, My Family, and Me	U	RF	250+	Derby, Pat	Sunburst
Grand Canyon Adventure	N	I	250+	Windows on Literacy	National Geographic
Grand Canyon Day	J	I	97	Larkin, Bruce	Wilbooks
Grand Canyon Doesn't Scare Me, The	R	RF	250+	Pair-It Books	Steck-Vaughn
Grand Canyon Journey, A: Tracing Time in Stone	W	I	250+	A First Book	Franklin Watts
Grand Canyon National Park	O	I	250+	A True Book	Children's Press
Grand Canyon, The	N	I	509	Lightning Bolt Books	Lerner Publishing Group
Grand Central Terminal: Gateway to New York City	U	I	250+	Bookshop	Mondo Publishing
Grand Coulee Dam, The	Q	I	793	Leveled Readers Social Studies	Houghton Mifflin Harcourt
Grand Duchess Anastasia Romanov	T	B	250+	Queens and Princesses	Capstone Press
Grand Escape, The	S	F	250+	Naylor, Phyllis Reynolds	Bantam Books
*Grand Mothers: Poems, Reminiscences, and Short Stories About Keepers of Our Traditions	Y	B	250+	Giovanni, Nikki	Henry Holt & Co.
Grand Plan to Fix Everything, The	U	RF	250+	Krishnaswami, Uma	Atheneum Books
Grand Street Theater Robbery, The	M	RF	250+	PM Extensions	Rigby
Grand Trees of America: Our State and Champion Trees	T	I	250+	Jorgenson, Lisa	Roberts Rinehart
Grandad	L	RF	250+	Literacy 2000	Rigby

G

TITLE	LEVEL	GENRE	WORD COUNT	AUTHOR / SERIES	PUBLISHER / DISTRIBUTOR
Grandad's Dinosaur	K	F	250+	Storyteller-Shooting Stars	Wright Group/McGraw Hill
Grandad's Mask	K	RF	250+	PM Collection	Rigby
Grandad's Wild Stories	O	F	250+	Tristars	Richard C. Owen
Granddad's Dinosaur	J	F	250+	I Am Reading	Kingfisher
Grandfather Buffalo	L	F	250+	Arnosky, Jim	G.P. Putnam's Sons
Grandfather Counts	N	RF	250+	Cheng, Andrea	Lee & Low Books Inc.
Grandfather Horned Toad	K	F	250+	Little Celebrations	Pearson Learning Group
Grandfather Tang's Story: A Tale Told With Tangrams	N	RF	250+	Parker, Robert Andrew	Crown Publishers
Grandfathers	F	I	49	Families	Capstone Press
Grandfathers	C	I	41	Pebble Books	Capstone Press
Grandfather's Dance	R	HF	250+	MacLachlan, Patricia	HarperTrophy
Grandfather's Dream	M	RF	250+	Keller, Holly	Hampton Brown
Grandfather's Ghost	M	F	250+	Sunshine	Wright Group/McGraw Hill
Grandfather's Journey	P	HF	250+	Say, Allen	Houghton Mifflin Harcourt
Grandfather's Mask	I	RF	245	Leveled Readers Language Support	Houghton Mifflin Harcourt
Grandma Alma's Special Room	H	RF	246	On Our Way to English	Rigby
Grandma and Calick	D	F	88	McAlpin, MaryAnn	Short Tales Press
Grandma and Me	D	I	68	Sun Sprouts	ETA/Cuisenaire
Grandma and the Pirate	F	RF	105	Lloyd, David	Crown Publishers
Grandma Betty's Banjo	R	RF	3968	Reading Street	Pearson
Grandma Book, The	G	I	147	Parr, Todd	Little Brown and Company
Grandma Carol's Plant	I	RF	250+	Home Connection Collection	Rigby
Grandma Chicken Legs	O	TL	250+	McCaughrean, Geraldine	Carolrhoda Books
Grandma Comes to Stay	E	RF	118	Sails	Rigby
Grandma Comes to Stay Again	I	F	389	Sails	Rigby
Grandma Go	R	RF	250+	Reading Safari	Mondo Publishing
Grandma Helps Out!	G	RF	202	Sails	Rigby
Grandma J	I	RF	170	Instant Readers	Harcourt School Publishers
Grandma Mixup, The	K	RF	250+	Little Readers	Houghton Mifflin Harcourt
Grandma Mix-Up, The	K	RF	250+	McCully, Emily Arnold	HarperTrophy
Grandma Moses	N	B	250+	Biography	Benchmark Education
Grandma Moses: Painter of Rural America	T	B	250+	O'Neal, Zibby	Penguin Group
Grandma Moves In	I	RF	250+	Greetings	Rigby
Grandma Pickleberry's Cold	I	RF	268	Springboard	Wright Group/McGraw Hill
Grandma Ruth Feeds Her Friends	D	F	57	Coulton, Mia	Maryruth Books
Grandma Ruth's Garden	C	F	33	Coulton, Mia	Maryruth Books
Grandma Ruth's Glasses	C	F	34	Coulton, Mia	Maryruth Books
Grandma U	M	RF	250+	Ransom, Jeanie Franz	Peachtree
Grandma's Glasses	F	RF	193	Leveled Literacy Intervention/ Green System	Heinemann
Grandmas At Bat	K	RF	250+	McCully, Emily Arnold	HarperTrophy
Grandmas at the Lake	K	RF	250+	McCully, Emily Arnold	HarperTrophy
Grandma's Attic	I	RF	250+	Windows on Literacy	National Geographic
Grandma's Bicycle	G	RF	74	Read Alongs	Rigby
Grandma's Bird	R	RF	250+	Sails	Rigby
Grandma's Birthday	G	RF	197	On Our Way to English	Rigby
Grandma's Button Box	K	RF	250+	Math Matters	Kane Press
Grandma's Cane	H	RF	250+	Story Box	Wright Group/McGraw Hill
Grandma's Christmas Tree	F	RF	105	McAlpin, MaryAnn	Short Tales Press
Grandma's Cookie Cutters	K	RF	577	Leveled Readers	Houghton Mifflin Harcourt
Grandma's Flying Adventure	O	RF	250+	Tristars	Richard C. Owen
Grandma's Garden	K	I	340	Rigby Focus	Rigby

G

TITLE	LEVEL	GENRE	WORD COUNT	AUTHOR / SERIES	PUBLISHER / DISTRIBUTOR
Grandma's Good Food	H	RF	200	InfoTrek	ETA/Cuisenaire
Grandma's Hearing Aids	K	RF	361	Sails	Rigby
Grandma's Heart	K	I	90	Wonder World	Wright Group/McGraw Hill
Grandma's House	D	RF	113	Jasper the Cat	Pioneer Valley
Grandma's Letter	D	RF	67	Foundations	Wright Group/McGraw Hill
Grandma's Memories	F	RF	102	Literacy 2000	Rigby
Grandma's Other Life	X	RF	2480	Leveled Readers	Houghton Mifflin Harcourt
Grandma's Other Life	X	RF	2480	Leveled Readers/CA	Houghton Mifflin Harcourt
Grandma's Other Life	X	RF	2480	Leveled Readers/TX	Houghton Mifflin Harcourt
Grandma's Patchy Pocket	F	RF	55	Polette, Nancy	Kaeden Books
Grandma's Pictures of The Past	J	RF	250+	Home Connection Collection	Rigby
Grandma's Present	F	RF	191	Foundations	Wright Group/McGraw Hill
Grandma's Project	L	RF	250+	On Our Way to English	Rigby
Grandma's Records	O	RF	250+	Velasquez, Eric	Scholastic
Grandma's Smile	M	RF	250+	PM Plus Chapter Books	Rigby
Grandma's Stick	H	RF	250+	Story Box	Wright Group/McGraw Hill
Grandma's Surprise	G	RF	220	Leveled Readers	Houghton Mifflin Harcourt
Grandma's Surprise	G	RF	220	Leveled Readers/CA	Houghton Mifflin Harcourt
Grandma's Surprise	G	RF	220	Leveled Readers/TX	Houghton Mifflin Harcourt
Grandma's Surprise	H	RF	216	Storyworlds	Heinemann
Grandma's Table	K	RF	287	Leveled Readers	Houghton Mifflin Harcourt
Grandmother	E	RF	60	Joy Readers	Pearson Learning Group
Grandmother and I	I	RF	250+	Buckley, Helen E.	Scholastic
Grandmother and I	C	RF	53	Home Connection Collection	Rigby
Grandmother Is Tired	C	RF	31	Joy Readers	Pearson Learning Group
Grandmother, Have the Angels Come?	L	F	250+	Vega, Denise	Little Brown and Company
Grandmothers	F	I	50	Families	Capstone Press
Grandmothers	C	I	50	Pebble Books	Capstone Press
Grandpa	C	RF	61	Literacy by Design	Rigby
Grandpa	S	RF	250+	Reading Safari	Mondo Publishing
Grandpa	C	RF	61	Rigby Literacy	Rigby
Grandpa	C	RF	69	Rigby Star	Rigby
Grandpa	E	RF	70	Sunshine	Wright Group/McGraw Hill
Grandpa	A	I	36	Vocabulary Readers	Houghton Mifflin Harcourt
Grandpa	A	I	36	Vocabulary Readers/CA	Houghton Mifflin Harcourt
Grandpa	A	I	36	Vocabulary Readers/TX	Houghton Mifflin Harcourt
Grandpa and I	C	RF	40	Home Connection Collection	Rigby
Grandpa and Me	E	RF	124	Gear Up!	Wright Group/McGraw Hill
Grandpa and Me	C	RF	86	Leveled Readers	Houghton Mifflin Harcourt
Grandpa and Me	C	RF	86	Leveled Readers/CA	Houghton Mifflin Harcourt
Grandpa and Me	C	RF	86	Leveled Readers/TX	Houghton Mifflin Harcourt
Grandpa and Me	D	I	36	Sun Sprouts	ETA/Cuisenaire
*Grandpa at the Beach	J	F	250+	Lewis, Rob	Mondo Publishing
Grandpa Book, The	G	I	141	Parr, Todd	Little Brown and Company
*Grandpa Comes To Stay	J	F	1083	Lewis, Rob	Mondo Publishing
Grandpa Knits Hats	E	RF	55	Wonder World	Wright Group/McGraw Hill
Grandpa Moves In	I	RF	158	InfoTrek	ETA/Cuisenaire
Grandpa Snored	F	RF	51	Literacy 2000	Rigby
Grandpa, Grandma, and the Tractor	H	RF	220	Ready Readers	Pearson Learning Group
Grandpa, Grandpa	G	RF	122	Story Box	Wright Group/McGraw Hill
Grandparents	G	I	140	Families	Heinemann Library
Grandparents Are Fun!	H	I	216	Leveled Readers Language Support	Houghton Mifflin Harcourt
Grandparents Are Great	I	I	257	Leveled Readers	Houghton Mifflin Harcourt

G

TITLE	LEVEL	GENRE	WORD COUNT	AUTHOR / SERIES	PUBLISHER / DISTRIBUTOR
Grandpa's Baseball Card	P	RF	1022	Leveled Readers	Houghton Mifflin Harcourt
Grandpa's Birthday	J	RF	250+	Literacy 2000	Rigby
Grandpa's Boat	E	RF	108	Developing Books	Pioneer Valley
Grandpa's Bright Ideas	J	RF	250+	Lighthouse	Ginn & Co.
Grandpa's Camera	P	RF	250+	HSP/Harcourt Trophies	Harcourt, Inc.
Grandpa's Candy Store	F	RF	65	Books for Young Learners	Richard C. Owen
Grandpa's Castanets	I	RF	250+	Windows on Literacy	National Geographic
Grandpa's Clues	F	RF	198	Rigby Literacy	Rigby
Grandpa's Cookies	F	F	193	Little Readers	Houghton Mifflin Harcourt
Grandpa's Corner Store	N	RF	250+	DiSalvo-Ryan, DyAnne	HarperCollins
Grandpa's Face	Q	RF	250+	Greenfield, Eloise	G.P. Putnam's Sons Books for Young Readers
Grandpa's Garden Shed	G	I	68	Windows on Literacy	National Geographic
Grandpa's Lemonade	G	RF	138	Storyteller Nonfiction	Wright Group/McGraw Hill
Grandpa's Mountain	T	RF	250+	Reeder, Carolyn	Avon Books
Grandpa's New Hip	M	RF	250+	Reading Safari	Mondo Publishing
Grandpa's Rail Tales	T	F	1730	Leveled Readers	Houghton Mifflin Harcourt
Grandpa's Scrapbook	M	HF	660	Reading Street	Pearson
Grandpa's Sign	I	RF	304	Reading Street	Pearson
Grandpa's Special Present	I	RF	286	Foundations	Wright Group/McGraw Hill
Grandpa's Tool Box	D	RF	52	Kaleidoscope Collection	Hameray Publishing Group
Grandpa's Train	E	RF	69	Early Emergent, Set 3	Pioneer Valley
Grandpa's Tricky Puzzles	J	RF	537	InfoTrek	ETA/Cuisenaire
Grandpa's Visit	H	RF	226	PM Stars	Rigby
Grandpa's Visit	C	RF	38	Vocabulary Readers	Houghton Mifflin Harcourt
Grandpop's Cabin	J	RF	250+	The Rowland Reading Program Library	Rowland Reading Foundation
Granny	R	SF	250+	Anthony Horowitz	Puffin Books
Granny	A	RF	36	Leveled Readers	Houghton Mifflin Harcourt
Granny	A	RF	36	Leveled Readers/CA	Houghton Mifflin Harcourt
Granny	A	RF	36	Leveled Readers/TX	Houghton Mifflin Harcourt
Granny	G	RF	186	Sails	Rigby
Granny and the Desperadoes	J	RF	250+	Parish, Peggy	Simon & Schuster
Granny Bundle's Boring Walk	H	RF	250+	Stepping Stones	Nelson/Michaels Assoc.
Granny Gadget	J	F	250+	Rigby Rocket	Rigby
Granny Garcia's Gifts	J	RF	366	Storyteller	Wright Group/McGraw Hill
Granny Lina's Bedtime Story	M	RF	250+	Springboard	Wright Group/McGraw Hill
Granny Torrelli Makes Soup	S	RF	250+	Creech, Sharon	Scholastic
Granny's Teeth	H	RF	169	Cambridge Reading	Pearson Learning Group
Granny's Visit	E	RF	144	Leveled Readers Language Support	Houghton Mifflin Harcourt
Grant Wood	R	B	250+	Venezia, Mike	Children's Press
Granville T. Woods	P	I	1344	Vocabulary Readers	Houghton Mifflin Harcourt
Granville T. Woods	P	B	1344	Vocabulary Readers/CA	Houghton Mifflin Harcourt
Grapes of Math, The	N	I	250+	Tang, Greg	Scholastic
Graph It	K	I	250+	Yellow Umbrella Books	Capstone Press
Graphing	C	I	32	Early Math	Lerner Publishing Group
Grass Circles Mystery, The	K	F	250+	Talking Points Series	Pearson Learning Group
Grass for Dinner	B	F	36	Sails	Rigby
Grass Is for Goats	D	RF	84	Joy Readers	Pearson Learning Group
Grasshopper and the Ants	K	TL	452	Sunshine	Wright Group/McGraw Hill
Grasshopper and the Flea, The	B	F	63	Springboard	Wright Group/McGraw Hill
Grasshopper Learns a Lesson: A Play	K	TL	250+	On Our Way to English	Rigby
Grasshopper on the Road	K	F	250+	Lobel, Arnold	HarperTrophy

* Collection of short stories   # Graphic text
^ Mature content with lower level text demands

TITLE	LEVEL	GENRE	WORD COUNT	AUTHOR / SERIES	PUBLISHER / DISTRIBUTOR
Grasshopper Summer	T	HF	250+	Turner, Ann	Aladdin
Grasshoppers	F	I	96	Animal Life Cycles	Lerner Publishing Group
Grasshoppers	K	I	224	Ashley, Susan/Let's Read About Insects	Weekly Reader Publishing
Grasshoppers	H	I	84	Bugs, Bugs, Bugs!	Red Brick Learning
Grasshoppers	F	I	50	Insects	Capstone Press
Grasshoppers	N	I	250+	Nature's Friends	Compass Point Books
Grasshopper's Song, The	T	TL	250+	Giovanni, Nikki	Candlewick Press
Grassland Food Chains	T	I	250+	Protecting Food Chains	Heinemann Library
Grassland Safari	Q	I	250+	InfoQuest	Rigby
Grasslands	O	I	250+	A True Book	Children's Press
Grasslands	Q	I	250+	Ecosystems	Red Brick Learning
Grasslands	Q	I	250+	First Reports	Compass Point Books
Grasslands Food Webs	Q	I	2062	Early Bird Food Webs	Lerner Publishing Group
Grateful Fred, The (Melvin Beederman, Superhero)	N	F	250+	Trine, Greg	Henry Holt & Co.
Gratefully Yours	T	HF	250+	Buchanan, Jane	Puffin Books
Grave Robber's Secret, The	W	HF	250+	Myers, Anna	Bloomsbury Children's Books
*Graven Images: Three Stories by Paul Fleischman	W	F	250+	Fleischman, Paul	HarperTrophy
Graveyard Book, The	X	F	250+	Gaiman, Neil	HarperCollins
Gravity	O	I	250+	Early Connections	Benchmark Education
Gravity	I	I	77	Forces and Motion	Lerner Publishing Group
^Gravity	P	I	250+	Our Physical World	Capstone Press
Gravity	N	I	485	Red Rocket Readers	Flying Start Books
Gravity	D	I	33	Wonder World	Wright Group/McGraw Hill
Gravity All Around	L	I	227	Physical Science	Capstone Press
Gravity and the Solar System	O	I	250+	PM Plus Story Books	Rigby
Gravity Pulls Us	K	I	165	Larkin, Bruce	Wilbooks
Gravity: Simple Experiments for Young Scientists	T	I	250+	White, Larry	Millbrook Press
Gray Blanket, The: Rabbits in Australia	V	I	1878	Leveled Readers Social Studies	Houghton Mifflin Harcourt
Gray Everywhere	K	I	329	Lightning Bolt Books	Lerner Publishing Group
*Gray Heroes Elder Tales from Around the World	Z	TL	250+	Yolen, Jane	Penguin Group
Gray Whales	P	I	828	Reading Street	Pearson
Gray Wolf, The	J	I	35	Readlings	American Reading Company
Gray Wolves	O	I	2281	Early Bird Nature Books	Lerner Publishing Group
*Great African Americans in Business	T	B	250+	Rediger, Pat	Crabtree
*Great African Americans in Civil Rights	T	B	250+	Rediger, Pat	Crabtree
*Great African Americans in Entertainment	T	B	250+	Rediger, Pat	Crabtree
*Great African Americans in Film	T	B	250+	Parker, Janice	Crabtree
*Great African Americans in Government	T	B	250+	Dudley, Karen	Crabtree
*Great African Americans in History	T	B	250+	Hacker, Carlotta	Crabtree
*Great African Americans in Jazz	T	B	250+	Hacker, Carlotta	Crabtree
*Great African Americans in Literature	T	B	250+	Rediger, Pat	Crabtree
*Great African Americans in Music	T	B	250+	Rediger, Pat	Crabtree
*Great African Americans in Sports	T	B	250+	Rediger, Pat	Crabtree
*Great African Americans in the Arts	T	B	250+	Hacker, Carlotta	Crabtree
*Great African Americans in the Olympics	T	B	250+	Hunter, Shaun	Crabtree
Great and Shining Road, The	R	I	250+	Orbit Chapter Books	Pacific Learning
Great and Terrible Beauty, A	Z+	F	250+	Bray, Libba	Delacorte Press
Great Apes	T	I	2309	Reading Street	Pearson
Great Apes, The	S	I	250+	A First Book	Franklin Watts
Great Astronomers	Y	B	250+	High-Fliers	Pacific Learning

G

TITLE	LEVEL	GENRE	WORD COUNT	AUTHOR / SERIES	PUBLISHER / DISTRIBUTOR
Great Attitude, A	F	B	196	Learn to Read	Creative Teaching Press
Great Barrier Reef	O	I	250+	Windows on Literacy	National Geographic
Great Basin Indians, The: Daily Life in the 1700s	O	I	250+	Native American Life	Capstone Press
Great Bay, The	M	RF	706	Leveled Readers	Houghton Mifflin Harcourt
Great Bay, The	M	RF	706	Leveled Readers/CA	Houghton Mifflin Harcourt
Great Bay, The	M	RF	706	Leveled Readers/TX	Houghton Mifflin Harcourt
Great Bean Race, The	K	RF	295	Pacific Literacy	Pacific Learning
Great Bear, The	N	F	175	Gleeson, Libby	Candlewick Press
Great Big Enormous Turnip, The	H	TL	355	Leveled Literacy Intervention/ Blue System	Heinemann
Great Big Enormous Turnip, The	H	TL	317	Reading Unlimited	Pearson Learning Group
Great Big Enormous Turnip, The	H	TL	250+	Tolstoi, Aleksei; Nikolaevich, Graf	Watts
Great Brain at the Academy, The	T	RF	250+	Fitzgerald, John D.	Yearling Books
Great Brain Does It Again, The	T	RF	250+	Fitzgerald, John D.	Yearling Books
Great Brain Reforms, The	T	RF	250+	Fitzgerald, John D.	Yearling Books
Great Brain, The	T	RF	250+	Fitzgerald, John D.	Language for Learning Assoc.
Great Bug Hunt, The	G	RF	96	Rookie Readers	Children's Press
Great Car Race, The	E	F	162	Carousel Readers	Pearson Learning Group
Great Chicago Fire, 1871, The	Z	HF	250+	Massie, Elizabeth	Pocket Books
Great Danes	R	I	250+	All About Dogs	Capstone Press
Great Danes	I	I	149	Dogs	Capstone Press
Great Danes Are the Best!	Q	I	1002	The Best Dogs Ever	Lerner Publishing Group
Great Day	G	RF	161	Alphakids	Sundance
Great Day for Snorkeling, A	K	RF	238	Leveled Readers	Houghton Mifflin Harcourt
Great Day for Up	J	F	180	Seuss, Dr.	Random House
Great Day in the City, A	H	I	198	Avenues	Hampton Brown
Great Day, A	C	F	94	Literacy by Design	Rigby
Great Death, The	U	HF	250+	Smelcer, John	Henry Holt & Co.
Great Depression, The	X	I	250+	Cornerstones of Freedom	Children's Press
Great Dimpole Oak, The	S	RF	250+	Lisle, Janet Taylor	Puffin Books
Great Dinosaur Hunt, The	M	F	250+	Woodland Mysteries	Wright Group/McGraw Hill
Great Dinosaur Race, The	L	F	250+	Popcorn	Sundance
Great Divide, The	N	I	347	Yellow Umbrella Books	Red Brick Learning
Great Divide, The: A Mathematical Marathon	N	F	250+	Dodds, Dayle Ann	Candlewick Press
Great Dog Wash, The	O	RF	250+	Rigby Focus	Rigby
Great Egg Problem, The	P	HF	250+	Bookweb	Rigby
Great Enormous Hamburger, The	B	F	36	Sunshine	Wright Group/McGraw Hill
Great Escape, The	P	RF	250+	In Step Readers	Rigby
Great Escape, The	L	RF	250+	Rigby Literacy	Rigby
Great Escapes & Amazing Tricks	V	I	250+	Boldprint	Steck-Vaughn
*Great Escapes of World War II	Z	I	250+	Sullivan, George	Scholastic
Great Estimations	Q	I	250+	Goldstone, Bruce	Henry Holt & Co.
Great Expectations	S	HF	250+	Bullseye Step Into Classics	Random House
Great Explorations	T	HF	250+	Neufeld, David	Scholastic
Great Fire of London, The	P	I	250+	Rigby Star Quest	Rigby
Great Fire, The	W	I	250+	Murphy, Jim	Scholastic
Great Franklin Debate, The	R	I	250+	Harcourt Trophies	Harcourt, Inc.
Great Gear	N	I	250+	Scooters	ETA/Cuisenaire
Great Genghis Khan Look-Alike Contest, The	L	RF	250+	Sharmat, Marjorie Weinman	Random House
Great Ghost Rescue, The	U	F	250+	Ibbotson, Eva	Penguin Group
Great Ghosts	L	F	250+	Cohen, Daniel	Scholastic
Great Gilly Hopkins, The	S	RF	250+	Paterson, Katherine	Hearst
Great Gobs of Gum!	N	I	250+	Rigby Literacy	Rigby

G

* Collection of short stories   # Graphic text
^ Mature content with lower level text demands

TITLE	LEVEL	GENRE	WORD COUNT	AUTHOR / SERIES	PUBLISHER / DISTRIBUTOR
Great Gracie Chase, Stop That Dog, The	K	RF	250+	Rylant, Cynthia	Scholastic
Great Graph Contest, The	M	F	250+	Leedy, Loreen	Holiday House
Great Great Grandfather's Railroad	J	HF	250+	Sunshine	Wright Group/McGraw Hill
Great Green Place, The	K	I	242	Story Box	Wright Group/McGraw Hill
Great Grumbler and the Wonder Tree, The	K	F	250+	Mahy, Margaret	Pacific Learning
Great Hearts: Heroes of Special Olympics	S	I	250+	High-Fliers	Pacific Learning
Great Houdini, The: World Famous Magician and Escape Artist	M	B	250+	Kulling, Monica	Random House
Great Ice Battle, The	M	F	250+	Abbott, Tony	Scholastic
Great Ice Battle, The: The Secrets of Droon	O	F	250+	Abbott, Tony	Scholastic
Great Idea!	S	I	250+	Boldprint	Steck-Vaughn
Great Interactive Dream Machine, The	Y	SF	250+	Peck, Richard	Puffin Books
Great Invention, The	H	RF	108	City Stories	Rigby
Great Inventions and Where They Came From	P	I	250+	Navigators Social Studies Series	Benchmark Education
Great Inventor, A: An Wang	J	B	207	Leveled Readers Social Studies	Houghton Mifflin Harcourt
Great Joy	O	RF	250+	DiCamillo, Kate	Candlewick Press
Great Kapok Tree, The	R	I	250+	Cherry, Lynne	Scholastic
Great Lakes, The	N	I	555	Lightning Bolt Books	Lerner Publishing Group
Great Little Madison, The	X	B	250+	Fritz, Jean	G.P. Putnam's Sons
Great Math Tattle Battle, The	N	RF	250+	Bowen, Anne	Albert Whitman & Co.
Great Migration, The	R	I	250+	Lawrence, Jacob	HarperCollins
Great Migration, The	V	I	250+	Reading Expeditions	National Geographic
Great Moments in American Auto Racing	U	I	250+	Christopher, Matt	Little Brown and Company
Great Moments in Basketball History	T	I	250+	Christopher, Matt	Little Brown and Company
Great Monsieur Vertelli, The	O	I	250+	Wonder World	Wright Group/McGraw Hill
Great Nursery Rhyme Disaster, The	M	F	250+	Conway, David	Tiger Tales
Great Ocean, The	K	I	250+	Spyglass Books	Compass Point Books
Great Outdoor Camping Trip, The	L	RF	250+	Book Blazers	ETA/Cuisenaire
Great Outdoors, The	G	I	111	Red Rocket Readers	Flying Start Books
Great Partnership, A	T	I	2132	Vocabulary Readers	Houghton Mifflin Harcourt
Great Partnership, A	T	I	2132	Vocabulary Readers/CA	Houghton Mifflin Harcourt
Great Piano Hoist, The	O	RF	250+	Orbit Chapter Books	Pacific Learning
Great Plague, The	T	HF	250+	Story Surfers	ETA/Cuisenaire
Great Plains Indians, The: Daily Life in the 1700s	O	I	250+	Native American Life	Capstone Press
Great Plains, The	T	I	250+	Theme Sets	National Geographic
Great Pumpkin, The	I	F	239	Sunshine	Wright Group/McGraw Hill
Great Pyramid, The	T	I	250+	Lighthouse	Ginn & Co.
Great Pyramid, The	S	I	250+	Windows on Literacy	National Geographic
Great Quarterback Switch, The	Q	RF	250+	Christopher, Matt	Little Brown and Company
Great Race, The	G	F	250+	McPhail, David	Scholastic
Great Riddle Mystery, The	M	RF	250+	MacClean, James R.	Pearson Learning Group
Great Rivers	R	I	250+	InfoQuest	Rigby
#Great San Francisco Earthquake and Fire, The	S	I	250+	Disasters in History	Capstone Press
Great Sand Dunes National Monument	O	I	250+	A True Book	Children's Press
Great Scientist Detectives at Work	N	I	643	Reading Street	Pearson
Great Shakes: The Science of Earthquakes	X	I	250+	Headline Science	Compass Point Books
Great Shape-up, The	L	RF	1610	Science Solves It!	Kane Press
Great Smoky Mountains Encyclopedia	R	I	250+	Literacy by Design	Rigby
Great Snake Escape, The	J	F	250+	Coxe, Molly	HarperTrophy
Great Snake Swindle, The	O	RF	250+	Klooz	Stone Arch Books
Great Snakes!	I	I	161	Robinson, Fay	Scholastic
Great Sporting Events	R	I	250+	PM Nonfiction-Ruby	Rigby
Great Storyteller, The	O	RF	1095	Leveled Readers/TX	Houghton Mifflin Harcourt

TITLE	LEVEL	GENRE	WORD COUNT	AUTHOR / SERIES	PUBLISHER / DISTRIBUTOR
Great Tomato Battle, The	S	RF	250+	Story Surfers	ETA/Cuisenaire
Great Trash Bash, The	M	F	250+	Leedy, Loreen	Holiday House
Great Tree Mouse Adventure, The	J	F	250+	Rigby Rocket	Rigby
Great Wall of China, The	R	I	250+	Explorer Books-Pathfinder	National Geographic
Great Wall of China, The	P	I	250+	Explorer Books-Pioneer	National Geographic
Great Wall of China, The	Q	I	250+	Fisher, Leonard Everett	Aladdin
Great Wall of China, The	Q	I	250+	Rosen Real Readers	Rosen Publishing Group
Great Wall of China, The	N	I	141	Vocabulary Readers	Houghton Mifflin Harcourt
Great Wall of Lucy Wu, The	W	RF	250+	Shang, Wendy Wan-Long	Scholastic
Great Whales: The Gentle Giants	W	I	250+	Lauber, Patricia	Henry Holt & Co.
Great Wheel, The	U	RF	250+	Lawson, Robert	Scholastic
^Great White Shark	N	I	250+	Shark Zone	Capstone Press
Great White Shark	J	I	157	Sharks	Capstone Press
Great White Shark, The	E	I	79	Bonnell, Kris/Animals in Danger	Reading Reading Books
Great White Sharks	P	I	1633	Animal Predators	Lerner Publishing Group
Great White Sharks	O	I	1853	Early Bird Nature Books	Lerner Publishing Group
Great White Sharks	F	I	98	Pair-It Books	Steck-Vaughn
Great White Sharks	U	I	250+	The Untamed World	Steck-Vaughn
Great, Big, Giant Turnip, The	J	TL	610	Early Connections	Benchmark Education
Greatest Baseball Records, The	S	I	250+	Sports Records	Capstone Press
Greatest Basketball Records, The	S	I	250+	Sports Records	Capstone Press
Greatest Binnie in the World, The	M	RF	709	Sunshine	Wright Group/McGraw Hill
Greatest Digger of All, The	M	F	250+	Pair-It Turn and Learn	Steck-Vaughn
Greatest Electrician in the World, The	W	B	1926	Leveled Readers	Houghton Mifflin Harcourt
Greatest Football Records, The	S	I	250+	Sports Records	Capstone Press
Greatest Hockey Records, The	S	I	250+	Sports Records	Capstone Press
Greatest of All, The: A Japanese Folktale	L	TL	250+	Kimmel, Eric A.	Holiday House
Greatest Player, The	V	B	250+	WorldScapes	ETA/Cuisenaire
Greatest Wall of All, The	Q	I	250+	WorldScapes	ETA/Cuisenaire
Greatest, The	R	I	250+	Literacy 2000	Rigby
Greatest, The: Muhammad Ali	Z	B	250+	Myers, Walter Dean	Scholastic
Great-Grandpa	G	RF	130	Voyages	SRA/McGraw Hill
Great-Grandpa's in the Litter Box	N	F	250+	The Zack Files	Grosset & Dunlap
Greebies	I	F	171	Gear Up!	Wright Group/McGraw Hill
Greece	W	I	250+	Countries and Cultures	Capstone Press
Greece	P	I	1758	Country Explorers	Lerner Publishing Group
Greece	W	I	250+	Primary Source Readers	Teacher Created Materials
Greece	W	I	250+	Theme Sets	National Geographic
Greece in the Past and Present	T	I	250+	Reading Expeditions	National Geographic
Greece: A Question and Answer Book	P	I	250+	Question and Answer Countries	Capstone Press
Greece: Civilizations Past to Present	S	I	250+	Reading Expeditions	National Geographic
Greece: Everyday Kids Now and Then	S	HF	250+	Reading Expeditions	National Geographic
Greece: The Culture	U	I	250+	Kalman, Bobbie	Crabtree
Greece: The Land	U	I	250+	Kalman, Bobbie	Crabtree
Greece: The People	U	I	250+	Kalman, Bobbie	Crabtree
Greedy Apostrophe: A Cautionary Tale	O	F	250+	Carr, Jan	Holiday House
Greedy Cat	G	F	166	Pacific Literacy	Pacific Learning
Greedy Cat and the Birthday Cake	M	F	250+	Cowley, Joy	Pacific Learning
Greedy Cat Is Hungry	D	RF	103	Pacific Literacy	Pacific Learning
Greedy Cat's Breakfast	E	F	53	Story Basket	Wright Group/McGraw Hill
Greedy Crows, The	M	TL	250+	Story Vines	Wright Group/McGraw Hill
Greedy Dog, The	H	F	148	New Way Blue	Steck-Vaughn
Greedy Giant	LB	RF	14	Rigby Rocket	Rigby
Greedy Goat, The	L	TL	250+	Bookshop	Mondo Publishing

G

* Collection of short stories   # Graphic text
^ Mature content with lower level text demands

TITLE	LEVEL	GENRE	WORD COUNT	AUTHOR / SERIES	PUBLISHER / DISTRIBUTOR
Greedy Gray Octopus, The	G	F	195	Tadpoles	Rigby
Greedy Gus the Pirate	J	F	447	Red Rocket Readers	Flying Start Books
Greedy King, The	J	RF	250+	Lighthouse	Rigby
Greedy Mouse	G	F	187	Sails	Rigby
Greek and Roman Eras, The	R	I	250+	Journey Through History	Barron's Educational
Greek Civilization	Y	I	250+	Reading Expeditions	National Geographic
Greek Myths	Y	TL	250+	Coolidge, Olivia	Houghton Mifflin Harcourt
Greek News, The	W	I	250+	The History News	Candlewick Press
Greek Warriors	S	I	250+	Fierce Fighters	Raintree
Greeks, The	O	I	250+	Footsteps in Time	Children's Press
Greeks, The: Life in Ancient Greece	V	I	1940	Ancient Civilizations	Millbrook Press
Green	B	I	53	Bookworms	Marshall Cavendish
Green	B	I	26	Colors	Lerner Publishing Group
Green	LB	I	32	Seeger, Laura Vaccaro	Roaring Brook Press
Green	N	I	250+	Trackers	Pacific Learning
Green All Around	A	I	60	Color My World	American Reading Company
Green and Blue, Yellow, Too!	B	I	38	Little Celebrations	Pearson Learning Group
Green and Growing	M	I	250+	Rigby Focus	Rigby
Green and Growing: A Book About Plants	M	I	250+	Growing Things	Picture Window Books
Green Angel	Z	RF	250+	Hoffman, Alice	Scholastic
Green Bananas	F	F	49	Tadpoles	Rigby
Green Bay Packers, The	S	I	250+	Team Spirit	Norwood House Press
Green Beans, Potatoes, and Even Tomatoes: What Is in the Vegetables Group?	N	I	487	Food is CATegorical	Millbrook Press
Green Berets	T	I	250+	Warriors of History	Capstone Press
^Green Berets, The	T	I	250+	Elite Military Forces	Capstone Press
Green Book, The	V	SF	250+	Walsh, Jill Paton	Farrar, Straus, & Giroux
Green Boy	W	F	250+	Cooper, Susan	Aladdin
Green Bread, The	J	RF	338	Storyteller	Wright Group/McGraw Hill
Green Dog, The	M	RF	1022	Science Solves It!	Kane Press
Green Dragon, The	I	F	131	Sunshine	Wright Group/McGraw Hill
Green Dragons, The	J	RF	250+	PM Story Books	Rigby
Green Eggs and Ham	J	F	250+	Seuss, Dr.	Random House
Green Everywhere	K	I	319	Lightning Bolt Books	Lerner Publishing Group
Green Eyes	F	RF	111	Literacy 2000	Rigby
Green Footprints	E	RF	42	Literacy 2000	Rigby
Green Glass Sea, The	W	HF	250+	Klages, Ellen	Viking/Penguin
Green Grass	B	F	26	Story Box	Wright Group/McGraw Hill
Green Grass Grows All Around, The	H	TL	144	Instant Readers	Harcourt School Publishers
Green Grasshoppers	K	F	229	Sunshine	Wright Group/McGraw Hill
Green Green Green	E	F	218	Instant Readers	Harcourt School Publishers
Green Iguanas	N	I	250+	World of Reptiles	Capstone Press
Green in the Trees	A	I	24	Bonnell, Kris	Reading Reading Books
Green Living: No Action Too Small	T	I	250+	Green Generation	Compass Point Books
Green Means Go	D	I	25	Yellow Umbrella Books	Red Brick Learning
Green Men of Gressingham, The	O	F	250+	Ardagh, Philip	Stone Arch Books
Green Planet	W	I	10723	Dominoes two	Oxford University Press
Green Plants	H	RF	213	Foundations	Wright Group/McGraw Hill
^#Green Queen of Mean, The	R	F	250+	Dahl, Michael & Nickel, Scott	Stone Arch Books
Green Scene, The	T	I	250+	InfoQuest	Rigby
Green Snake	N	I	250+	Life Cycles	Creative Teaching Press
Green Snake, The	D	I	131	Twig	Wright Group/McGraw Hill
Green Team, The	L	RF	957	Leveled Readers	Houghton Mifflin Harcourt
Green Team, The	L	RF	957	Leveled Readers/CA	Houghton Mifflin Harcourt

G

TITLE	LEVEL	GENRE	WORD COUNT	AUTHOR / SERIES	PUBLISHER / DISTRIBUTOR
Green Team, The	L	RF	957	Leveled Readers/TX	Houghton Mifflin Harcourt
Green Technology	W	I	2470	Leveled Readers	Houghton Mifflin Harcourt
Green Technology	W	I	2470	Leveled Readers/CA	Houghton Mifflin Harcourt
Green Technology	W	I	2470	Leveled Readers/TX	Houghton Mifflin Harcourt
Green Thumbs	Q	I	250+	Literacy 2000	Rigby
Green Thumbs, Everyone	N	RF	250+	Giff, Patricia Reilly	Bantam Books
Green Toenails Gang, The (Olivia Sharp)	L	RF	250+	Sharmat, Marjorie Weinman	Yearling Books
Green Transportation	V	I	2575	Vocabulary Readers	Houghton Mifflin Harcourt
Green Transportation	V	I	2575	Vocabulary Readers/CA	Houghton Mifflin Harcourt
Green Transportation	V	I	2575	Vocabulary Readers/TX	Houghton Mifflin Harcourt
Green Tree Pythons	K	I	212	Colorful World of Animals	Capstone Press
Green Turtle Rescue	J	RF	279	Gear Up!	Wright Group/McGraw Hill
Green Wilma	I	F	252	Arnold, Tedd	Scholastic
Green with Red Spots Horrible	N	RF	250+	Supa Doopers	Sundance
Green, Green	D	RF	114	Little Readers	Houghton Mifflin Harcourt
Green: Seeing Green All Around Us	L	I	250+	Colors	Capstone Press
Green: Seeing Green All Around Us	I	I	78	Colors	Capstone Press
Greenland's Ocean Region	Q	I	250+	Theme Sets	National Geographic
Greenwitch	X	F	250+	Cooper, Susan	Scholastic
Greeting Card Making: Sending Your Personal Message	Q	I	250+	Crafts	Capstone Press
Gregor and the Code of the Claw	V	F	250+	Collins, Suzanne	Scholastic
Gregor and the Curse of the Warmbloods	V	F	250+	Collins, Suzanne	Scholastic
Gregor and the Marks of Secret	V	F	250+	Collins, Suzanne	Scholastic
Gregor and the Prophecy of Bane	V	F	250+	Collins, Suzanne	Scholastic
Gregor Mendel: Genetics Pioneer	V	B	250+	Science Readers	Teacher Created Materials
Gregor Mendel: The Friar Who Grew Peas	T	B	250+	Bardoe, Cheryl	Harry N. Abrams
Gregor the Grumblesome Giant	G	F	212	Literacy 2000	Rigby
Gregor the Overlander	V	F	250+	Collins, Suzanne	Scholastic
Gregory, the Mean Dragon	I	F	250+	Phonics and Friends	Hampton Brown
Gregory, the Terrible Eater	L	F	250+	Sharmat, Marjorie Weinman	Scholastic
Gregory's Dog	C	RF	23	Cat on the Mat	Oxford University Press
Gregory's Garden	F	RF	70	Cat on the Mat	Oxford University Press
Greg's Microscope	K	I	250+	Selsam, Millicent E.	HarperTrophy
Gremlins Don't Chew Bubble Gum	M	F	250+	Dadey, Debbie; Jones, Marcia Thornton	Scholastic
Grey King, The	X	F	250+	Cooper, Susan	Simon & Schuster
Grey Lady and the Strawberry Snatcher, The	WB	F	0	Bang, Molly	Aladdin
Greyhounds	Q	I	250+	All About Dogs	Capstone Press
Gribblegrot from Outer Space, The	N	F	250+	Literacy 2000 Satellites	Rigby
Griffin Comes to Visit	J	F	308	McAlpin, MaryAnn	Short Tales Press
Griffin, the School Cat	I	RF	160	Sunshine	Wright Group/McGraw Hill
Grigory Rasputin: Holy Man or Mad Monk?	Z	B	250+	A Wicked History	Scholastic
Grilled Cheese Sandwich	G	I	61	Windows on Literacy	National Geographic
Grilled Pizza Sandwich and Other Vegetarian Recipes	S	I	250+	Fun Food for Cool Cooks	Capstone Press
Grim Grotto, The	V	F	250+	Snicket, Lemony	HarperCollins
Grim Legacy, The	W	F	250+	Shulman, Polly	G.P. Putnam's Sons
Grimms' Fairy Tales	X	B	2480	Leveled Readers	Houghton Mifflin Harcourt
Grimms' Fairy Tales	X	B	2402	Leveled Readers/CA	Houghton Mifflin Harcourt
Grimms' Fairy Tales	X	B	2402	Leveled Readers/TX	Houghton Mifflin Harcourt
Grin and Bear It: Zoo Jokes to Make You Roar	O	F	1762	Make Me Laugh!	Lerner Publishing Group
^Grind	U	RF	250+	Orca Soundings	Orca Books
Grist	Z+	RF	250+	Waldorf, Heather	Fitzhenry & Whiteside

G

* Collection of short stories   # Graphic text
^ Mature content with lower level text demands

TITLE	LEVEL	GENRE	WORD COUNT	AUTHOR / SERIES	PUBLISHER / DISTRIBUTOR
Gristmill, The	T	I	250+	Historic Communities	Crabtree
Grizzled Bill Turns Over a New Leaf	U	HF	9080	Reading Street	Pearson
Grizzlies	M	I	250+	Phonics Plus	Educators Publishing Service
Grizzly and the Bumble-Bee	I	F	183	Sunshine	Wright Group/McGraw Hill
Grizzly Bear, The	R	I	250+	Wildlife of North America	Red Brick Learning
Grizzly Bears	S	I	2053	Animal Predators	Lerner Publishing Group
Grizzly Bears	K	I	250+	Bears	Capstone Press
Grizzly Bears	R	I	250+	Predators in the Wild	Red Brick Learning
Grizzly Bears	N	I	250+	Woolley, M.; Pigdon, K.	Mondo Publishing
^Grizzly Bears on the Hunt	N	I	250+	Killer Animals	Capstone Press
Grizzly Bears Return to Yellowstone	S	I	2009	Leveled Readers	Houghton Mifflin Harcourt
Grizzly Bears Return to Yellowstone	S	I	2009	Leveled Readers/CA	Houghton Mifflin Harcourt
Grizzly Bears Return to Yellowstone	S	I	2009	Leveled Readers/TX	Houghton Mifflin Harcourt
*Grizzly Mistake and Other Cases, The	O	RF	250+	Simon, Seymour	Avon Books
Grizzly Toothache, A	O	F	250+	Tristars	Richard C. Owen
Grizzwold	I	F	250+	Hoff, Syd	HarperTrophy
Grocer	D	I	35	Benchmark Rebus	Marshall Cavendish
Grocers	M	I	610	Pull Ahead Books	Lerner Publishing Group
Grocery Shopping	D	RF	34	Yannone, Deborah	Kaeden Books
Groing Around the Sun: Some Planetary Fun	M	F	838	Sharing Nature with Children	Dawn Publications
Groovy Gran and the Karaoke Kid	R	RF	250+	Storyteller-Whispering Pines	Wright Group/McGraw Hill
Gross Out!: Animals That Do Disgusting Things	O	I	250+	All Aboard Science Reader	Grosset & Dunlap
Groundhog Day!	N	I	250+	Gibbons, Gail	Holiday House
Groundhog's New Home	N	TL	1070	Leveled Readers/TX	Houghton Mifflin Harcourt
Grouping	C	I	35	Early Math	Lerner Publishing Group
Grouping Shells	H	RF	344	PM Math Readers	Rigby
Groups of Animals	N	I	250+	Windows on Literacy	National Geographic
Grover Cleveland	U	B	250+	Profiles of the Presidents	Compass Point Books
Grover Cleveland: Twenty-second and Twenty-fourth President	R	B	250+	Getting to Know the U.S. Presidents	Children's Press
Grow a Bean Plant!	I	I	220	Vocabulary Readers	Houghton Mifflin Harcourt
Grow a Bean Plant!	I	I	220	Vocabulary Readers/CA	Houghton Mifflin Harcourt
Grow a Bean Plant!	I	I	220	Vocabulary Readers/TX	Houghton Mifflin Harcourt
Grow a Plant Inch by Inch	H	I	142	Rosen Real Readers	Rosen Publishing Group
Grow a Tomato!	J	I	315	Reading Street	Pearson
^Grow Up, Dad!	Q	F	5022	Dhami, Narinder	Stone Arch Books
Grow Up: Verbs in Action	K	I	250+	Bookworms	Marshall Cavendish
Grow York Own Bean Plant	K	I	250+	Rigby Star Quest	Harcourt, Inc.
Grow, Seed, Grow	E	I	36	Discovery Links	Newbridge
Grow: A Novel in Verse	S	RF	250+	Havill, Juanita	Peachtree
Growin'	R	RF	250+	Grimes, Nikki	Puffin Books
Growing	B	I	22	Little Celebrations	Pearson Learning Group
Growing	A	I	15	On Our Way to English	Rigby
Growing	C	I	42	Story Steps	Rigby
Growing	B	I	23	Windmill Books	Wright Group/McGraw Hill
Growing a Kitchen Garden	O	I	250+	Navigators How-To Series	Benchmark Education
Growing a Plant	G	I	115	Discovery World	Rigby
Growing a Plant	C	I	43	Early Connections	Benchmark Education
Growing a Salad	E	RF	59	Gear Up!	Wright Group/McGraw Hill
Growing and Changing	O	I	250+	InfoTrek	ETA/Cuisenaire
Growing and Changing	N	I	869	Springboard	Wright Group/McGraw Hill
Growing Beans	G	I	92	Little Blue Readers	Sundance
Growing Colors	LB	I	14	McMillan, Bruce	HarperTrophy

G

TITLE	LEVEL	GENRE	WORD COUNT	AUTHOR / SERIES	PUBLISHER / DISTRIBUTOR
Growing Cotton	M	I	581	Rigby Flying Colors	Rigby
Growing Frogs	L	RF	250+	French, Vivian	Candlewick Press
Growing Ideas	O	B	250+	Meet The Author	Richard C. Owen
Growing in my Garden	I	I	208	Dominie Factivity Series	Pearson Learning Group
Growing Like Me	J	RF	160	Rockwell, Anne	Harcourt, Inc.
Growing Older	I	I	216	Early Connections	Benchmark Education
Growing Peas	I	I	346	Rigby Flying Colors	Rigby
Growing Radishes and Carrots	I	I	125	Bookshop	Mondo Publishing
Growing Sprouts and Eva's Sprout Diary	J	RF	250+	Voyages	SRA/McGraw Hill
Growing Tomatoes	G	I	87	Alphakids	Sundance
Growing Tomatoes	M	I	626	Leveled Readers Science	Houghton Mifflin Harcourt
Growing Up	D	I	47	Dominie Factivity Series	Pearson Learning Group
Growing Up	P	I	250+	It's Science	Children's Press
Growing Up Abenaki	N	B	250+	On Our Way to English	Rigby
Growing Up in a New Century	V	I	250+	Our America	Lerner Publishing Group
Growing Up in a New World	T	I	8949	Our America	Lerner Publishing Group
Growing Up in China	U	I	2537	Reading Street	Pearson
Growing Up in Coal Country	X	I	250+	Bartoletti, Susan Campbell	Houghton Mifflin Harcourt
Growing Up in Pioneer America	T	I	8785	Our America	Lerner Publishing Group
Growing Up in Revolution and the New Nation	T	I	7946	Our America	Lerner Publishing Group
Growing Up in the Civil War	V	I	250+	Our America	Lerner Publishing Group
Growing Up in the Great Depression	W	I	250+	Our America	Lerner Publishing Group
Growing Up in the Pond	N	I	799	Vocabulary Readers	Houghton Mifflin Harcourt
Growing Up in the Pond	N	I	799	Vocabulary Readers/CA	Houghton Mifflin Harcourt
Growing Up in World War II	V	I	7922	Our America	Lerner Publishing Group
Growing Up Is Fun	C	I	87	The Candid Collection	Pearson Learning Group
*Growing Up Stories	T	RF	250+	Byars, Betsy	Kingfisher
Growing Up, Up, Up Book	F	RF	120	First Start	Troll Associates
Growing Vegetables	K	RF	423	Reading Street	Pearson
Grown-Ups Get to Do All the Driving	P	RF	226	Steig, William	Carolrhoda Books
Grown-ups Make You Grumpy	J	RF	250+	Lighthouse	Ginn & Co.
Grown-ups Say the Silliest Things	J	F	250+	Lighthouse	Rigby
Growth	K	I	250+	InfoTrek Plus	ETA/Cuisenaire
Gruesome Ghosts	N	RF	250+	Damian Drooth Supersleuth	Stone Arch Books
Gruesome Halloween	H	F	202	The Joy Cowley Collection	Hameray Publishing Group
Gruesome House	H	F	233	The Joy Cowley Collection	Hameray Publishing Group
Gruesome Song	I	F	259	The Joy Cowley Collection	Hameray Publishing Group
Gruff Brothers, The	I	TL	250+	Hooks, William H.	Bantam Books
Grumbles, Growls, and Roars	F	I	133	Twig	Wright Group/McGraw Hill
Grump, The	F	RF	73	Literacy 2000	Rigby
Grumpus Under the Rug, The	K	F	250+	Jackson, Ellen	Pearson Learning Group
Grumputer, The	G	F	235	Story Basket	Wright Group/McGraw Hill
Grumpy Bear	I	F	367	Gear Up!	Wright Group/McGraw Hill
Grumpy Elephant	E	F	100	Story Box	Wright Group/McGraw Hill
Grumpy Grizzly	C	RF	40	Learn to Read	Creative Teaching Press
Grumpy Millionaire, The	O	RF	250+	Bookweb	Rigby
Grumpy Rella	I	TL	251	Literacy by Design	Rigby
#Guan Yu: Blood Brothers to the End	V	TL	3684	Graphic Myths and Legends	Lerner Publishing Group
#Guard Dog	U	RF	250+	Wooderson, Philip	Stone Arch Books
Guard Dog Diggory	L	RF	250+	Pacific Literacy	Pacific Learning
Guard the House, Sam!	G	RF	46	Rookie Readers	Children's Press
Guardian of the Dark	W	F	250+	Spencer, Bev	Scholastic
Guardian of the Everglades	R	I	1441	Leveled Readers	Houghton Mifflin Harcourt
Guardian of the Everglades	R	I	1441	Leveled Readers/CA	Houghton Mifflin Harcourt

G

* Collection of short stories   # Graphic text
^ Mature content with lower level text demands

TITLE	LEVEL	GENRE	WORD COUNT	AUTHOR / SERIES	PUBLISHER / DISTRIBUTOR
Guardian of the Everglades	R	I	1441	Leveled Readers/TX	Houghton Mifflin Harcourt
Guardian, The	Z	RF	250+	Sweeney, Joyce	Henry Holt & Co.
Guatemala	O	I	250+	Countries of the World	Red Brick Learning
Guatemala	P	I	1718	Country Explorers	Lerner Publishing Group
Guatemala	Q	I	250+	Theme Sets	National Geographic
Guatemala in Colors	N	I	250+	World of Colors	Capstone Press
Guatemala: A Question and Answer Book	P	I	250+	Question and Answer Countries	Capstone Press
Guess How Many	N	I	250+	Rosen Real Readers	Rosen Publishing Group
Guess How Many I Have	A	I	24	Early Connections	Benchmark Education
Guess How Much I Love You	J	F	250+	McBratney, Sam	Candlewick Press
Guess What Kind of Ball	E	RF	219	Urmston, Kathleen; Evans, Karen	Kaeden Books
Guess What the Moon Saw?	C	RF	38	Home Connection Collection	Rigby
Guess What the Sun Saw?	C	RF	36	Home Connection Collection	Rigby
Guess What Today Is?	I	F	250+	Popcorn	Sundance
Guess What!	E	RF	28	Literacy 2000	Rigby
Guess What?	E	RF	120	Foundations	Wright Group/McGraw Hill
Guess Who Bites	G	I	162	Book Worms	Marshall Cavendish
Guess Who Changes	G	I	140	Book Worms	Marshall Cavendish
Guess Who Dives	F	I	156	Book Worms	Marshall Cavendish
Guess Who Grabs	F	I	129	Book Worms	Marshall Cavendish
Guess Who Grunts	F	I	111	Book Worms	Marshall Cavendish
Guess Who Hides	F	I	140	Book Worms	Marshall Cavendish
Guess Who Hisses	G	I	166	Book Worms	Marshall Cavendish
Guess Who Hops	G	I	151	Book Worms	Marshall Cavendish
Guess Who Hunts	F	I	130	Book Worms	Marshall Cavendish
Guess Who Jumps	F	I	124	Book Worms	Marshall Cavendish
Guess Who Purrs	F	I	108	Book Worms	Marshall Cavendish
Guess Who Roars	F	I	150	Book Worms	Marshall Cavendish
Guess Who Runs	F	I	133	Book Worms	Marshall Cavendish
Guess Who Snaps	G	I	159	Book Worms	Marshall Cavendish
Guess Who Spins	G	I	174	Book Worms	Marshall Cavendish
Guess Who Stings	F	I	120	Book Worms	Marshall Cavendish
Guess Who Swims	F	I	122	Book Worms	Marshall Cavendish
Guess Who Swoops	F	I	125	Book Worms	Marshall Cavendish
Guess Who We Saw	F	RF	170	Windows on Literacy	National Geographic
Guess Who?	L	I	250+	Home Connection Collection	Rigby
Guess Who?	J	I	133	Miller, Margaret	HarperCollins Publishers
Guess Who?	A	RF	40	Rigby Star	Rigby
Guess Who's Coming to Dinner?	F	RF	130	Literacy 2000	Rigby
Guessing Game, The	H	RF	183	InfoTrek	ETA/Cuisenaire
Guessing Games	E	I	144	InfoTrek	ETA/Cuisenaire
Guessing Jar, The	K	I	395	Early Connections	Benchmark Education
Guests	T	HF	250+	Dorris, Michael	Hyperion
Guests from Japan	I	RF	205	The King School Series	Townsend Press
Guide Book to the Great Tree, A: Guardians of Ga'Hoole	V	F	250+	Lasky, Kathryn	Scholastic
Guide Dog School	J	I	348	Leveled Readers/TX	Houghton Mifflin Harcourt
Guide Dog, The	K	I	338	Foundations	Wright Group/McGraw Hill
Guide Dogs	H	I	107	Rosen Real Readers	Rosen Publishing Group
Guide to the Planets, A	N	I	250+	Windows on Literacy	National Geographic
Guilty by a Hair!	W	I	250+	24/7 Science Behind the Scenes	Scholastic
Guilty!: The Complicated Life of Claudia Cristina Cortez	S	RF	250+	Gallagher, Diana G.	Stone Arch Books
Guinea Dog	P	RF	250+	Jennings, Patrick	Egmont USA

TITLE	LEVEL	GENRE	WORD COUNT	AUTHOR / SERIES	PUBLISHER / DISTRIBUTOR
Guinea Pig for You, A: Caring for Your Guinea Pig	M	I	250+	Pet Care	Picture Window Books
Guinea Pig Gang	O	RF	250+	Baglio, Ben M.	Scholastic
Guinea Pig Grass	I	RF	140	Literacy 2000	Rigby
Guinea Pig Scientists: Bold Self Experimenter in Science and Medicine	Y	B	250+	Dendy, Leslie and Boring, Mel	Henry Holt & Co.
Guinea Pigs	E	I	50	All About Pets	Capstone Press
Guinea Pigs	S	I	250+	Hansen, Elvig	Carolrhoda Books
Guinea Pigs	K	I	180	Macken, JoAnn Early/Let's Read About Pets	Weekly Reader Publishing
Guinea Pigs	J	I	250+	PM Animal Facts: Orange	Rigby
Guinea Pigs	C	I	34	Sun Sprouts	ETA/Cuisenaire
Guinea Pigs Add Up	N	RF	250+	Cuyler, Margery	Walker & Company
Guji Guji	K	F	250+	Chen, Chih-Yuan	Kane/Miller Book Publishers
Gulf	X	F	250+	Westfall, Robert	Scholastic
Gulliver's Stories	Q	F	250+	Dolch, E. W.; Marguerite, P.	Scholastic
#Gulliver's Travels	U	F	250+	Lemke, Donald (Retold)	Stone Arch Books
Gulliver's Travels	Z+	F	250+	Swift, Jonathan	Penguin Group
Gulls	D	I	32	The Rowland Reading Program Library	Rowland Reading Foundation
Gulp!	D	F	103	Story Box	Wright Group/McGraw Hill
Gulps, The	M	F	250+	Wells, Rosemary	Little Brown and Company
Gum on the Drum, The	E	F	41	Start to Read	School Zone
Gumball, The	E	RF	67	Bonnell, Kris	Reading Reading Books
Gumby Shop, The	I	F	359	Read Alongs	Rigby
Gumshoe Goose Private Eye	K	F	250+	Kwitz, Mary DeBall	Puffin Books
Gun, The	Y	RF	250+	Langan, Paul	Townsend Press
Gung Hay Fat Choy	N	I	250+	Behrens, June	Children's Press
Gunpowder and Tea	W	HF	3290	Leveled Readers	Houghton Mifflin Harcourt
Guns for General Washington	U	HF	250+	Reit, Seymour	Harcourt Achieve
Gurgles and Growls: Learning About Your Stomach	L	I	250+	Amazing Body	Picture Window Books
Gus and Grandpa	J	RF	250+	Mills, Claudia	Sunburst
Gus and His Bus	D	F	72	Reading Street	Pearson
Gus, the Duck-Billed Platypus	I	F	250+	The Rowland Reading Program Library	Rowland Reading Foundation
Gusts and Gales: A Book About Wind	M	I	250+	Amazing Science	Picture Window Books
Guttersnipe	R	HF	250+	Cutler, Jane	Farrar, Straus, & Giroux
*Guys Write for Guys Read	Z	B	250+	Scieszka, Jon	Scholastic
Gwen Torrence	P	B	250+	Stewart, Mark	Children's Press
Gwendolyn Brooks: A Life of Poetry	R	B	811	Leveled Readers	Houghton Mifflin Harcourt
Gym Candy	Z+	RF	250+	Deuker, Carl	Houghton Mifflin Harcourt
Gym Teacher from the Black Lagoon, The	K	F	250+	Thaler, Mike	Scholastic
Gymnastics	M	I	466	Nonfiction Crimson	Pioneer Valley
Gymnastics Competitions: On Your Way to Victory	S	I	250+	Gymnastics	Capstone Press
Gymnastics Essentials: Safety and Equipment	S	I	250+	Gymnastics	Capstone Press
Gymnastics Events: Floor, Vault, Bars, and Beam	S	I	250+	Gymnastics	Capstone Press
Gymnastics for Fun!	S	I	250+	Sports for Fun!	Compass Point Books
Gymnastics Skills: Beginning Tumbling	S	I	250+	Gymnastics	Capstone Press
Gymnastics Training and Fitness: Being Your Best	S	I	250+	Gymnastics	Capstone Press
Gypsy Game, The	U	RF	250+	Snyder, Zilpha Keatly	Yearling Books

* Collection of short stories   # Graphic text
^ Mature content with lower level text demands

G

TITLE	LEVEL	GENRE	WORD COUNT	AUTHOR / SERIES	PUBLISHER / DISTRIBUTOR
H	LB	I	14	Readlings	American Reading Company
H for Horrible	Q	RF	250+	PM Extensions	Rigby
Habibi	V	B	250+	Nye, Naomi Shihab	Simon & Schuster
Habitat Is Where We Live, A	F	I	132	Twig	Wright Group/McGraw Hill
Habitat Rescue	O	I	250+	Navigators Social Studies Series	Benchmark Education
Habitat Spy	N	I	172	Kieber-King, Cynthia	Sylvan Dell Publishing
Habitats in Need of Help	T	I	2357	Reading Street	Pearson
Habitats of Africa	P	I	250+	Navigators Social Studies Series	Benchmark Education
Habitats of Australia	P	I	250+	Navigators Social Studies Series	Benchmark Education
Habitats of South America	P	I	250+	Navigators Social Studies Series	Benchmark Education
Hachiko Waits	S	HF	250+	Newman, Leslea	Square Fish
Haddie's Caps	D	F	90	Ready Readers	Pearson Learning Group
^Hades	W	I	250+	World Mythology	Capstone Press
Ha-Ha Party, The	J	RF	250+	Sunshine	Wright Group/McGraw Hill
Haiku for You	O	I	250+	Books for Young Learners	Richard C. Owen
Hailstorm, The	J	RF	386	PM Collection	Rigby
Hair	A	RF	32	Carousel Earlybirds	Pearson Learning Group
Hair	B	I	37	Foundations	Wright Group/McGraw Hill
Hair	C	RF	35	Little Celebrations	Pearson Learning Group
Hair	A	I	28	Springboard	Wright Group/McGraw Hill
Hair	C	I	60	Sun Sprouts	ETA/Cuisenaire
Hair	I	I	237	The Rowland Reading Program Library	Rowland Reading Foundation
Hair Ball From Outer Space	Q	F	250+	Wiley & Grampa's Creature Features	Little Brown and Company
Hair Party, The	J	RF	250+	Literacy 2000	Rigby
Hair Scare	N	RF	250+	Girlz Rock!	Mondo Publishing
Haircut, The	D	RF	27	Hartley, Susan; Armstrong, Shane	Scholastic
Haircuts	G	RF	307	Yukish, Joe	Kaeden Books
Haircuts for Bella & Rosie	E	F	129	Bella and Rosie Series	Literacy Footprints
Hairdresser, The	G	I	164	PM Nonfiction-Blue	Rigby
Hairem Scarem	K	TL	250+	Rigby Rocket	Rigby
Hairs Pelitos	L	RF	159	Cisneros, Sandra	Alfred A. Knopf
Hairy Bear	G	F	109	Story Box	Wright Group/McGraw Hill
Hairy Bear and the Door	I	F	270	The Joy Cowley Collection	Hameray Publishing Group
Hairy Bear on the Roof	F	F	193	The Joy Cowley Collection	Hameray Publishing Group
Hairy Caterpillars	I	I	164	Sails	Rigby
Hairy Harry	G	I	92	Windows on Literacy	National Geographic
Hairy Little Critters	O	I	250+	Literacy Tree	Rigby
Hairy Story, A	L	F	802	Springboard	Wright Group/McGraw Hill
Hairy, Scary, Ordinary: What is an Adjective?	O	I	337	Words Are CATegorical	Millbrook Press
Haiti	U	I	250+	Countries and Cultures	Red Brick Learning
Haiti: A Question and Answer Book	P	I	250+	Questions & Answers: Countries	Capstone Press
Half and Half	I	F	389	InfoTrek	ETA/Cuisenaire
Half Brother	Z	RF	250+	Oppel, Kenneth	Scholastic
Half Each	C	I	97	Red Rocket Readers	Flying Start Books
Half for You, Half for Me	K	TL	399	Literacy 2000	Rigby
Half Magic	T	F	250+	Eager, Edward	Harcourt
Half Marathon, The	S	RF	250+	Reading Safari	Mondo Publishing
Half Moon Investigations	U	RF	250+	Colfer, Eoin	Hyperion
Halfway Party, The	J	RF	506	PM Stars Bridge Books	Rigby
Halloween	Q	I	250+	Celebrate!	Capstone Press
Halloween	E	I	128	Fiesta Holiday Series	Pearson Learning Group

H

TITLE	LEVEL	GENRE	WORD COUNT	AUTHOR / SERIES	PUBLISHER / DISTRIBUTOR
Halloween	C	RF	87	Handprints C, Set 1	Educators Publishing Service
Halloween	Q	I	250+	Holiday Histories	Heinemann
Halloween	J	I	114	Holidays and Celebrations	Capstone Press
Halloween	M	I	250+	Holidays and Celebrations	Picture Window Books
Halloween	O	I	250+	Holidays and Festivals	Compass Point Books
Halloween	P	I	250+	Let's See	Compass Point Books
Halloween	C	RF	69	McAlpin, MaryAnn	Short Tales Press
Halloween	N	I	1209	On My Own Holidays	Lerner Publishing Group
Halloween	S	RF	250+	Seinfeld, Jerry	Little Brown and Company
Halloween	B	RF	44	Story Box	Wright Group/McGraw Hill
Halloween	H	RF	230	The King School Series	Townsend Press
Halloween	D	RF	32	Visions	Wright Group/McGraw Hill
Halloween Book of Facts & Fun, The	Q	I	250+	Old, Wendie	Albert Whitman & Co.
Halloween Caper, The	J	F	863	Spaceboy	Literacy Footprints
Halloween Danny	E	F	51	Coulton, Mia	Maryruth Books
Halloween Gotcha	N	RF	250+	Boyz Rule!	Mondo Publishing
*Halloween Horror and Other Cases, The	O	RF	250+	Simon, Seymour	Avon Books
Halloween House, The	M	F	250+	Slverman, Erica	Square Fish
Halloween Is…	M	I	250+	Gibbons, Gail	Holiday House
Halloween Mask for Monster	C	F	38	Mueller, Virginia	Whitman
Halloween Night	C	RF	58	Kaleidoscope Collection	Hameray Publishing Group
Halloween Parade	F	RF	101	Ziefert, Harriet	Puffin Books
Halloween Sky Ride	M	F	250+	Spurr, Elizabeth	Holiday House
Halloween: Why We Celebrate It the Way We Do	P	I	250+	Hintz, Martin & Kate	Red Brick Learning
Hamburger	H	RF	49	City Kids	Rigby
Hamburger Heaven	T	I	250+	The News	Richard C. Owen
#Hamlet	Z	F	250+	Manga Shakespeare	Amulet Books
Hamlet and the Tales of the Sniggery Woods	M	F	250+	Kneen, Maggie	Henry Holt & Co.
Hamlet the Hamster	G	RF	189	Breakthrough	Longman/Bow
^Hammerhead Shark	N	I	250+	Shark Zone	Capstone Press
Hammerhead Shark	J	I	146	Sharks	Capstone Press
Hammurabi and the Glory of Mesopotamia	Y	B	2564	Independent Readers Social Studies	Houghton Mifflin Harcourt
Hammurabi: Babylonian Ruler	X	B	250+	Primary Source Readers	Teacher Created Materials
Hamper's Great Escape	M	RF	250+	High-Fliers	Pacific Learning
#Hamster and Cheese	O	F	250+	Guinea Pig, Pet Shop Private Eye	Graphic Universe
Hamster Hotel	O	RF	250+	Baglio, Ben M.	Scholastic
Hamster in a Handbasket	Q	RF	250+	Baglio, Ben M.	Scholastic
Hamster of the Baskervilles, The: A Chet Gecko Mystery	Q	F	250+	Hale, Bruce	Harcourt Trade
Hamsters	D	I	39	All About Pets	Red Brick Learning
Hamster's Tale, A	M	RF	250+	Literacy by Design	Rigby
Hana's Suitcase	Y	I	250+	Levine, Karen	Albert Whitman & Co.
Hand Me Downs, The	G	RF	156	Little Readers	Houghton Mifflin Harcourt
Hand Tools	M	I	367	Wonder World	Wright Group/McGraw Hill
Hand, Hand, Fingers, Thumb	J	F	250+	Perkins, Al	Random House
Handbook for Boys	W	RF	250+	Myers, Walter Dean	HarperTrophy
Handful of Time, A	U	F	250+	Pearson, Kit	Puffin Books
Handle with Care	S	I	250+	Orbit Collections	Pacific Learning
Hands	D	I	90	Big Cat	Pacific Learning
Hands	C	RF	39	Literacy 2000	Rigby
Hands	C	I	24	Rookie Readers	Children's Press
Hands	B	I	15	Twig	Wright Group/McGraw Hill

* Collection of short stories   # Graphic text
^ Mature content with lower level text demands

TITLE	LEVEL	GENRE	WORD COUNT	AUTHOR / SERIES	PUBLISHER / DISTRIBUTOR
Hands and Feet, Fingers and Toes	F	I	83	Factivity Series	Pearson Learning Group
Hands at Work	C	I	50	Windows on Literacy	National Geographic
Hands of the Rain Forest: The Embera People of Panama	Q	I	250+	Crandell, Rachel	Henry Holt & Co.
Hands Up, Wolf	L	F	250+	Pacific Literacy	Pacific Learning
Hands, Hands, Hands	F	I	85	Bookshop	Mondo Publishing
Hands, Hands, Hands	B	RF	17	Little Celebrations	Pearson Learning Group
^Handwriting Evidence	T	I	250+	Forensic Crime Solvers	Capstone Press
Handy Dragon, A	H	F	159	Literacy 2000	Rigby
Handy Handbook for Harrowing Events	R	I	250+	Sails	Rigby
Hang a Left at Venus	N	F	250+	The Zack Files	Grosset & Dunlap
Hang in There, Oscar Martin!	N	RF	250+	Orbit Chapter Books	Pacific Learning
Hanged Man, The	Z	RF	250+	Block, Francesca Lia	HarperCollins
Hanging on to Max	Z+	RF	250+	Bechard, Margaret	Millbrook Press
Hanging Out with Mom	H	RF	209	Black, Sonia W.	Scholastic
Hank Aaron	O	B	877	Leveled Readers	Houghton Mifflin Harcourt
Hank Aaron	O	B	877	Leveled Readers/CA	Houghton Mifflin Harcourt
Hank Aaron	O	B	877	Leveled Readers/TX	Houghton Mifflin Harcourt
Hank Aaron	U	B	250+	Sports Heroes and Legends	Lerner Publishing Group
Hank Hammer	G	F	241	Stone Arch Readers	Stone Arch Books
Hanna Hippo's Horrible Hiccups	J	F	442	Animal Antics A To Z	Kane Press
Hannah	P	HF	250+	Book Blazers	ETA/Cuisenaire
Hannah	I	RF	250+	Stepping Stones	Nelson/Michaels Assoc.
Hannah	N	RF	250+	Whelan, Gloria	Random House
Hannah and Her Dad	J	RF	250+	Voyages	SRA/McGraw Hill
Hannah and the Angels	Q	F	250+	Lowery, Linda	Random House
Hannah and the Golden Thread	Q	HF	250+	Book Blazers	ETA/Cuisenaire
Hannah Brown, Union Army Spy	V	HF	2231	Leveled Readers	Houghton Mifflin Harcourt
Hannah Is My Name	P	RF	250+	Yang, Belle	Candlewick Press
Hannah of Fairfield	Q	HF	250+	Pioneer Daughters	Puffin Books
Hannah's Fancy Notions: A Story of Industrial New England	R	HF	250+	Ross, Pat	Penguin Group
Hannah's Halloween	LB	I	14	Little Books for Early Readers	University of Maine
Hannah's Helping Hands	Q	HF	250+	Van Leeuwen, Jean	Puffin Books
Hannah's Hiccups	G	RF	196	Home Connection Collection	Rigby
Hannah's Voyage	Q	HF	250+	Book Blazers	ETA/Cuisenaire
Hannah's Winter of Hope	Q	HF	250+	Van Leeuwen, Jean	Puffin Books
Hanna's Butterfly	I	RF	158	Start to Read	School Zone
Hannibal	T	B	250+	Green, Robert	Franklin Watts
Hans Christian Andersen: Prince of Storytellers	N	B	250+	Rookie Biographies	Children's Press
Hansel and Gretel	K	TL	250+	Enrichment	Wright Group/McGraw Hill
Hansel and Gretel	G	TL	451	Hunia, Fran	Ladybird Books
Hansel and Gretel	O	TL	250+	Morpurgo, Michael	Candlewick Press
Hansel and Gretel	K	TL	250+	Storyworlds	Heinemann
Hanukkah	N	I	250+	Festivals and Holidays	Children's Press
Hanukkah	K	I	206	Holidays and Celebrations	Capstone Press
Hanukkah	K	I	129	Holidays and Festivals	Heinemann Library
Hanukkah	P	I	250+	Let's See	Compass Point Books
Hanukkah	O	I	1443	On My Own Holidays	Lerner Publishing Group
Hanukkah at Valley Forge	T	HF	250+	Krensky, Stephen	Dutton Children's Books
Hanukkah Party, The	I	RF	250+	Early Transitional, Set 1	Pioneer Valley
Hap is Hot	B	F	30	Reading Street	Pearson
Happily Ever After	O	F	250+	Quindlen, Anna	Penguin Group
Happily Ever After!	K	TL	250+	Storyteller-Lightning Bolts	Wright Group/McGraw Hill

H

TITLE	LEVEL	GENRE	WORD COUNT	AUTHOR / SERIES	PUBLISHER / DISTRIBUTOR
Happiness Tree, The: Celebrating the Gifts of Trees We Treasure	O	F	250+	Gosline, Andrea Alban	Feiwel and Friends
Happy	D	I	13	Feelings	Lerner Publishing Group
Happy 100th Day!	C	RF	35	Little Celebrations	Pearson Learning Group
Happy Accidents!	Q	I	250+	Action Packs	Rigby
Happy and Sad	I	F	232	Sunshine	Wright Group/McGraw Hill
Happy Birthday	C	F	39	Brand New Readers	Candlewick Press
Happy Birthday	G	RF	130	First Start	Troll Associates
Happy Birthday	C	F	26	Instant Readers	Harcourt School Publishers
Happy Birthday	B	I	42	Red Rocket Readers	Flying Start Books
Happy Birthday America	L	RF	250+	Osborne, Mary Pope	Square Fish
Happy Birthday Book, The	P	I	250+	Sunshine	Wright Group/McGraw Hill
#Happy Birthday Dogtown	C	F	65	Dogtown Comics	American Reading Company
Happy Birthday Josie	LB	I	14	Rigby Rocket	Rigby
Happy Birthday Thomas!	G	F	213	Step into Reading	Random House
Happy Birthday to Me	D	RF	60	Bonnell, Kris	Reading Reading Books
Happy Birthday to Whooo?: A Baby Animal Riddle Book	N	F	190	Fisher, Doris	Sylvan Dell Publishing
Happy Birthday!	E	I	98	Early Connections	Benchmark Education
Happy Birthday!	C	RF	28	Literacy 2000	Rigby
Happy Birthday!	A	I	40	Vocabulary Readers	Houghton Mifflin Harcourt
Happy Birthday!	A	I	40	Vocabulary Readers/CA	Houghton Mifflin Harcourt
Happy Birthday!	A	I	40	Vocabulary Readers/TX	Houghton Mifflin Harcourt
Happy Birthday, Addy!	Q	HF	250+	The American Girls Collection	Pleasant Company
Happy Birthday, America!	L	I	388	Reading Street	Pearson
Happy Birthday, Anna, Sorpresa!	N	RF	250+	Giff, Patricia Reilly	Bantam Books
Happy Birthday, Bad Kitty	P	F	250+	Bruel, Nick	Roaring Brook Press
Happy Birthday, Brother!	A	I	24	Vocabulary Readers	Houghton Mifflin Harcourt
Happy Birthday, Danny and the Dinosaur	H	F	250+	Little Readers	Houghton Mifflin Harcourt
Happy Birthday, Danny and the Dinosaur!	H	F	250+	Hoff, Syd	HarperTrophy
Happy Birthday, Dear Dragon	E	F	290	Dear Dragon	Norwood House Press
Happy Birthday, Dear Duck	K	F	250+	Bunting, Eve	Clarion
Happy Birthday, Duckling	I	I	154	Literacy Tree	Rigby
Happy Birthday, Estela!	LB	RF	30	Pacific Literacy	Pacific Learning
Happy Birthday, Everyone	J	I	337	Leveled Readers	Houghton Mifflin Harcourt
Happy Birthday, Everyone	J	I	337	Leveled Readers/CA	Houghton Mifflin Harcourt
Happy Birthday, Everyone	J	I	337	Leveled Readers/TX	Houghton Mifflin Harcourt
Happy Birthday, Felicity!	Q	HF	250+	The American Girls Collection	Pleasant Company
Happy Birthday, Frog	C	F	87	Story Box	Wright Group/McGraw Hill
Happy Birthday, Josefina!	Q	HF	250+	The American Girls Collection	Pleasant Company
Happy Birthday, Kirsten!	Q	HF	250+	The American Girls Collection	Pleasant Company
Happy Birthday, Mallory!	O	RF	250+	Friedman, Laurie	Lerner Publishing Group
Happy Birthday, Martin Luther King	L	B	250+	Marzollo, Jean	Scholastic
Happy Birthday, Molly!	Q	HF	250+	The American Girls Collection	Pleasant Company
Happy Birthday, Monster!	J	F	98	Beck, Scott	Harry N. Abrams
Happy Birthday, Moon	L	F	345	Asch, Frank	Simon & Schuster
Happy Birthday, Mrs. Boedecker	L	RF	250+	Little Celebrations	Pearson Learning Group
Happy Birthday, Ronald Morgan!	J	RF	250+	Giff, Patricia Reilly	Viking/Penguin
Happy Birthday, Rosa!	B	RF	31	Brand New Readers	Candlewick Press
Happy Birthday, Sam	I	RF	213	Hutchins, Pat	Greenwillow Books
Happy Birthday, Sam!	I	RF	258	Leveled Readers	Houghton Mifflin Harcourt
Happy Birthday, Samantha!	Q	HF	250+	The American Girls Collection	Pleasant Company
Happy Birthday, Toad	E	F	144	Leveled Readers	Houghton Mifflin Harcourt
Happy Birthday,Toad	E	F	144	Leveled Readers/CA	Houghton Mifflin Harcourt

H

* Collection of short stories   # Graphic text
^ Mature content with lower level text demands

TITLE	LEVEL	GENRE	WORD COUNT	AUTHOR / SERIES	PUBLISHER / DISTRIBUTOR
Happy Birthday, Toad	E	F	144	Leveled Readers/TX	Houghton Mifflin Harcourt
Happy Café, The	I	RF	238	Story Box	Wright Group/McGraw Hill
Happy Day	E	RF	238	Joy Starters	Pearson Learning Group
Happy Day, A: Katie Woo	J	RF	250+	Manushkin, Fran	Picture Window Books
Happy Day, The	G	F	134	Krauss, Ruth	HarperCollins
Happy Dogs	A	I	18	Bonnell, Kris	Reading Reading Books
Happy Easter, Dear Dragon	F	F	257	Dear Dragon	Norwood House Press
Happy Egg	E	F	210	Kraus, Robert	Scholastic
Happy Endings	I	F	213	Sunshine	Wright Group/McGraw Hill
Happy Face, Sad Face	C	I	77	Foundations	Wright Group/McGraw Hill
Happy Faces	H	RF	210	Reading Unlimited	Pearson Learning Group
Happy Halloween, Mittens	G	RF	174	Schaefer, Lola M.	HarperCollins
Happy Hanukkah, Dear Dragon	F	F	250+	Dear Dragon	Norwood House Press
Happy Harriet	I	RF	326	Sails	Rigby
Happy Hector	J	F	193	Dunbar, Polly	Candlewick Press
Happy Holidays	B	I	27	Teacher's Choice Series	Pearson Learning Group
Happy House, The	F	RF	224	Sails	Rigby
Happy Jack	F	F	99	First Start	Troll Associates
Happy Monkey in the Shed	C	F	30	Joy Readers	Pearson Learning Group
Happy Monkey's Peanuts	D	F	63	Joy Readers	Pearson Learning Group
Happy Moon, The	D	F	81	Bonnell, Kris	Reading Reading Books
Happy Mother's Day!	G	RF	101	Teacher's Choice Series	Pearson Learning Group
Happy New Year!	M	I	114	Independent Readers Social Studies	Houghton Mifflin Harcourt
Happy New Year, Mallory!	O	RF	16726	Friedman, Laurie	Carolrhoda Books
Happy Pets, Healthy Pets	H	I	98	Spyglass Books	Compass Point Books
Happy Prince, The	L	TL	250+	Storybook Classics	Picture Window Books
Happy Valentine's Day, Dolores	M	RF	250+	Samuels, Barbara	Square Fish
Happy Valentine's Day, Miss Hildy!	K	RF	250+	Grambling, Lois	Random House
Happy's Hat	C	F	69	Joy Starters	Pearson Learning Group
Harbor Seal Pup Grows Up, A	K	I	449	Baby Animals	Lerner Publishing Group
Harbour, The	M	I	250+	Cambridge Reading	Pearson Learning Group
Hard at Work	B	RF	66	Early Emergent	Pioneer Valley
Hard Drive to Short	Q	RF	250+	Christopher, Matt	Little Brown and Company
Hard Soft	B	I	74	Bookworms	Marshall Cavendish
Hard Times	Y	HF	16450	Dominoes three	Oxford University Press
Hard Workers	J	I	186	Phonics Readers	Compass Point Books
Hardcourt Comeback	R	RF	250+	Bowen, Fred	Peachtree
Hardworking Puppies	L	RF	250+	Reiser, Lynn	Houghton Mifflin Harcourt
Hare and the Tortoise, The	J	TL	587	Aesop's Fables	Pearson Learning Group
Hare and the Tortoise, The	J	TL	531	Leveled Literacy Intervention/ Blue System	Heinemann
Hare and the Tortoise, The	K	TL	250+	Literacy 2000	Rigby
Hare and the Tortoise, The	K	TL	250+	PM Tales and Plays-Purple	Rigby
Hare and the Tortoise, The	D	TL	93	Storyworlds	Heinemann
Hare and the Tortoise, The	O	TL	395	Ward, Helen	Carolrhoda Books
Hare and Tortoise	H	TL	206	Red Rocket Readers	Flying Start Books
Hare and Tortoise Go to School	D	F	66	Rigby Rocket	Rigby
Hare's Big Tug-of-War	I	TL	207	Instant Readers	Harcourt School Publishers
Harlem	Y	I	3083	Vocabulary Readers	Houghton Mifflin Harcourt
Harlem	Y	I	3083	Vocabulary Readers/CA	Houghton Mifflin Harcourt
Harlem Globetrotters, The: Clown Princes of Basketball	T	I	250+	High Five Reading	Red Brick Learning

H

TITLE	LEVEL	GENRE	WORD COUNT	AUTHOR / SERIES	PUBLISHER / DISTRIBUTOR
Harlem Stomp! A Cultural History of the Harlem Renaissance	Z	I	250+	Hill, Laban Carrick	Little Brown and Company
Harlem Summer	X	HF	250+	Myers, Walter Dean	Scholastic
Harley-Davidson Motorcycles	M	I	250+	Horsepower	Capstone Press
Harold and the Purple Crayon	K	F	660	Johnson, Crockett	Harper & Row
Harold's Flyaway Kite	G	F	166	First Start	Troll Associates
Harp Seals	O	I	1669	Early Bird Nature Books	Lerner Publishing Group
Harriet and George's Christmas Treat	L	F	400	Carlson, Nancy	Carolrhoda Books
Harriet and the Garden	K	F	363	Carlson, Nancy	Carolrhoda Books
Harriet and the Roller Coaster	K	F	283	Carlson, Nancy	Carolrhoda Books
Harriet and Walt	K	F	376	Carlson, Nancy	Carolrhoda Books
Harriet Bean and the League of Cheats	O	RF	250+	Smith, Alexander McCall	Bloomsbury Children's Books
Harriet Beecher Stowe	T	B	250+	Amazing Americans	Wright Group/McGraw Hill
Harriet Beecher Stowe and the Beecher Preachers	X	B	250+	Fritz, Jean	Penguin Group
Harriet Higby	J	F	250+	Howard-Hess, Susan	Kaeden Books
Harriet the Hamster Fairy: Rainbow Magic	L	F	250+	Meadows, Daisy	Scholastic
Harriet the Spy	T	RF	250+	Fitzhugh, Louise	HarperCollins
Harriet Tubman	P	B	250+	Early Biographies	Compass Point Books
Harriet Tubman	S	B	3390	History Maker Bios	Lerner Publishing Group
Harriet Tubman	U	B	250+	Let Freedom Ring	Red Brick Learning
Harriet Tubman	N	B	239	Pebble Books	Capstone Press
Harriet Tubman	S	B	2185	People to Remember Series	January Books
Harriet Tubman	P	B	250+	Photo-Illustrated Biographies	Red Brick Learning
Harriet Tubman	Q	B	250+	Primary Source Readers	Teacher Created Materials
Harriet Tubman and the Freedom Train	O	B	250+	Stories of Famous Americans	Aladdin
#Harriet Tubman and the Underground Railroad	T	B	250+	Graphic Library	Capstone Press
Harriet Tubman and the Underground Railroad	X	B	2159	Leveled Readers	Houghton Mifflin Harcourt
Harriet Tubman, Secret Agent: How Daring Slaves and Free Blacks Spied for the Union During the Civil War	W	B	250+	Allen, Thomas B.	National Geographic
Harriet Tubman: A Lesson in Bravery	M	B	250+	Rosen Real Readers	Rosen Publishing Group
Harriet Tubman: A Woman of Courage	K	B	170	Independent Readers Social Studies	Houghton Mifflin Harcourt
^Harriet Tubman: The Path to Freedom	T	B	250+	Hameray Biography Series	Hameray Publishing Group
Harriet's Halloween Candy	K	F	285	Carlson, Nancy	Carolrhoda Books
Harriet's Hare	O	F	250+	King-Smith, Dick	Alfred A. Knopf
Harriet's Horrible Hair Day	L	F	250+	Stewart, Dawn Lesley	Peachtree
Harriet's Recital	K	F	196	Carlson, Nancy	Carolrhoda Books
Harris and Me	V	RF	250+	Paulsen, Gary	Bantam Books
Harry	P	RF	1868	Take Two Books	Wright Group/McGraw Hill
Harry and Chicken	S	F	250+	Sheldon, Dyan	Candlewick Press
Harry and Shellburt	I	TL	250+	Van Woerkom, Dorothy O.	Macmillan
Harry and the Lady Next Door	J	F	250+	Zion, Gene	HarperTrophy
Harry and the Terrible Whatzit	K	F	250+	Gackenbach, Dick	Clarion Books
Harry and Willy and Carrothead	K	RF	250+	Caseley, Judith	Scholastic
Harry Cat and Tucker Mouse: Harry to the Rescue!	K	F	250+	Feldman, Thea (Retold)	Macmillan
Harry Cat and Tucker Mouse: Starring Harry	J	F	250+	Feldman, Thea (Retold)	Macmillan
Harry Cat and Tucker Mouse: Tucker's Beetle Band	K	F	250+	Feldman, Thea (Retold)	Macmillan
Harry Cat's Pet Puppy	R	F	250+	Selden, George	Bantam Books
Harry Gets Ready for School	G	F	170	Ziefert, Harriet	Puffin Books
Harry Goes to Day Camp	F	F	250+	Ziefert, James	Puffin Books

H

* Collection of short stories   # Graphic text
^ Mature content with lower level text demands

TITLE	LEVEL	GENRE	WORD COUNT	AUTHOR / SERIES	PUBLISHER / DISTRIBUTOR
Harry Goes to Fun Land	F	F	166	Ziefert, Harriet	Puffin Books
Harry Hates Shopping!	K	F	250+	Armitage, Ronda & David	Scholastic
Harry Houdini	S	B	3389	History Maker Bios	Lerner Publishing Group
Harry Houdini: Master of Magic	R	B	250+	Kraske, Robert	Scholastic
^Harry Houdini: The Great Escape Artist	S	B	250+	Hameray Biography Series	Hameray Publishing Group
Harry Houdini: The Legend of the World's Greatest Escape Artist	W	B	250+	Weaver, Janice	Harry N. Abrams
Harry Houdini: The Man and His Magic	P	B	863	Reading Street	Pearson
Harry Houdini: Wonderdog!	N	RF	250+	Orbit Chapter Books	Pacific Learning
Harry Houdini: Young Magician	O	B	250+	Childhood of Famous Americans	Aladdin
Harry Kitten and Tucker Mouse	P	F	250+	Selden, George	Farrar, Straus, & Giroux
Harry On Vacation	S	SF	250+	Sheldon, Dyan	Candlewick Press
Harry Potter and the Chamber of Secrets	V	F	250+	Rowling, J. K.	Scholastic
Harry Potter and the Deathly Hallows	Z	F	250+	Rowling, J. K.	Scholastic
Harry Potter and the Goblet of Fire	W	F	250+	Rowling, J. K.	Scholastic
Harry Potter and the Half-Blood Prince	W	F	250+	Rowling, J. K.	Scholastic
Harry Potter and the Order of the Phoenix	W	F	250+	Rowling, J. K.	Scholastic
Harry Potter and the Prisoner of Azkaban	V	F	250+	Rowling, J. K.	Scholastic
Harry Potter and the Sorcerer's Stone	V	F	250+	Rowling, J. K.	Scholastic
Harry S. Truman	U	B	250+	Profiles of the Presidents	Compass Point Books
Harry S. Truman: Thirty-third President	R	B	250+	Getting to Know the U.S. Presidents	Children's Press
Harry Takes a Bath	G	F	132	Ziefert, Harriet	Puffin Books
Harry the Dirty Dog	J	F	250+	Zion, Gene	HarperTrophy
Harry the Explorer	S	F	250+	Sheldon, Dyan	Candlewick Press
Harry's Caterpillars	I	RF	381	Gear Up!	Wright Group/McGraw Hill
Harry's Elephant	H	F	250+	Storyworlds	Heinemann
Harry's Garden	H	I	138	Big Cat	Pacific Learning
Harry's Great Big Burp	J	RF	361	Springboard	Wright Group/McGraw Hill
Harry's Hat	B	RF	45	Little Books	Sadlier-Oxford
Harry's Hats	D	F	49	Teacher's Choice Series	Pearson Learning Group
Harry's Hiccups	J	F	439	Rigby Gigglers	Rigby
Harry's House	F	RF	83	Medearis, Angela; Keeter, Susan	Scholastic
Harry's Mad	P	F	250+	King-Smith, Dick	Alfred A. Knopf
Harry's Monkey	H	F	250+	Storyworlds	Heinemann
Harry's New Hat	F	RF	171	PM Stars	Rigby
Harry's Seal	H	F	250+	Storyworlds	Heinemann
Harry's Snake	H	F	250+	Storyworlds	Heinemann
Harvest Festivals	O	I	250+	Windows on Literacy	National Geographic
Harvest Holidays	J	RF	399	Reading Street	Pearson
Harvest of Light	M	I	986	Ofanansky, Allison	Kar-Ben Publishing
Harvest Time	J	I	228	Spyglass Books	Compass Point Books
Harvest Time	H	I	184	Yellow Umbrella Books	Red Brick Learning
Harvesting Medicine on the Hill	U	HF	2388	Reading Street	Pearson
Hassan's New Friend	K	RF	591	PM Stars Bridge Books	Rigby
Hat	I	RF	116	Hoppe, Paul	Bloomsbury Children's Books
Hat Came Back, The	K	RF	250+	Literacy 2000	Rigby
Hat Chat	H	I	124	Storyteller	Wright Group/McGraw Hill
Hat Day at the Zoo	B	F	63	Early Connections	Benchmark Education
Hat for Alf, A	F	RF	246	The Rowland Reading Program Library	Rowland Reading Foundation
Hat for Cat, A	C	F	85	Leveled Readers	Houghton Mifflin Harcourt
Hat for Cat, A	C	F	85	Leveled Readers/CA	Houghton Mifflin Harcourt

H

TITLE	LEVEL	GENRE	WORD COUNT	AUTHOR / SERIES	PUBLISHER / DISTRIBUTOR
Hat for Hippo, A	C	F	137	Sails	Rigby
Hat for Me, A	J	F	642	InfoTrek	ETA/Cuisenaire
Hat for Monster, A	LB	F	14	Handprints A	Educators Publishing Service
Hat That Wore Clara B., The	N	RF	250+	Turner-Denstaedt, Melanie	Farrar, Straus, & Giroux
Hat Trick	C	RF	38	Literacy 2000	Rigby
Hat, The	B	TL	43	Leveled Literacy Intervention/ Orange System	Heinemann
Hat, The	M	RF	250+	Literacy by Design	Rigby
Hat, The	LB	F	12	Ready Readers	Pearson Learning Group
Hat, The	B	RF	35	Sails	Rigby
Hatchet	R	RF	250+	Paulsen, Gary	Aladdin
Hatching Chickens at School	H	RF	94	City Kids	Rigby
Hatching Chicks	H	I	132	Nonfiction Set 6	Literacy Footprints
Hatching Eggs	C	RF	110	Red Rocket Readers	Flying Start Books
Hatchling, The	J	F	516	Sun Sprouts	ETA/Cuisenaire
Hatchling, The: Guardians of Ga'Hoole	V	F	250+	Lasky, Kathryn	Scholastic
Hate List	Z+	RF	250+	Brown, Jennifer	Little Brown and Company
Hate That Cat	T	RF	250+	Creech, Sharon	HarperCollins
Hats	E	RF	70	Dominie Readers	Pearson Learning Group
Hats	C	RF	35	Joy Readers	Pearson Learning Group
Hats	C	RF	43	Little Readers	Houghton Mifflin Harcourt
Hats	B	F	30	Sails	Rigby
Hats	F	I	88	Talk About Books	Pearson Learning Group
Hats	C	I	27	Twig	Wright Group/McGraw Hill
Hats	LB	I	46	Williams, Deborah	Kaeden Books
Hats	F	I	114	Wonder World	Wright Group/McGraw Hill
Hats Around the World	B	I	59	Charlesworth, Liza	Scholastic
Hats for the Carnival	H	RF	231	Lighthouse	Rigby
Hats Hats Hats	E	I	35	Morris, Ann	Scholastic
Hats Off to Hair	N	RF	250+	Kroll, Virginia	Charlesbridge
Hats On!	E	I	120	Early Connections	Benchmark Education
Hats!	E	RF	59	Early Readers	Compass Point Books
Hats!	C	F	28	Learn to Read	Creative Teaching Press
Hats, Hats, Hats	LB	I	14	Shutterbug Books	Steck-Vaughn
Hatshepsut and Nerfertiti: Egyptian Queens	X	B	2135	Leveled Readers Social Studies	Houghton Mifflin Harcourt
Hatshepsut Egypt's Woman King	Y	I	250+	iOpeners	Pearson Learning Group
Hatshepsut: First Female Pharaoh	X	B	250+	Primary Source Readers	Teacher Created Materials
Hattie and the Fox	I	TL	321	Fox, Mem	Bradbury/Trumpet
Hattie Big Sky	W	HF	250+	Larson, Kirby	Delacorte Press
Hattie: The Backstage Bat	M	F	250+	Freeman, Don	Puffin Books
Hatty and Tatty and the Bumping Boats	G	F	235	Gear Up!	Wright Group/McGraw Hill
Hatty and Tatty and the Deep Blue Sea	H	F	199	Gear Up!	Wright Group/McGraw Hill
Hatty and Tatty and the Greedy Gull	F	F	165	Gear Up!	Wright Group/McGraw Hill
Hatty and Tatty and the Polar Bear	I	F	291	Gear Up!	Wright Group/McGraw Hill
Hatupatu and the Birdwoman	J	F	250+	Story Box	Wright Group/McGraw Hill
Hau Kola Hello Friend	O	B	250+	Meet The Author	Richard C. Owen
Haunted	Q	F	250+	Ragged Island Mysteries	Wright Group/McGraw Hill
Haunted	J	F	383	Take Two Books	Wright Group/McGraw Hill
Haunted Bike, The	L	F	250+	Herman, Gail	Grosset & Dunlap
Haunted Halloween, The	M	F	250+	Woodland Mysteries	Wright Group/McGraw Hill
Haunted Hotel, The	N	RF	250+	A to Z Mysteries	Random House
Haunted House, The	N	RF	250+	Parish, Peggy	Yearling Books
Haunted House, The	M	RF	937	Springboard	Wright Group/McGraw Hill

* Collection of short stories   # Graphic text
^ Mature content with lower level text demands

TITLE	LEVEL	GENRE	WORD COUNT	AUTHOR / SERIES	PUBLISHER / DISTRIBUTOR
Haunted House, The	E	F	77	Story Box	Wright Group/McGraw Hill
^Haunted Houses: The Unsolved Mystery	R	I	250+	Mysteries of Science	Capstone Press
^Haunted Playground, The	S	F	250+	Tan, Shaun	Stone Arch Books
#Haunted Surfboard, The	T	F	3639	Masters, Anthony	Stone Arch Books
Haunting of Grade Three, The	O	RF	250+	Maccarone, Grace	Scholastic
#Haunting of Julia, The	T	F	250+	Hooper, M.	Stone Arch Books
Have a Ball!	K	I	456	Gear Up!	Wright Group/McGraw Hill
Have a Cookout	A	RF	21	Little Books for Early Readers	University of Maine
Have Numbers, Will Travel	WB	I	0	Gosset, Rachel	Scholastic
Have Wheels, Will Travel	Q	RF	250+	Mazer, Anne	Scholastic
Have You Ever Found a Beetle?	F	I	94	Voyages	SRA/McGraw Hill
Have You Ever Seen a Shell Walking?	M	I	460	Springboard	Wright Group/McGraw Hill
Have You Ever Seen a Sneep?	I	F	173	Pym, Tasha	Farrar, Straus, & Giroux
Have You Ever?	E	F	33	Big Cat	Pacific Learning
Have You Got Everything, Colin?	E	RF	72	Rigby Literacy	Rigby
Have You Got Everything, Colin?	E	RF	76	Rigby Star	Rigby
Have You Read It?	O	RF	250+	Sails	Rigby
Have You Seen a Javelina?	K	F	250+	Literacy 2000	Rigby
Have You Seen Birds?	K	I	250+	Oppenheim, Joanne; Reid, Barbara	Scholastic
Have You Seen Hyacinth Macaw?	R	RF	250+	Giff, Patricia Reilly	Dell
Have You Seen Joe?	D	RF	57	Home Connection Collection	Rigby
Have You Seen Lucy?	K	RF	537	InfoTrek	ETA/Cuisenaire
Have You Seen My Cat?	B	F	93	Carle, Eric	G.P. Putnam's Sons Books for Young Readers
Have You Seen My Duckling?	WB	F	0	Tafuri, Nancy	Greenwillow Books
Have You Seen the Crocodile?	F	F	150	West, Colin	Harper & Row
Have You Seen the Tooth Fairy?	E	RF	187	Visions	Wright Group/McGraw Hill
Have You Seen?	C	RF	38	Literacy 2000	Rigby
Haven't Got a Clue	W	I	250+	Boldprint	Steck-Vaughn
Having a Ball	U	I	250+	Rigby Literacy	Rigby
Having a Haircut	J	RF	298	City Kids	Rigby
Having a Hearing Test	J	I	250+	Growing Up	Heinemann Library
Having an Eye Test	J	I	250+	Growing Up	Heinemann Library
Having Fun	B	RF	35	Early Emergent	Pioneer Valley
Having Fun	D	I	78	Windows on Literacy	National Geographic
Having Fun Then and Now	R	I	250+	PM Extensions	Rigby
Having Healthful Habits	Q	I	250+	Navigators How-to Series	Benchmark Education
Having My Hair Washed	I	RF	171	City Kids	Rigby
Hawaii	T	I	250+	Hello U.S.A.	Lerner Publishing Group
Hawaii	S	I	250+	Land of Liberty	Red Brick Learning
Hawaii	T	I	250+	Sea to Shining Sea	Children's Press
Hawaii	R	I	250+	This Land Is Your Land	Compass Point Books
Hawaii	L	I	240	Windows on Literacy	National Geographic
Hawaii and Alaska: Apart, But Still a Part	N	I	394	Avenues	Hampton Brown
Hawaii: Facts and Symbols	O	I	250+	The States and Their Symbols	Capstone Press
Hawaii: The Aloha State	Q	I	250+	Rosen Real Readers	Rosen Publishing Group
Hawaiian Magic	R	I	250+	Orbit Chapter Books	Pacific Learning
Hawaiian Sea Life	R	I	1386	Vocabulary Readers/CA	Houghton Mifflin Harcourt
Hawaiin Sea Life	R	I	1386	Vocabulary Readers	Houghton Mifflin Harcourt
Hawk Drum, The	D	RF	81	Adams, Lorraine & Bruvold, Lynn	Eaglecrest Books
Hawk Eyes	K	I	250+	Trackers	Pacific Learning
Hawk, & Drool: Gross Stuff in Your Mouth	U	I	4595	Gross Body Science	Millbrook Press
Hawkers' Amazing Machines, The: A Play	K	F	250+	Phonics and Friends	Hampton Brown

TITLE	LEVEL	GENRE	WORD COUNT	AUTHOR / SERIES	PUBLISHER / DISTRIBUTOR
Hawks	R	I	250+	Predators in the Wild	Red Brick Learning
Hawks	F	RF	87	Seedlings	Continental Press
Hay for Ambrosia	G	I	86	Pacific Literacy	Pacific Learning
Hay Making	F	I	62	Wonder World	Wright Group/McGraw Hill
Hay Ride, The	A	I	16	Leveled Readers	Houghton Mifflin Harcourt
Hay Ride, The	A	I	16	Leveled Readers/CA	Houghton Mifflin Harcourt
Hayley the Rain Fairy: Rainbow Magic	L	F	250+	Meadows, Daisy	Scholastic
Haymeadow, The	T	RF	250+	Paulsen, Gary	Dell
Haystack, The	L	HF	250+	Cambridge Reading	Pearson Learning Group
He Bear, She Bear	J	F	250+	Berenstain, Stan & Jan	Random House
He Who Listens	K	RF	250+	Literacy 2000	Rigby
Head Above Water	Z+	RF	250+	Rottman, S. L.	Peachtree
Head For the Hills!	O	I	250+	Walker, Paul Robert	Random House
Head Full of Notions, A: A Story about Robert Fulton	S	B	250+	Russell Bowen, Andy	Carolrhoda Books
Head Lice	K	I	250+	Health Matters	Capstone Press
Head of the Class: Have You Got What It Takes to Be an Early Childhood Teacher?	T	I	250+	On the Job	Compass Point Books
Head to Toe: The Human Body	S	I	250+	Boldprint	Steck-Vaughn
Headache, The	B	RF	20	Oxford Reading Tree	Oxford University Press
Headfirst into the Oatmeal	L	TL	250+	Rigby Literacy	Rigby
Headfirst into the Porridge	L	TL	250+	Rigby Star Plus	Rigby
Headgear	I	I	362	Sails	Rigby
^Headless Ghost, The	V	F	250+	The Extraordinary Files	Hameray Publishing Group
Headless Horseman, The	L	TL	250+	Standiford, Natalie	Random House
Headline News	J	F	357	Sails	Rigby
Headlines	Y	I	250+	Boldprint	Steck-Vaughn
Headlines from Space	Q	I	250+	Rigby Focus	Rigby
Heads and Tails	LB	I	29	Windmill Books	Rigby
Heads or Tails	O	RF	250+	On Our Way to English	Rigby
*Heads or Tails: Stories from the Sixth Grade	U	RF	250+	Gantos, Jack	Farrar, Straus, & Giroux
Heads Up, Horses!	N	F	250+	Wind Dancers	Feiwel and Friends
Healthy and Happy	J	I	251	Gear Up!	Wright Group/McGraw Hill
Healthy Choices	L	I	250+	InfoTrek	ETA/Cuisenaire
Healthy Earth, A	M	I	394	Early Explorers	Benchmark Education
Healthy Food	I	I	162	PM Plus Nonfiction	Rigby
Healthy Habits	L	I	203	Health and Your Body	Capstone Press
Healthy Visit, A	E	I	44	New Way Red	Steck-Vaughn
Hear Hear	T	I	250+	Science Alive	Rigby
Hear Our Stories	Y	I	250+	iOpeners	Pearson Learning Group
Hearing	J	I	107	Pebble Books	Capstone Press
Hearing	G	I	212	PM Science Readers	Rigby
Hearing	E	I	86	Senses	Lerner Publishing Group
Hearing	M	I	250+	The Senses	Capstone Press
Heart and Lungs, The	Q	I	697	Time for Kids	Teacher Created Materials
Heart of a Champion	Z	RF	250+	Deuker, Carl	Little Brown and Company
Heart of a Chief, The	U	RF	250+	Bruchac, Joseph	Puffin Books
Heart of a Samurai	W	HF	250+	Preus, Margi	Amulet Books
Heart of Glass	Z+	RF	250+	Dean, Zoey	Little Brown and Company
Heart of Glass, The	S	F	250+	French, Vivian	Candlewick Press
Heart to Heart with Mallory	O	RF	250+	Friedman, Laurie	Carolrhoda Books
Heartbeat	W	RF	250+	Creech, Sharon	HarperCollins
*Heartbreak and Roses: Real Life Stories of Troubled Love	Z+	RF	250+	Bode, Janet & Mack, Stan	Grolier

* Collection of short stories   # Graphic text
^ Mature content with lower level text demands

TITLE	LEVEL	GENRE	WORD COUNT	AUTHOR / SERIES	PUBLISHER / DISTRIBUTOR
Hearts at Stake: The Drake Chronicles	Z+	F	250+	Harvey, Alyxandra	Walker & Company
Heart's Blood	X	F	250+	Yolen, Jane	Harcourt Trade
Heat	Q	I	2290	Early Bird Energy	Lerner Publishing Group
Heat	I	I	203	Early Connections	Benchmark Education
Heat	V	RF	250+	Lupica, Mike	Puffin Books
Heat	J	I	146	Take Two Books	Wright Group/McGraw Hill
Heat all Around	E	I	120	Leveled Readers Science	Houghton Mifflin Harcourt
Heat and Eat!	C	I	79	Independent Readers Science	Houghton Mifflin Harcourt
Heat Changes Things	G	I	101	Instant Readers	Harcourt School Publishers
Heat Changes Things	E	I	46	Windows on Literacy	National Geographic
Heat Is On, The	U	I	250+	Tanaka, Shelley	Firefly Books
Heat Wave	N	RF	250+	Spinelli, Eileen	Harcourt, Inc.
Heather and the Pink Poodles	Q	RF	250+	Engle, Marion	Magic Attic
Heather at the Barre	Q	RF	250+	Sinykin, Sheri Cooper	Magic Attic
Heather Goes to Hollywood	Q	RF	250+	Sinykin, Sheri Cooper	Magic Attic
Heather Takes the Reins	Q	RF	250+	Sinykin, Sheri Cooper	Magic Attic
Heather the Violet Fairy: Rainbow Magic	L	F	250+	Meadows, Daisy	Scholastic
Heather, Belle of the Ball	Q	RF	250+	Sinykin, Sheri Cooper	Magic Attic
Heather's Book	K	RF	250+	Ready Readers	Pearson Learning Group
Heather's Story	R	I	250+	Orbit Double Takes	Pacific Learning
Heating	C	I	23	Changing Matter	Lerner Publishing Group
Heating Earth	T	I	2023	Science Support Readers	Houghton Mifflin Harcourt
Heaven	U	RF	250+	Johnson, Angela	Scholastic
Heaven Looks a Lot Like the Mall	Z+	RF	250+	Mass, Wendy	Little Brown and Company
Heaven Shop, The	Z	RF	250+	Ellis, Deborah	Fitzhenry & Whiteside
Heaviest Pumpkin Contest, The	J	RF	689	InfoTrek	ETA/Cuisenaire
Heavy and Light: An Animal Opposites Book	J	I	250+	Animal Opposites	Capstone Press
Heavy Bombers: The B-52 Stratofortresses	V	I	250+	War Planes	Capstone Press
Heavy Hippo,The	H	RF	211	Windows on Literacy	National Geographic
*Heavy Weight and Other Cases, The	O	RF	250+	Simon, Seymour	Avon Books
Heavy-Duty Trucks	L	I	250+	Step into Reading	Random House
Heavyweights	O	I	250+	Take Two Books	Wright Group/McGraw Hill
Hector and the Cello	J	F	440	Big Cat	Pacific Learning
Hedgehog Bakes a Cake	J	F	250+	Bank Street	Bantam Books
Hedgehog Day	I	I	121	Seedlings	Continental Press
Hedgehog in the Hall	Q	RF	250+	Daniels, Lucy	Barron's Educational
Hedgehog Is Hungry	C	RF	48	PM Story Books	Rigby
Hedgehog Mountain	K	F	489	Rigby Gigglers	Rigby
Hedgehogs	F	I	94	Bonnell, Kris	Reading Reading Books
Hedgehogs	J	I	192	Nocturnal Animals	Capstone Press
Hedgehogs	I	I	286	Sails	Rigby
#Hedy Lamarr and a Secret Communication System	T	B	250+	Inventions and Discovery	Capstone Press
Heights, The	Z+	RF	250+	James, Brian	Feiwel and Friends
Heir of Mistmantle, The: The Mistmantle Chronicles	X	F	250+	McAllister, M.I.	Hyperion
Helen Keller	K	B	250+	Adler, David A.	Holiday House
Helen Keller	N	B	250+	Davidson, Margaret	Scholastic
Helen Keller	R	B	3393	History Maker Bios	Lerner Publishing Group
Helen Keller	N	B	1884	On My Own Biography	Lerner Publishing Group
Helen Keller	S	B	2815	People to Remember Series	January Books
Helen Keller	P	B	250+	Photo-Illustrated Biographies	Red Brick Learning
Helen Keller: A Life of Adventure	O	B	250+	Orbit Chapter Books	Pacific Learning
Helen Keller: A Light for the Blind	R	B	250+	Kudlinski, Kathleen V.	Penguin Group

H

TITLE	LEVEL	GENRE	WORD COUNT	AUTHOR / SERIES	PUBLISHER / DISTRIBUTOR
Helen Keller: Courage in Darkness	Y	B	250+	Sterling Biographies	Sterling Publishing
Helen Keller: Courage in the Dark	N	B	250+	Hurwitz, Johanna	Random House
#Helen Keller: Courageous Advocate	S	B	250+	Graphic Library	Capstone Press
Helen Keller: Crusader for the Blind and Deaf	P	B	250+	Graff, Stewart & Polly Anne	Bantam Books
Helen Keller: From Tragedy to Triumph	O	B	250+	Childhood of Famous Americans	Aladdin
Helen Keller's Lifelong Friend	S	I	1377	Leveled Readers	Houghton Mifflin Harcourt
Helen Keller's Lifelong Friend	S	I	1377	Leveled Readers/CA	Houghton Mifflin Harcourt
Helen Keller's Lifelong Friend	S	I	1377	Leveled Readers/TX	Houghton Mifflin Harcourt
Helen Keller's Special Friend	S	I	1472	Leveled Readers	Houghton Mifflin Harcourt
Helen Keller's Special Friend	S	I	1472	Leveled Readers/CA	Houghton Mifflin Harcourt
Helen Keller's Special Friend	S	I	1472	Leveled Readers/TX	Houghton Mifflin Harcourt
Helen Keller's Teacher	Q	B	250+	Davidson, Margaret	Scholastic
Helen of Troy	T	B	250+	Queens and Princesses	Capstone Press
Helena the Horse-Riding Fairy: Rainbow Magic	L	F	250+	Meadows, Daisy	Scholastic
Helen's Job	A	RF	24	Phonics and Friends	Hampton Brown
Helga and the Ogre	J	F	495	Sun Sprouts	ETA/Cuisenaire
Helga's Secret	J	RF	250+	Rigby Literacy	Rigby
Helicopter Over Hawaii	LB	I	21	Twig	Wright Group/McGraw Hill
Helicopters	O	I	250+	A True Book	Children's Press
Helicopters	M	I	250+	Horsepower	Capstone Press
Helicopters	V	I	4384	Military Hardware in Action	Lerner Publishing Group
Helicopters	L	I	294	Pull Ahead Books	Lerner Publishing Group
Helicopters	T	I	250+	The World's Fastest	Red Brick Learning
Helicopters on the Move	L	I	294	Lightning Bolt Books	Lerner Publishing Group
Hello	C	F	63	Story Box	Wright Group/McGraw Hill
Hello Chick!	D	I	54	Leveled Readers Language Support	Houghton Mifflin Harcourt
Hello Creatures!	K	I	250+	Literacy 2000	Rigby
Hello Doctor	C	RF	43	Rookie Readers	Children's Press
Hello Flower	B	RF	20	Bebop Books	Lee & Low Books Inc.
Hello Goodbye	B	F	29	Literacy 2000	Rigby
Hello Hello	J	F	164	Takeshita, Fumiko	Kane/Miller Book Publishers
Hello Ocean	N	RF	302	Ryan, Pam Munoz	Charlesbridge
Hello Puppet	C	I	26	Voyages	SRA/McGraw Hill
Hello Sun!	L	F	1201	Wilhelm, Hans	Carolrhoda Books
Hello Tilly: A Tilly and Friends Book	I	F	118	Dunbar, Polly	Candlewick Press
Hello Twins	I	RF	180	Voake, Charlotte	Candlewick Press
Hello!	F	I	17	Chessen, Betsey; Bergen, Samantha	Scholastic
Hello, Bingo!	C	RF	42	PM Stars	Rigby
Hello, Cat: You Need a Hat	I	F	250+	Gelman, Rita	Scholastic
Hello, Dad!	D	RF	16	Pacific Literacy	Pacific Learning
Hello, Duck!	C	I	31	Avenues	Hampton Brown
Hello, First Grade	I	RF	250+	Ryder, Joanne	Troll Associates
Hello, Friend	C	F	39	Instant Readers	Harcourt School Publishers
Hello, Goodbye, I Love You: The Story of Aloha, A Guide Dog for the Blind	S	RF	250+	Mueller, Pamela Bauer	Pinata Publishing
Hello, Hello, Hello	E	RF	56	Sunshine	Wright Group/McGraw Hill
Hello, I'm Joe	J	RF	652	Rigby Flying Colors	Rigby
Hello, Little Chick!	D	I	56	Leveled Readers	Houghton Mifflin Harcourt
*Hello, Mrs. Piggle-Wiggle	O	F	250+	MacDonald, Betty	HarperTrophy
Hello, My Name Is Scrambled Eggs	R	RF	250+	Gilson, Jamie	Pocket Books
Hello, Neighbor!	J	F	456	InfoTrek	ETA/Cuisenaire
Hello, Peter-Bonjour, Remy	L	F	250+	Little Celebrations	Pearson Learning Group

* Collection of short stories   # Graphic text
^ Mature content with lower level text demands

TITLE	LEVEL	GENRE	WORD COUNT	AUTHOR / SERIES	PUBLISHER / DISTRIBUTOR
Help for Dear Dragon	E	F	304	Dear Dragon	Norwood House Press
Help for Eyes	H	I	156	Sails	Rigby
Help for Loc: A Play	H	RF	202	Literacy by Design	Rigby
Help for Loc: A Play	H	RF	202	On Our Way to English	Rigby
Help for Rhino!	E	F	131	Sails	Rigby
Help for Rosie	H	F	165	Bella and Rosie Series	Pioneer Valley
Help for Santa	F	F	147	Little Elf	Literacy Footprints
Help Is on the Way	Q	I	372	Vocabulary Readers	Houghton Mifflin Harcourt
Help Me	D	RF	107	Emergent	Pioneer Valley
*Help Me	H	TL	196	Story Box	Wright Group/McGraw Hill
Help Me!	C	F	55	New Way Red	Steck-Vaughn
Help the Forest	G	I	122	Reading Street	Pearson
Help with the Herd	T	RF	1830	Leveled Readers	Houghton Mifflin Harcourt
Help Yourself to Health	L	I	538	Springboard	Wright Group/McGraw Hill
Help!	H	RF	82	Giant Step Readers	Educational Insights
Help!	C	I	57	Reading Corners	Pearson Learning Group
Help!	C	RF	57	Rigby Literacy	Rigby
Help! A Vampire's Coming!	L	RF	250+	Klein, Abby	Scholastic
Help! Help!	LB	RF	14	Joy Readers	Pearson Learning Group
Help! I'm a Prisoner in the Library	Q	RF	250+	Clifford, Eth	Scholastic
Help! I'm Stuck!	J	F	250+	Little Celebrations	Pearson Learning Group
Help! I'm Trapped in an Alien's Body	Q	F	250+	Strasser, Todd	Scholastic
Help! I'm Trapped in My Lunch Lady's Body	Q	F	250+	Strasser, Todd	Scholastic
Help! I'm Trapped in My Teacher's Body	Q	F	250+	Strasser, Todd	Scholastic
Help! I'm Trapped in Obedience School	Q	F	250+	Strasser, Todd	Scholastic
Help! I'm Trapped in Obedience School Again	Q	F	250+	Strasser, Todd	Scholastic
Help! I'm Trapped in Santa's Body	Q	F	250+	Strasser, Todd	Scholastic
Help! I'm Trapped in the First Day of School	Q	F	250+	Strasser, Todd	Scholastic
Help! I'm Trapped in the First Day of Summer Camp	Q	F	250+	Strasser, Todd	Scholastic
Help! I'm Trapped in the President's Body	Q	F	250+	Strasser, Todd	Scholastic
Help! Said Jed	C	TL	35	Instant Readers	Harcourt School Publishers
Help! Somebody Get Me Out of Fourth Grade!	R	RF	250+	Winkler, Henry and Oliver, Lin	Grosset & Dunlap
Helper Monkeys	L	I	499	Leveled Readers	Houghton Mifflin Harcourt
Helper Monkeys	L	I	499	Leveled Readers/CA	Houghton Mifflin Harcourt
Helper Monkeys	L	I	499	Leveled Readers/TX	Houghton Mifflin Harcourt
Helper, The	A	I	31	InfoTrek	ETA/Cuisenaire
Helpers	D	RF	57	Joy Starters	Pearson Learning Group
Helpers	C	I	36	Kaleidoscope Collection	Hameray Publishing Group
Helpers	C	RF	31	Storyworlds	Heinemann
Helpful Becky	J	RF	250+	Phonics Readers Plus	Steck-Vaughn
Helpful Change, A	L	RF	250+	Behr, Alexandra	Hampton Brown
*Helpful Harry and Other Stories	L	RF	250+	New Way Literature	Steck-Vaughn
Helpful Hints for Boring Moments	R	I	250+	Sails	Rigby
Helpful or Harmful?	O	I	250+	Orbit Double Takes	Pacific Learning
Helping	F	RF	79	Bookshop	Mondo Publishing
Helping	A	RF	22	Johns, Linda	Scholastic
Helping	D	RF	79	Joy Readers	Pearson Learning Group
Helping	C	RF	74	Leveled Literacy Intervention/Orange System	Heinemann
Helping	A	I	36	Leveled Readers	Houghton Mifflin Harcourt
Helping	A	I	36	Leveled Readers/CA	Houghton Mifflin Harcourt
Helping	A	I	36	Leveled Readers/TX	Houghton Mifflin Harcourt
Helping	F	RF	103	Well-Being Series	Pearson Learning Group

TITLE	LEVEL	GENRE	WORD COUNT	AUTHOR / SERIES	PUBLISHER / DISTRIBUTOR
Helping Animals	E	I	119	Early Explorers	Benchmark Education
Helping at Home	E	I	157	Vocabulary Readers	Houghton Mifflin Harcourt
Helping at Home	C	I	86	Vocabulary Readers	Houghton Mifflin Harcourt
Helping at Home	E	I	157	Vocabulary Readers/CA	Houghton Mifflin Harcourt
Helping at Home	B	I	86	Vocabulary Readers/CA	Houghton Mifflin Harcourt
Helping at Home	E	I	157	Vocabulary Readers/TX	Houghton Mifflin Harcourt
Helping Dad	B	RF	31	Storyteller	Wright Group/McGraw Hill
Helping Dad	C	RF	34	Sunshine	Wright Group/McGraw Hill
Helping Each Other	C	RF	80	Literacy by Design	Rigby
Helping Each Other	C	RF	80	On Our Way to English	Rigby
Helping Friends	C	I	73	Early Explorers	Benchmark Education
Helping Grandma	G	RF	164	Adams, Lorraine & Bruvold, Lynn	Eaglecrest Books
Helping Hand, A	P	I	250+	Rigby Focus	Rigby
Helping Hands	K	I	372	Gear Up!	Wright Group/McGraw Hill
Helping Hands	I	RF	350	Rigby Flying Colors	Rigby
Helping Hands	J	I	387	Vocabulary Readers	Houghton Mifflin Harcourt
Helping Hands	J	I	387	Vocabulary Readers/CA	Houghton Mifflin Harcourt
Helping Hands	P	I	250+	WorldScapes	ETA/Cuisenaire
Helping Hands	J	I	250+	Yellow Umbrella Books	Red Brick Learning
Helping Hannah	C	RF	51	Neighborhood Readers	Rosen Publishing Group
Helping Mom	E	RF	165	Leveled Literacy Intervention/ Green System	Heinemann
Helping Mom and Dad	E	RF	121	Learn to Read	Creative Teaching Press
Helping Mr. Horse	D	F	82	Leveled Readers	Houghton Mifflin Harcourt
Helping Mr. Horse	D	F	82	Leveled Readers/CA	Houghton Mifflin Harcourt
Helping My Dad	D	RF	90	Teacher's Choice Series	Pearson Learning Group
Helping Out	L	RF	317	Independent Readers Social Studies	Houghton Mifflin Harcourt
Helping Out	F	I	121	Sails	Rigby
Helping Paws: Dogs That Serve	O	I	250+	Luke, Melinda	Scholastic
Helping the Everglades	J	I	369	In Step Readers	Rigby
Helping the Hoiho	S	I	250+	Literacy 2000	Rigby
Helping the Zookeeper	E	RF	108	Red Rocket Readers	Flying Start Books
Helping Toby's Team	E	RF	98	Windows on Literacy	National Geographic
Helping Wild Animals	T	I	2126	Leveled Readers	Houghton Mifflin Harcourt
Helping Wild Animals	T	I	2126	Leveled Readers/CA	Houghton Mifflin Harcourt
Helping Wild Animals	T	I	2126	Leveled Readers/TX	Houghton Mifflin Harcourt
Helping Wild Animals	R	I	582	Vocabulary Readers	Houghton Mifflin Harcourt
Helping With Baby	E	RF	115	Adams, Lorraine & Bruvold, Lynn	Eaglecrest Books
Helping You	D	I	53	Interaction	Rigby
Helping You Heal: A Book About Nurses	H	I	145	Community Workers	Picture Window Books
Helping You Learn: A Book About Teachers	H	I	147	Community Workers	Picture Window Books
Helter-Skelter	J	F	250+	Rigby Rocket	Rigby
^Hemingway Tradition, The	Z	RF	250+	Orca Soundings	Orca Books
Hen Can, A	E	F	159	Tiger Cub	Peguis
Hen, The Rooster, and the Bean, The	I	TL	250+	Kratky, Lada Josefa	Hampton Brown
Henny Penny	I	TL	582	Galdone, Paul	Clarion
Henny Penny	H	TL	292	New Way Green	Steck-Vaughn
Henny Penny	I	TL	250+	Zimmerman, H. Werner	Scholastic
Henri de Toulouse-Lautrec	R	B	250+	Venezia, Mike	Children's Press
Henri Matisse	R	B	250+	Venezia, Mike	Children's Press
Henri Rousseau	T	B	250+	Rabott, Ernest	HarperTrophy
Henrietta Hornbuckle's Circus of Life	U	RF	250+	de Guzman, Michael	Farrar, Straus, & Giroux
Henrietta There's No One Better	Q	F	250+	Murray, Martine	Scholastic

* Collection of short stories   # Graphic text
^ Mature content with lower level text demands

TITLE	LEVEL	GENRE	WORD COUNT	AUTHOR / SERIES	PUBLISHER / DISTRIBUTOR
Henry	T	RF	250+	Bawden, Nina	Bantam Books
Henry	E	RF	77	Books for Young Learners	Richard C. Owen
Henry	F	F	141	Instant Readers	Harcourt School Publishers
Henry and Beezus	O	RF	250+	Cleary, Beverly	Avon Books
Henry and Hala Build a Haiku	N	RF	1100	Poetry Builders	Norwood House Press
Henry and Mudge and Annie's Good Move	J	RF	250+	Rylant, Cynthia	Aladdin
Henry and Mudge and Annie's Perfect Pet	J	RF	250+	Rylant, Cynthia	Aladdin Paperbacks
Henry and Mudge and the Bedtime Thumps	J	RF	250+	Rylant, Cynthia	Aladdin
Henry and Mudge and the Best Day of All	J	RF	250+	Rylant, Cynthia	Aladdin
Henry and Mudge and the Careful Cousin	J	RF	250+	Rylant, Cynthia	Aladdin
Henry and Mudge and the Forever Sea	J	RF	250+	Rylant, Cynthia	Aladdin
Henry and Mudge and the Funny Lunch	I	RF	250+	Rylant, Cynthia	Scholastic
Henry and Mudge and the Happy Cat	J	RF	250+	Rylant, Cynthia	Aladdin
Henry and Mudge and the Long Weekend	J	RF	250+	Rylant, Cynthia	Aladdin
Henry and Mudge and the Sneaky Crackers	J	RF	250+	Rylant, Cynthia	Aladdin
Henry and Mudge and the Snowman Plan	J	RF	250+	Rylant, Cynthia	Aladdin
Henry and Mudge and the Starry Night	J	RF	250+	Rylant, Cynthia	Aladdin
Henry and Mudge and the Wild Goose Chase	J	RF	250+	Rylant, Cynthia	Aladdin Paperbacks
Henry and Mudge and the Wild Wind	J	RF	250+	Rylant, Cynthia	Aladdin
Henry and Mudge Get the Cold Shivers	J	RF	250+	Rylant, Cynthia	Aladdin
Henry and Mudge in Puddle Trouble	J	RF	250+	Rylant, Cynthia	Aladdin
Henry and Mudge in the Family Trees	J	RF	250+	Rylant, Cynthia	Aladdin
Henry and Mudge in the Green Time	J	RF	250+	Rylant, Cynthia	Aladdin
Henry and Mudge in the Sparkle Days	J	RF	250+	Rylant, Cynthia	Aladdin
Henry and Mudge Take the Big Test	J	RF	250+	Rylant, Cynthia	Aladdin
Henry and Mudge Under the Yellow Moon	J	RF	250+	Rylant, Cynthia	Aladdin
Henry and Mudge: The First Book	J	RF	250+	Rylant, Cynthia	Aladdin
Henry and Ribsy	O	RF	250+	Cleary, Beverly	Hearst
Henry and the Buccaneer Bunnies	M	F	250+	Crimi, Carolyn	Candlewick Press
Henry and the Clubhouse	O	RF	250+	Cleary, Beverly	Avon Books
Henry and the Fox	K	RF	388	Leveled Readers	Houghton Mifflin Harcourt
Henry and the Helicopter	D	RF	58	Literacy 2000	Rigby
Henry and the Paper Route	O	RF	250+	Cleary, Beverly	Hearst
Henry Ford	T	B	250+	Amazing Americans	Wright Group/McGraw Hill
Henry Ford	L	B	216	Famous People in Transportation	Red Brick Learning
Henry Ford	R	B	3726	History Maker Bios	Lerner Publishing Group
Henry Ford	P	B	250+	Photo-Illustrated Biographies	Red Brick Learning
Henry Ford and His Idea	L	I	473	Leveled Readers Social Studies	Houghton Mifflin Harcourt
Henry Ford and the Automobile Industry	R	B	250+	On Deck	Rigby
Henry Ford and the Car	P	I	250+	Windows on Literacy	National Geographic
#Henry Ford and the Model T	T	B	250+	Inventions and Discovery	Capstone Press
^Henry Ford: The Man Who Put the World on Wheels	S	B	250+	Hameray Biography Series	Hameray Publishing Group
Henry Ford: Young Man with Ideas	O	B	250+	Childhood of Famous Americans	Aladdin
Henry Gonzales, U.S. Representative	N	B	491	Leveled Readers Social Studies	Houghton Mifflin Harcourt
Henry Helps with the Baby	F	RF	160	Henry Helps	Picture Window Books
Henry Helps with the Dog	F	RF	128	Henry Helps	Picture Window Books
Henry Huggins	O	RF	250+	Cleary, Beverly	Avon Books
Henry Keeps Score	J	RF	250+	Math Matters	Kane Press
Henry Morgan, the Pirate	Q	B	947	Springboard	Wright Group/McGraw Hill
Henry Reed, Inc.	X	F	250+	Robertson, Keith	Puffin Books
Henry Runs Away	F	RF	150	Books for Young Learners	Richard C. Owen
Henry the Impatient Heron	N	F	1098	Love, Donna	Sylvan Dell Publishing
Henry VIII and His Six Wives	Z	B	250+	Oxford Bookworms Library	Oxford University Press

H

* Collection of short stories   # Graphic text
^ Mature content with lower level text demands

| --- | --- | --- | --- | --- | --- |
Henry VIII: Royal Beheader	Z	B	250+	A Wicked History	Scholastic
Henry's Busy Day	E	F	112	Campbell, Rod	Penguin Group
Henry's Choice	M	RF	527	Reading Unlimited	Pearson Learning Group
Henry's New Friend	I	RF	250+	Leveled Readers Language Support	Houghton Mifflin Harcourt
Henry's Show and Tell	K	F	307	Carlson, Nancy	Carolrhoda Books
Henry's Tricks	H	RF	162	Books for Young Learners	Richard C. Owen
Her Name Is Amira	U	RF	2510	Leveled Readers/CA	Houghton Mifflin Harcourt
Her Name Is Amira	U	RF	2510	Leveled Readers/TX	Houghton Mifflin Harcourt
Her Name Is Amira	U	RF	2510	Leveled Readers	Houghton Mifflin Harcourt
Her Piano Sang: A Story About Clara Schumann	R	B	250+	Allman, Barbara	Carolrhoda Books
Her Seven Brothers	O	TL	250+	Goble, Paul	Aladdin
Herbert Fieldmouse, Secret Agent	R	F	250+	Bookshop	Mondo Publishing
Herbert Hoover	U	B	250+	Profiles of the Presidents	Compass Point Books
Herbert Hoover: Thirty-first President	R	B	250+	Getting to Know the U.S. Presidents	Children's Press
Herbert: The True Story of a Brave Sea Dog	L	HF	250+	Belton, Robyn	Candlewick Press
Herbie Jones	N	RF	250+	Kline, Suzy	Penguin Group
Herbie Jones and Hamburger Head	N	RF	250+	Kline, Suzy	Penguin Group
Herbie Jones and the Birthday Showdown	N	RF	250+	Kline, Suzy	Penguin Group
Herbie Jones and the Class Gift	N	RF	250+	Kline, Suzy	Penguin Group
Herbie Jones and the Dark Attic	N	RF	250+	Kline, Suzy	Puffin Books
Herbie Jones and the Monster Ball	N	RF	250+	Kline, Suzy	Penguin Group
^Hercules	W	I	250+	World Mythology	Capstone Press
*Hercules and Other Greek Legends	T	TL	250+	Wildcats	Wright Group/McGraw Hill
Hercules Doesn't Pull Teeth	M	F	250+	Dadey, Debbie; Jones, Marcia Thornton	Scholastic
Hercules: Superhero	Q	TL	1809	Big Cat	Pacific Learning
#Hercules: The Twelve Labors	W	TL	250+	Edge	Hampton Brown
#Hercules: The Twelve Labors	W	TL	3741	Graphic Myths and Legends	Lerner Publishing Group
Here Are My Hands	H	I	127	Bobber Book	SRA/McGraw Hill
Here Come the Bison!	L	I	212	Sunshine	Wright Group/McGraw Hill
Here Come the Puffins	I	I	260	Classroom Library Set A	Options Publishing Inc.
Here Come the Shapes	E	F	118	PM Plus Story Books	Rigby
Here Comes a Bus	F	F	171	Ziefert, Harriet	Penguin Group
Here Comes a Storm	O	I	1021	Reading Street	Pearson
Here Comes Annette!	E	RF	143	Voyages	SRA/McGraw Hill
Here Comes Everyone	F	RF	78	Cambridge Reading	Pearson Learning Group
Here Comes Jack Frost	J	F	269	Kohara, Kazuno	Roaring Brook Press
Here Comes Kate!	J	RF	250+	Real Reading	Steck-Vaughn
Here Comes Little Chimp	D	F	69	PM Plus Story Books	Rigby
Here Comes McBroom	O	F	250+	Fleischman, Sid	Beech Tree Books
Here Comes the Bus	B	RF	21	Bebop Books	Lee & Low Books Inc.
Here Comes the Bus	D	RF	143	Rigby Flying Colors	Rigby
Here Comes the Cat	LB	RF	24	Asch, Frank	Scholastic
Here Comes the Parade!	B	RF	32	Pair-It Books	Steck-Vaughn
Here Comes the Rain!	C	I	47	Little Books	Sadlier-Oxford
Here Comes the Strikeout	K	RF	250+	Kessler, Leonard	HarperTrophy
Here Comes the Strikeout	I	RF	250+	Little Readers	Houghton Mifflin Harcourt
Here Comes Trouble	N	RF	250+	High-Fliers	Pacific Learning
Here Comes Winter	G	RF	134	First Start	Troll Associates
Here I Am!	B	RF	36	First Stories	Pacific Learning
Here Is . . .	B	I	49	Carousel Earlybirds	Pearson Learning Group

H

* Collection of short stories   # Graphic text
^ Mature content with lower level text demands

TITLE	LEVEL	GENRE	WORD COUNT	AUTHOR / SERIES	PUBLISHER / DISTRIBUTOR
Here Is a Bird	A	RF	24	Sails	Rigby
Here Is a Box	B	I	91	Rigby Literacy	Rigby
Here Is a Carrot	C	I	96	Foundations	Wright Group/McGraw Hill
Here Is a Seed	C	RF	23	Science	Outside the Box
Here Is Hen	A	F	21	Leveled Readers Language Support	Houghton Mifflin Harcourt
Here Is Rosa!	B	RF	20	Brand New Readers	Candlewick Press
Here Is the Butter	D	I	48	Rigby Flying Colors	Rigby
Here Is the Tropical Rain Forest	N	I	250+	Dunphy, Madeleine	Web of Life Children's Books
Here It Is!	B	RF	64	Literacy by Design	Rigby
Here It Is!	B	RF	64	On Our Way to English	Rigby
Here Lies the Librarian	V	RF	250+	Peck, Richard	Puffin Books
*Here There Be Dragons	Y	F	250+	Yolen, Jane	Harcourt Trade
Here There Be Monsters: The Legendary Kraken and the Giant Squid	W	I	250+	Newquist, H. P.	Houghton Mifflin Harcourt
*Here There Be Witches	Y	F	250+	Yolen, Jane	Harcourt Trade
Here We All Are	N	B	250+	DePaola, Tomie	Penguin Group
Here We Go Round the Mulberry Bush	D	TL	187	Little Readers	Houghton Mifflin Harcourt
Here We Go Round the Mulberry Bush	F	TL	208	PM Readalongs	Rigby
Here We Go Round the Mulberry Bush	L	TL	250+	Trapani, Iza	Charlesbridge
Here's a House	C	I	45	Windmill Books	Wright Group/McGraw Hill
Here's Bobby's World! How a TV Cartoon Is	L	I	250+	Little Celebrations	Pearson Learning Group
Here's Looking At Me: How Artists See Themselves	S	I	2768	Raczka, Bob	Millbrook Press
Here's My Home Page	N	RF	250+	InfoTrek	ETA/Cuisenaire
Here's Skipper	B	RF	28	Salem, Lynn; Stewart, Josie	Continental Press
Here's to Hats	L	I	250+	Sunshine	Wright Group/McGraw Hill
Here's to You, Rachel Robinson	T	RF	250+	Blume, Judy	Bantam Books
Here's What I Made	C	RF	38	Literacy 2000	Rigby
Heretic's Daughter, The	Y	HF	250+	Kent, Kathleen	Little Brown and Company
Herman and Marguerite: An Earth Story	N	F	250+	O'Callahan, Jay	Peachtree
Herman Henry's Dog	I	F	250+	Little Readers	Houghton Mifflin Harcourt
Herman the Helper	J	F	94	Kraus, Robert	Simon & Schuster
Herman the Helper Lends a Hand	F	F	198	Kraus, Robert	Windmill
Herman's Tooth	H	F	210	Foundations	Wright Group/McGraw Hill
Hermie the Crab	J	RF	250+	PM Plus Story Books	Rigby
Hermit Crab	E	I	111	PM Story Books	Rigby
Hermit Crab, The	G	RF	119	Sunshine	Wright Group/McGraw Hill
Hermit Crabs	S	I	250+	Keeping Unsual Pets	Heinemann Library
Hero	W	F	250+	Lupica, Mike	Philomel
Hero	Z+	F	250+	Moore, Perry	Hyperion
Hero	X	RF	250+	Rottman, S. L.	Peachtree
Hero Ain't Nothin' but a Sandwich, A	Z+	RF	250+	Childress, Alice	Puffin Books
Hero and the Crown, The	Z	F	250+	McKinley, Robin	Puffin Books
Hero Dad	L	RF	93	Hardin, Melinda	Marshall Cavendish
Hero in the Mirror, The	M	RF	250+	Rigby Literacy	Rigby
Hero of Lesser Causes	W	RF	250+	Johnston, Julie	Tundra Books
#Hero of Little Street, The	WB	F	0	Rogers, Gregory	Roaring Brook Press
Hero of the Poor	W	I	2410	Leveled Readers	Houghton Mifflin Harcourt
Hero of the Poor	W	I	2410	Leveled Readers/CA	Houghton Mifflin Harcourt
Hero of the Poor	W	I	2410	Leveled Readers/TX	Houghton Mifflin Harcourt
Hero of Ticonderoga, The	V	HF	250+	Gauthier, Gail	Scholastic
#Hero Twins, The: Against the Lords of Death	U	TL	2460	Graphic Myths and Legends	Lerner Publishing Group

H

TITLE	LEVEL	GENRE	WORD COUNT	AUTHOR / SERIES	PUBLISHER / DISTRIBUTOR
Hero Weighs In, A	S	SF	1488	Leveled Readers	Houghton Mifflin Harcourt
Hero Weighs In, A	S	SF	1488	Leveled Readers/CA	Houghton Mifflin Harcourt
Hero Weighs In, A	S	SF	1488	Leveled Readers/TX	Houghton Mifflin Harcourt
Hero, The	T	RF	250+	Woods, Ron	Dell
Heroes	N	I	250+	Wildcats	Wright Group/McGraw Hill
Heroes & Idealists	U	B	250+	Real Lives	Troll Associates
Heroes for Civil Rights	S	B	250+	Adler, David A.	Holiday House
Heroes in the Sky	K	I	204	Literacy by Design	Rigby
Heroes of the American Revolution	P	B	626	Reading Street	Pearson
Heroes of the Antarctic	V	I	1994	Leveled Readers	Houghton Mifflin Harcourt
Heroes of the Antarctic	V	I	1994	Leveled Readers/CA	Houghton Mifflin Harcourt
Heroes of the Antarctic	V	I	1994	Leveled Readers/TX	Houghton Mifflin Harcourt
Heroes of the Holocaust	Z	I	250+	The Holocaust	Compass Point Books
*Heroes of the Holocaust: True Stories of Rescues by Teens	Y	I	250+	Zullo, Allan & Bovsun, Mara	Scholastic
Heroes of the Revolution	S	B	250+	Adler, David A.	Holiday House
Heroic Animals	U	I	2926	Reading Street	Pearson
Herons	H	I	106	Wetland Animals	Capstone Press
Heros and Heroines	S	I	250+	Literacy 2000	Rigby
Hero's Guide to Deadly Dragons, A: The Heroic Misadventures of Hiccup the Viking	T	F	250+	Cowell, Cressida	Little Brown and Company
Hexagon	C	I	31	Shapes	Lerner Publishing Group
Hey Coach!	C	RF	37	TOTTS	Tott Publications
Hey Diddle Diddle	D	F	53	Seedlings	Continental Press
Hey Diddle Diddle: A Food Chain Tale	M	F	390	Kapchinske, Pam	Sylvan Dell Publishing
Hey Kid, Want to Buy a Bridge?	P	F	250+	Scieszka, Jon	Penguin Group
Hey There, Bear!	C	F	39	Little Celebrations	Pearson Learning Group
*Hey World, Here I Am!	S	RF	250+	Little, Jean	HarperTrophy
Hey! You're Eating My Homework	H	RF	250+	Bebop Books	Lee & Low Books Inc.
Hey, Al	N	F	250+	Yorinks, Arthur	Farrar, Straus, & Giroux
Hey, Daddy!: Animals Fathers and Their Babies	N	I	250+	Batten, Mary	Peachtree
Hey, Diddle, Diddle!	D	TL	30	Sunshine	Wright Group/McGraw Hill
Hey, Four-Eyes!	K	RF	469	Rigby Flying Colors	Rigby
Hey, New Kid!	N	RF	250+	Duffey, Betsy	Penguin Group
Hi Dog	D	RF	137	Ready Readers	Pearson Learning Group
Hi! Fly Guy	I	F	250+	Arnold, Tedd	Scholastic
Hi, Clouds	D	RF	56	Rookie Readers	Children's Press
Hiawatha, American Leader	M	B	535	Leveled Readers Social Studies	Houghton Mifflin Harcourt
Hibernation	H	I	91	Discovering Nature's Cycles	Lerner Publishing Group
Hibernation	I	I	170	Patterns in Nature	Capstone Press
Hiccup Cake, A	G	RF	97	Dominie Readers	Pearson Learning Group
Hiccupotamus, The	M	F	168	Zenz, Aaron	Marshall Cavendish
Hiccups	I	F	250+	Bookshop	Mondo Publishing
Hiccups for Elephant	I	F	250+	Preller, James	Scholastic
Hiccups for Hippo	I	F	100	Sunshine	Wright Group/McGraw Hill
Hiccups for Rachel	I	RF	250+	Scooters	ETA/Cuisenaire
Hiccups Would Not Stop, The	H	F	177	Ready Readers	Pearson Learning Group
Hickory Dickory Dock	D	F	20	Instant Readers	Harcourt School Publishers
Hickory, Dickory Pizza Clock	C	F	92	Little Celebrations	Pearson Learning Group
Hidden	X	RF	250+	Frost, Helen	Farrar, Straus, & Giroux
Hidden Animals	C	I	32	Gear Up!	Wright Group/McGraw Hill
Hidden Army: Clay Soldiers of Ancient China	Q	I	250+	All Aboard Reading	Grosset & Dunlap
Hidden Cave, The	P	RF	1739	Gear Up!	Wright Group/McGraw Hill
Hidden Flower	T	B	250+	WorldScapes	ETA/Cuisenaire

* Collection of short stories   # Graphic text
^ Mature content with lower level text demands

TITLE	LEVEL	GENRE	WORD COUNT	AUTHOR / SERIES	PUBLISHER / DISTRIBUTOR
Hidden Gallery, The (The Incorrigible Children of Ashton Place)	V	F	250+	Wood, Mayrose	HarperCollins
Hidden Hand, The	M	RF	250+	Woodland Mysteries	Wright Group/McGraw Hill
Hidden Heritage	T	I	250+	WorldScapes	ETA/Cuisenaire
Hidden Hippo	K	F	145	Gannij, Joan & Beaton, Clare	Barefoot Books
Hidden in the Midden	N	I	250+	Books for Young Learners	Richard C. Owen
Hidden Insects	I	I	244	Sails	Rigby
Hidden on the Mountain: Stories of Children Sheltered from the Nazis in Le Chambon	Z	I	250+	DeSaix, Deborah and Ruelle, Karen Gray	Holiday House
Hidden Spiders	I	I	239	Sails	Rigby
Hidden Stairs and the Magic Carpet, The	O	F	250+	Abbott, Tony	Scholastic
Hidden Voices: The Orphan Musicians of Venice	Z+	HF	250+	Collins, Pat Lowery	Candlewick Press
Hidden World	R	I	250+	Explorers	Wright Group/McGraw Hill
Hidden World of Mold, The	U	I	1541	Vocabulary Readers	Houghton Mifflin Harcourt
Hidden World of Mold, The	U	I	1541	Vocabulary Readers/CA	Houghton Mifflin Harcourt
Hidden World of Mold, The	U	I	1541	Vocabulary Readers/TX	Houghton Mifflin Harcourt
Hide & Seek	H	I	138	Wonder World	Wright Group/McGraw Hill
Hide and Seek	K	I	250+	World Quest Adventures	World Quest Learning
Hide and Seek	I	I	337	Avenues	Hampton Brown
Hide and Seek	B	F	19	Avenues	Hampton Brown
Hide and Seek	D	F	63	Brown, Roberta; Carey, Sue	Scholastic
Hide and Seek	H	RF	215	Foundations	Wright Group/McGraw Hill
Hide and Seek	E	F	60	Instant Readers	Harcourt School Publishers
Hide and Seek	J	F	398	Leveled Literacy Intervention/ Blue System	Heinemann
Hide and Seek	B	RF	38	Literacy 2000	Rigby
Hide and Seek	D	RF	98	McAlpin, MaryAnn	Short Tales Press
Hide and Seek	D	RF	49	New Way Red	Steck-Vaughn
Hide and Seek	I	I	250+	Phonics and Friends	Hampton Brown
Hide and Seek	D	RF	108	PM Extensions-Red	Rigby
Hide and Seek	C	F	78	Reed, Janet	Scholastic
Hide and Seek	LB	F	24	Rigby Star	Rigby
Hide and Seek	A+	F	38	Smart Start	Rigby
Hide and Seek	D	RF	49	Start to Read	School Zone
Hide and Seek	H	F	171	Storyworlds	Heinemann
Hide and Seek	E	F	228	Sun Sprouts	ETA/Cuisenaire
Hide and Seek	D	RF	78	The King School Series	Townsend Press
Hide and Seek Buddy	E	F	78	McGougan, Kathy	Buddy Books Publishing
#Hide and Seek Moon: The Moon Phases	M	I	250+	First Graphics	Capstone Press
Hide and Seek With Allie Alligator	G	F	174	Springboard	Wright Group/McGraw Hill
Hide and Seek: Nature's Best Vanishing Acts	T	I	250+	Helman, Andrea	Walker & Company
Hide and Sneak	S	I	250+	Underwater Encounters	Hameray Publishing Group
Hide from Max Monkey	G	F	189	Red Rocket Readers	Flying Start Books
Hide to Survive	L	I	250+	Home Connection Collection	Rigby
Hide!	C	F	81	Sun Sprouts	ETA/Cuisenaire
Hide, Spider!	G	F	179	Momentum Literacy Program	Troll Associates
Hide-and-Go-Seek	C	F	66	First Stories	Pacific Learning
Hide-and-Seek	C	F	30	Brand New Readers	Candlewick Press
Hide-and-Seek	H	F	546	Leveled Readers	Houghton Mifflin Harcourt
Hide-and-Seek	H	F	250+	Momentum Literacy Program	Troll Associates
Hide-and-Seek All Week	I	RF	250+	DePaola, Tomie	Grosset & Dunlap
*Hide-and-Seek with Grandpa	J	F	250+	Lewis, Rob	Mondo Publishing
Hi-De-Hi	E	F	110	Little Celebrations	Pearson Learning Group

TITLE	LEVEL	GENRE	WORD COUNT	AUTHOR / SERIES	PUBLISHER / DISTRIBUTOR
Hide-Out, The	K	RF	250+	The Rowland Reading Program Library	Rowland Reading Foundation
Hiders, The	M	I	250+	Sails	Rigby
Hides-It, The	J	F	250+	Schoder, Judy	Pearson Publishing Group
Hiding	E	I	97	Foundations	Wright Group/McGraw Hill
Hiding	A	F	28	KinderReaders	Rigby
Hiding	B	F	57	Leveled Literacy Intervention/ Orange System	Heinemann
Hiding	B	I	56	Sails	Rigby
Hiding from Bella	D	RF	114	PM Photo Stories	Rigby
Hiding in Deserts	M	I	250+	Creature Camouflage	Heinemann Library
Hiding in Forests	M	I	250+	Creature Camouflage	Heinemann Library
Hiding in Grasslands	M	I	250+	Creature Camouflage	Heinemann Library
Hiding in Mountains	M	I	250+	Creature Camouflage	Heinemann Library
Hiding in Oceans	M	I	250+	Creature Camouflage	Heinemann Library
Hiding in Plain Sight	I	I	173	Instant Readers	Harcourt School Publishers
Hiding in Rain Forests	M	I	250+	Creature Camouflage	Heinemann Library
Hiding in the Polar Regions	M	I	250+	Creature Camouflage	Heinemann Library
Hiding in Wetlands	M	I	250+	Creature Camouflage	Heinemann Library
Hiding Places	J	I	250+	Storyteller-Night Crickets	Wright Group/McGraw Hill
Hiding Toads	K	I	438	Pull Ahead Books	Lerner Publishing Group
^Hieroglyphs	S	I	250+	Ancient Egypt	Capstone Press
High- Altitude Spy Planes: The U-2s	V	I	250+	War Planes	Capstone Press
High and Inside	U	RF	250+	South Side Sports	Orca Books
High and Low: An Animal Opposites Book	J	I	355	Animal Opposites	Capstone Press
High Flying	R	I	250+	Explorers	Wright Group/McGraw Hill
High King, The: The Chronicles of Prydain-Book 5	X	F	250+	Alexander, Lloyd	Henry Holt & Co.
High Life, The	T	I	250+	WorldScapes	ETA/Cuisenaire
High Noon	P	F	250+	Storyteller Chapter Books	Wright Group/McGraw Hill
High Tech	P	I	250+	Trackers	Pacific Learning
High Tide	X	I	2084	Independent Readers Science	Houghton Mifflin Harcourt
High Wire	N	RF	250+	Orbit Double Takes	Pacific Learning
Higher Power of Lucky, The	W	RF	250+	Patron, Susan	Atheneum Books
Highest Tide, The	Z+	RF	250+	Lynch, Jim	Bloomsbury Children's Books
High-Flying Contest, The: An African American Trickster Tale	N	TL	639	Leveled Readers	Houghton Mifflin Harcourt
Highland Cattle, The	J	RF	250+	Storyworlds	Heinemann
Highland Games, The	J	RF	250+	Storyworlds	Heinemann
High-Water Heroes	T	RF	2242	Leveled Readers	Houghton Mifflin Harcourt
Highway Turtles, The	K	RF	250+	PM Plus Story Books	Rigby
High-Wheeler Race, The	O	RF	250+	Windows on Literacy	National Geographic
Hike at Day Camp, The	C	RF	32	Visions	Wright Group/McGraw Hill
Hiking	S	I	250+	The Great Outdoors	Capstone Press
Hiking for Fun!	S	I	250+	Sports for Fun!	Compass Point Books
Hiking in the Wilds	P	I	1894	Take Two Books	Wright Group/McGraw Hill
Hiking the Appalachian Trail	R	I	250+	Explore More	Wright Group/McGraw Hill
Hiking Together	K	RF	250+	On Our Way to English	Rigby
Hiking with Dad	H	RF	189	Wonder World	Wright Group/McGraw Hill
Hilary and the Lions	M	F	250+	Desaix, Frank	Farrar, Straus, & Giroux
Hill of Fire	L	RF	1099	Lewis, Thomas P.	HarperCollins
Hillary Clinton	M	I	298	First Ladies	Capstone Press
Hillary Rodham Clinton	Y	B	250+	A&E Biography	Lerner Publishing Group
Hillary Rodham Clinton: A New Kind of First Lady	S	B	250+	Guernsey, JoAnn Bren	Lerner Publishing Group

* Collection of short stories   # Graphic text
^ Mature content with lower level text demands

TITLE	LEVEL	GENRE	WORD COUNT	AUTHOR / SERIES	PUBLISHER / DISTRIBUTOR
Hindu Holiday	P	I	494	Independent Readers Social Studies	Houghton Mifflin Harcourt
Hinduism	Y	I	250+	World Religions	Compass Point Books
Hip Hop	Z	I	250+	Boldprint	Steck-Vaughn
Hip Hop	LB	F	19	Rigby Star	Rigby
Hip Hop Dancing	S	I	250+	Dance	Capstone Press
Hippo	C	I	31	Zoozoo-Into the Wild	Cavallo Publishing
Hippo from Another Planet	M	F	250+	Little Celebrations	Pearson Learning Group
Hippo in June's Tub, A	H	F	85	Little Books	Sadlier-Oxford
Hippo Lesson	T	RF	8031	Reading Street	Pearson
Hippo Pot and Hippo Tot	G	F	88	Supersonics	Rigby
Hippocrates: Father of Medicine	W	B	250+	Mission: Science	Compass Point Books
Hippocrates: Making the Way for Medicine	T	B	250+	Science Readers	Teacher Created Materials
Hippopotamus Ate the Teacher, A	J	F	250+	Thaler, Mike	Avon Books
Hippopposites	LB	I	34	Coat, Janik	Harry N. Abrams
Hippos	O	I	1595	Early Bird Nature Books	Lerner Publishing Group
Hippos	U	I	5579	Nature Watch Books	Lerner Publishing Group
Hippos	K	I	250+	PM Animal Facts: Turquoise	Rigby
Hippos	H	I	394	Sails	Rigby
Hippos	H	I	117	Story Steps	Rigby
Hippo's Hiccups	G	F	208	Literacy 2000	Rigby
Hiram Fong, Hawaii's First Senator	S	B	1726	Leveled Readers Social Studies	Houghton Mifflin Harcourt
Hiroshima	S	HF	250+	Yep, Laurence	Scholastic
His Majesty the King	J	F	250+	Little Celebrations	Pearson Learning Group
Hispaniola: Island of Two Nations	T	I	1871	Independent Readers Social Studies	Houghton Mifflin Harcourt
Hiss Me Deadly: A Chet Gecko Mystery	R	F	250+	Hale, Bruce	Harcourt, Inc.
Historic Santa Fe Trail, The	V	I	2546	Vocabulary Readers	Houghton Mifflin Harcourt
Historic Santa Fe Trail, The	V	I	2546	Vocabulary Readers/CA	Houghton Mifflin Harcourt
Historic Santa Fe Trail, The	V	I	2546	Vocabulary Readers/TX	Houghton Mifflin Harcourt
History Behind the Holidays	N	I	250+	Early Connections	Benchmark Education
History Nook, The	O	SF	1075	Avenues	Hampton Brown
History Nook, The	O	SF	250+	Phonics and Friends	Hampton Brown
History of Baseball	S	I	1203	Time for Kids	Teacher Created Materials
History of Bread, The	P	I	951	Springboard	Wright Group/McGraw Hill
History of Communication, The	U	I	250+	Major Inventions Through History	Lerner Publishing Group
History of Electricity, A	S	I	794	Leveled Readers Science	Houghton Mifflin Harcourt
History of Energy, The	U	I	250+	Major Inventions Through History	Lerner Publishing Group
History of Everyday Life, The	U	I	250+	Major Inventions Through History	Lerner Publishing Group
History of Firefighting, The	T	I	2304	Leveled Readers	Houghton Mifflin Harcourt
History of Firefighting, The	T	I	2304	Leveled Readers/CA	Houghton Mifflin Harcourt
History of Food, The	U	I	250+	Major Inventions Through History	Lerner Publishing Group
History of Guitars, The	S	I	250+	Literacy by Design	Rigby
History of Guitars, The	S	I	250+	On Our Way to English	Rigby
History of Hip-Hop, A: The Roots of Rap	R	I	250+	High Five Reading	Red Brick Learning
History of Machines, The	O	I	250+	Home Connection Collection	Rigby
History of Medicine, The	U	I	250+	Major Inventions Through History	Lerner Publishing Group
History of Money	S	I	250+	Time for Kids	Teacher Created Materials
History of Money, The	N	I	515	Gear Up!	Wright Group/McGraw Hill
History of Photography	K	I	353	Red Rocket Readers	Flying Start Books

H

TITLE	LEVEL	GENRE	WORD COUNT	AUTHOR / SERIES	PUBLISHER / DISTRIBUTOR
History of Pirates, The: From Privateers to Outlaws	T	I	250+	The Real World of Pirates	Capstone Press
History of School	R	I	1249	Time for Kids	Teacher Created Materials
History of the Blues, The	S	I	250+	Rosen Real Readers	Rosen Publishing Group
History of the Flu, A	R	I	250+	High-Fliers	Pacific Learning
History of the Fur Trade	V	I	2295	Leveled Readers	Houghton Mifflin Harcourt
History of the Fur Trade	V	I	2295	Leveled Readers/CA	Houghton Mifflin Harcourt
History of the Fur Trade	V	I	2200	Leveled Readers/TX	Houghton Mifflin Harcourt
History of Transportation, The	U	I	250+	Major Inventions Through History	Lerner Publishing Group
History of Weapons, The	V	I	250+	Major Inventions Through History	Lerner Publishing Group
History Walk	M	RF	250+	Pacific Literacy	Pacific Learning
Hit and Run	Z	RF	250+	Misfits Inc.	Peachtree
Hit by a Blade	K	RF	250+	Foundations	Wright Group/McGraw Hill
#Hit It!	S	RF	3445	Hardcastle, Michael	Stone Arch Books
^Hit Squad	Z+	RF	250+	Orca Soundings	Orca Books
Hit the Beach	N	RF	250+	Boyz Rule!	Mondo Publishing
Hit-Away Kid, The	M	RF	250+	Christopher, Matt	Little Brown and Company
Hitler Youth: Growing up in Hitler's Shadow	Z	I	250+	Bartoletti, Susan Cambell	Scholastic
Hitler's Daughter	W	RF	250+	French, Jackie	Scholastic
^Hitmen Triumph	V	RF	250+	Orca Sports	Orca Books
Hitty: Her First Hundred Years	U	F	250+	Field, Rachel	Aladdin
Hive Detectives, The	W	I	250+	Scientists in the Field	Houghton Mifflin Harcourt
Hiyomi and the Moon Men	S	HF	250+	Orbit Chapter Books	Pacific Learning
HMMWV Humvee, The	U	I	250+	Cross-Sections	Capstone Press
*Ho Yi the Archer and Other Classic Chinese Tales	X	TL	250+	Fu, Shelley	Linnet Books
Ho, Ho, Benjamin, Feliz Navidad	N	RF	250+	Giff, Patricia Reilly	Bantam Books
Hoang Anh: A Vietnamese-American Boy	T	B	250+	Hoyt-Goldsmith, Diane	Scholastic
Hoaxes	Z	I	6559	The Unexplained	Lerner Publishing Group
Hobbit, The	Z	F	250+	Tolkien, J.R.R.	Ballantine Books
Hobby: The Young Merlin Trilogy	V	F	250+	Yolen, Jane	Scholastic
Hobnob the Troll	H	F	165	Supersonics	Rigby
Hobson Family Vacation, The	H	RF	250+	Momentum Literacy Program	Troll Associates
Hockey for Fun!	S	I	250+	Sports for Fun	Compass Point Books
Hockey Machine, The	S	RF	250+	Christopher, Matt	Norwood House Press
Hockey Practice	G	RF	134	Geddes, Diana	Kaeden Books
Hocus Focus	L	RF	250+	Science Solves It!	Kane Press
Hocus Pocus	M	I	250+	Wildcats	Wright Group/McGraw Hill
Hocus-Pocus Hound	M	F	250+	I Am Reading	Kingfisher
Hofus the Stonecutter	N	TL	250+	Literacy by Design	Rigby
Hogboggit, The	D	RF	65	Pacific Literacy	Pacific Learning
Hoggee	T	RF	250+	Myers, Anna	Walker & Company
Hoiho's Chicks	D	I	38	Pacific Literacy	Pacific Learning
Hoketichee and the Manatee	I	RF	113	Books for Young Learners	Richard C. Owen
Hold on Tight!	B	I	60	Sails	Rigby
Holdup	Z	RF	250+	Fields, Terri	Square Fish
Hole in Harry's Pocket, The	I	RF	250+	Little Readers	Houghton Mifflin Harcourt
Hole in My Life	Z+	B	250+	Edge	Hampton Brown
Hole in the Garden, The	G	RF	277	Sails	Rigby
Hole in the Hedge, The	F	F	188	Sunshine	Wright Group/McGraw Hill
Hole in the Hill, The	N	RF	250+	Action Packs	Rigby
Hole in the Tub, The	F	F	174	The Story Basket	Wright Group/McGraw Hill

* Collection of short stories   # Graphic text
^ Mature content with lower level text demands

TITLE	LEVEL	GENRE	WORD COUNT	AUTHOR / SERIES	PUBLISHER / DISTRIBUTOR
Hole Is a Great Home, A	F	RF	236	Avenues	Hampton Brown
Hole Is A Great Home, A	F	RF	236	Phonics and Friends	Hampton Brown
Hole, The	A	F	24	Sails	Rigby
Holes	V	RF	250+	Sachar, Louis	Random House
Holiday Howlers: Jokes for Punny Parties!	O	F	1701	Make Me Laugh!	Lerner Publishing Group
Holiday!: Celebration Days Around the World	L	I	250+	DK Readers	DK Publishing
Holidays	G	I	98	Leveled Readers Language Support	Houghton Mifflin Harcourt
Holidays	I	I	195	Time for Kids	Teacher Created Materials
Holidays	C	I	23	We Are Alike and Different	Lerner Publishing Group
Holidays	J	I	191	Windows on Literacy	National Geographic
Holidays Around the World	O	I	250+	Navigators Social Studies Series	Benchmark Education
Holidays at Our Home	I	RF	88	Leveled Readers Social Studies	Houghton Mifflin Harcourt
Hollow Log, The	J	RF	361	Leveled Readers	Houghton Mifflin Harcourt
Hollow Log, The	J	RF	361	Leveled Readers/CA	Houghton Mifflin Harcourt
Holly & Mac	N	RF	250+	Supa Doopers	Sundance
Holly the Christmas Fairy: Rainbow Magic	L	F	250+	Meadows, Daisy	Scholastic
Holly's Surprise	C	RF	50	Adams, Lorraine & Bruvold, Lynn	Eaglecrest Books
Hollywood Royalty	Z+	RF	250+	Dean, Zoey	Little Brown and Company
Hollywood Special Effects	V	I	2667	Reading Street	Pearson
Holocaust Rescuers	Y	I	1941	Reading Street	Pearson
Holy Enchilada!	R	RF	250+	Winkler, Henry and Oliver, Lin	Grosset & Dunlap
Holy Guacamole and Other Scrumptious Snacks	R	I	250+	Kids Dish	Picture Window Books
Home	J	I	143	Shelley Rotner's Early Childhood Library	Millbrook Press
Home	L	F	250+	Smith, Alex T.	Tiger Tales
Home	M	RF	250+	Voyages	SRA/McGraw Hill
Home Alone	E	F	70	Potato Chip Books	American Reading Company
Home and School	B	I	48	Leveled Readers Social Studies	Houghton Mifflin Harcourt
Home at Last	D	F	94	Sun Sprouts	ETA/Cuisenaire
Home at Mount Vernon, A	W	I	2941	Leveled Readers	Houghton Mifflin Harcourt
Home at Mount Vernon, A	W	I	2941	Leveled Readers/CA	Houghton Mifflin Harcourt
Home at Mount Vernon, A	W	I	2941	Leveled Readers/TX	Houghton Mifflin Harcourt
Home Crafts	T	I	250+	Historic Communities	Crabtree
Home for a Dog, A	G	RF	146	Book Bus	Creative Edge
Home for a Puppy	G	RF	194	First Start	Troll Associates
Home for Curly, A	A	F	30	Rigby Star	Rigby
Home for Diggory, A	K	RF	250+	Pacific Literacy	Pacific Learning
Home for Flap the Cat, A	E	RF	100	Reading Street	Pearson
Home for Humans in Outer Space, A: Is It Possible?	U	I	1989	Reading Street	Pearson
Home for Little Teddy, A	D	F	153	PM Extensions-Red	Rigby
Home for Mindy, A	H	I	250+	Rigby Literacy	Rigby
Home for Star and Patches, A	J	RF	250+	PM Plus Story Books	Rigby
Home for the Howl-idays	S	F	250+	Regan, Dian Curtis	Scholastic
Home Front During World War II, The	W	I	250+	Reading Expeditions	National Geographic
Home Green Home	U	I	250+	Literacy by Design	Rigby
Home in the Sky	K	RF	250+	Baker, Jeannie	Scholastic
Home in the Wilderness, A	O	HF	948	Reading Street	Pearson
Home Invaders	P	I	250+	Trackers	Pacific Learning
^Home Invasion	Z+	RF	250+	Orca Soundings	Orca Books
Home Is Beyond the Mountains	U	HF	250+	Lottridge, Celia Barker	Groundwood Books
Home of the Brave	W	RF	250+	Applegate, Katherine	Feiwel and Friends

H

TITLE	LEVEL	GENRE	WORD COUNT	AUTHOR / SERIES	PUBLISHER / DISTRIBUTOR
Home of the Brave	R	I	958	Reading Street	Pearson
Home of the Braves	Z+	RF	250+	Klass, David	HarperCollins
Home on the Earth: A Song About Earth's Layers	M	I	250+	Science Songs	Picture Window Books
Home on the Range	P	I	851	Reading Street	Pearson
Home on the Range: Down Girl and Sit	M	F	250+	Nolan, Lucy	Marshall Cavendish
Home Run!	B	RF	42	Peters, Catherine	Scholastic
Home Run, The	E	RF	92	Teacher's Choice Series	Pearson Learning Group
Home Safety	F	I	44	Safety	Lerner Publishing Group
Home Sweet Home	K	RF	250+	HSP/Harcourt Trophies	Harcourt, Inc.
Home Sweet Home	G	F	299	Leveled Literacy Intervention/ Green System	Heinemann
Home Sweet Home	N	I	250+	Literacy 2000	Rigby
Home Sweet Home	T	RF	250+	Reading Expeditions	National Geographic
Home Sweet Home	I	F	250+	Rigby Rocket	Rigby
Home Sweet Home	E	I	172	Roffey, Maureen	Bodley
Home Sweet Home	M	F	250+	Use Your Imagination	Steck-Vaughn
Home Sweet Home, Goodbye	R	RF	250+	Stowe, Cynthia	Scholastic
Home Team	R	RF	250+	Orca Young Readers	Orca Books
Home Technology	O	I	250+	Bookweb	Rigby
Home Then and Now	I	I	110	Then and Now	Lerner Publishing Group
Home Windmills	U	I	6490	A Great Idea	Norwood House Press
Home, A	D	I	40	Instant Readers	Harcourt School Publishers
Home, A	LB	F	12	Sails	Rigby
Home: A Journey Through America	R	I	250+	Locker, Thomas	Voyager Books
Home-Alone Kids	S	I	250+	Rigby Literacy	Rigby
Homeboyz	Z+	RF	250+	Sitomer, Alan Lawrence	Hyperion
Homecoming	X	RF	250+	Voigt, Cynthia	Ballantine Books
Homegirl on the Range (Sister Sister)	S	RF	250+	Quin-Harkin, Janet	Pocket Books
Homeless Bird	X	RF	250+	Whelan, Gloria	HarperCollins
*Homer Price	Q	RF	250+	McCloskey, Robert	Puffin Books
Home-Run King, The	O	B	856	Leveled Readers	Houghton Mifflin Harcourt
Home-Run King, The	O	B	856	Leveled Readers/CA	Houghton Mifflin Harcourt
Home-Run King, The	O	B	856	Leveled Readers/TX	Houghton Mifflin Harcourt
Homes	D	I	42	Avenues	Hampton Brown
Homes	C	I	34	Basic Human Needs	Lerner Publishing Group
Homes	B	I	63	Bookshop	Mondo Publishing
Homes	A	I	35	Handprints A	Educators Publishing Service
Homes	C	I	90	Leveled Literacy Intervention/ Green System	Heinemann
Homes	D	I	42	Rise & Shine	Hampton Brown
Homes	C	I	69	Storyteller Nonfiction	Wright Group/McGraw Hill
Homes	I	I	244	Yellow Umbrella Books	Red Brick Learning
Homes Are for Living	M	I	417	Cumpiano, Ina	Hampton Brown
Homes Around the World	C	I	73	Early Connections	Benchmark Education
Homes Around the World	D	I	192	iOpeners	Pearson Learning Group
Homes Around the World	I	I	192	Rigby Focus	Rigby
Homes Around the World	J	I	294	Time for Kids	Teacher Created Materials
Homes for Birds	A	I	36	Bonnell, Kris/About	Reading Reading Books
Homes for People	B	I	40	Early Connections	Benchmark Education
Homes in Many Cultures	I	I	98	Life Around the World	Capstone Press
Homes on Wheels	M	I	788	Rigby Flying Colors	Rigby
Homes That Move	L	I	250+	The Big Picture	Capstone Press

* Collection of short stories   # Graphic text
^ Mature content with lower level text demands

TITLE	LEVEL	GENRE	WORD COUNT	AUTHOR / SERIES	PUBLISHER / DISTRIBUTOR
Homes Through Time	N	I	755	Rigby Flying Colors	Rigby
Homes: From Caves to Eco-Pods	U	I	250+	Timeline History	Heinemann Library
Homesick, My Own Story	X	B	250+	Fritz, Jean	Penguin Group
Homesteaders in Nebraska	T	HF	4356	Reading Street	Pearson
Homesteading Community of the 1880s, A	T	I	250+	Reading Expeditions	National Geographic
Hometown Turtles	P	RF	1175	Leveled Readers	Houghton Mifflin Harcourt
Homework	F	RF	57	City Stories	Rigby
Homework	E	RF	154	Emergent Set 4	Pioneer Valley
Homework	M	F	250+	Yorinks, Arthur	Walker & Company
Homework Machine, The	R	RF	250+	Gutman, Dan	Aladdin Paperbacks
Hondo & Fabian	J	RF	146	McCarty, Peter	Square Fish
Honest Ashley	L	RF	250+	The Way I Act	Albert Whitman & Co.
Honestly, Mallory!	O	RF	16726	Friedman, Laurie	Carolrhoda Books
Honest-to-Goodness Truth, The	O	RF	250+	McKissack, Fredrick & Patricia	Aladdin Paperbacks
Honesty	L	I	250+	Character Education	Red Brick Learning
Honesty	L	I	250+	Everyday Character Education	Capstone Press
Honey Bees	D	I	61	Honeybees	Capstone Press
Honey Bees	M	I	250+	Kahkonen, Sharon	Steck-Vaughn
Honey Bees and Flowers	G	I	67	Honeybees	Capstone Press
Honey Bees and Hives	E	I	58	Honeybees	Capstone Press
Honey Bees and Honey	F	I	57	Honeybees	Capstone Press
Honey for Baby Bear	F	F	200	PM Story Books	Rigby
Honey for Wolf	I	F	246	Sun Sprouts	ETA/Cuisenaire
Honey Hunt	E	RF	63	Sunshine	Wright Group/McGraw Hill
Honey Tree, The	L	TL	250+	Literacy 2000	Rigby
Honey, Honey	E	F	53	Sails	Rigby
Honey, My Rabbit	E	RF	56	Voyages	SRA/McGraw Hill
Honey: A Gift From Nature	N	I	250+	Fujiwara, Yumiko	Kane/Miller Book Publishers
HoneyàHoneyàLion!: A Story from Africa	M	F	250+	Brett, Jan	G.P. Putnam's Sons
Honeybees	L	I	379	Leveled Readers	Houghton Mifflin Harcourt
Honeybees	L	I	379	Leveled Readers/CA	Houghton Mifflin Harcourt
Honeybees	L	I	379	Leveled Readers/TX	Houghton Mifflin Harcourt
Honeybees Help Flowers	J	I	286	Early Explorers	Benchmark Education
Honk!	B	F	36	Bookshop	Mondo Publishing
Honk, Honk, Goose!: Canada Geese Start a Family	L	RF	250+	Sayre, April Pulley	Henry Holt & Co.
Honolulu, Hawaii	Q	I	250+	Theme Sets	National Geographic
Honorable Prison, The	W	HF	250+	Becerra de Jenkins, Lyll	Penguin Group
*Honoring Our Ancestors: Stories and Pictures by Fourteen Artists	T	B	250+	Rohmer, Harriet	Children's Book Press
Honus & Me	T	F	250+	Gutman, Dan	HarperTrophy
Hooey Higgins and the Shark	N	RF	250+	Voake, Steve	Candlewick Press
Hoofprints	D	RF	62	Teacher's Choice Series	Pearson Learning Group
Hook	K	RF	91	Young, Ed	Roaring Brook Press
Hoop Crazy	S	RF	250+	Orca Young Readers	Orca Books
Hoop Dancers	L	I	702	Avenues	Hampton Brown
Hoop Dancers	L	I	250+	Phonics and Friends	Hampton Brown
Hoop Dreams: A True Story	Z+	B	250+	Edge	Hampton Brown
Hoops	U	I	250+	Boldprint	Steck-Vaughn
Hoops	X	RF	250+	Myers, Walter Dean	Bantam Books
Hoops and Me	K	RF	929	Books for Young Learners	Richard C. Owen
Hoops with Swoopes	J	I	87	Avenues	Hampton Brown
Hoops!	L	RF	250+	On Our Way to English	Rigby
Hoopstars: Go to the Hoop!	M	RF	250+	Hughes, Dean	Random House

H

TITLE	LEVEL	GENRE	WORD COUNT	AUTHOR / SERIES	PUBLISHER / DISTRIBUTOR
Hooray for Hollywood	U	I	1725	Vocabulary Readers	Houghton Mifflin Harcourt
Hooray for Hollywood	U	I	1725	Vocabulary Readers/CA	Houghton Mifflin Harcourt
Hooray for Midsommar!	J	RF	250+	Greetings	Rigby
Hooray for Snail	F	F	102	Stadler, John	HarperCollins
Hooray for Snow	D	RF	15	Voyages	SRA/McGraw Hill
Hooray for the Golly Sisters!	K	RF	250+	Byars, Betsy	HarperTrophy
Hooray! 100 Days	G	I	184	Early Explorers	Benchmark Education
Hoot	W	RF	250+	Hiaasen, Carl	Alfred A. Knopf
Hoover Dam	N	I	934	Pair-It Turn and Learn	Steck-Vaughn
Hoover Dam, The	N	I	531	Lightning Bolt Books	Lerner Publishing Group
Hop and Stop	C	RF	35	Books for Young Learners	Richard C. Owen
Hop In!	D	F	23	Small-Gamby, Julie	Scholastic
Hop Jump	I	F	132	Walsh, Ellen Stoll	Houghton Mifflin Harcourt
Hop on Pop	J	F	250+	Seuss, Dr.	Random House
Hop on Top!	C	F	42	Reading Street	Pearson
Hop to It, Minty!	O	RF	250+	PM Collection	Rigby
Hop! Spring! Leap! Animals That Jump	H	I	150	Bayrock, Fiona	Scholastic
Hop, Hop, Hop	B	F	51	Leveled Literacy Intervention/ Orange System	Heinemann
Hop, Skip, and Jump	A	RF	22	Cherrington, Janelle	Scholastic
Hop, Skip, Run	E	RF	109	Real Kids Readers	Millbrook Press
Hop: The Chapter Book	N	F	250+	Paul, Cinco & Daurio, Ken	Little Brown and Company
Hope Not	D	RF	83	Salem, Lynn; Stewart, Josie	Continental Press
Hope Was Here	W	RF	250+	Bauer, Joan	G.P. Putnam's Sons
Hopes and Dreams: A Story from Northern Thailand	S	RF	250+	Reading Expeditions	National Geographic
Hopeville Book of Records, The	L	RF	250+	Rigby Gigglers	Rigby
Hopi, The	P	I	250+	Native Peoples	Red Brick Learning
Hopi, The	S	I	250+	The Heinle Reading Library	Thomson Learning
Hopper	L	F	250+	Pfister, Marcus	Scholastic
Hopper Grass	Z+	HF	250+	Brown, Chris Carlton	Henry Holt & Co.
Hopping Henry	O	F	1216	Leveled Readers	Houghton Mifflin Harcourt
Hopping Henry	O	F	1216	Leveled Readers/CA	Houghton Mifflin Harcourt
Hopping Henry	O	F	1216	Leveled Readers/TX	Houghton Mifflin Harcourt
Hopping Up and Down	C	F	31	Brand New Readers	Candlewick Press
Hoppity Hop	B	F	51	Red Rocket Readers	Flying Start Books
Hopscotch	P	I	250+	Games Around the World	Compass Point Books
Hopscotch	D	F	61	Reading Street	Pearson
Horace	D	F	56	Story Box	Wright Group/McGraw Hill
Horace's Home Helpers	K	RF	250+	Windows on Literacy	National Geographic
Horacio's Hiccups	G	RF	205	In Step Readers	Rigby
Horatio Whale	J	F	165	Book Bus	Creative Edge
Horned Dinosaurs	P	I	967	Meet the Dinosaurs	Lerner Publishing Group
Horned Lizards	K	I	171	Reptiles	Capstone Press
Horned Toad Prince, The	P	TL	250+	Hopkins, Jackie Mims	Peachtree
Hornets: Incredible Insect Architects	T	I	3366	Insect World	Lerner Publishing Group
Horns	I	I	157	Animal Spikes and Spines	Heinemann Library
Horns	C	I	102	Sails	Rigby
Horns, Scales, Claws, and Tales	I	I	208	Story Steps	Rigby
*Horrakapotchkin	M	F	250+	Pacific Literacy	Pacific Learning
Horrible Big Black Bug, The	D	RF	50	Tadpoles	Rigby
Horrible Harry and the Ant Invasion	L	RF	250+	Kline, Suzy	Scholastic
Horrible Harry and the Christmas Surprise	L	RF	250+	Kline, Suzy	Scholastic
Horrible Harry and the Drop of Doom	L	RF	250+	Kline, Suzy	Puffin Books

* Collection of short stories   # Graphic text
^ Mature content with lower level text demands

TITLE	LEVEL	GENRE	WORD COUNT	AUTHOR / SERIES	PUBLISHER / DISTRIBUTOR
Horrible Harry and the Dungeon	L	RF	250+	Kline, Suzy	Penguin Group
Horrible Harry and the Green Slime	L	RF	250+	Kline, Suzy	Penguin Group
Horrible Harry and the Kickball Wedding	L	RF	250+	Kline, Suzy	Penguin Group
Horrible Harry and the Purple People	L	F	250+	Kline, Suzy	Puffin Books
Horrible Harry in Room 2B	L	RF	250+	Kline, Suzy	Penguin Group
Horrible Harry Moves Up to Third Grade	L	RF	250+	Kline, Suzy	Puffin Books
Horrible Harry's Secret	L	RF	250+	Kline, Suzy	Penguin Group
Horrible Thing with Hairy Feet	H	TL	208	Read Alongs	Rigby
Horrible Urktar of Or, The	G	F	143	Sunshine	Wright Group/McGraw Hill
*Horrid Henry	N	RF	5200	Simon, Francesca	Sourcebooks
*Horrid Henry and the Abominable Snowman	N	RF	5200	Simon, Francesca	Sourcebooks
*Horrid Henry and the Mega-Mean Time Machine	N	RF	7500	Simon, Francesca	Sourcebooks
*Horrid Henry and the Mummy's Curse	N	RF	250+	Simon, Francesca	Sourcebooks
*Horrid Henry and the Soccer Fiend	N	RF	250+	Simon, Francesca	Sourcebooks
*Horrid Henry Tricks the Tooth Fairy	N	RF	7300	Simon, Francesca	Sourcebooks
*Horrid Henry's Evil Enemies	N	RF	5200	Simon, Francesca	Sourcebooks
*Horrid Henry's Stink Bomb	N	RF	6200	Simon, Francesca	Sourcebooks
*Horrid Henry's Wicked Ways	N	RF	5200	Simon, Francesca	Sourcebooks
Horrie the Hoarder	K	RF	250+	Voyages	SRA/McGraw Hill
#Horror in Space	U	F	250+	Twisted Journeys	Graphic Universe
Horrors of the Haunted Museum	Q	RF	250+	Stine, R. L.	Scholastic
Horse	W	I	250+	Eyewitness Books	DK Publishing
Horse	M	I	250+	Life Cycles	Creative Teaching Press
Horse	B	I	30	Zoozoo-Animal World	Cavallo Publishing
Horse and His Boy, The	T	F	250+	Lewis, C. S.	Collier Books
Horse and the Bell, The	J	TL	250+	PM Plus Story Books	Rigby
*Horse and the Donkey, The	I	F	382	New Way Green	Steck-Vaughn
Horse Called Sky, A	M	RF	250+	Leveled Readers Language Support	Houghton Mifflin Harcourt
Horse Can, A	A	I	24	Bonnell, Kris/About	Reading Reading Books
Horse Feathers	D	I	41	Pair-It Books	Steck-Vaughn
Horse Happy: A Brisa Story	N	F	250+	Wind Dancers	Feiwel and Friends
*Horse Heroes: True Stories of Amazing Horses	S	I	250+	DK Readers	DK Publishing
Horse in Harry's Room, The	J	F	425	Hoff, Syd	HarperCollins
Horse in the House, A	Q	I	250+	Ablow, Gail	Candlewick Press
Horse Must Go On, The!: A Sumatra Story	N	F	250+	Wind Dancers	Feiwel and Friends
Horse of Her Own, A	W	RF	250+	Wedekind, Annie	Square Fish
Horse on the Hill, The: A Story of Ancient India	O	HF	250+	Historical Tales	Picture Window Books
^Horse Power	S	RF	250+	Orca Currents	Orca Books
Horse Power	O	I	250+	Pacific Literacy	Pacific Learning
Horse Rescue!	K	I	344	Reading Street	Pearson
Horse Show	L	I	250+	Hayden, Kate/DK Readers	DK Publishing
Horse, of Course!, A	N	F	250+	Wind Dancers	Feiwel and Friends
Horse, of Course, The	Q	I	250+	Action Packs	Rigby
Horseback Riding for Fun!	S	I	250+	Activities for Fun	Compass Point Books
Horsepower	Q	I	250+	InfoQuest	Rigby
Horses	N	I	250+	A New True Book	Children's Press
Horses	D	I	43	All About Pets	Red Brick Learning
Horses	R	I	250+	Boldprint	Steck-Vaughn
Horses	P	I	250+	Crabapples	Crabtree
Horses	O	I	2279	Early Bird Nature Books	Lerner Publishing Group
Horses	G	I	92	Farm Animals	Lerner Publishing Group
Horses	E	I	104	Nonfiction Set 4	Literacy Footprints

TITLE	LEVEL	GENRE	WORD COUNT	AUTHOR / SERIES	PUBLISHER / DISTRIBUTOR
Horses	E	I	131	Pebble Books	Capstone Press
Horses	L	I	250+	PM Animal Facts: Purple	Rigby
Horses	K	I	417	Springboard	Wright Group/McGraw Hill
Horses	L	I	438	Time for Kids	Teacher Created Materials
Horses	F	I	131	Twig	Wright Group/McGraw Hill
Horses as Pets	D	I	57	Bonnell, Kris/About	Reading Reading Books
Horses Have Foals	M	I	250+	Animals and Their Young	Compass Point Books
Horses Her Way	N	F	250+	Wind Dancers	Feiwel and Friends
Horse's Hiccups	F	F	83	Storyteller-Moon Rising	Wright Group/McGraw Hill
Horses' Holiday	J	F	302	Big Cat	Pacific Learning
Horses in North America	R	I	1007	Vocabulary Readers	Houghton Mifflin Harcourt
Horses in North America	R	I	1007	Vocabulary Readers/CA	Houghton Mifflin Harcourt
Horses in North America	R	I	1007	Vocabulary Readers/TX	Houghton Mifflin Harcourt
Horses' Night Out: A Sirocco Story	N	F	250+	Wind Dancers	Feiwel and Friends
Horses of the Air	N	I	250+	Little Celebrations	Pearson Learning Group
Horses of the Sea	P	I	250+	Lighthouse	Ginn & Co.
Horses of the Sea	P	I	250+	Rigby Literacy	Rigby
Horses on the Farm	I	I	120	Pebble Books	Red Brick Learning
Horses You Can Draw	R	I	1511	Ready, Set, Draw!	Millbrook Press
Horseshoe Crabs and Shorebirds: The Story of the Food Web	S	I	250+	Crenson, Victoria	Marshall Cavendish
Horsing Around	N	RF	250+	Girlz Rock!	Mondo Publishing
Horsing Around	S	I	250+	WorldScapes	ETA/Cuisenaire
Horsing Around: Jokes to Make Ewe Smile	O	F	1667	Make Me Laugh!	Lerner Publishing Group
Horton Halfpott: or The Fiendish Mystery of Smugwick Manor or The Loosening of M'Lady Luggertuck's Corset	V	HF	2501	Angleberger, Tom	Amulet Books
Hospital Party, The	H	RF	237	PM Plus Story Books	Rigby
Hospitals	L	I	177	Bookshop	Mondo Publishing
Hostile Hospital, The	V	F	250+	Snicket, Lemony	Scholastic
Hosting Grandpa Joseph	O	RF	1424	Reading Street	Pearson
#Hot Air	Q	RF	1993	Masters, Anthony	Stone Arch Books
Hot Air Balloons	E	I	95	Bonnell, Kris/About	Reading Reading Books
Hot Air Balloons	L	I	479	Pair-It Books	Steck-Vaughn
Hot and Cold	F	I	219	Sails	Rigby
Hot and Cold	C	I	47	Windows on Literacy	National Geographic
Hot and Cold Summer	O	RF	250+	Hurwitz, Johanna	Scholastic
Hot and Cold Weather	K	I	922	Sunshine	Wright Group/McGraw Hill
Hot Chocolate for Sale	H	F	242	Gear Up!	Wright Group/McGraw Hill
Hot Competition	R	RF	250+	Story Surfers	ETA/Cuisenaire
Hot Day at the Farm	H	F	321	Springboard	Wright Group/McGraw Hill
Hot Day, A	C	RF	86	Handprints B	Educators Publishing Service
Hot Day, A	E	I	61	Pebble Books	Capstone Press
Hot Day, The	N	RF	647	Leveled Literacy Intervention/Blue System	Heinemann
Hot Desert Sun, The	C	F	60	Bonnell, Kris	Reading Reading Books
Hot Dogs	I	RF	196	City Kids	Rigby
Hot Dogs (Sausages)	C	RF	84	PM Story Books	Rigby
Hot Fudge Hero	L	RF	250+	Brisson, Pat	Henry Holt & Co.
Hot Hand	S	RF	250+	Lupica, Mike	Puffin Books
^Hot Iron: The Adventure of a Civil War Powder Boy	T	HF	250+	Burgan, Michael	Stone Arch Books
Hot Moose Stew	H	RF	251	Adams, Lorraine & Bruvold, Lynn	Eaglecrest Books
Hot or Cold?	F	I	106	Yellow Umbrella Books	Red Brick Learning

* Collection of short stories   # Graphic text
^ Mature content with lower level text demands

TITLE	LEVEL	GENRE	WORD COUNT	AUTHOR / SERIES	PUBLISHER / DISTRIBUTOR
Hot Potato and Cold Potato	C	I	77	Foundations	Wright Group/McGraw Hill
Hot Rod Harry	E	RF	66	Rookie Readers	Children's Press
Hot Rods	D	I	72	Bonnell, Kris/About	Reading Reading Books
Hot Rods	M	I	250+	Horsepower	Capstone Press
Hot Rods	W	I	6714	Motor Mania	Lerner Publishing Group
^Hot Rods	N	I	199	Rev It Up!	Capstone Press
Hot Sidewalks	C	RF	28	Visions	Wright Group/McGraw Hill
Hot Stuff to Help Kids Cheer Up: The Depression and Self-Esteem Workbook	X	I	13200	Wilde, Ph.D., Jerry	Sourcebooks
Hot Sunny Days	F	I	122	PM Plus Nonfiction	Rigby
Hot Surprise, A	H	RF	162	Rigby Literacy	Rigby
Hot-Air Balloon Day	F	I	115	Springboard	Wright Group/McGraw Hill
Hottest Week in Sun City, The	I	F	250+	Reading Safari	Mondo Publishing
Houdini Box, The	S	HF	250+	Selznick, Brian	Aladdin
#Houdini: The Handcuff King	V	HF	250+	Lutes, Jason	Hyperion
#Houdini: The Life of the Great Escape Artist	T	B	250+	Graphic Library	Capstone Press
Houdini: World's Greatest Mystery Man and Escape King	S	B	250+	Krull, Kathleen	Walker & Company
Houdini's Last Trick	O	B	250+	Hass, Elizabeth	Random House
Hound Dog True	R	F	250+	Urban, Linda	Harcourt, Inc.
Hound from the Pound, The	P	RF	250+	Swaim, Jessica	Candlewick Press
Hound of Rowan, The: The Tapestry Book I	X	F	250+	Neff, Henry H.	Random House
#Hound of the Baskervilles, The	U	HF	250+	Doyle, Sir Arthur Conan	Stone Arch Books
Houndsley and Catina	K	F	250+	Howe, James	Candlewick Press
Houndsley and Catina and the Birthday Surprise	K	F	250+	Howe, James	Candlewick Press
Houndsley and Catina and the Quiet Time	K	F	250+	Howe, James	Candlewick Press
Houndsley and Catina Plink and Plunk	K	F	250+	Howe, James	Candlewick Press
Hour of the Olympics	M	F	250+	Osborne, Mary Pope	Random House
Hours, Minutes, and Seconds	H	I	171	Measuring Time	Heinemann Library
House	WB	I	0	Felix, Monique	Stewart, Tabori & Chang
House	C	I	47	Little Celebrations	Pearson Learning Group
House Book, The	LB	I	17	Windows on Literacy	National Geographic
House Called Awful End, A	U	F	250+	Ardagh, Philip	Scholastic
House Cleaning	LB	RF	19	Book Bank	Wright Group/McGraw Hill
House for a Mouse, A	E	F	182	On Our Way to English	Rigby
House for a Mouse, A	LB	RF	21	Pacific Literacy	Pacific Learning
House for a Mouse, A	E	F	124	Sails	Rigby
House for Hickory, A	H	F	174	Bookshop	Mondo Publishing
House for Little Red	F	RF	78	Just Beginning	Pearson Learning Group
House for Little Red, A	E	RF	283	Easy Stories	Norwood House Press
House for Me, A	E	F	134	Kaleidoscope Collection	Hameray Publishing Group
House for Me, A	C	I	71	Twig	Wright Group/McGraw Hill
House for My Fish, A	D	RF	34	Reading Street	Pearson
House for Sergin, A	M	RF	250+	Greetings	Rigby
House for Squirrel, A	C	F	55	Bonnell, Kris	Reading Reading Books
House for the Alien, A	C	F	158	Sails	Rigby
House Gobbaleen, The	P	F	250+	Alexander, Lloyd	Penguin Group
House Hunting	G	RF	223	PM Story Books	Rigby
House in the Snow, The	S	RF	250+	Engh, M. J.	Scholastic
House in the Tree, The	F	RF	202	PM Story Books	Rigby
House of Dies Drear, The	V	HF	250+	Hamilton, Virginia	Aladdin
House of Dies Drear, The	V	HF	250+	Edge	Hampton Brown
House of Dolls	U	F	250+	Block, Francesca Lia	HarperCollins

TITLE	LEVEL	GENRE	WORD COUNT	AUTHOR / SERIES	PUBLISHER / DISTRIBUTOR
House of Funny Mirrors, The	G	RF	206	The Joy Cowley Collection	Hameray Publishing Group
House of History	N	I	470	Pair-It Turn and Learn	Steck-Vaughn
House of Mirrors, The	M	F	250+	Take Two Books	Wright Group/McGraw Hill
House of Power, The	U	F	250+	Carman, Patrick	Little Brown and Company
House of Stairs	Z	F	250+	Sleator, William	Puffin Books
House of the Horrible Ghosts	M	F	250+	Hayes, Geoffrey	Random House
House of the Scorpion, The	Z+	SF	250+	Farmer, Nancy	Simon & Schuster
House of Wings, The	R	RF	250+	Byars, Betsy	Penguin Group
House on Mango Street, The	W	RF	250+	Cisneros, Sandra	Alfred A. Knopf
House on the Hill, The	F	F	189	PM Plus Story Books	Rigby
House on Walenska Street, The	N	RF	250+	Herman, Charlotte	Penguin Group
House on Winchester Lane, The	O	RF	2042	Brown, Beverly Swerdlow	January Books
^House Party	Z+	RF	250+	Orca Soundings	Orca Books
House Sitters, The	G	RF	211	Sails	Rigby
House Spider's Life, A	K	I	230	Himmelman, John	Scholastic
House that Jack Built, The	I	TL	201	Cat on the Mat	Oxford University Press
House that Jack Built, The	J	TL	250+	Peppe, Rodney	Delacorte Press
House That Jack's Friends Built, The	J	RF	254	Pair-It Books	Steck-Vaughn
House that Stood on Booker Hill, The	J	RF	250+	Ready Readers	Pearson Learning Group
House Through the Ages	U	I	250+	Steele, Philip	Troll Associates
House with a Clock in its Walls, The	S	F	250+	Bellairs, John	Penguin Group
House with Herbie House	C	RF	27	Ballenger, Joy	Reading Matters
^House with No Name, The	Q	F	4864	Goodhart, P.	Stone Arch Books
House, A	A	I	32	PM Starters	Rigby
House, A	A	F	30	Sails	Rigby
Houseful of Christmas, A	L	RF	250+	Joosse, Barbara	Square Fish
Houses	G	I	51	Learn to Read	Creative Teaching Press
Houses	C	I	35	Little Celebrations	Pearson Learning Group
Houses	B	I	64	Rigby Literacy	Rigby
Houses	C	I	64	Story Box	Wright Group/McGraw Hill
Houses	C	RF	38	Windmill Books	Wright Group/McGraw Hill
Houses	I	I	103	Windows on Literacy	National Geographic
Houses	M	I	279	Wonder World	Wright Group/McGraw Hill
Houses and Homes	G	RF	250+	PM Plus Poetry	Rigby
Houses and Homes	E	I	125	Red Rocket Readers	Flying Start Books
Houses of Bark	T	I	163	Native Dwellings	Tundra Books
Houses of Hide and Earth	T	I	157	Native Dwellings	Tundra Books
Houses That Move	K	I	250+	Voyages	SRA/McGraw Hill
Houses, Then and Now	L	I	407	Take Two Books	Wright Group/McGraw Hill
Houses: Past and Present	Q	I	1751	Reading Street	Pearson
Houston Astros, The	S	I	250+	Team Spirit	Norwood House Press
Houston Astros, The (Revised Edition)	S	I	250+	Team Spirit	Norwood House Press
Houston Rockets, The	S	I	4644	Team Spirit	Norwood House Press
Houston Texans, The	S	I	250+	Team Spirit	Norwood House Press
Hovercrafts	M	I	250+	Horsepower	Capstone Press
Hovering Hummingbirds	K	I	407	Pull Ahead Books	Lerner Publishing Group
How & Why Animals Are Poisonous	M	I	250+	How & Why	Creative Teaching Press
How & Why Animals Grow New Parts	M	I	250+	How & Why	Creative Teaching Press
How & Why Animals Hatch From Eggs	M	I	250+	How & Why	Creative Teaching Press
How & Why Animals Hide	M	I	250+	How & Why	Creative Teaching Press
How & Why Animals Prepare for Winter	M	I	250+	How & Why	Creative Teaching Press
How & Why Birds Use Their Bills	M	I	250+	How & Why	Creative Teaching Press
How & Why Insects Grow and Change	M	I	250+	How & Why	Creative Teaching Press
How & Why Insects Visit Flowers	M	I	250+	How & Why	Creative Teaching Press

Organized Alphabetically by Title
Storable Database at www.fountasandpinnellleveledbooks.com

* Collection of short stories   # Graphic text
^ Mature content with lower level text demands

TITLE	LEVEL	GENRE	WORD COUNT	AUTHOR / SERIES	PUBLISHER / DISTRIBUTOR
How & Why Plants Eat Insects	M	I	250+	How & Why	Creative Teaching Press
How & Why Seeds Travel	M	I	250+	How & Why	Creative Teaching Press
How & Why Spiders Spin Silk	M	I	250+	How & Why	Creative Teaching Press
How 100 Dandelions Grew	E	I	173	Instant Readers	Harcourt School Publishers
How a Book Gets Published	S	I	1765	Vocabulary Readers	Houghton Mifflin Harcourt
How a Book Gets Published	S	I	1765	Vocabulary Readers/CA	Houghton Mifflin Harcourt
How a Book Gets Published	S	I	1765	Vocabulary Readers/TX	Houghton Mifflin Harcourt
How a Book Is Made	N	I	250+	Aliki	Harper & Row
How a Butterfly Farm Works	J	I	392	Sun Sprouts	ETA/Cuisenaire
How a Frog Grows	I	I	136	Phonics Readers	Compass Point Books
How a House Is Built	M	I	250+	Gibbons, Gail	Scholastic
How a Plant Grows	O	I	250+	Kalman, Bobbie	Crabtree
How a Seed Grows	J	I	250+	Let's Read and Find Out About	HarperCollins
How a Volcano Is Formed	M	I	135	Wonder World	Wright Group/McGraw Hill
How Advertising Works: The Amazing Adventures of the GOB Mob and the Gang From OWW!	U	I	250+	Bookshop	Mondo Publishing
*How Angel Peterson Got His Name: And Other Outrageous Tales About Extreme Sports	U	RF	250+	Paulsen, Gary	Random House
How Animals Change and Grow	K	I	374	Early Explorers	Benchmark Education
How Animals Change: The Interaction of Animals and Scientists	U	I	250+	Reading Street	Pearson
How Animals Hide	F	I	98	Wonder World	Wright Group/McGraw Hill
How Animals Move	L	I	250+	Animal Behavior	Capstone Press
How Animals Move	G	I	132	Discovery Links	Newbridge
How Animals Move	L	I	132	Discovery World	Rigby
How Animals Move	J	I	401	Leveled Readers	Houghton Mifflin Harcourt
How Animals Move	J	I	401	Leveled Readers/CA	Houghton Mifflin Harcourt
How Animals Move	J	I	401	Leveled Readers/TX	Houghton Mifflin Harcourt
How Animals Move	M	I	700	Springboard	Wright Group/McGraw Hill
How Animals Move	F	I	44	Windows on Literacy	National Geographic
How Animals Move Around	L	I	593	PM Plus Nonfiction	Rigby
How Ants Live	I	I	159	Sunshine	Wright Group/McGraw Hill
How Are Magnets Used?	I	I	166	Windows on Literacy	National Geographic
How Are We the Same?	D	I	100	Teacher's Choice Series	Pearson Learning Group
How Barbed Wire Changed the West	V	I	3269	Leveled Readers	Houghton Mifflin Harcourt
How Barbed Wire Changed the West	V	I	3269	Leveled Readers/CA	Houghton Mifflin Harcourt
How Barbed Wire Changed the West	V	I	3269	Leveled Readers/TX	Houghton Mifflin Harcourt
How Bat Learned to Fly	H	TL	168	Storyteller-Night Crickets	Wright Group/McGraw Hill
How Bear Lost His Tail	K	TL	492	Leveled Literacy Intervention/ Blue System	Heinemann
How Bees Make Honey	L	I	250+	The Big Picture	Capstone Press
How Ben Franklin Stole the Lightning	R	B	250+	Schanzer, Rosalyn	HarperCollins
How Beth Feels	I	RF	272	Reading Street	Pearson
How Big Is a Foot?	K	F	250+	Myller, Rolf	Bantam Books
How Big Is Big?	F	I	158	Ziefert, Harriet	Puffin Books
How Big Is Big?: Comparing Plants	N	I	250+	Measuring and Comparing	Heinemann Library
How Big Is It?	J	RF	250+	Lighthouse	Rigby
How Big? How Heavy? How Dense?: A Look at Matter	M	I	250+	Lightning Bolt Books	Lerner Publishing Group
How Big? How Much?	H	I	134	Hutchins, Jeannie	Scholastic
How Birds Live	I	I	1090	Sunshine	Wright Group/McGraw Hill
How Bizarre	R	I	250+	Orbit Collections	Pacific Learning
How Bullfrog Found His Sound	M	TL	250+	Michaels, Eric	Pearson Learning Group
How Can I Help?	E	RF	73	Learn to Read	Creative Teaching Press

H

TITLE	LEVEL	GENRE	WORD COUNT	AUTHOR / SERIES	PUBLISHER / DISTRIBUTOR
How Can I Help?	D	I	65	Questions & Answers	Pearson Learning Group
How Can We See in the Dark?	H	I	157	Sunshine	Wright Group/McGraw Hill
How Can You Fix It?	B	I	56	Rigby Literacy	Rigby
How Can You Sort?	I	I	197	Early Explorers	Benchmark Education
How Chocolate Is Made	L	I	250+	Lighthouse	Rigby
How Could You?	Q	I	250+	Kids Talk	Picture Window Books
How Coyote Stole Fire	K	TL	544	Leveled Readers	Houghton Mifflin Harcourt
How Coyote Stole Fire	K	TL	544	Leveled Readers/CA	Houghton Mifflin Harcourt
How Coyote Stole Fire	K	TL	544	Leveled Readers/TX	Houghton Mifflin Harcourt
How Coyote Stole the Summer	N	TL	1653	On My Own Folklore	Millbrook Press
How Did Ancient Greece Get So Great?	Y	I	2402	Reading Street	Pearson
How Did Slaves Find a Route to Freedom?: And Other Questions about the Underground Railroad	T	I	5357	Six Questions of American History	Lerner Publishing Group
How Did the Lights Go Out? The Story of the New York City Blackout	R	I	1175	Independent Readers Science	Houghton Mifflin Harcourt
How Did They Do That?	Q	I	250+	On Our Way to English	Rigby
How Did This City Grow?	M	I	250+	Early Connections	Benchmark Education
How Do Airplanes Fly?	Q	I	250+	Rosen Real Readers	Rosen Publishing Group
How Do Animal Babies Live?	M	I	250+	I Like Reading About Animals!	Enslow Publishers, Inc.
How Do Animals Keep Clean?	M	I	250+	I Like Reading About Animals!	Enslow Publishers, Inc.
How Do Animals Stay Alive?	I	I	193	Early Connections	Benchmark Education
How Do Animals Stay Safe?	M	I	250+	I Like Reading About Animals!	Enslow Publishers, Inc.
How Do Dinosaurs Go to School?	J	F	191	Yolen, Jane	Blue Sky Press
How Do Dinosaurs Learn to Read?	J	F	156	Yolen, Jane	Scholastic
How Do Fish Breathe Underwater?	S	I	250+	Tell Me Why, Tell Me How	Marshall Cavendish
How Do Fish Live?	I	I	1242	Sunshine	Wright Group/McGraw Hill
How Do Flies Walk Upside Down?	R	I	250+	Berger, Melvin & Gilda	Scholastic
How Do Frogs Grow?	G	I	42	Discovery Links	Newbridge
How Do Frogs Swallow with Their Eyes?	R	I	250+	Berger, Melvin	Scholastic
How Do I Become a Firefighter?	P	I	250+	The Heinle Reading Library	Thomson Learning
How Do I Feel?	D	I	64	Questions & Answers	Pearson Learning Group
How Do I Put It On?	H	I	168	Watanabe, Shiego	Penguin Group
How Do Plants Get Food?	L	I	250+	Goldish, Meish	Steck-Vaughn
How Do Plants Grow Here?	K	I	250+	Explorations	Okapi Educational Materials
How Do Plants Grow Here?	K	I	250+	Explorations	Eleanor Curtain Publishing
How Do Plants Grow?	L	I	250+	Rosen Real Readers	Rosen Publishing Group
How Do Plants Grow?	S	I	250+	Tell Me Why, Tell Me How	Marshall Cavendish
How Do Seeds Travel?	J	I	179	Windows on Literacy	National Geographic
How Do Trees Grow?	N	I	281	Early Explorers	Benchmark Education
How Do Trees Grow?	L	I	250+	Rosen Real Readers	Rosen Publishing Group
How Do We Use Water?	O	I	250+	Reading Expeditions	National Geographic
How Do You Count a Dozen Ducklings?	K	F	250+	Chae, In Seon	Albert Whitman & Co.
How Do You Feel Today?	C	I	71	Gear Up!	Wright Group/McGraw Hill
How Do You Feel Today?	L	I	250+	Rosen Real Readers	Rosen Publishing Group
How Do You Make a Bubble?	G	RF	250+	Hooks, William H.	Bantam Books
How Do You Measure a Dinosaur?	M	I	257	Pacific Literacy	Pacific Learning
How Do You Move?	E	F	160	Red Rocket Readers	Flying Start Books
How Do You Move?	J	I	250+	Yellow Umbrella Books	Red Brick Learning
How Do You Say Hello to A Ghost?	F	F	149	Tiger Cub	Peguis
How Do You Sleep?	H	I	188	On Our Way to English	Rigby
How Do You Spell g-e-e-k?	T	RF	250+	Peters, Julie Anne	Little Brown and Company
How Do You Train a Goldfish?	N	I	250+	Scooters	ETA/Cuisenaire
How Do Your Lungs Work?	P	I	250+	Rookie Read-About Health	Children's Press

* Collection of short stories   # Graphic text
^ Mature content with lower level text demands

TITLE	LEVEL	GENRE	WORD COUNT	AUTHOR / SERIES	PUBLISHER / DISTRIBUTOR
How Does a Cactus Grow?	J	I	189	Early Explorers	Benchmark Education
How Does a Plant Grow?	I	I	115	Instant Readers	Harcourt School Publishers
How Does a Tree Help?	B	I	69	Literacy by Design	Rigby
How Does It Breathe?	K	I	250+	Home Connection Collection	Rigby
How Does It Change?	F	I	127	InfoTrek	ETA/Cuisenaire
How Does It Feel?	B	I	28	Properties of Matter	Lerner Publishing Group
How Does It Feel?	LB	I	11	Windows on Literacy	National Geographic
How Does It Grow?	L	I	250+	Home Connection Collection	Rigby
How Does It Work?	O	I	694	Big Cat	Pacific Learning
How Does My Bike Work?	J	I	127	Windows on Literacy	National Geographic
How Does My Garden Grow?	H	I	73	Windows on Literacy	National Geographic
How Does Sound Travel?	J	I	148	Instant Readers	Harcourt School Publishers
How Does the Mail Work?	H	I	169	Reading Street	Pearson
How Does the Wind Blow?	S	I	250+	Tell Me Why, Tell Me How	Marshall Cavendish
How Does This Sound?	L	I	260	Independent Readers Science	Houghton Mifflin Harcourt
How Does Water Change?	J	I	176	Rigby Star Quest	Rigby
How Does Your Garden Grow?	Q	I	250+	PM Extensions	Rigby
How Does Your Salad Grow?	H	I	136	Alexander, Francie	Scholastic
How Dog Lost His Bone	E	TL	100	Leveled Readers Language Support	Houghton Mifflin Harcourt
How Far Is Far?: Comparing Geographical Distances	O	I	250+	Measuring and Comparing	Heinemann Library
How Far Is It?	L	I	250+	Rosen Real Readers	Rosen Publishing Group
How Far Will I Fly?	F	RF	94	Oyama, Sachi	Scholastic
How Far Would You Have Gotten If I Hadn't Called You Back?	Z+	RF	250+	Hobbs, Valerie	Scholastic
How Far?	F	I	86	Windows on Literacy	National Geographic
How Fire Came to Earth	K	TL	250+	Literacy 2000	Rigby
How Flamingos Came to Have Red Legs: A South American Folk Tale	M	TL	250+	Take Two Books	Wright Group/McGraw Hill
How Flexible Are You?	M	I	250+	Take Two Books	Wright Group/McGraw Hill
How Flies Live	I	I	448	Sunshine	Wright Group/McGraw Hill
How Flowers Grow	E	I	68	Rosen Real Readers	Rosen Publishing Group
How Fly Saved the River	J	TL	426	Rigby Flying Colors	Rigby
How Fox Became Red	I	TL	163	Books for Young Learners	Richard C. Owen
How Frogs Grow	G	I	116	Leveled Literacy Intervention/ Green System	Heinemann
How Full Is Full?: Comparing Bodies of Water	N	I	250+	Measuring and Comparing	Heinemann Library
*How Glooskap Found Summer and Other Curious Tales	Q	TL	250+	Literacy by Design	Rigby
How Goods Are Moved	K	I	250+	People, Spaces & Places	Rand McNally
How Grandmother Spider Got the Sun	J	TL	115	Little Readers	Houghton Mifflin Harcourt
How Grapes Become Raisins	F	I	81	Bonnell, Kris/About	Reading Reading Books
How Has It Changed?	D	I	103	Rigby Literacy	Rigby
How Have I Grown	G	RF	235	Reid, Mary	Scholastic
How Heavy Is Heavy?: Comparing Vehicles	N	I	250+	Measuring and Comparing	Heinemann Library
How Helicopters Help	F	I	104	Bonnell, Kris/About	Reading Reading Books
How I Came to Be a Writer	W	B	250+	Naylor, Phyllis Reynolds	Scholastic
How I Fixed the Year 1000 Problem	N	F	250+	The Zack Files	Grosset & Dunlap
How I Go	F	I	138	Early Connections	Benchmark Education
How I Met Archie	M	RF	250+	Kenna, Anna	Pacific Learning
How I Met Einstein: A Character Comes to Life	S	I	250+	Orbit Chapter Books	Pacific Learning
How I Move	A	RF	21	Leveled Readers Science	Houghton Mifflin Harcourt
How I Went from Bad to Verse	N	F	250+	The Zack Files	Grosset & Dunlap

H

TITLE	LEVEL	GENRE	WORD COUNT	AUTHOR / SERIES	PUBLISHER / DISTRIBUTOR
How I, Nicky Flynn, Finally Get a Life (and a Dog)	T	RF	250+	Corriveau, Art	Amulet Books
How Is a Crayon Made?	P	I	250+	Oz, Charles	Scholastic
How Is a Moose Like a Goose?	I	I	408	Silly Millies	Millbrook Press
How Kittens Grow	L	I	250+	Selsam, Millicent E.	Scholastic
How Leaves Change Color	M	I	250+	Rosen Real Readers	Rosen Publishing Group
How Living Things Help Each Other	I	I	221	Literacy by Design	Rigby
How Lizard Lost His Colors	J	TL	197	Literacy Tree	Rigby
How Lizard Lost His Colors	F	TL	139	Shapiro, Sara	Scholastic
How Long Do Animals Live?	D	I	65	Pacific Literacy	Pacific Learning
How Long Is a Dog's Tail?	H	RF	209	InfoTrek	ETA/Cuisenaire
How Long Is a Foot?	M	I	250+	Twig	Wright Group/McGraw Hill
How Long Is a Piece of String?	L	RF	250+	Voyages	SRA/McGraw Hill
How Long Is Long?: Comparing Animals	N	I	250+	Measuring and Comparing	Heinemann Library
How Long or How Wide?: A Measuring Guide	M	I	437	Math is CATegorical	Millbrook Press
How Loud Can You Burp?	W	I	250+	Murphy, Glenn	Roaring Brook Press
How Machines Help	D	I	143	Sunshine	Wright Group/McGraw Hill
How Magic Tricks Work	P	I	250+	PM Extensions	Rigby
How Many Animals?	LB	I	27	Big Cat	Pacific Learning
How Many Animals?	A	I	25	Vocabulary Readers	Houghton Mifflin Harcourt
How Many Ants in an Anthill?	T	I	250+	Reading Expeditions	National Geographic
How Many Ants?	E	RF	35	Rookie Readers	Children's Press
How Many Are in the Crowd?	J	I	214	Windows on Literacy	National Geographic
How Many Are Left?	I	I	225	Early Connections	Benchmark Education
How Many Baby Pandas?	N	I	250+	Markle, Sandra	Walker & Company
How Many Bugs in a Box?	LB	F	126	Carter, David	Simon & Schuster
How Many Can Play?	D	I	46	Canizares, Susan; Chessen, Betsey	Scholastic
How Many Climates Does One Island Need?	R	RF	250+	Pair-It Books	Steck-Vaughn
How Many Days to America?	P	HF	1072	Avenues	Hampton Brown
How Many Days to America?: A Thanksgiving Story	P	I	250+	Bunting, Eve	Houghton Mifflin Harcourt
How Many Ducks?	F	F	88	Chapman, Cindy	Scholastic
How Many Ducks?	A	I	22	Vocabulary Readers	Houghton Mifflin Harcourt
How Many Ducks?	A	I	22	Vocabulary Readers/CA	Houghton Mifflin Harcourt
How Many Feet? How Many Tails?	F	RF	157	Burns, Marilyn	Scholastic
How Many Fish in the Sea?	N	I	250+	Why In the World?	Capstone Press
How Many Fish?	B	F	30	Gosset, Rachel; Ballinger, Margaret	Scholastic
How Many Fish?	F	I	114	Yellow Umbrella Books	Red Brick Learning
How Many Frogs?	C	I	44	Leveled Readers Language Support	Houghton Mifflin Harcourt
How Many Hats?	C	I	57	On Our Way to English	Rigby
How Many Hot Dogs?	E	I	115	Story Box	Wright Group/McGraw Hill
How Many Jelly Beans	B	RF	61	Phonics and Friends	Hampton Brown
How Many Kisses Do You Want Tonight?	J	F	250+	Bajaj, Varsha	Little Brown and Company
How Many Kittens?	C	I	37	Twig	Wright Group/McGraw Hill
How Many Legs?	D	I	74	Bookshop	Mondo Publishing
How Many Legs?	E	I	104	Early Connections	Benchmark Education
How Many Legs?	D	I	103	Sails	Rigby
How Many Legs?	C	F	47	Science	Outside the Box
How Many Legs?	B	I	19	Windmill Books	Wright Group/McGraw Hill
How Many Monkeys?	B	F	16	Pair-It Books	Steck-Vaughn
How Many Muffins?	K	I	229	Early Explorers	Benchmark Education
How Many Pennies?	H	I	180	Shutterbug Books	Steck-Vaughn

* Collection of short stories   # Graphic text
^ Mature content with lower level text demands

TITLE	LEVEL	GENRE	WORD COUNT	AUTHOR / SERIES	PUBLISHER / DISTRIBUTOR
How Many Pets?	D	RF	37	Bookshop	Mondo Publishing
How Many Sandwiches?	K	RF	463	In Step Readers	Rigby
How Many Seeds?	E	I	42	Pair-It Books	Steck-Vaughn
How Many Toes?	B	I	48	Sails	Rigby
How Many Walruses?	A	F	32	Early Connections	Benchmark Education
How Many Ways Can You Catch a Fly?	R	I	250+	Jenkins, Steve & Page, Robin	Houghton Mifflin Harcourt
How Many Wheels?	D	I	102	Red Rocket Readers	Flying Start Books
How Many?	E	I	147	Early Connections	Benchmark Education
How Many?	C	I	45	Gear Up!	Wright Group/McGraw Hill
How Many?	C	I	45	Learn to Read	Creative Teaching Press
How Many?	B	I	49	Nonfiction Set 2	Literacy Footprints
How Many?	WB	I	0	Reading Street	Pearson
How Many?	C	I	39	Windows on Literacy	National Geographic
How Maps Came to Be	M	I	250+	HSP/Harcourt Trophies	Harcourt, Inc.
How Moon Tricked Sun	H	TL	241	Rigby Rocket	Rigby
How Mountains Are Made	P	I	250+	Let's-Read-and-Find-Out Science	HarperTrophy
How Much Bigger?	I	RF	250+	Windows on Literacy	National Geographic
How Much Can a Bare Bear Bear?: What are Homonyms and Homophones?	O	I	421	Words Are CATegorical	Millbrook Press
How Much Does It Weigh?	I	I	253	On Our Way to English	Rigby
How Much Does This Hold?	K	RF	179	Coulton, Mia	Kaeden Books
How Much Is A Million?	M	I	250+	Schwartz, David M.	Scholastic
How Much Is That Guinea Pig in the Window?	L	RF	250+	Rocklin, Joanne	Scholastic
How Much Money?	L	I	360	Yellow Umbrella Books	Red Brick Learning
How Music Came to Earth	P	TL	250+	WorldScapes	ETA/Cuisenaire
How Music is Made	K	I	250+	Rigby Star Quest	Rigby
How My Family Lives in America	O	I	250+	Kuklin, Susan	Aladdin
How My Pet Grew	I	RF	235	Leveled Readers Science	Houghton Mifflin Harcourt
How News Travels	M	I	250+	PM Plus Nonfiction	Rigby
*How Not to Catch the Moon	N	TL	250+	Storyteller Summer Skies	Wright Group/McGraw Hill
How Old Are You?	E	I	107	Red Rocket Readers	Flying Start Books
How Oliver Olson Changed the World	L	RF	250+	Mills, Claudia	Farrar, Straus, & Giroux
How Owl Changed His Hoot	I	TL	227	Sunshine	Wright Group/McGraw Hill
How Paper Is Made	M	I	514	Red Rocket Readers	Flying Start Books
How People Got Fire	K	TL	580	Leveled Readers	Houghton Mifflin Harcourt
How People Got Fire	K	TL	580	Leveled Readers/CA	Houghton Mifflin Harcourt
How People Got Fire	K	TL	580	Leveled Readers/TX	Houghton Mifflin Harcourt
How People Got Wisdom: An Ashanti Tale	N	TL	891	Leveled Readers	Houghton Mifflin Harcourt
How People Move Around	L	I	541	PM Plus Nonfiction	Rigby
How Plants Grow	O	I	250+	Plants	Heinemann
How Plants Grow	F	I	69	Time for Kids	Teacher Created Materials
How Plants Survive	P	I	250+	Science Links	Chelsea Clubhouse
How Popcorn Pops	F	I	81	Bonnell, Kris/About	Reading Reading Books
How Raven Became Black and Owl Got Its Spots	F	TL	193	Early Connections	Benchmark Education
How Robin Saved Spring	N	TL	250+	Ouellet, Debbie	Henry Holt & Co.
How Small Is Small?: Comparing Body Parts	N	I	250+	Measuring and Comparing	Heinemann Library
How Smart Are Animals?	U	I	2123	Vocabulary Readers	Houghton Mifflin Harcourt
How Smart Are Animals?	U	I	2123	Vocabulary Readers/CA	Houghton Mifflin Harcourt
How Spider Tricked Snake	K	TL	250+	Real Reading	Steck-Vaughn
How Spiders Catch Their Food	K	I	250+	Explorations	Eleanor Curtain Publishing
How Spiders Catch Their Food	K	I	250+	Explorations	Okapi Educational Materials
How Spiders Got Eight Legs	L	TL	884	Pair-It Books	Steck-Vaughn
How Spiders Live	F	I	145	Sunshine	Wright Group/McGraw Hill

TITLE	LEVEL	GENRE	WORD COUNT	AUTHOR / SERIES	PUBLISHER / DISTRIBUTOR
How Tadpoles Become Frogs	D	I	43	Bonnell, Kris/About	Reading Reading Books
How Tall Is It?	K	F	522	Dominie Math Stories	Pearson Learning Group
How Tall Is Tall?: Comparing Structures	N	I	250+	Measuring and Comparing	Heinemann Library
How Tall?	A	I	31	Red Rocket Readers	Flying Start Books
How Tfa Lola Saved the Summer	R	RF	250+	Alvarez, Julia	Alfred A. Knopf
How the Animals Got Their Tails	L	TL	250+	Cambridge Reading	Pearson Learning Group
*How the Camel Got His Hump and Other Stories	K	TL	250+	Storyteller- Shooting Stars	Wright Group/McGraw Hill
How the Chick Tricked the Fox	G	F	167	Ready Readers	Pearson Learning Group
How the Dinosaurs Disappeared	L	I	250+	Rosen Real Readers	Rosen Publishing Group
How the Elephant Got His Trunk	J	TL	250+	Rigby Rocket	Rigby
How the Gator's Snout Grew Out	I	TL	135	Dominie Readers	Pearson Learning Group
How the Giraffe Became a Giraffe	M	TL	648	Sunshine	Wright Group/McGraw Hill
How the Government Works	S	I	1142	Vocabulary Readers	Houghton Mifflin Harcourt
How the Government Works	S	I	1142	Vocabulary Readers/CA	Houghton Mifflin Harcourt
How the Guinea Fowl Got Her Spots	L	TL	635	Knutson, Barbara	Carolrhoda Books
How the Leaves Got Their Colors	K	F	474	Leveled Readers/TX	Houghton Mifflin Harcourt
How the Moon Regained Her Shape	N	TL	584	Heller, Janet Ruth	Sylvan Dell Publishing
How the Mouse Got Brown Teeth	I	TL	250+	Bookshop	Mondo Publishing
How the Rattlesnake Got Its Rattle	L	TL	1006	Pair-It Books	Steck-Vaughn
How the Sky Got Its Stars	G	TL	208	Instant Readers	Harcourt School Publishers
How the Three Great Mountains Came to Be	N	TL	710	Gear Up!	Wright Group/McGraw Hill
*How the Tortoise Got His Shell and Other Stories	K	TL	250+	New Way Literature	Steck-Vaughn
How the Walrus Got to the Arctic	Q	TL	250+	Reading Safari	Mondo Publishing
How the Water Got to the Plains	L	TL	250+	Home Connection Collection	Rigby
How Things Move	H	I	214	Yellow Umbrella Books	Red Brick Learning
How Things Work	R	I	250+	Explorers	Wright Group/McGraw Hill
How Tia Lola Came to Stay	R	RF	250+	Alvarez, Julia	Yearling Books
How to Be a Detective	N	RF	4197	Damian Drooth Supersleuth	Stone Arch Books
How to Be a Friend	M	I	250+	Brown, Laurie Krasny, & Marc	Little Brown and Company
How to Be a Pirate by Hiccup Horrendous Haddock III	T	F	250+	Cowell, Cressida	Little Brown and Company
How to Be a Pirate in 10 Easy Stages	N	F	1077	Big Cat	Pacific Learning
How to Be Cool in the Third Grade	N	RF	250+	Duffey, Betsy	Penguin Group
How to Be Healthy	K	I	250+	Rosen Real Readers	Rosen Publishing Group
How To Be Nice… And Other Lessons I Didn't Learn	Q	RF	250+	Bookshop	Mondo Publishing
How to Build a Tornado in a Bottle	K	I	147	Hands-On Science Fun	Capstone Press
How to Build a Dinosaur	L	I	457	Pair-It Turn and Learn	Steck-Vaughn
How to Build a Fizzy Rocket	M	I	210	Hands-On Science Fun	Capstone Press
How to Build a Robot	T	I	1660	Leveled Readers	Houghton Mifflin Harcourt
How to Build a Robot	T	I	1660	Leveled Readers/CA	Houghton Mifflin Harcourt
How to Build a Robot	T	I	1660	Leveled Readers/TX	Houghton Mifflin Harcourt
How to Build Flipsticks	L	I	180	Hands-On Science Fun	Capstone Press
How to Cheat a Dragons's Curse: The Heroic Misadventures of Hiccup the Viking	T	F	250+	Cowell, Cressida	Little Brown and Company
How to Choose a Pet	L	I	250+	Discovery World	Rigby
How to Clean a Dinosaur	G	F	208	Windmill Books	Rigby
How to Cook Scones	J	I	250+	Bookshop	Mondo Publishing
How to Ditch Your Fairy	W	F	250+	Larbalestier, Justine	Bloomsbury Children's Books
How to Draw Amazing Letters	Q	I	250+	Drawing Fun	Capstone Press
How to Draw Amazing Motorcycles	Q	I	250+	Drawing Cool Stuff	Capstone Press
How to Draw Cartoons	N	I	944	Big Cat	Pacific Learning

* Collection of short stories   # Graphic text
^ Mature content with lower level text demands

TITLE	LEVEL	GENRE	WORD COUNT	AUTHOR / SERIES	PUBLISHER / DISTRIBUTOR
How to Draw Comic Heroes	Q	I	250+	Drawing Cool Stuff	Capstone Press
How to Draw Cool Fashions	Q	I	250+	Drawing Fun	Capstone Press
How to Draw Cool Kids	Q	I	250+	Drawing Fun	Capstone Press
How to Draw Crazy Fighter Planes	Q	I	250+	Drawing Cool Stuff	Capstone Press
How to Draw Cute Animals	Q	I	250+	Drawing Fun	Capstone Press
How to Draw Disgusting Aliens	Q	I	250+	Drawing Cool Stuff	Capstone Press
How to Draw Faces	Q	I	250+	Drawing Fun	Capstone Press
How to Draw Ferocious Animals	Q	I	250+	Drawing Cool Stuff	Capstone Press
How to Draw Ferocious Dinosaurs	Q	I	250+	Drawing Cool Stuff	Capstone Press
How to Draw Flowers	Q	I	250+	Drawing Fun	Capstone Press
How to Draw Grotesque Monsters	Q	I	250+	Drawing Cool Stuff	Capstone Press
How to Draw Horses	Q	I	250+	Drawing Fun	Capstone Press
How to Draw Incredible Cars	Q	I	250+	Drawing Cool Stuff	Capstone Press
How to Draw Indestructible Tanks	Q	I	250+	Drawing Cool Stuff	Capstone Press
How to Draw Manga Warriors	Q	I	250+	Drawing Cool Stuff	Capstone Press
How to Draw Monster Trucks	Q	I	250+	Drawing Cool Stuff	Capstone Press
How to Draw Mythical Creatures	Q	I	250+	Drawing Fun	Capstone Press
How to Draw Terrifying Robots	Q	I	250+	Drawing Cool Stuff	Capstone Press
How to Draw Unreal Spaceships	Q	I	250+	Drawing Cool Stuff	Capstone Press
How to Eat Fried Worms	R	RF	250+	Rockwell, Thomas	Bantam Books
How to Grow a Plant	E	I	172	Visions	Wright Group/McGraw Hill
How to Grow Crystals	P	I	250+	Bookshop	Mondo Publishing
How to Have a Party	F	I	85	Big Cat	Pacific Learning
How to Heal a Broken Wing	I	RF	80	Graham, Bob	Candlewick Press
How to Help Your Community	P	I	1190	Vocabulary Readers	Houghton Mifflin Harcourt
How to Help Your Community	P	I	1190	Vocabulary Readers/CA	Houghton Mifflin Harcourt
How to Make a Bird Feeder	E	I	80	Rigby Literacy	Rigby
How to Make a Bird Feeder	E	I	84	Rigby Star Quest	Rigby
How to Make a Bouncing Egg	L	I	208	Hands-On Science Fun	Capstone Press
How to Make a Card	G	I	69	Urmston, Kathleen; Evans, Karen	Kaeden Books
How to Make a Clown Costume	G	I	90	Rigby Rocket	Rigby
How to Make a Crocodile	H	F	62	Little Books	Sadlier-Oxford
How to Make a Family Tree	N	I	929	Leveled Readers	Houghton Mifflin Harcourt
How to Make a Family Tree	N	I	929	Leveled Readers/CA	Houghton Mifflin Harcourt
How to Make a Family Tree	N	I	929	Leveled Readers/TX	Houghton Mifflin Harcourt
How to Make a Hen House	B	I	25	Ready Readers	Pearson Learning Group
How to Make a Hot Dog	C	I	48	Story Box	Wright Group/McGraw Hill
How to Make a Kite	M	I	250+	Take Two Books	Wright Group/McGraw Hill
How to Make a Lion Mask	G	I	133	Instant Readers	Harcourt School Publishers
How to Make a Liquid Rainbow	L	I	204	Hands-On Science Fun	Capstone Press
How to Make a Mud Pie	H	RF	127	Little Readers	Houghton Mifflin Harcourt
How to Make a Mudpie	A	I	32	Learn to Read	Creative Teaching Press
How to Make a Mystery Smell Balloon	M	I	216	Hands-On Science Fun	Capstone Press
How to Make a Paper Frog	I	I	140	Windows on Literacy	National Geographic
How to Make a Salad	A	I	12	Vocabulary Readers	Houghton Mifflin Harcourt
How to Make a Sandwich	C	I	27	Visions	Wright Group/McGraw Hill
How to Make a Scarecrow	WB	I	0	Big Cat	Pacific Learning
How to Make a Sun Hat	E	I	87	Home Connection Collection	Rigby
How to Make a Wind Sock	B	F	20	Tarlow, Ellen	Scholastic
How to Make Bubbles	K	I	189	Hands-On Science Fun	Capstone Press
How to Make Can Stilts	C	I	28	Story Box	Wright Group/McGraw Hill
How to Make Cheese Muffins	K	I	220	Voyages	SRA/McGraw Hill
How to Make Paper	L	I	250+	On Our Way to English	Rigby
How to Make Pop-Up Cards	I	I	434	Big Cat	Pacific Learning

* Collection of short stories   # Graphic text
^ Mature content with lower level text demands

H

TITLE	LEVEL	GENRE	WORD COUNT	AUTHOR / SERIES	PUBLISHER / DISTRIBUTOR
How To Make Salsa	J	I	192	Bookshop	Mondo Publishing
How to Make Slime	K	I	179	Hands-On Science Fun	Capstone Press
How to Make Smoothies!	E	I	75	Literacy by Design	Rigby
How to Make Snack Mix	C	I	47	Oppenlander, Meredith	Kaeden Books
How to Make Sock Puppets	H	I	229	Bookshop	Mondo Publishing
How to Ride a Dragon's Storm: The Heroic Misadventures of Hiccup the Viking	T	F	250+	Cowell, Cressida	Little Brown and Company
How to Ride a Giraffe	I	F	191	Little Readers	Houghton Mifflin Harcourt
How to Rock Your Baby	J	F	250+	Fleming, Sibley	Peachtree
How to Scratch a Wombat	R	I	250+	French, Jackie	Clarion Books
How to Speak Dolphin in Three Easy Lessons	N	F	250+	The Zack Files	Grosset & Dunlap
How to Speak Dragonese: The Heroic Misadventures of Hiccup the Viking	T	F	250+	Cowell, Cressida	Little Brown and Company
How to Start Your Own Business	U	I	250+	Bookshop	Mondo Publishing
How to Stay Safe at Home and On-Line	M	I	250+	Rosen Real Readers	Rosen Publishing Group
How to Steal a Dog	T	RF	250+	O'Connor, Barbara	Square Fish
How to Survive a Flood	T	I	250+	Prepare to Survive	Capstone Press
How to Survive a Tornado	T	I	250+	Prepare to Survive	Capstone Press
How to Survive a Totally Boring Summer	N	RF	250+	Delacroix, Alice	Holiday House
How to Survive an Earthquake	T	I	250+	Prepare to Survive	Capstone Press
How to Survive Being Lost at Sea	T	I	250+	Prepare to Survive	Capstone Press
How to Survive in Antarctica	U	I	250+	Bledsoe, Lucy Jane	Holiday House
How to Survive in the Wilderness	T	I	250+	Prepare to Survive	Capstone Press
How to Survive on a Deserted Island	T	I	250+	Prepare to Survive	Capstone Press
How to Take the Ex Out of Ex-Boyfriend	Y	RF	250+	Rallison, Janette	Speak
How to Talk to Your Cat	Q	I	250+	George, Jean Craighead	HarperCollins
How to Talk to Your Dog	Q	I	250+	George, Jean Craighead	HarperCollins
How to Train Your Dragon by Hiccup Horrendous Haddock III	T	F	250+	Cowell, Cressida	Little Brown and Company
How to Twist a Dragon's Tale: The Heroic Misadventures of Hiccup Horrendous Haddock III	T	F	250+	Cowell, Cressida	Little Brown and Company
How to Weigh an Elephant	K	TL	390	Pacific Literacy	Pacific Learning
How Turtle Got His Tail	H	F	248	Rigby Literacy	Rigby
How Turtle Raced Beaver	J	TL	182	Literacy 2000	Rigby
How We Can Help the Earth	K	I	159	Larkin's Little Readers	Wilbooks
How We Get Food	G	I	291	Leveled Readers	Houghton Mifflin Harcourt
How We Get Food	G	I	291	Leveled Readers/CA	Houghton Mifflin Harcourt
How We Get Food	G	I	291	Leveled Readers/TX	Houghton Mifflin Harcourt
How We Group Animals	M	I	627	Early Explorers	Benchmark Education
How We Know What We Know About Our Changing Climate: Scientists and Kids Explore Global Warming	Y	I	250+	Cherry, Lynne & Braasch, Gary	Dawn Publications
How We Learn About Space	N	I	250+	Windows on Literacy	National Geographic
How We Make Music	H	I	104	Rosen Real Readers	Rosen Publishing Group
How We Use Wool	M	I	654	Leveled Readers	Houghton Mifflin Harcourt
How We Use Wool	M	I	654	Leveled Readers/CA	Houghton Mifflin Harcourt
How We Use Wool	M	I	654	Leveled Readers/TX	Houghton Mifflin Harcourt
How We Vote	L	I	314	Independent Readers Social Studies	Houghton Mifflin Harcourt
How Will I Get to Grandma's House?	D	F	103	Blevins, Wiley	Scholastic
How Wisdom Came to the World: An Ashanti Tale	M	TL	250+	Khan, Benjamin	Houghton Mifflin Harcourt
How Women Got the Vote	U	I	1760	Vocabulary Readers	Houghton Mifflin Harcourt
How Women Got the Vote	U	I	1760	Vocabulary Readers/CA	Houghton Mifflin Harcourt
How Your Body Works	M	I	218	Health and Your Body	Capstone Press

H

* Collection of short stories   # Graphic text
^ Mature content with lower level text demands

TITLE	LEVEL	GENRE	WORD COUNT	AUTHOR / SERIES	PUBLISHER / DISTRIBUTOR
Howard Carter: Searching for King Tut	W	B	250+	Ford, Barbara	W. H. Freeman & Co.
Howie Has a Stomachache	E	F	100	Moore, Johnny R.	Continental Press
Howie Merton and the Magic Dust	M	F	250+	Reeves, Faye Couch	Random House
Howler Monkey	L	I	250+	A Day in the Life: Rain Forest Animals	Heinemann Library
Howliday Inn	P	F	250+	Howe, James	Atheneum Books
Howling at the Hauntly's	M	RF	250+	Dadey, Debbie; Jones, Marcia Thornton	Scholastic
*Howling Dog and Other Cases, The	O	RF	250+	Simon, Seymour	Avon Books
Howling Hurricanes	T	I	250+	Awesome Forces of Nature	Heinemann Library
How's the Weather	B	I	29	Learn to Read	Creative Teaching Press
How's the Weather?	N	I	250+	Berger, Melvin & Gilda	Ideals Children's Books
How's the Weather?	R	I	250+	On Our Way to English	Rigby
Hubba Dubba	I	F	209	The Joy Cowley Collection	Hameray Publishing Group
Hubble Space Telescope, The	Q	I	250+	A True Book	Children's Press
#Hubbub, A	M	F	250+	Mr. Badger and Mrs. Fox	Graphic Universe
Hubert and Frankie	K	F	572	Reading Street	Pearson
Hubert the Sad Giant	J	F	602	InfoTrek	ETA/Cuisenaire
Huberta the Hiking Hippo	L	RF	250+	Literacy 2000	Rigby
Huckleberry Finn	U	RF	6180	Oxford Bookworms Library	Oxford University Press
Hudson: Henry Hudson Searches for a Passage to Asia	U	B	250+	Exploring the World	Compass Point Books
Hue Boy	M	RF	250+	Mitchell, Rita Phillips	Penguin Group
Huff & Puff	F	TL	95	Rueda, Claudia	Harry N. Abrams
Huff and Puff!	I	TL	394	Red Rocket Readers	Flying Start Books
Hug Bug	F	F	65	Start to Read	School Zone
Hug Is Warm, A	C	F	60	Sunshine	Wright Group/McGraw Hill
Hug, The	E	F	162	Leveled Literacy Intervention/ Blue System	Heinemann
Huge Carrot, The	D	F	50	Leveled Readers	Houghton Mifflin Harcourt
Huge Paintings of Thomas Hart Benton, The	Q	B	1182	Reading Street	Pearson
Huge Ship, The	H	I	132	Windows on Literacy	National Geographic
Huggles at School	G	F	240	The Joy Cowley Collection	Hameray Publishing Group
Huggles' Breakfast	LB	F	14	Sunshine	Wright Group/McGraw Hill
Huggles Can Juggle	LB	F	15	Sunshine	Wright Group/McGraw Hill
Huggles' Cold	F	F	184	The Joy Cowley Collection	Hameray Publishing Group
Huggles Goes Away	LB	F	14	Sunshine	Wright Group/McGraw Hill
Huggles' Hug, The	F	F	201	The Joy Cowley Collection	Hameray Publishing Group
Huggly, Snuggly Pets	F	RF	142	Giant Step Readers	Educational Insights
Huggly's Pizza	L	F	250+	Ted Arnold	Scholastic
Hugo and Splot	O	F	250+	Bookweb	Rigby
Hugo Hogget: Story Based on an Ecuadoran Legend	K	TL	528	Cumpiano, Ina	Hampton Brown
Hullabaloo at the Zoo	G	F	172	Lighthouse	Rigby
Human Barriers - The Walls of the World	T	I	250+	Connectors	Pacific Learning
Human Body	Z	I	250+	Kingfisher Knowledge	Kingfisher
Human Body	U	I	250+	Navigators Science Series	Benchmark Education
Human Body Math	T	I	250+	Navigators Math Series	Benchmark Education
Human Body Systems	R	I	1831	Science Support Readers	Houghton Mifflin Harcourt
Human Body, The	Q	I	250+	Explorers	Wright Group/McGraw Hill
Human Body, The	Y	I	250+	Mission Science	Compass Point Books
Human body: Train It Right	R	I	250+	iScience	Norwood House Press
Human Emotions	Q	I	250+	Navigators Science Series	Benchmark Education
Human Growth	T	I	250+	Sun Sprouts	ETA/Cuisenaire
Human Head, The	R	I	250+	Anatomy Class	Capstone Press

H

TITLE	LEVEL	GENRE	WORD COUNT	AUTHOR / SERIES	PUBLISHER / DISTRIBUTOR
Human Life Cycle, The	S	I	1193	Time for Kids	Teacher Created Materials
Human Machine, The	X	I	250+	Reading Expeditions	National Geographic
Human Muscles	R	I	250+	Anatomy Class	Capstone Press
Human Organs	R	I	250+	Anatomy Class	Capstone Press
Human Skeleton, The	R	I	250+	Anatomy Class	Capstone Press
Hummingbird	N	I	250+	Life Cycles	Creative Teaching Press
Hummingbird Garden	K	RF	252	Story Box	Wright Group/McGraw Hill
Hummingbird, The	I	I	189	Sails	Rigby
Humongous Cat, The	I	F	250+	Sunshine	Wright Group/McGraw Hill
Humpback Teddy, The	E	RF	144	Take Two Books	Wright Group/McGraw Hill
Humpback Whale, The	E	I	106	Bonnell, Kris/Animals in Danger	Reading Reading Books
Humpback Whale, The	S	I	250+	Frahm, Randy	Red Brick Learning
Humpback Whales	E	I	48	Pair-It Books	Steck-Vaughn
Humpback Whales	F	I	72	Ready Readers	Pearson Learning Group
Humpback Whales Up Close	M	I	250+	First Facts-Whales and Dolphins Up Close	Capstone Press
Humphrey	M	RF	250+	Literacy Tree	Rigby
Humpity-Bump!	C	F	36	Little Celebrations	Pearson Learning Group
Humpty Dumpty	D	F	28	Instant Readers	Harcourt School Publishers
Humpty Dumpty	D	TL	26	Jumbled Tumbled Tales & Rhymes	Rigby
Humpty Dumpty	D	TL	27	Peppe, Rodney	Penguin Group
Humpty Dumpty	C	F	42	Seedlings	Continental Press
Humpty Dumpty Jr: Hardboiled Detective, in the Case of the Fiendish Flapjack Flop	Q	F	11470	Evans, Nate and Hindman, Paul	Sourcebooks
Humpty Dumpty Jr: Hardboiled Detective, in the Mystery of Merlin and the Gruesome Ghost	Q	F	14000	Evans, Nate and Hindman, Paul	Sourcebooks
Humvees	J	I	87	Mighty Machines	Capstone Press
Humvees	N	I	432	Pull Ahead Books	Lerner Publishing Group
#Hunchback of Notre Dame, The	W	HF	1627	Owens, L.L. (Retold)	Stone Arch Books
#Hundred- Dollar Robber, The: A Mystery with Money	P	RF	2522	Manga Math Mysteries	Graphic Universe
Hundred Dresses, The	P	RF	250+	Estes, Eleanor	Scholastic
Hundred Hugs, A	I	F	229	Sunshine	Wright Group/McGraw Hill
Hundred Penny Box, The	P	RF	250+	Mathis, Sharon Bell	Puffin Books
Hunger For Learning: A Story About Booker T. Washington, A	R	B	8474	Creative Minds Biographies	Carolrhoda Books
Hunger Games, The	Z	SF	250+	Collins, Suzanne	Scholastic
Hungry Animals	G	I	127	Little Readers	Houghton Mifflin Harcourt
Hungry as a Horse	N	F	250+	Wind Dancers	Feiwel and Friends
Hungry Bear	C	F	22	Smart Start	Rigby
Hungry Brown Bears	F	I	96	Bonnell, Kris/About	Reading Reading Books
Hungry Cat	D	RF	45	Brand New Readers	Candlewick Press
Hungry Chameleon, The	D	I	57	Bonnell, Kris	Reading Reading Books
Hungry Chickens, The	G	F	107	Literacy Tree	Rigby
Hungry Dragon, The	B	F	26	Rigby Rocket	Rigby
Hungry Farmer, The	E	RF	149	Learn to Read	Creative Teaching Press
Hungry Fox, The	E	F	158	Early Connections	Benchmark Education
Hungry Fox, The	LB	RF	12	Rigby Literacy	Rigby
Hungry Giant, The	F	F	183	Story Box	Wright Group/McGraw Hill
Hungry Giant's Baby, The	I	F	214	The Joy Cowley Collection	Hameray Publishing Group
Hungry Giant's Birthday Cake, The	G	F	241	Story Basket	Wright Group/McGraw Hill
Hungry Giant's Lunch, The	F	F	140	Story Box	Wright Group/McGraw Hill
Hungry Giant's Shoe, The	I	F	243	The Joy Cowley Collection	Hameray Publishing Group
Hungry Giant's Soup, The	G	F	42	Story Basket	Wright Group/McGraw Hill

* Collection of short stories   # Graphic text
^ Mature content with lower level text demands

TITLE	LEVEL	GENRE	WORD COUNT	AUTHOR / SERIES	PUBLISHER / DISTRIBUTOR
Hungry Goat, The	D	F	30	Ray's Readers	Outside the Box
Hungry Goat, The	C	F	33	Rise & Shine	Hampton Brown
Hungry Happy Monkey	E	F	77	Joy Readers	Pearson Learning Group
Hungry Hedgehog	C	F	79	Story Steps	Rigby
Hungry Holidays for Bella and Rosie	I	F	586	Bella and Rosie Series	Literacy Footprints
Hungry Hoppers: Grasshoppers in Your Backyard	M	I	250+	Backyard Bugs	Picture Window Books
Hungry Horse	E	RF	35	Literacy 2000	Rigby
Hungry Kitten	C	F	50	Teacher's Choice Series	Pearson Learning Group
Hungry Kitten, The	D	F	95	PM Story Books	Rigby
Hungry Ladybugs	L	I	388	Pull Ahead Books	Lerner Publishing Group
Hungry Little Birds, The	D	I	67	Bonnell, Kris	Reading Reading Books
Hungry Monster	H	F	241	Story Box	Wright Group/McGraw Hill
Hungry Puppy, A	D	F	103	Bella and Rosie Series	Literacy Footprints
Hungry Red Fox	F	F	125	Adams, Lorraine & Bruvold, Lynn	Eaglecrest Books
Hungry Red Hawk, A	K	I	2312	Independent Readers Science	Houghton Mifflin Harcourt
Hungry Sea Star, The	I	I	69	Books for Young Learners	Richard C. Owen
Hungry Spiders	G	I	97	Gear Up!	Wright Group/McGraw Hill
Hungry Squirrel, The	C	RF	77	PM Stars	Rigby
Hungry Thing, The	M	F	250+	Slepian, Jan & Seidler, Ann	Scholastic
Hungry Turtle	F	I	173	Handprints D, Set 1	Educators Publishing Service
Hungry! Hungry! Hungry!	K	F	151	Doyle, Malachy	Peachtree
Hungry, Hungry Jack	I	RF	173	Lighthouse	Rigby
Hungry, Hungry Sharks	L	I	250+	Cole, Joanna	Random House
Hunt for Clues, A	G	RF	157	Ready Readers	Pearson Learning Group
Hunt for Pirate Gold, The	M	F	250+	Woodland Mysteries	Wright Group/McGraw Hill
Hunt, The	G	RF	162	The Rowland Reading Program Library	Rowland Reading Foundation
Hunted, The	O	I	250+	Rigby Focus	Rigby
Hunted: (House of Night)	Z+	F	250+	Cast, P. C. & Kristin	St. Martin's Griffin
Hunter and the Animals, The	WB	RF	0	DePaola, Tomie	Holiday House
Hunterman and the Crocodile, The	P	TL	250+	Diakite, Baba Wague	Scholastic
Hunter's Moon	R	RF	5887	Townsend, John	Stone Arch Books
Hunters of the Dusk: The Saga of Darren Shan	Y	F	250+	Shan, Darren	Little Brown and Company
Hunting for Mummies	T	RF	250+	Reading Expeditions	National Geographic
Hunting for Treasure	I	RF	359	Red Rocket Readers	Flying Start Books
Hunting Sharks	M	I	250+	Pull Ahead Books	Lerner Publishing Group
Hunting Squirrels	I	F	254	Jack and Daisy	Pioneer Valley
Hunting the Horned Lizard	R	I	250+	Orbit Chapter Books	Pacific Learning
Hunting with My Camera	S	I	250+	Literacy 2000	Rigby
Hup Pups	F	F	89	Supersonics	Rigby
Hurdles and Jumps	M	I	250+	Take Two Books	Wright Group/McGraw Hill
*Hurray For Ali Baba Bernstein	O	RF	250+	Hurwitz, Johanna	Scholastic
Hurricane	S	HF	250+	Duey, Kathleen; Bale, Karen A.	Simon & Schuster
Hurricane	D	RF	36	Joy Readers	Pearson Learning Group
Hurricane at the Zoo!	N	I	250+	Literacy by Design	Rigby
Hurricane Diary	T	RF	3392	Leveled Readers Science	Houghton Mifflin Harcourt
Hurricane Dog	G	RF	175	Kaleidoscope Collection	Hameray Publishing Group
Hurricane Hunters	R	I	250+	Explorer Books-Pathfinder	National Geographic
Hurricane Hunters	P	I	250+	Explorer Books-Pioneer	National Geographic
Hurricane Katrina Dogs	K	I	250+	All About Dogs	Literacy Footprints
*Hurricane Machine and Other Cases, The	O	RF	250+	Simon, Seymour	Avon Books

H

TITLE	LEVEL	GENRE	WORD COUNT	AUTHOR / SERIES	PUBLISHER / DISTRIBUTOR
Hurricane Music	Y	RF	2564	Leveled Readers	Houghton Mifflin Harcourt
Hurricane On Its Way!	N	I	250+	Greetings	Rigby
Hurricane on Seashell Island	O	F	250+	Reading Safari	Mondo Publishing
Hurricane Opal: Into the Storm	U	RF	1931	Leveled Readers	Houghton Mifflin Harcourt
^Hurricane Power	X	RF	250+	Orca Sports	Orca Books
Hurricane Wolf	K	RF	250+	Paterson, Diane	Albert Whitman & Co.
Hurricane!	M	RF	250+	InfoTrek Plus	ETA/Cuisenaire
Hurricane!	N	RF	250+	London, Jonathan	Hampton Brown
Hurricanes	F	I	107	Bonnell, Kris/About	Reading Reading Books
Hurricanes	W	I	250+	Disasters Up Close	Lerner Publishing Group
Hurricanes	Q	I	250+	Discovery Links	Newbridge
Hurricanes	M	I	160	Earth in Action	Capstone Press
Hurricanes	T	I	250+	iOpeners	Pearson Learning Group
Hurricanes	S	I	250+	Natural Disasters	Capstone Press
Hurricanes	M	I	564	Pull Ahead Books	Lerner Publishing Group
Hurricanes	S	I	250+	Theme Sets	National Geographic
Hurricanes	N	I	250+	Weather Update	Capstone Press
Hurricanes & Tornadoes	R	I	250+	The Wonders of Our World	Crabtree
Hurricanes and Storms	M	I	250+	Rosen Real Readers	Rosen Publishing Group
Hurricanes!	N	I	250+	Hopping, Jean	Scholastic
Hurricanes: Earth's Mightiest Storms	T	I	250+	Lauber, Patricia	Scholastic
Hurry Squirrel!	E	RF	72	Start to Read	School Zone
Hurry Up	D	RF	49	Voyages	SRA/McGraw Hill
Hurry Up!	D	I	81	Explorations	Okapi Educational Materials
Hurry Up!	D	RF	81	Explorations	Eleanor Curtain Publishing
Hurry Up!	J	RF	250+	Literacy by Design	Rigby
Hurry Up!	G	RF	131	Rookie Readers	Children's Press
Hurry Up, Hippo!	B	F	54	Literacy by Design	Rigby
Hurry Up, Lucy!	I	RF	340	Sun Sprouts	ETA/Cuisenaire
Hurry! Hurry!	I	RF	810	Spirn, Michele	January Books
Hurt Go Happy	W	RF	250+	Rorby, Ginny	Tom Doherty
Hush	U	RF	250+	Woodson, Jacqueline	Scholastic
Hush Harbor: Praying in Secret	T	HF	1945	Evans, Freddi Williams	Carolrhoda Books
Hush Up!	L	F	250+	Little Celebrations	Pearson Learning Group
Hush, Little Ones	J	F	172	Butler, John	Peachtree
Hushtown: A Peaceful Community	Q	RF	250+	Massie, Elizabeth	Steck-Vaughn
Husky in a Hut	Q	RF	250+	Baglio, Ben M.	Scholastic
Hut in the Old Tree, The	I	RF	250+	PM Plus Story Books	Rigby
Huzzard Buzzard	F	F	112	Reese, Bob	Children's Press
Hybrid Cars	U	I	7534	A Great Idea	Norwood House Press
Hydroelectric Power	V	I	250+	Energy at Work	Capstone Press
Hydroplanes	M	I	250+	Horsepower	Capstone Press
Hyena	L	I	250+	A Day in the Life: Grassland Animals	Heinemann Library
Hyena Tricks Vulture	N	F	1472	Take Two Books	Wright Group/McGraw Hill
Hyenas	P	I	1999	Animal Scavengers	Lerner Publishing Group
Hyenas	O	I	250+	Holmes, Kevin J.	Red Brick Learning
^Hypnotized	Z	RF	250+	Orca Currents	Orca Books
*Hypnotized Frog and Other Cases, The	O	RF	250+	Simon, Seymour	Avon Books
Hyrax of Top-Knot Island, The	S	I	1762	Leveled Readers	Houghton Mifflin Harcourt
Hyrax, The: An Interesting Puzzle	R	I	250+	Leveled Readers Language Support	Houghton Mifflin Harcourt

H

* Collection of short stories   # Graphic text
^ Mature content with lower level text demands

TITLE	LEVEL	GENRE	WORD COUNT	AUTHOR / SERIES	PUBLISHER / DISTRIBUTOR
I Almost Love You, Eddie Clegg	W	RF	250+	Supplee, Audra	Peachtree
I Am	A	RF	21	Klein, Adria	Scholastic
I Am	B	RF	32	Little Readers	Houghton Mifflin Harcourt
I Am	D	RF	27	Rookie Readers	Children's Press
I Am	B	RF	32	Seedlings	Continental Press
I Am . . .	A	RF	20	Sunshine	Wright Group/McGraw Hill
I Am a Bee	A	F	24	Sails	Rigby
I Am a Book	M	F	730	Silly Millies	Millbrook Press
I Am a Bookworm	C	F	32	Sunshine	Wright Group/McGraw Hill
I Am a Dancer	O	RF	247	Collins, Pat Lowery	Millbrook Press
I Am a Dentist	C	I	20	Read-More Books	Pearson Learning Group
I Am a Drummer	E	I	32	iOpeners	Pearson Learning Group
I Am a Fireman	D	I	45	Read-More Books	Pearson Learning Group
I Am a Gypsy Pot	K	F	220	Evangeline Nicholas Collection	Wright Group/McGraw Hill
I Am a Leader	I	I	120	Character Values	Capstone Press
I Am a Leaf	L	I	250+	Marzollo, Jean	Scholastic
I Am a Painter	A	F	24	Sails	Rigby
I Am a Pencil	M	F	778	Silly Millies	Millbrook Press
I Am a Photographer	E	I	32	Read-More Books	Pearson Learning Group
I Am a Rock	J	I	250+	Marzollo, Jean	Scholastic
I Am a Sea Horse: The Life of a Dwarf Sea Horse	N	I	250+	I Live in the Ocean	Picture Window Books
I Am a Star	B	RF	32	Little Readers	Houghton Mifflin Harcourt
I Am a Star	I	I	195	Marzollo, Jean	Scholastic
I Am a Star: Child of the Holocaust	W	I	250+	Auerbacher, Inge	Penguin Group
I Am a Tiger!	B	I	35	Rigby Flying Colors	Rigby
I Am a Train Driver	D	I	32	Read-More Books	Pearson Learning Group
I Am Alive!	D	I	109	Literacy by Design	Rigby
I Am America	N	I	140	Smith Jr., Charles R.	Scholastic
I Am an American: A True Story of Japanese Internment	Z	I	250+	Stanley, Jerry	Scholastic
I Am an Apple	H	I	166	Marzollo, Jean	Scholastic
I Am an Artist	C	I	30	Rosen Real Readers	Rosen Publishing Group
I Am an Explorer	D	RF	32	Rookie Readers	Children's Press
I Am Apache	Y	HF	250+	Landman, Tanya	Candlewick Press
I Am Blind	G	I	160	PM Science Readers	Rigby
I Am Bored	D	RF	65	The King School Series	Townsend Press
I Am Busy	C	RF	43	Windows on Literacy	National Geographic
I Am Cold	E	RF	136	Foundations	Wright Group/McGraw Hill
I Am Courageous	I	I	110	Character Values	Capstone Press
I Am Danny	A	RF	23	Coulton, Mia	Maryruth Books
I Am Deaf	H	I	227	PM Science Readers	Rigby
I Am Fire	G	I	162	Marzollo, Jean	Scholastic
I Am Friendly	G	I	103	Character Values	Capstone Press
I Am Frightened	B	RF	41	Story Box	Wright Group/McGraw Hill
I Am Generous	G	I	89	Pebble Books	Capstone Press
I Am Going	B	RF	31	Sun Sprouts	ETA/Cuisenaire
I Am Here	B	F	36	Sails	Rigby
I Am Hot	E	RF	123	Foundations	Wright Group/McGraw Hill
I Am Jumping	A	RF	18	Sails	Rigby
I Am Jumping	A	RF	24	Sun Sprouts	ETA/Cuisenaire
I Am King!	E	F	57	My First Reader	Grolier
I Am Mad!	E	RF	112	Real Kids Readers	Millbrook Press
I Am Not Afraid	K	RF	250+	Mann, Kenny	Bantam Books

TITLE	LEVEL	GENRE	WORD COUNT	AUTHOR / SERIES	PUBLISHER / DISTRIBUTOR
I Am Not Esther	Z+	RF	250+	Beale, Fleur	Hyperion
I Am Patriotic	H	I	76	Pebble Books	Red Brick Learning
I Am Planet Earth	G	I	124	Marzollo, Jean	Scholastic
I Am Polite	G	I	76	Pebble Books	Capstone Press
I Am Regina	U	HF	250+	Keehn, Sally	Bantam Books
I Am Rene, the Boy	M	RF	250+	Lafnez, RenT Colato	Pinata Publishing
I Am Rosa Parks	O	B	250+	Parks, Rosa	Dial/Penguin
I Am Running	A	I	24	PM Plus Starters	Rigby
I Am Six	F	I	75	Avenues	Hampton Brown
I Am Special	C	RF	38	Learn to Read	Creative Teaching Press
I Am Tama, Lucky Cat: A Japanese Legend	P	TL	14570	Henrichs, Wendy	Peachtree
I Am Thankful	A	RF	42	Carousel Earlybirds	Pearson Learning Group
I Am the Cheese	Z	RF	250+	Cormier, Robert	Laurel-Leaf Books
I Am the Ice Worm	S	F	250+	Easley, Mary Ann	Yearling Books
I Am the Walrus	R	I	250+	Storyteller-Autumn Leaves	Wright Group/McGraw Hill
I Am Tolerant	H	I	132	Pebble Books	Red Brick Learning
I Am Too Absolutely Small for School	M	RF	250+	Child, Lauren	Candlewick Press
I Am Water	A	I	25	Independent Readers Science	Houghton Mifflin Harcourt
I Am Water	A	I	25	Science Support Readers	Houghton Mifflin Harcourt
I Am Working	A	F	18	Sails	Rigby
I and You and Don't Forget Who: What is a Pronoun?	O	I	382	Words Are CATegorical	Millbrook Press
I Bought My Lunch Today	I	I	90	City Kids	Rigby
I Can	A	RF	21	Carousel Earlybirds	Pearson Learning Group
I Can	B	I	40	InfoTrek	ETA/Cuisenaire
I Can	B	RF	54	Little Readers	Houghton Mifflin Harcourt
I Can	B	RF	21	New Way	Steck-Vaughn
I Can	B	RF	40	Ready Readers	Pearson Learning Group
I Can	A	F	18	Sails	Rigby
I Can	C	RF	27	Visions	Wright Group/McGraw Hill
I Can Be Anything	E	RF	242	Pair-It Books	Steck-Vaughn
I Can Be Anything!	L	F	84	Spinelli, Jerry	Little Brown and Company
I Can Breathe Underwater	G	RF	44	Windows on Literacy	National Geographic
I Can Build a House	D	I	52	Watanabe, Shiego	Viking/Penguin
I Can Change Things!	A	RF	29	Leveled Readers Science	Houghton Mifflin Harcourt
I Can Dig	C	I	45	Can You Do This?	SRA/McGraw Hill
I Can Do Anything!	C	RF	21	Sunshine	Wright Group/McGraw Hill
I Can Do It	I	RF	200	Bookshop	Mondo Publishing
I Can Do It Myself	H	RF	266	Adams, Diane	Peachtree
I Can Do It Myself	C	RF	37	Literacy 2000	Rigby
I Can Do It Myself	E	RF	150	Visions	Wright Group/McGraw Hill
I Can Do It!	D	RF	74	Early Learning Modules	Steck-Vaughn
I Can Do It!	A	RF	30	Gear Up!	Wright Group/McGraw Hill
I Can Do It!	Q	I	250+	Kids Talk	Picture Window Books
I Can Do It, I Really Can	G	RF	195	Teacher's Choice Series	Pearson Learning Group
I Can Do Lots of Stuff!	E	RF	72	Reading Street	Pearson
I Can Do Many Things	C	RF	43	Carousel Readers	Pearson Learning Group
I Can Draw	C	RF	75	Carousel Earlybirds	Pearson Learning Group
I Can Draw	C	RF	57	Gear Up!	Wright Group/McGraw Hill
I Can Draw	C	RF	37	Learn to Read	Creative Teaching Press
I Can Draw	A	I	35	Pacific Literacy	Pacific Learning
I Can Draw	A	I	33	Sun Sprouts	ETA/Cuisenaire
I Can Eat	C	I	51	Can You Do This?	SRA/McGraw Hill
I Can Find	E	I	131	Teacher's Choice Series	Pearson Learning Group

* Collection of short stories   # Graphic text
^ Mature content with lower level text demands

TITLE	LEVEL	GENRE	WORD COUNT	AUTHOR / SERIES	PUBLISHER / DISTRIBUTOR
I Can Fly	F	F	107	Carousel Readers	Pearson Learning Group
I Can Fly	B	RF	86	InfoTrek	ETA/Cuisenaire
I Can Fly	C	F	68	Lighthouse	Rigby
I Can Fly	B	F	21	Sunshine	Wright Group/McGraw Hill
I Can Hear	A	RF	32	TOTTS	Tott Publications
I Can Help	C	RF	73	McAlpin, MaryAnn	Short Tales Press
I Can Help	A	F	30	Sails	Rigby
I Can Help	D	RF	65	Teacher's Choice Series	Pearson Learning Group
I Can Hop. Can You?	B	I	41	Independent Readers Science	Houghton Mifflin Harcourt
I Can Jump	C	F	40	Sunshine	Wright Group/McGraw Hill
I Can Laugh	A	RF	18	Sails	Rigby
I Can Make a Flower	A	I	32	InfoTrek	ETA/Cuisenaire
I Can Make Music	B	I	41	Little Red Readers	Sundance
I Can Make You Red	B	F	43	The Book Project	Sundance
I Can Measure an Elephant	R	I	521	Independent Readers Science	Houghton Mifflin Harcourt
I Can Mix Colors	B	I	49	Bonnell, Kris	Reading Reading Books
I Can Move!	B	I	39	Leveled Readers Science	Houghton Mifflin Harcourt
I Can Move!	A	I	18	Vocabulary Readers	Houghton Mifflin Harcourt
I Can Paint	A	RF	35	Book Bank	Wright Group/McGraw Hill
I Can Paint a Picture	C	I	26	Rosen Real Readers	Rosen Publishing Group
I Can Play	C	I	45	Can You Do This?	SRA/McGraw Hill
I Can Play	B	RF	32	Handprints B	Educators Publishing Service
I Can Play Soccer	F	I	120	Welcome Books	Children's Press
I Can Play Tangram	E	I	99	Pacific Literacy	Pacific Learning
I Can Push	A	RF	29	Bookshop	Mondo Publishing
I Can Read	A	I	35	Learn to Read	Creative Teaching Press
I Can Read	A	I	47	Leveled Literacy Intervention/ Orange System	Heinemann
I Can Read	A	RF	35	Pacific Literacy	Pacific Learning
I Can Read	C	RF	38	Teacher's Choice Series	Pearson Learning Group
I Can Read Anything	C	F	42	Sunshine	Wright Group/McGraw Hill
I Can Read with My Eyes Shut	J	F	250+	Seuss, Dr.	Random House
I Can Read! I Can Read!	L	RF	250+	Little Celebrations	Pearson Learning Group
I Can Ride	C	I	66	Can You Do This?	SRA/McGraw Hill
I Can Ride	A	I	66	Sun Sprouts	ETA/Cuisenaire
I Can Ride My Bike	E	RF	224	Rigby Flying Colors	Rigby
I Can See	A	F	40	Carousel Earlybirds	Pearson Learning Group
I Can See	E	RF	38	Cervantes, Jesus	Scholastic
I Can See	A	I	35	Independent Readers Science	Houghton Mifflin Harcourt
I Can See	B	RF	36	Rigby Focus	Rigby
I Can See	C	I	35	Science Support Readers	Houghton Mifflin Harcourt
I Can See My Shadow	F	I	55	Windows on Literacy	National Geographic
I Can See the Leaves	K	RF	368	Pacific Literacy	Pacific Learning
I Can See You	D	RF	66	Sun Sprouts	ETA/Cuisenaire
I Can Spell Dinosaur	F	RF	82	Predictable Storybooks	SRA/McGraw Hill
I Can Squeak	E	RF	154	Windmill Books	Wright Group/McGraw Hill
I Can Swim	D	RF	61	Ready Readers	Pearson Learning Group
I Can Swim	A	F	18	Sails	Rigby
I Can Take Care of the Earth	C	I	72	Independent Readers Science	Houghton Mifflin Harcourt
I Can Talk with My Hands	G	RF	146	Learn to Read	Creative Teaching Press
I Can Taste	C	I	31	Teacher's Choice Series	Pearson Learning Group
I Can Use a Computer	D	RF	52	Teacher's Choice Series	Pearson Learning Group
I Can Wash	C	RF	66	Carousel Earlybirds	Pearson Learning Group

TITLE	LEVEL	GENRE	WORD COUNT	AUTHOR / SERIES	PUBLISHER / DISTRIBUTOR
I Can Write	A	RF	40	Learn to Read	Pacific Learning
I Can Write, Can You?	B	RF	30	Stewart, Josie; Salem, Lynn	Continental Press
I Can!	B	I	26	Time for Kids	Teacher Created Materials
I Can!	F	I	131	Twig	Wright Group/McGraw Hill
I Can!	A	I	15	Vocabulary Readers	Houghton Mifflin Harcourt
I Can!	A	I	15	Vocabulary Readers/CA	Houghton Mifflin Harcourt
I Can, Can You	B	RF	35	Springboard	Wright Group/McGraw Hill
I Can, I Can!	A	I	21	Little Readers	Houghton Mifflin Harcourt
I Can't Find It!	WB	RF	0	Rigby Literacy	Rigby
I Can't Open It!	E	F	76	Rigby Literacy	Rigby
I Can't Said the Ant	M	F	250+	Cameron, Polly	Scholastic
I Can't See	C	RF	36	Little Celebrations	Pearson Learning Group
I Can't Sleep	D	F	71	Learn to Read	Creative Teaching Press
I Can't Wait to Read	H	RF	185	Adventures in Reading	Pearson Learning Group
I Can't Whistle	D	F	133	Red Rocket Readers	Flying Start Books
I Care: American Reformers	S	I	914	Independent Readers Social Studies	Houghton Mifflin Harcourt
I Climb	C	I	57	This Is the Way I Go	SRA/McGraw Hill
I Could Be	D	RF	71	Sun Sprouts	ETA/Cuisenaire
I Could Be	B	RF	40	Visions	Wright Group/McGraw Hill
I Could Eat You Up!	I	RF	74	Harper, Jo	Holiday House
I Crawl	C	I	56	This Is the Way I Go	SRA/McGraw Hill
I Did It!	E	RF	213	Handprints D, Set 1	Educators Publishing Service
I Did It, Dear Dragon	E	F	251	Dear Dragon	Norwood House Press
I Did That!	I	RF	250+	Momentum Literacy Program	Troll Associates
I Do Not Like Peas	D	RF	32	Visions	Wright Group/McGraw Hill
I Don't Believe It!	L	RF	250+	Home Connection Collection	Rigby
I Don't Care	H	F	250+	Reading Friends	Pearson Learning Group
I Don't Care!	H	RF	250+	TOTTS	Tott Publications
I Don't Like Peas	F	RF	89	Start to Read	School Zone
I Don't Think It's Fair	G	RF	147	Teacher's Choice Series	Pearson Learning Group
I Don't Want a Posh Dog!	I	RF	119	Dodd, Emma	Little Brown and Company
I Don't Want To	E	RF	144	Rigby Rocket	Rigby
I Double Dare You	S	RF	1910	Leveled Readers	Houghton Mifflin Harcourt
I Dream	K	RF	583	Sunshine	Wright Group/McGraw Hill
I Dress Up Like Mama	C	RF	35	Visions	Wright Group/McGraw Hill
I Eat Leaves	C	I	47	Bookshop	Mondo Publishing
I Feel Cold	C	RF	57	Home Connection Collection	Rigby
I Feel Hot	C	RF	58	Home Connection Collection	Rigby
I Feel Like a Dummy	H	RF	211	The King School Series	Townsend Press
I Feel Sick	A	RF	15	Science	Outside the Box
I Fixed Breakfast	H	RF	176	Teacher's Choice Series	Pearson Learning Group
I Fly	C	I	57	This Is the Way I Go	SRA/McGraw Hill
I Follow Rules at School	A	I	21	Early Explorers	Benchmark Education
I Found a Can	C	I	33	Twig	Wright Group/McGraw Hill
I Get Ready for School	C	RF	37	Visions	Wright Group/McGraw Hill
I Get the Creeps	K	RF	250+	Reading Corners	Pearson Learning Group
I Get Tired	B	RF	37	Carousel Earlybirds	Pearson Learning Group
I Go to Gymnastics	D	I	58	Sun Sprouts	ETA/Cuisenaire
I Go with Grandpa	E	RF	100	Landman, Yael	Scholastic
I Go, Go, Go	B	F	21	Sunshine	Wright Group/McGraw Hill
I Got a "D" in Salami	R	RF	250+	Winkler, Henry and Oliver, Lin	Grosset & Dunlap
I Got a Goldfish	E	F	92	Ready Readers	Pearson Learning Group

* Collection of short stories   # Graphic text
^ Mature content with lower level text demands

TITLE	LEVEL	GENRE	WORD COUNT	AUTHOR / SERIES	PUBLISHER / DISTRIBUTOR
I Grow Too!	C	I	30	Start to Read	School Zone
I Had Seen Castles	Z+	HF	250+	Rylant, Cynthia	Harcourt, Inc.
I Hadn't Meant to Tell You This	Z	RF	250+	Woodson, Jacqueline	Bantam Books
I Hate Camping	M	RF	250+	Petersen, P. J.	Penguin Group
I Hate Company	M	RF	250+	Petersen, P. J.	Penguin Group
I Hate English	L	RF	250+	Levine, Ellen	Scholastic
I Hate My Best Friend	L	RF	250+	Rosner, Ruth	Hyperion
I Have 10	A	RF	29	InfoTrek	ETA/Cuisenaire
I Have a Coin	B	I	64	Early Explorers	Benchmark Education
I Have a Dream	Q	B	250+	Davidson, Margaret	Scholastic
I Have a Home	E	RF	79	Sunshine	Wright Group/McGraw Hill
I Have a New Baby Brother	F	F	163	Learn to Read	Creative Teaching Press
I Have a Paper Route	I	I	90	City Kids	Rigby
I Have a Pet	B	RF	35	Reading Corners	Pearson Learning Group
I Have a Question, Grandma	G	RF	124	Literacy 2000	Rigby
I Have a Watch!	C	RF	60	Williams, Deborah	Kaeden Books
I Have Another Language	F	RF	92	Instant Readers	Harcourt School Publishers
I Have Feelings!	J	F	250+	Bookshop	Mondo Publishing
I Have Fifty Cents	J	I	156	Early Explorers	Benchmark Education
I Have Five Senses	D	I	89	Literacy by Design	Rigby
I Have Five Senses	D	I	89	On Our Way to English	Rigby
I Have Heard of a Land	Q	HF	250+	Thomas, Joyce Carol	HarperTrophy
I Have Lived a Thousand Years	Y	B	250+	Bitton-Jackson, Livia	Simon & Schuster
I Have Not Yet Begun to Fight: A Story About John Paul Jones	R	B	8692	Creative Minds Biographies	Carolrhoda Books
I Have Self-Respect	I	I	112	Character Values	Capstone Press
I Have Shoes	C	RF	24	Visions	Wright Group/McGraw Hill
I Hear!	A	I	33	Early Connections	Benchmark Education
I Heard the Owl Call My Name	Z	RF	250+	Craven, Margaret	Random House
I Heard, Said the Bird	J	F	250+	Berends, Polly Berrien	Dial/Penguin
I Help in the Garden	B	RF	34	Windows on Literacy	National Geographic
I Help My Dad	A	I	24	Windows on Literacy	National Geographic
I Hope It Floats!	R	I	250+	Literacy by Design	Rigby
I Jump	C	I	56	This Is the Way I Go	SRA/McGraw Hill
I Just Forgot	G	F	250+	Mayer, Mercer	Scholastic
I Know a Lady	L	RF	221	Zolotow, Charlotte	Penguin Group
I Know an Old Lady	H	F	82	Readalong Rhythms	Wright Group/McGraw Hill
I Know an Old Lady	K	TL	250+	Traditional Songs	Picture Window Books
I Know an Old Lady Who Swallowed a Fly	J	TL	250+	Westcott, Nadine Bernard	Little Brown and Company
I Know an Old Teacher	N	TL	476	Bowen, Anne	Carolrhoda Books
I Know It Is Living	E	I	26	Living or Nonliving	Lerner Publishing Group
I Know It Is Nonliving	E	I	34	Living or Nonliving	Lerner Publishing Group
I Know Karate	E	RF	62	Packard, Mary	Scholastic
I Know Someone Who Is Obese	M	I	250+	Understand Health Issues	Heinemann Library
I Know Someone Who Uses a Wheelchair	M	I	250+	Understand Health Issues	Heinemann Library
I Know Someone with a Hearing Impairment	M	I	250+	Understand Health Issues	Heinemann Library
I Know Someone with a Visual Impairment	M	I	250+	Understand Health Issues	Heinemann Library
I Know Someone with ADHD	M	I	250+	Understand Health Issues	Heinemann Library
I Know Someone with Allergies	M	I	250+	Understand Health Issues	Heinemann Library
I Know Someone with Asthma	M	I	250+	Understand Health Issues	Heinemann Library
I Know Someone with Autism	M	I	250+	Understand Health Issues	Heinemann Library
I Know Someone with Cancer	N	I	250+	Understand Health Issues	Heinemann Library
I Know Someone with Diabetes	N	I	250+	Understand Health Issues	Heinemann Library
I Know Someone with Down Syndrome	M	I	250+	Understand Health Issues	Heinemann Library

TITLE	LEVEL	GENRE	WORD COUNT	AUTHOR / SERIES	PUBLISHER / DISTRIBUTOR
I Know Someone with Dyslexia	M	I	250+	Understand Health Issues	Heinemann Library
I Know Someone with Eczema	N	I	250+	Understand Health Issues	Heinemann Library
I Know Someone with Epilepsy	N	I	250+	Understand Health Issues	Heinemann Library
I Know Someone with HIV/AIDS	N	I	250+	Understand Health Issues	Heinemann Library
I Know That Tune!	F	RF	201	Foundations	Wright Group/McGraw Hill
I Know That!	I	I	99	Sunshine	Wright Group/McGraw Hill
I Know What You Did Last Summer	Z+	RF	250+	Duncan, Lois	Little Brown and Company
I Know Why the Caged Bird Sings	Z+	B	250+	Angelou, Maya	Bantam Books
I Know, I Know!	U	RF	1820	Leveled Readers	Houghton Mifflin Harcourt
I Like	B	RF	53	Early Connections	Benchmark Education
I Like	C	RF	24	Literacy 2000	Rigby
I Like	A	RF	24	Sunshine	Wright Group/McGraw Hill
I Like Apples	A	RF	12	Windows on Literacy	National Geographic
I Like Balloons	A	RF	27	Reading Corners	Pearson Learning Group
I Like Being Outdoors	WB	I	0	Windows on Literacy	National Geographic
I Like Bikes	A	I	24	Sun Sprouts	ETA/Cuisenaire
I Like Books	D	F	168	Browne, Anthony	Random House
I Like Boxes	B	F	30	Sails	Rigby
I Like Cars	B	RF	36	Rigby Rocket	Rigby
I Like Cheese	G	I	105	Welcome Books	Children's Press
I Like Dogs	C	RF	35	Rigby Literacy	Rigby
I Like Elephants	A	F	18	Sails	Rigby
I Like Farm Animals	B	I	32	Reach	National Geographic
I Like Flowers	B	F	35	Coulton, Mia	Maryruth Books
I Like Fruit	LB	RF	18	Visions	Wright Group/McGraw Hill
I Like Green	C	RF	47	Literacy 2000	Rigby
I Like Green	B	F	28	The Book Project	Sundance
I Like Hats	A	RF	18	Sails	Rigby
I Like It Like That: Gossip Girl	Z+	RF	250+	von Ziegesar, Cecily	Little Brown and Company
I Like It When . . .	E	RF	82	Ready Set Read	Steck-Vaughn
I Like Jam	B	F	30	Sails	Rigby
I Like Me	A	RF	31	Visions	Wright Group/McGraw Hill
I Like Mess	E	RF	74	Real Kids Readers	Millbrook Press
I Like My Picture!	D	RF	160	Teacher's Choice Series	Pearson Learning Group
I Like My Stuff	C	F	56	Potato Chip Books	American Reading Company
I Like Painting	C	RF	42	Little Red Readers	Sundance
I Like Playing	B	RF	38	Rigby Flying Colors	Rigby
I Like Red	A	RF	18	Sails	Rigby
I Like Rice	B	I	36	First Stories	Pacific Learning
I Like Riding	A	F	18	Sails	Rigby
I Like Salad	A	I	24	InfoTrek	ETA/Cuisenaire
I Like School	C	I	107	Vocabulary Readers	Houghton Mifflin Harcourt
I Like School	C	I	107	Vocabulary Readers/CA	Houghton Mifflin Harcourt
I Like Shapes	LB	RF	21	Armstrong, Shane	Scholastic
I Like Shopping	J	RF	287	Sunshine	Wright Group/McGraw Hill
I Like That Horse	B	RF	68	First Stories	Pacific Learning
I Like Things	F	RF	250+	Let's Play	Norwood House Press
I Like to Count	C	RF	40	Ready Readers	Pearson Learning Group
I Like to Eat	A	RF	41	Reading Corners	Pearson Learning Group
I Like to Eat...	C	RF	56	Sunshine	Wright Group/McGraw Hill
I Like to Find Things	C	I	40	Sunshine	Wright Group/McGraw Hill
I Like to Have Fun!	A	RF	24	Bonnell, Kris	Reading Reading Books
I Like to Help	E	I	137	In Step Readers	Rigby
I Like to Help	B	RF	46	Little Books for Early Readers	University of Maine

TITLE	LEVEL	GENRE	WORD COUNT	AUTHOR / SERIES	PUBLISHER / DISTRIBUTOR
I Like to Jump	C	F	50	Rigby Literacy	Rigby
I Like to Jump	C	F	50	Rigby Star	Rigby
I Like to Paint	A	RF	29	Reading Corners	Pearson Learning Group
I Like to Paint	C	I	91	Red Rocket Readers	Flying Start Books
I Like to Play	C	RF	50	Carousel Readers	Pearson Learning Group
I Like to Read	A	RF	44	Early Emergent	Pioneer Valley
I Like to Read	B	RF	49	Little Books for Early Readers	University of Maine
I Like to Ride	C	RF	72	Little Readers	Houghton Mifflin Harcourt
I Like to Win!	E	RF	96	Real Kids Readers	Millbrook Press
I Like to Write	C	RF	62	Carousel Readers	Pearson Learning Group
I Like Worms!	D	F	213	Sunshine	Wright Group/McGraw Hill
I Listen	F	RF	84	Windows on Literacy	National Geographic
I Live in a House	D	I	51	Read-More Books	Pearson Learning Group
I Live in an Apartment	D	I	41	Read-More Books	Pearson Learning Group
I Live in an Apartment Building	I	I	111	City Kids	Rigby
I Live in the Rockies	L	I	259	Windows on Literacy	National Geographic
I Live on a Farm	C	I	42	Read-More Books	Pearson Learning Group
I Lost My Tooth in Africa	N	RF	250+	Diakite, Penda	Scholastic
I Lost Something	C	RF	74	The King School Series	Townsend Press
I Love a Parade	C	I	38	Yellow Umbrella Books	Red Brick Learning
I Love Bugs	C	RF	40	Bookshop	Mondo Publishing
I Love Camping	E	RF	83	Carousel Readers	Pearson Learning Group
I Love Camping	B	RF	34	Early Emergent	Pioneer Valley
I Love Cats	I	RF	104	Bookshop	Mondo Publishing
I Love Cats	E	RF	116	Rookie Readers	Children's Press
I Love Chickens	D	F	67	Story Box	Wright Group/McGraw Hill
I Love Fishing	D	RF	37	Rookie Readers	Children's Press
I Love Guinea Pigs	M	I	250+	Read and Wonder	Candlewick Press
I Love Ladybugs	C	RF	68	Van Allen, Roach	Wright Group/McGraw Hill
I Love Mud and Mud Loves Me	D	RF	121	Stephens, Vicki	Scholastic
I Love Music	C	RF	41	Carousel Readers	Pearson Learning Group
I Love My Family	B	I	31	Bonnell, Kris	Reading Reading Books
I Love My Family	B	RF	34	Foundations	Wright Group/McGraw Hill
I Love My Family	B	RF	31	Sunshine	Wright Group/McGraw Hill
I Love My Grandma	D	RF	36	Rise & Shine	Hampton Brown
I Love My Hair!	M	RF	250+	Tarpley, Natasha Anastasia	Little Brown and Company
I Love Our Earth	I	I	68	Martin Jr., Bill & Sampson, Michael	Charlesbridge
I Love Rocks	G	RF	150	Rigby Rocket	Rigby
I Love Rocks	F	RF	95	Rookie Readers	Children's Press
I Love the Beach	M	I	250+	Literacy 2000	Rigby
I Love the Beach!	E	RF	57	Windows on Literacy	National Geographic
I Love to Sleep	C	RF	46	Potato Chip Books	American Reading Company
I Love to Sneeze	J	F	250+	Bank Street	Bantam Books
I Love to Write!	F	RF	131	Mader, Jan	Kaeden Books
I Love You	E	F	121	Teacher's Choice Series	Pearson Learning Group
I Love You Book, The	H	I	197	Parr, Todd	Little Brown and Company
I Love You So Much	J	F	250+	Norac, Carl	Scholastic
I Love You, Dear Dragon	E	F	278	Dear Dragon	Norwood House Press
I Love You, Mom	L	RF	250+	Arno, Iris Hiskey	Troll Associates
I Made a Picture	B	I	39	Storyteller	Wright Group/McGraw Hill
I Made a Trail	I	RF	191	InfoTrek	ETA/Cuisenaire
I Make Clay Pots	C	I	29	Bebop Books	Lee & Low Books Inc.
I Meowed	D	RF	58	Books for Young Learners	Richard C. Owen

TITLE	LEVEL	GENRE	WORD COUNT	AUTHOR / SERIES	PUBLISHER / DISTRIBUTOR
I Miss Grandpa	E	RF	65	InfoTrek	ETA/Cuisenaire
I Need . . .	C	RF	23	Ray's Readers	Outside the Box
I Need a Book	F	RF	113	Sunshine	Wright Group/McGraw Hill
I Need a Lunch Box	H	RF	216	Caines, Jeannette	Scholastic
I Need a Rest	F	RF	119	Home Connection Collection	Rigby
I Need Glasses: My Visit to the Optometrist	M	RF	250+	Bookshop	Mondo Publishing
I Need Something Round	H	RF	239	On Our Way to English	Rigby
I Need to Clean My Room	F	RF	157	Learn to Read	Creative Teaching Press
I Need You	F	RF	121	Rookie Readers	Children's Press
I Never Promised You a Rose Garden	Z+	RF	250+	Greenberg, Joanne	Penguin Group
I Paint	A	RF	26	Bookshop	Mondo Publishing
I Paint	A	I	22	Literacy 2000	Rigby
I Picked a Flower	C	RF	33	Science	Outside the Box
I Play Soccer	C	RF	31	Bebop Books	Lee & Low Books Inc.
I Play Soccer	J	RF	97	City Kids	Rigby
I Pledge Allegiance	Q	I	250+	Martin Jr., Bill & Sampson, Michael	Candlewick Press
I Pledge Allegiance	O	I	1421	On My Own History	Lerner Publishing Group
I Push, I Pull	B	I	40	On Our Way to English	Rigby
I Read	A	RF	38	Reading Corners	Pearson Learning Group
I Read Signs	LB	I	12	Hoban, Tana	Greenwillow Books
I Read Symbols	LB	I	14	Hoban, Tana	Greenwillow Books
I Remember	C	RF	26	Literacy 2000	Rigby
I Remember Abuelito: A Day of the Dead Story	M	RF	250+	Levy, Janice	Albert Whitman & Co.
"I Remember!" Cried Grandma Pinky	O	F	250+	Wahl, Jan	Troll Associates
I Ride the Waves	I	RF	61	Books for Young Learners	Richard C. Owen
I Rode a Horse of Milk White Jade	V	HF	250+	Wilson, Diane Lee	HarperTrophy
I Run	B	RF	22	Carousel Earlybirds	Pearson Learning Group
I Run	C	I	56	This Is the Way I Go	SRA/McGraw Hill
I Said to Sam	M	F	250+	Molnar, Gwen	Scholastic
I Saw a Dinosaur	E	F	98	Book Bus	Creative Edge
I Saw a Dinosaur	G	F	55	Literacy 2000	Rigby
I Saw a Sign	F	RF	100	Literacy Tree	Rigby
I Saw the Boston Tea Party	J	HF	273	Independent Readers Social Studies	Houghton Mifflin Harcourt
I Saw You in the Bathtub	J	TL	250+	Schwartz, Alvin	HarperTrophy
I Say, You Say	Q	I	250+	Orbit Collections	Pacific Learning
I See	B	F	29	Bookshop	Mondo Publishing
I See	A	I	32	Early Connections	Benchmark Education
I See	A	I	32	Sun Sprouts	ETA/Cuisenaire
I See	C	RF	29	Teacher's Choice Series	Pearson Learning Group
I See Animals Hiding	M	I	250+	Arnosky, Jim	Scholastic
I See Bugs	A	I	30	Blevins, Wiley	Scholastic
I See Colors	B	I	23	Learn to Read	Creative Teaching Press
I See Colors	B	RF	50	Little Readers	Houghton Mifflin Harcourt
I See Cubes	B	I	52	Early Explorers	Benchmark Education
I See Dad	A	RF	24	Literacy by Design	Rigby
I See Fall	I	RF	120	I See	Picture Window Books
I See Fish	B	I	45	Curry, Don L.	Scholastic
I See Flags	C	I	31	Blevins, Wiley	Scholastic
I See Monkeys	C	RF	39	Williams, Deborah	Kaeden Books
I See Patterns	A	I	42	Learn to Read	Creative Teaching Press
I See Patterns	C	I	43	Yellow Umbrella Books	Red Brick Learning
I See Shapes	B	I	37	Learn to Read	Creative Teaching Press

* Collection of short stories   # Graphic text
^ Mature content with lower level text demands

TITLE	LEVEL	GENRE	WORD COUNT	AUTHOR / SERIES	PUBLISHER / DISTRIBUTOR
I See Spring!	A	I	18	Vocabulary Readers	Houghton Mifflin Harcourt
I See Tails	B	I	42	Avenues	Hampton Brown
I See Tails!	B	I	42	Rise & Shine	Hampton Brown
I See Teeth	A	I	28	Look! I'm Reading!	Abrams & Company
I See Winter	I	RF	121	I See	Picture Window Books
I See You	C	I	56	Twig	Wright Group/McGraw Hill
I See, You Saw	E	F	112	Karlin, Nurit	Scholastic
I Sell	A	I	32	The Rowland Reading Program Library	Rowland Reading Foundation
I Sense the Seasons	C	I	48	Reach	National Geographic
I Shop with My Daddy	G	RF	131	Maccarone, Grace	Scholastic
I Smell Smoke!	E	RF	49	Sunshine	Wright Group/McGraw Hill
I Speak English and Chinese	F	RF	159	On Our Way to English	Rigby
I Spy	R	I	250+	Bookweb	Rigby
I Spy	A	RF	31	Lighthouse	Rigby
I Spy	I	RF	302	Literacy 2000	Rigby
I Spy	C	RF	29	Literacy Tree	Rigby
I Spy	D	RF	103	Red Rocket Readers	Flying Start Books
I Spy	B	RF	30	Story Steps	Rigby
I Spy a Fly	I	I	132	Wonder World	Wright Group/McGraw Hill
I Spy on the Farm	D	RF	110	Powell, Richard	Puffin Books
I Swim	C	I	57	This Is the Way I Go	SRA/McGraw Hill
I Take Care	E	I	88	Joy Starters	Pearson Learning Group
I Take Care of My Dog	WB	RF	0	Rigby Literacy	Rigby
I Take Care of My Dog	D	I	121	Rigby Star Quest	Rigby
I Thought I Couldn't	C	RF	40	Visions	Wright Group/McGraw Hill
I Try to Be a Good Person	H	RF	192	Learn to Read	Creative Teaching Press
I Use My Senses	B	I	28	On Our Way to English	Rigby
I Used to Be Naughty	G	F	112	McGougan, Kathy	Buddy Books Publishing
I Walk and Read	LB	I	16	Hoban, Tana	Greenwillow Books
I Want a Dog	C	RF	53	Potato Chip Books	American Reading Company
I Want a Dog	F	RF	192	Sun Sprouts	ETA/Cuisenaire
I Want a Pet	C	RF	46	Little Readers	Houghton Mifflin Harcourt
I Want a Pet	C	RF	46	Start to Read	School Zone
I Want a Pet!	H	F	167	Big Cat	Pacific Learning
I Want a Red Ball	B	F	29	The Book Project	Sundance
I Want Ice Cream	C	RF	18	Story Box	Wright Group/McGraw Hill
I Want My Lights On!: A Little Princess Story	J	F	323	Ross, Tony	Andersen Press USA
I Want My Own Room!	LB	RF	25	Visions	Wright Group/McGraw Hill
I Want Some Honey	E	F	152	Take Two Books	Wright Group/McGraw Hill
I Want to be a Ballerina	D	RF	66	Teacher's Choice Series	Pearson Learning Group
I Want to Be a Clown	F	RF	82	Start to Read	School Zone
I Want to Be an Astronaut	I	RF	79	Barton, Byron	HarperCollins
I Want to Be Me	I	F	214	Sun Sprouts	ETA/Cuisenaire
I Want to Be…	B	F	46	The Book Project	Sundance
I Want to Go Camping	I	RF	407	Leveled Readers	Houghton Mifflin Harcourt
I Want to Live: The Diary of a Young Girl in Stalin's Russia	Z	B	250+	Lugovskaya, Nina	Houghton Mifflin Harcourt
I Want Two Birthdays!	L	F	665	Ross, Tony	Andersen Press USA
I Was a Sixth Grade Alien	S	F	250+	Coville, Bruce	Pocket Books
I Was a Third Grade Science Project	N	RF	250+	Auch, Mary Jane	Yearling Books
I Was at the Zoo	J	I	250+	Literacy Tree	Rigby
I Was Just About to Go to Bed	E	RF	107	Instant Readers	Harcourt School Publishers
I Was So Mad	J	RF	232	Mayer, Mercer	Donovan

TITLE	LEVEL	GENRE	WORD COUNT	AUTHOR / SERIES	PUBLISHER / DISTRIBUTOR
I Was Walking Down the Road	H	F	299	Barchas, Sarah	Scholastic
I Wash	B	RF	33	First Stories	Pacific Learning
I Went to the Beach	C	RF	25	Books for Young Learners	Richard C. Owen
I Went to the Dentist	K	RF	152	City Kids	Rigby
I Went to the Movies	J	RF	120	City Kids	Rigby
I Went to Visit a Friend One Day	F	F	111	Voyages	SRA/McGraw Hill
I Went Walking	C	RF	105	Williams, Sue	Harcourt Trade
I Will Never Not Ever Eat a Tomato	M	RF	250+	Child, Lauren	Candlewick Press
I Will Not Eat That!	R	RF	1344	Leveled Readers	Houghton Mifflin Harcourt
I Will Not Eat That!	R	RF	1344	Leveled Readers/CA	Houghton Mifflin Harcourt
I Will Not Eat That!	R	RF	1344	Leveled Readers/TX	Houghton Mifflin Harcourt
I Will Plant You a Lilac Tree	Z	B	250+	Edge	Hampton Brown
I Will Plant You a Lilac Tree: A Memoir of a Schindler's List Survivor	Z	B	250+	Hillman, Laura	Atheneum Books
I Wish I Had a Dinosaur	D	F	46	Little Celebrations	Pearson Learning Group
I Wish I Was a Bat	C	F	31	Rigby Rocket	Rigby
I Wish I Was Sick, Too	G	RF	94	Brandenburg, Franz	Morrow
I Wish, I Wish	O	F	250+	High-Fliers	Pacific Learning
I Wonder	H	I	151	Green Light Readers	Harcourt
I Wonder	C	RF	49	Little Celebrations	Pearson Learning Group
I Wonder	F	RF	67	Sunshine	Wright Group/McGraw Hill
I Wonder Why	E	RF	73	Foundations	Wright Group/McGraw Hill
I Wonder Why Records Are Broken and Other Questions About Amazing Facts and Figures	P	I	250+	I Wonder Why	Kingfisher
I Wonder Why Snakes Shed Their Skins and Other Questions About Reptiles	O	I	250+	O'Neill, Amanda	Scholastic
I Wonder Why the Sky Is Blue	O	I	250+	Rosen Real Readers	Rosen Publishing Group
I Wonder Why There's a Hole in the Sky and Other Questions About the Environment	R	I	250+	I Wonder Why	Kingfisher
I Wonder Why Whales Sing	R	I	250+	I Wonder Why	Kingfisher
I Wonder Why?	F	I	95	Wonder World	Wright Group/McGraw Hill
I Work at Night	D	RF	49	Windows on Literacy	National Geographic
I Write	B	RF	40	Little Books for Early Readers	University of Maine
I Write	C	RF	19	Sunshine	Wright Group/McGraw Hill
I Write for the Newspaper	I	I	145	Rosen Real Readers	Rosen Publishing Group
I, Amber Brown	O	RF	250+	Danziger, Paula	Scholastic
I, Dred Scott	U	HF	250+	Moses, Sheila P.	Margaret K. McElderry Books
I, Emma Freke	T	RF	47364	Atkinson, Elizabeth	Carolrhoda Books
I, Juan de Pareja	Y	HF	250+	de Trevino, Elizabeth Borton	Square Fish
I. M. Pei	M	B	250+	Biography	Benchmark Education
^I.D.	Z+	RF	250+	Orca Soundings	Orca Books
I.M. Pei	S	B	250+	Amazing Americans	Wright Group/McGraw Hill
I.M. Pei	T	B	250+	On Our Way to English	Rigby
Iain's Eagle Eye	M	RF	250+	Lighthouse	Ginn & Co.
Ibis: A True Whale Story	K	I	250+	Himmelman, John	Scholastic
Ice	B	I	34	Gear Up!	Wright Group/McGraw Hill
Ice	Q	I	250+	Theme Sets	National Geographic
Ice	I	I	92	Windows on Literacy	National Geographic
Ice - A Cold Blanket	S	I	250+	Connectors	Pacific Learning
Ice Age Safari	P	I	250+	Rigby Focus	Rigby
Ice and Snow	D	I	71	Explorations	Eleanor Curtain Publishing
Ice and Snow	D	I	71	Explorations	Okapi Educational Materials
Ice Bear: In the Steps of the Polar Bear	N	I	250+	Davies, Nicola	Candlewick Press
Ice Climbing	M	I	250+	To the Extreme	Capstone Press

* Collection of short stories   # Graphic text
^ Mature content with lower level text demands

TITLE	LEVEL	GENRE	WORD COUNT	AUTHOR / SERIES	PUBLISHER / DISTRIBUTOR
Ice Cream	D	I	46	Benchmark Rebus	Marshall Cavendish
Ice Cream	O	I	1078	Big Cat	Pacific Learning
Ice Cream	N	I	250+	Gibbons, Gail	Holiday House
Ice Cream	B	F	36	Sails	Rigby
Ice Cream	L	I	450	Springboard	Wright Group/McGraw Hill
Ice Cream	C	RF	49	Sunshine	Wright Group/McGraw Hill
Ice Cream Dream	I	F	250+	Rigby Rocket	Rigby
Ice Cream for You	J	I	214	Windows on Literacy	National Geographic
Ice Cream Line, The	J	F	506	Pawprints Teal	Pioneer Valley
Ice Cream Man, The	E	RF	155	Joy Starters	Pearson Learning Group
Ice Cream Supreme	N	RF	250+	Book Blazers	ETA/Cuisenaire
Ice Cream Truck, The	K	RF	553	Math Stories	Pearson Learning Group
*Ice Dove and Other Stories, The	M	RF	250+	deAnda, Diane	Arte Publico
Ice Fishing	H	I	140	Ready Readers	Pearson Learning Group
Ice Fishing	S	I	250+	The Great Outdoors	Red Brick Learning
Ice Fishing Fun	Q	RF	996	Red Rocket Readers	Flying Start Books
Ice Hockey	L	I	458	Nonfiction Crimson	Pioneer Valley
Ice Hockey	K	I	250+	On Deck	Rigby
Ice Hockey	C	I	55	Readlings	American Reading Company
Ice Hockey	H	I	109	Readlings/ Sports	American Reading Company
Ice Is . . . Whee!	D	RF	59	Rookie Readers	Children's Press
Ice Magic	Q	RF	250+	Christopher, Matt	Little Brown and Company
Ice Man, The: A Traditional Native American Tale	L	TL	250+	Rigby Literacy	Rigby
Ice Mummies: Frozen in Time	V	I	250+	Mummies	Capstone Press
Ice Mummy: The Discovery of a 5,000-Year-Old Man	P	I	250+	Dubowski, Mark & Cathy East	Random House
Ice on the Move	K	I	362	Rigby Focus	Rigby
Ice Skates for Quack	K	F	625	Pawprints Teal	Pioneer Valley
Ice Storm Birthday, The	R	RF	250+	HSP/Harcourt Trophies	Harcourt, Inc.
Ice Storm, The	A	I	48	Getting Around	American Reading Company
Ice Storms	Q	I	250+	Natural Disasters	Red Brick Learning
Iceberg Ahead!	R	I	1240	Vocabulary Readers	Houghton Mifflin Harcourt
Iceberg Ahead!	R	I	1240	Vocabulary Readers/CA	Houghton Mifflin Harcourt
Iceberg Ahead!	R	I	1240	Vocabulary Readers/TX	Houghton Mifflin Harcourt
Iceberg Hermit, The	X	RF	250+	Roth, Arthur	Scholastic
Iceberg Rescue	N	HF	464	Leveled Readers	Houghton Mifflin Harcourt
Icebergs	K	I	188	Red Rocket Readers	Flying Start Books
Icebergs	L	I	250+	Sunshine	Wright Group/McGraw Hill
Ice-Cream Factory, The	J	I	250+	Rigby Literacy	Rigby
Ice-Cream Factory, The	J	I	250+	Rigby Star Quest	Rigby
Ice-Cream Stick	B	RF	35	Story Box	Wright Group/McGraw Hill
Iceland	P	I	1693	Country Explorers	Lerner Publishing Group
Iceman	Z	RF	250+	Lynch, Chris	HarperCollins
Ice-Skating	G	RF	219	Rigby Flying Colors	Rigby
Ichiro Suzuki	P	B	1546	Amazing Athletes	Lerner Publishing Group
Ichiro Suzuki	U	B	250+	Sports Heroes and Legends	Lerner Publishing Group
Ichthyosaurus	N	I	250+	Discovering Dinosaurs	Red Brick Learning
Icky Bug Alphabet Book, The	N	I	250+	Pallotta, Jerry	Charlesbridge
Icky on the Run	H	RF	203	The Rowland Reading Program Library	Rowland Reading Foundation
Icy Adventure, An	R	I	1176	Leveled Readers	Houghton Mifflin Harcourt
Icy Adventure, An	R	I	1176	Leveled Readers/CA	Houghton Mifflin Harcourt
Icy Adventure, An	R	I	1176	Leveled Readers/TX	Houghton Mifflin Harcourt

TITLE	LEVEL	GENRE	WORD COUNT	AUTHOR / SERIES	PUBLISHER / DISTRIBUTOR
Icy Cold	O	I	250+	Infotrek Plus	ETA/Cuisenaire
Icy Hand, The: Something Wickedly Weird	R	F	250+	Mould, Chris	Roaring Brook Press
*Icy Question and Other Cases, The	O	RF	250+	Simon, Seymour	Avon Books
I'd Tell You I Love You, But Then I'd Have to Kill You	W	RF	250+	Carter, Ally	Hyperion
Ida B. Wells	T	B	250+	Amazing Americans	Wright Group/McGraw Hill
Ida B . . . and Her Plans to Maximize Fun, Avoid Disaster, and (Possibly) Save the World	T	RF	250+	Hannigan, Katherine	HarperTrophy
Ida Lewis and the Lighthouse	S	I	973	Leveled Readers	Houghton Mifflin Harcourt
Idaho	T	I	250+	Hello U.S.A.	Lerner Publishing Group
Idaho	S	I	250+	Land of Liberty	Red Brick Learning
Idaho	R	I	250+	This Land Is Your Land	Compass Point Books
Idaho: Facts and Symbols	O	I	250+	The States and Their Symbols	Capstone Press
Idea Seed, An - Inventions That Change Our Lives	S	I	250+	Connectors	Pacific Learning
Ideas to Inventions	O	I	1009	Reading Street	Pearson
Iditarod, The: Story of the Last Great Race	S	I	250+	High Five Reading	Red Brick Learning
Iditarod: Dogsled Race Across Alaska	Q	I	250+	Sunshine	Wright Group/McGraw Hill
If	H	F	83	Sunshine	Wright Group/McGraw Hill
If a Chicken Stayed for Supper	K	F	250+	Weston, Carrie	Holiday House
If a Dolphin Were a Fish	N	I	358	Wlodarski, Loran	Sylvan Dell Publishing
If a Tree Could Talk	G	F	62	Learn to Read	Creative Teaching Press
If a Tree Falls at Lunch Period	Z	RF	250+	Choldenko, Gennifer	Houghton Mifflin Harcourt
If Animals Came to School	F	F	125	Learn to Read	Creative Teaching Press
If Anything Ever Goes Wrong at the Zoo	L	F	250+	Hendrick, Mary Jean	Harcourt Trade
If Dogs Ruled the World	J	F	250+	McNulty, Faith	Scholastic
If Germs Were Purple	D	F	53	Carousel Readers	Pearson Learning Group
If Horses Could Talk!	E	RF	32	Teacher's Choice Series	Pearson Learning Group
If I Could: A Mother's Promise	K	F	112	Milord, Susan	Candlewick Press
If I Forget, You Remember	V	RF	250+	Williams, Carol Lynch	Bantam Books
If I Found a Wistful Unicorn: A Gift of Love	M	F	250+	Ashford, Ann	Peachtree
If I Had a Hammer: Building Homes and Hope with Habitat for Humanity	W	I	250+	Rubel, David	Candlewick Press
If I Had an Alligator	H	F	214	Mayer, Mercer	Dial/Penguin
If I Had an Elephant	F	F	90	Teacher's Choice Series	Pearson Learning Group
If I Should Die Before I Wake	Z+	F	250+	Nolan, Han	Harcourt, Inc.
If I Stay	Z+	RF	250+	Forman, Gayle	Speak
If I Were a Ballerina	K	I	144	Dream Big	Capstone Press
If I Were a Major League Baseball Player	K	I	268	Dream Big	Capstone Press
If I Were a Penguin	H	RF	159	Goeneil, Heidi	Little Brown and Company
If I Were an Ant	I	F	51	Rookie Readers	Children's Press
If I Were an Astronaut	L	I	250+	Dream Big!	Picture Window Books
If I Were the President	L	I	250+	Dream Big!	Picture Window Books
If I Were You	K	RF	250+	Hamilton, Richard	Bloomsbury Children's Books
If I Were You	E	RF	77	Wildsmith, Brian	Oxford University Press
If I Were You...	S	F	250+	Power Up!	Steck-Vaughn
If Maps Could Talk: Using Symbols and Keys	N	I	250+	Map Mania	Capstone Press
If the Shoe Fits	K	RF	250+	Bell, Krista	Charlesbridge
If the Shoe Fits	H	F	252	Dominie Math Stories	Pearson Learning Group
If the Witness Lied	Z	RF	250+	Cooney, Caroline B.	Delacorte Press
If We Could Do What the Animals Do	G	F	188	Learn to Read	Creative Teaching Press
If Wishes Were Horses: A Kona Story	N	F	250+	Wind Dancers	Feiwel and Friends
If Wishes Were Horses: Ridgeview Riding Club	P	RF	250+	Kelly, Bernadette	Stone Arch Books
If You Come Softly	Y	RF	250+	Woodson, Jacqueline	G.P. Putnam's Sons

* Collection of short stories   # Graphic text
^ Mature content with lower level text demands

TITLE	LEVEL	GENRE	WORD COUNT	AUTHOR / SERIES	PUBLISHER / DISTRIBUTOR
If You Could Be Anything	Q	I	250+	Power Up!	Steck-Vaughn
If You Give a Cat a Cupcake	K	F	250+	Numeroff, Laura	HarperCollins
If You Give A Moose a Muffin	K	F	250+	Numeroff, Laura Joffe	HarperCollins
If You Give A Mouse a Cookie	K	F	291	Numeroff, Laura Joffe	HarperCollins
If You Give a T-Rex a Bone	N	I	842	Myers, Tim	Dawn Publications
If You Give an Author a Pencil	O	B	250+	Meet the Author	Richard C. Owen
If You Grew Up with Abraham Lincoln	Q	I	250+	McGovern, Ann	Scholastic
If You Grew Up with George Washington	Q	I	250+	Gross, Ruth Belov	Scholastic
If You Like Strawberries, Don't Read this Book	H	RF	101	Literacy 2000	Rigby
If You Lived 100 Years Ago	Q	I	250+	McGovern, Ann	Scholastic
If You Lived at the Time of Martin Luther King	Q	I	250+	Levine, Ellen	Scholastic
If You Lived at the Time of the American Revolution	Q	I	250+	Moore, Kay	Scholastic
If You Lived at the Time of the Civil War	Q	I	250+	Moore, Kay	Scholastic
If You Lived at the Time of the Great San Francisco Earthquake	Q	I	250+	Levine, Ellen	Scholastic
If You Lived Here You'd Be Home By Now	WB	F	0	Briant, Ed	Roaring Brook Press
If You Lived in Colonial Times	Q	I	250+	McGovern, Ann	Scholastic
If You Lived in the Alaska Territory	Q	I	250+	Levinson, Nancy Smiler	Scholastic
If You Lived with the Cherokee	Q	I	250+	Roop, Peter & Connie	Scholastic
If You Lived with the Hopi	Q	I	250+	Kamma, Anne	Scholastic
...If You Lived With the Indians of the Northwest Coast	Q	I	250+	Kamma, Anne	Scholastic
If You Lived with the Iroquois	Q	I	250+	Levine, Ellen	Scholastic
If You Lived with the Sioux Indians	Q	I	250+	McGovern, Ann	Scholastic
If You Meet a Dragon	C	F	31	Story Box	Wright Group/McGraw Hill
If You Miss Your Bus	F	F	160	Leveled Readers	Houghton Mifflin Harcourt
If You Sailed on the Mayflower in 1620	Q	I	250+	McGovern, Ann	Scholastic
If You See a Kitten	K	RF	81	Butler, John	Peachtree
If You Take a Mouse to the Movies	K	F	250+	Numeroff, Laura	HarperCollins
If You Traveled on the Underground Railroad	Q	I	250+	Levine, Ellen	Scholastic
If You Traveled West in a Covered Wagon	Q	I	250+	Levine, Ellen	Scholastic
If You Were a Bat	K	I	227	Gear Up!	Wright Group/McGraw Hill
If You Were a Bat	F	F	78	Instant Readers	Harcourt School Publishers
If you Were a Capital Letter	L	I	250+	Word Fun	Picture Window Books
If You Were a Circle	O	I	250+	Math Fun	Picture Window Books
If You Were a Comma	L	I	250+	Word Fun	Picture Window Books
If You Were a Contraction	L	I	250+	Word Fun	Picture Window Books
If You Were a Divided-By Sign	M	I	250+	Math Fun	Picture Window Books
If You Were a Minute	L	I	250+	Math Fun	Picture Window Books
If You Were a Parrot	M	I	250+	Rawson, Katherine	Sylvan Dell Publishing
If You Were a Period	L	I	250+	Word Fun	Picture Window Books
If You Were a Plural Word	L	I	250+	Word Fun	Picture Window Books
If You Were a Plus Sign	L	I	250+	Math Fun	Picture Window Books
If You Were a Polygon	N	I	250+	Math Fun	Picture Window Books
If You Were a Pound or a Kilogram	L	I	250+	Math Fun	Picture Window Books
If You Were a Quadrilateral	Q	I	250+	Math Fun	Picture Window Books
If You Were a Quart or a Liter	L	I	250+	Math Fun	Picture Window Books
If You Were a Question Mark	L	I	284	Word Fun	Picture Window Books
If You Were a Times Sign	M	I	250+	Math Fun	Picture Window Books
If You Were a Triangle	N	I	250+	Math Fun	Picture Window Books
If You Were an Apostrophe	N	I	250+	Word Fun	Picture Window Books
If You Were an Exclamation Point	L	I	247	Word Fun	Picture Window Books
If You Were an Inch or a Centimeter	L	I	250+	Math Fun	Picture Window Books

TITLE	LEVEL	GENRE	WORD COUNT	AUTHOR / SERIES	PUBLISHER / DISTRIBUTOR
If You Were My Baby	L	F	338	Hodgkins, Fran	Dawn Publications
If You Were Quotation Marks	L	I	250+	Word Fun	Picture Window Books
If You Were There in 1492: Everyday Life in the Time of Columbus	U	I	250+	Brenner, Barbara	Aladdin
If You Were There When They Signed the Constitution	Q	I	250+	Levy, Elizabeth	Scholastic
If You Won 100 Dollars	P	I	250+	Literacy by Design	Rigby
If Your Name was Changed at Ellis Island	Q	I	250+	Levine, Ellen	Scholastic
If You're Reading This, It's Too Late	U	F	250+	Bosch, Pseudonymous	Little Brown and Company
Iggie's House	R	RF	250+	Blume, Judy	Bantam Books
Iggy Iguana's Trip	B	F	43	Phonics and Friends	Hampton Brown
Iggy Peck, Architect	O	F	250+	Beaty, Andrea	Harry N. Abrams
Igloo	L	I	157	Bookworms	Marshall Cavendish
Igloos and Inuit Life	L	I	250+	The Big Picture	Capstone Press
Ignatius MacFarland: Frequenaut!	W	F	250+	Feig Paul	Little Brown and Company
Igneous Rocks	S	I	250+	Let's Rock	Heinemann Library
Igneous Rocks	Q	I	250+	On Deck	Rigby
Iguanodon	N	I	250+	Discovering Dinosaurs	Capstone Press
Iguanodon and Other Leaf-Eating Dinosaurs	N	I	250+	Dinosaur Find	Picture Window Books
*Ike Flies a Kite, Ike Fixes His Kite, Ivan	K	F	421	Easy-for-Me Reading	Child 1st Publications
Ike in the Spotlight	M	RF	992	Leveled Readers	Houghton Mifflin Harcourt
Ike in the Spotlight	M	RF	992	Leveled Readers/CA	Houghton Mifflin Harcourt
Ike in the Spotlight	M	RF	992	Leveled Readers/TX	Houghton Mifflin Harcourt
Ileana Ros-Lehtinen: Lawmaker	N	B	250+	Beginning Biographies	Pearson Learning Group
Iliad, The	Z+	TL	250+	Homer	Penguin Group
I'll Be a Pirate	E	F	53	Eifrig, Kate	Kaeden Books
I'll Be Good	K	RF	862	Rigby Gigglers	Rigby
I'll Be There	Y	RF	250+	Sloan, Holly Goldberg	Little Brown and Company
I'll Be There	H	RF	77	Stott, Ann	Candlewick Press
I'll Do It Later	I	RF	574	Real Kids Readers	Millbrook Press
I'll Make You a Card	G	RF	180	Early Readers	Compass Point Books
I'll Run Away	D	RF	53	Home Connection Collection	Rigby
I'll Teach My Dog 100 Words	J	F	250+	Frith, Michael	Random House
Illegal	Z	RF	250+	Restrepo, Bettina	Katherine Tegan Books
Illinois	T	I	250+	Hello U.S.A.	Lerner Publishing Group
Illinois	S	I	250+	Land of Liberty	Red Brick Learning
Illinois	Q	I	250+	One Nation	Capstone Press
Illinois: Facts and Symbols	O	I	250+	The States and Their Symbols	Capstone Press
#Illuminating World of Light with Max Axiom, Super Scientist; The	V	I	250+	Graphic Library	Capstone Press
I'm a Caterpillar	G	I	169	Marzollo, Jean	Scholastic
I'm a Chef	M	I	250+	Literacy 2000	Rigby
I'm a Girl!	J	RF	186	Jukes, Lila	Cool Kids Press
I'm a Good Reader	H	RF	188	Carousel Readers	Pearson Learning Group
I'm a Little Seed	D	F	30	Pair-It Books	Steck-Vaughn
I'm a Little Teapot	L	TL	250+	Trapani, Iza	Charlesbridge
I'm a Pill Bug	M	I	640	Tokuda, Yukihisa	Kane/Miller Book Publishers
I'm a Seed	G	F	181	Marzollo, Jean	Scholastic
I'm a Wimp!	R	RF	250+	Sails	Rigby
I'm an Artist	N	I	250+	Literacy 2000	Rigby
I'm an Astronaut	H	F	162	Voyages	SRA/McGraw Hill
I'm an Entrepreneur	N	B	501	Independent Readers Social Studies	Houghton Mifflin Harcourt
I'm and Won't, They're and Don't: What's a Contraction?	O	I	277	Words Are CATegorical	Millbrook Press

* Collection of short stories   # Graphic text
^ Mature content with lower level text demands

TITLE	LEVEL	GENRE	WORD COUNT	AUTHOR / SERIES	PUBLISHER / DISTRIBUTOR
I'm Bigger Than You!	C	F	48	Sunshine	Wright Group/McGraw Hill
I'm Brave	D	RF	51	Sunshine	Wright Group/McGraw Hill
I'm Glad I'm Me	F	RF	147	Windmill Books	Rigby
I'm Glad to Say	H	RF	165	Sunshine	Wright Group/McGraw Hill
I'm Going to Washington to Visit the President	F	RF	124	I'm Going to Read!	Sterling Publishing
I'm Heading to the Rodeo	I	RF	160	Bebop Books	Lee & Low Books Inc.
I'm Hungry	B	I	25	Fitros, Pamela	Kaeden Books
I'm Hungry	D	RF	84	Tuer, Judy	Scholastic
I'm Hungry	C	RF	37	Visions	Wright Group/McGraw Hill
I'm in the Fish Tank	M	I	865	Springboard	Wright Group/McGraw Hill
I'm King of the Castle	F	F	184	Watanabe, Shigeo	Philomel
I'm King of the Mountain	G	F	285	Pacific Literacy	Pacific Learning
I'm Looking for My Hat	F	RF	89	Book Bank	Wright Group/McGraw Hill
I'm No One Else But Me	M	RF	1010	Book Bank	Wright Group/McGraw Hill
I'm Not Afraid of This Haunted House	K	F	512	Friedman, Laurie	Carolrhoda Books
I'm Not Jess	I	RF	174	Gear Up!	Wright Group/McGraw Hill
I'm Not Scared	J	F	408	Rigby Gigglers	Rigby
I'm Not Scared Book, The	H	RF	256	Parr, Todd	Little Brown and Company
I'm Not, I'm Not	C	RF	19	Windmill Books	Wright Group/McGraw Hill
I'm Out of My Body . . . Please Leave a Message	N	F	250+	The Zack Files	Grosset & Dunlap
I'm Red	B	F	25	The Book Project	Sundance
I'm Sick Today	H	RF	150	Carousel Readers	Pearson Learning Group
I'm So Hungry and Other Plays	M	F	250+	Orbit Chapter Books	Pacific Learning
I'm Still Scared	P	B	250+	DePaola, Tomie	Puffin Books
I'm Telling	E	RF	71	Teacher's Choice Series	Pearson Learning Group
I'm Too Fond of My Fur!	O	F	250+	Stilton, Geronimo	Scholastic
I'm Too Tall	I	RF	206	The King School Series	Townsend Press
Images of Nikki Grimes, The	Y	B	1974	Leveled Readers	Houghton Mifflin Harcourt
Images of War	Z	I	250+	Boldprint	Steck-Vaughn
Imagination	O	B	250+	Meet The Author	Richard C. Owen
Imagine That	J	F	250+	Story Box	Wright Group/McGraw Hill
Imagine This, James Robert	P	F	250+	Action Packs	Rigby
Immigrant Children in New York City	V	I	1614	Reading Street	Pearson
Immigrant Community of the 1900s, An	T	I	250+	Reading Expeditions	National Geographic
Immigrants	T	I	250+	Sandler, Martin W.	HarperTrophy
Immigrants at Work: A Look at Migrant Labor	V	I	2264	Reading Street	Pearson
Immigrants Today	V	I	250+	Reading Expeditions	National Geographic
Immigrants: Coming to America	R	I	250+	Thompson, Gare	Children's Press
Immigration	U	I	250+	Primary Source Readers	Teacher Created Materials
Immi's Gift	M	F	250+	Littlewood, Karin	Peachtree
Immortal	S	HF	250+	Tristars	Richard C. Owen
Imogene's Antlers	L	F	191	Small, David	Scholastic
Important Years, The : The 1980s	P	I	1023	Leveled Readers Language Support	Houghton Mifflin Harcourt
*Impossible Bend and Other Cases, The	O	RF	250+	Simon, Seymour	Avon Books
Impossible Bridge, The	N	I	250+	Pacific Literacy	Pacific Learning
Impossible Patriotism Project, The	N	RF	250+	Skeers, Linda	Puffin Books
^Impossible Victory: The Battle of Stalingrad	X	I	250+	Bloodiest Battles	Capstone Press
Impressionism	Z	I	250+	Eyewitness Books	DK Publishing
Imran and the Watch	J	RF	415	Cambridge Reading	Pearson Learning Group
In a Cave	LB	I	11	Animal Homes	Lerner Publishing Group
*In a Dark, Dark Room	J	TL	250+	Schwartz, Alvin	HarperTrophy
In a Dark, Dark Wood	E	TL	168	Carter, David	Simon & Schuster
In a Dark, Dark Wood	E	TL	81	Story Box	Wright Group/McGraw Hill

TITLE	LEVEL	GENRE	WORD COUNT	AUTHOR / SERIES	PUBLISHER / DISTRIBUTOR
In a Faraway Forest	K	F	347	Kratky, Lada Josefa	Hampton Brown
In a Muddle	G	RF	93	Voyages	SRA/McGraw Hill
In a New Land	L	I	378	Sunshine	Wright Group/McGraw Hill
In a Nutshell	L	I	250+	Sharing Nature with Children	Dawn Publications
In a Painting	E	I	52	Canizares, Susan; Moreton, Daniel	Scholastic
In a Pickle	M	RF	250+	Supa Doopers	Sundance
In a Town	E	RF	47	Little Celebrations	Pearson Learning Group
In a Tree	LB	I	12	Animal Homes	Lerner Publishing Group
In a Tree	M	I	250+	Look Once Look Again	Creative Teaching Press
In a Tropical Rain Forest	K	I	336	Early Explorers	Benchmark Education
In Abby's Hands	Q	RF	250+	Lewis, Wendy A.	Red Deer Press
In and Out	C	RF	38	Brand New Readers	Candlewick Press
In and Out	C	I	41	Location	Lerner Publishing Group
In and Out	I	I	254	Where Words	Capstone Press
In Arctic Waters	L	F	288	Crawford, Laura	Sylvan Dell Publishing
In Aunt Lucy's Kitchen	M	RF	250+	Rylant, Cynthia	Aladdin
In Black Bear Country	N	I	250+	Books for Young Learners	Richard C. Owen
In Business with Mallory	O	RF	250+	Friedman, Laurie	Lerner Publishing Group
In City Gardens	L	I	250+	Little Celebrations	Pearson Learning Group
In Control, Ms. Wiz?	O	F	250+	Blacker, Terence	Marshall Cavendish
In Crowd, The: Dealing with Peer Pressure	Z	I	250+	What's the Issue?	Compass Point Books
In Danger	M	I	250+	Home Connection Collection	Rigby
In Defense of Liberty: The Story of America's Bill of Rights	Z	I	250+	Freedman, Russell	Holiday House
In Flight	U	I	250+	The News	Richard C. Owen
In Front of the Ant: Walking with Beetles and Other Insects	K	I	166	Kuwahara, Ryuichi	Kane/Miller Book Publishers
In Grandma Rita's Garden	K	RF	191	Books for Young Learners	Richard C. Owen
In Grandma's Garden	H	RF	244	Sunshine	Wright Group/McGraw Hill
In Her Stride	T	B	250+	WorldScapes	ETA/Cuisenaire
In Hiding, Animals Under Cover	L	I	250+	Burke, Melissa Blackwell	Steck-Vaughn
In Jail, Ms. Wiz?	O	F	250+	Blacker, Terence	Marshall Cavendish
In My Backyard	M	I	308	Giogas, Valarie	Sylvan Dell Publishing
In My Backyard	LB	RF	18	Visions	Wright Group/McGraw Hill
In My Bag	H	RF	237	Windows on Literacy	National Geographic
In My Bed	C	RF	57	Literacy 2000	Rigby
In My Bucket	F	RF	94	Carousel Readers	Pearson Learning Group
In My Country	G	I	119	My World	Capstone Press
In My Desert	D	I	24	Little Celebrations	Pearson Learning Group
In My Family	B	I	35	Explorations	Okapi Educational Materials
In My Family	B	I	35	Explorations	Eleanor Curtain Publishing
In My Family	D	RF	61	Windows on Literacy	National Geographic
In My Garden	B	RF	35	Bookshop	Mondo Publishing
In My Garden	C	RF	36	Carousel Readers	Pearson Learning Group
In My Garden	A	I	36	Getting Around	American Reading Company
In My Garden	I	I	250+	Momentum Literacy Program	Troll Associates
In My Head	G	RF	74	Voyages	SRA/McGraw Hill
In My Home	E	I	126	My World	Capstone Press
In My Lunchbox	C	I	88	Red Rocket Readers	Flying Start Books
In My Neighborhood	E	I	110	My World	Capstone Press
In My Pocket	E	RF	195	Carousel Readers	Pearson Learning Group
In My Pocket	B	RF	34	Instant Readers	Harcourt School Publishers
In My Pocket	A	I	28	Sun Sprouts	ETA/Cuisenaire

* Collection of short stories   # Graphic text
^ Mature content with lower level text demands

TITLE	LEVEL	GENRE	WORD COUNT	AUTHOR / SERIES	PUBLISHER / DISTRIBUTOR
In My Room	C	I	74	Leveled Literacy Intervention/ Blue System	Heinemann
In My Room	C	F	44	Literacy 2000	Rigby
In My Room	D	RF	58	Seedlings	Continental Press
In My School	A	I	27	Little Books for Early Readers	University of Maine
In My State	G	I	137	My World	Capstone Press
In My Toolbox	B	I	36	Foundations	Wright Group/McGraw Hill
In My Town	F	I	111	My World	Capstone Press
In My World	H	I	120	My World	Capstone Press
In My Yard	A	I	28	Leveled Readers	Houghton Mifflin Harcourt
In My Yard	A	I	28	Leveled Readers/CA	Houghton Mifflin Harcourt
In Nonna's Kitchen	C	I	32	Home Connection Collection	Rigby
In One Ear, Out the Other	K	F	250+	Dahl, Michael	Picture Window Books
In One Tidepool	P	I	937	Sharing Nature with Children	Dawn Publications
In Our Classroom	A	I	33	PM Plus Starters	Rigby
In Our Classroom	F	I	89	Windows on Literacy	National Geographic
In Our Country	F	I	63	Canizares, Susan; Moreton, Daniel	Scholastic
In Our Own Words: Teen Art and Writing	W	RF	250+	Power Up!	Steck-Vaughn
In Our Yard	G	RF	150	Reed, Janet	Scholastic
In Ravi's Fort	C	RF	78	Lighthouse	Rigby
In School	A	I	21	On Our Way to English	Rigby
In Search of Food	M	SF	923	Springboard	Wright Group/McGraw Hill
In Search of Something Delicious	G	F	202	Seedlings	Continental Press
In Search of the Giant Pandas	P	RF	250+	Reading Safari	Mondo Publishing
In Search of the Grand Canyon	W	I	250+	Fraser, Mary Ann	Henry Holt & Co.
In Search of the Great Bears	S	I	250+	Literacy 2000	Rigby
In Search of the Mummy	Q	I	250+	Scooters	ETA/Cuisenaire
In Search of Treasure	L	TL	250+	PM Story Books	Rigby
*In Short: A Collection of Brief Creative Nonfiction	Z	I	250+	Kitchen, J.; Jones, M. P.	W. W. Norton
In Spring	B	I	15	Discovery Links	Newbridge
In Spring	B	I	34	Science	Outside the Box
In Summer	D	I	36	Discovery Links	Newbridge
In the Afternoon	H	I	156	PM Nonfiction-Green	Rigby
In the Air	D	I	38	Berger, Samantha & Chessen, Betsey	Scholastic
In the Air	B	I	54	Sails	Rigby
In the Air	B	I	20	Sunshine	Wright Group/McGraw Hill
In the Arctic	C	I	43	Science	Outside the Box
In the Army	G	RF	157	The King School Series	Townsend Press
In the Backyard	L	I	480	Early Explorers	Benchmark Education
In the Backyard	H	F	197	Little Celebrations	Pearson Learning Group
In the Bank	H	I	140	Independent Readers Social Studies	Houghton Mifflin Harcourt
In the Barn	D	I	38	Vocabulary Readers	Houghton Mifflin Harcourt
In the Barrio	J	RF	130	Ada, Alma Flor	Scholastic
In the Bathroom	B	RF	24	Smart Start	Rigby
In the Boat	LB	F	30	Big Cat	Pacific Learning
In the Box	C	RF	64	Leveled Readers Emergent	Houghton Mifflin Harcourt
In the Box	C	RF	33	Phonics and Friends	Hampton Brown
In the Box	D	I	36	Sun Sprouts	ETA/Cuisenaire
In the Box	B	F	64	The Book Project	Sundance
In the Car	B	RF	32	First Stories	Pacific Learning
In the Chicken Coop	D	I	56	Twig	Wright Group/McGraw Hill

TITLE	LEVEL	GENRE	WORD COUNT	AUTHOR / SERIES	PUBLISHER / DISTRIBUTOR
In the City	LB	RF	22	Home Connection Collection	Rigby
In the City	A	I	20	Leveled Readers	Houghton Mifflin Harcourt
In the City	A	I	20	Leveled Readers/CA	Houghton Mifflin Harcourt
In the City	C	RF	45	Pasternac, Susana	Scholastic
In the City	C	RF	50	Rise & Shine	Hampton Brown
In the City of Rome	J	TL	250+	Literacy 2000	Rigby
In the Clouds	M	RF	250+	Literacy 2000	Rigby
In the Clouds	H	RF	192	Literacy by Design	Rigby
In the Country	D	RF	21	Home Connection Collection	Rigby
In the Country	D	I	54	Vocabulary Readers	Houghton Mifflin Harcourt
In the Country, In the City	B	I	71	Rigby Literacy	Rigby
In the Dark	B	RF	36	Big Cat	Pacific Learning
In the Dark Forest	C	I	24	Pacific Literacy	Pacific Learning
In the Days of Missions and Ranchos	T	I	1029	Vocabulary Readers	Houghton Mifflin Harcourt
In the Days of Missions and Ranchos	T	I	1029	Vocabulary Readers/CA	Houghton Mifflin Harcourt
In the Days of Missions and Ranchos	T	I	1029	Vocabulary Readers/TX	Houghton Mifflin Harcourt
In the Days of the Dinosaur	V	I	3182	Leveled Readers Science	Houghton Mifflin Harcourt
In the Days of the Dinosaurs: Arky, the Dinosaur With Feathers	K	HF	250+	PM Plus Story Books	Rigby
In the Days of the Vaqueros: America's First True Cowboys	X	I	250+	Freedman, Russell	Sandpiper Books
In the Desert	D	I	109	Leveled Readers	Houghton Mifflin Harcourt
In the Desert	D	I	109	Leveled Readers/CA	Houghton Mifflin Harcourt
In the Desert	M	I	250+	Look Once Look Again	Creative Teaching Press
In the Desert	D	I	51	Pacific Literacy	Pacific Learning
In the Desert	H	I	138	Shutterbug Books	Steck-Vaughn
In the Desert	D	I	62	Sunshine	Wright Group/McGraw Hill
In the Desert	N	I	558	Time for Kids	Teacher Created Materials
In the Dinosaur's Paw	M	RF	250+	Giff, Patricia Reilly	Bantam Books
In the Doghouse	K	RF	250+	Kimmelman, Leslie	Holiday House
In the Fall	H	I	286	Leveled Readers	Houghton Mifflin Harcourt
In the Fall	H	I	286	Leveled Readers/CA	Houghton Mifflin Harcourt
In the Fall	H	I	286	Leveled Readers/TX	Houghton Mifflin Harcourt
In the Fast Lane	R	I	250+	Literacy 2000	Rigby
In the Forest	B	I	48	Adams, Lorraine & Bruvold, Lynn	Eaglecrest Books
In the Forest	E	I	116	Early Explorers	Benchmark Education
In the Forest	L	I	581	Leveled Readers	Houghton Mifflin Harcourt
In the Forest	N	I	250+	Look Once Look Again	Creative Teaching Press
In the Forest	C	F	71	Schiller, Melissa	Scholastic
In the Forest	B	I	38	Science	Outside the Box
In the Forest	M	I	556	Time for Kids	Teacher Created Materials
In the Forest	C	RF	42	Twig	Wright Group/McGraw Hill
In the Forest	G	RF	95	Voyages	SRA/McGraw Hill
In the Forest	B	RF	38	Windows on Literacy	National Geographic
In the Forest with the Elephants	U	I	250+	Smith, Roland & Schmidt, Michael J.	Harcourt Brace
In the Garage	Z+	RF	250+	Fullerton, Alma	Fitzhenry & Whiteside
In the Garden	LB	RF	18	Big Cat	Pacific Learning
In the Garden	K	I	250+	HSP/Harcourt Trophies	Harcourt, Inc.
In the Garden	A	I	20	Leveled Readers	Houghton Mifflin Harcourt
In the Garden	A	I	20	Leveled Readers/CA	Houghton Mifflin Harcourt
In the Garden	D	I	90	Literacy 2000	Rigby
In the Garden	M	I	250+	Look Once Look Again	Creative Teaching Press
In the Garden	A	I	32	PM Plus Starters	Rigby

* Collection of short stories   # Graphic text
^ Mature content with lower level text demands

TITLE	LEVEL	GENRE	WORD COUNT	AUTHOR / SERIES	PUBLISHER / DISTRIBUTOR
In the Garden	A	F	24	Sails	Rigby
In the Garden	E	I	0	Sun Sprouts	ETA/Cuisenaire
In the Garden	WB	I	0	Windows on Literacy	National Geographic
In the Garden: Who's Been Here?	K	RF	250+	George, Lindsay Barrett	Greenwillow Books
In the Green Room	Q	RF	250+	Reading Safari	Mondo Publishing
In the Hen House	G	RF	82	Oppenlander, Meredith	Kaeden Books
In the Hole	J	RF	128	Larkin's Little Readers	Wilbooks
In the Jungle	F	F	247	Dominie Math Stories	Pearson Learning Group
In the Jungle River	I	I	214	Sails	Rigby
In the Kitchen	N	I	250+	Bookweb	Rigby
In the Kitchen	C	I	16	Canizares, Susan; Chessen, Betsey	Scholastic
In the Land of the Polar Bear	J	RF	250+	Robinson, F. R.	Steck-Vaughn
*In the Line of Fire: Eight Women War Spies	U	B	250+	Sullivan, George	Scholastic
In the Meadow	M	I	250+	Look Once Look Again	Creative Teaching Press
In the Middle of the Night	I	RF	250+	Sunshine	Wright Group/McGraw Hill
In the Mirror	B	RF	26	Story Box	Wright Group/McGraw Hill
In the Morning	H	I	218	PM Nonfiction-Green	Rigby
In the Mountains	U	I	250+	iOpeners	Pearson Learning Group
In the Mountains	LB	I	14	Twig	Wright Group/McGraw Hill
In the Mud	B	F	30	Sails	Rigby
In the Name of God	Z+	RF	250+	Jolin, Paula	Square Fish
In the News	Q	I	250+	Wildcats	Wright Group/McGraw Hill
In the News	O	I	250+	Wonder World	Wright Group/McGraw Hill
In the Ocean	A	I	36	The Places I Go	American Reading Company
In the Ocean	LB	I	14	Yoon, Salina	Feiwel and Friends
In the Paint	U	RF	250+	South Side Sports	Orca Books
In the Park	D	RF	65	Foundations	Wright Group/McGraw Hill
In the Park	B	I	37	Gear Up!	Wright Group/McGraw Hill
In the Park	F	I	96	Literacy 2000	Rigby
In the Park	M	I	250+	Look Once Look Again	Creative Teaching Press
In the Park	A	I	35	On Our Way to English	Rigby
In the Park With Ranger Rosa	F	RF	109	Run to Reading	Discovery Peak
In the Path of Lewis & Clark: Traveling the Missouri	V	I	250+	Lourie, Peter	Silver Burdett Press
In the Pond	B	RF	32	Gear Up!	Wright Group/McGraw Hill
In the Pool	E	RF	158	Joy Starters	Pearson Learning Group
In the Rain	E	RF	121	On Our Way to English	Rigby
In the Rain	B	F	19	Ready Readers	Pearson Learning Group
In the Rain Forest	B	I	65	Leveled Readers	Houghton Mifflin Harcourt
In the Rain Forest	B	I	65	Leveled Readers/CA	Houghton Mifflin Harcourt
In the Rain Forest	E	I	57	Twig	Wright Group/McGraw Hill
In the Rain Forest	Q	I	250+	Wildcats	Wright Group/McGraw Hill
In the Rainforest	M	I	567	Time for Kids	Teacher Created Materials
In the Sea	D	I	87	Leveled Readers	Houghton Mifflin Harcourt
In the Sea	D	I	87	Leveled Readers/CA	Houghton Mifflin Harcourt
In the Sea	D	I	87	Leveled Readers/TX	Houghton Mifflin Harcourt
In the Sea	B	I	41	Little Red Readers	Sundance
In the Sea	C	I	41	Sunshine	Wright Group/McGraw Hill
In the Shade of the Nispero Tree	S	HF	250+	Bernier-Grand, Carmen T.	Orchard Books
In the Shadow of the Lamp	Z	HF	250+	Dunlap, Susanne	Bloomsbury Children's Books
In the Shopping Cart	A	I	24	PM Starters	Rigby
In the Sky	E	I	121	Factivity Series	Pearson Learning Group

TITLE	LEVEL	GENRE	WORD COUNT	AUTHOR / SERIES	PUBLISHER / DISTRIBUTOR
In the Sky	B	I	42	Little Red Readers	Sundance
In the Sky	B	I	96	Vocabulary Readers	Houghton Mifflin Harcourt
In the Sky	A	I	20	Vocabulary Readers	Houghton Mifflin Harcourt
In the Sky	A	I	20	Vocabulary Readers/CA	Houghton Mifflin Harcourt
In the Sky	B	I	96	Vocabulary Readers/CA	Houghton Mifflin Harcourt
In the Sky	B	I	96	Vocabulary Readers/TX	Houghton Mifflin Harcourt
In the Small	Z	F	250+	Hague, Michael	Little Brown and Company
In the Small, Small Pond	K	RF	65	Fleming, Denise	Scholastic
In the Summer	A	I	36	Gear Up!	Wright Group/McGraw Hill
In the Sun	C	F	95	Phonics and Friends	Hampton Brown
In the Supermarket	A	RF	24	Smart Start	Rigby
In the Teacup	A	F	35	KinderReaders	Rigby
In the Toy Shop	C	F	29	The Book Project	Sundance
In the Tree	C	I	110	Leveled Readers	Houghton Mifflin Harcourt
In the Tree	B	RF	48	Leveled Readers Emergent	Houghton Mifflin Harcourt
In the Tree	C	I	110	Leveled Readers/CA	Houghton Mifflin Harcourt
In the Tree	B	I	36	Windows on Literacy	National Geographic
In the Tree	B	F	36	Zoozoo-Into the Wild	Cavallo Publishing
In the Trees, Honey Bees	M	I	81	Mortensen, Lori	Dawn Publications
In the Treetops	J	I	250+	Explorations	Okapi Educational Materials
In the Treetops	J	I	250+	Explorations	Eleanor Curtain Publishing
In the Treetops	M	I	250+	Woolley, M.; Pigdon, K.	Mondo Publishing
In the Van	C	RF	55	Leveled Readers	Houghton Mifflin Harcourt
In the Water	LB	I	12	Animal Homes	Lerner Publishing Group
In the Woods	B	I	48	Bookshop	Mondo Publishing
In the Woods	WB	I	0	Christini, Ermanno; Puricelli, Luigi	Scholastic
In the Woods	B	F	25	Gibson, Akimi	Scholastic
In the Woods	B	I	60	Literacy by Design	Rigby
In the Woods	B	I	60	On Our Way to English	Rigby
In the Woods	G	I	304	Reading Corners	Pearson Learning Group
In the Woods	A	I	40	Readlings	American Reading Company
In the Woods	A	I	36	The Places I Go	American Reading Company
In the Yard	E	RF	40	Avenues	Hampton Brown
In the Yard	F	RF	40	Early Readers	Compass Point Books
In the Yard	D	RF	88	Rigby Literacy	Rigby
In the Year of the Boar and Jackie Robinson	S	HF	250+	Lord, Bette Bao	HarperTrophy
In The Zoo	H	F	252	Lane, Jerry	Ginn & Co.
In Times Long Ago	G	I	196	Learn to Read	Creative Teaching Press
In Too Deep (The 39 Clues)	U	F	250+	Watson, Jude	Scholastic
In Went Goldilocks	C	TL	30	Literacy 2000	Rigby
In Winter	H	RF	263	Leveled Literacy Intervention/ Green System	Heinemann
In-Between Days, The	P	RF	250+	Bunting, Eve	HarperTrophy
Inca, The	U	I	250+	Navigators Social Studies Series	Benchmark Education
Incantation	Y	HF	250+	Hoffman, Alice	Little Brown and Company
Inch by Inch	K	F	183	Lionni, Leo	Scholastic
Inchworm and a Half	L	F	250+	Pinczes, Elinor J.	Houghton Mifflin Harcourt
Incident at Hawk's Hill	V	F	250+	Eckert, Allen W.	Little Brown and Company
Inclined Plane, The	K	I	237	Reading Street	Pearson
Inclined Planes and Wedges	Q	I	1869	Early Bird Energy Physics Books	Lerner Publishing Group
Inclined Planes to the Rescue	O	I	250+	Simple Machine to the Rescue	Capstone Press
Incognito	S	RF	2619	Leveled Readers	Houghton Mifflin Harcourt
Incognito	S	RF	2619	Leveled Readers/CA	Houghton Mifflin Harcourt

* Collection of short stories   # Graphic text
^ Mature content with lower level text demands

TITLE	LEVEL	GENRE	WORD COUNT	AUTHOR / SERIES	PUBLISHER / DISTRIBUTOR
Incognito	S	RF	2619	Leveled Readers/TX	Houghton Mifflin Harcourt
*Incredible Animal Adventures	N	I	250+	George, Jean Craighead	HarperCollins
Incredible Cells	Q	I	250+	Discovery Links	Newbridge
Incredible Creatures	P	I	250+	Explorers	Wright Group/McGraw Hill
Incredible Hulk Pop-up, The	U	F	250+	Marvel Comics	Candlewick Press
Incredible Insects	M	I	250+	Sunshine	Wright Group/McGraw Hill
Incredible Journey of Thor Heyerdahl and the Kon-Tiki Raft, The	T	I	2415	Reading Street	Pearson
Incredible Journey, The	V	F	250+	Burnford, Sheila	Bantam Books
Incredible Places	P	I	250+	Wildcats	Wright Group/McGraw Hill
Incredible Rescue of Apollo 13, The	O	I	521	Springboard	Wright Group/McGraw Hill
Incredible Sea Journey, The	R	HF	2921	Reading Street	Pearson
Incredible Shrinking Kid, The	P	F	250+	Abbott, Tony	Scholastic
*Incredible Shrinking Machine and Other Cases, The	O	RF	250+	Simon, Seymour	Avon Books
Incredible Shrinking Teacher, The	K	F	250+	Passen, Lisa	Square Fish
Incredible, Edible Plants	L	I	250+	Early Connections	Benchmark Education
Independence Day	J	I	131	American Holidays	Lerner Publishing Group
Independence Day	Q	I	250+	Holiday Histories	Heinemann
Independence Day	M	I	224	Holidays and Festivals	Heinemann Library
Independence Day	L	I	182	Pebble Books	Red Brick Learning
Independence Hall	I	I	77	Leveled Readers	Houghton Mifflin Harcourt
Independence Hall: I, Q	Z	RF	250+	Smith, Roland	Sleeping Bear Press
India	S	I	250+	A True Book	Children's Press
India	W	I	250+	Countries and Cultures	Capstone Press
India	O	I	250+	Countries of the World	Red Brick Learning
India	P	I	2187	Country Explorers	Lerner Publishing Group
India	S	I	250+	First Reports: Countries	Compass Point Books
India	W	I	250+	Primary Source Readers	Teacher Created Materials
India	LB	I	14	Readlings	American Reading Company
India and China	W	I	250+	Navigators Social Studies Series	Benchmark Education
India in Colors	N	I	250+	World of Colors	Capstone Press
India in the Past and Present	T	I	250+	Reading Expeditions	National Geographic
India the Moonstone Fairy: Rainbow Magic	L	F	250+	Meadows, Daisy	Scholastic
India: Civilizations Past to Present	S	I	250+	Reading Expeditions	National Geographic
Indian Captive, The Story of Mary Jemison	V	HF	250+	Lenski, Lois	HarperTrophy
Indian Chiefs	Y	B	250+	Freedman, Russell	Scholastic
Indian in the Cupboard, The	R	F	250+	Banks, Lynne Reid	Avon Books
Indian Ocean, The	N	I	250+	Oceans	Capstone Press
Indian School, The	P	RF	250+	Whelan, Gloria	HarperTrophy
Indian Wars, The	Q	I	250+	On Deck	Rigby
Indian Winter, An	X	I	250+	Freedman, Russell	Holiday House
Indiana	T	I	250+	Hello U.S.A.	Lerner Publishing Group
Indiana	S	I	250+	Land of Liberty	Red Brick Learning
Indiana	R	I	250+	This Land Is Your Land	Compass Point Books
Indiana Pacers, The	S	I	250+	Team Spirit	Norwood House Press
Indiana: Facts and Symbols	O	I	250+	The States and Their Symbols	Capstone Press
Indianapolis Colts, The	S	I	5063	Team Spirit	Norwood House Press
*Indian-Head Pennies and Other Cases, The	O	RF	250+	Simon, Seymour	Avon Books
India's Amazing Geography	Y	I	1953	Leveled Readers	Houghton Mifflin Harcourt
India's Amazing Geography	Y	I	1953	Leveled Readers/CA	Houghton Mifflin Harcourt
India's Amazing Geography	Y	I	1953	Leveled Readers/TX	Houghton Mifflin Harcourt
India's Monsoons	X	I	1124	Leveled Readers	Houghton Mifflin Harcourt
India's Monsoons	X	I	1124	Leveled Readers/CA	Houghton Mifflin Harcourt

TITLE	LEVEL	GENRE	WORD COUNT	AUTHOR / SERIES	PUBLISHER / DISTRIBUTOR
India's Monsoons	X	I	1124	Leveled Readers/TX	Houghton Mifflin Harcourt
Indigo Jackal, The	N	TL	250+	WorldScapes	ETA/Cuisenaire
Indigo's Star	W	RF	250+	McKay, Hilary	Aladdin
Indonesia	O	I	1546	A Ticket to …	Carolrhoda Books
Indonesia	O	I	250+	Countries of the World	Red Brick Learning
Indonesia	P	I	2010	Country Explorers	Lerner Publishing Group
Indonesia	T	I	250+	First Reports: Countries	Compass Point Books
Indonesia: A Question and Answer Book	P	I	250+	Questions & Answers: Countries	Capstone Press
Indonesia's Rain Forests	Q	I	250+	Theme Sets	National Geographic
Indoor S'mores and Other Tasty Treats for Special Occasions	R	I	250+	Kids Dish	Picture Window Books
Indoor Sports	N	I	250+	Trackers	Pacific Learning
Industrial Giants	U	B	250+	Primary Source Readers	Teacher Created Materials
Industrial Revolution	U	I	250+	Primary Source Readers	Teacher Created Materials
Industrial Revolution, The	U	I	250+	Reading Expeditions	National Geographic
Industry Changes America	S	I	250+	Reading Expeditions	National Geographic
Indy Cars	M	I	250+	Horsepower	Capstone Press
Indy Cars	T	I	250+	The World's Fastest	Red Brick Learning
Indy Race Cars	W	I	6090	Motor Mania	Lerner Publishing Group
Infinite Imagination, The	S	I	250+	Kids Discover Reading	Wright Group/McGraw Hill
Inkheart	W	F	250+	Funke, Cornelia	Scholastic
Inky the Indigo Fairy: Rainbow Magic	L	F	250+	Meadows, Daisy	Scholastic
Inland Valleys Missions in California	V	I	5494	Exploring California Missions	Lerner Publishing Group
In-Line Skates, The	F	RF	137	Foundations	Wright Group/McGraw Hill
Inn Keeper's Apprentice	Z	B	250+	Say, Allen	Penguin Group
Innocent Prisoners!: Life in a Japanese American Internment Camp	T	HF	1621	Reading Street	Pearson
Innocent's Story, The	Z	F	250+	Singer, Nicky	Holiday House
Innovations from Ancient China	Y	I	2264	Leveled Readers	Houghton Mifflin Harcourt
Innovations from Ancient China	Y	I	2264	Leveled Readers/CA	Houghton Mifflin Harcourt
Innovations from Ancient China	Y	I	2264	Leveled Readers/TX	Houghton Mifflin Harcourt
Inquisitor's Apprentice, The	Y	F	250+	Moriarty, Chris	Houghton Mifflin Harcourt
Insect	W	I	250+	Eyewitness Books	DK Publishing
Insect and Spider	C	F	50	Science	Outside the Box
Insect Army, The	O	I	250+	InfoQuest	Rigby
^Insect Evidence	S	I	250+	Forensic Crime Solvers	Capstone Press
Insect Luck	G	RF	131	Appleton-Smith, Laura	Flyleaf Publishing
Insect or Arachnid?	K	I	284	Reading Street	Pearson
Insect Pets	M	I	250+	The Rowland Reading Program Library	Rowland Reading Foundation
Insect-Eaters	J	I	213	Rigby Focus	Rigby
Insectigations	V	I	250+	Blobaum, Cindy	Chicago Review Press
Insects	N	I	250+	A New True Book	Children's Press
Insects	U	I	250+	Bird, Bettina; Short, Joan	Mondo Publishing
Insects	M	I	250+	Exploring the Animal Kingdom	Capstone Press
Insects	R	I	250+	Eyewitness Explorers	DK Publishing
Insects	J	I	171	MacLulich, Carolyn	Scholastic
Insects	A	I	28	Nonfiction Set 1	Literacy Footprints
Insects	G	I	107	Rigby Focus	Rigby
Insects & Spiders	U	I	250+	World Book Looks at Science	World Book
Insects & Spiders	R	I	250+	Worldwise	Franklin Watts
Insects All Around	K	I	229	Early Connections	Benchmark Education
Insects and Spiders	H	I	150	Time for Kids	Teacher Created Materials
Insects Change	J	I	202	Shutterbug Books	Steck-Vaughn

TITLE	LEVEL	GENRE	WORD COUNT	AUTHOR / SERIES	PUBLISHER / DISTRIBUTOR
Insects That Bother Us	G	I	87	Foundations	Wright Group/McGraw Hill
Insects That Use Color	I	I	310	Sails	Rigby
Insects Up Close	D	I	85	Shutterbug Books	Steck-Vaughn
Insects You Can Draw	R	I	1659	Ready, Set, Draw!	Millbrook Press
Insects, Insects, Insects	G	I	167	Appleton-Smith, Laura	Flyleaf Publishing
Insects: Six-Legged Animals	N	I	250+	Amazing Science	Picture Window Books
Insects: Which One Doesn't Belong?	O	I	250+	iScience	Norwood House Press
Inside a Cave	J	I	331	In Step Readers	Rigby
Inside a Cell	S	I	1651	Leveled Readers Science	Houghton Mifflin Harcourt
Inside a Rain Forest	M	I	353	Pair-It Books	Steck-Vaughn
Inside All	K	I	110	Sharing Nature with Children	Dawn Publications
Inside an Ant Colony	K	I	250+	Rookie Read-About Science	Children's Press
Inside Caves	L	I	306	Sails	Rigby
Inside Caves	P	I	250+	Scooters	ETA/Cuisenaire
Inside Ecosystems and Biomes	T	I	250+	Science Readers	Teacher Created Materials
Inside Insects	G	I	89	Sails	Rigby
Inside Look at Zoos, An	S	I	1864	Leveled Readers	Houghton Mifflin Harcourt
Inside Look at Zoos, An	S	I	1864	Leveled Readers/CA	Houghton Mifflin Harcourt
Inside Look at Zoos, An	S	I	1864	Leveled Readers/TX	Houghton Mifflin Harcourt
Inside Nests	D	I	115	Sails	Rigby
Inside or Outside?	E	RF	57	Literacy 2000	Rigby
Inside Out & Back Again	U	HF	250+	Lai, Thanhha	HarperCollins
Inside School	A	I	35	Little Books for Early Readers	University of Maine
Inside Story, The	E	RF	43	Teacher's Choice Series	Pearson Learning Group
Inside Story, The: The Sisters Grimm	U	F	250+	Buckley, Michael	Amulet Books
Inside the Cage: The Greatest Fights of Mixed Martial Arts	T	I	250+	The World of Mixed Martial Arts	Capstone Press
Inside the Castle Walls	N	I	250+	Scooters	ETA/Cuisenaire
Inside the Game - Rex Jones	P	SF	1649	Zucker, Jonny	Stone Arch Books
Inside the Internet	T	I	250+	Reading Expeditions	National Geographic
Inside the Sun	O	I	250+	Rosen Real Readers	Rosen Publishing Group
Inside the Volcano	T	F	2272	Leveled Readers	Houghton Mifflin Harcourt
Inside the Volcano	T	F	2272	Leveled Readers/CA	Houghton Mifflin Harcourt
Inside the Volcano	T	F	2272	Leveled Readers/TX	Houghton Mifflin Harcourt
Inside the Water Cycle	U	I	250+	Science Readers	Teacher Created Materials
Inside the World of Matter	Y	I	250+	Science Readers	Teacher Created Materials
Inside the Zoo	R	I	1322	Leveled Readers	Houghton Mifflin Harcourt
Inside the Zoo	R	I	1322	Leveled Readers/CA	Houghton Mifflin Harcourt
Inside the Zoo	R	I	1322	Leveled Readers/TX	Houghton Mifflin Harcourt
Inside, Outside, Upside Down	E	F	118	Berenstain, Stan & Jan	Random House
Inside-Outside Book of London, The	WB	I	0	Monro, Roxie	Dutton Children's Books
Inside-Outside Book of Washington, DC, The	WB	I	0	Monro, Roxie	Dutton Children's Books
Inside-Outside Dinosaurs	LB	I	19	Munro, Roxie	Marshall Cavendish
Inspector Grub and the Fizzer-X Spy	S	RF	250+	Bookweb	Rigby
Inspector Grub and the Gourmet Mystery	Q	RF	250+	Bookweb	Rigby
Inspector Grub and the Jelly Bean Robber	L	RF	250+	Bookweb	Rigby
Inspiration of Art, The	V	I	2437	Reading Street	Pearson
*Inspirational Artists	T	I	250+	Take Two Books	Wright Group/McGraw Hill
Instead of a Car	H	RF	250+	Reading Safari	Mondo Publishing
*Instead of Three Wishes: Magical Short Stories	Y	F	250+	Turner, Megan Whalen	Penguin Group
Instrument Families	O	I	250+	Bookweb	Rigby
Interactions of Living Things	Q	I	1588	Science Support Readers	Houghton Mifflin Harcourt
Intergalactic : 150 Cosmic Jokes About Space	P	F	250+	Sidesplitters	Kingfisher
International Children's Day	U	I	250+	WorldScapes	ETA/Cuisenaire

TITLE	LEVEL	GENRE	WORD COUNT	AUTHOR / SERIES	PUBLISHER / DISTRIBUTOR
International Day	D	I	47	Home Connection Collection	Rigby
International Food Fair, An	K	RF	381	Reading Street	Pearson
International Space Station, The	M	I	560	Rigby Flying Colors	Rigby
International Space Station, The	V	I	2708	Vocabulary Readers	Houghton Mifflin Harcourt
International Space Station, The	O	I	798	Vocabulary Readers	Houghton Mifflin Harcourt
International Space Station, The	V	I	2708	Vocabulary Readers/CA	Houghton Mifflin Harcourt
International Space Station, The	O	I	798	Vocabulary Readers/CA	Houghton Mifflin Harcourt
International Space Station, The	V	I	2708	Vocabulary Readers/TX	Houghton Mifflin Harcourt
Internet	S	I	250+	Theme Sets	National Geographic
Interrupted Journey: Saving Endangered Sea Turtles	U	I	250+	Lasky, Kathryn	Candlewick Press
Interrupting the Big Sleep	P	RF	250+	Orbit Chapter Books	Pacific Learning
Interruptions	F	F	81	Bookshop	Mondo Publishing
Interview with Alan Ant, An	L	I	441	Springboard	Wright Group/McGraw Hill
Interview with Cindy Centipede	N	I	864	Springboard	Wright Group/McGraw Hill
Into Space	J	I	250+	Momentum Literacy Program	Troll Associates
Into the Eye of a Hurricane	T	I	2712	Leveled Readers Science	Houghton Mifflin Harcourt
Into the Gauntlet (The 39 Clues)	U	F	250+	Haddix, Margaret Peterson	Scholastic
Into the Jungle: Searching for the Rare Mountain Gorilla	L	I	250+	World Quest Adventures	World Quest Learning
Into the Land of the Lost: The Secrets of Droon	O	F	250+	Abbott, Tony	Scholastic
Into the Sea	L	I	208	Leveled Literacy Intervention/ Blue System	Heinemann
Into the Unknown	P	RF	250+	Windows on Literacy	National Geographic
Into the Unknown	V	I	250+	WorldScapes	ETA/Cuisenaire
Into the Wild: Warriors, Book 1	U	F	250+	Hunter, Erin	Avon Books
Into the Woods	W	F	250+	Gardner, Lyn	David Fickling Books
Introducing Arkansas	O	I	156	Larkin, Bruce	Wilbooks
Introducing New York	O	I	251	Larkin, Bruce	Wilbooks
Introducing the Euro	W	I	1930	Leveled Readers Social Studies	Houghton Mifflin Harcourt
Introducing Vermont	O	I	218	Larkin, Bruce	Wilbooks
Introduction to Energy	U	I	250+	Reading Expeditions	National Geographic
Introduction to Weather	S	I	250+	Reading Expeditions	National Geographic
Inuit of Arctic Canada, The	X	I	2714	Vocabulary Readers	Houghton Mifflin Harcourt
Inuit of Arctic Canada, The	X	I	2714	Vocabulary Readers/CA	Houghton Mifflin Harcourt
Inuit, The	S	I	250+	A True Book	Children's Press
Invaders!	Y	I	3289	Leveled Readers	Houghton Mifflin Harcourt
Invasion from Planet Dork (Melvin Beederman, Superhero)	N	F	250+	Trine, Greg	Henry Holt & Co.
Invasion of the Boy Snatchers	X	RF	250+	Harrison, Lisi	Little Brown and Company
Invasive Species	T	I	250+	Connectors	Pacific Learning
Inventing Oatmeal	P	F	784	Reading Street	Pearson
Inventing the Telephone	L	I	250+	iOpeners	Pearson Learning Group
Invention of Hugo Cabret, The	W	RF	250+	Selznick, Brian	Scholastic
Inventions	W	I	250+	Kingfisher Knowledge	Kingfisher
Inventions	N	I	167	Windows on Literacy	National Geographic
Inventions from Space Travel	T	I	2639	Reading Street	Pearson
Inventions Help Us	I	I	169	Red Rocket Readers	Flying Start Books
Inventions in Communication	O	I	789	Pair-It Turn and Learn	Steck-Vaughn
Inventions in Communications	R	I	1045	Time for Kids	Teacher Created Materials
Inventions in the Clothing Industry	R	I	1049	Time for Kids	Teacher Created Materials
Inventions in the Food Industry	R	I	1039	Time for Kids	Teacher Created Materials
Inventions of Alexander Graham Bell, The	Q	B	250+	On Deck	Rigby
Inventions of Amanda Jones, The	Q	B	250+	On Deck	Rigby

* Collection of short stories   # Graphic text
^ Mature content with lower level text demands

TITLE	LEVEL	GENRE	WORD COUNT	AUTHOR / SERIES	PUBLISHER / DISTRIBUTOR
Inventions of Eli Whitney, The	Q	B	250+	On Deck	Rigby
Inventions of Granville Woods, The	Q	B	250+	On Deck	Rigby
Inventions of Martha Coston, The	Q	B	250+	On Deck	Rigby
Inventions of Thomas Alva Edison, The	Q	B	250+	On Deck	Rigby
Inventions of Thomas Edison, The	O	I	250+	Rigby Star Quest	Rigby
Inventions That Changed the World	O	I	250+	Reading Expeditions	National Geographic
Inventions That Changed the World	P	I	250+	Reading Expeditions	National Geographic
Inventions: Great Ideas and Where They Came From	U	I	250+	High Five Reading	Red Brick Learning
Inventions: Stonger, Faster, Better	U	I	250+	Kids Discover Reading	Wright Group/McGraw Hill
Inventive Mind of Jules Verne, The	X	B	1828	Leveled Readers	Houghton Mifflin Harcourt
Inventor of the Telephone	M	B	448	Leveled Readers	Houghton Mifflin Harcourt
Inventor of the Telephone	M	B	448	Leveled Readers/CA	Houghton Mifflin Harcourt
Inventor of the Telephone	M	B	448	Leveled Readers/TX	Houghton Mifflin Harcourt
Inventors	T	I	250+	Sandler, Martin W.	HarperTrophy
Inventors at Work	U	I	2596	Reading Street	Pearson
Inventor's Diary, The	M	RF	271	Pacific Literacy	Pacific Learning
Inventor's Vision, An	V	B	250+	WorldScapes	ETA/Cuisenaire
Inventors: Making Things Better	M	I	250+	Pair-It Books	Steck-Vaughn
Invertebrates	Q	I	943	Time for Kids	Teacher Created Materials
Investigating Electricity	Q	I	1469	Searchlight Books	Lerner Publishing Group
Investigating Electromagnetism	Y	I	250+	Science Readers	Teacher Created Materials
Investigating Forces and Motion	W	I	250+	Science Readers	Teacher Created Materials
Investigating Heat	Q	I	1633	Searchlight Books	Lerner Publishing Group
Investigating Inverterbrates	N	I	964	Rigby Flying Colors	Rigby
Investigating Landforms	T	I	250+	Science Readers	Teacher Created Materials
Investigating Light	Q	I	1736	Searchlight Books	Lerner Publishing Group
#Investigating Machu Picchu: An Isabel Soto Archaeology Adventure	S	F	250+	Graphic Expeditions	Capstone Press
Investigating Magnetism	Q	I	1701	Searchlight Books	Lerner Publishing Group
Investigating Matter	Q	I	1181	Searchlight Books	Lerner Publishing Group
Investigating Plate Tectonics	W	I	250+	Science Readers	Teacher Created Materials
Investigating Simple Organisms	Y	I	250+	Science Readers	Teacher Created Materials
Investigating Sound	Q	I	1716	Searchlight Books	Lerner Publishing Group
Investigating Storms	S	I	250+	Science Readers	Teacher Created Materials
Investigating the Chemistry of Atoms	Y	I	250+	Science Readers	Teacher Created Materials
Investigating the Human Body	U	I	250+	Science Readers	Teacher Created Materials
#Investigating the Scientific Method with Max Axiom, Super Scientist	T	I	250+	Graphic Library	Capstone Press
Invincible Iron Man	M	F	250+	Too Cool	Pacific Learning
Invincible Louisa	Z	B	250+	Meigs, Cornelia	Scholastic
Invisible	I	F	111	Read Alongs	Rigby
Invisible Clues	W	I	250+	Sails	Rigby
Invisible Dog, The	M	F	250+	King-Smith, Dick	Alfred A. Knopf
Invisible Fran, The	N	SF	250+	Benton, Jim	Aladdin
Invisible in the Third Grade	M	RF	250+	Cuyler, Margery	Scholastic
#Invisible Man, The	W	F	250+	Davis, Terry (Retold)	Stone Arch Books
Invisible Spy, The	J	F	227	Foundations	Wright Group/McGraw Hill
Invisible Stanley	N	F	250+	Brown, Jeff	HarperTrophy
Invitation to Ballet: A Celebration of Dance and Degas	V	I	250+	Vaughn, Carolyn	Harry N. Abrams
Invitations	K	F	615	Red Rocket Readers	Flying Start Books
Iowa	T	I	250+	Hello U.S.A.	Lerner Publishing Group
Iowa	S	I	250+	Land of Liberty	Red Brick Learning

TITLE	LEVEL	GENRE	WORD COUNT	AUTHOR / SERIES	PUBLISHER / DISTRIBUTOR
Iowa	T	I	250+	Sea to Shining Sea	Children's Press
Iowa	R	I	250+	This Land Is Your Land	Compass Point Books
Iowa Is the Hawkeye State	O	I	232	Larkin, Bruce	Wilbooks
Iowa: Facts and Symbols	O	I	250+	The States and Their Symbols	Capstone Press
Iqbal	X	RF	250+	D'Adamo, Francesco	Atheneum Books
Iran	P	I	2458	Country Explorers	Lerner Publishing Group
Iran	T	I	250+	First Reports: Countries	Compass Point Books
Iraq: A Question and Answer Book	P	I	250+	Questions and Answers: Countries	Capstone Press
Ireland	W	I	250+	Countries and Cultures	Capstone Press
Ireland	P	I	1478	Country Explorers	Lerner Publishing Group
Ireland: A Question and Answer Book	P	I	250+	Question and Answer Countries	Capstone Press
Iris and Walter	J	RF	250+	Guest, Elissa Haden	Harcourt, Inc.
Iris and Walter and Baby Rose	J	RF	250+	Guest, Elissa Haden	Harcourt, Inc.
Iris and Walter and Cousin Howie	J	RF	250+	Guest, Elissa Haden	Harcourt, Inc.
Iris and Walter and the Birthday Party	J	RF	250+	Guest, Elissa Haden	Harcourt, Inc.
Iris and Walter and the Field Trip	J	RF	250+	Guest, Elissa Haden	Harcourt, Inc.
Iris and Walter and the Substitute Teacher	J	RF	250+	Guest, Elissa Haden	Harcourt, Inc.
Iris and Walter: Lost and Found	J	RF	250+	Guest, Elissa Haden	Harcourt, Inc.
Iris and Walter: The School Play	J	RF	250+	Guest, Elissa Haden	Harcourt, Inc.
Iris and Walter: The Sleepover	J	RF	250+	Guest, Elissa Haden	Harcourt, Inc.
Iris and Walter: True Friends	J	RF	250+	Guest, Elissa Haden	Harcourt, Inc.
Iris Rose Maple	O	RF	1913	Take Two Books	Wright Group/McGraw Hill
Irish Experience, The	U	I	250+	Literacy by Design	Rigby
^Irish Immigrants in America: An Interactive History Adventure	V	HF	250+	You Choose Books	Capstone Press
Irish Immigration	V	I	250+	Theme Sets	National Geographic
Irish Step Dancing	S	I	250+	Dance	Capstone Press
Irish Wolfhounds Are the Best!	Q	I	1393	The Best Dogs Ever	Lerner Publishing Group
Irma Imogen: Inventor	R	RF	250+	Take Two Books	Wright Group/McGraw Hill
Irniq and the Eagles	M	TL	250+	Orbit Chapter Books	Pacific Learning
Iron	T	I	250+	Navigators Science Series	Benchmark Education
Iron Giant, The	O	SF	250+	Hughes, Ted	Alfred A. Knopf
Iron Hans: A Grimms' Fairy Tale	S	TL	250+	Mitchell, Stephen	Candlewick Press
Iron Horse, The	A	F	21	Smart Start	Rigby
Iron Mikkos the Magnet Man	T	F	250+	Reading Safari	Mondo Publishing
Iron Ring, The	W	F	250+	Alexander, Lloyd	Puffin Books
Ironkid	N	RF	250+	PM Plus Chapter Books	Rigby
Ironman	Z	RF	250+	Crutcher, Chris	Laurel-Leaf Books
Iroquois Indians, The	P	I	250+	Native Peoples	Red Brick Learning
Iroquois League, The	Q	I	250+	Rosen Real Readers	Rosen Publishing Group
Iroquois, The	R	I	250+	First Reports	Compass Point Books
Iroquois, The	T	I	4385	Native American Histoies	Lerner Publishing Group
Iroquois, The: People of the Longhouse	S	I	250+	Explore More	Wright Group/McGraw Hill
Iroquois, The: People of the Northeast	S	I	250+	Theme Sets	National Geographic
Irrational Season, The	Z	B	250+	L'Engle, Madeleine	HarperCollins
Irritating Irma	N	F	250+	Literacy 2000	Rigby
Is a Dollar Enough?	D	RF	75	Visions	Wright Group/McGraw Hill
Is Anyone Home?	F	RF	65	Maris, Ron	Greenwillow Books
Is it a Fish?	K	I	606	Sunshine	Wright Group/McGraw Hill
Is it a Fruit?	G	I	101	Rigby Literacy	Rigby
Is It Alive?	C	RF	26	Learn to Read	Creative Teaching Press
Is It Almost Ready?	C	RF	53	Book Bus	Creative Edge
Is It Almost Time?	H	RF	252	InfoTrek	ETA/Cuisenaire

* Collection of short stories   # Graphic text
^ Mature content with lower level text demands

TITLE	LEVEL	GENRE	WORD COUNT	AUTHOR / SERIES	PUBLISHER / DISTRIBUTOR
Is It an Insect?	C	I	85	First Stories	Pacific Learning
Is It Better to Be Judged by a Jury of Your Peers Than by a Judge? (Flipsides)	W	I	250+	Bookshop	Mondo Publishing
Is It Big or Little?	B	I	31	Properties of Matter	Lerner Publishing Group
Is It Floating?	E	I	146	Sunshine	Wright Group/McGraw Hill
Is It Heavy or Light?	B	I	25	Properties of Matter	Lerner Publishing Group
Is It Hot? Is It Not?	C	I	30	Phonics Readers	Compass Point Books
Is It Living or Nonliving?	E	I	30	Living or Nonliving	Lerner Publishing Group
Is It Metal?	C	I	19	Rigby Focus	Rigby
Is It Night or Day?	X	HF	250+	Chapman, Fern Schumer	Farrar, Straus, & Giroux
Is It Night or Day?	Y	HF	250+	Chapman, Fern Schumer	Farrar, Straus, & Giroux
Is It Odd or Even?	K	I	344	Yellow Umbrella Books	Red Brick Learning
Is It Possible?	F	F	115	Dominie Math Stories	Pearson Learning Group
Is It Red? Is It Yellow? Is It Blue?	WB	F	0	Hoban, Tana	Greenwillow Books
Is it Rough? Is it Smooth?	D	I	45	Rosen Real Readers	Rosen Publishing Group
Is It Time Yet?	G	RF	162	Foundations	Wright Group/McGraw Hill
Is It Time?	C	RF	52	Campbell, J. G.	Scholastic
Is Jim In?	F	RF	106	Supersonics	Rigby
Is Singing for You?	T	I	4300	Ready to Make Music	Lerner Publishing Group
Is That a Bear?	H	RF	225	Sunshine	Wright Group/McGraw Hill
Is That Fair?	W	I	250+	WorldScapes	ETA/Cuisenaire
Is the Bermuda Triangle Really a Dangerous Place?: And Other Questions About the Ocean	U	I	4483	Is That a Fact?	Lerner Publishing Group
Is the Clarinet for You?	T	I	4178	Ready to Make Music	Lerner Publishing Group
Is the Flute for You?	T	I	4077	Ready to Make Music	Lerner Publishing Group
Is the Saxophone for You?	T	I	4002	Ready to Make Music	Lerner Publishing Group
Is the Spaghetti Ready?	E	F	80	New Reader Series	Bungalo Books
Is the Trumpet for You?	T	I	4175	Ready to Make Music	Lerner Publishing Group
Is the Wise Owl Wise?	I	F	250+	Literacy by Design	Rigby
Is the Wise Owl Wise?	I	F	250+	Rigby Literacy	Rigby
Is the Wise Owl Wise?	I	F	250+	Rigby Star	Rigby
Is There Anyone Out There?	O	I	1625	Big Cat	Pacific Learning
Is There Life in Outer Space	O	I	250+	Branley, Franklyn M.	HarperCollins
Is There Life on Other Planets?: And Other Questions About Space	U	I	4219	Is That a Fact?	Lerner Publishing Group
Is This a Collection?	F	I	88	Gear Up!	Wright Group/McGraw Hill
Is This a Monster?	C	F	93	Bookshop	Mondo Publishing
Is This a Moose?	G	I	150	Armstrong, Jenny	Scholastic
Is This My Dinner?	I	F	162	Black/Fry	Whitman
Is This You?	F	RF	250+	Krauss, Ruth	Scholastic
Is Tomorrow My Birthday?	E	RF	87	Blaxland, Wendy	Scholastic
Is Your Mama a Llama?	L	F	250+	Guarino, Deborah	Scholastic
Is Your Pail Full?	F	RF	162	Mishica, Clare	Continental Press
Is Your Pet a Mammal?	K	I	267	Larkin, Bruce	Wilbooks
Isaac Asimov	W	I	1575	Vocabulary Readers	Houghton Mifflin Harcourt
Isaac Asimov	W	B	1575	Vocabulary Readers/CA	Houghton Mifflin Harcourt
Isaac Newton	Y	B	250+	Krull, Kathleen	Scholastic
Isaac Newton and His Laws of Motion	X	I	250+	Navigators Science Series	Benchmark Education
#Isaac Newton and the Laws of Motion	V	B	250+	Graphic Library	Capstone Press
Isaac Newton and the Laws of the Universe	X	B	250+	Science Readers	Teacher Created Materials
Isaac Newton: Groundbreaking Physicist and Mathematician	X	B	250+	Mission Science	Compass Point Books
Isabel Allende	X	B	3430	Leveled Readers	Houghton Mifflin Harcourt
Isabel Allende	X	B	3430	Leveled Readers/CA	Houghton Mifflin Harcourt

TITLE	LEVEL	GENRE	WORD COUNT	AUTHOR / SERIES	PUBLISHER / DISTRIBUTOR
Isabel Allende	X	B	3430	Leveled Readers/TX	Houghton Mifflin Harcourt
Isabella: A Wish for Miguel	Q	HF	250+	Childhood Journeys	Aladdin
Isabelle's Boyfriend	Y	RF	250+	Hickey, Caroline	Roaring Brook Press
Isabel's Car Wash	L	RF	250+	Bair, Sheila	Albert Whitman & Co.
Isabel's Day	C	I	88	Literacy by Design	Rigby
Isabel's Day	C	I	88	On Our Way to English	Rigby
Isabel's Story: From Guatemala to Georgia	V	HF	250+	Reading Expeditions	National Geographic
Isadora Duncan	O	B	915	Leveled Readers	Houghton Mifflin Harcourt
Isadora Duncan	O	B	915	Leveled Readers/CA	Houghton Mifflin Harcourt
Isadora Duncan	O	B	915	Leveled Readers/TX	Houghton Mifflin Harcourt
Ish	L	RF	250+	Reynolds, Peter H.	Candlewick Press
Ishi's Tale of Lizard	P	TL	250+	Hinton, Leanne; Roth, Susan L.	Farrar, Straus, & Giroux
#Isis & Osiris: To the Ends of the Earth	W	TL	2567	Graphic Myths and Legends	Lerner Publishing Group
Islam	Y	I	250+	World Religions	Compass Point Books
Islamic World, The	Y	I	250+	Reading Expeditions	National Geographic
Island Baby	M	RF	250+	Keller, Holly	Scholastic
Island Far From Home, An	W	HF	250+	Donahue, John	Carolrhoda Books
Island Keeper	T	RF	250+	Mazer, Harry	Language for Learning Assoc.
Island Life	R	I	250+	iOpeners	Pearson Learning Group
*Island Like You, An: Stories of the Barrio	Z	RF	250+	Cofer, Judith Ortiz	Penguin Group
Island of the Blue Dolphins	V	HF	250+	O'Dell, Scott	Bantam Books
Island of the Skog, The	M	F	250+	Kellogg, Steven	Dial/Penguin
Island of Wingo, The	N	F	250+	Sails	Rigby
Island on Bird Street, The	X	HF	250+	Orlev, Uri	Houghton Mifflin Harcourt
Island Picnic, The	H	RF	236	PM Story Books	Rigby
Island to Island	K	RF	250+	Ready to Read	Pacific Learning
Island, The	X	RF	250+	Paulsen, Gary	Bantam Books
Island, The	D	RF	24	Wildsmith, Brian	Oxford University Press
Islander, The	T	F	250+	Rylant, Cynthia	Random House
Islands	J	I	294	Landforms	Lerner Publishing Group
^Islands	M	I	198	Natural Wonders	Capstone Press
Isn't It Cool?	R	I	250+	Action Packs	Rigby
Isn't It Strange?	H	I	128	Polette, Nancy	Kaeden Books
Israel	O	I	2096	A Ticket to …	Carolrhoda Books
Israel	O	I	250+	Countries of the World	Red Brick Learning
Israel	P	I	2361	Country Explorers	Lerner Publishing Group
Israel	Q	I	250+	First Reports: Countries	Compass Point Books
Israel ABCs: A Book About the People and Places of Israel	Q	I	250+	Country ABCs	Picture Window Books
It All Adds Up	J	I	329	Pair-It Turn and Learn	Steck-Vaughn
It Came From Ohio!: My Life as a Writer	R	B	250+	Stine, R. L.	Scholastic
It Came from Outer Space	K	RF	864	Science Solves It!	Kane Press
It Came Through the Wall	O	F	1182	Healey, Tim	Mondo Publishing
It Can Fly	LB	I	8	Windows on Literacy	National Geographic
It Could Be Worse	E	F	108	Home Connection Collection	Rigby
It Didn't Frighten Me	D	F	250+	Bookshop	Mondo Publishing
It Had to Be You: The Gossip Girl Prequel	Z+	RF	250+	von Ziegesar, Cecily	Little Brown and Company
It Happened to Nancy	Z+	B	250+	Sparks, Beatrice (Ed.)	Avon Books
It Is Halloween!	J	RF	404	Appleton-Smith, Laura	Flyleaf Publishing
It Is My Birthday, Too!	E	RF	50	Pair-It Turn and Learn	Steck-Vaughn
It Is Raining	F	I	56	PM Plus Nonfiction	Rigby
It Looked Like Spilt Milk	E	RF	172	Shaw, Charles	Harper & Row
It Must Be Clay	H	I	173	Independent Readers Science	Houghton Mifflin Harcourt

* Collection of short stories   # Graphic text
^ Mature content with lower level text demands

TITLE	LEVEL	GENRE	WORD COUNT	AUTHOR / SERIES	PUBLISHER / DISTRIBUTOR
It Never Rains in Antarctica and Other Freaky Facts About Climate, Land, and Nature	S	I	250+	Seuling, Barbara	Capstone Press
It Only Looks Easy	T	RF	250+	Swallow, Pamela Curtis	Scholastic
It Smells Like Friday	L	F	250+	Popcorn	Sundance
It Sounds Like Music	D	I	56	Pair-It Books	Steck-Vaughn
It Started As a Seed	F	I	126	Learn to Read	Creative Teaching Press
It Started As an Egg	G	I	179	Learn to Read	Creative Teaching Press
It Starts as a Seed	E	I	36	Rosen Real Readers	Rosen Publishing Group
It Takes a Village	L	RF	250+	Cowen-Fletcher, J.	Scholastic
It Takes All Kinds	N	I	250+	Voyages	SRA/McGraw Hill
It Takes Balance	M	I	250+	Rigby Literacy	Rigby
It Takes Three	K	F	501	Silly Millies	Millbrook Press
It Takes Time to Grow	H	RF	57	Sunshine	Wright Group/McGraw Hill
It Takes Two	N	I	250+	Wonderwise	Franklin Watts
*It Was on Fire When I Lay Down on It	Z	I	250+	Fulghum, Robert	Ballantine Books
It Wasn't My Fault	L	RF	250+	Lester, Helen	Houghton Mifflin Harcourt
It Would Be Fun!	F	F	203	Start to Read	School Zone
It's Halloween, You 'Fraidy Mouse!	O	F	250+	Stilton, Geronimo	Scholastic
Italy	H	I	34	Canizares, Susan; Chessen, Betsey	Scholastic
Italy	O	I	250+	Countries of the World	Red Brick Learning
Italy	P	I	1919	Country Explorers	Lerner Publishing Group
Italy	Q	I	250+	First Reports: Countries	Compass Point Books
Italy	R	I	250+	Theme Sets	National Geographic
Itch & Ooze: Gross Stuff on Your Skin	U	I	4729	Gross Body Science	Millbrook Press
Itch! Itch!	C	RF	76	Bookshop	Mondo Publishing
Itchy Mitch	U	RF	250+	Bookshop	Mondo Publishing
Itchy, Itchy Chicken Pox	F	RF	131	Maccarone, Grace	Scholastic
Ithaka	Z+	TL	250+	Geras, Adele	Harcourt
It'll Be All Right on the Night!	Q	I	250+	Orbit Chapter Books	Pacific Learning
It's a Beautiful Day!	H	F	229	Silly Millies	Millbrook Press
It's a Big Country	Q	I	250+	WorldScapes	ETA/Cuisenaire
It's a Bit Tricky	G	RF	250+	Home Connection Collection	Rigby
It's a Blizzard!	L	I	250+	Rosen Real Readers	Rosen Publishing Group
It's a Butterfly's Life	O	I	250+	Kelly, Irene	Holiday House
It's a Dog's Life	R	I	250+	Explore More	Wright Group/McGraw Hill
It's a Fair Swap	P	I	393	Reading Street	Pearson
It's a Fiesta, Benjamin	N	RF	250+	Giff, Patricia Reilly	Bantam Books
It's a Frog's Life	Q	I	250+	Literacy 2000 Satellites	Rigby
It's a Gift	H	I	156	Lighthouse	Rigby
It's a Goal!	V	I	250+	WorldScapes	ETA/Cuisenaire
It's a Good Game, Dear Dragon	E	F	160	Dear Dragon	Norwood House Press
It's a Good Thing That There Are Insects	H	I	250+	Fowler, Allan	Scholastic
It's a Mall World After All	X	RF	250+	Rallison, Jeanette	Walker & Company
It's a Mammal!	Q	I	250+	iOpeners	Pearson Learning Group
It's a Party	D	I	24	Berger, Samantha; Moreton, Daniel	Scholastic
It's a Party!	A	F	15	Leveled Readers	Houghton Mifflin Harcourt
It's a Party!	A	F	15	Leveled Readers/CA	Houghton Mifflin Harcourt
It's a Pattern!	H	I	133	Pebble Math	Capstone Press
It's a Robot!	K	I	250+	The Rowland Reading Program Library	Rowland Reading Foundation
It's a Rule	E	I	128	Yellow Umbrella Books	Red Brick Learning
It's a Shape!	H	I	157	Pebble Math	Capstone Press

TITLE	LEVEL	GENRE	WORD COUNT	AUTHOR / SERIES	PUBLISHER / DISTRIBUTOR
It's a World of Time Zones	R	I	2055	Reading Street	Pearson
It's a Zoo!	H	RF	100	City Stories	Rigby
It's About Time	Q	I	250+	Orbit Collections	Pacific Learning
It's About Time	M	I	481	Storyteller Nonfiction	Wright Group/McGraw Hill
It's About Time	B	I	39	Twig	Wright Group/McGraw Hill
It's About Time	K	I	250+	Yellow Umbrella Books	Capstone Press
It's About Time!	I	I	224	In Step Readers	Rigby
It's About Time!	X	I	2675	Reading Street	Pearson
It's About Time, Max!	K	RF	250+	Math Matters	Kane Press
It's Addition!	H	I	187	Pebble Math	Capstone Press
It's Alive!	L	I	432	Reading Street	Pearson
It's Alive: Earth's Plants and Animals	T	I	250+	Kids Discover Reading	Wright Group/McGraw Hill
It's All Greek to Me	P	F	250+	Scieszka, Jon	Penguin Group
It's All in the Soil	Q	I	250+	iOpeners	Pearson Learning Group
It's All in Your Mind, James Robert	P	F	250+	Literacy 2000	Rigby
It's Alright to Cry	F	RF	138	Teacher's Choice Series	Pearson Learning Group
*It's Back to School We Go: First Day Stories From Around the World	Q	I	3508	Jackson, Ellen	Millbrook Press
It's Bedtime, Dear Dragon	F	F	177	Hillert, Margaret/Dear Dragon	Norwood House Press
It's Broken	E	RF	88	Dominie Phonics Reader	Pearson Learning Group
It's Circus Time, Dear Dragon	F	F	322	Dear Dragon	Norwood House Press
It's Cloudy Today	K	I	264	Lightning Bolt Books	Lerner Publishing Group
It's Cold Where I Live	H	RF	98	Windows on Literacy	National Geographic
It's Dinner Time	WB	I	0	Windows on Literacy	National Geographic
It's Earth Day!	N	I	601	Early Explorers	Benchmark Education
It's Easy!	O	RF	250+	Leveled Readers Language Support	Houghton Mifflin Harcourt
It's Electric!	T	I	250+	Rosen Real Readers	Rosen Publishing Group
It's Fall!	K	RF	875	Glaser, Linda	Millbrook Press
It's Fall, Dear Dragon	F	F	232	Dear Dragon	Norwood House Press
It's Football Time	C	RF	24	Geddes, Diana	Kaeden Books
It's Fun to Exercise	J	I	250+	Rosen Real Readers	Rosen Publishing Group
It's Game Day	D	RF	65	Salem, Lynn; Stewart, Josie	Continental Press
It's George!	H	RF	250+	Cohen, Miriam	Bantam Books
It's Going to Be Perfect!	K	RF	421	Carlson, Nancy	Carolrhoda Books
It's Groundhog Day, Dear Dragon	F	F	236	Hillert, Margaret/Dear Dragon	Norwood House Press
It's Halloween!	K	RF	250+	Prelutsky, Jack	Scholastic
It's Halloween, Dear Dragon	F	F	309	Dear Dragon	Norwood House Press
It's Hanukkah!	J	RF	109	Modesitt, Jeanne	Scholastic
It's Hot	D	RF	54	Ready Readers	Pearson Learning Group
It's in the Air	Z	I	2025	Independent Readers Science	Houghton Mifflin Harcourt
It's Israel's Birthday!	M	RF	282	Dietrick, Ellen	Kar-Ben Publishing
It's Just a Trick	O	RF	250+	Literacy 2000	Rigby
It's Justin Time, Amber Brown	K	RF	250+	Danziger, Paula	Puffin Books
It's Magic	H	F	204	Start to Read	School Zone
It's Magic!	L	I	250+	Trackers	Pacific Learning
It's Melting	C	RF	16	Learn to Read	Creative Teaching Press
It's Mine!	P	F	250+	Lionni, Leo	Scholastic
It's My Bread	B	F	43	Pacific Literacy	Pacific Learning
It's New, It's Improved, It's Terrible!	Q	RF	250+	Manes, Stephen	Bantam Books
It's Noisy at Night	E	RF	80	Wonder World	Wright Group/McGraw Hill
It's Not All Ancient History	Y	I	250+	iOpeners	Pearson Learning Group
It's Not Easy Being a Bunny	I	F	250+	Sadler, Marilyn	Random House
It's Not Easy Being George	S	RF	250+	Smith, Janice Lee	HarperTrophy

* Collection of short stories   # Graphic text
^ Mature content with lower level text demands

TITLE	LEVEL	GENRE	WORD COUNT	AUTHOR / SERIES	PUBLISHER / DISTRIBUTOR
It's Not Easy Being Mean: The Clique	X	RF	250+	Harrison, Lisi	Little Brown and Company
It's Not Fair	F	RF	51	Tadpoles	Rigby
It's Not Fair!	I	F	267	Harper, Anita	Holiday House
It's Not Going to Rain	J	F	363	Gear Up!	Wright Group/McGraw Hill
It's Not My Fault!	J	F	407	Carlson, Nancy	Carolrhoda Books
It's Not the End of the World	T	RF	250+	Blume, Judy	Dell
It's Not the Same	I	RF	250+	Sunshine	Wright Group/McGraw Hill
It's Not Worth Making a Tzimmes Over!	L	F	250+	Rosenthal, Betsy R.	Albert Whitman & Co.
It's Okay to Be Different	I	I	224	Parr, Todd	Little Brown and Company
It's Our Right	V	I	2676	Reading Street	Pearson
It's Our World	Q	I	250+	Orbit Collections	Pacific Learning
It's Our World, Too!	T	I	250+	Hoose, Phillip	Sunburst
It's Pumpkin Time!	J	RF	234	Hall, Zoe	Scholastic
It's Raining	E	I	86	Teacher's Choice Series	Pearson Learning Group
It's Raining!	C	I	32	Pair-It Books	Steck-Vaughn
It's Rainy Today	K	I	263	Lightning Bolt Books	Lerner Publishing Group
It's Shearing Time, Max!	H	F	225	Sun Sprouts	ETA/Cuisenaire
It's Show Time	S	I	250+	InfoQuest	Rigby
It's Snowing!	C	F	39	Brand New Readers	Candlewick Press
It's Snowing!	L	RF	158	Dunrea, Olivier	Farrar, Straus, & Giroux
It's Snowing!	J	I	193	Find Out Readers	Continental Press
It's Snowy Today	J	I	306	Lightning Bolt Books	Lerner Publishing Group
It's Spring	A	I	24	Vocabulary Readers	Houghton Mifflin Harcourt
It's Spring!	H	F	124	Berger, Samantha; Chanko, Pamela	Scholastic
It's Spring!	K	RF	941	Glaser, Linda	Millbrook Press
It's Spring, Dear Dragon	F	F	236	Dear Dragon	Norwood House Press
It's St. Patrick's Day, Dear Dragon	F	F	250+	Dear Dragon	Norwood House Press
It's Subtraction!	H	I	206	Pebble Math	Capstone Press
It's Summer!	K	RF	972	Glaser, Linda	Millbrook Press
It's Summer, Dear Dragon	F	F	224	Dear Dragon	Norwood House Press
It's Sunny Today	K	I	249	Lightning Bolt Books	Lerner Publishing Group
It's Super Mouse!	C	F	40	Brand New Readers	Candlewick Press
It's Taco Time	F	I	56	Teacher's Choice Series	Pearson Learning Group
It's Test Day, Tiger Turcotte	M	RF	4628	Flood, Pansie Hart	Carolrhoda Books
It's the Fashion	V	I	250+	Literacy 2000	Rigby
It's Time	F	F	283	Dominie Math Stories	Pearson Learning Group
It's Time for Bed	E	RF	126	Visions	Wright Group/McGraw Hill
It's Time to Eat!	C	I	49	Davidson, Avelyn	Scholastic
It's Time to Get Up	E	RF	143	Visions	Wright Group/McGraw Hill
It's Time to Rhyme	B	I	56	Harrison, Pat	Blueberry Hill Books
It's Time to Sleep, My Love	L	F	197	Tillman, Nancy	Feiwel and Friends
It's Time!	A	I	24	Early Connections	Benchmark Education
It's Time!	H	I	175	Yellow Umbrella Books	Red Brick Learning
It's Too Loud	C	I	53	Independent Readers Science	Houghton Mifflin Harcourt
It's Up to Me	T	I	250+	InfoTrek	ETA/Cuisenaire
It's Windy Today	K	I	287	Lightning Bolt Books	Lerner Publishing Group
It's Winter!	K	RF	250+	Glaser, Linda	Millbrook Press
It's Winter, Dear Dragon	F	F	254	Dear Dragon	Norwood House Press
It's Your First Day of School, Annie Claire	I	F	250+	Carlstrom, Nancy White	Harry N. Abrams
Itsy Bitsy Spider, The	K	TL	225	Trapani, Iza	Charlesbridge
I've Been Working on the Railroad	J	TL	250+	Traditional Songs	Picture Window Books
I've Got an Elephant	K	F	250+	Ginkel, Anne	Peachtree

TITLE	LEVEL	GENRE	WORD COUNT	AUTHOR / SERIES	PUBLISHER / DISTRIBUTOR
I've Got Mail	N	RF	250+	InfoTrek	ETA/Cuisenaire
I've Got New Sneakers	H	RF	111	City Kids	Rigby
I've Lost My Boot	C	RF	18	Windmill Books	Wright Group/McGraw Hill
I've Seen Santa!	K	F	250+	Bedford, David	Tiger Tales
Ivy & Bean	M	RF	250+	Barrows, Annie	Chronicle Books
Ivy & Bean and the Ghost That Had to Go	M	RF	250+	Barrows, Annie	Scholastic
Ivy & Bean Break the Fossil Record	M	RF	250+	Barrows, Annie	Chronicle Books
Ivy & Bean Take Care of the Babysitter	M	RF	250+	Barrows, Annie	Chronicle Books
Ivy's Journal: A Trip to the Yucatán	R	RF	250+	Bookshop	Mondo Publishing
Izzy Impala's Imaginary Illnesses	K	F	541	Animal Antics A To Z	Kane Press
Izzy, Willy-Nilly	X	RF	250+	Voigt, Cynthia	Aladdin
Izzy's Move	D	F	129	Leveled Readers	Houghton Mifflin Harcourt
Izzy's Move	D	F	129	Leveled Readers/CA	Houghton Mifflin Harcourt
Izzy's Move	D	F	129	Leveled Readers/TX	Houghton Mifflin Harcourt

* Collection of short stories   # Graphic text
^ Mature content with lower level text demands

TITLE	LEVEL	GENRE	WORD COUNT	AUTHOR / SERIES	PUBLISHER / DISTRIBUTOR
J	LB	I	14	Readlings	American Reading Company
J. K. Rowling	W	B	250+	A&E Biography	Lerner Publishing Group
^J. Pierpont Morgan and Wall Street	R	I	250+	On Deck	Rigby
J. R. R. Tolkien	X	B	250+	Just the Facts Biographies	Lerner Publishing Group
J. T.	Q	RF	250+	Wagner, Jane	Bantam Books
*J.J. Rabbit and the Monster	K	F	250+	I Am Reading	Kingfisher
J: My Name Is Jess	C	RF	61	Little Books	Sadlier-Oxford
Jace, Mace, and the Big Race	F	RF	124	Start to Read	School Zone
Jack	D	TL	11	Jumbled Tumbled Tales & Rhymes	Rigby
*Jack Adrift : Fourth Grade Without a Clue	U	RF	250+	Gantos, Jack	Farrar, Straus, & Giroux
Jack and Billy	C	RF	50	PM Plus Story Books	Rigby
Jack and Billy and Rose	G	RF	179	PM Plus Story Books	Rigby
Jack and Chug	I	F	337	PM Story Books-Orange	Rigby
Jack and Jill	D	TL	25	Jumbled Tumbled Tales & Rhymes	Rigby
Jack and Jill	D	F	40	Seedlings	Continental Press
Jack and Jill	E	TL	51	Sunshine	Wright Group/McGraw Hill
Jack and the Ball	D	F	100	Jack and Daisy	Pioneer Valley
Jack and the Bean Stalk	D	TL	109	Folk Tales	Pioneer Valley
Jack and the Bean Stalk	D	TL	109	Traditional Tales	Pioneer Valley
Jack and the Beanstalk	M	TL	250+	Crews, Nina	Henry Holt & Co.
Jack and the Beanstalk	K	TL	901	Hunia, Fran	Ladybird Books
Jack and the Beanstalk	L	TL	664	Leveled Literacy Intervention/ Blue System	Heinemann
Jack and the Beanstalk	I	TL	250+	Literacy 2000	Rigby
Jack and the Beanstalk	K	TL	250+	Storyworlds	Heinemann
Jack and the Beanstalk	H	TL	170	Sunshine	Wright Group/McGraw Hill
Jack and the Beanstalk	K	TL	250+	Weisner, David	Scholastic
#Jack and the Beanstalk: The Graphic Novel	M	TL	250+	Graphic Spin	Stone Arch Books
#Jack and the Box	J	F	250+	Spiegelman, Art	Toon Books
Jack and the Fox	I	F	226	Jack and Daisy	Pioneer Valley
Jack and the Magic Harp	K	TL	250+	PM Tales and Plays-Gold	Rigby
Jack DePert at the Supermarket	G	RF	188	Wonder World	Wright Group/McGraw Hill
Jack in the Box	I	F	250+	Story Box	Wright Group/McGraw Hill
Jack Plays the Violin	H	RF	250+	Schultz, Jessica	Scholastic
Jack Prelutsky	M	B	690	Leveled Readers	Houghton Mifflin Harcourt
Jack Prelutsky	M	B	690	Leveled Readers/CA	Houghton Mifflin Harcourt
Jack Prelutsky	M	B	690	Leveled Readers/TX	Houghton Mifflin Harcourt
Jack Russell Dog Detective: Dog Den Mystery	N	F	250+	Odgers, Darrel & Sally	Kane/Miller Book Publishers
Jack Russell Dog Detective: The Awful Pawful	N	F	250+	Odgers, Darrel & Sally	Kane/Miller Book Publishers
Jack Russell Dog Detective: The Lying Postman	N	F	250+	Odgers, Darrel & Sally	Kane/Miller Book Publishers
Jack Russell Dog Detective: The Mugged Pug	N	F	250+	Odgers, Darrel & Sally	Kane/Miller Book Publishers
Jack Russell Dog Detective: The Phantom Mudder	N	F	250+	Odgers, Darrel & Sally	Kane/Miller Book Publishers
Jack Russell Dog Detective: The Sausage Situation	N	F	250+	Odgers, Darrel & Sally	Kane/Miller Book Publishers
Jack Russell Terriers	R	I	250+	All About Dogs	Capstone Press
Jack Russell Terriers	I	I	161	Dogs	Capstone Press
Jack the Puppy	M	I	250+	How Your Pet Grows!	Random House
Jack Tumor	Z+	RF	250+	McGowan, Anthony	Farrar, Straus, & Giroux
Jackals	P	I	1812	Animal Scavengers	Lerner Publishing Group
Jackaroo	Y	RF	250+	Voigt, Cynthia	Scholastic
Jacket, The	R	RF	250+	Clements, Andrew	Aladdin Paperbacks
Jackets	C	RF	42	Joy Readers	Pearson Learning Group

JK

TITLE	LEVEL	GENRE	WORD COUNT	AUTHOR / SERIES	PUBLISHER / DISTRIBUTOR
Jackie & Me	T	F	250+	Gutman, Dan	HarperTrophy
Jackie Mitchell: Baseball Player	N	B	250+	Beginning Biographies	Pearson Learning Group
Jackie Robinson	T	B	250+	Amazing Americans	Wright Group/McGraw Hill
Jackie Robinson	T	B	250+	Christopher, Matt	Little Brown and Company
Jackie Robinson	P	B	250+	Early Biographies	Compass Point Books
Jackie Robinson	N	B	235	First Biographies	Capstone Press
Jackie Robinson	S	B	3421	History Maker Bios	Lerner Publishing Group
Jackie Robinson	O	B	1991	On My Own Biography	Lerner Publishing Group
Jackie Robinson	P	B	250+	Photo-Illustrated Biographies	Red Brick Learning
Jackie Robinson	R	B	1789	Reading Street	Pearson
Jackie Robinson	N	B	250+	Soar To Success	Houghton Mifflin Harcourt
Jackie Robinson and the Big Game	J	B	250+	Childhood of Famous Americans	Aladdin
Jackie Robinson and the Breaking of the Color Barrier	S	B	250+	Shorto, Russell	Millbrook Press
Jackie Robinson and the Story of All-Black Baseball	N	B	250+	O'Connor, Jim	Random House
Jackie Robinson Breaks the Color Line	V	B	250+	Cornerstones of Freedom	Children's Press
Jackie Robinson Breaks Through	Q	B	1350	Vocabulary Readers	Houghton Mifflin Harcourt
Jackie Robinson Breaks Through	Q	B	1350	Vocabulary Readers/CA	Houghton Mifflin Harcourt
Jackie Robinson Story, The	P	B	250+	Windows on Literacy	National Geographic
Jackie Robinson, Breaking Barriers	X	B	2907	Vocabulary Readers	Houghton Mifflin Harcourt
Jackie Robinson, Breaking Barriers	X	B	2907	Vocabulary Readers/CA	Houghton Mifflin Harcourt
Jackie Robinson: Baseball's First Black Major Leaguer	O	B	250+	Greene, Carol	Children's Press
#Jackie Robinson: Baseball's Great Pioneer	T	B	250+	Graphic Library	Capstone Press
^Jackie Robinson: Breaking the Color Barrier	S	B	250+	Hameray Biography Series	Hameray Publishing Group
Jackie Robinson: He Led the Way	K	B	250+	All Aboard Reading	Grosset & Dunlap
Jackie's New Friend	F	I	168	O'Connor, C. M.	Continental Press
Jack-in-the-Box	B	RF	34	Literacy 2000	Rigby
Jacko of Baker Street	I	RF	369	Sails	Rigby
Jacko, the Dreamer	I	F	306	Sails	Rigby
Jack-O-Lantern	B	I	37	Twig	Wright Group/McGraw Hill
Jack-O-Lanterns	D	I	47	Pebble Books	Capstone Press
Jacks	P	I	250+	Games Around the World	Compass Point Books
Jacks and More Jacks	F	F	79	Little Celebrations	Pearson Learning Group
Jack's Balloon	D	RF	69	Reading Safari	Mondo Publishing
Jack's Birthday	C	RF	89	PM Plus Story Books	Rigby
*Jack's Black Book	W	RF	250+	Gantos, Jack	Farrar, Straus, & Giroux
Jack's Boat	I	I	172	Windows on Literacy	National Geographic
*Jack's New Power: Stories From a Caribbean Year	W	RF	250+	Gantos, Jack	Sunburst
Jack's New Skates	E	RF	148	Developing Books	Pioneer Valley
Jack's Pack	C	I	22	KinderReaders	Rigby
Jack's Road	C	RF	59	PM Stars	Rigby
Jack's Run	X	RF	250+	Smith, Roland	Hyperion
Jackson and Bud's Bumpy Ride: America's First Cross-Country Automobile Trip	N	HF	1733	Koehler-Pentacoff, Elizabeth	Millbrook Press
Jackson Pollock in Action	S	B	1263	Leveled Readers	Houghton Mifflin Harcourt
Jackson Pollock in Action	S	B	1263	Leveled Readers/CA	Houghton Mifflin Harcourt
Jackson Pollock in Action	S	B	1263	Leveled Readers/TX	Houghton Mifflin Harcourt
Jackson's Bear	K	F	678	Springboard	Wright Group/McGraw Hill
Jackson's Monster	I	F	250+	Little Readers	Houghton Mifflin Harcourt
Jacksonville Jaguars, The	S	I	250+	Team Spirit	Norwood House Press
Jacob Have I Loved	X	RF	250+	Paterson, Katherine	HarperTrophy
Jacob Two-Two and the Dinosaur	P	F	250+	Richler, Mordecai	Tundra Books

JK

* Collection of short stories   # Graphic text
^ Mature content with lower level text demands

TITLE	LEVEL	GENRE	WORD COUNT	AUTHOR / SERIES	PUBLISHER / DISTRIBUTOR
Jacob Two-Two Meets the Hooded Fang	P	F	250+	Richler, Mordecai	Seal Books
Jacob's Day	F	RF	51	Windows on Literacy	National Geographic
Jacob's Rescue: A Holocaust Story	Y	HF	250+	Drucker, M.; Halperin, M.	Bantam Books
Jacqueline Kennedy	M	B	229	First Ladies	Capstone Press
Jacques Cousteau	L	B	250+	Biography	Benchmark Education
^Jacques Cousteau: Guardian of the Sea	S	B	250+	Hameray Biography Series	Hameray Publishing Group
Jacques Cousteau: In Love with the Sea	R	B	250+	Explore More	Wright Group/McGraw Hill
Jada's Adventure	K	F	250+	Windows on Literacy	National Geographic
Jade Dragon, The	P	RF	250+	Marsden, Carolyn & Shin-Mui Loh, Virginia	Candlewick Press
Jade Dragon, The: A Story of Ancient China	O	HF	250+	Historical Tales	Picture Window Books
Jade Emperor and the Four Dragons, The	K	TL	250+	Lighthouse	Rigby
Jade Green	Z	F	250+	Naylor, Phyllis Reynolds	Simon & Schuster
Jaguar	L	I	250+	A Day in the Life: Rain Forest Animals	Heinemann Library
^Jaguar	O	I	250+	Fast Cars	Capstone Press
Jaguar	W	RF	250+	Smith, Roland	Hyperion
Jaguar Attack!	P	RF	250+	Bookweb	Rigby
Jaguars	O	I	250+	First Reports	Compass Point Books
Jaguars	T	I	250+	High Performance	Red Brick Learning
Jaguars	U	I	6508	Nature Watch Books	Lerner Publishing Group
Jaguars	J	I	78	Pebble Books	Red Brick Learning
Jaguar's Jewel, The	N	RF	250+	A to Z Mysteries	Random House
Jaime Escalante	T	B	250+	Literacy by Design	Rigby
Jaime Escalante, A Great Teacher	M	B	273	Independent Readers Social Studies	Houghton Mifflin Harcourt
Jake	A	I	35	Little Books for Early Readers	University of Maine
Jake and the Big Fish	E	RF	130	PM Photo Stories	Rigby
Jake and the Copycats	J	RF	250+	Rocklin, Joanne	Bantam Books
#Jake Burton Carpenter and the Snowboard	S	B	250+	Graphic Library	Capstone Press
Jake Can Play	B	RF	42	Little Books for Early Readers	University of Maine
Jake Drake Bully Buster	O	RF	250+	Clements, Andrew	Aladdin Paperbacks
Jake Drake Class Clown	O	RF	250+	Clements, Andrew	Aladdin Paperbacks
Jake Drake Know-It-All	O	RF	250+	Clements, Andrew	Aladdin
Jake Drake Teacher's Pet	O	RF	250+	Clements, Andrew	Aladdin Paperbacks
Jake Greenthumb	J	F	250+	Bookshop	Mondo Publishing
Jake Kicks a Goal	D	RF	87	PM Photo Stories	Rigby
Jake Makes a Map	D	RF	55	Leveled Readers	Houghton Mifflin Harcourt
Jake Reynolds: Chicken or Eagle?	Q	RF	250+	Orca Young Readers	Orca Books
Jake Starts School	K	RF	250+	Wright, Michael	Feiwel and Friends
Jake Stays Awake	K	F	250+	Wright, Michael	Feiwel and Friends
Jake the Ballet Dog	M	F	250+	LeFrak, Karen	Walker & Company
Jake the Snake	K	F	250+	Supersonics	Rigby
Jake Was a Pirate	M	F	250+	Voyages	SRA/McGraw Hill
Jake, the Juggler	J	RF	403	Sails	Rigby
Jake's 100th Day of School	M	RF	250+	Laminack, Lester L.	Peachtree
Jake's Bird Feeder	J	RF	514	Kanninen, Barbara	Kaeden Books
Jake's Car	D	RF	80	PM Photo Stories	Rigby
Jake's Dream	N	RF	846	Reading Street	Pearson
Jake's First Word	H	RF	204	Books for Young Learners	Richard C. Owen
Jake's Lemonade Stand	H	RF	294	Kanninen, Barbara	Kaeden Books
Jake's Map	C	RF	63	Leveled Readers Language Support	Houghton Mifflin Harcourt
Jake's Plane	E	RF	137	PM Photo Stories	Rigby

JK

TITLE	LEVEL	GENRE	WORD COUNT	AUTHOR / SERIES	PUBLISHER / DISTRIBUTOR
Jake's Toad House	I	RF	382	Kanninen, Barbara	Kaeden Books
Jamaica	O	I	1895	A Ticket to …	Carolrhoda Books
Jamaica	P	I	1534	Country Explorers	Lerner Publishing Group
Jamaica	G	I	97	Nonfiction Set 4	Literacy Footprints
Jamaica	Q	I	250+	Theme Sets	National Geographic
Jamaica and Brianna	K	RF	250+	Little Readers	Houghton Mifflin Harcourt
Jamaica Tag-Along	K	RF	250+	Havill, Juanita	Scholastic
Jamaica's Find	K	RF	250+	Havill, Juanita	Scholastic
Jamall's City Garden	I	I	250+	Rigby Literacy	Rigby
Jamal's Busy Day	J	RF	207	Hudson, Wade	Just Us Books
Jamberry	J	F	111	Degen, Bruce	Harper & Row
Jambo, Joshua	K	RF	820	InfoTrek	ETA/Cuisenaire
James A. Garfield	U	B	250+	Profiles of the Presidents	Compass Point Books
James A. Garfield: Twentieth President	R	B	250+	Getting to Know the U.S. Presidents	Children's Press
^James and the Alien Experiment	P	SF	9643	Prue, S	Stone Arch Books
James and the Giant Peach	Q	F	250+	Dahl, Roald	Penguin Group
James Beckwourth: Legendary Mountain Man	V	B	250+	Trailblazer Biographies	Carolrhoda Books
James Buchanan	U	B	250+	Profiles of the Presidents	Compass Point Books
James Buchanan: Fifteenth President	R	B	250+	Getting to Know the U.S. Presidents	Children's Press
James Earl Carter, Jr.	U	B	250+	Profiles of the Presidents	Compass Point Books
James Is Hiding	A	RF	24	Windmill Books	Wright Group/McGraw Hill
James K. Polk	U	B	250+	Profiles of the Presidents	Compass Point Books
James K. Polk: Eleventh President	R	B	250+	Getting to Know the U.S. Presidents	Children's Press
James Madison	U	B	250+	Amazing Americans	Wright Group/McGraw Hill
James Madison	T	B	3473	Presidential Series	January Books
James Madison	S	B	250+	Primary Source Readers	Teacher Created Materials
James Madison	U	B	250+	Profiles of the Presidents	Compass Point Books
James Madison: Founding Father	Q	B	250+	Rosen Real Readers	Rosen Publishing Group
James Madison: Fourth President	R	B	250+	Getting to Know the U.S. Presidents	Children's Press
James Monroe	T	B	3311	Presidential Series	January Books
James Monroe	U	B	250+	Profiles of the Presidents	Compass Point Books
James Monroe: Fifth President	R	RF	250+	Getting to Know the U.S. Presidents	Children's Press
James Stewart	P	B	2116	Amazing Athletes	Lerner Publishing Group
James Stuart: Motocross Great	Q	B	250+	Dirt Bikes	Capstone Press
Jamestown and the Virginia Colony	U	I	250+	Reading Expeditions	National Geographic
Jamestown Colony, The	V	I	250+	Cornerstones of Freedom	Children's Press
Jamestown Colony, The	V	I	250+	Let Freedom Ring	Capstone Press
Jamestown Colony, The	T	I	250+	We The People	Compass Point Books
Jamestown, 1607	W	I	250+	Cooper, Michael L.	Holiday House
Jamestown: New World Adventure	T	I	250+	Adventures in Colonial America	Troll Associates
*Jamie and Angus Stories, The	N	RF	250+	Fine, Anne	Candlewick Press
*Jamie and Angus Together	N	RF	250+	Fine, Anne	Candlewick Press
Jamie the Lifeguard	F	RF	81	Seedlings	Continental Press
Jamila Joins the Team	K	RF	509	Springboard	Wright Group/McGraw Hill
Jan and the Jacket	E	RF	74	Oxford Reading Tree	Oxford University Press
Jan Can Juggle	B	RF	25	Ready Readers	Pearson Learning Group
Jan Matzeliger, Inventor	T	B	1916	Leveled Readers Science	Houghton Mifflin Harcourt
Jane Addams	U	B	250+	Amazing Americans	Wright Group/McGraw Hill
Jane Addams	P	B	250+	Community Builders	Children's Press

JK

* Collection of short stories   # Graphic text
^ Mature content with lower level text demands

TITLE	LEVEL	GENRE	WORD COUNT	AUTHOR / SERIES	PUBLISHER / DISTRIBUTOR
Jane Addams	Q	B	250+	Early Biographies	Compass Point Books
Jane Addams	O	B	586	Leveled Readers Social Studies	Houghton Mifflin Harcourt
Jane Addams: A Life of Cooperation	P	B	592	Pull Ahead Books	Lerner Publishing Group
Jane and the Beanstalk	Q	TL	1534	Leveled Readers	Houghton Mifflin Harcourt
Jane Eyre	Z	RF	250+	Bronte, Charlotte	Scholastic
Jane Eyre	W	RF	250+	Edge	Hampton Brown
Jane Eyre	Z	RF	250+	High-Fliers	Pacific Learning
Jane Goodall	N	B	250+	Biography	Benchmark Education
Jane Goodall	M	B	250+	First Biographies	Capstone Press
Jane Goodall	R	B	3883	History Maker Bios	Lerner Publishing Group
Jane Goodall	O	B	250+	Leveled Readers	Houghton Mifflin Harcourt
Jane Goodall	E	B	183	Leveled Readers Science	Houghton Mifflin Harcourt
Jane Goodall	R	B	1298	Time for Kids	Teacher Created Materials
Jane Goodall and the Chimps	L	B	250+	Twig	Wright Group/McGraw Hill
Jane Goodall and the Wild Chimpanzees	L	B	250+	Birnbaum, Bette	Steck-Vaughn
Jane Goodall: A Chimp's Best Friend	K	B	247	Shutterbug Books	Steck-Vaughn
Jane Goodall: A Good and True Heart	S	B	250+	Pair-It Books	Steck-Vaughn
Jane Goodall: A Life of Loyalty	N	B	522	Pull Ahead-Biographies	Lerner Publishing Group
^Jane Goodall: A Voice for Wild Chimpanzees	R	B	250+	Hameray Biography Series	Hameray Publishing Group
Jane Goodall: Animal Scientist and Friend	R	B	250+	Science Readers	Teacher Created Materials
Jane Goodall: Finding Hope in the Wilds of Africa	R	B	250+	High Five Reading	Red Brick Learning
Jane Goodall: Living With Chimpanzees	E	B	162	Leveled Readers Science	Houghton Mifflin Harcourt
Jane Goodall: Living With the Chimpanzees	M	B	250+	Rigby Literacy	Rigby
Jane Goodall: Living with the Chimpanzees	M	B	250+	Rigby Star Quest	Rigby
Jane Goodall: Primatologist and Animal Activist	U	B	250+	Mission: Science	Compass Point Books
Jane Goodall: Protecting Primates	T	I	250+	Reading Expeditions	National Geographic
Jane in Bloom	W	RF	250+	Lytton, Deborah	Dutton Children's Books
Jane Mt. Pleasant	H	B	134	Leveled Readers Science	Houghton Mifflin Harcourt
Jane's Car	F	RF	121	PM Story Books	Rigby
Jane's Mansion	N	I	250+	Literacy 2000	Rigby
Janey Crane	J	F	356	Let's Read Together	Kane Press
Janitor's Boy, The	S	RF	250+	Clements, Andrew	Aladdin Paperbacks
Jan's New Fan	C	RF	34	KinderReaders	Rigby
January to March	N	RF	2082	Take Two Books	Wright Group/McGraw Hill
Japan	Q	I	250+	A True Book	Children's Press
Japan	O	I	250+	Countries of the World	Red Brick Learning
Japan	P	I	2162	Country Explorers	Lerner Publishing Group
Japan	Q	I	250+	First Reports: Countries	Compass Point Books
Japan	P	I	250+	Many Cultures, One World	Capstone Press
Japan	M	I	488	Pair-It Books	Steck-Vaughn
Japan	R	I	250+	Theme Sets	National Geographic
Japan ABCs: A Book About the People and Places of Japan	Q	I	250+	Country ABCs	Picture Window Books
Japan in Colors	N	I	250+	World of Colors	Capstone Press
Japan: A Question and Answer Book	P	I	250+	Questions and Answers: Countries	Capstone Press
Japan: Civilizations Past to Present	S	I	250+	Reading Expeditions	National Geographic
Japan: Land of Contrasts	R	I	250+	Orbit Chapter Books	Pacific Learning
^Japanese American Internment, The: An Interactive History Adventure	W	HF	250+	You Choose Books	Capstone Press
Japanese Garden, The	K	RF	250+	PM Plus Story Books	Rigby
Japanese Giant Hornet, The	M	I	250+	Literacy by Design	Rigby
Japanese Language, The	R	I	1945	Reading Street	Pearson

JK

TITLE	LEVEL	GENRE	WORD COUNT	AUTHOR / SERIES	PUBLISHER / DISTRIBUTOR
Jar of Dreams, A	R	HF	250+	Uchida, Yoshiko	Aladdin
Jar, The	E	RF	107	Bonnell, Kris	Reading Reading Books
Jasmine's Duck	H	RF	207	Lighthouse	Rigby
Jason & Marceline	Z	RF	250+	Spinelli, Jerry	Little Brown and Company
Jason and the Aliens Down the Street	O	F	250+	Greer, Greg; Ruddick, Bob	HarperTrophy
Jason and the Blind Puppy	I	RF	605	Rigby Flying Colors	Rigby
Jason and the Space Creature	K	F	643	Leveled Readers	Houghton Mifflin Harcourt
Jason and the Space Creature	K	F	643	Leveled Readers/CA	Houghton Mifflin Harcourt
Jason and the Space Creature	K	F	643	Leveled Readers/TX	Houghton Mifflin Harcourt
Jason Kidd Story, The	P	RF	250+	Moore, David	Scholastic
#Jason: Quest for the Golden Fleece	V	TL	3286	Graphic Myths and Legends	Graphic Universe
Jason's Bus Ride	G	F	117	Ziefert, Harriet	Penguin Group
Jason's Gold	T	HF	250+	Hobbs, Will	William Morrow
Jason's Journey	N	RF	250+	InfoTrek	ETA/Cuisenaire
Jasper	F	RF	107	Books for Young Learners	Richard C. Owen
Jasper and the Bully	K	F	250+	Jasper the Cat	Pioneer Valley
Jasper and the Kitten	I	F	647	Jasper the Cat	Pioneer Valley
Jasper the Fat Cat	C	RF	68	Jasper the Cat	Pioneer Valley
Javed's Pet	K	RF	250+	Reading Safari	Mondo Publishing
Javelinas	P	I	2056	Early Bird Nature Books	Lerner Publishing Group
Jaws of Life, The	T	I	4144	A Great Idea	Norwood House Press
Jazmin's Notebook	Z	RF	250+	Grimes, Nikki	Penguin Group
Jazz Age Poet: A Story About Langston Hughes	R	B	8795	Creative Minds Biographies	Carolrhoda Books
Jazz Baby	J	RF	125	Bebop Books	Lee & Low Books Inc.
Jazz Band, The	E	RF	95	Reading Street	Pearson Learning Group
Jazz Dance	S	I	250+	Dance	Capstone Press
Jazz Great	U	RF	3296	Leveled Readers	Houghton Mifflin Harcourt
Jazz Kid, The	Y	RF	250+	Collier, James Lincoln	Penguin Group
Jazz Man, The	T	RF	250+	Weik, Mary Hays	Simon & Schuster
Jazz, Jazz, Jazz	V	I	1696	Reading Street	Pearson
Jazz, Pizzazz, and the Silver Threads	P	RF	250+	Quattlebaum, Mary	Bantam Books
Jazzy Jewelry, Pretty Purses, and More!	P	I	3233	Ross, Kathy	Millbrook Press
Jean Baptiste Pointe du Sable: Father of Chicago	T	B	250+	Literacy by Design	Rigby
Jean Batten: Pioneer of the Sky	P	B	250+	Wonder World	Wright Group/McGraw Hill
Jean Craighead George	S	B	250+	Cary, Alice	Creative Teaching Press
Jean Fritz Comes Home	X	B	2268	Leveled Readers	Houghton Mifflin Harcourt
Jeanie's Valentines	L	RF	250+	Rarick, Carrie	Pearson Learning Group
Jeans From Mines to Malls	P	I	250+	Explorer Books-Pioneer	National Geographic
Jeans: From Mines to Malls	Q	I	250+	Explorer Books-Pathfinder	National Geographic
Jeb's Barn	G	RF	86	Little Celebrations	Pearson Learning Group
Jeepers	L	RF	250+	Books for Young Learners	Richard C. Owen
Jeff Gordon	P	B	1580	Amazing Athletes	Lerner Publishing Group
Jeff Gordon	R	B	250+	Sports Heroes	Red Brick Learning
Jefferson Davis	U	B	250+	Let Freedom Ring	Red Brick Learning
Jefferson Davis and the Confederacy	Y	B	250+	The Civil War	Carus Publishing Company
Jeff's Hero	U	RF	7218	Reading Street	Pearson
Jeff's Magnets	I	I	168	Instant Readers	Harcourt School Publishers
Jelly Beans	M	I	250+	Early Connections	Benchmark Education
Jellybean Jar, The	F	RF	107	InfoTrek	ETA/Cuisenaire
Jellybean Tree, The	H	F	231	Sunshine	Wright Group/McGraw Hill
Jellybeans and the Big Book Bonanza, The	K	F	250+	Numeroff, Laura & Evans, Nate	Harry N. Abrams
Jellybeans and the Big Camp Kickoff, The	K	F	250+	Numeroff, Laura & Evans, Nate	Harry N. Abrams
Jellybeans and the Big Dance, The	K	F	250+	Numeroff, Laura & Evans, Nate	Harry N. Abrams

JK

* Collection of short stories   # Graphic text
^ Mature content with lower level text demands

TITLE	LEVEL	GENRE	WORD COUNT	AUTHOR / SERIES	PUBLISHER / DISTRIBUTOR
Jellyfish	L	I	250+	A Day in the Life: Sea Animals	Heinemann Library
Jellyfish	O	I	1188	Early Bird Nature Books	Lerner Publishing Group
Jellyfish	I	I	58	Pebble Books	Red Brick Learning
Jellyfish	F	I	125	Sails	Rigby
Jellyfish	M	I	250+	Scooters	ETA/Cuisenaire
Jellyfish	J	I	95	Under the Sea	Capstone Press
Jem and Jan Win!	D	RF	93	Reading Street	Pearson Learning Group
Jemma Hartman, Camper Extraordinaire	T	RF	250+	Ferber, Brenda A.	Farrar, Straus, & Giroux
Jemma's Big Leap	K	RF	542	Rigby Gigglers	Rigby
Jen and Max	E	RF	93	Reading Street	Pearson Learning Group
Jen and Max Build a House	E	RF	109	Reading Street	Pearson Learning Group
Jen and Max Fix It!	E	RF	106	Reading Street	Pearson Learning Group
Jen and Max Say Good Night	E	RF	121	Reading Street	Pearson Learning Group
Jeni's Lettuce	G	RF	194	Rigby Flying Colors	Rigby
Jenius: The Amazing Guinea Pig	N	F	250+	King-Smith, Dick	Hyperion
Jenna and the Three R's	L	RF	250+	Read-it! Readers	Picture Window Books
Jenna's Pet	E	RF	179	Windows on Literacy	National Geographic
Jennifer Murdley's Toad	R	F	250+	Coville, Bruce	Harcourt, Inc.
Jennifer Pockets	I	RF	205	Book Bank	Wright Group/McGraw Hill
Jennifer, Hecate, Macbeth, William McKinley, and Me, Elizabeth	R	RF	250+	Konigsburg, E. L.	Yearling Books
Jennifer, Too	L	RF	250+	Havill, Juanita	Hyperion
Jenny and the Cornstalk	L	TL	890	Pair-It Books	Steck-Vaughn
Jenny Archer to the Rescue	M	RF	250+	Conford, Ellen	Little Brown and Company
Jenny Archer, Author	M	RF	250+	Conford, Ellen	Little Brown and Company
Jenny in Bed	D	RF	76	Lighthouse	Rigby
Jenny Lives on Hunter Street	H	RF	141	Book Bank	Wright Group/McGraw Hill
Jenny's Garden	E	RF	45	Leveled Readers Science	Houghton Mifflin Harcourt
Jenny's Socks	G	RF	94	Rookie Readers	Children's Press
Jenny's Yellow Ribbon	J	RF	103	Dominie Readers	Pearson Learning Group
Jen's Best Gift Ever	I	RF	310	Appleton-Smith, Laura	Flyleaf Publishing
Jeremy and the Enchanted Theater	M	F	250+	Orca Echoes	Orca Books
Jeremy Draws a Monster	I	F	210	McCarty, Peter	Henry Holt & Co.
Jeremy Fink and the Meaning of Life	U	RF	250+	Mass, Wendy	Little Brown and Company
Jeremy Jackrabbit's Jumping Journey	K	F	595	Animal Antics A To Z	Kane Press
Jeremy Thatcher, Dragon Hatcher	R	F	250+	Coville, Bruce	Aladdin
Jeremy's Cake	F	RF	97	Storyteller-Moon Rising	Wright Group/McGraw Hill
Jericho	T	RF	250+	Hickman, Janet	Hearst
Jericho Walls	V	HF	250+	Collier, Kristi	Henry Holt & Co.
Jericho's Journey	U	RF	250+	Wisler, G. Clifton	Penguin Group
Jerry on the Line	R	RF	250+	Seabrooke, Brenda	Puffin Books
Jerry Yang, Chief Yahoo	T	B	250+	Bookshop	Mondo Publishing
Jess in the Snow	E	RF	109	Handprints C, Set 2	Educators Publishing Service
Jesse	A	RF	38	Leveled Literacy Intervention/ Green System	Heinemann
Jesse	Y	RF	250+	Soto, Gary	Scholastic
Jesse Jackson	P	B	250+	Simon, Charnan	Children's Press
Jesse Owens	N	B	200	First Biographies	Capstone Press
Jesse Owens	X	B	250+	Just the Facts Biographies	Lerner Publishing Group
Jesse Owens	P	B	1746	On My Own Biography	Lerner Publishing Group
Jesse Owens An American Hero	R	B	1336	Vocabulary Readers/CA	Houghton Mifflin Harcourt
Jesse Owens An American Hero	R	B	1336	Vocabulary Readers	Houghton Mifflin Harcourt
Jesse Owens: Olympic Hero	P	B	250+	Sabin, Francene	Troll Associates

JK

* Collection of short stories   # Graphic text
^ Mature content with lower level text demands

TITLE	LEVEL	GENRE	WORD COUNT	AUTHOR / SERIES	PUBLISHER / DISTRIBUTOR
Jesse's Star	R	HF	250+	Orca Young Readers	Orca Books
Jessica	L	RF	250+	Henkes, Kevin	Scholastic
Jessica in the Dark	I	RF	362	PM Story Books-Orange	Rigby
Jessica's Dress-Ups	F	RF	130	Voyages	SRA/McGraw Hill
Jessie's Flower	G	F	132	Read Alongs	Rigby
Jet Fighter Planes	Q	I	250+	Wild Rides!	Capstone Press
Jets	M	I	250+	Horsepower	Capstone Press
Jets	H	I	88	Mighty Machines	Capstone Press
Jets	L	I	337	Pull Ahead Books	Lerner Publishing Group
Jets and the Rockets, The	J	RF	250+	PM Plus Story Books	Rigby
Jetty's Journey to Freedom	S	HF	250+	Pair-It Books	Steck-Vaughn
Jewel of the Desert	V	HF	2994	Leveled Readers	Houghton Mifflin Harcourt
Jewelers to the Palace	O	HF	250+	Windows on Literacy	National Geographic
Jewels of the Sea	M	I	250+	Rigby Flying Colors	Rigby
Jewish Comedy Stars: Classic to Cutting Edge	Y	B	16329	Kar-Ben Biographies	Kar-Ben Publishing
J-Files, The	L	RF	250+	Bookweb	Rigby
Jigaree, The	E	F	128	Story Box	Wright Group/McGraw Hill
Jigaree's Breakfast, The	I	F	203	The Story Basket	Wright Group/McGraw Hill
Jill Jumps	C	F	35	Ray's Readers	Outside the Box
Jill the Pill	M	RF	250+	The Rowland Reading Program Library	Rowland Reading Foundation
Jillian Jiggs	J	RF	250+	Gilman, Phoebe	Scholastic
Jilly the Kid	M	RF	250+	Krailing, Tessa	Barron's Educational
Jilly's Ball	F	RF	137	Kaleidoscope Collection	Hameray Publishing Group
Jim Abbott: Making the Most of It	X	B	2451	Leveled Readers	Houghton Mifflin Harcourt
Jim Boy	W	HF	250+	Earley, Tony	Little Brown and Company
Jim Henson, the Puppet Man	E	B	93	Leveled Readers	Houghton Mifflin Harcourt
Jim Henson, the Puppet Man	E	B	93	Leveled Readers/CA	Houghton Mifflin Harcourt
Jim Henson, the Puppet Man	E	B	93	Leveled Readers/TX	Houghton Mifflin Harcourt
Jim Meets the Thing	I	F	250+	Cohen, Miriam	Bantam Books
^Jim Morrison	Z	B	250+	Rock Music Library	Capstone Press
Jim Thorpe	U	B	250+	Sports Heroes and Legends	Lerner Publishing Group
Jim Thorpe	N	I	528	Vocabulary Readers	Houghton Mifflin Harcourt
Jim Thorpe	N	I	528	Vocabulary Readers/CA	Houghton Mifflin Harcourt
Jim Thorpe	N	I	528	Vocabulary Readers/TX	Houghton Mifflin Harcourt
#Jim Thorpe: Greatest Athlete in the World	R	B	250+	Graphic Library	Capstone Press
Jim Thorpe: The Greatest Athlete in the World	S	B	2443	Reading Street	Pearson
Jim Ugly	Q	RF	250+	Fleischman, Sid	Bantam Books
Jimi Hendrix	Z	B	250+	Just the Facts Biographies	Lerner Publishing Group
Jimmy	D	RF	83	Foundations	Wright Group/McGraw Hill
Jimmy Carter	R	B	4103	History Maker Bios	Lerner Publishing Group
Jimmy Carter: A Life of Friendship	N	B	532	Pull Ahead-Biographies	Lerner Publishing Group
Jimmy Carter: Thirty-ninth President	R	B	250+	Getting to Know the U.S. Presidents	Children's Press
Jimmy Lee Did It	J	RF	250+	Cummings, Pat	Lothrop
Jimmy McRay Was Different	J	RF	175	Dominie Readers	Pearson Learning Group
Jimmy Parker's New Job	J	RF	250+	Voyages	SRA/McGraw Hill
Jimmy the Gymnast	K	RF	250+	Foundations	Wright Group/McGraw Hill
Jimmy Zangwow's Out-of-This-World Moon Pie Adventure	N	F	250+	DiTerlizzi, Tony	Aladdin Paperbacks
Jimmy's Birthday Balloon	F	RF	95	Foundations	Wright Group/McGraw Hill
Jimmy's Goal	E	RF	159	Foundations	Wright Group/McGraw Hill
Jimmy's Jeans	D	RF	69	Joy Starters	Pearson Learning Group
Jim's Dog Muffins	K	RF	250+	Cohen, Miriam	Bantam Books

JK

* Collection of short stories   # Graphic text
^ Mature content with lower level text demands

TITLE	LEVEL	GENRE	WORD COUNT	AUTHOR / SERIES	PUBLISHER / DISTRIBUTOR
Jim's Trumpet	H	RF	304	Sunshine	Wright Group/McGraw Hill
Jim's Visit to Kim	G	RF	149	Ready Readers	Pearson Learning Group
Jingle Bells: How the Holiday Classic Came to Be	Q	HF	250+	Harris, John	Peachtree
Jingo Django	V	RF	250+	Fleischman, Sid	Bantam Books
Jinx	Z+	F	250+	Cabot, Meg	HarperCollins
Jinx	Z	RF	250+	Wild, Margaret	Walker & Company
Jip the Pirate	F	F	142	New Way Blue	Steck-Vaughn
Jip: His Story	V	HF	250+	Paterson, Katherine	Penguin Group
*JJ Rabbit and the Monster	K	F	250+	Storyteller-Shooting Stars	Wright Group/McGraw Hill
Jo and the Spider	D	RF	78	Sun Sprouts	ETA/Cuisenaire
Jo Jo Winnie Again	O	RF	250+	Sachs, Marilyn	Dutton Children's Books
Jo Jo's Flying Side Kick	M	RF	250+	Soar To Success	Houghton Mifflin Harcourt
Jo MacDonald Saw a Pond	J	TL	412	Quattlebaum, Mary	Dawn Publications
Jo the Model Maker	K	I	250+	Lighthouse	Rigby
Joan of Arc	W	B	250+	Demi	Marshall Cavendish
Joan of Arc	Y	B	250+	DK Readers	DK Publishing
Joan of Arc: Heavenly Warrior	Y	B	250+	Sterling Biographies	Sterling Publishing
Joanie's House Becomes a Home	M	RF	860	Reading Street	Pearson
Joan's Garden	B	F	34	Sun Sprouts	ETA/Cuisenaire
Joan's Hat	F	F	174	Sun Sprouts	ETA/Cuisenaire
Job at the Zoo, A	K	RF	525	Rigby Gigglers	Rigby
Job for a Day, A	K	RF	250+	On Our Way to English	Rigby
Job for Giant Jim, A	I	RF	298	Sunshine	Wright Group/McGraw Hill
Job for Jenny Archer, A	M	RF	250+	Conford, Ellen	Random House
Job for Jojo, A	J	F	326	Leveled Readers	Houghton Mifflin Harcourt
Job for Jojo, A	J	F	326	Leveled Readers/CA	Houghton Mifflin Harcourt
Job for Jojo, A	J	F	326	Leveled Readers/TX	Houghton Mifflin Harcourt
Job for Little Elf, A	F	F	197	Little Elf	Literacy Footprints
Job For Pup, A	F	F	89	Pair-It Turn and Learn	Steck-Vaughn
Job for You, A	D	I	56	Independent Readers Social Studies	Houghton Mifflin Harcourt
Job Sense	P	I	1472	Vocabulary Readers	Houghton Mifflin Harcourt
Job Sense	P	I	1472	Vocabulary Readers/CA	Houghton Mifflin Harcourt
Job Sense	P	I	1472	Vocabulary Readers/TX	Houghton Mifflin Harcourt
Job to Do, A	T	I	250+	Connectors	Pacific Learning
Job Well Done, A	Q	I	250+	Orbit Collections	Pacific Learning
Jobs	C	I	30	Basic Human Needs	Lerner Publishing Group
Jobs	E	F	112	Benger, Wendy	Kaeden Books
Jobs	B	I	29	Bookshop	Mondo Publishing
Jobs	I	I	112	Canizares, Susan; Chessen, Betsey	Scholastic
Jobs	D	I	71	Leveled Readers	Houghton Mifflin Harcourt
Jobs	F	I	55	Windows on Literacy	National Geographic
Jobs Around Town	A	I	31	Leveled Readers Social Studies	Houghton Mifflin Harcourt
Jobs at Home	C	I	35	Leveled Readers Language Support	Houghton Mifflin Harcourt
Jobs at School	D	I	101	Early Explorers	Benchmark Education
Jobs for Dogs	H	I	188	Rigby Focus	Rigby
Jobs for Everyone	E	I	51	Pair-It Turn and Learn	Steck-Vaughn
Jobs for Some People	E	I	146	Sails	Rigby
Jobs in a Community	E	I	120	Early Explorers	Benchmark Education
Jobs in Our Community	C	I	40	Reach	National Geographic
Jobs on a Farm	F	I	111	World of Farming	Heinemann Library

JK

TITLE	LEVEL	GENRE	WORD COUNT	AUTHOR / SERIES	PUBLISHER / DISTRIBUTOR
Jobs on the Farm	D	I	107	Leveled Readers	Houghton Mifflin Harcourt
Jobs on the Farm	D	I	107	Leveled Readers/CA	Houghton Mifflin Harcourt
Jobs People Do	LB	I	17	Reach	National Geographic
Jobs People Do	F	I	115	Red Rocket Readers	Flying Start Books
Jobs to Do	J	I	368	Vocabulary Readers	Houghton Mifflin Harcourt
Jobs to Do	J	I	368	Vocabulary Readers/CA	Houghton Mifflin Harcourt
Jobs Up High	C	I	62	Early Connections	Benchmark Education
Jobs: Making and Helping	E	I	63	Windows on Literacy	National Geographic
Jock Jerome	E	F	99	Voyages	SRA/McGraw Hill
Jody's Beans	K	RF	250+	Doyle, Malachy	Candlewick Press
Joe and Betsy the Dinosaur	K	F	250+	Hoban, Lillian	HarperTrophy
Joe and Sparky Get New Wheels	L	F	250+	Candlewick Sparks	Candlewick Press
Joe and Sparky, Superstars!	L	F	250+	Candlewick Sparks	Candlewick Press
Joe and the BMX Bike	E	RF	91	Oxford Reading Tree	Oxford University Press
Joe and the Mouse	F	RF	138	Oxford Reading Tree	Oxford University Press
Joe Cocker Spaniel	N	RF	250+	Supa Doopers	Sundance
Joe Joe	LB	RF	22	Montezinos, Nina	McElderry
Joe Lion's Big Boots	L	F	250+	I Am Reading	Kingfisher
Joe Makes a House	G	RF	174	PM Plus Story Books	Rigby
Joe Mauer	P	B	250+	Amazing Athletes	Lerner Publishing Group
Joe Mauer (Revised Edition)	P	B	1825	Amazing Athletes	Lerner Publishing Group
Joe on the Go	I	F	250+	Anderson, Peggy Perry	Houghton Mifflin Harcourt
Joe's Blue Shoes	G	RF	130	Books for Young Learners	Richard C. Owen
Joe's Father	E	RF	138	Book Bank	Wright Group/McGraw Hill
Joe's Letter	G	RF	219	Springboard	Wright Group/McGraw Hill
Joe's Pizza Parlor	I	RF	113	City Stories	Rigby
Joey	G	RF	243	PM Extensions-Green	Rigby
Joey Goat	J	F	356	Let's Read Together	Kane Press
Joey Pigza Loses Control	T	RF	250+	Gantos, Jack	Farrar, Straus, & Giroux
Joey Pigza Swallowed the Key	T	RF	250+	Gantos, Jack	HarperTrophy
Joey's Head	L	F	250+	Cretan, G.	Simon & Schuster
Joey's Rowboat	H	RF	83	Little Books	Sadlier-Oxford
Jog, Frog, Jog	F	F	72	Start to Read	School Zone
Joha Makes a Wish: A Middle Eastern Tale	L	TL	250+	Kimmel, Eric A.	Marshall Cavendish
Johan Reinhard: Discovering Ancient Civilizations	T	I	250+	Reading Expeditions	National Geographic
#Johann Gutenberg and the Printing Press	T	B	250+	Inventions and Discovery	Capstone Press
Johann Sebastian Bach: Great Man of Music	O	B	250+	Greene, Carol	Children's Press
John & Abigail Adams: An American Love Story	W	B	250+	St. George, Judith	Scholastic
John A. Macdonald	X	B	250+	The Canadians	Fitzhenry & Whiteside
John Adams	S	B	3770	History Maker Bios	Lerner Publishing Group
John Adams	Q	B	250+	Photo-Illustrated Biographies	Red Brick Learning
John Adams	U	B	250+	Profiles of the Presidents	Compass Point Books
John Adams and the Boston Massacre	Y	B	2307	Leveled Readers	Houghton Mifflin Harcourt
John Adams: Second President	R	B	250+	Getting to Know the U.S. Presidents	Children's Press
John Brown	P	B	1609	On My Own Biography	Lerner Publishing Group
John Brown: His Fight for Freedom	U	B	250+	Hendrix, John	Harry N. Abrams
#John Brown's Raid on Harper's Ferry	U	B	250+	Graphic Library	Capstone Press
^John Cena	T	B	250+	Stars of Pro Wrestling	Capstone Press
John Chapman: The Man Who Was Johnny	N	B	250+	Rookie Biographies	Children's Press
John Charles and Jessie Fremont: Pathfinders of the West	V	B	2453	Leveled Readers Social Studies	Houghton Mifflin Harcourt

* Collection of short stories   # Graphic text
^ Mature content with lower level text demands

JK

TITLE	LEVEL	GENRE	WORD COUNT	AUTHOR / SERIES	PUBLISHER / DISTRIBUTOR
John D. Rockefeller and the Oil Industry	R	I	250+	On Deck	Rigby
John Deere	R	B	3640	History Maker Bios	Lerner Publishing Group
John F. Kennedy	S	B	250+	Amazing Americans	Wright Group/McGraw Hill
John F. Kennedy	P	B	250+	Early Biographies	Compass Point Books
John F. Kennedy	N	B	250+	First Biographies	Red Brick Learning
John F. Kennedy	S	B	3373	History Maker Bios	Lerner Publishing Group
John F. Kennedy	X	B	250+	Just the Facts Biographies	Lerner Publishing Group
John F. Kennedy	N	B	250+	Pebble Books	Capstone Press
John F. Kennedy	Q	B	250+	Photo-Illustrated Biographies	Red Brick Learning
John F. Kennedy	U	B	250+	Profiles of the Presidents	Compass Point Books
John F. Kennedy	V	B	250+	World Leaders: Past and Present	Chelsea House
John F. Kennedy and the Stormy Sea	J	B	250+	Childhood of Famous Americans	Aladdin
#John F. Kennedy: American Visionary	R	B	250+	Graphic Library	Capstone Press
John F. Kennedy: America's Youngest President	O	B	250+	Childhood of Famous Americans	Aladdin
John F. Kennedy: Thirty-fifth President	R	B	250+	Getting to Know the U.S. Presidents	Children's Press
John Glenn	X	B	250+	A&E Biography	Lerner Publishing Group
^John Glenn	N	B	250+	Explore Space!	Capstone Press
John Glenn	W	B	250+	Just the Facts Biographies	Lerner Publishing Group
John Greenwood's Journey to Bunker Hill	S	HF	4574	History Speaks	Millbrook Press
John H. Johnson, Business Leader	K	B	130	Independent Readers Social Studies	Houghton Mifflin Harcourt
John Hancock	S	B	3514	History Maker Bios	Lerner Publishing Group
John Henry	N	TL	1865	On My Own Folklore	Lerner Publishing Group
John Henry	N	TL	250+	Tall Tales	Compass Point Books
John Henry and the Steam Drill	Q	TL	1203	Leveled Readers	Houghton Mifflin Harcourt
John Henry: An American Legend	O	TL	1196	Avenues	Hampton Brown
John Jacob Astor and the Fur Trade	R	B	250+	On Deck	Rigby
John James Audubon	M	B	250+	Biography	Benchmark Education
John James Audubon, American Painter	M	B	538	Leveled Readers Social Studies	Houghton Mifflin Harcourt
John James Audubon: Wildlife Artist	V	B	250+	A First Book	Franklin Watts
John Jay	Q	B	250+	Primary Source Readers	Teacher Created Materials
^John Lennon	Z	B	250+	Rock Music Library	Capstone Press
John Lewis	W	B	3390	Vocabulary Readers	Houghton Mifflin Harcourt
John Lewis	W	B	3390	Vocabulary Readers/CA	Houghton Mifflin Harcourt
John Muir: A Man of the Wilderness	T	B	2317	Reading Street	Pearson
John Muir: America's First Environmentalist	S	B	250+	Lasky, Kathryn	Candlewick Press
John Muir: Man of the Wild Places	N	B	250+	Rookie Biographies	Children's Press
John Paul Jones	X	B	2828	Vocabulary Readers	Houghton Mifflin Harcourt
John Paul Jones	X	B	2828	Vocabulary Readers/CA	Houghton Mifflin Harcourt
John Paul Jones	X	B	2828	Vocabulary Readers/TX	Houghton Mifflin Harcourt
John Paul Jones and the Battle at Sea	W	B	2095	Independent Readers Social Studies	Houghton Mifflin Harcourt
John Peter Zenger and Freedom of the Press	V	B	2213	Leveled Readers Social Studies	Houghton Mifflin Harcourt
John Philip Duck	O	HF	250+	Polacco, Patricia	Scholastic
John Philip Sousa: The March King	N	B	250+	Rookie Biographies	Children's Press
John Quincy Adams	U	B	250+	Profiles of the Presidents	Compass Point Books
John Quincy Adams in Paris	W	I	3091	Vocabulary Readers	Houghton Mifflin Harcourt
John Quincy Adams in Paris	W	I	3091	Vocabulary Readers/CA	Houghton Mifflin Harcourt
John Quincy Adams in Paris	W	I	3091	Vocabulary Readers/TX	Houghton Mifflin Harcourt
John Quincy Adams: Sixth President	R	B	250+	Getting to Know the U.S. Presidents	Children's Press
#John Sutter and the California Gold Rush	S	I	250+	Graphic Library	Capstone Press
John Tyler	U	B	250+	Profiles of the Presidents	Compass Point Books

JK

TITLE	LEVEL	GENRE	WORD COUNT	AUTHOR / SERIES	PUBLISHER / DISTRIBUTOR
John Tyler: Tenth President	R	B	250+	Getting to Know the U.S. Presidents	Children's Press
John Wesley Powell	O	B	888	Leveled Readers	Houghton Mifflin Harcourt
John Wesley Powell	O	B	888	Leveled Readers/CA	Houghton Mifflin Harcourt
John Wesley Powell	O	B	888	Leveled Readers/TX	Houghton Mifflin Harcourt
John Williams: Musical Storyteller	S	B	250+	Explore More	Wright Group/McGraw Hill
John Winthrop: Governor of the Massachusetts Bay Colony	U	B	250+	Let Freedom Ring	Red Brick Learning
Johnny Appleseed	J	B	250+	All Aboard Reading	Grosset & Dunlap
Johnny Appleseed	M	B	250+	First Biographies	Red Brick Learning
Johnny Appleseed	Q	TL	250+	Kellogg, Steven	Scholastic
Johnny Appleseed	O	B	622	Leveled Readers	Houghton Mifflin Harcourt
Johnny Appleseed	Q	B	250+	Lindbergh, Reeve	Little Brown and Company
Johnny Appleseed	M	TL	250+	Moore, Eva	Scholastic
Johnny Appleseed	N	B	1453	On My Own Biography	Lerner Publishing Group
Johnny Appleseed	N	TL	250+	Tall Tales	Compass Point Books
Johnny Kelley's Tale	X	HF	2162	Leveled Readers	Houghton Mifflin Harcourt
Johnny Lion's Book	J	F	250+	Hurd, Edith Thacher	HarperCollins
Johnny Lion's Rubber Boots	F	F	80	Hurd, Edith Thacher	HarperCollins
Johnny Long Legs	R	RF	250+	Christopher, Matt	Little Brown and Company
Johnny Mohawk: The Horses of Half Moon Ranch	S	RF	20000	Oldfield, Jenny	Sourcebooks
Johnny Moore and the Wright Brothers' Flying Machine	R	HF	3756	History Speaks	Millbrook Press
Johnny Tremain	Z	HF	250+	Forbes, Esther	Bantam Books
Johnston Flood, The	V	HF	250+	Reading Expeditions	National Geographic
Join Us	D	RF	54	InfoTrek	ETA/Cuisenaire
Jojo and the Robot	J	F	250+	Sunshine	Wright Group/McGraw Hill
Joke Book, The	H	I	143	Vocabulary Readers	Houghton Mifflin Harcourt
Joke, The	H	F	186	Little Readers	Houghton Mifflin Harcourt
Jokers	H	F	190	Breakthrough	Longman/Bow
Jokes About Sports	K	I	236	Joke Books	Capstone Press
Jokes and Riddles	O	I	250+	Literacy 2000	Rigby
Jolly Jumping Jelly Beans	E	F	121	Sunshine	Wright Group/McGraw Hill
Jolly Postman or Other People's Letters, The	N	F	250+	Ahlberg, Janet & Allan	Little Brown and Company
Jolly Roger and the Spyglass	G	F	200	PM Stars	Rigby
Jolly Roger and the Treasure	E	F	129	PM Plus Story Books	Rigby
Jolly Roger, the Pirate	D	F	138	PM Extensions-Yellow	Rigby
Jon Scieszka Gets Kids Reading	Q	B	1155	Leveled Readers	Houghton Mifflin Harcourt
Jon Sleeps On	G	RF	147	Little Red Readers	Sundance
#Jonas Salk and the Polio Vaccine	T	B	250↓	Inventions and Discovery	Capstone Press
Jonathan and His Mommy	L	RF	250+	Smalls, Irene	Scholastic
Jonathan Buys a Present	J	RF	353	PM Story Books-Turquoise	Rigby
Jono's Rescue	O	RF	250+	PM Plus	Rigby
Jordan and the Northside Reps	K	RF	250+	PM Story Books-Silver	Rigby
Jordan at the Big Game	I	RF	250+	PM Plus Story Books	Rigby
Jordan Is Hiding	A	RF	24	Little Books for Early Readers	University of Maine
Jordan's Catch	J	RF	250+	PM Story Books	Rigby
Jordan's Lucky Day	K	RF	466	PM Story Books-Turquoise	Rigby
Jordan's Soccer Ball	G	RF	210	PM Plus Story Books	Rigby
Jordan's Zoo	G	RF	90	City Stories	Rigby
Jo's Triumph	R	HF	250+	Orca Young Readers	Orca Books
Jo's Troubled Heart	Q	HF	250+	The Little Women Journals	Avon Books
Josefina Learns a Lesson	Q	HF	250+	The American Girls Collection	Pleasant Company

* Collection of short stories   # Graphic text
^ Mature content with lower level text demands

JK

TITLE	LEVEL	GENRE	WORD COUNT	AUTHOR / SERIES	PUBLISHER / DISTRIBUTOR
Josefina Saves the Day	Q	HF	250+	The American Girls Collection	Pleasant Company
Josefina Story Quilt	L	F	250+	Coerr, Eleanor	HarperTrophy
Josefina's Surprise	Q	HF	250+	The American Girls Collection	Pleasant Company
Joseph Brant: Iroquois Leader in the Revolution	Y	B	1743	Leveled Readers	Houghton Mifflin Harcourt
Joseph Warren An American Hero	U	B	2577	Leveled Readers/CA	Houghton Mifflin Harcourt
Joseph Warren An American Hero	U	B	2577	Leveled Readers/TX	Houghton Mifflin Harcourt
Joseph Warren, An American Hero	U	B	2577	Leveled Readers	Houghton Mifflin Harcourt
Joseph, the Greedy Octopus	H	F	290	Springboard	Wright Group/McGraw Hill
Joseph: 1861 - A Rumble of War	V	HF	250+	Pryor, Bonnie	Avon Books
Josephine's Imagination	L	RF	250+	Dobrin, Arnold	Scholastic
Josh	I	RF	582	Rigby Flying Colors	Rigby
Josh and Scruffy	C	RF	48	PM Photo Stories	Rigby
Josh and the Bad Hair Day	K	RF	837	Rigby Flying Colors	Rigby
Josh and the Big Boys	C	RF	82	PM Photo Stories	Rigby
Josh and the Kite	C	RF	58	PM Photo Stories	Rigby
Josh Hamilton	T	B	2065	Amazing Athletes	Lerner Publishing Group
Josh Rides a Skateboard	D	RF	107	PM Photo Stories	Rigby
Joshua James Likes Trucks	C	RF	50	Rookie Readers	Children's Press
Joshua Poole and Sunrise	L	RF	250+	Rigby Literacy	Rigby
Joshua T. Bates	Q	RF	250+	Shreve, Susan	Alfred A. Knopf
Joshua T. Bates in Trouble Again	Q	RF	250+	Shreve, Susan	Alfred A. Knopf
Joshua T. Bates Takes Charge	Q	RF	250+	Shreve, Susan	Alfred A. Knopf
Josie and the Baby	C	RF	62	Rigby Star	Rigby
Josie and the Bully	E	RF	149	Rigby Rocket	Rigby
Josie and the Cake Sale	D	RF	91	Rigby Rocket	Rigby
Josie and the Juke Box	B	RF	28	Rigby Star	Rigby
Josie and the Parade	B	RF	49	Rigby Star	Rigby
Josie and the Play	F	RF	185	Rigby Star	Rigby
Josie and the Puppy	G	RF	206	Rigby Star	Rigby
Josie Cleans Up	I	RF	213	Little Readers	Houghton Mifflin Harcourt
Josie Goes on Holiday	F	RF	240	Rigby Star	Rigby
Josie Helps Out	E	RF	71	Rigby Star	Rigby
Josie's New Coat	F	RF	189	Rigby Star	Rigby
Journal of Douglas Allen Deeds, The: The Donner Party Expedition, 1846	W	HF	250+	My Name is America	Scholastic
Journal of James Edmond Pease, The	V	HF	250+	Dear America	Scholastic
Journal of Patrick Seamus Flaherty, The	Z	HF	250+	White, Ellen Emerson	Scholastic
Journal of Sean Sullivan, The	W	HF	250+	Dear America	Scholastic
Journal, The: Dear Future II	Q	SF	250+	Literacy 2000	Rigby
Journals of the West	R	I	1300	Vocabulary Readers/TX	Houghton Mifflin Harcourt
Journery into an Estuary, A	T	I	2444	Biomes of North America	Lerner Publishing Group
Journey	S	RF	250+	MacLachlan, Patricia	Yearling Books
Journey Home	Q	RF	250+	McKay, Jr., Lawrence	Lee & Low Books Inc.
Journey Home	V	RF	250+	Uchida, Yoshika	Aladdin
Journey Home, The	S	RF	250+	Holland, Isabelle	Scholastic
Journey into a Lake, A	T	I	2317	Biomes of North America	Lerner Publishing Group
Journey into a River, A	T	I	2598	Biomes of North America	Lerner Publishing Group
Journey into a Wetland, A	T	I	2256	Biomes of North America	Lerner Publishing Group
#Journey Into Adaptation with Max Axiom, Super Scientist; A	T	I	250+	Graphic Library	Capstone Press
Journey Into Terror	U	RF	250+	Wallace, Bill	Simon & Schuster
Journey into the Deep: Discovering New Ocean Creatures	X	I	250+	Johnson, Rebecca L.	Millbrook Press
Journey into the Earth	I	F	250+	Storyworlds	Heinemann

JK

TITLE	LEVEL	GENRE	WORD COUNT	AUTHOR / SERIES	PUBLISHER / DISTRIBUTOR
Journey of a Butterfly, The	P	I	250+	Scrace, Carolyn	Scholastic
Journey of the Kon-Tiki	O	I	1036	Leveled Readers	Houghton Mifflin Harcourt
Journey of the Kon-Tiki	O	I	1036	Leveled Readers/CA	Houghton Mifflin Harcourt
Journey of the Kon-Tiki	O	I	1036	Leveled Readers/TX	Houghton Mifflin Harcourt
Journey of the Red Wolf	U	I	250+	Smith, Roland	Dutton Children's Books
Journey on a Patriotic Path	R	I	250+	In Step Readers	Rigby
Journey Outside	V	F	250+	Steele, Mary Q.	Penguin Group
#Journey Through the Digestive System with Max Axiom Super Scientist, A	U	I	250+	Graphic Library	Capstone Press
Journey Through the Earth	T	SF	4548	Reading Street	Pearson
Journey to a Free Town	S	HF	1747	Leveled Readers	Houghton Mifflin Harcourt
Journey to a New Land	M	HF	250+	Rigby Literacy	Rigby
Journey to a New Land: An Oral History	R	B	250+	Bookshop	Mondo Publishing
Journey to America	U	HF	250+	Levitin, Sonia	Simon & Schuster
Journey to an 800 Number	V	RF	250+	Konigsburg, E. L.	Aladdin
Journey to Antarctica	V	I	250+	PM Collection	Rigby
Journey to Ellis Island: How My Father Came to America	T	B	250+	Bierman, Carol	Scholastic
Journey to Jo'burg	S	HF	250+	Naidoo, Beverly	HarperTrophy
Journey to Kansas	R	HF	250+	Leveled Readers Language Support	Houghton Mifflin Harcourt
Journey to Mars	T	I	644	Vocabulary Readers	Houghton Mifflin Harcourt
Journey to Nowhere	T	HF	250+	Auch, Mary Jane	Bantam Books
Journey to Statehood	T	I	2596	Reading Street	Pearson
#Journey to the Center of the Earth	V	F	250+	Miller, Davis W. & Brevard, Katherine M. (Retold)	Stone Arch Books
Journey to the Center of the Earth, A	X	SF	250+	Verne, Jules	HarperCollins
Journey to the New World	S	HF	250+	Action Packs	Rigby
Journey to the New World	V	HF	250+	My America	Scholastic
Journey to the Undersea Gardens	Q	I	250+	iOpeners	Pearson Learning Group
Journey to the Volcano Palace: The Secrets of Droon	O	F	250+	Abbott, Tony	Scholastic
Journey to Topaz	U	HF	250+	Uchida, Yoshiko	Creative Arts Book Co.
Journey West, The	N	I	250+	Rigby Literacy	Rigby
Journey, The; Guardians of Ga'Hoole	V	F	250+	Lasky, Kathryn	Scholastic
Journeying into Rain Forests	S	I	250+	Reading Expeditions	National Geographic
Journeys of Courage on the Underground Railroad	T	I	250+	Pair-It Books	Steck-Vaughn
Journeys of Sojourner Truth, The	R	B	1217	Leveled Readers Social Studies	Houghton Mifflin Harcourt
Joy Crowley Writes	K	B	250+	Sunshine	Wright Group/McGraw Hill
Joy Luck Club, The	Z+	HF	250+	Tan, Amy	Random House
Joy of Making Music, The	N	I	280	Vocabulary Readers	Houghton Mifflin Harcourt
Joy the Summer Vacation Fairy: Rainbow Magic	L	F	250+	Meadows, Daisy	Scholastic
Joyride	Z	RF	250+	Ehrlich, Amy	Candlewick Press
Joy's Close Call: Butterfly Meadow	M	F	250+	Moss, Olivia	Scholastic
Joy's Great Idea	M	RF	250+	Ellis, Veronica Freeman	Houghton Mifflin Harcourt
Joy's Planet Patrol Plan	M	RF	889	Leveled Readers	Houghton Mifflin Harcourt
Joy's Planet Patrol Plan	M	RF	889	Leveled Readers/CA	Houghton Mifflin Harcourt
Joy's Planet Patrol Plan	M	RF	889	Leveled Readers/TX	Houghton Mifflin Harcourt
Juan	H	RF	77	City Kids	Rigby
Juan Bobo	E	TL	55	Leveled Readers	Houghton Mifflin Harcourt
Juan Bobo Goes Up and Down the Hill	K	TL	250+	Montes, Marisa	Hampton Brown
Juan Ponce De Leon	Q	B	250+	Biographies-Great Explorers	Capstone Press
Juan Ponce de Leon	S	B	3232	History Maker Bios	Lerner Publishing Group
Juan's Journey	T	RF	1980	Reading Street	Pearson

Organized Alphabetically by Title
Storable Database at www.fountasandpinnellleveledbooks.com

* Collection of short stories   # Graphic text
^ Mature content with lower level text demands

JK

TITLE	LEVEL	GENRE	WORD COUNT	AUTHOR / SERIES	PUBLISHER / DISTRIBUTOR
Juan's Three Wishes	V	F	1842	Leveled Readers	Houghton Mifflin Harcourt
Judaism	Y	I	250+	World Religions	Compass Point Books
Judge Rabbit Helps the Fish	N	TL	250+	Story Vines	Wright Group/McGraw Hill
Judges and Courts: A Look at the Judicial Branch	S	I	2194	Searchlight Books	Lerner Publishing Group
Judo	P	I	1644	Take Two Books	Wright Group/McGraw Hill
Judy Baca: Artist	N	B	250+	Beginning Biographies	Pearson Learning Group
Judy Moody	M	RF	250+	McDonald, Megan	Candlewick Press
*Judy Moody & Stink: The Holly Joliday	M	RF	250+	McDonald, Megan	Candlewick Press
Judy Moody and Stink: The Mad, Mad, Mad, Mad Treasure Hunt	M	RF	250+	McDonald, Megan	Candlewick Press
Judy Moody Around the World in 8 1/2 Days	M	RF	250+	McDonald, Megan	Candlewick Press
Judy Moody Declares Independence	M	RF	250+	McDonald, Megan	Candlewick Press
Judy Moody Gets Famous!	M	RF	250+	McDonald, Megan	Candlewick Press
Judy Moody Goes to College	M	RF	250+	McDonald, Megan	Candlewick Press
Judy Moody Predicts the Future	M	RF	250+	McDonald, Megan	Candlewick Press
Judy Moody Saves the World	M	RF	250+	McDonald, Megan	Candlewick Press
Judy Moody was in a Mood. Not a Good Mood. A Bad Mood.	M	RF	250+	McDonald, Megan	Candlewick Press
Judy Moody, Girl Detective	M	RF	250+	McDonald, Megan	Candlewick Press
Judy Moody, M.D. The Doctor Is In!	M	RF	250+	McDonald, Megan	Candlewick Press
Juggling	P	I	250+	Games Around the World	Compass Point Books
Juggling	LB	RF	15	Rigby Literacy	Rigby
Juggling	LB	RF	15	Rigby Star	Rigby
Juice	B	RF	38	Bonnell, Kris	Reading Reading Books
^Juice	T	RF	250+	Orca Soundings	Orca Books
Juicy Peach	C	RF	18	Bebop Books	Lee & Low Books Inc.
Julia Alvarez, Storyteller	L	B	515	In Step Readers	Rigby
Julia Alvarez: One Author, Two Cultures	Q	B	1029	Leveled Readers	Houghton Mifflin Harcourt
Julia Gillian (and the Art of Knowing)	R	RF	250+	McGhee, Alison	Scholastic
Julian Rodriguez: Trash Crisis on Earth	R	SF	250+	Stadler, Alexander	Scholastic
Julian, Dream Doctor	O	RF	250+	Cameron, Ann	Random House
Julian, Secret Agent	O	RF	250+	Cameron, Ann	Random House
Julian's Glorious Summer	O	RF	250+	Cameron, Ann	Random House
Julia's Lists	D	RF	47	Little Celebrations	Pearson Learning Group
Julia's New Home	R	RF	1950	Reading Street	Pearson
Julie	U	RF	250+	George, Jean Craighead	HarperTrophy
Julie Gets Lost	T	RF	3624	Reading Street	Pearson
Julie Krone	Y	B	250+	The Achievers	Lerner Publishing Group
Julie of the Wolves	U	RF	250+	George, Jean Craighead	HarperCollins
Julie of the Wolves	U	RF	250+	inZone Books	Hampton Brown
Julie Rescues Big Mack	M	RF	250+	Voyages	SRA/McGraw Hill
Julie Taymor: Art on Stage and Screen	W	B	250+	Explore More	Wright Group/McGraw Hill
Julie the Rockhound	O	RF	591	Karowski, Gail Langer	Sylvan Dell Publishing
Julie's Mornings	K	F	250+	Ready Readers	Pearson Learning Group
Julie's Wolf Pack	U	RF	250+	George, Jean Craighead	HarperTrophy
Juliet Dove, Queen of Love	S	F	250+	Coville, Bruce	Harcourt, Inc.
Juliet the Valentine Fairy: Rainbow Magic	L	F	250+	Meadows, Daisy	Scholastic
Juliet's Moon	Y	HF	250+	Rinaldi, Ann	Houghton Mifflin Harcourt
Juliette Low	R	B	3484	History Maker Bios	Lerner Publishing Group
Juliette: The Modern Art Monkey	Q	F	250+	Bookweb	Rigby
#Julius Caesar	Z	F	250+	Manga Shakespeare	Amulet Books
Julius Caesar: Roman General and Statesman	Y	B	250+	Signature Lives	Compass Point Books
Julius Caesar: Roman Leader	W	B	250+	Primary Source Readers	Teacher Created Materials

JK

TITLE	LEVEL	GENRE	WORD COUNT	AUTHOR / SERIES	PUBLISHER / DISTRIBUTOR
Julius: The Baby of the World	N	F	250+	Henkes, Kevin	Scholastic
July 4th	C	RF	20	Instant Readers	Harcourt School Publishers
July Fourth!	F	I	137	In Step Readers	Rigby
Jumanji	R	F	250+	Van Allsburg, Chris	Houghton Mifflin Harcourt
Jumbaroo, The	H	F	173	Story Basket	Wright Group/McGraw Hill
Jumble Power	L	F	250+	Cambridge Reading	Pearson Learning Group
Jumble Sale, The	E	RF	81	Oxford Reading Tree	Oxford University Press
Jumbo	E	RF	133	PM Plus Story Books	Rigby
Jump	A	F	30	Leveled Literacy Intervention/ Green System	Heinemann
Jump and Swim	H	RF	293	Leveled Readers	Houghton Mifflin Harcourt
Jump and Thump!	C	RF	18	Home Connection Collection	Rigby
Jump Ball!: You Can Play Basketball	M	I	250+	Game Day	Picture Window Books
Jump for Joy	A	I	32	Red Rocket Readers	Flying Start Books
Jump in the Pool, A	H	RF	243	Leveled Readers Language Support	Houghton Mifflin Harcourt
Jump Jets: The AV-88 Harriers	U	I	250+	War Planes	Capstone Press
Jump Right In	D	RF	50	Ready Readers	Pearson Learning Group
Jump Rope	B	RF	18	Bebop Books	Lee & Low Books Inc.
Jump Rope, The	H	RF	241	PM Plus Story Books	Rigby
Jump Serve	P	RF	250+	Maddox, Jake	Stone Arch Books
Jump Ship to Freedom	U	HF	250+	Collier, James & Christopher	Bantam Books
Jump the Broom	L	RF	119	Books For Young Learners	Richard C. Owen
*Jump!: The Adventures of Brer Rabbit	T	TL	250+	Harris, Joel Chandler	Harcourt Brace
Jump, Frog	C	F	33	Stewart, Josie; Salem, Lynn	Continental Press
Jump, Jump, Jump	I	F	236	Sunshine	Wright Group/McGraw Hill
Jump, Jump, Kangaroo	B	F	31	Story Box	Wright Group/McGraw Hill
Jump, Trundle, Climb, Slither, Flap, Snap!	N	I	565	Springboard	Wright Group/McGraw Hill
Jumped	Z+	RF	250+	Williams-Garcia, Rita	HarperCollins
Jumper	E	RF	125	Literacy Tree	Rigby
^Jumper	T	RF	250+	Orca Sports	Orca Books
Jumper for James, A	C	RF	34	Rigby Rocket	Rigby
Jumpers	B	F	21	Sunshine	Wright Group/McGraw Hill
Jumping Fish, The	D	F	114	Rigby Flying Colors	Rigby
Jumping Game, The	C	F	29	Brand New Readers	Candlewick Press
Jumping Into Nothing	M	RF	250+	Willner-Pardo, Gina	Houghton Mifflin Harcourt
Jumping into the Flames	P	I	675	Vocabulary Readers	Houghton Mifflin Harcourt
Jumping Jack	J	F	250+	Rigby Literacy	Rigby
Jumping Jack	J	F	250+	Rigby Star	Rigby
Jumping Jenny	L	RF	250+	Bari, Ellen	Kar-Ben Publishing
Jumping Jesters, The	H	F	217	Rigby Rocket	Rigby
Jumping Kangaroos	K	I	377	Pull Ahead Books	Lerner Publishing Group
Jumping Shoes	C	RF	34	Joy Readers	Pearson Learning Group
Jumping Spider	O	I	250+	Life Cycles	Creative Teaching Press
Jumping Spiders	A	I	84	Readlings/ Predator Bugs	American Reading Company
Jumping Spiders	I	I	404	Sails	Rigby
Jumping Spiders	N	I	250+	Spiders	Capstone Press
Jumping the Nail	Y	RF	250+	Bunting, Eve	Harcourt, Inc.
Jumping Tree, The	Y	RF	250+	Saldana, Jr., Rene	Scholastic
Jumprope	D	RF	31	Visions	Wright Group/McGraw Hill
Jun and Pepper Grow Up	J	RF	362	Reading Street	Pearson
June and August	K	F	250+	Walsh, Vivian	Harry N. Abrams
June Bacon-Bercey: A Meteorologist Talks About the Weather	K	I	192	Leveled Readers Science	Houghton Mifflin Harcourt

JK

* Collection of short stories   # Graphic text
^ Mature content with lower level text demands

TITLE	LEVEL	GENRE	WORD COUNT	AUTHOR / SERIES	PUBLISHER / DISTRIBUTOR
June Vacation	C	I	86	Leveled Readers	Houghton Mifflin Harcourt
June Vacation	C	I	86	Leveled Readers/CA	Houghton Mifflin Harcourt
Junebug	S	RF	250+	Mead, Alice	Bantam Books
Junebug and the Reverend	S	RF	250+	Mead, Alice	Dell
Junebug in Trouble	T	RF	250+	Mead, Alice	Dell
Juneteenth	J	I	106	American Holidays	Lerner Publishing Group
Juneteenth	Q	I	250+	Holiday Histories	Heinemann
Juneteenth	O	I	1632	On My Own Holidays	Lerner Publishing Group
Juneteenth: Celebrating the End of Slavery	Q	I	250+	Rosen Real Readers	Rosen Publishing Group
Juneteenth: Jubilee for Freedom	M	I	250+	Holidays and Culture	Capstone Press
Jungle	V	I	250+	Eyewitness Books	DK Publishing
Jungle Animals	L	I	250+	I Wonder Why	Kingfisher
Jungle Book, The	U	F	250+	Kipling, Rudyard	Scholastic
Jungle Book, The	S	F	6570	Oxford Bookworms Library	Oxford University Press
Jungle Crossing	W	RF	250+	Salter, Sydney	Houghton Mifflin Harcourt
Jungle Drums	N	F	250+	Base, Graeme	Harry N. Abrams
Jungle Friends	I	RF	250+	Reading Safari	Mondo Publishing
Jungle Frogs	G	F	195	PM Plus Story Books	Rigby
Jungle Grapevine, The	L	F	250+	Beard, Alex	Harry N. Abrams
Jungle Jack Hanna's What Zoo-Keepers Do	M	I	250+	Hanna, Jack	Scholastic
Jungle Jenny	M	F	250+	Literacy by Design	Rigby
Jungle Law	S	RF	250+	Sails	Rigby
Jungle Life	K	I	268	Spyglass Books	Compass Point Books
Jungle of Colors, A	A	I	40	Color My World	American Reading Company
Jungle Parade: A Singing Game	D	F	105	Little Celebrations	Pearson Learning Group
Jungle Picture Pops	M	I	250+	Priddy, Roger	Priddy Books
^Jungle Scout: A Vietnam War Story	W	HF	250+	Hoppey, Tim	Stone Arch Books
Jungle Spots	B	F	28	Little Celebrations	Pearson Learning Group
Jungle Sun, The	M	F	250+	Sails	Rigby
Jungle Tiger Cat	G	F	120	Frankford, Marilyn	Kaeden Books
Jungle Trek	S	RF	250+	PM Extensions	Rigby
Jungle Walk	WB	RF	0	Tafuri, Nancy	Greenwillow Books
Jungle, The	LB	F	12	Sails	Rigby
Junie B. Jones and a Little Monkey Business	M	RF	250+	Park, Barbara	Random House
Junie B. Jones and Her Big Fat Mouth	M	RF	250+	Park, Barbara	Random House
Junie B. Jones and Some Sneaky Peeky Spying	M	RF	250+	Park, Barbara	Random House
Junie B. Jones and that Meanie Jim's Birthday	M	RF	250+	Park, Barbara	Random House
Junie B. Jones and the Mushy Gushy Valentine	M	RF	250+	Park, Barbara	Random House
Junie B. Jones and the Stupid Smelly Bus	M	RF	250+	Park, Barbara	Random House
Junie B. Jones and the Yucky Blucky Fruitcake	M	RF	250+	Park, Barbara	Random House
Junie B. Jones Has a Monster Under Her Bed	M	RF	250+	Park, Barbara	Random House
Junie B. Jones Has a Peep in Her Pocket	M	RF	250+	Park, Barbara	Random House
Junie B. Jones Is (almost) a Flower Girl	M	RF	250+	Park, Barbara	Random House
Junie B. Jones Is a Beauty Shop Guy	M	RF	250+	Park, Barbara	Random House
Junie B. Jones Is a Party Animal	M	RF	250+	Park, Barbara	Random House
Junie B. Jones Is Not a Crook	M	RF	250+	Park, Barbara	Random House
Junie B. Jones Loves Handsome Warren	M	RF	250+	Park, Barbara	Random House
Junie B. Jones Smells Something Fishy	M	RF	250+	Park, Barbara	Random House
Junie B., First Grader (at last!)	M	RF	250+	Park, Barbara	Random House
Junior Concert, The	J	RF	266	PM Math Readers	Rigby
Junior Gymnasts: Katie's Big Move	M	RF	250+	Slater, Teddy	Scholastic
Junior Superstars	K	RF	765	PM Stars Bridge Books	Rigby
Juniper Berry	W	F	250+	Kozlowsky, M.P.	HarperCollins
Junk Art	K	I	250+	InfoTrek Plus	ETA/Cuisenaire

JK

TITLE	LEVEL	GENRE	WORD COUNT	AUTHOR / SERIES	PUBLISHER / DISTRIBUTOR
Junk Box, The	B	RF	84	Red Rocket Readers	Flying Start Books
Junk Box, The	C	RF	54	Windmill Books	Rigby
Junk Food	T	I	5222	Where's the Science Here?	Lerner Publishing Group
Junk into Art	K	RF	587	Leveled Readers	Houghton Mifflin Harcourt
Junk Sculpture	O	I	250+	PM Extensions	Rigby
Junk-Food Files, The	S	F	250+	Power Up!	Steck-Vaughn
Junkpile Robot, The	L	F	250+	Ready Readers	Pearson Learning Group
Junkyard Dog, The	N	RF	250+	PM Collection	Rigby
Juno Loves Barney	I	RF	249	Voyages	SRA/McGraw Hill
Junonia	S	RF	250+	Henkes, Kevin	Greenwillow Books
Jupiter	Q	I	250+	A True Book	Children's Press
Jupiter	Q	I	1714	Early Bird Astronomy	Lerner Publishing Group
Jupiter	J	I	131	Exploring the Galaxy	Capstone Press
Jupiter	S	I	250+	Our Solar System	Compass Point Books
Jupiter	N	I	785	Our Universe	Lerner Publishing Group
Jupiter	Q	I	250+	The Galaxy	Capstone Press
Jupiter	M	I	250+	The Solar System	Capstone Press
Jupiter	R	I	250+	Theme Sets	National Geographic
Jupiter Spiders and Other Scary Creatures	K	SF	250+	Popcorn	Sundance
Jupiter: The Moon King	Q	I	250+	Explorer Books-Pathfinder	National Geographic
Jupiter: The Moon King	P	I	250+	Explorer Books-Pioneer	National Geographic
Jurassic Grampa	Q	F	250+	Wiley & Grampa's Creature Features	Little Brown and Company
Jurassic Park	Z+	SF	250+	Crichton, Michael	Ballantine Books
Just a Box	J	RF	424	Appleton-Smith, Laura	Flyleaf Publishing
Just a Few Words, Mr. Lincoln	N	I	250+	Fritz, Jean	G.P. Putnam's Sons Books for Young Readers
Just a Mess	I	F	206	Mayer, Mercer	Donovan
Just a Seed	E	I	74	Blaxland, Wendy	Scholastic
Just Add Water	C	I	41	Discovery World	Rigby
Just As Long As We're Together	T	RF	250+	Blume, Judy	Bantam Books
Just Call Me Joe	Q	HF	250+	Orca Young Readers	Orca Books
Just Call Me Stupid	R	RF	250+	Birdseye, Tom	Puffin Books
Just Clowning Around: Two Stories	E	F	62	Green Light Readers	Harcourt
Just Desserts	O	RF	250+	Durand, Hallie	Atheneum Books
Just Ella	Y	F	250+	Haddix, Margaret Peterson	Simon & Schuster
Just Enough	G	RF	107	Salem, Lynn; Stewart, Josie	Continental Press
Just for Fun	J	F	250+	Literacy 2000	Rigby
Just for Fun	Q	I	250+	Orbit Collections	Pacific Learning
Just for the Fun of It	W	RF	2792	Leveled Readers	Houghton Mifflin Harcourt
Just for the Fun of It	W	RF	2792	Leveled Readers/CA	Houghton Mifflin Harcourt
Just for the Fun of It	W	RF	2792	Leveled Readers/TX	Houghton Mifflin Harcourt
Just for You	G	F	160	Mayer, Mercer	Donovan
Just Grace	O	RF	250+	Harper, Charise Mericle	Houghton Mifflin Harcourt
Just Grace and the Double Surprise	O	RF	250+	Harper, Charise Mericle	Houghton Mifflin Harcourt
Just Grace and the Flower Girl Power	O	RF	250+	Harper, Charise Mericle	Houghton Mifflin Harcourt
Just Grace and the Snack Attack	O	RF	250+	Harper, Charise Mericle	Houghton Mifflin Harcourt
Just Grace and the Terrible Tutu	O	RF	250+	Harper, Charise Mericle	Houghton Mifflin Harcourt
Just Grace Goes Green	O	RF	250+	Harper, Charise Mericle	Sandpiper Books
Just Grace Walks the Dog	O	RF	250+	Harper, Charise Mericle	Houghton Mifflin Harcourt
Just Grace, Star on Stage	O	RF	250+	Harper, Charise Mericle	Houghton Mifflin Harcourt
Just Grandma and Me	I	F	186	Mayer, Mercer	Donovan
Just Graph It!	G	I	156	Learn to Read	Creative Teaching Press

JK

* Collection of short stories   # Graphic text
^ Mature content with lower level text demands

TITLE	LEVEL	GENRE	WORD COUNT	AUTHOR / SERIES	PUBLISHER / DISTRIBUTOR
Just Hanging Around	J	I	223	Storyteller-Night Crickets	Wright Group/McGraw Hill
Just in Passing	WB	RF	0	Bonners, Susan	Lothrop, Lee & Shepard
Just Juice	Q	RF	250+	Hesse, Karen	Scholastic
Just Like Dad	D	RF	44	Hiris, Monica	Kaeden Books
Just Like Daddy	F	F	93	Asch, Frank	Simon & Schuster
Just Like Everyone Else	I	RF	225	Kuskin, Karla	HarperCollins
Just Like Grandpa	E	RF	81	Literacy 2000	Rigby
Just Like Grandpa	C	RF	49	Little Celebrations	Pearson Learning Group
Just Like Heaven	J	F	275	McDonnell, Patrick	Little Brown and Company
Just Like Mama	L	RF	250+	Newman, Leslea	Harry N. Abrams
Just Like Me	F	RF	86	First Start	Troll Associates
Just Like Me	G	RF	108	Learn to Read	Creative Teaching Press
Just Like Me	F	RF	115	Reading Street	Pearson
Just Like Me	E	RF	138	Rookie Readers	Children's Press
*Just Like Me	J	F	2154	Story Box	Wright Group/McGraw Hill
Just Like Me!	D	RF	62	Sunshine	Wright Group/McGraw Hill
Just Like Mom	D	RF	56	Hiris, Monica	Kaeden Books
Just Like Mom and Dad	O	I	1099	Leveled Readers Science	Houghton Mifflin Harcourt
Just Like My Grandpa	D	RF	48	Rise & Shine	Hampton Brown
Just Like Us	E	RF	55	Ready Readers	Pearson Learning Group
Just Like You	D	F	160	Dominie Readers	Pearson Learning Group
Just Like You!	C	F	28	Instant Readers	Harcourt School Publishers
Just Look at You	B	RF	16	Sunshine	Wright Group/McGraw Hill
*Just Mabel	K	RF	250+	I Am Reading	Kingfisher
Just Me	C	RF	51	Literacy 2000	Rigby
Just Me and My Babysitter	H	F	182	Mayer, Mercer	Donovan
Just Me and My Dad	H	F	161	Mayer, Mercer	Donovan
Just Me and My Puppy	H	F	190	Mayer, Mercer	Donovan
Just My Luck	G	RF	136	Literacy 2000	Rigby
Just One Fish Would Do	I	RF	250+	Home Connection Collection	Rigby
Just One Guinea Pig	I	RF	339	PM Story Books-Orange	Rigby
Just One More, Mom	I	F	423	Grady, Kit S.	Kaeden Books
Just One of the Family	M	F	250+	Use Your Imagination	Steck-Vaughn
Just One Seed	H	RF	182	Ada, Alma Flor	Hampton Brown
Just One Wish	W	RF	250+	Rallison, Janette	G.P. Putnam's Sons
Just Plain Cat	O	RF	250+	Robinson, Nancy K.	Scholastic
Just Right	C	F	35	Brand New Readers	Candlewick Press
Just Right for the Night	E	RF	69	Voyages	SRA/McGraw Hill
Just Right!	C	F	75	Leveled Readers	Houghton Mifflin Harcourt
Just Right!	G	RF	105	Sunshine	Wright Group/McGraw Hill
Just Tell Me When We're Dead!	O	RF	250+	Clifford, Eth	Scholastic
Just the Bee's Knees	K	I	250+	Story Steps	Rigby
Just the Best	I	RF	250+	The Rowland Reading Program Library	Rowland Reading Foundation
Just the Facts	K	F	536	Dominie Math Stories	Pearson Learning Group
Just the Right Size	T	I	250+	Davies, Nicola	Candlewick Press
Just This Once	H	F	252	Sunshine	Wright Group/McGraw Hill
Just Us Women	J	RF	250+	Caines, Jeannette	Scholastic
Just Wait and See	F	F	185	Leveled Literacy Intervention / Green System	Heinemann
Justice	Z+	RF	10420	Oxford Bookworms Library	Oxford University Press
Justin and the Best Biscuits in the World	P	RF	250+	Pitts, Walter & Mildred	Alfred A. Knopf
Justin Case: School, Drool, and Other Daily Disasters	O	RF	250+	Vail, Rachel	Feiwel and Friends

JK

TITLE	LEVEL	GENRE	WORD COUNT	AUTHOR / SERIES	PUBLISHER / DISTRIBUTOR
Justin Morgan Had a Horse	R	HF	250+	Henry, Marguerite	Scholastic
Justin's Big Fish	I	RF	509	Pair-It Turn and Learn	Steck-Vaughn
Justin's New Bike	G	RF	150	Hill, Barbara	Scholastic
Just-Right House, The	F	F	201	Leveled Readers	Houghton Mifflin Harcourt
Juvenile Diabetes	N	I	250+	Health Matters	Capstone Press
K	LB	I	14	Readlings	American Reading Company
K. C. at the Bat	U	F	1939	Leveled Readers	Houghton Mifflin Harcourt
K-9 Team on Patrol	G	I	138	Literacy by Design	Rigby
Kabuki Kid, The	P	RF	773	Leveled Readers	Houghton Mifflin Harcourt
Kabuki Kid, The	P	RF	773	Leveled Readers/CA	Houghton Mifflin Harcourt
Kabuki Kid, The	P	RF	773	Leveled Readers/TX	Houghton Mifflin Harcourt
Ka-Ha-Si and the Loon: An Eskimo Legend	R	TL	250+	Native American Legends	Troll Associates
Kakapo Rescue: Saving the World's Strangest Parrot	W	I	250+	Scientists in the Field	Houghton Mifflin Harcourt
Kaleidoscope Eyes	W	HF	250+	Bryant, Jen	Yearling Books
Kali and the Rat Snake	O	RF	250+	Whitaker, Zai	Kane/Miller Book Publishers
Kalpana Chawla, Astronaut	T	B	250+	Independent Readers Science	Houghton Mifflin Harcourt
Kalulu's Pumpkins	K	TL	250+	Rigby Literacy	Rigby
Kamala's Art	G	I	150	Vocabulary Readers	Houghton Mifflin Harcourt
Kamala's Art	G	I	150	Vocabulary Readers/CA	Houghton Mifflin Harcourt
Kamala's Art	G	I	150	Vocabulary Readers/TX	Houghton Mifflin Harcourt
Kama's Lei	H	RF	134	Bebop Books	Lee & Low Books Inc.
Kandake, The: Queens of Kush	X	I	2040	Independent Readers Social Studies	Houghton Mifflin Harcourt
Kangaroo from Wooloomooloo	H	F	254	Jellybeans	Rigby
Kangaroo in the Kitchen	D	F	72	Ready Readers	Pearson Learning Group
Kangaroo Joey Grows Up, A	K	I	397	Baby Animals	Lerner Publishing Group
Kangaroo, The	M	I	250+	Crewe, Sabrina	Steck-Vaughn
Kangaroos	N	I	250+	A New True Book	Children's Press
Kangaroos	J	I	163	Australian Animals	Capstone Press
Kangaroos	K	I	230	Pawprints Teal	Pioneer Valley
Kangaroos	K	I	250+	PM Animal Facts: Turquoise	Rigby
Kangaroos	F	I	111	Springboard	Wright Group/McGraw Hill
Kangaroos Have Joeys	M	I	250+	Animals and Their Young	Compass Point Books
Kangaroos in the Land Down Under	M	I	250+	Rosen Real Readers	Rosen Publishing Group
Kangaroo's Pouch	C	F	36	Sails	Rigby
Kansas	T	I	250+	Hello U.S.A.	Lerner Publishing Group
Kansas	S	I	250+	Land of Liberty	Red Brick Learning
Kansas	R	I	250+	This Land Is Your Land	Compass Point Books
Kansas City Chiefs, The	S	I	250+	Team Spirit	Norwood House Press
Kansas City Royals, The	S	I	250+	Team Spirit	Norwood House Press
Kansas City Royals, The (Revised Edition)	S	I	250+	Team Spirit	Norwood House Press
Kansas: Facts and Symbols	O	I	250+	The States and Their Symbols	Capstone Press
Kantjil and Tiger	M	TL	250+	Story Vines	Wright Group/McGraw Hill
Kapuapua's Magic Shell	O	TL	1374	Reading Street	Pearson
Karate Kick	Q	RF	250+	Christopher, Matt	Little Brown and Company
Karate Mouse, The	O	F	250+	Stilton, Geronimo	Scholastic
Karina	D	RF	40	Step-By-Step Series	Pearson Learning Group
Karma Club, The	Z+	RF	250+	Brody, Jessica	Farrar, Straus, & Giroux
Kart Crash	Q	RF	250+	Maddox, Jake	Stone Arch Books
Kartchner Caverns	K	I	142	Larkin's Little Readers	Wilbooks
Kat Kong	O	F	250+	Pilkey, Dav	Harcourt, Inc.
Kat the Curious	R	RF	1723	Leveled Readers	Houghton Mifflin Harcourt
Katarina	X	HF	250+	Winter, Kathryn	Scholastic

* Collection of short stories   # Graphic text
^ Mature content with lower level text demands

JK

TITLE	LEVEL	GENRE	WORD COUNT	AUTHOR / SERIES	PUBLISHER / DISTRIBUTOR
Kate Shelley and the Midnight Express	M	B	250+	On My Own History	Carolrhoda Books
Kate, Who Was Always Late	M	RF	250+	Tristars	Richard C. Owen
Kate's Truck	C	RF	92	Leveled Literacy Intervention/ Green System	Heinemann
Kate's Surprise	F	RF	143	Rookie Readers	Children's Press
Katharine Graham: American Publisher	P	B	250+	On Deck	Rigby
Katherine Dunham, Black Dancer	N	B	250+	Rookie Biographies	Children's Press
Katherine Paterson	S	B	250+	Cary, Alice	Creative Teaching Press
Kathleen, Please Come Home	Z+	RF	250+	O'Dell, Scott	Marshall Cavendish
Katie and Kimble: A Ghost Story	Q	F	15250	Thieman, Linda	Pale Silver Rainplop Press
Katie and Kimble: The Magic Wish	Q	F	14675	Thieman, Linda	Pale Silver Rainplop Press
Katie Couldn't	F	RF	176	Rookie Readers	Children's Press
Katie Did It	G	RF	105	Rookie Readers	Children's Press
Katie in the Kitchen: Katie Woo	J	RF	250+	Manushkin, Fran	Picture Window Books
Katie Kazoo Switcheroo: No Messin' with My Lesson	M	F	250+	Krulik, Nancy	Scholastic
Katie Saves Thanksgiving: Katie Woo	J	RF	250+	Manushkin, Fran	Picture Window Books
Katie the Kitten Fairy: Rainbow Magic	L	F	250+	Meadows, Daisy	Scholastic
Katie's Butterfly	H	RF	222	PM Plus Story Books	Rigby
Katie's Caterpillar	E	RF	149	PM Plus Story Books	Rigby
Katie's Lucky Birthday: Katie Woo	J	RF	250+	Manushkin, Fran	Picture Window Books
Kat's Mystery Gift (Jon Scieszka's Trucktown)	G	F	123	Scieszka, Jon	Aladdin
Katy and the Big Snow	L	F	250+	Burton, Virginia L.	Scholastic
Katydids	E	I	20	Books for Young Learners	Richard C. Owen
Katydid's Life, A	M	I	250+	Twig	Wright Group/McGraw Hill
Katy's Inventions	N	F	804	Leveled Readers	Houghton Mifflin Harcourt
Katy's Inventions	N	F	804	Leveled Readers/CA	Houghton Mifflin Harcourt
Katy's Inventions	N	F	804	Leveled Readers/TX	Houghton Mifflin Harcourt
Katy's Last-Minute Book Report	M	RF	831	Reading Street	Pearson
Kawi, Pawi, Po	K	RF	472	Take Two Books	Wright Group/McGraw Hill
Kayaking	Q	I	250+	Extreme Sports	Red Brick Learning
Kayaking at Blue Lake	J	RF	250+	PM Plus Story Books	Rigby
Kayla Chronicles, The	Z+	RF	250+	Winston, Sherri	Little Brown and Company
Kay's Birthday	C	RF	26	KinderReaders	Rigby
Kazam All Wet	D	RF	40	Brand New Readers	Candlewick Press
Kazam's Birds	D	F	38	Brand New Readers	Candlewick Press
Kazam's Cards	D	F	34	Brand New Readers	Candlewick Press
Kazam's Coins	D	F	35	Brand New Readers	Candlewick Press
Kazam's Rabbit	D	RF	40	Brand New Readers	Candlewick Press
Kazam's Scarf	D	RF	41	Brand New Readers	Candlewick Press
Kazam's Wand	D	F	29	Brand New Readers	Candlewick Press
Keeker and the Crazy, Upside-Down Birthday	M	F	250+	Higginson, Hadley	Chronicle Books
Keeker and the Horse Show Show-Off	M	F	250+	Higginson, Hadley	Chronicle Books
Keeker and the Not-So- Sleepy Hollow	M	F	250+	Higginson, Hadley	Chronicle Books
Keeker and the Pony Camp Castastrophe	M	F	250+	Higginson, Hadley	Chronicle Books
Keeker and the Springtime Surprise	M	F	250+	Higginson, Hadley	Chronicle Books
Keeker and the Sugar Shack	M	F	250+	Higginson, Hadley	Chronicle Books
Keelboat Annie	N	TL	250+	Johnson, Janet P.	Troll Associates
Keening, The	Y	HF	250+	LaFaye, A.	Milkweed Editions
Keep Calm!	Q	RF	250+	Bookweb	Rigby
Keep Ms. Sugarman in the Fourth Grade	M	RF	250+	Levy, Elizabeth	HarperTrophy
Keep on Rollin' Meatballs and Other Delicious Dinners	R	I	250+	Kids Dish	Picture Window Books

TITLE	LEVEL	GENRE	WORD COUNT	AUTHOR / SERIES	PUBLISHER / DISTRIBUTOR
Keep On!: The Story of Matthew Henson, Co-Discoverer of the North Pole	S	B	250+	Hopkinson, Deborah	Peachtree
Keep Out!	B	RF	19	Ready Readers	Pearson Learning Group
Keep Out: Our Dog Buries What It Can't Eat	P	RF	250+	Beale, Fleur	Pacific Learning
Keep Rivers Clean	M	I	405	Sun Sprouts	ETA/Cuisenaire
Keep Smiling Through	V	RF	250+	Rinaldi, Ann	Harcourt Trade
Keep the Beat	D	RF	48	Little Celebrations	Pearson Learning Group
Keep the Lights Burning Abbie	K	HF	250+	On My Own History	Scholastic
Keep Your Cool!: What You Should Know about Stress	V	I	7034	Health Zone	Lerner Publishing Group
Keep Your Distance!	L	RF	250+	Math Matters	Kane Press
Keep Your Eye on Amanda!	R	F	250+	Avi	Avon Books
Keeper	U	F	250+	Appelt, Kathi	Atheneum Books
Keeper	W	F	250+	Edge	Hampton Brown
Keeper and the Crows, The	P	F	250+	Orca Young Readers	Orca Books
Keeper of Soles	Q	F	250+	Bateman, Teresa	Holiday House
Keeper of the Night	Z+	RF	250+	Holt, Kimberly Willis	Henry Holt & Co.
Keeping Baby Animals Safe	C	I	56	Little Books	Sadlier-Oxford
Keeping Clean	I	I	220	Sails	Rigby
Keeping Clean	WB	I	0	Windows on Literacy	National Geographic
Keeping Cool	D	I	18	Foundations	Wright Group/McGraw Hill
Keeping Cool	C	I	18	Pacific Literacy	Pacific Learning
Keeping Count	Q	I	250+	WorldScapes	ETA/Cuisenaire
Keeping Days, The	Z	HF	250+	Johnston, Norma	Puffin Books
Keeping Fit	U	I	250+	Reading Expeditions	National Geographic
Keeping Fit	H	I	61	Windows on Literacy	National Geographic
Keeping Fit with Sports	I	I	250+	Time for Kids	Teacher Created Materials
Keeping Fit!	E	F	36	Little Celebrations	Pearson Learning Group
Keeping Ice Cold	L	I	567	Sun Sprouts	ETA/Cuisenaire
Keeping in Touch	S	I	250+	Connectors	Pacific Learning
Keeping in Touch	K	I	328	Gear Up!	Wright Group/McGraw Hill
Keeping Israel Safe: Serving in the Israel Defense Forces	X	I	7210	Sofer, Barbara	Kar-Ben Publishing
Keeping Records	V	I	250+	WorldScapes	ETA/Cuisenaire
Keeping Room, The	V	HF	250+	Myers, Anna	Puffin Books
Keeping Safe in an Earthquake	O	I	949	Vocabulary Readers	Houghton Mifflin Harcourt
Keeping Safe in an Earthquake	O	I	949	Vocabulary Readers/CA	Houghton Mifflin Harcourt
Keeping Safe in an Earthquake	O	I	949	Vocabulary Readers/TX	Houghton Mifflin Harcourt
Keeping Score	J	I	240	Early Connections	Benchmark Education
Keeping Score	U	HF	250+	Park, Linda Sue	Sandpiper Books
Keeping Tadpoles	N	I	250+	Discovery World	Rigby
Keeping the Balance	P	I	250+	WorldScapes	ETA/Cuisenaire
Keeping the Night Watch	W	RF	250+	Smith, Hope Anita	Henry Holt & Co.
Keeping the Promise: A Torah's Journey	R	I	1277	Lehman-Wilzig, Tami	Kar-Ben Publishing
Keeping Time	J	I	231	Early Connections	Benchmark Education
Keeping Time	S	I	250+	InfoQuest	Rigby
Keeping Time	P	I	250+	Tristars	Richard C. Owen
Keeping Up with Claire	O	RF	250+	On Our Way To English	Rigby
Keeping Warm	E	I	105	Yellow Umbrella Books	Red Brick Learning
Keeping Warm in Winter	P	I	516	Vocabulary Readers	Houghton Mifflin Harcourt
Keeping Warm! Keeping Cool!	K	I	946	Sunshine	Wright Group/McGraw Hill
Keeping Watch	J	F	520	Bella and Rosie Series	Literacy Footprints
Keeping Water Clean	I	I	117	Pebble Books	Red Brick Learning
Keeping You a Secret	Z+	RF	250+	Peters, Julie Anne	Little Brown and Company

* Collection of short stories   # Graphic text
^ Mature content with lower level text demands

TITLE	LEVEL	GENRE	WORD COUNT	AUTHOR / SERIES	PUBLISHER / DISTRIBUTOR
Keeping You Healthy: A Book About Doctors	I	I	185	Community Workers	Picture Window Books
Keeping You Safe: A Book About Police Officers	I	I	112	Community Workers	Picture Window Books
Keesha's Bright Idea	L	RF	250+	Social Studies Connects	Kane Press
Keisha Discovers Harlem	Q	RF	250+	Lewis, Zoe	Magic Attic
Keisha Leads the Way: Magic Attic Club	Q	RF	250+	Reed, Teresa	Magic Attic
Keisha the Fairy Snow Queen: Magic Attic Club	Q	RF	250+	Reed, Teresa	Magic Attic
Keisha to the Rescue: Magic Attic Club	Q	RF	250+	Reed, Teresa	Magic Attic
Keisha's Maze Mystery: Magic Attic Club	Q	RF	250+	Benson, Lauren	Magic Attic
Kelly the Rescue Dog	S	HF	250+	High-Fliers	Pacific Learning
Kelly's Trip	L	RF	250+	Sunshine	Wright Group/McGraw Hill
Ken Griffey, Jr. & Ken Griffey, Sr.	T	B	250+	Star Families	Crestwood House
Kendria's Watch	S	SF	2316	Leveled Readers	Houghton Mifflin Harcourt
Kendria's Watch	S	SF	2316	Leveled Readers/CA	Houghton Mifflin Harcourt
Kendria's Watch	S	SF	2316	Leveled Readers/TX	Houghton Mifflin Harcourt
Kenji's Haircut	D	RF	105	Lighthouse	Rigby
Kenny and the Little Kickers	J	F	250+	Marzollo, Claudio	Scholastic
Kenny's Big Present	H	RF	181	Leveled Readers	Houghton Mifflin Harcourt
Kensuke's Kingdom	V	RF	250+	Morpurgo, Michael	Scholastic
Kent State Shootings, The	X	I	250+	We the People	Compass Point Books
Kentucky	T	I	250+	Hello U.S.A.	Lerner Publishing Group
Kentucky	S	I	250+	Land of Liberty	Red Brick Learning
Kentucky	R	I	250+	This Land Is Your Land	Compass Point Books
Kentucky: Facts and Symbols	O	I	250+	The States and Their Symbols	Capstone Press
Kenya	O	I	2440	A Ticket to …	Carolrhoda Books
Kenya	O	I	250+	Countries of the World	Red Brick Learning
Kenya	P	I	1993	Country Explorers	Lerner Publishing Group
Kenya	Q	I	250+	First Reports: Countries	Compass Point Books
Kenya	LB	I	14	Readlings	American Reading Company
Kenya ABCs: A Book About the People and Places of Kenya	Q	I	250+	Country ABCs	Picture Window Books
Kenya in Colors	N	I	250+	World of Colors	Capstone Press
Kenya: A Question and Answer Book	P	I	250+	Questions & Answers: Countries	Capstone Press
Kenya's Word	L	RF	250+	Trice, Linda	Charlesbridge
Kermit and Robin's Scary Story	J	F	250+	Muntean, Michaela	Puffin Books
Kerplunk!	J	I	250+	Spyglass Books	Compass Point Books
Kerri Strug: Heart of Gold	L	B	250+	Strug, K.; Brown, G.	Scholastic
Kerry	K	RF	250+	PM Story Books-Silver	Rigby
Kerry's Double	K	RF	250+	PM Story Books-Silver	Rigby
Ketchup Deal, The	T	F	250+	Orbit Chapter Books	Pacific Learning
Kevin and Lucy	E	RF	130	Leveled Readers	Houghton Mifflin Harcourt
Kevin and Lucy	E	RF	130	Leveled Readers/CA	Houghton Mifflin Harcourt
Kevin Counts	D	RF	83	Seedlings	Continental Press
Kevin Durant	P	B	1977	Amazing Athletes	Lerner Publishing Group
Kevin Garnett	P	B	1501	Amazing Athletes	Lerner Publishing Group
Kevin Garnett (Revised Edition)	P	B	1639	Amazing Athletes	Lerner Publishing Group
Kevin Garnett	R	B	250+	Sports Heroes	Red Brick Learning
Key Lardo: A Chet Gecko Mystery	R	F	250+	Hale, Bruce	Harcourt, Inc.
Key to Maps, The	K	I	222	Windows on Literacy	National Geographic
Key to the Playhouse, The	O	RF	250+	York, Carol	Scholastic
Key to the Treasure	N	RF	250+	Parish, Peggy	Bantam Books
Key, The	L	F	250+	On Our Way to English	Rigby
Keys	B	I	31	Ready Readers	Pearson Learning Group
Khyber Pass in Asia, The	U	I	2227	Leveled Readers Language Support	Houghton Mifflin Harcourt

TITLE	LEVEL	GENRE	WORD COUNT	AUTHOR / SERIES	PUBLISHER / DISTRIBUTOR
Khyber Pass, The	W	I	1993	Leveled Readers Social Studies	Houghton Mifflin Harcourt
Kiboko and the Water Snake	I	F	250+	Storyworlds	Heinemann
Kick	Y	RF	250+	Myers, Walter Dean & Workman, Ross	HarperCollins
Kick, Pass, and Run	J	RF	250+	Kessler, Leonard	HarperTrophy
Kick-a-Lot Shoes, The	H	F	433	Story Box	Wright Group/McGraw Hill
Kickball	F	RF	148	Handprints D, Set 1	Educators Publishing Service
Kickboxing	M	I	250+	To the Extreme	Capstone Press
Kickboxing	S	I	250+	X-Sports	Capstone Press
^Kicked Out	Z	RF	250+	Orca Soundings	Orca Books
^Kicker	T	RF	250+	Orca Sports	Orca Books
Kickin' It	Y	I	250+	Boldprint	Steck-Vaughn
Kid Coach, The	P	RF	250+	Bowen, Fred	Peachtree
Kid Heroes of the Environment	Q	I	250+	Dee, Catherine	Scholastic
Kid in the Red Jacket, The	O	RF	250+	Park, Barbara	Random House
Kid Next Door, The	N	RF	250+	Smith, Janice Lee	HarperTrophy
Kid Power	P	RF	250+	Pfeffer, Susan Beth	Scholastic
Kid vs. Squid	S	F	250+	van Eekhout, Greg	Bloomsbury Children's Books
Kid Who Only Hit Homers, The	P	RF	250+	Christopher, Matt	Little Brown and Company
Kid Who Ran For President, The	T	RF	250+	Gutman, Dan	Language for Learning Assoc.
#Kidnap!	T	RF	2600	Dominoes starter	Oxford University Press
Kidnapped	U	RF	12435	Oxford Bookworms Library	Oxford University Press
Kidnapped at the Capital	N	RF	250+	Roy, Ron	Random House
Kidnapped King, The	N	RF	250+	A to Z Mysteries	Random House
^Kids Against Hunger	P	RF	250+	We Are Heroes	Stone Arch Books
Kids Are Citizens: Kids Make a Difference	S	I	250+	Reading Expeditions	National Geographic
Kids Are Consumers: Kids Make a Difference	S	I	250+	Reading Expeditions	National Geographic
Kids Around the World	K	I	294	Time for Kids	Teacher Created Materials
Kids at Our School	I	RF	107	City Kids	Rigby
Kids at Work: Lewis Hine and the Crusade Against Child Labor	T	B	250+	Freedman, Russell	Clarion
Kids Can Be Safe!	D	I	65	On Our Way to English	Rigby
Kids Can Cook	M	I	250+	Literacy 2000	Rigby
Kids Can Read	C	RF	158	Sails	Rigby
Kids Care Club, The	I	RF	414	Reading Street	Pearson
Kids Care for the Earth: Kids Make a Difference	S	I	250+	Reading Expeditions	National Geographic
Kids Communicate: Kids Make a Difference	S	I	250+	Reading Expeditions	National Geographic
Kids from Quiller's Bend	P	RF	250+	Action Packs	Rigby
Kids' Guide to Mummies	U	I	250+	Kids' Guides	Capstone Press
Kids' Guide to Aliens, The	R	I	250+	Kids' Guides	Capstone Press
Kids' Guide to Balloon Twisting, The	R	I	250+	Kids' Guides	Capstone Press
Kids' Guide to Building Cool Stuff, The	R	I	250+	Kids' Guides	Capstone Press
Kids' Guide to Classic Games, The	R	I	250+	Kids' Guides	Capstone Press
Kids' Guide to Collecting Stuff, The	R	I	250+	Kids' Guides	Capstone Press
Kids' Guide to Family Reunions, A	O	I	351	Vocabulary Readers	Houghton Mifflin Harcourt
Kids' Guide to Jumping Rope, The	R	I	250+	Kids' Guides	Capstone Press
Kids' Guide to Military Vehicles, The	T	I	250+	Kids' Guides	Capstone Press
Kids' Guide to Monster Trucks, The	R	I	250+	Kids' Guides	Capstone Press
Kids' Guide to Paper Airplanes, The	R	I	250+	Kids' Guides	Capstone Press
Kids' Guide to Pranks, Tricks, and Practical Jokes, The	R	I	250+	Kids' Guides	Capstone Press
Kids' Guide to Robots, The	R	I	250+	Kids' Guides	Capstone Press

* Collection of short stories   # Graphic text
^ Mature content with lower level text demands

JK

TITLE	LEVEL	GENRE	WORD COUNT	AUTHOR / SERIES	PUBLISHER / DISTRIBUTOR
Kid's Guide to Social Action	V	I	250+	Lewis, Barbara A.	Free Spirit Publishing
Kids Have Jobs	G	I	142	Early Explorers	Benchmark Education
Kids in a Booth	J	RF	109	Dominie Readers	Pearson Learning Group
Kids in Ms. Colman's Class: Author Day	M	RF	250+	Martin, Ann M.	Scholastic
Kids in Pioneer Times	Q	I	250+	Kids Throughout History	Rosen Publishing Group
Kids in the Circus	L	I	250+	Sunshine	Wright Group/McGraw Hill
Kids in the Kitchen	C	RF	127	Sails	Rigby
^Kids in the Medieval World	R	I	250+	The Middle Ages	Capstone Press
Kids' Invention Book, The	T	I	250+	Erlbach, Arlene	Lerner Publishing Group
Kids Manage Money: Kids Make a Difference	S	I	250+	Reading Expeditions	National Geographic
Kids Rule!	O	I	250+	Bookshop	Mondo Publishing
Kids Say	N	F	250+	Sails	Rigby
Kids to the Rescue	W	I	2421	Vocabulary Readers	Houghton Mifflin Harcourt
Kids to the Rescue	W	I	2421	Vocabulary Readers/CA	Houghton Mifflin Harcourt
Kids to the Rescue	W	I	2421	Vocabulary Readers/TX	Houghton Mifflin Harcourt
*Kids You Ought to Know	U	B	250+	Bookshop	Mondo Publishing
Kiki Strike: Empress's Tomb, The	W	F	250+	Miller Kirsten	Bloomsbury Children's Books
Kiki Strike: Inside the Shadow City	W	F	250+	Miller Kirsten	Bloomsbury Children's Books
Killer Bees	S	I	250+	Blau, Melinda	Steck-Vaughn
Killer Creatures	V	I	250+	Navigators	Kingfisher
Killer Lipstick	W	I	250+	24/7 Science Behind the Scenes	Scholastic
Killer Pizza	V	F	250+	Taylor, Greg	Feiwel and Friends
Killer Plants	K	I	469	Explorations	Eleanor Curtain Publishing
Killer Plants	K	I	469	Explorations	Okapi Educational Materials
^Killer Robot	T	SF	250+	The Extraordinary Files	Hameray Publishing Group
Killer Sharks	Q	SF	250+	Cullimore, Stan	Stone Arch Books
Killer Whale	B	I	45	Zoozoo-Animal World	Cavallo Publishing
Killer Whales	P	I	1678	Animal Predators	Lerner Publishing Group
Killer Whales	R	I	250+	Predators in the Wild	Red Brick Learning
Killer Whales	K	I	250+	Simon, Seymour	Chronicle Books
Killer Whales Up Close	M	I	250+	First Facts-Whales and Dolphins Up Close	Capstone Press
Killers of the Dawn: The Saga of Darren Shan	Y	F	250+	Shan, Darren	Little Brown and Company
Killing Germs	K	I	677	Pull Ahead Books	Lerner Publishing Group
Killing Mr. Griffin	Z	RF	250+	Duncan, Lois	Little Brown and Company
Kilmer's Pet Monster	L	RF	250+	Dadey, Debbie; Jones, Marcia Thornton	Scholastic
Kim and the Computer Giant	J	F	250+	Storyworlds	Heinemann
Kim and the Computer Mouse	J	F	250+	Storyworlds	Heinemann
Kim and the Missing Paint Pot	J	F	250+	Storyworlds	Heinemann
Kim and the Shape Dragon	J	F	250+	Storyworlds	Heinemann
Kim Carries the Flag	H	RF	130	Pair-It Turn and Learn	Steck-Vaughn
Kim Does It	P	RF	250+	Reading Safari	Mondo Publishing
Kim's New Shoes	G	RF	234	Leveled Literacy Intervention/ Blue System	Heinemann
Kimiko Quest	O	F	250+	Literacy by Design	Rigby
Kind Child, The	I	RF	250+	Hechinger, Nancy	Scholastic
Kind Emma	I	F	224	Big Cat	Pacific Learning
Kind of Friends We Used to Be, The	V	RF	250+	Dowell, Frances O'Roark	Atheneum Books
Kind of Thief, A	U	RF	250+	Alcock, Vivien	Bantam Books
*Kind Prince and Rupert, The	L	F	250+	New Way Literature	Steck-Vaughn
Kindergarten	D	RF	118	Carousel Readers	Pearson Learning Group
Kindest Family, The	K	TL	536	PM Plus Story Books	Rigby

TITLE	LEVEL	GENRE	WORD COUNT	AUTHOR / SERIES	PUBLISHER / DISTRIBUTOR
Kindling, The (Fire-Us Trilogy: Book 1)	Y	SF	250+	Armstrong, Jennifer; Butcher, Nancy	HarperCollins
Kinds of Environments	I	I	382	Science Support Readers	Houghton Mifflin Harcourt
King Arthur	M	F	250+	Brown, Marc	Little Brown and Company
#King Arthur and the Knights of the Round Table	W	TL	2595	Hall, M. C. (Retold)	Stone Arch Books
King Arthur and the Knights of the Round Table (Abridged)	S	TL	12000	Hear It Read It	Sourcebooks
#King Arthur: Exalibur Unsheathed	W	TL	3883	Graphic Myths and Legends	Lerner Publishing Group
King Beast's Birthday	L	F	250+	Literacy 2000	Rigby
King Bidgood's in the Bathtub	L	F	250+	Wood, Audrey	Scholastic
King Crab is Coming!	J	F	250+	Rigby Rocket	Rigby
King Dork	Z+	RF	250+	Portman, Frank	Delacorte Press
King Emmett the Second	R	RF	250+	Stolz, Mary	Bantam Books
King Glitter and the Stars	J	F	318	Talking Point Series	Pearson Learning Group
King Horace's Treasure Hunt	M	F	250+	Tristars	Richard C. Owen
#King Lear	Z	HF	250+	Manga Shakespeare	Amulet Books
King Max	Q	F	250+	King-Smith, Dick	Troll Associates
King Midas and the Golden Touch	K	TL	721	PM Collection	Rigby
King Midas and the Golden Touch	J	TL	250+	Traditional Tales	Pearson Learning Group
King of Egypt, The	R	HF	250+	Rigby Literacy	Rigby
King of Shadows	Z	F	250+	Cooper, Susan	McElderry
King of the Birds	J	TL	476	PM Stars Bridge Books	Rigby
King of the Birds, The	J	F	250+	Rigby Literacy	Rigby
King of the Birds, The	J	F	250+	Rigby Star	Rigby
King of the Mild Frontier: An Ill-Advised Autobiography	Z+	B	250+	Crutcher, Chris	HarperCollins
King of the Mountain	J	F	288	Dominie Readers	Pearson Learning Group
King of the Pygmies	Z+	RF	250+	Fuqua, Jonathon Scott	Candlewick Press
King of the Screwups	Z+	RF	250+	Going, K. L.	Houghton Mifflin Harcourt
King of the Sky	J	RF	250+	Foundations	Wright Group/McGraw Hill
King of the Wind	R	HF	250+	Henry, Marguerite	Aladdin
King of the Zoo	B	I	72	Red Rocket Readers	Flying Start Books
King Philip	V	B	250+	Amazing Americans	Wright Group/McGraw Hill
King Tut	R	I	250+	Explorer Books-Pathfinder	National Geographic
King Tut	Q	I	250+	Explorer Books-Pioneer	National Geographic
King Tut: Tales from the Tomb	W	I	250+	High Five Reading	Red Brick Learning
^King Tut's Tomb	S	I	250+	Ancient Egypt	Capstone Press
King Who Could Knit, The	J	F	250+	The Wright Skills	Wright Group/McGraw Hill
King Who Had Dirty Feet, The: A Play	M	TL	250+	Rigby Literacy	Rigby
King Who Loved to Dance, The	F	F	82	Instant Readers	Harcourt School Publishers
*King with Horse's Ears and Other Irish Folktales, The	U	TL	250+	Burns, Batt	Sterling Publishing
King, the Mice, and the Cheese, The	K	F	250+	Gurney, Nancy	Random House
Kingdom of Kush, The	Z	I	3395	Leveled Readers	Houghton Mifflin Harcourt
Kingdom of the Golden Dragon	X	F	250+	Allende, Isabel	HarperTrophy
*Kingfisher Treasury of Ghost Stories, The	R	F	250+	Ireland, Kenneth	Kingfisher
Kingfisher's Gift, The	W	F	250+	Beckhorn, Susan Williams	Penguin Group
Kingfisher's Tale, The	Z	RF	250+	Misfits Inc.	Peachtree
King's Big Foot, The	I	F	249	On Our Way to English	Rigby
King's Birthday, The	B	F	35	Ray's Readers	Outside the Box
King's Crossing	G	RF	258	Handprints D	Educators Publishing Service
King's Dream and Sammy's New Yellow Sweater, The	L	TL	250+	New Way Literature	Steck-Vaughn

* Collection of short stories   # Graphic text
^ Mature content with lower level text demands

JK

TITLE	LEVEL	GENRE	WORD COUNT	AUTHOR / SERIES	PUBLISHER / DISTRIBUTOR
King's Equal, The	O	TL	250+	Paterson, Katherine	HarperTrophy
King's Job	F	F	155	Handprints C, Set 2	Educators Publishing Service
King's Mapmaker, The	K	TL	720	Early Explorers	Benchmark Education
Kings of Persia, The	X	I	2093	Leveled Readers	Houghton Mifflin Harcourt
Kings of Persia, The	X	I	2093	Leveled Readers/CA	Houghton Mifflin Harcourt
Kings of Persia, The	X	I	2093	Leveled Readers/TX	Houghton Mifflin Harcourt
King's Pudding, The	I	F	214	Literacy Tree	Rigby
*King's Race and Other Stories, The	L	F	250+	New Way Literature	Steck-Vaughn
King's Ring, The	C	F	38	KinderReaders	Rigby
King's Slippers, The	E	F	107	Sun Sprouts	ETA/Cuisenaire
King's Surprise, The	D	F	54	Stewart, Josie; Salem, Lynn	Continental Press
King's Warrior, The: A Story of Ancient India	O	HF	250+	Historical Tales	Picture Window Books
Kink the Mink	C	F	18	KinderReaders	Rigby
Kip and Tip	C	I	24	KinderReaders	Rigby
Kipper's Birthday	E	RF	64	Oxford Reading Tree	Oxford University Press
Kira-Kira	T	RF	250+	Kadohata, Cynthia	Aladdin Paperbacks
Kirsten Learns a Lesson	Q	HF	250+	The American Girls Collection	Pleasant Company
Kirsten Saves the Day	Q	HF	250+	The American Girls Collection	Pleasant Company
Kirsten's Surprise	Q	HF	250+	The American Girls Collection	Pleasant Company
Kishina: A True Story of Gorilla Survival	V	I	250+	Rock, Maxine	Peachtree
Kiss	Z	RF	250+	Wilson, Jacqueline	Roaring Brook Press
Kiss for Little Bear, A	H	F	250+	Minarik, Else H.	HarperTrophy
Kiss Me, I'm Perfect	L	F	250+	Munsch, Robert	Scholastic
Kiss the Cow!	L	F	250+	Root, Phyllis	Candlewick Press
Kiss the Dust	W	RF	250+	Laird, Elizabeth	Penguin Group
Kiss! Kiss! Yuck! Yuck!	K	RF	250+	Mewburn, Kyle	Peachtree
Kisses on the Wind	L	HF	250+	Moser, Lisa	Candlewick Press
*Kissing Game, The	Z+	RF	250+	Chambers, Aidan	Amulet Books
Kissing Hand, The	I	F	250+	Penn, Audrey	Scholastic
Kit Carson: Mountain Man	V	B	250+	Let Freedom Ring	Capstone Press
Kit Finds a Mitt	H	RF	198	Leveled Readers	Houghton Mifflin Harcourt
Kitchen Garden	F	I	174	Explorations	Okapi Educational Materials
Kitchen Garden	F	I	174	Explorations	Eleanor Curtain Publishing
Kitchen Knight, The	T	TL	250+	Hodges, Margaret	Holiday House
Kitchen Rules	J	I	153	Windows on Literacy	National Geographic
Kitchen Science	P	I	958	Independent Readers Science	Houghton Mifflin Harcourt
Kitchen Science	O	I	250+	Infotrek Plus	ETA/Cuisenaire
Kitchen Science	M	I	552	Vocabulary Readers	Houghton Mifflin Harcourt
Kitchen Science	M	I	552	Vocabulary Readers/CA	Houghton Mifflin Harcourt
Kitchen Science	M	I	552	Vocabulary Readers/TX	Houghton Mifflin Harcourt
Kitchen Science	M	I	250+	Windows on Literacy	National Geographic
Kitchen Scientist	M	I	792	Sun Sprouts	ETA/Cuisenaire
Kitchen Table Science	M	I	250+	Literacy by Design	Rigby
Kitchen Tools	E	I	104	Foundations	Wright Group/McGraw Hill
Kitchen, The	T	I	250+	Historic Communities	Crabtree
Kite and the Butterflies, The	I	F	364	Book Bank	Wright Group/McGraw Hill
Kite Contest, The	I	RF	346	Leveled Readers	Houghton Mifflin Harcourt
Kite Contest, The	I	RF	346	Leveled Readers/CA	Houghton Mifflin Harcourt
Kite Contest, The	I	RF	346	Leveled Readers/TX	Houghton Mifflin Harcourt
Kite Dance	E	RF	65	Danforth, Audrey	Continental Press
Kite Day	E	RF	120	Springboard	Wright Group/McGraw Hill
Kite Fighters, The	S	HF	250+	Park, Linda Sue	Houghton Mifflin Harcourt
Kite Flying	E	I	190	Vocabulary Readers	Houghton Mifflin Harcourt

JK

TITLE	LEVEL	GENRE	WORD COUNT	AUTHOR / SERIES	PUBLISHER / DISTRIBUTOR
Kite Flying	E	I	190	Vocabulary Readers/CA	Houghton Mifflin Harcourt
Kite Flying	E	I	190	Vocabulary Readers/TX	Houghton Mifflin Harcourt
Kite Race, The	J	RF	939	Spirn, Michele	January Books
Kite Shapes	C	I	31	Little Celebrations	Pearson Learning Group
Kite That Flew Away, The	H	RF	279	Ready Readers	Pearson Learning Group
Kite That Got Away, The	I	RF	250+	PM Plus Story Books	Rigby
Kite, The	D	RF	59	My First Reader	Grolier
Kite, The	J	RF	468	Springboard	Wright Group/McGraw Hill
Kites	I	I	166	Explorations	Okapi Educational Materials
Kites	I	I	166	Explorations	Eleanor Curtain Publishing
Kites	C	RF	41	Joy Readers	Pearson Learning Group
Kites	C	RF	42	Ling, Bettina	Scholastic
Kites	N	I	250+	Literacy 2000	Rigby
Kites	B	F	41	Phonics and Friends	Hampton Brown
Kites	O	I	250+	PM Nonfiction-Emerald	Rigby
Kites, The	B	RF	36	Sails	Rigby
Kitesurfing	O	I	250+	Sails	Rigby
Kit's Castle	L	RF	250+	Storyteller-Shooting Stars	Wright Group/McGraw Hill
Kit's Wilderness	Y	RF	250+	Almond, David	Random House
Kitten Castle	K	RF	250+	Math Matters	Kane Press
Kitten Chased a Fly	C	RF	57	Windmill Books	Wright Group/McGraw Hill
Kitten Crowd	O	RF	250+	Baglio, Ben M.	Scholastic
Kitten for Kate, A	E	RF	137	On Our Way to English	Rigby
Kitten in the Cold	Q	RF	250+	Baglio, Ben M.	Scholastic
Kitten Is a Baby Cat, A	D	I	64	Blevins, Wiley	Scholastic
Kitten That Won First Prize, The	Q	RF	250+	Baglio, Ben M.	Scholastic
Kitten, The	A	RF	40	Sun Sprouts	ETA/Cuisenaire
Kittens	LB	I	32	Bright Baby	Priddy Books
Kittens	B	RF	33	Curry, Don L.	Scholastic
Kittens	G	I	107	Discovery Links	Newbridge
Kittens	J	I	181	Let's Read About Pets	Weekly Reader Publishing
Kittens	C	I	87	Leveled Literacy Intervention/ Blue System	Heinemann
Kittens	C	RF	22	Literacy 2000	Rigby
Kittens	E	I	32	Pair-It Turn and Learn	Steck-Vaughn
Kittens in the Kitchen	Q	RF	250+	Daniels, Lucy	Barron's Educational
Kitty and the Birds	C	F	64	PM Story Books	Rigby
Kitty Cat	C	RF	57	PM Plus Story Books	Rigby
Kitty Cat and Fat Cat	D	F	98	PM Plus Story Books	Rigby
Kitty Cat and the Bird	C	RF	78	PM Stars	Rigby
Kitty Cat and the Fish	D	F	73	PM Plus Story Books	Rigby
Kitty Cat and the Paint Can	F	F	165	PM Plus Story Books	Rigby
Kitty Cat Plays Inside	E	F	134	PM Plus Story Books	Rigby
Kitty Cat Runs up a Tree	E	F	134	PM Stars	Rigby
Kitty Goes on Vacation	I	RF	354	Rigby Flying Colors	Rigby
Kitty Goes Splash	E	RF	112	Books for Young Learners	Richard C. Owen
Kitty's Cuddles	I	F	108	Cabrera, Jane	Holiday House
Kitzikuba	G	F	198	Story Basket	Wright Group/McGraw Hill
Klondike Gold Rush, The	S	I	250+	A First Book	Franklin Watts
Klutzy Cat, The	M	F	250+	Storyteller Summer Skies	Wright Group/McGraw Hill
Knee Knock Rise	S	F	250+	Babbitt, Natalie	Farrar, Straus, & Giroux
Knife, The	N	RF	250+	Orbit Chapter Books	Pacific Learning
Knight	X	I	250+	Eyewitness Books	DK Publishing
Knight at Dawn, The	M	F	250+	Osborne, Mary Pope	Random House

* Collection of short stories   # Graphic text
^ Mature content with lower level text demands

JK

TITLE	LEVEL	GENRE	WORD COUNT	AUTHOR / SERIES	PUBLISHER / DISTRIBUTOR
Knight in Armor, A	U	I	1224	Vocabulary Readers	Houghton Mifflin Harcourt
Knight in Armor, A	U	I	1224	Vocabulary Readers/CA	Houghton Mifflin Harcourt
Knight in Armor, A	U	I	1224	Vocabulary Readers/TX	Houghton Mifflin Harcourt
Knightly News	P	RF	250+	Kenna, Anna	Pacific Learning
Knights	T	I	250+	Warriors of History	Capstone Press
Knights & Armor	Q	I	250+	Worldwise	Franklin Watts
Knight's Castle	T	F	250+	Eager, Edward	Harcourt
Knights Don't Teach Piano	M	F	250+	Dadey, Debbie; Jones, Marcia Thornton	Scholastic
Knights in Shining Armor	O	I	250+	Gibbons, Gail	Little Brown and Company
Knights of the Kitchen Table	P	F	250+	Scieszka, Jon	Penguin Group
#Knights of the Lunch Table, The: Dodgeball Chronicles	T	F	250+	Cammuso, Frank	Scholastic
Knit, Knit, Knit, Knit	J	F	250+	Literacy 2000	Rigby
Knitting for Fun!	S	I	250+	For Fun! Crafts	Compass Point Books
Knitting for Penguins	J	I	179	Storyteller	Wright Group/McGraw Hill
Knitting of Elizabeth Amelia, The	N	F	250+	Gauch, Patricia Lee	Henry Holt & Co.
Knitty Kitty	K	F	158	Elliott, David	Candlewick Press
Knitwits	Q	RF	250+	Taylor, William	Scholastic
Knobby Knuckles, Knobby Knees	I	F	236	Sunshine	Wright Group/McGraw Hill
Knock! Knock!	K	RF	250+	Carter, Jackie	Scholastic
Knock, Knock	B	F	22	Kaleidoscope Collection	Hameray Publishing Group
Knock, Knock	E	RF	96	Leveled Readers	Houghton Mifflin Harcourt
Knock, Knock	C	F	56	Little Celebrations	Pearson Learning Group
Knock, Knock!	I	TL	388	Red Rocket Readers	Flying Start Books
*Knot in the Grain (and Other Stories)	X	F	250+	McKinley, Robin	HarperTrophy
Knots in My Yo-yo String: The Autobiography of a Kid	U	B	250+	Spinelli, Jerry	Alfred A. Knopf
Knots on a Counting Rope	P	RF	250+	Martin, Jr., B.; Archambault, J.	Henry Holt & Co.
Know Where to Go	M	I	250+	Pacific Literacy	Pacific Learning
Know Your Birthday Manners	D	F	38	Instant Readers	Harcourt School Publishers
Know Your Noodles	K	I	115	Gear Up!	Wright Group/McGraw Hill
Know-Nothing Birthday, A	K	RF	250+	Spirn, Michele Sobel	HarperTrophy
Know-Nothings, The	K	RF	250+	Spirn, Michele Sobel	HarperTrophy
Knucklehead: Tall Tales & Mostly True Stories About Growing Up Scieszka	R	B	250+	Scieszka, Jon	Viking/Penguin
Knuffle Bunny	K	RF	212	Willems, Mo	Scholastic
Knuffle Bunny Free: An Unexpected Diversion	K	RF	250+	Willems, Mo	HarperCollins
Koala Bears	D	I	37	Rosen Real Readers	Rosen Publishing Group
Koala Is Not a Bear, A	P	I	250+	Crabapples	Crabtree
Koala Joey Grows Up, A	K	I	728	Baby Animals	Carolrhoda Books
Koalas	N	I	250+	A New True Book	Children's Press
Koalas	J	I	166	Australian Animals	Capstone Press
Koalas	O	I	2111	Early Bird Nature Books	Lerner Publishing Group
Koalas	R	I	250+	Explorer Books-Pathfinder	National Geographic
Koalas	P	I	250+	Explorer Books-Pioneer	National Geographic
Koalas	E	I	36	Literacy 2000	Rigby
Koalas	F	I	45	Pebble Books	Capstone Press
Kobe Bryant	P	B	1474	Amazing Athletes	Lerner Publishing Group
Kobe Bryant	T	B	250+	Sports Heroes	Red Brick Learning
Koi's Python	P	RF	250+	Moore, Miriam	Hyperion
Koko Communicates	O	I	822	Leveled Readers	Houghton Mifflin Harcourt
Koko Communicates	O	I	822	Leveled Readers/CA	Houghton Mifflin Harcourt
Koko Communicates	O	I	822	Leveled Readers/TX	Houghton Mifflin Harcourt

JK

TITLE	LEVEL	GENRE	WORD COUNT	AUTHOR / SERIES	PUBLISHER / DISTRIBUTOR
Komodo Dragons	R	I	250+	Predators in the Wild	Red Brick Learning
Komodo Dragons	A	I	33	Readlings/ Animals of Asia	American Reading Company
Komodo Dragons	K	I	161	Reptiles	Capstone Press
Komodo Dragons	I	I	238	Sails	Rigby
Komodo Dragons	R	I	250+	Theme Sets	National Geographic
^Komodo Dragons on the Hunt	N	I	250+	Killer Animals	Capstone Press
Kon-Tiki	Z+	I	250+	Heyerdahl, Thor	Simon & Schuster
Kon-Tiki, The	O	I	1201	Leveled Readers	Houghton Mifflin Harcourt
Kon-Tiki, The	O	I	1201	Leveled Readers/CA	Houghton Mifflin Harcourt
Kon-Tiki, The	O	I	1201	Leveled Readers/TX	Houghton Mifflin Harcourt
#Kooks in the Cafeteria: Comic Guy	N	RF	250+	Roland, Timothy	Scholastic
Kori Bustard	L	I	250+	A Day in the Life: Grassland Animals	Heinemann Library
Korka the Mighty Elf	H	F	250+	Rigby Literacy	Rigby
Korka the Mighty Elf	H	F	250+	Rigby Star	Rigby
Korky Paul: Biography of an Illustrator	M	B	250+	Discovery World	Rigby
Koya DeLaney and the Good Girl Blues	P	RF	250+	Greenfield, Eloise	Scholastic
Krakus and the Dragon: A Polish Folktale	J	TL	250+	Leveled Readers Language Support	Houghton Mifflin Harcourt
Kristen: The Clique Summer Collection	X	RF	250+	Harrison, Lisi	Little Brown and Company
Kristy and the Walking Disaster	O	RF	250+	Martin, Ann M.	Scholastic
Kudzu Invasion, The	T	I	1438	Reading Street	Pearson
#Kung Fu Masters	U	F	12258	Twisted Journeys	Graphic Universe
#Kung Fu Puzzle, The: A Mystery with Time and Temperature	P	RF	2755	Manga Math Mysteries	Graphic Universe
^Kurt Cobain	Z	B	250+	Rock Music Library	Capstone Press
Kwanza	J	I	143	Holidays and Celebrations	Capstone Press
Kwanzaa	Q	I	250+	Celebrate!	Capstone Press
Kwanzaa	O	I	250+	Chocolate, Deborah M. Newton	Children's Press
Kwanzaa	K	I	247	Holidays and Festivals	Heinemann Library
Kwanzaa	O	I	1518	On My Own Holidays	Lerner Publishing Group
Kwanzaa	K	I	225	Visions	Wright Group/McGraw Hill
Kwasi: A Storysong	J	RF	250+	Greetings	Rigby
Kyle's First Kwanzaa	L	RF	250+	Little Celebrations	Pearson Learning Group
Kylie Kangaroo's Karate Kickers	J	F	590	Animal Antics A to Z	Kane Press
Kylie the Carnival Fairy: Rainbow Magic	L	F	250+	Meadows, Daisy	Scholastic

* Collection of short stories   # Graphic text
^ Mature content with lower level text demands

TITLE	LEVEL	GENRE	WORD COUNT	AUTHOR / SERIES	PUBLISHER / DISTRIBUTOR
L	LB	I	14	Readlings	American Reading Company
L8r, g8r	Z+	RF	250+	Myracle, Lauren	Amulet Books
La Causa: The Migrant Farmworkers' Story	U	I	250+	deRuiz, Dana Catharine	Steck-Vaughn
La Mariposa	P	RF	250+	Jimenez, Franciso	Scholastic
La Salle: La Salle and the Mississippi River	U	B	250+	Exploring the World	Compass Point Books
Labor Day	J	I	106	American Holidays	Lerner Publishing Group
Labor Day	Q	I	250+	Holiday Histories	Heinemann
Labor Day	M	I	203	Holidays and Festivals	Heinemann Library
Labor Day	L	I	125	National Holidays	Red Brick Learning
Labracadabra	K	F	250+	Nelson, Jessie & Hopkins, Karen Leigh	Viking/Penguin
Labradoodles	R	I	250+	All About Dogs	Capstone Press
Labrador Retrievers	R	I	250+	All About Dogs	Capstone Press
Labrador Retrievers Are the Best!	Q	I	1794	The Best Dogs Ever	Lerner Publishing Group
Labradors	I	I	157	Dogs	Capstone Press
Lacey's Loud Voice	L	RF	589	Leveled Readers	Houghton Mifflin Harcourt
Lacrosse Face-Off	P	RF	250+	Christopher, Matt	Little Brown and Company
Lacrosse Firestorm	Q	RF	250+	Christopher, Matt	Little Brown and Company
Lacrosse for Fun!	S	I	250+	Sports for Fun!	Compass Point Books
Lad Who Went to the North Wind, The	J	F	250+	Bookshop	Mondo Publishing
LaDainian Tomlinson	P	B	2203	Amazing Athletes	Lerner Publishing Group
Ladders	G	I	162	Sails	Rigby
Ladies and Gentlemen	G	RF	120	Early Readers	Compass Point Books
*Ladies First	U	B	250+	Rappaport, Ken	Peachtree
Ladies of the Lake, The: Gilda Joyce	W	F	250+	Allison, Jennifer	Puffin Books
Lady Bird Johnson	Q	B	250+	Simon, Charnan	Children's Press
Lady Liberty	J	I	229	Twig	Wright Group/McGraw Hill
Lady Liberty: A Biography	T	B	250+	Rappaport, Doreen	Candlewick Press
Lady Lollipop	P	F	250+	King-Smith, Dick	Candlewick Press
Lady Lupin's Book of Etiquette	L	F	229	Cole, Babette	Peachtree
Lady Macbeth's Daughter	Z+	F	250+	Klein, Lisa	Bloomsbury Children's Books
Lady Red Rose and the Woods	S	RF	2621	Reading Street	Pearson
Lady with the Alligator Purse	F	F	218	Wescott, Nadine Bernard	Little Brown and Company
Lady with the Hat, The	Z	HF	250+	Orlev, Uri	Penguin Group
Ladybug	N	I	250+	Life Cycles	Creative Teaching Press
Ladybug and the Cricket, The	J	F	388	Leveled Literacy Intervention/ Blue System	Heinemann
Ladybug and the Legislature, The	O	I	484	Independent Readers Social Studies	Houghton Mifflin Harcourt
Ladybug, Ladybug	D	I	118	Rigby Flying Colors	Rigby
Ladybug, The	O	I	250+	Crewe, Sabrina	Steck-Vaughn
Ladybug, The	O	I	250+	Exploring History & Geography	Rigby
Ladybugs	K	I	232	Ashley, Susan/Let's Read About Insects	Weekly Reader Publishing
Ladybugs	E	I	99	Bonnell, Kris/About	Reading Reading Books
Ladybugs	G	I	98	Bugs, Bugs, Bugs	Red Brick Learning
Ladybugs	D	I	42	Insects	Capstone Press
Ladybugs	F	I	163	Leveled Readers	Houghton Mifflin Harcourt
Ladybugs	F	I	163	Leveled Readers/CA	Houghton Mifflin Harcourt
Ladybugs	F	I	163	Leveled Readers/TX	Houghton Mifflin Harcourt
Ladybugs	N	I	250+	Minibeasts	Franklin Watts
Ladybugs	N	I	250+	Nature's Friends	Compass Point Books
Ladybugs: Red, Fiery, and Bright	M	I	735	Posada, Mia	Carolrhoda Books
Lady's Big Surprise: Lucky Foot Stable Series	R	RF	36261	Dawson, JoAnn S.	Sourcebooks

TITLE	LEVEL	GENRE	WORD COUNT	AUTHOR / SERIES	PUBLISHER / DISTRIBUTOR
^Laggan Lard Butts	V	RF	250+	Orca Currents	Orca Books
Lake and Pond Food Webs	Q	I	2205	Early Bird Food Webs	Lerner Publishing Group
Lake Critter Journal	O	RF	250+	Little Celebrations	Pearson Learning Group
Lake Life	Q	I	250+	Orbit Chapter Books	Pacific Learning
Lake of Secrets	V	RF	250+	Little, Lael	Henry Holt & Co.
Lake of Souls, The: The Saga of Darren Shan	Y	F	250+	Shan, Darren	Little Brown and Company
Lake of Stars, The	F	F	248	Storyworlds	Heinemann
Lake, The	G	I	53	Windows on Literacy	National Geographic
Lakes	H	I	240	Rigby Flying Colors	Rigby
Lamb in the Laundry	Q	RF	250+	Baglio, Ben M.	Scholastic
Lamb Lessons	O	RF	250+	Baglio, Ben M.	Scholastic
Lamb Who Came for Dinner, The	M	F	250+	Smallman, Steve	Scholastic
^Lamborghini	O	I	250+	Fast Cars	Capstone Press
Lamborghinis	T	I	250+	High Performance	Red Brick Learning
Lamby's Breakfast	D	RF	105	PM Photo Stories	Rigby
Lamp from the Warlock's Tomb, The	S	F	250+	Bellairs, John	Puffin Books
Lampfish of Twill, The	U	F	250+	Lisle, Janet Taylor	Scholastic
Lan Xang, Kingdom of the Million Elephants	Y	I	2056	Leveled Readers Social Studies	Houghton Mifflin Harcourt
Lana and Miguel's Park	J	RF	381	Leveled Readers	Houghton Mifflin Harcourt
Lana and Miguel's Park	J	RF	381	Leveled Readers/CA	Houghton Mifflin Harcourt
Lana and Miguel's Park	J	RF	381	Leveled Readers/TX	Houghton Mifflin Harcourt
Lana Llama's Little Lamb	J	F	638	Animal Antics A to Z	Kane Press
Lance Armstrong	P	B	2052	Amazing Athletes	Lerner Publishing Group
Lance Armstrong	L	I	444	Leveled Readers	Houghton Mifflin Harcourt
Lance Armstrong	L	I	444	Leveled Readers/CA	Houghton Mifflin Harcourt
Lance Armstrong	L	I	444	Leveled Readers/TX	Houghton Mifflin Harcourt
Lance Armstrong	U	B	250+	Sports Heroes and Legends	Lerner Publishing Group
Lance Armstrong: Champion for Life!	S	B	250+	High Five Reading	Red Brick Learning
Land	C	I	12	Geography	Lerner Publishing Group
Land	D	I	50	Time for Kids	Teacher Created Materials
Land and Water	K	I	106	Independent Readers Social Studies	Houghton Mifflin Harcourt
Land and Water of the United States, The: A Dictionary,	K	I	219	Literacy by Design	Rigby
Land Around Us, The	J	I	249	Explorations	Okapi Educational Materials
Land Around Us, The	J	I	249	Explorations	Eleanor Curtain Publishing
Land I Lost, The	P	I	250+	Nhuong, Huynh Quang	HarperTrophy
*Land of Big Dreams, A: Voices of Courage in America	T	B	2092	Waldman, Neil	Millbrook Press
Land of Opportunity, The	T	I	2550	Reading Street	Pearson
Land of the Dragons	P	I	250+	Orbit Chapter Books	Pacific Learning
Land of the Great Big "No!"	L	RF	250+	Trussell-Cullen, Alan	Pearson Learning Group
Land Predators of North America	T	I	250+	Animals in Order	Franklin Watts
Land, The	Z	HF	250+	Taylor, Mildred D.	Penguin Group
Land: Earth Matters	L	I	250+	Bookworms	Marshall Cavendish
Landforms	V	I	250+	Mission Science	Compass Point Books
Landforms	T	I	250+	Pair-It Books	Steck-Vaughn
Landry News, The	R	RF	250+	Clements, Andrew	Simon & Schuster
Lands of Ice and Snow	Q	I	250+	InfoQuest	Rigby
Lands of Mystery	Z	I	6907	The Unexplained	Lerner Publishing Group
Lands of Rock	Q	I	250+	InfoQuest	Rigby
Lands of the Rainforest	T	I	1698	Leveled Readers Social Studies	Houghton Mifflin Harcourt
Landslides	R	I	1127	Leveled Readers	Houghton Mifflin Harcourt
Landslides	Q	I	250+	Natural Disasters	Red Brick Learning

L

* Collection of short stories   # Graphic text
^ Mature content with lower level text demands

TITLE	LEVEL	GENRE	WORD COUNT	AUTHOR / SERIES	PUBLISHER / DISTRIBUTOR
Landslides	M	I	609	Pull Ahead Books	Lerner Publishing Group
Landslides, Slumps & Creep	U	I	250+	A First Book	Franklin Watts
Langston Hughes	L	B	168	Vocabulary Readers	Houghton Mifflin Harcourt
Langston Hughes: An Illustrated Edition	X	B	250+	Meltzer, Milton	Millbrook Press
Langston Hughes: Young Black Poet	O	B	250+	Childhood of Famous Americans	Aladdin
Lara Ladybug	C	F	68	Rookie Readers	Children's Press
Lara Saves the Concert	J	RF	250+	Rigby Flying Colors	Rigby
Larabee	I	F	119	Luthardt, Kevin	Peachtree
Lara's Team	H	RF	287	Take Two Books	Wright Group/McGraw Hill
Large American Plant Eaters	N	I	321	Larkin, Bruce	Wilbooks
Lark Sings in Many Colors, The	T	TL	2159	Leveled Readers	Houghton Mifflin Harcourt
Lark Sings in Many Colors, The	T	TL	2159	Leveled Readers/CA	Houghton Mifflin Harcourt
Lark Sings in Many Colors, The	T	TL	2159	Leveled Readers/TX	Houghton Mifflin Harcourt
Larklight: A Rousing Tale of Dauntless Pluck in the Farthest Reaches of Space	Y	F	250+	Reeve, Philip	Bloomsbury Children's Books
Larry and Rita Dance	C	F	24	Brand New Readers	Candlewick Press
Larry and the Cookie	E	RF	56	Rookie Readers	Children's Press
Larry and the Crab	C	F	38	Brand New Readers	Candlewick Press
Larry the Singing Chicken	J	F	333	Leveled Readers	Houghton Mifflin Harcourt
Larry the Singing Chicken	J	F	333	Leveled Readers/CA	Houghton Mifflin Harcourt
Larry the Singing Chicken	J	F	333	Leveled Readers/TX	Houghton Mifflin Harcourt
Laser Shows	M	I	250+	Rigby Literacy	Rigby
Lasers	V	I	250+	Sunshine	Wright Group/McGraw Hill
Lassie Come-Home	T	RF	250+	Knight, Eric	Square Fish
Last Best Days of Summer, The	V	RF	250+	Hobbs, Valerie	Farrar, Straus, & Giroux
Last Book in the Universe, The	W	SF	250+	Philbrick, Rodman	Scholastic
Last Castaway, The	P	F	250+	Horse, Harry	Peachtree
Last Chance for Magic	P	F	250+	Chew, Ruth	Scholastic
Last Cowboys, The	P	F	250+	Horse, Harry	Peachtree
Last Dance, The	R	HF	250+	Deedy, Carmen Agra	Peachtree
Last Day Blues	M	RF	250+	Danneberg, Julie	Charlesbridge
Last Exit to Normal, The	Z+	RF	250+	Harmon, Michael	Alfred A. Knopf
Last Game, The	G	RF	89	Start to Read	School Zone
Last Gold Diggers, The	P	F	250+	Horse, Harry	Peachtree
Last Gosling Is Missing!, The	E	F	107	Bonnell, Kris	Reading Reading Books
Last Gosling, The	E	I	68	Bonnell, Kris	Reading Reading Books
Last Holiday Concert, The	R	RF	250+	Clements, Andrew	Aladdin Paperbacks
Last Inca Emperor, The	V	I	1642	Leveled Readers/CA	Houghton Mifflin Harcourt
Last Inca Emperor, The	V	I	1642	Leveled Readers/TX	Houghton Mifflin Harcourt
Last Inca Emporer, The	V	I	1642	Leveled Readers	Houghton Mifflin Harcourt
Last Laugh, The	WB	F	0	Aruego, Jose & Dewey, Ariane	Dial/Penguin
Last Look	P	RF	250+	Bulla, Clyde Robert	Puffin Books
Last of the Mohicans, The	W	HF	10650	Dominoes three	Oxford University Press
Last One in Is a Rotten Egg	J	RF	250+	Kessler, Leonard	HarperTrophy
Last Polar Bears, The	P	F	250+	Horse, Harry	Peachtree
Last Princess, The: The Story of Princess Ka'iulani of Hawaii	T	B	250+	Stanley, Fay	Aladdin Paperbacks
Last Puppy, The	K	F	244	Asch, Frank	Simon & Schuster
^Last Rider, The: The Final Days of the Pony Express	T	HF	3357	Gunderson, J.	Stone Arch Books
Last Summer with Maizon	Q	RF	250+	Woodson, Jacqueline	G.P. Putnam's Sons
Last Treasure, The	W	F	250+	Anderson, Janet S.	Puffin Books
Last-Minute Rescue	M	RF	250+	Rigby Rocket	Rigby
Late for School	L	F	250+	Reiss, Mike	Peachtree

L

TITLE	LEVEL	GENRE	WORD COUNT	AUTHOR / SERIES	PUBLISHER / DISTRIBUTOR
Late for School!	J	RF	251	Calmenson, Stephanie	Carolrhoda Books
Late for Soccer (Football)	G	RF	185	PM Story Books	Rigby
Late for the Party	H	RF	235	PM Photo Stories	Rigby
Late One Night	D	RF	97	Mader, Jan	Kaeden Books
Later	D	RF	106	Teacher's Choice Series	Pearson Learning Group
Later, Gator	R	RF	250+	Yep, Laurence	Hyperion
Later, Rover	G	RF	200	Ziefert, Harriet	Puffin Books
*Latino Legends: Hispanics in Major League Baseball	S	B	250+	High Five Reading	Red Brick Learning
Laugh Stand, The: Adventures in Humor	U	I	1597	Cleary, Brian P.	Millbrook Press
Laughing Cake, The	G	RF	89	Reading Corners	Pearson Learning Group
Laughing Hyena	I	F	250+	Lighthouse	Rigby
Laughing Place, The	K	F	250+	Story Steps	Rigby
Laughter Is the Best Medicine	P	I	250+	Literacy Tree	Rigby
Laundromat, The	D	RF	25	Sunshine	Wright Group/McGraw Hill
Laundromat, The	B	RF	25	Visions	Wright Group/McGraw Hill
Laundry Day	C	RF	28	Bebop Books	Lee & Low Books Inc.
Laura and Mr. Edwards	M	HF	250+	Wilder, Laura Ingalls	HarperTrophy
Laura and Nellie	M	HF	250+	Wilder, Laura Ingalls	HarperTrophy
Laura Bush	M	I	248	First Ladies	Capstone Press
Laura Ingalls Wilder	O	B	250+	Allen, Thomas B.	G.P. Putnam's Sons Books for Young Readers
Laura Ingalls Wilder	L	B	250+	Biography	Benchmark Education
Laura Ingalls Wilder	P	B	250+	Blair, Gwenda; Allen, Thomas	Lerner Publishing Group
Laura Ingalls Wilder	R	B	1477	Leveled Readers	Houghton Mifflin Harcourt
Laura Ingalls Wilder	R	B	1477	Leveled Readers/CA	Houghton Mifflin Harcourt
Laura Ingalls Wilder	R	B	1477	Leveled Readers/TX	Houghton Mifflin Harcourt
Laura Ingalls Wilder	M	B	1439	On My Own Biography	Lerner Publishing Group
Laura Ingalls Wilder	R	B	250+	Primary Source Readers	Teacher Created Materials
Laura Ingalls Wilder	N	B	326	Rookie Biographies	Children's Press
Laura Ingalls Wilder: A Biography	R	B	250+	Anderson, William	HarperTrophy
Laura Ingalls Wilder: An Author's Story	N	B	250+	Pair-It Books	Steck-Vaughn
Laura Ingalls Wilder: Author of the Little House Books	O	B	250+	Greene, Carol	Children's Press
Laura Ingalls Wilder: Growing Up in the Little House	P	B	250+	Giff, Patricia Reilly	Puffin Books
Laura's Ma	M	HF	250+	Wilder, Laura Ingalls	HarperTrophy
Laura's Pa	M	HF	250+	Wilder, Laura Ingalls	HarperTrophy
Lauren Helps Sammy	M	F	823	Leveled Readers	Houghton Mifflin Harcourt
Lauren Helps Sammy	M	F	823	Leveled Readers/CA	Houghton Mifflin Harcourt
Lauren Helps Sammy	M	F	817	Leveled Readers/TX	Houghton Mifflin Harcourt
Lauren Otter	N	F	772	Leveled Readers	Houghton Mifflin Harcourt
Lauren Otter	N	F	772	Leveled Readers/CA	Houghton Mifflin Harcourt
Lauren Otter	N	F	785	Leveled Readers/TX	Houghton Mifflin Harcourt
Lauren the Puppy Fairy: Rainbow Magic	L	F	250+	Meadows, Daisy	Scholastic
Lavender	O	RF	250+	Hesse, Karen	Henry Holt & Co.
Lavender the Library Cat	K	RF	418	Jellybeans	Rigby
Law and Order	K	I	250+	Spyglass Books	Compass Point Books
Lawn Boy	V	RF	250+	Paulsen, Gary	Scholastic
Lawn Boy Returns	V	RF	250+	Paulsen, Gary	Yearling Books
Layla, Queen of Hearts	O	RF	250+	Millard, Glenda	Farrar, Straus, & Giroux
Lazily, Crazily, Just a Bit Nasally: More about Adverbs	O	I	342	Words Are CATegorical	Millbrook Press
Lazy Bones Jones	P	F	250+	Orbit Chapter Books	Pacific Learning
Lazy Fox	I	F	268	Leveled Readers	Houghton Mifflin Harcourt

L

Organized Alphabetically by Title
Storable Database at www.fountasandpinnellleveledbooks.com

* Collection of short stories   # Graphic text
^ Mature content with lower level text demands

TITLE	LEVEL	GENRE	WORD COUNT	AUTHOR / SERIES	PUBLISHER / DISTRIBUTOR
Lazy Jackal, The	M	F	561	Sunshine	Wright Group/McGraw Hill
Lazy Lions, Lucky Lambs	M	RF	250+	Giff, Patricia Reilly	Bantam Books
Lazy Little Loafers	L	RF	250+	Orlean, Susan	Harry N. Abrams
Lazy Mary	D	RF	191	Story Box	Wright Group/McGraw Hill
Lazy Moon, The	I	F	242	Take Two Books	Wright Group/McGraw Hill
Lazy Pig, The	C	F	78	PM Story Books	Rigby
Lazy Sailor Sam	G	F	227	Sails	Rigby
Lazy Sloth	I	F	418	Sails	Rigby
LCAC Military Hovercraft, The	U	I	250+	Cross-Sections	Capstone Press
L'Chaim!: To Jewish Life in America!	Z	I	250+	Rubin, Susan Goldman	Harry N. Abrams
Leader for All, A	U	B	1500	Leveled Readers/CA	Houghton Mifflin Harcourt
Leader for All, A	U	B	1500	Leveled Readers	Houghton Mifflin Harcourt
Leader for All, A	U	B	1500	Leveled Readers/TX	Houghton Mifflin Harcourt
Leader of the Pack	U	RF	2770	Leveled Readers	Houghton Mifflin Harcourt
Leader of the Pack	U	RF	2770	Leveled Readers/CA	Houghton Mifflin Harcourt
Leader of the Pack	U	RF	2770	Leveled Readers/TX	Houghton Mifflin Harcourt
Leader of the Pack	L	RF	250+	Martha Speaks	Houghton Mifflin Harcourt
Leaders Can Help	D	I	81	Early Explorers	Benchmark Education
Leaders of Middle East	U	B	250+	Primary Source Readers	Teacher Created Materials
Leaders of the People	U	B	250+	Real Lives	Troll Associates
Leaders: People Who Make a Difference	R	B	250+	You Are There	Children's Press
Leading the Way	P	B	250+	InfoQuest	Rigby
Leaf	WB	F	0	King, Stephen Michael	Roaring Brook Press
Leaf Boats, The	E	RF	132	PM Plus Story Books	Rigby
Leaf Jumpers	J	RF	207	Gerber, Carole	Charlesbridge
Leaf Rain	F	RF	82	Book Bank	Wright Group/McGraw Hill
Leaf Raker, The	M	RF	250+	Voyages	SRA/McGraw Hill
Leafcutter Ant, The	H	I	77	Vocabulary Readers	Houghton Mifflin Harcourt
Leafcutter Ants	J	I	425	Sails	Rigby
Leaf-Cutter Ants	M	I	462	Springboard	Wright Group/McGraw Hill
Leafy Sea Dragons	F	I	183	Sun Sprouts	ETA/Cuisenaire
Leanin' Dog, The	T	RF	250+	Nuzum, K.A.	HarperCollins
Leap Day	Z	RF	250+	Mass, Wendy	Little Brown and Company
Leap Frog	WB	RF	0	Ready to Read	Pacific Learning
Leaping Grasshoppers	K	I	389	Pull Ahead Books	Lerner Publishing Group
Leaping Lena	L	F	250+	Rigby Literacy	Rigby
Leaping Lizards	M	I	250+	Early Connections	Benchmark Education
Leaps and Bounds	R	I	250+	WorldScapes	ETA/Cuisenaire
Learn to Estimate	M	I	408	Early Explorers	Benchmark Education
Learn to Write Your Numbers	I	I	260	Priddy, Roger	Priddy Books
Learning About Alabama	O	I	188	Larkin, Bruce	Wilbooks
Learning About Art	K	I	401	Rigby Flying Colors	Rigby
Learning About Bears	L	I	249	Larkin, Bruce	Wilbooks
Learning About Clouds	D	I	18	Rosen Real Readers	Rosen Publishing Group
Learning About Leaves	D	I	37	Rosen Real Readers	Rosen Publishing Group
Learning About Logerheads	P	I	250+	In Step Readers	Rigby
Learning About Missouri	O	I	212	Larkin, Bruce	Wilbooks
Learning about Ocean Animals	S	I	250+	Reading Expeditions	National Geographic
Learning About Rain	E	I	26	Rosen Real Readers	Rosen Publishing Group
Learning About Sand	E	I	42	Rosen Real Readers	Rosen Publishing Group
Learning About Snow	F	I	42	Rosen Real Readers	Rosen Publishing Group
Learning About the Library	I	I	164	Rosen Real Readers	Rosen Publishing Group
Learning from Fossils	P	I	870	Leveled Readers	Houghton Mifflin Harcourt
Learning from Fossils	Q	I	3234	Leveled Readers Science	Houghton Mifflin Harcourt

L

TITLE	LEVEL	GENRE	WORD COUNT	AUTHOR / SERIES	PUBLISHER / DISTRIBUTOR
Learning from Fossils	P	I	870	Leveled Readers/CA	Houghton Mifflin Harcourt
Learning from Fossils	P	I	870	Leveled Readers/TX	Houghton Mifflin Harcourt
Learning from Ms. Liang	T	RF	2968	Reading Street	Pearson
Learning New Things	H	RF	156	Foundations	Wright Group/McGraw Hill
Learning the Rules	I	I	187	Early Explorers	Benchmark Education
Learning to Play the Game	R	RF	2614	Reading Street	Pearson
Learning to Swim	I	RF	234	My World	Steck-Vaughn
Leather Boat, The	V	B	250+	WorldScapes	ETA/Cuisenaire
Leatherback Sea Turtle, The	E	I	93	Bonnell, Kris/Animals in Danger	Reading Reading Books
Leave It to Beavers	F	RF	102	Leveled Readers Science	Houghton Mifflin Harcourt
Leave, Bees!	K	TL	250+	MacDonald, Margaret Read & Vathanaprida, Supaporn & Tossa, Wajuppa	Hampton Brown
Leaves	C	I	34	Explorations	Okapi Educational Materials
Leaves	C	I	34	Explorations	Eleanor Curtain Publishing
Leaves	C	I	29	Hoenecke, Karen	Kaeden Books
Leaves	I	I	250+	Momentum Literacy Program	Troll Associates
Leaves	E	I	29	Parts of Plants	Lerner Publishing Group
Leaves	K	I	236	Pebble Books	Capstone Press
Leaves	I	I	130	Plant Parts	Capstone Press
Leaves	H	I	155	Spot the Difference	Heinemann Library
Leaves in Fall	F	I	86	All About Fall	Capstone Press
Leaves, Fruits, Seeds, and Roots	C	I	26	Pacific Literacy	Pacific Learning
Leaving a Mark - Dinosaur Discoveries	U	I	250+	Connectors	Pacific Learning
Leaving Glorytown: One Boy's Stuggle Under Castro	Z	B	250+	Calcines, Eduardo F.	Farrar, Straus, & Giroux
Leaving Home	N	F	727	Gear Up!	Wright Group/McGraw Hill
Leaving Home	R	I	250+	InfoQuest	Rigby
*Leaving Home	Z	RF	250+	Keillor, Garrison	Penguin Group
Leaving Home	K	RF	509	Pair-It Turn and Learn	Steck-Vaughn
*Leaving Home: 15 Distinguished Authors Explore Personal Journeys	Z	RF	250+	Rochman, Hazel; McCampbell, Darlene	HarperTrophy
Leaving the Bellweathers	T	F	250+	Venuti, Kristin Clark	Egmont USA
Lebanon: A Question and Answer Book	P	I	250+	Questions & Answers: Countries	Capstone Press
LeBron James	Q	B	1791	Amazing Athletes	Lerner Publishing Group
LeBron James: King of the Court	V	B	250+	High Five Reading	Capstone Press
LeBron James: Revised Edition	Q	B	1840	Amazing Athletes	Lerner Publishing Group
Leeches	P	I	1861	Early Bird Nature Books	Lerner Publishing Group
Left and Right	C	I	43	Location	Lerner Publishing Group
Left Behind	L	RF	250+	Carrick, Carol	Clarion
Left Behind: An Alaska Legend of Betrayal, Courage, and Survival	U	TL	250+	Edge	Hampton Brown
Left for Dead!: Lincoln Hall's Story of Survival	S	I	250+	True Tales of Survival	Capstone Press
Left Hand of Darkness, The	Z+	SF	250+	Le Guin, Ursula K.	Ace Books
Left or Right	H	I	154	Rehm, Karl & Koike, Kay	Scholastic
Left, Right	G	RF	182	Sunshine	Wright Group/McGraw Hill
Leftovers, The: Catch Flies!	N	RF	250+	Howard, Tristan	Scholastic
Leftovers, The: Fast Break	N	RF	250+	Howard, Tristan	Scholastic
Leftovers, The: Get Jammed	N	RF	250+	Howard, Tristan	Scholastic
Leftovers, The: Reach Their Goal	N	RF	250+	Howard, Tristan	Scholastic
Leftovers, The: Strike Out!	N	RF	250+	Howard, Tristan	Scholastic
Leftovers, The: Use Their Heads!	N	RF	250+	Howard, Tristan	Scholastic
Legacy of Blood	Y	F	250+	Ford, Michael	Walker & Company
Legacy of the Holocaust, The	Z	I	250+	The Holocaust	Compass Point Books
Legend of Dirty Bert the Bandit, The	M	TL	250+	Lighthouse	Ginn & Co.

L

* Collection of short stories   # Graphic text
^ Mature content with lower level text demands

TITLE	LEVEL	GENRE	WORD COUNT	AUTHOR / SERIES	PUBLISHER / DISTRIBUTOR
Legend of Old Befana, The	M	TL	250+	DePaola, Tomie	Harcourt, Inc.
Legend of Scarface, The	Q	I	900	Books for Young Learners	Richard C. Owen
#Legend of Sleepy Hollow, The	T	F	250+	Hoena, Blake A. (Retold)	Stone Arch Books
Legend of the Bluebonnet, The	O	TL	250+	DePaola, Tomie	Scholastic
Legend of the Bluebonnet, The	N	TL	250+	On Our Way to English	Rigby
Legend of the Golden Snail, The	N	F	250+	Base, Graeme	Harry N. Abrams
Legend of the Hummingbird, The	K	TL	250+	Folk Tales	Mondo Publishing
Legend of the Indian Paintbrush, The	O	TL	250+	DePaola, Tomie	Scholastic
Legend of the Lonesome Bear, The	M	TL	2047	Take Two Books	Wright Group/McGraw Hill
Legend of the Red Bird, The	K	TL	389	Sunshine	Wright Group/McGraw Hill
Legend of the Underwater Cave, The	Q	RF	250+	Reading Safari	Mondo Publishing
Legendary Heroes	P	B	1448	Take Two Books	Wright Group/McGraw Hill
Legendary Places	N	I	250+	Wildcats	Wright Group/McGraw Hill
Legends	S	TL	250+	Goodman, R.; Pierce, R.; Wagner, Betty Jane	Houghton Mifflin Harcourt
*Legends of the Blues	T	B	2196	Reading Street	Pearson
*Legends of the Past	S	TL	4820	Take Two Books	Wright Group/McGraw Hill
Legends of the Wild West	R	B	250+	Storyteller-Autum Leaves	Wright Group/McGraw Hill
LEGO Toys	T	I	4953	A Great Idea	Norwood House Press
Legs	B	F	15	Gosset, Rachel; Ballinger, Margaret	Scholastic
Legs	D	I	21	Literacy 2000	Rigby
Legs	B	I	36	Sails	Rigby
Legs	LB	I	21	Twig	Wright Group/McGraw Hill
Legs	B	I	36	Windows on Literacy	National Geographic
Legs, Legs, Legs	C	I	36	Wonder World	Wright Group/McGraw Hill
Legs, No Legs	H	I	167	Sails	Rigby
Leif Eriksson	Q	B	250+	Biographies-Great Explorers	Capstone Press
Leif Eriksson	P	B	1419	On My Own Biography	Lerner Publishing Group
Leigh Ann's Civil War	Y	HF	250+	Rinaldi, Ann	Houghton Mifflin Harcourt
Lemon Tree, The	D	RF	28	Harry's Math Books	Outside the Box
Lemonade	C	I	27	Bonnell, Kris	Reading Reading Books
Lemonade	F	F	140	Learn to Read	Creative Teaching Press
Lemonade Crime, The	S	RF	250+	Davies, Jacqueline	Houghton Mifflin Harcourt
Lemonade for Gilbert	H	F	144	Gilbert the Pig	Pioneer Valley
Lemonade for Sale	D	F	36	Brand New Readers	Candlewick Press
Lemonade for Sale	K	RF	1343	Real Kids Readers	Millbrook Press
Lemonade Mouth	Z	RF	250+	Hughes, Mark Peter	Delacorte Press
Lemonade on the Double	H	RF	204	On Our Way to English	Rigby
Lemonade Stand, The	G	RF	148	City Stories	Rigby
Lemonade Stand, The	I	RF	357	Dominie Math Stories	Pearson Learning Group
Lemonade Stand, The	J	I	166	Early Connections	Benchmark Education
Lemonade Stand, The	L	RF	385	Leveled Readers	Houghton Mifflin Harcourt
Lemonade Stand, The	L	RF	385	Leveled Readers/CA	Houghton Mifflin Harcourt
Lemonade Stand, The	L	RF	385	Leveled Readers/TX	Houghton Mifflin Harcourt
Lemonade Trick, The	Q	RF	250+	Corbett, Scott	Scholastic
Lemonade War, The	S	RF	250+	Davies, Jacqueline	Sandpiper Books
Lemony Snicket: The Unauthorized Autobiography	W	F	250+	Snicket, Lemony	HarperCollins
Lemuel the Fool	M	TL	250+	Uhlberg, Myron	Peachtree
Lemur	L	I	250+	A Day in the Life: Rain Forest Animals	Heinemann Library
Lemurs	M	I	250+	The Wild World of Animals	Capstone Press
Lena's Garden	J	F	302	Leveled Readers	Houghton Mifflin Harcourt

L

TITLE	LEVEL	GENRE	WORD COUNT	AUTHOR / SERIES	PUBLISHER / DISTRIBUTOR
Lena's Garden	J	F	302	Leveled Readers/CA	Houghton Mifflin Harcourt
Lena's Garden	J	F	302	Leveled Readers/TX	Houghton Mifflin Harcourt
Lend a Hand	E	I	26	iOpeners	Pearson Learning Group
Lend a Hand	K	F	250+	Kratky, Lada	Hampton Brown
Lenny and Tweek	K	F	250+	Bookshop	Mondo Publishing
Len's Tomato Plant	L	RF	294	Leveled Readers	Houghton Mifflin Harcourt
Len's Tomato Plant	L	RF	294	Leveled Readers/CA	Houghton Mifflin Harcourt
Len's Tomato Plant	L	RF	294	Leveled Readers/TX	Houghton Mifflin Harcourt
Len's Tomatoes	L	RF	289	Leveled Readers	Houghton Mifflin Harcourt
Len's Tomatoes	L	RF	289	Leveled Readers/CA	Houghton Mifflin Harcourt
Len's Tomatoes	L	RF	289	Leveled Readers/TX	Houghton Mifflin Harcourt
Lenses and Light	V	I	250+	Literacy By Design	Rigby
Lentil	M	RF	250+	McCloskey, Robert	Scholastic
Leo and Lester	L	F	250+	Bookshop	Mondo Publishing
Leo and the Butterflies	K	I	250+	Bebop Books	Lee & Low Books Inc.
Leo and the School of Fish	K	F	393	Reading Street	Pearson
Leo the Fat Cat	K	RF	457	Red Rocket Readers	Flying Start Books
Leo the Late Bloomer	I	F	164	Kraus, Robert	Simon & Schuster
Leo, You Are a Star	I	RF	401	Rigby Flying Colors	Rigby
Leon and Bob	K	RF	250+	James, Simon	Candlewick Press
Leona Goes Home	N	F	952	Leveled Readers	Houghton Mifflin Harcourt
Leona Goes Home	N	F	952	Leveled Readers/CA	Houghton Mifflin Harcourt
Leona Goes Home	N	F	952	Leveled Readers/TX	Houghton Mifflin Harcourt
Leonard Bernstein	R	B	250+	Venezia, Mike	Children's Press
Leonardo and His Times	Y	I	250+	Eyewitness Books	DK Publishing
Leonardo Da Vinci	W	HF	250+	Augarde, Steve	Kingfisher
Leonardo Da Vinci	Z	B	250+	Krull, Kathleen	Scholastic
Leonardo da Vinci	U	B	1623	Leveled Readers	Houghton Mifflin Harcourt
Leonardo da Vinci	T	B	1776	Leveled Readers Science	Houghton Mifflin Harcourt
Leonardo da Vinci	U	B	1623	Leveled Readers/CA	Houghton Mifflin Harcourt
Leonardo da Vinci	U	B	1623	Leveled Readers/TX	Houghton Mifflin Harcourt
Leonardo da Vinci	S	B	250+	Masterpieces: Artists and Their Works	Capstone Press
Leona's Sneakers	M	RF	1691	In Step Readers	Rigby
Leon's Story	T	B	250+	Tillage, Leon Walter	Farrar, Straus, & Giroux
Leontyne Price: Opera Superstar	N	B	250+	Williams, Sylvia B.	Children's Press
Leopard Seal	L	I	250+	A Day in the Life: Polar Animals	Heinemann Library
Leopard Seals	R	I	2107	Animal Predators	Lerner Publishing Group
Leopards	I	I	119	African Animals	Capstone Press
Leopards	A	I	70	Readlings/ Predator Animals	American Reading Company
Leopards	K	I	343	Vocabulary Readers	Houghton Mifflin Harcourt
Leopards	K	I	343	Vocabulary Readers/CA	Houghton Mifflin Harcourt
Leo's Italian Lesson	R	RF	1041	Leveled Readers	Houghton Mifflin Harcourt
Leo's Italian Lesson	R	RF	1041	Leveled Readers/CA	Houghton Mifflin Harcourt
Leo's Tree	H	F	135	Pearson, Debora	Annick Press
Leprechauns Don't Play Basketball	M	F	250+	Dadey, Debbie; Jones, Marcia Thornton	Scholastic
LeRoy and the Old Man	Z+	RF	250+	Butterworth, W.E.	Scholastic
Les Paul: Master of the Electric Guitar	S	B	250+	Literacy By Design	Rigby
Leslie Ludel's Apple Strudel	M	RF	250+	Literacy by Design	Rigby
Lesson Before Dying, A	Z+	HF	250+	Gaines, Ernest J.	Vintage Books
Lesson for Martin Luther King Jr., A	K	B	250+	Childhood of Famous Americans	Aladdin
Lesson of Icarus, The	Q	TL	325	Reading Street	Pearson
Lesson, The	H	RF	133	Cummings, Pat	Scholastic

* Collection of short stories   # Graphic text
^ Mature content with lower level text demands

L

TITLE	LEVEL	GENRE	WORD COUNT	AUTHOR / SERIES	PUBLISHER / DISTRIBUTOR
Lessons About Lightning	N	I	850	Leveled Readers	Houghton Mifflin Harcourt
Lessons About Lightning	N	I	850	Leveled Readers/CA	Houghton Mifflin Harcourt
Lessons About Lightning	N	I	850	Leveled Readers/TX	Houghton Mifflin Harcourt
Lessons from Lester	J	F	250+	Rigby Rocket	Rigby
#Lessons in Science Safety with Max Axiom, Super Scientist	U	I	250+	Graphic Library	Capstone Press
Lester's Bedtime	B	F	39	Lester the Lion Series	Pioneer Valley
Lester's Haircut	I	F	250+	Lester the Lion Series	Pioneer Valley
Lester's Song	F	F	155	Lester the Lion Series	Pioneer Valley
Let Art Do the Talking	T	I	250+	Rigby Literacy	Rigby
Let It Begin Here!	S	HF	250+	Fradin, Dennis Brindell	Scholastic
Let It Rain!	I	I	257	Vocabulary Readers	Houghton Mifflin Harcourt
Let It Rain!	I	I	257	Vocabulary Readers/CA	Houghton Mifflin Harcourt
Let It Rain!	I	I	257	Vocabulary Readers/TX	Houghton Mifflin Harcourt
Let Me Help!	I	RF	451	Real Kids Readers	Millbrook Press
Let Me In	E	F	63	Potato Chip Books	American Reading Company
*Let Me In	I	TL	1814	Story Box	Wright Group/McGraw Hill
Let the Circle Be Unbroken	X	HF	250+	Taylor, Mildred D.	Penguin Group
Let the Fun Begin: Wacky What-Do-You-Get-Jokes, Playful Puns, and More	O	F	1793	Make Me Laugh!	Lerner Publishing Group
Let the Games Begin	T	I	250+	The News	Richard C. Owen
Let the Games Begin: History of the Olympics	S	I	979	Reading Street	Pearson
Let the River Run Silver Again!	V	I	250+	Burk, Sandy	The McDonald & Woodward Publishing Co.
Let's Make Pancakes	J	I	349	Red Rocket Readers	Flying Start Books
Let's All Dance!	G	I	148	Vocabulary Readers	Houghton Mifflin Harcourt
Let's Bake	G	I	195	Discovery Links	Newbridge
Let's Be Enemies	J	RF	250+	Sendak, Maurice	Harper & Row
Let's Be Friends	D	I	23	Pair-It Books	Steck-Vaughn
Let's Be Safe and Healthy	I	I	291	InfoTrek	ETA/Cuisenaire
Let's Brush Our Teeth	F	I	78	Rosen Real Readers	Rosen Publishing Group
Let's Build a Playground	O	I	250+	Myers, Edward	Pearson Learning Group
Let's Build a Tower	LB	RF	15	Literacy 2000	Rigby
Let's Camp at Crescent Lake	J	RF	262	Reading Street	Pearson
Let's Celebrate	T	I	250+	News Extra	Richard C. Owen
Let's Celebrate	C	I	33	Rise & Shine	Hampton Brown
Let's Clean Up	K	I	326	Gear Up!	Wright Group/McGraw Hill
Let's Clean Up!	H	F	181	Anderson, Peggy Perry	Houghton Mifflin Harcourt
Let's Climb!	A	I	19	Leveled Readers	Houghton Mifflin Harcourt
Let's Climb!	A	I	19	Leveled Readers/CA	Houghton Mifflin Harcourt
Let's Compare	K	I	567	In Step Readers	Rigby
Let's Dance	J	I	131	Gear Up!	Wright Group/McGraw Hill
Let's Do Karate!	I	I	119	Sports and Activities	Capstone Press
Let's Downhill Ski!	H	I	131	Sports and Activities	Capstone Press
Let's Draw!	F	I	21	Rosen Real Readers	Rosen Publishing Group
Let's Eat	D	I	110	Sails	Rigby
Let's Eat	E	RF	63	Teacher's Choice Series	Pearson Learning Group
Let's Eat in the Funny Zone	O	F	250+	The Funny Zone	Norwood House Press
Let's Eat!	M	RF	250+	Zamorano, Ana	Scholastic
Let's Eat: Foods of Our World	K	I	250+	Spyglass Books	Compass Point Books
Let's Explore Antarctica!	T	I	2356	Reading Street	Pearson
Let's Find Out about Money	O	I	250+	Barabas, Kathy	Scholastic
Let's Find Shapes	A	I	30	Gear Up!	Wright Group/McGraw Hill
Let's Get a Pet	F	RF	22	Jellybeans	Rigby

TITLE	LEVEL	GENRE	WORD COUNT	AUTHOR / SERIES	PUBLISHER / DISTRIBUTOR
Let's Get a Pup! Said Kate	L	RF	250+	Graham, Bob	Candlewick Press
Let's Get Dressed: What People Wear	K	I	250+	Spyglass Books	Compass Point Books
Let's Get Moving	M	I	250+	Literacy 2000	Rigby
Let's Get Set	D	RF	73	The Rowland Reading Program Library	Rowland Reading Foundation
Let's Get Those Stingers Out of Here!	L	RF	901	Springboard	Wright Group/McGraw Hill
Let's Get to Know the Incas	S	I	1264	Reading Street	Pearson
Let's Go	B	I	81	Early Connections	Benchmark Education
Let's Go	A	RF	32	Reading Corners	Pearson Learning Group
Let's Go	C	RF	30	Windmill Books	Wright Group/McGraw Hill
Let's Go Camping	A	I	56	Readlings	American Reading Company
Let's Go Camping	A	I	41	The Places I Go	American Reading Company
Let's Go Camping	E	I	44	Vocabulary Readers	Houghton Mifflin Harcourt
*Let's Go Camping and Other Stories	H	F	250+	New Way Literature	Steck-Vaughn
Let's Go Camping!	L	I	692	Rigby Flying Colors	Rigby
Let's Go Camping!	H	I	114	Sports and Activities	Capstone Press
Let's Go Downtown	F	RF	85	City Stories	Rigby
Let's Go Fishing	M	RF	250+	Voyages	SRA/McGraw Hill
Let's Go Have Fun!	P	I	1516	Reading Street	Pearson
Let's Go in the Funny Zone	O	F	250+	The Funny Zone	Norwood House Press
Let's Go Marching	E	RF	94	Ready Readers	Pearson Learning Group
Let's Go Rock Climbing!	I	I	128	Vocabulary Readers	Houghton Mifflin Harcourt
Let's Go Rock Collecting	N	I	250+	Soar To Success	Houghton Mifflin Harcourt
Let's Go Shopping	C	I	34	Rise & Shine	Hampton Brown
Let's Go Shopping!	G	I	120	Pair-It Turn and Learn	Steck-Vaughn
Let's Go Shopping!	N	I	250+	Rigby Focus	Rigby
Let's Go Skating! (After-School Sports Club)	G	RF	256	Heller, Alyson	Aladdin
Let's Go to a Fair	F	I	139	Welcome Books	Children's Press
Let's Go to a Museum	E	RF	181	Blevins, Wiley	Scholastic
Let's go to Mars	N	I	782	Big Cat	Pacific Learning
Let's Go to the Bank	I	I	233	Rosen Real Readers	Rosen Publishing Group
Let's Go to the Store!	LB	I	15	Reach	National Geographic
Let's Go to the Supermarket	I	I	198	Rosen Real Readers	Rosen Publishing Group
Let's Go to the Theater!	N	I	320	Vocabulary Readers	Houghton Mifflin Harcourt
Let's Go!	B	I	28	On Our Way to English	Rigby
Let's Go!	L	I	250+	Trackers	Pacific Learning
Let's Go!	A	I	30	Vocabulary Readers	Houghton Mifflin Harcourt
Let's Go, Dear Dragon	E	F	293	Dear Dragon	Norwood House Press
Let's Go, Philadelphia!	M	RF	250+	Giff, Patricia Reilly	Bantam Books
Let's Grab It!	D	RF	60	Leveled Readers	Houghton Mifflin Harcourt
Let's Graph	M	I	239	Yellow Umbrella Books	Capstone Press
Let's Graph It!	S	I	250+	Rosen Real Readers	Rosen Publishing Group
Let's Grow!	C	I	36	Reach	National Geographic
Let's Have a Play	F	RF	250+	Let's Play	Norwood House Press
Let's Have a Swim	C	F	74	Sunshine	Wright Group/McGraw Hill
Let's Have Fun!	A	I	20	Vocabulary Readers	Houghton Mifflin Harcourt
Let's Have Fun!	A	I	20	Vocabulary Readers/CA	Houghton Mifflin Harcourt
Let's Have Lunch	H	I	159	The Rowland Reading Program Library	Rowland Reading Foundation
Let's Hear It for Ears!	L	I	501	Avenues	Hampton Brown
Let's Hibernate	J	RF	223	The King School Series	Townsend Press
Let's Jump Rope	D	RF	83	The King School Series	Townsend Press
Let's Look After Our World	L	I	250+	Sunshine	Wright Group/McGraw Hill
Let's Look at Animal Bottoms	H	I	131	Looking At Animal Parts	Capstone Press

L

* Collection of short stories   # Graphic text
^ Mature content with lower level text demands

TITLE	LEVEL	GENRE	WORD COUNT	AUTHOR / SERIES	PUBLISHER / DISTRIBUTOR
Let's Look at Animal Ears	H	I	132	Looking At Animal Parts	Capstone Press
Let's Look at Animal Eyes	H	I	137	Looking At Animal Parts	Capstone Press
Let's Look at Animal Feathers	H	I	136	Looking At Animal Parts	Capstone Press
Let's Look at Animal Feet	H	I	113	Looking At Animal Parts	Capstone Press
Let's Look at Animal Legs	H	I	124	Looking At Animal Parts	Capstone Press
Let's Look at Animal Noses	H	I	134	Looking At Animal Parts	Capstone Press
Let's Look at Animal Tails	I	I	129	Looking At Animal Parts	Capstone Press
Let's Look at Animal Teeth	H	I	133	Looking At Animal Parts	Capstone Press
Let's Look at Animal Wings	H	I	137	Looking At Animal Parts	Capstone Press
Let's Look at Armadillos	K	I	376	Lightning Bolt Books	Lerner Publishing Group
Let's Look at Bats	K	I	311	Lightning Bolt Books	Lerner Publishing Group
Let's Look at Brown Bears	K	I	270	Lightning Bolt Books	Lerner Publishing Group
Let's Look at Earthworms	K	I	375	Lightning Bolt Books	Lerner Publishing Group
Let's Look at Fall	H	I	106	Investigate the Seasons	Capstone Press
Let's Look at Iguanas	K	I	382	Lightning Bolt Books	Lerner Publishing Group
Let's Look at Leopards	H	I	155	Rosen Real Readers	Rosen Publishing Group
Let's Look at Monarch Butterflies	K	I	394	Lightning Bolt Books	Lerner Publishing Group
Let's Look at Pigeons	K	I	454	Lightning Bolt Books	Lerner Publishing Group
Let's Look at Prairie Dogs	K	I	373	Lightning Bolt Books	Lerner Publishing Group
Let's Look at Rocks	I	I	186	Yellow Umbrella Books	Red Brick Learning
Let's Look at Sea Otters	K	I	470	Lightning Bolt Books	Lerner Publishing Group
Let's Look at Sharks	K	I	326	Lightning Bolt Books	Lerner Publishing Group
Let's Look at Sloths	K	I	454	Lightning Bolt Books	Lerner Publishing Group
Let's Look at Snails	K	I	385	Lightning Bolt Books	Lerner Publishing Group
Let's Look at Spring	H	I	104	Investigate the Seasons	Capstone Press
Let's Look at Summer	H	I	110	Investigate the Seasons	Capstone Press
Let's Look at Venus	L	I	250+	Rosen Real Readers	Rosen Publishing Group
Let's Look at Winter	H	I	113	Investigate the Seasons	Capstone Press
Let's Look for Words	D	RF	61	The King School Series	Townsend Press
Let's Look Outside	B	I	38	Early Connections	Benchmark Education
Let's Make a Club Hut	G	RF	119	Reading Street	Pearson
Let's Make a Kite	J	I	250+	Bookshop	Mondo Publishing
Let's Make a Trade!	L	I	450	Reading Street	Pearson
Let's Make a Volcano	J	I	166	Red Rocket Readers	Flying Start Books
Let's Make Butter	I	I	224	Yellow Umbrella Books	Red Brick Learning
Let's Make Music	J	I	220	iOpeners	Pearson Learning Group
Let's Make Music!	I	I	185	Leveled Readers	Houghton Mifflin Harcourt
Let's Make Music!	I	I	185	Leveled Readers/CA	Houghton Mifflin Harcourt
Let's Make Music!	I	I	185	Leveled Readers/TX	Houghton Mifflin Harcourt
Let's Make Something New	G	I	116	Discovery Links	Newbridge
Let's Measure It!	D	F	100	Learn to Read	Creative Teaching Press
Let's Measure It!	G	I	252	Shutterbug Books	Steck-Vaughn
Let's Move!	B	RF	29	Ready Readers	Pearson Learning Group
Let's Move!	B	I	55	Vocabulary Readers	Houghton Mifflin Harcourt
Let's Move!	B	I	55	Vocabulary Readers/CA	Houghton Mifflin Harcourt
Let's Paint	C	RF	51	Rise & Shine	Hampton Brown
Let's Paint!	D	RF	42	Windows on Literacy	National Geographic
Let's Party	L	I	476	Explorations	Okapi Educational Materials
Let's Party	L	I	476	Explorations	Eleanor Curtain Publishing
Let's Play	B	RF	40	Little Books for Early Readers	University of Maine
Let's Play	B	RF	37	Peters, Catherine	Scholastic
Let's Play Ball	C	F	68	New Way Red	Steck-Vaughn
Let's Play Ball	B	RF	41	Red Rocket Readers	Flying Start Books
Let's Play Baseball!	H	RF	157	Reading Street	Pearson

* Collection of short stories   # Graphic text
^ Mature content with lower level text demands

L

TITLE	LEVEL	GENRE	WORD COUNT	AUTHOR / SERIES	PUBLISHER / DISTRIBUTOR
Let's Play Basketball	E	RF	46	Geddes, Diana	Kaeden Books
Let's Play Football!	H	I	117	Sports and Activities	Capstone Press
Let's Play Games Around the World	O	I	250+	iOpeners	Pearson Learning Group
Let's Play in the Forest	E	F	209	Rueda, Claudia	Scholastic
Let's Play Soccer	E	I	100	Douglas, Ian	Scholastic
Let's Play Today	D	RF	68	Leveled Readers Language Support	Houghton Mifflin Harcourt
Let's Pretend	B	RF	40	Home Connection Collection	Rigby
Let's Pretend	C	RF	82	PM Plus Story Books	Rigby
Let's Pretend	G	RF	186	The Rowland Reading Program Library	Rowland Reading Foundation
Let's Race	E	F	77	Reading Street	Pearson
Let's Recycle!	I	I	154	Caring For The Earth	Capstone Press
Let's Reduce Garbage!	I	I	141	Caring For The Earth	Capstone Press
Let's Reuse!	I	I	120	Caring For The Earth	Capstone Press
Let's Ride	G	RF	90	Reading Street	Pearson
Let's Save Energy	I	I	136	Caring For The Earth	Capstone Press
Let's Save Money	N	RF	583	Reading Street	Pearson
Let's Save Water	I	I	121	Caring For The Earth	Capstone Press
Let's Sell Things!	A	I	28	Leveled Readers	Houghton Mifflin Harcourt
Let's Sell Things!	A	I	28	Leveled Readers/CA	Houghton Mifflin Harcourt
Let's Skip-Count	I	I	197	Shutterbug Books	Steck-Vaughn
Let's Sleep	D	I	73	Sails	Rigby
Let's Sort	F	I	100	Yellow Umbrella Books	Red Brick Learning
Let's Swim	A	I	19	Leveled Readers	Houghton Mifflin Harcourt
Let's Swim	A	I	19	Leveled Readers/CA	Houghton Mifflin Harcourt
Let's Take a Trip	H	F	178	Leveled Readers	Houghton Mifflin Harcourt
Let's Take Care of the Earth	E	I	121	Learn to Read	Creative Teaching Press
Let's Take the Bus	H	RF	250+	Real Reading	Steck-Vaughn
Let's Talk: How We Communicate	K	I	250+	Spyglass Books	Compass Point Books
Let's Travel North!	J	I	106	Larkin, Bruce	Wilbooks
Let's Visit the Circus	J	I	338	The Rowland Reading Program Library	Rowland Reading Foundation
Let's Visit the Moon	E	F	130	Instant Readers	Harcourt School Publishers
Let's Wash Up	F	I	69	Rosen Real Readers	Rosen Publishing Group
Letter Carriers	L	I	250+	Community Workers	Compass Point Books
Letter from Fish Bay, A	N	B	250+	Cowley, Joy	Pacific Learning
Letter from Phoenix Farm, A	O	B	250+	Meet The Author	Richard C. Owen
Letter to a Friend	L	I	250+	Early Connections	Benchmark Education
Letter to Amy, A	K	RF	250+	Keats, Ezra Jack	Harper & Row
Letter to Mrs. Roosevelt, A	R	HF	250+	DeYoung, C. Coco	Delacorte Press
Letter Writer, The	Z	HF	250+	Rinaldi, Ann	Houghton Mifflin Harcourt
Letter, The	E	I	76	Little Celebrations	Pearson Learning Group
Letter, The	LB	RF	15	Twig	Wright Group/McGraw Hill
Letter, the Witch, and the Ring, The	S	F	250+	Bellairs, John	Penguin Group
Letters for Mr. James	H	RF	203	Sunshine	Wright Group/McGraw Hill
Letters from a Mill Town	T	HF	1662	Leveled Readers Social Studies	Houghton Mifflin Harcourt
Letters from a Slave Girl: The Story of Harriet Jacobs	X	HF	250+	Lyons, Mary E.	Simon & Schuster
Letters from Camp: A Mystery	V	RF	250+	Klise, Kate	HarperTrophy
Letters from Rifka	S	HF	250+	Hesse, Karen	Puffin Books
Letters from the Front	W	HF	2118	Leveled Readers	Houghton Mifflin Harcourt
Letters from the Front	W	HF	2118	Leveled Readers/CA	Houghton Mifflin Harcourt
Letters from the Front	W	HF	2118	Leveled Readers/TX	Houghton Mifflin Harcourt

* Collection of short stories   # Graphic text
^ Mature content with lower level text demands

L

Letters from the Sea	S	I	250+	Voyages in Time	Wright Group/McGraw Hill
Letters from the War	V	HF	1998	Leveled Readers	Houghton Mifflin Harcourt
Letters from the War	V	HF	1998	Leveled Readers/CA	Houghton Mifflin Harcourt
Letters from the War	V	HF	1998	Leveled Readers/TX	Houghton Mifflin Harcourt
Letters to a Soldier	U	I	250+	Falvey, First Lieutenant David and Hutt, Julie	Marshall Cavendish
Letters to Cupid	Z	RF	250+	Lantz, Francess	Pleasant Company
Letters to Julia	W	RF	250+	Holmes, Barbara Ware	HarperTrophy
Letters to Leah	U	RF	250+	Book Blazers	ETA/Cuisenaire
Lettie's North Star	T	HF	250+	Bookshop	Mondo Publishing
Letting Swift River Go	M	HF	250+	Yolen, Jane	Little Brown and Company
Lettuce Grows on the Ground	K	I	155	How Fruits and Vegetables Grow	Capstone Press
Leukemia: True Survival Stories	Z	I	3423	Powerful Medicine	Lerner Publishing Group
Levers	Q	I	1736	Early Bird Energy Physics Books	Lerner Publishing Group
Levers to the Rescue	O	I	250+	Simple Machine to the Rescue	Capstone Press
Levi Sings	C	RF	29	Teacher's Choice Series	Pearson Learning Group
Levi Strauss	R	B	250+	Amazing Americans	Wright Group/McGraw Hill
Levi Strauss	P	B	250+	Early Biographies	Compass Point Books
Levi Strauss	R	B	3244	History Maker Bios	Lerner Publishing Group
#Levi Strauss and Blue Jeans	R	B	250+	Graphic Library	Capstone Press
Lewis & Clark	S	I	250+	Primary Source Readers	Teacher Created Materials
Lewis & Clark: Explorers of the American West	S	I	250+	Kroll, Steven	Holiday House
Lewis and Clark	Q	B	250+	Biographies-Great Explorers	Capstone Press
Lewis and Clark	V	B	250+	Cornerstones of Freedom	Children's Press
Lewis and Clark	S	B	250+	History Maker Bios	Lerner Publishing Group
Lewis and Clark	R	I	250+	Navigators Social Studies Series	Benchmark Education
Lewis and Clark	S	B	1476	Reading Street	Pearson
Lewis and Clark	N	B	250+	Rookie Biographies	Children's Press
Lewis and Clark	T	B	250+	Santella, Andrew	Franklin Watts
Lewis and Clark	T	HF	250+	Sullivan, George	Scholastic
#Lewis and Clark Expedition, The	R	I	250+	Graphic Library	Capstone Press
Lewis and Clark Expedition, The	V	I	250+	Let Freedom Ring	Red Brick Learning
Lewis and Clark Expedition, The	T	I	250+	We The People	Compass Point Books
Lewis and Clark's Packing List	Q	I	936	Vocabulary Readers	Houghton Mifflin Harcourt
Lewis and Clark's Packing List	Q	I	936	Vocabulary Readers/CA	Houghton Mifflin Harcourt
Lewis and Clark's Packing List	Q	I	936	Vocabulary Readers/TX	Houghton Mifflin Harcourt
Lewis and Clark's Voyage of Discovery	S	I	250+	The Library of the Westward Expansion	Rosen Publishing Group
Lexie	R	RF	250+	Couloumbis, Audrey	Random House
Lexington and Concord	V	I	250+	Cornerstones of Freedom	Children's Press
Liang and the Magic Paintbrush	M	TL	250+	Demi	Henry Holt & Co.
Liar	Z+	F	250+	Larbalestier, Justine	Bloomsbury Children's Books
Liar, Liar Pants on Fire	I	RF	250+	Cohen, Miriam	Bantam Books
Liar, Liar, Pants on Fire	O	RF	250+	Korman, Gordon	Scholastic
Liar, Liar: The Theory, Practice and Destructive Properties of Deception	V	RF	250+	Paulsen, Gary	Wendy Lamb Books
Libby's New Friend	L	F	403	Leveled Literacy Intervention/Blue System	Heinemann
#Liberty	V	I	250+	Cartoon Nation	Capstone Press
Liberty	Q	I	250+	HSP/Harcourt Trophies	Harcourt, Inc.
Liberty Bell, The	N	I	250+	American Symbols	Capstone Press
Liberty Bell, The	V	I	250+	Cornerstones of Freedom	Children's Press
Liberty Bell, The	P	I	669	Pull Ahead Books	Lerner Publishing Group
Liberty Bell, The	S	I	250+	Symbols of America	Marshall Cavendish

L

TITLE	LEVEL	GENRE	WORD COUNT	AUTHOR / SERIES	PUBLISHER / DISTRIBUTOR
Liberty or Death: A Story about Patrick Henry	S	B	8519	Creative Minds Biographies	Lerner Publishing Group
Librarian Who Measured the Earth, The	S	B	250+	Lasky, Kathryn	Scholastic
Librarians	J	I	186	Bookworms	Marshall Cavendish
Librarians	M	I	250+	Community Helpers	Red Brick Learning
Librarians	L	I	250+	Community Workers	Compass Point Books
Librarians	L	I	363	Pull Ahead Books	Lerner Publishing Group
Librarians: Then and Now	O	I	250+	Primary Source Readers	Teacher Created Materials
Library	D	I	29	Community Buildings	Lerner Publishing Group
Library Card, The	R	RF	250+	Spinelli, Jerry	Scholastic
Library Comes to Town, A	I	HF	136	Reading Street	Pearson
Library Day	J	F	250+	Sunshine	Wright Group/McGraw Hill
Library Dragon, The	P	F	250+	Deedy, Carmen Agra	Peachtree
Library Mouse	L	F	250+	Kirk, Daniel	Harry N. Abrams
Library Mouse: A Friend's Tale	L	F	250+	Kirk, Daniel	Harry N. Abrams
Library Mouse: A World to Explore	M	F	250+	Kirk, Daniel	Harry N. Abrams
Library of Congress, The	V	I	250+	Cornerstones of Freedom	Children's Press
Library, The	C	RF	33	Carousel Readers	Pearson Learning Group
Library, The	D	RF	96	Emergent	Pioneer Valley
Library, The	H	RF	195	McAlpin, MaryAnn	Short Tales Press
License Plates	J	RF	411	PM Collection	Rigby
Lick, Lick, Drip, Drip	B	F	40	Brand New Readers	Candlewick Press
Licken Chicken	I	TL	250+	Tiger Cub	Peguis
Lid, The	G	RF	111	Books for Young Learners	Richard C. Owen
Liddy's Sayings	N	RF	880	Leveled Readers/CA	Houghton Mifflin Harcourt
Liddy's Sayings	N	RF	880	Leveled Readers/TX	Houghton Mifflin Harcourt
Life Among the Redwoods	S	I	1410	Leveled Readers	Houghton Mifflin Harcourt
Life Among the Redwoods	S	I	1410	Leveled Readers/CA	Houghton Mifflin Harcourt
Life Among the Redwoods	S	I	1410	Leveled Readers/TX	Houghton Mifflin Harcourt
Life and Death of Crazy Horse, The	X	B	250+	Freedman, Russell	Holiday House
Life and Death of Martin Luther King, Jr.,The	Y	B	250+	Haskins, James	Beech Tree Books
Life and Death of Stars, The	Y	I	250+	Spangenburg, Ray and Moser, Kit	Franklin Watts
Life and Times of Corn, The	R	I	250+	Micucci, Charles	Houghton Mifflin Harcourt
Life and Times of Frederick Douglass, The	Z+	B	250+	Douglass, Frederick	Dover Publications
Life and Times of the Ant, The	Q	I	250+	Micucci, Charles	Houghton Mifflin Harcourt
Life and Times of the Honeybee, The	Q	I	250+	Micucci, Charles	Houghton Mifflin Harcourt
Life and Times of the Peanut, The	Q	I	250+	Micucci, Charles	Houghton Mifflin Harcourt
Life and Words of Martin Luther King, Jr., The	W	B	250+	Peck, Ira	Scholastic
Life As We Knew It	Z	SF	250+	Pfeffer, Susan Beth	Harcourt
Life at Plimoth	L	I	210	Leveled Readers Social Studies	Houghton Mifflin Harcourt
Life at the Beach	A	I	28	Early Explorers	Benchmark Education
Life at the Bottom of the Sea	U	I	250+	Leveled Readers Language Support	Houghton Mifflin Harcourt
Life Birds	N	RF	250+	Sails	Rigby
Life Cycle of a Bean, The	I	I	117	Plant Life Cycles	Capstone Press
Life Cycle of a Butterfly, The	J	I	94	Life Cycles	Capstone Press
Life Cycle of a Carrot, The	I	I	115	Plant Life Cycles	Capstone Press
Life Cycle of a Cat, The	J	I	108	Life Cycles	Capstone Press
Life Cycle of a Chicken, The	J	I	103	Life Cycles	Capstone Press
Life Cycle of a Cow, The	J	I	108	Life Cycles	Capstone Press
Life Cycle of a Dog, The	J	I	110	Life Cycles	Capstone Press
Life Cycle of a Frog, The	J	I	115	Life Cycles	Capstone Press
Life Cycle of a Kangaroo, The	J	I	155	Life Cycles	Capstone Press
Life Cycle of a Pine Tree, The	I	I	111	Plant Life Cycles	Capstone Press
Life Cycle of a Plant	G	I	147	Red Rocket Readers	Flying Start Books

L

* Collection of short stories   # Graphic text
^ Mature content with lower level text demands

TITLE	LEVEL	GENRE	WORD COUNT	AUTHOR / SERIES	PUBLISHER / DISTRIBUTOR
Life Cycle of a Salmon, The	K	I	121	Life Cycles	Capstone Press
Life Cycle of a Sunflower, The	I	I	90	Plant Life Cycles	Capstone Press
Life Cycle of a Swan	J	I	250+	Rigby Rocket	Rigby
Life Cycle of a Whale, The	J	I	135	Life Cycles	Capstone Press
Life Cycle of an Apple Tree, The	I	I	128	Plant Life Cycles	Capstone Press
Life Cycle of an Oak Tree, The	I	I	109	Plant Life Cycles	Capstone Press
Life Cycle of Plants, The	R	I	250+	Navigators Science Series	Benchmark Education
Life Cycle of Trees, The	R	I	250+	Navigators Science Series	Benchmark Education
Life Cycle of Water Plants, The	R	I	250+	Navigators Science Series	Benchmark Education
Life Cycles	M	I	891	Cycles	Lerner Publishing Group
Life Cycles	J	I	226	Explorations	Eleanor Curtain Publishing
Life Cycles	J	I	226	Explorations	Okapi Educational Materials
Life Cycles	U	I	250+	Reading Expeditions	National Geographic
Life Cycles of a Wolf, The	P	I	250+	Kalman, Bobbie and Bishop, Amanda	Crabtree
Life Cycles of Animals	L	I	121	Windows on Literacy	National Geographic
Life During Winter	J	I	128	Larkin, Bruce	Wilbooks
Life in a Cave	U	I	250+	The Heinle Reading Library	Thomson Learning
Life in a City	K	I	248	Larkin, Bruce	Wilbooks
Life in a Coral Reef	L	I	250+	Rosen Real Readers	Rosen Publishing Group
Life in a Desert	I	I	123	Living in a Biome	Capstone Press
Life in a Forest	I	I	124	Living in a Biome	Capstone Press
Life in a Hot, Dry Place	L	I	187	Larkin's Little Readers	Wilbooks
Life in a Polar Region	H	I	133	Living in a Biome	Capstone Press
Life in a Pond	I	I	147	Living in a Biome	Capstone Press
Life in a Pond	I	I	158	Systems Set	Newbridge
Life in a Rain Forest	I	I	146	Living in a Biome	Capstone Press
Life in a Rural Community	K	I	246	Larkin, Bruce	Wilbooks
Life in a Shell	K	I	206	Gear Up!	Wright Group/McGraw Hill
Life in a Sioux Village	S	I	250+	Picture the Past	Heinemann
Life in a Stream	H	I	109	Living in a Biome	Capstone Press
Life in a Wetland	I	I	140	Living in a Biome	Capstone Press
Life in an Ocean	H	I	109	Living in a Biome	Capstone Press
Life in Ancient Egypt	U	I	1473	Vocabulary Readers	Houghton Mifflin Harcourt
Life in Ancient Egypt	U	I	1473	Vocabulary Readers/CA	Houghton Mifflin Harcourt
Life in Ancient Egypt	U	I	1473	Vocabulary Readers/TX	Houghton Mifflin Harcourt
Life in Colonial America	L	I	405	Leveled Readers Social Studies	Houghton Mifflin Harcourt
Life in Hot Places	I	I	247	PM Science Readers	Rigby
Life in the 1950s	U	I	1576	Vocabulary Readers/CA	Houghton Mifflin Harcourt
Life in the 1950s	U	I	1576	Vocabulary Readers/TX	Houghton Mifflin Harcourt
Life in the 1950's	U	I	1576	Vocabulary Readers	Houghton Mifflin Harcourt
Life In the Arctic	K	I	293	Leveled Readers Science	Houghton Mifflin Harcourt
Life in the Arctic	T	I	250+	Reading Street	Pearson
Life in the Arctic	M	I	250+	Rosen Real Readers	Rosen Publishing Group
Life in the Arctic	U	I	1518	Vocabulary Readers	Houghton Mifflin Harcourt
Life in the Arctic	U	I	1518	Vocabulary Readers/CA	Houghton Mifflin Harcourt
Life in the Arctic	U	I	1518	Vocabulary Readers/TX	Houghton Mifflin Harcourt
Life in the Boreal Forest	R	I	250+	Guiberson, Brenda Z.	Henry Holt & Co.
Life in the City	J	I	307	Early Connections	Benchmark Education
Life in the City	E	RF	184	Handprints D, Set 1	Educators Publishing Service
Life in the Colonies	T	I	250+	Primary Source Readers	Teacher Created Materials
Life in the Colonies: A Diary	O	RF	826	Gear Up!	Wright Group/McGraw Hill

L

* Collection of short stories   # Graphic text
^ Mature content with lower level text demands

TITLE	LEVEL	GENRE	WORD COUNT	AUTHOR / SERIES	PUBLISHER / DISTRIBUTOR
Life in the Coral Reefs	G	I	198	Leveled Readers	Houghton Mifflin Harcourt
Life in the Coral Reefs	G	I	198	Leveled Readers/CA	Houghton Mifflin Harcourt
Life in the Coral Reefs	G	I	198	Leveled Readers/TX	Houghton Mifflin Harcourt
Life in the Desert	K	I	326	Gear Up!	Wright Group/McGraw Hill
Life in the Desert	M	I	250+	Pair-It Books	Steck-Vaughn
Life in the Desert	L	I	250+	Sails	Rigby
Life in the Mangroves	I	I	172	Home Connection Collection	Rigby
Life in the Ocean	M	I	250+	Windows on Literacy	National Geographic
Life in the Ocean Depths	T	I	2165	Leveled Readers Science	Houghton Mifflin Harcourt
Life in the Oceans: Animals, People, Plants	T	I	250+	Baker, Lucy	Scholastic
Life in the Rain Forest	L	I	250+	Rosen Real Readers	Rosen Publishing Group
Life in the Rain Forests: Animals, People, Plants	T	I	250+	Baker, Lucy	Scholastic
Life in the Rainforest	L	I	250+	The Big Picture	Capstone Press
Life in the Sahara	U	I	1804	Leveled Readers Social Studies	Houghton Mifflin Harcourt
Life in the Sea	T	I	2027	Reading Street	Pearson
Life in the Suburbs	K	I	284	Larkin, Bruce	Wilbooks
Life in the Trees	I	I	340	Rigby Flying Colors	Rigby
Life in the Trees	F	I	147	Springboard	Wright Group/McGraw Hill
Life in Their Hands, A	T	RF	250+	Power Up!	Steck-Vaughn
Life in Tide Pools	K	I	383	Leveled Readers	Houghton Mifflin Harcourt
Life in Tide Pools	K	I	383	Leveled Readers/CA	Houghton Mifflin Harcourt
Life in Tide Pools	K	I	383	Leveled Readers/TX	Houghton Mifflin Harcourt
Life Inside the Arctic Circle	T	I	2632	Reading Street	Pearson
Life Is Fun	J	F	178	Carlson, Nancy	Carolrhoda Books
Life Long Ago	K	I	250+	Spyglass Books	Compass Point Books
Life of a Bean, The	J	I	201	Independent Readers Science	Houghton Mifflin Harcourt
Life of a Butterfly, The	E	I	46	Vocabulary Readers	Houghton Mifflin Harcourt
Life of a Comet	V	I	250+	Navigators Science Series	Benchmark Education
Life of a Continental Soldier, The	W	I	3160	Vocabulary Readers	Houghton Mifflin Harcourt
Life of a Continental Soldier, The	W	I	3160	Vocabulary Readers/CA	Houghton Mifflin Harcourt
Life of a Continental Soldier, The	W	I	3160	Vocabulary Readers/TX	Houghton Mifflin Harcourt
Life of a Dollar Bill, The	N	I	301	Leveled Readers Social Studies	Houghton Mifflin Harcourt
Life of a Lion, The	E	I	28	Rosen Real Readers	Rosen Publishing Group
Life of a Miner	T	I	250+	Life in the Old West	Crabtree
Life of a Star	V	I	250+	Navigators Science Series	Benchmark Education
Life of Abraham Lincoln, The	M	B	250+	Rosen Real Readers	Rosen Publishing Group
Life of B. B. King, The	U	B	2522	Leveled Readers/CA	Houghton Mifflin Harcourt
Life of B. B. King, The	U	B	2522	Leveled Readers/TX	Houghton Mifflin Harcourt
Life of B.B. King, The	U	B	2522	Leveled Readers	Houghton Mifflin Harcourt
Life of Cesar Chavez	U	B	2568	Reading Street	Pearson
Life of Emily Pauline Johnson, The	Y	B	2363	Leveled Readers	Houghton Mifflin Harcourt
Life of Emily Pauline Johnson, The	Y	B	2363	Leveled Readers/CA	Houghton Mifflin Harcourt
Life of Emily Pauline Johnson, The	Y	B	2363	Leveled Readers/TX	Houghton Mifflin Harcourt
Life of George Washington Carver, The	O	B	991	Leveled Readers	Houghton Mifflin Harcourt
Life of George Washington Carver, The	O	B	991	Leveled Readers/CA	Houghton Mifflin Harcourt
Life of George Washington Carver, The	O	B	991	Leveled Readers/TX	Houghton Mifflin Harcourt
Life of Jack London, The	T	B	1643	Leveled Readers	Houghton Mifflin Harcourt
Life of Jack London, The	T	B	1643	Leveled Readers/CA	Houghton Mifflin Harcourt
Life of Jack London, The	T	B	1643	Leveled Readers/TX	Houghton Mifflin Harcourt
Life of Jack Prelutsky, The	M	B	631	Leveled Readers	Houghton Mifflin Harcourt
Life of Jack Prelutsky, The	M	B	631	Leveled Readers/CA	Houghton Mifflin Harcourt
Life of Jack Prelutsky, The	M	B	631	Leveled Readers/TX	Houghton Mifflin Harcourt
Life of Jackson Pollock, The	S	B	1155	Leveled Readers	Houghton Mifflin Harcourt
Life of Jackson Pollock, The	S	B	1155	Leveled Readers/CA	Houghton Mifflin Harcourt

L

* Collection of short stories   # Graphic text
^ Mature content with lower level text demands

TITLE	LEVEL	GENRE	WORD COUNT	AUTHOR / SERIES	PUBLISHER / DISTRIBUTOR
Life of Jackson Pollock, The	S	B	1155	Leveled Readers/TX	Houghton Mifflin Harcourt
Life of Langston Hughes, The	P	B	1003	Leveled Readers	Houghton Mifflin Harcourt
Life of Langston Hughes, the	P	B	1003	Leveled Readers/CA	Houghton Mifflin Harcourt
Life of Langston Hughes, The	P	B	1003	Leveled Readers/TX	Houghton Mifflin Harcourt
Life of Phillis Wheatley, The	T	B	2202	Leveled Readers	Houghton Mifflin Harcourt
Life of Phillis Wheatley, The	T	B	2202	Leveled Readers/CA	Houghton Mifflin Harcourt
Life of Phillis Wheatley, The	T	B	2202	Leveled Readers/TX	Houghton Mifflin Harcourt
Life of Rice, The: From Seedling to Supper	U	I	250+	Sobol, Richard	Candlewick Press
Life on a Farm	A	I	24	Early Connections	Benchmark Education
Life on a Plantation	T	I	250+	Historic Communities	Crabtree
Life on a Ranch	P	I	1202	Vocabulary Readers	Houghton Mifflin Harcourt
Life on a Ranch	P	I	1202	Vocabulary Readers/CA	Houghton Mifflin Harcourt
Life on a Space Station	U	I	2670	Leveled Readers	Houghton Mifflin Harcourt
Life on a Space Station	U	I	2670	Leveled Readers/CA	Houghton Mifflin Harcourt
Life on a Space Station	U	I	2670	Leveled Readers/TX	Houghton Mifflin Harcourt
Life on a Wagon Train	Q	I	250+	Rosen Real Readers	Rosen Publishing Group
Life On Land, Water, And Air	N	I	781	Pair-It Turn and Learn	Steck-Vaughn
Life on Mars: The Real Story	R	RF	1834	Reading Street	Pearson
Life on the Edge	Y	I	6699	Cool Science	Lerner Publishing Group
Life on the Farm	WB	I	0	Reach	National Geographic
Life on the Mayflower	M	I	250+	Thanksgiving	Picture Window Books
Life on the Mississippi	Z+	HF	250+	Twain, Mark	Bantam Books
Life on the Oregon Trail	W	I	2967	Vocabulary Readers	Houghton Mifflin Harcourt
Life on the Oregon Trail	W	I	2967	Vocabulary Readers/CA	Houghton Mifflin Harcourt
Life on the Oregon Trail	W	I	2967	Vocabulary Readers/TX	Houghton Mifflin Harcourt
Life on the Ranch	M	RF	1733	Reading Street	Pearson
Life on the Serengeti	V	I	1811	Independent Readers Science	Houghton Mifflin Harcourt
Life Savers	H	I	198	Sails	Rigby
Life Savers at Point Reyes	W	I	2992	Vocabulary Readers	Houghton Mifflin Harcourt
Life Savers at Point Reyes	W	I	2992	Vocabulary Readers/CA	Houghton Mifflin Harcourt
Life Savers at Point Reyes	W	I	2992	Vocabulary Readers/TX	Houghton Mifflin Harcourt
Life Stinks	L	F	250+	Rigby Gigglers	Rigby
Life with Mammoth (Ogg and Bob)	L	F	250+	Fraser, Ian	Marshall Cavendish
Life: Earth Matters	L	I	250+	Bookworms	Marshall Cavendish
Lifeboat in Space	Z	I	3358	Leveled Readers	Houghton Mifflin Harcourt
Lifeguards	M	I	250+	Community Helpers	Red Brick Learning
Lifesavers: Discoveries in Medicine	Y	I	250+	High-Fliers	Pacific Learning
#Lifesaving Adventure of Sam Deal, Shipwreck Rescuer, The	O	HF	565	History's Kid Heroes	Graphic Universe
Lifetimes	Q	I	250+	Sharing Nature with Children	Dawn Publications
Lift Off!	G	I	121	Pair-It Books	Steck-Vaughn
Lift off!: The Story of Space Flight	O	I	669	Rigby Flying Colors	Rigby
Lift the Sky Up	H	RF	133	Little Celebrations	Pearson Learning Group
Lift the Sky Up	H	RF	133	Little Readers	Houghton Mifflin Harcourt
Lifting the Sky	X	F	250+	d'Arge, Mackie	Bloomsbury Children's Books
Lift-Off!	I	SF	141	Pacific Literacy	Pacific Learning
Light	Q	I	1781	Early Bird Energy	Lerner Publishing Group
Light	J	I	150	Early Connections	Benchmark Education
Light	Z	I	250+	Eyewitness Books	DK Publishing
Light	J	I	250+	Momentum Literacy Program	Troll Associates
^Light	P	I	250+	Our Physical World	Capstone Press
Light	Q	I	1063	Science Support Readers	Houghton Mifflin Harcourt
Light	T	I	250+	The News	Richard C. Owen

L

TITLE	LEVEL	GENRE	WORD COUNT	AUTHOR / SERIES	PUBLISHER / DISTRIBUTOR
Light	C	I	30	Twig	Wright Group/McGraw Hill
Light	Q	I	250+	Windows on Literacy	National Geographic
Light and Color	T	I	250+	Straightforward Science	Franklin Watts
Light and Shade	X	I	250+	iOpeners	Pearson Learning Group
Light and Shadow	G	I	138	Discovery Links	Newbridge
Light and Shadow	F	I	82	Yellow Umbrella Books	Red Brick Learning
Light and Sound	P	I	250+	Science Kids	Kingfisher
Light and Sound Technology	T	I	250+	Navigators Science Series	Benchmark Education
Light at Tern Rock, The	N	RF	250+	Sauer, Julia L.	Scholastic
Light Bulb, The	P	I	250+	Great Inventions	Red Brick Learning
Light in the Forest, The	Y	HF	250+	Richter, Conrad	Random House
Light in the Storm, A	T	HF	250+	Hesse, Karen	Scholastic
Light: Shadows, Mirrors, and Rainbows	M	I	250+	Amazing Science	Picture Window Books
Light-Bearer's Daughter, The	Y	F	250+	Melling, O.R.	Amulet Books
Lighter on the Moon	N	I	250+	Windows on Literacy	National Geographic
Lighter Than Air	S	I	1494	Vocabulary Readers	Houghton Mifflin Harcourt
Lighter Than Air	S	I	1494	Vocabulary Readers/CA	Houghton Mifflin Harcourt
Lighter Than Air	S	I	1494	Vocabulary Readers/TX	Houghton Mifflin Harcourt
Lighthouse Children, The	I	F	250+	Hoff, Syd	HarperTrophy
Lighthouse Keepers, The	Y	SF	250+	McKinty, Adrian	Amulet Books
Lighthouse Mermaid, The	M	F	250+	Karr, Kathleen	Hyperion
Lighthouse People, The	N	RF	250+	Orbit Chapter Books	Pacific Learning
Lighthouse War, The	Y	SF	250+	McKinty, Adrian	Amulet Books
Lightning	T	I	250+	Kramer, Stephen	Carolrhoda Books
Lightning	S	I	1110	Leveled Readers	Houghton Mifflin Harcourt
Lightning	S	I	250+	Simon, Seymour	Scholastic
Lightning	L	I	279	Weather	Capstone Press
Lightning Bugs	E	RF	45	Ketch, Ann	Kaeden Books
Lightning Liz	F	F	41	Rookie Readers	Children's Press
Lightning Strikes	R	I	250+	Explorer Books-Pathfinder	National Geographic
Lightning Strikes	P	I	250+	Explorer Books-Pioneer	National Geographic
Lightning Thief, The	W	F	250+	Riordan, Rick	Scholastic
Lights	E	I	65	Big Cat	Pacific Learning
Lights and Switches	F	I	76	Factivity Series	Pearson Learning Group
Lights Are Out, The	D	RF	92	The King School Series	Townsend Press
Lights at Night	LB	I	33	Pacific Literacy	Pacific Learning
Lights Go On	C	I	45	Windows on Literacy	National Geographic
Lights in the Mine	M	RF	250+	PM Plus Chapter Books	Rigby
Lights in the Night	J	RF	368	Leveled Readers	Houghton Mifflin Harcourt
Lights in the Night	J	RF	368	Leveled Readers/CA	Houghton Mifflin Harcourt
Lights On!	S	I	1450	Independent Readers Science	Houghton Mifflin Harcourt
Lights Out	K	RF	250+	Math Matters	Kane Press
Lights! Camera! Magic!: Making Movies	S	I	250+	Explore More	Wright Group/McGraw Hill
Lights, Camera, Amalee	W	RF	250+	Williams, Dar	Scholastic
*Lightweight Rocket and Other Cases, The	O	RF	250+	Simon, Seymour	Avon Books
Like Jake and Me	O	RF	250+	Jukes, Mavis	Alfred A. Knopf
Like Me	D	RF	20	Book Bank	Wright Group/McGraw Hill
Like My Daddy	E	RF	129	Visions	Wright Group/McGraw Hill
Like Pickle Juice on a Cookie	O	RF	250+	Sternberg, Julie	Amulet Books
Like Sisters on the Homefront	Z+	RF	250+	Williams-Garcia, Rita	Penguin Group
Lila the Fair	L	RF	250+	Social Studies Connects	Kane Press
Lilacs, Lotuses, and Ladybugs	L	RF	402	Evangeline Nicholas Collection	Wright Group/McGraw Hill
Lili the Brave	N	RF	250+	Armstrong, Jennifer	Random House
Lili's Breakfast	F	RF	156	Storyteller-Setting Sun	Wright Group/McGraw Hill

L

* Collection of short stories   # Graphic text
^ Mature content with lower level text demands

TITLE	LEVEL	GENRE	WORD COUNT	AUTHOR / SERIES	PUBLISHER / DISTRIBUTOR
Lillian the Librarian	I	RF	315	Seedlings	Continental Press
Lillian's Fish	P	F	250+	Menk, James	Peachtree
Lilly-Lolly-Little-Legs	H	RF	129	Literacy 2000	Rigby
Lilly's Purple Plastic Purse	N	F	250+	Henkes, Kevin	Scholastic
Lily and Miss Liberty	N	HF	250+	Stephens, Carla	Scholastic
Lily and the Leaf Boats	C	RF	55	PM Photo Stories	Rigby
Lily and the Wigwogs	F	RF	142	The Rowland Reading Program Library	Rowland Reading Foundation
Lily B. on the Brink of Love	U	RF	250+	Kimmel, Elizabeth Cody	HarperTrophy
Lily Dale: Awakening	Z	F	250+	Staub, Wendy Corsi	Walker & Company
Lily Dale: Believing	Z	F	250+	Staub, Wendy Corsi	Walker & Company
Lily Dale: Connecting	Z	F	250+	Staub, Wendy Corsi	Walker & Company
Lily's Crossing	S	HF	250+	Giff, Patricia Reilly	Delacorte Press
Lily's Fantastic Animals	F	RF	175	The Rowland Reading Program Library	Rowland Reading Foundation
Lily's New Home	J	RF	557	Rigby Flying Colors	Rigby
Lily's Playhouse	D	RF	69	PM Photo Stories	Rigby
Lily's Special Garden	E	RF	156	Reading Safari	Mondo Publishing
Limbo, Limbo	D	F	48	Brand New Readers	Candlewick Press
Lime, a Mime, a Pool of Slime, A: More About Nouns	O	I	252	Words Are CATegorical	Millbrook Press
Limestone Cave	N	I	250+	Habitats	Children's Press
Limestone Caves	N	I	250+	A First Book	Franklin Watts
Lincoln Memorial, The	V	I	250+	Cornerstones of Freedom	Children's Press
Lincoln Memorial, The	N	I	395	Lightning Bolt Books	Lerner Publishing Group
Lincoln Memorial, The	Q	I	250+	National Landmarks	Red Brick Learning
Lincoln Memorial, The	P	I	661	Pull Ahead Books	Lerner Publishing Group
Lincoln Shot: A President's Life Remembered	Y	B	250+	Denenberg, Barry	Feiwel and Friends
Lincoln Through the Lens: How Photography Revealed and Shaped an Extraordinary Life	X	B	250+	Sandler, Martin W.	Walker & Company
Lincoln: A Photobiography	V	B	250+	Freedman, Russell	Clarion
Lincoln-Douglas Debates, The	W	I	250+	Cornerstones of Freedom	Children's Press
Ling & Ting: Not Exactly the Same	K	RF	250+	Lin, Grace	Little Brown and Company
Ling and the Turtle	D	F	65	Rigby Star	Rigby
Lingospeak	S	I	250+	Rigby Literacy	Rigby
Ling's Monster	I	RF	274	Sun Sprouts	ETA/Cuisenaire
Ling's New Friend	F	RF	164	Sun Sprouts	ETA/Cuisenaire
Links in the Food Chain	L	I	284	Reading Street	Pearson
Lin-Lin and the Gulls	J	TL	478	Appleton-Smith, Laura	Flyleaf Publishing
Linney Twins Get Cooking, The	M	SF	968	Leveled Readers	Houghton Mifflin Harcourt
Linney Twins Get Cooking, The	M	SF	968	Leveled Readers/CA	Houghton Mifflin Harcourt
Linney Twins Get Cooking, The	M	SF	968	Leveled Readers/TX	Houghton Mifflin Harcourt
Lin's Backpack	C	RF	49	Little Celebrations	Pearson Learning Group
Lion	C	I	39	Zoozoo-Into the Wild	Cavallo Publishing
Lion and the Hare, The	N	TL	1655	On My Own Folklore	Millbrook Press
Lion and the Mouse	E	TL	87	Herman, Gail	Random House
Lion and the Mouse, The	I	TL	499	Aesop's Fables	Pearson Learning Group
Lion and the Mouse, The	E	SF	91	Cambridge Reading	Pearson Learning Group
Lion and the Mouse, The	J	TL	427	Leveled Literacy Intervention/ Green System	Heinemann
Lion and The Mouse, The	G	TL	250+	Literacy 2000	Rigby
Lion and the Mouse, The	J	TL	325	Little Books	Sadlier-Oxford
*Lion and the Mouse, The	F	TL	115	New Way Red	Steck-Vaughn
Lion and the Mouse, The	K	TL	557	Pair-It Books	Steck-Vaughn
Lion and the Mouse, The	G	TL	125	PM Story Books	Rigby

L

TITLE	LEVEL	GENRE	WORD COUNT	AUTHOR / SERIES	PUBLISHER / DISTRIBUTOR
Lion and the Mouse, The	I	TL	250+	Storyworlds	Heinemann
Lion and the Mouse, The	J	TL	285	Sunshine	Wright Group/McGraw Hill
Lion and the Mouse, The	G	TL	250+	Traditional Tales & More	Rigby
Lion and the Rabbit, The	F	TL	99	PM Story Books	Rigby
Lion Cubs	E	I	57	Bonnell, Kris/About	Reading Reading Books
Lion Dancer: Ernie Wan's Chinese New Year	N	B	250+	Waters, Kate; Slovenz-Low, Madeline	Scholastic
Lion in the Grass, The	G	I	72	Benchmark Rebus	Marshall Cavendish
Lion in the Night, The	J	F	250+	Momentum Literacy Program	Troll Associates
Lion Roars, The	I	RF	270	Ready Readers	Pearson Learning Group
Lion Roars, The	B	F	23	Zoozoo-Into the Wild	Cavallo Publishing
Lion Talk	I	I	216	Storyteller-Night Crickets	Wright Group/McGraw Hill
*Lion Tamer's Daughter And Other Stories, The	Z	F	250+	Dickinson, Peter	Laurel-Leaf Books
Lion to Guard Us, A	P	HF	250+	Bulla, Clyde Robert	HarperTrophy
Lion Vs. Gazelle	L	I	250+	Predator Vs. Prey	Raintree
Lion, The	A	I	20	Vocabulary Readers	Houghton Mifflin Harcourt
Lion, The	A	I	20	Vocabulary Readers/CA	Houghton Mifflin Harcourt
Lion, the Witch, and the Wardrobe, The	T	F	250+	Lewis, C. S.	HarperTrophy
Lionel and Amelia	L	F	250+	Bookshop	Mondo Publishing
*Lionel and His Friends	K	RF	250+	Krensky, Stephen	Puffin Books
*Lionel and Louise	K	RF	250+	Krensky, Stephen	Puffin Books
*Lionel at Large	K	RF	250+	Krensky, Stephen	Puffin Books
*Lionel in the Fall	K	RF	250+	Krensky, Stephen	Puffin Books
*Lionel in the Spring	K	RF	250+	Krensky, Stephen	Puffin Books
*Lionel in the Summer	K	RF	250+	Krensky, Stephen	Puffin Books
*Lionel in the Winter	K	RF	250+	Krensky, Stephen	Puffin Books
Lions	I	I	111	African Animals	Capstone Press
Lions	P	I	1662	Animal Predators	Lerner Publishing Group
Lions	O	I	250+	Holmes, Kevin J.	Red Brick Learning
Lions	N	I	250+	Meadows, Graham; Vial, Claire	Pearson Learning Group
Lions	L	I	644	Pair-It Books	Steck-Vaughn
Lions & Tigers	K	I	250+	PM Animals in the Wild-Yellow	Rigby
Lions and the Water Buffaloes, The	I	RF	250+	PM Plus Story Books	Rigby
Lions at Lunchtime	M	F	250+	Osborne, Mary Pope	Random House
Lion's Birthday	K	F	445	Pawprints Teal	Pioneer Valley
Lions' Dinner, The	E	F	111	Rigby Literacy	Rigby
Lions Dinner, The: A Play	E	F	110	Rigby Star	Rigby
Lion's Dinner, The: A Play	E	F	111	Literacy By Design	Rigby
Lion's Lunch	F	F	201	Lighthouse	Rigby
Lions of Africa	A	I	55	Readlings/ Animals of Africa	American Reading Company
^Lions on the Hunt	N	I	250+	Killer Animals	Capstone Press
Lion's Share, The: A Tale of Halving Cake and Eating It, Too	M	F	250+	McElligott, Matthew	Walker & Company
Lion's Tail, The	F	F	147	Reading Unlimited	Pearson Learning Group
Lipizzan Horses	I	I	250+	Horses	Capstone Press
Lipizzans Are My Favorite!	O	I	250+	My Favorite Horses	Lerner Publishing Group
Liquids	K	I	240	Gear Up!	Wright Group/McGraw Hill
Liquids and Gases	R	I	250+	Navigators Science Series	Benchmark Education
Liquids and Solids	L	I	250+	InfoTrek	ETA/Cuisenaire
Lisa Leftover	N	RF	250+	PM Extensions	Rigby
Lisa, Bright and Dark	Z+	RF	250+	Neufeld, John	Penguin Group
Lisa's Diary	L	RF	250+	Home Connection Collection	Rigby
Lisa's Ices	G	RF	106	City Stories	Rigby
Lise Meitner	Y	B	3362	Leveled Readers Science	Houghton Mifflin Harcourt

L

* Collection of short stories   # Graphic text
^ Mature content with lower level text demands

TITLE	LEVEL	GENRE	WORD COUNT	AUTHOR / SERIES	PUBLISHER / DISTRIBUTOR
List, The	D	RF	82	The Rowland Reading Program Library	Rowland Reading Foundation
Listen	D	RF	35	Visions	Wright Group/McGraw Hill
*Listen Children: An Anthology of Black Literature	U	RF	250+	Strickland, Dorothy S.	Bantam Books
Listen to Me	E	RF	113	Rookie Readers	Children's Press
Listen to Me	I	F	327	Springboard	Wright Group/McGraw Hill
Listen to That	B	I	42	Red Rocket Readers	Flying Start Books
Listening in Bed	M	RF	116	Book Bank	Wright Group/McGraw Hill
Listening to Crickets: A Story About Rachel Carson	R	B	7387	Creative Minds Biographies	Carolrhoda Books
Listening to Sound	T	I	250+	Navigators Science Series	Benchmark Education
Little Acorn, The	J	I	327	Bonnell, Kris	Reading Reading Books
Little Adventure, A	J	RF	250+	PM Story Books-Silver	Rigby
Little and Big	B	I	77	InfoTrek	ETA/Cuisenaire
Little and Big	C	I	57	Little Red Readers	Sundance
Little Animals	A	F	22	Reed, Janet	Scholastic
Little Ant, The	J	TL	329	Avenues	Hampton Brown
Little Ant, The: A Folktale From New Mexico	J	TL	250+	Costigan, Shirleyann	Hampton Brown
Little Ballerina, The	L	RF	250+	DK Readers	DK Publishing
Little Bat	E	F	196	Leveled Literacy Intervention/ Blue System	Heinemann
Little Bear	J	F	1664	Minarik, Else H.	HarperCollins
Little Bear	D	F	77	My First Reader	Grolier
Little Bear and the Bee	E	F	184	Rigby Flying Colors	Rigby
Little Bears	A	I	37	Bookshop	Mondo Publishing
*Little Bear's Friend	J	F	250+	Minarik, Else H.	HarperTrophy
*Little Bear's Visit	J	F	250+	Minarik, Else H.	HarperTrophy
Little Beauty	I	F	250+	Browne, Anthony	Candlewick Press
Little Bike, The	C	F	29	Joy Readers	Pearson Learning Group
Little Bill	L	RF	250+	Cosby, Bill	Scholastic
Little Bird	E	TL	42	Sunshine	Wright Group/McGraw Hill
Little Bit Hotter Can't Hurt, A	L	RF	466	Leveled Readers	Houghton Mifflin Harcourt
Little Black Lies	Z+	RF	250+	Cohen, Tish	Egmont USA
Little Black: A Pony	J	RF	250+	Farley, Walter	Random House
Little Blue and Little Yellow	J	F	250+	Lionni, Leo	Scholastic
Little Blue Fish	C	RF	58	Evans, Lynette	Scholastic
Little Blue Horse, The	I	RF	250+	PM Plus Story Books	Rigby
Little Blue, Big Blue	K	RF	250+	Rigby Literacy	Rigby
Little Blue, Big Blue	K	RF	250+	Rigby Star	Rigby
Little Boat, The	D	F	77	Bonnell, Kris	Reading Reading Books
Little Book of Street Rods, The	H	I	79	Books for Young Learners	Richard C. Owen
Little Bo-Peep	C	F	48	Seedlings	Continental Press
Little Box, The	L	F	250+	Rigby Gigglers	Rigby
Little Boy and the Balloon Man	E	F	16	Tiger Cub	Peguis
Little Boy Blue	D	TL	32	Sunshine	Wright Group/McGraw Hill
*Little Boy with Three Names and Other Short Stories	S	TL	250+	Clark, Ann Nolan	Kiva Publishing
Little Brother	Z+	RF	250+	Doctorow, Cory	Tom Doherty
Little Brother	C	RF	31	Story Box	Wright Group/McGraw Hill
Little Brother	A	RF	14	Sunshine	Wright Group/McGraw Hill
Little Brother's Haircut	J	RF	250+	Story Box	Wright Group/McGraw Hill
Little Brown House	H	RF	266	Jellybeans	Rigby
Little Brown Jay, The: A Tale from India	K	TL	366	Claire, Elizabeth	Mondo Publishing
Little Buddy in the Tub	D	F	49	McGougan, Kathy	Buddy Books Publishing

L

TITLE	LEVEL	GENRE	WORD COUNT	AUTHOR / SERIES	PUBLISHER / DISTRIBUTOR
Little Bulldozer	E	F	170	PM Story Books	Rigby
Little Bulldozer Helps Again	F	F	197	PM Extensions-Blue	Rigby
Little Car	F	F	181	Sunshine	Wright Group/McGraw Hill
Little Caribou	N	I	250+	Fox-Davies, Sarah	Candlewick Press
Little Cat Big Cat	L	I	472	Leveled Literacy Intervention/ Blue System	Heinemann
Little Cat Goes Fast	D	F	80	Early Connections	Benchmark Education
Little Cats	P	I	250+	Crabapples	Crabtree
Little Chick	F	F	161	Early Connections	Benchmark Education
Little Chick	I	F	250+	Hest, Amy	Candlewick Press
Little Chick's Friend Duckling	I	F	572	Kwitz, Mary Deball	HarperTrophy
Little Chicks Sing, The	E	F	52	Instant Readers	Harcourt School Publishers
Little Chief	K	F	250+	Hoff, Syd	HarperCollins
Little Chimp	C	F	50	PM Plus Story Books	Rigby
Little Chimp and Baby Chimp	E	F	184	PM Plus Story Books	Rigby
Little Chimp and Big Chimp	C	RF	66	PM Plus Story Books	Rigby
Little Chimp and the Bees	F	F	160	PM Plus Story Books	Rigby
Little Chimp and the Buffalo	G	F	195	PM Stars	Rigby
Little Chimp and the Termites	H	F	192	PM Plus Story Books	Rigby
Little Chimp Finds Some Fruit	G	F	192	PM Stars	Rigby
Little Chimp Is Brave	D	F	92	PM Stars	Rigby
Little Chimp Runs Away	D	F	104	PM Plus Story Books	Rigby
Little Clearing in the Woods	Q	HF	250+	Wilkes, Maria D.	HarperTrophy
Little Cookie, The	E	TL	310	Fairy Tales and Folklore	Norwood House Press
Little Cousins' Visit, The	C	RF	123	Emergent	Pioneer Valley
Little Cowboy and the Big Cowboy, The	E	RF	275	Easy Stories	Norwood House Press
Little Creatures	F	I	151	PM Science Readers	Rigby
Little Critter Sleeps Over	H	F	267	Mayer, Mercer	Random House
Little Critters	I	RF	127	Books for Young Learners	Richard C. Owen
Little Cub	A	F	24	Leveled Literacy Intervention/ Orange System	Heinemann
Little Dan	H	F	205	The Joy Cowley Collection	Hameray Publishing Group
*Little Dancer and Other Short Stories, The	K	F	250+	New Way Literature	Steck-Vaughn
Little Danny Dinosaur	G	F	195	First Start	Troll Associates
Little Dinosaur	D	F	55	The Vocabulary Development Collection	Pearson Learning Group
Little Dinosaur	K	F	250+	Voyages	SRA/McGraw Hill
Little Dinosaur Escapes	J	HF	389	PM Collection	Rigby
Little Dinosaur Runs Away	J	F	847	Little Dinosaur	Literacy Footprints
Little Dinosaur, the Hero	E	F	159	Little Dinosaur	Literacy Footprints
Little Dinosaur's Skateboard	H	F	186	Little Dinosaur	Literacy Footprints
Little Dog Moon	Q	RF	250+	Trottier, Maxine	Stoddart Kids
Little Dragon Boats	I	RF	250+	Literacy by Design	Rigby
Little Dragon Boats	I	RF	250+	On Our Way to English	Rigby
Little Duchess, The	T	B	250+	WorldScapes	ETA/Cuisenaire
Little Duck and Little Goose	D	F	60	Seedlings	Continental Press
Little Duck for Lily, A	C	RF	42	PM Photo Stories	Rigby
Little Duckling Is Lost	C	F	66	Nelson, May	Scholastic
Little Ducklings	B	RF	56	First Stories	Pacific Learning
Little Dump Truck, The	J	F	198	Cuyler, Margery	Henry Holt & Co.
Little Dutch Boy, The	J	TL	250+	Jumbled Tumbled Tales & Rhymes	Rigby
Little Egg, The	F	F	78	Big Cat	Pacific Learning
Little Elephant	G	F	192	New Way Blue	Steck-Vaughn

Organized Alphabetically by Title
Storable Database at www.fountasandpinnellleveledbooks.com

* Collection of short stories   # Graphic text
^ Mature content with lower level text demands

L

TITLE	LEVEL	GENRE	WORD COUNT	AUTHOR / SERIES	PUBLISHER / DISTRIBUTOR
Little Elephant Thunderfoot	O	RF	250+	Grindley, Sally	Peachtree
Little Elephant's Trunk	L	F	250+	Lincoln, Hazel	Albert Whitman & Co.
Little Farm in the Ozarks	R	HF	250+	MacBride, Roger Lea	HarperTrophy
Little Fawn Grows Up, A	D	I	90	Bonnell, Kris	Reading Reading Books
Little Firefighter, The	M	RF	867	Sunshine	Wright Group/McGraw Hill
Little Fireman	J	RF	250+	Brown, Margaret Wise	HarperCollins
Little Fish	C	F	106	Sails	Rigby
Little Fish	C	F	192	Tiger Cub	Peguis
Little Fish that Got Away	I	F	250+	Cook, Bernadine	Scholastic
Little Fox Goes to the End of the World	L	F	250+	Tompert, Ann	Marshall Cavendish
#Little Friends	K	RF	250+	Tukel, Onur	Marshall Cavendish
Little Frog, Big Pond	J	F	250+	The Wright Skills	Wright Group/McGraw Hill
Little Frog's Monster Story	E	F	144	Ready Readers	Pearson Learning Group
Little Frogs of Puerto Rico, The	J	RF	143	Books for Young Learners	Richard C. Owen
Little Ghost Goes to School	G	F	210	TOTTS	Tott Publications
Little Ghost's Baby Brother	G	F	221	TOTTS	Tott Publications
Little Ghost's Vacation	G	F	118	TOTTS	Tott Publications
Little Giraffe, The	C	RF	70	PM Stars	Rigby
Little Girl and Her Beetle, The	I	TL	250+	Literacy 2000	Rigby
Little Girl and the Bear, The	K	TL	250+	Storyworlds	Heinemann
Little Gorilla	J	F	167	Bornstein, Ruth	Clarion
Little Green Car, The	G	RF	252	Rigby Flying Colors	Rigby
Little Green Dandelion, A	H	RF	191	Books for Young Learners	Richard C. Owen
Little Green Frog	F	F	121	Learn to Read	Creative Teaching Press
Little Green Frogs	I	I	85	Fold Out and Find Out	Candlewick Press
Little Green Man Visits a Farm, The	E	F	183	Learn to Read	Creative Teaching Press
Little Green Witch, The	K	F	250+	McGrath, Barbara Barbieri	Charlesbridge
Little Half Chick	K	F	250+	Literacy Tree	Rigby
Little Hare and the Thundering Earth	S	HF	1426	Leveled Readers	Houghton Mifflin Harcourt
Little Hare and the Thundering Earth	S	HF	1426	Leveled Readers/CA	Houghton Mifflin Harcourt
Little Hare and the Thundering Earth	S	HF	1426	Leveled Readers/TX	Houghton Mifflin Harcourt
Little Hawk's New Name	M	HF	250+	Bolognese, Don	Scholastic
Little Hearts	C	RF	44	Story Box	Wright Group/McGraw Hill
Little Help, A	M	F	250+	Pair-It Turn and Learn	Steck-Vaughn
Little Helpers	I	I	203	Sails	Rigby
Little Hen, The	D	F	107	Ready Readers	Pearson Learning Group
Little Horse and Big Horse	D	F	162	Rigby Flying Colors	Rigby
Little House	LB	F	14	Ready Readers	Pearson Learning Group
Little House Birthday, A	J	HF	250+	Wilder, Laura Ingalls	HarperCollins
Little House by Boston Bay	Q	HF	250+	Wiley, Melissa	HarperTrophy
Little House Farm Days	M	HF	250+	Wilder, Laura Ingalls	HarperTrophy
Little House Friends	M	HF	250+	Wilder, Laura Ingalls	HarperTrophy
Little House in Brookfield	Q	HF	250+	Wilkes, Maria D.	HarperTrophy
Little House in the Big Woods	Q	HF	250+	Wilder, Laura Ingalls	HarperTrophy
Little House in the Highlands	Q	HF	250+	Wiley, Melissa	HarperTrophy
Little House on Rocky Ridge	R	HF	250+	MacBride, Roger Lea	HarperTrophy
Little House on the Prairie	Q	HF	250+	Wilder, Laura Ingalls	HarperTrophy
Little House, The	I	TL	391	Pacific Literacy	Pacific Learning
Little Icicle	O	RF	250+	Szymanski, Lois	Avon Books
Little Iguana	C	RF	28	Reading Street	Pearson
Little Jack Horner	D	TL	29	Jumbled Tumbled Tales & Rhymes	Rigby
Little Kid	H	F	169	Literacy 2000	Rigby
Little Kittens	B	F	27	Ready Readers	Pearson Learning Group

L

TITLE	LEVEL	GENRE	WORD COUNT	AUTHOR / SERIES	PUBLISHER / DISTRIBUTOR
Little Klein	T	HF	250+	Ylvisaker, Anne	Candlewick Press
Little Knight and the Kitten	L	F	648	Pawprints Teal	Pioneer Valley
Little Knight Goes Shopping	A	F	23	Tiny Treasures	Pioneer Valley
Little Knight Runs Away	L	F	549	Pawprints Teal	Pioneer Valley
Little Knight, The	K	F	250+	Reading Unlimited	Pearson Learning Group
Little Knight's Feather	C	F	76	Tiny Treasures	Pioneer Valley
Little Lady, The	C	RF	37	Ray's Readers	Outside the Box
Little Larry: Attentiveness	K	RF	1858	Salerno, Tony Character Classics	Character Building Company
Little Leaf- Leaper, The	O	RF	250+	WorldScapes	ETA/Cuisenaire
*Little Leaf's Journey and the Lost Tooth, The	K	F	564	New Way Orange	Steck-Vaughn
Little Lefty	P	RF	250+	Christopher, Matt	Little Brown and Company
Little Lion, The	A	I	29	Phonics and Friends	Hampton Brown
Little Lizard's First Day	E	F	88	Stone Arch Readers	Stone Arch Books
Little Lizard's New Bike	E	F	103	Stone Arch Readers	Stone Arch Books
Little Lizard's New Pet	C	F	95	Stone Arch Readers	Stone Arch Books
Little Match Girl, The	M	TL	250+	Lighthouse	Ginn & Co.
Little Meanie's Lunch	D	F	90	Story Box	Wright Group/McGraw Hill
Little Mermaid, The	S	TL	250+	Bookshop	Mondo Publishing
Little Mermaid, The	M	TL	735	Springboard	Wright Group/McGraw Hill
Little Miss Muffet	D	TL	26	Jumbled Tumbled Tales & Rhymes	Rigby
Little Miss Muffet	F	TL	146	Literacy 2000	Rigby
Little Miss Muffet	D	RF	59	Seedlings	Continental Press
Little Miss Stoneybrook and Dawn	O	RF	250+	Martin, Ann M.	Scholastic
Little Monkey	I	F	250+	Alphakids	Sundance
Little Monkey Is Stuck	E	F	251	Foundations	Wright Group/McGraw Hill
Little Monkeys	A	I	21	Windows on Literacy	National Geographic
Little Monsters	F	F	38	Pienkowski, Jan	Candlewick Press
Little Mouse	C	F	59	Handprints B	Educators Publishing Service
Little Mouse	E	RF	74	Hoenecke, Karen	Kaeden Books
#Little Mouse Gets Ready	J	F	161	Smith, Jeff	Toon Books
Little Mouse's Trail Tale	I	F	250+	Bookshop	Mondo Publishing
Little Number Stories: Addition	G	I	154	Learn to Read	Creative Teaching Press
Little Number Stories: Subtraction	G	I	133	Learn to Read	Creative Teaching Press
Little Old Lady Who Danced on the Moon, The	M	RF	711	Sunshine	Wright Group/McGraw Hill
Little One Inch	K	TL	384	Gibson, Akimi	Scholastic
Little Overcoat, The	F	TL	237	Bookshop	Mondo Publishing
Little Painter of Sabana Grande, The	M	RF	250+	Soar To Success	Houghton Mifflin Harcourt
Little Panda	G	F	143	Books for Young Learners	Richard C. Owen
Little Panda, The	D	I	40	Windows on Literacy	National Geographic
Little Peach Boy, The	M	TL	250+	Sun Sprouts	ETA/Cuisenaire
*Little Pear	O	HF	250+	Lattimore, Eleanor F.	Harcourt Trade
*Little Pear and His Friends	O	HF	250+	Lattimore, Eleanor F.	Harcourt Trade
Little Peep's Birdhouse	H	F	328	Bonnell, Kris	Reading Reading Books
Little Penguin Is Lost	D	F	56	Reading Safari	Mondo Publishing
Little Penguin: The Emperor of Antarctica	N	RF	250+	London, Jonathan	Marshall Cavendish
Little Penguin's Tale	L	F	250+	Wood, Audrey	Scholastic
Little Pickle	WB	F	0	Collington, Peter	Dutton Children's Books
Little Pig	B	F	24	Coulton, Mia	Maryruth Books
Little Pig	C	F	63	Story Box	Wright Group/McGraw Hill
Little Pig Gets Stuck	D	RF	62	Coulton, Mia	Maryruth Books
Little Piggies	F	F	65	Dominie Readers	Pearson Learning Group

* Collection of short stories   # Graphic text
^ Mature content with lower level text demands

L

TITLE	LEVEL	GENRE	WORD COUNT	AUTHOR / SERIES	PUBLISHER / DISTRIBUTOR
Little Pinto of Mustang Canyon	N	RF	250+	London, Jonathan	Candlewick Press
Little Polar Bear and the Brave Little Hare	K	F	250+	de Beer, Hans	North-South Books
Little Porro	N	F	250+	Sun Sprouts	ETA/Cuisenaire
Little Prairie House, A	J	HF	250+	Wilder, Laura Ingalls	HarperCollins
Little Prince, The	X	F	250+	De Saint-Exupery, Antoine	Harcourt Trade
Little Princess	E	F	99	Seedlings	Continental Press
Little Princess, A	L	RF	250+	All Aboard Reading	Grosset & Dunlap
Little Princess, A	S	RF	5840	Oxford Bookworms Library	Oxford University Press
Little Puff	F	F	297	Easy Stories	Norwood House Press
Little Puffer Fish	H	F	133	Books for Young Learners	Richard C. Owen
Little Puppy Rap	I	F	211	Sunshine	Wright Group/McGraw Hill
Little Quack	I	F	250+	Woods, Ruth	Pearson Publishing Group
Little Quack's New Friend	J	F	250+	Thompson, Lauren	Scholastic
Little Rabbit	E	TL	202	Storyworlds	Heinemann
Little Rabbit Goes to School	J	F	250+	Horse, Harry	Peachtree
Little Rabbit Is Sad	D	F	97	Williams, Deborah	Kaeden Books
Little Rabbit Lost	J	F	250+	Horse, Harry	Peachtree
Little Rabbit Runaway	J	F	250+	Horse, Harry	Peachtree
Little Rabbit Who Wanted Red Wings, The	K	F	364	Seedlings	Continental Press
Little Rabbit's Christmas	J	F	250+	Horse, Harry	Peachtree
Little Rabbit's New Baby	J	F	250+	Horse, Harry	Peachtree
Little Rat Makes Music	L	F	250+	Bang-Campbell, Monika	Harcourt
Little Rat Rides	L	F	250+	Bang-Campbell, Monika	Harcourt
Little Rat Sets Sail	L	F	250+	Bang-Campbell, Monika	Harcourt
Little Red and the Wolf	I	TL	316	Pair-It Books	Steck-Vaughn
Little Red Bat	N	F	1284	Gerber, Carole	Sylvan Dell Publishing
Little Red Bus, The	H	RF	222	PM Story Books	Rigby
Little Red Hen	I	TL	250+	Hunia, Fran	Ladybird Books
Little Red Hen	H	TL	255	New Way Green	Steck-Vaughn
Little Red Hen, The	I	TL	250+	Berg, Jean Horton	Pearson Publishing Group
Little Red Hen, The	G	TL	250+	Cambridge Reading	Pearson Learning Group
Little Red Hen, The	D	TL	200	Cherrington, Janelle	Scholastic
Little Red Hen, The	B	TL	96	Folk Tales	Pioneer Valley
Little Red Hen, The	C	TL	93	Leveled Literacy Intervention/ Blue System	Heinemann
Little Red Hen, The	I	TL	250+	Literacy 2000	Rigby
Little Red Hen, The	G	TL	206	Literacy by Design	Rigby
Little Red Hen, The	L	TL	250+	Pinkney, Jerry	Dial/Penguin
Little Red Hen, The	I	TL	250+	PM Traditional Tales Orange	Rigby
Little Red Hen, The	G	TL	256	Storyteller-Moon Rising	Wright Group/McGraw Hill
Little Red Hen, The	H	TL	250+	Storyworlds	Heinemann
Little Red Hen, The	I	TL	226	Sunshine	Wright Group/McGraw Hill
Little Red Hen, The	C	TL	96	Traditional Tales	Pioneer Valley
Little Red Hen, The	H	TL	375	Traditional Tales	Pearson Learning Group
Little Red Hen, The	B	TL	87	Windmill Books	Wright Group/McGraw Hill
Little Red Hen, The	G	TL	250+	Ziefert, Harriet	Puffin Books
Little Red Pig, The	G	F	214	Ready Readers	Pearson Learning Group
Little Red Riding Hood	E	TL	140	Bookshop	Mondo Publishing
Little Red Riding Hood	K	TL	250+	Enrichment	Wright Group/McGraw Hill
Little Red Riding Hood	E	TL	355	Fairy Tales and Folklore	Norwood House Press
Little Red Riding Hood	G	TL	140	Folk Tales	Pioneer Valley
Little Red Riding Hood	WB	TL	0	Goodall, John	McElderry
Little Red Riding Hood	H	TL	250+	Hunia, Fran	Ladybird Books
Little Red Riding Hood	N	TL	250+	Hyman, Trina Schart	Houghton Mifflin Harcourt

L

TITLE	LEVEL	GENRE	WORD COUNT	AUTHOR / SERIES	PUBLISHER / DISTRIBUTOR
Little Red Riding Hood	I	TL	250+	Jumbled Tumbled Tales & Rhymes	Rigby
Little Red Riding Hood	J	TL	250+	PM Tales and Plays-Turquoise	Rigby
Little Red Riding Hood	H	TL	250+	Shapiro, Sara	Scholastic
Little Red Riding Hood	M	TL	250+	Spirin, Gennady	Marshall Cavendish
Little Red Riding Hood	K	TL	250+	Story Steps	Rigby
Little Red Riding Hood	I	TL	250+	Storyworlds	Heinemann
Little Red Riding Hood	G	TL	140	Sun Sprouts	ETA/Cuisenaire
Little Red Riding Hood and the Wolf	I	TL	461	Traditional Tales	Pioneer Valley
Little Red Riding Hood: A Newfangled Prairie Tale	O	TL	250+	Ernst, Lisa Campbell	Scholastic
Little Red Sports Car	G	F	231	The Story Basket	Wright Group/McGraw Hill
Little Rock Nine Stand Up for Their Rights, The	T	HF	3655	History Speaks	Millbrook Press
Little Round Husband, The	M	F	250+	Sunshine	Wright Group/McGraw Hill
Little Runaway, The	F	F	196	Easy Stories	Norwood House Press
Little Runner of the Longhouse	K	HF	250+	Baker, Betty	HarperTrophy
Little School	J	RF	216	Norling, Beth	Kane/Miller Book Publishers
Little Sea Pony, The	N	F	250+	Cresswell, Helen	HarperTrophy
Little Seed, A	B	I	18	Smart Start	Rigby
Little Seeds	C	I	75	First Stories	Pacific Learning
Little Shapes and Big Shapes	A	I	40	InfoTrek	ETA/Cuisenaire
Little Shopping, A	M	RF	250+	Rylant, Cynthia	Aladdin
Little Sibu	M	F	250+	Grindley, Sally	Peachtree
Little Sima and the Giant Bowl	N	TL	1645	On My Own Folklore	Millbrook Press
Little Sister	C	RF	40	Mitchell, Robin	Scholastic
Little Sister	H	RF	213	More Adventures with Colin	Short Tales Press
Little Skink's Tail	L	F	395	Halfmann, Janet	Sylvan Dell Publishing
Little Snowman, The	C	RF	59	PM Extensions-Red	Rigby
Little Soup's Birthday	K	HF	250+	Peck, Robert Newton	Bantam Books
Little Sparrow, The: A Cinderella Story From Italy	O	TL	795	Leveled Readers	Houghton Mifflin Harcourt
Little Spider, The	K	F	250+	Literacy 2000	Rigby
Little Sprout, The	E	F	105	Bonnell, Kris	Reading Reading Books
Little Swan	M	RF	250+	Geras, Adele	Random House
Little Teddy and the Monkey	C	F	50	PM Stars	Rigby
Little Things	A	I	40	Leveled Literacy Intervention/ Orange System	Heinemann
Little Things	A	I	33	PM Starters	Rigby
Little Tin Soldier,The	M	TL	766	Tales from Hans Andersen	Wright Group/McGraw Hill
Little Tommy Tucker	E	TL	30	Jumbled Tumbled Tales & Rhymes	Rigby
Little Town at the Crossroads	Q	HF	250+	Wilkes, Maria D.	HarperTrophy
Little Town in the Ozarks	R	HF	250+	MacBride, Roger Lea	HarperTrophy
Little Town on the Prairie	Q	HF	250+	Wilder, Laura Ingalls	HarperTrophy
Little Tree, The	K	F	222	Dominie Readers	Pearson Learning Group
Little Tree, The	D	I	114	Vocabulary Readers	Houghton Mifflin Harcourt
Little Tree, The	D	I	114	Vocabulary Readers/CA	Houghton Mifflin Harcourt
Little Tuppen	I	TL	250+	Galdone, Paul	Houghton Mifflin Harcourt
Little Turtle	WB	RF	0	Books for Young Learners	Richard C. Owen
Little Turtle, The	D	F	57	Lindsay, Vachel	Scholastic
Little Vampire and the Midnight Bear	L	F	250+	Kwitz, Mary DeBall	Puffin Books
Little Walrus Rising	K	F	250+	Young, Carol	Scholastic
Little Whale, The	M	F	1057	Sunshine	Wright Group/McGraw Hill
Little Wheels	D	F	115	Stone Arch Readers	Stone Arch Books
Little White Hen, The	E	F	159	PM Plus Story Books	Rigby

* Collection of short stories   # Graphic text
^ Mature content with lower level text demands

TITLE	LEVEL	GENRE	WORD COUNT	AUTHOR / SERIES	PUBLISHER / DISTRIBUTOR
Little Witch Goes to School	K	F	250+	Hautzig, Deborah	Random House
Little Witch's Big Night	K	F	250+	Hautzig, Deborah	Random House
Little Wolf's New Home	F	F	253	Leveled Literacy Intervention/ Blue System	Heinemann
Little Women	Z	HF	250+	Alcott, Louisa May	Aladdin
Little Women	M	HF	250+	Bullseye	Random House
Little Work Plane, The	I	F	250+	PM Plus Story Books	Rigby
Little Yellow Chicken, The	I	F	322	Sunshine	Wright Group/McGraw Hill
Little Yellow Chicken's House, The	F	F	287	Story Basket	Wright Group/McGraw Hill
Little Zoot	E	F	33	Little Celebrations	Pearson Learning Group
Little, Little Man, The	M	F	741	Book Bank	Wright Group/McGraw Hill
Littles and the Great Halloween Scare, The	M	F	250+	Peterson, John	Scholastic
Littles and the Lost Children, The	M	F	250+	Peterson, John	Scholastic
Littles and the Terrible Tiny Kid, The	M	F	250+	Peterson, John	Scholastic
Littles and the Trash Tinies, The	M	F	250+	Peterson, John	Scholastic
Littles Give a Party, The	M	F	250+	Peterson, John	Scholastic
Littles Go Exploring, The	M	F	250+	Peterson, John	Scholastic
Littles Go to School, The	M	F	250+	Peterson, John	Scholastic
Littles Have a Wedding, The	M	F	250+	Peterson, John	Scholastic
Littles Take a Trip, The	M	F	250+	Peterson, John	Scholastic
Littles to the Rescue, The	M	F	250+	Peterson, John	Scholastic
Littles, The	M	F	250+	Peterson, John	Scholastic
Littlest Dinosaur, The	K	F	250+	Foreman, Michael	Walker & Company
Littlest Dinosaur's Big Adventure, The	K	F	250+	Foreman, Michael	Walker & Company
Littlest Glowworm, The	N	F	1517	Take Two Books	Wright Group/McGraw Hill
Lives of Ants, The	O	I	1054	Leveled Readers	Houghton Mifflin Harcourt
Lives of Ants, The	O	I	1054	Leveled Readers/CA	Houghton Mifflin Harcourt
Lives of Ants, The	O	I	1054	Leveled Readers/TX	Houghton Mifflin Harcourt
*Lives of Extraordinary Women: Rulers, Rebels, (and What the Neighbors Thought)	V	B	250+	Krull, Kathleen	Houghton Mifflin Harcourt
Lives of Social Insects, The	P	I	886	Leveled Readers	Houghton Mifflin Harcourt
Lives of Social Insects, The	P	I	886	Leveled Readers/CA	Houghton Mifflin Harcourt
Lives of Social Insects, The	P	I	886	Leveled Readers/TX	Houghton Mifflin Harcourt
*Lives of the Artists: Masterpieces, Messes, (and What the Neighbors Though)	V	B	250+	Krull, Kathleen	Sandpiper Books
*Lives of the Musicians: Good Times, Bad Times (and What the Neighbors Thought)	V	B	250+	Krull, Kathleen	Sandpiper Books
*Lives of the Presidents: Fame, Shame (and What the Neighbors Thought)	V	B	250+	Krull, Kathleen	Houghton Mifflin Harcourt
*Lives of the Writers: Comedies, Tragedies (and What the Neighbors Thought)	V	B	250+	Krull, Kathleen	Sandpiper Books
Living Abroad	S	I	1619	Reading Street	Pearson
Living and Growing	J	I	250+	PM Plus Nonfiction	Rigby
Living and Nonliving	I	I	132	Nature Basics	Capstone Press
Living and Working in Space	J	I	383	Leveled Readers	Houghton Mifflin Harcourt
Living and Working in Space	J	I	383	Leveled Readers/CA	Houghton Mifflin Harcourt
Living and Working in Space	J	I	383	Leveled Readers/TX	Houghton Mifflin Harcourt
Living Desert, The	J	I	230	On Our Way to English	Rigby
Living Desert, The	I	I	123	Pair-It Turn and Learn	Steck-Vaughn
Living Dinosaurs	O	I	641	Big Cat	Pacific Learning
Living Green	V	I	250+	Sally Ride Science	Roaring Brook Press
Living History	V	I	250+	iOpeners	Pearson Learning Group
Living in a City	F	I	133	Communities	Capstone Press
Living in a Desert	K	I	333	Red Rocket Readers	Flying Start Books
Living in a Rural Area	G	I	129	Communities	Capstone Press

L

TITLE	LEVEL	GENRE	WORD COUNT	AUTHOR / SERIES	PUBLISHER / DISTRIBUTOR
Living in a Small Town	F	I	117	Communities	Capstone Press
Living in a Suburb	G	I	114	Communities	Capstone Press
Living in Alaska	C	I	101	In Step Readers	Rigby
Living in Alaska	C	I	101	Literacy by Design	Rigby
Living in an Igloo	H	RF	181	Bebop Books	Lee & Low Books Inc.
Living in Groups	O	I	250+	Rigby Flying Colors	Rigby
Living in Hard Times	S	I	594	Vocabulary Readers	Houghton Mifflin Harcourt
Living in Harsh Lands	X	I	250+	iOpeners	Pearson Learning Group
Living in Rural Communities	I	I	243	Communities	Lerner Publishing Group
Living in Space	V	I	2329	Leveled Readers	Houghton Mifflin Harcourt
Living in Space	U	I	250+	Leveled Readers Language Support	Houghton Mifflin Harcourt
Living in Space	V	I	2329	Leveled Readers/CA	Houghton Mifflin Harcourt
Living in Space	V	I	2329	Leveled Readers/TX	Houghton Mifflin Harcourt
Living in Space	O	I	250+	Nayer, Judy	Pearson Learning Group
Living in Space	M	I	250+	Rigby Star Quest	Rigby
Living in Space	O	I	250+	Scooters	ETA/Cuisenaire
Living in Space	R	I	1121	Time for Kids	Teacher Created Materials
Living in Suburban Communities	I	I	279	Communities	Lerner Publishing Group
Living in the Extreme	O	I	250+	Literacy by Design	Rigby
Living in the Ocean	G	I	212	Dominie Factivity Series	Pearson Learning Group
Living in the Rain Forest	N	I	818	Rigby Flying Colors	Rigby
Living in the Sky	K	RF	328	Sunshine	Wright Group/McGraw Hill
Living in Trees	Q	I	1328	Leveled Readers	Houghton Mifflin Harcourt
Living in Trees	Q	I	1328	Leveled Readers/CA	Houghton Mifflin Harcourt
Living in Trees	Q	I	1328	Leveled Readers/TX	Houghton Mifflin Harcourt
Living in Trees	B	I	36	Sails	Rigby
Living in Two Worlds	N	I	250+	InfoQuest	Rigby
Living in Urban Communities	I	I	212	Communities	Lerner Publishing Group
Living It Up in Space	R	I	250+	Explorer Books-Pathfinder	National Geographic
Living it Up in Space	P	I	250+	Explorer Books-Pioneer	National Geographic
Living Lights: Fireflies in Your Backyard	M	I	250+	Backyard Bugs	Picture Window Books
Living Ocean, The	U	I	250+	Pair-It Books	Steck-Vaughn
Living on the Edge	R	I	250+	High-Fliers	Pacific Learning
Living on the Farm	D	I	155	Early Connections	Benchmark Education
Living or Nonliving	B	I	27	Instant Readers	Harcourt School Publishers
Living Rain Forest, The	S	I	250+	Orbit Chapter Books	Pacific Learning
Living Things	E	I	75	Avery, Dorothy	Scholastic
Living Things	C	I	57	Independent Readers Science	Houghton Mifflin Harcourt
Living Things	C	I	43	Leveled Readers Science	Houghton Mifflin Harcourt
Living Things	G	I	151	Rosen Real Readers	Rosen Publishing Group
Living Things	I	I	383	Science Support Readers	Houghton Mifflin Harcourt
Living Things	K	I	250+	The Rowland Reading Program Library	Rowland Reading Foundation
Living Things Are Everywhere!	H	I	130	Life Science	Abrams & Company
Living Things Need Food	H	I	66	Windows on Literacy	National Geographic
Living Things Need Water	C	I	26	Windows on Literacy	National Geographic
Living Through a Natural Disaster	W	I	250+	iOpeners	Pearson Learning Group
*Living to Tell the Tale—Survival Stories	T	I	250+	Connectors	Pacific Learning
Living Together	L	I	284	Gear Up!	Wright Group/McGraw Hill
Living Together	F	I	176	Sails	Rigby
Living Underground	I	I	185	Red Rocket Readers	Flying Start Books
*Living Up the Street	Y	RF	250+	Soto, Gary	Bantam Books
Living with Hurricanes	S	I	250+	Harcourt Trophies	Harcourt, Inc.
Living with Llamas	R	I	250+	WorldScapes	ETA/Cuisenaire

* Collection of short stories   # Graphic text
^ Mature content with lower level text demands

L

TITLE	LEVEL	GENRE	WORD COUNT	AUTHOR / SERIES	PUBLISHER / DISTRIBUTOR
Living With Others	J	I	250+	PM Plus Nonfiction	Rigby
Living with Salties	P	I	250+	Orbit Double Takes	Pacific Learning
^Living With Vampires	O	F	3653	Strong, Jeremy	Stone Arch Books
Liz Makes a Rainbow: The Magic School Bus	L	F	250+	West, Tracey	Scholastic
Liz on the Move: The Magic School Bus	L	F	250+	West, Tracey	Scholastic
Lizard	E	RF	80	Foundations	Wright Group/McGraw Hill
Lizard Loses His Tail	D	RF	54	PM Story Books	Rigby
Lizard Music	T	F	250+	Pinkwater, D. Manus	Bantam Books
Lizard on a Stick	C	RF	38	Wonder World	Wright Group/McGraw Hill
Lizard on the Loose	K	RF	667	In Step Readers	Rigby
Lizard Tongue	Q	RF	250+	PM Extensions	Rigby
Lizards	H	I	106	Desert Animals	Capstone Press
Lizards	S	I	250+	Keeping Unsual Pets	Heinemann Library
Lizards	G	I	228	Sails	Rigby
Lizards	L	I	356	Wonder World	Wright Group/McGraw Hill
Lizards and Salamanders	M	I	250+	Reading Unlimited	Pearson Learning Group
Lizards and Snakes	O	I	250+	Rigby Literacy	Rigby
Lizard's Grandmother	J	F	336	Sunshine	Wright Group/McGraw Hill
Lizard's Song	M	TL	250+	Voyages	SRA/McGraw Hill
Lizzie Bright and the Buckminster Boy	X	HF	250+	Schmidt, Gary D.	Clarion Books
Lizzie Newton and the San Francisco Earthquake	Q	HF	3613	History Speaks	Millbrook Press
Lizzie's Lizard	L	I	289	Storyteller Nonfiction	Wright Group/McGraw Hill
Lizzie's Lunch	I	F	118	Literacy Tree	Rigby
Lizzy	E	RF	155	Leveled Literacy Intervention/ Green System	Heinemann
Llama in the Family, A	O	RF	250+	Hurwitz, Johanna	Scholastic
Llama Pajamas	N	RF	250+	Clymer, Susan	Scholastic
Llamas	O	I	1297	Early Bird Nature Books	Lerner Publishing Group
Lluvia and Christopher	F	RF	74	Larkin's Little Readers	Wilbooks
Loading the Airplane	G	RF	140	Windows on Literacy	National Geographic
Loans for the Poor	W	I	2313	Leveled Readers	Houghton Mifflin Harcourt
Loans for the Poor	W	I	2313	Leveled Readers/CA	Houghton Mifflin Harcourt
Loans for the Poor	W	I	2313	Leveled Readers/TX	Houghton Mifflin Harcourt
Lobster	I	I	132	Under the Sea	Capstone Press
Lobster Fishing at Dawn	I	I	104	Ready Readers	Pearson Learning Group
Lobstering	LB	I	14	Little Books for Early Readers	University of Maine
Lobster's Tale, A	W	I	2114	Leveled Readers	Houghton Mifflin Harcourt
*Local News	W	RF	250+	Soto, Gary	Scholastic
Loch Ness Monster Mystery, The	S	I	250+	Literacy 2000	Rigby
^Loch Ness Monster, The	V	I	250+	The Unexplained	Capstone Press
Loch Ness Monster, The	L	I	359	Vocabulary Readers	Houghton Mifflin Harcourt
Loch Ness Monster, The	L	I	359	Vocabulary Readers/CA	Houghton Mifflin Harcourt
Loch Ness Monster, The	I	I	359	Vocabulary Readers/TX	Houghton Mifflin Harcourt
^Loch Ness Monster, The: The Unsolved Mystery	R	I	250+	Mysteries of Science	Capstone Press
Lockdown: Escape from Furnace	Z	SF	250+	Smith, Alexander Gordon	Farrar, Straus, & Giroux
Lock the Gate!	D	RF	41	Leveled Readers	Houghton Mifflin Harcourt
Locked In	J	F	250+	Coulton, Mia	Maryruth Books
Locked In	H	RF	228	PM Plus Story Books	Rigby
Locked in the Library!	M	F	250+	Brown, Marc	Little Brown and Company
Locked Out	G	RF	15	PM Story Books	Rigby
Locked Out!	B	RF	15	Twig	Wright Group/McGraw Hill
Lockgate Mystery, The	P	RF	250+	Storyteller-Raging Rivers	Wright Group/McGraw Hill
Locomotion	V	RF	250+	Woodson, Jacqueline	Penguin Group
Locusts: Insects on the Move	T	I	2877	Insect World	Lerner Publishing Group

* Collection of short stories   # Graphic text
^ Mature content with lower level text demands

Organized Alphabetically by Title   **445**

L

TITLE	LEVEL	GENRE	WORD COUNT	AUTHOR / SERIES	PUBLISHER / DISTRIBUTOR
Log Cabin	I	I	157	Bookworms	Marshall Cavendish
Log Cabin in the Woods	R	HF	250+	Henry, Joanne Landers	Scholastic
Log Cabin Wedding, The	O	HF	250+	Howard, Ellen	Holiday House
Log Garfish	M	TL	114	Books for Young Learners	Richard C. Owen
Log Hotel	J	RF	261	Schreiber, Anne	Scholastic
Log Hotel, The	A	F	22	Little Celebrations	Pearson Learning Group
Log, The	C	RF	29	New Way Red	Steck-Vaughn
Log, The	E	RF	179	Sails	Rigby
Logan West, Printer's Devil	T	HF	250+	Bookshop	Mondo Publishing
Lois Lowry	T	B	250+	Markham, Lois	Creative Teaching Press
Lola and Miss Kitty	H	RF	250+	Little Readers	Houghton Mifflin Harcourt
Lola at the Library	I	RF	288	McQuinn, Anna	Charlesbridge
Lola Loves Stories	J	F	245	McQuinn, Anna	Charlesbridge
Lola, the Muddy Dog	D	RF	107	Leveled Readers	Houghton Mifflin Harcourt
Lola, the Muddy Dog	D	RF	107	Leveled Readers/CA	Houghton Mifflin Harcourt
Lollipop	G	F	59	Watson, Wendy	Crowell
Lollipop Please, A	H	RF	73	Literacy 2000	Rigby
Lon Po Po: A Red-Riding Hood Story from China	S	TL	250+	Young, Ed	Scholastic
London	T	I	4800	Oxford Bookworms Library	Oxford University Press
London Eye Mystery, The	X	RF	250+	Dowd, Siobhan	Yearling Books
London: From Roman Capital to Olympic City	T	I	250+	Through Time	Kingfisher
Lone Wolf	Y	RF	2697	Leveled Readers	Houghton Mifflin Harcourt
Lonely Bull, The	E	F	116	Pacific Literacy	Pacific Learning
Lonely Dragon, The	J	F	250+	Momentum Literacy Program	Troll Associates
Lonely Giant, The	K	F	449	Literacy 2000	Rigby
Lonely Giant, The	J	F	590	Red Rocket Readers	Flying Start Books
Lonely Man, The	P	TL	767	Leveled Readers	Houghton Mifflin Harcourt
Lonely Man, The	P	TL	767	Leveled Readers/CA	Houghton Mifflin Harcourt
Lonely Man, The	P	TL	767	Leveled Readers/TX	Houghton Mifflin Harcourt
Long Way Gone: Memoirs of a Boy Soldier	Z	B	250+	Beah, Ishmael	Macmillan
Long Ago	G	I	53	Discovery Links	Newbridge
Long Ago	D	I	105	Early Connections	Benchmark Education
Long Ago and Far Away	T	I	250+	Wildcats	Wright Group/McGraw Hill
Long Ago and Today	D	I	72	Learn to Read	Creative Teaching Press
Long Ago and Today	E	I	64	Shutterbug Books	Steck-Vaughn
Long and Short	D	RF	108	PM Math Readers	Rigby
Long and Short	I	F	228	Sunshine	Wright Group/McGraw Hill
Long and Short: An Animal Opposites Book	K	I	250+	Animal Opposites	Capstone Press
Long Arrow and the Elk Dogs	Q	TL	250+	Leveled Readers Language Support	Houghton Mifflin Harcourt
Long Bike Ride, The	G	RF	183	PM Photo Stories	Rigby
Long Cattle Drive, The	T	HF	2463	Leveled Readers	Houghton Mifflin Harcourt
Long Cattle Drive, The	T	HF	2463	Leveled Readers/CA	Houghton Mifflin Harcourt
Long Cattle Drive, The	T	HF	2463	Leveled Readers/TX	Houghton Mifflin Harcourt
Long Grass of Tumbledown Road	M	F	283	Read Alongs	Rigby
Long Hair	B	I	30	Sails	Rigby
Long Limousines	L	I	160	On Deck	Rigby
Long Live the Queen	Z+	RF	250+	White, Ellen Emerson	Feiwel and Friends
Long May She Reign	Z+	RF	250+	White, Ellen Emerson	Feiwel and Friends
Long Road to Freedom: Journey of the Hmong	V	I	250+	High Five Reading	Red Brick Learning
Long Shot	S	RF	250+	Lupica, Mike	Puffin Books
Long Shot	S	RF	250+	Orca Young Readers	Orca Books
Long Shot for Paul	Q	RF	250+	Christopher, Matt	Little Brown and Company

Organized Alphabetically by Title
Storable Database at www.fountasandpinnellleveledbooks.com

* Collection of short stories   # Graphic text
^ Mature content with lower level text demands

TITLE	LEVEL	GENRE	WORD COUNT	AUTHOR / SERIES	PUBLISHER / DISTRIBUTOR
Long Texas Trail, The	R	HF	250+	Literacy by Design	Rigby
Long Time Ago, A	H	I	112	Sails	Rigby
Long Trail Home, The	S	HF	250+	On Our Way to English	Rigby
Long Trip West, The	R	I	633	Reading Street	Pearson
Long Wait, The	L	RF	250+	Math Matters	Kane Press
Long Walk Home, The	P	RF	250+	Action Packs	Rigby
Long Walk to Water, A	W	RF	250+	Park, Linda Sue	Clarion Books
Long Walk, A	E	I	131	Twig	Wright Group/McGraw Hill
Long Way from Chicago, A	V	HF	250+	Peck, Richard	Puffin Books
Long Way Home, The	G	RF	94	Rookie Readers	Children's Press
Long Way to a New Land, A	L	HF	250+	Sandin, Joan	HarperTrophy
Long Way to Go, A	R	I	250+	O'Neal, Zibby	Penguin Group
Long Way Westward, The	L	HF	250+	Sandin, Joan	HarperTrophy
Long Winter, The	Q	HF	250+	Wilder, Laura Ingalls	HarperTrophy
Long, Long Ago	M	I	250+	Literacy 2000	Rigby
Long, Long Ago	M	TL	250+	Literacy by Design	Rigby
Long, Long Ride, The	J	RF	462	Red Rocket Readers	Flying Start Books
Long, Long Tail, The	B	F	33	Sunshine	Wright Group/McGraw Hill
Long-Arm Quarterback	S	RF	250+	Christopher, Matt	Norwood House Press
Long-Distance Dispatch Between Lydia Goldblatt & Julie Graham-Chan, The	T	RF	250+	Ignatow, Amy	Amulet Books
Longest Necklace, The	B	RF	64	InfoTrek	ETA/Cuisenaire
Longest Noodle in the World, The	D	F	66	Joy Readers	Pearson Learning Group
Longest Shortcut, The	O	RF	250+	Literacy by Design	Rigby
Longest Shortcut, The	O	RF	250+	On Our Way to English	Rigby
Longest Yawn, The	M	RF	1220	Science Solves It!	Kane Press
Long-Lost Friends, The	M	RF	250+	Woodland Mysteries	Wright Group/McGraw Hill
Long-Neck: The Adventure of Apatosaurus	N	I	250+	Dinosaur World	Picture Window Books
Long-Range Bombers: The B-1B Lancers	V	I	250+	War Planes	Capstone Press
Loni's Town	J	RF	353	Reading Street	Pearson
Look	A	F	20	Sunshine	Wright Group/McGraw Hill
Look Again	C	I	47	Bookshop	Mondo Publishing
Look and See	G	I	208	Learn to Read	Creative Teaching Press
Look Around!	LB	I	7	Reading Street	Pearson
Look at All the Money!	F	I	110	InfoTrek	ETA/Cuisenaire
Look at Australia, A	M	I	185	Pebble Books	Red Brick Learning
Look at Bix	B	I	25	Reading Street	Pearson
Look at Both Sides	K	I	236	Yellow Umbrella Books	Capstone Press
Look at Canada, A	M	I	180	Pebble Books	Red Brick Learning
Look at China, A	M	I	178	Our World	Capstone Press
Look at Conor	A	RF	27	Little Books for Early Readers	University of Maine
Look at Cuba, A	M	I	149	Our World	Capstone Press
Look at Danny	C	RF	39	Coulton, Mia	Maryruth Books
Look at Dogs, A	M	I	551	Pair-It Books	Steck-Vaughn
Look at Egypt, A	M	I	179	Our World	Capstone Press
Look at France, A	M	I	152	Pebble Books	Red Brick Learning
Look at Germany, A	M	I	162	Our World	Capstone Press
Look at Japan, A	M	I	185	Pebble Books	Red Brick Learning
Look at Kenya, A	M	I	161	Our World	Capstone Press
Look at Kyle	B	I	46	Little Books for Early Readers	University of Maine
Look at Lady Liberty, A	M	B	250+	Rosen Real Readers	Rosen Publishing Group
Look at Me	D	RF	67	Carousel Readers	Pearson Learning Group
Look at Me	C	RF	62	Early Connections	Benchmark Education
Look at Me	B	I	24	InfoTrek	ETA/Cuisenaire

L

TITLE	LEVEL	GENRE	WORD COUNT	AUTHOR / SERIES	PUBLISHER / DISTRIBUTOR
Look at Me	F	RF	104	Literacy 2000	Rigby
Look at Me	LB	I	17	Little Books for Early Readers	University of Maine
Look at Me	B	RF	48	PM Starters	Rigby
Look at Me	LB	I	13	Windows on Literacy	National Geographic
Look at Me Fly	B	F	35	Brand New Readers	Candlewick Press
Look at Me!	B	F	59	In Step Readers	Rigby
Look at Me!	A	F	27	KinderReaders	Rigby
Look at Me!	A	RF	27	Leveled Readers Emergent	Houghton Mifflin Harcourt
Look at Me!	B	RF	35	Lighthouse	Rigby
Look at Me!	D	F	94	Rigby Rocket	Rigby
Look at Me!	B	F	62	Sails	Rigby
Look at Me!	A	I	19	Vocabulary Readers	Houghton Mifflin Harcourt
Look at Me!	A	I	19	Vocabulary Readers/CA	Houghton Mifflin Harcourt
Look at Mexico, A	M	I	159	Our World	Capstone Press
Look at Minerals, A: From Galena to Gold	S	I	250+	A First Book	Franklin Watts
Look at Monkey	C	F	95	Sails	Rigby
Look at My Eggs!	C	F	39	Sails	Rigby
Look at My Friends	A	RF	32	In Step Readers	Rigby
Look At My Home	A	I	32	Red Rocket Readers	Flying Start Books
Look at My Weaving	C	I	69	First Stories	Pacific Learning
Look at Pets, A	J	I	250+	Rigby Rocket	Rigby
Look at Pickles	B	RF	90	Pickles the Dog Series	Pioneer Valley
Look at Rocks, A: From Coal to Kimerlite	S	I	250+	A First Book	Franklin Watts
Look at Russia, A	M	I	161	Our World	Capstone Press
Look at Snakes, A	M	I	250+	Pair-It Books	Steck-Vaughn
Look at Spiders, A	M	I	785	Pair-It Books	Steck-Vaughn
Look at That Cat!	I	RF	407	Reading Street	Pearson
Look at the Animals	B	I	64	Early Connections	Benchmark Education
Look at the Animals	B	RF	49	Little Readers	Houghton Mifflin Harcourt
Look at the Animals	B	RF	24	Sails	Rigby
Look at the Ball	B	I	58	Storyteller	Wright Group/McGraw Hill
Look at the Bears	A	F	28	Leveled Readers	Houghton Mifflin Harcourt
Look at the Bears	A	F	28	Leveled Readers/CA	Houghton Mifflin Harcourt
Look at the Calendar, A	H	I	139	Rosen Real Readers	Rosen Publishing Group
Look at the Clock, Max!	C	F	28	Reading Street	Pearson
Look at the Garden	A	I	43	Windmill Books	Rigby
Look at the House	B	F	53	PM Plus Starters	Rigby
Look at the Leaves	I	I	350	Rigby Flying Colors	Rigby
Look at the Leaves	B	I	27	Windows on Literacy	National Geographic
Look at the Lizard	A	I	33	Bookshop	Mondo Publishing
Look at the Moon	N	I	250+	Bookshop	Mondo Publishing
Look at the Ocean, A	B	I	50	Little Books for Early Readers	University of Maine
Look at the Robot	A	F	24	Sails	Rigby
Look at the Signs	A	I	71	Getting Around	American Reading Company
Look at the Signs	A	I	98	Readlings	American Reading Company
Look at the Stars	H	I	144	Rigby Focus	Rigby
Look at the Tree	B	I	22	Windows on Literacy	National Geographic
Look at This	B	I	57	Carousel Earlybirds	Pearson Learning Group
Look at This Mess!	C	RF	50	First Stories	Pacific Learning
Look at This!	B	I	71	Literacy by Design	Rigby
Look at Us	B	RF	42	Johns, Linda	Scholastic
Look at Vietnam, A	M	I	163	Our World	Capstone Press
Look at What I Can Do!	C	I	57	Bonnell, Kris	Reading Reading Books
Look Before You Leap	Q	RF	250+	Mazer, Anne	Scholastic

* Collection of short stories   # Graphic text
^ Mature content with lower level text demands

L

TITLE	LEVEL	GENRE	WORD COUNT	AUTHOR / SERIES	PUBLISHER / DISTRIBUTOR
Look Closer	A	I	21	Ready Readers	Pearson Learning Group
Look Down Low	F	I	66	Early Readers	Compass Point Books
Look Down!	B	I	51	Early Connections	Benchmark Education
Look for Bugs	A	RF	35	Leveled Readers	Houghton Mifflin Harcourt
Look for Bugs	A	RF	35	Leveled Readers/CA	Houghton Mifflin Harcourt
Look For It!	C	I	49	Bonnell, Kris	Reading Reading Books
Look for Me	D	RF	71	Story Box	Wright Group/McGraw Hill
Look for Me!	F	I	208	Little Readers	Houghton Mifflin Harcourt
Look for Pony	D	F	47	Coulton, Mia	Maryruth Books
Look Here!	E	RF	67	Wonder World	Wright Group/McGraw Hill
Look How Tall I Am!	E	RF	108	Windows on Literacy	National Geographic
Look How We Cook	B	I	49	Red Rocket Readers	Flying Start Books
Look in Mom's Purse	D	RF	60	Carousel Readers	Pearson Learning Group
Look in the Garden	G	RF	208	PM Plus Story Books	Rigby
Look in the Garden	D	I	115	Rigby Flying Colors	Rigby
Look in the Rainforest, A	A	I	29	Bonnell, Kris	Reading Reading Books
Look in the Tree	D	I	97	Springboard	Wright Group/McGraw Hill
Look in the Waterhole	I	TL	357	Red Rocket Readers	Flying Start Books
Look in the Woods	C	RF	71	Leveled Readers	Houghton Mifflin Harcourt
Look in the Woods	C	RF	71	Leveled Readers/CA	Houghton Mifflin Harcourt
Look Inside	E	I	77	Sails	Rigby
Look Inside	J	I	168	Storyteller Nonfiction	Wright Group/McGraw Hill
Look Inside a Log Cabin	J	I	163	Look Inside	Capstone Press
Look Inside a Pyramid	L	I	160	Look Inside	Capstone Press
Look Inside a Tepee	J	I	163	Look Inside	Capstone Press
Look Inside an Igloo	J	I	173	Look Inside	Capstone Press
Look into Space, A	D	I	71	Discovery World	Rigby
Look Out - Minibeasts About!	N	I	250+	Rigby Rocket	Rigby
Look Out for Bingo	E	RF	138	PM Plus Story Books	Rigby
Look Out for Space Monster	C	F	54	Spaceboy	Literacy Footprints
Look Out for Your Tail	J	F	250+	Literacy 2000	Rigby
Look Out the Window	C	RF	67	Story Steps	Rigby
Look Out!	B	F	15	Literacy 2000	Rigby
Look Out!	I	RF	250+	PM Plus Story Books	Rigby
Look Out!	B	F	29	Rigby Rocket	Rigby
Look Out!	D	F	53	Sunshine	Wright Group/McGraw Hill
Look Out, Butterfly!	WB	I	0	Big Cat	Pacific Learning
Look Out, Dan!	B	F	34	Story Box	Wright Group/McGraw Hill
Look Out, Fish!	C	F	65	Lighthouse	Rigby
Look Out, Fox!	B	F	32	Sails	Rigby
Look Out, Suzy Goose	J	F	232	Horacek, Petr	Candlewick Press
Look Out, Washington D.C.!	O	RF	250+	Giff, Patricia Reilly	Bantam Books
Look Up	C	I	25	Bonnell, Kris	Reading Reading Books
Look Up	R	I	250+	iOpeners	Pearson Learning Group
Look Up	E	I	44	Little Celebrations	Pearson Learning Group
Look Up!	A	I	25	Leveled Readers	Houghton Mifflin Harcourt
Look Up!	A	I	25	Leveled Readers/CA	Houghton Mifflin Harcourt
Look Up!	WB	I	0	Reach	National Geographic
Look Up, Look Down	D	I	165	PM Nonfiction-Red	Rigby
Look What Came from China	O	I	250+	Harvey, Miles	Franklin Watts
Look What Came from Egypt	O	I	250+	Harvey, Miles	Franklin Watts
Look What Came from France	O	I	250+	Harvey, Miles	Franklin Watts
Look What Came from Italy	O	I	250+	Harvey, Miles	Franklin Watts
Look What Came from Mexico	O	I	250+	Harvey, Miles	Franklin Watts

L

TITLE	LEVEL	GENRE	WORD COUNT	AUTHOR / SERIES	PUBLISHER / DISTRIBUTOR
Look What Came from Russia	O	I	250+	Harvey, Miles	Franklin Watts
Look What Came from the United States	O	I	250+	Davis, Kevin	Franklin Watts
Look What Feet Can Do	P	I	1546	Look What Animals Can Do	Lerner Publishing Group
Look What I Can Do	WB	F	0	Aruego, Jose	Macmillan
Look What I Can Read!	E	RF	49	Instant Readers	Harcourt School Publishers
Look What I Found!	B	RF	29	Lighthouse	Rigby
Look What I Found!	B	RF	29	Science	Outside the Box
Look What I Made!	D	I	40	Gear Up!	Wright Group/McGraw Hill
Look What I Made!	M	I	250+	Literacy 2000	Rigby
Look What Mouths Can Do	P	I	2123	Look What Animals Can Do	Lerner Publishing Group
Look What Tails Can Do	P	I	1963	Look What Animals Can Do	Lerner Publishing Group
Look What Whiskers Can Do	P	I	1970	Look What Animals Can Do	Lerner Publishing Group
Look What You Can Make!	G	I	203	Story Steps	Rigby
Look Who Is at the Zoo	C	I	59	Bonnell, Kris	Reading Reading Books
Look Who Is Eating	C	I	41	Bonnell, Kris	Reading Reading Books
Look Who's Playing First Base	P	RF	250+	Christopher, Matt	Little Brown and Company
Look Who's Talking!	L	I	250+	Rigby Literacy	Rigby
Look!	A	F	31	Leveled Literacy Intervention/ Green System	Heinemann
Look!	C	RF	43	Little Celebrations	Pearson Learning Group
Look! Bugs!	C	I	32	Seedlings	Continental Press
Look! I Can Read!	F	RF	124	Hood, Susan	Grosset & Dunlap
Look! Now Look!	B	I	9	Rigby Literacy	Rigby
Look! Snow!	LB	RF	14	Montezinos, Nina	McElderry
Look, Bear	D	F	51	Sun Sprouts	ETA/Cuisenaire
Look, Listen, and Learn	E	I	49	Canizares, Susan; Chanko, Pamela	Scholastic
Look, Listen, Taste, Touch, and Smell: Learning About Your Five Senses	M	I	250+	Amazing Body	Picture Window Books
Look, We Can Fly Too	I	F	250+	Phonics Readers Plus	Steck-Vaughn
Look-Alike Animals	H	I	130	Bernard, Robin	Scholastic
Look-Alikes	J	RF	164	Dominie Readers	Pearson Learning Group
Look-and-Find Shapes	B	I	42	Blevins, Wiley	Scholastic
Looking After a Dog	C	I	58	Sun Sprouts	ETA/Cuisenaire
Looking After Baby	E	I	143	Storyteller Nonfiction	Wright Group/McGraw Hill
Looking After Eggs	M	I	250+	Explorations	Eleanor Curtain Publishing
Looking After Eggs	M	I	250+	Explorations	Okapi Educational Materials
Looking After Grandpa	D	RF	91	Foundations	Wright Group/McGraw Hill
Looking After Our World	S	I	250+	Connectors	Pacific Learning
Looking after Suzie	G	RF	209	Well-Being Series	Pearson Learning Group
Looking at Animals in Cold Places	O	I	250+	Butterfield, Moira	Steck-Vaughn
Looking at Animals in Hot Places	N	I	250+	Butterfield, Moira	Steck-Vaughn
Looking at Animals in the Ocean	O	I	250+	Butterfield, Moira	Steck-Vaughn
Looking at Ants	I	I	250+	Yellow Umbrella Books	Red Brick Learning
Looking at Art	Q	I	250+	PM Plus Nonfiction	Rigby
Looking at Baby Animals	E	I	54	Teacher's Choice Series	Pearson Learning Group
Looking at Bugs	A	I	37	Red Rocket Readers	Flying Start Books
Looking at Cities	E	I	30	iOpeners	Pearson Learning Group
Looking at Fish	A	I	35	Bonnell, Kris	Reading Reading Books
Looking at Fish	D	I	148	Sails	Rigby
Looking at Insects	L	I	250+	Discovery World	Rigby
Looking at Insects	E	I	110	Rigby Flying Colors	Rigby
Looking at Light	S	I	250+	Navigators Science Series	Benchmark Education
Looking at Light	T	I	250+	Orbit Chapter Books	Pacific Learning

L

* Collection of short stories   # Graphic text
^ Mature content with lower level text demands

TITLE	LEVEL	GENRE	WORD COUNT	AUTHOR / SERIES	PUBLISHER / DISTRIBUTOR
Looking at Light	S	I	250+	Reading Expeditions	National Geographic
Looking at Low Tide	M	RF	642	Leveled Readers	Houghton Mifflin Harcourt
Looking at Maps and Globes	K	I	250+	Brederson, Carmen	Scholastic
Looking at Materials	F	I	137	Rigby Rocket	Rigby
Looking at Matter	J	I	175	Early Explorers	Benchmark Education
Looking at Our World	I	I	188	Early Connections	Benchmark Education
Looking at Pets	C	I	99	Vocabulary Readers	Houghton Mifflin Harcourt
Looking at Pets	C	I	99	Vocabulary Readers/CA	Houghton Mifflin Harcourt
Looking at Pictures	V	I	250+	Richardson, Joy	Harry N. Abrams
Looking at Plants	C	I	44	Leveled Readers Science	Houghton Mifflin Harcourt
Looking at Scorpions	K	I	119	Larkin, Bruce	Wilbooks
Looking at Shapes	G	I	235	Yellow Umbrella Books	Red Brick Learning
Looking at Snails	D	I	90	Rigby Flying Colors	Rigby
Looking at the Birds	F	I	155	PM Science Readers	Rigby
Looking at the Moon	I	I	228	PM Science Readers	Rigby
Looking at Worms	D	I	94	Rigby Flying Colors	Rigby
Looking at X-Rays	A	I	20	Bonnell, Kris/About	Reading Reading Books
Looking Back: A Book of Memories	X	B	250+	Lowry, Lois	Delacorte Press
Looking Down	E	I	130	Early Connections	Benchmark Education
Looking Down	B	RF	64	First Stories	Pacific Learning
Looking Down	C	RF	70	PM Starters	Rigby
Looking for a Letter	F	RF	223	New Way Green	Steck-Vaughn
Looking for a Moose	K	RF	250+	Root, Phyllis	Candlewick Press
Looking for a New House	I	RF	250+	Windows on Literacy	National Geographic
Looking for Alaska	Z+	RF	250+	Green, John	Speak
Looking for Amelia	S	RF	250+	PM Plus Chapter Books	Rigby
Looking for Angus	H	F	99	Ready Readers	Pearson Learning Group
Looking for Bears	H	RF	80	Books for Young Learners	Richard C. Owen
Looking for Birds	D	I	74	Leveled Readers	Houghton Mifflin Harcourt
Looking for Buddy	N	RF	250+	Leveled Readers Language Support	Houghton Mifflin Harcourt
Looking for Dad	M	RF	250+	Supa Doopers	Sundance
Looking for Easter	J	F	250+	Chaconas, Dori	Albert Whitman & Co.
Looking for Eggs	C	RF	47	Windmill Books	Rigby
^Looking for Fingerprints	S	I	250+	Crime Solvers	Capstone Press
Looking for Frogs	D	I	50	Leveled Readers	Houghton Mifflin Harcourt
Looking for Halloween	LB	RF	49	Urmston, Kathleen; Evans, Karen	Kaeden Books
Looking for Home	B	I	63	In Step Readers	Rigby
Looking for Leo	G	RF	253	Rigby Flying Colors	Rigby
Looking for Lions	L	I	250+	World Quest Adventures	World Quest Learning
Looking for Luke	I	RF	250+	Sunshine	Wright Group/McGraw Hill
Looking for Luna	L	RF	250+	Myers, Tim	Marshall Cavendish
Looking for Numbers	D	I	91	Early Connections	Benchmark Education
Looking for Patterns	J	I	160	Early Connections	Benchmark Education
Looking for Shapes	K	I	289	Early Connections	Benchmark Education
Looking for Symmetry	I	I	224	Windows on Literacy	National Geographic
Looking for Taco	C	F	94	Leveled Literacy Intervention/Green System	Heinemann
Looking for the Queen	N	I	711	Avenues	Hampton Brown
Looking for the Queen	N	I	250+	Frederick, Shirley	Hampton Brown
Looking Great	V	I	250+	10 Things You Need to Know About	Capstone Press
Looking in Mirrors	L	I	316	Explorations	Eleanor Curtain Publishing
Looking in Mirrors	L	I	316	Explorations	Okapi Educational Materials

L

TITLE	LEVEL	GENRE	WORD COUNT	AUTHOR / SERIES	PUBLISHER / DISTRIBUTOR
Looking Inside Cells	Y	I	250+	Science Readers	Teacher Created Materials
Looking into Space	L	I	345	Early Connections	Benchmark Education
Looking Like Me	R	RF	250+	Myers, Walter Dean	Egmont USA
Looking the Part	X	I	2322	Leveled Readers	Houghton Mifflin Harcourt
Looking Through a Telescope	K	I	250+	Rookie Read-About Science	Children's Press
Looks Like Rain!	C	RF	24	Science	Outside the Box
Loon Chase	N	RF	1296	Diehl, Jean H.	Sylvan Dell Publishing
Loony Little: An Environmental Tale	L	F	250+	Aston, Dianna Hutts	Candlewick Press
Loose Bolts	O	SF	250+	Sunshine	Wright Group/McGraw Hill
Loose Laces	J	RF	209	Reading Unlimited	Pearson Learning Group
Loose Tooth	B	RF	51	Bebop Books	Lee & Low Books Inc.
Loose Tooth	G	I	147	Healthy Teeth	Capstone Press
Loose Tooth	F	RF	123	Schaefer, Lola M.	Scholastic
Loose Tooth, The	H	RF	168	Breakthrough	Longman/Bow
Loose Tooth, The	E	F	134	Galaxy Girl	Literacy Footprints
Loose-Tooth Luke	K	RF	1304	Real Kids Readers	Millbrook Press
Lord Loss (The Demonata Series)	Z+	F	250+	Shan, Darren	Little Brown and Company
Lord Mount Dragon, The	M	TL	250+	Cambridge Reading	Pearson Learning Group
Lord of the Nutcracker Men	Z	HF	250+	Lawrence, Iain	Random House
Lord of the Rings, The	Z	F	250+	Tolkien, J.R.R.	Houghton Mifflin Harcourt
Lord of the Shadows: The Saga of Darren Shan	Y	F	250+	Shan, Darren	Little Brown and Company
#Lords of the Sea: The Vikings Explore the North Atlantic	S	I	250+	Graphic Library	Capstone Press
Lorenzo's Secret Mission	W	HF	250+	Guzman Lila and Rick	Pinata Publishing
Los Angeles Angels of Anaheim, The	S	I	250+	Team Spirit	Norwood House Press
Los Angeles Angels of Anaheim, The (Revised Edition)	S	I	250+	Team Spirit	Norwood House Press
Los Angeles Area Missions	V	I	5485	Exploring California Missions	Lerner Publishing Group
Los Angeles Clippers, The	S	I	4173	Team Spirit	Norwood House Press
Los Angeles Dodgers, The	S	I	250+	Team Spirit	Norwood House Press
Los Angeles Dodgers, The (Revised Edition)	S	I	250+	Team Spirit	Norwood House Press
Los Angeles Lakers, The	S	I	250+	Team Spirit	Norwood House Press
Loser	U	RF	250+	Spinelli, Jerry	HarperCollins
Losing Joe's Place	Y	RF	250+	Korman, Gordon	Scholastic
Lost	Z+	HF	250+	Davies, Jacqueline	Marshall Cavendish
Lost	E	RF	82	Literacy Tree	Rigby
Lost	C	RF	38	Story Box	Wright Group/McGraw Hill
Lost	E	RF	29	Sun Sprouts	ETA/Cuisenaire
Lost	P	RF	2082	Take Two Books	Wright Group/McGraw Hill
Lost	A	RF	29	TOTTS	Tott Publications
Lost and Found	G	RF	203	Adams, Lorraine & Bruvold, Lynn	Eaglecrest Books
Lost and Found	D	RF	64	Carousel Readers	Pearson Learning Group
Lost and Found	R	RF	250+	Clements, Andrew	Simon & Schuster
Lost and Found	G	F	55	Instant Readers	Harcourt School Publishers
*Lost and Found	D	RF	55	New Way Red	Steck-Vaughn
Lost and Found	I	RF	534	Real Kids Readers	Millbrook Press
Lost and Found	Z	RF	250+	Schraff, Anne	Townsend Press
Lost and Found Game, The	M	RF	250+	Nayer, Judy	Pearson Learning Group
Lost and Found Pony, The	M	F	250+	Dockray, Tracy	Feiwel and Friends
Lost At Sea!: Tami Oldham Ashcraft's Story of Survival	S	I	250+	True Tales of Survival	Capstone Press
Lost at the Fun Park	F	RF	192	PM Extensions-Blue	Rigby
Lost at the White House: A 1909 Easter Story	L	HF	250+	Griest, Lisa	Carolrhoda Books
Lost at the Zoo	F	RF	174	Red Rocket Readers	Flying Start Books

L

* Collection of short stories   # Graphic text
^ Mature content with lower level text demands

TITLE	LEVEL	GENRE	WORD COUNT	AUTHOR / SERIES	PUBLISHER / DISTRIBUTOR
Lost Autobot, The	K	SF	250+	Transformers: Dark of the Moon	Little Brown and Company
Lost Ball, The	D	F	73	Tiny Treasures	Pioneer Valley
Lost Cat!	E	RF	156	Bookshop	Mondo Publishing
Lost Children, The	M	TL	250+	Goble, Paul	Aladdin
Lost Cities	T	I	250+	Navigators Social Studies Series	Benchmark Education
Lost Cities	Q	I	1581	Take Two Books	Wright Group/McGraw Hill
Lost Cities, The: A Drift House Voyage	U	F	250+	Peck, Dale	Bloomsbury Children's Books
Lost City (Dinotopia)	T	F	250+	Ciencin, Scott	Random House
Lost City of Faar, The: Pendragon	X	F	250+	MacHale, D.J.	Aladdin
Lost Coat, The	D	RF	98	Storyworlds	Heinemann
Lost Colony of Roanoke, The	T	I	1081	Leveled Readers Social Studies	Houghton Mifflin Harcourt
Lost Comic Book, The	S	RF	2655	Leveled Readers/CA	Houghton Mifflin Harcourt
Lost Comic Book, The	S	RF	2655	Leveled Readers/TX	Houghton Mifflin Harcourt
*Lost Continent and Other Cases, The	O	RF	250+	Simon, Seymour	Avon Books
Lost Costume, The	I	RF	250+	Storyworlds	Heinemann
Lost Dog, The	N	RF	908	Reading Street	Pearson
Lost Flower Children, The	Q	RF	250+	Lisle, Janet Taylor	Philomel
Lost Garden, The	W	B	250+	Yep, Laurence	Beech Tree Books
Lost Glasses	G	RF	270	Rigby Flying Colors	Rigby
Lost Glove, The	D	RF	105	Foundations	Wright Group/McGraw Hill
Lost Goat Lane	W	RF	250+	Jordan, Rosa	Peachtree
*Lost Hikers and Other Cases, The	O	RF	250+	Simon, Seymour	Avon Books
Lost in a Cave	P	RF	250+	On Our Way to English	Rigby
Lost in Cyberspace	Y	SF	250+	Peck, Richard	Puffin Books
Lost in English	N	RF	999	Springboard	Wright Group/McGraw Hill
Lost in Lexicon: An Adventure in Words and Numbers	W	F	250+	Noyce, Pendred	Tumblehome Press
Lost in Space	M	SF	250+	Pacific Literacy	Pacific Learning
Lost in Space	P	SF	960	Springboard	Wright Group/McGraw Hill
Lost in the Dark	Q	I	250+	Orbit Double Takes	Pacific Learning
Lost in the Fog	D	F	59	Ready Readers	Pearson Learning Group
Lost in the Forest	I	HF	298	PM Story Books-Orange	Rigby
Lost in the Forest	K	RF	250+	Sunshine	Wright Group/McGraw Hill
Lost in the Jungle	E	F	131	Little Dinosaur	Literacy Footprints
Lost in the Mist	J	RF	250+	Storyworlds	Heinemann
Lost in the Museum	I	RF	250+	Cohen, Miriam	Bantam Books
Lost in the Store	H	RF	198	The King School Series	Townsend Press
Lost in the Wilderness!	Q	I	660	Vocabulary Readers	Houghton Mifflin Harcourt
Lost in the Woods	D	F	120	Bella and Rosie Series	Pioneer Valley
Lost in Time	V	B	250+	WorldScapes	ETA/Cuisenaire
Lost in Yonkers	W	RF	250+	Simon, Neil	Penguin Group
Lost Island of Tamarind, The	W	F	250+	Aguiar, Nadia	Feiwel and Friends
#Lost Key, The: A Mystery with Whole Numbers	P	RF	1920	Manga Math Mysteries	Graphic Universe
Lost Keys, The	G	RF	223	PM Plus Story Books	Rigby
Lost Lake, The	M	RF	250+	Soar To Success	Houghton Mifflin Harcourt
#Lost Lunch, The	K	RF	250+	My 1st Graphic Novel	Stone Arch Books
Lost Money, The	E	F	100	Georgie Giraffe	Literacy Footprints
Lost Mother, The	E	RF	112	Alphakids	Sundance
Lost Necklace, The	E	RF	132	Adams, Lorraine & Bruvold, Lynn	Eaglecrest Books
Lost of Comic Bok, The	S	RF	2655	Leveled Readers	Houghton Mifflin Harcourt
Lost on a Mountain in Maine	R	RF	250+	Fendler, Donn	Peter Smith Publications
Lost Pirate, The	J	F	311	Early Explorers	Benchmark Education
Lost Reward, The	N	RF	878	Red Rocket Readers	Flying Start Books

L

TITLE	LEVEL	GENRE	WORD COUNT	AUTHOR / SERIES	PUBLISHER / DISTRIBUTOR
Lost Sandals, The	N	RF	250+	Bennett, Jean	Pacific Learning
Lost Scroll, The	K	RF	253	Pair-It Turn and Learn	Steck-Vaughn
Lost Sheep, The	I	F	219	Little Readers	Houghton Mifflin Harcourt
Lost Sight: True Survival Stories	Y	I	3220	Powerful Medicine	Lerner Publishing Group
Lost Socks	F	RF	159	PM Plus Story Books	Rigby
Lost Star: The Story of Amelia Earhart	T	B	250+	Lauber, Patricia	Language for Learning Assoc.
Lost Storybook, The	F	RF	172	Storyworlds	Heinemann
Lost Stuff, The	D	RF	60	The Rowland Reading Program Library	Rowland Reading Foundation
Lost Tales of Ga'Hoole: Guardians of Ga'Hoole	V	F	250+	Lasky, Kathryn	Scholastic
Lost Toy, The	G	F	184	Storyworlds	Heinemann
Lost Treasure of the Emerald Eye	O	F	250+	Stilton, Geronimo	Scholastic
Lost Underground	T	RF	250+	Reading Safari	Mondo Publishing
Lost Valentines, The	G	RF	159	Developing Set 4	Pioneer Valley
Lost Warrior, The: Warriors Manga	U	F	250+	Hunter, Erin	HarperCollins
Lost World of the Olmec	V	I	2149	Independent Readers Social Studies	Houghton Mifflin Harcourt
Lost World, The	U	F	9435	Dominoes two	Oxford University Press
Lost Worlds	X	I	250+	Howe, John	Kingfisher
Lost!	J	RF	452	Gear Up!	Wright Group/McGraw Hill
Lost!	F	F	82	Green Light Readers	Harcourt
Lost!	D	RF	57	Harry's Math Books	Outside the Box
Lost!	L	F	57	Home Connection Collection	Rigby
Lost!	J	F	356	McPhail, David	Little Brown and Company
Lost!	B	RF	18	Smart Start	Rigby
Lost: One Cat!	N	RF	250+	Tristars	Richard C. Owen
Lot Happened Today, A	I	RF	193	Ready Readers	Pearson Learning Group
Lots and Lots of Stairs	B	RF	33	Little Books for Early Readers	University of Maine
Lots of Balloons	F	RF	72	Early Readers	Compass Point Books
Lots of Birds	A	I	25	Vocabulary Readers	Houghton Mifflin Harcourt
Lots of Birds	A	I	25	Vocabulary Readers/CA	Houghton Mifflin Harcourt
Lots of Boats	K	I	468	Vocabulary Readers	Houghton Mifflin Harcourt
Lots of Boats	K	I	468	Vocabulary Readers/CA	Houghton Mifflin Harcourt
Lots of Caps	G	F	205	New Way Blue	Steck-Vaughn
Lots of Clocks	G	I	88	Gear Up!	Wright Group/McGraw Hill
Lots of Dogs	C	I	68	Teacher's Choice Series	Pearson Learning Group
Lots of Dolls!	C	I	61	The Candid Collection	Pearson Learning Group
Lots of Feelings	J	I	72	Shelley Rotner's Early Childhood Library	Millbrook Press
Lots of Flowers	A	I	28	Leveled Readers	Houghton Mifflin Harcourt
Lots of Flowers	A	I	28	Leveled Readers/CA	Houghton Mifflin Harcourt
Lots of Grandparents	J	I	156	Shelley Rotner's Early Childhood Library	Millbrook Press
Lots of Helpers	C	I	92	Leveled Readers	Houghton Mifflin Harcourt
Lots of Helpers	C	I	92	Leveled Readers/CA	Houghton Mifflin Harcourt
Lots of Legs	E	F	140	Red Rocket Readers	Flying Start Books
Lots of Socks	B	I	30	Gear Up!	Wright Group/McGraw Hill
Lots of Things	B	RF	23	Reading Corners	Pearson Learning Group
Lots of Toys	B	I	47	Carousel Earlybirds	Pearson Learning Group
Lottery Winner, The	Y	RF	5655	Oxford Bookworms Library	Oxford University Press
Lottie Goat & Donny Goat	H	F	145	Ready Readers	Pearson Learning Group
^Lotus	O	I	250+	Fast Cars	Capstone Press
Lotus Seed, The	P	HF	250+	Garland, Sherry	Harcourt Trade
Lou Gehrig	U	B	250+	Sports Heroes and Legends	Lerner Publishing Group

L

* Collection of short stories   # Graphic text
^ Mature content with lower level text demands

TITLE	LEVEL	GENRE	WORD COUNT	AUTHOR / SERIES	PUBLISHER / DISTRIBUTOR
Lou Gehrig: A Life of Dedication	N	B	614	Pull Ahead-Biographies	Lerner Publishing Group
Lou Gehrig: One of Baseball's Greatest	O	B	250+	Childhood of Famous Americans	Aladdin
Lou Gehrig: The Luckiest Man	O	B	2200	Adler, David A.	Harcourt, Inc.
Louanne Pig in Making the Team	K	F	325	Carlson, Nancy	Carolrhoda Books
Louanne Pig in The Mysterious Valentine	K	F	490	Carlson, Nancy	Carolrhoda Books
Louanne Pig in The Perfect Family	L	F	588	Carlson, Nancy	Carolrhoda Books
Louanne Pig in The Talent Show	K	F	302	Carlson, Nancy	Carolrhoda Books
Louanne Pig in Witch Lady	L	F	489	Carlson, Nancy	Carolrhoda Books
Loud and Quiet: An Animal Opposites Book	K	I	250+	Animal Opposites	Capstone Press
Loud or Soft? High or Low?: A Look at Sound	L	I	250+	Lightning Bolt Books	Lerner Publishing Group
Loud Silence of Francine Green, The	Y	HF	250+	Cushman, Karen	Clarion Books
Loud Sounds, Quiet Sounds	B	I	26	Rosen Real Readers	Rosen Publishing Group
Loudmouth George and the Big Race	L	F	531	Carlson, Nancy	Carolrhoda Books
Loudmouth George and the Cornet	L	F	460	Carlson, Nancy	Carolrhoda Books
Loudmouth George and the Fishing Trip	K	F	455	Carlson, Nancy	Carolrhoda Books
Loudmouth George and the New Neighbors	K	F	336	Carlson, Nancy	Carolrhoda Books
Loudmouth George and the Sixth-Grade Bully	L	F	544	Carlson, Nancy	Carolrhoda Books
Louie's Hat	C	RF	53	Adams, Lorraine & Bruvold, Lynn	Eaglecrest Books
Louis Agassiz Fuertes, Painter of the Bird	L	B	250+	Independent Readers Science	Houghton Mifflin Harcourt
Louis Armstrong	Z	B	250+	Brown, Sandford	Franklin Watts
Louis Armstrong	S	B	3775	History Maker Bios	Lerner Publishing Group
Louis Armstrong: Jazz Legend	P	B	250+	Great African Americans	Capstone Press
Louis Braille	G	B	132	Independent Readers Science	Houghton Mifflin Harcourt
Louis Braille: Boy Who Invented Books for the Blind	N	B	250+	Davidson, Margaret	Scholastic
Louis Is Hungry	C	RF	31	Bonnell, Kris	Reading Reading Books
Louis Pasteur	N	B	250+	Biography	Benchmark Education
Louis Pasteur	P	B	250+	Photo-Illustrated Biographies	Red Brick Learning
#Louis Pasteur and Pasteurization	V	B	250+	Graphic Library	Capstone Press
Louis Pasteur and the Fight Against Germs	S	B	250+	Science Readers	Teacher Created Materials
Louis Riel	X	B	250+	The Canadians	Fitzhenry & Whiteside
Louisa May Alcott: Young Novelist	O	B	250+	Childhood of Famous Americans	Aladdin
Louisa: The Life of Louisa May Alcott	S	B	250+	McDonough, Yona Zeldis	Henry Holt & Co.
Louise Arner Boyd and Glaciers	V	B	2384	Leveled Readers	Houghton Mifflin Harcourt
Louise Arner Boyd and Glaciers	V	B	2384	Leveled Readers/CA	Houghton Mifflin Harcourt
Louise Arner Boyd and Glaciers	V	B	2384	Leveled Readers/TX	Houghton Mifflin Harcourt
Louise the Lily Fairy: Rainbow Magic	L	F	250+	Meadows, Daisy	Scholastic
Louisiana	T	I	250+	Hello U.S.A.	Lerner Publishing Group
Louisiana	S	I	250+	Land of Liberty	Red Brick Learning
Louisiana	R	I	250+	This Land Is Your Land	Compass Point Books
Louisiana Purchase, The	V	I	250+	Cornerstones of Freedom	Children's Press
Louisiana Purchase, The	V	I	250+	Let Freedom Ring	Red Brick Learning
Louisiana: Facts and Symbols	O	I	250+	The States and Their Symbols	Capstone Press
Love	B	RF	24	Handprints A	Educators Publishing Service
Love 101	Z	I	250+	Boldprint	Steck-Vaughn
Love Among the Haystacks	Z	RF	7030	Oxford Bookworms Library	Oxford University Press
Love and Roast Chicken: A Trickster Tale From the Andes Moutains	N	TL	1221	Knutson, Barbara	Lerner Publishing Group
Love Curse of the Rumbaughs, The	W	F	250+	Gantos, Jack	Square Fish
Love from Your Friend, Hannah	Y	HF	250+	Skolsky, Mindy Warshaw	HarperTrophy
Love Is	LB	RF	11	Visions	Wright Group/McGraw Hill
Love Me, Love My Broccoli	S	RF	250+	Peters, Julie Anne	Avon Books
Love of a King, The	W	I	6150	Oxford Bookworms Library	Oxford University Press

TITLE	LEVEL	GENRE	WORD COUNT	AUTHOR / SERIES	PUBLISHER / DISTRIBUTOR
Love or Money?	Y	RF	6010	Oxford Bookworms Library	Oxford University Press
Love That Dog	T	RF	250+	Creech, Sharon	HarperCollins
Love That Puppy!: The Story of a Boy Who Wanted to Be a Dog	K	RF	213	Jarka, Jeff	Henry Holt & Co.
Love Those Bugs!	T	I	1798	Leveled Readers	Houghton Mifflin Harcourt
Love Those Bugs!	T	I	1798	Leveled Readers/CA	Houghton Mifflin Harcourt
Love Those Bugs!	T	I	1798	Leveled Readers/TX	Houghton Mifflin Harcourt
Love You, Soldier	R	HF	250+	Hest, Amy	Puffin Books
Love, Football, and Other Contact Sports	X	RF	250+	Carter, Alden R.	Holiday House
Love, from the Fifth-Grade Celebrity	Q	RF	250+	Giff, Patricia Reilly	Bantam Books
Love, Ruby Lavender	U	RF	250+	Wiles, Deborah	Harcourt Achieve
Love, Ruby Valentine	K	F	589	Friedman, Laurie	Carolrhoda Books
Love, Star Girl	V	RF	250+	Spinelli, Jerry	Alfred A. Knopf
Loveykins	K	F	250+	Blake, Quentin	Peachtree
Low Riders	L	I	110	On Deck	Rigby
Lowriders	M	I	250+	Horsepower	Capstone Press
Lowriders	W	I	4919	Motor Mania	Lerner Publishing Group
^Lowriders	N	I	160	Rev It Up!	Capstone Press
Lowriders	Q	I	250+	Wild Rides!	Capstone Press
Luca's Scary Dream	I	RF	274	McAlpin, MaryAnn	Short Tales Press
Lucas the Lizard	K	F	474	Rigby Gigglers	Rigby
Luciano Pavarotti	W	B	1706	Leveled Readers	Houghton Mifflin Harcourt
Luciano Pavarotti	W	B	1706	Leveled Readers/CA	Houghton Mifflin Harcourt
Luciano Pavarotti	W	B	1706	Leveled Readers/TX	Houghton Mifflin Harcourt
Luck of the Buttons, The	T	HF	250+	Ylvisaker, Anne	Candlewick Press
Lucky	Z+	B	250+	Sebold, Alice	Little Brown and Company
Lucky Baseball Bat, The	M	RF	250+	Christopher, Matt	Little Brown and Company
Lucky Buster	M	F	250+	Rigby Gigglers	Rigby
Lucky Candlesticks, The	N	RF	764	Leveled Readers	Houghton Mifflin Harcourt
Lucky Cap	P	RF	250+	Jennings, Patrick	Egmont USA
Lucky Chuck's Least Favorite Cousin	V	HF	5761	Reading Street	Pearson
Lucky Day for Little Dinosaur, A	F	HF	135	PM Extensions-Yellow	Rigby
Lucky Duck	J	F	287	Let's Read Together	Kane Press
Lucky Duck, The	E	F	73	Ready Readers	Pearson Learning Group
Lucky Feather, The	L	F	250+	Literacy 2000	Rigby
Lucky Goes to Dog School	E	RF	127	PM Story Books	Rigby
Lucky Grub, The	E	F	71	Award Reading	School Specialty Publishing
Lucky Last Luke	M	RF	250+	Clark, Margaret	Sundance
#Lucky Leaf	M	RF	174	O'Malley, Kevin	Walker & Company
Lucky Me!	K	RF	1573	Real Kids Readers	Millbrook Press
Lucky Penny, The	G	RF	259	Leveled Literacy Intervention/Green System	Heinemann
Lucky Pony, A	D	F	76	Coulton, Mia	Maryruth Books
Lucky Socks	K	RF	250+	Literacy by Design	Rigby
Lucky Socks	K	RF	250+	On Our Way to English	Rigby
Lucky Stars	L	RF	250+	Adler, David A.	Random House
Lucky Stone, The	Q	RF	250+	Clifton, Lucille	Bantam Books
Lucky Thursday	M	RF	250+	PM Extensions	Rigby
Lucky Tucker	I	F	250+	McGuirk, Leslie	Candlewick Press
Lucky We Have a Station Wagon	F	RF	259	Foundations	Wright Group/McGraw Hill
Lucky Whale, The	J	RF	351	Springboard	Wright Group/McGraw Hill
Lucky's Mountain	Q	RF	250+	Orca Young Readers	Orca Books
Lucy and Billy	L	RF	317	Leveled Readers/TX	Houghton Mifflin Harcourt
Lucy Loses Red Ted	E	RF	187	Storyworlds	Heinemann

L

* Collection of short stories   # Graphic text
^ Mature content with lower level text demands

TITLE	LEVEL	GENRE	WORD COUNT	AUTHOR / SERIES	PUBLISHER / DISTRIBUTOR
Lucy Maud Montgomery	Q	B	250+	Wallner, Alexandra	Holiday House
Lucy Meets a Dragon	L	F	250+	Literacy 2000	Rigby
Lucy Rose: Big on Plans	O	RF	250+	Kelly, Katy	Yearling Books
Lucy Rose: Busy Like You Can't Believe	O	RF	250+	Kelly, Katy	Yearling Books
Lucy Rose: Here's the Thing About Me	O	RF	250+	Kelly, Katy	Yearling Books
Lucy Rose: Working Myself to Pieces and Bits	O	RF	250+	Kelly, Katy	Delacorte Press
Lucy Takes a Holiday	M	F	250+	Bookshop	Mondo Publishing
Lucy the Diamond Fairy: Rainbow Magic	L	F	250+	Meadows, Daisy	Scholastic
Lucy's Boot	F	F	210	Dominie Readers	Pearson Learning Group
Lucy's Box	E	F	108	Cambridge Reading	Pearson Learning Group
Lucy's Garden	I	RF	303	PM Math Readers	Rigby
Lucy's Loose Tooth	D	RF	88	Springboard	Wright Group/McGraw Hill
Lucy's Quiet Book	I	RF	237	Green Light Readers	Harcourt
Lucy's Sore Knee	F	RF	93	Windmill Books	Wright Group/McGraw Hill
Ludwig van Beethoven: Musical Pioneer	N	B	250+	Rookie Biographies	Children's Press
Luis Alvarez	S	B	871	Leveled Readers Science	Houghton Mifflin Harcourt
Luis Munoz Marin: Father of Modern Puerto Rico	P	B	250+	Community Builders	Children's Press
Luis Rodriguez	S	B	250+	Schwartz, Michael	Steck-Vaughn
Luis W. Alvarez	R	B	250+	Hispanic Stories	Steck-Vaughn
Luka Plays Baseball	H	RF	328	Rigby Flying Colors	Rigby
Luka's Campout	I	RF	384	Rigby Flying Colors	Rigby
Luka's New Kite	C	RF	104	Rigby Flying Colors	Rigby
Luka's Tortoise	F	RF	178	Rigby Flying Colors	Rigby
Luke and Leo Build a Limerick	N	RF	1100	Poetry Builders	Norwood House Press
Luke Lively and the Castle of Sleep	P	F	250+	High-Fliers	Pacific Learning
#Luke on the Loose	K	F	250+	Bliss, Harry	Toon Books
Luke's Adventures	H	F	98	City Stories	Rigby
Luke's Bully	N	RF	250+	Winthrop, Elizabeth	Puffin Books
Luke's Go-cart	L	RF	656	PM Collection	Rigby
Lullabob, The	N	I	250+	Sails	Rigby
Lulu Goes to Witch School	K	F	250+	O'Connor, Jane	HarperTrophy
Lulu the Big Little Chicken	K	F	250+	Bogan, Paulette	Bloomsbury Children's Books
Lulu's Lemonade	M	RF	250+	Math Matters	Kane Press
Lulu's Lost Shoes	LB	F	43	We Both Read	Treasure Bay
Lumberjacks	P	I	1110	Reading Street	Pearson
Lumberjacks	M	I	255	Vocabulary Readers	Houghton Mifflin Harcourt
Lump in My Bed, A	D	RF	48	Book Bank	Wright Group/McGraw Hill
Lumpy Rug	D	RF	86	Dominie Phonics Reader	Pearson Learning Group
Luna	L	F	371	Leveled Readers	Houghton Mifflin Harcourt
Luna	Z+	RF	250+	Peters, Julie Anne	Little Brown and Company
Luna and the Well of Secrets: The Fairy Chronicles	Q	F	11900	Sweet, J.H.	Sourcebooks
Luna Moths: Masters of Change	T	I	2731	Insect World	Lerner Publishing Group
Lunch	C	RF	42	Harry's Math Books	Outside the Box
Lunch	F	RF	156	Urmston, Kathleen; Evans, Karen	Kaeden Books
Lunch at the Joy House Cafe	K	RF	250+	Blackaby, Susan	Hampton Brown
Lunch at the Joy House Cafe	K	RF	424	Avenues	Hampton Brown
Lunch at the Park	E	I	132	Rigby Flying Colors	Rigby
Lunch at the Pond	E	F	146	Foundations	Wright Group/McGraw Hill
Lunch at the Zoo	B	RF	64	Blaxland, Wendy; Brimage, C.	Scholastic
Lunch at the Zoo	A	RF	32	Bookshop	Mondo Publishing
Lunch Bunch, The	I	RF	594	Real Kids Readers	Millbrook Press

L

TITLE	LEVEL	GENRE	WORD COUNT	AUTHOR / SERIES	PUBLISHER / DISTRIBUTOR
Lunch Bunch, The	I	I	169	Storyteller-Moon Rising	Wright Group/McGraw Hill
Lunch for Baby Elephant	LB	RF	12	Coulton, Mia	Maryruth Books
Lunch for Carl	B	RF	36	Bonnell, Kris	Reading Reading Books
Lunch in Space	G	RF	156	Instant Readers	Harcourt School Publishers
Lunch in the Park	D	F	108	Springboard	Wright Group/McGraw Hill
Lunch Money	R	RF	250+	Clements, Andrew	Aladdin Paperbacks
Lunch Orders	C	RF	18	Tadpoles	Rigby
Lunch Room, The	M	F	259	Leveled Readers	Houghton Mifflin Harcourt
Lunch Time	C	RF	69	Carousel Readers	Pearson Learning Group
Lunch Walks Among Us	N	SF	250+	Benton, Jim	Aladdin
Lunch with Cat and Dog	F	F	122	Learn to Read	Creative Teaching Press
Lunchbox and the Aliens	S	F	250+	Fields, Bryan W.	Square Fish
Lunch-Box Dream	X	HF	250+	Abbott Tony	Farrar, Straus, & Giroux
Lunchbox Mystery, The	N	RF	250+	Lohans, Alison	Scholastic
Lunchbox, The	H	RF	90	Pacific Literacy	Pacific Learning
Lunchroom, The	F	RF	80	City Stories	Rigby
Lunchtime	D	RF	82	Rigby Literacy	Rigby
Lunchtime at the Zoo	B	RF	53	First Stories	Pacific Learning
Lunchtime Rules	L	RF	250+	Go Girl!	Feiwel and Friends
Luther Burbank	O	B	250+	Faber, Doris	Garrard Publishing Co.
Luv Ya Bunches	U	RF	250+	Myracle, Lauren	Amulet Books
Luz and the Garden	J	RF	446	Leveled Readers	Houghton Mifflin Harcourt
Luz and the Garden	J	RF	446	Leveled Readers/CA	Houghton Mifflin Harcourt
Luz and the Garden	J	RF	446	Leveled Readers/TX	Houghton Mifflin Harcourt
Lyddie	V	HF	250+	Paterson, Katherine	Penguin Group
Lydia and Her Cat	G	RF	77	Oxford Reading Tree	Oxford University Press
Lydia and Her Garden	G	RF	88	Oxford Reading Tree	Oxford University Press
Lydia and Her Kitten	G	RF	77	Oxford Reading Tree	Oxford University Press
Lydia and the Ducks	G	RF	87	Oxford Reading Tree	Oxford University Press
Lydia and the Letters	F	RF	84	Oxford Reading Tree	Oxford University Press
Lydia and the Present	F	RF	77	Oxford Reading Tree	Oxford University Press
Lydia at the Shops	G	RF	72	Oxford Reading Tree	Oxford University Press
Lying as Still as I Can	L	RF	250+	Greetings	Rigby
Lying Down Mountain: The Buffalo Woman Trilogy, Book Three	Z	HF	250+	Merrifield, Heyoka	Atria Books
Lyla and the New Piano	D	F	85	Lester the Lion Series	Pioneer Valley
Lyndon B. Johnson: Thirty-sixth President	R	B	250+	Getting to Know the U.S. Presidents	Children's Press
Lyndon Baines Johnson	U	B	250+	Profiles of the Presidents	Compass Point Books
Lynxes	O	I	2051	Early Bird Nature Books	Lerner Publishing Group

L

* Collection of short stories   # Graphic text
^ Mature content with lower level text demands

BOOK PUBLISHERS AND DISTRIBUTORS

ABDO Publishing Company
P.O. Box 398166
Minneapolis, MN 55439
1-800-800-1312
www.abdopub.com

Abrams & Company/Abrams Learning Trends
16310 Bratton Lane Suite 250
Austin, TX 78728
1-800-227-9120
www.abramslearningtrends.com

Abrams Comicarts
115 West 18th Street 6th Floor
New York, NY 10011
(212) 206-7715
www.abramsbooks.com/comicarts

Ace Books
375 Hudson Street
New York, NY 10014
212-366-2000
www.us.penguingroup.com/pages
/publishers/adult/ace.html

Aladdin Paperbacks
1230 Avenue of the Americas
New York, NY 10020
(212) 698-7000
http://imprints.simonandschuster.biz
/aladdin

Albert Whitman & Co.
250 South Northwest Highway, Suite 320
Park Ridge, IL 60068
800-255-7675
http://www.albertwhitman.com/

Alfred A. Knopf
1745 Broadway
New York, NY 10019
212-782-9000
http://knopfdoubleday.com/imprint
/knopf/

American Reading Company
201 South Gulph Rd.
King of Prussia, PA 19406
1-866-810-2665
http://www.americanreading.com/

Amulet Books
115 West 18th Street 6th Floor
New York, NY 10011
(212) 206-7715
www.abramsbooks.com/comicarts

Andersen Press USA
241 First Ave N
Minneapolis, MN 55401
1-800-328-4929
https://www.lernerbooks.com/about
-lerner/Pages/Andersen-Press-USA.aspx

Andre Deutsch
387 Park Avenue South
New York, NY 10016
(800) 367 9692
http://www.carltonbooks.co.uk/imprints
/andredeutsch

Annick Press
15 Patricia Avenue
Toronto, ON M2M 1H9
Canada
416-221-4802
http://www.annickpress.com/

Arcade Publishing
307 West 36th Street, 11th Floor
New York, NY 10018
(212) 643-6816
http://www.arcadepub.com/

Arte Publico
University of Houson, 4902 Gulf Fwy, Bldg
19, Rm 100
Houston, TX 77204
1-800-633-ARTE
http://www.latinoteca.com/arte-publico
-press/

Arthur A. Levine Books
557 Broadway
New York, NY 10012
http://www.arthuralevinebooks.com/

Atheneum Books
1230 Avenue of the Americas
New York, NY 10020
(212) 698-7000
http://imprints.simonandschuster.biz
/atheneum

Atman Press
2104 Cherokee Avenue
Columbus, GA 31906
706-323-6377
http://www.atmanpress.com/

Atria Books
1230 Avenue of the Americas
New York, NY 10020
(212) 698-7000
http://imprints.simonandschuster.biz/atria

August House Publishers
3500 Piedmont Road, ste. 310
Atlanta, GA 30305
800.284.8784
http://www.augusthouse.com/

Avon Books
10 East 53rd Street
New York, NY 10022
212-207-7000
http://www.avonromance.com/

Ballantine Books
1745 Broadway
New York, NY 10019
212-782-9000
http://ballantine.atrandom.com/

Bantam Books
1745 Broadway
New York, NY 10019
212-782-9000
http://bantam-dell.atrandom.com/

Barefoot Books
2067 Massachusetts Avenue
Cambridge, MA 02140
866.215.1756
www.barefootbooks.com

Barron's Educational
250 Wireless Blvd
Hauppauge, NY 11788
1-800-645-3476
http://www.barronseduc.com/

Beech Tree Books
4 Redwood Rd
Sag Harbor, NY 11963
(631) 725-7722
http://beechtreebooks.com/

Belle River Readers, Inc.
P.o. Box 1224
Lapeer, MI 48446

Bellwether Media
5357 Penn Ave S
Minneapolis, MN 55419
(800) 679-8068
http://www.bellwethermedia.com/

Benchmark Education
629 FIFTH AVENUE
Pelham, NY 10803
1-877-236-2465
http://www.benchmarkeducation.com/

Berkley Books
375 Hudson Street
New York, NY 10014
212-366-2000
www.us.penguingroup.com/static/pages
/publishers/adult/berkley.html

Beyond Words
20827 NW Cornell Rd, Suite 500
Hillsboro, OR 97124
(503) 531.8700
http://www.beyondword.com/

Blackbirch Press
27500 Drake Rd
Farmington Hills, MI 48331
1-800-877-4253
http://www.gale.cengage.com/greenhaven
/blackbirch.htm

Bloomsbury Children's Books
1385 Broadway, Fifth Floor
New York, NY 10018
(212) 419 5300
http://www.bloomsbury.com/us/childrens/

Blue Sky Press
557 Broadway Avenue
New York, NY 10012
1-800-724-6527
http://www.scholastic.com/home/

Blueberry Hill Books
11 Donna Place
East St. Paul, MB R2E 0H6
Canada
780-489-1736
http://www.blueberryhillbooks.com/

Bluefish Bay Publishing
1093 A1A BEACH BLVD
St. Augustine, FL 32080
904-471-3142

Books for a Cause, Inc.
1334 W Chester Pike
West Chester, PA 19382

Boyds Mills Press
815 Church Street
Honesdale, PA 18431
1-800-490-5111
http://www.boydsmillspress.com/

Buddy Books Publishing
PO Box 3354
Pinehurst, NC 28374
910-295-2876
http://www.buddybookspublishing.com/

Bungalo Books
829 Norwest Rd, Ste. 337
Kingston, ON K7P 2N3
Canada
613-374-1243
http://bungalobooks.com/

C Unique Creations Inc.
Site 707, Box 71, RR7
Saskatoon, SK S7K 1N2
306-241-1638
http://www.seeabook.com/index.htm

Candlewick Press
99 Dover St.
Somerville, MA 02144
http://www.candlewick.com/

Capstone Press
1710 Roe Crest Drive
North Mankato, MN 56003
800-747-4992
http://www.capstonepub.com/

Carolrhoda Books
241 First Ave N
Minneapolis, MN 55401
1-800-328-4929
https://www.lernerbooks.com/About
-Lerner/pages/carolrhoda-books.aspx

Carus Publishing Company
30 Grove Street, Suite C
Peterborough, NH 03458
800-821-0115
http://www.cricketmag.com/

Cavallo Publishing
2633 Lincoln Blvd., #617
Santa Monica, CA 90405
866-311-0111
http://www.cavallopublishing.com/

Cengage/National Geographic
10650 Toebben Drive
Independence, KY 41051
1-800-487-8488
http://www.cengage.com/us/

Chariot Victor Publishing
4050 Lee Vance View
Colorado Springs, CO 80918
719-536-0100

Charlesbridge
85 Main St.
Watertown, MA 02472
800-225-3214
http://www.charlesbridge.com/

Checkerboard
P.O. Box 398166
Minneapolis, MN 55439
1-800-800-1312
http://www.abdopub.com/shop/pc
/viewCategories.asp?idCategory=203

Chelsea House
132 West 31st Street, 17th Floor
New York, NY 10001
1-800-322-8755
http://www.infobasepublishing.com/
Default.aspx

Chicago Review Press
814 N. Franklin St
Chicago, IL 60610
312.337.0747
http://www.chicagoreviewpress.com/

Child 1st Publications
3907 Fraser ST. NE
Rockford, MI 49341
800.881.0912
http://www.child-1st.com/new_site/index
.html

Child's Play Ltd
250 Minot Avenue
Auburn, ME 04210
207-784-7252
http://www.childs-play.com/usa/home
-page.html

Children's Book Press
95 MADISON AVENUE, SUITE # 1205
New York, NY 10016
212-779-4400
http://www.leeandlow.com/p/overview
_cbp.mhtml

Children's Press
557 Broadway Avenue
New York, NY 10012
1-800-724-6527
http://www.scholastic.com/
internationalschools/childrenspress.htm

Chronicle Books
680 Second Street
San Fransisco, CA 94107
415-537-4200
http://www.chroniclebooks.com/

Cinco Puntos Press
701 Texas Ave
El Paso, TX 79901
1-800-566-9072
http://www.cincopuntos.com/

Clarion
222 Berkeley Street
Boston, MA 02116
800.225.5425
http://www.houghtonmifflinbooks.com
/hmh/site/hmhbooks/home/kids

Clarion Books
222 Berkeley Street
Boston, MA 02116
800.225.5425
http://www.houghtonmifflinbooks.com
/hmh/site/hmhbooks/home/kids

Collins Publishing Group (see HarperColins)

Compass Point Books
1710 Roe Crest Drive
North Mankato, MN 56003
800-747-4992
http://www.capstonepub.com/category
/LIB_PUBLISHER_CPB

Continental Press
520 East Bainbridge Street
Elizabethtown, PA 17022
800.233.0759
https://www.continentalpress.com/

Crabtree
PMB 59051, 350 Fifth Avenue, 59th Floor
New York, NY 10118
1-800-387-7650
http://www.crabtreebooks.com/

Creative Education
PO Box 1066
Falls Church, VA 22041
703-856-7005
http://www.
creativeeducationandpublishing.com
/store/

Creative Teaching Press
PO Box 2723
Huntington Beach, CA 92647
800-287-8879
http://www.creativeteaching.com/

Cricket Books
30 Grove Street, Suite C
Peterborough, NH 03458
800-821-0115
http://www.cricketmag.com/

Crown Publishers
1745 Broadway
New York, NY 10019
212-782-9000
http://crownpublishing.com/

Curriculum Press
PO Box 177
Carlton South, VIC 3053
Australia
+61 3 9207 9600
http://www.curriculumpress.edu.au/

Cypress
P.O. Box 2636
Tallahassee, FL 32316
(850) 576-8820
http://www.cypresspublications.com/

Darby Creek Publishing
241 First Ave N
Minneapolis, MN 55401
1-800-328-4929
https://www.lernerbooks.com/About
-Lerner/pages/darby-creek.aspx

David Fickling Books
31 Beaumont Street
Oxford, OX1 2NP
Canada
http://www.davidficklingbooks.com/

David R. Godine
PO Box 450
Jaffrey, NH 03452
800-344-4771
http://www.godine.com/

Dawn Publications
12402 Bitney Springs Rd
Nevada City, CA 95959
1-800-545-7475
http://www.dawnpub.com/

Delacorte Press
1745 Broadway
New York, NY 10019
212-782-9000
http://bantam-dell.atrandom.com/

Dell
1745 Broadway
New York, NY 10019
212-782-9000
http://bantam-dell.atrandom.com/

Dial/Penguin
375 Hudson Street
New York, NY 10014
212-366-2000
www.us.penguingroup.com/static/pages
/publishers/yr/dial.html

Disney Book Group
44 S Broadway
White Plains, NY 10601
(212) 807-5875

DK Publishing
375 Hudson St
New York, NY 10014
(646) 674-4000
http://us.dk.com/

Dog Ear Publishing
4010 West 86th Street, Suite H
Indianapolis, IN 46268
888-568-8411
http://dogearpublishing.net/

Donovan
28 South Street, Suite 4
Hingham, MA 02043
781.741.8182
http://donovanpublishing.net/

Doubleday Books
1745 Broadway
New York, NY 10019
212-782-9000
http://knopfdoubleday.com/imprint
/doubleday/

Douglas & McIntyre
4437 Rondeview Road
Madeira Park, BC V0N 2H0
Canada
1-800-667-2988
http://www.dmpibooks.com/home

Dover Publications
31 East 2nd Street
Mineola, NY 11501
http://store.doverpublications.com/

Dragonfly Books
112 W Water Street
Decorah, IA 52101
563.382.4275
http://www.dragonflybooks.com/

Dutton Children's Books
375 Hudson Street
New York, NY 10014
212-366-2000
www.us.penguingroup.com/static/pages
/publishers/yr/dutton.html

Eaglecrest Books
#209B-5462 Trans Canada Hwy
Duncan, BC V9L 6W4
Canada
250.748.3744
http://www.eaglecrestbooks.com/home
.htm

EDC Publishing
P.O. Box 470663
Tulsa, OK 74147
800-475-4522
http://www.edcpub.com/

Educational Insights
18730 S. Wilmington Avenue
Rancho Dominguez, CA 90220
(800) 995 4436
http://www.educationalinsights.com

Educators Publishing Service
625 Mt. Auburn Street, 3rd Floor
Cambridge, MA 02138
800-225-5750
http://eps.schoolspecialty.com/

Eerdman's Books for Young Readers
2140 Oak Industrial Dr. NE
Grand Rapids, MI 49505
800-253-7521
http://www.eerdmans.com/youngreaders/

Egmont USA
443 Park Avenue South, Suite 806
New York, NY 10016
212-685-0102
http://www.egmontusa.com/blog/books/

Eleanor Curtain Publishing
Level 1, Suite 3, 102 Toorak Road
South Yarra, VIC 3141
Australia
+613 9867 4880
http://ecpublishing.com.au/

Enslow Publishers, Inc.
Box 398, 40 Industrial Road, F61
Berkeley Heights, NJ 07922
1-800-398-2504
www.enslow.com/

ETA/Cuisenaire
500 Greenview Court
Vernon Hills, IL 60061
800-445-5985
http://www.hand2mind.com/

FaithWords
3 CENTER PLAZA
BOSTON, MA 02108
(800) 759-0190
http://www.faithwords.com/

Farrar, Straus, & Giroux
18 West 18th Street
New York, NY 10011
212-741-6900
http://us.macmillan.com/FSG.aspx

Feiwel and Friends
175 Fifth Avenue
New York, NY 10010
888.330.8477
http://us.macmillan.com/MacKids.aspx

Firefly Books
c/o Frontier Distributing, 1000 Young
Street, Suite 160
Tonawanda, NY 14150
800-387-5085
http://www.fireflybooks.com/

Fitzhenry & Whiteside
195 Allstate Parkway
Markham, ON L3R 4T8
Canada
1-800-387-9776
http://www.fitzhenry.ca/

Flying Start Books
8345 NW 66th St. #6695
Miami, FL 33166
1-888-269-4059
http://www.flyingstartbooks.com/

Flyleaf Publishing
400 Bedford Street, 1st floor SW-03
Manchester, NH 03101
800-449-7006
http://www.flyleafpublishing.com/

Follett
2233 West Street
River Grove, IL 60171
800.621.4345
http://www.follett.com/

Four Winds
PO Box 21597
Charleston, SC 29413
(843) 323-6822
http://fourwindsbooks.org/

Frances Lincoln
74-77 White Lion Street, Islington
London, N1 9PF
UK
020 7284 9300
http://www.franceslincoln.com/

Franklin Watts
557 Broadway Avenue
New York, NY 10012
1-800-724-6527
http://www.hachettechildrens.co.uk
/homepage_franklinwatts.page

Free Spirit Publishing
217 Fifth Avenue North, Suite 200
Minneapolis, MN 55401
1.800.735.7323
http://www.freespirit.com/

Front Street Press
815 Church Street
Honesdale, PA 18431
1-800-490-5111
http://www.boydsmillspress.com/reviews
/front-street

Fulcrum Publishing
4690 Table Mountain Drive, Suite 100
Golden, CO 80403
800-992-2908
http://www.fulcrum-books.com/

G.P. Putnam's Sons
375 Hudson Street
New York, NY 10014
212-366-2000
www.us.penguingroup.com/static/pages
/publishers/adult/putnam.html

G.P. Putnam's Sons Books for Young Readers
375 Hudson Street
New York, NY 10014
212-366-2000
www.us.penguingroup.com/static/pages
/publishers/yr/putnam.html

Gallopade International
PO Box 2779
Peachtree City, GA 30269
800.536.2438
http://www.gallopade.com/

Gecko Press
PO Box 9335, Marion Square
Wellington, 6141
New Zealand
+64 (0)4 801 9333
http://www.geckopress.co.nz/

Ginn & Co. (see also Silver Burdett or Pearson
Education)
Halley Court Jordan Hill
Oxford, OX2 8EJ
UK
(01865) 888044

Golden
1745 Broadway
New York, NY 10019
212-782-9000
http://www.randomhouse.com/golden/

Good Books
PO Box 419
Intercourse, PA 17534
(800) 762-7171
http://www.goodbooks.com/

Grand Central Publishing
3 CENTER PLAZA
BOSTON, MA 02108
(800) 759-0190
http://www.hachettebookgroup.com
/publishers/grand-central-publishing/

Graphia
222 Berkeley Street
Boston, MA 02116
800.225.5425
http://www.houghtonmifflinbooks.com
/graphia/

Graphic Universe
241 First Ave N
Minneapolis, MN 55401
1-800-328-4929
https://www.lernerbooks.com/About
-Lerner/pages/graphic-universe.aspx

Green Tiger Press
3645 Interlake N
Seattle, WA 98103
(800) 354-0400
http://greentigerpress.com/

Greenwillow Books
10 East 53rd Street
New York, NY 10022
212-207-7000
http://harpercollins.com/imprints/index
.aspx?imprintid=517996

Greystone Books
Suite 201, 343 Railway Street
Vancouver, BC V6A 1A4
Canada
(604) 875-1550
http://www.greystonebooks.com/

Grolier
90 Sherman Turnpike
Danbury, CT 06816
800-621-1115
http://teacher.scholastic.com/products
/grolier/index.htm

Grosset & Dunlap
375 Hudson Street
New York, NY 10014
212-366-2000
www.us.penguingroup.com/static/pages
/publishers/yr/grosset.html

Grosset & Dunlap
375 Hudson Street
New York, NY 10014
212-366-2000
http://www.us.penguingroup.com/static
/pages/publishers/yr/grosset.html

Groundwood Books
110 Spadina Ave., Suite 801
Toronto, ON M5V 2K4
Canada
41-363-4343
http://www.houseofanansi.com/

Gulf
P.O. Box 2608
Houston, TX 77252
(713) 529-4301
http://www.gulfpub.com/

Hameray Publishing Group
11545 Sorrento Valley Road, Suite 310
San Diego, CA 92121
1-866-918-6173
http://www.hameraypublishing.com/

Hampton Brown
1 Lower Ragsdale, Building 1, Suite 200
Monterey, CA 93940
888-915-3276
http://www.hbedge.net/

Harcourt School Publishers
5513 North Cumberland Avenue
Chicago, IL 60656
(773) 594- 5110
http://www.harcourtschool.com/

Harper & Row (see HarperCollins)
10 East 53rd Street
New York, NY 10022
212-207-7000
http://www.harpercollins.com/

Harper Tempest
10 East 53rd Street
New York, NY 10022
212-207-7000
http://www.harpercollins.com/imprints
/index.aspx?imprintid=518004

HarperCollins Publishers
10 East 53rd Street
New York, NY 10022
212-207-7000
http://www.harpercollins.com/

HarperPerennial
10 East 53rd Street
New York, NY 10022
212-207-7000
http://www.harpercollins.com/imprints
/index.aspx?imprintid=517986

HarperTrophy
10 East 53rd Street
New York, NY 10022
212-207-7000
http://harpercollins.com/imprints/index
.aspx?imprintid=517987

Harry N. Abrams
115 West 18th Street, 6th Floor
New York, NY 10011
(212) 206-7715
http://www.abramsbooks.com/

Health Communications
3201 S.W. 15th Street
Deerfield Beach, FL 33442
1.800.441.5569
http://www.hcibooks.com/

Heinemann
P. O. Box 6926
Portsmouth, NH 03802
800.225.5800
http://www.heinemann.com/

Henry Holt & Co.
175 Fifth Avenue
New York, NY 10010
646-307-5095
http://us.macmillan.com/HenryHolt.aspx

Herald Press
490 Dutton Drive, Unit C8
Waterloo, ON N2L 6H7
Canada
1-800-245-7894
http://www.heraldpress.com/

Heritage House
#340 - 1105 Pandora Ave.
Victoria, BC V8V 3P9
250.360.0829
http://www.heritagehouse.ca/

High Noon Books
20 Commercial Boulevard
Novato, CA 94949
(800) 422-7249
http://www.highnoonbooks.com/index
-hnb.tpl

Hohm Press
PO BOX 4410
CHINO VALLEY, AZ 86323
1-800-381-2700
http://www.hohmpress.com/

Holiday House
425 Madison Avenue
New York, NY 10017
212-421-6134
http://www.holidayhouse.com/

Houghton Mifflin Harcourt
222 Berkeley Street
Boston, MA 02116
(617) 351-5000
http://www.hmhco.com/

Hyperion
1500 Broadway, 3rd Floor
New York, NY 10036
http://www.hyperionbooks.com/

Hyperion Books for Children
44 S Broadway
White Plains, NY 10601
(212) 807-5875

Hyperion/Madison Press
18321 SE McLoughlin Blvd
Portland, OR 97267
http://www.exodusbooks.com/publisher
.aspx?id=214

Ideals Children's Books
39 Old Ridgebury Road, Ste. 2AB
Danbury, CT 06810
800-586-2572
http://www.idealsbooks.com/

Ideals Publications Inc.
39 Old Ridgebury Road, Ste. 2AB
Danbury, CT 06810
800-586-2572
http://www.idealsbooks.com/

Imagination Stage
4908 Auburn Avenue
Bethesda, MD 20814
301-961-6060
http://www.imaginationstage.org/

Intercultural Center for Research in
Education
366 Massachusetts Avenue, 2nd flr.
Arlington, MA 02474
(781) 643-2142
http://www.incre.org/

Jamestown Publishers
PO Box 182605
Columbus, OH 43218
877-833-5524
http://www.glencoe.com/gln/jamestown/

Jumping Cow Press
P.O. Box 8982
Scarborough, NY 10510
914-373-9816
http://www.jumpingcowpress.com/

Just Us Books
356 Glenwood Ave.
East Orange, NJ 07017
(973) 672-7701
http://justusbooks.blogspot.com/

Kaeden Books
P.O. Box 16190
Rocky River, OH 44116
1-800-890-7323
http://www.kaeden.com/

Kane Press
350 Fifth Avenue, Suite 7206
New York, NY 10118
212-268-1435
http://www.kanepress.com/

Kane/Miller Book Publishers
4901 Morena Blvd Ste 213
San Diego, CA 92117
1-800-611-1655
http://www.kanemiller.com/

Kar-Ben Publishing
241 First Ave N
Minneapolis, MN 55401
1-800-328-4929
https://www.lernerbooks.com/About
-Lerner/pages/kar-ben-publishing.aspx

Katherine Tegan Books
10 East 53rd Street
New York, NY 10022
212-207-7000
http://www.harpercollinschildrens.com
/Home/ImprintBooks.aspx?TCId=
100&SIId=9452&ST=7

Keep Books
1100 Kinnear Rd.
Columbus, OH 43212
800-678-6484
http://www.keepbooks.org/

Kids Can Press
2250 Military Road
Tonawanda, NY 14150
416-479-7000
http://www.kidscanpress.com/

Kim.FIG.Fern
P.O. Box 415
Oakmont, PA 15139
412-828-0394
http://www.kimfigfern.com/

Kingfisher
175 Fifth Avenue
New York, NY 10010
646-307-5151
http://us.macmillan.com/kingfisher.aspx

Kiva Publishing
21731 E. Buckskin Dr.
Walnut, CA 91789
1-800-634-5482
http://www.kivapub.com/

Ladybird Books
80 Strand
London, WC2R 0RL
UK
0845 313 4444
http://www.ladybird.co.uk/

Language for Learning Assoc.
Shoppenhangers Road, Maidenhead
Berkshire, SL6 2QL
UK
http://mcgraw-hill.co.uk/sra
/languageforlearning.htm

Laurel-Leaf Books
18321 SE McLoughlin Blvd
Portland, OR 97267
http://www.exodusbooks.com/publisher
.aspx?id=71

Lee & Low Books Inc.
95 MADISON AVENUE, SUITE # 1205
New York, NY 10016
212-779-4400
http://www.leeandlow.com/

Lerner Publishing Group
241 First Ave N
Minneapolis, MN 55401
1-800-328-4929
https://www.lernerbooks.com/Pages
/Home.aspx

Linnet Books
2 Linsley Street
North Haven, CT 06473
203-239-2702
http://www.shoestringpress.com/linnet
.html

Little Brown and Company
237 Park Avenue
New York, NY 10017
(800) 759-0190
http://www.littlebrown.com/

Llumina Press
7580 NW 5th Street, #16535
Fort Lauderdale, FL 33318
866-229-9244
http://www.llumina.com/

London Town Press
P.O. Box 585
Montrose, CA 91011
(818) 248-4000
http://www.londontownpress.com/

Longman
Edinburgh Gate, Harlow
Essex, CM20 2JE
UK
+44(0) 1279 623925
http://www.pearsonelt.com/

Longman Group UK
Edinburgh Gate, Harlow
Essex, CM20 2JE
UK
+44(0) 1279 623925
http://www.pearsonelt.com/

Longman/Bow
Edinburgh Gate, Harlow
Essex, CM20 2JE
UK
+44(0) 1279 623925
http://www.pearsonelt.com/

Lost Coast Press
155 Cypress St
Fort Bragg, CA 95437
707-964-9520

Lothian Books
Level 2, 437 St Kilda Rd
Melbourne, VIC 3004
Australia
03 9694 4900
http://www.lothian.com.au/

Lothrop, Lee & Shepard
1350 Avenue of the Americas
New York, NY 10019
212-261-6641

MacAdam/Cage Publishing
155 Sansome Street
San Fransisco, CA 94104
415-986-7503
http://macadamcage.com/

Macmillan
175 Fifth Avenue
New York, NY 10010
888.330.8477
http://us.macmillan.com/

Macmillan/McGraw Hill
PO Box 182605
Columbus, OH 43218
800-334-7344
https://www.mheonline.com/

Margaret K. McElderry Books
1230 Avenue of the Americas
New York, NY 10020
(212) 698-7000
http://imprints.simonandschuster.biz
/margaret-k-mcelderry-books

Marimba Books
356 Glenwood Ave.
East Orange, NJ 07017
(973) 672-7701
http://www.justusbooksonlinestore.com
/categories/Marimba-Books/

Marshall Cavendish
99 White Plains Road
Tarrytown, NJ 10591
(914) 332 8888
www.marshallcavendish.us

Maryruth Books
18660 Ravenna Road, Building 2
Chagrin Falls, OH 44023
877-834-1105
http://www.maryruthbooks.com/

McElderry
1230 Avenue of the Americas
New York, NY 10020
(212) 698-7000
http://imprints.simonandschuster.biz
/margaret-k-mcelderry-books

Meadowbrook Press
6110 Blue Circle Drive, Suite 237
Minnetonka, MN 55343
800-338-2232
http://www.meadowbrookpress.com/

Milkweed Editions
1011 Washington Avenue South, Open
Book Building, Suite 300
Minneapolis, MN 55415
(800) 520-6455
http://milkweed.org/

Millbrook Press
241 First Ave N
Minneapolis, MN 55401
1-800-328-4929
https://www.lernerbooks.com/About
-Lerner/pages/millbrook-press.aspx

Millmark Education
7101 Wisconsin Avenue, Suite 1204
Bethesda, MD 20814
1-877-322-8020
http://www.millmarkeducation.com/

Modern Curriculum
1550 Oak Industrial Lane, Suite F
Cumming, GA 30041
800-401-9931
http://www.learningthings.com/articles
/mcp-modern-curriculum-press.aspx

Mondo Publishing
980 Avenue of the Americas
New York, NY 10018
888-886-6636
http://www.mondopub.com/

Montana Magazine
317 Cruse
Helena, MT 59604
1-888-666-8624
http://www.montanamagazine.com/

Morning Glory Press
6595 San Haroldo Way
Buena Park, CA 90620
1-888-612-8254
http://www.morningglorypress.com/

National Geographic (see Cengage)
10650 Toebben Drive
Independence, KY 41051
1-800-487-8488
http://www.cengage.com/us/

New Directions
80 Eighth Avenue
New York, NY 10011
http://ndbooks.com/

Newbridge
33 Boston Post Road West, Suite 440
Marlborough, MA 01752
800-867-0307
http://www.newbridgeonline.com/

Newmark Learning
629 Fifth Ave
Pelham, NY 10803
1-855-232-1960
http://www.newmarklearning.com/

North-South Books
350 7th Avenue Room 1400
New York, NY 10001
212-706-4545
http://www.northsouth.com/

NorthWord Press
18705 Lake Dr. E
Chanhassen, MN 55317
(952)936-4700

Norwood House Press
P.O. Box 316598
Chicago, IL 60631
1-866-565-2900
http://www.norwoodhousepress.com/

Okapi Educational Materials
42381 Rio Nedo
Temecula, CA 92590
(866) 652-7436
http://myokapi.com/

Options Publishing Inc.
PO Box 1749
Merrimack, NH 03054
603-424-1176
http://www.triumphlearning.com/

Orca Book Publishers
PO Box 468
Custer, WA 98240
800.210.5277
http://www.orcabook.com

Orca Books
PO Box 468
Custer, WA 98240
1.800.210.5277

Orchard Books
557 Broadway Avenue
New York, NY 10012
1-800-724-6527
http://www.hachettechildrens.co.uk
/homepage_orchardbooks.page

Oxford University Press
198 Madison Avenue
New York, NY 10016
800-445-9714
http://www.oup.com/us/

Pacific Learning
PO Box 2723
Huntington Beach, CA 92647
800-276-0737
http://www.pacificlearning.com/

Pantheon
1745 Broadway
New York, NY 10019
212-782-9000
http://knopfdoubleday.com/imprint/
pantheon/

Peachtree
1700 Chattahoochee Avenue
Atlanta, GA 30318
1-800-241-0113
http://peachtree-online.com/

Pearson
One Lake Street
Upper Saddle River, NJ 07458
http://www.pearson.com/

Pearson Learning Group
One Lake Street
Upper Saddle River, NJ 07459
http://www.k12pearson.com/teach_learn
_cycle/PLG/plg.html

Pearson Publishing Group
One Lake Street
Upper Saddle River, NJ 07460
http://www.k12pearson.com/teach_learn
_cycle/PLG/plg.html

Pelican Publishing Company
1000 Burmaster Street
Gretna, LA 70053
1-800-843-1724
http://www.pelicanpub.com/

Penguin Group
375 Hudson Street
New York, NY 10014
212-366-2000
www.us.penguingroup.com/

Persea Books
277 Broadway, Suite 708
New York, NY 10007
(212) 260-9256
http://www.perseabooks.com/index.php

Peter Smith Publications
5 Lexington Ave.
Glouchester, MA 01930
(978)525-3562

Philomel
375 Hudson Street
New York, NY 10014
212-366-2000
www.us.penguingroup.com/static/pages
/publishers/yr/philomel.html

Picture Window Books
1710 Roe Crest Drive
North Mankato, MN 56003
800-747-4992
http://www.capstonepub.com/category
/LIB_PUBLISHER_PWB

Pinata Publishing
University of Houson, 4902 Gulf Fwy, Bldg
19, Rm 100
Houston, TX 77204
1-800-633-ARTE
http://www.latinoteca.com/arte-publico
-press/

Pioneer Valley
155A Industrial Drive
Northampton, MA 01060
888-482-3906
http://www.pioneervalleybooks.com/

Play In A Book
P.O. Box 25629
Chicago, IL 60625
(773) 329-0920
www.playinabook.com/

Pleasant Company Publications
P.O. Box 620991
Middleton, WI 53562
1-800-233-0264
http://www.americangirlpublishing.com/

Pocket Books
1230 Avenue of the Americas
New York, NY 10020
(212) 698-7000
http://imprints.simonandschuster.biz
/gallery-books

Portage and Main
100-318 McDermot Avenue
Winnipeg, MB R3A 0A2
Canada
1-800-667-9673
http://www.portageandmainpress.com
/index.cfm

Prentice-Hall
375 Hudson Street
New York, NY 10014
212-366-2000
http://www.phschool.com/

Priddy Books
175 Fifth Avenue
New York, NY 10010
888.330.8477
http://us.macmillan.com/MacKids.aspx

Puffin Books
375 Hudson Street
New York, NY 10014
212-366-2000
www.us.penguingroup.com/static/pages
/publishers/yr/puffin.html

Raincoast Books
2440 Viking Way
Richmond, BC V6V 1N2
Canada
604-448-7100
http://www.raincoast.com/

Raintree
Brunel Road, Houndmills
Basingstoke Hants, RG21 6XS
UK
+44 (0) 1865 312262
http://www.raintreepublishers.co.uk/

Rand McNally
9855 Woods Drive
Skokie, IL 60077
http://www.randmcnally.com/

Random House
1745 Broadway
New York, NY 10019
212-782-9000
http://www.randomhouse.com/

Ransom Publishing
8 St. Cross Road, Winchester
Hampshire, SO23 9HX
UK
+44 (0) 1962 862307
http://www.ransom.co.uk/

Reader's Digest Children's Books
44 S Broadway
White Plains, NY 10601
(914) 238-1000
http://www.rdtradepublishing.com/

Reading Matters
806 Main Street
Akron, PA 17501
(888) 255-6665
http://readingmatters.net/

Reading Reading Books
PO Box 6654
Reading, PA 19610

Red Brick Learning
P.O. Box 669
Mankato, MN 56002
888-262-6135
http://www.capstoneclassroom.com
/content/RedBrick

Red Cygnet Press
2245 Enterprise St. Suite 110
Escondido, CA 92029
http://www.redcygnet.com/

Red Deer Press
195 Allstate Parkway
Markham, ON L3R 4T8
UK
1-800-387-9776 Ext. 225
http://www.reddeerpress.com/

Reflections Publishing
5395 Foxhound Way
San Diego, CA 92130
http://www.reflectionspublishing.com/

Richard C. Owen
PO Box 585
Katonah, NY 10536
800/262-0787
http://www.rcowen.com/

Rigby
Specialized Curriculum Group, 9205
Southpark Center Loop
Orlando, FL 32819
800-225-5425
www.rigby.com

Rising Moon
4501 Forbes Blvd.
Lanham, MD 20706
928-774-5251
http://www.nbnbooks.com/

Rising Star Studios
5251 W 73rd St, Suite C
Edina, MN 55439
952-831-8532
http://www.risingstarstudios.com/

Roaring Brook Press
Edinburgh Gate, Harlow
New York, NY 10010
888.330.8477
http://us.macmillan.com/MacKids.aspx

Roberts Rinehart
4501 Forbes Boulevard Suite 200
Lanham, MD 20706
303-543-7835 x 318
http://www.rowmanlittlefield.com/

Rosen Publishing Group
29 East 21st St.
New York, NY 10010
800-237-9932
https://www.rosenpublishing.com/

Rourke Classroom Resources
P.O. Box 643328
Vero Beach, FL 32964
800-380-2289
http://rourkeclassroom.com/

Rowland Reading Foundation
6120 University Avenue
Middleton, WI 53562
888-378-9258
http://www.rowlandreading.org/

Sadlier-Oxford
9 Pine Street
New York, NY 10005
800-221-5175
http://www.sadlier-oxford.com/

Sandpiper Books
222 Berkeley Street
Boston, MA 02116
800.225.5425
http://www.houghtonmifflinbooks.com
/hmh/site/hmhbooks/home/kids

Scholastic
557 Broadway Avenue
New York, NY 10012
1-800-724-6527
http://www.scholastic.com/home/

School Specialty Publishing
PO Box 35665
Greensboro, NC 27425
800-321-0943
http://www.carsondellosa.com/cd2/default
.aspx

School Zone
1819 Industrial Drive, PO Box 777
Grand Haven, MI 49417
616-846-5030
http://www.schoolzone.com/

Schwartz & Wade Books
1745 Broadway
New York, NY 10019
(212) 782-9000
https://www.facebook.com
/schwartzandwadebooks

Scribner
1230 Avenue of the Americas
New York, NY 10020
(212) 698-7000
http://imprints.simonandschuster.biz
/scribner

Sea-to-Sea Publications
P.O. Box 3263
North Mankato, MN 56002
507-388-1607
http://www.blackrabbitbooks.com/

Seal Press
1700 4th Street
Berkeley, CA 94710
(510) 595-3664
http://www.sealpress.com/home.php

SeaScape Press
5717 TANNER RIDGE AVE
WESTLAKE VILLAGE, CA 91362
805-963-7878

SeaStar Books
875 Sixth Avenue
New York, NY 10001

Secret Passage Press
814 N. Franklin Street
Chicago, IL 60610
(800) 888-4741
http://www.ipgbook.com/secret-passage
-press-publisher-SEC.php

Seven Footer Press
247 West 30th Street, 11th Floor
New York, NY 10001
(212) 710-9340
http://www.sevenfooterpress.com/

Seven Stories Press
140 Watts Street
New York, NY 10013

Short Tales Press
75 Barret Drive, PO Box 1524
Webster, NY 14580
585-509-1600
http://shorttalespress.com/

Shortland Publications
PO Box 11-904
Auckland, 5
New Zealand
(09) 687-0128

Signet Classics
375 Hudson Street
New York, NY 10014
212-366-2000
http://www.us.penguingroup.com/static
/pages/signetclassics/

Silver Burdett Press
One Lake Street
Upper Saddle River, NJ 07459
http://www.k12pearson.com/teach_learn
_cycle/PLG/plg.html

Simon & Schuster
1230 Avenue of the Americas
New York, NY 10020
(212) 698-7000
http://www.simonandschuster.com/

Simon Pulse
1230 Avenue of the Americas
New York, NY 10020
(212) 698-7000
http://imprints.simonandschuster.biz
/simon-pulse

Skylark
13866 Geranium Pl
West Palm Beach, FL 33414
(561) 792-0630
http://www.skylarkpubl.com/

Sleeping Bear Press
315 Eisenhower Parkway, Suite 200
Ann Arbor, MI 48108
800-487-2323
http://sleepingbearpress.com/

Smithsonian
P.O. Box 37012, MRC 513, Capital Gallery,
Suite 6001
Washington, DC 20013
http://www.smithsonianbooks.com
/uscrscction/Home.aspx

Sourcebooks
1935 Brookdale Road, Suite 139
Naperville, IL 60563
(800) 432-7444
http://www.sourcebooks.com/

Speak
375 Hudson Street
New York, NY 10014
212-366-2000
www.us.penguingroup.com/static/pages
/publishers/yr/speak.html

Square Fish
175 Fifth Avenue
New York, NY 10010
888.330.8477
http://us.macmillan.com/MacKids.aspx

SRA/McGraw Hill
PO Box 182605
Columbus, OH 43218
800-334-7344
https://www.mheonline.com/program
_sort_list/view/1

St. Martin's Press
175 Fifth Avenue
New York, NY 10010
888.330.8477
http://us.macmillan.com/SMP.aspx

Star Bright Books
13 Landsdowne Street
Cambridge, MA 02139
617 354 1300
http://www.starbrightbooks.org/

Steck-Vaughn
222 Berkeley Street
Boston, MA 02116
(617) 351-5000
http://steckvaughn.hmhco.com/en
/steckvaughn.htm

Sterling Publishing
387 Park Avenue South
New York, NY 10016
(800) 367 9692
http://www.sterlingpublishing.com/

Stewart, Tabori & Chang
115 West 18th Street 6th Floor
New York, NY 10011
(212) 206-7715
www.abramsbooks.com/comicarts

Stillwater Publishing
Bloxham Mill Business Centre, Barford
Road, Bloxham
BANBURY, OX15 4FF
UK
http://www.stillwaterpublishing.co.uk/

Stoddart Kids
195 Allstate Parkway
Markham, ON L3R 4T8
Canada
1-800-387-9776
http://www.fitzhenry.ca/

Stone Arch Books
1710 Roe Crest Drive
North Mankato, MN 56003
800-747-4992
http://www.capstonepub.com/category
/LIB_PUBLISHER_SAB

Sunburst Books
18 West 18th Street
New York, NY 10011
212-741-6900
http://us.macmillan.com
/FSGYoungReaders.aspx

Sundance
33 Boston Post Road West, Suite 440
Marlborough, MA 01752
800-343-8204
http://www.sundancepub.com/

Sylvan Dell Publishing
612 Johnnie Dodds Blvd., Suite A2
Mt. Pleasant, SC 29464
877-243-3457
http://www.sylvandellpublishing.com/

Teacher Created Materials
5301 Oceanus Drive
Huntington Beach, CA 92649
800 858-7339
http://www.teachercreatedmaterials.com

The McDonald & Woodward Publishing Co.
431 East College Street
Granville, OH 43023
800-233-8787
http://www.mwpubco.com/

The O'Brien Press
12 Terenure Road East, Rathgar
Dublin, 6
Ireland
353-1-4923333
http://www.obrien.ie/

Thomas Y. Crowell (see Harper & Row)
10 East 53rd Street
New York, NY 10022
212-207-7000
http://www.harpercollins.com/

Thomson Learning (see Cengage)
10650 Toebben Drive
Independence, KY 41051
1-800-487-8488
http://www.cengage.com/us/

Three Trees, Inc.
P.O. Box 92
Cottleville, MO 63338
1-877-707-9465
http://petalwink.com/

Thunderbolt Publishing
PO Box 294
The Dalles, OR 97058
541-296-3202
http://www.thunderboltpublishing.com/

Tiger Tales
5 River Road, Suite 128
Wilton, CT 06897
920-387-2333
http://www.tigertalesbooks.com/

Time Inc.
1271 Avenue of the Americas
New York, NY 10020
212.522.1212
http://www.timeinc.com/home/

Tom Doherty Associates
175 Fifth Avenue
New York, NY 10010
888.330.8477
http://us.macmillan.com/TorForge.aspx

Toon Books
27 Greene Street
New York, NY 10013
(212) 431-5756
http://www.toon-books.com/

Tor
175 Fifth Avenue
New York, NY 10010
888.330.8477
http://us.macmillan.com/TorForge.aspx

Tott Publications
513 Land Drive
Dayton, OH 45440
937-426-7636

Townsend Press
439 Kelley Drive
West Berlin, NJ 08091
1-800-772-6410
http://www.townsendpress.com/

Treasure Bay
P.O. Box 119
Novato, CA 94948
800-476-6416
http://www.webothread.com

Tricycle Press
2625 Alcatraz Avenue PO Box 50
Berkeley, CA 94705
510-285-3000
http://www.randomhousekids.com/

Troll Associates
100 Corporate Drive
Mahwah, NJ 07430

Tumblehome Press
201 Newton Street
Weston, MA 02493
781-894-8993
http://tumblehomelearning.com/

Tundra Books
P.O. Box 1030
Plattsburgh, NY 12901
1-800-788-1074
http://www.tundrabooks.com/

Two-Can Publishing
4501 Forbes Blvd., Suite 200
Lanham, MD 20706
301-459-3366
http://www.nbnbooks.com/

University of Maine Press
126A College Avenue
Orono, ME 04473
(207) 866-0573
http://umaine.edu/umpress/

University of New Mexico Press
MSC05 3185, 1 University of New Mexico
Albuquerque, NM 87131
505.277.2346
http://www.unmpress.com/

Usborne Publishing Ltd.
10302 E. 55th Place
Tullsa, OK 74146
800-611-1655
http://www.myubam.com/

Viking/Penguin
375 Hudson Street
New York, NY 10014
212-366-2000
www.us.penguingroup.com/static/pages
/publishers/adult/viking.html

Vintage Books
1745 Broadway
New York, NY 10019
(212) 782-9000
http://knopfdoubleday.com/imprint
/vintage/

Voyager Books
10 East 53rd Street
New York, NY 10022
212-207-7000
http://harpervoyagerbooks.com/

W. H. Freeman & Co.
175 Fifth Avenue
New York, NY 10010
888.330.8477
http://www.whfreeman.com/catalog/

W. W. Norton
500 Fifth Avenue
New York, NY 10110
(212) 354-5500
http://books.wwnorton.com/books/index
.aspx

Walker & Company
175 Fifth Avenue
New York, NY 10010

Warner Books
237 Park Avenue
New York, NY 10017
(800) 759-0190
http://www.hachettebookgroup.com/

WaterBrook Press
12265 Oracle Blvd., Suite 200
Colorado Springs, CO 80921
(719) 590.4999
http://waterbrookmultnomah.com/

Watts Publishing Group
338 Euston Road
London, NW1 3BH
england
020 7873 6000
http://wattspublishinggroup.com/

Web of Life Children's Books
366 61st Street
Oakland, CA 94618
(510) 589-7814
http://www.weboflifebooks.com/

Web Of Life Children's Books
366 61st Street
Oakland, CA 94618
(510) 589-7814
http://www.weboflifebooks.com/

Weekly Reader Publishing
PO Box 7502
Jefferson City, MO 65102
1-800-446-3355
http://www.weeklyreader.com/

Weinstein Books
44 Farnsworth Street, 3rd Floor
Boston, MA 02210
http://www.weinsteinbooks.com/

Wendy Lamb Books
1745 Broadway
New York, NY 10019
(212) 782-9000
www.randomhousekids.com

Wilbooks
1311 West Chester Pike
West Chester, PA 19382
(610) 436-8755
http://www.wilbooks.com/

William Morrow
10 East 53rd Street
New York, NY 10022
212-207-7000
http://www.harpercollins.com/imprints
/index.aspx?imprintid=518003

Willow Bend Publishing
P.O. Box 304
Goshen, MA 01032
413.268.3461
http://www.willowbendpublishing.com/

Winslow Press
36 West 20th Street, Third Floor
New York, NY 10011
212-366-4160
http://www.winslowpress.com/

World Book
233 North Michigan Avenue, Suite 2000
Chicago, IL 60601
800-967-5325
http://www.worldbook.com

Wright Group/McGraw Hill
PO Box 182605
Columbus, OH 43218
800-334-7344
https://www.mheonline.com/program
_sort_list/view/2

Yearling Books
1745 Broadway
New York, NY 10019
(212) 782-9000
www.randomhousekids.com